THE

TRUE CHRISTIAN RELIGION:

CONTAINING

THE UNIVERSAL THEOLOGY

OF THE

NEW CHURCH,

FORETOLD BY THE LORD IN DANIEL VII. 13, 14; AND IN REVELATION XXI. 1, 2.

BY EMANUEL SWEDENBORG,

SERVANT OF THE LORD JESUS CHRIST.

A new Translation

FROM THE ORIGINAL LATIN EDITION, PRINTED AT AMSTERDAM, IN THE YEAR 1771.

PHILADELPHIA:

J. B. LIPPINCOTT & CO.

1875.

DANIEL VII. 13, 14.

I was seeing in the visions of the night; and behold, with the clouds of the heavens, as it were, THE SON OF MAN *was coming. And unto Him was given dominion, and glory, and a kingdom; and all people, nations and tongues shall worship Him. His dominion is the dominion of an age which will not pass away, and his kingdom one which will not perish.*

REVELATION XXI. 1, 2, 5, 9, 10.

I John saw a new heaven and a new earth. And I saw the holy city, New Jerusalem, descending from God out of heaven, prepared as a bride adorned for her husband. And an angel spoke with me, saying, Come, I will show thee THE BRIDE, THE LAMB'S WIFE. *And he carried me away in spirit upon a great and high mountain, and showed me the great city, the holy Jerusalem, descending out of heaven from God.*

He who sat upon the throne said, Behold, I MAKE ALL THINGS NEW, *And He said to me, Write, because these words are true and faithful.*

ADVERTISEMENT.

THE public is now presented with a New Translation of the work of EMANUEL SWEDENBORG originally entitled "VERA RELIGIO CHRISTIANA, CONTINENS UNIVERSAM THEOLOGIAM NOVÆ ECCLESIÆ, A DOMINO APUD DANIELEM, CAP. VII. 13, 14, ET IN APOCALYPSI XXI. 1, 2, PREDICTÆ:" *The True Christian Religion, containing the Universal Theology of the New Church, foretold by the Lord in Daniel* vii. 13, 14, *and in Revelation* xxi. 1, 2. This is the last work that was published by the Author; and it comprises, as the title indicates, a general summary of the doctrines of the New Church, reduced to a regular system of theology. It was originally written in Latin, and published at Amsterdam in 1771, the year before the Author's death. It was first translated into English by the Rev. John Clowes, and published in England in the year 1781. After several editions of this version had been printed in England, and one in America, it was revised by the Rev. Samuel Noble and others, and republished in London in the year 1819. Some time since, a design was formed of stereotyping it in Boston, and it was then thought proper that it should be again revised; but after further consideration, it was deemed advisable that it should undergo a new translation; and, accordingly, the whole work has been translated anew.

The Translator has endeavored to express the meaning of the original Latin, as literally and accurately as possible, in plain English; but he has not, in all instances, done it to his own satisfaction. The style of the original is, in general, remarkably simple and perspicuous; yet there are some sentences, and some particular phrases, which seem obscure and difficult; and, although the Translator has endeavored to render them faithfully, he is not sure that he has always either apprehended or expressed the true meaning. He hopes, however, that the present translation will be found not only more literal and accurate than the former, but also more simple in its phraseology, and consequently more intelligible to common readers.

One remarkable characteristic of the style of our Author, is the frequent use of adjectives as substantives; as, for example, *Divinum* the Divine;' *Humanum*, 'the Human;' *bonum*, 'the good;' *verum* 'the true;' *malum*, 'the evil;' *falsum*, 'the false;' *spirituale*, 'the spiritual;' *naturale*, 'the natural,' &c. In the present translation, the word 'nature' or 'principle' is sometimes added to 'the Divine' and 'the Human,' but not generally. *Jucundum*, which properly means 'pleasant, agreeable, delightful,' &c., is commonly rendered 'delight,' but sometimes 'delightful.' *Proprium*, which properly signifies 'what is proper, peculiar or appropriated to any one,' is retained and used as a noun, for want of a more proper word. The Latin verbs *esse* and *existere* are also retained, in several instances; particularly in the second part of the first chapter, where they seemed to denote abstract ideas, which could not be conveniently expressed by other words. *Esse* properly means 'to be,' but it is used to denote 'BEING itself, in the abstract,' or 'the inmost essence of things;' and *existere* properly means 'to exist,' but it is used to denote 'BEING as it is manifested,' or 'the sensible existence of things.' The phrase *liberum arbitrium*, which was formerly translated 'free will,' is now rendered 'free agency.' The passages quoted from the Sacred Scripture are generally translated very literally, and they sometimes vary considerably from the corresponding passages in the common version of the Bible.

T. G. W

Cambridge, December 1, 1832.

CHAPTER II.

CONCERNING THE LORD THE REDEEMER.

CHAPTER III.

CONCERNING THE HOLY SPIRIT, AND CONCERNING THE DIVINE OPERATION. *n.* 138.

Concerning the Divine Trinity. n. 163.

CHAPTER IV.

CONCERNING THE SACRED SCRIPTURE, OR WORD OF THE LORD.

CHAPTER V.

THE CATECHISM OR DECALOGUE EXPLAINED AS TO ITS EXTERNAL AND INTERNAL SENSE. *n.* 282.

CHAPTER VI.

CONCERNING FAITH.

CHAPTER VII.

CONCERNING CHARITY OR LOVE TOWARDS THE NEIGHBOR; AND CONCERNING GOOD WORKS.

CHAPTER VIII.

CONCERNING FREE AGENCY.

CHAPTER IX.

CONCERNING REPENTANCE.

CHAPTER X.

CONCERNING REFORMATION AND REGENERATION.

CHAPTER XI.

CONCERNING IMPUTATION.

CHAPTER XII.

CONCERNING BAPTISM.

CHAPTER XIII.

CONCERNING THE HOLY SUPPER.

VII. That those who come to the Holy Supper worthily are in the Lord, and the Lord in them; consequently, that by the Holy Supper there is made a Conjunction with the Lord. *n.* 725 to 727.

VIII. That the Holy Supper is, to those who come worthily, a Sign and Seal that they are the Sons of God. *n.* 728 to 730.

CHAPTER XIV.

CONCERNING THE CONSUMMATION OF THE AGE; CONCERNING THE COMING OF THE LORD; AND CONCERNING THE NEW CHURCH.

I. That the Consummation of the Age is the Last Time or End of the Church *n.* 753 to 756.

II. That at this day is the Last Time of the Church, which was foretold and described by the Lord in the Evangelists, and in the Revelation. *n.* 757 to 759.

III. That this Last Time of the Christian Church is the Night itself, in which former Churches have come to an end. *n.* 760 to 763.

IV. That after this Night follows the Morning; and that the Coming of the Lord is that. *n.* 764 to 767.

V. That the Coming of the Lord is not his coming to destroy the visible Heaven and the habitable Earth, and to create a new Heaven and a new Earth, as many hitherto, from not understanding the Spiritual Sense of the Word, have supposed. *n.* 768 to 771

VI. That this Coming of the Lord, which is the Second, takes place in order that the Evil may be separated from the Good, and that those may be saved who have believed and do believe in Him, and that by these a New Angelic Heaven and a New Church on earth may be formed; and that, without it, no flesh could be saved, Matt. xxiv. 22. *n.* 772 to 775.

VII. That this Second Coming of the Lord is not in Person, but that it is in the Word, which is from Him, and thus Himself. *n.* 776 to 778.

VIII. That this Second Coming is made through a Man, before whom He has manifested Himself, and whom He has filled with his Spirit, to teach the Doctrines of the New Church by means of the Word from Him. *n.* 779, 780.

IX. That this is meant by the New Heaven and the New Jerusalem, in the Revelation, xxi. *n.* 781 to 785.

X. That this Church is the Crown of all the Churches which have been hitherto in the world. *n.* 786 to 791.

SUPPLEMENT.

1. Concerning THE SPIRITUAL WORLD, what it is. *n.* 792 to 795.
2. Concerning LUTHER in the spiritual world. *n.* 796.
3. Concerning MELANCHTHON in the spiritual world. *n.* 797.
4. Concerning CALVIN in the spiritual world. *n.* 798, 799.
5. Concerning THE DUTCH in the spiritual world. *n.* 800 to 805.
6. Concerning THE ENGLISH in the spiritual world. *n.* 806 to 812.
7. Concerning THE GERMANS in the spiritual world. *n.* 813 to 816.
8. Concerning THE PAPISTS in the spiritual world. *n.* 817 to 821.
9. Concerning THE POPISH SAINTS in the spiritual world. *n.* 822 to 827.
10. Concerning THE MAHOMETANS in the spiritual world. *n.* 828 to 834.
11. Concerning THE AFRICANS in the spiritual world, and also something concerning the GENTILES. *n.* 835 to 840.
12. Concerning THE JEWS in the spiritual world. *n.* 841 to 845.

THE TRUE CHRISTIAN RELIGION

CONTAINING

The Universal Theology

OF THE

NEW HEAVEN AND THE NEW CHURCH.

THE FAITH OF THE NEW HEAVEN AND THE NEW CHURCH.

1. THE Faith, in a universal and a particular form, is prefixed, that it may be as a face before the work which follows; and as a gate, through which entrance is made into a temple; and a summary, in which the particulars which follow are in their own measure contained. It is said, *the Faith of the New Heaven and the New Church*, because the heaven where angels are, and the church in which men are, make one, as the internal and the external with man. Thence it is, that, as to the interiors of his mind, the man of the church, who is in the good of love from the truths of faith, and in the truths of faith from the good of love, is an angel of heaven; wherefore, after death, he also comes into heaven, and there enjoys felicity according to the state of their conjunction. It should be known, that this faith is in the New Heaven, which the Lord is at this day establishing, its face gate and summary.

2. THE FAITH OF THE NEW HEAVEN AND THE NEW CHURCH, IN THE UNIVERSAL FORM, is this: That the Lord from eternity, who is Jehovah, came into the world, that he might subjugate the hells and glorify his Human; and that, without this, no mortal could have been saved; and that those are saved who believe in Him.

It is said, *in the universal form*, because this is the universal of faith; and a universal of faith is that which will be in the whole and every part. It is a universal of faith, that God is one in essence and in person, in whom is a divine Trinity, and that the Lord God the Savior Jesus Christ is He. It is a universal of faith, that no mortal could have been saved, unless the Lord had come into the world. It is a universal of faith, that He came into the world that He might remove hell from man, and that He did remove it, by means of combats against it and victories over it; thus He subjugated it and reduced it to order and under obedience to Himself. It is a universal of faith, that He came into the world, that He might glorify his Human, which He assumed in the world, that is, might unite it with the Divine, from which it proceeded; thus He holds hell in order and under obedience to Himself forever. Since this could not have been done but by means of temptations admitted into his Human, even to the last of them, and the last of them was the passion of the cross, therefore He underwent that. These are the universals of faith concerning the Lord.

The universal of faith, on the part of man, is, That he should believe in the Lord; for by believing in Him, conjunction with Him is effected, by which is salvation. To believe in Him, is to have confidence that He saves: and because no one can have this confidence, except those who live well, therefore this also is meant by believing in Him. This the Lord also says in John: *This is the will of the Father, that every one, who believeth in the Son, may have eternal life*, vi. 40; and in another place, *He who believeth in the Son, hath eternal life; but he who believeth not the Son, shall not see life, but the anger of God abideth on him*, iii. 36.

3. The Faith of the New Heaven and the New Church, in the particular Form, is this: That Jehovah God is Love itself and Wisdom itself, or that he is Good itself and Truth itself: and that He, as to Divine Truth, which is the Word, and which was God with God, descended and assumed the Human, to the end that He might reduce to order all things which were in heaven, and all things which were in hell, and all things which were in the church; since, at that time, the power of hell prevailed over the power of heaven, and, upon earth, the power of evil over the power of good, and thence a total damnation stood before the door and threatened. This impending damnation Jehovah God removed by means of his Human, which was Divine Truth, and thus He redeemed angels and men; and afterwards He united, in his Human, Divine Truth with Divine Good, or Divine Wisdom with Divine Love, and thus, together with and in his glorified Human, returned into his Divine, in which He was from eternity. These things are meant by this passage in John, *The Word was with God, and the Word was God: and the Word became flesh*, i. 1, 14; and in the same, *I proceeded from the Father, and came into the world: again I leave the world, and go to the Father*, xvi. 28: and also by this, *We know that the Son of God hath come, and given us understanding, that we might know the True; and we are in the True, in his Son Jesus Christ: This is the true God and eternal Life*, 1 John v. 20, 21. From these it is manifest that, without the coming of the Lord into the world, no one could have been saved. It is similar at this day: wherefore, unless the Lord should again come into the world, in Divine Truth, no one can be saved.

The particulars of the faith, on the part of man, are, 1. That God is One, in whom is a Divine Trinity, and that He is the Lord God the Savior Jesus Christ; 2. That saving faith is to believe in Him; 3. That evils should not be done, because they are of the devil and from the devil; 4. That goods should be done, because they are of God and from God; 5. And that these should be done by man as from himself; but that it should be believed, that they are from the Lord, with him and through him. The two first are of faith, the two next are of charity, and the fifth is of the conjunction of charity and faith, thus of the Lord and man.

CHAPTER I.

CONCERNING GOD THE CREATOR.

4. THE Christian Church, since the time of the Lord, had passed through the several stages from infancy to extreme old age. Its infancy was in the time when the apostles lived, and preached, throughout the world, repentance and faith in the Lord God the Savior. That they preached these two things, is evident from these words in the Acts of the Apostles: *Paul proclaimed, both to the Jews and to the Greeks, repentance towards God, and faith in our Lord Jesus Christ*, xx. 21. It is memorable, that the Lord, some months ago, called together his twelve disciples, now angels, and sent them forth into all the spiritual world, with the command that they should there preach the gospel anew, since the church which was instituted by the Lord through them, has at this day come to such a state of consummation, that scarcely any relics of it remain; and that this has come to pass, because they divided the Divine Trinity into three persons, each one of whom is God and Lord; and that thence a sort of phrensy has issued forth into the whole of theology, and thus into the church, which, from the name of the Lord, is called Christian. It is said *a phrensy*, because the minds of men have been driven by it into such a delirium, that they do not know whether God be one, or whether there be three; there is one in the speech of their lips, but three in the thought of their mind, wherefore there is a disagreement between their mind and lips, or between their thought and speech; from which disagreement results the idea that there is no God. The naturalism which reigns at this day is from no other source. Consider, if you please, while the lips speak of one, and the mind thinks of three, whether one does not, inwardly, in the midst of the way, by turns expel the other; thence it is that man scarcely thinks otherwise concerning God, if he thinks at all, than from the mere word *God*, without any sense of its meaning which implies a knowledge of Him. Since the idea concerning God, with every notion of it, is thus torn to pieces, I propose to treat, in their order, of God the Creator, of the Lord the Redeemer, and of the Holy Spirit the Operator, and lastly of the Divine Trinity; to the end that what is torn to pieces may again be made whole, which is effected while the reason of man is convinced, from the Word and the light thence proceeding, that there is a Divine Trinity, and that it is in the Lord God the Savior Jesus Christ, like the soul, body and proceeding operation in man; and thus that this article in the Athanasian Creed is true;—*That in Christ, God and Man, or the Divine and the Human, are not two, but in one person; and that, as the rational soul and flesh is one man so God and Man is one Christ*

CONCERNING THE UNITY OF GOD.

5. SINCE the acknowledgment of God from a knowledge of him, is the very essence and soul of all things in universal theology, it is necessary that an exordium should be made concerning the UNITY of God, which will be demonstrated in order by these articles: I. *That the whole Sacred Scrip-*

ture, and thence the doctrines of churches in the Christian world, teach that God is one. II. *That there is a universal influx into the souls of men, that there is a God, and that He is one.* III. *Thence it is that, in all the world, there is no nation, possessed of religion and sound reason, which does not acknowledge that there is a God, and that He is one.* IV. *That as to what the one God is, nations and people have differed, and still differ, from several causes.* V. *That human reason, from many things in the world, may, if it will, perceive or conclude, that there is a God, and that he is one.* VI. *That unless God were one, the universe could not have been created and preserved.* VII. *That the man who does not acknowledge a God, is excommunicated from the church and condemned.* VIII. *That with the man who does not acknowledge one God, but several, nothing of the church coheres.* But these articles shall be explained one by one.

6. I. That the whole Sacred Scripture, and thence all the Doctrines of the Churches in the Christian world, teach that there is a God, and that He is one.

That the whole Sacred Scripture teaches that there is a God, is because, in its inmost, it is no other than God, that is, the Divine which proceeds from God; for it was dictated by God, and nothing else can proceed from God, than that which is Himself, and is called Divine; this the Sacred Scripture is in its inmost. But in its derivatives, which are below and from the inmost, the Sacred Scripture is accommodated to the perception of angels and men; in these it is also Divine, but in another form, in which it is called the Celestial Divine, the Spiritual Divine and the Natural Divine, which are no other than coverings of God; since God himself, such as He is in the inmost of the Word, cannot be seen by any creature. For he said to Moses, when he prayed that he might see the glory of Jehovah, that *no one can see God and live.* It is similar with the inmost of the Word, where God is in his esse [to be] and in his essence. But still the Divine, which is the inmost, and is covered with such things as are accommodated to the perceptions of angels and men, shines forth, like light through crystalline forms, but variously, according to the state of mind which man has formed for himself, from God or from himself. To every one who has formed the state of his mind from God, the Sacred Scripture is like a mirror, in which he sees God; but each one in his own way. The truths which he learns from the word, and imbues by a life according to them compose that mirror. From these things, in the first place, it is evident, that the Sacred Scripture is the fulness of God. That it not only teaches that there is a God, but also that God is one, is evident from the truths, which, as was said, compose that mirror, in that they cohere in one series, and make man incapable of thinking of God but as one. Thence it is, that every one, whose reason is imbued with any sanctity from the Word, knows as of himself, that God is one, and perceives that it is like madness to say that there are more. The angels cannot open their lips to pronounce the word *Gods*, for the celestial aura, in which they live, opposes it. That God is one, the Sacred Scripture teaches not only thus universally, as was said, but also in many particular passages, as in the following: *Hear, O Israel; Jehovah our God is one Jehovah*, Deut. vi. 4; and in like manner, Mark xii. 29. *Surely in thee is God, and there is no other God beside*, Isai. xlv. 14. *Am not I Jehovah? and there is no other God beside Me*, xlv. 21. *I am Jehovah thy God, and thou shalt acknowledge no God beside Me*, Hosea xiii. 4. *Thus saith Jehovah, the King of Israel, I am the First and the Last, and beside Me there is no God*, Isai. xliv. 6. *In that day, Jehovah shall be King over all the earth; in that day, Jehovah shall be one, and his name one* Zech. xiv. 9.

7. It is known, that the doctrines of the churches in the Christian world teach, that God is one; they teach this because all their doctrines are derived

from the Word, and they cohere so far as one God is acknowledged not only with the lips, but also in the heart. Those who confess one God only with the lips, and in heart three, as is the case with very many at this day in Christendom, have no other apprehension of God, than of something uttered by the lips; and every thing relating to theology is, to them, no other than as it were an idol of gold enclosed in a shrine, the key of which is in possession of the priests only; and when they read the Word, they do not perceive any light in it or from it, not even that God is one. The Word, with such persons, is as if it were stained with blots; and, as to the unity of God, entirely covered. These are they who are described by the Lord in Matthew: *Hearing ye shall hear, and shall not understand; and seeing ye shall see, and shall not perceive: they have shut up their eyes, lest they should see with their eyes, and hear with their ears, and understand with their heart, and turn themselves about, and I should heal them*, xiii. 14, 15. All such persons are like those who shun the light, and enter chambers where there are no windows, and feel about the walls, and search for food and for money, and at length acquire a vision like that of owls, and see in darkness. They are like a woman, having several husbands, who is not a wife, but a lascivious harlot; and like a virgin, who accepts rings from several suitors, and after the nuptials, bestows her favors upon one, and also upon the others.

8. II. That there is a universal Influx into the Souls of Men, that there is a God, and that He is one.

That there is an influx from God into man, is evident from the confession of all, that all good which in itself is good, and is in man, and is done by him, is from God; in like manner all of charity and all of faith; for it is read, *A man cannot take any thing, unless it be given him from heaven*, John iii. 27; and Jesus said, *Without Me ye cannot do any thing*, xv. 5; that is, not any thing which is of charity and of faith. That this influx is into the souls of men, is because the soul is the inmost and highest part of man, and the influx from God enters into that, and thence descends into those things which are beneath, and vivifies them according to reception. The truths which will be of faith, indeed, flow in by hearing, and so are implanted in the mind, thus below the soul. But man, by these truths, is only disposed for receiving the influx from God through the soul; and as the disposition is, such is the reception, and such the transformation of natural faith into spiritual faith. That there is an influx from God into the souls of men, that God is one, is because all the Divine, taken universally as well as particularly, is God; and because all the Divine coheres as one, it cannot but inspire into man the idea of one God; and this idea is corroborated daily, as man is elevated by God into the light of heaven; for the angels, in their light, cannot force themselves to utter the word *Gods;* wherefore, also, their speech, at the close of every sentence, terminates as to accent in unity, which is from no other cause, than from the influx into their souls, that God is one. The reason that, although it flows into the souls of all, that God is one, still many think that his divinity is divided into several of the same essence, is because, when that influx descends, it falls into forms not correspondent, and the form itself varies it, as is the case in all the subjects of the three kingdoms of nature. It is the same God that vivifies every beast, that vivifies man; but the recipient form causes beast to be beast, and man to be man. It is similar with man while he induces on his mind the form of a beast. There is a similar influx from the sun into every plant, but it is varied according to the form of each what flows into the vine is similar to what flows into the thorn; but if the thorn is ingrafted into a vine, that influx is inverted, and proceeds according to the form of the thorn. The case is similar in the subjects of the mineral kingdom; the light flowing into a lime-stone and into a diamond, is the same, but it becomes bright in the latter, and dark in the former. As to human minds, they are varied according to their forms, which inwardly are spiritual according to faith in God, and at the same time a life from God, and those forms become bright and angelic by faith in one God; but on the contrary, they become dark and bestial by faith in several Gods, which differs but little from faith in no God.

9. III. THENCE IT IS, THAT, IN ALL THE WORLD, THERE IS NO NATION, POSSESSED OF RELIGION AND SOUND REASON, WHICH DOES NOT ACKNOWLEDGE A GOD, AND THAT GOD IS ONE.

From the divine influx into the souls of men, treated of just above, it follows, that there is an internal dictate with every man, that there is a God, and that He is one. That there are still those who deny God, and who acknowledge nature instead of God, and who acknowledge several Gods, and also who worship images as Gods, is because they have filled up the interiors of their reason or understanding with worldly and corporeal things, and thereby have obliterated their primitive idea, or the idea of their infancy concerning God, and at the same time, they then rejected religion from the breast to the back. That Christians do, in a certain manner, acknowledge one God, appears from the general Confession of their faith, which is as follows: *The Catholic faith is this, that we should worship one God in a trinity, and the Trinity in unity; there are three Divine Persons, the Father, the Son and the Holy Ghost, and yet there are not three Gods, but there is one God; and there is one person of the Father, another of the Son, and another of the Holy Ghost, and their divinity is one, their glory equal, and their majesty coeternal; thus the Father is God, the Son is God, and the Holy Ghost is God: but although we are compelled by Christian verity to confess each person, one by one, to be God and Lord, yet we are forbidden by the Catholic religion to say there are three Gods, and three Lords.* Such is the Christian faith concerning the unity of God; but that the trinity of God and the unity of God, in that Confession, are inconsistent with each other, will be seen in the chapter on the DIVINE TRINITY. The other nations in the world, who are in possession of religion and sound reason, agree in acknowledging that God is one; all the Mahometans in their several empires; the Africans in many kingdoms of their continent; and also the Asiatics in many of theirs; and moreover the Jews at this day. The most ancient people in the golden age, such as had any religion, worshipped one God, whom they called Jehovah; in like manner the ancient people in the following age, before monarchical governments were formed, when worldly and at length corporeal loves began to close up the superior parts of their understanding, which before were open, and then as temples and sacred recesses for the worship of one God. But the Lord God, that he might open them, and so restore the worship of one God, instituted a church among the posterity of Jacob, and prefixed to all the precepts of their religion this commandment, *Thou shalt have no other God before my face*, Exod. xx. 3. *Jehovah*, also, the name which he assumed anew before them, signifies the supreme and only Being from whom every thing is, that is and exists in the universe. The ancient gentiles acknowledged Jove as the supreme God, so called perhaps from Jehovah; and many others, who composed his court, they also clothed with divinity; but the wise men in the following age, as Plato and Aristotle, confessed that these were not gods, but so many properties, qualities and attributes of one God, which were called gods, because in each of them there was divinity.

10. All sound reason, although not imbued with religion, sees that every thing which is divided, unless it depend upon one, would of itself fall to pieces; for instance, man, composed of so many members, viscera and organs of motion and sensation, unless he expended upon one soul; and the body itself, unless upon one heart In like manner, a kingdom, unless it

depended upon one king; a family, unless upon one master; and every office, of which there are many kinds in every kingdom, unless upon one officer. What would an army avail against the enemy, without a leader, who has supreme power, and officers subordinate to him, each of whom has his proper command over the soldiers. It would be similar with the church, unless it acknowledged one God, and also with the angelic heaven, which is as a head to the church upon earth, in both which the Lord is the soul itself. Wherefore, heaven and the church are called his body; which, unless they acknowledged one God, would both of them be like a lifeless corpse, which, being of no use, would be cast away and buried.

11. IV. That as to what the one God is, Nations and People have differed, and still differ, from several Causes.

The first cause is, that the knowledge of God, and thence an acknowledgment of Him, are not attainable without revelation; and a knowledge of the Lord and thence an acknowledgment, that *in Him dwelleth all the fullness of the Godhead bodily*, are not attainable except from the Word, which is the crown of revelations; for man, by the revelation which is given, is able to approach God, and to receive influx, and so from natural to become spiritual. The first revelation pervaded all the world, and the natural man had perverted it in many ways; whence arose the disputes, dissensions, heresies and schisms of religions. The second cause is, that the natural man cannot perceive and apply to himself the things of God, but only the things of the world; wherefore it is among the established doctrines of the church, that the natural man is contrary to the spiritual, and that they fight against each other. Thence it is, that those who have learnt from the Word, or other revelation, that there is a God, have differed, and still differ, concerning his quality, and also concerning his unity. Wherefore, those whose mental sight depended on the senses of the body, and who still wished to see God, formed for themselves artificial images, of gold, silver, stone, and wood, that under these, as objects of sight, they might worship God; and that others, who rejected from their religious worship artificial images, formed for themselves ideal images of God in the sun and moon, in the stars, and in various things upon the earth. But those who supposed themselves to be wise above the common people, and who still remained natural, from the immensity and omnipresence of God in creating the world, acknowledged nature as God, some in its inmost, some in its outmost parts: and some, that they might separate God from nature, conceived an idea of something most universal, which they called the Being [*Ens*] of the universe; and because they know nothing more concerning God, this Being becomes with them a being of reason, which does not signify any thing. Who cannot comprehend, that knowledges concerning God are mirrors of God, and that those who know nothing concerning God, do not see God in a mirror with its face turned towards their eyes, but in a mirror with its back towards them, which, being covered with mercury, or some dark, glutinous substance, does not reflect, but suffocates the image? The faith of God enters into man through a prior way, which is from the soul into the superior parts of the understanding; but knowledges concerning God enter through a posterior way, because they are imbibed from the revealed Word, by the understanding, through the senses of the body, and there is a meeting of the influxes in the understanding, as a common centre; and there natural faith, which is only persuasion, becomes spiritual, which is real acknowledgment; wherefore the human understanding is as a refining vessel, in which the change is effected.

12. V. That human Reason, from many Things in the World, may, if it will, perceive, or conclude, that there is a God, and that He is One.

This truth may be confirmed by in

numerable things in the visible world; for the universe is like a theatre, upon which are continually exhibited testimonies, that there is a God, and that He is one. But to illustrate this, I will adduce this memorable relation from the spiritual world. Once, while I was conversing with the angels, there arrived some novitiate spirits from the natural world, to whom I wished a happy arrival, and related many things, before unknown, concerning the spiritual world; and after this relation, I inquired of them what theory they brought with them from the world, concerning God and nature. They said this, that nature operates all things that take place in the created universe; and that God, after creation, induced and impressed upon nature that faculty and power; and that God only sustains and preserves them lest they should perish; wherefore all things which exist, which are produced and reproduced upon the earth, are at this day ascribed to nature. But I replied, that nature, of itself, does not operate any thing, but God through nature; and because they asked for proof, I said, those who believe the divine operation to be in every thing of nature, can, from very many things which they see in the world, confirm themselves in favor of God, much more than in favor of nature; for those who confirm themselves in favor of the divine operation in every thing of nature, attend to the wonderful things which are conspicuous in the productions of vegetables as well as of animals.—In the Productions of Vegetables. They observe that, from a little seed sown in the ground, there goes forth a root, and by means of the root, a stem, and successively branches, buds, leaves, flowers, and fruits, even to new seeds, just as if the seed knew the order of succession, or the process by which it was about to renew itself. What rational man can suppose that the sun, which is pure fire, knows this, or that it can instruct its heat and light to effect such things, or that it can intend uses. The man whose rational faculty is elevated while he sees and properly considers those things, cannot think otherwise, than that they are from him who has infinite wisdom, thus from God. Those who acknowledge the divine operation in every thing of nature, also confirm themselves in it when they see those things; but, on the contrary those who do not acknowledge it, do not see such things with the eyes of their reason in their forehead, but in the back of their head; who are such as derive all the ideas of their thought from the senses of the body and confirm their fallacies, saying, "Do you not see the sun by its heat and light operating all those things; what is that which you do not see; is it any thing?"—Those who confirm themselves in favor of the Divine, attend to the wonderful things which they see in the Productions of Animals. In the first place, it is remarkable in eggs, that in them the chicken is concealed in its seed with every thing requisite for its formation, and also for its future growth after its exclusion, even until it becomes a bird of its own species. Moreover, if we attend to winged creatures in general, such things are presented to the mind, which thinks deeply, as excite astonishment; as that in the least as well as in the greatest of them, in the invisible as well as in the visible, that is, in little insects as well as in birds, and great beasts, there are the organs of the senses, which are seeing, smelling, tasting, and feeling, and also the organs of motion, which are muscles, for they fly and walk; as also viscera adhering to the heart and lungs, which are actuated by the brain. They who ascribe all things to nature see, indeed, such things, but they think only that they exist, and say that nature produces them; and they say this because they have turned away their mind from thinking of the Divine. and those who have turned themselves away from the Divine, while they behold the wonderful things in nature, cannot think rationally concerning them, still less spiritually; but they think sensually and materially; and then, at length, they think in nature from nature, and not above it. They differ from beasts only in being endued with rationality; that is, they could understand if they would. Those who have averted themselves from thinking of the Divine, and hereby have become sensual corporeal, do not consider that the sight of the eye is so gross and material, that it sees many little insects as one obscure object, and yet every one of them is endued with organs of motion and sensation, and consequently with fibres and vessels, and also with a little heart, pulmonary tubes, little viscera and brains; and that these are contextures of the purest things in nature, and that those contextures correspond to life in its lowest degree, by which the minutest of them are distinctly actuated. Since the sight of the eye is so gross, that many insects, with the innumerable parts of each, appear to it as a small, obscure spot, and yet sensual men think and conclude from that vision, it appears how very gross their mind is, and thence in what darkness they are with respect to spiritual things.

Every man, if he will, may confirm himself in favor of the Divine, from the things visible in nature; and also he does confirm himself, who thinks concerning God, and his omnipotence in creating the universe, and concerning his omnipresence in preserving it: whilst, for instance, he observes the fowls of the air, and how each species of them knows its proper food, and where it is; how it distinguishes those of its own kind by their voice and figure; how, among the birds, they can distinguish which are their friends, and which their enemies; how they unite in pairs, and celebrate connubial rites; how they artfully build their nests where they lay their eggs, and sit upon them during the proper time of incubation, when they hatch their young, which they love most tenderly; how they cherish them under their wings, procure food, and nourish them, until they are able to provide for themselves, and to do similar things. Every man, who is disposed to think of the Divine influx through the spiritual world into the natural, may see it in those things; and he may also say in his heart, if he will, that such science cannot be given to them from the sun by its heat and light; for the sun, from which nature derives its origin and essence, is pure fire; and thence the effluxes of its heat and light are altogether dead; and thus they may conclude that such things are from the Divine influx through the spiritual world into the ultimates of nature.

Every man may, from the things visible in nature, confirm himself in favor of the Divine, while he sees worms, how, from the delight of a certain love, they seek and aspire after a change of their earthly state into one analogous to the heavenly state; and how, for this purpose, they crawl into suitable places, envelope themselves with a covering, and thus put themselves into the womb, that they may be born again, and thus become chrysalises, aureliæ, nymphs, and at length butterflies; and when they have undergone these changes of form, and, according to their species, have been clothed with beautiful wings, they fly abroad into the open air, as into their heaven, and there indulge in pleasant sports, celebrate connubial rites, lay eggs, and provide for themselves a posterity; and then they nourish themselves with sweet and pleasant food extracted from flowers. Whoever confirms himself in favor of the Divine, from the things visible in nature, may see in them, while worms, an image of the earthly state of man, and when butterflies, an image of his heavenly state; but those who confirm themselves in favor of nature, see them indeed, but, because they have rejected the heavenly state of man from their mind, they call them mere operations of nature.

Every man may, from the things visible in nature, confirm himself in favor of the Divine, while he attends to the things which are known concerning bees, that they know how to gather wax, and suck honey out of roses and flowers, and to build cells like little houses, and arrange them in the form of a city, with streets through which they come in and go out; that at a distance they smell the herbs and flowers from which they gather wax for their houses and honey for their food; and that, thus loaded, they fly back in the right direction to their hive, and thus provide for themselves food for the approaching winter, as if they foresaw it. They also appoint over themselves a ruler like a queen, from whom their posterity is propagated; they build for her, as it were, a palace in an elevated situation, and furnish it with proper guards. When the time of procreation arrives, she goes, accompanied by her satellites, called drones, from cell to cell, and lays her eggs, which her attendants cover with a sort of ointment, that they may not be injured by the air. Hence arises a new race; and afterwards, when it has arrived at the proper age, and is able to do similar things, it is expelled from the hive; the swarm first collects itself into a band, that it may not be divided and dispersed, and afterwards flies abroad to seek for itself a habitation. About the time of autumn, those drones, because they have brought in nothing of wax or honey, are led forth and deprived of their wings, that they may not return and consume the food, which they took no pains to provide. Many other things might be added; whence it is evident, that, on account of the use which they perform to the human race, they have, from the Divine influx through the spiritual world, a form of government such as there is among men on earth, yea, among the angels in the heavens. What person of enlightened reason does not see, that such things, with them, are not from the natural world? What has the sun of the natural world in common with a government similar and analogous to the government of heaven? From these and similar things observable in brute animals, the advocate and worshipper of nature confirms himself in favor of nature; whilst the advocate and worshipper of God, from the same things, confirms himself in favor of God: for the spiritual man sees in them spiritual things, and the natural man sees in them natural things; thus each according to his quality. As to myself, such things have been to me evident indications of the influx of the spiritual world into the natural from God. Consider also whether you can think analytically concerning any form of government, or concerning any civil law, or concerning any moral virtue, or concerning any spiritual truth, unless the Divine, from his wisdom, flow in through the spiritual world. As to myself, I never could, nor can I now; for I have perceptibly and sensibly observed that influx now for twenty-six years, continually; wherefore I say this from experience.

Can nature regard use as an end, and dispose uses into their orders and forms? This can be done only by a wise being; and the universe could be thus ordered and formed only by God, whose wisdom is infinite. Who else could foresee and provide for men their food and clothing; their food from the harvests of the field, the fruits of the earth, and from animals; and their clothing from the same. It is among those wonderful things, that those vile worms, called silk worms, should clothe with silk, and magnificently adorn, both men and women, from kings and queens, even to servants and maids; and that those vile insects, called bees, should furnish wax for lights, by which temples and palaces are illuminated. These and many other things are standing proofs that God, from Himself through the spiritual world, operates all things which are done in nature.

To these things it is proper to add, that, in the spiritual world, have been seen those, who, from the things visible in the world, have confirmed themselves in favor of nature to such a degree, that they became atheists; and that their understanding in spiritual light appeared open below and closed above, because, in their thoughts, they had looked downwards to the earth, and not upwards to heaven. Above their sensual principle, which is the lowest region of the understanding there appeared, as it were, a veil sparkling with infernal fire: in some cases, black as soot; in others, livid like a corpse. Let every one, therefore, beware of confirming himself in favor of nature; but, since there is no want of means, let him confirm himself in favor of God.

13. VI. That unless God were one, the Universe could not have been created and preserved.

That the unity of God may be inferred from the creation of the universe, is because the universe is a work cohering as one from firsts to lasts, depending upon one God, as the body on the soul. The universe is so created, that God may be every where present, and hold all and every part of it under his direction, and hold it together as one, perpetually, which is to preserve it. Hence also it is, that Jehovah God says, *That he is the First and the Last, the Beginning and the Ending, the Alpha and the Omega*, Isai. xliv. 6; Rev. i. 8, 17; and, in another place, *That he maketh all things, spreadeth out the heavens, and stretcheth out the earth by himself*, Isai. xliv. 24. This great system, which is called the *universe*, is a work cohering as one from firsts to lasts, because God, in creating it, had one end in view, which was an angelic heaven from the human race; and the means to that end are all things of which the earth is composed; for he who wills an end, also wills the means; wherefore he who contemplates the world as a work containing means to that end, may contemplate the created universe as a work cohering as one, and may see that the world is a complex of uses, in successive order, for the human race, from which is the angelic heaven. The Divine Love can intend no other end than the eternal blessedness of men from its own Divine. Divine Wisdom can produce nothing else than uses which are means to that end. By contemplating the world in this universal idea, every wise man may perceive that the Creator of the universe is one, and that his essence is Love and Wisdom: wherefore there is not a single thing in the universe, which does not contain a use, more or less remote, for man.

Those who contemplate some things in the world separately, and not all as united in a series in which are ends, mediate causes and effects, and who do not deduce creation from the Divine Love through the Divine Wisdom, cannot see that the universe is the work of one God, and that he dwells in every use, because he dwells in the end; for every one who is in the end, is also in the means; for the end is inwardly in all the means, actuating and directing them. Those who do not contemplate the universe as the work of God, and as the habitation of his love and wisdom, but as the work of nature, and the habitation of the heat and light of the sun, close the superior parts of their mind towards God, and open the inferior parts of it for the devil; and thence they put off the nature of man, and put on the nature of beasts, and not only think themselves like beasts, but also become so; for they become foxes in cunning, wolves in fierceness, leopards in treachery, tigers in cruelty, and crocodiles, serpents, owls and bats, according to the nature of those animals. Those who are such also appear, in the spiritual world, at a distance, like those wild beasts; their love of evil thus exhibits itself.

14. VII. That the Man who does not acknowledge a God, is excommunicated from the Church, and condemned.

That the man who does not acknowledge a God, is excommunicated from the church, is because God is the all of the church, and divine things, which are called theological, constitute the church; wherefore a denial of God is a denial of all things of the church; and this denial itself excommunicates him; thus the man himself, and not God, is the author of his excommunication. He is also condemned, because whosoever is excommunicated from the church, is also excommunicated from heaven; for the church upon earth, and the angelic heaven, make one, like the internal and external, and ike the spiritual and natural in man For man was so created by God that, as to his internal, he may be in the spiritual world, and as to his external, in the natural world; thus he is created a native of both worlds, in order that the spiritual, which is of heaven, may be implanted in the natural, which is of the earth, as is the case with seed in the ground; and thus man may acquire a fixed and everlasting existence. The man who, by a denial of God, has excommunicated himself from the church, and thus from heaven, has closed up his internal man as to the will, and thus as to his genial love; for the will of man is the receptacle of his love, and becomes its habitation. But he cannot close up his internal man, as to the understanding; for, if he could and should do this, the man would be no longer man. But the love of the will infatuates the superior parts of the understanding; whence the understanding becomes, as it were, closed as to the truths which are of faith, and as to the goods which are of charity; thus more and more against God, and, at the same time, against the spiritual things of the church; and thus he is excluded from communion with the angels of heaven; and, when thus excluded, he enters into communion with the satans of hell, and thinks in unity with them; and as all satans deny a God, and think foolishly concerning God and the spiritual things of the church, so also does the man who is conjoined with them. When he is in his spirit, as he is when left to himself at home, he suffers his thoughts to be led by the delights of the evil and the false, which he has conceived and brought forth in himself; and then he thinks that there is no God, but that what is called God is only a word resounding from pulpits, to bind the common people to obedience to the laws of justice, which are laws of society. He also thinks that the Word, from which ministers proclaim a God, is a collection of visionary stories, the sanctity of which is derived from authority; and that the Decalogue, or Catechism, is a little book, which, after it has been handled by children, may be thrown away; for it teaches that we should honor our parents, that we should not do murder, nor commit adultery, nor steal, nor bear false testimony; and who does not know the same things from the civil law? Concerning the church, he thinks it is a congregation of weak, simple and credulous people, who see what they do not see. Respecting man, and himself as a man, he thinks as he does of a beast; concerning his life after death, he thinks it will be like that of a beast after death. Thus his internal man thinks, however differently the external man speaks; for, as was said, every man has an internal and an external; and his internal constitutes the man, which is called the *spirit*, and lives after death; and the external, in which, by a semblance of morality, he plays the hypocrite, is buried, and then, on account of his denial of God, he is condemned. Every man, as to his spirit, is consociated with his like in the spiritual world, and is as one with them; and it has often been given me to see the spirits of persons still living, some in angelic societies, and some in infernal societies; and I have also been permitted to converse with them for several days; and have wondered that man himself, while he lives in his body, should know nothing at all of this. Thence it appeared, that whoever denies a God, is already among the condemned; and, after death, he is gathered to his companions.

15. VIII. That with Men who do not acknowledge one God, but several, nothing of the Church coheres.

He who in faith acknowledges, and in heart worships, one God, is in the communion of saints on earth, and in the communion of angels in heaven; they are called *communions*, and they are so because they are in one God, and one God is in them. The same are also in conjunction with the whole angelic heaven, and I might venture to say with all and every one there, for they are all as the children and posterity of one father, whose minds, manners and faces are similar, so that they mutually recognise each other. The angelic heaven is arranged into societies according to all the varieties of the love of good; which varieties aim at one most universal love, which is love to God; from this love are propagated all those who in faith acknowledge, and in heart worship, one God, the Creator of the universe, and at the same time the Redeemer and Regenerator. But the case is altogether different with those who do not approach and worship one God, but several; and also with those who profess one with their lips, and at the same time think of three, as do those in the church at this day, who distinguish God into three persons, and declare that each person by himself is God, and attribute to each separate qualities or properties, which do not belong to either of the others. Hence it comes to pass, that not only the unity of God is actually divided, but also theology itself, and likewise the human mind, in which it should reside; what thence can result but perplexity and incoherency in the things of the church? That such is the state of the church at this day, will be demonstrated in the Appendix to this work. The truth is, that the division of God, or of the Divine essence, into three persons, each of which, by himself, or singly, is God, leads to the denial of God. It is as if any one should enter a temple in order to worship, and should see, in a picture upon the altar, one God painted as the Ancient of days, another as the High Priest, and a third as the flying Æolus, with this inscription, "*These three are one God;*" or as if he should there see the Unity and Trinity painted as a man with three heads upon one body, or with three bodies under one head, which is the form of a monster. If any one should enter heaven with such an idea, he would certainly be cast out headlong, although he should say that the head or heads signified essence, and he body or bodies. distinct properties.

16. To the above I shall add one RELATION [MEMORABILE]. I saw some new comers from the natural into the spiritual world, talking together about three Divine Persons from eternity; they were dignitaries of the church, and one of them a bishop. They came up to me, and, after some conversation concerning the spiritual world, of which they before had not known any thing, I said, "I heard you talking about three Divine Persons from eternity; and I beseech you to open to me this great mystery, according to your ideas which you conceived in the natural world, whence you have lately come." Then the primate, looking at me, said, "I see that you are a layman; wherefore I will open the ideas of my thought concerning this mystery, and teach you. My ideas always have been, and still are, that God the Father, God the So., and God the Holy Ghost, sit in the midst of heaven, upon magnificent and lofty seats or thrones; God the Father, upon a throne of the finest gold, with a sceptre in his hand; God the Son, at his right hand, upon a throne of the purest silver, with a crown on his head; and God the Holy Ghost, near them, upon a throne of shining crystal, holding a dove in his hand; and that lamps, hanging round about them in triple order, were glittering with precious stones; and that, at a distance from this circus, were standing innumerable angels, all worshipping, and singing praises; and, moreover, that God the Father is continually conversing with his Son concerning those who are to be justified; and that they together decree and determine who, upon earth, were worthy to be received among the angels, and crowned with eternal life; and that God the Holy Ghost, having heard their names, instantly hastens to them over all parts of the earth, carrying with him the gifts of righteousness, as so many tokens of salvation for those who are to be justified; and, as soon as he arrives, and breathes upon them, he disperses their sins, as a ventilator disperses the smoke out of a furnace, and makes it

white; and also he takes away from their hearts the hardness of stone, puts into them the softness of flesh; and, at the same time, he renews their spirits or minds, and regenerates them, and induces upon them the countenances of infants; and, at last, marks their foreheads with the sign of the cross,' and calls them the *elect*, and *children of God*." The primate, having finished this discourse, said to me, "Thus I unravelled this great mystery in the world; and, because most of our order there applauded my sentiments on this subject, I am persuaded that you also, who are a layman, will acquiesce in them." After these things were said by the primate, I looked at him, and, at the same time, at the dignitaries with him, and observed that they all favored him with their full assent: wherefore I began to reply, and said, "I have well considered the exposition of your faith, and have thence collected, that you have conceived, and still cherish, a merely natural and sensual, yea, material idea concerning the triune God, whence inevitably flows the idea of three Gods. Is it not to think sensually of God the Father, that He sits upon a throne with a sceptre in his hand? and of the Son, that He sits upon his throne with a crown on his head? and of the Holy Ghost, that He sits upon his, with a dove in his hand, and that, in obedience to the decrees of the two former, He runs over all the world? And because such an idea thence results, I cannot believe what you have declared; for, from my infancy, I have not been able to admit into my mind any other idea than that of ONE GOD, and since I have received, and still retain, this idea only, all that you have said has no weight with me. And then I saw that, by the throne upon which, according to the Scripture, Jehovah is said to sit, is meant the kingdom; by the sceptre and crown, government and dominion; by sitting on the right hand, the omnipotence of God by means of his Human; and by those things which are related of the Holy Spirit, the operations of the Divine omnipresence. Assume, sir, if you please, the idea of ONE GOD, and revolve it well in your rational mind [*ratiocinio*], and you will at length clearly perceive that it is so. Indeed, you also say, that there is one God, and this because you make the essence of those three persons one and indivisible; yet you do not allow any one to say, that the one God is one person, but that there are still three; and this you do, lest the idea of three Gods, such as yours is, should be lost; and you also ascribe to each a character separate from that of another: do you not thus divide your Divine essence? Since it is so, how can you, at the same time, think that God is one? I could forgive you, if you should say, that the Divine is one. When any one hears, that *the Father is God, the Son is God, the Holy Ghost is God, and that each Person singly is God*, how can he conceive that God is one? Is it not a contradiction which can never be believed? That they cannot be said to be one God, but to be of a similar Divine, may be illustrated by these examples:—It cannot be said of several men, who compose one senate, synod, or council, that they are one man; but while they are all and each of them of one opinion, it may be said, that they think one thing. Neither can it be said of three diamonds of one substance, that they are one diamond, but that they are one as to substance, and also each diamond differs from the others in value, according to its own weight; but it would not be so, if they were one, and not three. But I perceive that the reason why you say, that the three persons, each of whom, by himself, or singly, is God, are one God, and why you insist, that every one in the church should thus speak, is, that sound and enlightened reason, throughout the whole world, acknowledges that God is one; and therefore you would be covered with shame, if you should not also speak in like manner. But even while you utter with your lips one God, although you entertain the idea of three, still that shame does not keep those two forms of expression within your lips, but you speak them out." After this conversation, the bishop retired with his clerical attendants, and, in retiring, he turned about, and wished to exclaim, "There is one God;" but he could not, because his thought drew back his tongue; and then, with open mouth, he breathed out, "three Gods." Those who were standing by, laughed at the strange sight, and departed.

17. Afterwards, I inquired where I might find, amongst the learned, those who are of the most acute genius, and who stand for a Divine Trinity, divided into three persons: and there came three, to whom I said, "How can you divide the Divine Trinity into three persons, and assert that each person, by himself, or singly, is God and Lord? Is not such a confession of the mouth, that God is one, as distant from the thought, as the south is from the north?" To which they replied, "It is not, in the least, because the three persons have one essence, and the Divine Essence is God. We were, in the world, tutors of a Trinity of persons; and the pupil under our care was our faith, in which each divine person has his office: God the Father, the office of imputation and donation; God the Son, that of intercession and mediation; and God the Holy Ghost, that of effecting the uses of imputation and mediation." But I asked, "What do you mean by the Divine Essence?" They said, "We mean omnipotence, omniscience, omnipresence, immensity, eternity, equality of majesty." To which I said, "If that essence out of several Gods makes One, you may add still more, as for example, a fourth, who is mentioned in Moses, Job, and Ezekiel, and is called God Schaddai. In like manner also did the ancients in Greece and Italy, who ascribed equal attributes and a similar essence to their gods, as to Saturn, Jupiter, Neptune, Pluto, Apollo, Juno, Diana, Minerva, yea, even to Mercury and Venus; but still they could not say that all those were one God. And also you, who are three, and, as I perceive, of similar learning, and so of similar essence as to that, still are not able to combine yourselves into one learned man." But at this they laughed, saying, "You are jesting it is otherwise with the Divine Essence; this is one, and not tripartite, and it is indivisible, and so not divided, it is not a subject of partition and division." To this I rejoined, "Let us descend into this arena, and dispute;" and I asked, "What do you mean by *person*, and what does that word signify?" And they said, "*The name of a person signifies not any part or quality in another, but what subsists in one's own self* [proprie subsistit]. Thus all the principal doctors of the church define *person*, and we agree with them." And I said, "Is this the definition of *person?*" And they replied, "It is." To which I answered, "Then there is not any part of the Father in the Son, nor any of either in the Holy Ghost; whence it follows, that each has his peculiar choice, right and power; and so there is not any thing which joins them together except the will, which is proper to each, and thus communicable at pleasure: are not the three persons thus three distinct Gods? Again, you have also defined *person*, that it is what subsists in one's own self: consequently it follows that there are three substances into which you divide the Divine Essence; and yet this, as you also say, is incapable of division, because it is one and indivisible; and, moreover, to each substance, that is, to each person, you attribute properties which are not in another, and which cannot be communicated to another, such as imputation, mediation and operation; and what else thence results, than that the three persons are three Gods?" At these words they withdrew, saying, "We will canvass [*ventilabimur*] these things, and, having canvassed, we will answer." There stood by a certain wise man, who, hearing these things, said, "I do not wish, by such subtle speculations [*subtiles transennas*], to look into this high subject; but without those subtilties, I see in clear light, that, in the ideas of your thought, there are three Gods; but, because it would be to your shame to publish them to all the world (for if you should publish

them, you would be called madmen and idiots), therefore, to avoid that disgrace, it is expedient for you to confess with your lips one God." But the three disputants, still tenacious of their own opinion, paid no attention to these words; and, in going away, they muttered out some terms borrowed from the science of metaphysics, whence I perceived, that that science was their tripod, from which they wished to give answers.

CONCERNING THE DIVINE ESSE, WHICH IS JEHOVAH.

18. WE shall treat first of the Divine Esse, and afterwards of the Divine Essence. It appears as if these two were one and the same; but still *esse* is more universal than *essence*, for an *essence* supposes an *esse*, and from *esse* essence is derived. The Esse of God, or the Divine Esse, cannot be described, because it is above every idea of human thought, into which nothing else falls, than what is created and finite, but not what is uncreate and infinite, thus not the Divine Esse. The Divine Esse is Esse itself, from which all things are, and which must be in all things, that they may be. A further notion of the Divine Esse may flow in from the following articles: I. *That the one God is called Jehovah from Esse, thus from this, because He alone is, was, and will be, and because He is the First and the Last, the Beginning and the End, the Alpha and the Omega.* II. *That the one God is Substance itself and Form itself, and that angels and men are substances and forms from Him, and that as far as they are in Him and He in them, so far they are images and likenesses of Him.* III. *That the Divine Esse is Esse in itself, and at the same time Existere in itself.* IV. *That the Divine Esse and Existere in itself cannot produce another Divine, that is Esse and Existere in itself; consequently, that another God of the same essence is not possible* [dabilis]. V. *That a plurality of gods amongst the ancients, and also amongst the moderns, existed from no other cause, than from not understanding the Divine Esse.* But these articles are to be elucidated one by one

19. I. THAT THE ONE GOD IS CALLED JEHOVAH FROM ESSE, THUS FROM THIS, BECAUSE HE ALONE IS AND WILL BE; AND BECAUSE HE IS THE FIRST AND THE LAST, THE BEGINNING AND THE END, THE ALPHA AND THE OMEGA.

That *Jehovah* signifies I AM and TO BE, is known; and that God was so called from the most ancient times, is evident from the book of creation, or Genesis, where, in the first chapter, He is called *God*, but in the second and the following, *Jehovah God;* and afterwards, when the descendants of Abraham by Jacob, during their sojourning in Egypt, forgot the name of God, it was recalled to their remembrance; concerning which it is thus written: *Moses said unto God What is thy name? God said, I AM THAT I AM. Thus shalt thou say to the children of Israel, I AM hath sent me unto you; and thou shalt say, Jehovah, the God of your fathers, hath sent me to you; this is my name forever, and this my memorial from generation to generation*, Exod. iii. 14, 15. Since God alone is the I AM, and the Esse or Jehovah, therefore there is not any thing in the created universe, which does not derive its esse from Him; but in what manner, will be seen below. The same is also meant by these words: *I am the First and the Last, the Beginning and the End, the Alpha and the Omega*, Isaiah xliv. 6; and Rev. i. 8, 11; xxii. 13; by which is signified, Who is the Itself and the Only from firsts to lasts, from which are all things.

That God is called the Alpha and the Omega, the Beginning and the End, is because Alpha is the first, and Omega is the last letter in the Greek alphabet; and thence they signify all things in the complex: the reason is, because every alphabetic letter, in the spiritual world, signifies some thing; and a vowel, which serves for sound, something of affection or love: from this origin is spiritual or angelic speech, and also writing, there. But this is an arcanum hitherto unknown; for there is a universal language, in which all angels and spirits are; and this has nothing in common with any language of men in the world: every man comes into this language after death, for it is implanted in every man from creation; wherefore all can understand each other throughout the whole spiritual world. It has been given me often to hear that language, and I have compared it with languages in the world, and have found that it does not, even in the least degree, make one with any natural language upon earth: it differs from them in its first principle, which is, that every letter of every word signifies a thing. Thence, now, it is, that God is called the Alpha and the Omega, by which is signified, that He is the Itself and the Only from firsts to lasts, from which are all things. But concerning this language, and the writing of it, flowing from the spiritual thought of angels, see in the work concerning CONJUGIAL LOVE, n. 326 to 329, and also in the following pages.

20. II. THAT THE ONE GOD IS SUBSTANCE ITSELF AND FORM ITSELF, AND THAT ANGELS AND MEN ARE SUBSTANCES AND FORMS FROM HIM; AND AS FAR AS THEY ARE IN HIM AND HE IN THEM, SO FAR THEY ARE IMAGES AND LIKENESSES OF HIM.

Since God is *Esse*, He is also Substance, for an *esse*, unless it be a substance, is only an ideal entity [*ens rationis*]; for substance, is a subsisting entity; and whoever is a substance is also a form, for substance unless it be a form, is an ideal entity; wherefore both can be predicated of God, but so that He may be the only, the very, and the first Substance and Form. That this form is the very Human, that is, that God is very Man, all things of whom are infinite, is demonstrated in the ANGELIC WISDOM CONCERNING THE DIVINE LOVE AND THE DIVINE WISDOM, published at Amsterdam in the year 1763: in like manner, that angels and men are substances and forms, created and organized for receiving the Divine, flowing into them through heaven; wherefore, in the book of Creation, they are called *images* and *likenesses of God*, i. 26, 27; and in other places, *His sons*, and *born of Him:* but in the course of this work, it will be fully demonstrated, that, in proportion as man lives under the Divine auspices, that is, suffers himself to be led by God, so far he becomes an image of Him, more and more interiorly. Unless an idea be formed of God, that he is the first substance and form, and of his form, that it is the very human, the minds of men would readily imbibe idle fancies, like spectres, concerning God himself, the origin of man, and the creation of the world: of God they would conceive no other notion than as of the nature of the universe in its firsts, thus of the expanse of the universe, or as of emptiness or nothing; of the origin of men, as of the conflux of the elements into such a form by chance; of the creation of the world, that the origin of its substances and forms is from points, then from geometrical lines, which, because they are of no predication, are therefore in themselves not any thing. With such persons, every thing of the church is like the Styx, or the darkness of Tartarus.

21. III. THAT THE DIVINE ESSE IS ESSE IN ITSELF, AND, AT THE SAME TIME, EXISTERE IN ITSELF.

That Jehovah God is Esse in itself, is because He is the I AM, the Itself, the Only and the First, from eternity to eternity, from which every thing is which is, that it may be something; and thus, and not otherwise, He is the Beginning and the End, the First and the Last, and the Alpha and the Omega. It cannot be said that his Esse is from itself, because THIS FROM ITSELF supposes what is prior, and thus time, which is not applicable to Infinite, which is called from eternity; and also it supposes another God, who is God in himself, thus a God from God, or that God formed himself, and so could not be uncreate or infinite, because thus He made himself finite from himself or from another. From this, that God is Esse in itself, it follows, that He is Love in itself, Wisdom in itself, and Life in itself, and that He is the Itself, from which are all things, and to which all things refer themselves, that they may be something. That God is Life in itself, and thus God, is evident from the words of the Lord in John, v. 26; and in Isaiah, *I Jehovah make all things, and spread out the heavens alone, and stretch out the earth by myself*, xliv. 24; and that *He alone is God, and beside Him there is no God*, xlv. 14, 15, 20, 21; Hosea, xiii. 4.

That God is not only Esse in itself, but also Existere in itself, is because an esse, unless it exist, is not any thing; and, in like manner, an existere, unless it be from an esse; wherefore, one being given, the other is given: in like manner, a substance is not any thing, unless it be also a form; of a substance, unless it be a form, nothing can be predicated; and this, because it has no quality, is in itself nothing. The reason why *Esse* and *Existere* are here used, and not *Essence* and *Existence*, is because a distinction is to be made between *Esse* and *Essence*, and thence between *Existere* and *Existence*, as between what is prior and what is posterior; and what is prior is more universal than what is posterior. Infinity and eternity are applicable to the Divine Esse, but to the Divine Essence and Existence divine love and divine wisdom are applicable, and, by means of these two, omnipotence and omnipresence; of which, therefore, we shall treat in their order.

22. That God is the Itself, the Only, and the First, which is called Esse and Existere in itself, from which are all things that are and exist, the natural man, by his own reason, cannot possibly discover; for the natural man by his own reason, can apprehend nothing else than what is of nature; for this squares with his essence, because, from his infancy and childhood, nothing else has entered into it. But since man is so created that he may also be spiritual, because he is about to live after death, and then amongst the spiritual in their world, therefore God has provided the Word, in which He has not only revealed himself, but also that there is a heaven and a hell; and that in one or the other of these every man is about to live to eternity, each according to his life and his faith at the same time. He has also revealed in the Word, that He is the I AM, or the Esse, and the Itself, and the Only, which is in itself, and so the First or the Beginning, from which are all things. It is by means of this revelation, that the natural man can elevate himself above nature, thus above himself, and see such things as are of God; but yet only as at a distance, although God is nigh to every man, for He is in him with his essence, and, because it is so, He is nigh to those who love Him; and those love Him who live according to his commandments, and believe in Him these, as it were, see Him; for what is faith, but a spiritual sight that He is? And what is a life according to his commandments, but an actual acknowledgment that from Him is salvation and eternal life? But those who have not spiritual faith, but natural, which is only science, and thence a similar life, see God, indeed, but at a distance, and this only when they are speaking of Him. The difference between the former and the latter, is like that between those who stand in clear light, and see men, and touch them, and those who stand in a thick cloud, from which they cannot distinguish men from trees or stones. Or it is like the difference between those who stand upon a high mountain, where there is a city, and who go hither and thither and talk with their fellow citizens, and those who look down from that mountain and know not whether the objects which they see are men, or beasts, or statues. Nay

it is like that between those who stand upon some planetary orb, and see their companions there; and those who are in another planetary orb, with optical glasses in their hands, and look thither, and say that they see men there, when yet they only see, in general, the earthy parts, as lunar brightness, and the watery parts, as dark spots. Such is the difference between seeing God and the divine things which proceed from Him, as they are in the minds of those who are in faith, and at the same time in the life of charity, and of those who are only in science concerning those things; consequently, such is the difference between natural and spiritual men. But those who deny the divine sanctity of the Word, and still carry the things, which are of religion, as it were, in a sack upon their back, do not see God, but only talk about Him, in a manner but little different from parrots.

23. IV. THAT THE DIVINE ESSE AND EXISTERE IN ITSELF, CANNOT PRODUCE ANOTHER DIVINE, THAT IS ESSE AND EXISTERE IN ITSELF; CONSEQUENTLY, THAT ANOTHER GOD OF THE SAME ESSENCE IS NOT POSSIBLE.

That the one God, who is the Creator of the universe, is Esse and Existere in itself, thus God in himself, has already been shown: thence it follows, that a God from God is not possible, because the very essential Divine, which is Esse and Existere itself, is in him incommunicable. It is the same, whether he be said to be begotten by God, or to proceed from Him; in either case, he would be produced by God, and this differs but little from being created. Wherefore, to introduce into the church the faith that there are three divine persons, each of whom singly is God, and of the same essence, and one born from eternity, and a third proceeding from eternity, is altogether to abolish the idea of the unity of God, and with this all notion of Divinity, and so to cause all the SPIRITUAL of reason to be banished into exile; thence man becomes no longer man, but altogether natural, and differs from a beast only in possessing the power of speech; and he is opposed to all the spiritual things of the church, for these the natural man calls foolishness; hence, and hence alone, have originated such enormous heresies concerning God. Wherefore a Divine Trinity, divided into persons, has brought into the church not only night, but also death. That an identity of three Divine Essences is an offence to reason, appeared evident to me from the angels, who said, that they could not even utter *three equal Divinities;* and if any one should come to them, and wish to utter that expression, he could not but turn away himself; and after having given it utterance, he would become like the trunk of a man, and would be cast out, and afterwards would go away to those in hell who do not acknowledge any God. The truth is, that, to implant in infants and children an idea of three divine persons, to which inevitably adheres the idea of three Gods, is to take away from them all spiritual milk, and afterwards all spiritual meat, and lastly all spiritual reason, and to induce upon those, who confirm themselves in it, spiritual death. Those, who in faith and in heart worship one God, the Creator of the universe, and Him at the same time the Redeemer and Regenerator, are as the city of Zion was in the time of David, and as the city of Jerusalem in the time of Solomon, after the temple was built; but the church which believes in three persons, and in each as a distinct God, is like the city of Zion and Jerusalem destroyed by Vespasian, and the temple there burnt. Moreover, the man who worships one God, in whom is the Divine Trinity, thus who is one Person, becomes more and more a living and angelic man; but he who confirms himself in a plurality of Gods, from a plurality of persons, becomes, by degrees, like a statue made with movable joints, in the midst of which Satan stands, and speaks through its artificial mouth.

24. V. THAT A PLURALITY OF GODS, IN ANCIENT AND ALSO IN MODERN TIMES, ORIGINATED FROM NO

OTHER CAUSE THAN FROM NOT UNDERSTANDING THE DIVINE ESSE.

That the unity of God is most intimately inscribed on the mind of every man, since it is in the midst of all things which flow into the soul of man from God, has been shown above, n. 8.; but that still, it has not descended into the human understanding, is because there was a want of the knowledges by means of which man ought to ascend to meet God; for every one should prepare the way for God, that is, should prepare himself for reception, and this should be done by means of knowledges. The knowledges which have hitherto been wanting to enable the human understanding to penetrate where it might see that God is one, and that only one Divine Esse is possible, and that all things of nature are from that Esse, are the following: 1. That hitherto no one has known any thing concerning the spiritual world, where spirits and angels are, and into which every man comes after death. 2. Also that in that world, there is a sun, which is pure love from Jehovah God, who is in the midst of it. 3. That from that sun proceeds heat, which in its essence is love, and light, which in its essence is wisdom. 4. That thence all things, which are in that world, are spiritual, and affect the internal man, and form his will and understanding. 5. That Jehovah God, out of his sun, not only produced the spiritual world, and all the spiritual things of it, which are innumerable and substantial, but that he also produced the natural world, and all the natural things of it, which are also innumerable, but material. 6. That hitherto no one has known the distinction between what is spiritual and what is natural, nor even what the spiritual is, in its essence. 7. Nor that there are three degrees of love and wisdom, according to which the angelic heavens are arranged. 8. And that the human mind is distinguished into the same number of degrees, to the end that it may be elevated after death into one of the heavens, which is effected according to his life and faith conjointly. 9. And, finally, that not a single particle of all those things could have existed, but from the Divine Esse, which is the Itself in itself, and so the First, and the Beginning, from which are all things. These knowledges have hitherto been wanting; yet they are the means by which man may ascend and know the Divine Esse. It is said, that man ascends; but it is meant that he is elevated by God; for man has free will, and the faculty of procuring for himself knowledges, and as he procures them for himself from the Word, by means of the understanding, he thus prepares a way by which God may descend, and elevate him. The knowledges by means of which the human understanding ascends, being upheld and led by God, may be compared to the steps of the ladder seen by Jacob, which was *set upon the earth, whose head reached to heaven, and by which the angels ascended, and Jehovah stood above it*, Genesis xxviii. 12, 13. But it is quite otherwise when those knowledges are wanting, or when man despises them; then the elevation of the understanding may be compared to a ladder, raised from the ground to the windows of the first story of a magnificent palace, where men have their habitations, and not to the windows of the second story, where spirits are, and still less to the windows of the third story, where angels are. Thence it is, that man abides in the atmospheres and material things of nature, in which he keeps his eyes, ears and nostrils; from which he derives no other ideas of heaven, and of the Esse and Essence of God, than such as are atmospherical and material; and whilst a man thinks from these, he does not form any judgment concerning God, whether He exists or not, or whether He is one or more; and still less what He is as to his Esse and as to his Essence. Thence arose a plurality of gods in ancient and also in modern times.

---

25. To the above I shall add this RELATION [*Memorabile*]. Some time since, being awaked from sleep, I fell into profound meditation concerning

God; and when I looked up, I saw above me, in heaven, a very bright light, in an oval form; and when I fixed my eyes upon that light, the light receded to the sides, and entered into the circumferences; and then, lo, heaven was opened to me, and I saw magnificent things, and angels standing in the form of a circle on the southern side of the opening, and they were talking together; and because I had an ardent desire to hear what they were talking about, it was therefore given me first to hear a sound, which was full of heavenly love, and afterwards their speech, which was full of wisdom from that love. They were talking together about the ONE GOD, and about CONJUNCTION WITH HIM, and thence SALVATION. They spoke ineffable things, most of which cannot be expressed in the words of any natural language; but because I had sometimes been in company with angels in that heaven, and then in a similar speech with them, because in a similar state, I was therefore able now to understand them, and to select from their discourse some things which may be rationally expressed in the words of natural language. They said that the DIVINE ESSE IS ONE, THE SAME, THE ITSELF, AND INDIVIDUAL. This they illustrated by spiritual ideas, saying that the Divine Esse cannot be communicated to several, each of whom has the Divine Esse, and still that be One, the Same, the Itself, and Indivisible; for each one would think from his own Esse from himself, and singly by himself; if then from others and by others, unanimously, there would be several unanimous Gods, and not one God; for unanimity, because it is the agreement of several, and at the same time of each one from himself, and by himself, does not agree with the unity of God, but with a plurality—they did not say *of Gods*, because they could not; for the light of heaven, from which was their thought, and the aura in which their discourse was uttered, opposed it. They said also, that when they wished to pronounce the word *Gods*, and each one as a person by himself, the effort of pronouncing was instantly directed to One, yea, to the Only God. To this they added, that the Divine Esse is a DIVINE ESSE IN ITSELF, not from itself; because *from itself* supposes an Esse in itself, from another prior; thus it supposes a God from God, which is not possible. What is from God is not called *God*, but is called *Divine;* for what is a God from God? thus, what is a God born of God from eternity? and what is a God proceeding from God through a God born from eternity, but words in which there is nothing of light from heaven? They said, moreover, that the Divine Esse, which in itself is God, is the SAME, not the same simple, but infinite; that is, the Same from eternity to eternity: it is the Same every where, and the Same with every one, and in every one; but that all variableness and changeableness is in the recipient; the state of the recipient causes this. That the Divine Esse, which is God in himself, is the ITSELF, they illustrated thus: God is the Itself, because He is Love itself and Wisdom itself, or because He is Good itself and Truth itself, and thence Life itself, which, unless they were the Itself in God, they would not be any thing in heaven and the world, because there would not be any thing of them relative to the Itself. Every quality has its quality from that which is the Itself from which it is, and to which it refers itself that it may be such. This Itself, which is the Divine Esse, is not in place, but with those, and in those, who are in place, according to reception; since of Love and Wisdom, or of Good and Truth, and thence of Life, which are the Itself in God, yea, God himself, place cannot be predicated, nor progression from place to place, whence is Omnipresence; wherefore, the Lord says, that *He is in the midst of them;* also that *He is in them, and they in Him.* But because He cannot be received by any, as He is in Himself, He appears as He is in his essence, as a sun above the angelic heavens; the proceeding from which, as light, is Himself as to wisdom, and the proceeding as heat, is Himself as to love; that sun is not Himself, but the Divine Love and the Divine Wisdom, emanating from Him proximately round about Him, appear to the angels as a sun. He within the sun is MAN; He is OUR LORD JESUS CHRIST, both as to the DIVINE FROM WHICH [ARE ALL THINGS], and also as to the DIVINE HUMAN; since the *Itself*, which is Love itself and Wisdom itself, was a soul to Him from the Father; thus the divine life, which is life in itself. It is otherwise in every man; in him the soul is not life, but a recipient of life. The Lord also teaches this, saying, *I am the way, the truth, and the* LIFE*;* and in another place, *As the Father* HATH LIFE IN HIMSELF, *so also hath he given to the Son* TO HAVE LIFE IN HIMSELF, John v. 26. *Life in Himself* is God. To this they added, that those who are in any spiritual light, may perceive from these things, that the Divine Esse, because it is One, the Same, the Itself, and thence Indivisible, cannot be in several; and that, if it should be said to be, manifest contradictions would result.

26. When I had heard these things, the angels perceived in my thought the common ideas of the Christian church, concerning a trinity of persons in unity, and their unity in the trinity relating to God; and also concerning the birth of the Son of God from eternity; and then they said, "What are you thinking? Do you not derive those thoughts from natural light, with which our spiritual light does not agree? Wherefore, unless you remove them from your mind, we shut heaven to you, and depart." But then I said, "Enter, I beseech you, more deeply into my thought, and perhaps you will see an agreement." They did so, and saw that, by three persons, I understood three proceeding divine attributes, which are CREATION, REDEMPTION, and REGENERATION; and that those are attributes of one God; and that, by the birth of the Son of God from eternity, I understood his birth foreseen from eternity, and provided in time; and that it is not above what is natural and rational, but contrary to what is natural and rational, to conceive that any Son was born of God from eternity; but not so, to conceive that the Son, born of God by the Virgin Mary in time, is the only, and the only begotten; and that to believe otherwise is an enormous error. And then I told them that my natural thought concerning the trinity of persons and their unity, and concerning the birth of a Son of God from eternity, was from the doctrine of faith of the church, which has its name from Athanasius. Then the angels said, "Well." And they requested me to say from their mouth, that if any one does not approach the very God of heaven and earth, he cannot come into heaven, because heaven is heaven from Him, the only God, and that this God is Jesus Christ, who is the Lord Jehovah, from eternity Creator, in time Redeemer, and to eternity Regenerator; thus who is the Father, the Son, and the Holy Spirit; and that this is the gospel, which is to be preached. After these things, the heavenly light, which was before seen, returned over the opening, and, by degrees, descended thence, and filled the interiors of my mind, and illustrated my ideas concerning the trinity and unity of God And then I saw the ideas, which I had at first entertained concerning them, and which were merely natural, separated, as chaff is separated from wheat by winnowing, and carried away, as by a wind, to the northern region of heaven, and there dispersed.

CONCERNING THE INFINITY OF GOD, OR HIS IMMENSITY AND ETERNITY.

27. THERE are two things peculiar to the natural world, which cause all things there to be finite: one is SPACE, and the other is TIME; and because that world was created by God, and spaces and times were created togeth-

er with that world, and make it finite, therefore, it is proper to treat of their two beginnings, which are Immensity and Eternity; for the immensity of God has relation to spaces, and his eternity, to times; and his INFINITY comprehends both immensity and eternity. But because infinity transcends what is finite, and the knowledge of it a finite mind, therefore, that it may in some manner be perceived, it is expedient to treat of it in this series: I. *That God is infinite, since He is and exists in Himself, and all things in the universe are and exist from Him.* II. *That God is infinite, since He was before the world, thus before spaces and times arose.* III. *That God, since the world was made, is in space without space, and in time without time.* IV. *That infinity, in relation to spaces, is called immensity, and in relation to times, is called eternity; and that, although there are these relations, still there is nothing of space in his immensity, and nothing of time in his eternity.* V. *That enlightened reason, from very many things in the world, may see the infinity of God the Creator.* VI. *That every created thing is finite, and that the infinite is in finite things, as in its receptacles, and in men as in its images.* But these things shall be explained one by one.

28. I. THAT GOD IS INFINITE, SINCE HE IS AND EXISTS IN HIMSELF, AND ALL THINGS IN THE UNIVERSE ARE AND EXIST FROM HIM.

It has already been shown, that God is One, and that He is the Itself, and that He is the first Esse of all things, and that all things which are, exist, and subsist in the universe, are from Him; thence it follows, that He is infinite. That human reason may see this from very many things in the created universe, will be demonstrated in the sequel. But, although the human mind, from those things, may acknowledge, that the first Being, or the first Esse, is infinite, still it cannot know what that is, and, therefore, it cannot define it otherwise, than that it is the Infinite All, and that it subsists in itself, and thence that it is the very and the only Substance, and, because nothing is predicable of a substance, unless it be a form, that it is the very and the only Form. But still what are these things? It does not thus appear what the Infinite is; for the human mind, however highly analytical and elevated, is itself finite, and what is finite in it cannot be removed; wherefore, it is by no means capable of seeing the infinity of God, as it is in itself, thus God; but it may see Him in the shade behind, as it was said to Moses, while he prayed to see God, that he was put in the hole of a rock, and saw his back parts, *Exod.* xxxiii. 20 to 28. By the *back parts* of God are meant the things visible in the world, and, in particular, the things perceptible in the Word. Hence it appears, that it is vain to wish to know what God is in his *esse* or in his *substance;* but that it is enough to acknowledge Him from finite, that is created things, in which He is infinitely. Whosoever is anxious to know more, may be compared to a fish drawn out into the air, or to a bird put into the receiver of an air-pump, which, as the air is pumped out, gasps for breath, and at last expires. He may also be compared to a ship, which, when it is overcome by a tempest, and does not obey the rudder, is carried upon the rocks and quicksands. So it is with those who wish to know the infinity of God from within, not contented that they may acknowledge it from without, from manifest tokens. It is related of a certain philosopher amongst the ancients, that he cast himself into the sea, because he could not see, in the light of his mind, or comprehend, the eternity of the world; what would he have done, if he had desired to comprehend the infinity of God?

29. II. THAT GOD IS INFINITE, SINCE HE WAS BEFORE THE WORLD, THUS BEFORE SPACES AND TIMES AROSE.

In the natural world, there are times and spaces, but in the spiritual world, not so actually, but still apparently. The reason why times and spaces were introduced into the worlds, was, that one thing might be distinguished from another, great from small, many from few; thus quantity from quantity, and so quality from quality; and that, by means of them, the senses of the body might be able to distinguish their objects, and the senses of the mind theirs, and thus might be affected, think and choose. Times were introduced into the natural world by the rotation of the earth about its axis, and by the progression of those rotations, from station to station, along the zodiac; while these changes appear to be made by the sun, from which the whole terraqueous globe derives its heat and light. Thence are the times of the day, which are morning, noon, evening and night; and the times of the year, which are spring, summer, autumn, and winter; the times of days, according to light and darkness, and the times of years, according to heat and cold. But spaces were introduced into the natural world, by the earth's being formed into a globe, and filled with various kinds of matter, the parts of which were distinguished from each other, and at the same time extended. But in the spiritual world, there are not material spaces, and times corresponding with them; but still there are appearances of them, which appearances are according to the differences of the states, in which are the minds of spirits and angels there; wherefore, times and spaces there conform themselves to the affections of their will, and thence to the thoughts of their understanding; but those appearances are real, because constant, according to their state. The common opinion concerning the state of souls after death, and thence also of angels and spirits, is, that they are not in any extense, and, consequently, not in space and time; according to which idea, it is said of souls after death, that they are in an undetermined somewhere, and that spirits and angels are aërial beings [*pneumata*], of which no other idea is entertained, than as of ether, air, vapor, or wind; when, nevertheless, they are substantial men, and live together, like men of the natural world, upon spaces and in times, which, as was said, are determined according to the states of their minds. If it were not so, that is, if there were no spaces and times, that whole world, where souls are gathered after death, and where spirits and angels dwell, might be drawn through the eye of a needle, or concentrated upon the point of a single hair. This would be possible, if there were no substantial extense there; but since this is there, therefore angels dwell as separately and distinctly from each other, yea, more distinctly, than men who have a material extense. But times there are not distinguished into days, weeks, months and years, because the sun there does not appear to rise and set, nor to revolve, but it remains stationary in the east, in the middle degree between the zenith and the horizon. They also have spaces, because all things in that world are substantial, as in the natural world they are material; but concerning these things, more will be said in the Lemma of this chapter concerning Creation. From what has been said above, it may be comprehended, that spaces and times make finite all and every thing in both worlds, and thence that men are finite, not only as to their bodies, but also as to their souls; and in like manner angels and spirits. From all these things it may be concluded, that God is infinite, that is, not finite; because He, as the Creator, Maker and Former of the universe, made all things finite; and He made them finite by means of his sun, in the midst of which He is, and which consists of the divine essence, which proceeds as a sphere from Him. There and thence is the first of finiteness, and its progression extends even to ultimates in the nature of the world. It follows, that He in Himself is infinite, because He is uncreated. But what is infinite appears to man as not any thing, because man is finite, and thinks from what is finite; wherefore, if what is finite which adheres to his thought, were taken away, it would seem to him as if the residue were not any thing: yet the truth is, that God is infinitely all, and that man, respectively, is of himself not any thing.

30. III. THAT GOD, SINCE THE WORLD WAS MADE, IS IN SPACE WITHOUT SPACE, AND IN TIME WITHOUT TIME.

That God, and the Divine which proceeds immediately from him, is not in space, although he is omnipresent, and with every man in the world, and with every angel in heaven, and with every spirit under heaven, cannot be comprehended by a merely natural idea, but it may, in some degree, by a spiritual idea. The reason why it cannot be comprehended by a merely natural idea, is because in that idea there is space; for it is formed from such things as are in the world, in all and in every one of which, that is visible to the eye, there is space: every thing great and small there is of space; every thing long, broad and high there is of space; in a word, every measure, figure, and form there is of space. But still man may, in some degree, comprehend this by natural thought, provided he admit into it something of spiritual light. But, in the first place, something shall be said concerning an idea of spiritual thought; this derives nothing from space, but it derives its all from state. State is predicated of love, of life, of wisdom, of affections, of joys, in general of good and truth; a truly spiritual idea concerning those things has nothing in common with space; it is above, and looks down upon the ideas of space under it, as heaven looks down upon the earth The reason why God is present in space without space, and in time without time, is because God is always the same from eternity to eternity; thus such before the world was created as after it; and in God, and in the sight of God, there were no spaces nor times before creation, but after it; wherefore, because He is the same, He is in space without space, and in time without time: thence it follows that nature is separate from Him, and yet He is omnipresent in it; scarcely otherwise than as life is in every substantial and material part of man, although it does not mingle itself with them; comparatively as light in the eye, sound in the ear, taste in the tongue, or as ether in the land and water, by means of which the terraqueous globe is held together, and made to revolve, and so on; and if these agents should be taken away, the substantial and material subjects would in a moment fall to pieces or be destroyed; yea, the human mind, if God were not every where and at all times present in it, would be dissipated, like a bubble in the air, and both spheres of the brain, in which it acts from its principles, would go off into froth, and thus every thing human would become dust of the earth, or an odor flying in the atmosphere. Since God is in all time without time, therefore, in his Word, He speaks of the past, and of the future, in the present, as in Isaiah; *A Child is born to us; a Son is given to us, whose name is Hero, the Prince of Peace*, ix. 6; and in David; *I will announce concerning the statute, Jehovah said to me, Thou art my Son; to-day have I begotten Thee*, Psalm ii. 7. These words are concerning the Lord, who was about to come: wherefore it is also said in the same, *A thousand years in thy sight are as yesterday*, Psalm xc. 4. That God is every where present in the whole world, and yet not any thing proper to the world is in Him, that is, not any thing which is of space and time, may be clearly seen from very many other passages in the Word, by those who see and search, as from this passage in Jeremiah: *Am not I a God at hand, and not a God afar off? Will a man be hidden in coverts, that I may not see him? Do not I fill all heaven and all the earth?* xxiii. 23, 24.

31. IV. THAT THE INFINITY OF GOD IN RELATION TO SPACES IS CALLED IMMENSITY, AND IN RELATION TO TIMES IT IS CALLED ETERNITY; AND THAT, ALTHOUGH THERE ARE THESE RELATIONS, STILL THERE IS NOTHING OF SPACE IN HIS IMMENSITY, AND NOTHING OF TIME IN HIS ETERNITY.

That the infinity of God, in relation to spaces, is called *immensity*, is because *immense* is predicated of whatsoever is great and large, and also of what is extended, and in this of what is spacious. But that the infinity of God, in relation to times, is called *eternity*, is because the phrase "*to eternity*" is predicated of things progressive without end, which are measured by times; as for example, the things which are of space are predicated of the terraqueous globe viewed in itself; and the things which are of time are predicated of its rotation and progression; the latter also make times, and the former make spaces; and they are thus presented by the senses in the perception of reflecting minds. But in God there is nothing of space and time, as was shown above; and yet their beginnings are from God; thence it follows, that his infinity, in relation to spaces, is meant by immensity; and his infinity, in relation to times, is meant by eternity. But in heaven, the angels understand by the immensity of God, his Divinity as to Esse, and by eternity, his Divinity as to Existere; and also by immensity, the Divinity as to love, and by eternity, the Divinity as to wisdom. The reason is, because the angels abstract spaces and times from the Divinity, and then those notions result. But since man cannot think otherwise than from ideas derived from such things as are of space and time, he cannot perceive any thing concerning the immensity of God before spaces, and of his eternity before times; yea, if he wishes to perceive them, it is as if his mind were falling into a swoon; almost like one, who, having fallen into the water, is in the state of drowning, or like one, in an earthquake, on the eve of being overwhelmed; yea, if he should persist in penetrating into those things he might easily fall into a delirium, and from this be led to a denial of God. I also was once in a similar state, while thinking what God was from eternity, what he did before the world was created; whether he deliberated concerning creation, and contrived the plan of it; whether deliberate thought were possible in a pure vacuum, beside other vain things. But lest, by such things, I should become delirious, I was elevated by the Lord into the sphere and light in which the interior angels are; and, after the idea of space and time, in which my thought was before, was there a little removed, it was given me to comprehend, that the eternity of God is not an eternity of time, and that because time was not before the world, it was utterly vain to think such things concerning God; and also because the Divine from eternity, thus abstracted from all time, does not involve days, years and ages, but that all these are to God an instant, I concluded, that the world was created by God, not in time, but that times were introduced by God with creation. To these things I shall add this memorable circumstance: There appear, at one extremity of the spiritual world, two statues, in a monstrous human form, with their mouths wide open, and their jaws dilated, by which those seem to themselves to be devoured, who think vain and foolish things concerning God from eternity; but they are the fantasies, into which those cast themselves, who think absurdly and improperly concerning God before the world was created.

32. V. That enlightened Reason, from very many Things in the World, may see the Infinity of God.

Some things shall be enumerated, from which human reason may see the infinity of God, which are, I. That in the created universe there are not two things which are the same: that such identity does not exist in simultaneous things, human learning, by means of human reason, has seen and proved; and yet the substantial and material things in the universe, considered individually, are infinite in number. And that there is not an identity of two effects in things which are successive in the world, may be concluded from the rotation of the earth, in that its eccentricity at the poles causes that not any thing should ever return the same

That it is so, is evident from human faces, in that throughout the whole world there is not any one face altogether similar, or the same with another, neither can there be to eternity; this infinite variety could not by any means exist, but from the infinity of God the Creator. II. That the mind of one is never exactly similar to that of another; wherefore it is said, *many men, many minds;* consequently the will and the understanding of one is never exactly similar and the same with those of another; hence, also, neither is the speech of one, as to the sound and as to the thought whence it proceeds, nor his action, as to the gesture and as to the affection, exactly similar to that of another; from which infinite variety, also, the infinity of God the Creator may be seen as in a mirror. III. That there is a kind of immensity and eternity innate in every seed, as well of animals as of vegetables; an *immensity*, in that it may be multiplied to infinity; and an *eternity*, in that such multiplication has continued hitherto, without interruption, from the creation of the world, and may continue perpetually. From the animal kingdom take, for example, the fishes of the sea, which, if they should multiply according to the abundance of their seed, within 20 or 30 years would fill the ocean so that it would consist of fish only; thence the water of it would overflow and thus destroy all the earth; but, lest this should take place, it was provided by God that one fish should be food for another. It is similar with the seeds of vegetables; if as many of them, as annually arise from one, should be planted, within 20 or 30 years they would cover the surface not only of one earth, but also of several; for there are shrubs of which every single seed produses a hundred and a thousand others. Try it by calculation, multiplying the product of one, successively, into 20 or 30, and you will see. From both cases, of vegetables and animals, the divine immensity and eternity, from which a resemblance cannot but be produced, may be seen as in a common face. IV. The infinity of God may appear to the eye of enlightened reason, from the infinity to which every science may grow, and thence the intelligence and wisdom of every man; both of which may grow as a tree from seeds, and as forests and gardens from trees; for there is no end of them; the memory of man is their ground, and the understanding is where their germination, and the will is where their fructification, is effected; and these two faculties, the understanding and the will, are such that they may be cultivated and perfected in the world to the end of life, and afterwards to eternity. V. The infinity of God the Creator may also be seen from the infinite number of stars, which are so many suns; and thence there are as many worlds. That in the starry heaven, also, there are earths, upon which are men, beasts, birds and vegetables, has been shown in a little work written from things seen. VI. The infinity of God appeared still more evident to me, from the angelic heaven, and also from hell, seeing that they are both of them orderly divided and subdivided into innumerable societies or congregations, according to all the varieties of the love of good and evil, and that every one obtains a place according to his love; for there all of the human race, since the creation of the world, are collected, and are to be collected, to ages of ages; and that, although every one has his own place or habitation, still all there are so joined together, that the whole angelic heaven represents one divine man, and all hell one monstrous devil. From these two, and from the infinite wonders in them, the immensity, together with the omnipotence of God, is manifestly exhibited to view. VII. Who also cannot perceive, if he elevates a little the rational powers of his mind, that the life to eternity, which every man has after death, is not communicable but from an eternal God. VIII. Besides those things, there is a sort of infinity in many things, which fall into natural light and into spiritual light with man

Into natural light—that there are various series in geometry which go on to infinity; that, between the three degrees of altitude, there is a progress to infinity, in that the first degree, which is called *natural*, cannot be perfected and elevated to the perfection of the second degree, which is called *spiritual*, nor this to the perfection of the third, which is called *celestial*. The case is similar with respect to the end, cause and effect; as that the effect cannot be perfected so that it may become as its cause, nor the cause, so that it may become as its end. This may be illustrated by the atmospheres, of which there are three degrees; for the highest is the aura; under this is the ether; and below this is the air; and no quality of the air can be elevated to any quality of the ether, nor any of this to any quality of the aura; and yet an elevation of perfections to infinity is possible in each. *Into spiritual light*—that natural love, which is that of a beast, cannot be elevated into spiritual love, which, from creation, was implanted in man: the case is similar with the natural intelligence of a beast, in relation to the spiritual intelligence of a man; but these things, because they are as yet unknown, will be explained in another place. From these things it is evident, that the universals of the world are perpetual types of the infinity of God the Creator; but in what manner particulars resemble universals, and represent the infinity of God, is an abyss; and it is an ocean, in which the human mind may, as it were, sail; but it must beware of the tempest, arising from the natural man, which may overwhelm the ship, with the masts and sails, from the stern, where the natural man stands confiding in himself.

33. VI. THAT EVERY CREATED THING IS FINITE, AND THAT THE INFINITE IS IN FINITE THINGS AS IN RECEPTACLES, AND IN MEN AS IN ITS IMAGES.

That every created thing is finite, is because all things are from Jehovah God, by means of the sun of the spiritual world, which proximately encompasses Him; and that sun is of the substance which proceeded from Him, the essence of which is love; out of that sun, by means of its heat and light, the universe was created, from the firsts to the lasts of it. But to explain in order the progress of creation, does not belong to this place: some scheme of it will be given in the following pages. It is important here only to know, that one thing was formed from another, and that thence were made degrees, three in the spiritual world, and three, corresponding to them, in the natural world, and as many in the quiescent things of which the terraqueous globe consists. But whence and what those degrees are, has been fully explained in the ANGELIC WISDOM CONCERNING THE DIVINE LOVE AND THE DIVINE WISDOM, published at Amsterdam in the year 1763; and in a small treatise concerning THE INTERCOURSE OF THE SOUL AND BODY, published at London in the year 1769.—It is by means of these degrees, that all posterior things are receptacles of prior things, and these of things still prior, and thus in order receptacles of the primitives of which the sun of the angelic heaven consists, and thus that finite things are receptacles of the infinite. This also coincides with the wisdom of the ancients, according to which all and every thing is divisible to infinity. The common idea is, that, because what is finite does not comprehend what is infinite, finite things cannot be receptacles of the infinite. But, from those things which are said in MY WORKS concerning the creation, it is evident that God first made his infinity finite, by substances emitted from Himself, from which exists his proximate encompassing sphere, which makes the sun of the spiritual world; and that afterwards, by means of that sun, He perfected other encompassing spheres, even to the last, which consists of things quiescent; and that thus, by means of degrees, He made the world finite more and more. These things are adduced in order that human reason may be satisfied, which does not rest unless it see the cause.

34. That the Infinite Divine is in men, as in its images, is evident from the Word, where this is read: *At length God said, Let us make man in our image, after our likeness; therefore God created man into his own image, into the image of God He created him*, Gen. i. 26, 27: from which it follows, that man is an organ recipient of God, and that he is an organ according to the quality of reception. The human mind, from which and according to which man is man, is formed into three regions, according to three degrees: in the first degree, it is celestial, in which also are the angels of the highest heaven; in the second degree, it is spiritual, in which also are the angels of the middle heaven; and in the third degree, it is natural, in which also are the angels of the lowest heaven. The human mind, organized according to those three degrees, is a receptacle of the divine influx; but still the Divine flows in no further than as man prepares the way, or opens the door; if he does this even to the highest, or celestial degree, then man becomes truly an image of God, and after death he becomes an angel of the highest heaven; but if he prepares the way, or opens the door, only to the middle or spiritual degree, then, indeed, man becomes an image of God, but not in that perfection, and after death he becomes an angel of the middle heaven; but if he prepares the way, or opens the door, only to the lowest or natural degree, then man, if he acknowledges a God, and worships him with actual piety, becomes an image of God in the lowest degree, and after death he becomes an angel of the lowest heaven. But if he does not acknowledge a God, and does not worship him with actual piety, he puts off the image of God, and becomes like an animal, except that he enjoys the faculty of understanding and thence of speech. If he then shuts up the highest natural degree, which corresponds to the highest celestial, he becomes, as to love, like a beast of the earth; but if he shuts up the middle natural degree, which corresponds to the middle spiritual, he becomes, as to love, like a fox, and as to the sight of the understanding, like a bird of the evening: but if he also shuts up the lowest natural degree, as to its spiritual part, he becomes, as to love, like a wild beast, and as to the understanding of truth, like a fish. The divine life which, by influx from the sun of the angelic heaven, actuates man, may be compared with the light from the sun of the world, and with the influx of it into a transparent object; the reception of life in the highest degree, with the influx of light into a diamond; the reception of life in the second degree, with the influx of light into a crystal; and the reception of life in the lowest degree, with the influx of light into glass, or into a transparent membrane; but if this degree, as to its spiritual part, be entirely shut up, which is done when God is denied and Satan is worshipped, the reception of life from God may be compared with the influx of light into the opaque things of the earth, as into rotten wood, or into the turf of a bog, or into dung, &c.; for man then becomes a spiritual carcass.

---

35. To the above I shall add this Relation. I was once in great astonishment at the vast multitude of men, who ascribe creation, and thence all things which are under the sun, and all things which are above the sun, to nature; saying, from an acknowledgment of the heart, when they see any thing, "Is not this of nature?" And when they are asked, why they say that those things are of nature, and why not of God, when, nevertheless, they sometimes say, with the rest of the world, that God created nature, and thence they may just as well say, that those things which they see are of God, as that they are of nature, they answer with an internal tone scarcely audible, "What is God but nature?" All such, from the persuasion of the creation of the universe by nature, and from that insanity as from wisdom, appear so elated, that they look upon all who acknowledge the creation of the universe by God, as

ants which creep upon the ground, and tread the beaten path, and upon some as butterflies, which fly in the air, calling their opinions dreams, because they see what they do not see, saying, "Who has seen God, and who does not see nature." While I was in astonishment at the multitude of such persons, an angel stood at my side, and said to me, "What are you meditating about?" and I replied, "About the multitude of such persons as believe that nature is of itself, and thus the creator of the universe." And the angel said to me, "All hell is of such, and they are called there *satans* and *devils; satans*, who have confirmed themselves in favor of nature, and thence have denied God; *devils*, who have lived wickedly, and thus have rejected from their hearts all acknowledgment of God. But I will conduct you to the gymnasiums, which are in the south-western quarter, where such are, who are not yet in hell." And he took me by the hand, and led me along, and I saw small houses, in which were gymnasiums, and, in the midst of them, one which was like a palace to the rest: it was built of pitch-colored stones, which were covered with little plates, as of glass, sparkling as it were with gold and silver, like those which are called *selenites*, or stones used instead of glass; and here and there were interspersed glittering shells. Hither we came, and knocked; and presently one opened the door and said, "Welcome;" and he ran to the table, and brought four books, and said, "These books are the wisdom which is at this day applauded by many kingdoms; this book, or wisdom, is applauded by many in France; this, by many in Germany; this, by some in Holland; and this, by some in Britain:" he said, moreover, "If you wish to see it, I will make these books shine before your eyes;" and then he poured forth and around the glory of his fame, and the books instantly shone as from light, but this light, before our eyes, immediately vanished; and then we asked what he was now writing; and he replied, that he was producing, and bringing forth from his treasures, things which are of inmost wisdom, which in a summary are these: I. WHETHER NATURE BE OF LIFE, OR WHETHER LIFE BE OF NATURE. II. WHETHER THE CENTRE BE OF THE EXPANSE, OR WHETHER THE EXPANSE BE OF THE CENTRE. III. CONCERNING THE CENTRE OF THE EXPANSE AND OF LIFE. Having said this, he placed himself again upon the seat at the table, but we walked in his gymnasium, which was spacious. He had a candle upon the table, because the light of the sun was not there, but the nocturnal light of the moon; and what appeared to me wonderful, the candle seemed to be carried round about there, and to give light; but because it had not been snuffed, it gave but little light. And when he wrote, we saw images in various forms, flying from the table to the walls, which, in that nocturnal light of the moon, appeared like beautiful Indian birds; but when we opened the door, they appeared, in the day-light of the sun, like those birds of the evening, which have wings of network; for they were appearances of truth, which, by confirmations, became fallacies, which had been ingeniously connected by him in a series. After we had seen them, we came up to the table, and asked him what he was now writing. He said, concerning the first question: WHETHER NATURE BE OF LIFE, OR WHETHER LIFE BE OF NATURE; and of this he said that he could confirm both sides, and cause them to be true; but because something was concealed within, which he feared, he durst confirm only this, *That nature is of life*, that is, from life, and not *That life is of nature*, that is, from nature. We asked him, courteously, what it was that was concealed within, which he feared. He replied, that it was that he should be called by the clergy a naturalist, and thus an atheist, and by the laity a man of unsound reason, since both the former and the latter, either believe from a blind faith, or see from the sight of those who confirm it. But then, from an indignation of zeal for the truth, we addressed him, saying "Friend, you are very much deceived;

your wisdom, which is an ingenuity of writing, has seduced you, and the glory of fame has induced you to confirm what you do not believe. Do you not know, that the human mind is capable of being elevated above the sensual things, which are in the thoughts, from the senses of the body, and that when it is elevated, it sees those things which are of life above, and those things which are of nature below? What else is life, but love and wisdom? and what else is nature but their receptacle, by which they may produce their effects or uses? Can these be one, except as the principal and instrumental are so? Can light be one with the eye, or sound with the ear? Whence are the sensations of these but from life? whence their forms, but from nature? What is the human body but an organ of life? Is not all, and every thing there, organically formed for producing those things which the love wills, and the understanding thinks? Are not the organs of the body from nature, and love and thought from life? And are not these entirely distinct from each other? Elevate the keen sight of your genius yet a little higher, and you will see that it is of life to be affected and to think, and that it is of love to be affected, and of wisdom to think, and both are of life; for, as was said, love and wisdom are life. If you elevate the faculty of understanding a little higher still, you will see, that love and wisdom could not exist, unless they had an origin somewhere, and that their origin is Love itself, and Wisdom itself, and thence Life itself; and these are God from whom nature is." Afterwards we conversed with him about the second, WHETHER THE EXPANSE BE OF THE CENTRE, OR WHETHER THE CENTRE BE OF THE EXPANSE; and we asked him why he canvassed this. He replied, to the end that he might conclude concerning the centre, and the expanse of nature, and of life; and thus concerning the origin of the one and the other. And when we asked him what was his opinion, he replied concerning these, just as before, that he could confirm both sides, but that for fear of the loss of fame, he would confirm that the expanse is of the centre, that is, from the centre; "although I know, that before the sun, there may have been something, and this every where in the expanse; and that this, from itself, flowed together into order, thus into the centre." But then we again addressed him, from an indignant zeal, and said, "Friend, you are beside yourself." And when he heard this, he drew back the seat from the table, and looked timidly at us, and then listened, but smiling: we, however, continued the discourse by saying, "What is more indicative of insanity than to say that the centre is from the expanse? By your *centre*, we understand the *sun*, and by your *expanse*, we understand the *universe*, and thus that the universe may have existed without the sun. Does not the sun make nature, and all its properties, which depend solely on the light and heat proceeding from the sun, through the atmospheres? Where these are, we have said before; but whence they are, we will say in the following discussion. Are not the atmospheres, and all things which are upon the earth as surfaces, and the sun as their centre? What would all those things be without the sun? Could they subsist a moment? How, then, could all those things have existed before the sun? Is not subsistence perpetual existence? Since, therefore, the subsistence of all things of nature is from the sun, it follows, that the existence of all things is so too. Every one sees this, and from his own perception acknowledges it. Does not what is posterior subsist also, as well as exist, from what is prior? If the surface were prior, and the centre posterior, would not the prior subsist from the posterior, which yet is contrary to the laws of order? How can posterior things produce prior, or exterior, interior, or grosser, purer? Thence, how can surfaces, which make the expanse, produce the centre? Who does not see that this is contrary to the laws of nature? We have adduced these arguments from the analysis of reason, to prove that the expanse exists from the centre, and not the centre from the expanse, although every one, who thinks justly, sees this without those arguments. You said that the expanse flowed together into the centre from itself; did it by chance flow thus into such wonderful and stupendous order, that one thing is for the sake of another, and all and every thing for the sake of man and his eternal life? Can nature, from any love, by any wisdom, intend ends, provide causes, and thus produce effects, that such things may exist in their order? Can nature make angels of men, and a heaven of angels, and cause those who are there to live forever? Propose and consider these things, and your idea concerning the existence of nature from nature will fall." After this, we asked him what he had thought, and what he then thought, concerning the third, CONCERNING THE CENTRE AND THE EXPANSE OF NATURE AND OF LIFE; whether he believed, that the centre and the expanse of life is the same with the centre and the expanse of nature. He said that he hesitated, and that he formerly thought, that the interior activity of nature was life, and that love and wisdom, which essentially make the life of man, were thence; and that the fire of the sun, by heat and light, through the medium of the atmospheres, produced it; but that now, from what he had heard concerning the life of men after death, he was in doubt; and that this doubt carried his mind sometimes upwards, and sometimes downwards; and when upwards, he acknowledged a centre, of which he before had not known any thing; and when downwards, he saw the centre, which he believed the only one, and that life was from the centre, of which he before had not known any thing, and that nature was from the centre, which he before believed to be the only one, and that each centre had an expanse around it. To this we said, "Well;" if he would only look also at the centre and the expanse of nature, from the centre and the expanse of life, and not conversely. And we instructed him that, above the angelic heaven there is a sun, which is pure love, to appearance fiery, as the sun of the world; and that from the heat which proceeds from that sun, angels and men have will and love, and that from the light thence, they have understanding and wisdom; and that those things which are thence, are called *spiritual*; and that those things, which proceed from the sun of the world, are containers or receptacles of life, and are called *natural*; then, that the expanse of the centre of life is called the SPIRITUAL WORLD, which subsists from its sun: and that the expanse of the centre of nature is called the NATURAL WORLD, which subsists from its sun. Now, because spaces and times cannot be predicated of love and wisdom, but instead of them, states, it follows, that the expanse around the sun of the angelic heaven, is not an extense, but still in the extense of the natural sun, and with the living subjects there according to reception, and the reception is according to forms and states. But then he asked, "Whence is the fire of the sun of the world, or of nature?" We replied, that it is from the sun of the angelic heaven, which is not fire, but divine love proximately proceeding from God, who is in the midst of it; and because he wondered at this, we demonstrated it thus: "Love, in its essence, is spiritual fire; thence it is, that *fire*, in the Word, in its spiritual sense, signifies love; wherefore priests in the temples pray, that heavenly fire may fill the hearts, by which they mean love. The fire of the altar, and the fire of the candlestick, in the tabernacle, amongst the Israelites, represented no other than the divine love. The heat of the blood, or the vital heat of men, and of animals in general, is from no other source than from the love which makes their life; thence it is, that man is enkindled, grows warm, and is inflamed, whilst his love is exalted to zeal, or excited to anger and indignation Wherefore from this, that spiritual heat, which is love, produces natural heat with men, to such a degree that it enkindles their faces and limbs, it may be evident, that the fire of the natural sun existed from no other source, than from the fire of the spiritual sun, which is Divine Love. Now, because the expanse arises from the centre, and not the centre from the expanse, as we said above, and the centre of life, which is the sun of the angelic heaven, is the Divine Love, proximately proceeding from God, who is in the midst of that sun; and because the expanse of that centre, which is called the *spiritual world*, is thence; and because the sun of the world existed from that sun, and from this, its expanse, which is called the *natural world*, it is manifest, that the universe was created by God." After this we departed, and he accompanied us out of the court of his gymnasium, and talked with us concerning heaven and hell, and concerning the divine auspices, with new sagacity of genius.

CONCERNING THE ESSENCE OF GOD, WHICH IS DIVINE LOVE AND DIVINE WISDOM.

36. We have distinguished between the Esse of God and the Essence of God, because there is a distinction between the infinity of God and the love of God; and infinity is applicable to the Esse of God, and love to the Essence of God; for the Esse of God, as was said above, is more universal than the Essence of God: in like manner, the infinity is more universal than the love of God; wherefore, *infinite* is an adjective belonging to the essentials and attributes of God, all which are called infinite; as it is said of the Divine Love, that it is infinite, of the Divine Wisdom, that it is infinite, and of the Divine Power, in like manner; not that the Esse of God existed before, but because it enters into the Essence, as an adjunct, cohering with, determining, forming, and, at the same time, elevating it. But this member of this chapter, like the former, shall be divided into the following articles: I. *That God is Love itself and Wisdom itself, and that these two make his Essence.* II. *That God is Good itself and Truth itself; because Good is of Love, and Truth is of Wisdom.* III. *That Love itself and Wisdom itself are Life itself, which is Life in itself.* IV. *That Love and Wisdom, in God, make one.* V. *That the Essence of Love is, to love others out of itself, to desire to be one with them, and to make them happy from itself.* VI. *That these properties of the Divine Love were the cause of the creation of the universe, and that they are the cause of its preservation.* But of these one by one.

37. I. That God is Love itself and Wisdom itself, and that these two make His Essence.

That love and wisdom are the two essentials, to which all the infinite things which are in God, and which proceed from Him, refer themselves, the first antiquity saw; but the ages following successively, as they withdrew their minds from heaven, and immersed them in worldly and corporeal things, could not see it; for they began not to know what love is, in its essence, and thence what wisdom is, in its essence; not knowing that love, abstracted from form, cannot exist, and that it operates in a form, and by a form. Now, because God is the very, and the only, and thus the first Substance and Form, whose essence is love and wisdom; and because out of Him all things were made, that were made; it follows, that He created the universe, with all and every thing of it, out of love by wisdom; and that thence the Divine Love, together with the Divine Wisdom, is in all and every created subject. Love, moreover, is not only the essence, which forms all things, but it also unites and conjoins them, and thus keeps them, when formed, in connexion. These things may be illustrated by innumerable things in the world; as by the HEAT and LIGHT from the sun, which are the two essentials and universals, by means of which all and every thing, upon the earth, exists and subsists: these are there, because they correspond to the Divine Love and the Divine Wisdom; for the heat, which proceeds from the sun of the spiritual world, in its essence, is love; and the light thence, in its essence, is wisdom. They may also be illustrated by the two essentials and universals, by which human minds exist and subsist, which are THE WILL and THE UNDERSTANDING; for of these two the mind of every one consists; and those two are and operate in all and every thing of it. The reason is, because the will is the receptacle and habitation of love, and the understanding, of wisdom; wherefore those two faculties correspond to the Divine Love and the Divine Wisdom, from which they originate. Moreover, those same things may be illustrated by the two essentials and universals, by which human bodies exist and subsist, which are THE HEART and THE LUNGS; or the systole and diastole of the heart, and the respiration of the lungs: that these two operate in all and every thing there, is known; the reason is, because the heart corresponds to love, and the lungs to wisdom; which correspondence is fully demonstrated in the ANGELIC WISDOM CONCERNING THE DIVINE LOVE AND DIVINE WISDOM, published at Amsterdam. That love as the bridegroom or husband, produces or begets all forms, but by wisdom as the bride or wife, may be proved by innumerable things, both in the spiritual and the natural world; this only is to be observed, that the whole angelic heaven is arranged into its form, and preserved in it, from the Divine Love by the Divine Wisdom. Those who deduce the creation of the world from any other source than from the Divine Love by the Divine Wisdom and do not know that those two make the Divine Essence, descend from the sight of reason to the sight of the eye, and kiss nature as the creator of the universe, and thence conceive chimeras, and bring forth phantoms; they think fallacies, reason from them, and conclude eggs, in which are birds of night. Such cannot be called *minds*, but eyes and ears without understanding, or thoughts without a soul; they speak of colors, as if they existed without light, of the existence of trees, as if without seed, and of all the things of the world, as if without a sun; since they make derivatives, primitives, and effects, causes; and so they turn every thing upside down, and lull to sleep the powers of reason, and thus see dreams.

38. II. THAT GOD IS GOOD ITSELF AND TRUTH ITSELF, BECAUSE GOOD IS OF LOVE, AND TRUTH IS OF WISDOM.

It is universally known, that all things refer themselves to good and truth; a proof that all things derived their existence from love and wisdom; for all that proceeds from love is called *good*—for this is sensibly perceived—and the delight by which love manifests itself, is every one's good; but all that which proceeds from wisdom is called *truth*—for wisdom consists of nothing but truths, and affects its objects with the pleasantness of light; and this pleasantness, while it is perceived, is truth from good. Wherefore love is the complex of all goodnesses, and wisdom is the complex of all truths; but both the former and the latter are from God, who is Love itself, and thence Good itself, and Wisdom itself, and thence Truth itself. Thence it is, that in the church there are two essentials, which are called *charity* and *faith*, of which all and every thing of the church consists, and which will be in all and every thing of it: the reason is, because all the goods of the church are of charity, and are called charity; and all its truths are of faith, and are called faith. The delights of love, which are also the delights of charity, cause what is good to be called good; and the pleasantness of wisdom, which is also the pleasantness of faith, causes what is true to be called true; for delights and pleasantnesses make their life, and without life from them, goods and truths are like inanimate things, and they are also unfruitful. But the delights of love are of two kinds, as are also the pleasantnesses, which appear as of wisdom; for there are the delights of the love of good, and the delights of the love of evil, and thence there are the pleasantnesses of the faith of truth, and the pleasantnesses of the faith of the false. Those two delights of love, from the sensation of them in the subjects in which they are, are called good; and those two pleasantnesses of faith, from the perception of them, are also called good; but because they are in the understanding, they are no other than true; although they are opposite to each other; and the good of one love is good, and the good of the other love is evil; also the truth of one faith is true, and the truth of the other faith is false. But the love whose delights are essentially good, is like the heat of the sun, fructifying, vivifying and operating in fertile grounds, in useful plants, and fields of corn; and where it operates, there is produced, as it were, a paradise, a garden of the Lord, and, as it were, the land of Canaan; and the pleasantness of its truth is as the light of the sun in the time of spring, and as the influx of light into a crystal vessel, in which are beautiful flowers, and from which, when opened, there breathes forth a fragrant perfume; but the delight of the love of evil is as the heat of the sun, parching, killing, and operating in barren ground, in noxious plants, as in thorns and briers; and where it operates, there is produced a desert of Arabia, where are hydras and venomous serpents; and the pleasantness of its false is as the light of the sun in the time of winter, and as light flowing into a bottle, in which there are worms, swimming in vinegar, and reptiles of a noisome smell. It should be known, that every good forms itself by truths, and also clothes itself with them, and thus distinguishes itself from other goods; and also, that the goods of one stock or kind bind themselves into bundles, and, at the same time, clothe them, and thus distinguish themselves from others: that thus formations are effected, is manifest from all and every thing in the human body; and that similar formations are effected in the human mind, is evident, because there is a perpetual correspondence of all things of the mind with all things of the body Thence it follows, that the human mind is organized, inwardly, of spiritual substances, and outwardly of natural substances, and lastly of material substances. The mind, the delights of whose love are good, consists, inwardly, of spiritual substances, such as are in heaven; but the mind, the delights of whose love are evil, consists, inwardly, of spiritual substances, such as are in hell; and the evils of the latter are bound into bundles by falses, and the goods of the former are bound into bundles by truths. Since there are such bindings of goods and evils into bundles, therefore the Lord says, *That the tares are to be bound together into bundles, to be burnt, and in like manner all things that offend,* Matt. xiii 30, 40, 41. John xv. 6.

39. III. That God, because He is Love itself and Wisdom itself, is Life itself, which is Life in itself.

It is said in John, *The Word was with God, and the Word was God; in Him was life, and the life was the light of men,* i. 1, 4. By *God*, there, is meant the Divine Love, and by the *Word*, the Divine Wisdom; and Divine Wisdom is properly life, and life is properly the light which proceeds from the sun of the spiritual world, in the midst of which is Jehovah God. Divine Love forms life, as fire forms light. There are two properties in fire, that of burning, and that of shining; from its burning property proceeds heat, and from its shining property proceeds light. In like manner, there are two things in love; one, to which the burning property of fire corresponds, which is something most intimately affecting the will of man; and another, to which the shining property of fire corresponds, which is something most intimately affecting the understanding of man. Thence man has love and intelligence; for, as has been several times said above, from the sun of the spiritual world proceeds heat, which, in its essence, is love; and light, which, in its essence, is wisdom; and those two flow into all and every thing of the universe, and affect them most intimately; and with men, into their will and understanding, which two were created receptacles of the influx; the will, the receptacle of love, and the understanding, the receptacle of wisdom. Thence it is manifest, that the life of man dwells in his understanding, and that it is such as his wisdom is, and that the love of the will modifies it.

40. It is also read in John, *As the Father hath life in Himself, so hath He given to the Son to have life in Himself*, v. 26; by which is meant, that as the Divine, which was from eternity, lives in itself, so also the Human, which it assumed in time, lives in itself. Life in itself is the very and the only life, from which all angels and men live. Human reason may see this from the light which proceeds from the sun of the natural world, in that this is not creatable, but that forms, receiving it, are created; for eyes are its recipient forms, and the light, flowing in from the sun, causes them to see. It is similar with life, which, as was said, is the light proceeding from the sun of the spiritual world, that it is not creatable, but that it flows in continually, and, as it enlightens, it also enlivens the understanding of man; consequently, that, because light, life and wisdom are one, wisdom is not creatable; so neither is faith, nor truth, nor love, nor charity, nor good; but that forms receiving them are created; human and angelic minds are those forms. Let every one, therefore, be cautious how he persuades himself, that he lives from himself; and also, that he is wise, believes, loves, perceives truth, and wills and does good from himself; for so far as any one indulges such a persuasion, he casts down his mind from heaven to earth, and from spiritual becomes natural, sensual, and corporeal; for he shuts up the superior regions of his mind, whence he becomes blind, as to all the things which are of God and heaven and the church; and then, all that he may by chance think, reason and speak concerning them, is done in foolishness because in darkness, and then, at the same time, he is confident that they are of wisdom; for when the superior regions of the mind, where the true light of life dwells, are shut up, the region below them opens itself, into which only the light of the world is admitted; and this light separate from the light of the superior regions, is a fallacious light in which falses appear as truths, and truths as falses, and reasoning from falses as wisdom, and from truths as madness; and then he believes himself to be endued with the keen sight of an eagle, although he sees the things which are of wisdom no more than a bat sees in the light of day.

41. IV. That Love and Wisdom in God, make one.

Every wise man in the church knows, that all the good of love and charity is from God; in like manner, all the truth of wisdom and faith: that it is so, human reason may also see, if it only knows that the origin of love and wisdom is from the sun of the spiritual world, in the midst of which is Jehovah God; or, what is the same, that it is from Jehovah God, through the sun, which is round about Him; for the heat proceeding from that sun, in its essence, is love, and the light thence proceeding, in its essence, is wisdom. thence it is manifest, as in clear daylight, that love and wisdom, in that origin, are one; consequently in God, from whom is the origin of that sun. This may be illustrated, also, from the sun of the natural world, which is pure fire, in that heat proceeds from its fiery property, and light proceeds from the splendor of its fiery property; and thus that both are, in their origin, one. But that they are divided in proceeding, is evident from the subjects, some of which receive more of heat, and some, more of light: this is the case, especially with men; in them, the light of life, which is intelligence, and the heat of life, which is love, are divided, which is done because man is to be reformed and regenerated; and this cannot be done, unless the light of life, which is intelligence, teaches him what ought to be willed and loved. It should, however, be known, that God is continually operating the conjunction of love and wisdom in man, but that man, unless he looks to God, and believes in Him, continually operates to effect their division; wherefore, as far as those two, the good of love or charity, and the truth of wisdom or faith, are conjoined in man, so far man is an image of God, and is elevated to heaven, and into heaven, where the angels are; and, on the contrary, as far as those two are divided by man, so far he becomes an image of Lucifer and the dragon, and is cast down from heaven to earth, and then under the earth into hell. From the conjunction of those two, the state of man becomes like the state of a tree in the time of spring, when the heat conjoins itself equally with the light; whence it produces buds, blossoms, and fruit; but, on the other hand, from the division of those two, the state of man becomes like the state of a tree in the time of winter, when the heat recedes from the light, whence it is stripped and divested of all its foliage and verdure. When spiritual heat, which is love, separates itself from spiritual light, which is wisdom, or, what is the same, charity from faith, the man becomes like sour and rotten ground, in which worms are bred, and, if it produces shrubs, their leaves are covered with lice, and are consumed. For the allurements of the love of evil, which, in themselves, are concupiscences, burst forth, which the understanding, instead of subduing and restraining, loves, pampers and cherishes. In a word, to divide love and wisdom, or charity and faith, which two God continually endeavors to join together, is comparatively like depriving the face of its redness, whence comes a death-like paleness; or like taking away the whiteness from the redness, whence the face beomes like a burning torch. It is like like dissolving the marriage connection between two partners and so making the wife a harlot, and the husband an adulterer; for love, or charity, is as the husband, and wisdom, or faith, is as the wife; and when those two are separated, spiritual whoredom and adultery ensue, which are the falsification of truth, and the adulteration of good.

42. Moreover, it should be known, that there are three degrees of love and wisdom, and thence three degrees of life, and that the human mind, according to these degrees, is formed, as it were, into regions, and that life, in the highest region, is in the highest degree, and in the second region, in a lower degree, and in the last region, in the lowest degree. These regions are successively opened in man; the last region, where life is in the lowest degree, is opened from infancy to childhood, and this is done by the sciences; the second region, where life is in a higher degree, from childhood to youth, and this is done by knowledges from the sciences; and the highest region, where life is in the highest degree, from youth to manhood and onwards, and this is done by the perception of truths, both moral and spiritual. It should be further known, that the perfection of life consists not in thought, but in the perception of truth from the light of truth; the differences of life with men may be thence ascertained; for there are some, who, as soon as they hear the truth, perceive that it is truth; these are represented in the spiritual world by eagles: there are others, who do not perceive truth, but conclude it from confirmations, by appearances; and these are represented by singing birds: there are others, who believe a thing to be true, because it was asserted by a man of authority; these are represented by magpies: and, also, there are others, who are not willing, and then not able, to perceive truth, but only the false; the reason is, because they are in the light of infatuation, in which light, the false appears as truth, and the truth appears, either as something above the head, hid in a thick cloud, or as a meteor, or as the false; the thoughts of these are represented by owls, and their speech by

screech-owls. Those amongst them, who have confirmed their falses, cannot bear to hear truths; and as soon as any truth strikes the drum of their ears, they repel it with aversion, just as the stomach, when loaded with bilious matter, nauseates and vomits out food.

43. V. THAT THE ESSENCE OF LOVE IS TO LOVE OTHERS OUT OF ITSELF, TO DESIRE TO BE ONE WITH THEM, AND TO MAKE THEM HAPPY FROM ITSELF.

There are two things which make the essence of God—love and wisdom; but there are three things which make the essence of his love—to love others out of itself, to desire to be one with them, and to make them happy from itself: the same three things also make the essence of his wisdom, because love and wisdom, in God, make one, as was shown above; but love wills those things, and wisdom produces them. THE FIRST ESSENTIAL, *which is, to love others out of itself*, is acknowledged from the love of God towards the whole human race; and for their sake God loves all the things which he has created, because they are means; for he who loves the end also loves the means; and all persons and all things are out of God, because they are finite, and God is infinite. The love of God goes and extends itself, not only to good persons and good things, but also to evil persons and evil things; consequently, not only to those persons and things which are in heaven, but also to those which are in hell; thus not only to Michael and Gabriel, but also to the devil and Satan; for God is every where, and from eternity to eternity the same. He says also, *that He maketh his sun rise on the good and the evil, and that He sendeth rain upon the just and the unjust*, Matt. v. 45. But the reason, that evil persons and evil things are still evil, is in the subjects and objects themselves, in that they do not receive the love of God, as it is, and according to its inmost influx, but as they themselves are, just as the thorn and the nettle do with the heat of the sun and the rain of heaven. THE SECOND ESSENTIAL OF THE LOVE OF GOD, *which is to desire to be one with them*, is acknowledged also from his conjunction with the angelic heaven, with the church upon earth, with every one there, and with every good and truth which enter into and make man and the church; love also, viewed in itself, is nothing but an effort to conjunction; wherefore, that this object of the essence of love might be obtained, God created man into his image and likeness, with which conjunction may be effected. That the Divine Love continually intends conjunction, is manifest from the words of the Lord, that *He wills that they may be one, He in them and they in Him, and that the love of God may be in them*, John xvii. 21, 22, 23, 26. THE THIRD ESSENTIAL OF THE LOVE OF GOD, *which is to make them happy from itself*, is acknowledged from eternal life, which is blessedness, happiness, and felicity without end, which God gives to those who receive his love in themselves; for God, as He is love itself, is also blessedness itself; for every love breathes forth from itself a delight, and the Divine Love, blessedness itself, happiness, and felicity to eternity. Thus God makes angels happy from Himself, and also men after death, which is effected by conjunction with them.

44. That such is the Divine Love, is known from its sphere, which pervades the universe, and affects every one according to his state; it especially affects parents, from which it is that they tenderly love their children, who are out of themselves, that they desire to be one with them, and that they desire to make them happy from themselves. This sphere of Divine Love affects not only the good, but also the evil; and not only men, but also beasts and birds of every kind. For what else does a mother think of, when she has brought forth her child, than that she may, as it were, unite herself with it, and provide for its good? What other concern has a bird, when she has hatched her young, than to cherish them under her wings, and through their little mouths to put food into their throats? That dragons and

vipers also love their young, is known. That universal sphere affects, in a special manner, those who receive that love of God in themselves, who are such as believe in God and love their neighbor; charity with them is an image of that love. Friendship amongst the good also resembles that love; for a friend, at his table, gives to a friend the better things; he kisses and caresses him, takes him by the hand, and proffers useful offices. The sympathies and efforts of homogeneous and similar things to conjunction, derive their origin from no other source. That same divine sphere operates also into inanimate things, as into trees and plants, but through the sun of the world and its heat and light; for the heat enters them from without, conjoins itself with them, and causes them to bud, blossom, and bear fruit, which things are in the place of blessedness in animals; that heat does this, because it corresponds to spiritual heat, which is love. Representations of the operation of this love are also exhibited in various subjects of the mineral kingdom; types of it are presented in their exaltation to uses, and thence to corresponding values.

45. From the description of the essence of Divine Love, it may be seen what is the essence of diabolical love; this may be seen from the opposite. Diabolical love is the love of self; and this is called love, but, viewed in itself, it is hatred, for it does not love any one out of itself, nor does it desire to be conjoined to others, that it may do good to them, but only that it may do so to itself; from its inmost, it continually desires to rule over others, to possess the goods of others, and at last to be worshipped as a god. This is the reason why those who are in hell do not acknowledge God, but worship, as gods, those who have power over others; thus inferior and superior, or lesser and greater gods, according to the extent of their power; and because every one there desires that in heart he also burns with hatred against his god, and the god against those who are under his power; and he reputes them as vile slaves, with whom, indeed, he speaks courteously, as long as they adore him, but he rages as from fire against others, and also inwardly, or in his heart, against his dependents for the love of self is the same with the love of robbers, who mutually kiss each other, while they are engaged in robberies, but afterwards they burn with the desire of killing each other, that they may also rob each other of their booty. This love causes its lusts to appear at a distance, in hell where it reigns, like various species of wild beasts, some like foxes and leopards, some like wolves and tigers, and some like crocodiles and venomous serpents; and the deserts where they live, to consist only of heaps of stones, or of naked gravel, with bogs interspersed, in which frogs croak, and also dismal birds fly over their cottages and scream. The ochim, tziim and jiim, which are mentioned in the prophetical parts of the Word, where the love of ruling from the love of self is spoken of, are nothing else. *Isaiah* xiii. 21. *Jerem* l. 39. *Psalm* lxxiv. 15.

46. VI. That these Properties of the Divine Love were the Cause of the Creation of the Universe, and that they are the Cause of its Preservation.

That those three essentials of the Divine Love were the cause of creation, may be clearly seen from an attentive examination of them. That this first, *which is to love others out of itself*, was a cause, is evident from the universe, which is out of God, as the world is out of the sun; and therefore He can extend his love into the universe, and exercise it in it, and so rest. It is read also, that after God had created the heaven and the earth, he rested; and that thence the day of the Sabbath was made. *Gen.* ii. 2, 3. That the second, *which is to will to be one with them*, was a cause, is evident from the creation of man into the image and likeness of God; by which is meant, that man was made a form receptive of love and wisdom from God, so that God can unite himself with him, and, for the sake of him, with all and every thing of the universe which are no other than mediums; for conjunction with a final cause, is also a conjunction with the mediate causes. That all things were created for the sake of man, is manifest also from the book of Creation, or Genesis, i. 28, 29, 30. THAT THE THIRD, *which is to make them happy from itself*, is a cause, is evident from the angelic heaven, which is provided for every man who receives the love of God, where all are made happy from God alone. That those three essentials of the love of God, are also the cause of the preservation of the universe, is because preservation is perpetual creation, as subsistence is perpetual existence; and the Divine Love, from eternity to eternity, is the same; thus such as it was in creating the world, such it is and continues to be, in the created world.

47. From these things, rightly perceived, it may be seen, that the universe is a work cohering from firsts to lasts, because it is a work continent of ends, causes and effects, in an indissoluble connection; and because in all love there is an end, and in all wisdom the promotion of an end by mediate causes, and through them to effects, which are uses, it follows also, that the universe is a work continent of divine love, divine wisdom, and uses, and thus a work altogether coherent from firsts to lasts. That the universe consists of perpetual uses produced by wisdom and originated by love, every wise man may see as in a mirror, while he procures to himself a general idea of the creation of the universe, and in that views the particulars; for the particular parts adapt themselves to the whole, and the whole disposes them into such a form that they may agree. That it is so, will be more fully illustrated in the following pages.

---

48. To this I shall add this RELATION. I was once conversing with two angels; one was from the eastern heaven, and the other from the southern heaven. When they perceived that I was meditating arcana of wisdom concerning love, they said, "Do you know any thing about the exercises of wisdom in our world?" I replied, that I did not; and they said, "There are many, and that those who love truths from spiritual affection, or truths because they are truths, and because by them is wisdom, meet together at a given signal, and canvass and determine those questions which are of deeper understanding." They then took me by the hand, saying, "Follow us and you shall see and hear, for the signal of the meeting has been given to-day." I was led over a plain to a hill, and behold, at the foot of the hill, a portico of palm trees, continued even to its top; we entered it, and ascended; and upon the top or summit of the hill, there appeared a grove, and between the trees, the ground, being elevated, formed as it were a theatre, within which was a smooth floor, paved with little stones of various colors. Around it, in the form of a square, were placed seats, upon which the lovers of wisdom were sitting; and in the midst of the theatre, there was a table, upon which lay a paper sealed with a seal. Those who sat on the seats invited us to the seats still vacant; and I replied that I was led hither by two angels, that I might see and hear, and not that I might sit. And then those two angels went into the middle of the floor to the table, and loosed the seal of the paper, and read, in the presence of those who were sitting, the arcana of wisdom written on the paper, which they were now to canvass and unfold. They were written by angels of the third heaven, and let down upon the table. There were three arcana: THE FIRST—"*What is the image of God, and what the likeness of God, into which man was created?*" THE SECOND—"*Why is not man born into the science of any love, when yet beasts and birds, noble as well as ignoble, are born into the sciences of all their loves?*" THE THIRD—"*What does the tree of life signify; and what the tree of the knowledge of good and evil; and what the eating from them?*" Underneath was written—"Join those three together into one sentence, and write it upon a new paper, and put it back upon this table, and we will see it; if the sentence appear true and just on the bal-

ance, to each of you shall be given the prize of wisdom." The two angels, having read this, retired, and were carried up into their heavens. And then those who sat upon the seats began to canvass and unfold the arcana proposed to them; and they spoke in order; first, those who sat towards the North, then those towards the West, afterwards those towards the South, and lastly those towards the East. And they took up the first subject of investigation, which was, "WHAT IS THE IMAGE OF GOD, AND WHAT THE LIKENESS OF GOD, INTO WHICH MAN WAS CREATED?" And then, in the first place, these words from the book of Creation, were read to them all: *God said, Let us make man in* OUR IMAGE, *according to* OUR LIKENESS; *and God created man into* HIS OWN IMAGE; *He made him in the* LIKENESS OF GOD, Gen. i. *In the day when God created man, He made him in the* LIKENESS OF GOD, Gen. v. 1.

Those who sat towards the NORTH spoke first, saying, that "The image of God and the likeness of God are the two lives breathed into man by God, which are the life of the will, and the life of the understanding; for it is read, *Jehovah God breathed into the nostrils of Adam the breath of* LIVES, *and man was made into a living soul,* Gen. ii. 7. By which seems to be meant, that there was breathed into him the will of good, and the perception of truth, and thus the soul of lives; and because life from God was breathed into him, an image and a likeness signify integrity from love and wisdom, and from justice and judgment in him." Those who sat towards the WEST favored these, adding however this, that "The state of integrity breathed into him by God, is continually breathed into every man after him; but that it is in man as in a receptacle, and that man, as he is a receptacle, is an image and likeness of God." After wards the third in order, who were those who sat towards the SOUTH, said, "The image of God and the likeness of God are two distinct things, but united in man by creation; and we see, as from a kind of interior light, that the image of God may be lost by man, but not the likeness of God. This appears as it were, through a veil, from this, that Adam retained the likeness of God after he had lost the image of God; for it is read after the curse, *Behold the man is become as one of us, in knowing good and evil,* Gen. iii. 22. And afterwards he is called a likeness of God, and not an image of God, Gen. v. 1. But let us leave to our companions, who sit towards the east, and are thence in superior light, to say what is properly the image of God, and what is properly the likeness of God." And then, after silence was made, those who sat towards the EAST rose up from their seats, and looked up to the Lord; and afterwards they sat down again upon their seats and said, that "An image of God is a receptacle of God; and because God is Love itself and Wisdom itself, an image of God is the reception of love and wisdom from God in it; but that a likeness of God is a perfect likeness and a full appearance, as if love and wisdom were in man, and thence as if they were altogether his; for man, by the senses, perceives no otherwise than that he loves from himself, and is wise from himself; or that he wills good and understands truth from himself; when, nevertheless, nothing of this is from himself, but from God. God alone loves from himself, and is wise from himself, because God is Love itself and Wisdom itself; the likeness or appearance that love and wisdom, or good and truth, are in man, as his, causes that man may be man, and that he may be conjoined to God, and thus live to eternity; whence it flows, that man is man from this, that he can will good and understand truth, altogether as from himself, and still know and believe that it is from God; for as he knows and believes this, God puts his image in man; it would be otherwise, if he should believe it is from himself, and not from God." When these things were said, there came upon them a zeal from the love of truth, from which they spoke these words: "How can man receive any thing of love and wisdom, and retain it, and re-produce it, unless he sensibly perceives it as his own? And how can conjunction with God, by means of love and wisdom, be effected, unless there be given to man something reciprocal of conjunction? For without reciprocation, no conjunction is possible, and the reciprocation of conjunction is, that man should love God, and do those things which are of God, as from himself, and yet believe that it is from God. Besides, how can man live to eternity, unless he be conjoined to the eternal God? Consequently, how can man be man, without that likeness in him?" To these words all assented, and said, "Let a conclusion be made from them;" and this was made: "Man is a receptacle of God, and a receptacle of God is an image of God; and because God is Love itself and Wisdom itself, man is a receptacle of them; and a receptacle becomes an image of God according as it receives; and man is also a likeness of God from this, that he sensibly perceives in himself that those things which are from God, are in him as his; but still so much of that likeness is an image of God, as acknowledges that love and wisdom, or good and truth, are not in him his, and thence neither from him, but only in God, and thence from God." After this, they took up the next object of investigation, "WHY MAN IS NOT BORN INTO THE SCIENCE OF ANY LOVE, WHEN YET BEASTS AND BIRDS, NOBLE AS WELL AS IGNOBLE, ARE BORN INTO THE SCIENCES OF ALL THEIR LOVES." First they confirmed the truth of the proposition from various things; as, concerning man, that he is born into no science, not even into the science of conjugial love; and they inquired and heard from examiners, that an infant does not even know the breast of its mother, from any innate science, but that it learns this by being applied to it by its mother or nurse; and that it only knows how to suck, and that it derives this from continual suction in the mother's womb; and that, afterwards, it does not know how to walk, nor to articulate sound into any human voice, yea nor to sound the affections of its love, as beasts do moreover, that it knows not what food is suitable for it, as beasts do, but that it lays hold of whatever comes in its way, whether clean or unclean, and puts it into its mouth. The examiners said, that "Man, without instruction, knows nothing at all about the modes of loving the sex, and that not even virgins and young men know any thing of this, without instruction from others. In a word, man is born corporeal, like a worm, and continues corporeal, unless he acquires knowledge, intelligence and wisdom from others." After this, they proved that animals, noble as well as ignoble, such as the beasts of the earth, the fowls of the air, the reptiles, the fishes, and the little worms which are called insects, are born into all the sciences of the loves of their life, as into all things concerning nourishment, into all things concerning habitation, into all things concerning the love of the sex and prolification, and into all things concerning the education of their young. These things they confirmed by the wonderful things which they recalled to remembrance, from what they had seen, heard and read in the natural world, in which they once lived, and in which there are not representative, but real beasts. After the truth of the proposition was thus established, they applied their minds to investigate and discover the causes by means of which they might unfold and lay open this mystery; and they all said that those things could not but exist from the Divine Wisdom, that man may be man, and beast may be beast; and that thus the imperfection of man's nativity is his perfection, and the perfection of a beast's nativity is its imperfection.

Then those on the NORTH began first to open their minds, and said, that "Man was born without sciences, that he might be able to receive them all; but, if he were born into sciences, he would not be able to receive any, except those into which he was born, and then he would not be able to appropriate any to himself;" which they illus trated by this comparison: "Man, at first, is born like ground in which no seeds have been sown, but which can yet receive all, and bring them forth, and cause them to bear fruit; but a beast is like ground already sown, and covered over with grass and herbs, which receives no other seeds than those which have been sown; and, if others should be sown, they would be suffocated. Thence it is, that man is many years in coming to his growth, during which he may be cultivated like the ground, and produce grain of every kind, flowers and trees; but a beast comes to its growth in a few years, during which it can be cultivated for no other things than those which are born with it." Afterwards, those on the WEST spoke, and said, that "Man is not born science, like a beast, but that he is born a faculty, and an inclination; a faculty to know, and an inclination to love; and that he is born a faculty, not only for loving those things which are of self and the world, but also those which are of God and heaven; consequently, that man is born an organ, which scarcely lives by the external senses, except obscurely, but by no internal senses, to the intent, that he may, by degrees, live, and become a man; first, a natural man; afterwards, a rational man; and, lastly, a spiritual man; which would not be the case, if he were born into sciences and loves, as beasts are; for the sciences and affections of love, which are born with one, limit that progression; but mere faculties and inclinations, born with one, limit nothing; wherefore, man may be perfected in science, intelligence and wisdom, to eternity." Those on the SOUTH took up the subject, and declared their opinion, saying, that "It is impossible for man to derive any science from himself, but he may derive it from others, since no science was born with him; and because he cannot derive any science from himself, neither can he any love, since, where there is no science, there is no love; science and love are inseparable companions; they can no more be separated, than the will and understanding, or affection and thought; yea, no more than essence and form; wherefore, as man receives science from others, love adjoins itself to it, as its companion. The universal love, which adjoins itself, is the love of knowing, and afterwards of understanding and becoming wise; and these loves are in man only, and not in beasts, and they flow in from God. We agree with our companions from the West, that man is not born into any love, and thence not into any science; but that he is only born into an inclination to love, and thence into a faculty to receive sciences, not from himself, but from others, that is, through others: it is said, *through others*, because neither did those receive any thing from themselves, but originally from God. We agree also with our companions towards the North, that man, at first, is born like ground, in which not any seeds have been sown, but in which all seeds, as well noble as ignoble, may be sown: thence it is, that man was called man from the ground, and Adam from *Adama*, which is the ground. To this we add, that beasts are born into natural loves, and thence into the sciences corresponding to them; but still from the sciences they do not derive any knowledge, nor thought, nor intelligence, nor wisdom, but that they are led to them from their loves, almost in the same manner as blind men are led through the streets by dogs; for, as to the understanding, they are blind; or rather like persons walking in sleep, who do what they do from a blind science, while the understanding is fast asleep." Lastly, those on the EAST spoke, and said, "We consent to those things which our brethren have spoken, that man knows nothing from himself, but from others, and through others, that he may know and acknowledge that all science, intelligence and wisdom are from God, and that man could not otherwise be born and begotten of God, and become an image and likeness of Him; for he becomes an image of God, by acknowledging and believing, that all the good of love and charity, and all the truth of wisdom and faith, were received, and are received, by him from God, and nothing from himself; and he is a likeness of God, in that he sensibly perceives those things in himself, as if from himself; and he sensibly perceives this, because he is not born into sciences, but receives them; and what he receives, appears to him as from himself. To perceive thus, is given to man by God, that he may be a man, and not a beast; since by this, that he wills, thinks, loves, knows, understands, and is wise, as from himself, he receives sciences, and exalts them into intelligence, and by their uses into wisdom; thus God conjoins man to himself, and man conjoins himself to God. These things could not have been effected, unless it had been provided by God, that man should be born in total ignorance." After this declaration, all desired that a conclusion should be made from the things canvassed; and this was made: "That man is born into no science, in order that he may be able to come into them all, and advance to intelligence, and through this to wisdom; and that man is born into no love, in order that he may be able to come into all, by applications of the sciences from intelligence, and into love to God through love towards the neighbor, and thus to be conjoined to God, and by that means to become a man, and to live to eternity."

After this, they took the paper, and read the third object of investigation, which was, WHAT DOES THE TREE OF LIFE SIGNIFY; WHAT THE TREE OF THE KNOWLEDGE OF GOOD AND EVIL; AND WHAT THE EATING FROM THEM? And they all requested, that those who were from the East would unfold this mystery, because it is of deeper understanding, and because those who are from the East are in flammeous light, that is, in the wisdom of love; and this wisdom is meant by the garden of Eden, in which those two trees were placed. And they answered, "We will speak; but, because man does not take any from himself, but from God, we will speak from Him, but still from ourselves, as from ourselves." And then they said, "A tree signifies man, and its fruit, the good of life; thence, by the tree of life, is signified man living from God; and because love and wisdom and charity and faith, or good and truth, make the life of God in man, by the tree of life is signified the man in whom those things are from God, and who has thence eternal life. Similar things are signified by the tree of life, from which it will be given to eat, *Rev.* ii. 7, xxii. 2, 14. By the tree of the knowledge of good and evil, is signified man believing that he lives from himself, and not from God; thus, that love and wisdom, charity and faith, that is, good and truth, are in man, his, and not God's; believing this, because he thinks, and wills, and speaks, and acts, in all likeness and appearance, as from himself; and because man thence persuades himself that he is a God, therefore the serpent said, *God doth know, that, in the day when ye shall eat of the fruit of that tree, your eyes will be opened, and ye will be as God, knowing good and evil*, Gen. iii. 5. By eating from those trees is signified reception and appropriation; by eating from the tree of life, the reception of eternal life; by eating from the tree of the knowledge of good and evil, the reception of damnation. By the serpent is meant the devil, as to the love of self, and the pride of one's own intelligence; and that love is the possessor of that tree, and the men who are in pride from that love, are those trees. They are, therefore, in an enormous error, who believe that Adam was wise, or did good from himself, and that this was his state of integrity; when, yet, Adam himself on account of that belief, was cursed; for this is signified by eating of the tree of the knowledge of good and evil; wherefore, he then fell from the state of integrity which he had from this, that he believed that he was wise and did good from God, and not at all from himself; for this is meant by eating from the tree of life. The Lord alone, when He was in the world, was wise from Himself, and did good from Himself, because the Divine Itself, from nativity, was in Him, and was his; wherefore also by his own power, He became a Redeemer and Savior." From all these things, they made this conclusion; that "By the tree of life, and by the tree of the knowledge of good and evil, and by eating from them, is meant, that the life of man is God in him, and that then he has heaven and eternal life, and that the death of man is the persuasion and belief that the life of man is not God, but himself, whence he has hell and eternal death, which is damnation."

After this, they looked at the paper which was left by the angels upon the table, and saw written underneath, JOIN THOSE THREE TOGETHER INTO ONE SENTENCE; and then they collected them, and saw that those three cohered in one series, and that that series or sentence is this; that "Man was created, that he might receive love and wisdom from God, and yet in all likeness as from himself, and this for the sake of reception and conjunction; and that, therefore, man is not born into any love, nor into any science, nor even into any power of loving and becoming wise from himself; wherefore, if he ascribes all the good of love, and all the truth of wisdom, to God, he becomes a living man; but if he ascribes them to himself, he becomes a dead man." This they wrote on a new paper, and laid it upon the table; and lo, suddenly the angels came in a bright cloud, and carried the paper away into heaven; and, after it was read there, those who sat upon the seats heard thence the words, "Well, well, well." And immediately there appeared one thence, as it were flying, who had, as it were, two wings about the feet, and two about the temples, bringing the prizes, which were robes, caps, and wreaths of laurel; and he alighted, and gave to those towards the North, robes of an opaline color; to those towards the West, robes of a scarlet color; to those towards the South, caps, whose borders were adorned with bands of gold and pearls, and the elevations of the left side with diamonds, cut in the form of flowers; but to those towards the East he gave wreaths of laurel in which were rubies and sapphires. And they all, decorated with these rewards, left the school of wisdom, and went home with joy

CONCERNING THE OMNIPOTENCE, OMNISCIENCE AND OMNIPRESENCE OF GOD.

49. WE have treated of THE DIVINE LOVE AND THE DIVINE WISDOM, and shown that these two are the DIVINE ESSENCE: it follows now to treat of the Omnipotence, Omniscience and Omnipresence of God, because these three proceed from the Divine Love and the Divine Wisdom, scarcely otherwise than the power and presence of the sun in this world, and in all and every part of it, by means of light and heat. The heat also from the sun of the spiritual world, in the midst of which is Jehovah God, in its essence, is Divine Love, and the light thence is Divine Wisdom; whence it is manifest, that as infinity, immensity and eternity appertain to the Divine Esse, so omnipotence, omniscience and omnipresence appertain to the Divine Essence. But because those three universal predicables of the Divine Essence have not hitherto been understood, because their progression, according to their own ways, which are the laws of order, was unknown, it is proper to exhibit them here by distinct articles, which will be, I. *That Omnipotence, Omniscience and Omnipresence are of the Divine Wisdom from the Divine Love.* II. *That the Omnipotence, Omniscience and Omnipresence of God can not be known, unless it be known what Order is, and unless these properties of it be known, that God is Order, and that, at the creation, He introduced Or-*

der into the universe, and into all and every part of it. III. *That the Omnipotence of God in the universe, and in all and every part of it, proceeds and operates according to the laws of his Order.* IV. *That God is omniscient, that is, perceives, sees and knows all and every thing, even to the most minute, which is done according to Order; and thence also whatever is done contrary to Order.* V. *That God is omnipresent from the firsts to the lasts of his Order.* VI. *That man was created a form of Divine Order.* VII. *That man is so far in power against the evil and the false from the Divine Omnipotence, and that he is so far in wisdom concerning the good and the true from the Divine Omniscience, and that he is so far in God from the Divine Omnipresence, as he lives according to Divine Order.* But these articles are to be explained one by one.

50. I. THAT OMNIPOTENCE, OMNISCIENCE AND OMNIPRESENCE ARE OF THE DIVINE WISDOM FROM THE DIVINE LOVE.

That omnipotence, omniscience and omnipresence are of the Divine Wisdom from the Divine Love, is an arcanum from heaven, which has not hitherto shone in the understanding of any one; because no one has yet known what love is in its essence, nor what wisdom thence is in its essence, and still less concerning the influx of one into the other, which is, that love, with all and every thing of it, flows into wisdom, and resides in it, as a king in his kingdom, or as a master in his house, and relinquishes all the government of justice to judgment; and because justice is of love, and judgment is of wisdom, he relinquishes all the government of love to his wisdom; but this arcanum will receive additional light in what follows: in the mean time, let it serve for a canon. That God is omnipotent, omniscient, and omnipresent, by means of the wisdom of his love, is also meant by these words in John; *In the beginning was the Word, and the Word was with God, and the Word was God. All things were made by Him, and without Him there was nothing made that was made In Him was life, and the life was the light of men; and the world was made by Him; and the Word became flesh,* i. 1, 3, 4, 10, 14. By the *Word* there, is meant the Divine Truth, or, what amounts to the same, the Divine Wisdom; wherefore it is also called life and light; and life and light are no other than wisdom.

51. Since, in the Word, justice is predicated of the Divine Love, and judgment of the Divine Wisdom, therefore some passages shall be adduced to prove, that the government of God is effected in the world by means of those two; which passages are—JEHOVAH, JUSTICE *and* JUDGMENT *are the support of thy throne*, Psalm lxxxix. 15. *Let him who glorieth, glory in this, that* JEHOVAH *doeth* JUDGMENT *and* JUSTICE *in the earth*, Jerem. ix. 23. *Let* JEHOVAH *be exalted, because He hath filled the earth with* JUDGMENT *and* JUSTICE, Isaiah xxxiii. 5. JUDGMENT *shall flow as water, and* JUSTICE *as a mighty torrent*, Amos v. 24. JEHOVAH, *thy* JUSTICE *is as the mountains of God, thy* JUDGMENTS *are as a great abyss*, Psalm xxxvi. 7. JEHOVAH *will bring forth his* JUSTICE *as the light, and his* JUDGMENT *as the noonday*, Psalm xxxvii. 6. JEHOVAH *will judge his people in* JUSTICE, *and his miserable ones in* JUDGMENT, Psalm lxxii. 2. *When I shall have learned the* JUDGMENTS *of thy* JUSTICE, Psalm cxix. 7, 164. *I will betroth thee unto Me in* JUSTICE *and* JUDGMENT, Hosea ii. 19. *Zion shall be redeemed in* JUSTICE, *and her converts in* JUDGMENT, Isaiah i. 27. *He shall sit upon the throne of David, and upon his kingdom, to establish it in* JUDGMENT *and* JUSTICE, Isaiah ix. 7. *I will raise unto David a righteous branch, who shall reign as king, and shall do* JUDGMENT and JUSTICE *in the earth*, Jerem. xxiii. 5; xxxiii. 15: and in other places it is said, that they ought to do JUSTICE and JUDGMENT, as in Isaiah i. 21 v. 16; lviii. 2; Jerem. iv. 1: xxii. 3, 13, 15; Ezekiel xviii. 5; xxxiii. 14, 16, 19; Amos vi. 12; Mich. vii. 9; Deut. xxxiii. 21; John xvi. 8, 10, 11

52. II. That the Omnipotence, Omniscience and Omnipresence of God cannot be known, unless it be known what Order is, and unless these Properties of it be known, that God is Order, and that, at the Creation, He introduced Order into the Universe, and into all and every Part of it.

How many and how great absurdities have crept into the minds of men, and thence, through the heads of innovators, into the church, in consequence of their not understanding the Order in which God created the universe, and all and every part of it, will be evident from the bare mention of them in the following pages. But here we will first explain *Order*, by a general definition of it. *Order is the quality of the disposition, determination and activity of the parts, substances or entities which make the form, whence is the state, whose perfection wisdom from its love produces, or whose imperfection the insanity of reason from cupidity forges.* In this definition, substance, form and state are mentioned; and by *substance*, we at the same time mean *form*, because every substance is a form, and the quality of the form is its state, the perfection or imperfection of which results from order. But these things, because they are metaphysical, cannot but be in darkness; but this will be dispersed in what follows by applications to examples, which will illustrate the subject.

53. That God is Order, is because He is Substance itself and Form itself; *Substance*, because all things which subsist, existed and exist from Him; *Form*, because every quality of substances arose and arises from Him: quality is derived from no other source than from form. Now, because God is the very, the only, and the first Substance and Form, and, at the same time, the very and the only Love, and the very and the only Wisdom, and because wisdom from love makes form, and the state and quality of this is according to the order therein, it follows that God is Order itself, and that, from Himself, He introduced order into the universe, and also into all and every part of it, and that He introduced the most perfect order, because all things which He created were good, as it is read in the book of Creation. It will be demonstrated in its proper place, that evils began to exist at the same time with hell, thus after creation. But now to such things as more readily enter, more clearly enlighten, and more gently affect, the understanding.

54. But what the order is, in which the universe was created, cannot be fully explained but by many pages: some sketch of it will be exhibited in the following Lemma concerning creation. It is to be held, that all things in the universe were created in their orders, so that they may subsist each one by itself, and that from the beginning they were so created, that they may conjoin themselves with the universal order, to the intent, that each particular order may subsist in the universal, and thus make one. But to refer to some examples: Man is created according to his order, and also every particular part of him, according to its order; as the head and the body, each according to its order; the heart, the lungs, the liver, the pancreas, the stomach, according to their orders; every organ of motion, which is called a muscle, according to its order; and every organ of sense, as the eye, the ear, the tongue, each respectively, according to its order; nay, there is not the smallest artery or fibril there, which is not according to its order; and yet these innumerable parts conjoin themselves with the whole, and so insert themselves in it, that they together make one. The case is similar with other things, the bare mention of which is sufficient for illustration; every beast of the earth, every bird of the air, every fish of the sea, every reptile, nay, every worm, even to the moth, is created according to its order; in like manner, every tree, every grove, every shrub, and every herb, according to its order; and moreover every stone and every mineral, even to every particle

of the dust of the earth, is according to its order.

55. Who does not see, that there is not an empire, kingdom, dukedom, republic, state, or family, which is not established by laws, which make the order, and thus the form, of its government? In each of them, the laws of justice are in the highest place, political laws in the second, and economical laws in the third: if these are compared with man, the laws of justice make his head, political laws his body, and economical laws his dress; wherefore also these, like the dress, may be changed. But as to what concerns the order, according to which the church is established by God, it is this; that God is in all and every part of it; and the neighbor is he towards whom order is to be exercised. The laws of that order are as many as there are truths in the Word; the laws which relate to God will make its head, the laws which relate to the neighbor will make its body, and the ceremonies will make the dress; for unless these hold the others together, in their order, it would be as if the body were stripped naked, and exposed to the heat in summer, and to the cold in winter; or as if the walls and roof should be removed from a temple, and thus the sacred asylum, the altar, and the pulpit, should stand without protection, exposed to various violences.

56. III. That the Omnipotence of God, as well in the Universe as in all and every Part of it, proceeds and operates according to the Laws of his Order.

God is omnipotent, because He has all power from Himself, and all others from Him. His power and will are one; and because He wills nothing but what is good, therefore He can do nothing but what is good. In the spiritual world, no one can do any thing contrary to his own will; this they derive there from God, whose power and will are one. God also is Good itself; wherefore, whilst He does good, He is in Himself, and He cannot go out of Himself. Thence it appears, that his omnipotence proceeds and operates within the sphere of the extension of good, which is infinite; for this sphere, from the inmost, fills the universe and all and every thing there; and, from the inmost, governs those things which are without, as far as they conjoin themselves according to their orders; and if they do not conjoin themselves, still it sustains them, and with all effort labors to bring them into order, according to the universal order in which God is in his omnipotence; and if this is not effected, they are cast out from Him, where, nevertheless, He sustains them from the inmost. From this it is evident, that the Divine Omnipotence can by no means go out from itself to the contact of any thing evil, nor promote it from itself, for evil turns itself away; thence it is, that evil is entirely separated from Him, and cast into hell, between which and heaven, where He is, there is a great gulf. From these few things it may be seen how delirious they are, who think, and more so who believe, and still more so who teach, that God can condemn any one, curse any one, cast any one into hell, predestinate the soul of any one to eternal death, avenge injuries, be angry, or punish. He cannot even turn away his face from any one, or look at him with a stern countenance; these and similar things are contrary to his essence, and what is contrary to this, is contrary to Himself.

57. It is, at this day, a prevailing opinion, that the omnipotence of God is like the absolute power of a king in the world, who can at his pleasure do whatever he wills, absolve and condemn whom he pleases, make the guilty innocent, declare the faithless faithful, exalt the unworthy and undeserving above the worthy and deserving; nay, that he can, under any pretext, deprive his subjects of their goods, and sentence them to death; besides other similar things. From this infatuated opinion, faith and doctrine, concerning the divine omnipotence, as many falsities, fallacies and chimeras have flowed into the church, as there are changes, articulations, and generations of faith therein; and as many more may yet

flow in, as would equal the number of pitchers which might be filled with water from a large lake, or of serpents which creep out of their holes, and regale on a sunny day in the desert of Arabia. What need is there of more than two words, *omnipotence* and *faith;* and then to spread before the vulgar conjectures, fables and trifles, such as fall into the senses of the body? For reason is utterly banished, and when reason is banished, in what does the thought of man excel that of a bird that flies over his head; or what is the spirituality, which man has above the beasts, but something like the stench in the dens of beasts, which is agreeable to the wild beasts, but not to man, unless he be like them? If the extension of the divine omnipotence were to do evil as well as good, what would be the distinction between God and the devil? Would it be any other than that between two monarchs, one of whom is a king, and at the same time a tyrant, and the other a tyrant, whose power is restrained, whence he is not to be called a king; or that between two shepherds, one of whom is permitted to act the part of a sheep, and also of a leopard; and the other is not permitted to do so? Who may not know that good and evil are opposites, and that if God, from his omnipotence, could will the one and the other, and, from willing, could do them, He could do nothing at all? Thus He would have no power, much less omnipotence. This would be as if two wheels, in a contrary motion, should mutually act against each other, from which re-action, both wheels would stop and be entirely at rest; or like a ship in a torrent driving it contrary to its course, which, unless it rest at anchor, would be carried away and lost; or like a man who has two wills opposed to each other, one of which must necessarily be at rest, while the other acts; but if both should act at the same time, delirium or giddiness would seize his mind.

58. If the omnipotence of God were, according to the faith at this day, absolute for doing evil as well as good, would it not be possible, nay, easy, for God to elevate all hell into heaven, and to convert devils and satans into angels, and to purify every sinner upon earth in a moment from his sins, to renew, sanctify and regenerate him, and from a child of wrath to make a child of grace, that is, to justify him; which would be done merely by the application and imputation of the righteousness of his Son? But God by his omnipotence cannot do this, because it is contrary to the laws of his order in the universe, and at the same time contrary to the laws of order prescribed to every man, which are, that they should conjoin themselves by a mutual inclination; that it is so, will be seen in the sequel of this work. From that infatuated opinion and faith concerning the omnipotence of God, it would result, that God could convert every man-goat into a man-sheep, and, of his good pleasure, remove him from his left to his right side; also, that He could change the spirits of the dragon into the angels of Michael, and that He could give to a man, whose understanding is like that of a mole, the sight of an eagle; in a word, from a man-owl, make a man-dove. These things God cannot do, because they are contrary to the laws of his own order, although He continually wills and endeavors to effect them. If He could have done such things, He would not have permitted Adam to obey the serpent, and take fruit from the tree of the knowledge of good and evil, and put it to his mouth; if He could have done it, He would not have permitted Cain to kill his brother, David to number the people, Solomon to build temples to idols, and the kings of Judah and Israel to profane the temple, as they so often did; nay, if He could have done it, He would have saved the whole human race, without exception, through the redemption of his Son, and would have extirpated all hell. The ancient gentiles ascribed such omnipotence to their gods and goddesses, whence arose their fabulous stories, as concerning Deucalion and Pyrrha, that the stones thrown behind

them became men and women; concerning Apollo, that he changed Daphne into a laurel; concerning Diana, that she changed a hunter into a stag; and that another of their gods turned the virgins of Parnassus into magpies. There is, at this day, a similar belief concerning the divine omnipotence, whence so many fanatical, and thence heretical opinions, have been introduced into the world, in every country where there is any religion.

59. IV. THAT GOD IS OMNISCIENT, THAT IS, PERCEIVES, SEES AND KNOWS ALL AND EVERY THING, EVEN TO THE MOST MINUTE, WHICH IS DONE ACCORDING TO ORDER, AND THENCE ALSO WHAT IS DONE CONTRARY TO ORDER.

That God is omniscient, that is, perceives, sees and knows all things, is, because he is Wisdom itself, and Light itself; and Wisdom itself perceives all things, and Light itself sees all things. That God is Wisdom itself, was shown above; that He is Light itself, is because He is the sun of the angelic heaven, which enlightens the understandings of all angels and all men; for, as the eye is enlightened by the light of the natural sun, so the understanding is enlightened by the light of the spiritual sun; nor is it only enlightened, but it is also filled with intelligence, according to the love of receiving it, since this light, in its essence, is wisdom; wherefore in David it is said, that *God dwelleth in light inaccessible;* and in the Revelation, that, *in the New Jerusalem, they have no need of a candle, because the Lord God enlighteneth them:* and in John, that *the Word which was in the beginning with God, and was God, is the light, which enlighteneth every man that cometh into the world.* By the *Word* is meant the Divine Wisdom. Thence it is, that the angels, as far as they are in wisdom, are so far in the brightness of light; and thence also it is, that in the Word, where light is mentioned, wisdom is meant.

60. That God perceives, sees and knows all things, even to the most minute, which are done according to order, is, because order is universal from all the several parts; for the several parts, taken together, are called a *universal,* as the particulars are called a *general;* and a universal, together with all its several parts, is a work cohering as one, so that one part cannot be touched and affected, without communicating to the rest some sensible perception of it. It is from this quality of order in the universe, that there is something similar in all created things in the universe; but this will be illustrated by comparisons taken from visible things. In the whole man, there are general things and particular things, and the general include the particular therein, and unite themselves together by such a connection, that one depends upon another: this is done by this, that there is a general covering about every member there, and that this insinuates itself into every part therein, so that they make one in every office and use. For example, the covering of every muscle enters into every moving fibre, and from itself clothes them; in like manner, the coverings of the liver, the pancreas and the spleen, enter into all the particular parts which are within; in like manner the covering of the lungs, which is called the *pleura,* into the interior parts of the lungs; and in like manner the pericardium, into all and every part of the heart; and, generally, the peritonæum, by anastomoses, with the coverings of all the viscera; in like manner the meninges of the brain; these, by threads emitted from them, enter into all the glands below them and, through these, into all the fibres, and, through these, into all parts of the body; thence it is, that the head, from the brains, governs all and every thing subject to itself. These things are adduced, merely for the purpose that, from visible things, some idea may be formed, how God perceives, sees and knows all things, even to the most minute, which are done according to order.

61. That God, from those things which are according to order, perceives, sees and knows all and every thing, even to the most minute, which is done contrary to order, is, because God does

not hold man in evil, but withholds him from evil; thus he does not lead him, but strives with him. From that perpetual striving, struggling, resistance, repugnance, and reaction of the evil and the false, against his good and truth, thus against Himself, He perceives both their quantity and quality. This follows from the omnipresence of God, in all and every part of his order, and, at the same time, from his perfect knowledge of all and every thing there; comparatively, as he who has an ear for music and harmony, accurately notices every discordant and unharmonious sound, as soon as it enters; in like manner, he whose senses are in their delight, readily perceives what is undelightful; or, as the eye, which is looking at a beautiful object, sees it distinctly while any thing ugly is at the side of it; wherefore it is customary for painters to place an ugly face at the side of a handsome one. It is similar with the good and the true, while they strive against the evil and the false; for they are distinctly perceived from their opposites; for every one, who is in good, can perceive what is evil; and he who is in truth, can see what is false; the cause is, because good is in the heat of heaven, and truth in its light; but evil is in the cold of hell, and the false in its darkness; which may be illustrated by this, that the angels of heaven can see whatever is done in hell, and what monsters are there; but, on the other hand, the spirits of hell cannot see any thing at all that is done in heaven, and not even the angels, any more than a blind man, or more than an eye looking into the naked air, or ether. Those whose understandings are in the light of wisdom, are like those who, at noon-day, stand upon a mountain, and see clearly all things that are below; and those who are in still superior light, are, comparatively, like those who, through telescopes, see the objects around and below them, as if they were present; but those who are in the infatuated light of hell, from the confirmation of falsities, are like those who stand upon the same mountain, in the time of night, with lanterns in their hands, and see nothing but the nearest objects, and the forms of these indistinctly, and their colors confusedly. A man who is in some light of truth, and yet in evil of life, while he is in the delight of his love of evil, does not at first see truths, otherwise than as a bat sees linen, hanging in a garden, to which it flies, as to its place of refuge; and afterwards he becomes as a bird of night, and at length as an owl; and then he becomes like a chimney-sweeper, sticking close to a black chimney, who, when he raises his eyes upwards, sees the sky beyond the smoke, and when he looks downwards, he sees the fire from which the smoke arises.

62. It is to be observed, that the perception of opposites differs from the perception of relatives; for opposites are without, and contrary to those things which are within; for an opposite begins to be, when one thing entirely ceases to be any thing, and another thing rises up with the effort of counteracting the former, as a wheel which acts against a wheel, or a stream against a stream; but relatives have respect to the disposition of many and various things in convenient and agreeable order, as of precious stones of divers colors in the stomacher of a queen, or of different colored flowers in an ornamental garland. There are, therefore, relatives in each opposite, in the good as well as in the evil, and in the true as well as in the false; thus in heaven as well as in hell; but the relatives in hell are all opposite to the relatives in heaven. Now, because God perceives and sees, and thence knows, all the relatives in heaven, from the order in which He is, and thence perceives, sees and knows all the opposite relatives in hell, as it follows from what was said above, it is manifest that God is omniscient in hell as well as in heaven, and likewise among men in the world; thus that He perceives, sees and knows their evils and falses, from the good and the true, in which He is, and which, in their essence, are Himself; for it is read, *If I ascend into heaven, Thou art there: if I lay me down in hell, be-*

hold Thou art there, Psalm cxxxix. 8; and in another place, *If they dig through into hell, thence shall my hand take them*, Amos ix. 2, 3.

63. V. THAT GOD IS OMNIPRESENT, FROM THE FIRSTS TO THE LASTS OF HIS ORDER.

That God is omnipresent, from the firsts to the lasts of his order, is by means of the heat and light of the sun of the spiritual world, in the midst of which He is: by means of this sun, order was made, and from it He sends forth heat and light, which pervade the universe, from the firsts to the lasts of it, and produce the life of men and every animal, and also the vegetative soul in every germ upon the earth; and those two flow into all and every thing, and cause every thing to live and grow, according to the order impressed upon them at the creation; and because God is not extended, and yet fills all the extenses of the universe, He is omnipresent. That God is in all space without space, and in all time without time, and that thence the universe, as to essence and order, is the fullness of God, has been elsewhere shown; and because it is so, by omnipresence He perceives all things; by omniscience He provides all things; and by omnipotence He operates all things; whence it is manifest, that omnipresence, omniscience and omnipotence make one, or that one supposes another, and thus that they cannot be separated.

64. The divine omnipresence may be illustrated by the wonderful presence of angels and spirits in the spiritual world. In this world, because there is no space, but only an appearance of space, an angel or a spirit may, in a moment, become present to another, provided he comes into a similar affection of love, and thence thought, for these two make the appearance of space. That such is the presence of all there, was manifest to me from this, that I could see Africans and Indians there very near me, although they are so many miles distant upon earth; nay, that I could become present to those who are in other planets of this system, and also to those who are in the planets in other systems, out of this solar system. By virtue of this presence, not of place, but of the appearance of place, I have conversed with apostles, deceased popes, emperors and kings; with the founders of the present church, Luther, Calvin and Melancthon; and with others from distant countries. Since such is the presence of angels and spirits, what limits can be set to the Divine presence in the universe, which is infinite! The reason that angels and spirits have such presence, is, because every affection of love, and thence every thought of the understanding, is in space without space, and in time without time; for any one can think of a brother, relation or friend in the Indies, and then have him, as it were, present to him; in like manner, he may be affected with their love by recollection. By these things, because they are familiar to every one, the divine omnipresence may, in some degree, be illustrated; and also by human thoughts, as, when any one recalls to his remembrance what he has seen upon a journey in various places, he is, as it were, present at those places. Nay, the sight of the body emulates that same presence; the eye does not perceive distances, except by intermediate objects, which, as it were, measure them. The sun itself would be near the eye, nay, in the eye, unless intermediate objects discovered that it is so distant: that it is so, writers on optics have also observed in their books. Such presence has each sight of man, both intellectual and corporeal, because his spirit sees through his eyes; but no beast has similar presence, because they have not any spiritual sight. From these things, it is evident, that God is omnipresent, from the firsts to the lasts of his order: that He is also omnipresent in hell, was shown in the preceding article.

65. VI. THAT MAN WAS CREATED A FORM OF DIVINE ORDER.

That man was created a form of divine order, is because he was created an image and likeness of God, and because God is Order itself, he was created an image and likeness of order. There are two things from which order exists, and by which it subsists—Divine Love and Divine Wisdom; and man was created a receptacle of them; wherefore, also, he was created in the order according to which those two act in the universe, and principally according to which they act in the angelic heaven; thence all that heaven is, in the greatest effigy, a form of divine order; and that heaven is, in the sight of God, as one man; and, also, there is a plenary correspondence between that heaven and man; for there is not any society in heaven, which does not correspond to some member, viscus or organ in man. Wherefore it is said in heaven, that this society is either in the province of the liver, or the pancreas, or the spleen, or the stomach, or the eye, or the ear, or the tongue, &c.; the angels themselves also know in what jurisdiction of any part of man they dwell. That it is so, has been given me to know to the life. I have seen a society, consisting of several thousands of angels, as one man; whence it was manifest, that heaven, in the complex, is an image of God, and an image of God is a form of divine order.

66. It is to be observed, that all things which proceed from the sun of the spiritual world, in the midst of which is Jehovah God, have some resemblance to man, and that thence, whatsoever things exist in that world, conspire to the human form, and, in their inmost, they exhibit it; whence all the objects, which are presented to the eyes there, are representatives of man. There appear there animals of every kind, and they are likenesses of the affections of the love, and thence of the thoughts, of the angels; and likewise shrubberies, flower-gardens, and green fields there; and it is given to know what affection this and that object represents; and, what is wonderful, when their inmost sight is opened, they know their own image in those things; and this is the case, because every man there is his own love, and thence his own thought; and because the affections, and thence the thoughts, in every man, are various and manifold, and some of them represent the affection of one animal, and some of another; therefore, images of their affections are thus exhibited. But more will be seen concerning these things in the following member concerning Creation. From these things also appears the truth, that the end of creation was an angelic heaven from the human race; consequently man, in whom God may dwell as in his receptacle; thence is the reason why man was created a form of divine order.

67. God, before the creation, was Love itself and Wisdom itself, and these two in the effort of doing uses; for love and wisdom, without use, are only volatile things of reason, and they also fly away, unless they apply themselves to use. The two former also, separate from the third, are like birds which are flying over a great ocean, and at length, being wearied with flying, they fall down, and are drowned. Thence it is evident, that the universe was created by God, that uses might exist; wherefore also the universe may be called a *theatre of uses;* and because man was the principal end of creation, it follows, that all and every thing was created for the sake of man and thence that all and every thing of order was brought together into him, and concentrated in him, that God might do primary uses through him. Love and wisdom, without their third, which is use, may be compared to the heat and light of the sun, which, unless they operated upon men, animals and vegetables, would be empty things; but they become real, by influx into them, and operation in them. There are also three things, which follow each other in order, end, cause and effect; and it is known, in the learned world, that the end is not any thing, unless it have respect to the efficient cause, and that the end and this cause are not any thing, unless the effect be produced; the end and the cause may, indeed, be abstractly contemplated in the mind, but still for the sake of some effect, which the end intends and the

cause procures. It is similar with love, wisdom and use; and use is what love intends and produces by the cause; and when the use is produced, love and wisdom really exist, and make for themselves a habitation and abode in it, and rest, as it were, in their own house. It is similar with the man in whom are the love and wisdom of God, while he is doing uses; and that he may do the uses of God, he is created an image and likeness, that is, a form, of divine order.

68. VII. That Man is so far in Power against the Evil and the False, from the Divine Omnipotence, and that he is so far in Wisdom concerning the Good and the True, from the Divine Omniscience, and that he is so far in God from the Divine Omnipresence, as he lives according to Divine Order.

The reason that man is so far in power against the evil and the false, from the divine omnipotence, as he lives according to divine order, is, because no one can resist evils, and the falses thence, but God alone; for all evils, and the falses thence, are from hell; and in hell they cohere as one, just as all goods, and the truths thence, do in heaven; for, as was said above, the whole heaven is, in the sight of God, as one man, and, on the other hand, hell as one giant, which is a monster; wherefore, to act against one evil and one false thence, is to act against that monstrous giant, or hell; and this no one can do but God, because He is omnipotent; whence it is manifest, that man, unless he goes to the omnipotent God, has, from himself, no more power against the evil, and the false thence, than a fish has against the ocean, than a flee against a whale, or than a particle of dust against a falling mountain, and much less than a locust has against an elephant, or a fly against a camel. And, moreover, man has still less power against the evil, and the false thence, because he is born in evil, and evil cannot act against itself. Hence it follows, that unless a man lives according to divine order, that is, unless he acknowledges God and his omnipotence, and from this, protection against hell; and, moreover, unless man, on his part, fights with the evil in himself (for this together with that is of order), he cannot but be immersed and overwhelmed in hell, and there be driven about by evils, one after another, as a boat on the sea is driven about by tempests.

69. The reason that man is so far in wisdom, concerning the good and the true, from the divine omniscience, as he lives according to divine order, is, because all the love of good, and all the wisdom of truth, or all the good of love, and all the truth of wisdom, are from God. That it is so, is also according to the confession of all the churches in the Christian world; whence it follows, that man cannot be interiorly in any truth of wisdom unless from God, because God is Omniscience, that is, infinite wisdom. The human mind is distinguished into three degrees, like the angelic heaven, and thence it may be elevated to a degree higher and higher, and also it may be let down to a degree lower and lower; but as far as it is elevated to the higher degrees, so far it is elevated into wisdom, because into the light of heaven; and this cannot be done, except by God; and as far as it is elevated thither, so far it is a man; and as far as it is let down to the lower degrees, so far it is in the infatuated light of hell, and so far it is not a man, but a beast. Man, also, for this reason, stands erect upon his feet, and looks towards heaven with his face, and can elevate it to the zenith; but a beast stands upon his feet, in a posture parallel with the earth, and with his whole countenance looks thither; nor can he, without difficulty, raise it up towards heaven. The man who elevates his mind to God, and acknowledges that all the truth of wisdom is from Him, and, at the same time, lives according to order, is like one who stands upon a high tower, and sees a populous city below him, and, at the same time, whatever is done there in the streets; but the man who confirms in himself the idea, that all the truth of wisdom

is from the natural light with him, thus from himself, is like one who stays in a cavern under that tower, and looks, through the holes there, into the same city; he sees nothing but the walls of one house in that city, and how the bricks there cohere. Again, the man who derives wisdom from God, is like a bird flying aloft, which looks about upon all things that are in the gardens, woods and villages, and flies to those things which are of use to it; but the man who derives such things as are of wisdom, from himself, without a belief that they are still from God, is like a hornet, which flies along near the ground, and when it sees a heap of dung, it flies to it, and regales itself with its stench. Every man, as long as he lives in the world, walks in the midst between heaven and hell, and thence is in equilibrium, so that he has freedom of will to look upwards to God, or downwards to hell: if he looks upwards to God, he acknowledges that all wisdom is from God, and he, as to his spirit, is actually with the angels in heaven; but he who looks downwards, as every one does who is in the false from evil, is, as to his spirit, actually with the devils in hell.

70. That man is so far in God, from the divine omnipresence, as he lives according to order, is because God is omnipresent, and because where He is, in his order, there He is as in Himself; because He is Order itself, as was shown above. Now, because man was created a form of divine order, God is in him, and, so far as he lives according to divine order, fully; but if he does not live according to divine order, still God is in him, but in the highest parts of him, and gives him the power to understand truth and to will good; that is, He gives him a faculty for understanding, and an inclination for loving; but as far as man lives contrary to order, so far he shuts up the lower parts of his mind, or spirit, and thus prevents God from descending and filling the lower parts of him with his presence; thence God is in him, but he not in God. It is a general canon in heaven, that God is in every man, evil as well as good, but that man is not in God, unless he lives according to order; for the Lord says, that *He willeth that man should be in Him, and He in man*, John xv. 4. That man is in God, by a life according to order, is because God is omnipresent in the universe, and in all and every part of it, in the inmost of those parts, for these are in order; but in those things which are contrary to order, which are such only as are out of the inmost, God is omnipresent by a continual struggle with them, and by a continual effort to bring them back to order; wherefore, as far as man allows himself to be brought back to order, so far God is omnipresent in the whole of him; consequently, so far God is in him and he in God. The absence of God from man is no more possible than the absence of the sun, by means of heat and light, from the earth; the objects of the earth, however, are not affected by the sun's virtue, except so far as they receive the light and heat proceeding from it, as is done in the time of spring and summer. These things may be thus applied to the omnipresence of God; that man is so far in spiritual heat, and, at the same time, in spiritual light, that is, in the good of love and in the truth of wisdom, as he is in order. Spiritual heat and light, however, are not like natural heat and light; for natural heat recedes from the earth in the time of winter, and light in the time of night; and this is the case, because the earth, by its rotations about its axis, and its revolutions about the sun, makes those times. But spiritual heat and light are not so; for God, by means of his sun, is present with both, and does not undergo changes, as the sun of the world apparently does. Man himself turns himself away, comparatively, as the earth turns from its sun; and when he turns himself away from the truths of wisdom, he is like the earth turned from its sun in the time of night; and when he turns himself away from the goods of love, he is like the earth turned from its sun in the time of winter. Such is the correspondence between

the effects and uses from the sun of the spiritual world, and the effects and uses from the sun of the natural world.

---

71. To the above shall be added three Relations. First. I once heard under me, as it were, a roaring of the sea; and I asked, "What is this?" And some one said to me, that it was a tumult amongst those who are gathered together in the lower part of the earth, which is next above hell; and presently the ground, which made a covering over them, opened wide, and lo through the opening, there flew out in flocks, birds of night, which spread themselves to the left hand; and immediately after them, rose up locusts, which leaped upon the grass of the ground, and made a desert wherever they came; and a little afterwards, I heard alternately from those birds of night, as it were a howling, and at the side a horrid screaming, as it were from spectres in the woods. After this, I saw beautiful birds from heaven, which spread themselves to the right hand: those birds were remarkable for their wings as of gold, interspersed with streaks and spots as of silver, and upon the heads of some of them were crests in the form of crowns. Whilst I was looking and wondering at these things, suddenly a spirit raised himself up from the lower part of the earth where that tumult was, who could transform himself into an angel of light; and he cried, "Where is he who speaks and writes concerning the order, to which the omnipotent God has tied himself, in relation to man? We have heard these things below, through the covering." While he was above that earth, he ran through a paved street, and at length came to me, and immediately feigned himself an angel of heaven, and speaking in a tone not his own, he said, "Are you the man who thinks and speaks concerning order? Tell me, briefly, what order is, and some things which are of order." And I replied, "I will tell you the general things, but not the particulars, because you cannot comprehend them." And I said, "I. That God is Order itself II. That He created man from order in order and to order. III. That He created his rational mind according to the order of the whole spiritual world, and his body according to the order of the whole natural world; wherefore man was called, by the ancients, a *little heaven*, and a *little world* IV. That thence it is a law of order, that man, from his little heaven, or little spiritual world, should govern his little world, or his little natural world, as God, from his great heaven, or spiritual world, governs the great world, or natural world, in all and every part of it. V. That it is a law of order thence resulting, that man ought to introduce himself into faith by truths from the Word, and into charity by good works, and thus to reform and regenerate himself. VI. That it is a law of order, that man should purify himself from sins by his own labor and power, and not stand still in a belief of his inability, and expect that God should immediately wipe away his sins. VII. It is also a law of order, that man should love God with all his soul, and with all his heart, and his neighbor as himself, and not wait and expect that such love should be infused into his mind and his heart, immediately, by God, as bread from the baker is put into his mouth; besides many similar things." When the satan had heard these things, he replied, with a mild voice, in which there was inwardly craft, "What is it that you say? that man, of his own power, is to introduce himself into order, by obeying its laws? Do you not know, that man is not under the law, but under grace? that all things are given to him freely? and that he cannot take any thing to himself, unless it be given him from heaven? and that man, of himself, has no more power to act than the statue, Lot's wife, or no more than Dagon, the idol of the Philistines at Ekron? and that thus it is impossible for man to justify himself, which must be done by faith and charity?" In reply to these questions, I only said, "It is also a law of order, that man, by his own

labor and power, should procure to himself faith, by means of truths from the Word, and yet he should believe, that not a grain of faith is from himself, but from God; and also that man, by his own labor and power, should justify himself, and yet he should believe, that not a jot of justification is from himself, but from God. Is it not commanded, that man should believe in God, and love God with all his strength, and his neighbor as himself? Think, and say how these things could have been commanded by God, if man had no power to obey and do them." When the satan had heard this, he was changed as to his face, which from white became at first dark, and then black; and, speaking from his own mouth, he said, "You have spoken paradoxes against paradoxes;" and then he instantly sunk down to his companions, and disappeared. And the birds on the left hand, together with the spectres, uttered unusual sounds, and cast themselves into the sea, which is there called the Sea *Suph*, and the locusts followed them by leaps; and the air was purified, and the earth was cleared of those wild creatures, and the tumult below ceased, and it became tranquil and serene.

72. Second Relation. I once heard an unusual murmur at a distance, and I, in the spirit, followed the direction of the sound, and approached to it. When I came to the beginning of it, behold there was a company of spirits reasoning about Imputation and Predestination. They were Dutchmen and Englishmen; and some from other nations were intermixed, who, at the conclusion of every argument, exclaimed, "Wonderful! Wonderful!" The question discussed was, "Why God does not impute the merit and righteousness of his Son to all and every one created and afterwards redeemed by Him. Is He not omnipotent? Could He not, if He would, make Lucifer, the dragon, and all the goats, archangels? Is He not omnipotent? Why does He permit the injustice and impiety of the devil to triumph over the righteousness of his Son, and over the piety of the worshippers of God? What is easier for God than to bestow faith, and thus salvation, upon all? What is necessary for this but a single word? And if all are not saved, does He not act contrary to his own words, which are, that He desires the salvation of all, and the death of none? Say, therefore, from whom, and in whom, is the cause of the damnation of those who perish." And then one of the Dutchmen, a Supralapsarian Predestinarian, said, "Is not this according to the good pleasure of the Almighty? Shall the clay find fault with the potter, because he has made of it a vessel of dishonor?" And another said, "The salvation of every one is in His hand as a balance in the hand of him who uses it." There stood at the sides some who were simple in faith and upright in heart, some of them inflamed in their eyes, some as it were amazed, some as it were intoxicated, and some as it were suffocated, muttering amongst themselves, "What have we to do with those deliriums? Their faith has infatuated them, which is, that God the Father imputes the righteousness of his Son to whomsoever and whensoever He pleases, and sends the Holy Spirit to give assurances of that righteousness; and, lest man should claim any thing to himself, in the work of salvation, he must be altogether like a stone in the business of justification, and like a stock in spiritual things." And one of them thrust himself into the company, and speaking with a loud voice, he said, "O you simpletons, your reasoning is futile. You are totally ignorant that the omnipotent God is Order itself, and that the laws of order are myriads, even as many as there are truths in the Word, and that God cannot act contrary to them, because to act contrary to them, would be to act contrary to Himself, and thus not only contrary to his justice, but also contrary to his omnipotence." And he saw at his right hand, as it were a sheep, and a lamb, and a dove flying; and at his left hand, as it were a goat, a wolf, and a vulture; and he

said, "Do you suppose that God, by virtue of his omnipotence, could change that goat into a sheep, or that wolf into a lamb, or that vulture into a dove, or the contrary? No; for it is contrary to the laws of his order, of which not even a tittle can fall to the ground, according to his own words. How, then, can He insert the righteousness of his Son's redemption into any one who rebels against the laws of his righteousness? How can Righteousness itself commit unrighteousness, predestinate any to hell, cast any into the fire, at which the devil stands with torches in his hand to feed it? O simpletons, destitute of the spirit! your faith has seduced you. Is it not as a snare in your hands for catching doves?" A certain magician, hearing these words, formed a snare, as it were, from that faith, and hung it upon a tree saying, "You will see that I shall catch that dove." And presently a hawk flew up, and put his neck into the snare, and was caught; and the dove, seeing the hawk, flew away. The by-standers wondered, and exclaimed, "Even this sport is a proof of justice."

73. The next day there came to me several from the company who were in the faith of predestination and imputation, and they said, "We are, as it were, drunken, not with wine, but with the discourse of that man yesterday. He spoke concerning omnipotence, and, at the same time, concerning order; and concluded that, as there is divine omnipotence, so also there is divine order, nay, that God himself is Order; and he said, that there are as many laws of order as there are truths in the Word, which are not only thousands, but myriads of myriads, and that God is bound to his laws there, and man to his. What, then, is the divine omnipotence, if it is tied up by laws? for thus all that is absolute recedes from omnipotence; and, in that case, is not the power of God less than that of a king in the world, who is a monarch? for he can change the laws of justice at his pleasure, and act absolutely, like Octavius Augustus, and also like Nero. After we began to think of omnipotence tied up by laws, we became, as it were, drunken and are ready to fall into a swoon, unless a remedy be quickly applied; for, according to our faith, we have prayed that God the Father would have mercy on us, for the sake of his Son; and we believed, that He could have mercy on whom He would, and remit sins to whom He pleased, and save whom He would; and we durst not take away the least particle from his omnipotence. Wherefore, to bind God with the chains of any of his own laws, we regarded as great wickedness, because it seemed contradictory to his omnipotence.' Having said these words, they looked at me, and I at them, and I saw that they were amazed; and I said, "I will pray to the Lord, and thence will bring to you a remedy, by illustrating this subject; but now only by examples." And I said, "The omnipotent God created the world, from the order in Himself, and thus into the order in which He is, and according to which He governs; and He stamped upon the universe, and upon all and every part of it, its proper order; upon man, beast, bird, fish, worm and tree of every kind; nay, upon the grass its own order. But, to illustrate by examples, I will briefly adduce the following: The laws of order, prescribed to man, are, that man should acquire for himself truths from the Word and think of them naturally, and, as far as he can, rationally, and thus procure for himself natural faith: the laws of order, then, on the part of God, are, that He should approach and fill the truths with his divine light, and thus man's natural faith, which is only science and persuasion, with his divine essence; thus, and not otherwise, saving faith is produced. The case is similar with charity; but we will mention some particulars. God cannot, according to the laws of his order, remit sins to any man, except so far as man, according to his laws, ceases from them. God cannot spiritually regenerate man, except so far as man according to his laws, naturally regen

erates himself. God is in the perpetual effort of regenerating, and thus of saving man; but this He cannot effect, except as man prepares himself a receptacle, and thus prepares the way for God, and opens the door; a bridegroom cannot enter into the chamber of a virgin not betrothed to him; she shuts the door, and keeps the key with her within; but after the virgin has been betrothed, she gives the key to the bridegroom. God could not, by his omnipotence, have redeemed men, unless He had become man; nor could He have made his Human Divine, unless his Human had been, at first, as the human of an infant, and afterwards as the human of a boy; and unless the Human afterwards had formed itself into a receptacle and habitation, into which its Father might enter; which was done by fulfilling all things of the Word, that is, all the laws of order there; and as far as He did this, so far He united Himself to the Father, and the Father united Himself to Him. But these are a few things, adduced for the sake of illustration, that you may see, that the divine omnipotence is in order, and that its government, which is called *Providence*, is according to order; and that it acts continually and eternally according to the laws of its order; and that it cannot act contrary to them nor change them, as to a single tittle, because order, with all its laws, is Himself." When these words were spoken, a radiant light, of a golden color, flowed in through the roof, and formed cherubs flying in the air; and the effulgence thence enlightened the temples of some towards the occiput, but not as yet towards the forehead; for they muttered, "We are still ignorant what order is." And I said, "It will be revealed to you, when the things hitherto said to you shall have received some light."

74. Third Relation. I saw, at a distance, several gathered together, with caps on their heads; some with caps bound around with silk and who were of the ecclesiastic order; some with caps whose borders were adorned with bands of gold, who were of the civil order; all these were men of science and erudition; and, moreover I saw some with turbans, who were illiterate. I approached, and heard them conversing together concerning Divine Power without limits, saying, that if it proceeded according to any established laws of order, it could not be without limits, but limited, and thus power, and not omnipotence. But who does not see, that no law of necessity can compel omnipotence to do so, and not otherwise? Certainly, while we think of omnipotence, and at the same time of the laws of order, according to which it is obliged to proceed, our preconceived ideas concerning omnipotence fall, like a hand when its staff is broken. When they saw me near them, some of them ran up to me, and, with some vehemence, said, "Are you the man that has circumscribed God with laws, as with bonds? How insolent this is! Thus you have also torn to pieces our faith, upon which our salvation is founded, in the midst of which we place the righteousness of the Redeemer; upon that, the omnipotence of God the Father; and we make the operation of the Holy Spirit an appendage; and the efficacy of it is in the absolute impotency of man, in spiritual things, for whom it is enough to speak of the fullness of justification, which is in that faith, from the omnipotence of God. But we have heard that you see vanity in it, because there is in it nothing of divine order on the part of man." On hearing these words, I opened my mouth, and, speaking with a loud voice, I said, "Learn the laws of divine order, and afterwards open that faith, and you will see a vast desert, and in it an oblong and crooked Leviathan, and all around it, nets, as it were, entangled into an inexplicable knot; but do you, as it is read of Alexander, when he saw the Gordian knot, that he drew his sword, and cut it in two, and thus loosed its entanglements, and threw its thongs on the ground, and trampled them under his feet." At these words, the congregation bit their tongues, wishing to sharpen them for invectives; but

they durst not, because they saw heaven open above me, and heard a voice thence—"Listen with moderation to hear, for the first time, what is the order, according to the laws of which the omnipotent God acts. God from Himself, as Order, in order and into order, created the universe, and likewise man, in whom He fixed the laws of his order, by which he became an image and likeness of God; which laws, in the sum, are, that he should believe in God and love his neighbor, and as far as he does those two things by natural power, so far he makes himself a receptacle of the divine omnipotence, and so far God conjoins Himself to him, and him to Himself; thence his faith becomes living and saving, and his practice becomes charity, also living and saving. But it should be known, that God is perpetually present, and continually strives and acts in man, and also touches his free will, but never violates it; for if He should violate the free will of man, man's dwelling in God would perish, and there would be that of God only in man; and this dwelling is in all, as well in those who are upon the earth as in those who are in the heavens, and also in those who are in the hells; for thence is their power to will and understand. But there is no reciprocal dwelling of man in God, except with those who live according to the laws of order prescribed in the Word; and these become images and likenesses of Him, and to them paradise is given for a possession, and the fruit of the tree of life for food. But the rest gather themselves together around the tree of the knowledge of good and evil, and talk with the serpent there, and eat; but afterwards they are driven out of paradise; yet God does not leave them, but they leave God." Those in caps understood and approved these words; but those in turbans denied, and said, "Is not omnipotence thus limited? and is not limited omnipotence a contradiction?" But I replied, "It is not a contradiction to act omnipotently according to the laws of justice, and with judgment, or according to the laws inscribed on love from wisdom but it is a contradiction, that God can act contrary to the laws of his own justice and love; and this would not be from judgment and wisdom. Such a contradiction is implied in your faith, which is, that God can, out of mere grace, justify the unjust, and endow him with all the gifts of salvation and the rewards of life. But I will say, in a few words, what the omnipotence of God is. God, by his omnipotence, created the universe, and, at the same time, introduced order into all and every part of it; God also, by his omnipotence, preserves the universe, and watches over the order there, with all its laws, perpetually, and when any thing gets out of order, He puts it back again, and re-establishes it. Moreover, God, by his omnipotence, established the church, and revealed the laws of its order in the Word; and when it fell from order, He re-established it, and when it fell totally, He came down into the world, and, by assuming the Human He clothed himself with omnipotence, and restored it. God, by his omnipotence, and also his omniscience, examines every one after death, and prepares the righteous, or the sheep, for their places in heaven, and forms heaven from them; and He prepares the unrighteous, or the goats, for their places in hell, and forms hell from them; and He disposes both heaven and hell into societies and congregations, according to all the varieties of their love, which, in heaven, are as many as the stars in the firmament of the world; and He joins the societies in heaven together into one, that they may be as one man in his sight; in like manner, the congregations in hell, that they may be as one devil; and He separates the former from the latter by a gulf, lest hell should do violence to heaven, and lest heaven should occasion torment in hell; for those who are in hell are tormented in proportion as heaven flows in. Unless God, by his omnipotence, should every instant act in heaven and in hell, the bestial nature would enter into men to such a degree, that they could no longer be restrained by the laws of any order, and thus the human race would perish. These and similar things would happen, unless God were Order, and omnipotent in order." On hearing these words, those who wore caps went away, with their caps under their arms, praising God; for in that world, the intelligent wear caps Not so those who wore turbans, because they are bald, and baldness signifies dullness or stupidity; and these went away to the left, but those to the right.

CONCERNING THE CREATION OF THE UNIVERSE.

75. Since, in this first chapter, we treat of God the Creator, we ought also to treat of the creation of the universe by Him; as, in the following chapter concerning the Lord the Redeemer, we shall also treat of Redemption. But no one can obtain for himself a just idea concerning the creation of the universe, unless some universal knowledges, previously acquired, put the understanding into a state of perception; which knowledges will be the following: I. That there are two worlds, the spiritual world, in which angels and spirits are; and the natural world, in which men are. II. That in each world there is a sun, and that the sun of the spiritual world is pure love from Jehovah God, who is in the midst of it; and that from that sun proceed heat and light; and that the heat thence proceeding, in its essence, is love, and that the light thence proceeding, in its essence, is wisdom, and that those two affect the will and understanding of man, the heat his will, and the light his understanding; but that the sun of the natural world is pure fire, and that therefore the heat thence is dead: in like manner, the light; and that they serve for clothing and support to spiritual heat and light, that they may pass to man. III. Then, that those two things, which proceed from the sun of the spiritual world, and thence all the things which exist there by means of them, are substantial, and are called *spiritual;* and that the two similar things, which proceed from the sun of the natural world, and thence all the things which exist here by means of them, are material, and are called *natural.* IV. That in each world there are three degrees, which are called *degrees of altitude,* and thence three regions, according to which the three angelic heavens are arranged, and according to which human minds are arranged, which thus correspond to the three angelic heavens; and that other things are arranged in like manner, both here and there. V. That there is a correspondence between those things which are in the spiritual world, and those things which are in the natural world. VI. That there is an order, into which all and every thing in both worlds was created. VII. That an idea concerning these things ought first of all to be obtained; and, unless this be done, the human mind, from mere ignorance concerning them, may easily fall into the idea of the creation of the universe by nature, and say, only from the authority of the church, that nature was created by God; but because it knows not how, if it inquires into it more interiorly, it falls headlong into naturalism, which denies God. But because it would be the work of a large volume, to explain and demonstrate those things in a proper manner, one by one, and, also, as it does not properly enter into such a system of theology as this, as a lemma, or an argument, I will only adduce some Relations, from which an idea of the creation of the universe by God may be conceived, and from conception, some birth, representing it, may be produced.

---

76. First Relation. On a certain day, I was engaged in meditation about the creation of the universe; and

because this was perceived by the angels who were above me on the right side, where were some who had several times meditated and reasoned on the same subject, therefore one descended and invited me, and I became in the spirit, and accompanied him; and after I entered, I was conducted to the prince, in whose palace I saw several hundreds assembled, and the prince in the midst of them. And then one of them said, "We perceived here, that you were meditating about the creation of the universe, and we have several times been in a similar meditation, but could never come to a conclusion, since in our thoughts was fixed the idea of a chaos; that this was, as it were, a great egg, out of which proceeded all and every thing of the universe in their order; when yet we now perceive, that so great a universe could not have been thus produced. Then, also, there was fixed in our minds another idea, which was, that all things were created by God out of nothing; and yet we now perceive, that nothing is made out of nothing; and our minds have not yet been able to extricate themselves from these two ideas, and to see creation in any light, how it was effected; wherefore, we have called you out from the place where you were, that you may disclose your meditation concerning this subject." On hearing these words, I replied, "I will do so." And I said, "I meditated on this subject for a long time, but to no purpose; but afterwards, when I was admitted by the Lord into your world, I perceived that it would be vain to conclude any thing concerning the creation of the universe, unless it be first known, that there are two worlds, one in which angels are, and another in which men are; and that men, at death, pass out of their world into the other; and then also I saw, that there were two suns, one from which all spiritual things proceed, and the other from which all natural things proceed; and that the sun, from which all spiritual things proceed, is pure love from Jehovah God, who is in the midst of it; and that the sun, from which all natural things proceed, is pure fire. Knowing these things, on a certain time, when I was in illustration, I was enabled to perceive that the universe was created by Jehovah God, by means of the sun in the midst of which He is; and because love cannot exist, except together with wisdom, that the universe was created by Jehovah God, from his love by his wisdom. That it is so, is evinced by all and every thing that I have seen in the world where you are, and that I have seen in the world where I am, as to the body. But to explain how the progress of creation was made, from its beginning, would be too prolix; but, when I was in illustration, I perceived, that by means of the light and heat from the sun of your world, spiritual atmospheres, which in themselves are substantial, were created one from another; and because there were three, and thence three degrees of them, three heavens were made; one for the angels who are in the highest degree of love and wisdom, another for the angels who are in the second degree, and the third for the angels who are in the lowest degree: but, because this spiritual universe cannot exist without a natural universe, in which it may produce its effects and uses, that then the sun, from which all natural things proceed, was created at the same time, and by this, in like manner, by means of light and heat, three atmospheres, encompassing the former, as the shell does the kernel, or the bark of a tree the wood; and at last, by means of these, the terraqueous globe, where are men, beasts and fishes, also trees, shrubs and herbs, was formed of different kinds of earths, which consist of loom, stones and minerals. But this is a very general sketch of the creation and its progression; but the particulars and singulars cannot be explained, except by volumes of books; but all things lead to the conclusion, that God did not create the universe out of nothing, because, as you said, *Nothing is made out of nothing;* but by means of the sun of the angelic heaven, which is from his

Esse, and thence is pure love, together with wisdom. That the universe, by which is meant both worlds, the spiritual and the natural, was created from the divine love, by the divine wisdom, all and every part of it testifies and proves; and you, if you consider the parts of the universe in their order and connection, from the light in which the perceptions of your understandings are, may clearly see it. But it should be kept in mind, that the love and wisdom, which in God make one, are not love and wisdom, in an abstract sense, but in Him as a substance; for God is the very, the only, and thence the first Substance and Essence, which is and subsists in itself. That all and every thing was created from the divine love and the divine wisdom, is meant by these words in John; *The Word was with God, and the Word was God; all things were made by Him; and the world was made by Him*, i. 1, 3, 10. *God* there, signifies the divine love, and the *Word* signifies the divine truth, or the divine wisdom; wherefore the Word there is called *light*, and by light, when spoken of God, is meant the divine wisdom." After this, when I was saying farewell, rays of light, from the sun there, descended through the angelic heavens, into their eyes, and through them into the habitations of their mind; and, when thus illustrated, they favored the things that had been said by me, and afterwards followed me into the outer court, and my former companion to the house where I was, and from thence he reascended to his society.

77 Second Relation. One morning, when I had awaked from sleep, and was meditating in the serene twilight of the morning, before it was broad day-light, I saw through the window, as it were a flash of lightning, and presently I heard, as it were, a clap of thunder. While I was wondering whence this was, I heard from heaven, that there were some not far from me, who were reasoning sharply concerning God and Nature, and that the flashing of the light, like lightning, and the clapping of the air, like thunder, were correspondences, and thence appearances of the conflict and collision of arguments, on one side in favor of *God*, and on the other in favor of *nature*. The beginning of this spiritual combat was this: There were some satans in hell, who said amongst themselves, "O that we might be allowed to speak with the angels of heaven, and we would completely and fully demonstrate, that what they call God, from whom are all things, is nature; thus, that God is only a word, unless nature be meant." And because those satans believed this, with the whole heart, and the whole soul, and wished to speak with the angels of heaven, it was given to them to ascend out of the filth and darkness of hell, and to speak with two angels then descending from heaven. They were in the world of spirits, which is in the midst, between heaven and hell. The satans, when they saw the angels there, ran quickly to them, and cried with a furious voice, "Are you the angels of heaven, with whom we are allowed to engage in reasoning concerning God and nature? You are called wise, because you acknowledge God; but oh, how simple you are! Who has ever seen God? or who understands what God is? Who can conceive that God reigns, and that He can govern the universe, and all and every part of it? Who, except the vulgar and the lowest of the people, acknowledges what he does not see and understand? What is more evident than that nature is all in all? Who has seen any thing with the eye, but nature? Who has heard any thing with the ear, but nature? Who has smelt any thing with the nose, but nature? Who has tasted any thing with the tongue, but nature? Who has perceived any thing with the touch of the hand or body, but nature? Are not the senses of the body our witnesses of truths? Who cannot swea from those things, that it is so? Is not respiration, by which our body lives, also a witness? What else do we breathe, but nature? Are not our heads and yours in nature? Whence is there

influx into the thoughts of our heads, but from nature? And if nature be taken away, can you think any thing?" Beside many other things of a similar kind. The angels, on hearing these things, replied, "You speak in this manner, because you are merely sensual. All in hell have the ideas of their thoughts immersed in the senses of the body, nor are they able to elevate their minds above them; wherefore we forgive you. The life of evil, and the faith of the false, have so closed up the interiors of your minds, that elevation above sensual things, with you, is not possible, except in a state removed from evils of life and falses of faith; for a satan can understand the truth, when he hears it, as well as an angel, but he does not retain it, because evil obliterates the truth and induces the false. But we perceive that you are in a state thus removed, and so you can understand the truth which we speak; wherefore attend to those things which we shall say." And they said, "You have been in the natural world, and you have departed thence, and now you are in the spiritual world; did you ever before know any thing concerning a life after death? Did you not before deny it, and make yourselves like the beasts? Did you before know any thing concerning heaven and hell? or any thing concerning the light and heat of this world? or concerning this, that you are no longer within nature, but above it? For this world, and all the things of it, are spiritual; and spiritual things are above natural things, so that not even the least thing of nature, in which you were, can flow into this world. But you, because you believed nature to be a god or a goddess, also believe the light and heat of this world to be the light and heat of the natural world, when yet it is not so; for natural light here is darkness, and natural heat here is cold. Did you know any thing concerning the sun of this world, from which our light and our heat proceed? Did you know that this sun is pure love, and that the sun of the natural world is pure fire? and that the sun of the world, which is pure fire, is that from which nature exists and subsists? and that the sun of heaven, which is pure love, is that from which life itself, which is love together with wisdom, exists and subsists? and thus, that nature, which you make a god or a goddess, is entirely dead? You can, if a guard be given to you, ascend with us into heaven; and we can, if a guard be given, descend with you into hell; and you will see in heaven magnificent and splendid things, but in hell, vile and filthy things; that difference is, because all in heaven worship God, and all in hell worship nature; and those magnificent and splendid things in the heavens are correspondences of the affections of the love of good and truth; but those vile and filthy things in the hells are correspondences of the affections of the love of the evil and the false. From all these things now conclude, whether God or whether nature be all in all." To this the satans replied, "In the state in which we are now, we can conclude, from what we have heard, that there is a God; but when the delight of evil fills our minds, we see nothing but nature." Those two angels and the satans were standing not far from me, wherefore I saw and heard them; and, behold, I saw around them many who had been celebrated for erudition in the natural world, and I wondered, that those scholars should stand now near the angels, and now near the satans, and that they should favor those near whom they were standing; and it was said to me, that the changes of their situation were changes of the state of their mind, which sometimes favored one side, and sometimes the other; for they were, as to faith, like *Vertumni*, or changelings. "And we will tell you a secret: we looked down upon the earth at those who were celebrated for erudition, and we found six hundred in a thousand in favor of nature, and the rest in favor of God: and these in favor of God, because they had frequently said,—not from the understanding, but from what they had heard,—

that nature is from God; for the practice of speaking from memory and recollection, although not at the same time from thought and intelligence, produces an appearance of faith." After this, a guard was given to the satans, and they ascended with the two angels into heaven, and they saw magnificent and splendid things; and then, in the illustration from the light of heaven there, they acknowledged that there is a God, and that nature was created to be subservient to the life which is from God; and that nature in itself is dead; and that thus it does nothing from itself, but is actuated by life. Having seen and perceived these things, they descended; and, while they were descending, the love of evil returned, and closed their understanding above, and opened it below; and then there appeared above it, as it were, a dark shade, sparkling from infernal fire; and, as soon as they touched the earth with their feet, the ground under them opened, and they sunk down again to their companions.

78. Third Relation. The next day, an angel came to me from another society of heaven, and said, "We have heard there, that, in consequence of meditating on the creation of the universe, you were invited into a society near ours, and that there you said such things about the creation as they favored then, and have since recollected with pleasure. I will now show you how animals and vegetables of every kind were produced by God." And he led me along into a large green field, and said, "Look around." And I looked around, and saw birds of the most beautiful colors, some flying, some perching upon the trees, and some upon the ground, plucking little leaves from the roses; amongst the birds were also doves and swans. After these things vanished from my sight, I saw, not far from me, flocks of sheep with lambs, and of goats and kids; and round about those flocks, I saw herds of cows and calves, and also of camels and mules; and in a certain grove, stags with high horns; and also unicorns. After these things were seen, he said, "Turn your face towards the east." And I saw a garden, in which were fruit-trees, as orange-trees, citrons, olives, vines, fig-trees, pomegranates, and also shrubs, which bore berries. Afterwards he said, "Look now towards the south." And I saw fields of grain of various kinds—wheat, oats, barley and beans; and round about them, beds of roses, exhibiting colors beautifully variegated; but, towards the north, groves full of chestnut-trees, palm-trees, linden-trees, plane-trees, and other trees, all in the richest foliage. When I had seen these, he said, "All those things which you have seen are correspondences of the affections of the love of the angels, who are in the vicinity." And they told me to what affections every thing corresponded; and, moreover, that not only those things, but also all the other things which are presented to our eyes as objects of sight, are correspondences; such as houses and the furniture in them, tables and meats and clothes, and also coins of gold and silver, as also diamonds and other precious stones, with which wives and virgins in heaven are adorned. "From all these things, we perceive what each one is as to love and wisdom. Those things which are in our houses, and serve for uses, constantly remain there; but to the eyes of those who wander from one society to another, such things are changed according to consociation. These things have been shown to you, in order that you might see the whole creation in a particular type; for God is Love itself and Wisdom itself; and the affections of his love are infinite, and the perceptions of his wisdom are infinite; and of these, all and every thing that appears upon the earth are correspondences; thence are birds and beasts, thence trees and shrubs, thence corn and other grain, thence herbs and grass of every kind, for God is not extended, but still He is in the extense every where; thus in the universe from its firsts to its lasts; and because He is omnipresent, such correspondences of the affections of his love and wisdom are in the whole

natural world; but in our world, which is called the spiritual world, there are similar correspondences with those who receive affections and perceptions from God; the difference is, that such things, in our world, are created by God instantaneously, according to the affections of the angels; but in your world, they were created in like manner at the beginning; but it was provided, that, by generations of one from another, they should be perpetually renewed, and thus that creation should be continued. The reason why creation, in our world, is instantaneous, and in yours continued by generations, is, because the atmospheres and earths of our world are spiritual, and the atmospheres and earths of your world are natural; and natural things were created that they might clothe spiritual things, as the skin clothes the bodies of men and animals, and the rind and bark clothe the trunks and branches of trees, the *maters* and *meninges* the brain, the coats the nerves, and the delicate membranes, the nervous fibres, &c. Thence it is, that all those things which are in your world are constant, and constantly return every year." To this the angel added, "Relate these things, which you have seen and heard, to the inhabitants of your world, because hitherto they have been in entire ignorance concerning the spiritual world; and without some knowledge of it, no one can know, nor even guess, that creation is continual in our world, and that it was similar to this in yours, while the universe was created by God."

After this, we talked upon various subjects, and at last concerning hell; as, that no such things as are in heaven appear there, but only the opposites; since the affections of their love, which are the lusts of evil, are opposite to the affections of the love in which the angels of heaven are. Wherefore, with those in hell, and generally in their deserts, there appear birds of night, as bats, and various kinds of owls, and also wolves, leopards, tigers, rats and mice; moreover, venomous serpents of every kind, such as dragons and crocodiles; and where there is any spot of grass, there grow briers, nettles, thorns and thistles, and some poisonous plants, which at times vanish, and then appear only heaps of stones, and bogs in which frogs croak. All these things are also correspondences; but, as was said, correspondences of the affections of their love, which are the lusts of evil. Yet such things were not created there by God, nor were they created in the natural world, where similar things exist; for all things that God created and creates, were and are good; but such things upon the earth arose together with hell, which exists from men, who, by aversion from God, after death became devils and satans. But because these direful things began to hurt our ears, we averted our thoughts from them, and recollected the things which we had seen in the heavens.

79. Fourth Relation. Once, when I was engaged in thinking of the creation of the universe, there came to me some from the Christian world, who, in their time, were philosophers among the most celebrated, and reputed wise above the rest; and they said, "We perceive that you are thinking of the creation; tell us what your mind is about it." But I replied, "Tell first what yours is." And one said, "My mind is, that creation is from nature, and thus that nature created itself, and that it was from eternity; for there is not, and cannot be, a vacuum. But what do we see with our eyes, hear with our ears, smell with our nostrils, and receive into our breast by respiration, except nature, which, because it is without us, is also within us?" Another, hearing these words, said, "You talk of nature, and make it the creator of the universe; but you do not know how nature operates in producing the universe; wherefore I will tell you. It folded up itself into vortexes, which dashed against each other, like clouds, or like houses when they fall together in an earthquake; and, by means of that collision, the denser parts collected themselves together, whence was formed the earth; and the looser parts separated themselves from these

and also collected themselves together, whence were formed seas; and the parts still lighter separated themselves from these, whence were formed the air and ether; and from the lightest of these, the sun. Have you not seen, that when oil, water and dust of the earth are mixed together, they separate of their own accord, and arrange themselves in order, one above another?" Then another, hearing that, said, "You speak from fancy. Who does not know, that the first origin of all things was chaos, which, in magnitude, filled a fourth part of the universe; and that in the midst of it was fire; and round about it, ether; and around this, matter; and that that chaos was shivered, and through the chinks burst out fire, as from Ætna and Vesuvius, whence originated the sun; and that, after this, the ether evolved and diffused itself, whence originated the atmosphere: and at last the residue of matter collected itself into a globe, whence originated the earth? As to the stars, they are only luminaries in the expanse of the universe, which sprung from the sun and its fire and light; for the sun, at first, was, as it were, an ocean of fire, which, lest it should burn the earth, severed from itself little shining flames, which, being located in the circumference, completed the universe; thence originated its firmament." But there stood one among them who said, "You are mistaken; you appear to yourselves to be wise, and I appear to you simple; but still, in my simplicity, I have believed, and do believe, that the universe was created by God; and because nature is of the universe, that all nature was then created at the same time. If nature created itself, would it not have been from eternity? But oh, what folly!" And then one of those wise men, so called, ran up nearer and nearer to him who spoke, and put his left ear to his mouth, for his right ear was stopped up, as it were with cotton, and asked what he said; and he repeated the same; and then he who ran up, looked around to see whether any priest were present; and he saw one at the side of him who spoke; and then he replied, saying, "I also confess, that all nature is from God, but"—And then he went away, and, whispering to his companions, he said, "I said this because the priest was present; but you and I know that nature is from nature; and because thus nature is God, I said that all nature is from God. But"—Then the priest, hearing their whispering, said, "Your wisdom, which is merely philosophical, has seduced you, and has so closed the interiors of your minds, that no light from God and from his heaven could flow in and enlighten you; you have extinguished it. Consider," said he, "and decide among yourselves, whence are your souls, which are immortal, whether they were from nature, or whether they were at the same time in that great chaos." On hearing this, the former went away to his companions, requesting that they, together with him, would solve this knot of a question; and they concluded, that the human soul is nothing but ether, and that thought is nothing but a modification of ether, by means of the sun's light; and ether is of nature. And they said, "Who does not know that we speak by means of the air, and that thought is nothing but speech in a purer air, which is called ether; thence it is, that thought and speech make one. Who cannot perceive this from man while he is an infant? He first learns to speak, and, by degrees, to speak with himself, and this is to think. What then is thought, but a modification of ether? and what else is the sound of speech, but a modulation of air? Whence we conclude, that the soul, which thinks, is of nature." But some of them dissented not, indeed, from the rest, but illustrated the state of the question, saying, that "Souls sprung into existence when the ether gathered itself together from that great chaos, and then, in the highest region, divided itself into innumerable individual forms, which infuse themselves into men, while they begin to think from purer air, which are then called *souls*." Hearing this, another said,

"I grant that the individual forms, formed by the ether in the higher region, may have been innumerable; but still the men born since the creation of the world, have exceeded their number; how, then, could those ethereal forms suffice? Wherefore I have thought with myself, that the souls, which go out of the mouth of men when they die, may return to the same, and begin and end a life similar to the former; that many of the wise men believe similar things and a metempsychosis, is known." Besides these, other conjectures were broached by the rest, which, because they were utterly foolish, I pass by. After an hour or so, the priest returned; and then he, who before spoke of the creation of the universe by God, told him their decisions concerning the soul; on hearing which, the priest said to them, "You have spoken just as you thought in the world, not knowing that you are not in that world, but in another, which is called the *spiritual world;* all those who have become sensual corporeal, by confirmations in favor of nature, know no otherwise than that they are in the same world in which they were born and educated: the reason is, because there they were in a material body, but here they are in a substantial body; and a substantial man sees himself and his companions around him, just as a material man sees himself and his companions around him; for the substantial is the primitive of the material; and because you think, see, smell, taste and speak in like manner as in the natural world, therefore you suppose, that the same nature is here, when yet the nature of this world is as different and distant from the nature of that world, as the substantial is from the material, or the spiritual from the natural, or the prior from the posterior; and because the nature of the world in which you before lived is respectively dead, therefore you, by confirmations in favor of it, are become, as it were, dead; but in respect to those things which are of God, heaven and the church, and also in respect to that which relates to your souls. But still every man, the bad as well as the good, may, as to the understanding, be elevated even into the light in which the angels of heaven are, and then see that there is a God, and that there is a life after death, and that the soul of man is not ethereal, and thus from the nature of that world, but spiritual, and therefore that it will live to eternity. The understanding may be in that angelic light, provided natural loves, which are from the world, and for it and its nature, and from the body, and for it and its proprium, be removed;"—and then, in an instant, those loves were removed by the Lord; and it was given them to speak with the angels, and from their conversation, while in that state, they perceived that there is a God, and that, after death, they live in another world; wherefore they were covered with shame, and exclaimed "We have been mad, we have been mad!" But because this was not their proper state, and thence, after some minutes, it became tedious and irksome, they turned themselves away from the priest, and would not hear his speech any longer; and thus they returned into their former loves, which were merely natural, worldly and corporeal; and they went away to the left, from society to society, and at length came to a way where the delights of their loves blew upon them, and they said, "Let us go this way;" and they went, and descended, and at length came to those who were in the delights of similar loves, and farther. And because their delight was the delight of doing evil, and in the way they also did evil to many, they were imprisoned, and became demons: and then their delight was changed into what is undelightful, because they were curbed and restrained, by punishments and the fears of them, from their former delight, which made their nature; and they asked those who were in the same prison, whether they were about to live so to eternity. Some there replied, "We have been here several ages, and we are to remain for ages of ages; since the nature, which we contracted in the world, cannot be changed nor expelled by punishments; and whenever it is expelled by them, still, after a short lapse of time, it returns.

80. Fifth Relation. Once a satan, by permission, ascended out of hell, together with a woman, and came to the house where I was; on seeing whom, I shut the window, but yet through it I talked with them, and asked the satan whence he came. He said, "From the company of his associates." And I asked, "Whence came the woman?" He said, "From the same." She was from a company of Sirens, who know how to induce upon themselves, by means of fantasies, all the habits and figures of beauty and ornament: at one time, they figure the beauty of Venus; at another, gracefulness of person, as it were of a nymph of Parnassus; at another, they adorn themselves, as it were, with the crowns and robes of a queen, and walk magnificently, leaning upon a silver cane. Such, in the world of spirits, are harlots, and they study fantasies. Fantasy is produced by sensual thought, whilst ideas from any interior thought are shut up. I asked the satan whether she was his wife. He replied, "What is a wife? I do not know what a wife is, nor does my society. She is my harlot." And then she breathed lascivious desire into the man, which also Sirens know how to do dexterously; and he, on receiving it, kissed her, and said, "Ah, my Adonis!" But to proceed to serious things: I asked the satan what was his employment; and he said, "My employment is the pursuit of learning: do you not see the laurel upon my head?" for this his Adonis had formed by her art, and, standing behind, she placed it upon his head. And I said, "Since you are come from a society where there are schools of learning, tell me what you believe, and what your associates believe, concerning God." He replied, "Our God is the universe, which also we call *nature*, and which the simple amongst us call the *atmosphere*, which to them is air; but the wise call it the *atmosphere*, which also is ether. God, heaven, angels, and the like, about which many tell many stories in this world, are empty words and fictions taken from meteors, which play before the eyes of many here. Are not all the things which appear upon the earth created by the sun? Are not worms, with wings and without wings, produced at every coming of the sun, in the time of spring? And do not the birds, from his heat, mutually love each other, and breed?

"Does not the earth, warmed by his heat, bring forth seeds into plants, and at length into fruits, as an offspring? Is not thus the universe a God, and nature a Goddess; and does not she, as a wife, conceive, bring forth, educate and nourish them?" Moreover, I asked what he and his society believed concerning religion. He replied, that "Religion, with those of us who are learned above the vulgar, is nothing but a charm for the common people, which, about the sensitive and imaginative powers of their mind, is as it were, an aura, in which the ideas of piety fly like butterflies in the air; and their faith, which connects those ideas, as it were, into a chain, is like a silkworm, in a silken envelope, from which it flies forth as the king of butterflies. For the common herd of the illiterate love images above the sensual things of the body and of the thought thence, on account of a strong desire that they may fly; thus, also, they make for themselves wings, that they may elevate themselves like eagles, and boast before the inhabitants of the earth, saying, 'Look at me.' But we believe what we see, and love what we touch." And then he touched his harlot, and said, "I believe this, because I see and touch it; but as for such ludicrous things, we cast them out through our windows, and drive them away with a blast of ridicule." Afterwards, I asked what he, together with his associates, believed concerning heaven and hell. He replied, with a loud laugh, "What is heaven, but the ethereal firmament in its light? and what are the angels there, but spots wandering about the sun? and the archangels, but comets with a long tail? And what is hell, but bogs, where are frogs and crocodiles, which, in the imagination of those people, are devils? Besides these ideas concerning heaven and hell, all the rest are trifles, introduced by some primate, for the purpose of acquiring glory from an ignorant populace." But all these things he spoke just as he had thought concerning them in the world, not knowing that he was living after death, and having forgotten all that he heard, when he first entered the world of spirits; wherefore, to the question concerning a life after death, he replied, that "It is an imaginary entity; and that perhaps some effluvia, arising from a dead body in the tomb, in form as a man, or something which is called a *spectre*, about which some people tell fabulous stories, had introduced some such thing into the imaginations of men." On hearing these words, I could no longer restrain my laughter from bursting forth, and I said, "Satan, you are raving mad Why, now, are you not in form a man? Do you not speak, see, hear and walk? Recollect that you once lived in another world, which you have forgotten, and that now, after death, you live, and that you have been talking just as you did before." And recollection was given to him, and he remembered, and then he was ashamed, and cried, "I am mad: I have seen heaven above, and heard the angels there speaking ineffable things; but this when I had recently arrived here; but now I will retain this in order to relate it to my companions, from whom I came, and perhaps they likewise will then be ashamed." And he kept in his mouth, that he would call them mad; but, as he descended, forgetfulness expelled recollection, and when he was there, he was as mad as ever, and called those things which he heard from me nonsense. Such is the state of thought and speech of satans after death. Those are called *satans*, who have confirmed themselves in the belief of falses; and those *devils*, who have confirmed evils in themselves by life.

CHAPTER II.

CONCERNING THE LORD THE REDEEMER.

81. In the former chapter, we have treated of God the Creator, and at the same time of creation; but in this chapter we are to treat of the Lord the Redeemer, and at the same time also of redemption; and in the following chapter, of the Holy Spirit, and at the same time of the divine operation. By the Lord the Redeemer, we mean Jehovah in the Human; for that Jehovah himself descended and assumed the Human, for the purpose of accomplishing redemption, will be demonstrated in what follows. The reason why it is said the *Lord*, and not *Jehovah*, is because *Jehovah*, in the Old Testament, is called the *Lord* in the New, as is evident from these passages: It is said in Moses, *Hear, O Israel,* Jehovah *your God is one Jehovah; and thou shalt love* Jehovah *thy God with all thy heart and with all thy soul,* Deut. vi. 4, 5; but in Mark; *The* Lord *your God is one* Lord, *and thou shalt love the* Lord *thy God with all thy heart and with all thy soul,* xii. 29, 30. Also in Isaiah; *Prepare a way for* Jehovah; *make smooth in the desert a path for our God,* xl. 3; but in Luke; *Thou shalt go before the face of the* Lord, *to prepare a way for Him,* i. 76; besides in other passages. And also the Lord commanded his disciples to call Him *Lord,* and therefore He was so called by the apostles, in their Epistles, and afterwards by the apostolic church, as appears from their creed, which is called the "Apostles' Creed." The reason was, because the Jews durst not use the name *Jehovah,* on account of its sanctity; and also, by *Jehovah* is meant the Divine Esse, which was from eternity, and the Human, which He assumed in time, was not that Esse. What the Divine Esse, or Jehovah, is, was shown in the foregoing chapter, n. 18 to 26, and n. 27 to 35. For this reason, here and in what follows, by the *Lord,* we mean *Jehovah in his Human.* Now, because knowledge concerning the Lord exceeds, in excellence, all the knowledges which are given in the church, and even those which are in heaven, the arrangement shall be so ordered, that that knowledge may come into the light, which therefore will be this: I. *That Jehovah, the Creator of the universe, descended and assumed the Human, that He might redeem and save men.* II. *That He descended as the Divine Truth, which is the Word, and yet that He did not separate the Divine Good.* III. *That He assumed the Human according to his divine order.* IV. *That the Human, by which He sent Himself into the world, is what is called the Son of God.* V. *That the Lord, by acts of redemption, made Himself righteousness.* VI. *That by the same acts, He united Himself to the Father, and the Father Himself to Him; also according to divine order.* VII. *That thus God became Man, and Man God, in one person.* VIII. *That the progression to union was the state of his exinanition, (or humiliation,) and that the union itself is the state of his glorification.* IX. *That hereafter no one among Christians can come into heaven, unless he believes in the Lord God the Savior, and goes to Him alone.* But these things shall be explained one by one.

82. I. That Jehovah, the Creator of the Universe, descended and assumed the Human, that He might redeem and save Men.

In the Christian churches at this day, it is believed that God, the Creator of the universe, begat a Son from eternity, and that this Son descended and assumed the Human, to redeem and save men; but this is erroneous, and falls of itself to the ground, while it is considered that God is one, and that it is more than fabulous in the eye of reason, that the one God should have begotten a Son from eternity, and also that God the Father, together with the Son and the Holy Ghost, each of whom singly is God, should be one God. This fabulous representation is entirely dissipated, while it is demonstrated from the Word, that Jehovah God himself descended, and became MAN, and also Redeemer. As it regards the first–*That Jehovah God himself descended and became Man*, is evident from these passages: *Behold a Virgin shall conceive and bring forth a Son, who shall be called* GOD WITH US, Isaiah vii. 14. Matt. i. 22, 23. *A Child is born to us, a Son is given to us, upon whose shoulder shall be the government, and his name shall be called Wonderful,* GOD, *Hero,* FATHER OF ETERNITY, *the Prince of Peace*, Isaiah ix. 6. *It shall be said in that day, Lo, this is our* GOD, *whom we have expected to deliver us; this is* JEHOVAH, *whom we have expected; let us exult and rejoice in his salvation*, xxv. 9. *The voice of one crying in the wilderness, Prepare a way for* JEHOVAH; *make smooth in the desert a path for our* GOD; *and all flesh shall see together*, xl. 3, 5. *Behold, the* LORD JEHOVAH *is coming in the mighty one, and his arm shall rule for Him; behold, his reward is with Him, and he shall feed his flock like a* SHEPHERD, xl. 10, 11. JEHOVAH *said, Sing and rejoice, O daughter of Zion; behold, I am coming to dwell in the midst of thee; then many nations shall cleave to* JEHOVAH *in that day*, Zech. ii. 14, 15. I JEHOVAH *have called thee in righteousness, and I will give thee for a covenant of the people;* I AM JEHOVAH; THIS IS MY NAME, AND MY GLORY I WILL NOT GIVE TO ANOTHER, Isaiah xii. 6, 7, 8. *Behold, the days are coming, when I will raise up unto David a righteous* BRANCH, *who shall reign king, and do judgment and justice in the earth, and this is his name,* JEHOVAH OUR RIGHTEOUSNESS, Jerem. xxiii. 5, 6. xxxiii 15, 16: besides in many passages, where the coming of the Lord is called THE DAY OF JEHOVAH, as Isaiah xiii. 6, 9, 13, 22. Ezek. xxxi. 25. Joel i. 15. ii. 1, 2, 11 iii. 24. iv. 1, 4, 18. Amos v. 13, 18, 20. Zeph. i. 7 to 18. Zech. xiv. 1, 4 to 21; and in other places. That Jehovah himself descended and assumed the Human, is very evident in Luke, where are these words: *Mary said to the angel, How shall this be done, since I know not a man? To whom the angel replied, The Holy Spirit shall come upon thee, and the virtue of the Most High shall overshadow thee; whence the Holy Thing that is born of thee, shall be called the Son of God*, i. 34, 35. And in Matthew: *The angel said to Joseph, the bridegroom of Mary, in a dream, That which is born in her is of the Holy Spirit; and Joseph knew her not, until she brought forth a Son, and called his name Jesus*, i. 20, 25. That by the *Holy Spirit* is meant the Divine which proceeds from Jehovah, will be seen in the third chapter of this work. Who does not know, that the child has the soul and life from the father, and that the body is from the soul? What, therefore, is said more plainly, than that the Lord had his soul and life from Jehovah God? and, because the Divine cannot be divided, that the Divine itself was his soul and life? Wherefore the Lord so often called Jehovah God his *Father*, and Jehovah God called Him his *Son*. What, then, can be heard more ludicrous, than that the soul of our Lord was from the mother Mary, as both the Roman Catholics and the Reformed at this day dream, not having as yet been awaked by the Word.

83. That a Son, born from eternity, descended and assumed the Human, evidently appears as erroneous, and is dissipated, from the passages in the Word, in which Jehovah himself says, that He himself is the Savior and the Redeemer, which are the following: *Am not I* JEHOVAH? *and there is no God else besides Me; a just God and a* SAVIOR THERE IS NOT BESIDES ME, Isaiah xlv. 21, 22. *I am* JEHOVAH, *and* BESIDES ME THERE IS NO SAVIOR, xliii. 11. *I am*

JEHOVAH THY GOD, *and thou shalt not acknowledge a God besides Me;* THERE IS NO SAVIOR BESIDES ME, Hosea xiii. 4. *That all flesh may know that* I JEHOVAH *am thy* SAVIOR *and thy* REDEEMER, Isaiah xlix. 26. lx. 16. *As for* OUR REDEEMER, JEHOVAH OF HOSTS IS HIS NAME, xlvii. 4. THEIR REDEEMER IS MIGHTY; JEHOVAH OF HOSTS IS HIS NAME, Jerem. l. 34. JEHOVAH, *my Rock and my* REDEEMER, Psalm xix. 15. *Thus said* JEHOVAH, THY REDEEMER, *the Holy One of Israel, I am* JEHOVAH THY GOD, Isaiah xlviii. 17. xliii. 24. xlix. 7. *Thus said* JEHOVAH *thy* REDEEMER, *I am* JEHOVAH, *that maketh all things, even alone by myself,* xliv. 24. *Thus said* JEHOVAH, *the King of Israel, and his* REDEEMER, JEHOVAH OF HOSTS, *I am the First and the Last, and besides Me there is no God,* xliv. 6. THOU, JEHOVAH, *art our Father, our* REDEEMER *from eternity is thy name,* lxiii. 16. *With the mercy of eternity I will have mercy, thus said Jehovah thy* REDEEMER, liv. 8. THOU HAST REDEEMED *me,* JEHOVAH, GOD OF TRUTH, Psalm xxxi. 6. *Let Israel hope in* JEHOVAH, *because in* JEHOVAH *is mercy, and with Him is plenteous* REDEMPTION, *and He will* REDEEM *Israel from all his iniquities,* cxxx. 7, 8. JEHOVAH GOD, *and* THY REDEEMER *the Holy One of Israel,* THE GOD OF THE WHOLE EARTH SHALL HE BE CALLED, Isaiah liv. 5. From these passages and very many others, every man who has eyes, and a mind opened by means of them, may see that God, who is one, descended and became Man, for the purpose of accomplishing the work of redemption. Who cannot see this, as in the morning light, while he attends to those very divine declarations, which have been adduced? But those who are in the shade of night, from confirmation in favor of the birth of another God from eternity, and concerning his descent and redemption, close their eyelids at those divine declarations, and in that state think how they may apply them to their falses, and pervert them.

84. There are several reasons, which will be explained in the course of the following pages, why God could not redeem men, that is, deliver them from damnation and hell, except by the assumed Human; for redemption was the subjugation of the hells, and the establishment of order in the heavens, and, after this, the institution of a church: these things, God by his omnipotence could not effect, except by means of the Human; as no one can work unless he has an arm; also his Human is called in the Word, *the Arm of Jehovah,* Isaiah xl. 10; liii. 1; and also as no one can attack a fortified city, and destroy the temples of the idols which are therein, except by means of proper powers. That, in this divine work, God had omnipotence by means of his Human, also is manifest from the Word; for God, who is in the inmost, and thus the purest things, otherwise might have passed in vain into the ultimates in which the hells are, and in which the men of that time were, comparatively as the soul cannot do any thing without a body, or as no one can conquer enemies, which do not come into his sight, or to which he cannot come and approach with any arms, as spears, shields, or muskets. To accomplish the work of redemption without the Human, was as impossible for God, as it is for man to subjugate the Indies, and not transport soldiers thither by means of ships, or as it is to make trees grow only by the heat and light of the sun, unless the air were created, through which the heat and light might pass, and unless the earth were created, out of which they might be produced; nay, it is as impossible, as to cast nets into the air, and catch fishes there, and not in the water; for Jehovah, as He is in Himself, cannot, by his omnipotence, touch any devil in hell, nor any devil upon earth, and repress him and his fury, and subdue his violence, unless He be in the lasts, as He is in the firsts: He is in the lasts in his Human; wherefore, in the Word, He is called the First and the Last, the Alpha and the Omega, the Beginning and the End.

85. II. THAT JEHOVAH DESCENDED AS THE DIVINE TRUTH, WHICH IS THE WORD, AND YET THAT HE DID NOT SEPARATE THE DIVINE GOOD.

There are two things which make the essence of God, the Divine Love and the Divine Wisdom; or, what is the same, the Divine Good and the Divine Truth. That these two are the essence of God, was demonstrated above, n. 36 to 48. These two, in the Word, are meant also by *Jehovah God;* by *Jehovah*, the Divine Love or the Divine Good, and by *God*, the Divine Wisdom or the Divine Truth; thence it is, that, in the Word, they are distinguished in various ways, and sometimes only Jehovah is named, and sometimes only God; for where it is treated of the Divine Good, there it is said *Jehovah;* and where of the Divine Truth, there *God;* and where of both, there *Jehovah God.* That Jehovah God descended as the Divine Truth, which is the Word, is evident in John, where are these words; *In the beginning was the Word, and the Word was with God, and the Word was God. All things were made by Him, and without Him was nothing made that was made. And the Word became flesh, and dwelt amongst us*, i. 1, 3, 14. That by the *Word* is there meant the Divine Truth, is because the Word, which is in the church, is the Divine Truth itself; for it was dictated by Jehovah Himself, and what is dictated by Jehovah, is purely the Divine Truth,and can be no other; but, because that passed through the heavens, even into the world, it became accommodated to the angels in heaven, and also to men in the world. Thence there is, in the Word, a spiritual sense, in which Divine Truth is in the light, and a natural sense, in which Divine Truth is in the shade; wherefore the Divine Truth, in this Word, is what is meant in John. This appears still more clearly from this, that the Lord came into the world that He might fulfill all things of the Word; wherefore it is so often read, that this and that was done by Him that the Scripture might be fulfilled. No other than the Divine Truth is meant by the Messiah or Christ; nor any other by the Son of Man; nor any other by the Comforter, the Holy Spirit, which the Lord sent after his departure. That He represented Himself as that Word, in his transfiguration before the three disciples on the mount (*Matt.* xii. *Mark* ix. and *Luke* ix.), and also before John (*Rev.* i, 12 to 16), will be seen in the chapter concerning the SACRED SCRIPTURE. That the Lord, in the world, was the Divine Truth, appears from his own words: *I am the Way the* TRUTH *and the Life*, John xiv 6; and from these, *We know that the Son of God hath come, and given us understanding, that we may know the* TRUTH, *and we are in the* TRUTH, IN HIS SON JESUS CHRIST: *This is the true God and eternal life*, 1 John v 20, 21; and still further by his being called the LIGHT, as in these passages: *He was the* TRUE LIGHT, *which enlighteneth every man that cometh into the world*, John i. 4, 9. *Jesus said, Yet for a little while the* LIGHT *is with you: walk while ye have* LIGHT, *lest darkness overtake you: while ye have* LIGHT, *believe in the* LIGHT, *that ye may be sons of the* LIGHT, xii. 35, 36, 46. *I am the* LIGHT *of the world*, ix. 5. Simeon said, *Mine eyes have seen thy salvation, a* LIGHT *for the revelation of the gentiles*, Luke ii. 30, 31, 32. *This is the judgment, that* LIGHT *hath come into the world; he who doeth the* TRUTH, *cometh to the* LIGHT, John iii. 19, 21: besides other places, where by the *light* is meant the Divine Truth.

86. The reason why Jehovah God descended into the world as the Divine Truth was, that He might do the work of redemption; and redemption was the subjugation of the hells, the establishment of order in the heavens, and, after this, the institution of a church. The Divine Good is not competent to effect those things, but the Divine Truth from the Divine Good: the Divine Good, considered in itself, is as the round hilt of a sword, or as blunt wood, or as a naked bow; but the Divine Truth from the Divine Good, is as a sharp sword, and as wood in the form of a spear, and as a bow with arrows, which are serviceable against an enemy. By swords, spears, and bows, in the spiritual sense of the Word, also are meant truths fighting: see

"Apocalypse Revealed," n. 52, 298, 436, where this is demonstrated: nor could the falses and evils in which the hells were and perpetually are, be attacked, conquered and subjugated otherwise than by the divine truth from the Word; nor could the new heaven, which also was then made, be founded, formed and arranged in order by any other means; nor could the New Church upon earth be instituted by any other means. Moreover, all the strength, all the virtue, and all the power of God, is of the divine truth from the divine good. This was the reason why Jehovah God descended as divine truth, which is the Word; therefore it is said in David, *Gird thy sword upon thy thigh, O* MIGHTY, *and in thy honor ascend;* RIDE UPON THE WORD OF TRUTH; *thy right hand will teach thee wonderful things; thine arrows are sharp; thine enemies shall fall under thee*, Psalm xlv. 4, 5, 6. These words are concerning the Lord, and concerning his combats with the hells, and concerning his victories over them.

87. What good without truth is, and what truth from good is, appears manifestly from man; all his good resides in the will, and all his truth in the understanding; and the will from its good cannot do any thing except by the understanding; it cannot work, it cannot speak, it cannot feel; all its virtue and power is by means of the understanding, consequently by means of truth, for the understanding is the receptacle and habitation of truth. The case is similar with these as with the operation of the heart and lungs in the body; the heart, without the respiration of the lungs, does not produce any motion or any sensation, but the respiration of the lungs from the heart does both; which is evident in swoons with those who are suffocated and drowned in water, in whom respiration ceases, while the systolic activity of the heart still continues; that such have neither motion nor sensation, is known. It is similar with embryos in the womb of the mother; the reason is, because the heart corresponds to the will and its goods, and the lungs to the understanding and its truths. In the spiritual world, the power of truth is most conspicuous; an angel who is in divine truths from the Lord, although, as to the body, he is as weak as an infant, can put to flight, pursue to hell, and thrust into the caverns there, even a troop of infernal spirits, who appear as the Anakim and the Nephalim, that is, as giants; and when they go out of the caverns, they dare not approach the angel. Those who are in divine truths from the Lord are in that world as lions, although, as to their bodies, they are no stronger than sheep. It is similar with men who are in divine truths from the Lord, against evils and falses, consequently against phalanxes of devils, who, considered in their essence, are no other than evils and falses. The reason why there is such strength inherent in divine truth is, because God is Good itself and Truth itself, and He created the universe by the divine truth; and all the laws of order, by which He preserves the universe, are truths. Wherefore it is said in John, that *By the Word all things were made, and without it nothing was made that was made*, i. 3, 10; and in David, *By the Word of Jehovah the heavens were made, and all the host of them by the breath of his mouth*, Psalm xxxiii. 6.

88. That God, although He descended as the divine truth, still did not separate the divine good, is evident from the conception, concerning which it is read, that *The virtue of the Most High overshadowed Mary*, Luke i. 35; and by the virtue of the Most High, is meant the divine good. The same is evident from the passages, where He says that the Father is in Him, and He in the Father; that all things of the Father are his; and that the Father and He are one; besides many other things; by the *Father* is meant the Divine Good.

89. III. THAT GOD ASSUMED THE HUMAN ACCORDING TO HIS DIVINE ORDER.

In the section concerning the divine omnipotence and omniscience, it was shown, that God, at the creation, introduced order into the universe, and into all and every part of it; and that therefore the omnipotence of God, in the universe and in all and every part of it, proceeds and operates according to the laws of his divine order, concerning which we have treated above in a series from n. 47 to 74. Now, because God descended, and because He is Order itself, as also was there demonstrated, in order that He also might actually become Man, He could not but be conceived, carried in the womb, brought forth, educated, and successively learn the sciences, and by them be introduced into intelligence and wisdom. Wherefore, as to the Human, He was an infant as an infant, a boy as a boy, &c.; with this difference only, that He perfected those progressive states sooner, more fully and more perfectly, than others. That He advanced thus progressively according to order, is evident from these words in Luke; *And the Child Jesus grew, and was strengthened in spirit, and increased in wisdom, in age, and in favor with God and man*, ii. 43, 50. That He did so sooner, more fully and more perfectly, than others, appears from those things which are said of Him in the same Evangelist; as that when He was *a Boy of twelve years, He sat in the temple in the midst of the doctors, and taught; and that all who heard Him were astonished at his intelligence and answers*, ii. 46, 47; and afterwards, iv. 16 to 22, 32. This was done, because the divine order is, that man should prepare himself for the reception of God; and as he prepares himself, so God enters into him, as into his habitation and house; and that preparation is made by means of knowledges concerning God, and concerning the spiritual things which are of the church, and thus by intelligence and wisdom; for it is a law of order, that as far as man accedes and approaches to God, which he should do altogether as from himself, so far God accedes and approaches to man, and in the midst of him conjoins Himself with him. That the Lord proceeded according to this order, even to union with his Father, will be further demonstrated in what follows

90. Those who do not know, that the divine omnipotence proceeds and operates according to order, may hatch out of their fancy many things opposite and contradictory to sound reason, as why God did not assume the Human immediately, without such a progression; why He did not create or compose for Himself a body out of the elements, from the four quarters of the world, and thus exhibit himself to be seen as God-Man, before the Jewish people, nay, before the whole world; or, if He would be born, why He did not infuse into the embryo itself, or into Himself as an infant, all his Divine; or why He did not, after his birth, raise Himself up to the stature of a perfect man, and speak immediately from the divine wisdom. Such and similar things those may conceive and bring forth, who think concerning the divine omnipotence without order; and thus may fill the church with deliriums and trifles, as also has been done; as that God could beget a Son from eternity, and cause that a third God also should then proceed from Himself and the Son; then that He could be angry with the human race, give them over to execration, and be willing to be brought back to mercy by his Son, and this by his intercession and the remembrance of his cross; and, moreover, that He could put into man the righteousness of his Son, and insert it in his heart, as a simple substance, according to Wolfius, in which, as the author himself says, are all things of the Son's merit; but that it cannot be divided, since, if it be divided, it falls into nothing; and, moreover, that He can, as by a papal bull, remit sins to whomsoever He will, or purify the most impious person from his black evils, and thus make one who is black as a devil, white as an angel of light, without man's moving himself any more than a stone, or while he stands still as a statue or as an idol; besides many other foolish notions, which those who maintain that the divine power is absolute, without any knowledge or acknowledgment of order, may scatter about as a winnower scatters chaff in

the air. These, in spiritual things, which are of heaven and the church, and thence of eternal life, may wander from divine truths, like a blind man in the woods, who now falls upon stones, now dashes his forehead against a tree, now entangles his hair in its branches.

91. Divine miracles also have been done according to divine order, but according to the *Order of the Influx of the Spiritual World into the Natural;* concerning which order no one has hitherto known any thing, because no one has known any thing of the spiritual world. But what that order is, will be made manifest in its time, when we treat of DIVINE MIRACLES, and of MAGICAL MIRACLES.

92. IV. THAT THE HUMAN, BY WHICH GOD SENT HIMSELF INTO THE WORLD, IS THE SON OF GOD.

The Lord frequently said, that the Father sent Him into the world, and that He was sent by the Father; as Matt. x. 40. xv. 24. John iii. 17, 24. v. 23, 24, 36, 37, 38. vi. 29, 39, 40, 44, 57. vii. 16, 18, 28, 29. viii. 16, 18, 29, 42. ix. 4; and in many other places; and this He says, because by being sent into the world, is meant to descend and come amongst men; and this was done by the Human, which He assumed by means of the virgin Mary; and also the Human is actually the Son of God, because it was conceived of Jehovah God, as a Father, according to Luke, i. 32, 35. He is called the Son of God, the Son of Man, and the Son of Mary; and by the Son of God is meant Jehovah God in his Human; by the Son of Man, the Lord as to the Word; and by the Son of Mary, properly the Human, which He assumed. That by the Son of God, and by the Son of Man, those two things are meant, will be demonstrated in what follows; that by the Son of Mary is meant the merely Human, is manifest from the generation of men, that the soul is from the father, and the body from the mother; for the soul is in the seed of the father, and it is clothed with a body in the mother; or, what is the same, all the spiritual that man has, is from the father, and all the material is from the mother; as to the Lord, the Divine which He had was from Jehovah, the Father, and the human was from the mother; these two united are the Son of God. That it is so, appears clearly from the nativity of the Lord, concerning which this is written in Luke: *The angel Gabriel said to Mary, The Holy Spirit shall come upon thee, and the virtue of the Most High shall overshadow thee; whence the Holy Thing that is born of thee shall be called the Son of God,* i. 35. The Lord called Himself *Sent by the Father,* also for this reason, because by *sent* is signified the like as by *angel;* for *angel,* in the original language, is *sent:* for it is said in Isaiah, THE ANGEL OF THE FACES OF JEHOVAH *delivered them; in his love and his pity he redeemed them,* lxiii. 9; and in Malachi; THE LORD, *whom ye seek, shall suddenly come to his temple,* AND THE ANGEL OF THE COVENANT, *whom ye desire,* iii. 1; besides other places. That the Divine Trinity, God the Father, the Son, and the Holy Spirit, is in the Lord, and that the Father in Him is the Divine from which [are all things], the Son, the Divine Human, and the Holy Spirit, the proceeding Divine, will be seen in the third chapter of this work, where we shall treat of the Divine Trinity.

93. Since it was said to Mary, by the angel Gabriel, *the Holy Thing which shall be born of thee shall be called the Son of God,* passages shall be adduced from the Word to show that the Lord, as to the Human, is called THE HOLY ONE OF ISRAEL, which are *I was seeing in visions; lo, a watcher and a* HOLY ONE *descending from heaven,* Dan. iv. 10, 20. *God will come from Teman, and* THE HOLY ONE *from mount Paran,* Hab. iii. 3. *I Jehovah,* THE HOLY ONE, *the Creator of Israel,* YOUR HOLY ONE, Isaiah xliv. 11, 15. *Thus said Jehovah, the Redeemer of Israel,* HIS HOLY ONE, xlii. 7. *I Jehovah thy God,* THE HOLY ONE OF ISRAEL, *thy Savior,* xliii. 3. *As for our Redeemer, Jehovah of hosts is his name,* THE HOLY ONE OF ISRAEL, xlvii

4. *Said Jehovah your Redeemer*, THE HOLY ONE OF ISRAEL, xliii. 13. xlviii. 17 *Jehovah of hosts is his name, and thy Redeemer*, THE HOLY ONE OF ISRAEL, liv. 5. *They tempted God and* THE HOLY ONE OF ISRAEL, Psalm lxxviii. 41. *They forsook Jehovah, and provoked* THE HOLY ONE OF ISRAEL, Isaiah l. 4. *They said, Make* THE HOLY ONE OF ISRAEL *cease from our faces; therefore, thus said* THE HOLY ONE OF ISRAEL, xxx. 11, 12. *Who say, Let him hasten his work, that we may see, and let the counsel of* THE HOLY ONE OF ISRAEL *approach and come*, v. 19. *In that day they shall lean upon* JEHOVAH, THE HOLY ONE OF ISRAEL, *in truth*, x. 20. *Cry out and sing aloud, O daughter of Zion, because great in the midst of thee is* THE HOLY ONE OF ISRAEL, xii. 6. *The saying of the God of Israel; In that day his eyes shall look to* THE HOLY ONE OF ISRAEL, xvii. 7. *The poor of men shall exult in* THE HOLY ONE OF ISRAEL, xxix. 19. xli. 16. *The earth is full of guiltiness against* THE HOLY ONE OF ISRAEL, Jerem. l. 29; and, moreover, Isaiah lv. 5. lx. 9, and in other places. By THE HOLY ONE OF ISRAEL is meant the Lord as to the Divine Human; for the angel said to Mary, THE HOLY THING *which shall be born of thee shall be called* THE SON OF GOD, Luke i. 35. That JEHOVAH and THE HOLY ONE OF ISRAEL are one, although they are distinctly named, may be evident from the passages also here adduced to show that Jehovah is that Holy One of Israel. That the Lord is called the GOD OF ISRAEL, is evident also from very many passages, as Isaiah xvii. 6. xxi. 10, 17. xxiv. 15. xxix. 23. Jerem. vii. 3. ix. 14. xi. 3. xiii. 12. xvi. 9. xix. 3, 15. xxiii. 2. xxiv. 5. xxv. 15, 27. xxix. 4, 8, 21, 25. xxx. 2. xxxi. 29. xxxii. 14, 15, 36. xxxiii. 4. xxxiv. 2, 13. xxxv. 13, 17, 18, 19. xxxvii. 7. xxxviii. 17. xxxix. 16. xlii. 9, 15, 18. xliii. 10. xliv. 2, 7, 11, 25. xlviii. 1. l. 18. li. 33. Ezek. viii. 4. ix. 3. x. 19, 20. xi. 2. xliii. 2. xliv. 2. Zeph. ii. 9. Psalm xli. 13. lix. 6. lxviii. 9.

94. In the Christian churches at the present time, it is common to call the Lord, our Savior, the *Son of Mary* and rarely the *Son of God*, unless they then mean a Son of God, born from eternity: the reason of this is, because the Roman Catholics have sanctified Mary, the mother, above the rest, and have exalted her as a goddess, or queen over all their saints; when yet the Lord, when He glorified his Human, put off all of his mother, and put on all of the Father, which will be fully demonstrated in the following parts of this work. From this common saying in the mouth of all, that He is called the *Son of Mary*, many enormities have flowed into the church; especially with those who have not admitted into their judgment those things which are said in the Word concerning the Lord, as that *the Father and He are one; that He is in the Father, and the Father in Him; that all things of the Father are his; that He called Jehovah his Father, and Jehovah the Father called Him his Son.* The enormities which have flowed into the church from this, that they name Him the Son of Mary, and not the Son of God, are, that concerning the Lord, the idea of divinity is lost, and with this, all that which is said in the Word concerning Him as the Son of God; then that through that enters Judaism, Arianism, Socinianism, Calvinism, such as it was in the beginning, and at length Naturalism, and with this the fancy that He was the Son of Mary by Joseph, and also that he had his soul from the mother, and thence that He is called the Son of God, and is not so. Let every one, clergyman as well as layman, consult himself, whether he has conceived and cherishes any other idea concerning the Lord, as the Son of Mary, than as of a mere man. Since such an idea began to prevail amongst Christians in the third century, when the Arians arose, therefore the Nicene council, to vindicate the divinity of the Lord, feigned a Son of God born from eternity; but, by this fiction, the Human of the Lord was indeed elevated then, and with many also at this day it is elevated, to the Divine; but not with those who, by the *hypostatic union*, understand

a union as between two, of whom one is above, and the other is below. But what else results thence than that the whole Christian church should perish, which was founded solely upon the worship of Jehovah in the Human, consequently upon God-Man. That no one can see the Father, nor know Him, nor come to Him, nor believe in Him, unless through his Human, the Lord declares in many passages. If this is not done, all the noble seed of the church is turned into ignoble seed; the seed of the olive into the seed of the pine; the seed of the orange, the citron, the apple and the pear, into the seed of the willow, the elm, the linden and the holm-oak; the vine into the bulrush of the bog; the wheat and barley into chaff; nay, all spiritual food becomes as the dust which serpents eat; for in man the spiritual light becomes natural, and at length sensual corporeal, which, viewed in itself, is the light of infatuation; yea, man then becomes as a bird, which, while it flies on high, when its wings are clipped will fall to the earth, where walking, it sees no more around it than what lies before its feet; and then concerning the spiritual things of the church, which will be for eternal life, he thinks no otherwise than a soothsayer. These things take place while man regards the Lord God, the Redeemer and Savior, as the mere Son of Mary, thus as a mere man.

95. V. That the Lord, by Acts of Redemption, made Himself Righteousness.

That the Lord alone had merit and righteousness by the obedience which He yielded to the Father, and especially by the passion of the cross, is said and believed at this day in Christian churches; but it is supposed, that the passion of the cross was the very act of redemption, when yet that was not the act of redemption, but the act of the glorification of his Human, of which we shall treat in the following Lemma concerning Redemption.—The acts of redemption, by which the Lord made Himself righteousness, were that He executed a last judgment, which was done in the spiritual world, and then separated the evil from the good, and the goats from the sheep, and expelled from heaven those who made one with the beasts of the dragon, and of the worthy He founded a new heaven, and of the unworthy a hell, and successively reduced all things in both to order; and, moreover, instituted a new church. These acts were the acts of redemption, by which the Lord made Himself righteousness; for righteousness is to do all things according to divine order; and to reduce to order those things which have fallen out of order; for righteousness is divine order itself. Those things are meant by these words of the Lord: *It is meet for Me to fulfill all the* RIGHTEOUSNESS OF GOD, Matt. iii. 15; and by these in the Old Testament; *Behold the days will come, when I shall raise unto David a* RIGHTEOUS BRANCH, *who shall reign King, and* DO RIGHTEOUSNESS *in the earth, and this is his name,* JEHOVAH OUR RIGHTEOUSNESS, Jerem. xxiii. 5, 6. xxxiii. 15, 16. *I speak in* RIGHTEOUSNESS, *great to save*, Isaiah lxiii. 1. *He shall sit upon the throne of David, to establish it in judgment and* RIGHTEOUSNESS, ix. 7. *Zion shall be redeemed in* RIGHTEOUSNESS, i. 27.

96. Our countrymen who bear rule in the church, describe the righteousness of the Lord quite differently; and also, by the inscription of it upon man, they make their faith saving; when yet the truth is, that the righteousness of the Lord, because it is such and thence, and in itself purely divine, cannot be conjoined to any man, and thus cannot produce any salvation, any more than the divine life, which is the divine love and the divine wisdom. The Lord with these enters into every man; but, unless man lives according to order, that life is in him, indeed, but it contributes nothing at all to his salvation; it only gives the faculty of understanding truth, and of doing good To live according to divine order, is to live according to the commandments of God; and when man so lives and does, then he procures for himself righteousness; not the righteousness of the re-

demption of the Lord, but the Lord himself as righteousness. These are they, who are meant by these words: *Unless* YOUR RIGHTEOUSNESS *shall abound above that of the Scribes and Pharisees, ye shall not enter into the kingdom of the heavens* Matt. v. 20. *In the consummation of the age, the angels will go forth, and separate the wicked from the midst of the righteous,* xiii. 49; besides other places. By the RIGHTEOUS, in the Word, are meant those who have lived according to divine order, since the divine order is righteousness. The righteousness itself, which, by acts of redemption, the Lord became, cannot be ascribed to man, inscribed upon him, adapted and conjoined to him, otherwise than light can be to the eye, sound to the ear, will to the muscles of one acting, thought to the lips of one speaking, air to the lungs of one breathing, heat to the blood, &c., which, that they flow in and adjoin themselves, besides that they conjoin themselves, every one of himself perceives. But righteousness is acquired so far as man exercises righteousness; and he exercises righteousness as far as he acts with his neighbor from the love of what is just and true: in the good itself, or in the use itself, which he does, righteousness dwells; for the Lord says, that every tree may be known by its fruit. Who does not know another by his works, if he attends to them, from what end and purpose of the will, and from what cause and intention they are done? All the angels attend to these things, and also all the wise men in our world. In general, every shrub and plant is known by its flower and seed, and by its use; every metal, by its goodness; every stone by its quality; every field, every kind of food, every animal of the earth, and every bird of the air, by their quality: why not man? But concerning the quality of the works of man, whence it is, will be opened in the chapter concerning faith.

97. VI. THAT THE LORD, BY THE SAME ACTS, UNITED HIMSELF TO THE FATHER, AND THE FATHER HIMSELF TO HIM.

That the union was effected by acts of redemption, is because the Lord performed them by means of his Human and as He operated, so the Divine, which is meant by the Father, came nearer, assisted and co-operated, and at length They so conjoined Themselves, that They were not two, but one; and this union is the glorification, of which in the following pages.

98. That the Father and the Son, that is, the Divine and the Human in the Lord, are united like the soul and body, is, indeed, according to the faith of the church at this day, and also according to the Word; but still scarcely five in a hundred, or fifty in a thousand know this: the reason is, the doctrine of justification by faith alone, which most of the clergy, who seek the reputation of learning, on account of honors and riches, have embraced with all zeal, until that doctrine has got complete possession of the minds of those at this day; and because this has intoxicated their thoughts, like the vinous spirit called alcohol, therefore, like men intoxicated, they have not seen this most essential thing of the church, that Jehovah God descended and assumed the Human; when yet, solely by this union, is given to man conjunction with God; and by conjunction, salvation. That salvation depends on the knowledge and acknowledgment of God, may appear evident to every one who considers that God is all in all of heaven, and thence all in all of the church; consequently, all in all of theology. But first it shall here be demonstrated, that the union of the Father and the Son, or of the Divine and the Human in the Lord, is as the union of the soul and the body; and afterwards, that that union is reciprocal. A union like that of the soul and the body has been established in the Athanasian creed, which is received, in all the Christian world, for the doctrine concerning God. There these words are read: *Our Lord Jesus Christ is God and Man, still there are not two, but there is one Christ: He is one, because the Divine took the Human to itself; yea, He is*

altogether one, and He is one person; for as the soul and body is one man, so God and Man is one Christ. But here it is meant that there is such a union of a Son of God from eternity with the Son born in time; but, because God is one, and not three, while that union is meant with the one God from eternity, that doctrine agrees with the Word. In the Word these things are read, that *He was conceived of Jehovah, the Father,* Luke i. 34, 35; thence his soul and life; wherefore He says, that *He and the Father are one,* John x. 30; that *He who seeth and knoweth Him, seeth and knoweth the Father,* xiv. 9; *If ye had known me, ye would also have known my Father,* viii. 19; *He who receiveth me, receiveth Him who sent me,* xiii. 20. that *He is in the bosom of the Father,* i. 18; that *All things whatsoever the Father hath are his,* xvi. 15; that *He is called the Father of eternity,* Isaiah ix. 6; that *Thence He hath power over all flesh,* John xvii. 2; *and all power in heaven and in earth,* Matt. xxviii. 18. From these and several other passages in the Word, it may be clearly seen, that the union of the Father and Him is like that of the soul and body; wherefore also, in the Old Testament, He is often named *Jehovah, Jehovah of hosts,* and *Jehovah the Redeemer:* see above, n. 83.

99. That that union is reciprocal, is very evident from these passages in the Word: *Philip, believest thou not that I am in the Father, and the Father in Me? Believe Me, that I am in the Father, and the Father in Me.* John xiv. 6, 11; *That ye may know and believe that the Father is in Me, and I in the Father,* x. 36, 38; *That they all may be one, as Thou, Father, art in Me, and I in Thee,* xvii. 21; *Father, all mine are thine, and thine are mine,* xvii. 10. That the union is reciprocal, is because no union or conjunction between two is given, unless one mutually accedes to the other: every conjunction in the universal heaven, in the universal world, and in the whole of man, is from no other source than from the reciprocal accession of one to another, and then that both will one thing; thence is effected something homogeneous, sympathetic, unanimous and concordant in every part of each. Such is the reciprocal conjunction of the soul and body with every man; such is the conjunction of the spirit of man with the organs of sensation and motion of his body; such is the conjunction of the heart and lungs; such is the conjunction of the will and understanding; such is the conjunction of all the members and viscera in and amongst each other in man; such is the conjunction of minds, amongst all those who inwardly love each other, for it is inscribed on all love and friendship, for love wishes to love, and wishes to be loved. There is a reciprocal conjunction of all things in the world, that are fully conjoined with each other; similar is the conjunction of the heat of the sun with the heat of wood and of stone; of the vital heat with the heat of all the animal fibres in animals; similar is that of a tree with its root, by the root with the tree, and by the tree with the fruit; such is that of the magnet with iron, &c. Unless conjunction be effected reciprocally and mutually by the accession of one to another, only an external conjunction is effected, and not an internal one; and this in time is spontaneously and mutually dissolved, and sometimes so that they no longer know each other.

100. Now, because a conjunction which is a conjunction, cannot be effected, unless it be done mutually and reciprocally, therefore the conjunction of the Lord and man is no other, as is very manifest from these passages: *He that eateth my flesh, and drinketh my blood,* ABIDETH IN ME, AND I IN HIM, John vi. 56. ABIDE IN ME, AND I IN YOU: HE THAT ABIDETH IN ME, AND I IN HIM, *beareth much fruit,* xv. 4, 5. *Whosoever openeth the door, I will come in to him, and* WILL SUP WITH HIM, AND HE WITH ME, Rev. iii. 20; besides other places. This conjunction is effected by man's acceding to the Lord, and the Lord to him; for it is a fixed and immutable law, that as far as man accedes to the Lord, so far

the Lord accedes to man: but more will be seen concerning this in the chapters concerning CHARITY and FAITH.

101. VII. THAT THUS GOD BECAME MAN, AND MAN GOD, IN ONE PERSON.

That Jehovah God became Man, and Man God, in one person, follows as a conclusion from all the preceding articles of this chapter, particularly from these two; that *Jehovah, the Creator of the universe, descended and assumed the Human, that He might redeem and save men;* of which above, n. 82, 83, 84; and that *The Lord, by acts of redemption, united Himself to the Father, and the Father Himself to Him, thus reciprocally and mutually;* of which above, n. 97 to 100. From that reciprocal union, it is very manifest, that God became Man, and Man God, in one person. The same also follows as a consequence of the union of both, that it is like that of the soul and body: that this is according to the faith of the church at this day, according to the creed of Athanasius, may be seen above, n. 89; also according to the faith of the evangelical Protestants, in their chief book of orthodoxy, which is called the FORMULA CONCORDIÆ, where it is strongly confirmed, both from the Sacred Scripture, and from the fathers, and also by rational arguments, that the human nature of Christ is exalted to divine majesty, omnipotence and omnipresence; and also that, in Christ, Man is God, and God Man; concerning this, see there, p. 607, 765. Besides, in this chapter it has been proved, that Jehovah God, as to his Human, in the Word, is called *Jehovah, Jehovah God, Jehovah of hosts,* and also the *God of Israel;* wherefore Paul says, that *In Jesus Christ all the fullness of the Godhead dwelleth bodily,* Col. ii. 9; and John, that *Jesus Christ, the Son of God, is the true God and eternal life,* 1 John v. 20, 21. That by the *Son of God* is properly meant his Human, may be seen above, n. 92, and the following. And, moreover, Jehovah God calls both Himself and Him *Lord;* for it is read, *The Lord said unto my Lord, Sit on my right hand,* Psalm cx. 1; and in Isaiah, *A Child is born to us a Son is given to us, whose name is God the Father of eternity,* ix. 5, 6. By *Son,* also, is meant the Lord, as to the Human, in David; *I will announce concerning the statute, Jehovah said, Thou art my Son; to-day I have begotten thee. Kiss the Son, lest He be angry, and ye perish in the way,* Psalm ii. 7, 12. Here is not meant a Son from eternity, but the Son born in the world; for it is prophetical of the Lord, who was about to come; wherefore it is called the statute concerning which Jehovah announced to David; and in that Psalm it is written before, *I have anointed my King upon Zion,* verse 6; and it follows, *I will give to Him the nations for an inheritance,* verse 8; wherefore TO-DAY, there, is not from eternity, but in time, for with Jehovah the future is present.

102. It is believed that the Lord, as to the Human, not only was, but also is the Son of Mary; but in this the Christian world is under a delusion. That he was the Son of Mary, is true; but that He is so still, is not true; for by acts of redemption, He put off the Human from the mother, and put on a Human from the Father; thence it is, that the Human of the Lord is Divine, and that, in Him, God is Man, and Man God. That He put off the Human from the mother, and put on a Human from the Father, which is the Divine Human, may be seen from this, that He never called Mary his mother, as may be evident from these passages: *The mother of Jesus said to Him, They have no wine. Jesus said to her,* WOMAN, *what is it to Me and thee? My hour is not yet come,* John ii. 4. And in another place; *Jesus from the cross, seeing his mother, and the disciple standing by, whom He loved, saith to his mother,* WOMAN, *behold thy Son! Then He saith to the disciple, Behold thy mother!* xix. 26, 27; and once that He did not acknowledge her; *It was told Jesus by some, saying, Thy mother and thy brethren are standing without, and wish to see Thee. Jesus, answering, said, My mother and my brethren are those who hear the Word*

of God, and do it, Luke viii. 20, 21; Matt. xii. 46 to 49; Mark iii. 31 to 35. Thus the Lord did not call her *mother*, but *woman*, and gave her to John as a mother; in other places, she is called his mother, but not by his own mouth. This also is confirmed by this, that He did not acknowledge Himself to be the Son of David, for it is read in the Evangelists, *Jesus asked the Pharisees, saying, What think ye of Christ? Whose son is He? They say to Him, David's. He saith to them, How, then, doth David, in the spirit, call Him his Lord, saying, The Lord said to my Lord, Sit on my right hand, until I make thine enemies thy footstool. If, then, David calleth Him Lord, how is He his Son? And no one was able to answer Him a word*, Matt. xxii. 39 to 44; Mark xii. 35, 36, 37; Luke xx. 41 to 44; Psalm cx. 1. To the above I shall add this news. It was once given me to speak with Mary the mother. She passed by some time since, and appeared in heaven over my head, in white raiment, as of silk; and then, stopping a little while, she said that she was the mother of the Lord, because He was born of her, but that, when He became God, He put off all the Human which he had from her, and that therefore she worships Him as her God, and that she is not willing that any one should acknowledge Him for her son, because in Him all is divine. From these things, this truth shines forth, that thus Jehovah is Man, as in the firsts, also in the lasts, according to these words; *I am the Alpha and the Omega, the Beginning and the End, He who is, and who was, and who is to come, the Almighty*, Rev. i. 8, 11. *John, when he saw the Son of Man in the midst of the seven candlesticks, fell at his feet as dead; but He put his right hand upon him, saying, I am the First and the Last*, Rev. i. 13, 17; xxi. 6. *Behold, I come quickly, that I may give to every one according to his work. I am the Alpha and the Omega, the Beginning and the End, the First and the Last*, xxii. 12, 13. And in Isaiah, *Thus said Jehovah, the King of Israel, and his Redeemer, Jehovah of hosts, I am the First and the Last*, xliv. 6; xlviii. 12.

103. To the above I shall add this arcanum, that the soul, which is from the father, is the very man, and that the body, which is from the mother, is not man in itself, but from the soul; the body is only a covering of the soul, composed of such things as are of the natural world. Every man, after death, puts off the natural, which he had from the mother, and retains the spiritual, which he had from the father, together with a kind of border [or circumambient accretion] from the purest things of nature, around it; but this border, with those who come into heaven, is below, and the spiritual above; but that border with those who come into hell is above, and the spiritual below; thence it is, that a man-angel speaks from heaven, thus what is good and true; but that a man-devil speaks from hell, while from his heart, and, as it were, from heaven, while from his mouth; he does this abroad, but that at home. Since the soul of man is the very man, and is spiritual from its origin, it is manifest whence it is that the mind, soul, disposition, inclination and affection of the love of the father dwells in his offspring, and returns and renders itself conspicuous from generation to generation. Thence it is, that many families, yea, nations, are known from their first father; there is a general image in the face of each descendant, which manifests itself; and this image is not changed, except by the spiritual things of the church. The reason that a general image of Jacob and Judah still remains in their posterity, by which they may be distinguished from others, is, because they have hitherto adhered firmly to their religious principles; for there is in the seed of every one, from which he is conceived, a graft or offset of the father's soul, in its fullness, within a certain covering from the elements of nature, by which the body is formed in the womb of the mother; which may be made according to the likeness of the father, or according to

the likeness of the mother, the image of the father still remaining within it, which continually endeavors to bring itself forth, and if it cannot do it in the first generation, it effects it the following. The reason that the image of the father is in its fullness in the seed, is, because, as was said, the soul is spiritual from its origin, and what is spiritual has nothing in common with space; wherefore it is similar to itself in a small, as well as in a large compass. With respect to the Lord, He, while He was in the world, by acts of redemption, put off the human from the mother, and put on a Human from the Father, which is the Divine Human; thence it is, that in Him, Man is God, and God Man.

104. VIII. THAT THE PROGRESS TO UNION WAS THE STATE OF HIS EXINANITION [OR HUMILIATION], AND THAT THE UNION ITSELF IS THE STATE OF HIS GLORIFICATION.

That the Lord, while He was in the world, had two states, which are called states of exinanition and glorification, is known in the church; the former state, which was that of exinanition, is described in many passages in the Word, especially in the Psalms of David, and also in the prophets, and particularly in Isaiah liii., where it is said, that *He poured out his soul unto death*, verse 12. This same state was the state of his humiliation before the Father, for in it he prayed to the Father, and He says that He does his will, and ascribes all that He did or said to the Father. That He prayed to the Father, is evident from these passages, Matt. xvii. 43; Mark i. 35; vi. 46; xiv. 32 to 39; Luke v. 15; vi. 12; xxii. 41 to 44; John xvii. 9, 15, 20. That He did the will of the Father, John iv. 34; v. 30. That He ascribed all that He did and said to the Father, John viii. 26, 27, 28; xii. 49, 50; xiv. 10. Yea, upon the cross He cried out, *My God, My God, why hast Thou forsaken Me?* Matt. xxvii. 47; Mark xv. 34; and, moreover, without this state, He could not have been crucified. The state of glorification is also a state of union. He was in this state when He was transfigured before his three disciples, and when He did miracles, and whenever He said that the Father and He were one; that the Father is in Him, and He in the Father; that all things of the Father are his; and when the union was fully completed, that *He had power over all flesh*, John xvii. 2; and *all power in heaven and in earth*, Matt. xxviii. 18; besides many other things.

105. The reason that the Lord had those two states of exinanition and glorification, was, because there is no other possible way of attaining to union, since it is according to the divine order, which is unchangeable. The *divine order* is, that man should dispose himself for the reception of God, and prepare himself for a receptacle and habitation, into which God may enter and dwell, as in his temple. Man should do this from himself, but still he should acknowledge that it is from God; he should acknowledge this, because he does not perceive the presence and operation of God, although God, being most perfectly present, operates in man all the good of love, and all the true of faith. According to this order every man proceeds and must proceed, that he may, from natural, become spiritual. In like manner the Lord, that He might make his Natural Divine; thence it is, that He prayed to the Father; that He did his will; and that all that He did and said, He attributed to Him; and that upon the cross He said, *My God, my God, why hast Thou forsaken Me?* for in this state, God appears absent. But after this state, comes another, which is a state of conjunction with God; in this man acts in like manner, but then from God; nor has he then need, in like manner as before, to ascribe to God all the good which he wills and does, and all the truth which he thinks and speaks, because this is inscribed upon his heart, and thence it is inwardly in all his actions and speech. In like manner, the Lord united Himself to his Father and the Father Himself to Him; in a word, the Lord glorified his Human, that is, made it divine, in the same

manner that the Lord regenerates man, that is, makes him spiritual.

That every man, who from natural becomes spiritual, undergoes two states, and that through the first he enters into the other, and thus from the world to heaven, will be fully demonstrated in the chapters concerning FREE-WILL, concerning CHARITY and FAITH, and concerning REFORMATION and REGENERATION; here only, that in the first state, which is called the state of reformation, man is in full liberty of acting according to the rational of his understanding; and that in the second, which is the state of regeneration, he is also in similar liberty, but that then he wills and acts, and thinks and speaks, from a new love and a new intelligence, which are from the Lord; for, in the first state, the understanding acts the first part, and the will the second; in the other, the will acts the first, and the understanding the second; but the understanding from the will, and not the will by the understanding. The conjunction of the good and the true, of charity and faith, and of the internal and the external man, is not otherwise effected.

106. Those two states are represented by various things in the universe; the reason is, because they are according to divine order, and divine order fills all and every thing, even to the minutest things in the universe. The first state is represented with every man by the state of his infancy and childhood, even to his youth, adolescence and manhood, which is the state of his humiliation before his parents, and then of obedience, and also of instruction from masters and ministers; but the other state is represented by the state of the same person when he becomes his own master, and freely exercises his own will and understanding, in which he has absolute power in his own house. The first state is also represented by the state of a prince, or the son of a king, or of a duke, before he becomes a king or a duke; in like manner, by the state of every citizen before he becomes the person of a magistrate; of every subject before he obtains any office; of every student who is preparing for the ministry, before he becomes a priest; and of every priest before he becomes a pastor; and then of every pastor before he becomes a primate; also of every virgin before she becomes a wife; and of every maid before she becomes a mistress; in general, of every clerk before he becomes a merchant; of every soldier before he becomes an officer; of every servant before he becomes a master. The first of these is a state of servitude, the other of one's own will, and thence understanding. Those two states are represented also by various things in the animal kingdom; the first, by beasts and birds as long as they are with their mothers and fathers, which they then follow constantly, and are nourished and led by them; and the other state, when they leave them, and look out for themselves: in like manner by worms; the first, while they crawl and are nourished by leaves, the second, when they cast off their skins, and become butterflies. Those two states are represented also in the subjects of the vegetable kingdom; the first, when the vegetable springs up from the seed, and is adorned with branches, buds and leaves: the other, when it bears fruit, and produces new seeds; this may be compared to the conjunction of the good and the true, since all things which belong to a tree correspond to truths, and the fruit to good. But the man, who stops in the first state, and does not enter the second, is like a tree which bears only leaves, and not fruit, concerning which it is said in the Word, that it is to be pulled up, and cast into the fire. Matt. xxi. 19; Luke xiii. 6 to 10, John xv. 5, 6. And he is like a servant, that is not willing to be free, concerning whom it was commanded, that *He should be brought to the door, or to the door-post, and his ear should be bored through with an awl*, Exod. xxi. 6. Servants are those who are not conjoined to the Lord, but the free are those who are conjoined to Him; for the Lord says, *If the Son makes you free, ye are truly free*, John viii. 36

107 IX. THAT, HEREAFTER, NO ONE CAN COME FROM CHRISTIANS INTO HEAVEN, UNLESS HE BELIEVES IN THE LORD GOD THE SAVIOR, AND GOES TO HIM ALONE.

It is read in Isaiah, *Behold, I create a new heaven, and a new earth, and the former shall not be mentioned, nor come upon the heart; and behold, I am about to create Jerusalem an exultation, and her people a joy*, lxv. 17. And in the Revelation; *I saw a new heaven and a new earth, and I saw the holy Jerusalem descending from God out of heaven, prepared as a bride for her husband; and one sitting upon the throne said, Behold, I make all things new*, xxi. 1, 2, 5. And it is often said, that *No others will enter into heaven, than those who are written in the Lamb's book of life*, Rev. xiii. 8; xvii. 8; xx. 12, 15; xxi. 26. By *heaven* there, is not meant the heaven which is visible to our eyes, but the angelic heaven; by *Jerusalem*, not any city from heaven, but the church, which will descend out of that heaven from the Lord; and by *the Lamb's book of life*, is not meant any book written in heaven, which will be opened, but the Word, which is from the Lord and concerning Him. That Jehovah God, who is called the Creator and Father, descended and assumed the Human, also for the purpose of enabling man to approach Him, and to be conjoined to Him, has been proved, confirmed, and established, in the preceding articles of this chapter. For who, that comes to a man, goes to his soul? and who can do this? But he goes to the man himself, whom he sees face to face, and with whom he speaks mouth to mouth. The case is similar with God the Father and the Son, for God the Father is in the Son, as the soul in its body. That it is necessary to believe in the Lord God the Savior, is evident from these passages in the Word: *God so loved the world, that He gave his only begotten Son, that every one who believeth in Him may not perish, but have eternal life*, John iii. 15, 16. *He who* BELIEVETH IN THE SON *is not judged, but he who believeth not, is already judged, because he hath not believed in the name of the only* BEGOTTEN SON OF GOD, iii. 18. *He who* BELIEVETH IN THE SON *hath eternal life, but he who believeth not the Son shall not see life, but the anger of God shall abide upon him*, iii. 36. *The bread of God is He that descended from heaven, and giveth life to the world; he who cometh to Me shall never hunger, and he who believeth in Me shall never thirst*, vi. 33, 35. *This is the will of Him who sent Me, that every one who seeth the Son, and* BELIEVETH IN HIM, *may have eternal life, and I will resuscitate him at the last day*, vi. 40. *They said to Jesus, What shall we do that we may work the works of God? Jesus answered, This is the work of God, that ye* BELIEVE IN HIM *whom the Father hath sent*, vi. 28, 29. *Verily I say unto you, He who* BELIEVETH IN ME *hath eternal life*, vi. 47. *Jesus cried, saying, If any one thirst, let him come to Me and drink; whosoever* BELIEVETH IN ME, *out of his belly shall flow rivers of living water*, vii. 37, 38. *Unless ye believe that I am, ye shall die in your sins*, viii. 24. *Jesus said, I am the resurrection and the life; he who believeth in Me, although he die, shall live; but every one who liveth and believeth in Me, shall never die*, xi. 25, 26. *Jesus said, I am come a light into the world, that every one who believeth in Me may not abide in darkness*, xii. 46, viii. 12. *As long as ye have light, believe in the light, that ye may be sons of the light*, xii. 36. *That they shoul abide in the Lord, and the Lord in them*, xiv. 20, xv. 1 to 5, xvii. 23 which is done by faith. *Paul testified, both to the Jews and to the Greeks, repentance towards God, and* FAITH IN OUR LORD JESUS CHRIST, Acts xx. 21 *I am the way, the truth and the life; no one cometh to the Father, but by Me*, John xiv. 6. That he who believes in the Son, believes in the Father (since, as above said, the Father is in Him, as the soul in the body), is evident from these passages *If ye had known Me, ye would also have known my Father*, John viii. 19; xiv. 7. *He who seeth*

Me, seeth Him who sent Me, xii. 45. *He who receiveth Me, receiveth Him who sent Me*, xiii. 20. The reason is, because *No one can see the Father and live*, Exod. xxxiii. 20. Wherefore the Lord says, *No one hath ever seen God; the only begotten Son, who is in the bosom of the Father, He hath manifested Him*, John i. 18. *No one hath seen the Father, but He who is with the Father, He hath seen the Father*, vi. 46. *Ye have never heard the voice of the Father, nor seen his shape*, v. 37. But those who do not know any thing concerning the Lord, as most of those in the two parts of the world, Asia and Africa, and also in the Indies, these, if they believe in one God, and live according to the precepts of their religion, are saved by means of their faith and life; for imputation is to those who know, and not to those who know not, as it is not to the blind, when they stumble; for the Lord says, *If ye were blind, ye would not have sin; but now ye say that ye see, therefore your sin remaineth*, John ix. 41.

108. To confirm this further, I will relate what I know, because I have seen, and therefore I can testify what follows; that the Lord, at this day, is forming a new angelic heaven, and that it is formed of those who believe in the Lord God the Savior, and go immediately to Him; and that the rest are rejected. Wherefore, if any hereafter comes from Christendom into the spiritual world, into which every man does come after death, and does not believe in the Lord, and go to Him alone, and then is not able to receive this, because he has lived wickedly, or has confirmed himself in falses, he is repelled at his first approach towards heaven, and his face is thence averted, and turned towards the lower earth, whither he also goes, and conjoins himself with those there, who are meant in the Revelation by the dragon and the false prophet. Every man also in Christian countries, who does not believe in the Lord, is not hereafter heard with acceptance; his prayers, in heaven, are like ill-scented odors, and like eructations from ulcerated lungs; and if he thinks that his prayer is like the perfume of incense, still it does not ascend to the angelic heaven, otherwise than as the smoke of a fire, which is driven back by a violent tempest, into his eyes, or as the perfume from a censer under a monk's cloak: thus, after this time, it is with all piety which is determined to a divided trinity, and not to one conjoined. That the divine trinity is conjoined in the Lord, is the principal object of this work. Here I will add this news; that some months since, the twelve apostles were called together by the Lord, and sent forth into all the spiritual world, as before they were into the natural world, with the command, that they should preach this gospel; and then every apostle had his province assigned to him; which command, also, they are executing with all zeal and industry. But concerning this subject, we shall treat particularly in the last chapter of this work, where we shall speak concerning THE CONSUMMATION OF THE AGE, concerning THE COMING OF THE LORD, and concerning THE NEW CHURCH.

109. A COROLLARY. All the churches which had been before the coming of the Lord, were representative churches, which could not see divine truths, but as in the shade; but, after the coming of the Lord into the world, a church was instituted by Him, which saw, or rather was able to see, divine truths in the light. The difference is like that between evening and morning; the state of the church before the coming of the Lord is also in the Word called *evening*, and the state of the church after his coming, is called *morning*. The Lord, before his coming into the world, was indeed present with the men of the church, but mediately through angels, who represented Him; but since his coming, He is present with the men of the church immediately; for, in the world, He put on also the NATURAL DIVINE, in which He is present with men. The glorification of the Lord is the glorification of his Human, which He assumed in the world, and the glorified Human of the Lord is the NATURAL DIVINE. That it is so, is evident from this, that

the Lord rose from the sepulchre with his whole body, which He had in the world; nor did He leave any thing in the sepulchre; consequently, that He took thence with Him, the natural human itself, from the firsts to the lasts of it; wherefore He said to the disciples, after the resurrection, when they supposed that they saw a spirit, *See my hands and my feet, that it is I myself; feel of Me, and see; for a spirit hath not flesh and bones, as ye see Me have,* Luke xxiv. 37, 39. Whence it is manifest, that his natural body, by glorification, was made divine. Wherefore Paul says, that *In Christ dwelleth all the fullness of the God-head bodily,* Coloss. ii. 9; and John, that *The Son of God, Jesus Christ, is the true God,* 1 Epist. v. 20, 21. Hence the angels know, that the Lord alone, in the whole spiritual world, is fully MAN. It is known in the church, that all the worship amongst the Israelitish and Jewish nation was merely external, and that it shadowed forth the internal worship which the Lord opened, and that thus worship, before the coming of the Lord, consisted in types and figures, which represented true worship in its just effigy. The Lord himself, indeed, appeared amongst the ancients; for He said to the Jews, *Abraham, your father, exulted that he might see my day, and he saw and rejoiced; I say unto you, before Abraham was, I am,* John viii. 56, 58. But because the Lord then was only represented, which was done by means of angels, therefore all the things of the church with them were made representative; but after He came into the world, those representations vanished; the interior reason of which was, because the Lord, in the world, put on also the NATURAL DIVINE, and from this He illustrates not only the internal spiritual man, but also the external natural; which two, unless they are at the same time illustrated, man is, as it were, in the shade; but while both are at the same time illustrated, he is, as it were, in the day; for while the internal man alone is illustrated, and not the external at the same time; or while only the external, and not, at the same time, the internal, he is like one that sleeps and dreams, and presently, when he awakes, he recollects the dream, and from it he concludes various things, which nevertheless, are imaginary. And he is also like one walking in sleep, who thinks the objects which he sees are seen in day-light. The difference between the state of the church before the coming of the Lord, and after his coming, is like the difference between reading a writing in the night by the light of the moon and stars, and reading it by the light of the sun; that the eye, in the former light, which is only pale, is liable to mistake, and in the latter, which is also flammeous, is not liable to mistake, is well known. Wherefore it is read concerning the Lord, *The God of Israel said, the Rock of Israel spoke to me, He is as the light of the morning while the sun arises, of a morning without clouds,* 2 Sam. xxiii. 3, 4. The *God of Israel* and the *Rock of Israel* is the Lord. And in another place, *The light of the moon shall be as the light of the sun, and the light of the sun shall be seven-fold, as the light of seven days, in the day when Jehovah shall bind up the breach of his people,* Isaiah xxx. 25, 26. These things are said concerning the state of the church, after the coming of the Lord. In a word, the state of the church before the coming of the Lord, may be compared to an old woman, whose face has been painted, and who, from the bright color of the paint, has appeared to herself beautiful; but the state of the church after the coming of the Lord, may be compared to a virgin, beautiful from the native brightness of her complexion. And also the state of the church, before the coming of the Lord, may be compared to the rind of any sort of fruit, as of an orange, an apple, a pear, or a grape, and to its flavor; but the state of the church after his coming, may be compared to the inner parts of those fruits, and to their flavor, besides with other similar things. The reason of this difference is, because the Lord, since He put on also the Natural Divine, illustrates the internal spiritual man, and the external natural, at the same time; for while only the internal man is illustrated, and not at the same time the external, there is made a shade; in like manner, while only the external, and not at the same time the internal.

---

110. Here the following RELATIONS will be adduced. FIRST. Once, in the spiritual world, I saw an *ignis fatuus* in the air, falling to the earth, and a lucid circumference around it; it was a meteor, which the vulgar call a *dragon.* I observed the place where it fell; but this disappeared in the morning twilight, before sunrise, as is the case with every *ignis fatuus.* In the morning, I went to the place where I saw it fall in the night, and behold! the ground there was a mixture of sulphur, iron-filings and clay; and suddenly there appeared two tents, one directly over the place, and the other at the side towards the south: and I looked up, and saw a spirit falling down from heaven, like lightning, and cast into the tent which stood directly over the place where the meteor fell; and I in the other, which was near it towards the south: in the door of this I stood, and saw the spirit in the other also standing in the door of his tent; and then I asked him why he thus fell down from heaven; to which he replied, that he was cast down, as an angel of the dragon, by the angels of Michael, "because I spoke some things concerning my faith, in which I confirmed myself in the world; amongst which was this, that God the Father and God the Son are two, and not one; for all in the heavens at this day believe that they are one, like the soul and body; and every word spoken against that, is like a sting in their nostrils, and like an awl boring through their ears, whence they have emotion and pain; and, therefore, whoever contradicts their belief, is commanded to go out, and, if he is backward, he is cast down headlong." On hearing this, I said to him, "Why did you not believe as they did?" He answered, that, "After departure out of the world, no one can believe any thing else, than what he had by confirmation impressed upon himself; this remains fixed in him, and cannot be torn away especially that which any one has confirmed in himself concerning God, since every one in the heavens has a place according to his idea of God." Then I asked, "By what he had confirmed the idea, that the Father and the Son were two." He said, "By these things in the Word; that the Son prayed to the Father, not only before the passion of the cross, but also upon the cross; as also that He humbled Himself before his Father; how, then, can they be one, as the soul and body are one in man? Who prays, as to another, and humbles himself as before another, while he himself is that other? No one does so, much less the Son of God; and, besides, the whole Christian church, in my time, divided the God-head into persons, and each person is one by himself, and is defined to be *what subsists in itself.*" When I had heard these things from him, I replied, "I have perceived from your discourse, that you know nothing at all how God the Father and the Son are one; and because you know not how, you had confirmed yourself in the falses, in which the church as yet is concerning God. Do you not know that the Lord, when He was in the world, had a soul, as every other man has? Whence had He this soul, but from God the Father? That it is so, appears abundantly from the Word of the Evangelists. What, then, is that which is called the *Son,* but the Human, which was conceived from the Divine of the Father, and born of the virgin Mary? A mother cannot conceive a soul; this is totally repugnant to the order, according to which every man is born; nor can God the Father impart a soul from Himself, and then recede from it, as every father in the world can, since God is his own divine essence, and this is one and individual, and because it is individual, it is Himself. Thence it is, that the Lord says, that *The Father and He are one; and that the Father is in Him and He in the*

Father; besides many similar things. The composers of the Athanasian creed also saw this at a distance; wherefore, after they divided God into three persons, still they say, that In Christ, God and Man, that is, the Divine and the Human, are not two, but one, like the soul and body in man. That the Lord, in the world, prayed to the Father as to another, and that he humbled Himself before the Father, as before another, was according to the order established from creation, which is immutable, according to which every one must proceed to conjunction with God. That order is, that as man, by a life according to the laws of order, which are the commandments of God, conjoins himself to God, so God conjoins Himself to man, and from natural makes him spiritual. In like manner, the Lord united Himself to his Father, and God the Father Himself to Him. Was not the Lord, while an infant, like an infant, and while a boy, like a boy? Is it not read, that *He increased in wisdom and favor;* and afterwards, that He asked the Father that He would glorify his name, that is, his Human? To glorify is to make divine by union with Himself. Thence it is manifest, that the Lord, in the state of his exinanition, which was the state of his progress to union, prayed to the Father. That same order, from creation, is inscribed on every man; that is, as man, by means of truths from the Word, prepares his understanding, so he adapts it to the reception of faith from God; and as, by works of charity, he prepares his will, so he accommodates it to the reception of love from God; for as an artist cuts a diamond, so he applies it to receive and emit the splendor of light, &c. To prepare one's self for the reception of God and conjunction, is to live according to divine order; and the laws of order are all the commandments of God; these the Lord fulfilled to every tittle, and thus made himself a receptacle of the God-head in all fullness. Wherefore Paul says, that *In Jesus Christ all the fullness of the God-head dwelleth bodily;* and the Lord himself, that *All things of the Father are His.* It is further to be held that the Lord alone is active with every man, and that man of himself is merely passive; but that, by an influx of life from the Lord, he is also active; from this perpetual influx from the Lord, it appears to man as if he were active from himself; and because it is so, he also has free will, and this is given him, that he may prepare himself for receiving the Lord, and thus for conjunction, which is not practicable, unless it be reciprocal, and it becomes reciprocal, while man acts from his liberty, and yet from faith attributes all activity to the Lord."

After this, I asked whether he, like others his companions, confessed that God is one. He replied that he did; and then I said, "But I am afraid that the confession of your heart is, that there is no God. Does not all the speech of the mouth proceed from the thought of the mind? Wherefore it cannot be otherwise, than that the confession of the mouth *that God is one* should expel from the mind the thought *that there are three;* and reciprocally, that the thought of the mind should expel from the mouth the confession *that He is one.* What else thence results, than that there is no God? Is not all the intermediate region, which is from the thought to the mouth, and from the mouth back to the thought, thus rendered an empty void? And what else is then concluded by the mind concerning God, but that nature is God, and concerning the Lord, but that his soul was either from the mother, or from Joseph; from which two things, as horrid and abominable, all the angels of heaven turn themselves away." When these things were said, that spirit was sent away into the abyss, mentioned in the Revelation, ix. 2, and the following, where the angels of the dragon discuss the mysteries of their faith. The next day, when I looked towards the same place, I saw, instead of the tents, two statues in the likeness of human beings, made of the dust of the earth, which was a mixture of sulphur, iron and clay; and one statue seemed to have a sceptre in the left hand, a crown on the head, and a book in the right hand, and also a stomacher obliquely tied across, and set with precious stones, and behind, a robe flowing to the other statue; but these things were induced upon that statue by fantasy; and then a voice was heard thence, from a certain dragonist:—"This statue represents our faith as a queen; and the other behind it, charity as her maid-servant." This was composed of a similar mixture of dust, and placed at the extremity of the robe flowing down from the back of the queen; and she held in her hand a paper, upon which it was written, "Beware lest you approach nearer and touch the robe." But then, on a sudden, a shower fell from heaven, and penetrated both the statues, which, because they were composed of a mixture of sulphur, iron and clay, began to bubble, as is the case with a mixture of those ingredients while water is poured upon it; and being thus inflamed by an intestine fire, they were reduced to ashes, and became heaps, which afterwards lay upon the ground there like sepulchral mounds.

111. Second Relation. In the natural world, the speech of man is two-fold, because his thought is two-fold, external and internal; for man can speak from internal thought, and at the same time from external thought, and he can speak from external thought and not from the internal, yea, contrary to the internal; thence originate dissimulation, flattery and hypocrisy. But, in the spiritual world, the speech of man is not two-fold, but single; he speaks there as he thinks; or else the sound grates, and hurts the ear; but still he can be silent, and so not divulge the thoughts of his mind. Wherefore a hypocrite, when he comes among the wise, either goes away, or gets himself into a corner of the room, and makes himself unobserved, and sits in silence. Once there were many assembled in the world of spirits, and were conversing together upon this subject, saying, that "Not to be able to speak, except as one thinks, is hard for those in company with the good, who have not thought justly concerning God and concerning the Lord." In the middle of the assembly were the reformed, and many of the clergy, and next to them, the papists, with the monks; and the former and the latter at first said, that "This is not hard: what necessity is there for one to speak otherwise than he thinks? and, if by chance he does not think justly, can he not close his lips, and keep silence?" And one of the clergy said, "Who does not think justly concerning God and concerning the Lord?" But some of the congregation said, "Let us try them." And they said to those who had confirmed themselves in a trinity of persons concerning God, that they from thought should say, *One God;* but they could not. They twisted and folded their lips into many folds, and could not articulate sound into other words than such as were consonant to the ideas of their thought, which were those of three persons, and thence of three Gods. Then it was said to those who confirmed faith separate from charity, that they should name Jesus; but they could not, although they all could say *Christ*, and also *God the Father.* They wondered at this, and inquired the reason, and found it to be this; that they had prayed to God the Father, for the sake of the Son, and had not prayed to the Savior himself; and *Jesus* signifies Savior. Moreover, it was said to them, that they should, from their thought concerning the Human of the Lord, say Divine Human; but no one of the clergy who was present there could do it, although some of the laity could; wherefore this was submitted to a serious discussion; and then, I. These passages in the evangelists were read to them: *The Father hath given all things into the hand of the Son,* John iii. 35. *The Father hath given to the Son power over all flesh,* xvii. 2. *All things are delivered to Me by the Father,* Matt. xi. 7. *All power is given to Me in heaven and in earth,* xxviii 18. And it was said to them, "Keep thence in your thought, that Christ, as to his Human, as well as to his Divine, is the God of heaven and earth, and thus pronounce Divine Human;" but

still they could not; and they said, that, indeed, they held thence something of thought from the understanding concerning it, but still not any thing of acknowledgment, and that therefore they could not. II. Afterwards it was read to them from Luke i. 32, 34, 35, that the Lord, as to the Human, was the Son of Jehovah God, and that he is there called the *Son of the Most High*, and, in various other places, the *Son of God*, and also the *Only-begotten;* and they requested that they would keep this in their thought, and also that the Only-begotten Son of God born in the world, could not but be God, as the Father is God, and speak out DIVINE HUMAN. But they said, "We cannot, because our spiritual thought, which is interior, does not admit into the thought next to the speech other than similar ideas, and that thence they perceived, that now it was not allowable for them to divide their thoughts, as in the natural world." III. Then were read to them these words of the Lord to Philip—*Philip said, Lord, show us the Father; and the Lord said, He who seeth Me seeth the Father; believest thou not that I am in the Father, and the Father in Me*, John xiv. 8 to 11; and also other passages, *That the Father and He are one*, as John x. 30. And it was said to them, that they should keep that in their thought, and thus say, DIVINE HUMAN; but, because that thought was not rooted in the acknowledgment, that the Lord was God even as to the Human, they twisted their lips into folds, even to indignation, and wished to force their mouth to speak out, but they could not do it: the reason was, because the ideas of thought, which flow from acknowledgment, make one with the words of the tongue, with those who are in the spiritual world; and where those ideas are not, words are not given, for ideas become words in speech. IV. Moreover, there were read to them, from the doctrine received in all the Christian world, these words; that *The Divine and the Human in the Lord are not two, but one; yea, one Person, united as the soul and body in man* These words are from the Confession of Faith, named from Athanasius, and acknowledged by councils. And it was said to them, "You can from this, certainly, have an idea from acknowledgment, that the Human of the Lord is divine, because His soul is divine; for it is from the doctrine of your church, which you acknowledged in the world; besides, the soul is the very essence of man, and the body is its form, and essence and form make one, as *esse* and *existere*, and as the cause producing an effect, and the effect itself." They retained that idea, and wished, from it, to pronounce DIVINE HUMAN; but they could not; for their interior idea concerning the Human of the Lord exterminated and expunged this new adscititious idea, as they called it. V. Then this passage from John was read to them; *The Word was with God, and the Word was God, and the Word became flesh*, i. 1, 14; and also this; *Jesus Christ is the true God, and eternal Life*, v. 21; and from Paul; *In Jesus Christ dwelleth all the fullness of the Godhead bodily*, Col. ii. 9: and it was said to them, that they should think in like manner; that is, that God, who was the Word, became Man, that He was the true God, and that all the fullness of the Godhead dwelt in Him bodily. And they did so, but only in external thought; wherefore they could not, on account of the resistance of the internal, speak out DIVINE HUMAN, saying openly that they could not have an idea of DIVINE HUMAN, because God is God, and man is man; and God is a Spirit, and concerning spirit we have thought no otherwise than as concerning wind or ether. VI. At length it was said to them, "You know that the Lord said, *Abide in Me, and I in you; he who abideth in Me, and I in him, beareth much fruit; because without Me, ye cannot do any thing*," John xv. 4, 5; and because some of the clergy of England were present, it was read to them, from one of their exhortations at the Holy Communion, "*For, when we spiritually eat the flesh of Christ, and drink the blood, then we dwell in Christ and Christ in us.*" "If now you think that this cannot be given, unless the Human of the Lord be Divine, say therefore DIVINE HUMAN from acknowledgment in thought;" but still they could not; for the idea was so deeply impressed on them, that the Divine could not be Human, and the Human could not be Divine, and that his Divine was from the Divine of a Son from eternity, and his Human similar to the human of another man. But it was said to them, "How can you think so? Can a rational mind ever think that any Son was born of God from eternity?" VII. Afterwards they turned themselves to the evangelical, saying, that the Augsburg Confession and Luther taught, that the Son of God and the Son of Man, in Christ, is one Person, and that He, even as to the human nature, is omnipotent and omnipresent; and that as to this, He sits at the right hand of God the Father, and governs all things in the heavens and in the earths, fills all things, is with us, dwells and operates in us; and that there is no difference of adoration; because, through the nature which is discerned, the Divinity which is not discerned is adored; and that, in Christ, God is Man and Man God. On hearing these things, they replied, "Is it so?" And they looked around, and presently said, "We did not know this before; wherefore we cannot say, DIVINE HUMAN." But one and another said, "We have read it, and we have written it, but still, when we thought about it in ourselves, they were only words, of which we had no interior idea." VIII. At last, turning about to the papists, they said, "Perhaps you can say DIVINE HUMAN, because you believe that, in your eucharist, Christ is entire in the bread and wine, and in every part of them; and also you adore Him, when you show and carry about the host, as the most holy God; also because you call Mary *Deipara*, or the Mother of God; consequently you acknowledge that she brought forth God, that is, the DIVINE HUMAN." And they then wished to speak it, but because there arose then a material idea concerning the body and blood of Christ, and also the faith, that his Human is separable from the Divine, and that it is actually separated with the pope, to whom only his human, and not his divine power was transferred they could not speak it. And then a monk arose and said, that he could think of a Divine Human in respec to the most holy virgin Mary, and also in respect to a saint of his monastery. And another monk came up, saying, "I can, from the idea of my thought which I now entertain, say DIVINE HUMAN, in respect to the most holy pope, rather than in respect to Christ." But then some of the papists pulled him back, and said, "For shame on you!" After this, heaven appeared open, and there appeared tongues like little flames, descending and flowing in with some; and then they celebrated the DIVINE HUMAN OF THE LORD, saying, "Remove the idea of three Gods, and believe that in the Lord dwells all the fullness of the Godhead bodily, and that the Father and He are one, as the soul and body are one, and that God is not wind and ether, but that He is Man, and then you will be conjoined to heaven, and, from the Lord, will be able to speak the name JESUS, and to say DIVINE HUMAN."

112. THIRD RELATION. Once, having awaked just after the dawn, I went out into the garden before the house, and saw the sun arising in his splendor, and round about him a girdle, at first faint, and afterwards more conspicuous, shining as if from gold, and under its edge a cloud ascending, which glittered like a carbuncle, from the flame of the sun; and then I fell into a meditation respecting the fables of the ancients, that they feigned Aurora with wings of silver feathers, and in her face displaying the lustre of gold. When my mind was delighted in these things, I became in the spirit, and heard some talking among themselves, and saying, "O! that we might be allowed to speak with the innovator, who has thrown the apple of contention amongst the rulers of the church, which many of the laity have run after; and, having picked it up, they have presented it to our eyes." By that ap-

ple, they meant a little pamphlet, entitled, A BRIEF EXPOSITION OF THE DOCTRINE OF THE NEW CHURCH. And they said, "It is indeed a schismatical thing, which no one ever before conceived." And I heard then one of them exclaiming, "What! schismatical? it is heretical." But some at his side replied, "Hush, hold your tongue; it is not heretical; he quotes a great many passages of the Word, to which our strangers, by whom we mean the laity, attend and assent." When I heard these things, because I was in the spirit, I went to them, and said, "Here I am; what is the subject?" And presently one of them, who, as I afterwards heard, was a German, a native of Saxony, speaking in a tone of authority, said, "Whence had you the audacity to change the worship in the Christian world, established for so many ages, which was, that God the Father should be invoked as the Creator of the universe, and his Son as the Mediator, and the Holy Ghost as the Operator? And you separate the first and last God from our personality, when yet the Lord himself says, *When ye pray, pray thus; Our Father, who art in the heavens, hallowed be thy name, thy kingdom come.* Thus is it not commanded, that we should invoke God the Father?" These things being said, silence was made, and all who favored him, stood like brave soldiers upon ships of war when they see a hostile fleet, ready to cry, Let us fight now; the victory is certain. And then I began to speak, and said, "Which of you does not know, that God descended from heaven, and became man? for it is read, *The Word was with God, and the Word was God; and the Word became flesh:* also, which of you does not know (and I looked at the evangelical, amongst whom was that dictator who had just addressed me) that in Christ, who was born of the virgin Mary, God is Man, and Man God?" But at these words, the assembly made a great noise; wherefore I said, "Do you not know this? It is according to the doctrine of your confession, which is called the FORMULA CONCORDIÆ, where this is said and corroborated by many things." Then that dictator turned himself towards the assembly, and asked whether they knew this. And they replied, "We have studied very little in that book concerning the PERSON of CHRIST, but we have sweat upon the article there concerning JUSTIFICATION *by faith alone.* But still, if that is read there, we acquiesce." And then one of them, recollecting, said, "It is read; and what is still more, that the human nature of Christ is exalted to divine majesty, and to all its attributes, and also that in it Christ sits at the right hand of the Father." Having heard these words, they were silent; and after this consent, I spoke again, saying, "Since it is so, what then is the Father, but the Son, and what the Son, but the Father also?" But because this again made an unpleasant noise in their ears, I continued, saying, "Hear the very words of the Lord, to which, if you have not attended before, attend now; for He said, *The Father and I are one; the Father is in Me, and I in the Father; Father, all mine are thine, and all thine mine; he who seeth Me, seeth the Father.* What else do those words mean, than that the Father is in the Son, and the Son in the Father, and that they are one, as the soul and body in man, and thus that they are one person? This also will be of your faith, if you believe the Athanasian creed, where similar things are said. But take from the words adduced only this declaration of the Lord; *Father, all mine are thine, and all thine are mine;* what else is this than that the Divine of the Father belongs to the Human of the Son, and the Human of the Son to the Divine of the Father? consequently that, in Christ, God is man, and man God? and thus that they are one, as the soul and body are one. Every man also may say the like concerning his soul and his body, viz. 'All thine are mine, and all mine thine; thou in me, and I in thee; he who sees me, sees thee; we are one as to person and as to life;' the reason is, because the soul is in the whole and in every part of man; for the life of the soul is the life of the body, and there is a mutuality between them. Hence it is manifest, that the Divine of the Father is the soul of the Son, and that the Human of the Son is the body of the Father. Whence is the soul of a son but from the father? and whence is his body, but from the mother? It is said, *the Divine of the Father*, and the Father himself is meant since He and his Divine are the same; this also is one and individual. That it is so, is evident also from these words of the angel Gabriel to Mary; *The virtue of the Most High shall overshadow thee, and the Holy Spirit come upon thee, and the holy Thing that shall be born of thee, shall be called the Son of God;* and just above He is called *the Son of the Most High*, and elsewhere, *the only-begotten Son*. But you, who only call Him the *Son of Mary*, lose the idea of his divinity; but no others lose it, except the learned of the clergy, and scholars among the laity, who, while they elevate their thoughts above the sensual things of the body, look at the glory of their own fame, which not only overshadows, but also extinguishes the light, by which the glory of God enters. But let us return to the Lord's prayer, where it is said, *Our Father who art in the heavens, hallowed be thy name, thy kingdom come.* You who are here understand, by those words, the Father in his Divine alone; but I, Him in his Human, and this also is the name of the Father; for the Lord said, *Father, glorify thy Name*; that is, thy Human; and when this is done, the kingdom of God comes; and this prayer was commanded for this time, in order that God the Father may be approached through his Human. The Lord also said, *No one cometh to the Father but by me;* and in the prophet, *A Child is born to us, a Son is given to us, whose name is God, Hero, the Father of eternity;* and in another place, *Thou Jehovah, our Father, our Redeemer from an age is thy name;* and in a thousand other places, where the Lord our Savior is called *Jehovah* This is the true explanation of the words of that prayer." After these things were said, I looked at them, and observed the changes of their countenances, according to the changes of the state of their minds; some favoring and looking at me, and some not favoring, and turning themselves away from me; and then, on the right, I saw a cloud of an opal color, and on the left, a dusky cloud, and under each, as it were, a shower, and under the latter, as it were, a shower of rain in the end of autumn, and under the former, as it were, a shower of dew at the beginning of spring; and suddenly then I came from the spirit into the body, and thus returned from the spiritual world into the natural world.

113. Fourth Relation. I looked into the spiritual world, and saw an army upon red and black horses Those who sat upon them appeared like apes, turned, as to the face and breast, towards the loins and tails of the horses, and as to the back of the head and the back towards their necks and heads, and the bridles were hanging about the necks of the riders, and they were crying against those who rode upon white horses, and shaking the bridles with both their hands, and thus were pulling the horses back from the battle, and this continually. Then two angels descended from heaven, and came to me, and said, "What do you see?" And I replied, that I saw so ludicrous a company of horsemen; and I asked, "What is this, and who are they?" And the angels answered, "They are from the place which is called Armageddon (*Rev.* xii. 16), in which are gathered several thousands to fight against those who are of the Lord's New Church, which is called the New Jerusalem. They were talking in that place about the church and religion; and yet with them there was not any thing of the church, because not any spiritual truth; nor any thing of religion, because not any spiritual good. They were talking there with the mouth and lips about the former and the latter, but to the end that they might, by means of them, have dominion. They learnt, in their youth, to

confirm faith alone, and something concerning God; but when they were promoted to higher offices in the church, for a while they retained those things; but because then they began to think no more concerning God and concerning heaven, but about themselves and about the world, thus not concerning eternal blessedness and felicity, but about temporal eminence and opulence, they rejected the doctrinals, which they learnt in their youth, from the interiors of the rational mind, which communicate with heaven, and thence are in the light of heaven, to the exteriors of the rational mind, which communicate with the world, and thence are in the light of the world; and at length they thrust them down into the sensual natural region; whence the doctrinals of the church, with them, became things of the mouth only, and no longer of thought from reason, and still less of affection from love; and because they have made themselves such, they do not admit any divine truth, which is of the church, nor any genuine good, which is of religion; the interiors of their mind are become comparatively like bottles filled with iron filings, mixed with the flour of sulphur, into which if water is poured, there is at first a heat and afterwards a flame, by which those bottles are burst; in like manner they, when they hear any thing concerning living water, which is the genuine truth of the Word, and this enters through their ears, are violently heated and inflamed, and reject it, as something that would burst their heads. These are they who appeared to you like apes, riding backwards upon red and black horses, with the bridles about their necks; since those who do not love the truth and good of the church from the Word, do not wish to look at the fore-parts of a horse, but at his back-parts; for *horse* signifies the understanding of the Word; a *red horse*, the understanding of the Word, lost as to good; and a *black horse*, the understanding of the Word, lost as to truth. That they cried to battle against those who were riding upon white horses, is because a *white horse* signifies the understanding of the Word as to truth and good; that they seemed, by their neck, to pull back their horses, was, because they feared the battle, lest the truth of the Word should come to many, and thus into the light. This is the interpretation."

The angels further said, "We are from the society of heaven, which is called Michael, and we were commanded by the Lord to descend into the place called Armageddon, whence issued that company of horsemen, which you saw. By *Armageddon*, amongst us in heaven, is signified the state and disposition of fighting from falsified truths, arising from the love of dominion and eminence over all; and because we perceive in you a desire of knowing about that battle, we will relate something. After our descent from heaven, we came to the place called Armageddon, and saw there several thousands assembled; we did not, indeed, enter into their assembly, but there were some houses on the southern side of that place, where were boys, with their masters; we entered into them, and were courteously received. We were delighted with their company; they were all, as to the face, beautiful from the life in their eyes, and from the zeal in their discourse; the life in their eyes was from the perception of truth, and the zeal in their discourse from the affection of good; wherefore, also, we gave them caps, the borders of which were adorned with bands of golden threads interwoven with pearls; and also we gave them garments variegated with white and blue." We asked them whether they ever looked into the neighboring place, which is called Armageddon: they said that they had looked through a window, which is under the roof of the house, and that they saw there an assembly, but under various figures; sometimes as tall men, and sometimes not as men, but as statues and carved idols, and around them a multitude of people bending their knees: these also appeared to us under various forms; some like men, some like leopards, and some like goats, and these with horns pointing downwards, with which they dug up the ground. We interpreted those metamorphoses, whom they represented, and what they signified. But to the point:—Those who were assembled, when they heard that we had entered into those houses, said amongst themselves, "What business have they amongst those boys? Let us send some of our company to turn them out." So they sent; and when they came, they said to us, "Why have you entered into these houses? Whence are you! We, by authority, command you to depart." But we replied, "You cannot command that by authority. You are, indeed, in your own eyes, like the Anakim, and those who are here are like dwarfs; but still you have no power and authority here, except by means of cunning, which yet will not avail; wherefore go and tell your companions, that we were sent hither from heaven, to see whether there is any religion with you or not; if there is not, you will be cast out from this place. Wherefore, propose to them this, in which is the very essential of the church and of religion—how they understand these words in the Lord's prayer, OUR FATHER, WHO ART IN THE HEAVENS, HALLOWED BE THY NAME, THY KINGDOM COME." When they had heard these words, they said at first, "What is this?" and afterwards, that they would propose it. And they went away, and told those things to their companions, who replied, "What and of what quality is that proposition?" But they understood the secret which they wished to know, whether those words confirm the way of our faith to God the Father; wherefore they said, "The words are clear, that we ought to pray to God the Father; and because Christ is our Mediator, that we ought to pray to God the Father for the sake of the Son." And then, in indignation, they determined that they would go to us, and dictate that, face to face, saying also that they would pull our ears. So they went out of that place, and entered into a grove near those houses in which the boys were with their masters, in the middle of which grove there was a plain, elevated like a place of exercise; and they held each other by their hands, and entered into that place of exercise where we were, and we waited for them. There were there green sods raised from the ground like little hillocks: upon them they seated themselves, for they said one to another, "We will not stand in their presence, but we will sit down." And then one of them, who could speak so that he would appear as an angel of light, and who was appointed, by the rest, to speak with us, said, "You have proposed to us that we should open our minds concerning the first words of the Lord's prayer, as we understand them. I say, therefore, to you, that we understand them thus; that we should pray to God the Father; and because Christ is our Mediator, and we are saved by his merit, that we should pray to God the Father from faith in his merit." But then we said to them, "We are from a society of heaven which is called Michael, and we were sent to visit and to inquire whether you, who are assembled in this place, have any religion or not; for the idea of God enters into every thing of religion, and by it conjunction is effected, and by conjunction salvation. We in heaven read that prayer daily, as men do on earth; and then we do not think concerning God the Father, because He is invisible, but concerning Him in his Divine Human, because in this He is visible; and He in this is called by you *Christ*, but by us the *Lord;* and thus to us the Lord is the Father in the heavens. The Lord also taught, that He and the Father are one; that the Father is in Him, and He in the Father; and that he who sees Him, sees the Father; also, that no one comes to the Father, except through Him; and, also, that it is the will of the Father, that men should believe in the Son; and that he who does not believe in the Son, does not see life; yea, that the anger of God abideth on him; from which it is manifest, that the Father should be approached through Him and in Him;

and because it is so, He also taught that all power is given to Him in heaven and in earth. It is said in that prayer, HALLOWED BE THY NAME, THY KINGDOM COME. We have demonstrated from the Word, that his Divine Human is the name of the Father, and that the kingdom of the Father then is, when the Lord is approached immediately, and not when God the Father is approached immediately. Wherefore, also, the Lord commanded the disciples, that they should preach the kingdom of God; and this is the kingdom of God." Having heard these words, the antagonists said, "You recite many things from the Word, and we, perhaps, have read such things there, but we do not remember; wherefore open the Word before us, and read them from it, especially this, That the kingdom of the Father then comes when the kingdom of the Lord does" And then they said to the boys, "Bring hither the Word." And they brought it; and we read from it the following passages: *John, preaching the gospel of the kingdom, said, The time is fulfilled; the kingdom of God has come near*, Mark i. 14, 15. Matt. iii. 2. *Jesus himself preached the gospel of the kingdom, and that the kingdom of God was approaching*, Matt. v. 17, 23; ix. 35. *Jesus commanded the disciples, that they should preach and tell the good news of the kingdom of God*, Mark xvi. 15; Luke viii. 1, ix. 6; in like manner the seventy whom He sent forth, x. 9, 11; besides other places, as Matt. xi. 5; xvi. 27, 28. Mark viii. 35; ix. 1, 27; x. 29, 30; xi. 10. Luke i. 19; ii. 10, 11; iv. 43; vii. 22; xxi. 30, 31; xxii. 18. The kingdom of God, which was proclaimed, was the kingdom of the Lord, and thus the kingdom of the Father: that it is so, is manifest from these passages: *The Father hath given all things into the hand of the Son*, John iii. 35. *The Father hath given to the Son power over all flesh*, John xvii. 2. *All things are delivered to Me by the Father*, Matt. xi. 27. *All power is given to Me in heaven and in earth*, xxviii. 18. And moreover from these: *Jehovah of hosts is his name; and the Redeemer, the Holy One of Israel, shall be called the God of the whole earth*, Isaiah liv. 5. *I saw, and, behold, one like the Son of man, to whom was given dominion, glory, and a kingdom, and all people and nations shall worship Him; his dominion is the dominion of an age which shall not pass away, and his kingdom that which shall not be destroyed*, Dan. vii. 13, 14. *When the seventh angel sounded, great voices were uttered in the heavens, saying, The kingdoms of the world have become the kingdom of our Lord and of his Christ, and He shall reign to ages of ages*, Rev. xi. 15; xii. 10. And, besides, we instructed them from the Word, that the Lord came into the world not only that He might redeem angels and men, but also that they might be united to God the Father by Him and in Him; for He taught that He is in those who believe in Him, and that they are in Him, John vi. 56; xiv. 20; xv. 4, 5. Having heard these things, they asked, "How, then, can your Lord be called Father?" We said, "From those passages which have been read, and also from these: *A Child is born to us, a Son is given to us, whose name is God, Hero, the Father of eternity*, Isaiah ix. 6. *Thou art our Father; Abraham doth not know us, and Israel doth not acknowledge us; Thou, Jehovah, art our Father, our Redeemer from an age is thy name*, Isaiah lxiii. 16. Did He not say to Philip, who wished to see the Father, *Philip, hast thou not known Me? He who seeth Me, seeth the Father*, John xiv. 9, xii. 45. Who else, then, is the Father, but He whom Philip saw with his eyes?" To which we added this: "It is said in the whole Christian world, that those who are of the church, make the body of Christ, and are in his body: how, then, can the man of the church go to God the Father, except through Him in whose body He is? If otherwise, he must go entirely out of the body, and go to Him." At last we informed them, that the Lord is at this day instituting a NEW CHURCH, which is meant by the New Jerusalem in the Revelation, in which will be the worship of the Lord alone, as in heaven, and that thus every thing will be fulfilled, which is contained in the Lord's prayer from the beginning to the end. We confirmed all from the Word, in the evangelists, and in the prophets, and from the Revelation, in which that church is treated of from the beginning to the end, in so great abundance that they were tired of hearing.

While hearing these things with indignation, the Armageddons desired, at every turn, to interrupt our discourse; and at length they broke it, and exclaimed, "You have spoken contrary to the doctrine of our church, which is, that we should go to God the Father immediately, and believe in Him: thus you have made yourselves guilty of a violation of our faith; wherefore, go out from this place; and if not, you shall be cast out." And, their minds being inflamed, they came from threatening to attempting violence: but then, by a power given to us, we struck them with blindness, in consequence of which, not seeing us, they rushed forth, and, in their wandering, they ran in different directions, and some fell into the abyss, which is mentioned in the Rev. ix. 2, which is now in the southern region towards the east, where those are who confirm justification by faith alone; and those there who confirm it from the Word, are sent forth into a desert, in which they are brought even to the extremity of the Christian world, and mixed with pagans.

CONCERNING REDEMPTION.

114. That there are in the Lord two offices, the office of priest and the office of king, is known in the church; but few know in what the one and in what the other consists; wherefore it shall be told. The Lord, from the office of priest, is called *Jesus;* and from the office of king, *Christ:* and also, from the office of priest, He is called in the Word, *Jehovah* and *Lord;* and from the office of king, *God*, and the *Holy One of Israel*, as also *King*. These two offices are distinguished from each other, as love and wisdom, or, what is the same, as good and truth, are distinguished from each other; wherefore, whatever the Lord did and operated from divine love or divine good, He did and operated from his priestly office; but whatever from divine wisdom or divine truth, from his kingly office. In the Word, also, *priest* and *priesthood* signify divine good; and *king* and *royalty* signify divine truth: those two things the priests and kings in the Israelitish church represented. As to what concerns redemption, that pertains to both offices; but what part of it to the one, and what part of it to the other, will be shown in what follows. But, that every thing may be distinctly perceived, the exposition of it will be divided into canons or articles, which will be, I. *That redemption itself was a subjugation of the hells, and an establishment of order in the heavens, and thereby a preparation for a New Spiritual Church.* II. *That without that redemption no man could have been saved, nor could the angels have subsisted in a state of integrity.* III. *That the Lord thus redeemed not only men, but also angels.* IV. *That redemption was a work purely divine.* V. *That this redemption itself could not have been effected but by God incarnate.* VI. *That the passion of the cross was the last temptation which He, as the greatest Prophet, sustained; and that it was the means of the glorification of his Human, that is, of union with the Divine of his Father, and not redemption.* VII. *That the passion of the cross is believed to have been redemption itself, is a fundamental error of the church; and that that error, together with the error concerning three divine persons from eternity has per*

verted the whole church, so that not any thing spiritual is left remaining in it. These things will now be unfolded one by one.

115. I. That Redemption itself was a Subjugation of the Hells, and an Establishment of Order in the Heavens, and thereby a Preparation for a New Spiritual Church.

That these three things are redemption, I can say in all certainty, since the Lord also at this day is performing a redemption, which He commenced in the year 1757, together with the Last Judgment, which was then performed. This redemption has continued from that time even to this: the reason is, because at this time is the Second Coming of the Lord; and a New Church is to be instituted which cannot be instituted unless there be first a subjugation of the hells, and an establishment of order in the heavens; and because it was given to me to see all, I can describe how the hells were subjugated, and how the new heaven was ordered and established; but this would be the subject of a whole work. But how the last judgment was performed I have made known in a small volume, published at London in the year 1758. That the subjugation of the hells, the establishment of order in the heavens, and the institution of a New Church, were redemption, is because without these no man could have been saved: they follow, also, in order; for first the hells are to be subjugated before a new angelic heaven can be formed; and this is to be formed before a New Church upon earth can be instituted; for men in the world are so conjoined with the angels of heaven and the spirits of hell, that, in the interiors of the mind on both sides, they make one: but concerning this we shall speak in the last chapter of this work, where we shall treat, specifically, of the Consummation of the Age, of the Coming of the Lord, and of the New Church.

116. That the Lord, while he was in the world, fought against the hells, and conquered, and subjugated them, and thus reduced them under obedience to Him, is evident from many passages in the Word, of which I shall select these few in Isaiah: *Who is this that cometh from Edom, sprinkled as to his garments from Bozrah, who is honorable in his apparel, marching in the multitude of his strength? I who speak in righteousness, great to save. Wherefore art Thou red as to thy garment, and thy garment as of one treading in the wine-press? I have trodden the wine-press alone, and of the people not a man with Me; therefore I trod them in my anger, and trampled them in my wrath; thence their victory was sprinkled upon my garments; for the day of vengeance is in my heart, and the year of my redeemed is come; my arm brought salvation to me; I made their victory descend to the earth. He said, Behold my people, they are children; therefore He became to them for a Savior; for his love and for his pity He redeemed them;* lxiii. 1 to 9. These things are concerning the battle of the Lord against the hells; by *the garment in which He was honorable, and which was red,* is meant the Word, to which violence was offered by the Jewish people. The battle itself against the hells, and the victory over them, is described by this, that *He trod them in his anger, and trampled them in his wrath.* That He fought alone, and from his own power, is described by these words: *Of the people not a man with me; my arm brought salvation to me; I made their victory descend to the earth.* That thereby He saved and redeemed, by these: *Therefore He became to them for a Savior; for his love and for his pity He redeemed them.* That this was the cause of his coming, is meant by these: *The day of vengeance is in my heart, and the year of my redeemed is come.* Again in Isaiah: *He saw that there was not any one, and was astonished that there was none interceding; therefore his arm brought salvation to Him, and righteousness roused Him up; thence He put on righteousness as a breastplate, and the helmet of salvation upon his head, and He put on garments of vengeance, and covered himself with*

zeal as with a cloak; then He came to Zion a Redeemer, lix. 16, 17, 20. In Jeremiah: *They were dismayed, their strong ones were knocked down; they fled apace, neither did they look back; that day is to the Lord Jehovah of hosts a day of revenge, that he may take vengeance on his enemies, that the sword may devour and be satiated*, xlvi. 5, 10. The latter and the former are concerning the battle of the Lord against the hells, and concerning the victory over them. In David: *Gird thy sword upon thy thigh, O Mighty; thy arrows are sharp, the people shall fall under Thee, from the heart enemies of the King. Thy throne is for an age and forever. Thou hast loved righteousness, therefore God hath anointed Thee*, Psalm xlv. 4 to 7; besides in many other places. Since the Lord alone conquered the hells, without help from any angel, therefore He is called a HERO, AND A MAN OF WARS, Isaiah xliv. 15; ix. 6; THE KING OF GLORY, JEHOVAH THE MIGHTY, THE HERO OF WAR, Psalm xiv. 8, 10; THE MIGHTY ONE OF JACOB, cxxxii. 2; and in many places, JEHOVAH SABAOTH, that is, JEHOVAH OF HOSTS. And also his advent is called *the day of Jehovah, terrible, cruel, of indignation, of wrath, of anger, of vengeance, of ruin, of war, of a trumpet, of a loud noise, of tumult*, &c. In the evangelists these things are read: *Now is the judgment of this world; the prince of this world shall be cast out*, John xii. 31. *The prince of this world is judged*, xvi. 11. *Have confidence; I have overcome the world*, xvii. 33. *I saw Satan as lightning falling from heaven*, Luke x. 18. By the *world*, the *prince of the world*, *Satan* and the *devil*, is meant *hell*. Besides these things, it is described in the Revelation, from the beginning to the end, what the Christian church is at this day, and also that the Lord is about to come again, and subjugate the hells, and make a new angelic heaven, and then to establish a New Church upon earth. All these things are there predicted, but they have not been discovered till the present time: the reason is, because the Revelation, as also all the prophetical parts of the Word, was written by mere correspondences; and unless these had been made known by the Lord, scarcely any one would have been able rightly to understand a single verse there: but now, for the sake of the New Church, all the things which are there, are made known in the APOCALYPSE REVEALED, published at Amsterdam, in the year 1766; and those will see them who believe the Word of the Lord in Matt. xxiv. concerning the state of the church at the present time, and concerning his coming. But this belief is, as yet, only wavering with those who have so deeply impressed on their hearts the faith of the present church, concerning a trinity of divine persons from eternity, and concerning the passion of Christ, that it was redemption itself, that it cannot be eradicated. But these (as was said in the RELATION above, n. 113) are like bottles filled with iron-filings and flour of sulphur, into which if water be poured, there is first produced a heat, and afterwards a flame, by which those bottles are burst: they also, in like manner, when they hear any thing concerning living water, which is the genuine truth of the Word, and this enters through their eyes or ears, are violently heated and inflamed, and reject it, as that which would burst their heads.

117. The subjugation of the hells, the establishment of order in the heavens, and afterwards the institution of a church, may be illustrated by various similitudes. The hells may be illustrated by a comparison with an army of robbers or rebels, who invade a kingdom or a city, and then set fire to the houses, plunder the goods of the inhabitants, and divide the spoil amongst themselves, and then exult and triumph; but redemption itself may be illustrated by a comparison with a just king, who marches against them with his army, puts a part of them to the sword, shuts a part up in prisons, takes away their spoil, and restores it to his subjects, and establishes order in the kingdom, and renders it safe from similar invasions. It may also be illustrated by a comparison with a herd of wild beasts, issuing out together from a for-

est, which attacks flocks and herds, and also men; on account of which, no man dares go out from the walls of his city to till the ground; whence the fields will be deserted, and the inhabitants of the city will perish by famine: and redemption may be illustrated by the destruction and dispersion of those wild beasts, and the protection of the fields and plains from further invasion of such animals. It may also be illustrated by locusts consuming every green thing on the surface of the ground; and by the means of preventing their further progress: also, by the little worms in the first part of summer, which deprive the trees of leaves, and thus, also, of fruits, so that they stand naked as in the midst of winter; and by shaking them off, and thus restoring the garden to the state of its bloom and fruitfulness. The case would be similar with the church, unless the Lord, by redemption, had separated the good from the evil, and cast the latter into hell, and raised the former into heaven. What would become of an empire or a kingdom, if there were no justice nor judgment, by which the evil might be taken away from the midst of the good, and the good protected from violence, so that every one might live securely in his own house, and, as it is said in the Word, might sit under his own fig-tree and vine in tranquillity?

118. II. That without that Redemption, no Man could have been saved, nor could the Angels have subsisted in a State of Integrity.

In the first place, it shall be told what redemption is. To redeem signifies to liberate from damnation, to deliver from eternal death, to rescue from hell, and take away captives and prisoners out of the hand of the devil. This was done by the Lord, in that He subjugated the hells, and formed a new heaven. That man could not otherwise have been saved, is because the spiritual world has such a connection with the natural world that they cannot be separated. This connection is principally with the interiors of men, which are called their souls and minds: those of the good are connected with the souls and minds of angels, and those of the evil, with the souls and minds of infernal spirits. They have such union, that, if they were removed from man, he would fall down dead as a stock; in like manner, angels and spirits could not subsist, if men were withdrawn from them. Thence it is manifest why redemption was performed in the spiritual world, and why heaven and hell were first to be restored to order before the church on earth could be established. That it is so, is very manifest from what is said in the Revelation, that, after the new heaven was made, the New Jerusalem, which is the New Church, came down out of that heaven; xxi. 1, 2.

119. The reason that angels could not have subsisted in a state of integrity unless redemption had been performed by the Lord, is because the whole angelic heaven, together with the church on earth, is before the Lord as one man, whose internal is the angelic heaven, and whose external is the church; or, more particularly, the highest heaven constitutes the head; the second and the last constitute the breast and middle region of the body; and the church on earth, the loins and feet; and the Lord Himself is the soul and life of the whole of this man: wherefore, unless the Lord had performed redemption, this man would have been destroyed, as to the feet and loins, by the seceding of the church on earth; as to the gastric region, by the seceding of the lowest heaven; as to the breast, by the seceding of the second heaven; and then the head, having no correspondence with the body, would fall into a swoon. But this shall be illustrated by similitudes. It is as when a mortification attacks the feet, and, in its ravages, gradually ascends, and infects first the loins, then the viscera of the abdomen, and at length it invades the vicinity of the heart; and it is known, that man then falls a victim to death. It may also be illustrated by a comparison with diseases of the viscera, which are below the diaphragm, that when they have any breach or rupture, the heart begins to

palpitate, and the lungs to pant heavily, and at length they both cease. It may also be illustrated by a comparison with the internal and external man, in that the internal man is well, as long as the external man obediently performs its functions; but if the external does not obey, but resists the internal, and still more if it assaults it, at length the internal is weakened and finally carried away by the delights of the external, until it even favors and assents to it.

It may also be illustrated by a comparison with a man standing upon a mountain, who sees below him the country inundated, and that the waters are rising higher and higher; and when they reach the summit on which he stands, he also is inundated, unless he can secure his safety by a boat which comes to him through the flood: in like manner, if any one from a mountain sees a thick cloud rising higher and higher from the earth, and hiding the fields, villages, and cities; and afterwards, when that cloud reaches even to him, he does not see any thing, not even himself where he is. The case is similar with the angels when the church on earth perishes; that then the inferior heavens also pass away. The reason is, because the heavens consist of men from the earth; and when there no longer remains any good of the heart and truth of the Word, the heavens are inundated with the evils which rise up, and are suffocated by them as by Stygian waters; but still they are concealed by the Lord somewhere, and are reserved to the day of the last judgment, and are then raised up into a new heaven. These are they who are meant in the Revelation by these: *I saw under the altar the souls of those who were slain for the Word of God, and for the testimony which they had; and they cried with a loud voice, saying, How long, O Lord, who art holy and true, dost thou not judge and avenge our blood upon those who dwell upon the earth? And white robes were given to every one of them; and it was said to them, that they should rest yet for a little time, until their fellow servants also, and their brethren, who were to be killed as they had been, should be fulfilled*, vi. 9, 10, 11.

120. That without redemption by the Lord, iniquity and wickedness would spread through the whole Christian orb, in both worlds, the natural and the spiritual, is, amongst several other reasons, because every man, after death, comes into the world of spirits, and then is altogether similar to himself, such as he was before; and at his entrance, he cannot be restrained from conversing with deceased parents, brothers, relations and friends; every husband, then, first seeks his wife, and every wife her husband; and by the former and the latter they are introduced into various companies of such as outwardly appear like sheep, and inwardly are like wolves; and by these even those are perverted, who have been devoted to piety: from this cause, and from abominable arts, unknown in the natural world, the spiritual world is so full of the wicked and cunning, that it is like a pond green with the spawn of frogs. That intercourse with the wicked there also effects this, may be rendered manifest from these considerations, that whoever associates with robbers or pirates, at length becomes like them; and whoever lives with adulterers and harlots, at length regards adulteries as nothing; and, also, whoever connects himself with rebellious persons, at length does not scruple to do violence to any one. For all evils are contagious, and may be compared to the plague, which an infected person communicates by breath or perspiration; and also to a cancer or gangrene, which spreads, and putrefies the parts near it, and successively those more distant, until the whole body perishes. The delights of evil, into which every one is born, cause wickedness to be contagious. From these things it may appear evident, that without redemption by the Lord, no one could be saved, nor could the angels subsist in a state of integrity. The only refuge from destruction, for any one, is in the Lord; for He says, *Abide in Me, and I in you; as the branch cannot bear fruit*

of itself, unless it abide in the vine, so ye, unless ye abide in Me. I am the vine, ye are the branches: he who abideth in Me, and I in him, beareth much fruit; because without Me ye cannot do any thing. If any one abide not in Me, he is cast away, and, being dried, is thrown into the fire and burned, John xv. 4, 5, 6.

121. III THAT THE LORD THUS REDEEMED NOT ONLY MEN, BUT ALSO ANGELS.

This follows from what was said in the preceding article, *That without redemption by the Lord, the angels could not have subsisted.* To the reasons above mentioned, these may be added: I. That, at the time of the first coming of the Lord, the hells had grown up to such a height, that they filled all the world of spirits, which is in the middle, between heaven and hell, and thus not only confused the heaven which is called the last or lowest, but also assaulted the middle heaven, which they infested in a thousand ways, and which would have gone to destruction, unless the Lord had protected it. Such insurrection of the hells is meant by the tower built in the land of Shinar, the head of which should reach even to heaven; but the design of the builders was frustrated by the confusion of languages, and they were dispersed, and the city was called *Babel*, Gen. xi, 1 to 9 What is there meant by the tower and by the confusion of languages, is explained in the ARCANA CŒLESTIA, published at London. The reason that the hells had grown up to such a height, was, that at the time when the Lord came into the world, the whole world had entirely alienated itself from God, by idolatries and magic; and the church which had been amongst the sons of Israel, and at length amongst the Jews, by falsification and adulteration of the Word, was utterly destroyed; and both the former and the latter after death flocked into the world of spirits, where at length they so increased and multiplied, that they could not be expelled thence, but by the descent of God Himself, and then by the strength of his divine arm. How this was done is described in a little treatise concerning the LAST JUDGMENT, published at London in the year 1758. This was accomplished by the Lord when He was in the world. The like, also, at this day, has been done by the Lord, since, as was said above, at this day is his second coming, which was predicted in the Revelation in various places; and in Matt. xxiv. 3, 30; in Mark xiii. 26; in Luke xxi. 27; and in the Acts of the Apostles, i. 11; and in other places. The difference is, that, at his first coming, the hells had grown to such a degree from the multitude of idolaters, magicians, and falsifiers of the Word; but at this second coming, from Christians so called, both such as are imbued with naturalism, and also such as have falsified the Word, by confirmations of their fabulous faith concerning three Divine Persons from eternity, and concerning the passion of the Lord, that it was redemption itself; for these are they who are meant by the dragon and his two beasts in the Revelation, xii. and xiii. II. The second reason why the Lord also redeemed angels, is, that not only every man, but also every angel, is withheld by the Lord from evil, and held in good; for no one, whether angel or man, is in good from himself, but all good is from the Lord: when, therefore, the footstool of the angels, which is in the world of spirits, was taken away from them, it was then with them, as with one sitting upon a throne, when its pedestals are removed. That the angels are not pure in the sight of God, is evident from the prophetical parts of the Word, and also from Job; and likewise from this, that there is not any angel who had not previously been a man. Hereby are confirmed those things which are said in the FAITH OF THE NEW HEAVEN AND THE NEW CHURCH IN A UNIVERSAL AND A PARTICULAR FORM, prefixed to this work, viz.: "That the Lord came into the world that He might remove hell from man, and that He did remove it by combats against it and by victories over it; thus He subjugated it, and reduced it under obedience to Himself." And also by these things there, "That Jehovah God descended and assumed the Human, to the end that He might reduce into order all things which were in heaven, and all things which were in the church; since, at that time, the power of the devil, that is, of hell, prevailed over the power of heaven, and upon earth the power of evil over the power of good, and thence a total damnation stood before the door and threatened. This impending damnation Jehovah God removed by means of his Human, and thus redeemed men and angels: from which it is manifest, that without the coming of the Lord, no one could have been saved. It is similar at this day; wherefore, unless the Lord again come into the world, no one can be saved." See above, n. 2, 3.

122. That the Lord has delivered the spiritual world, and, by this, is about to deliver the church, from universal damnation, may be illustrated by comparison with a king, who, by victories over the enemy, liberates the princes, his sons, who had been taken by the enemy, confined in prisons, and bound with chains, and brings them back to his palace; also by comparison with a shepherd, who, like Samson and David, rescues his sheep from the jaws of a lion or a bear, or drives away those wild beasts when they come out of the forest into the pastures, and pursues them even to the utmost limits, and at last forces them into ponds or deserts, and afterwards returns to the sheep, and feeds them in safety, and gives them drink from fountains of pure water. It may also be illustrated by comparison with one who sees a serpent coiled up, lying in the way and intending to inflict a wound upon the heel of a traveller, and seizes its head, and, although it twists itself about his hand, he carries it home, and there cuts off its head, and throws the rest into the fire. It may also be illustrated by comparison with a bridegroom or a husband, who, when he sees an adulterer attempting to do violence to his bride, or wife, attacks him, and either wounds his hand with a sword, or covers his legs and loins with blows, or casts him into the streets by means of his servants, who with clubs pursue him even to his house; and having thus liberated his beloved, he leads her away into his chamber. By a bride and wife, also, in the Word, is meant the church of the Lord; and by adulterers are meant the violators of it, who are those who adulterate his Word; and because the Jews did this, they were called by the Lord an adulterous generation.

123. IV. That Redemption was a Work purely Divine.

He who knows what hell is, and what was its height and inundation over all the world of spirits, at the time of the Lord's coming, and also with what power the Lord cast down and dispersed hell, and afterwards reduced it, together with heaven, into order, cannot but be astonished, and exclaim, that all those things were a work purely divine. First, *as to what hell is:* it consists of myriads of myriads, since it consists of all those who, from the creation of the world, by evils of life and falses of faith, have alienated themselves from God. Secondly, *as to the height and inundation of hell over all the world of spirits, at the time of the Lord's coming*, something has been stated in the preceding articles. What it was at the time of the first coming, was not made known to any one, because it is not revealed in the sense of the letter of the Word. But what it was at the time of his second coming, it was given to see with my eyes; from which it may be concluded concerning the former; and this is described in a little treatise concerning the Last Judgment, published at London in the year 1758. There also it is described, *with what power the Lord cast down and dispersed hell;* but to transfer hither those things which are described from personal observation in that little treatise, is a needless work, because that is extant, and there are yet copies in abundance at the booksellers' in London. Every one who reads that treatise may clearly see, that this was the work of God Almighty. Fourthly, *how the Lord afterwards reduced all things both in heaven and in hell, into order,* has not yet been described by me, since the establishment of order in the heavens and the hells, has continued in progress from the day of the last judgment to the present time, and still continues; but after this book is published, if it be desired, it shall be given to the public. As to myself, I have seen, and do see every day, the divine omnipotence of the Lord in this thing, as in the face. This last properly belongs to redemption, but the former properly belongs to the last judgment; those who view these two things distinctly, may see many things which, in the prophetical parts of the Word, are concealed under figures; and yet they are described, when, by an explanation of the correspondences, they are brought forth into the light of the understanding. The former and the latter divine work cannot be illustrated otherwise than by comparisons, and so but imperfectly. They may be illustrated by comparison with a battle against the armies of all the nations in the whole world, armed with spears, shields, swords, muskets and cannon, having skilful and cunning generals and other officers: this is said, because many in hell are skilled in arts unknown in our world, in which they exercise themselves with each other, how they may attack, ensnare, beset, and assault those who are from heaven. The battle of the Lord with hell may also be compared, but yet imperfectly, with a battle with the wild beasts of the whole world, and with the slaughter and subjugation of them, until not one of them dares to come forth and make an assault upon any man who is in the Lord; whence, if any one shows a threatening aspect, he suddenly shrinks back, as if he felt a vulture in his bosom, endeavoring to eat through even to the heart. By wild beasts, also, in the Word, are described infernal spirits: these also are meant in Mark i. 13, by the wild beasts with which the Lord was forty days. It may also be compared with resistance to the whole ocean, rushing with its billows into countries and cities, when the dikes are demolished. The subjugation of hell by the Lord is also meant by his calming the sea, by saying, *Peace, be still,* Mark iv. 38, 39, Matt. viii. 26; Luke viii. 23, 24. For by the *sea* there, as in many other places, is signified *hell.* The Lord, with similar divine power, at this day fights against hell in every man who is being regenerated; for hell assaults all those with diabolical fury; and unless the Lord resisted and subdued it, man could not but yield. For hell is like one monstrous man, and like a huge lion, with which also it is compared in the Word. Wherefore, unless the Lord should keep that lion, or that monster, bound with manacles and fetters, it could not be otherwise than that man, when rescued from one evil, would of himself fall into another, and then into many more.

124. V. That this Redemption itself could not have been performed, but by God incarnate.

In the preceding article it was shown, that redemption was a work purely divine; consequently, that it could not have been performed but by an omnipotent God. The reason that it could not have been performed but by God incarnate, that is, made Man, is because Jehovah God, such as He is, in his infinite essence, cannot approach to hell, much less enter into it; for He is in the purest and first things. Wherefore, Jehovah God, being in himself such, if He should only blow upon those who are in hell, He would kill them in a moment; for He said to Moses, when He wished to see Him, *Thou wilt not be able to see my face, because no man will see Me and live,* Exod. xxxiii. 20. Since, therefore, Moses could not, still less could those who are in hell, where all are in the last and grossest things, and thus in those most remote; for they are in the lowest degree natural. Wherefore, unless Jehovah God had assumed the Human, and thus clothed himself with a body which is in the lowest things, He might have undertaken any redemption in vain. For who can attack any enemy, unless he approach and be furnished with arms for the battle? Or who can drive away and destroy dragons, hydras and basilisks in any desert, unless he surround his body with a coat of mail and his head with a helmet, and have a spear in his hand? Or who can catch whales in the sea, without a ship and the proper implements for catching them? By these and similar things may be illustrated, though not justly compared, the battle of the omnipotent God with the hells, which battle He could not have entered, unless He had before put on the Human. But it should be known, that the battle of the Lord with the hells, was not an oral battle, as between reasoners and wranglers; such a battle would have effected nothing at all there: but it was a spiritual battle, which is of divine truth from divine good, which was the very vital principle of the Lord: the influx of this, by means of sight, no one in hell can resist. There is in it such power, that the infernal genii, only at the perception of it, fly away and cast themselves down into the deep and creep into caverns, that they may hide themselves. This is the same that is described in Isaiah; *They shall enter into caverns of the rocks, and into clefts of the dust, for fear of Jehovah, when He shall arise to terrify the earth*, ii. 19; and in the Revelation; *All shall hide themselves in the caves of the rocks, and in the rocks of the mountains, and shall say to the mountains and to the rocks, Fall upon us, and hide us from the face of Him who sitteth upon the throne, and from the anger of the Lamb*, vi. 15, 16, 17. What the power of the Lord, which He has from the divine good was, when He performed the last judgment in the year 1757, may be evident from those things which are described in a little treatise concerning that judgment; as that He tore up from their places the hills and mountains, which the infernals in the spiritual world occupied, and removed them to distant places, and made some sink down; and that He deluged their cities, villages and fields with a flood, and tore up their lands, and cast them, together with the inhabitants, into whirlpools, bogs and fens; besides many other things; and all these were done by the Lord alone, through the power of divine truth from divine good.

125. That Jehovah God could not have operated and effected these things except by his Human, may be illustrated by various comparisons; as that those who are invisible to each other cannot shake hands, or converse together; an angel or a spirit cannot with a man, although he should stand close to his body and before his face Neither can the soul of any one speak and act with any one, except through his body. The sun cannot with its light and heat enter into any man, beast or tree, unless it first enter the air, and act through this; nor can it enter into fishes, except through the water; for it must act by means of the element in which the subject is. No one can scale a fish without a knife, nor pick the feathers from a crow without fingers, nor descend to the bottom of a lake without a diving-bell. In a word, one thing must be accommodated to another, before there can be effected any communication and operation against it or with it.

126. VI. That the Passion of the Cross was the last Temptation which the Lord, as the greatest Prophet, sustained; and that it was the Means of the Glorification of his Human, that is, of uniting it with the Divine of his Father, and not Redemption.

There are two things for which the Lord came into the world, and by which He saved men and angels, viz. redemption and the glorification of his Human. These two are distinct from each other, but yet they make one with respect to salvation. What Redemption is, has been shown in the preceding articles, as that it was a battle with the hells, a subjugation of them, and afterwards an establishment of order in the heavens. But glorification is the unition of the Human of the Lord with the Divine of his Father. This was done successively, and was fully completed by the passion of the cross; for every man ought, on his part, to approach to God, and as far as man approaches, so far God, on his part, enters. This is the same as with a temple; it is first to be built, and this is done by the hands of men; and afterwards it is to be consecrated, and finally prayer offered that God may be present, and unite himself with the church there. The reason why the union itself was fully effected by the passion of the cross, is, because that was the last temptation, which the Lord underwent in the world, and conjunction is effected by temptations; for in them man, to appearance, is left to himself alone, although he is not left, for God is then most really present in the inmost of him, and supports him; wherefore, when any one conquers in temptation, he is most intimately conjoined to God; and the Lord then was most intimately united to God his Father. That the Lord in the passion of the cross was left to himself, is evident from this his exclamation upon the cross; *O God, why hast thou forsaken Me?* and also from these words of the Lord; *No one taketh life from Me, but I lay it down of myself; I have the power of laying it down, and I have the power of taking it again; this commandment I have received from my Father*, John x. 18. From these passages, now, it may be evident, that the Lord did not suffer as to the Divine, but as to the Human; and that then an inmost and thus a complete union was effected. This may be illustrated by this, that while a man suffers as to the body, his soul does not suffer, but only grieves; and God takes away this grief after the victory, and wipes it away as one wipes away tears from the eyes.

127. These two things, redemption and the passion of the cross, should be distinctly perceived, otherwise the human mind, like a ship, falls into quicksands, or upon rocks, and is lost, together with the pilot, captain and sailors; that is, it errs in all those things which are of salvation by the Lord; for a man without a distinct idea concerning those two things is as one who dreams, and sees imaginary things, and draws conclusions from those things which he thinks to be real, when, nevertheless, they are ludicrous; or he is as one who walks in the night, and, while he takes hold of the leaves of some tree, he thinks them to be the hair of a man, and comes nearer, and entangles his own hair in the branches. But although redemption and the passion of the cross are two distinct things, yet they make one with respect to salvation; since the Lord, by union with his Father, which was completed by the passion of the cross, became Redeemer to eternity.

128. Concerning the Glorification, by which is meant the unition of the Divine Human of the Lord with the Divine of the Father, that it was fully completed by the passion of the cross, the Lord thus speaks; *After Judas went out, Jesus said, Now the Son of Man is glorified, and God is glorified in Him; if God be glorified in Him, God will also glorify Him in himself, and will presently glorify Him*, John xiii. 31, 32. Here glorification is said both of God the Father and of the Son, for it is said, God is glorified in Him, and God will glorify Him in Himself: that this is to be united is manifest. *Father, glorify thy Son, that thy Son also may glorify Thee*, xvii. 1, 5. It is thus said, because the unition was reciprocal, and as it is said, *The Father in Him and He in the Father. Now my soul is troubled; and He said, Father, glorify thy name; and a voice came out from heaven, I have both glorified, and will glorify again*, xii. 27, 28. This was said because the unition was effected successively. *Ought not Christ to suffer this, and enter into his glory?* Luke xxiv. 26. *Glory*, in the Word, when it is used concerning the Lord, signifies divine truth united to divine good. From these it is very manifest, that the Human of the Lord is Divine.

129. The reason why the Lord was willing to be tempted even to the passion of the cross, was, because He was The Prophet and prophets formerly

signified the doctrine of the church from the Word, and thence they represented the church, such as it was, by various things, and also by things unjust, grievous, and even wicked, which were enjoined on them by God. But the Lord, because He was the Word itself, by the passion of the cross, as THE PROPHET, represented the Jewish church, how it had profaned the Word itself. To this reason this other may be added, that thus He might be acknowledged in the heavens as the Savior of both worlds; for all the things of his passion signified such things as are of the profanation of the Word, and the angels understand them spiritually, while the men of the church understand them naturally. That the Lord was THE PROPHET, is evident from these passages: *The Lord said, A* PROPHET *is not less honored than in his own country and in his own house*, Matt. xiii. 57; Mark vi. 4; Luke iv. 24. *Jesus said, It is not fitting that a* PROPHET *should perish out of Jerusalem*, Luke xiii. 33. *Fear seized them all, praising God, and saying, that a* GREAT PROPHET *was raised up amongst them*, Luke vii. 16. *They said concerning Jesus, This is that* PROPHET *of Nazareth*, Matt. xxi. 11; John vii. 40, 41. *That a* PROPHET *should be raised up from the midst of the brethren, whose words they should obey*, Deut. xviii. 15 to 19.

130. That prophets represented the state of their church as to doctrine from the Word, and as to a life according to it, is evident from these passages:—It was commanded the prophet Isaiah, that *he should loose the sackcloth from off his loins, and the shoe from off his foot, and should go naked and barefoot three years, for a sign and a prodigy*, Isaiah xx. 2, 3. It was commanded the prophet Ezekiel, that *he should represent the state of the church by making vessels for removing, and that he should remove to another place, in the eyes of the sons of Israel, and should bring forth the vessels by day, and should go out in the evening through a hole dug in the wall, and should cover his face that he might not see the earth, and that thus he should be a prodigy to the house of Israel, and should say, Behold, I am your prodigy; as I have done, so shall it be done to you*, Ezek. xii. 3 to 7, 11. It was commanded the prophet Hosea, that he should represent the state of the church, *by taking to himself a harlot to wife; and also he took her, and she brought forth to him three sons, one of whom he called Jezreel, another Not-to-be-pitied, and the third Not-a-people.* And again it was commanded him that *he should go and love a woman beloved by her companion, and an adulteress, whom also he bought for himself*, Hosea i. 2 to 9; iii. 2, 3. It was also enjoined upon a certain prophet, that *he should put ashes upon his eyes, and suffer himself to be smitten and beaten*, 1 Kings xx. 35, 37. It was enjoined upon the prophet Ezekiel, that he should represent the state of the church *by taking a tile, and that he should engrave upon it Jerusalem, lay siege, and cast a trench and mound against it, should put a frying pan of iron between himself and the city, and should lie upon the left side and upon the right side. Also, that he should take wheat, barley, lentiles, millet and fitches, and make bread of them, and also a cake with man's dung; and because he prayed that this might not be, it was permitted that he should make it with cow's dung.* It was said to him, *Lie thou upon the left side, and lay the* INIQUITY OF THE HOUSE OF ISRAEL *upon it: the number of days that thou shalt lie upon it,* THOU SHALT BEAR THEIR INIQUITY; *for I will give thee the years of their iniquity according to the number of the days, three hundred and ninety days, that* THOU MAYEST BEAR THE INIQUITY OF THE HOUSE OF ISRAEL; *and when thou shalt have accomplished them, thou shalt lie upon thy right side, that thou mayest bear the iniquity of the house of Judah*, Ezek. iv. 1 to 15. That the prophet by these things bore the iniquities of the house of Israel, and of the house of Judah, and did not take them away, and thus expiate them, but only represented and pointed them out, is manifest from

what follows there. *Thus saith Jehovah, The sons of Israel shall eat their unclean bread; behold, I will break the staff of bread, that they may want bread and water, and be desolated, a man and his brother, and consume away for their iniquity*, iv. 13, 16, 17. The like, therefore, is meant concerning the Lord, where it is said, *He* HATH CARRIED *our sicknesses and* BORNE *our sorrows; Jehovah hath made the iniquities of us all to fall upon Him. By his knowledge He hath justified many, because* HE HATH BORNE THEIR INIQUITIES, Isaiah liii. 1, where, in the whole chapter, the passion of the Lord is treated of. That the Lord, as THE PROPHET, represented the state of the Jewish church, as to the Word, is manifest from the particulars of his passion; *as that He was betrayed by Judas; that He was taken and condemned by the chief priests and by the elders; that they buffeted Him; that they smote his head with a reed; that they put on him a crown of thorns; that they divided his garments, and cast the lot for his vesture; that they crucified Him; that they gave Him vinegar to drink; that they pierced his side; that He was buried; and that on the third day He rose again.* His being betrayed by Judas, signified that He was betrayed by the Jewish nation, with whom the Word then was, for Judas represented that nation: his being taken and condemned by the chief priests and elders, signified that he was so by all that church: their buffeting Him, spitting in his face, scourging Him, and smiting his head with a reed, signified that they did in like manner to the Word, as to its divine truths: their putting on Him a crown of thorns, signified that they had falsified and adulterated those truths: their dividing his garments, and casting the lot upon his vesture, signified that they had dispersed all the truths of the Word, but not its spiritual sense; this the vesture of the Lord signified: their crucifying Him, signified that they had destroyed and profaned the whole Word: their offering Him vinegar to drink, signified that the truths of the Word were all falsified; wherefore He did not drink it: their piercing his side, signified that they had totally extinguished all the truth of the Word and all the good of it: his being buried, signified the rejection of what remained from the mother: his rising again on the third day, signified the glorification or the union of his Human with the Divine of the Father. Hence, now, it is manifest, that to bear iniquities, does not mean to take them away, but to represent the profanation of the truths of the Word.

131. These things, also, may be illustrated by comparisons, which is done for the sake of the simple, who see better by means of comparisons than by deductions formed analytically from the Word, and at the same time from reason. Every citizen or subject is united to the king by doing his commands and precepts, and more so if he suffers hardships for him, and still more if he undergoes death for him, which is done in skirmishes and battles. In like manner, a friend is united to a friend, a son to his father, and a servant to his master, by doing those things which are agreeable to their will, and more so if they defend them against their enemies, and still more if they fight for their honor. Who is not united to the virgin whom he is courting for a bride, when he fights with those who defame her, and contends with his rival even to wounds? That they should be united by such means, is according to the law inscribed upon nature. The Lord says, *I am the good Shepherd; the good Shepherd layeth down his life for the sheep, for which reason the Father loveth Me*, John x. 11, 17.

132. VII. THAT THE PASSION OF THE CROSS IS BELIEVED TO HAVE BEEN REDEMPTION ITSELF, IS A FUNDAMENTAL ERROR OF THE CHURCH; AND THAT THAT ERROR, TOGETHER WITH THE ERROR CONCERNING THREE DIVINE PERSONS FROM ETERNITY, HAS PERVERTED THE WHOLE CHURCH, SO THAT NOT ANY THING SPIRITUAL IS LEFT REMAINING IN IT.

What at this day more fills and crams the books of the orthodox, o what is more zealously taught and inculcated in the schools, and more frequently preached and proclaimed from the pulpits, than that God the Father, being enraged against the human race, not only removed it from himself, but also concluded it under a universal damnation, and thus excommunicated it; but, because He is gracious, that He persuaded or excited his Son to descend, and take upon himself the determined damnation, and thus appease the anger of his Father; and that thus, and not otherwise, He could look upon man with some favor? Then that this, also, was done by the Son, who, in taking upon himself the damnation of the human race, suffered himself to be scourged by the Jews, to be spit upon in the face, and then to be crucified as the *accursed of God*, Deut. xxi. 23; and that the Father, after this was done, became propitious, and from love towards his Son, cancelled the sentence of damnation, but only in respect to those for whom He should intercede; and that He thus became a Mediator in the presence of his Father forever. These and similar things, at this day, sound in temples, and are reverberated from the walls, like an echo from the woods, and fill the ears of all there. But cannot any one, whose reason is enlightened and made sound by the Word, see that God is mercy and pity itself, because He is love itself and good itself, and that those are his essence; and that hence it is a contradiction to say, that mercy itself, or goodness itself, can look upon man with anger, and decree his damnation, and still continue to be his own divine essence? Such things are scarcely ever ascribed to a good man or an angel of heaven, but only to a wicked man or to a spirit of hell; wherefore it is abominable to ascribe them to God. But, if the cause be investigated, it is this, that they have taken the passion of the cross for redemption itself: thence have flowed those opinions, as, from one falsity, falses flow in a continued series, or as from a cask of vinegar, nothing comes but vinegar, or from an insane mind, nothing but what is insane; for from one established principle, theorems of the same sort are deduced: they are included in it, and proceed from it one after another; and from this, concerning the passion of the cross, that it is redemption, still many more things, scandalous and dishonorable to God, may be derived, until it comes to pass, as Isaiah says: *The priest and the prophet err through strong drink; they stumble in judgment; all the tables are full of things vomited,* xxviii. 7, 8.

133. From this idea concerning God and concerning redemption, all theology has, from spiritual, become to the lowest degree natural; which is the case, because merely natural properties are attributed to God; and yet on the idea of God, and on the idea of redemption, which makes one with salvation, every thing of the church depends. For that idea is like the head, from which all parts of the body are derived; wherefore, when that is spiritual, all things of the church become spiritual, and when that is natural, all things of the church become natural; hence, because the idea concerning God and concerning redemption has become merely natural, that is, sensual and corporeal, therefore all things, which the heads and members of the church have delivered and still deliver, in their dogmatical theology, are merely natural. The reason why nothing but falses can be derived thence, is, because the natural man continually acts against the spiritual, and thence he regards spiritual things as ghosts and phantoms in the air. Wherefore it may be said, that on account of tha sensual idea concerning redemption, and thence concerning God, the ways to heaven, which are ways to the Lord God the Savior, are beset with thieves and robbers, John x. 1, 8, 9; and that, in the temples, the doors are thrown down, so that dragons and owls, the tzjim and the jiim, have entered, and sing together in horrible discord That this idea concerning redemption, and concerning God, pervades the faith of the present age, is known; for that faith is, that men should pray to God

the Father, that He would remit their sins for the sake of the cross and blood of his Son, and to God the Son, that He would pray and intercede for them; and to God the Holy Ghost, that He would justify and sanctify them. And what else is this, than to make supplication to three Gods in their order? And how, then, is the thought concerning the divine government different from that concerning an aristocratical or hierarchical government, or from that concerning a triumvirate such as there was once at Rome? But instead of a triumvirate, it may be called a *tripersonate.* And what, then, is easier for the devil than to do, as is said, *divide and rule;* that is, to distract the minds of men, and excite rebellious motions, now against one God, now against another, as has been done from the time of Arius to the present day; and thus to cast down from the throne the Lord God the Savior, who has all power in heaven and earth, Matt. xxviii. 18, and to set upon it some one of his minions, and to ascribe worship to him; or, because it is taken away from him, to take it away also from the Lord himself?

---

134. To the above will be added these RELATIONS—FIRST. I once entered into a temple in the world of spirits, where many were assembled; and, before the sermon, they reasoned among themselves concerning REDEMPTION. The temple was square, and there were not windows in the walls, but a large opening above in the middle of the roof, through which light from heaven entered, and illuminated it better than if there had been windows at the sides. And behold, suddenly, while they were talking about redemption, a black cloud, coming from the north, covered the opening; whence it became so dark, that one could not see another, and scarcely any one could see the palm of his hand. While they stood amazed on account of this, lo, that black cloud was divided in the middle, and through the aperture were seen angels descending from heaven; and they dispersed the cloud on each side, whence it became again light in the temple; and then the angels sent down one of their number, who, in the name of the rest, asked the congregation what they were contending about, since so thick a cloud came over them, and took away the light, and brought on darkness. They replied, that it was about redemption, and that this was made by the Son of God, by the passion of the cross, and that by this He made expiation, and delivered the human race from damnation and eternal death But to this the deputed angel said, "How by the passion of the cross? Explain why it was effected by that." And then a priest came and said, "I will explain, in order, what we know and believe, which is, that God the Father, being enraged against the human race, condemned it, and excluded it from his clemency, and declared them accursed and reprobate, and doomed them to hell; and that He wished that his Son would take upon himself that condemnation, and that the Son consented, and, for that purpose, descended, and assumed the Human, and suffered himself to be crucified, and thus the condemnation of the human race to be transferred to himself; for it is written, *Cursed is every one who hangeth on the wood of a cross;* and that the Son thus appeased the Father by interceding and mediating; and that then the Father, from love towards the Son, and moved with the misery seen in Him upon the cross, determined that He would forgive; 'but only those to whom I impute thy righteousness; these I will make, from sons of wrath and curse, sons of grace and blessing, and will justify and save; but the rest may remain, as was before determined, sons of wrath:' this is our faith, and these things are the righteousness which God the Father inserts into our faith, which alone justifies and saves." The angel, having heard these words, was silent for a long time, for he was fixed in astonishment: and afterwards he broke silence, and spoke these words: "Can the Christian world be so infatuated, and wander from sound reason into such

deliriums, and conclude the fundamental article of salvation from such paradoxes? Who cannot see that those things are diametrically contrary to the very divine essence, that is, contrary to its divine love and its divine wisdom, and, at the same time, contrary to its omnipotence and omnipresence? No good master can deal thus with his servants and maids; nay, a wild beast is not so cruel to its cubs, or a bird of prey to its young. Is it not contrary to the divine essence to annul the call which has been made to all and every one of the human race? Is it not contrary to the divine essence to change the order established from eternity, which is, that every one should be judged according to his life? Is it not contrary to the divine essence to withdraw love and mercy from any man, and much more from the whole human race? Is it not contrary to the divine essence to be brought back to mercy from the misery seen in the Son; and because mercy is the very essence of God, to be brought back to his own essence? And is it not abominable to think that He ever went out of it? for it is Himself from eternity to eternity. Is it not also impossible to insert, in any thing such as your faith is, the righteousness of redemption, which, in itself, is of the divine omnipotence, and to impute and ascribe it to man, and to declare him righteous, pure and holy without any other means? Is it not impossible to remit sins to any one, and to renew, regenerate and save any one by imputation alone, and thus to turn unrighteousness into righteousness, and the curse into a blessing? Is it not, in such a case, possible to turn hell into heaven and heaven into hell, and the dragon into Michael and Michael into the dragon, and thus to end the battle between them? What is necessary but to take away the imputation of your faith from one, and put it into the other? thus we who are in heaven shall be in trepidation forever. It is not according to justice and judgment that one should take upon himself the wickedness of another, and the wicked should become innocent, and that wickedness should thus be washed away. Is not this contrary to justice, both divine and human? The Christian world is yet ignorant that there is order, and still more what the order is which God introduced into the world, when He created it, and that God cannot act contrary to it, since, in that case, He would act contrary to Himself; for God is Order itself." The priest understood the things said by the angel, because the angels who were above, infused light from heaven; and then he groaned, and said, "What is to be done? All, at this day, thus preach, and pray, and believe. This is in the mouth of all; 'Good Father, have mercy on us, and remit to us our sins for the sake of thy Son's blood, which He shed for us on the cross;' and to Christ, 'Lord, intercede for us;' to which we priests add, 'Send to us the Holy Spirit.'" And then the ange said, "I have observed that the priests prepare eye-salve from the Word not interiorly understood, which they put upon the eyes which are blinded by their faith, or they make of it a sort of plaster for themselves, which they put upon the wounds inflicted by their dogmas, but still they do not heal them, because they are inveterate; wherefore go to him who stands there (and he pointed with the finger to me), he will teach you from the Lord, that the passion of the cross was not redemption, but that it was the unition of the Human of the Lord with the Divine of the Father; but that redemption was the subjugation of the hells, and the establishment of order in the heavens; and that, unless those things had been performed by the Lord, when He was in the world, there would have been no salvation for any on earth, nor for any in the heavens; and he will teach you also the order introduced at the creation, according to which men should live, that they may be saved, and that those who do live according to it are numbered among the redeemed, and are called the *elect*." These things being said, windows were made in the temple at the sides, through which light flowed in from the four quarters of the world, and cherubs appeared flying in the splendor of the light; and the angel was taken up to his companions above the aperture, and we retired full of joy.

135. SECOND RELATION. One morning, as I awaked from sleep, the sun of the spiritual world appeared to me in its splendor, and under it I saw the heavens, distant as the earth is from its sun; and then were heard from the heavens unspeakable words, which, being collected together, were articulated into this expression, that "There is one God, who is Man, whose habitation is in that sun." This articulate sentence descended through the middle heavens to the lowest, and from this into the world of spirits, where I was; and I perceived that the idea of one God, which the angels had, was changed, according to the degrees of descent, into an idea of three Gods. When I observed this, I began to speak with those who thought of three Gods, saying, "Oh, what an enormity! Whence did you get that?" And they replied, "We think of three, from the idea which we entertain concerning the triune God; but still this does not fall into our mouth; when we speak, we always say roundly, that 'God is one;' if in our minds there is another idea, let it be so, provided it do not flow down and divide the unity of God in the mouth; but still, from time to time, it does flow down, because it is within; and then, if we should speak out, we should say 'three Gods;' but we cautiously avoid this, lest we should be exposed to the ridicule of those who hear us." And then they spoke openly from their thought, saying, "Are there not three Gods, because there are three divine persons, each one of whom is God? We cannot think otherwise, since the leader of our church, from the desk of his holy dogmas, ascribes creation to one, redemption to another, and sanctification to the third; and, especially, since he attributes to each of them his peculiar properties, which, he asserts, are incommunicable, and which are not only creation, redemp ion and sanctification, but also imputation, mediation and operation. Is there not, then, one who created us, and he also imputes? another who redeemed us, and he also mediates? and a third who operates the mediated imputation, and he also sanctifies? Who does not know that the Son of God was sent by the Father into the world, that he might redeem the human race, and thus become an Expiator, Mediator, Propitiator and Intercessor? And, because he is one with the Son of God from eternity, are there not two persons distinct from each other? and because these two are in heaven, one sitting at the right hand of the other, should there not be a third person, who may execute in the world what is decreed in heaven?" Having heard this, I was silent, but thought with myself, Oh, what infatuation! They do not know any thing at all what is meant in the Word by *mediation.* And then, by the command of the Lord, three angels descended from heaven and were associated with me, in order that from an interior perception, I might speak with those who were in the idea of three Gods; and particularly concerning mediation, intercession, propitiation and expiation, which are attributed by them to the second person, or the Son, but not until after He became man, many ages since the creation, when those four means of salvation were not before in existence: and thus God the Father was not propitiated, the human race not expiated, nor was any one sent from heaven, who interceded and mediated. Then, from the inspiration afforded me, I spoke with them, saying, "Come here as many of you as can, and hear what is meant in the Word by mediation, intercession, expiation and propitiation. Those are four predications of the grace of the one God in his Human. God the Father can never be approached, nor can He come to any man, because He is infinite, and in his esse, which is Jehovah; from which esse, if He should come to man, He would consume him, as fire consumes wood, and reduces it to ashes. This is manifest from these considerations: that He said to Moses

who wished to see Him, that *No one can see Him and live*, Exod. xxxiii. 20. And the Lord said, *No one hath ever seen God, except the Son, who is in the bosom of the Father*, John i. 18; Matt. xi. 27; also that *No one hath heard the voice of the Father, nor seen his shape*, John v. 37. It is read, indeed, that Moses saw Jehovah face to face, and spoke with Him mouth to mouth; but this was done through an angel; in like manner, with Abraham and Gideon. Now, because God the Father, in himself, is such, He was pleased to assume the Human, and, in this, to admit men to Himself, and thus to hear them, and to speak with them; and this Human is what is called *the Son of God;* and this is what mediates, intercedes, propitiates, and expiates. I will tell, therefore, what those four things, predicated of the Human of God the Father, signify. MEDIATION signifies that the Human is the medium through which man may come to God the Father, and God the Father to man, and thus teach and lead him, that he may be saved; wherefore the Son of God, by whom is meant the Human of God the Father, is called *Savior;* and in the world, *Jesus*, that is, salvation. INTERCESSION signifies perpetual mediation; for love itself, the properties of which are mercy, clemency and grace, perpetually intercedes, that is, mediates for those who do his commandments, whom He loves. EXPIATION signifies the removal of sins, into which man would rush if he should approach the naked Jehovah. PROPITIATION signifies the operation of clemency and grace, lest man, by means of sins, should bring himself into condemnation; likewise protection, lest he should profane holiness; this was signified by the propitiatory over the ark in the tabernacle. It is known that God spoke in the Word according to appearances, as that He is angry, avenges, tempts, punishes, casts into hell, condemns, yea, that He does evil; when yet He is angry with no one, He does not avenge, tempt, punish, cast into hell, or condemn: these hings are as far from God as heaven is from hell, and infinitely farther; wherefore they are forms of speech, according to appearance; such, also, in another sense, are expiation, propitiation, intercession and mediation, by which are meant the ways and means of access to God, and of receiving grace from God through his Human; which not being understood, men have divided God into three, and upon these three have founded every doctrine of the church, and thus have falsified the Word: hence THE ABOMINATION OF DESOLATION, foretold by the Lord in Daniel, and again in Matt. xxiv." When I had said this, the company of spirits retired from around me, and I observed that those who actually entertained an idea of three Gods, looked towards hell, and those who entertained an idea of one God, in whom is a divine Trinity, and that this is in the Lord God the Savior, looked towards heaven; and to these appeared the sun of heaven, in which Jehovah is in his Human.

136. THIRD RELATION. I saw, at a distance, five gymnasiums, each of which was surrounded with light from heaven. The first gymnasium was surrounded with purple light, such as is in the clouds in the morning, before sunrise, on earth; the second gymnasium was surrounded with a yellow light, like that of the morning after sunrise; the third gymnasium was surrounded with a bright light like that of noonday in the world; the fourth gymnasium was surrounded with a middle kind of light, such as there is when it begins to be mixed with the shade of the evening; and the fifth gymnasium stood in the very shade of the evening. The gymnasiums in the world of spirits are spacious halls, where the learned assemble, and discuss various arcana, which serve for their science, intelligence and wisdom On seeing them, I felt a strong desire of going to one of them, and I went in the spirit to that which was surrounded with a middle kind of light; and I entered, and there was seen a company of learned men assembled, who were together investigating what that in-

volves, which is said concerning the Lord, that, *being taken up into heaven, He sitteth at the right hand of God,* Mark xvi. 19. Most of the company assembled, said that those things should be understood exactly according to the words, that the Son thus sits beside the Father. But it was asked, "Why so?" Some said, that the Son was placed by the Father at the right hand, on account of the redemption which He accomplished; some, that He sits thus out of love; some, that it was in order that He might be his counsellor, and because He is so, that He may receive honor from the angels; and some that it was for this reason, that it was given to Him by the Father to reign in his stead, for it is read, that *All power is given to Him in heaven and in earth;* but a great part, that He may hear those on the right hand, for whom He intercedes; for all in the church, at this day, go to God the Father, and pray that He would have mercy for the sake of the Son; and this causes the Father to turn himself to Him, that He may receive his mediation. But some said, that only the Son of God from eternity sits at the right hand of the Father, that He may communicate his divinity to the Son of man, born in the world. On hearing these words, I wondered exceedingly, that learned men, although they had been some time in the spiritual world, should still be so ignorant of heavenly things; but I perceived the cause, that, by reason of confidence in their own intelligence, they did not suffer themselves to be instructed by the wise. But that they might not continue any longer in ignorance concerning the sitting of the Son on the right hand of the Father, I raised my hand, requesting that they would listen to a few words, which I wished to speak on that subject. And because they assented, I said, "Do you not know from the Word, that the Father and the Son are one, and that the Father is in the Son and the Son in the Father? This the Lord openly says in John x. 30, and xiv. 10, 11. If you do not believe these words, you divide God into two, which being done, you cannot think otherwise than naturally, sensually, yea, materially, concerning God, which has also been done in the world, ever since the Nicene council, which introduced three divine persons from eternity, and thereby turned the church into a theatre, ornamented with painted scenery, within which the actors represented new scenes. Who does not know and acknowledge that God is one? If you acknowledge this in heart and spirit, all that you have said is dissipated of itself, and rebounds into the air, like idle words from the ear of a wise man." At these words, many were enraged, and longed to pull my ears, and to command silence; but the president of the assembly, in a fit of indignation, said, "The discussion here is not concerning the unity and the plurality of God, because we believe both; but concerning this—What does it involve that the Son sits at the right hand of the Father? If you know any thing concerning this, speak." And I replied, "I will speak; but, I beseech you, stop the noise." And I said, "*By sitting on the right hand,* is not meant sitting on the right hand; but by that expression is meant the omnipotence of God by means of the Human, which He assumed in the world; by this He is in the lasts, as well as in the firsts; by this He entered, destroyed and subjugated the hells; by this He established order in the heavens; thus by this He redeemed both angels and men, and continues to redeem forever.

"If you consult the Word, and are such that you can be illuminated, you will perceive, that, by *the right hand* there, is meant omnipotence, as in Isaiah; MY HAND *founded the earth, and* MY RIGHT HAND *spanned the heavens,* xlviii. 13; and in David, *God hath sworn by his* RIGHT HAND, *and by the strength of* HIS ARM, Psalm lxii. 8. THY RIGHT HAND *holdeth me up,* xviii. 35. *Look to the Son, whom Thou hast strengthened for Thee; let* THY HAND *be for the man of* THE RIGHT HAND, *for the Son of Man whom Thou hast strengthened for thee,* lxxx. 17. Thence it is evident, how this is to be understood;

The saying of Jehovah to my Lord; Sit Thou at MY RIGHT HAND, *until I shall have made thine enemies thy footstool. Jehovah will send the sceptre of thy strength out of Zion; rule Thou in the midst of thine enemies*, Psalm cx. 1, 2. That whole psalm treats concerning the battle of the Lord with the hells, and concerning their subjugation. Since the right hand of God signifies omnipotence, therefore the Lord says, that *He is about to sit at* THE RIGHT HAND OF POWER, Matt. xxvi. 63, 64, *and at* THE RIGHT HAND OF THE POWER OF GOD, Luke xxii. 69." But at these words the company became tumultuous; and I said, "Take heed to yourselves; perhaps a hand may appear from heaven, which, when it appears, as it once did to me, strikes an incredible terror of power; which was to me a confirmation, that the right hand of God signifies omnipotence." Scarcely was this said, when a hand was stretched out under heaven, at the sight of which, so great a terror seized them, that they rushed in crowds to the gates, and some to the windows, that they might cast themselves out, and some, losing their breath, fainted away. But I remained not terrified, and, after them, slowly went away; and, at some distance thence, I turned about, and saw that gymnasium covered over with a dark cloud; and it was told me from heaven, that it was so covered, because they spoke from the belief of three Gods, and that the former light would return when those of a sounder mind should assemble there.

137. FOURTH RELATION. I heard that a council was convened of those who were celebrated for their writings and learning, concerning the faith of the present time, and concerning the justification of the elect by it. This was in the world of spirits; and it was given me to be present in the spirit; and I saw convened some of the clergy who were of the established churches, and some dissenters; on the right side stood those, who, in the world, were called *Apostolic Fathers*, and lived in the ages before the Nicene council; and on the left side stood men, who, since those ages, have been renowned for their books, printed or written. Many of these had their faces shaved, and their heads covered with wigs made of women's hair, and some of them had collars of twisted intestines, and some had collars of other stuff, but the former had long beards, and wore their natural hair. Before both parties there stood a man, a judge and critic of the writings of this age, with a staff in his hand, who struck the ground, and commanded silence; he ascended to the highest step of the pulpit, and breathed out a groan; and from that he wished to raise his voice aloud, but the groaning breath drew his voice back into his throat; but at length, speaking, he said, "Oh! my brethren, what an age! There has risen up one from the herd of the laity, having neither gown, cap, nor laurel, who has pulled down our faith from heaven, and cast it into the Styx. Oh, horrible! and yet that alone is our star, which shines like Orion in the night, and like Lucifer in the morning. That man, although advanced in years, is entirely blind in respect to the mysteries of our faith, because he has not opened it, and seen in it the righteousness of the Lord the Savior, and his mediation and atonement; and since he has not seen those, he has neither seen the wonders of his justification, which are the remission of sins, regeneration, sanctification and salvation. This man, instead of our faith, which is in the highest degree saving, because it is in three divine persons, thus in the whole Deity, has transferred faith to the second person; and not to him, but to his Human, which, indeed, we call Divine from the incarnation of the Son from eternity; but who thinks of it as any thing more than merely human? And what else can thence result, but a faith from which, as from a fountain, naturalism flows? And such a faith, because it is not spiritual, differs but little from faith in a pope or a saint. You know what Calvin said in his time, concerning worship from this faith, and I beseech you, tell me, one of you, whence is faith? Is it not immediately

from God, and thus does it not contain all things belonging to salvation?" At these words, his companions on the left side, whose faces were shaven, and who wore wigs and collars, clapped their hands, and exclaimed, "You have spoken most wisely! We know that we cannot take any thing which is not given us from heaven. Let that prophet tell us whence faith is, and what it is, if that be not faith. It is impossible that there should be any other, or from any other source; and to produce any other faith, which is faith, than this, is as impossible as it is for a man to ride on horseback to a constellation in heaven, and take thence a star, and put it in his pocket, and bring it down." This he said, that his companions might laugh at every new faith. On hearing these words, the men on the right side, who had long beards, and wore their natural hair, were filled with indignation; and one of them rose up (an old man, but still he seemed like a young man afterwards, for he was an angel from heaven, where every age becomes youthful), and spoke, saying, "I have heard what your faith is, which the man in the pulpit has so magnified. But what is that faith but the sepulchre of our Lord, after the resurrection, again closed by the soldiers of Pilate? I have opened it, and have seen nothing there but the rods of jugglers, with which the magicians in Egypt did miracles. Truly your faith, externally, in your eyes, is like a chest made of gold, and set with precious stones, which, when it is opened, is empty, except, perhaps, in the corners of it there may be dust from the relics of Roman Catholics; for these, also, have the same faith, only at this day it is covered over by them with external sanctities. It is also (that I may use comparisons) like the vestal virgin amongst the ancients, buried under the ground, because she let the sacred fire go out; and I can solemnly declare, that to my eyes it is like the golden calf, around which the children of Israel danced, after Moses departed and ascended into mount Sinai to Jehovah. Do not wonder that I should speak of your faith by such comparisons, because we speak so of it in heaven. But our faith is, was, and will be forever, in the Lord God the Savior, whose Human is Divine, and whose Divine is Human, thus accommodated to reception, and by means of which the spiritual Divine is united to the natural of man, and faith becomes spiritual in the natural, whence the natural becomes, as it were, transparent, from the spiritual light in which our faith is. The truths of which it consists are as many as the verses in the sacred volume; those truths are all like stars which manifest and form that faith. Man takes it from the Word by means of his natural light, in which it is science, thought and persuasion; but the Lord causes it to become, in such as believe in Him, conviction, trust and confidence; thus natural faith becomes spiritual, and by means of charity, it becomes living. This faith, with us, is like a queen, adorned with as many precious stones as the wall of the holy Jerusalem, Rev. xxi 17 to 20. But lest you should suppose that these things which I have said, are only words of exaltation, which may therefore be despised, I will read to you some things from the holy Word, from which it will be manifest, that our faith is not in a man, as you suppose, but in the true God, in whom is all the Divine. John says, *Jesus Christ is the true God and eternal life*, 1 John v. 20; Paul, *In Christ dwelleth all the fullness of the Godhead bodily*, Col. ii. 9; and in the Acts of the Apostles, that *he preached, both to the Jews and to the Greeks, repentance towards God, and faith in our Lord Jesus Christ*, xx. 21; and the Lord himself, that *All power is given to Him in heaven and in earth*, Matt. xxviii. 18; but these are a few." After this, the angel looked at me, and said, "You know what the Evangelical believe, or are about to believe, concerning the Lord the Savior: recite, therefore, some things, that we may know whether they are in such infatuation as to believe that his Human is merely human, or whether they ascribe to it something of the Divine, or how they do believe." Then in the presence of all the assembly, I read the following passages from those which I had collected from their book of orthodoxy, called FORMULA CONCORDIÆ, and printed at Leipzic in the year 1756: *That in Christ the divine and human natures are so united, that they make one person*, p. 606, 762. *That Christ is truly God and Man, in an undivided person, and continues to be so forever*, p. 609, 673, 762. *That in Christ God is Man, and Man God*, pp. 607, 765. *That the human nature of Christ is exalted to all divine majesty; this also from many of the fathers*, p. 844 to 852, 860 to 865, 869 to 878. *That Christ, as to the human nature, is omnipresent, and fills all things*, p. 768, 783, 784, 785. *That Christ, as to the human nature, has all power in heaven and in earth*, p. 775, 776, 780. *That Christ, as to the human nature, sits at the right hand of the Father*, p. 608, 764. *That Christ, as to the human nature, is to be invoked, confirmed by quotations from the Scripture there*, p. 226. *That the Augsburg confession very highly approves of that worship*, p. 19." After these passages were read, I turned myself to the president, and said, "I know that all here are consociated with their like in the natural world; tell me, I pray, whether you know with whom you are consociated." He replied in a grave tone, "I do know; I am consociated with a famous man, a leader of illustrious bands from the army of the church." And because he answered in so grave a tone, I said, "Allow me to ask whether you know where that famous leader lives." And he said, "Yes, I do; he lives not far from Luther's tomb." At this I smiled, and said, "Why do you speak of his tomb? Do you not know that Luther has risen again, and that he has now renounced his erroneous opinions concerning justification by faith in three divine persons from eternity, and is therefore transferred to a place amongst the happy of the new heaven, and that he sees and laughs at those who are running mad after him." And he rejoined, "I do know it; but what is that to me?" And then I addressed him in a tone similar to his own, saying, "Please to inform your famous companion with whom you are consociated, that I am afraid, that, contrary to the orthodoxy of his church, he robbed the Lord of his divinity, or suffered his pen to make a furrow, in which he thoughtlessly sowed naturalism, at the very time when he wrote against the worship of the Lord our Savior." To this he replied, "I cannot do this, because I and he, as to this thing, make almost one mind. But he does not understand the things that I say; but I understand clearly all that he says; for the spiritual world enters into the natural world, and perceives the thoughts of men there; but not *vice versâ*: this is the state of the consociation of spirits and men." Now, because I had begun to speak with the president, I said, "I will ask, if you please, another question. Do you know that the orthodoxy of the Evangelical, in the manual of their church, called the FORMULA CONCORDIÆ, teaches, that in Christ God is Man, and Man God, and that his Divine and Human are, and continue to be forever, in an undivided person? How, then, could he, and how can you, defile the worship of the Lord with naturalism?" To which he replied, "I know that, and yet I do not know it." Wherefore I continued, by saying, "I ask him, although he is absent, or you in his stead, Whence was the soul of our Lord? If you answer, that it was from the mother, you talk insanely; if from Joseph, you profane the Word; but if from the Holy Spirit, you say rightly, if only by the Holy Spirit, you mean the Divine, proceeding and operating, so that He is the Son of Jehovah God. Again, I ask, What is the hypostatic union? If you answer that it is a union as between two, one above and the other below, you talk insanely; for, in that case, you might have made God the Savior two, as you have made God three: but if you say that it is a personal union, like that of the soul and body, you say rightly; this also is according to your doctrine and also to that of the fathers. Consult the FORMULA CONCORDIÆ, p. 765 to 768; also the creed of Athanasius, where are these words; *The right faith is, that we believe and confess that our Lord Jesus Christ is God and Man; who, although He is God and Man, yet is not two, but one Christ; one altogether, not by confusion of substance, but unity of person; for, as the rational soul and flesh is one man, so God and Man is one Christ.* I ask, moreover, What else was the damnable heresy of ARIUS (on account of whom the Nicene council was convened by the emperor Constantine the Great) than that he denied the divinity of the Lord's Human. Again, tell me whom you understand by these words in Jeremiah, *Behold the days will come, when I will raise up unto David a righteous branch, who shall reign a king; and this shall be his name,* JEHOVAH OUR RIGHTEOUSNESS, xxiii. 5, 6; xxxiii. 15, 16. If you say, the Son from eternity, you talk insanely; that was not the Redeemer; but if you say, the Son born in time, who was the only-begotten Son of God, John i. 18, iii. 16, you say rightly; this by redemption became righteousness, of which you make your faith. Read also Isaiah ix. 6; besides other passages, in which it is foretold, that Jehovah himself was about to come into the world." At these words, the president was silent, and turned himself away.

After these things were done, the president wished to close the council with prayer; but suddenly a man then started up from the company on the left, who had a tiara on his head, and a cap over that; and he touched the cap with his finger, and spoke, saying, "I am also consociated with a man in your world, who is there placed in high honor: this I know, because I speak from him, as he does from me." And I asked, "Where does that eminent person stay?" He replied, "At Gottenburg; and I once thought from him, that your new doctrine savored of Mahometanism" On hearing which, I saw all on the right hand, where the apostolic fathers stood, were astonished, and changed their color; and I heard exclamations from their minds through their mouths, "Oh, horrible! Oh, what an age!" But to appease their just resentment, I put forth my hands, and requested a hearing; which being granted, I said, "I know that a man of that eminence wrote some such thing in a letter, which he afterwards printed; but if he had at that time known what a blasphemy that is, he would have torn it in pieces with his fingers, or committed it to the flames It is such contumely as that which is meant by these words of the Lord to the Jews, who said that Christ did miracles by other power than the divine, Matt. xii. 22 to 32: besides this, He also says in the same place, *Whosoever is not with Me, is against Me; and whosoever gathereth not with Me, scattereth abroad,* verse 30." At these words, the consociated spirit hung down his head; but presently he raised it up, and said, "I have heard severer things from you than ever." But I rejoined, "The cause of it is the two charges, naturalism and Mahometanism, which are wicked lies, invented by craft, and two deadly stigmas, designed to avert and deter the minds of men from the holy worship of the Lord." And I turned myself to the latter consociated spirit, and said, "Tell him at Gottenburg, if you can, to read what was said by the Lord in the Revelation, iii. 18; and also ii 16." At these words, a noise was made, but it was stilled by light descending from heaven; in consequence of which many of those on the left side went over to those on the right, those only remaining who think only vain things, and therefore depend on the authority of some master, and also those who believe that the Lord was only a mere man; from these and those the light which descended from heaven seemed to be reflected, and to flow into those who had passed from the left to the right side

CHAPTER III.

CONCERNING THE HOLY SPIRIT, AND CONCERNING THE DIVINE OPERATION.

138. All of the sacred order, who have entertained any just idea concerning the Lord our Savior, on their entrance into the spiritual world, which is generally on the third day after their decease, are first instructed concerning the Divine Trinity; and particularly concerning the Holy Spirit, that it is not a God by itself, but that by it, in the Word, is meant the Divine Operation, proceeding from one omnipresent God. The reason why they are particularly instructed concerning the Holy Spirit, is, because most enthusiasts, after death, fall into the wild fancy, that they themselves are the Holy Spirit; and also because many of the church, who, in the world, believed that the Holy Spirit spoke through them, terrify others, by the words of the Lord in Matthew, that to speak against those things which the Holy Spirit inspired into them, is the unpardonable sin, xii. 31, 32. Those who, after instruction, recede from the faith that the Holy Spirit is a God by itself, are informed afterwards, concerning the unity of God, that it is not divided into three persons, each one of whom, singly, is God and Lord, according to the Athanasian creed; but that the Divine Trinity is in the Lord the Savior, as the soul, the body and the proceeding virtue, with every man. These are then prepared for receiving the faith of the new heavens; and, after they are prepared, a way is opened for them to a society in heaven, where there is the like faith; and a mansion is given them amongst their brethren, with whom they live in blessedness forever. Now, because we have treated concerning God the Creator, and concerning the Lord the Redeemer, it is necessary that we should also treat concerning the Holy Spirit; and this subject, like the rest, is to be divided into its articles, which are the following: I. *That the Holy Spirit is the Divine Truth, and also the Divine Virtue and Operation, proceeding from the One God, in whom is a Divine Trinity, thus from the Lord God the Savior.* II. *That the Divine Virtue and Operation, which are meant by the Holy Spirit, are, in general, Reformation and Regeneration, and, according to these, Renovation, Vivification, Sanctification and Justification; and according to these, Purification from evils, and Remission of sins, and finally Salvation.* III. *That that Divine Virtue and Operation, which are meant by the sending of the Holy Spirit, are, with the clergy in particular, Illustration and Instruction.* IV. *That the Lord operates those virtues in those who believe in Him.* V. *That the Lord operates of Himself from the Father, and not* vice versâ. VI. *That the spirit of a man is his mind, and whatsoever proceeds from it.*

139. I. That the Holy Spirit is the Divine Truth, and also the Divine Virtue and Operation, proceeding from the One God, in whom is a Divine Trinity, thus from the Lord God the Savior.

By the Holy Spirit is properly signified the Divine Truth, thus also the Word; and in this sense the Lord himself is also the Holy Spirit; but because in the church, at this day, the divine operation, which is actual justification, is described by the Holy Spirit, therefore this is here taken for the Holy Spirit; and of this chiefly we speak, because the divine operation is effected by the divine truth, which proceeds from the Lord; and that which proceeds is of one and the same es sence with Him from whom it proceeds, like these three, the soul, the body, and the proceeding virtue, which together make one essence; with man, merely human, but with the Lord, divine and human also; these being, after the glorification, united together, like the prior with its posterior, and like essence with its form. Thus the three essentials, which are called the *Father*, the *Son*, and the *Holy Spirit*, in the Lord are one. That the Lord is the Divine True itself, or the Divine Truth, was shown above; and that the Holy Spirit is also the same, is manifest from these passages:—*A Rod shall go forth out of the trunk of Jesse, the Spirit of Jehovah shall rest upon Him, the Spirit of wisdom and intelligence, the Spirit of counsel and virtue; He shall smite the earth with the rod of his mouth, and He shall slay the wicked with the breath of his lips; righteousness shall be the girdle of his loins, and truth the girdle of his reins*, Isaiah xi. 1, 4, 5. *Affliction shall come like a flood, the Spirit of Jehovah shall bear the standard against it; then the Redeemer shall come to Zion*, lix. 19, 20. *The Spirit of the Lord Jehovah is upon Me, Jehovah hath anointed Me, He hath sent Me to announce good news to the poor*, lxi. 1; Luke iv.18. *This is my covenant; my Spirit which is upon thee, and my words shall not depart out of thy mouth, from this time and forever*, Isaiah lix. 21. Since the Lord is the Truth itself, therefore all that which proceeds from Him is truth; and this is meant by the Paraclete, which is also called the *Spirit of Truth*, and the *Holy Spirit;* this is manifest from these passages:—*I tell you the* TRUTH; *it is expedient for you that I go away; for, if I go not away, the Paraclete will not come to you; but if I go, I will send Him to you*, John xvi. 7. *When the Spirit of Truth shall have come, it shall lead you into* ALL THE TRUTH; *it shall not speak from itself, but whatsoever it shall hear it shall speak*, xvi. 13. *It shall glorify Me, because it shall receive of mine, and shall announce to you: all things, whatsoever the Father hath, are mine; on this account I said, it shall receive of mine, and shall announce to you*, xvi. 14, 15. *I will ask the Father to give you another Paraclete, the Spirit of Truth, which the world cannot receive, because it seeth it not, neither knoweth it; but ye know it, because it abideth with you, and shall be in you. I will not leave you orphans; I am coming to you, and ye shall see Me*, John xiv. 16, 17. *When the Paraclete shall have come, which I shall send to you from the Father, the Spirit of Truth, it shall testify of Me*, xv. 26. It is called the *Holy Spirit*, xiv. 26. That the Lord meant himself by the Paraclete or the Holy Spirit, is manifest from those words of the Lord, that *the world did not yet know Him, but ye know Him; I will not leave you orphans; I come to you; ye shall see Me.* And in another place, *Lo, I am with you all the days, even to the consummation of the age*, Matt xxviii. 20; also from these words, *It shall not speak from itself, but that it shall receive of mine.*

140. Now, because the Divine Truth is meant by the Holy Spirit, and this was in the Lord, and was the Lord himself, John xiv. 6, and thus because it could not proceed from any other source, therefore he said, *The Holy Spirit was not yet, because Jesus was not yet glorified*, vii. 39; and after the glorification, *He breathed into the disciples, and said, Receive ye the Holy Spirit*, xx. 22. The reason why the Lord breathed upon the disciples, and said that, was, because *aspiration* [or breathing upon] was an external representative sign of divine inspiration; but inspiration is an insertion into angelic societies. From these things, the understanding may comprehend this, which was said by the angel Gabriel, concerning the conception of the Lord; *The Holy Spirit shall come up on thee, and the virtue of the Most High shall overshadow thee; wherefore the Holy Thing which is born of thee shall be called the Son of God*, Luke i. 35. Also, *The angel of the Lord in a dream said to Joseph, Do not fear to take Mary for thy wife, for that which is born in her is of the Holy Spirit*

And Joseph did not touch her until she had brought forth her first-born son, Matt. i. 20, 25. The Holy Spirit there is the Divine Truth proceeding from Jehovah the Father; and this proceeding is the virtue of the Most High, which then overshadowed the mother. This, therefore, coincides with this in John; *The Word was with God, and the Word was God; and the Word became flesh*, i. 1, 14. That by the Word there is meant the Divine Truth, see in THE FAITH OF THE NEW CHURCH, above, n. 3.

141. That the Divine Trinity is in the Lord was demonstrated above, and will be demonstrated more fully in the sequel, when we come to treat professedly concerning it. Here, only some absurdities, following from that trinity divided into persons, will be adduced. This would be as if some minister of the church should teach from the pulpit what should be believed, and what should be done, and beside him another minister should stand and whisper in his ear, "You say this rightly; add also something more;" and they should say to a third, who stands upon the stairs, "Descend into the temple, and open their ears, and pour those things into their hearts, and, at the same time, cause them to be purities, sanctities, and pledges of righteousness." A Divine Trinity divided into persons, each of whom, singly, is God and Lord, is also similar to three suns in one world; one on high, near another, and the third beneath, which pours its rays around angels and men, and introduces the heat and light of the two into their minds, hearts and bodies, and subtilizes, clarifies and sublimates them, as fire does the matter in retorts. Who does not see, that, if it should be done so, man would be burnt even into ashes? The government of three divine persons in heaven, also, would be similar to the government of three kings in one kingdom, or to the government of three generals, of the same power, over one army; or rather to the Roman government before the times of the Cesars, when there were a consul, senate, and tribune of the people; among whom, indeed, the power was divided, but still the sovereignty was in them all together. Who does not see, that it is absurd, ludicrous and foolish, to introduce such a government into heaven; and it is introduced, when a power like that of a chief consul is ascribed to God the Father, a power like that of the senate to the Son, and a power like that of the tribune of the people to the Holy Spirit; which is the case, when a peculiar office is attributed to each one, and especially if it is added that those properties are not communicable.

142. II. THAT THE DIVINE VIRTUE AND OPERATION, WHICH ARE MEANT BY THE HOLY SPIRIT, ARE, IN GENERAL, REFORMATION AND REGENERATION; AND, ACCORDING TO THESE, RENOVATION, VIVIFICATION, SANCTIFICATION, AND JUSTIFICATION; AND, ACCORDING TO THESE, PURIFICATION FROM EVILS, AND REMISSION OF SINS, AND FINALLY SALVATION.

These are, in their order, the virtues which the Lord operates in those who believe in Him, and accommodate and dispose themselves for his reception and habitation; and this is done by means of divine truth, and with Christians by means of the Word; for this is the only medium through which man approaches to the Lord, and into which the Lord enters; for, as was said above, the Lord is the Divine Truth itself, and whatsoever proceeds from Him is divine truth. But the divine truth from good is to be understood, which is the same with faith from charity; for faith is no other than truth, and charity is no other than goodness. By means of divine truth from good, that is, by means of faith from charity, man is reformed and regenerated; also renovated, vivified, sanctified, justified; and, according to the progress and increase of these, is purified from evils; and purification from these is remission of sins. But all these operations of the Lord cannot be explained here, one by one, because each requires its analysis, confirmed from the Word, and illustrated by reason; and this does not belong to this place; wherefore the reader is referred to those things which follow in order in this work, which are concerning Charity, Faith, Free Agency Repentance, and also Reformation and Regeneration. It should be known, that the Lord is continually operating those saving graces with every man, for they are steps to heaven, for the Lord wills the salvation of all; wherefore the salvation of all is his end, and he who wills an end wills the means. His coming, redemption, and the passion of the cross, were for the sake of the salvation of men, Matt. xviii. 11; Luke xix. 10; and because the salvation of men was, and forever is his end, it follows that the above-mentioned operations are mediate ends, and salvation the ultimate end.

143. The operation of these virtues is the Holy Spirit, which the Lord sends to those who believe in Him, and dispose themselves to receive Him; and it is meant by the spirit in these passages: *I will give a new heart and* A NEW SPIRIT; MY SPIRIT *I will give in the midst of you, and I will cause you to walk in the way of salvation*, Isaiah xxxvi. 26, 27; Ezek. xi. 19. *Create in me a clean heart, O God, and renew* A FIRM SPIRIT *in the midst of me: restore to me the joy of thy salvation, and let* A FREE SPIRIT *sustain me*, Psalm li. 12. *Jehovah formeth* THE SPIRIT OF MAN *in the midst of him*, Zech. xii. 11. *In my soul I have waited for Thee in the night, and in* MY SPIRIT *in the midst of me I have waited for Thee in the morning*, Isaiah xxxvi. 9. *Make for you a new heart, and* A NEW SPIRIT: *why will ye die?* Ezek. xviii. 31: besides other passages. In those passages, by *a new heart* is meant the will of good, and by *a new spirit*, the understanding of truth. That the Lord operates these, in those who do what is good, and believe what is true, consequently in those who are in the faith of charity, is very manifest from these things there, *God gives a soul* to those who walk in it; and from this, that it is called *a free spirit:* and that man is to operate on his part, from these; *Make for you a new heart, and a new spirit; why will ye die, O house of Israel?*

144. It is read that, *when Jesus was baptized, the heavens were opened, and John saw the Holy Spirit descending like a dove*, Matt. iii. 16; Mark i. 10 Luke iii. 11; John i. 32, 33. This was done because baptism signifies regeneration and purification, as also does a dove. Who cannot perceive, that the dove was not the Holy Spirit, and that the Holy Spirit was not in the dove? Doves often appear in heaven, and as often as they appear, the angels know that they are correspondences of the affections, and thence the thoughts, concerning regeneration and purification, with some who stand in the vicinity; wherefore, as soon as they come up to them, and speak with them concerning any other thing than what was in their thoughts, when that appearance was presented, the doves instantly vanish. This is similar to many things which appeared to the prophets; as that a lamb appeared to John on Mount Zion, Rev. xiv. 1; and in other places. Who does not know, that the Lord was not that lamb, nor in the lamb, but that the lamb was a representation of his innocence? Thence appears manifest the error of those who, from the dove seen upon the Lord, when he was baptized, and from the voice then heard from heaven, *This is my beloved Son*, deduce the three persons of the trinity. That the Lord regenerates man by faith and charity, is meant by this, which John the Baptist said: *I baptize you with water unto repentance, but He who is to come after me will baptize with the* HOLY SPIRIT *and with fire*, Matt. iii. 15; Mark i. 8; Luke iii. 16. To baptize with the Holy Spirit and with fire, is to regenerate by the divine truth, which is of faith, and by the divine good, which is of charity. The like is signified by these words of the Lord: *Except a man be born of water and of the spirit, he cannot enter into the kingdom of God*, John iii. 5. By *water* here, as elsewhere in the Word, is signified truth, in the natural or external man, and by *the spirit*, truth from good, in the spiritual or internal man.

145. Now, because the Lord is Divine Truth itself from the Divine Good, and this is his very essence, and every one acts what he acts from his essence, it is evident that the Lord continually wills, nor can He will otherwise than to implant truth and good, or faith and charity, in every man. This may be illustrated by many things in the world, as by these: that every man wills and thinks, and, as far as it is allowable, speaks and acts, from his essence; as, for example, a faithful man thinks and intends faithful things; an honest, upright, pious and religious man, honest, upright, pious and religious things; and, on the contrary, a haughty, cunning, treacherous and covetous man, such things as make one with his essence. A fortune-teller wishes only to tell fortunes, and a fool only to prate against the things which are of wisdom; in a word, an angel meditates and practises only heavenly things, and a devil only infernal things. The case is similar with every subject of inferior rank in the animal kingdom, as with a bird, a beast, a fish, an insect, winged and not winged; every one is known by its essence or nature, from which and according to which is the instinct of each. In like manner, in the vegetable kingdom, every tree, every shrub and every herb, is known by its fruit and seed, in which its essence is innate; nor can any thing else be produced from thence, but what is similar to itself and its own; yea, every kind of ground, clay and stone, noble and ignoble, and every mineral and metal, is estimated according to its essence.

146. III. That that Divine Virtue and Operation, which is meant by the sending of the Holy Spirit, with the Clergy in particular, is Illustration and Instruction.

The operations of the Lord, enumerated in the preceding article, which are reformation, regeneration, renovation, vivification, sanctification, justification, purification, remission of sins, and finally salvation, flow in from the Lord, as well with the clergy as with the laity, and are received by those who are in the Lord, and the Lord in them, John vi. 56; xiv. 20; xv. 4, 5. But the reasons why illustration and instruction are for the clergy, in particular, are, because those belong to their office, and inauguration into the ministry brings them along with it; and also they believe that, while they are preaching from zeal, they are inspired, like the disciples of the Lord into whom the Lord breathed, saying, *Receive ye the Holy Spirit*, John xx. 22; and also Mark xiii. 11. Some also affirm that they have felt the influx. But they should be very cautious how they persuade themselves, that the zeal, by which many are actuated while they are preaching, is the divine operation in their hearts; for a similar and even a warmer zeal, is excited in the breasts of enthusiasts, and also in those who are in extreme falses of doctrine; yea, in those who despise the Word, and worship nature instead of God, and cast faith and charity, as it were, into a bag behind their back; and whilst they are preaching and teaching, they hang it before them, as a kind of ruminatory stomach, from which they select and disgorge such things as they know will serve for food to the hearers. For zeal, viewed in itself, is a violent heating of the natural man; if there is within it the love of truth, then it is like the sacred fire which flowed into the apostles, concerning which it is thus written in the Acts: *There appeared to them cloven tongues, as of fire, and sat upon every one of them, whence they all were filled with the Holy Spirit*, ii. 3, 4. But if the love of the false lies inwardly concealed in that zeal or heat, it is then like fire imprisoned in wood, which bursts forth and burns the house. You, who deny the sanctity of the Word and the divinity of the Lord, take off, I beseech you, your bag from your back, and open it, which you do freely at home, and you will see. I know that those who are meant by Lucifer in Isaiah, and who are of Babel, when they enter the temple, and especially when they ascend the pulpit, particularly those who call themselves of the society of Jesus are hurried away by a zeal which, in many cases, is from infernal love; and thence they scream more vehemently, and fetch deeper sighs from their breasts, than those who are in zeal from heavenly love. That there are two other spiritual operations with the clergy may be seen below, n. 155.

147. The church is yet almost ignorant, that in all the will and thought, and thence in all the action and speech of man, there is an internal and an external, and that man, from infancy, is taught to speak from the external, however the internal dissents; thence proceed dissimulation, flattery, and hypocrisy; consequently that he has duplicity; and he only has simplicity whose external thinks, and speaks, and wills, and acts, from the internal: these also are meant by the simple in the Word, as Luke viii. 15; xi. 34; and in other places; although they are wiser than persons of duplicity. That there is duplicity and triplicity in every created thing is evident from these things in the human body: every nerve there consists of fibres, and every fibre of fibrils; every muscle of little bundles of fibres, and these of moving fibres; every artery of coats in a triple series. It is similar in the human mind, whose spiritual organism is such; this is according to what was said above, that the human mind is distinguished into three regions, the highest of which, which is also the inmost, is called *celestial*, the middle *spiritual*, and the lowest *natural*. The minds of all men, who deny the sanctity of the Word and the divinity of the Lord, think in the lowest region; but, because from infancy they have learned also the spiritual things which are of the church, and receive them, but put them below natural things, which are various scientific, political, civil and moral things; because they sit lowest in the mind, and nearest to the speech, they speak from them in temples and in companies; and, what is wonderful, they then know no otherwise than that they speak and teach from the belief of them; when, nevertheless, as soon as they are at liberty, which is the case at home, the door is opened, which shuts up the internal of their mind, and then sometimes they laugh at those things which they have preached in public, saying in heart, that theological things are specious snares for catching doves.

148. The internal and external of such persons may be likened to poisons covered over with crusts of sugar; and also to the wild gourds which the boys of the prophets gathered and cast into the pottage, which while they were eating, they cried out, *There is death in the pot*, 2 Kings iv. 38 to 43. They may also be compared to the beast arising out of the sea, which had two horns as of a lamb, and spoke as a dragon, Rev. xiii. 11. In what follows, that beast is called the *false prophet*. And they are like robbers in a city where the citizens are moral, who in the city act morally and speak rationally, but when they return into the woods they are wild beasts; or they are also like pirates, who upon the land are men, but at sea crocodiles. The latter and the former walk about, while upon the land or in a city, like panthers clothed in sheep-skins, or like apes dressed in men's clothes, before whose face a mask is placed. They may also be likened to a harlot, who anoints herself with balsam, and paints her face with carmine, and clothes herself with white silk, ornamented with flowers; who, when she returns to her house, undresses herself in the presence of her paramours, and infects them with her loathsome disease. That those, who detract from the sanctity of the Word and the divinity of the Lord, are such, has been given me to know, by the experience of years in the spiritual world; for there all, at first, are kept in their externals, but afterwards, when these are removed, they are let into internals, and then their comedy becomes a tragedy.

149. IV. THAT THE LORD OPERATES THOSE VIRTUES IN THOSE WHO BELIEVE IN HIM.

That the Lord operates those virtues, which are meant by the sending of the Holy Spirit, in those who believe in

Him, that is, that he reforms, regenerates, renovates, vivifies, sanctifies, justifies, purifies from evils, and finally saves them, is evident from all those passages in the Word, which may be seen adduced above, n. 108, to prove that those have salvation and eternal life, who believe in the Lord; and, moreover, from this; *Jesus said, Whosoever* BELIEVETH IN ME, *as the Scripture saith, out of his belly shall flow rivers of living water; this He said concerning the* SPIRIT *which those who* BELIEVE IN HIM *were about to receive,* John vii. 38, 39; and also from this; THE TESTIMONY OF JESUS IS THE SPIRIT OF PROPHECY, Rev. xix. 10. By the *spirit of prophecy* is meant the truth of doctrine from the Word; *prophecy* signifies no other than doctrine, and to *prophesy,* to teach it; and by the *testimony of Jesus* is meant confession from faith in Him. The like is meant by his *testimony* in this passage: *The angels of Michael overcame the dragon, by the blood of the Lamb, and by the Word of* HIS TESTIMONY; *and the dragon went away to make war with the rest of her seed, who kept the commandments of God, and have the testimony of Jesus Christ,* Rev. xii. 11, 17.

150. The reason why those who believe in the Lord Jesus Christ are about to receive those spiritual virtues, is, because He is salvation and eternal life; salvation, because he is the Savior; this also is his name, *Jesus:* eternal life, because those in whom He is, and who are in Him, have eternal life; wherefore also He is called *eternal Life,* in 1 John v. 20. Now, because He is salvation and eternal life, it follows that He is all that by which salvation and eternal life are obtained; consequently, that he is the all of reformation, regeneration, renovation, vivification, sanctification, justification, purification from evils, and at length salvation. The Lord operates those virtues in every man; that is, He strives to introduce them; and when man accommodates and disposes himself for the reception, He does introduce them. The active power of accommodation and disposition is also from the Lord but if man does not receive them with a free spirit, then, notwithstanding the effort of the Lord, which constantly continues, He cannot introduce them

151. To believe in the Lord is not only to acknowledge him, but also to do his commandments; for only to acknowledge him is only of the thought, from some understanding; but to do his commandments is also of acknowledgment from the will. The mind of man consists of understanding and will, and it is the part of the understanding to think, and of the will to do; wherefore, while man only acknowledges from the thought of the understanding, he goes to the Lord only with half of the mind; but when he does his commandments, then with the whole; and this is to believe. Otherwise, a man may divide his heart, and compel its surface to raise itself upwards, while its flesh turns itself downwards; and thus he flies, like an eagle, between heaven and hell; and yet man does not follow his sight, but the delights of his flesh; and because this is in hell, therefore he flies down thither; and, after he has there sacrificed to his sensual pleasures, and poured out libations of wine to demons, he puts on a countenance of gayety, and causes his eyes to sparkle with fire, and thus counterfeits an angel of light. Such satans those become, after death, who acknowledge the Lord and do not obey his commandments.

152. It was shown, in the foregoing article, that the salvation and eternal life of men are the first and the last ends of the Lord; and, because the first and the last ends contain in them the mediate ends, it follows that the above-mentioned spiritual virtues are together in the Lord, and also from the Lord in man, but still they come forth successively; for the mind of man grows like his body; the body in stature, but the mind in wisdom. Thus, also, the latter is exalted from region to region; that is, from the natural to the spiritual, and from this to the celestial; and in this region man is called *wise,* in that *intelligent,* and in the

lowest *scientific;* but this exaltation of the mind is not effected except from time to time; and it is effected as man procures for himself truths, and conjoins them to good. This is similar to the case of one who is building a house; he first procures for himself the materials for it, as bricks, tiles, beams and rafters; and thus he lays the foundation, raises the walls, divides it into rooms, makes doors for them, and windows in the walls, and stairs from one story to another; all these things are together in the end, which is a commodious and elegant habitation, which he foresees and provides. It is similar with a temple; all things requisite for the building of this exist together in the end, which is the worship of God. It is similar with all other things, as with gardens and fields, and also with offices and employments, for which the end procures for itself the requisite means.

153. V. That the Lord operates of Himself from the Father, and not *vice versâ*.

By *operating* is here meant the same thing as by *sending the Holy Spirit*, since the above-mentioned operations, which are, in general, reformation, regeneration, renovation, vivification, sanctification, justification, purification from evils, and remission of sins, which are at this day attributed to the Holy Spirit, as to a God by Himself, are the operations of the Lord. That these are of the Lord from the Father, and not *vice versâ*, shall be first confirmed from the Word, and afterwards illustrated by many things which are of reason. From the Word by these: *When the Paraclete shall have come,* WHOM I AM ABOUT TO SEND FROM THE FATHER, *the Spirit of truth which proceedeth from the Father, He shall testify of Me*, John xv. 26. *If I go not away, the Paraclete will not come to you; but if I go,* I WILL SEND HIM TO YOU, xvi. 7. *The Paraclete, the Spirit of truth, will not speak from Himself, but He will receive of mine, and announce to you; all things, whatsoever the Father hath,* ARE MINE; *on account of this I said, that He shall receive* OF MINE, *and announce to you,* xvi. 13, 14, 15. *The Holy Spirit was not yet, because Jesus was not yet glorified*, vii. 39. *Jesus breathed into the disciples, and said, Receive ye the Holy Spirit*, xx. 22. *Whatsoever ye shall ask in my name,* THIS I WILL DO, *that the Father may be glorified in the Son. If ye shall ask any thing in my name,* I WILL DO IT, xiv. 13, 14. From these passages, it is very manifest that the Lord sends the Holy Spirit, that is, operates those things, which at this day are ascribed to the Holy Spirit, as to a God by himself; for He said that He was about to send him from the Father; that He was about to send him to you; that the Holy Spirit was not yet, because Jesus was not yet glorified; that after the glorification *He breathed into the disciples, and said, Receive ye the Holy Spirit;* and also that He said, *Whatsoever ye shall ask the Father in my name, I will do;* as also that *the Paraclete is about to receive of mine, what He will announce.* That the Paraclete is the same with the Holy Spirit, may be seen, John xiv. 26. That God the Father does not operate those virtues of Himself through the Son, but that the Son of Himself operates them from the Father, is evident from these words: *No one hath ever seen God; the only-begotten Son, who is in the bosom of the Father, He hath manifested Him*, John i. 18; and in another place, *Ye have not heard the voice of the Father at any time, nor seen his shape*, v. 37. From these, therefore, it follows, that God the Father operates in the Son, and into the Son, but not by the Son; but that the Lord operates of Himself from the Father; for He says, *All things of the Father are mine*, John xvi. 14; *that the Father hath given all things into the hand of the Son*, iii. 35; and also that, *As the Father hath life in Himself, so He hath given to the Son to have life in Himself*, v. 26; as also, *The words which I speak are spirit and life*, vi. 63. The reason why the Lord says that the Spirit of truth proceeds from the Father, John xv. 26, is, because it proceeds from God the Father into the Son, and out of the Son from the Father; wherefore also He says, *In that day ye shall know that the Father is in Me, and I in the Father, and ye in Me, and I in you*, xiv. 11, 20. From these plain declarations of the Lord, an error in the Christian world is very manifest, which is, that God the Father sends the Holy Spirit to man; and the error of the Greek church, that the Holy Spirit proceeds immediately from God the Father. This, that the Lord of Himself sends Him from the Father, and not *vice versâ*, is from heaven; and the angels call it an *arcanum*, because it was never before made known in the world.

154. These things may be illustrated by many things which are of reason, as by these: It is known that the apostles, after they had received the gift of the Holy Spirit from the Lord, preached the Gospel through a great part of the world, and that they promulgated it by speaking and writings; and they did this of themselves from the Lord; for Peter taught and wrote in one manner, James in another, John in another, and Paul in another; each according to his own intelligence; the Lord filled them all with his Spirit, but each took of it a portion according to the quality of his perception, and they exercised it according to the quality of their ability. All the angels in the heavens are filled by the Lord, for they are in the Lord and the Lord in them; but still each speaks and acts according to the state of his mind, some in simplicity, some in wisdom, so with an infinite variety; and yet every one speaks of himself from the Lord. It is similar with every minister of the church, whether he be in truths or in falsities; each has his own mouth and his own intelligence, and each speaks from his own mind, that is, from his spirit which he possesses. All the Protestants, whether they are called Evangelical or Reformed, after they have been instructed in the tenets delivered by Luther, Melancthon, or Calvin,—these leaders or their tenets do not of themselves speak through their followers, but their followers of themselves from them; every single tenet also may be explained in a thousand ways, for it is like a *cornucopia*, from which every one takes out what is favorable and adapted to his own genius, and explains it according to his own talent. This may be illustrated by the action of the heart in the lungs and into them, and by the re-action of the lungs of themselves from the heart; these are two distinct things, but still reciprocally united; the lungs respire of themselves from the heart, but not the heart by the lungs; if this should be done, both would stop. It is similar also with the action of the heart in the viscera and into the viscera of the whole body; the heart sends forth the blood in all directions, but the viscera receive it thence, each one its proper share, according to the kind of use which it performs, and also acts according to it; thus each acts differently. The same thing may be illustrated by these: Evil from parents, which is called *hereditary*, acts in man and into man; in like manner, good from the Lord; the latter from above or from within, the former from below or from without; if evil should act by man, he would not be capable of being reformed, nor would he be a subject of blame; in like manner, if good from the Lord should act by man, he would not be capable of being reformed; but because each depends on the free choice of man, he becomes guilty when he acts of himself from evil, and guiltless when he acts of himself from good. Now, because evil is the devil, and good is the Lord, he becomes guilty if he acts from the devil, and guiltless if he acts from the Lord. It is from that free choice, which every man has, that man is capable of being reformed. It is similar with all the internal and external of man; these are two distinct things, but still reciprocally united; the internal acts in the external and into it, but it does not act by the external; for the internal involves a thousand things, of which the external takes only such as are accommodated to use; for in the internal of man, by which is meant his mind, voluntary

and perceptive, there are great accumulations of ideas in a volume, which, if they should flow out through the mouth of man, would be like the rushing of wind from a pair of bellows. The internal, because it involves universals, may be compared to an ocean, a flower-bed, or a garden, from which the external takes out as much as is sufficient for use. The Word of the Lord is like an ocean, a flower-bed, or a garden; when the Word is in any degree of fullness in the internal of man, then man speaks and acts of himself from the Word, and not the Word through him. It is similar with the Lord, because He is the Word, that is, the Divine Truth and the Divine Good therein; the Lord of Himself, or from the Word, acts in man and into him, but not by him, because man acts and speaks freely from the Lord, while he acts and speaks from the Word. But this may be more familiarly illustrated by the mutual intercourse between the soul and body, which two are distinct, but reciprocally united; the soul acts in the body and into the body, but not by the body, but the body acts of itself from the soul. That the soul does not act by the body, is because they do not consult and deliberate with each other; nor does the soul command or request the body to do this or that, or to speak from its mouth; nor does the body require or ask the soul to give or supply any thing, for every thing of the soul is of the body, mutually and reciprocally. It is similar with the Divine and Human of the Lord; for the Divine of the Father is the soul of his Human, and the Human is his body; and the Human does not ask of its Divine to tell what it shall speak or do; wherefore the Lord says, *In that day ye shall ask in my name, and I do not tell you that I will ask the Father for you; for the Father himself loveth you, because ye have loved Me*, John xvi. 26, 27; *in that day*, is after the glorification, that is, after perfect and absolute union with the Father. This arcanum is from the Lord himself, for those who will be of his New Church

155. It was shown above, in the third article, that that divine virtue, which is meant by the operation of the Holy Spirit, with the clergy in particular, is illustration and instruction. But, in addition to these two, there are two intermediate ones, which are perception and disposition; wherefore there are four, which with the clergy follow in order—*Illustration*, *Perception*, *Disposition*, and *Instruction*. ILLUSTRATION is from the Lord. PERCEPTION is with man according to the state of his mind, formed by doctrinals; if these are true, the perception becomes clear from the light which illustrates; but if they are false, the perception becomes obscure, which, however, may appear as if it were clear from confirmations; but this is from the light of infatuation, which to merely natural sight is like clearness. But DISPOSITION is from the affection of the love of the will; the delight of this love disposes; if this be a delight of the love of evil and the false thence, it excites a zeal which outwardly is fierce, rough, burning, and flaming, and inwardly it is anger, rage, and unmercifulness; but if it be of good, and thence of truth, it is outwardly mild, smooth, thundering and glowing, and inwardly it is charity, grace and mercy. But INSTRUCTION follows as an effect from the preceding as causes. Thus illustration, which is from the Lord, is turned into various lights and into various heats, with every one, according to the state of his mind.

156. VI. THAT THE SPIRIT OF MAN IS HIS MIND, AND WHATEVER PROCEEDS FROM IT.

By the *spirit* of man, in the concrete, no other is meant than his mind; for it is this which lives after death, and then is called a spirit; if good, an angelic spirit, and afterwards an angel; if evil, a satanic spirit, and afterwards a satan. The mind of every man is his internal man, which actually is the man, and is within the external man, which makes its body; wherefore, when the body is rejected, which is done by death, it is in a complete human form. They err, therefore, who believe that the mind of man is only in the head; it is there only in the principles, from which first proceeds every thing that man thinks from the understanding, and acts from the will; but it is in the body, in the derivatives formed for sensation and action; and because inwardly it adheres to the things of the body, it imparts to them sense and motion, and inspires a sort of perception, that the body thinks and acts of itself; but every wise man knows that this is a fallacy. Now, because the spirit of man thinks from the understanding, and acts from the will, and the body not from itself, but from that, it follows, that by the spirit of man, is meant his intelligence and the affection of love, and whatever proceeds from them and operates. That the spirit of man signifies such things as are of the mind, is evident from many passages in the Word, which, while they are only adduced, it may be seen by any one that they are no other. Of the many these are a few:—*Bezaleel was filled with the spirit of wisdom, intelligence and science*, Exod. xxxi. 3. Nebuchadnezzar concerning Daniel, *That an excellent spirit of science, intelligence and wisdom was in him*, Dan. v. 12. *Joshua was filled with the spirit of wisdom*, Deut. xxxiv. 9. *Make for you a new heart and a new spirit*, Ezek. xviii. 31. *Blessed are the poor in spirit, because of such is the kingdom of the heavens*, Matt. v. 3. *I dwell in the contrite and humble spirit, to revive the spirit of the humble*, Isaiah lvii 15. *The sacrifices of God are a broken spirit*, Psalm li. 19. *I will give the robe of praise instead of a contracted spirit*, Isaiah lxi. 3; besides in other places. That *spirit* signifies such things as are of a perverted and wicked mind, is evident from these: *He said to the foolish prophets, who go away after their own spirit*, Ezek. xiii. 3. *Conceive chaff, bring forth stubble; as to your spirit, fire shall devour you*, Isaiah xxxiii. 11. *A man who wanders in spirit, and babbles falsehood*, Micah ii. 11. *A generation whose spirit was not steadfast with God*, Psalm lxxviii. 8. *The spirit of whoredoms*, Hosea v. 4; Zech. iv. 12. *That every heart may melt, and every spirit may be contracted*, Ezek. xxi. 7. *That which ascendeth upon your spirit shall never be done*, Ezek. xx. 32. *Only in his spirit there is no guile*, Psalm xxxii. 2. *The spirit of Pharaoh was troubled*, Gen. xli. 8. In like manner of *Nebuchadnezzar*, Dan ii. 3. From these and very many other passages, it is very manifest that *spirit* signifies the mind of man, and such things as are of the mind.

157. Since by the *spirit* of man is meant his mind, therefore, BY BEING IN THE SPIRIT, which is sometimes said in the Word, is meant a state of the mind separate from the body; and because, in that state, the prophets saw such things as exist in the spiritual world, therefore that is called the *vision of God*. Their state then was such as that of spirits themselves is, and angels in that world. In that state, the spirit of man, like his mind as to sight, may be transported from place to place, the body remaining in its own. This is the state in which I have now been for twenty-six years, with this difference, that I have been in the spirit and at the same time in the body, and only several times out of the body. That Ezekiel, Zechariah, Daniel, and John when he wrote the Revelation, were in that state, is evident from the following passages: EZEKIEL says, *The spirit took me up and brought me back into Chaldea, to the captivity, in the* VISION OF GOD, *in the* SPIRIT OF GOD; *so the vision which I saw ascended upon me*, xi. 1, 24. *That the spirit took him up, and he heard behind him an earthquake*, iii. 12, 14. *That the spirit lifted him up between the earth and the heaven, and carried him away to Jerusalem, and he saw abominations*, viii. 3, and following verses *That he saw four animals, which were cherubs, and various things with them*, i. and x. *And also a new earth, and a new temple, and an angel measuring them*, xl. to xlviii; that he was then in vision and in the spirit, xl. 2, xliii. 15 The case was similar with ZECHARIAH in whom there was then an angel

when he saw *a man riding on horseback among the myrtle-trees*, i. 8, and following verses. *Four horns, and a man in whose hand was a measuring line*, ii. 1, 5, and following verses. *Joshua, the high priest*, v. 1, 6. *Four chariots, going out between two mountains, and horses*, vi. 1, and following verses. In a similar state was DANIEL, when he saw *four beasts coming up out of the sea, and many more things concerning them*, vii. 1, and following verses; when he saw *the battles of the ram and the he-goat*, viii. 1, and following verses. That he saw those things *in vision*, vii. 1, 2, 7, 13; viii. 2; x. 1, 7, 8; *that the angel Gabriel appeared to him in vision, and talked with him.* The case was similar with JOHN, when he wrote the Revelation, who says *that he was in the spirit on the Lord's day*, Rev. i. 10. *That he was carried in the spirit* into the wilderness, xvii. 3; upon a high mountain *in the spirit*, xxi. 10. That he saw *in vision*, ix. 17; and in other places, that *he saw* those things which he described; as that he saw the Son of man in the midst of the seven candlesticks; a tabernacle, a temple, an ark, and an altar, in heaven; the book sealed with seven seals, and four horses going out of it; the four animals around the throne; the twelve thousand chosen out of each tribe; the Lamb on Mount Zion; locusts ascending out of the abyss; the dragon and his battle with Michael; a woman bringing forth a male child, and fleeing into the wilderness on account of the dragon; two beasts, one ascending out of the sea, and the other out of the earth; a woman sitting upon a scarlet-colored beast; the dragon cast into a lake of fire and sulphur; a white horse, and a great supper; the holy city Jerusalem coming down, described as to the gates, the wall, and its foundations; the river of living water, and the trees of life yielding fruit every month; besides many other things. In a similar state were Peter, James, and John, when they saw Jesus transfigured; and Paul, when he heard from heaven ineffable things.

158. A COROLLARY. Since we have treated, in this chapter, concerning the HOLY SPIRIT, it deserves particularly to be observed, that, in the Word of the Old Testament, the Holy Spirit is nowhere named, but only the Spirit of Holiness, in three places; once in David, Psalm li. 13; and twice in Isaiah, lxiii. 10, 11; but in the Word of the New Testament, both in the Evangelists and in the Acts of the Apostles, and in their Epistles, frequently: the reason is, because the Holy Spirit was then for the first time, when the Lord came into the world, for it proceeds out of Him from the Father; for THE LORD ONLY IS HOLY, Rev. xv. 4; wherefore also it is said, by the angel Gabriel, to Mary the mother, *The Holy Thing which shall be born of thee*, Luke i. 35. The reason why it was said, *The Holy Spirit was not yet, because Jesus was not yet glorified*, John vii. 39, and yet it is said before, that the Holy Spirit filled Elisabeth, Luke i. 41, and Zechariah i. 67, as also Simeon, ii. 25, was, because the Spirit of Jehovah the Father filled them, which was called the Holy Spirit, on account of the Lord, who was already in the world. This is the reason why, in the Word of the Old Testament, it is nowhere said that the prophets spoke from the Holy Spirit, but from Jehovah; for every where it is said, *Jehovah spoke to me; The word of Jehovah came to me*; *Jehovah said: the saying of Jehovah.* That no one may doubt but that it is so, I will cite only from Jeremiah, where these things are said: i. 4, 7, 11, 12, 13, 14, 19; ii. 1, 2, 3, 4, 5, 9, 19, 22, 31; iii. 1, 6, 10, 12, 14, 16; iv. 1, 3, 9, 17, 27; v. 11, 14, 18, 22, 29; vi. 6, 9, 12, 15, 16, 21, 22; vii. 1, 3, 11, 13, 19, 20, 21; viii. 1, 3, 12, 13; ix. 2, 6, 8, 12, 14, 16, 21, 23, 24; x. 1, 2, 13; xi. 1, 6, 9, 11, 17, 18, 21, 22; xii. 14, 17; xiii. 1, 6, 9, 11, 12, 13, 14, 15, 25; xiv. 1, 10, 14, 15; xv. 1, 2, 3, 6, 11, 19, 20; xvi. 1, 3, 5, 9, 14, 16; xvii. 5, 9, 20, 21, 24; xviii. 1, 5, 6, 11, 13; xix. 1, 3, 6, 12, 16; xx. 4; xxi. 1, 4, 7, 8, 11, 12; xxii. 2, 5, 6, 11, 18, 24, 29, 30; xxiii. 2, 5, 7, 12, 15, 24, 29

31 38; xxiv. 3, 5, 8; xxv. 1, 3, 7, 8, 9, 15, 27, 28, 29, 32; xxvi. 1, 2, 18; xxvii. 1, 2, 4, 8, 11, 16, 19, 21, 22; xxviii. 2, 12, 14, 16; xxix. 4, 8, 9, 16, 19, 20, 21, 25, 30, 31; xxx. 1, 2, 3, 4, 5, 8, 10, 11, 12, 17, 18; xxxi. 1, 2, 7, 10, 15, 16, 17, 23, 27, 28, 31, 32, 33, 34, 35, 36, 37, 38; xxxii. 1, 6, 14, 15, 25, 26, 28, 30, 36, 41; xxxiii. 1, 2, 4, 10, 12, 13, 17, 19, 20, 23, 25; xxxiv. 1, 2, 4, 8, 12, 13, 17, 22; xxxv. 1, 13, 17, 18, 19; xxxvi. 1, 6, 27, 29, 30; xxxvii. 6, 7, 9; xxxviii. 2, 3, 17; xxxix. 15, 16, 17, 18; xl. 1; xlii. 7, 9, 15, 18, 19; xliii. 8, 10; xliv. 1, 2, 7, 11, 24, 25, 26, 30; xlv. 1, 2, 5; xlvi. 1, 23, 25, 28; xlvii. 1; xlviii. 1, 8, 12, 30, 35, 38, 40, 43, 44, 47; xlix. 2, 5, 6, 7, 12, 13, 16, 18, 26, 28, 30, 32, 35, 37, 38, 39; l. 1, 4, 10, 18, 20, 21, 30, 31, 33, 35, 40; li. 25, 33, 36, 39, 52, 58—these only in Jeremiah; the like is said in all the other prophets, and not that the Holy Spirit spoke, nor that Jehovah spoke to them by the Holy Spirit.

---

159. To the above I shall add the following RELATIONS. Once, when I was in company with the angels in heaven, I saw, at a distance below, a great smoke, and occasionally fire bursting out of it; and then I said to the angels who were talking with me, that few here know that the smoke, seen in the hells, arises from falses confirmed by reasonings, and that fire is anger kindling against those who contradict; to which I added, that this is as unknown in this world, as it is in the world where I live in the body, that flame is no other than smoke set on fire: that it is so, I have often proved by experiment, for I have seen smoke ascending from the wood in the fire-place, and when I applied fire to it by a lighted torch, I saw that smoke turned into flame, and this in a similar form with that; for each particle of smoke becomes a spark, and they all blaze together, as is also the case with lighted gunpowder. It is similar with the smoke which we see below; this consists of as many falses, and the fire bursting forth as a flame there, is the kindling of zeal in favor of them. Then the angels said to me, "Let us pray to the Lord, that we may descend and approach, so that we may perceive what are the falses, which with them thus smoke and burn." And leave was given; and lo, there appeared around us a pillar of light, extending to that place; and then we saw four companies of spirits who were strenuously maintaining that God the Father, because he is invisible, is to be approached and worshipped, and not his Son born in the world, because He is a man and visible. When I looked to the sides, at the left appeared the learned of the clergy, and behind them the unlearned; and at the right the learned of the laity, and behind them the unlearned; but between us and them there was a yawning gulf, which could not be passed. But we turned our eyes and ears to the left, where were the learned of the clergy, and behind them the unlearned, and we heard them reasoning concerning God after this manner: "We know from the doctrine of our church, which is one concerning God, in the whole European world, that God the Father, because He is invisible, is to be approached, and, at the same time, God the Son and God the Holy Ghost, who also are invisible, because coeternal with the Father; and because God the Father is the Creator of the universe, and thence in the universe, whithersoever we turn our eyes, He is present, and when we pray to Him, He graciously hears, and, after having accepted of the Son's mediation, he sends the Holy Ghost, who brings into our hearts the glory of his Son's righteousness, and blesses us: we, being appointed teachers of the church, while we preached, sensibly perceived the holy operation of that mission in our breasts, and were animated in devotion by his presence in our minds. We are affected thus because we direct all our senses towards the invisible God, who operates not singly in the sight of our understanding, but universally in the whole system of our mind and body, by his emis-

sary Spirit: such effects would not result from the worship of a visible God, or one who is conspicuous to our minds as a man." At these words, the unlearned of the clergy, who stood behind them, clapped their hands, and added this: "Whence is any thing holy but from the Divine, unseen and imperceptible; at this, as soon as it touches the drum of our ears, the features of our faces expand, and we are exhilarated, as it were, by the delights of an odoriferous aura, and also we beat our breasts; it is otherwise with the Divine seen and perceptible; this, when it enters the ear, becomes merely natural, and not divine. For a similar reason the Roman Catholics say their masses in Latin, and the hosts, concerning which they tell divine mystical things, they take out from the recesses of the altars and show, at which, as at the most sacred mysteries, the people fall upon their knees, and breathe out something holy." After this, we turned about towards the right, where stood the learned, and behind them the unlearned, of the laity; and from the learned I heard these things: "We know that the wisest amongst the ancients worshipped an invisible God, whom they called *Jehovah;* but that after these, in the age which succeeded, they made for themselves gods of deceased monarchs, amongst whom were Saturn, Jupiter, Neptune, Pluto, Apollo, and also Minerva, Diana, Venus, Themis, and built temples for them, and performed divine worship; from which worship, when in time it degenerated, arose idolatry, which at length filled the whole world with insanity. We therefore unanimously agree with our priests and elders, that there were and are three divine Persons from eternity, each of whom is God; and it is enough for us that they are invisible." To this the unlearned behind them added, "We agree. Is not God God, and man man? But we know that if any one should state the proposition, *that God is man*, the common herd of mankind, who have a sensual idea concerning God, would accede to it." After these words, their eyes were opened, and they saw us near them; and then, from indignation that we had heard them, they held their peace: but then the angels, by a power given to them, shut up the exterior or lower regions of their thoughts from which they spoke, and opened the interior or higher regions, and from these compelled them to speak concerning God; and then they spoke and said, "What is God? We have not seen his shape nor heard his voice. What then is God, but nature in its firsts and its lasts? This we have seen, for it shines in our eyes; and this we have heard, for it sounds in our ears." On hearing these words, we said to them, "Have you ever seen Socinus, who acknowledged only God the Father, or Arius, who denied the Divine of the Lord the Savior, or any of their followers?" To which they replied, "We have not." "They are," we said, "in the deep below you." And presently some were called up thence, and, being questioned concerning God, they spoke in like manner as those had before, and said, moreover, "What is God? We can make as many gods as we please." And then we said, "It is in vain to talk with you about the Son of God, born in the world; but still we will declare this, that, lest faith concerning God, in Him and from Him, which, because no one ever saw Him, was, in the first and second age, like a beautifully colored bubble of water in the air, in the third and following age should dwindle into nothing, it pleased Jehovah God to descend and assume the Human, and thus to exhibit Himself to view, and to evince, that God is not an imaginary Being, but the Itself, which was, is, and will be from eternity to eternity; and that God is not a word of three letters, but that He is all of reality from Alpha to Omega; consequently, that He is the life and salvation of all who believe in Him as visible, and not of those who say that they believe in an invisible God; for to believe, to see, and to know, make one; wherefore the Lord said to Philip, *He who seeth and knoweth Me, seeth and knoweth the Father;* and, in other places, that it is the will of the Father, that they should believe in the Son, and whosoever believeth in the Son hath eternal life, but he who believeth not the Son, shall not see life, but the anger of God abideth on him. The latter and the former He says in John iii. 15, 16, 36; xiv. 6 to 15." On hearing these things, many of the four companies were so enraged, that smoke and fire came out of their nostrils; wherefore we went away, and the angels, after they had accompanied me home, ascended into their heaven.

160. SECOND RELATION. Once, in company with angels, I walked in the world of spirits, which is in the middle between heaven and hell, into which all men after death first come, and are prepared, the good for heaven, and the bad for hell; and I conversed with them concerning many things, amongst which also concerning this, that in the world, where I am in the body, there appear, in the time of night, innumerable stars, greater and smaller, and that they are so many suns, which only transmit the light into the world of our sun; "and when I saw, that in your world, also, stars are to be seen, I conjectured that these may be as many as there are in the world where I am." The angels, being delighted with this discourse, said that "perhaps there may be as many, since every society of heaven, to those who are under heaven, sometimes shines like a star; and the societies of heaven are innumerable, all arranged in order, according to the varieties of the affections of the love of good, which in God are infinite, and thence from Him innumerable; and because these were foreseen before the creation, I suppose that, according to the number of them, were provided, that is, created, as many stars in the world where men were to live, who will be in a natural material body." When we were thus talking together, I saw in the north a paved way, so crowded with spirits, that there was scarcely room to step between two, and I said to the angels, that I had also seen this way before, and that I had heard that this was the way through which all pass, who depart from the natural world. The reason why that way was covered with so great a number of spirits, is because several myriads of men die every week, and all those after death pass into this world. To this the angels added, that that way is terminated in this world in the middle of it, where we now are; the reason why it is terminated in the middle of it, is, because on the side towards the east are the societies which are in love to God and towards the neighbor; and to the left, towards the west, the societies of those who are contrary to those loves; and forwards, in the south, the societies of those who are more intelligent than the rest. Thence it is, that new comers from the natural world first come hither. When they are here, they then are in the externals, in which they were last in the former world, and afterwards they are successively let into their internals, and are explored as to their quality, and, after exploration, are carried, the good to their places in heaven, and the bad to their places in hell.

We stopped in the middle, where the crowded way terminated, and said, "Let us stay here a little while, and speak with some of the new comers." And we chose twelve from the multitude; and, because they all had just come from the natural world, they knew no otherwise than that they were still there; and we asked them what they thought concerning HEAVEN and HELL, and what concerning A LIFE AFTER DEATH. To which ONE of them replied, that "Our sacred order impressed upon me the belief, that we shall live after death, and that there is a heaven and a hell; and thence I have believed that all who live morally come into heaven; and, because all do live morally, that none goes to hell, and thus that hell is a fable, invented by the clergy, that people may be deterred from living wickedly. What matter is it, if I think concerning God so or so? Thought is only like chaff, or a bubble upon the water, which bursts and goes off." ANOTHER near him said, "It is my belief, that there is a heaven and a hell, and that God governs heaven, and the devil hell; and because they are enemies, and thence opposed to each other, one calls evil what the other calls good; and that the moral man, who can dissemble, and cause evil to appear as good, and good as evil, stands on the side of both. What, then, is the difference, whether I am with the one or the other Lord, if he only favors me? Evil and good equally delight men." A THIRD at the side of him said, "Why should I believe that there is a heaven and a hell, for who has come thence and told? If every man lived after death why should not one out of so great a multitude have returned and told." A FOURTH near him said, "I will inform you why no one has ever returned and told: the reason is, because man, as soon as he expires and dies, then either becomes a spectre, and is dissipated, or is like the breath of the mouth, which is only wind. How can such a one return and speak with any one?" A FIFTH followed him, and said, "My friends, wait till the day of the last judgment, because all will then return into their own bodies, and you will see them, and talk with them, and then they will tell each other their destinies." A SIXTH, standing opposite, and smiling, said, "How can a spirit, which is wind, return into a body eaten up by worms, and, at the same time, into its skeleton, burnt up by the sun, and reduced to dust? and how can any one, made an Egyptian mummy, and mixed by the apothecary with various medicines, which have been eaten or drunk, return and relate any thing? Wherefore wait, if you have faith, till that last day; but you may wait forever and ever in vain." The SEVENTH after this said, "If I believed that there is a heaven and a hell, and thence a life after death, I should also believe that birds and beasts would likewise live. Are not some of them equally as moral and rational as men? It is denied that beasts live; wherefore I deny that men do: the reason is equal; one follows from the other. What is man but an animal?" An EIGHTH, standing behind him, came up, and said, "Believe there is a heaven, if you will; but I do not believe there is a hell. Is not God omnipotent? and is He not able to save every one?" Then a NINTH, patting his hand, said, "God is not only omnipotent, but also gracious, and cannot send any one into eternal fire; and if any one is there, He cannot but take him out thence, and lift him up." A TENTH ran out of his rank into the midst, and said, "Neither do I believe there is a hell. Did not God send his Son, and did not He make an atonement, and take away the sins of the whole world? What, then, can the devil avail against that? And because he cannot avail any thing, what then is hell?" An ELEVENTH, who was a priest, on hearing this, grew warm and said, "Do you not know, that those who have obtained the faith, on which the merit of Christ is inscribed, are saved, and that those whom God elects obtain that faith? Is not election according to the will of the Almighty? and is it not his prerogative to judge who are worthy? Who can do any thing against his will and judgment?" The TWELFTH, who was a politician, was silent; but, being asked to crown all with an answer, he said, "I shall not say any thing concerning heaven, hell, and a life after death, since no one knows any thing about them; but still allow the priests, without rebuke, to preach those things; for thus the minds of the vulgar are held bound by an invisible bond to the laws and rulers: does not the public safety depend on this?"

We were astonished at hearing such things, and said amongst ourselves, "These, although they are called Christians, are not men nor beasts, but men-beasts." But, in order to awaken them out of sleep, we said, "There is a heaven and a hell, and there is a life after death; you will be convinced that there is, when we dispel the ignorance concerning the state of life in which you now are; for every one, in the first days after death, knows no otherwise than that he still lives in the same world in which he lived before; for the time past is like a sleep from which, when any one is awaked, he perceives no otherwise than that he is where he was. It is similar with you now; wherefore you have spoken just as you thought in the former world." And the angels dispelled their ignorance, and then they saw themselves in another world, and amongst those whom they did not know; and then they exclaimed, "Oh, where are we?" And we said, "You are no longer in the natural world, but in the spiritual world, and we are angels." Then, after being awaked, they said, "If you are angels, show us heaven." And we replied, "Stay here a little while, and we will return." And on our return, after a half an hour, we saw them expecting us, and said, "Follow us into heaven." And they followed, and we ascended with them; and because we were with them, the keepers opened the gate, and let us in. And we said to those who at the threshold receive new comers, "Explore those." And they turned them about, and saw that the back parts of their heads were very hollow; and then they said, "Depart from hence, because the delight of your love is that of doing evil, and thence you are not conjoined to heaven, for in your hearts you have denied God and despised religion." And we then said to them, "Do not stay, because, if you do, you will be cast out." And they hastened down and departed.

In the way home, we spoke concerning the cause why the back parts of the heads of those who have the delight of doing evil, are in this world hollow; and I said this was the cause, that man has two brains, one in the back part of the head, which is called the *cerebellum*, and the other in the fore part, which is called the *cerebrum*, and that in the *cerebellum* dwells the love of the will, and in the *cerebrum* the thought of the understanding; and that, when the thought of the understanding does not lead the love of man's will, the inmost parts of the *cerebellum*, which in themselves are celestial, fall down flat, and thence there is a hollowness.

161. Third Relation. Once I heard in the spiritual world a sound like that of a mill; it was in the northern region of it. At first I wondered what this meant; but I recollected that by a mill, and grinding in a mill, is meant to search the Word for things serviceable for doctrine; wherefore I went up to the place where the sound was heard, and when I was near, the sound ceased; and then I saw a kind of arched roof above the ground, the entrance to which was through a cave; on seeing which, I descended and entered; and behold there was a vault, in which I saw an old man sitting amongst books, holding before him the Word, and searching in it for things serviceable for his doctrine. Little scraps of paper lay around, on which he wrote what was serviceable to his purpose. In a contiguous room there were scribes, who collected the little scraps, and transcribed those things which were written upon them on a whole sheet of paper. I inquired first concerning the books around him. He said that they all treated concerning justifying faith; those from Sweden and Denmark profoundly, those which were from Germany more profoundly, those which were from Britain still more profoundly, and those which were from Holland most profoundly. And he added, that in various points they differ, but in the article concerning justification, and salvation by faith alone, they all agree. Afterwards he said that he was now collecting from the Word this first article of justifying faith, that "God the Father fell out of favor towards mankind, on account of their iniquities; and that, therefore, in order to save men, there was a divine necessity that satisfaction, reconciliation, propitiation and mediation should be made by some one, who should take upon himself the sentence of justice, and that this could not possibly have been done but by his only Son; and that, after this was done, a way of access was opened to God the Father for his sake; for we say 'Father, have mercy on us for the sake of the Son.'" And he said, "I see and have seen that this is according to all reason and Scripture. How otherwise could God the Father have been

approached, but through faith in the merit of the Son?" I heard this, and was astonished that he should say that it was according to reason and according to Scripture, when yet it is contrary to reason and contrary to Scripture, which also I plainly told him. He then, in the heat of his zeal, rejoined, "How can you talk so?" Wherefore I opened my mind, saying, "Is it not contrary to reason, to think that God the Father fell out of favor [grace] towards mankind, and reprobated and excommunicated them? Is not divine grace [favor] an attribute of the Divine Essence? Wherefore, to fall out of favor [grace] would be to fall out of the Divine Essence; and to fall out of his Divine Essence would be to be no longer God. Can God be alienated from Himself? Believe me, that grace, on the part of God, as it is infinite, is also eternal; the grace of God, on the part of man, may be lost, if he does not receive it; if grace should recede from God, all heaven and all the human race would inevitably perish; wherefore grace remains on the part of God to eternity, not only towards angels and men, but also towards the devils in hell. Since this is according to reason, why do you say that the only way of access to God the Father is through faith in the merit of the Son, when yet there is perpetual access through grace? But why do you say access to God the Father *for the sake* of the Son, and not *through* the Son? Is not the Son the Mediator and Savior? Why do you not go to the Mediator and Savior himself? Is not He God and Man? Does any one on earth go immediately to any Cæsar, king or prince? Should there not be some one to procure admission and introduce him? Do you not know that the Lord came into the world that He might introduce us to the Father? and that no access is given except through Him? and that this access is perpetual, when you go immediately to the Lord himself, since He is in the Father and the Father in Him? Search now in the Scripture, and you will see that this is according to it, and that your way to the Father is as contrary to it as it is to reason. I tell you also that it is great effrontery to climb up to God the Father, and not through Him who is in the bosom of the Father, and alone with Him. Have you not read John xiv. 6?" On hearing these words, the old man was enraged to such a degree, that he sprang out of his seat, and called to his scribes that they should cast me out; and when I went out immediately, of my own accord, he threw after me, out of the doors, the book which his hand happened to seize, and that book was the Word.

162. Fourth Relation. A dispute arose amongst spirits, whether any one can see any doctrinal theological truth in the Word, except from the Lord. They all agreed in this, that no one can, except from God, because *no one can take any thing, unless it be given him from heaven*, John iii. 27. Wherefore it was disputed, whether any one can, unless he goes to the Lord immediately. They said, on one side, that the Lord ought to be approached directly, because He is the Word; on the other side, that doctrinal truth may also be seen when God the Father is approached immediately: wherefore the dispute came to this first principle, Whether it be lawful for any Christian to go to God the Father immediately, and thus to climb over the Lord, and whether this be not indecent and rash insolence and audacity, because the Lord says that *no one cometh to the Father except through Him*, John xiv. 6. But they left this and said, that man can see doctrinal truth from the Word by his own natural light; but this was rejected: wherefore they insisted that it may be seen by those who pray to God the Father. And something was read to them from the Word, and then they prayed upon their knees that God the Father would enlighten them; and to the words which were read to them from the Word, they said that this and that was true there; but it was false: thus several times, even till they were tired. At length they confessed that they could not. But those, on the other hand, who went to the Lord immediately,

saw truths, and informed the others. After this dispute was thus ended, there ascended from the abyss some who appeared at first like locusts, and afterwards like dwarfs; they were those who, in the world, prayed to God the Father, and confirmed justification by faith alone. They were the same that are treated of in the Revelation, ix. 1 to 11. These said that they saw this, *That man is justified by faith alone, without the works of the law*, in clear light, and also from the Word. Being asked, by what faith; they replied, "In God the Father." But after they were explored, it was told them from heaven, that they did not know even one doctrinal truth from the Word. But they rejoined, that they still saw their truths in the light; then it was said to them, that they saw them in the light of infatuation. They asked, "What is the light of infatuation?" and were informed that the light of infatuation is the light of the confirmation of the false, and that that light corresponds to the light in which owls and bats are, to which darkness is light, and light is darkness. This was confirmed by the fact, that, when they looked upwards to heaven, where light itself is, they saw darkness, and when they looked downwards to the abyss, whence they were, they saw light. Being indignant at this confirmation, they said, that thus light and darkness are not any thing, but only states of the eye, from which it is said, that light is light, and darkness is darkness. But it was shown that they had the light of infatuation, which is the light of the confirmation of the false, and that their light was only the activity of their mind, arising from the fire of concupiscences; not unlike the light of cats, whose eyes (in consequence of their burning appetite for mice) appear like candles in cellars in the night. On hearing this, they were angry, and said that they were not cats, nor like cats, because they could see, if they would; but, because they were afraid of being asked why they would not, they retired, and let themselves down into their abyss. Those who are there, and others like them, are also called, by the angels, owls and bats, and also locusts.

When they came to their companions in the abyss, and told that the angels said, that we "do not know any doctrinal truth, not even one, and that they called us owls, bats, and locusts," a tumult was made there; and they said, "Let us pray to God, that we may be permitted to ascend, and we will clearly demonstrate that we have many doctrinal truths, which the archangels themselves will acknowledge." And because they prayed to God, permission was given, and they ascended, to the number of three hundred. And when they appeared above the earth, they said, "We were in the world celebrated and renowned, because we knew and taught the mysteries of justification by faith alone: from confirmations, we not only saw the light, but we saw it like a glittering brightness, and in like manner we do now in our cells; and yet we have heard from our companions, who were with you, that that light was not light, but darkness, because we have not, as you said, any doctrinal truth from the Word. We know that every truth of the Word shines; and we believe that our coruscation, while we meditated profoundly on our mysteries, was thence derived. Wherefore we will demonstrate, that we have truths from the Word in great abundance." And they said, "Have we not this truth, that there is a Trinity, God the Father, the Son, and the Holy Spirit, and that we must believe in the Trinity? Have we not this truth, that Christ is our Redeemer and Savior? Have we not this truth, that Christ alone is righteousness, and that He alone has merit; and that he is unjust and wicked, who wishes to claim to himself any thing of his merit and righteousness? Have we not this truth, that no mortal can from himself do any spiritual good, and that all good, which in itself is good, is from God? Have we not this truth, that there is a meritorious and a hypocritical good, and that those goods are evils? Have we not this truth, that still good works should be done? Have we not this truth, that faith is, and that we ought to believe in God, and that every one has life according as he believes; besides many others from the Word? Can any of you deny one of those? And yet you said that we have not any truth in our schools, not even one. Did you not lay such things to our charge without any reason?" But then they were answered, that "All those things, which you have advanced, are in themselves truths, but with you they are truths falsified, which are falses, because they are derived from a false principle. That it is so, we will also demonstrate to the eye. There is a place, not far hence, into which the light from heaven flows directly; in the middle of it, there is a table; and when any paper, on which a truth from the Word is written, is laid upon it, that paper, from the truth written on it, shines like a star. Write, therefore, your truth on a paper, and let it be laid upon the table, and you will see." They did so, and gave it to the keeper, who laid it upon the table, and then said to them, "Move back, and look at the table." And they moved back, and looked; and, behold! that paper shone like a star; and then the keeper said, "You see that they are truths which you wrote on the paper; but come up nearer, and fix your eyes on the paper." And they did so, and then suddenly the light disappeared, and the paper became black, as if it were covered with the soot of a furnace. And, moreover, the keeper said, "Touch the paper with your hands, but beware that you do not touch the writing." And when they did so, a flame burst forth and consumed it. After these things were seen, it was told them, that if they had touched the writing, they would have heard a noise, and would have burnt their fingers. And then it was said to them, by those who stood behind, "You see now that the truths, which you have abused to confirm the mysteries of your justification, are truths in themselves, but that they are truths falsified in you." They then looked upwards, and heaven appeared to them like blood, and afterwards like thick darkness; and they appeared to the eyes of the angelic spirits, some like bats, some like owls, and some like other birds of night; and they fled away into their own darkness, which to their eyes shone with the light of infatuation.

The angelic spirits who were present wondered, because they did not know any thing before concerning that place, and the table there; and then a voice came to them from the southern region, saying, "Come up hither, and you will see something still more wonderful." And they came up, and entered into an arched room, whose walls glittered as it were from gold; and they saw there also a table, upon which the Word lay, decorated on all sides with precious stones, in a celestial form. Then the angel, who kept it, said, "Whenever the Word is opened, there darts from it a light of ineffable brightness; and then, at the same time, from the precious stones, there appears, as it were, a rainbow above and around the Word. When any angel from the third heaven comes thither, there appears, above and around the Word, a rainbow in a red ground; when an angel from the second heaven comes thither and looks, there appears a rainbow in a blue ground; when an angel from the lowest heaven comes thither and looks, there appears a rainbow in a white ground; when any good spirit comes thither and looks, there appears a variegation of light, as of marble." That it is so, was also shown to them to the eye. Moreover, the angel, who was the keeper, said, "If any one comes up, who had falsified the Word, then the splendor is immediately dissipated; and if he comes near, and fixes his eyes upon the Word, it becomes, as it were, covered with blood; and then he is admonished to depart, because there is danger." But a certain one, who in the world had been a great champion for the doctrine concerning justification by faith alone, came up boldly, and said, "I, while I was in the world, did not falsify the Word; I exalted charity, also, togeth er with faith, and taught that man, in a state of faith, in which he does charity and its works, is renewed, regenerated and sanctified by the Holy Spirit; and also that faith then does not exist alone, that is, without good works, as a good tree is not without fruit, the sun without light, or fire without heat; and also I blamed those who said that good works were not necessary, and moreover that the precepts of the decalogue need not be observed; and also I insisted much on repentance; and thus, in a wonderful manner, I applied all things of the Word to the article concerning faith, which yet I discovered and demonstrated to be the only saving virtue." He, in the confidence of his assertion, that he had not falsified the Word, came up to the table, and, contrary to the admonition of the angel, touched the Word; and then suddenly fire, with smoke, flowed out from the Word, and an explosion was made with a loud noise, by which he was thrown to a corner of the room, and there lay, for half an hour, as if he were dead. The angelic spirits wondered at this; but it was said to them, that this champion had, more than the rest, exalted the goods of charity, as proceeding from faith; but that still he meant no other works than political, which are also called moral and civil, which are to be done for the sake of the world, and prosperity there, and not at all for the sake of salvation; and also, that he supposed hidden works performed by the Holy Spirit, concerning which man knows nothing, which, in a state of faith, are ingenerated in faith.

Then the angelic spirits conversed with each other concerning the falsification of the Word; and in this they agreed, that to falsify the Word, is to take truths from it, and apply them to confirm falses, which is to drag them out of the Word, and to murder them; as, for example, to apply all those truths, which were adduced above by those from the abyss, to the faith now prevalent, and to explain them from it. That this faith is impregnated with falses, will be demonstrated in what follows. And also to take from the Word this truth, that charity should be exercised, and good to the neighbor should be done; if, then, any one attempts to prove that it should be done, but not for the sake of salvation, since all the good from man is not good, because it is meritorious, he drags that truth of the Word out of the Word, and murders it; since the Lord, in his Word, enjoins upon every man, who wishes to be saved, to love the neighbor, and from love to do him good; and so in other cases.

CONCERNING THE DIVINE TRINITY.

163. We have treated concerning God the Creator, and, at the same time, concerning Creation; and afterwards concerning the Lord the Redeemer, and, at the same time, concerning Redemption; and lastly concerning the Holy Spirit, and, at the same time, concerning the Divine Operation: and because we have thus treated concerning the triune God, it is necessary that we should also treat concerning the Divine Trinity, which is known in the Christian world, and yet is unknown. For by this alone a just idea concerning God may be obtained; and a just idea concerning God is, in the church, like the inmost sanctuary and altar in the temple, and like a crown on the head and a sceptre in the hand of a king, sitting upon the throne; for on this depends the whole body of theology, as a chain depends on the staple on which it hangs. And, if you will believe it, every one obtains his place in the heavens, according to the idea of God; for that is, as it were, the touchstone by which the gold and silver is tried; that is, the good and the

true, as to their quality with man; for there is not with him any saving good except from God, nor any truth which does not derive its quality from the bosom of good. But that it may be seen, with both eyes, what the Divine Trinity is, the exposition of it shall be divided into articles, which will be the following: I. *That there is a Divine Trinity, which is the Father, Son and Holy Spirit.* II. *That these three, the Father, Son, and Holy Spirit, are the three essentials of one God, which make one, like soul, body, and operation, with man.* III. *That, before the world was created, there was not this Trinity, but that after the world was created, when God became incarnate, it was provided and made, and then in the Lord God, the Redeemer and Savior, Jesus Christ.* IV. *That a Trinity of Divine Persons from eternity, or before the world was created, is, in the ideas of thought, a Trinity of Gods; and that this cannot be abolished by the oral confession of one God.* V. *That a Trinity of Persons was unknown in the Apostolic Church, but that it was first broached by the Nicene Council, and thence introduced into the Roman Catholic Church, and from this into the Churches separated from it.* VI. *That from the Nicene and Athanasian Trinity together, a faith arose, which had perverted the whole Christian Church* VII. *That thence is that abomination of desolation and affliction, such as has not been, nor will be, which the Lord had predicted in Daniel and the Evangelists, and in the Revelation.* VIII. *And also this, that, unless a New Heaven and a New Church be established by the Lord, no flesh could be saved.* IX. *That from a Trinity of Persons, each of whom singly is God, according to the Athanasian Creed, many absurd and heterogeneous ideas about God have existed, which are fantasies and abortions.* These will now be explained one by one.

164. I. THAT THERE IS A DIVINE TRINITY, WHICH IS THE FATHER, SON, AND HOLY SPIRIT.

That there is a Divine Trinity, the Father, the Son and the Holy Spirit, is very evident from the Word, and from these things there:—*The angel Gabriel said unto Mary, The* HOLY SPIRIT *shall come upon thee, and the* VIRTUE OF THE MOST HIGH *shall overshadow thee; wherefore the Holy Thing that is born of thee, shall be called* THE SON OF GOD, Luke i. 35. Here three are named, the Most High, who is God the Father, the Holy Spirit, and the Son of God. *When Jesus was baptized, behold, the heavens were opened, and John saw* THE HOLY SPIRIT *descending like a dove, coming upon Him; and a voice from heaven, saying, This is* MY BELOVED SON, *in whom I am well pleased,* Matt. iii. 16, 17; Mark i. 10, 11; John i. 32. And still more plainly from these words of the Lord to the disciples: *Go, make all nations disciples, baptizing them in the name of* THE FATHER, AND OF THE SON, AND OF THE HOLY SPIRIT, Matt. xxviii. 19; and moreover from these words in 1 John v. 7: *There are three who bear witness in heaven,* THE FATHER, THE WORD, *and* THE HOLY SPIRIT. And besides these things, that the Lord prayed to his Father, and spoke concerning Him and with Him; and that He said that He would send the Holy Spirit, and also that He did send Him; and moreover, that the apostles in their epistles frequently named the Father, and the Son, and the Holy Spirit. From these things it is manifest, that there is a Divine Trinity, which is the Father, Son, and Holy Spirit.

165. But how those are to be understood; whether that they are three Gods, who, in essence, and thence in name, are one God; or that they are three objects of one subject, so that they are only qualities or attributes of one God, which are so named; or that they are to be understood in some other manner, reason, left to it self, can by no means see. But what must be done? No other direction is given, than that man should go to the Lord God the Savior, and read the Word under his influence (for he is the God of the Word), and he will be enlightened, and will see truths which

reason also will acknowledge. But, surely, if you do not go to the Lord, although you should read the Word a thousand times, and should see there a Divine Trinity and Unity too, you would never understand any other, than that there are three Divine Persons, each one of whom, singly, is God, and thus three Gods. But because this is repugnant to the common perception of all men in the whole world, therefore, to avoid disgrace, they have invented this expedient—that, although there are in reality three Gods, still faith requires that not three Gods should be named, but one; and moreover, lest they should be overwhelmed with censures, as to this, especially, the understanding must be imprisoned, and held bound under obedience to faith; and this must be established as a law of Christian order in the Christian church hereafter. Such a paralytic birth was produced from this, that they did not read the Word under the influence of the Lord; and every one who does not read the Word under his influence, reads it under the influence of his own intelligence; and this is like an owl in respect to such things as are in spiritual light, as are all the essentials of the church; and he, while he reads such things in the Word as concern a Trinity, and from them thinks, that, although there are three, still they are one, this appears to him similar to the answer from a tripod, which, because he does not understand it, he rolls between his teeth; for if he should put it before his eyes, it would be an enigma, which the more he endeavors to unfold, the more he involves himself in darkness, until he begins to think concerning it without understanding, which is like seeing without an eye. In short, to read the Word under the influence of one's own intelligence, which is done by all who do not acknowledge the Lord as the God of heaven and earth, and thence approach and worship Him alone, may be likened to children playing, who tie a handkerchief before their eyes, and wish to walk on a straight line; and also they think that they do so, and yet, step by step, they turn aside, and at length proceed in the opposite direction, and strike against a stone, and fall down. And also they are like mariners, who sail without a compass, and direct the vessel against the rocks, and perish And also they are like one who walks over a wide plain, in a thick fog, and sees a scorpion, and believes it to be a bird, and wishes to catch it with his hand, and takes it up, and then is pierced with a deadly wound. They are also like a cormorant or a kite, which sees a little of the back of a great fish above the water, and flies upon it, and fixes its beak into it, and is drawn under by the fish, and is drowned. They are also like one who enters a labyrinth without a guide or a thread; and the further he goes in, the more he forgets the way out. The man who does not read the Word under the influence of the Lord, but under the influence of his own intelligence, believes himself to be a lynx and to have more eyes than Argus, when yet, interiorly, he does not see a particle of truth, but only the false; and when he has persuaded himself that this is true, it appears to him like the polar star, to which he directs all the sails of his thought; and then he sees truths no more than a mole; and if he does see any, he bends them in favor of his own fancy, and thus perverts and falsifies the holy things of the Word.

166. II. That these three, the Father, Son, and Holy Spirit, are the three Essentials of one God, which make one, like the Soul, Body, and Operation, with Man.

There are general and also particular essentials of one thing, and both together make one essence. The general essentials of one man are his soul, body, and operation. That these make one essence, may be seen from this, that one is from another, and for the sake of another, in a continual series; for man begins from the soul, which is the very essence of the seed: this not only initiates, but also produces in their order those things which are of the body, and afterwards the things which proceed from those two, the soul and body together, which are called *operations*: wherefore, from the production of one from another, and thence the insertion and conjunction, it is manifest that these three are of one essence, which are called three essentials.

167. That those three essentials, viz. the soul, body, and operation, were and are in the Lord God the Savior, every one acknowledges. That his soul was from Jehovah the Father, can be denied only by Antichrist, for in the Word of both Testaments He is called *the Son of Jehovah, the Son of the Most High God, the Only-begotten;* therefore the Divine of the Father, like the soul in man, is his first essential. That the Son, whom Mary brought forth, is the body of that divine soul, follows from this, that no other than the body, conceived and derived from the soul, is prepared in the womb of the mother; this, therefore, is another essential. That operations make the third essential, is because they proceed from the soul and body together; and those things which proceed are of the same essence with those which produce them. That the three essentials, which are the Father, Son, and Holy Spirit, are one in the Lord, like the soul, body, and operation, in man, is very evident from the words of the Lord, that the Father and He are one, and that the Father is in Him and He in the Father; in like manner, that He and the Holy Spirit are one, since the Holy Spirit is the Divine, proceeding out of the Lord from the Father, as was above, n. 153, 154, fully demonstrated from the Word; wherefore to demonstrate this again would be superfluous, and like loading a table with food, when the guests have eaten to satiety.

168. When it is said, that the Father, Son and Holy Spirit, are the three essentials of one God, like the soul, body and operation, in man, it appears to the human mind as if those three essentials were three persons, which is not possible; but when it is understood, that the Divine of the Father, which makes the soul, and the Divine of the Son, which makes the body, and the Divine of the Holy Spirit, or the proceeding Divine, which makes the operation, are the three essentials of one God, then it falls into the understanding. For the Father is his own Divine, the Son his from the Father, and the Holy Spirit his from both; which, because they are of one essence, and unanimous, make one God. But if those three divine essentials are called persons, and to each one is attributed his own property, as, to the Father imputation, to the Son mediation, and to the Holy Spirit operation, then the divine essence becomes divided, which yet is one and indivisible; so not any one of the three is God in fullness, but each in subtriplicate power, which a sound understanding cannot but reject.

169. Who, therefore, cannot perceive a trinity in the Lord from the trinity in every man? In every man there is a soul, body, and operation; in like manner in the Lord, *for in the Lord dwelleth all the fullness of the Godhead bodily*, according to Paul, Col. ii. 9; wherefore the trinity in the Lord is divine, but in man it is human. Who does not see, that, in the mystical notion, that there are three divine persons, and yet one God, and that this God, although he is one, still is not one person, reason has no part; but that, being lulled to sleep, it still compels the mouth to speak like a parrot? When reason is lulled to sleep, what, then, is the speech of the mouth but inanimate? When the mouth speaks that from which reason dissents and departs, what then is the speech but foolish? At this day, human reason is bound, as to the Divine Trinity, like a man bound with manacles and fetters in prison; and it may be compared to the vestal virgin, buried in the earth, because she let the sacred fire go out, when yet the Divine Trinity ought to shine like a lamp in the minds of the men of the church, since God, in his Trinity, and in its Unity, is all, in all the sanctities of heaven and the church For what else would it be, to make one God of the soul, another of the body, and a third of the operation, than to

make of those three essentials of one man, three parts distinct from each other? And what would this be but to behead and kill him?

170. III. That this Trinity was not before the World was created, but that after the World was created, when God became incarnate, it was provided and made; and then in the Lord God, the Redeemer and Savior, Jesus Christ.

In the Christian church, at this day, there is acknowledged a Divine Trinity, before the world was created, which is, that Jehovah God from eternity begat a Son, and that from both the Holy Spirit then proceeded, and that each one of those three is by himself, or singly, God, because each one is a person subsisting of himself. But this, because it does not fall into any reason, is called a mystery, into which entrance can be made only by this, that those three have one divine essence, by which is meant eternity, immensity, omnipotence, and thence equal divinity, glory, and majesty. But that this is a Trinity of three Gods, and thus not any Divine Trinity, will be demonstrated in what follows. But that the Trinity, which also is of the Father, Son, and Holy Spirit, which was provided and made after God became incarnate, consequently after the world was created, is a Divine Trinity, which is of one God, is evident from all the things which precede. That this Divine Trinity is in the Lord God, the Redeemer and Savior Jesus Christ, is, because the three essentials of one God, which make one essence, are in Him. That all the fullness of the Godhead is in Him, according to Paul, is evident also from the words of the Lord himself, that all things of the Father are His, and that the Holy Spirit does not speak from itself, but from Him; and besides, that He took from the sepulchre, when He arose, his whole human body, both as to the flesh and as to the bones, Matt. xxviii. 1 to 8; Mark xvi. 5, 6; Luke xxiv. 1, 2, 3; John xx. 11 to 15, otherwise than any other man; which also he testified to his disciples, to the life, saying, *See my hands and my feet, that it is I myself; feel of Me and see, for a spirit hath not flesh and bones, as ye see Me have*, Luke xxiv. 39. From this every man may be convinced, if he will, that the Human of the Lord is Divine; consequently, that in Him God is Man, and Man God.

171. The Trinity, which the present Christian church has embraced and introduced into its faith, is, that God the Father begat a Son from eternity, and that the Holy Spirit then proceeded from them both, and that each one is God by himself. This Trinity can be conceived by human minds no otherwise than as a triarchy, or a government of three kings in one kingdom, or of three generals over one army, or of three masters in one house, each of whom has equal power: what thence can ensue but destruction? And if any one wishes to figure or shadow forth this triarchy to the sight of his mind, and at the same time their unity, he cannot present it to his contemplation otherwise than as a man of three heads upon one body, or of three bodies under one head. Such a monstrous image of the Trinity must appear to those who believe there are three divine persons, and each one God by himself, and conjoin them into one God, and deny that God, because He is one, is one person. That a Son of God, born from eternity, descended and assumed the Human, may be compared to the fables of the ancients, that human souls were created at the beginning of the world, and that they enter into bodies and become men; and also to those absurd opinions, that the soul of one passes into another, as many in the Jewish church believed; as, that the soul of Elijah passed into the body of John the Baptist; and that David is to return into his own or another's body, and to reign over Israel and Judah; because it is said in Ezekiel, *I will raise up over them one shepherd, who shall feed them, my servant David; he shall be to them for a shepherd, and I Jehovah will be to them for a God, and David a prince in the midst of them*, xxxiv

23, 24, 25, besides other places; not knowing that by David there is meant the Lord.

172. IV. That a Trinity of Divine Persons from Eternity, or before the World was created, is, in the Ideas of Thought, a Trinity of Gods; and that this cannot be abolished by the oral Confession of one God.

That a Trinity of Divine Persons from eternity is a Trinity of Gods, is very evident from these words in the Athanasian Creed: "There is one person of the Father, another of the Son, and another of the Holy Ghost. The Father is God and Lord, the Son is God and Lord, and the Holy Ghost is God and Lord; but yet there are not three Gods and Lords, but one God and Lord; because, as we are compelled by Christian verity to confess each person singly God and Lord, so we are forbidden by the Catholic religion to say three Gods or three Lords." This creed is received as ecumenical or universal by the whole Christian church; and all that is, at this day, known and acknowledged concerning God, is thence. That no other Trinity than a Trinity of Gods, was understood by those who were in the Nicene council, from which the creed which is called the *Creed of Athanasius* proceeded, as a posthumous birth, every one who only reads it with open eyes, may see. That a Trinity of Gods was understood not only by them, but also that no other Trinity is understood in the Christian world, follows, because thence is all the knowledge concerning God, and every one remains in the belief of the words there. That no other Trinity than a Trinity of Gods, is at this day understood in the Christian world, I appeal to every one, both layman and clergyman, both laurelled masters and doctors, and consecrated bishops and archbishops, and also to purple cardinals, yea, to the Roman pontiff himself; let every one consult himself, and then speak out from the ideas of his own mind. From the words of this universally received doctrine concerning God, this is as manifest and clear as water through a crystal cup, both that there are three persons, and that each one of them is God and Lord, and also that from Christian verity or truth they ought to confess or acknowledge every person, singly, God and Lord, but that the Catholic or Christian religion or faith forbids them to say or name three Gods and Lords; and thus that *truth* and *religion*, or *truth* and *faith*, are not one thing, but two things contrary to each other. But as to what is added, that *there are not three Gods and Lords, but one God and Lord*, it was done lest they should be exposed to ridicule before the whole world; for who would not laugh at *three Gods?* But who does not see a contradiction in what is added? But if they had said, that the Father has the divine essence, the Son the divine essence, and the Holy Spirit the divine essence, but that there are not three divine essences, but that the divine essence is one and indivisible, then that mystery would be explicable; as when, by the Father, is understood the Divine from which [are all things], by the Son, the Divine Human thence, and by the Holy Spirit, the proceeding Divine, which three are of one God; or if by the Father the like is understood as by the soul with man, by the Divine Human, the like as by the body of that soul, and by the Holy Spirit, the like as by the operation which proceeds from both, then are understood three essences, which are of one and the same person, and thus they together make one and an indivisible essence.

173. The reason why the idea of three Gods cannot be abolished by the oral confession of one God, is, because that is implanted in the memory from childhood, and every man thinks from those things which are there. The memory with men, is like the ruminatory stomach with birds and beasts; into that stomach, they put the food by which they are to be nourished, and, by turns, take it out thence, and let it down into the stomach, in which it is digested, and dispensed to all the uses of the body. The human understand-

ing is this stomach, as the memory is the former. Every one may see, that the idea of three divine persons from eternity, which is the same with the idea of three Gods, cannot be abolished by the oral confession of one God, only from this, that it has not yet been abolished, and that there are, amongst the celebrated, those who are not willing that it should be abolished; for they insist that the three divine persons are one God, but obstinately deny that God, because He is one, is also one person. But what wise man does not think with himself, that by *person* is not meant person exactly, but the predication of some quality; but *what* quality, is not known; and because it is not known, that which was implanted in the memory from childhood remains, like the root of a tree in the earth, from which, if the tree is cut down, a shoot springs up. But, my friend, not only cut down that tree, but also pull up its root, and then plant in your garden trees of good fruit. Beware, therefore, lest there be fixed in your mind the idea of three Gods, and lest the mouth, which has in it no idea, sound *one God*. What, then, is the understanding above the memory, which thinks of three Gods, and the understanding below it, from which the mouth at the same time speaks out *one God*, but like an actor upon a theatre, who can act two persons, by running across from one side to the other, and on one side say something, and on the other contradict it, and, by such altercation, call himself here a wise man, and there a fool? What else results thence, than that, whilst he stands in the middle, and looks towards both sides, he should think that the one and the other is not any thing? and thus, perhaps, that there is not one God, and that there are not three, consequently none? The naturalism, reigning at this day, is from no other origin. In heaven, no one can say a *trinity of persons*, each one of whom singly is God; for the heavenly *aura*, in which their thoughts, like sounds in our air, fly and undulate, strives against it. But a hypocrite alone can do it there; but the sound of his voice, in the heavenly *aura*, grates like a tooth gnashing against a tooth, or croaks like a raven wishing to sing like a nightingale. I have heard, also, from heaven, that it is as impossible to abolish the faith established in the mind by confirmations in favor of a Trinity of Gods, by the oral confession of one God, as it is to draw a tree through its seed, or the chin of a man through a single hair of his beard.

174. V. That a Trinity of Persons was unknown in the Apostolic Church; but that it was first broached by the Nicene Council, and was thence introduced into the Roman Catholic Church, and from this into the Churches separated from it.

By the *Apostolic Church*, is meant not only the church which was in various places in the time of the apostles, but also in the two or three centuries after their times. But at length they began to pull off the door of the temple from its hinges, and to rush like thieves into its sacred recess. By the *temple* is meant the church, by the *door*, the Lord God the Redeemer, and by the *sacred recess*, his divinity; for Jesus says, *Verily I say unto you, he who entereth not through the door into the sheep-fold, but climbeth up any other way, is a thief and a robber. I am the door; if any one shall enter through Me, he shall be saved.* This wicked deed was done by Arius and his followers; wherefore a council was convened by Constantine the Great, at Nice, a city in Bithynia; and by those convened there, in order to cast out the damnable heresy of Arius, it was devised, concluded, and confirmed by sanctions, that there were three divine persons from eternity, the Father, the Son, and the Holy Spirit, each of whom had a personality, existence, and subsistence, by himself, and in himself; and also that the second person, or the Son, descended and assumed the Human, and performed redemption; and that thence his Human, by a hypostatic union, had divinity, and that by this union He had a close affinity with God the Father. From that time, heaps of abominable heresies, concerning God and concerning the person of Christ, began to spring out of the earth, and to exalt the head of Antichrist, and to divide God into three, and the Lord the Savior into two, and thus to destroy the temple erected by the Lord through the apostles, and this so effectually that one stone was not left upon another, which was not thrown down, according to his own words, Matt. xxiv. 2; where, by the *temple*, is not meant the temple at Jerusalem only, but also the church, the consummation or end of which is treated of in the whole of that chapter. But what else could be expected from that council, and the following ones, which in like manner divided the Godhead into three persons, and placed the incarnate God under them upon their footstool? For they removed the head of the church from its body by this, that they *climbed up another way;* that is, they passed by Him, and climbed up to God the Father as to another, only with the mention of Christ's merit in the mouth, that He would have mercy for the sake of that, and that thus might immediately flow in, justification with all its train, which is, the remission of sins, renovation, sanctification, regeneration, and salvation, and these without the use of any means on the part of man.

175. That the apostolic church did not know any thing at all concerning a trinity of persons, or concerning three divine persons from eternity, is very evident from the creed of that church, which is called the Apostles' Creed, where are these words: ***I believe in God the Father Almighty, the Creator of heaven and earth; and in Jesus Christ, his only Son, our Lord, who was conceived by the Holy Spirit, born of the Virgin Mary; and in the Holy Spirit.*** There no mention is made of any Son from eternity, but of the Son conceived by the Holy Spirit and born of the Virgin Mary; they knowing from the apostles that Jesus Christ was the true God, 1 John v. 21; and that in Him dwelt all the fullness of the Godhead bodily, Col. ii. 9; and that the apostles preached faith in Him, Acts xx. 21; and that he had all power in heaven and in earth, Matt. xxviii. 18.

176. What confidence is to be had in councils, whilst they do not go immediately to the God of the church? Is not the church the body of the Lord, and He its head? What is a body without a head? What sort of a body is that on which are placed three heads, under whose direction they hold consultations and make decrees? Does not illustration, which is spiritual, being from the Lord alone, who is the God of heaven and the church, and at the same time the God of the Word, become then more and more natural, and at length sensual? And then not any genuine theological truth is perceived in its internal form, but it is immediately cast out from the thought of the rational understanding, and dispersed like chaff into the air from the winnower's fan; in which state fallacies then succeed instead of truths, and darkness instead of the rays of light; and then they stand, as it were, in a cavern, with spectacles upon their noses, and a candle in their hands, and close their eye-lids to spiritual truths, which are in the light of heaven, and open them to sensual truths, which are in the false light of the senses of the body. The case is similar afterwards, whilst the Word is read; then the mind is asleep as to truths, and awake as to falses, and it becomes, as the beast from the sea is described, *as to the mouth like a lion, as to the body like a leopard, and as to the feet like a bear*, Rev. xiii. 2. It is said in heaven, that, when the Nicene council was closed, these things were accomplished, which the Lord foretold to the disciples—*The sun shall be darkened, and the moon shall not give her light, and the stars shall fall from heaven, and the virtues of the heavens shall be shaken*, Matt. xxiv. 29. And, indeed, the apostolic church was like a new star appearing in the starry heaven; but the church after the two Nicene councils, became like the same star afterwards, when it

is darkened and disappears, as also has sometimes happened in the natural world, according to the observations of astronomers. In the Word it is read, that Jehovah dwelleth in light inaccessible: who then can go to Him, unless He should dwell in light accessible; that is, unless He should descend and assume the Human, and in this should become the light of the world, John i. 9, xii. 46. Who cannot see, that to go to Jehovah the Father, in his light, is as impossible, as it is for one to take the wings of the morning, and to fly by means of them to the sun? or as it is to feed one's self with the rays of the sun, and not with elementary food? or as it is for a bird to fly in ether, or for a stag to run in air?

177. VI. That from the Nicene and Athanasian Trinity, together, a Faith arose which had perverted the whole Christian Church.

That the Nicene, and also the Athanasian Trinity, is a Trinity of Gods, may be seen above, shown from their creeds, n. 172. Thence arose the faith of the present church, which is in God the Father, God the Son, and God the Holy Spirit:—in God the Father, that He imputes the righteousness of the Savior, his Son, and ascribes it to man; in God the Son, that He intercedes and mediates; in the Holy Spirit, that He actually inscribes the imputed righteousness of the Son, and seals it, when established, by justifying, sanctifying and regenerating man. This is the faith of the present time, which alone can testify, that it is a Trinity of Gods which is acknowledged and worshipped. From the faith of every church is derived not only all its worship, but also all its doctrine; wherefore it may be said, that such as its faith is, such is its doctrine. That that faith, which is a faith in three Gods, has perverted every thing of the church, follows thence; for faith is the principle, and doctrinals are derivatives; and the derivatives derive their essence from the principle. If any one examines the doctrinals, one by one, as that which is concerning God, concerning the person of Christ, concerning charity, concerning repentance, concerning regeneration, concerning free will, concerning election, concerning the use of the sacraments, baptism and the holy supper, he will clearly see, that a Trinity of Gods is in every one of them; and if it does not actually appear to be in them, still they flow from it, as from their fountain. But because such an examination cannot be made here, and yet it is important that it should be made, in order to open the eyes, therefore an appendix will be added to this work, in which this will be demonstrated. The faith of the church concerning God, is like the soul of the body, and doctrinals are like its members; and, moreover, faith in God is like a queen, and doctrinal tenets are like the officers of her court; and as these depend on the authority of the queen, so doctrinal tenets depend on the declaration of faith. From that faith alone, it may be seen how the Word is understood in the church that possesses it; for faith applies to itself, and draws to itself, as it were by ropes, whatsoever it can. If the faith be false, it commits whoredom with every truth there, and perverts and falsifies it, and causes man to be insane in spiritual things; but if the faith be true, then the whole Word favors it, and the God of the Word, who is the Lord God the Savior, infuses light, gives the testimony of his divine assent, and makes man wise. That the faith of the present time, which, in the internal form, is that of three Gods, but in the external form, that of one God, has extinguished the light in the Word, and removed the Lord from the church, and thus precipitated its morning into night, will be seen also in the appendix. This was done by heretics before the Nicene council, and afterwards by the heretics of that council, and after it. But what confidence is to be placed in councils, who do not *enter through the door into the sheep-fold, but* CLIMB UP SOME OTHER WAY, according to the words of the Lord in John x. 1, 9? Their deliberation is not unlike the walking of a blind man in the day, or of a man who has good eyes in the night, neither of whom sees the pit before he has fallen into it. For example, what confidence ought we to place in the councils which established the vicarship of the pope, the canonization of the dead, and the invocation of them as deities, the worship of their images, the authority of indulgences, the division of the eucharist, besides other things? Also, what confidence ought we to place in the council which established an abominable predestination, and hung this up before the temples of their church, as the palladium of religion? But, my friend, go to the God of the Word, and thus to the Word, and so enter through the door into the sheep-fold, that is, into the church, and you will be enlightened; and then you will see, as from a mountain, not only those of many others, but your own former steps and wanderings, in the thick woods under the mountain.

178. The faith of every church is, as it were, the seed, from which all its dogmas spring; and it may be compared to the seed of a tree, from which all the parts of it, even to the fruit, are derived; and also to the seed of man, from which are produced children and families in a successive series. Wherefore, when the primary faith, which, from its predominance, is called *saving*, is known, it is perceived what is the quality of the church. This may be illustrated by this example: Let the faith be, that nature is the creator of the universe. From this, these things follow, that the universe is what is called *God;* that nature is his essence; that ether is the supreme God, whom the ancients called *Jupiter;* that the air is a goddess, whom the ancients called *Juno*, and made the wife of Jupiter; that the ocean is a God below them, who, with the ancients, may be called *Neptune;* and because the divinity of nature reaches even to the centre of the earth, that there also is a God, who, in conformity with the ancients, may be called *Pluto;* that the sun is the palace of all the gods, in which they assemble, whenever Jupiter summons a council; and, moreover, that fire is life from God; and thus that birds fly in God, beasts walk in God, and fishes swim in God; and, further, that thoughts are only modifications of ether, as words from them are only modulations of air; and that the affections of love are occasional changes of state, from the influx of the sun's rays into the ether and air: moreover, that a life after death, together with heaven and hell, is a fable, invented by the clergy, for the purpose of procuring honors and gains; but although it is a fable, that still it is useful, and ought not to be openly despised, because it is serviceable to the public for keeping the minds of the simple in the bond of obedience to magistrates; but that, still, those who are inveigled into religion, are abstract men, their thoughts phantasms, and their actions ludicrous, and that they are the drudges of the priests, who believe what they do not see, and see what exceeds the sphere of their mind. These consequences, and many others like them, are contained in that faith, that nature is the creator of the universe; and they proceed from it as soon as it is opened. These things are adduced, that it may be known that, in the faith of the present church, which, in its internal form, is in three Gods, and in its external form, in one, there are falsities in abundance; and that thence may be brought forth as many as there are little spiders in a heap of eggs laid by one spider. Any one, whose mind has been made truly rational by light from the Lord, may see this; but how will any other see it, when the door to that faith and its offspring is shut and barred by the statute, that it is unlawful for reason to look into its mysteries?

179. VII. That thence is that Abomination of Desolation and Affliction, such as has not been, nor will be, which the Lord had foretold in Daniel, and the Evangelists, and in the Revelation.

These words are read in Daniel: *At length upon the bird of abominations, desolation, and even to the consummation and decision, it shall drop upon the devastation*, ix. 27. In the evangelist Matthew, the Lord says these words: *Then many false prophets will rise up, and will seduce many: when, therefore, ye shall see the abomination of desolation, foretold by the prophet Daniel, standing in the holy place, let him who readeth note it well,* xxiv. 15: and afterwards in the same chapter, *There will then be great affliction, such as has not been since the beginning of the world until now, neither shall be,* 21. This affliction and that abomination are treated of in seven chapters in the Revelation, and they are what are meant by the black horse and by the pale horse, coming out of the book whose seal the Lamb opened, Rev. vi. 5 to 8; also by the beast coming up out of the abyss, which made war with the two witnesses, and slew them, ix. 7, and following verses; as also by the dragon which stood before the woman who was about to bring forth, that he might devour her child, and pursued her into the wilderness, and there cast out from his mouth water like a flood, that he might drown her, xii.; and also by the beasts of the dragon, one from the sea and the other from the earth, xiii.; also by the three spirits like frogs, which came out of the mouth of the dragon, out of the mouth of the beast, and out of the mouth of the false prophet, xvi. 13; and moreover by this, that, after the seven angels poured out the vials of the anger of God, in which were the seven last plagues, into the earth, into the sea, into the fountains and rivers, into the sun, into the throne of the beast, into the Euphrates, and at length into the air, there was a great earthquake, such as had not been since men were made, xvi. An earthquake signifies an inversion of the church, which is effected by falses and falsifications of the truth, which likewise is signified by the great affliction such as was not since the beginning of the world, Mat. xxiv. 21. Similar things are meant by these words: *The angel thrust in the sickle, and harvested the vine of the earth, and cast it into the great wine-press of the anger of God; and the wine-press was trodden, and blood came out even to the horses' bridles, for a thousand six hundred furlongs,* xiv. 19, 20; *blood* signifies truth falsified; besides many other things in those seven chapters.

180. In the evangelists, Matt. xxiv. Mark xiii. and Luke xxi., are described the successive declensions and corruptions of the Christian church; and there, by the great affliction such as was not since the beginning of the world, neither shall be, is meant, as every where else in the Word, the infestation of truth by falses, until there does not remain any truth which is not falsified and consummated: this also is meant by the abomination of desolation there; and this likewise is meant by the desolation upon the bird of abominations, and by the consummation and decision in Daniel; and this same thing is described in the Revelation by those passages which have just been adduced thence. This was effected by this, that the church did not acknowledge the Unity of God in Trinity, and his Trinity in Unity, in one person, but in three; and thence founded the church in the mind, upon the idea of three Gods, and in the mouth, upon the confession of one God; for thus they separated themselves from the Lord, and at length so far, that they had no idea of the divinity in his human nature remaining, when yet He is God the Father Himself in the Human; wherefore, also, He is called the Father of eternity, Isaiah ix. 5; and he says to Philip, ***He who seeth Me, seeth the Father***, John xiv. 7, 9.

181. But it is asked, Whence is the vein itself of the fountain, from which such abomination of desolation, as is described in Daniel, ix. 27, and such affliction as never was nor ever will be, Matt. xxiv. 21, has flowed? The answer is, From the faith which universally prevails in the Christian world, and from its influx, operation, and imputation, according to traditions. It is wonderful that the doctrine of justification by that faith alone, although it is not faith, but a chimera, should gain every point in Christian churches, that is, that it should reign there amongst the clergy, almost as the only essential of theology. It is that which all young students in theology eagerly learn, im-

imbibe and suck in at the universities; and which, afterwards, as if inspired with heavenly wisdom, they teach in the churches, and publish in books; by which also they seek and obtain the name of superior erudition, fame and glory; for which also degrees, diplomas and rewards are conferred: and these things are done, although by that faith alone, the sun is now darkened, the moon is deprived of her light, the stars of the heavens are fallen, and the virtues of the heavens are shaken, according to the words of the prediction by the Lord in Matt. xxiv. 29. That the doctrine of that faith has at this day blinded the minds of men to such a degree that they will not, and thence, as it were, they cannot, see any divine truth interiorly in the light of the sun, nor in the light of the moon, but only exteriorly, upon some rough surface, in the light of a fire by night, has been proved to me: wherefore I can say with confidence, that if divine truths concerning the genuine conjunction of charity and faith, concerning heaven and hell, concerning the Lord, concerning the life after death, and concerning eternal felicity, written in letters of silver, should be sent down from heaven, they would not be esteemed worth reading by the justifiers and sanctifiers by faith alone; but, on the other hand, if a treatise concerning justification by faith alone, should be sent from hell, this they would take up, kiss, and carry home in their bosom.

182. VIII. Also this, that unless a New Heaven and a New Church be established by the Lord, no Flesh would be saved.

It is read in Matthew, *Then there will be great affliction, such as has not been from the beginning of the world until now, nor ever will be: yea, unless those days should be shortened, no flesh would be saved*, xxiv. 21, 22. That chapter treats concerning the consummation of the age by which is meant the end of the present church: wherefore by shortening those days, is meant to put an end to that church, and to institute a new one. Who does not know, that, unless the Lord had come into the world and performed redemption, no flesh could have been saved? By performing redemption is meant, to establish a new heaven and a new church. That the Lord is to come again into the world, He foretold in the evangelists, Matt. xxiv. 30, 31; Mark xiii. 26; Luke xii. 40; xxi. 27; and in the Revelation, particularly in the last chapter. That he is also at this day performing a redemption, by establishing a new heaven and instituting a new church, in order that man may be saved, was shown above, in the lemma concerning redemption. The great arcanum, that unless a new church be instituted by the Lord, no flesh can be saved, is this, that, as long as the dragon with his crew continues in the world of spirits, into which he was cast, so long there cannot any divine truth united to divine good, pass through to the men of the earth, without being perverted and falsified, or destroyed It is that which is meant by this passage in the Revelation: *The dragon was cast out into the earth, and his angels were cast out with him. Wo to the inhabitants of the earth and the sea, because the devil has come down to them, having great anger*, xii. 9, 12, 13. But after the dragon was cast into hell, xx. 10, then John saw the new heaven and the new earth, and he saw the New Jerusalem coming down from God out of heaven, xxi. 1, 2. By the dragon, are meant those who are in the faith of the present church.

I have several times conversed, in the spiritual world, with the justifiers of men by faith alone, and have said that their doctrine is erroneous, and also absurd, and that it induces carelessness, blindness, sleep, and night, in spiritual things, and thence the death of the soul, and exhorted them to desist from it. But I have received for answer, "Why desist? Does not the excellence of the erudition of the clergy above that of the laity, depend on that alone?" But I replied, that thus they do not regard the salvation of souls as any end, but the excellence of their own fame; and that, because they have applied the truths of the Word to their fals-

principles, and thus have adulterated them, they are angels of the abyss, called *Abaddons* and *Apollyons*, Rev. ix. 11; by which are signified the destroyers of the church, by the total falsification of the Word. But they replied, "What of that? By our knowledge of the mysteries of that faith, we are oracles, and from it, as from the most sacred part of a temple, we give responses; wherefore we are not Apollyons, but APOLLOS." Being indignant at this, I said, "If you are Apollos, you are also LEVIATHANS; the first of you crooked Leviathans, and the second in rank, oblong Leviathans, which God will visit with his hard and great sword," Isaiah xxvii. 1. But they laughed at these words.

183. IX. THAT FROM A TRINITY OF PERSONS, EACH OF WHOM SINGLY IS GOD, ACCORDING TO THE ATHANASIAN CREED, MANY ABSURD AND HETEROGENEOUS IDEAS CONCERNING GOD HAVE EXISTED, WHICH ARE FANTASIES AND ABORTIONS.

From the doctrine of three divine persons from eternity, which, in itself, is the head of all the doctrinals in Christian churches, have arisen many unbecoming ideas concerning God, unworthy of the Christian world, which yet ought to be, and might be, a luminary to all the people and nations in the four parts of the earth, concerning God and his Unity. All who live out of the Christian church, as well Mahometans as Jews, and, besides these, the Gentiles of every worship, are averse to Christianity, solely on account of the faith of three Gods there. The propagators of it know this, and therefore they are very cautious not to teach openly a Trinity of persons such as it is in the Nicene and Athanasian creeds, since, in that case, they would forsake and ridicule them. The absurd, ludicrous and frivolous ideas, which have arisen from the doctrine of three divine persons from eternity, and which arise with every one, who remains in the belief of the words of that doctrine, and, from the eyes and ears, rise up into the sight of the thought, are these; That God the Father sits above the head on high, and the Son at his right hand, and the Holy Ghost before them, listening, and forthwith running over all the world; and, according to their decision, He dispenses the gifts of justification and inscribes them, and makes them, from sons of wrath, sons of grace, and from condemned, elect. I appeal to the learned of the clergy, and to the learned of the laity, whether they entertain any other than this ideal view in their minds; for that flows in of its own accord from the doctrine itself; see the RELATION above, n. 16. There also flows in a curiosity of conjecturing what they conversed about among themselves, before the world was created; whether about the world which was to be created, or whether also about those who were to be predestinated and justified, according to the Supralapsarians, or whether also about redemption; and likewise what they conversed about since the world was created; the Father from the authority and power of imputing, the Son from the power of mediating, and that imputation, which is election, is from the mercy of the Son interceding for all, and particularly for some, and that for them the Father has favor, being moved from love towards the Son, and from the misery seen in Him upon the wood of the cross. But who cannot see that such things are deliriums of the mind concerning God? And yet they are, in Christian churches, the holy things which are to be kissed with the mouth, but are not to be viewed with the eye of the mind, because they are things above reason, which, if they are elevated from the memory into the understanding, make a man insane. But still this does not remove the idea of three Gods, but induces a stupid faith, from which man thinks concerning God as if he were asleep in a dream, walking in the darkness of night, or like one blind from his birth in the light of day.

184. That a Trinity of Gods is fixed in the minds of Christians, although for shame they deny it, is very evident from the ingenuity of many in demonstrating that three are one, and one three, by various things in geometry,

stereometry, arithmetic, and natural philosophy, and likewise by the folding of pieces of cloth and paper; thus they play tricks among themselves, with the divine Trinity, like jugglers. Their juggling concerning it may be compared to the sight of the eye of persons in a fever, who see one object, whether it be a man, or a table, or a candle, as three, or three as one. It may also be compared with the mockery of those who turn soft wax between their fingers, and mould it into various forms, now into a triangular form, that they may show the Trinity; now into a spherical form, that they may show the Unity; saying, "Is it not still one and the same substance?" when yet the Divine Trinity is like a pearl of the greatest value; but, when divided into persons, it is like a pearl divided into three parts, whence it entirely loses its value.

---

185. To the above will be added these RELATIONS. FIRST. In the spiritual world, there are climates and zones, as well as in the natural world; there is not any thing given in the latter which is not also in the former; but they differ in origin. In the natural world, the varieties of climates are according to the distances of the sun from the equator; in the spiritual world, they are according to the distances of the affections of the will, and thence of the thoughts of the understanding, from true love and true faith; all the things there are correspondences of these. In the frigid zones, in the spiritual world, there appear similar things as in the frigid zones in the natural world; the lands there appear bound up with ice, and likewise the waters, and also snow upon them. Those come thither and dwell there, who, in the world, lulled their understandings to sleep by indolence in thinking about spiritual things, and who are thence, at the same time, indolent about doing any uses: they are called *boreal spirits*. Once I was seized with a desire of seeing some country in the frigid zone where those boreal spirits were; and therefore I was led in the spirit to the north, even to a region where all the land appeared covered with snow, and all the water congealed with ice. It was the day of the Sabbath; and I saw men, that is, spirits, of a similar stature with men of the world; but, on account of the cold, they were clad, as to the head, with the skin of a lion, whose mouth had been applied to their mouth; but as to the body, before and behind, as far as above the loins, they were covered with the skins of leopards; and as to the feet, with the skins of bears. And also I saw many riding in chariots, and some in chariots carved in the shape of a dragon, whose horns were extended forwards. Those chariots were drawn by little horses whose tails had been cut off; they were running like terrible wild beasts, and the driver, holding the reins in his hands, was continually impelling and urging them on their course. I saw, at length, that the multitudes were flocking to a temple, which, because it was covered with snow, had not been seen. But the keepers of the temple were loosening the snow, and, by digging, were preparing an entrance for the worshippers who had arrived; and they descended, and entered. It was given me also to see the temple within. It was illuminated with lamps and candles in abundance; the altar there was of hewn stone, behind which there was hanging a tablet, on which it was written, THE DIVINE TRINITY, FATHER, SON AND HOLY GHOST, WHO ESSENTIALLY ARE ONE GOD, BUT PERSONALLY THREE. At length the priest, standing at the altar, after he had kneeled thrice at the tablet of the altar, with a book in his hand, ascended the pulpit, and began a sermon by speaking of the Trinity, and exclaimed, "Oh, how great a mystery! that God in the Highest begat a Son from eternity, and by Him brought forth the Holy Ghost, which three joined themselves together by essence, but separated themselves by properties, which are imputation, redemption, and operation! but if we look into these things by reason, its sight is blinded, and a spot is made

before it, as before the eye of him who fixes his gaze upon the naked sun. Wherefore, my hearers, as to this, let us keep the understanding under obedience to faith." After this, he exclaimed again, "Oh, how great a mystery is our holy faith! which is this; that God the Father imputes the righteousness of the Son, and sends the Holy Ghost, who, by that imputed righteousness, operates the pledges of justification, which, in the sum, are the remission of sins, renovation, regeneration and salvation; concerning whose influx or act, man knows no more than the pillar of salt into which Lot's wife was turned, and concerning whose indwelling, or state, he knows no more than a fish in the sea. But, my friends, there is hid in it a treasure, so entirely covered and concealed, that not a grain of it appears. Wherefore, as to that also, let us keep the understanding under obedience to faith." After some sighs, he exclaimed again, saying, "Oh, how great a mystery is election! He is elected, to whom God imputes that faith, which, according to a free purpose, and of pure grace, He infuses into whomsoever He will, and when He will; and man is like a stock when it is being infused, but he becomes like a tree when it is infused; but the fruits, which are good works, hang, indeed, from that tree, which, in a representative sense, is our faith, but still they do not cohere; wherefore the value of that tree is not from the fruit. But, because this sounds like heterodoxy, and yet is a mystical truth, let us, my brethren, keep the understanding under obedience to this faith." And then, after a pause, standing as if he would yet extract something more from the memory, he continued, saying, "From the store of mysteries I will produce yet one more, which is, that man, in spiritual things, has not a grain of free will; for the primates and regular priests of our order, in their theological canons, say that man, in those things which are of faith and salvation, which are properly called *spiritual*, cannot will, think or understand any thing, and cannot even accommodate and apply himself to receive them wherefore I say of myself, that man of himself cannot think concerning those things from reason, and speak from thought, otherwise than like a parrot, a magpie or a raven; so that man, in spiritual things, is truly an ass, and a man only in natural things. But, my friends, lest this should trouble your reason, let us in this, as in the rest, keep the understanding under obedience to faith; for our theology is an abyss without a bottom, into which if you let your understanding look, you will be drowned and lost, as by shipwreck. But still hear: we are, nevertheless, in the very light of the gospel, which shines high above our heads; but, alas! the hair of our heads and the bones of our skulls prohibit and prevent it from penetrating into the inner chamber of our understanding.' Having said this, he descended; and after he had offered a prayer at the altar, and the service was ended, I went up to some who were talking together, where also was the priest in the midst of a circle; to whom those standing about him said, "We give you immortal thanks for a sermon so magnificent and full of wisdom." But then I said to them, "Did you understand any thing?" And they replied, "We received all with full ears; but why do you ask whether we understood it? Is not the understanding amazed in such things?" And the priest added this to what was said: "Because you have heard, and have not understood, you are blessed, since thence is your salvation." Afterwards I spoke with the priest, and asked him if he had a degree; and he replied, "I am a master of arts." And then I said, "Master, I have heard you preaching mysteries: if you know them, and not any thing which they contain, you know nothing; for they are just like caskets locked up with a triple lock which unless you open and look in, (which must be done by the understanding,) you know not whether the things therein are precious, or whether they are worthless, or whether they are noxious; they may be the eggs of an asp, or the web of a spider, according to the description in Isaiah lix. 5." As I spoke these words, the priest looked at me with a crabbed aspect, and the worshippers departed, and mounted their chariots, intoxicated with paradoxes, infatuated with empty words, and enveloped with darkness in all the things of faith, and the means of salvation.

186. Second Relation. I was once engaged in thinking in what region of the mind theological things reside with man, which, because they are spiritual and celestial, I at first supposed would reside in the highest region; for the human mind is distinguished into three regions, as a house is into three stories, and likewise as the habitations of the angels are into three heavens. And then an angel stood before me, and said, "Theological things, with those who love truth because it is truth, rise up even into the highest region, because there is their heaven, and they are in the light in which the angels are; but moral things, theoretically contemplated and perceived, place themselves under those in the second region, because they communicate with spiritual things; and political things under these in the first region; but scientifics, which are manifold, and may be referred to general and particular classes, make the door to those higher things. Those with whom spiritual, moral, political and scientific things are thus subordinated, think what they think, and do what they do, from justice and judgment; the reason is, because the light of truth, which also is the light of heaven, from the highest region, illuminates the things which are below, as the light of the sun, passing through the ethers and air, progressively, illuminates the eyes of men, beasts and fishes. But theological things are not so with those who do not love truth because it is truth, but only for the sake of the glory of their own fame. Theological things with these, reside in the lowest region, where scientifics are, with which, in some cases, they mingle themselves, and, in some cases, they cannot mingle themselves. Under these, in the same region, are political things and under these, moral; since with such persons the two higher regions are not opened on the right side, wherefore they have no interior reason of judgment, nor affection of justice, but only a sort of ingenuity, from which they can speak upon every subject, as if from intelligence, and confirm whatever occurs, as if from reason; but the objects of reason which they principally love are falses, because these cohere with the fallacies of the senses. Thence it is, that there are so many in the world who do not see the truths of doctrine from the Word, more than those who are born blind; and when they hear them, they press together their nostrils, lest their odor should offend them, and excite nausea; but they open all their senses to falses, and draw them in, as a whale does water."

187. Third Relation. Once, when I was meditating about the dragon, the beast and the false prophet, which are mentioned in the Revelation, an angelic spirit appeared to me, and asked, "What are you meditating about?" And I said, "About the false prophet." Then he said, "I will lead you to the place where they are, who are meant by the false prophet; and he said that they are the same that, in the 13th chapter of the Revelation, are meant by the beast from the earth, which had two horns like a lamb, and spoke like a dragon. I followed him, and lo, I saw a crowd, in the midst of which were the leaders of the church, who taught that nothing saves man, but faith in the merit of Christ; and that works are good, but not for salvation; and that still they should be taught from the Word, that the laity, especially the simple, may be kept more strictly in the bonds of obedience to the magistrates, and may be led, as from religion, thus more interiorly, to exercise moral charity. And then one of them, seeing me, said, "Do you wish to see our temple, in which there is an image representative of our faith?" I went and saw it; and lo, it was a magnificent edifice, and in the midst of it there was the image of a woman,

clothed in a scarlet garment, holding in her right hand a golden coin, and in her left a chain of pearls; but both the image and the temple were induced by fantasy; for by fantasies infernal spirits can represent magnificent things, by closing the interiors of the mind, and opening only its exteriors. But when I perceived that it was such a trick, I prayed to the Lord, and suddenly the interiors of my mind were opened; and then I saw, instead of the magnificent temple, a house full of chinks, from the top to the bottom, in which nothing cohered; and I saw in that house, instead of the woman, a pendent image, the head of which was like a dragon, the body like a leopard, the feet like those of a bear, and the mouth like that of a lion; thus in every respect as the beast from the sea is described, Rev. xiii. 2; and in place of a floor, there was a quagmire, in which was a multitude of frogs; and it was told me that under the quagmire there was a large hewn stone, under which lay the Word, entirely concealed. On seeing these things, I said to the juggler, "Is this your temple?" And he said that it was. But then suddenly his interior sight also was opened, from which he saw the same things that I did; on seeing which, he exclaimed, with a loud voice, "What is this? and whence is this?" And I said, "It is from the light of heaven, which discovers the quality of every form, and thus the quality of your faith separate from spiritual charity." And immediately an east wind blew, and carried away the temple, with the image, and also dried up the quagmire, and thus exposed the stone under which lay the Word. And after this, a warmth, like that of spring, breathed from heaven; and lo, then in the same place, there was seen a tabernacle, as to the external form simple; and the angels who were with me said, "Behold the tabernacle of Abraham, such as it was when the three angels came to him, and told concerning Isaac, who was about to be born. This appears to the eyes simple, but still, according to the influx of light from heaven, it becomes more and more magnificent." And it was given them to open the heaven in which were the spiritual angels, who are in wisdom, and then, from the light thence flowing in, that tabernacle appeared like a temple, similar to that at Jerusalem; and, on looking into it, I saw the stone of the foundation, under which the Word was deposited, set around with precious stones, from which bright rays like lightning, shone upon the walls upon which were the forms of cherubs, and beautifully variegated them with colors. When I was admiring these things, the angels said, "You will see something still more wonderful." Then it was given them to open the third heaven, in which were the celestial angels, who are in love; and then, from the flammeous light thence flowing in, the whole of that temple vanished, and instead of it the Lord alone was seen, standing upon the foundation stone, which was the Word, in the same form in which he appeared to John, Rev. i. But because a holy reverence then filled the interiors of the angels' minds, from which they had an inclination to fall prostrate on their faces, the way of light from the third heaven was closed by the Lord, and a way of light from the second heaven was opened; whence returned the former appearance of the temple, and also of the tabernacle, but this in the midst of the temple. Hereby was illustrated what is meant in the Revelation, xxi, by this passage: *The tabernacle of God is with men, and He will dwell with them*, ver. 3: and also by this: *I saw no temple in the New Jerusalem, because the Lord God Omnipotent is the temple of it, and the Lamb*, ver. 22.

188. Fourth Relation. Since it has been given me by the Lord to see the wonderful things which are in the heavens and under the heavens, I ought to relate, according to command, what has been seen. There was seen a magnificent palace, and in the inmost part of it a temple; in the midst of this, there was a table of gold, upon which was the Word, at which stood two angels. About the table there were

three rows of seats; the seats of the first row were covered with silk drapery of a purple color, the seats of the second row with silk drapery of a blue color, and the seats of the third row with white drapery. Under the roof, high above the table, there appeared a curtain spread out, glittering with precious stones, from the splendor of which shone forth, as it were, a rainbow, when the sky is becoming serene after a shower. Suddenly then were seen clergymen sitting upon all the seats, all clothed in the garments of the sacerdotal ministry. On one side there was a vestry, where stood an angel, who was the keeper, and in it lay splendid garments, in beautiful order. It was A COUNCIL CONVENED BY THE LORD; and I heard a voice from heaven, saying, "DELIBERATE." But they said, "On what?" It was said, "Concerning THE LORD THE SAVIOR, and concerning THE HOLY SPIRIT." But when they began to think concerning them, they were not in illustration; wherefore they made supplication, and then light flowed down out of heaven, and illuminated first the hinder parts of their heads, and afterwards their temples, and at last their faces; and then they began to deliberate, and, as it was commanded, FIRST CONCERNING THE LORD THE SAVIOR. The first thing proposed and canvassed was, "WHO ASSUMED THE HUMAN IN THE VIRGIN MARY?" And an angel, standing at the table, on which was the Word, read to them these words from Luke: *Behold, thou shalt conceive in the womb, and shalt bring forth a son, and shalt call his name Jesus; He shall be great, and shall be called* THE SON OF THE MOST HIGH. *And Mary said to the angel, How shall this be done, since I know not a man? And the angel, answering, said,* THE HOLY SPIRIT SHALL COME UPON THEE, AND THE VIRTUE OF THE MOST HIGH SHALL OVERSHADOW THEE; *wherefore* THE HOLY THING *that is born of thee shall be called* THE SON OF GOD, i. 31, 32, 34 35. Then also he read these in Matthew: *The angel said to Joseph in a dream, Joseph, son of David, fear not to take Mary for thy wife,* FOR THAT WHICH IS BORN IN HER IS OF THE HOLY SPIRIT. *And* JOSEPH KNEW HER NOT *until she had brought forth her first-born son, and she called his name Jesus,* i. 20, 25. And besides these passages, he read many more from the evangelists; as Matt. iii. 17, xvii. 5; John i. 18, iii. 16, xx. 31; and many other places, where the Lord, as to the Human, is called THE SON OF GOD, and where He, from his Human, calls Jehovah HIS FATHER; as also from the prophets, where it is foretold that Jehovah Himself was about to come into the world; among which also these two in Isaiah, *It shall be said in that day,* LO, THIS IS OUR GOD, *whom we have expected to deliver us; this is* JEHOVAH, WHOM WE HAVE EXPECTED; *let us be glad and rejoice in his salvation,* xxv. 9. *The voice of one crying in the wilderness, Prepare a way for* JEHOVAH, *make smooth in the desert a path for* OUR GOD; *for the* GLORY OF JEHOVAH *shall be revealed; and all flesh shall see together. Behold, the* LORD JEHOVAH WILL COME IN THE MIGHTY ONE; *He will feed his flock like a shepherd,* xl. 3, 5, 10, 11. And the angel said, "Since Jehovah Himself came into the world, and assumed the Human, therefore, in the prophets, He is called the SAVIOR and the REDEEMER." And then he read to them the following passages: *God is in thee only, and there is no God besides; truly thou art a* GOD *concealed, O* GOD OF ISRAEL THE SAVIOR, Isaiah xlv. 14, 15. *Am not I* JEHOVAH? *and there is no God else beside Me;* A JUST GOD AND A SAVIOR, THERE IS NOT BESIDE ME, xlv. 21, 22. I AM JEHOVAH, AND BESIDE ME THERE IS NO SAVIOR, xliii. 11. I JEHOVAH *am thy God, and thou shalt acknowledge no God beside Me,* AND THERE IS NO SAVIOR BESIDE ME, Hosea xiii. 4. *That all flesh may know that* I JEHOVAH AM THY SAVIOR AND THY REDEEMER, Isaiah xlix. 26; lx. 16. *As for* OUR REDEEMER, JEHOVAH OF HOSTS IS HIS NAME, xlvii. 4. THEIR REDEEMER IS MIGHTY; JEHOVAH OF HOSTS IS HIS NAME, Jerem. l 24. *Thus said Jehovah the King of*

Israel, and HIS REDEEMER, JEHOVAH OF HOSTS, *I am the First and the Last, and besides Me there is no God,* Isaiah xliv. 6. *Jehovah, my Rock and* MY REDEEMER, Psalm xix. 15. *Thus said* JEHOVAH THY REDEEMER, *the Holy One of Israel,* I JEHOVAH AM THY GOD, Isaiah xlviii. 17; xliii. 14; xlix. 7; liv. 8. *Thou* JEHOVAH *art our Father,* OUR REDEEMER *from an age is thy name,* lxiii. 16. *Thus said* JEHOVAH THY REDEEMER, *I am* JEHOVAH, *doing all things, even alone, by Myself,* xliv. 24. JEHOVAH OF HOSTS *is his name, and* THY REDEEMER, *the Holy One of Israel,* THE GOD OF THE WHOLE EARTH HE SHALL BE CALLED, liv. 5. *Behold the days will come when I shall raise unto David a righteous Branch, who shall reign a King; and this is his name,* JEHOVAH OUR RIGHTEOUSNESS, Jerem. xxiii. 5, 6; xxxiii. 15, 16. *In that day,* JEHOVAH *shall be for a King over all the earth;* IN THAT DAY, JEHOVAH SHALL BE ONE, AND HIS NAME ONE, Zech. xiv. 9. Those who sat on the seats, being confirmed by these and the former passages, unanimously said, that Jehovah Himself assumed the Human in order to redeem and save men. But then a voice was heard from the Roman Catholics, who had hid themselves behind the altar, saying, "How can Jehovah God become Man? Is he not the Creator of the universe?" And one of those who sat upon the seats of the second row, turned himself about, and said, "Who then?" And he behind the altar, standing close to the altar, replied, "THE SON FROM ETERNITY." But he was answered, "Is not the Son from eternity, according to your confession, also the Creator of the universe? And what is a Son and a God born from eternity? And how can the Divine Essence, which is one and indivisible, be separated, and one part of it descend, and not the whole together?" THE SECOND THING CANVASSED CONCERNING THE LORD WAS, Whether, according to this, the Father and He are not one, as the soul and body are one. They said that "This is a consequence, because the soul is from the Father." Then one of those who sat upon the seats of the third row, read from the confession of faith, which is called the Athanasian Creed, these words: "*Although our Lord Jesus Christ, the Son of God, is both God and Man, still there are not two, but there is one Christ; yea, He is altogether one; He is one person, since, as the soul and body make one man, so God and Man is one Christ.*" The reader said, that that creed where those words are, is received in the whole Christian world, even by the Roman Catholics. And they said, "What need is there of more proofs that God the Father and He are one, as the soul and body are one." And they said, "Because it is so, we see that the Human of the Lord is Divine, because it is the Human of Jehovah; and also that the Lord, as to the Divine Human, should be approached, and that thus, and not otherwise, the Divine may be approached, which is called the Father." This, their conclusion, the angel confirmed by many things from the Word, amongst which were these: *A Child is born to us, a Son is given to us, whose name is Wonderful, Counsellor,* GOD, *Hero,* THE FATHER OF ETERNITY, *the Prince of Peace,* Isaiah ix. 6. *Abraham doth not know us, and Israel doth not acknowledge us; Thou,* JEHOVAH, ART OUR FATHER, OUR REDEEMER; FROM AN AGE IS THY NAME, lxiii. 16: and in John; *Jesus said, He who believeth in Me, believeth in Him who sent Me; and he who seeth Me,* SEETH HIM WHO SENT ME, xii. 44, 45. *Philip said to Jesus, Show us the Father. Jesus saith to him,* HE WHO SEETH ME, SEETH THE FATHER; *how then sayest thou, Show us the Father? Believest thou not that* I AM IN THE FATHER, AND THE FATHER IN ME. *Believe Me,* THAT I AM IN THE FATHER, AND THE FATHER IN ME, xiv. 8, 9. *Jesus said,* I AND THE FATHER ARE ONE, x. 30; and also, *All things that the Father hath are mine, and all mine are the Father's,* xvi. 15; xvii. 10. Lastly, *Jesus said, I am the Way, the Truth and the Life; no one cometh to the Father but by Me,* xiv. 6. To this the reader added, that the same things that are here said by the Lord, concerning Himself and his Father, may also be said by man, concerning himself and his soul. Having heard these things, they all said, with one mouth and heart, that "The Human of the Lord is Divine, and that this is to be approached, in order that the Father may be approached; since Jehovah God, by it, sent Himself into the world, and made Himself visible to the eyes of men, and thus accessible. In like manner, He made Himself visible, and thus accessible, in a human form, to the ancients, but then by an angel; but because this form was representative of the Lord who was about to come, therefore all things of the church with the ancients were representative."

After this followed a deliberation concerning the Holy Spirit; and in the first place was disclosed the idea of most persons concerning God the Father, the Son and the Holy Spirit; which was, that God the Father sits on high, and the Son at his right hand, and that they send forth from them the Holy Spirit to enlighten, teach, justify and sanctify men. But then a voice was heard from heaven, saying, "We cannot endure that idea of thought. Who does not know, that Jehovah God is omnipresent? Whoever knows and acknowledges this, will also acknowledge, that He Himself enlightens, teaches, justifies and saves, and that there is not a mediating God distinct from Him, still less from two, as one person from another; wherefore let the former idea, which is vain, be removed, and let this, which is just, be received, and then you will see this clearly." But then a voice was heard from the Roman Catholics, who stood close to the altar of the temple, saying, "What then is the Holy Spirit, which is mentioned in the Word in the evangelists, and in Paul, by which so many learned men amongst the clergy, and especially of our church, say that they are led? Who, at this day, in the Christian world, denies the Holy Spirit and his operations?" At these words, one of those who sat upon the seats of the second row, turned himself about, and said, "You say that the Holy Spirit is a person by himself, and a God by himself; but what is a person going forth and proceeding from a person, but operation going forth and proceeding? One person cannot go forth and proceed from another, but operation can. Or what is a God going forth and proceeding from God, but the Divine going forth and proceeding? One God cannot go forth and proceed from another, but the Divine can from one God." On hearing these words, those who sat upon the seats unanimously concluded, that "The Holy Spirit is not a person by itself, thus neither a God by itself; but that it is the Holy Divine, going forth and proceeding from the one omnipresent God, who is the Lord." To this the angels, standing at the golden table upon which was the Word, said, "Well. It is not read any where in the Old Testament, that the prophets spoke the Word from the Holy Spirit, but from Jehovah; and wherever, in the New Testament, the Holy Spirit is mentioned, we are to understand the proceeding Divine, which is the Divine which enlightens, teaches, enlivens, reforms and regenerates." After this, there followed another question concerning the Holy Spirit, which was, From whom the Divine, which is meant by the Holy Spirit, proceeds; whether from the Father or from the Lord. And when they were canvassing this, there shone upon them a light from heaven, from which they saw that the Holy Divine, which is meant by the Holy Spirit, does not proceed out of the Father through the Lord, but out of the Lord from the Father; comparatively, as with man; his activity does not proceed from the soul through the body, but out of the body from the soul. This the angel standing at the table confirmed by these things from the Word: *He whom the Father hath sent, speaketh the words of God: He hath given Him the Spirit not by measure. The Father loveth the Son, and hath given all things into his hand,* John iii. 34, 35. *A Rod shall go out from the Trunk of Jesse, the spirit of Jehovah shall rest upon Him, the spirit of wisdom and intelligence, the spirit of counsel and virtue*, Isaiah xi. 1. That the spirit of Jehovah was given upon Him, and that it was in Him, xlii. 1; lix. 19,20; lxi. 1; Luke iv. 18. *When the Holy Spirit shall have come,* WHICH I SHALL SEND TO YOU FROM THE FATHER, John xv. 26. *He shall glorify Me*, BECAUSE HE SHALL RECEIVE OF MINE, AND ANNOUNCE UNTO YOU: ALL THINGS WHATSOEVER THE FATHER HATH ARE MINE; ON ACCOUNT OF THIS I SAID, THAT HE SHALL RECEIVE OF MINE, AND ANNOUNCE UNTO YOU, xvi. 14, 15. *If I go away*, I WILL SEND THE PARACLETE UNTO YOU, xvi. 7. *That the Paraclete is* THE HOLY SPIRIT, xiv. 26. THE HOLY SPIRIT WAS NOT YET, BECAUSE JESUS WAS NOT YET GLORIFIED, vii. 39. But after the glorification, JESUS BREATHED INTO, AND SAID TO THE DISCIPLES, RECEIVE THE HOLY SPIRIT, XX. 22. And in the Revelation, *Who shall not glorify thy name, O Lord? because* THOU ALONE ART HOLY, xv. 4. Since the divine operation of the Lord, from his divine omnipresence, is meant by the Holy Spirit, therefore, when He spoke to the disciples concerning the Holy Spirit, which He was about to send from the Father, He also said, *I will not leave you orphans;* I GO AWAY, AND COME UNTO YOU; *and in that day ye will know that* I AM IN MY FATHER, AND YE IN ME, AND I IN YOU, xiv. 18, 20, 28. And just before He departed out of the world, He said, *Lo, I am with you all the days, even to the consummation of the age*, Matt. xxviii. 20. Having read these words to them, the angel said, "From these and many other passages from the Word, it is manifest, that the Divine, which is called the Holy Spirit, proceeds out of the Lord, from the Father." To this those who sat upon the seats said, "THIS IS DIVINE TRUTH."

At last, this decree was made; that, "From what has been deliberated in this council, we have clearly seen, and thence acknowledge as holy truth, that in the Lord God, the Savior Jesus Christ, there is a Divine Trinity, which is, the Divine from which are all things, which is called the Father; the Divine Human, which is called the Son; and the proceeding Divine, which is called the Holy Spirit;" exclaiming together, that "IN JESUS CHRIST DWELLETH ALL THE FULLNESS OF THE GODHEAD BODILY," Coloss. ii. 9. Thus there is one God in the church.

After these things were concluded in that magnificent council, they rose up, and the angel who was keeper of the vestry came out of it, and brought to each of those who sat upon the seats splendid garments, interwoven here and there with threads of gold, and he said, "Receive THE WEDDING GARMENTS." And they were conducted, in glory, into the new Christian heaven, with which the church of the Lord upon earth, which is the New Jerusalem, will be conjoined.

CHAPTER IV.

CONCERNING THE SACRED SCRIPTURE, OR THE WORD OF THE LORD.

189. I. THAT THE SACRED SCRIPTURE, OR THE WORD, IS THE DIVINE TRUTH ITSELF.

It is in the mouth of all, that the Word is from God, divinely inspired, and thence holy; but still it has been hitherto unknown where in it the Divine is; for the Word, in the letter, appears as a common writing, in a foreign style, not sublime nor elegant, as are the writings of the world to appearance. Hence it is, that he who worships nature instead of God, or who worships it in preference to God, and thence thinks from himself and his *proprium*, and not out of heaven from the Lord, may easily fall into error concerning the Word, and into contempt of it, and may say with himself, when he reads it, "What is this? What is that? Is this Divine? Can God, who has infinite wisdom, speak so? Where and whence is its holiness, unless from superstition, and thence persuasion?"

190. But he who thinks so does not consider, that the Lord Jehovah, who is God of heaven and earth, spoke the Word by Moses and the prophets, and that thence it cannot be any thing else than Divine Truth; for that which the Lord Jehovah himself speaks is that; neither does he consider, that the Lord the Savior, who is the same with Jehovah, spoke the Word in the evangelists, many things from his own mouth, and the rest from the Spirit of his mouth, which is the Holy Spirit, by his twelve apostles. Thence it is, as He himself says, that in his words there is spirit and life; and that He himself is the Light which enlightens, and that He is the Truth; which is manifest from the following passages: *Jesus said, The words which I speak unto you are spirit and are life*, John vi. 63. *Jesus said to the woman at Jacob's well, If thou knewest the gift of God, and who it is that saith to thee, Give Me to drink, thou wouldst ask of Him, and He would give to thee living water. He who drinketh of the water that I shall give him, shall never thirst; but the water which I will give him shall become in him a fountain of water, springing up into eternal life*, John iv. 6, 10, 11. By *the fountain of Jacob*, is signified the Word, as also Deut. xxxiii. 28; wherefore also the Lord, because He is the Word, sat there, and spoke with the woman; and by *living water*, is signified the truth of the Word. *Jesus said, If any one thirst, let him come to Me and drink. Whosoever believeth in Me, as the Scripture saith, out of his belly shall flow rivers of living water*, John vii. 37, 38. *Peter said to Jesus, Thou hast the words of eternal life*, John vi. 63. *Jesus said, Heaven and earth shall pass away, but my words shall not pass away*, Mark xiii. 31. That the words of the Lord are truth and life, is, because He himself is the Truth and the Life, as He teaches in John; *I am the Way, the Truth, and the Life*, xiv. 6. And in the same; *In the beginning was the Word, and the Word was with God, and the Word was God; in Him was life, and the life was the light of men*, John i. 1, 2, 3. By the *Word*, is meant the Lord as to Divine Truth, in whom alone there is life and there is light. Thence it is that the Word, which is from the Lord, and which is the Lord, is called THE FOUNTAIN OF LIVING WATERS, Jer. ii. 13, xvii. 13, xxxi. 9; THE FOUNTAIN OF SALVATION, Isaiah xii. 3; A FOUNTAIN, Zech. xiii. 1;

and A RIVER OF THE WATER OF LIFE, Rev xxii. 1; and it is said, that *The Lamb, who is in the midst of the throne, shall feed them at living fountains of waters*, Rev. vii. 17; besides in other places, where the Word also is called a SANCTUARY, and a TABERNACLE, in which the Lord dwells with man.

191. But still the natural man cannot, from these things, be persuaded, that the Word is the Divine Truth itself, in which there is Divine Wisdom and Divine Life; for he regards it from the style, in which he does not see those things. But the style of the Word is the very divine style, with which no other style, however sublime and excellent it appears, can be compared. The style of the Word is such, that there is holiness in every sentence, and in every word, yea, in some instances, in the very letters: thence the Word conjoins man to the Lord, and opens heaven. There are two things which proceed from the Lord, Divine Love and Divine Wisdom, or, what is the same, Divine Good and Divine Truth: the Word, in its essence, is both of them; and because it conjoins man to the Lord, and opens heaven, as it was said, therefore the Word fills man with the goods of love and the truths of wisdom; his will with the goods of love, and his understanding with the truths of wisdom: thence man has life by the Word. But it should be well known, that those only have life from the Word, who read it for the purpose of deriving divine truths from it, as from their fountain, and, at the same time, for the purpose of applying the divine truths, thence derived, to life; and that the contrary happens to those who read it only for the sake of acquiring honors, and gaining the world.

192. Every person, who does not know that a spiritual sense is in the Word, as the soul is in the body, can judge concerning the Word only from the sense of the letter of it; when yet this is as a casket, containing precious things, which are its spiritual sense. When, therefore, this internal sense is not known, one cannot judge of the divine sanctity of the Word, otherwise than of a precious stone, from the matrix which envelopes it, and sometimes appears as a common stone; or as from the cabinet, made of jasper, lapis lazuli, amianthus, or agate, in which lie, in their order, diamonds, rubies, sardonyxes, oriental topazes, &c. While this is unknown, it is no wonder if the cabinet is esteemed no more than according to the price of its material, which appears to the eye. It is similar with the Word, as to the sense of its letter. Lest, therefore, mankind should be in doubt concerning the divinity and sanctity of the Word, its internal sense has been revealed to me, which in its essence is spiritual, and is in the external sense, which is natural, as the soul is in the body. That sense is the spirit, which vivifies the letter; wherefore, that sense can testify concerning the divinity and sanctity of the Word, and convince even the natural man, if he is willing to be convinced.

193. II. THAT IN THE WORD THERE IS A SPIRITUAL SENSE, HITHERTO UNKNOWN.

Who does not acknowledge and assent, when he hears it said that the Word, because it is divine, is in its bosom spiritual? But who has hitherto known what the spiritual is, and where it is concealed in the Word? But what *the spiritual* is, will be shown in a RELATION after this chapter; and where it is concealed in the Word, in what now follows. That the Word, in its bosom, is spiritual, is because it descended from the Lord Jehovah, and passed through the angelic heavens; and the Divine, which in itself is ineffable and imperceptible, became, in its descent, adequate to the perception of angels, and at last to the perception of men. Thence is the spiritual sense, which is within the natural, as the soul in man, the thought of the understanding in speech, and the affection of the will in action; and if it is allowable to compare it with such things as appear before the eyes in the natural world, there is a spiritual sense in the natural sense, as all the brains are within their *meninges* or *maters*, or as the shoots of a tree are within its inner and outer barks; yea, as all the requisites for producing the chicken are within the shell of the egg, &c. But that there is such a spiritual sense, in its natural sense, has hitherto been conjectured by no one; wherefore it is necessary that this mystery, which in itself is preeminent above all other mysteries hitherto revealed, should be made manifest to the understanding, which will be done while it is explained in this order. (1.) *What the spiritual sense is.* (2.) *That that sense is in all and every part of the Word.* (3.) *That thence it is, that the Word is divinely inspired, and holy in every expression.* (4.) *That that sense has been hitherto unknown.* (5.) *That hereafter it will not be given to any, but those who are in genuine truths from the Lord.* (6.) *Wonderful things concerning the Word, from its spiritual sense.* These things shall now be unfolded one by one.

194. (1.) *What the Spiritual Sense is.* The spiritual sense is not that which shines forth from the sense of the letter of the Word, when any one searches and explains the Word in order to confirm any tenet of the church: this sense may be called the literal and ecclesiastical sense of the Word; but if the spiritual sense does not appear in the sense of the letter, it is inwardly in it, as the soul in the body, as the thought of the understanding in the eyes, and as the affection of love in the face. It is principally that sense which makes the Word spiritual, not only for men, but also for angels; wherefore the Word, by that sense, communicates with the heavens. Since the Word is inwardly spiritual, therefore it is written by mere correspondences; and what is written by correspondences, is written, in the ultimate sense, in such a style as in the prophets, the evangelists and the Revelation; which, although it appears ordinary, still conceals within itself the divine wisdom, and all angelic wisdom. What correspondence is, may be seen in a work concerning HEAVEN AND HELL, published at London, 1758, where *the correspondence of all the things of heaven with all the things of man* is treated of, n. 87 to 102; and *the correspondence of all the things of heaven with all the things of the earth,* n. 103 to 115; and will be seen more fully from examples to be hereafter adduced from the Word.

195. From the Lord proceeds THE CELESTIAL DIVINE, THE SPIRITUAL DIVINE AND THE NATURAL DIVINE, one after another. Whatever proceeds from his Divine Love is called the CELESTIAL DIVINE, and all that is good; whatever proceeds from his Divine Wisdom is called SPIRITUAL DIVINE, and all that is truth. The NATURAL DIVINE is of both, and is their complex in the ultimate. The angels of the celestial kingdom, of whom is the third or highest heaven, are in the Divine which proceeds from the Lord, which is called *celestial;* for they are in the good of love from the Lord. The angels of the Lord's spiritual kingdom, of whom the second or middle heaven consists, are in the Divine which proceeds from the Lord, which is called *spiritual;* for they are in divine wisdom from the Lord. The angels of the Lord's natural kingdom, of which the first or lowest heaven consists, are in the Divine which proceeds from the Lord, which is called *natural Divine,* and they are in the faith of charity from the Lord. But the men of the church, according to their love, wisdom and faith, are in one of those kingdoms, and into that in which they are, they also come after death. Such as heaven is, such also is the Word of the Lord: in its ultimate sense it is natural, in its interior sense it is spiritual, and in its inmost sense it is celestial, and in every part divine; wherefore it is accommodated to the angels of the three heavens, and also to men.

196. (2.) *That the Spiritual Sense is in all and every Part of the Word,* cannot be seen better than from examples, such as the following John says, in the Revelation, *I saw heaven open, and behold, a white horse; and He who sat upon him was called the Faithful and True, who in righteousness judges and fights, and his eyes as a flame of fire, and upon his*

head many diadems; having a name written, which no one knoweth but Himself; and He was clothed in a vesture tinged with blood; and his name is called THE WORD OF GOD. *And his armies in heaven followed Him upon white horses, clothed in fine linen, white and clean. He has upon his vesture and upon his thigh a name written,* KING OF KINGS, AND LORD OF LORDS. *I saw, also, an angel standing in the sun, who cried with a loud voice, Come and gather yourselves together to the great supper, that ye may eat the flesh of kings, and the flesh of captains, and the flesh of the mighty, and the flesh of horses, and of those who sit upon them, and the flesh of all, free and bond, small and great*, xix. 11 to 18. What these things signify, no one can see, except from the spiritual sense of the Word; and no one can know the spiritual sense except from the science of correspondences; for all the expressions are correspondences, and no expression is without meaning. The science of correspondences teaches what is signified by the *white horse;* what by *Him who sat upon him;* what by the *eyes which were as a flame of fire;* what by the *diadems upon his head;* what by the *vesture tinged with blood*; what by the *white fine linen*, in which they who were of his army in heaven were clothed; what by the *angel standing in the sun;* and what by the *great supper* to which they came and were gathered together; and also what by the *flesh of kings and captains;* and of many other things which they should eat. But what each of those expressions, in the spiritual sense, signifies, may be seen explained in the APOCALYPSE REVEALED, from n. 820 to 838; and also in a little work concerning the WHITE HORSE; wherefore it is unnecessary to explain them further. It is there shown, that the Lord, as to the Word, is there described; and that by his eyes, which were as a flame of fire, is meant the divine wisdom of his divine love; and by the diadems which were upon his head, and by the name which no one knew but Himself, are meant the divine truths of the Word from Him and that what the Word is, in its spiritual sense, no one sees but the Lord and those to whom He reveals it; also, that by the vesture tinged with blood, is meant the natural sense of the Word, which is the sense of its letter, to which violence has been done. That it is the Word which is thus described, is very manifest; for it is said, HIS NAME IS CALLED THE WORD OF GOD. That it is the Lord who is meant, is also very manifest; for it is said, that *the name of him who sat upon the white horse was*, KING OF KINGS AND LORD OF LORDS; in like manner as in Rev. xvii. 14, where it is said, *And the Lamb shall overcome them, because* HE IS LORD OF LORDS AND KING OF KINGS. That the spiritual sense of the Word is to be opened at the end of the church, is signified not only by those things which are said concerning the white horse, and Him who sat upon him, but also by the great supper, to which the angel standing in the sun invited all to come, and eat the flesh of kings, and of captains, &c.; by which is signified the appropriation of all good things from the Lord. All the expressions there would be empty words, and without life and spirit, unless there was a spiritual sense within them, as the soul is in the body.

197. In Rev. xxi., the New Jerusalem is thus described: *That in it there was a luminary, like a very precious stone, as a jasper stone, shining like crystal. That it had a great and high wall, having twelve gates, and twelve angels upon the gates, and the names of the twelves tribes of the sons of Israel written. That the wall was of a hundred and forty-four cubits, which is the measure of a man, that is, of an angel. That the structure of the wall was jasper, and its foundations of every precious stone; of jasper, sapphire, chalcedony, emerald, sardonyx, sardius, chrysolite, beryl, topaz, chrysoprasus, hyacinth and amethyst. That the gates were twelve pearls. That the city itself was pure gold, like pure glass; and that it was four-cornered, the*

length, the breadth and the height equal; of twelve thousand furlongs; besides many other things. That all these things are to be understood spiritually, may be evident from this, that by the *New Jerusalem* is meant a New Church, which is to be instituted by the Lord, as is shown in the APOCALYPSE REVEALED, n. 880; and because by *Jerusalem* there, is signified the church, it follows, that all the things which are said of it as a city—of its gates, of its wall, of the foundations of the wall, also the things which are said of their measures—contain a spiritual sense, since those things which are of the church are spiritual; but what they signify has been demonstrated in the APOCALYPSE REVEALED, from n. 896 to 925; wherefore it would be superfluous to demonstrate them further. It is sufficient that it is thence known, that there is a spiritual sense in every part of that description, as the soul in the body; and that without that sense nothing of the church would be understood in those things which are written there; as that the city was of pure gold, its gates of pearls, the wall of jasper, the foundations of the wall of precious stones; that the wall was of a hundred and forty-four cubits, which is the measure of a man, that is, of an angel; and that the city was of the length, breadth and height of twelve thousand furlongs; besides many other things: but he who knows the spiritual sense, from the science of correspondences, understands those things; as that the wall and its foundations signify the doctrinals of that church, from the sense of the letter of the Word; and that the numbers, 12, 144, 12,000, signify all the things of it, or all the truths and goods of it, in one complex.

198. Where the Lord speaks to his disciples of the consummation of the age, which is the last time of the church, at the end of the predictions concerning its successive changes, He says: *Immediately after the affliction of those days, the sun shall be darkened, and the moon shall not give her light, and the stars shall fall from heaven, and the powers of the heavens shall be shaken; and then shall appear the sign of the Son of man in heaven; and then shall all the tribes of the earth mourn, and they shall see the Son of man coming in the clouds of heaven, with power and much glory. And He will send forth the angels, with a great sound of a trumpet, and they shall gather together his elect, from the four winds, from one end of the heavens even to the other,* Matt. xxiv. 29, 30, 31. By these words, in the spiritual sense, it is not meant that the sun and moon would be darkened, that the stars would fall from heaven, and that the sign of the Lord would appear in the heavens, and that they would see Him in the clouds, and, at the same time, the angels with trumpets; but by every one of the words there, are meant spiritual things, which are of the church, concerning the state of which, at the end, those things are said; for, in the spiritual sense, by the *sun*, which will be *darkened*, is meant love to the Lord; by the *moon*, which will *not give her light*, is meant faith in Him; by the *stars*, which will *fall from heaven*, are meant the knowledges of truth and good; by the *sign of the Son of man in heaven*, is meant the appearing of divine truth in the Word from Him; by the *tribes of the earth*, which shall *mourn*, is meant the want of all truth which is of faith, and of all good which is of love; by the *coming of the Son of man in the clouds of heaven with power and glory*, is meant the presence of the Lord in the Word, and revelation; by the *clouds of heaven*, is signified the sense of the letter of the Word, and by *glory*, the spiritual sense of the Word; by the *angels with a great sound of a trumpet*, is meant heaven, whence is divine truth; by *gathering together the elect from the four winds, from one end of the heavens to the other*, is meant a new heaven and a new church of those who have faith in the Lord, and live according to his commandments. That the darkening of the sun and moon, and the falling of the stars to the earth, are not meant, is very manifest from the prophets, by whom simi-

lar things are said concerning the state of the church, when the Lord was about to come into the world; as in Isaiah, *Behold, the day of Jehovah will come, cruel, and of the wrath of anger; the stars of heaven and the constellations of them will not shine with their light; the sun will be darkened in his rising, and the moon will not make her light shine. I will visit upon the world wickedness*, xxiv. 21, 23. In Joel, *The day of Jehovah cometh, a day of darkness and thick darkness; the sun and the moon will become black; the stars will withdraw their splendor*, iii. 4; iv. 15. In Ezekiel, *I will cover the heavens, and make black the stars; I will cover the sun with a cloud, and the moon will not make her light shine. All the luminaries of light I will cover over, and I will give darkness upon the earth*, xxii. 7, 8. By the *day of Jehovah*, is meant the coming of the Lord, which was when there was no longer any good of love and truth of faith remaining in the church, and not any knowledge of the Lord; therefore it is called a *day of darkness and thick darkness.*

199. That the Lord, when He was in the world, spoke by correspondences, thus also spiritually, when naturally, may be evident from his parables, in every word of which there is a spiritual sense. Let the parable of the ten virgins be for an example. He said, *The kingdom of the heavens is like ten virgins, who, taking their lamps, went out to meet the bridegroom; five of them were prudent, but five were foolish. Those who were foolish, taking their lamps, took no oil; but the prudent took oil in their lamps. While the bridegroom tarried, they all slumbered and slept. And at midnight a cry was made, Behold, the bridegroom is coming; go ye out to meet him. Then all those virgins awoke, and trimmed their lamps. But the foolish said to the prudent, Give us of your oil, for our lamps are going out. But the prudent answered, saying, Lest perhaps there be not enough for us and you, go ye rather to those who sell, and buy for yourselves. But while they were gone to buy, the bridegroom came, and those who were prepared went with him in to the wedding; and the door was shut And at length came also the other virgins, saying, Lord, Lord, open to us. But he, answering, said, Verily I say unto you, I know you not*, Matt. xxv. 1 to 12. That in every one of these words there is a spiritual sense, and thence a holy divine, no one sees but he who knows that there is a spiritual sense, and what it is. In the spiritual sense, by the *kingdom of the heavens* is meant heaven and the church; by the *bridegroom*, the Lord; by the *wedding*, the marriage of the Lord with them, by the good of love and the truth of faith; by *virgins*, those who are of the church; by *ten*, all; by *five*, a part; by *lamps*, those things which are of faith; by *oil*, those things which are of the good of love; by *sleeping* and *awaking*, the life of man in the world, which is natural, and his life after death, which is spiritual; by *buying*, to procure for themselves; by *going to those who sell and buying* oil, to procure for themselves the good of love from others after death; and because then it is no longer procurable, therefore, although they came with lamps, and the oil which they had bought, to the door where the wedding was, still it was said to them by the bridegroom, *I know you not.* The reason is, because man remains, after the life in the world, such as he had lived in the world. From these examples, it is manifest that the Lord spoke by mere correspondences, and this because from the Divine, which was in Him, and was His. Because virgins signify those who are of the church, therefore so often in the prophetical Word it is said, *the virgin*, and *the daughter* of Zion, of Jerusalem, of Judah, of Israel. And because oil signifies the good of love, therefore all the holy things of the church were anointed with oil. It is similar in the rest of the parables, and in all the words which the Lord spoke. Thence it is that the Lord says, that his *words are spirit and are life*, John vi. 63.

200. (3.) *That it is from the Spiritual Sense, that the Word is divine*

ly inspired, and holy in every Expression.

It is said in the church, that the Word is holy, and this because the Lord Jehovah spoke it; but because its holiness does not appear in the sense of the letter only, therefore he who, on that account, once doubts concerning its holiness, when he afterwards reads the Word, confirms himself by many things there; for he says with himself, "Is this holy? Is this divine?" Lest, therefore, such a thought should flow in with many, and afterwards be confirmed, and thence the Word should be rejected as a worthless writing, and the conjunction of the Lord with man, by means of it, should perish, it has pleased the Lord now to reveal its spiritual sense, in order that it may be known where in it the divine holiness is concealed. But let examples illustrate this. In the Word, we sometimes read of Egypt, sometimes of Assyria, sometimes of Edom, of Moab, of the sons of Ammon, of the Philistines, of Tyre and Zidon, and of Gog. He who does not know, that by the names of those are signified the things of heaven and the church, may be led into the error, that the Word treats much of people and nations, and but little of heaven and the church; thus much of worldly, and little of heavenly things; but when he knows what is signified by them, or by their names, he may be led back from error into the truth. In like manner, while he sees in the Word, that there are so often mentioned gardens, groves, forests, and their trees, as the olive, the vine, the cedar, the poplar, and the oak; and that so often a lamb, a sheep, a goat, a calf, an ox; and also mountains, hills, valleys, and there fountains, rivers, waters, and many such things; he who knows nothing of the spiritual sense of the Word, cannot think otherwise, than that it is only those things which are meant; for he does not know, that by a garden, grove and forest, are meant wisdom, intelligence and science; that by an olive, vine, cedar, poplar and oak, are meant the good and truth of the church, celestial, spiritual, rational, natural and sensual that by a lamb, a sheep, a goat, a calf, an ox, are meant innocence, charity and natural affection; that by mountains, hills and valleys, are meant the higher, lower and lowest things of the church: also that by Egypt is signified the scientific; by Assyria, the rational; by Edom, the natural; by Moab, the adulteration of good; by the sons of Ammon, the adulteration of truth; by the Philistines, faith without charity; by Tyre and Zidon, the knowledges of good and truth; by Gog, external worship without internal. In general, by Jacob, in the Word, is meant the natural church; by Israel, the spiritual church; and by Judah, the celestial church. When a man knows all these things, he may then think, that the Word treats only of heavenly things, and that those worldly things are only the subjects in which these are. But an example from the Word may illustrate this also. It is read in Isaiah, *In that day, there shall be a way from Egypt to Assyria, that Assyria may come into Egypt, and Egypt into Assyria; and the Egyptians may serve with the Assyrians. In that day, Israel shall be a third to Egypt and Assyria, a blessing in the midst of the land; which Jehovah of hosts shall bless, saying, Blessed be my people Egypt, and Assyria, the work of my hands, and Israel, my blessing*, xix. 23, 24, 25. By these words, in the spiritual sense, it is meant, that, at the time of the coming of the Lord, the scientific, the rational and the spiritual should make one, and that then the scientific will serve the rational, and both the spiritual; for, as it was said, by Egypt is signified the scientific, by Assyria the rational, and by Israel the spiritual; by the day twice mentioned, is meant the first and second coming of the Lord.

201. (4.) *That the Spiritual Sense of the Word has been hitherto unknown.*

That all and every thing, which is in nature, corresponds to spiritual things; in like manner, all and every thing in the human body; has been shown in a work concerning Heaven and Hell, n. 87 to 105. But what Correspondence is, has been hitherto unknown; but in the most ancient times, it was very well known; for, to those who then lived, the science of correspondences was the science of sciences, and so universal that all their tracts and books were written by correspondences. The book of Job, which is a book of the ancient church, is full of correspondences. The hieroglyphics of the Egyptians, and also the fables of the ancients, were no other. All the ancient churches were churches representative of spiritual things. Their rites, and also the statutes according to which their worship was instituted, consisted of mere correspondences; in like manner, all the things of the church with the sons of Israel. The whole burnt-offerings, sacrifices, meat-offerings, and drink-offerings, with every thing appertaining to them, were correspondences; in like manner, the tabernacle, with all the things in it; and also their feasts, as the feast of unleavened bread, the feast of tabernacles, and the feast of the first fruits; likewise the priesthood of Aaron and the Levites, as also their garments of holiness; but what the spiritual things were, to which those things respectively corresponded, has been shown in the Arcana Cœlestia, published at London. Besides these, also, all the statutes and judgments, which concerned their worship and life, were correspondences. Now, because divine things, in the world, present themselves in correspondences, therefore the Word was written by mere correspondences; wherefore the Lord, because He spoke from the Divine, spoke by correspondences; for what is from the Divine, this, in nature, falls into such things as correspond to divine things, and which then conceal, in their bosom, divine things, which are called *celestial* and *spiritual*.

202. I have been instructed, that the men of the most ancient church, which was before the flood, were of so heavenly a genius, that they conversed with the angels of heaven, and that they could converse with them by correspondences: thence the state of their wisdom became such, that whatever they saw in the earth, they thought of it not only naturally, but also spiritually, at the same time; thus also conjointly with the angels of heaven Moreover, I have been informed, that Enoch, of whom mention is made in Genesis v. 21 to 24, with his companions, collected correspondences from their mouth, and transmitted the science of them to posterity; in consequence of which, the science of correspondences was not only known, but also cultivated, in many kingdoms of Asia, especially in the land of Canaan, Egypt, Assyria, Chaldea, Syria, Arabia, Tyre, Zidon, and Nineveh; and that thence it was transferred into Greece; but there it was turned into fables, as is evident from the writings of the most ancient authors of that country.

203. That it may be seen, that the science of correspondences was for a long time preserved among the Gentile nations in Asia, but among those who were called *soothsayers* and *sages*, and by some *Magi*, I will adduce one example from 1 Sam. v. and vi. It is there related, that the ark, in which were the two tables, upon which the decalogue was written, was taken by the Philistines, and placed in the temple of Dagon, in Ashdod, and that Dagon fell before it to the ground, and afterwards his head, with the palms of his hands, severed from his body, lay upon the threshold of the temple; and that the Ashdodites and Ekronites, on account of the ark, were smitten with hemorrhoids, to the number of several thousands; and that their land was devastated by mice; and that, on account of those things, the Philistines called together the princes and soothsayers, and that they concluded, that, in order to prevent their destruction, they should make five hemorrhoids and five mice out of gold, and a new cart, and upon this they should place the ark, and by the side of the ark, the hemorrhoids and mice of gold; and by two cows, which lowed in the way be

fore the cart, they should send back the ark to the sons of Israel, by whom the cows and the cart were sacrificed, and thus the God of Israel was propitiated. That all these things, devised by the soothsayers of the Philistines, were correspondences, is evident from their signification, which is this:—The *Philistines* themselves signified those who are in faith separate from charity; *Dagon* represented that religion; the *hemorrhoids*, with which they were smitten, signified natural loves, which, separate from spiritual love, are unclean; and the *mice* signified the devastation of the church, by falsifications of the truth; the *new cart* signified natural doctrine of the church, for *chariot*, in the Word, signifies doctrine from spiritual truths; the *cows* signified good natural affections; the *hemorrhoids of gold* signified natural loves purified and made good; the *mice of gold* signified the vastation of the church removed by good, for *gold*, in the Word, signifies good; the *lowing* of the cows in the way, signified the difficult conversion of the natural man's concupiscences of evil into good affections; the offering of the cows with the cart for a whole burnt-offering, signified that thus the God of Israel was propitiated. All these things, which the Philistines did according to the advice of their soothsayers, were correspondences; from which it is manifest that that science was for a long time preserved among the Gentile nations.

204. Since the representative rites of the church, which were correspondences, in process of time began to be turned into things idolatrous, and also into things magical, then that science, by the Divine Providence of the Lord, was gradually lost, and amongst the Israelitish and Jewish nation, it was entirely obliterated. The worship of this nation, indeed, consisted of mere correspondences, and thence it was representative of heavenly things; but still they did not know what any thing signified, for they were altogether natural men, and thence they would not and could not know any thing concerning spiritual and heavenly things; consequently, not any thing concerning correspondences, for correspondences are representations of spiritual and heavenly things in natural things.

205. That the idolatries of the Gentile nations, in ancient times, derived their origin from the science of correspondences, was, because all things, which appear upon the earth, correspond; thus, not only trees, but also beasts and birds of every kind, also fishes and other things. The ancients who were in the science of correspondences, made for themselves images, which corresponded to heavenly things, and were delighted with them, because they signified such things as were of heaven and the church; and therefore they put them not only in their temples, but also in their houses; not for the sake of worshipping them, but of calling to mind the heavenly things which they signified. Thence in Egypt, and elsewhere, there were images of calves, oxen, serpents, also of boys, old men, and virgins; because calves and oxen signified the affections and powers of the natural man; serpents, the prudence and also the cunning of the sensual man; boys, innocence and charity; old men, wisdom; and virgins, affections of truth; and so on. Their posterity, when the science of correspondences was obliterated, began to worship as holy, and at length as deities, the images and resemblances set up by the ancients, because they were in their temples and about them. Thence, also, the ancients had worship in gardens and in groves, according to the sorts of trees; and also upon mountains and hills; for gardens and groves signified wisdom and intelligence, and every tree something of these; as the olive, the good of love; the vine, truth from that good; the cedar, rational good and truth; a mountain, the highest heaven; and a hill, the heaven under that. That the science of correspondences continued amongst many of the eastern nations, even to the coming of the Lord, is also evident from the wise men from the east, who came to the Lord when he was born; wherefore

a star went before them, and they carried with them gifts, gold, frankincense and myrrh, Matt. ii. 1, 2, 9, 10, 11; for the star which went before them signified knowledge from heaven; gold signified heavenly good; frankincense, spiritual good; and myrrh, natural good; of which three is all worship. But still the science of correspondences was not at all amongst the Israelitish and Jewish nation, although all the things of their worship, and all the statutes and judgments given to them by Moses, and all the things of the Word, were mere correspondences. The reason was, because they were in heart idolaters, and thence such that they were not even willing to know that any part of their worship signified any thing heavenly and spiritual; for they believed that all those things were holy of themselves; wherefore, if heavenly and spiritual things had been disclosed to them, they would not only have rejected, but would also have profaned them; wherefore heaven was so closed to them, that they scarcely knew that there was such a thing as eternal life. That it is so, is very manifest from this, that they did not acknowledge the Lord, although all the Sacred Scripture prophesied concerning Him, and foretold his coming. They rejected Him for this sole reason, that He taught them concerning a heavenly kingdom, and not concerning an earthly kingdom; for they wished for a Messiah who would exalt them above all the nations in the whole world, and not a Messiah who would provide for their eternal salvation.

206. The reason that the science of correspondences, by which is given the spiritual sense of the Word, was not disclosed after those times, was, because the Christians, in the primitive church, were very simple, so that it could not have been disclosed to them; for, if it had been disclosed, it would have been of no use to them, nor would it have been understood. After their times. darkness arose over all the Christian world; first by the heretical opinions of many spread about, and soon afterwards by the deliberations and decrees of the Nicene council concerning three divine persons from eternity, and concerning the person of Christ, as the Son of Mary, and not as the Son of Jehovah God. Thence originated the present faith of justification, in which three Gods are approached in their order; on which faith all and every thing of the church at this day depends, as the members of the body on their head; and because they applied all the things of the Word to confirm this erroneous faith, the spiritual sense could not be disclosed; for, if it had been, they would have applied to it also that sense, and thereby would have profaned the very holiness of the Word; and thus they would have entirely closed up heaven against themselves, and removed the Lord from the church.

207. The reason why the science of correspondences, by which the spiritual sense of the Word is given, has been at this time revealed, is, because now the divine truths of the church come forth into the light, and these are the things of which the spiritual sense of the Word consists; and while these are in man, the sense of the letter of the Word cannot be perverted; for the sense of the letter of the Word can be turned hither and thither; but if it is turned to the false, then its internal holiness is lost, and with this the external; but if it is turned to the true, its holiness remains. But, concerning these things, more will be said in the following pages. That the spiritual sense will, at this day, be opened, is meant by John's seeing heaven open, and then a white horse; and also by his seeing and hearing that an angel, standing in the sun, called all together to a great supper; concerning which, see Rev. xix. 11 to 18. But that it will not, for a long time, be acknowledged, is meant by the beast, and by the kings of the earth, who were about to make war with Him who sat upon the white horse, Rev. xix. 19; as also by the dragon, that he pursued the woman, who brought forth the son, even into the wilderness, and there cast forth out of his mouth wa-

ters, as a flood, that he might drown her, Rev. xii. 13 to 17.

208. (5.) *That the Spiritual Sense of the Word is not hereafter given to any, but those who are in genuine Truths from the Lord.*

The reason is, because no one can see the spiritual sense, except from the Lord alone, and unless he be in divine truths from the Lord; for the spiritual sense of the Word treats concerning the Lord alone, and concerning his kingdom; and that is the sense in which his angels in heaven are, for it is his divine truth there. This, man can violate, if he is in the science of correspondences, and wishes by it to explore the spiritual sense of the Word, from his own intelligence; for by means of some correspondences, known to him, he can pervert that sense, and even force it to confirm the false; and this would be to offer violence to divine truth, and thus also to heaven, in which it dwells. Wherefore, if any one wishes from himself, and not from the Lord, to open that sense, heaven is shut, which being shut, man either sees nothing of truth, or becomes spiritually insane. The reason also is, because the Lord teaches every one by the Word, and he teaches him from those knowledges which are with man, and does not immediately infuse new ones; wherefore, unless man be in divine truths, or if in only a few truths, and at the same time in falses, he can by these falsify truths, as is also done by every heretic, as to the sense of the letter of the Word. Lest, therefore, any one should enter into the spiritual sense, and the genuine truth which is of that sense, guards are placed by the Lord, which are meant in the Word by *cherubs.*

209. (6.) *Wonderful Things concerning the Word, from its Spiritual Sense.*

In the natural world, no wonderful things exist from the Word, because the spiritual sense does not there appear, nor is it inwardly received by man, such as it is in itself; but in the spiritual world, wonderful things appear from the Word, because all there are spiritual, and spiritual things affect the spiritual man, as natural things the natural man. The wonderful things which exist in the spiritual world, from the Word, are many; a few of which I shall here relate. The Word itself, in the inmost recesses of the temples there, shines before the eyes of the angels like a great star, and sometimes like the sun; and also, from the bright radiance round about it, there appear, as it were, most beautiful rainbows; this happens as soon as the sacred recess is opened. That all and every one of the truths of the Word shine, was made evident to me from this, that when any single verse of the Word is written out upon paper, and the paper is thrown into the air, the paper itself shines, in such a form as it was cut into; wherefore spirits are able to produce, by the Word, various shining forms, and also those of birds and fishes. And, what is still more wonderful, when any one rubs the face, the hands, or the clothes which he has on, with the Word open, applying the writing of it to them, the face itself, the hands and the clothes shine, as if he were standing in a star, surrounded with its light. This I have often seen and wondered at; thence it was evident to me, whence it was, that the face of Moses shone, when he brought down the tables of the covenant from mount Sinai.

Besides these, there are many other wonderful things there, which are from the Word, as, for instance, if any one, who is in falses, looks at the Word, lying in the holy place, there arises a thick darkness before his eyes, and thence the Word appears to him black, and sometimes, as it were, covered over with soot; but, if he also touches the Word, an explosion is made with a loud noise, and he is thrown to a corner of the room, and for an hour lies there as if he were dead. If any thing is written out of the Word upon paper, by any one who is in falses, and the paper is thrown up towards heaven, then a similar explosion is made in the air, between his eye and heaven, and the paper is torn into atoms, and vanishes: the like happens, if that paper is thrown towards an angel, who stands near: this I have often seen. Thence it was manifest to me, that those who are in falses of doctrine have no communication with heaven, by means of the Word; but that their reading is dispersed in the way, and perishes, like gunpowder enclosed in paper, when it is set on fire, and thrown into the air. The contrary happens with those who are in truths of doctrine, by means of the Word, from the Lord: the reading of the Word by those penetrates even into heaven, and makes conjunction with the angels there. The angels themselves, when they descend from heaven to execute any business below, appear encompassed with little stars, especially about the head, which is a sign that divine truths from the Word are in them.

Moreover, in the spiritual world there are things similar to those which are upon earth, but all and every thing there is from a spiritual origin; so there are also gold, and silver, and precious stones of every kind, and the spiritual origin of these is the sense of the letter of the Word. Thence it is, that, in the Revelation, the foundations of the wall of the New Jerusalem are described by twelve precious stones: the reason is, because, by the foundations of its wall are signified the doctrinals of the New Church, from the sense of the letter of the Word. Thence also it is, that, in the ephod of Aaron, there were also twelve precious stones, called *Urim* and *Thummim*, and that by these, answers were given from heaven. Besides these, there are many more wonderful things from the Word, which concern the power of truth there, which is so immense, that, if it should be described, it would exceed all belief; for the power is such, that it overturns mountains and hills there, removes them to a distance, and casts them into the sea; besides many other things. In short, the power of the Lord, from the Word, is infinite.

210. III. THAT THE SENSE OF THE LETTER OF THE WORD IS THE BASIS THE CONTINENT AND THE FIRMAMENT OF ITS SPIRITUAL AND CELESTIAL SENSE.

In every thing divine, there is a first, a middle, and a last; and the first goes through the middle to the last, and thus exists and subsists; thence the last is the BASIS. The first also, is in the middle, and, by the middle, in the last; thus the last is the CONTINENT; and because the last is the continent and the basis, it is also the FIRMAMENT. It is comprehended by the learned, that those three may be called *end*, *cause* and *effect;* and also *esse* [to be], *fieri* [to be done], and *existere* [to exist]; and that the end is the *esse*, the cause the *fieri*, and the effect the *existere;* consequently, that in every complete thing there is a trine, which is called *first*, *middle* and *last;* also *end*, *cause* and *effect*. When these things are comprehended, it is also comprehended that every divine work is complete and perfect in the last; and, likewise, that all are in the last, because the former are together in it.

211. It is from this, that by THREE, in the Word, in the spiritual sense, is meant what is complete and perfect, and also all together; and because these things are signified by that number, therefore it is used in the Word whenever such a thing is designated, as in these passages: *That Isaiah should go naked and barefoot* THREE YEARS, Isaiah xx. 3. *That Jehovah called Samuel* THREE TIMES, *and that Samuel ran* THREE TIMES *to Eli, and that Eli the* THIRD TIME *understood*, 1 Sam. iii. 1 to 8. *That David said to Jonathan, that he should hide himself in the field* THREE DAYS; *that Jonathan afterwards shot* THREE ARROWS *at the side of a stone; and that David then bowed himself* THREE TIMES *before Jonathan*, xx. 5, 12 to 42. *That Elijah stretched himself* THREE TIMES *upon the widow's son*, 1 Kings xvii. 21. *That Elijah commanded that they should pour water upon the whole burnt-offering* THREE TIMES, xviii. 34. *That Jesus said, that the kingdom of the*

heavens is like unto leaven, which a woman, taking, hid in THREE MEASURES OF MEAL, *till the whole was leavened,* Matt. xiii. 33. *That Jesus said to Peter, that he would deny him* THREE TIMES, xxvi. 34. *That Jesus said* THREE TIMES *to Peter, Lovest thou Me?* John xxi. 15, 16, 17. *That Jonah was in the belly of a whale* THREE DAYS AND THREE NIGHTS, Jon. ii. 2. *That Jesus said, Destroy this temple, and I will rebuild it in* THREE DAYS, John ii. 19; Matt. xxvi. 61. *That Jesus, in Gethsemane, prayed* THREE TIMES, Matt. xxvi. 39 to 44. *That Jesus rose again the* THIRD DAY, Matt. xxviii. 1: besides in many other places, where the number *three* is mentioned; and it is mentioned where a work finished and perfect is treated of, because this is signified by that number.

212. There are three heavens, the highest, the middle, and the lowest. The highest heaven makes the celestial kingdom of the Lord; the middle heaven makes his spiritual kingdom, and the lowest heaven makes his natural kingdom. As there are three heavens, so likewise there are three senses of the Word, the celestial, the spiritual, and the natural; with which also those things coincide which were said above, n. 210, viz. that the first is in the middle, and, by the middle, in the last; just as the end is in the cause, and, by the cause, in the effect. Thence it is manifest what the Word is, viz. that, in the sense of its letter, which is natural, there is an interior sense, which is spiritual, and in this an inmost sense, which is celestial; and thus that the last sense, which is natural, and is called the *sense of the letter*, is the continent, and so the basis and firmament, of the two interior senses.

213. Hence it follows, that the Word, without the sense of its letter, would be like a palace without a foundation, thus like a palace in the air, and not upon the earth, which would be only the shadow of a palace, that would vanish away; also that the Word, without the sense of its letter, would be like a temple in which are many holy things, and in the midst of it the most holy place, without a roof and walls, which are its continents, and if these should be wanting, or if they should be taken away, its holy things would be plundered by thieves, and violated by the beasts of the earth and the birds of the air, and thus they would be dissipated. It would likewise be like the tabernacle of the sons of Israel in the wilderness, in the inmost part of which was the ark of the covenant, and in the middle of it the golden candlestick, the golden altar, upon which incense was offered, and also the table upon which the bread of faces was placed, without its last things, which were the curtains, veils and columns. Yea, the Word, without the sense of its letter, would be like the human body without its coverings, which are called *skins*, and without its supporters, which are called *bones;* without the latter and the former, all the inner parts of it would be dispersed. It would also be like the heart and the lungs, in the thorax; without their covering, which is called the *pleura*, and their supporters, which are called the *ribs;* or like the brain without its coverings, which are called the *dura* and the *pia mater*, and without its common covering, continent and firmament, which is called the *skull.* It would be similar with the Word, without the sense of its letter; wherefore it is said in Isaiah, that *Jehovah creates upon all the glory a covering*, iv. 5.

214. IV. THAT DIVINE TRUTH, IN THE SENSE OF THE LETTER OF THE WORD, IS IN ITS FULLNESS, IN ITS HOLINESS, AND IN ITS POWER.

That the Word, in the sense of the letter, is in its fullness, in its holiness, and in its power, is because the two former, or interior senses, which are called the *spiritual* and the *celestial*, are together in the natural sense, which is the sense of the letter, as was said above, n. 210 and 212; but how they are together, shall be further told. There is in heaven and in the world, a successive order and a simultaneous order: in successive order, one thing succeeds and follows after another, from the highest even to the lowest; but in simultaneous order, one thing is next to another from the inmost even to the outermost. Successive order is like a column, with steps from the top to the bottom; but simultaneous order is like a work cohering with the circumference, from the centre even to the surface. It shall now be told, how successive order becomes, in the last, simultaneous order: it is done in this manner: the highest things of successive order become the inmost things of simultaneous order, and the lowest things of successive order become the outermost things of simultaneous order. It is, comparatively, like a column of steps, subsiding, and becoming a coherent body, in a plain. Thus, what is simultaneous is formed from what is successive, and this in all and every thing of the natural world, and in all and every thing of the spiritual world; for every where there is a first, a middle, and a last; and the first, by the middle, tends and goes to its last; but it should be well understood, that there are degrees of purity, according to which each order is made. Now to the Word: the celestial, the spiritual and the natural proceed from the Lord in successive order; and, in the last, they are in simultaneous order; so now the celestial and the spiritual senses of the Word are together in its natural sense. When this is comprehended, it may be seen how the natural sense of the Word is the continent, the basis and the firmament of its spiritual and celestial senses; and also how the divine good and the divine truth, in the sense of the letter of the Word, are in their fullness, in their holiness, and in their power. Hence it may be evident, that the Word is the Word itself, in its sense of the letter; for in this interiorly there is spirit and life: this is what the Lord says: *The words which I speak unto you are spirit and life*, John vi. 63; for the Lord spoke his words in the natural sense. The celestial and the spiritual senses are not the Word, without the natural sense, for they are like spirit and life without a body; and they are, as was said before, n. 213, like a palace which has no foundation.

215. The truths of the sense of the letter of the Word, as to a part, are not naked truths, but they are appearances of truth, and like similitudes and comparisons taken from such things as are in nature, and which thus are accommodated and adapted to the capacity of the simple, and also of children; but, because they are at the same time correspondences, they are the receptacles and habitations of genuine truth; and they are vessels which contain, as a crystal cup contains noble wine, a silver plate palatable food; and as garments used for clothing, as swaddling-bands for an infant, and a handsome dress for a virgin; they are also like the scientifics of the natural man, which comprehend in them the perceptions and affections of spiritual truth The naked truths themselves, which are included, contained, clothed and comprehended, are in the spiritual sense of the Word, and the naked goods are in its celestial sense. But this may be illustrated from the Word: *Jesus said, Wo unto you, scribes and Pharisees, because ye cleanse the outside of the cup and of the platter, but the insides are full of rapine and intemperance. Blind Pharisee, cleanse first the inside of the cup and of the platter, that the outside also may be clean*, Matt. xxiii. 25, 26. Here the Lord spoke by similitudes and comparisons, which at the same time are correspondences; and He said *cup* and *platter;* and by *cup* is not only meant, but also signified, the truth of the Word; for by the *cup* wine is meant, and truth is signified by *wine;* but by the *platter* meat is meant, and good is signified by *meat;* wherefore, by *cleansing the inside of the cup and of the platter*, is signified, to purify the interiors of the mind, which are of the will and the thought, by the Word; by *that thus the outside may be clean*, is signified, that thus the exteriors are purified, which are works and words, for the latter derive their essence from the former. Again, *Jesus said, There was*

a certain rich man, who was clothed in purple and fine linen, and fared sumptuously every day; and there was a certain poor man, named Lazarus, who was laid at his gate, full of sores, Luke xvi. 19, 20. Here also the Lord spoke by similitudes and comparisons, which were correspondences, and contained spiritual things; by the *rich man* is meant the Jewish nation, who are called *rich*, because they had the Word, in which are spiritual riches; by the *purple and fine linen*, with which he was clothed, is signified the good and truth of the Word; by *purple*, its good, and by *fine linen*, its truth; by *faring sumptuously every day*, is signified their delight in having it, and in hearing from it many things in the temples and synagogues; by the *poor man, Lazarus*, are meant the Gentiles, because they had not the Word; that they were despised and rejected by the Jews, is meant by Lazarus being *laid at the rich man's gate;* by *full of sores*, is meant that the Gentiles, from ignorance of the truth, were in many falses. That the Gentiles are meant by *Lazarus*, was because the Gentiles were loved by the Lord; as Lazarus, who was raised from the dead, was loved by the Lord, John xi. 3, 5, 36; and is called his *friend*, xi. 11; and sat at table with the Lord, xii. 2. From these two passages, it is manifest that the truths and goods of the sense of the letter of the Word, are like vessels, and like garments for the naked good and truth, which two are concealed in the spiritual and celestial senses of the Word. Since the Word, in the sense of the letter, is such, it follows, that those who are in divine truths, and in the belief that the Word, inwardly, in its bosom, is holy and divine, and especially those who are in the faith that the Word is such from its spiritual and celestial senses, while, in illustration from the Lord, they read the Word, see divine truths in natural light; for the light of heaven, in which the spiritual sense of the Word is, flows into natural light, in which the sense of the letter of the Word is, and illuminates the intellectual of man, which is called the *rational*, and makes him see and acknowledge divine truths, where they are obvious and where they are latent. These things, with the light of heaven, flow into some, on some occasions, even when they are unconscious of it.

216. Since the Word, in its inmost bosom, from its celestial sense, is like a gentle flame which enkindles, and in its middle bosom, from its spiritual sense, is like a light which enlightens, therefore the Word, in its last, from its natural sense, is like a transparent object receiving both, which, from the flame, is red like purple, and from the light, white like snow; thus it is respectively like a ruby and like a diamond; from the celestial flame, like a ruby, and from the spiritual light, like a diamond. Because the Word is such in the sense of the letter, therefore the Word in this sense is meant, (1.) *By the precious stones of which the foundations of the New Jerusalem consisted.* (2.) *Also by the Urim and Thummim upon the ephod of Aaron.* (3.) *And also by the garden of Eden, in which the king of Tyre is said to have been.* (4.) *As also by the curtains, veils and columns of the tabernacle.* (5.) *In like manner, by the externals of the temple at Jerusalem.* (6.) *That the Word in its glory was represented in the Lord, when He was transfigured.* (7.) *That the power of the Word, in its lasts or ultimates, was represented by the Nazarites.* (8.) *Of the ineffable power of the Word.* But these things are to be illustrated one by one.

217. (1.) *That the Truths of the Letter of the Word are meant by the precious Stones of which the Foundations of the New Jerusalem consisted, in the Revelation*, xxi. 17 to 21.

It was mentioned above, n. 209, that there are precious stones in the spiritual world, as well as in the natural world, and that their spiritual origin is from the truths in the sense of the letter of the Word; this appears incredible, but still it is a truth. Thence it is, that wheresoever in the Word precious stones are named, by them, in the spiritual sense, truths are meant. That by the *precious stones*, of which the foundations of the wall around the city New Jerusalem are said to be constructed, are signified the truths of the doctrine of the New Church, follows hence, because by the *New Jerusalem* is meant the New Church, as to doctrine from the Word; wherefore, by its *wall*, and by the *foundations of the wall*, no other can be meant than the external of the Word, which is the sense of its letter; for it is this from which doctrine is, and by doctrine the church; and this sense is like a wall with foundations, which encompasses and secures a city. Concerning the New Jerusalem and its doctrine, these words are read in the Revelation: *An angel measured the wall of the city Jerusalem, a hundred forty and four cubits, which was the measure of a man, that is, of an angel. And the wall had twelve foundations, adorned with every precious stone. The first foundation was a jasper; the second a sapphire; the third a chalcedony; the fourth an emerald; the fifth a sardonyx; the sixth a sardius; the seventh a chrysolite; the eighth a beryl; the ninth a topaz; the tenth a chrysoprasus; the eleventh a jacinth; the twelfth an amethyst*, xxi. 17 to 20. The reason why the foundations of the wall there were twelve, of as many precious stones, is, because the number *twelve* signifies all the things of truth from good; here, therefore, all things of doctrine. But these things, as also those which precede and follow in that chapter, may be seen particularly explained and confirmed by parallel passages from the Word, in OUR APOCALYPSE REVEALED.

218. (2.) *That the Goods and Truths of the Word, in the Sense of its Letter, are meant by the Urim and Thummim, upon the Ephod of Aaron.*

The Urim and Thummim were upon the ephod of Aaron, by whose priesthood the Lord was represented, as to the divine good, and as to the work of salvation. By the *garments of the priesthood*, or *of its holiness* were represented divine truths from the Lord; by the *ephod*, was represented the divine truth in its ultimate, and so the Word, in the sense of the letter, for this is divine truth in its ultimate; thence by the *twelve precious stones*, with the names of the twelve tribes of Israel, which were the Urim and Thummim, were represented divine truths from divine good in the whole complex. Concerning these, it is thus read in Moses: *They shall make the ephod of blue and purple, scarlet double dyed, and fine-twined linen; and afterwards they shall make the breastplate of judgment according to the work of the ephod; and thou shalt set it with settings of stone, four rows of stone; the first row, a ruby, a topaz and an emerald; the second row, a chrysoprasus, a sapphire and a diamond; the third row, a ligure, an agate and an amethyst; the fourth row, a beryl, a sardius and a jasper. These stones shall be according to the names of the sons of Israel; the engravings of a signet shall be according to their name for the twelve tribes of Israel; and Aaron shall carry upon the breastplate of judgment, the Urim and Thummim; and let them be upon the heart of Aaron, when he goeth in before Jehovah*, Exod. xxviii. 6, 15 to 20, 30. What was represented by the garments of Aaron, his *ephod, robe, coat, mitre* and *belt*, is explained in the ARCANA CŒLESTIA, published at London, upon that chapter, where it is shown, that by the *ephod* is represented divine truth in its ultimate; that by the *precious stones* there, are represented divine truths shining from good; by *twelve* in a fourfold order, all those truths from the firsts to the lasts; by the *twelve tribes*, all the things of the church; by the *breastplate*, divine truth from divine good in a universal sense; by the *Urim and Thummim*, the brilliancy of divine truth from divine good, in the lasts or ultimates; for *Urim* is shining fire, and *Thummim* is brilliancy, in the angelic language, and integrity in the Hebrew language: and also that answers were given by variegations of light, and, at the same time, by tacit perception, or by an audible voice; besides many other things. From these things, it may be evident, that by these stones, also, are signified divine truths from good, in the last or ultimate sense of the Word; nor are answers from heaven given by other means, because, in that sense, the proceeding divine is in its fullness.

219. (3.) *That similar Things are meant by the Precious Stones in the Garden of Eden, in which the King of Tyre is said to have been.*

It is read in Ezekiel, *King of Tyre, thou who sealest up thy measure, full of wisdom and perfect in beauty; thou hast been in Eden, the garden of God; every precious stone was thy covering; the ruby, the topaz and the diamond; the beryl, the sardonyx and the jasper; the sapphire, the chrysoprasus and the emerald; and gold*, xxviii. 12, 13. By *Tyre*, in the Word, is signified the church, as to the knowledges of the good and the true; by *king*, is signified the truth of the church; by the *garden of Eden*, is signified wisdom and intelligence from the Word; by *precious stones*, are signified truths shining from good, such as are in the sense of the letter of the Word; and because these things are signified by those stones, therefore they are called his *covering*. That the sense of the letter covers the interior things of the Word, may be seen above, n. 213.

220. (4.) *That Goods and Truths, in the Lasts or Ultimates, such as they are in the Sense of the Letter of the Word, were represented by the Curtains, Veils and Columns of the Tabernacle.*

By the *tabernacle* built by Moses in the wilderness, was represented heaven and the church; wherefore the form of it was shown by Jehovah upon mount Sinai; thence by all the things which were in that tabernacle, which were the *candlestick*, the *golden altar for incense*, and the *table* upon which was the bread of faces, were represented and signified the holy things of heaven and the church; and by the *holy of holies*, where was the ark of the covenant, was represented, and thence signified, the inmost of heaven and the church; and by the *law* itself, written upon the *two tables*, was signified the Word; and by the *cherubs* above it, were signified guards, lest the holy things of the Word should be violated. Now, because externals derive their essence from internals, and these and those from the inmost, which there was the law, therefore the holy things of the Word were represented and signified by all the things of the tabernacle; thence it follows, that by the last things, or ultimates, of the tabernacle, which were the *curtains, veils* and *columns*, which were the coverings, continents and firmaments, were signified the last things or ultimates of the Word, which are the truths and goods of the sense of its letter. Because those things were signified, therefore all the curtains and veils were made of fine-twined linen, and blue, and purple, and scarlet double dyed, with cherubs, Exod. xxvi. 1, 31, 36. What was represented and signified, in general and in particular, by the tabernacle and by all the things that were in it, is explained in the ARCANA CŒLESTIA, upon that chapter of Exodus: and it is there shown, that by the *curtains* and *veils*, were represented the externals of heaven and the church, and so likewise the externals of the Word; and also that by *fine linen*, was signified truth from a spiritual origin; by *blue*, truth from a celestial origin; by *purple*, celestial good; by *scarlet double dyed*, spiritual good; and by *cherubs*, the guards of the interiors of the Word.

221. (5.) *That the same was represented by the Externals of the Temple at Jerusalem.*

The reason is, because by the *temple*, as well as by the *tabernacle*, was represented heaven and the church, but by the *temple*, the heaven in which the spiritual angels are, and by the *tabernacle*, the heaven where the celestial angels are. The spiritual angels are they who are in wisdom from the Word, but the celestial angels are they who are in love from the Word

That by the *temple at Jerusalem*, in the highest sense, was signified the Divine Human of the Lord, He teaches in John: *Destroy this temple, and in three days I will raise it up; He spoke concerning the temple of his body*, ii. 19, 21; and where the Lord is meant, the Word also is meant, because He is the Word. Now, because by the interiors of the temple, were represented the interiors of heaven and the church, and so likewise of the Word, therefore, by its exteriors were represented and signified the exteriors of heaven and the church, and so likewise of the Word, which are the sense of its letter. Concerning the exteriors of the temple, it is read, that *They were built of whole stone, not hewn, and of cedar within; and that all its walls within were carved with cherubs, palm-trees, and openings of flowers; and that the floor was overlaid with gold*, 1 Kings vi. 7, 29, 30; by all which things, also, are signified the externals of the Word, which are the holy things of the sense of its letter.

222. (6.) *That the Word in its Glory was represented in the Lord, when He was transfigured.*

Concerning the Lord transfigured before Peter, James and John, it is read, *That his face shone like the sun; his garments became like the light; and that Moses and Elijah were seen talking with Him; and that a bright cloud overshadowed the disciples; and that a voice was heard from the cloud, saying, This is my beloved Son; hear Him*, Matt. xvii. 1 to 5. I have been instructed, that the Lord then represented the Word; by his *face*, which *shone like the sun*, was represented the divine good of his divine love; by the *garments*, which *became like the light*, the divine truth of his divine wisdom; by *Moses and Elijah*, the historical and prophetical Word; by *Moses*, the Word written by Him, and the historical Word in general; and by *Elijah*, all the prophetical Word; by the *bright cloud*, which *overshadowed the disciples*, the Word in the sense of the letter; wherefore, from this a voice was heard, saying, *This is my beloved Son; hear Him;* for all declarations and answers from heaven are always made by ultimates, such as are in the sense of the letter of the Word; for they are made by the Lord in fullness.

223. (7.) *That the power of the Word, in Ultimates, was represented by the Nazarites.*

It is read in the book of Judges concerning Samson, that he was a Nazarite from his mother's womb, and that his power consisted in hair. By *Nazarite*, and *Nazariteship*, also, is signified *hair*. That his power consisted in his hair, he himself made manifest, saying, *There hath not come a razor upon my head, because I am a Nazarite from my mother's womb; if I be shaved, then my strength will go from me, and I shall become weak, and shall be like any other man*, Judges xvi. 17. No one can know why the Nazariteship, by which is signified *hair*, was instituted, and whence it is that Samson had strength from his hair, unless he knows what is signified in the Word by the head. By the *head*, is signified the intelligence which angels and men have from the Lord by divine truth; thence, by *hair*, is signified intelligence in ultimates, or extremes, from divine truth. Because this was signified by hair, therefore it was a statute for the Nazarites, *that they should not shave the hair of their head, because that is the Nazariteship of God upon their head*, Num. vi. 1 to 21; and also it was for that reason ordained, *that the high priest and his sons should not shave their heads, lest they should die, and the whole house of Israel should be angry*, Lev. x. 6. Since the hair, on account of this signification from correspondence, was so holy, therefore the Son of Man, who is the Lord as to the Word, is described even as to the hair, *that it was like white wool, like snow*, Rev. i. 14; in like manner, *the Ancient of days*, Dan. vii. 9. Since *hair* signifies truth in the ultimates, and so the sense of the letter of the Word, therefore those who despise the Word, in the spiritual world become bald; and, on the contrary, those who have highly esteemed the Word, and have accounted it holy, appear in becoming hair. On account of this correspondence, it came to pass, that forty-two children, because they called Elisha bald, were torn in pieces by two she-bears, 2 Kings ii. 23, 24; for *Elisha* represented the church, as to doctrine from the Word, and *she-bears* signify the power of truth in the ultimates. That the power of divine truth, or of the Word, is in the sense of its letter, is because the Word there is in its fullness, and because the angels of both kingdoms of the Lord, and men, are together in that sense.

224. (8.) *Concerning the ineffable Power of the Word.*

Scarcely any one, at this day, knows that there is any power in truths; for it is supposed that it is only a word spoken by some one who is in authority, which ought, on that account, to be done; consequently, that truth is only like breath from the mouth, or sound in the ear; when yet truth and good are the constituent principles of all things in both worlds, the spiritual and the natural; and that they are the things by which the universe was created, and by which the universe is preserved, and also by which man was made; wherefore those two are all in all. That the universe was created by the Divine Truth, is openly said in John: *In the beginning was the Word, and the Word was God; all things were made by Him, that were made. And the world was made by Him*, i. 1, 3, 10. And in David, *By the Word of Jehovah the heavens were made*, Psalm xxxiii. 6. By the *Word*, in both passages, is meant the divine truth. Since the universe was created by it, therefore, also, the universe is preserved by it; for, as subsistence is perpetual existence, so preservation is perpetual creation. That man was made by the divine truth, is, because all the things of man refer themselves to the understanding and the will; and the understanding is the receptacle of divine truth, and the will, of divine good; consequently the human mind, which consists of those two principles, is no other than a form of divine truth and divine good, spiritually and naturally organized: the human brain is that form; and because the whole of man depends on his mind, all the things which are in his body are appendages, which are actuated and live from those two principles. Hence, now, it may be evident, why God came into the world, as the Word, and became Man; that this was for the sake of redemption; for then God, by the Human, which was divine truth, put on all power, and cast down, subjugated and reduced under obedience to Himself, the hells, which had grown up even to the heavens, where the angels were; and this not by an oral word, but by the divine Word, which is the divine truth; and afterwards He opened a great gulf between the hells and the heavens, which no one from hell can pass over; if any one attempts it, he is at the first step, tortured like a serpent, placed upon plates of red-hot iron, or upon a heap of ants; for devils and satans, as soon as they smell the divine truth, instantly precipitate themselves into the deep, cast themselves into caverns, and stop them up so closely, that not a crack may be open. The reason is, because their will is in evils, and their understanding in falses, and so in the opposites to divine good and divine truth; and because the whole man consists of those two principles of life, as was said, therefore they are so grievously tortured all over, from the head to the heel, on the sensible perception of the opposite. Hence it may be evident, that the power of divine truth is ineffable; and because the Word, which is in the Christian church, is the continent of divine truth, in the three degrees, it is manifest, that it is that which is meant in John i. 3, 10. That the power of this is ineffable, I can confirm by many documents of experience, in the spiritual world; but, because they exceed belief, or appear incredible, I forbear to adduce them; some, however, you may see related above, n. 209. From these things, this memorable inference will be deduced; That the church, which is in divine truths from the Lord, prevails over the hells, and that it is that, concerning which the Lord said to Peter, *Upon this rock I will build my church, and the gates of hell shall not prevail against it*, Matt xvi. 18. The Lord said these words, when Peter had confessed that *He was the Christ, the Son of the living God*, 16; this truth is meant there by *rock;* for by *rock*, every where in the Word, is meant the Lord as to divine truth.

225. V. THAT THE DOCTRINE OF THE CHURCH SHOULD BE DERIVED FROM THE SENSE OF THE LETTER OF THE WORD, AND CONFIRMED BY IT.

It was shown in the preceding articles, that the Word, in the sense of the letter, is in its fullness, in its holiness, and in its power; and because the Lord is the Word, and the First and the Last, as He says in the Revelation, i. 17, it follows that the Lord, in that sense, is most present, and that from that, He teaches and enlightens man; but these things are to be demonstrated in this order: (1.) *That the Word, without doctrine, is not understood.* (2.) *That doctrine should be derived from the sense of the letter of the Word.* (3.) *But that divine truth, which is of doctrine, does not appear to any others, than those who are in illustration from the Lord.*

226. (1.) *That the Word, without Doctrine, is not understood.*

The reason is, because the Word, in the sense of the letter, consists of mere correspondences, to the end that spiritual and celestial things may be in it together, and that every single word may be a continent and support of them; therefore divine truths, in the sense of the letter, are rarely naked, but clothed, which are called *appearances of truth;* and there are many things accommodated to the capacity of the simple, who do not elevate their thoughts above such things as they see before their eyes; and there are some things, which appear like contradictions, when yet, in the Word, viewed in its own spiritual light, there is no contradiction; and also in some passages in the prophets, there are names of places and persons brought together, from which no sense can be elicited. Since, therefore, the Word, in the sense of the letter, is such, it may be evident, that it cannot be understood without doctrine. But examples may illustrate. It is said that *Jehovah repenteth*, Exod. xxxii. 12, 14; Jonah iii. 9, iv. 2; and also it is said, that *Jehovah doth not repent*, Num. xxiii. 19; 1 Sam. xv. 29. These, without doctrine, are not conformable to each other. It is said that *Jehovah visiteth the iniquity of the fathers upon the children unto the third and fourth generation*, Num. xiv. 18; and also it is said, that *The father shall not die on account of the son, nor the son on account of the father; but every one in his own sin*, Deut. xxiv. 16. These do not disagree, but agree by doctrine. Jesus says, *Ask, and it shall be given to you; seek, and ye shall find; and to him that knocketh, it shall be opened*, Matt. vii. 7, 8; xxi. 21, 22. Without doctrine, it might be supposed that every one would receive what he asks; but from doctrine it is known, that whatever man asks of the Lord, this is given. This also the Lord teaches, *If ye abide in Me, and my words abide in you, whatever ye wish, ask, and it shall be done for you*, John xv. 7. The Lord says, *Blessed are the poor, because the kingdom of God is theirs*, Luke vi. 20. Without doctrine, it may be thought, that heaven is for the poor, and not for the rich; but doctrine teaches, that the poor in spirit are meant; for the Lord says, *Blessed are the poor in spirit, because the kingdom of the heavens is theirs*, Matt. v. 5. Again, the Lord says, *Judge not, lest ye be judged; with what judgment ye judge, ye shall be judged*, Matt. vii. 1, 2; Luke vi. 37. Without doctrine, any one might be led to conclude that we should not judge concerning a bad man, that he is bad; but from doctrine it is lawful to judge, but justly; for the Lord says, *Judge righteous judgment*, John vii. 24. Jesus says, *Be not ye called teacher; because one is your Teacher, Christ. Call no man your father on the earth; for one is your Father in the heavens. Neither be ye called masters; for one is your Master, Christ*, Matt. xxiii. 8, 9, 10. Without doctrine, it would be, that it is not lawful to call any one *teacher*, *father*, and *master;* but from doctrine, it is known, that it is lawful in a natural sense, but not in a spiritual sense. Jesus said to the disciples, *When the Son of man shall sit upon the throne of his glory, ye also shall sit upon twelve thrones, judging the twelve tribes of Israel*, Matt. xix. 28. From these words, it may be concluded, that the disciples of the Lord are also to judge, when yet they can judge no one; doctrine, therefore, will reveal this mystery, by this, that the Lord alone, who is omniscient, and knows the hearts of all, will judge, and is able to judge; and that, by his twelve *disciples*, is meant the church as to all the truths and goods which it has from the Lord by the Word; whence doctrine concludes, that those are to judge every one, according to the words of the Lord in John, iii. 17, 18; xii. 47, 48. There are many other things in the Word similar to these, from which it is very manifest, that the Word, without doctrine, is not understood.

227. The Word, by doctrine, is not only understood, but it also shines in the understanding; for doctrine is like a chandelier with lighted candles; a man then sees many things, which he had not seen before, and also understands those things, which he had not understood before: obscure and discordant passages he either does not see and passes by, or he sees and explains them so that they may be in accordance with doctrine. That the Word is seen from doctrine, and explained according to it, is testified by experience in the Christian world. All the Reformed see the Word from their doctrine, and they explain the Word according to it; in like manner, the Roman Catholics from theirs, and according to it; yea, the Jews from theirs, and according to it; consequently they see falses from false doctrine, and truths from true doctrine. Hence it is manifest, that true doctrine is like a lantern in the dark, and like a guide-post in the ways.

228. From these things, it may be evident, that those who read the Word, without doctrine, are in the dark concerning every truth, and that their mind is wandering and uncertain, prone to errors, and also inclinable to heresies, which they embrace, if favor and authority support them and their fame be not endangered; for the Word is to them like a candlestick without light, and they see in the shade, as it were, many things; and yet they see scarcely any thing, for doctrine alone is the candle. I have seen such explored by the angels, and it was found that they could confirm from the Word whatever they would, and that they do confirm, particularly, those things which are of their love, and of the love of those whom they favor. But I saw them stripped of their garments, a sign that they were without truths; garments there are truths.

229. (2.) *That Doctrine should be derived from the Sense of the Letter of the Word, and confirmed by it.*

The reason is, because the Lord is there present, and teaches and illustrates; for the Lord never performs any thing except in fullness, and the Word, in the sense of the letter, is in its fullness, as was shown above; thence it is, that doctrine should be derived from the sense of the letter. The doctrine of genuine truth may also be fully derived from the literal sense of the Word; for the Word, in that sense, is like a man clothed, whose face is bare, and whose hands also are bare. All the things which appertain to the faith and life of man, consequently to his salvation, are there naked or bare, but the rest are clothed; and in many places where they are clothed, they appear through the clothing as objects appear to a woman through thin silk before her face. The truths of the Word, also, as they are multiplied from the love of them, and as by this they are arranged in order, shine and appear more and more clearly.

230. It may be supposed, that the doctrine of genuine truth might be

obtained by the spiritual sense of the Word, which is given by the science of correspondences; but doctrine is not obtained by that, but it is only illustrated and corroborated; for, as was before said, n. 208, a man, by some correspondences which are known, may falsify the Word, by conjoining and applying them to confirm that which is fixed in his mind from a principle which he has imbibed. Besides, the spiritual sense is not given to any one, except by the Lord alone, and it is guarded by Him, as the angelic heaven is guarded; for this is in it.

231. (3.) *That genuine Truth, which should be of Doctrine, in the Sense of the Letter of the Word, does not appear to any others, than those who are in Illustration from the Lord.*

Illustration is from the Lord alone, and with those who love truths because they are truths, and make them uses of life; with others, illustration in the Word is not given. That illustration is from the Lord alone, is, because the Word is from Him, and thence He is in it. That those have illustration, who love truths because they are truths, and make them uses of life, is, because they are in the Lord, and the Lord in them; for the Lord is the Truth itself, as was shown in the chapter concerning the Lord; and the Lord is then loved, when man lives according to his divine truths, and so when uses are performed from them, according to these words in John: *In that day, ye shall know that ye are in Me, and I in you. He who hath my commandments, and doeth them, loveth Me; and I will love him, and will manifest Myself to him; and I will come to him, and make an abode with him*, xiv. 20, 21, 23. These are they who are in illustration, when they read the Word, and with whom the Word shines and becomes translucent. The reason why the Word, with those, shines and becomes translucent, is, because there is a spiritual and a celestial sense in every part of the Word, and these senses are in the light of heaven; wherefore, through these senses, and their light, the Lord flows into the natural sense of the Word, and into the light of this with man; thence man acknowledges the truth from an interior perception, and then sees it in his thought, and this as often as he is in the affection of truth, for the sake of truth; for perception comes from affection, and thought from perception, and thus acknowledgment is made, which is called *faith.*

232. The contrary happens to those who read the Word from the doctrine of a false religion, especially to those who confirm that doctrine from the Word, and then look to their own glory, and to the riches of the world. With these, the truths of the Word are as in the shade of night, and falses as in the light of day; they read truths, but they do not see them; and if they see the shadow of them, they falsify them. These are they, concerning whom the Lord says, that *They have eyes, and they do not see, and ears, and they do not understand*, Matt. xiii. 14, 15. Thence their light, in spiritual things, which are of the church, becomes merely natural, and the sight of their mind, like that of one who sees spectres in the bed when he wakes up; or like that of one walking in the night, who believes himself awake when he is asleep.

233. It has been given me to speak with many after death, who believed that they should shine like the stars in heaven, because, as they said, they had accounted the Word holy, had often read it through, had collected thence many things, by which they had confirmed the tenets of their faith, and therefore had been celebrated as learned men; whence they believed that they should be Michaels and Raphaels. But many of them were examined, as to the love from which they studied the Word; and it was found that some studied it from the love of themselves, that they might be worshipped as primates of the church; and some from the love of the world, that they might gain riches; when these, also, were examined, as to what

they knew from the Word, it was found that they knew nothing thence of genuine truth, but only such as is called *truth falsified*, which in itself is the false in a state of putridity, for in heaven it stinks; and it was said to them, that they had this because they themselves and the world were the ends, when they read the Word, and not the truth of faith and the good of life; and when self and the world become ends, then the mind, in reading the Word, is fixed in self and in the world; and thence they think continually from their proprium, and the proprium of man is in thick darkness, as to all the things which are of heaven and the church; in which state man cannot be led by the Lord, and elevated into the light of heaven; consequently he cannot receive any influx from the Lord through heaven. I have also seen these admitted into heaven, and when there they were found to be without truths, they were cast down; but still there remained with them a conceit that they were deserving. The case was different with those who had studied the Word from the affection of knowing truth, because it is truth, and serves for the uses of life, not only of their own, but also of their neighbor's: those I have seen elevated into heaven, and thus into the light in which the divine truth there is; and then, at the same time, exalted into angelic wisdom, and into its happiness, in which the angels of heaven are.

234. VI. That by the Sense of the Letter of the Word, there is Conjunction with the Lord, and Consociation with the Angels.

That by the Word, there is conjunction with the Lord, is, because He is the Word, that is, the Divine Truth itself and the Divine Good therein; that conjunction is by the sense of the letter, is, because the Word, in that sense, is in its fullness, in its holiness, and in its power, as was shown above, in its proper article. This conjunction does not appear to man, but it is in the affection of truth, and in the perception of it. That by the sense of the letter, there is consociation with the angels of heaven, is, because the spiritual sense and the celestial sense are within that sense, and the angels are in those senses; the angels of the Lord's spiritual kingdom, in the spiritual sense of the Word, and the angels of his celestial kingdom, in its celestial sense: these two senses are evolved from the natural sense of the Word, whilst man, who accounts the Word holy, is reading it. The evolution is instantaneous; consequently consociation is also.

235. That the spiritual angels are in the spiritual sense of the Word, and the celestial angels in its celestial sense, has been manifested to me by much experience. It was given to perceive, that, while I was reading the Word in the sense of its letter, communication was made with the heavens, now with this society there, now with that: the things which I understood according to the natural sense, the spiritual angels understood according to the spiritual sense, and the celestial angels according to the celestial sense, and this in an instant; and because this communication has been perceived several thousands of times, I have not any doubt left concerning it. There are also spirits who are below the heavens, and who abuse this communication; for they recite some sayings from the sense of the letter of the Word, and immediately observe and note the society with which communication is made: this, also, I have often seen and heard. From these things, it has been given to know by lively experience, that the Word, as to the sense of its letter, is a divine medium of conjunction with the Lord, and of consociation with the angels of heaven.

236. But it shall be illustrated by examples, how the spiritual angels perceive their sense, and the celestial angels theirs, from the natural sense, when man reads the Word. Let four commandments of the decalogue be for examples; as, the Fifth Commandment, *Thou shalt not kill.* By this, man not only understands *to kill*, but also to cherish hatred and breathe revenge even to death; a spiritual an-

gel, for *killing*, understands to act the devil and destroy the soul of man ; but a celestial angel, for *killing*, understands to cherish hatred towards the Lord and the Word. THE SIXTH COMMANDMENT, *Thou shalt not commit adultery.* Man, by *committing adultery*, understands to commit whoredom, to do obscene things, to speak lascivious words, and to entertain filthy thoughts ; a spiritual angel, for *committing adultery*, understands to adulterate the goods of the Word, and to falsify its truths; but a celestial angel, for *committing adultery*, understands to deny the Divine of the Lord, and to profane the Word. THE SEVENTH COMMANDMENT, *Thou shalt not steal.* Man, by *stealing*, understands, to steal, to defraud, and, under any pretence, to take away from the neighbor his goods; a spiritual angel, for *stealing*, understands to deprive others of the truths and goods of their faith, by falses and evils; but a celestial angel, for *stealing*, understands to attribute to himself those things which are the Lord's, and to claim to himself his righteousness and merit. THE EIGHTH COMMANDMENT, *Thou shalt not bear false witness.* Man, by *bearing false witness*, understands, also, to tell lies, and to defame any one ; a spiritual angel, for *bearing false witness*, understands to say, and to persuade others to believe, that the false is true, and evil is good, and *vice versâ ;* but a celestial angel, for *bearing false witness*, understands to blaspheme the Lord and the Word. From these examples, it may be seen how the spiritual and the celestial are evolved and extracted from the natural sense of the Word, within which they are; and, what is wonderful, the angels extract their senses, without knowing what the man is thinking; but still the thoughts of angels and men make one by correspondences, like end, cause and effect; ends, also, are actually in the celestial kingdom, causes in the spiritual kingdom, and effects in the natural kingdom ; thence, now, the consociation of men with angels is by means of the Word.

237. That a spiritual angel extracts and calls forth from the sense of the letter of the Word spiritual things, and a celestial angel, celestial things, is, because those things are according to their nature, and are homogeneous. That it is so, may be illustrated by similar things in the three kingdoms of nature, the animal, the vegetable and the mineral. In THE ANIMAL KINGDOM ; From the food, when it has become chyle, the vessels derive and call forth their blood, the nervous fibres, their juice, and the substances which are the origins of the fibres, their spirit. In THE VEGETABLE KINGDOM ; A tree, with its trunk, branches, leaves and fruit, stands upon its root; and from the ground, by means of the root, it extracts and calls forth a grosser juice for the trunk, branches and leaves, a purer, for the fleshy part of the fruit, and the purest, for the seeds within the fruit. In THE MINERAL KINGDOM ; In the bosom of the earth, in some places, there are minerals impregnated with gold, silver, copper and iron; from the vapors and effluvia from rocks, gold, silver and iron, respectively, derive their proper elements, and the watery element carries them round about.

238. The Word, in the letter, is like a cabinet, in which lie in order precious stones, pearls and diadems; and when a man accounts the Word holy, and reads it, for the sake of the uses of life, the thoughts of his mind are, comparatively, like one who holds such a cabinet in his hand, and sends it to heaven, and it is opened in its ascent, and the precious things therein come to the angels, who are interiorly delighted with seeing and examining them. This delight of the angels is communicated to man, and makes consociation, and also a communication of perceptions. For the sake of this consociation with angels, and, at the same time, conjunction with the Lord, the Holy Supper was instituted, in which the Bread becomes, in heaven, divine good, and the Wine becomes divine truth, both from the Lord. Such correspondence is from creation, to the end that the angelic heaven, and the church upon earth and the spiritual world in general

may make one with the natural world, and that the Lord may conjoin Himself with both at the same time.

239. The reason, also, why the consociation of men with angels is effected by the natural or literal sense of the Word, is, because, in every man, there are, from creation, three degrees of life, the celestial, the spiritual and the natural; but man is in the natural degree as long as he is in the world, and then so far in the angelic-spiritual as he is in genuine truths, and so far in the celestial as he is in a life according to them; but still he does not come into the spiritual and celestial themselves, till after death, because these two are included and concealed in his natural ideas; wherefore, when the natural goes off by death, the spiritual and the celestial remain, from which the ideas of his thought are then produced. From these things, it may be evident, that in the Word alone there is spirit and life, as the Lord says: *The words which I speak unto you are spirit and life,* John vi. 63. *The water which I will give unto you shall become a fountain of water, springing up into eternal life,* iv. 14. *Man doth not live by bread alone, but by every word proceeding from the mouth of God,* Matt. iv. 4. *Work for the meat which endureth unto eternal life, which the Son of Man will give to you,* John vi. 27.

240. VII. That the Word is in all the Heavens, and that thence is angelic Wisdom.

That the Word is in the heavens, has been hitherto unknown; nor could it be made known so long as the church was ignorant that angels and spirits are men, altogether similar, in face and body, to men in our world; and that there are with them things similar to the things which are with men, in all respects, with this difference only, that they are spiritual, and that all the things that are with them, are from a spiritual origin; and that men in the world are natural, and that all the things with them, are from a natural origin. As long as this was concealed, it could not be known, that the Word is also in the heavens, and that it is read by the angels there, and also by the spirits who are under the heavens. But lest this should be concealed forever, it has been given me to be in company with angels and spirits, and to speak with them, and to see the things that are with them, and afterwards to relate many things which I have seen and heard; this has been done in a work concerning Heaven and Hell, published at London in the year 1758; from which it may be seen, that angels and spirits are men, and that there are with them, in abundance, all the things that there are with men in the world. That angels and spirits are men, may be seen in that work, n. 73 to 77, and n. 453 to 456; that there are with them things similar to the things that are with men in the world, n. 170 to 190; and also that there is divine worship, and that there is preaching in the temples with them, n. 221 to 227; and that there are writings and also books, n. 253 to 264; and that the Sacred Scripture or the Word is there, n. 259.

241. As to what respects the Word in heaven, it is written in a spiritual style, which differs entirely from a natural style. The spiritual style consists of mere letters, each of which involves some particular sense; and there are little lines, curvatures and dots above and between the letters and in them, which exalt the sense. The letters with the angels of the spiritual kingdom are like the letters used in printing, in our world, and the letters with the angels of the celestial kingdom, are, with some, like Arabic letters, and with some like the old Hebrew letters, but inflected above and below, with marks above, between and within; each of these also involves an entire sense. Because their writing is such, therefore the names of persons and places in the Word with them are expressed by signs; thence it is understood by the wise, what spiritual and celestial thing is signified by each; as by Moses, the Word of God written by him, and in a general sense, the historical Word, by Elijah, the prophetical; by Abraham, Isaac and Jacob, the Lord as to the celestial Divine, the spiritual Di

vine and the natural Divine; by Aaron, the priestly office; by David, the kingly office, both of the Lord; by the names of the sons of Jacob, or of the twelve tribes of Israel, various things of heaven and the church; similar things by the names of the twelve disciples of the Lord; by Zion and Jerusalem, the church as to doctrine from the Word; by the land of Canaan, the church itself; by the places and cities there, on this side and beyond the Jordan, various things which are of the church and its doctrine. It is similar with numbers; these are not in the copies of the Word which are in heaven, but, instead of them, the things to which the numbers correspond. From these things it may be evident, that the Word, in heaven, is, as to the literal sense, similar, and at the same time corresponding to our Word, and thus that they are one. This is wonderful, that the Word in the heavens is so written, that the simple understand it in simplicity, and the wise in wisdom; for there are many curvatures and marks above the letters, which, as was said, exalt the sense; the simple do not attend to them, nor do they know them, but the wise attend, each one according to his wisdom, even to the highest. A copy of the Word, written by angels inspired by the Lord, is preserved amongst every larger society, in its sacred repository, lest the Word, as to some point, should in other places be altered. The Word which is in our world, is similar to the Word in heaven, in this, that the simple understand it in simplicity, and the wise in wisdom; but this is effected in a different manner.

242. That the angels have all their wisdom by the Word, they themselves confess; for as far as they are in the understanding of the Word, so far they are in light. The light of heaven is divine wisdom, which to their eyes is light. In the sacred repository in which a copy of the Word is laid up, the light is flammeous and bright, exceeding every degree of the light which is out of it in heaven. The wisdom of the celestial angels exceeds the wisdom of the spiritual almost as much as the wisdom of these angels exceeds the wisdom of men; and this because the celestial angels are in the good of love from the Lord, and the spiritual angels are in the truths of wisdom from the Lord; and where the good of love is, there wisdom resides at the same time; but where truths are, there resides no more of wisdom, than there does, at the same time, of the good of love. This is the reason why the Word, in the Lord's celestial kingdom, is written differently from the Word in his spiritual kingdom; for, in the Word of the celestial kingdom, the things expressed are the goods of love, and the marks are affections of love; but in the word of the spiritual kingdom, the things expressed are the truths of wisdom, and the marks are interior perceptions of truth. From these things it may be concluded, what wisdom there is concealed in the Word, which is in the world, for in it all angelic wisdom, which is ineffable, is concealed; and the man who is made an angel by the Lord, through the Word, comes into that wisdom after death.

243. VIII. That the Church is from the Word, and that it is such with Man as is his Understanding of the Word.

That the church is from the Word, does not fall into doubt; for it has been shown above, that the Word is the divine truth, n. 189 to 192; that the doctrine of the church is from the Word, n. 225 to 233; and that conjunction with the Lord is by the Word, n. 234 to 239; but that the understanding of the Word makes the church, may be a matter of doubt, because there are those who believe that they are of the church, because they have the Word, read it or hear it from a preacher, and know something of the sense of its letter; but how this and that in the Word is to be understood, they do not know, and some do not care; wherefore it will here be confirmed, that the Word does not make the church, but the understanding of it, and that the church is such, as is the understanding of the Word with those who are in the church.

244. That the church is according to the understanding of the Word, is, because the church is according to the truths of faith and the goods of charity, and these two are universals which are not only scattered about through all the literal sense of the Word, but they are also concealed within, like precious things in treasuries. Those things which are in its literal sense, appear to every man, because they flow in direcıly into the eyes; but those things which are hid in the spiritual sense do not appear, except to those who love truths because they are truths, and do goods because they are goods; to these the treasure is manifested, which the literal sense covers and guards; and these are the things which, essentially, make the church.

245. That the church is according to its doctrine, and that doctrine is from the Word, is known; but still doctrine does not make the church, but soundness and purity of doctrine, consequently the understanding of the Word; but doctrine does not institute and make the particular church, which is with every single man, but faith and a life according to it; in like manner, the Word does not institute and make the church, in particular, with every man, but a faith according to the truths, and a life according to the goods, which he derives thence and applies to himself. The Word is like a mine, in which gold and silver are at the bottom in all abundance; and like a mine in which, more and more interiorly, stones more and more precious are concealed: these mines are opened according to the understanding of the Word. Without an understanding of the Word, such as it is in itself, in its bosom and in its depth, it would no more make the church with man, than those mines in the continent of Asia could make an European rich, unless he were among those who possess and work them. The Word, with those who search for the truths of faith, and the goods of life thence, is like the treasures with the king of Persia, the Great Mogul, or the emperor of China; and the men of the church are like the officers placed over them, to whom permission is given to take thence, for their uses, as much as they please; but those who only possess the Word, and read it, and yet do not seek after genuine truths for faith, and genuine goods for life, are like those, who from hearsay, know that so great treasures are there, but do not receive from them any money. Those who possess the Word, and do not derive thence any understanding of genuine truth, and will of genuine good are like those who believe themselves to be rich, from having borrowed money of others, or having in possession the farms, houses and merchandise of others. that this is fanciful every one sees. They are also similar to those who go dressed in fine clothes, and ride in gilded chariots, with attendants before, behind and at the sides, and yet not any of those things are their own property.

246. Such was the Jewish nation: wherefore that nation, because it possessed the Word, was likened by the Lord to a rich man, who was clothed in purple and fine linen, and fared sumptuously every day; and yet he had not derived from the Word so much of good and truth, as to show mercy to poor Lazarus, who lay before his gate full of sores. That nation not only did not appropriate to itself any truths from the Word, but it appropriated falses in such abundance, that, at length, not any truth appeared to them; for truths are not only covered over by falses, but they are also obliterated and rejected: thence it was, that they did not acknowledge the Messiah, although all the prophets had announced his advent.

247. In many places in the prophets, the church, with the Israelitish and Jewish nation, is described as being entirely destroyed and annihilated by this, that they falsified the meaning or understanding of the Word; for nothing else destroys the church. The understanding of the Word, as well the true as the false, is described in the prophets by EPHRAIM, particularly in Hosea; for by *Ephraim*, in the Word, is signified the understanding of the Word in the church. Since the understanding of the Word makes the

church, therefore Ephraim is called in the Word A DEAR SON, and A PLEASANT CHILD, Jerem. xxxi. 21; THE FIRST-BORN, 20; THE STRENGTH OF THE HEAD OF JEHOVAH, Psalm lx. 9, cviii. 9; POWERFUL, Zech. x. 7; FILLED WITH THE BOW, ix. 13: and the sons of Ephraim are called ARMED, and SHOOTERS WITH THE BOW, Psalm lxxviii. 9; for by *the bow* is signified doctrine from the Word fighting against falses. Therefore, also, *Ephraim was removed to the right hand of Israel, and blessed; and also he was accepted instead of Reuben*, Gen. xlviii. 5, 11, and the following verses. And therefore *Ephraim, with his brother Manasseh, was exalted, by Moses, in the benediction of the sons of Israel, under the name of Joseph, their father, above all*, Deut. xxxiii. 13 to 17. But what the church is, when the understanding of the Word is lost, is also described by Ephraim, in the prophets, particularly in Hosea, as in these passages; *Israel and Ephraim will fall together. Ephraim will be for a wilderness. Ephraim is oppressed and shaken in judgment*, Hosea v. 5, 9, 11, 12, 13, 14. *What shall I do to thee, O Ephraim, because thy holiness, like the morning cloud, and like the early falling dew, goeth away?* vi. 4. *They shall not dwell in the land of Jehovah; Ephraim shall return into Egypt, and in Assyria he shall eat what is unclean*, ix. 3; the *land of Jehovah* is the church; *Egypt* is the scientific of the natural man; *Assyria* is reasoning thence; from which two together, the Word, as to the interior understanding of it, is falsified; therefore it is said, that Ephraim shall return into Egypt, and in Assyria he shall eat what is unclean. *Ephraim feedeth on the wind, and followeth after the east wind. Every day he multiplieth falsehood and vastation; he maketh a covenant with Assyria, and oil is carried into Egypt*, Hosea xii. 2. To *feed on the wind*, to *follow after the east wind*, and to *multiply falsehood and vastation*, is to falsify truths, and thus to destroy the church. The like is signified by the *whoredom* of Ephraim; for *whoredom* signifies the falsification of the understanding of the Word that is, of its genuine truth, as in these passages: *I know Ephraim, that he hath altogether committed whoredom, and Israel is defiled*, Hosea v. 3. *In the house of Israel, I have seen a horrible thing; there Ephraim committed whoredom, and Israel is defiled*, vi. 10. *Israel* is the church itself, and *Ephraim* is the understanding of the Word, from which and according to which the church is, wherefore it is said, *Ephraim has committed whoredom, and Israel is defiled.* Since the church, with the Israelitish and Jewish nation, was utterly destroyed by falsifications of the Word, therefore it is said concerning Ephraim, *I will give thee up, Ephraim, I will deliver thee up, Israel, like Admah, and I will set thee as Zeboim*, Hosea xi. 8. Now because the prophet Hosea, from the first chapter to the last, treats concerning the falsification of the genuine understanding of the Word, and concerning the destruction of the church thereby, and because by *whoredom* is signified the falsification of the truth there, therefore it was commanded that prophet, that he should represent the state of the church, by *taking to himself a harlot to wife, and begetting children of her*, Hosea i.; and again, that *he should take a woman, an adulteress*, iii. These passages have been cited, that it may be known and confirmed from the Word, that the church is such, as the understanding of the word in it; excellent and precious, if the understanding be from the genuine truths of the Word, but destroyed, yea, filthy, if from those that are falsified.

248. IX. THAT THE MARRIAGE OF THE LORD AND THE CHURCH, AND THENCE THE MARRIAGE OF THE GOOD AND THE TRUE, IS IN EVERY PART OF THE WORD.

That the marriage of the Lord and the church, and thence the marriage of the good and the true, is in every part of the Word, has not hitherto been seen; nor could it be seen, because the spiritual sense of the Word has not before been disclosed, and that marriage cannot be seen, except by that; for there are two senses in the Word concealed in the sense of its letter, which are called the spiritual and the celestial. In the spiritual sense, in the Word, those things which are of it refer themselves chiefly to the church; and in the celestial, chiefly to the Lord; and also in the spiritual sense, those things which are of it refer themselves to the divine truth, and in the celestial, to the divine good; thence, there is in the Word that marriage. But this does not appear to any one except to him, who, from the spiritual and celestial senses, knows the significations of words and names; for some words and names are predicated of good, and some of truth, and some include both; wherefore, without that knowledge, that marriage in every part of the Word cannot be seen; this is the reason, why this arcanum was never before discovered. Since there is such a marriage in every part of the Word, therefore many times, in the Word, there are two expressions, which appear like repetitions of one thing; but yet they are not repetitions, but one refers itself to good, and the other to truth, and both, taken together, make their conjunction, and so one thing. Thence also is the divine holiness of the Word; for, in every divine work, there is good conjoined to truth, and truth conjoined to good.

249. It is said, that the marriage of the Lord and the church, and thence the marriage of the good and the true, is in every part of the Word, because, where the marriage of the Lord and the church is, there also is the marriage of the good and the true, for this marriage is from that; for when the church, or the man of the church, is in truths, then the Lord flows into his truths with good, and vivifies them; or, what is the same, when the man of the church is in the understanding of truth, then the Lord, by the good of charity, flows into his understanding, and thus infuses life into him.

There are two faculties of life with every man, which are called the understanding and the will; the understanding is the receptacle of truth, and thence of wisdom; and the will is the receptacle of good, and thence of charity; these two faculties should make one, that man may be a man of the church; and they do make one when man forms the understanding from genuine truths and this is done to appearance as by himself, and when his will is filled with the good of love, this is done by the Lord; thence man has the life of truth, and the life of good; the life of truth in the understanding, and the life of good in the will, which, when they are united, do not make two, but one life. This is the marriage of the Lord and the church, and also the marriage of the good and the true with man.

250. That there are in the Word two expressions, which appear like repetitions of the same thing, may be seen by readers who attend to it; as, *brother* and *companion*, *poor* and *needy*, *wilderness* and *desert*, *void* and *emptiness*, *foe* and *enemy*, *sin* and *iniquity*, *anger* and *wrath*, *nation* and *people*, *joy* and *gladness*, *mourning* and *weeping*, *justice* and *judgment*, &c., which appear like synonymous expressions, when yet they are not so; for *brother*, *poor*, *wilderness*, *foe*, *sin*, *anger*, *nation*, *joy*, *mourning* and *justice*, are predicated of good, and in the opposite sense, of evil; but *companion*, *needy*, *desert*, *emptiness*, *enemy*, *iniquity*, *wrath*, *people*, *gladness*, *weeping* and *judgment*, are predicated of truth, and in the opposite sense, of the false; and yet it appears to the reader, who does not know this arcanum, that *poor* and *needy*, *wilderness* and *desert*, *void* and *emptiness*, &c., are one thing, and yet they are not; but they become one thing by conjunction. In the Word, also, many things are joined together, as *fire* and *flame*, *gold* and *silver*, *brass* and *iron*, *wood* and *stone*, *bread* and *wine*, *purple* and *fine linen*, &c.; because *fire*, *gold*, *brass*, *wood*, *bread* and *purple*, are predicated of good; but *flame*, *silver*, *iron*, *stone*, *water*, *wine*, and *fine linen*, are predicated of truth. In like manner, it is said, that men should love God with the whole heart and with the whole soul; and also, that God will create in man a new heart and a new spirit; for *heart* is predicated of the good of love, and *soul* and *spirit* of the truths of faith. There

are also words which, because they partake of both, as well of the good as the true, are used by themselves without others adjoined; but these and many more things are not apparent, except to the angels, and to those who, while they are in the natural sense, are also in the spiritual sense.

251. It would be tedious to show from the Word, that there are two such expressions in the Word, which appear like repetitions of the same thing, for it would fill many pages; but, that doubt may be removed, I will adduce the passages where *nation* and *people*, and where *joy* and *gladness* are used together. The passages where *nation* and *people* are named, are these; *Ah sinful* NATION, A PEOPLE *laden with iniquity*, Isaiah i. 4. THE PEOPLE *walking in darkness, saw a great light; thou hast multiplied* THE NATION, ix. 1, 2. *Assyria, the rod of mine anger; I will send him against a hypocritical* NATION, *I will give him a charge against* THE PEOPLE *of my wrath*, x. 5, 6. *It shall come to pass in that day,* THE NATIONS *shall seek the Root of Jesse, which standeth for a sign of* THE PEOPLE, xi. 10. *Jehovah, who smiteth* THE PEOPLE *with an incurable wound, ruling* THE NATIONS *with anger*, xiv. 6. *In that day shall be brought, as an offering to Jehovah of hosts,* A PEOPLE *distracted and peeled, and* A NATION *marked out and trampled upon*, xviii. 2. *The strong* PEOPLE *shall honor thee, the city of powerful* NATIONS *shall fear thee*, xxv. 3. *Jehovah will destroy the covering upon all* PEOPLE, *the veil upon all* NATIONS, xxv. 8. *Approach, ye* NATIONS, *and hearken, ye* PEOPLE, xxxiv. 1. *I have called thee for a covenant of* THE PEOPLE, *for a light of* THE NATIONS, xlii. 6. *Let all* THE NATIONS *be gathered together, and let* THE PEOPLE *come together*, xliii. 9. *Behold, I will lift up my hand towards* THE NATIONS, *and my standard towards* THE PEOPLE, xlix. 22. *I have given Him for a witness to* THE PEOPLE, *a Prince and a Lawgiver to* THE NATIONS, liv. 4, 5. *Behold* A PEOPLE *coming from the land of the north, and a great* NATION *from the sides of the land*, Jerem. vi. 22, 23. *I will not make thee hear the calumny of* THE NATIONS *any more, and thou shalt not bear the reproach of* THE PEOPLE *any more*, Ezek. xxxvi. 15. *All* PEOPLE *and* NATIONS *shall worship Him*, Dan. vii. 14. *Let not* THE NATIONS *make a by-word concerning them, and say among* THE PEOPLE, *Where is their God?* Joel ii. 7. *The remains of my* PEOPLE *shall spoil them, and the residue of my* NATION *shall inherit them*, Zeph. ii. 9. *Many* PEOPLE *and numerous* NATIONS *shall come to seek Jehovah in Jerusalem*, Zech. viii. 22. *Mine eyes have seen thy salvation, which thou hast prepared before the face of all* PEOPLE, *a light for the enlightening of the* NATIONS, Luke ii. 30, 31, 32. *Thou hast redeemed us by thy blood, out of every* PEOPLE *and* NATION, Rev. v. 9. *Thou must again prophesy over* PEOPLE *and* NATIONS, x. 11. *Thou wilt set me for the head of* THE NATIONS; A PEOPLE *which I had not known will serve me*, Psalm xviii. 43. *Jehovah frustrateth the counsel of* THE NATIONS, *He subverteth the thoughts of* THE PEOPLE, xxxiii. 10. *Thou settest us as a proverb among* THE NATIONS, *a shaking of the head among* THE PEOPLE, xliv. 14. Jehovah will subdue THE PEOPLE *under us, and* THE NATIONS *under our feet; Jehovah reigneth over* THE NATIONS, *the voluntary of* THE PEOPLE *are gathered together*, xlvii. 3, 8, 9. THE PEOPLE *will confess Thee, and* THE NATIONS *will sing praise, because Thou wilt judge* THE PEOPLE *in uprightness, and wilt lead* THE NATIONS *upon the earth*, lxvii. 3, 4. *Remember me, Jehovah, in the good pleasure of thy* PEOPLE, *that I may be glad in the joy of thy* NATIONS, cvi. 4, 5: besides in other places. The reason why *nations* and *people* are mentioned at the same time, is, because, by *nations*, are meant those who are in good, and in the opposite sense, those who are in evil; and by *people*, those who are in truths, and in the opposite sense, those who are in falses; wherefore those who are of the Lord's spiritual kingdom, are called *people*, and those who are of the Lord's celestial kingdom, are called *nations;* for all in the spiritual kingdom are in truths, and thence in intel-

igence; but all in the celestial kingdom are in goods, and thence in wisdom.

252. It is similar with many others; as that where JOY is mentioned, GLADNESS also is mentioned, as in these passages: *Behold* JOY *and* GLADNESS *to slay an ox*, Isaiah xxii. 13. *They shall obtain* JOY *and* GLADNESS, *and sorrow and sighing shall flee away*, xxxv. 10; li. 11. GLADNESS *and* JOY *are cut off from the house of our God*, Joel i. 16. *The voice of* JOY *shall cease, and the voice of* GLADNESS, Jerem. vii. 34; xxv. 10. *The fast of the tenth shall be to the house of Judah for* JOY *and* GLADNESS, Zech. viii. 19. BE GLAD *in Jerusalem, and* REJOICE *in her*, Isaiah lxvi. 10. REJOICE *and* BE GLAD, *O daughter of Edom*, Sam. iv. 21. *The heavens* SHALL BE GLAD, *and the earth* SHALL REJOICE, Psalm lxviii. 3. *They will make me hear* JOY *and* GLADNESS, li. 10. JOY *and* GLADNESS *shall be found in Zion, confession and the voice of singing*, Isaiah li. 3. *There shall be* GLADNESS, *and many shall* REJOICE *at his birth*, Luke i. 14. *I will make the voice of* JOY *and the voice of* GLADNESS *cease; the voice of the bridegroom and the voice of the bride*, Jerem. vii. 34; xvi. 9; xxv. 10. *There shall yet be heard, in this place, the voice of* JOY, *and the voice of* GLADNESS, *and the voice of the bridegroom, and the voice of the bride*, xxxiii. 10, 11: and in other places. The reason that both, *joy* as well as *gladness*, are mentioned, is, because *joy* is predicated of good, and *gladness* of truth, or *joy* of love, and *gladness* of wisdom; for joy is of the heart, and gladness of the spirit; or joy is of the will, and gladness is of the understanding. That the marriage of the Lord and the church is also in these, is manifest from this, that it is said, *The voice of joy and the voice of gladness, the voice of the bridegroom and the voice of the bride*, Jerem. vii. 34; xvi. 9; xxv. 10; xxxiii. 10, 11: and the Lord is the *bridegroom*, and the church is the *bride*. That the Lord is the bridegroom, may be seen in Matt. ix. 15; Mark ii. 19, 20: Luke v. 3: and that the church is the bride, Rev. xxi. 2, 9; xxii. 17. Wherefore John the Baptist said concerning Jesus, *He who hath the bride is the bridegroom*, John iii. 29.

253. On account of the marriage of divine good and divine truth, in every part of the Word, it is said, in very many places, *Jehovah God*, and also, *Jehovah* and *the Holy One of Israel*, as if they were two, when yet they are one; for by *Jehovah* is meant the Lord, as to the divine good of divine love, and by *God* and by the *Holy One of Israel* is meant the Lord, as to the divine truth of the divine wisdom. That *Jehovah* and *God*, and *Jehovah* and *the Holy One of Israel*, are mentioned in very many places, in the Word, and yet one is meant, may be seen in THE DOCTRINE CONCERNING THE LORD THE REDEEMER.

254. X. THAT HERESIES MAY BE TAKEN FROM THE SENSE OF THE LETTER OF THE WORD, BUT THAT TO CONFIRM THEM IS HURTFUL.

It was shown above, that the Word cannot be understood without doctrine, and that doctrine is like a candle, that genuine truths may be seen; and this because the Word was written by mere correspondences; thence it is, that many things there are appearances of truth, and not naked truths; and many things are written according to the capacity of the merely natural man, and yet so that the simple may understand them in simplicity, the intelligent in intelligence, and the wise in wisdom. Now, because the Word is such, appearances of truth, which are truths clothed, may be taken for naked truths, which, when they are confirmed, become fallacies, which in themselves are falses. From this, that appearances of truth may be taken for naked truths, and confirmed, have sprung all the heresies which have been and still are in the Christian world. Heresies themselves do not condemn men; but confirmations of the falsities, which are in a heresy, from the Word and by reasonings from the natural man and an evil life, do condemn. For every one is born into the religion of his country or of his parents, is initiated into it from infancy, and afterwards retains it; nor can he extricate himself from its falses, both on account of business in the world, and on account of the weakness of the understanding in perceiving truths of that sort; but to live wickedly and confirm falses, even to the destruction of genuine truth, this does condemn. For he who continues in his religion, and believes in God, and in Christendom believes in the Lord, and esteems the Word holy, and from religion lives according to the commandments of the decalogue, he does not swear to falses; wherefore, when he hears truths, and in his own way perceives them, he can embrace them, and thus be led out of falses; but not he who had confirmed the falses of his religion, for the false, when confirmed, remains, and cannot be extirpated; for a false, after confirmation, is as if one had sworn to it, particularly if it coheres with the love of himself, or with the pride of his own intelligence.

255. I have spoken with some in the spiritual world, who lived many ages ago, and confirmed themselves in the falses of their own religion, and I have found that they still remained firmly in the same; and I have also spoken with some there, who were in the same religion, and thought like those, but had not confirmed its falses in themselves; and I have found, that, when instructed by the angels, they have rejected falses and received truths; and that these were saved, but not those. Every man is instructed by the angels after death, and those are received who see truths, and from truths, falses; but those only see truths who have not confirmed themselves in falses; but those who have confirmed themselves are not willing to see truths; and if they do see, they turn themselves back, and then either laugh at them or falsify them; the genuine cause is, that confirmation enters the will, and the will is the man himself, and it disposes the understanding according to its pleasure; but bare knowledge only enters the understanding, and this has not any authority over the will, and so is not in man, otherwise than as one who stands in the entry, or at the door, and not as yet in the house.

256. But this may be illustrated by an example. In the Word, there is, in many places, attributed to God, anger, wrath, revenge, and that He punishes, casts into hell, tempts, and many like things; he who believes this in simplicity, and like a child, and on this account fears God, and takes heed to himself not to sin against Him, is not condemned on account of that simple belief. But he who confirms in himself those things to such a degree, as to believe that anger, wrath, revenge, and thus such things as are of evil, are with God, and that, from anger, wrath and revenge, He punishes man, and casts into hell, he is condemned, because he has destroyed the genuine truth, which is, that God is love itself, mercy itself, and goodness itself; and, being these, He cannot be angry, wrathful and revengeful. That these things are attributed to God, in the Word, is, because it appears so: such things are appearances of truth.

257. That many things, in the sense of the letter of the Word, are appearances of truth, in which genuine truths lie concealed; and that it is not hurtful to think and also to speak in simplicity, according to the appearances of truth; but that it is hurtful to confirm them, since, by confirmation, the divine truth, which is concealed within, is destroyed, may also be illustrated by an example in nature; which is presented, because what is natural more clearly illustrates and teaches, than what is spiritual. It appears to the eye as if the sun were carried around the earth every day, and also once every year; hence it is said, that the sun rises and sets; that it makes morning, noon, evening and night; and also the times of spring, summer, autumn and winter, and thus days and years: when yet the sun stands still, for it is an ocean of fire, and the earth revolves every day, and is carried about the sun every year The man who, from simplicity and

from ignorance, thinks that the sun is carried about the earth, does not destroy the natural truth, which is, that the earth is turned about its axis, and every year is carried along the ecliptic. But he who confirms the apparent motion of the sun, by reasonings from the natural man; and still more he who does so by the Word, because it is there said, that the sun rises and sets, weakens the truth and disperses it; and afterwards he can scarcely see it, although it should be shown to the eye, that the universal starry heaven is, in like manner, carried around every day and every year, to appearance, and yet not even one star is removed from its fixed place, in relation to another. That the sun is moved, is an apparent truth, but that it is not moved, is a genuine truth; yet every one speaks according to the apparent truth, in saying that the sun rises and sets; and this is allowable, because it cannot be otherwise; but to think according to that, from confirmation, blunts and darkens the rational understanding.

258. The reason why it is hurtful to confirm the appearances of truth, which are in the Word, since thereby fallacy is produced, and thus the divine truth, which is concealed within, is destroyed, is, because each and every part of the sense of the letter of the Word communicates with heaven; for, as was shown above, in each and every part of the sense of its letter, there is a spiritual sense, and this is opened when it passes from man to heaven; and all the things of the spiritual sense are genuine truths; wherefore, when man is in falses, and applies the sense of the letter to them, then falses are therein; and when falses enter, truths are dissipated, which is done in the way from man to heaven. And this is done, comparatively, as when a shining bladder, filled with gall, is thrown to another, which is burst in the air, before it comes to him, and the gall is scattered about; whereupon the other, when he perceives the air infected with the gall, turns himself away, and also shuts his mouth, lest it should touch his tongue. It is also like a bottle hooped with twigs of cedar, in which there is vinegar full of little worms; and the bottle is burst in the way, and its stench is perceived by another, who then immediately, from nausea, dissipates its stench by some ventilator, lest it should enter into his nostrils. It is also like an almond in the shell, within which, instead of the almond, is a snake just born, and the shell is broken, and the little snake appears to be carried by the wind towards the eyes of another; that this turns himself away, lest it should be done, is plain of itself. It is the same with the reading of the Word by a man who is in falses, and who applies to his falses some things of the sense of the letter of the Word; which is then rejected in its way to heaven, lest any such thing should flow in and infest the angels; for the false, when it touches the truth, is like the point of a needle when it touches the fibril of a nerve, or the pupil of the eye; that the fibril of the nerve instantly rolls itself back into a spiral, and betakes itself within itself, is known; and in like manner, that the eye, at the first touch, covers itself with its eyelids. From these things, it is manifest, that truth falsified takes away communication with heaven, and closes it. This is the cause that it is hurtful to confirm any heretical false.

259. The Word is like a garden, which may be called a heavenly paradise, in which are delicacies and delights of every kind; delicacies from the fruits, and delights from the flowers; in the middle of which are trees of life, and beside them fountains of living water, and around the garden are forest trees. The man who, from doctrine, is in divine truths, is in the middle, where are the trees of life, and he actually enjoys its delicacies and delights; but the man who is not in truths from doctrine, but only from the sense of the letter, is in the circumference, and sees only the things of the forest. But he who is in the doctrine of a false religion, and who

has confirmed its false in himself, is not even in the forest, but out of it, in a sandy plain, where there is not any grass. That such also is the state of those after death, is shown in a work CONCERNING HEAVEN AND HELL.

260. Moreover, it is to be known, that the sense of the letter of the Word is a guard for the genuine truths which are concealed within, lest they should be injured; and it is a guard in this, that this sense may be turned hither and thither, and explained according to apprehension, and yet its internal not be hurt or violated. For it does no hurt, that the sense of the letter is understood otherwise by one than by another; but it is hurtful, if a man introduces falses, which are contrary to divine truths, which is done only by those who have confirmed themselves in falses; by this, violence is done to the Word. Lest this should be done, the sense of the letter operates as a guard, and it operates as a guard with those who are in falses from religion, and do not confirm its falses. The sense of the letter of the Word, as a guard, is signified in the Word by cherubs, and it is also described there by them. This guard is signified by the cherubs, which, after Adam with his wife was cast out of the garden of Eden, were placed at its entrance, concerning which these things are read: *When Jehovah God had driven out the man, He caused* CHERUBS *to dwell at the east of the garden of Eden, and the flame of a sword, turning itself hither and thither, to guard the way of the tree of life*, Gen. iii. 23, 24. What these words signify, no one can see, unless he knows what is signified by *cherubs*, and what by the *garden of Eden*, and by the *tree of life* there, and then what by the *flame of a sword, turning itself hither and thither.* Each of these is explained in THE ARCANA CŒLESTIA, published at London, upon that chapter; where it is shown, that by *cherubs* is signified a guard; by the *way of the tree of life* is signified entrance to the Lord, which men have through the truths of the spiritual sense of the Word; by the *flame of a sword turning itself*, is signified divine truth in ultimates, which is like the Word in the sense of the letter, which can be so turned. The like is meant by the CHERUBS OF GOLD *placed upon the two extremities of the propitiatory, which was upon the ark in the tabernacle*, Exod. xxv. 18 to 21. By the *ark* was signified the Word, because the decalogue in it was the primitive of the Word; by the *cherubs* there was signified a guard; wherefore the Lord spoke with Moses between them, Exod. xxv. 22, xxxvi. 9; Num. vii. 89; and He spoke in the natural sense; for He does not speak with man, except in fullness; and in the sense of the letter, divine truth is in its fullness; see above, n. 214 to 224. Nor is any thing else signified by THE CHERUBS *upon the curtains of the tabernacle, and upon the veil*, Exod. xxvi. 31; for the *curtains and veils of the tabernacle* signified the ultimates of heaven and the church, and so also of the Word; see above, n. 220; in like manner, by THE CHERUBS *carved upon the walls, and upon the doors of the temple of Jerusalem*, 1 Kings vi. 29, 32, 35; see above, n. 221; and also by THE CHERUBS *in the new temple*, Ezek. xli. 18, 19, 20. Since by *cherubs* was signified a guard, that the Lord, heaven, and divine truth such as it is interiorly in the Word, may not be approached immediately, but mediately through ultimates, therefore it is thus said concerning the king of Tyre: *Thou, who sealest up the measure, who art full of wisdom, and perfect in beauty, hast been in the garden of Eden; every precious stone was thy covering. Thou,* O CHERUB, *art the outspreading of one that covereth; I have lost thee,* O COVERING CHERUB, *in the midst of the stones of fire*, Ezek. xxviii. 12, 13, 14, 16. By *Tyre*, is signified the church as to the knowledges of truth and good, and thence by the *king of Tyre*, the Word, where and whence those knowledges are. That the Word in its ultimate is here signified by him, and a guard by *cherub*, is manifest; for it is said, *Thou who sealest up the measure*

every precious stone was thy covering, thou cherub, the outspreading of one that covereth; as also, *O covering cherub.* That by *precious stones*, which are also there named, are meant those things which are of the sense of the letter, may be seen above, n. 217, 218. Since by *cherubs* is signified the Word in the ultimates, and also a guard, therefore it is said in David, *Jehovah bowed the heavens, and came down, and he rode upon* A CHERUB, Psalm xviii. 9, 10. *Shepherd of Israel, who sittest upon* THE CHERUBS, *shine forth*, lxxx. 1. *Jehovah sitteth upon* THE CHERUBS, xcix. 1. To *ride upon cherubs*, and to *sit upon them*, is upon the ultimate sense of the Word. Divine truth in the Word, and its quality, are described by the four animals which are also called *cherubs*, in Ezekiel, i., ix. and x.; and also by the four animals in the midst of the throne, and near the throne, Rev. iv. 6, and the following verses. See THE APOCALYPSE REVEALED, published by me at Amsterdam, n. 239, 275, 314.

261. XI. THAT THE LORD, IN THE WORLD, FULFILLED ALL THINGS OF THE WORD, AND THEREBY BECAME THE WORD, THAT IS, THE DIVINE TRUTH, EVEN IN ULTIMATES.

That the Lord, in the world, fulfilled all things of the Word, and that He thereby became the Divine Truth, or the Word, even in ultimates, is meant by these words in John: *And the Word became flesh, and dwelt among us, and we saw his glory, the glory as of the Only-begotten of the Father, full of grace and truth*, i. 14. To *become flesh* is to become the Word in ultimates. What the Lord was, as the Word in ultimates, He showed to the disciples, when He was transfigured, Matt. xvii. 2, and the following verses; Mark ix. 2, and the following; Luke ix. 28, and the following: and it is there said, that Moses and Elijah were seen in glory. By *Moses* is meant the Word which was written by him, and the historical Word in general; and by *Elijah*, the prophetical Word. The Lord, as the Word in ultimates, was also represented before John, Rev. i. 13 to 16; where all things of the description of Him signify the ultimates of divine truth, or of the Word. The Lord had indeed been the Word or the divine truth before, but in firsts; for it is said, *In the beginning was the Word, and the Word was with God*, AND GOD WAS THE WORD, John i. 1, 2; but when the Word became flesh, then the Lord became the Word, even in the ultimates: it is from this, that He is called THE FIRST *and* THE LAST, Rev. i. 8, 11, 17; ii. 8; xxi. 6; xxii. 12, 13; Isaiah xliv. 6.

262. That the Lord fulfilled all things of the Word, is manifest from the passages where it is said, that the law and the Scripture were fulfilled by Him, and that all things were accomplished; as from these: *Jesus said, Think not that I have come to destroy the law and the prophets; I have not come to destroy*, BUT TO FULFIL, Matt. v. 17, 18. *Jesus entered into the synagogue, and rose up to read; then was delivered to Him the book of Isaiah the prophet; and He opened the book, and found the place written, The Spirit of Jehovah is upon Me, because He hath anointed Me; He hath sent Me to bring good news to the poor, to heal the broken in heart, to preach deliverance to the bound, and sight to the blind; to proclaim the acceptable year of the Lord. Afterwards, closing the book, He said*, THIS DAY IS THIS SCRIPTURE FULFILLED IN YOUR EARS, Luke iv. 16 to 21. THAT THE SCRIPTURE MIGHT BE FULFILLED, *He that eateth bread with Me, hath lifted up his heel upon Me*, John xiii. 18. *No one of them is lost, except the son of perdition*, THAT THE SCRIPTURE MIGHT BE FULFILLED, xvii. 12. THAT THE WORD MIGHT BE FULFILLED, *which He spoke, Of those whom thou gavest Me, I have not lost one*, xviii. 19. *Jesus said to Peter, Put away thy sword into its place;* HOW THEN WOULD THE SCRIPTURE BE FULFILLED, *that thus it must be done? But this was done, that* THE SCRIPTURE MIGHT BE FULFILLED, Matt. xxvi. 52, 54, 56 *The Son of man goeth away*, AS IT IS WRITTEN *concerning Him*, THAT THE SCRIPTURES

MIGHT BE FULFILLED, Mark xiv. 21, 24. *Thus* THE SCRIPTURE WAS FULFILLED, *which said, He was reckoned with the impious,* Mark xv. 28; Luke xxii. 37. *That* THE SCRIPTURE MIGHT BE FULFILLED, *They divided to themselves my garments, and upon my vesture they cast lots,* John xix. 24. *After this, Jesus knowing that all things were now accomplished, that* THE SCRIPTURE MIGHT BE FULFILLED, xix. 28. *When Jesus had received the vinegar, He said,* IT IS FINISHED, *that is,* FULFILLED, xix. 30. *These things were done, that* THE SCRIPTURE MIGHT BE FULFILLED, *Ye shall not break a bone in Him; and again, another* SCRIPTURE SAITH, *They shall see Him whom they have pierced,* xix. 36, 37. That all the Word was written concerning Him, and that He came into the world that He might fulfill it, He also taught the disciples, before He went away, in these words: *He said to them, O fools, and slow of heart to believe all that the prophets have spoken; was it not necessary for Christ to suffer this, and enter into glory? And beginning with* MOSES AND ALL THE PROPHETS, *He expounded to them,* IN ALL THE SCRIPTURES CONCERNING HIMSELF, Luke xxiv. 25, 26, 27. Moreover, Jesus said, THAT ALL THE THINGS MUST BE FULFILLED, WHICH WERE WRITTEN IN THE LAW OF MOSES, AND IN THE PROPHETS, AND IN THE PSALMS, CONCERNING ME, xxiv. 44, 45. That the Lord, in the world, fulfilled all things of the Word, even to its least particulars, is manifest from these his words: *Verily, I say to you, until heaven and earth pass away,* ONE JOT OR ONE TITTLE SHALL NOT PASS AWAY FROM THE LAW, UNTIL ALL THINGS ARE DONE, Matt. v. 18. From these things, now, it may be clearly seen, that by this, that *the Lord fulfilled all things of the law,* is not meant, that He fulfilled all the precepts of the decalogue, but all things of the Word. That all things of the Word also are meant by the law, may be evident from these passages: *Jesus said, Is it not written in* YOUR LAW, *I said, Ye are gods,* John x. 34; this is written, Psalm lxxxii. 6; *The multitude answered, We have heard out of* THE LAW, *that Christ abideth forever,* John xii. 34; this is written, Psalm lxxxix. 29; cx. 4; Dan. vii. 14: *That the Word written in* THEIR LAW *might be fulfilled, They hated Me without a cause,* John xv. 25; this is written, Psalm xxxv. 19: *It is easier for heaven and earth to pass away, than for one tittle of the law to fail,* Luke xvi. 17. By the *law* there, as also every where else, is meant the whole Sacred Scripture.

263. How the Lord is the Word, is understood by few; for they think that the Lord can, by the Word, enlighten and teach men, and yet cannot thence be called the Word; but let them know, that every man is his own will, and his own understanding, and thus one distinct from another; and because the will is the receptacle of love, and thus of all the goods which are of that love, and the understanding is the receptacle of wisdom, and thus of all things of truth which are of that wisdom, it follows, that every man is his own love and his own wisdom; or, what is the same, his own good and his own truth. Man is not man from any thing else, and not any thing else with him is man. With respect to the Lord, He is Love itself and Wisdom itself, thus Good itself and Truth itself, which He became by means of his fulfilling all the good and all the truth which is in the Word; for he who thinks and speaks nothing but truth, becomes that truth; and he who wills and does nothing but good, becomes that good; and the Lord, because He fulfilled all the divine truth and the divine good which are in the Word, as well those which are in its natural sense as those which are in its spiritual sense, He became Good itself and Truth itself, consequently the Word.

264. XII. THAT BEFORE THIS WORD, WHICH AT THIS DAY IS IN THE WORLD, THERE WAS A WORD, WHICH IS LOST.

That before the Word given by Moses and the prophets to the Israelitish nation, worship by sacrifices was known, and that they prophesied from the mouth of Jehovah, may appear evident from what is related in the books of Moses. THAT WORSHIP BY SACRIFICES WAS KNOWN, is evident from these things: It was commanded, that the sons of Israel should overthrow the altars of the nations, and break in pieces their images, and cut down their groves, Exod. xxxiv. 13; Deut. vii. 5; xii. 3. That Israel in Shittim began to commit whoredom with the daughters of Moab, that they called the people to the SACRIFICES of their gods, and that the people did eat, Num. xxv. 1, 2, 3. That Balaam, who was from Syria, caused altars to be built, and SACRIFICED oxen and sheep, xxii. 40; xxiii. 1, 2, 14, 29, 30. That he also PROPHESIED CONCERNING THE LORD, saying, *That a star should arise from Jacob and a sceptre from Israel,* xxiv. 17. And THAT HE PROPHESIED FROM THE MOUTH OF JEHOVAH, xxii. 13, 18; xxiii. 3, 5, 8, 16, 26; xxiv. 1, 13. From which it is manifest, that there was among the nations divine worship, very similar to the worship instituted by Moses with the Israelitish nation. That it was also before the time of Abraham, appears evident from the words in Moses, Deut. xxxii. 7, 8; but more evidently from MELCHIZEDEK, king of Salem, in that he brought forth BREAD AND WINE, and blessed Abram; and that Abram gave him TITHES of all, Gen. xiv. 18 to 20; and that Melchizedek represented the Lord, for he is called a *priest to the Most High God,* Gen. xiv. 18; and it is said in David concerning the Lord, *Thou art a priest forever, after the manner of Melchizedek,* Psalm cx. 4. Thence it was, that Melchizedek brought forth bread and wine, as the most holy things of the church, as they are holy in the Sacred Supper. These, besides many other things, are standing proofs, that, before the Israelitish Word, there was a Word, from which were such revelations.

265. That there was a Word among the ancients, is evident in Moses, by whom it is mentioned, and something taken from it, Num. xxi. 14, 15, 27 to 30; and that the historicals of that Word were called THE WARS OF JEHOVAH, and the propheticals, THE ENUNCIATIONS. From the historicals of that Word, this passage was taken by Moses; *Therefore it is said in* THE BOOK OF THE WARS OF JEHOVAH, *I walked into (the sea) Suph, and the rivers of Arnon, and the channel of the rivers, which turned aside where Ar is inhabited, and stopped at the border of Moab,* Num. xxi. 14, 15. By *the wars of Jehovah,* in that Word, as in ours, are meant and described the combats of the Lord with the hells, and victories over them, when He was to come into the world. The same combats also are meant and described in many places in the historicals of our Word, as in the wars of Joshua with the nations of the land of Canaan, and in the wars of the judges and of the kings of Israel. From the propheticals of that Word, these things were taken; *Therefore* THE ENUNCIATORS *say, Go into Heshbon; the city of Sihon shall be built and strengthened; for a fire went out of Heshbon, and a flame out of the city of Sihon; it hath devoured Ar of Moab, the possessors of the heights of Arnon. Wo to thee, O Moab; thou hast perished, O people of Chemosh; he hath given his sons fugitives, and his daughters into captivity to Sihon, king of the Amorite. We have despatched them with weapons. Heshbon hath perished even to Dibon, and we have laid waste even to Nophah, which is even to Medebah,* Num. xxi. 27 to 30. The translators render them COMPOSERS OF PROVERBS; but they should be called ENUNCIATORS, or PROPHETICAL ENUNCIATIONS, as may appear evident from the signification of the word MOSHALIM in the Hebrew tongue, which means not only proverbs, but also prophetical enunciations, as in Num. xxiii. 7, 18. xxiv. 3, 15, where it is said, that Balaam uttered HIS ENUNCIATION, which was prophetical, even concerning the Lord His enunciation is called MOSHAL, in the singular. It may be added, that those things, taken thence by Moses, are not proverbs, but prophecies. That that Word was likewise divinely inspired, is manifest in Jeremiah, where almost the same things are said—

A fire has gone out from Heshbon, and a flame from among Sihon, which hath devoured the corner of Moab, and the crown of the head of the sons of Shaon. Wo to thee, O Moab; the people of Chemosh have perished; for thy sons have been carried into captivity, and thy daughters into captivity, xlviii. 45, 46. Besides those, a prophetical book of the ancient Word, called THE BOOK OF JASHER, or the book of the Upright, is mentioned by David and by Joshua. By David; *David lamented over Saul and over Jonathan, and wrote to teach the sons of Judah the bow; see what is written in* THE BOOK OF JASHER, 2 Sam. i. 17, 18; and by Joshua; *Joshua said, Sun, rest in Gibeon, and moon in the valley of Ajalon; is not this written in* THE BOOK OF JASHER? Joshua x. 12.

266. From these things it may be evident, that there was an ancient Word in the world, particularly in Asia, before the Israelitish Word. That this Word is preserved in heaven, with the angels, who lived in those ages, and also that it is still, at this day, among the nations in Great Tartary, may be seen in THE THIRD RELATION, after this chapter concerning the Sacred Scripture.

267. XIII. THAT BY THE WORD, THOSE ALSO HAVE LIGHT, WHO ARE OUT OF THE CHURCH, AND HAVE NOT THE WORD.

Conjunction with heaven cannot be given, unless there be somewhere in the earth a church, where the Word is, and the Lord is known by it; because the Lord is the God of heaven and earth, and without the Lord there is no salvation.

That by the Word, there is conjunction with the Lord and consociation with the angels, may be seen above, n. 234 to 240. It is enough that there be a church, where the Word is; although it be of few respectively, still, by the Word, the Lord is present in the whole world, for by it heaven is conjoined to the human race.

268. But how the presence and conjunction of the Lord and heaven is given in all countries, by means of the Word, shall be told. The whole angelic heaven, before the Lord, is as one man, and so also is the church upon earth. That they also actually appear as a man, may be seen in the Work concerning HEAVEN AND HELL, n. 59 to 87. In that man, the church where the Word is read and the Lord is known by it, is as the heart and as the lungs; the Lord's celestial kingdom as the heart, and his spiritual kingdom as the lungs. As, from these two fountains of life in the human body, all the rest of the members, viscera and organs subsist and live, so also all those in every part of the world, with whom there is religion, and one God is worshipped, and who live well, and thereby are in that man, and resemble the members and viscera out of the thorax, in which are the heart and lungs, subsist and live from the conjunction of the Lord and heaven with the church by means of the Word; for the Word, in the Christian church, is life to the rest from the Lord through heaven, just as the life of the members and viscera of the whole body is from the heart and lungs; there is also similar communication, which also is the reason why the Christians among whom the Word is read constitute the breast of that man; they are also in the midst of all, and around them are the Papists; around these are the Mahometans, who acknowledge the Lord as the greatest Prophet, and as the Son of God; after these are the Africans; and the people and nations in Asia and the Indies make the last circumference.

269. That it is so in the whole heaven may be concluded from the like in every society of heaven; for every society is a heaven in a less form, which also is like a man. That it is so, may be seen in the Work concerning HEAVEN AND HELL, n. 41 to 87. In every society of heaven, those who are in the middle of it, in like manner, resemble the heart and lungs, and with them is the greatest light; the light itself and the perception of truth thence, propagates

itself from that middle to the circumferences every way, thus to all who are in the society, and makes their spiritual life. It was shown, that when those who were in the middle and constituted the province of the heart and lungs, and with whom was the greatest light, were taken away, those who were around were in the shade of the understanding, and then in so little perception of truth, that they lamented; but as soon as those returned, the light was seen, and they had perception of truth as before. A comparison may be made with the heat and light from the sun of the world, which give vegetation to trees and shrubs, even to those which stand at the sides and under a cloud, provided the sun be risen. Thus the light and heat of heaven are from the Lord as the sun there, which light, in its essence, is divine truth, from which is all the intelligence and wisdom of angels and men. Wherefore it is said, concerning the Word, *that it was with God and was God; that it enlighteneth every man that cometh into the world; and that that light, also, appeareth in darkness*, John i. 1, 5, 9. By the word there, is meant the Lord as to Divine Truth.

270. From these things it may be evident, that the Word, which is with the Protestants and the Reformed, enlightens all nations and people, by spiritual communication; also that it is provided by the Lord, that there should always be on the earth a church, where the Word is read, and by it the Lord may be made known. Wherefore, when the Word was almost rejected by the Papists, by the divine providence of the Lord the Reformation took place; and thence the Word was drawn, as it were, from its concealment, and sent into use. When also the Word with the Jewish nation was entirely falsified and adulterated, and, as it were, made none, then it pleased the Lord to descend from heaven, and to come, as the Word, and to fulfill it and thereby to renew and restore it and again to give light to the inhabitants of the earth, according to these words of the Lord:—*The people sitting in darkness saw a great light; and to those sitting in the region and shadow of death, light hath arisen*, Isaiah ix. 2; and Matt. iv. 16.

271. Since it was foretold, that, at the end of this church, darkness also would arise from not knowing the Lord, that He is the God of heaven and earth, and from the separation of faith from charity, lest thereby the genuine understanding of the Word should perish, and so too the church, therefore it has pleased the Lord now to reveal THE SPIRITUAL SENSE OF THE WORD, and to show that the Word, in that sense, and from it, in the natural sense, contains innumerable things, by which the light of truth from the Word, almost extinguished, may be restored. That, at the end of this church, the light of truth would be almost extinguished, is foretold in many places in the Revelation, and also it is meant by these words of the Lord: *Immediately after the affliction of those days, the sun will be darkened, and the moon will not give her light, and the stars will fall from heaven, and the powers of the heavens will be shaken; and then they will see the Son of Man, coming in the clouds of heaven, with glory and virtue*, Matt. xxiv. 29, 30. By *sun* there is meant the Lord as to love; by *moon*, the Lord as to faith; by *stars*, as to the knowledges of truth and good; by the *Son of Man*, the Lord as to the Word; by *clouds*, the sense of the letter of the Word; by *glory*, the spiritual sense of the Word, and its transparence through the sense of its letter; and by *virtue* its power.

272. By much experience, it has been given me to know, that through the Word man has communication with heaven. While I read through the Word, from the first chapter of Isaiah even to the last of Malachi, and the Psalms of David, and kept the thought in their spiritual sense, it was given me to perceive clearly, that every verse communicated with some society of heaven, and thus the

Word with the universal heaven; from which it was manifest, that, as the Lord is the Word, heaven also is the Word, since heaven is heaven from the Lord, and the Lord by the Word, is the all in all of heaven.

273. XIV. That, unless there were a Word, no one would know God, Heaven and Hell, and Life after Death, and still less the Lord.

Since those who maintain, have also confirmed with themselves, that man, without the Word, might know the existence of God, and also of heaven and hell, and the other things which the Word teaches, therefore, it is not proper to argue with them from the Word, but from the natural light of reason; for they believe not the Word, but themselves. Inquire from the light of reason, and you will find, that there are two faculties of life with man, which are called the *understanding* and the *will;* and that the understanding is subject to the will, and not the will to the understanding; for the understanding only teaches and shows what is to be done from the will. Thence it is, that many, who are of an acute genius, and understand, better than others, the moral duties of life, still do not live according to them; it would be otherwise, if they willed them. Inquire, also, and you will find, that the will of man is his *proprium*, and that this from nativity is evil, and that thence is the false in the understanding. When you shall have found out these things, you will see, that man from himself, wishes not to understand any thing else, than what is from the proprium of his will; and that unless there be some other source, whence he may know it, man from the proprium of his will, would not wish to understand any thing, but what is of himself and the world. Whatever is above, is in thick darkness; as when he sees the sun, moon and stars, if by chance he should then think concerning their origin, he could not think otherwise than that they are from themselves. Could they think more deeply than many learned men in the world, who, although they know from the Word, that all things were created by God, still acknowledge nature? What, then, would these have done, if they had known nothing from the Word? Do you believe that the ancient philosophers, as Aristotle, Cicero, Seneca, and others, who have written concerning God and concerning the immortality of the soul, took it first from their own understanding? No; but from others, by tradition, from those who knew it first from the ancient Word, of which we have spoken above. Neither do writers on natural theology draw any such thing from themselves, but only confirm those things, which they know from the church in which the Word is, by rational arguments; and there may be those among them, who confirm, and yet do not believe them.

274. It has been given me to see people born in islands, rational as to civil affairs, who know nothing at all concerning God; those, in the spiritual world, appear like sphinxes; but, because they were born men, and thence in a capacity of receiving spiritual life, they are instructed by the angels; and by means of knowledges concerning the Lord, as Man, they are vivified. What man is of himself, evidently appears from those who are in hell, among whom are also some prelates and scholars, who are not willing even to hear concerning God, and, therefore, neither can they name God. I have seen these and conversed with them; and I have also conversed with those who came into the fire of anger and wrath, when they heard any one speaking concerning the Lord. Consider, therefore, what the man would be, who has heard nothing concerning the Lord, when such are some, who have talked about God, written about God, and preached about God. That they are such, is from the will, which is evil; and this, as was said before, leads the understanding, and takes away the truth, which is there from the Word. If man could, of himself, have known that there is a God, and that there is a life after death, why did he not know, that man is man after

death? Why does he believe that his soul or spirit is like wind or ether, which does not see with eyes, and hear with ears, and speak with a mouth, before it is conjoined and grows with its carcass and with its skeleton? Suppose, therefore, a doctrine hatched from rational light alone, would it not be, that self should be worshipped, as was done for ages, and also at this day is done by those who know, from the Word, that God alone is to be worshipped? Other worship cannot be given from the proprium of man, not even the worship of the sun and moon.

275. That from the most ancient times there was religion, and the inhabitants of the world everywhere knew concerning God, and something concerning life after death, was not from themselves, or from their own intelligence, but from the ancient Word, of which we have treated above, n. 264 to 266; and afterwards from the Israelitish Word. From these two Words, religions emanated into the Indies, and their islands, and through Egypt and Ethiopia into the kingdoms of Africa, and from the maritime parts of Asia into Greece, and thence into Italy. But, because the Word could not be written otherwise than by representatives, which are such things in the world as correspond to heavenly things, and thence signify them, therefore the religious things of the gentile nations were turned into idolatries, and in Greece, into fables; and the divine attributes and properties, into so many gods, over whom they made one supreme, whom they called *Jove*, perhaps from *Jehovah*. It is known that they had knowledge concerning paradise, concerning the deluge, concerning the sacred fire, and concerning the four ages, from the first, or the golden, to the last, or the iron, as in Daniel, ii. 31 to 35.

276. Those who believe that they can, from their own intelligence, procure for themselves knowledges concerning God, concerning heaven and hell, and concerning the spiritual things which are of the church, do not know that the natural man, viewed in himself, is contrary to the spiritual, and that, therefore, the spiritual things, which enter, he wishes to extirpate or involve in fallacies, that are like worms which consume the roots of herbs and grain. They may be likened to those who dream that they are sitting upon eagles, and borne up on high; or on winged horses, and are flying over mount Parnassus to Helicon; and they are actually like Lucifers in hell, who still call themselves there *sons of the morning*, Is. xiv. 12. And they are like those in the valley of the land of Shinah, who undertook to build a tower, whose head should be in heaven Gen xi. 2, 4; and they trust in themselves like Goliah, not foreseeing that they may, like him, be prostrated by a sling stone driven into the forehead. I will tell what lot awaits them after death, first they become as drunk; afterwards as insane, and at last sottish, and sit in darkness. Let them therefore beware of such a delirium.

---

277. To the above I shall add the following RELATIONS.—FIRST. One day, in the spirit, I rambled through various places in the spiritual world, in order that I might observe the representations of heavenly things which, in many places, are there exhibited; and in a certain house, where there were angels, I saw great purses, in which silver was stored up in great abundance; and because they were open, it was perceived as if every one might take out, yea, steal the silver there laid up; but near these purses sat two youths, who were guards. The place where they were deposited appeared like a manger in a stable. In the next room were seen modest virgins, with a chaste wife: and near that room stood two little children: and it was said, that they were not to be played with childishly, but were to be dealt with wisely. Afterwards there appeared a harlot, also a horse lying dead. After these things were seen, I was instructed, that by them was represented the natural sense of the Word in which there is a spir-

itual sense. Those great purses, full of silver, signified knowledges of truth in great abundance; that they were open and yet guarded by youths, signified, that every one might take thence the knowledges of truth, but that there should be care, lest any one violate the spiritual sense, in which are mere truths; the manger, as in a stable, signified spiritual nourishment for the understanding; a manger signifies this, because a horse, which eats out of it, signifies the understanding; the modest virgins, who were seen in the next room, signified the affections of truth; and the chaste wife, the conjunction of good and truth; the little children signified the innocence of wisdom, for the angels of the highest heaven, who are the wisest, from innocence, appear, at a distance, like little children, the harlot with the dead horse, signified the falsification of truth by many at this day, by which all understanding of truth perishes; a harlot signifies falsification, and a dead horse, no understanding of truth.

278. SECOND RELATION. There was once sent down to me from heaven a piece of paper, inscribed with Hebrew letters, but written as with the ancients, with whom those letters, which at this day are in some part linear, were curved with little horns turning upwards. And the angels, who were then with me, said that they knew entire senses from the letters themselves, and that they knew these, especially, from the flexures of the lines and of the points of the letter; and they explained what they signified separately, and what conjointly; saying that the H, which was added to the names of Abram and Sarai, signified infinite and eternal. They also explained to me the sense of the Word in Psalm xxxii. 2, from the letters only, or syllables; that the sense of them in the sum was, THAT THE LORD IS MERCIFUL, ALSO TO THOSE WHO DO EVIL. They informed me that writing, in the third heaven, consisted of letters, inflected and variously curved, of which each contained a certain sense; and that the vowels there were for sound, which corresponds to affection; and that, in that heaven, they cannot utter the vowels *i* and *e*, but instead of them, *y* and *eu;* and that the vowels *a*, *o* and *u* were in use with them, because they give a full sound; also that they did not express any of the consonants roughly, but softly; and that thence it is, that some Hebrew letters are pointed within, as a sign that they are uttered softly; saying that roughness in letters was in use in the spiritual heaven, because there they are in truths, and truth admits of the rough, but not good, in which the angels of the Lord's celestial kingdom, or third heaven, are. They also said, that they had with them the Word, written with inflected letters, with significant little horns and points; from which it was manifest, what these words of the Lord signify—*Not an iota nor a tittle* [or little horn] *shall pass from the law, until all things are done*, Matt. v. 18; also, *It is easier for heaven and earth to pass away, than for one point of the law to fail*, Luke xvi. 17.

279. THIRD RELATION. Seven years ago, when I was collecting the things which Moses wrote from those two books called THE WARS OF JEHOVAH, and THE ENUNCIATIONS, Num. xxi., some angels were present, and said to me, that those books were the ancient Word, THE HISTORICALS of which were called THE WARS OF JEHOVAH, and THE PROPHETICALS were called THE ENUNCIATIONS; and they said that that Word was still preserved in heaven, and in use among the ancients there, with whom that Word was when they were in the world. Those ancients, with whom that Word is still in use in heaven, were in part from the land of Canaan and from its confines, as from Syria, Mesopotamia, Arabia, Chaldea. Assyria, Egypt, Zidon, Tyre and Nineveh; the inhabitants of all which kingdoms were in representative worship, and thence in the science of correspondences. The wisdom of that

time was from that science, and by it they had interior perception and communication with the heavens. Those who knew the correspondences of that Word, were called wise and intelligent, and afterwards diviners and Magi. But because that Word was full of such correspondences as remotely signified celestial and spiritual things, and thence began to be falsified by many; therefore, by the divine providence of the Lord, in course of time that disappeared, and another Word, written by correspondences not so remote, was given, and this by the prophets among the sons of Israel. In this Word were retained many names of places, not only which were in the land of Canaan, but also which were round about in Asia, all which signified things and states of the church; but the significations were from that ancient Word. For that reason, Abram was commanded to go into that land, and his posterity from Jacob were introduced into it.

Concerning that ancient Word which had been in Asia before the Israelitish Word, it is permitted to relate this news, that it is still reserved there, among the people who live in Great Tartary. I have conversed with spirits and angels who were thence, in the spiritual world; who informed me that they possess the Word, and that they have possessed it from ancient times, and that they perform their divine worship according to this Word, and that it consists of mere correspondences. They said that in it also is the book of JASHER, which is mentioned in Joshua x. 12, 13, and in the second book of Samuel, i. 17, 18; and also, that with them are the books called THE WARS OF JEHOVAH, and THE ENUNCIATIONS, which are mentioned by Moses, Num. xxi. 14, 15, and 27 to 30; and when I read to them the words which Moses had taken thence, they looked to see if they were there, and found them; hence it was manifest to me, that the ancient Word is still with them. In conversing with them, they said that they worship Jehovah, some as an invisible God, and some as visible. They further told me, that they do not suffer foreigners to come among them, except the Chinese, with whom they cultivate peace, because the Chinese emperor is from their country; and also that they are so populous, that they do not believe any country in the whole world to be more populous; which also is credible, from the wall of so many miles, which the Chinese formerly built for their protection against invasion from them. Moreover, I heard from the angels, that the first chapters of Genesis, which treat concerning the creation, concerning Adam and Eve, concerning the garden of Eden, and concerning their sons and posterity till the flood, and likewise concerning Noah and his sons, are also in that Word; and thus that they were copied thence by Moses. The angels and spirits from Great Tartary appear in the southern quarter, on the side of the east, and are separated from the rest by their dwelling in a higher expanse, and by their not admitting any to them from the Christian world; and that if any ascend, they guard them, that they may not go away. The reason of this separation, is, because they possess another Word.

280. FOURTH RELATION. I once saw, at a distance, walks between rows of trees, and the youths collected there in groups, so many clubs of persons, conversing on the things of wisdom; this was in the spiritual world. I approached, and when I was near, I saw one whom the rest venerated as their primate, because he excelled them in wisdom. He, when he saw me, said, "I wondered, when I saw you in the way coming up, that you now passed into my sight, and now passed out of it, or that you was now seen by me, and suddenly not seen; certainly you are not in the same state of life as our people." Smiling at this, I replied, "I am not a puppetman, nor a Vertumnus (or a Proteus), but I am, by turns, now in your light, and now in your shade; thus a foreigner and also a native here." Upon this, that wise one looked at me, and said

"You speak strange and wonderful things; tell me who you are." And I said, "I am in the world in which you were, and from which you have departed, which is called the natural world; and I am also in the world in which you are, which is called the spiritual world. Thence it is, that I am in a natural state, and at the same time in a spiritual state; in a natural state with men of the earth, and in a spiritual state with you; and when I am in a natural state, I am not seen by you; but when in a spiritual state, I am seen: that I am such, has been given by the Lord. It is known to you, enlightened man, that a man of the natural world does not see a man of the spiritual world, nor the reverse; wherefore, when I had let my spirit into the body, I was not seen by you, but when I had let it out of the body, I was seen; and this exists from the distinction between spiritual and natural." When he heard *the distinction between spiritual and natural*, he said, "What is the distinction? Is it not as between more and less pure? Thus, what is the spiritual, but the purer natural?" And I replied, "The distinction is not such; the natural can never by subtilization approximate to the spiritual, so as to become the same; for the distinction is such as between prior and posterior, between which no finite ratio is given; for the prior is in the posterior, as the cause in its effect; and the posterior is from the prior, as the effect from its cause. Hence it is, that the one does not appear to the other." To this the wise one said, "I have meditated on this distinction, but hitherto in vain. Would that I might perceive it." And I said, "You shall not only perceive the distinction between spiritual and natural, but you shall also see it." And then I said this: "You are in a spiritual state when with your companions, but in a natural state with me; for you speak with your companions in spiritual language, which is common to every spirit and angel, but with me you speak in my native language: for every spirit and angel, speaking with man, speaks his own language; thus French with a Frenchman, Greek with a Grecian Arabic with an Arabian, and so forth. That you may know therefore the distinction between spiritual and natural, as to languages, do thus: Go in to your companions, and speak something there, and retain the words, and return with them in your memory, and utter them before me." And he did so, and returned to me with those words in his mouth, and uttered them; and they were words altogether foreign and strange, which are not given in any language of the natural world. From this experiment, several times repeated, it was clearly manifest, that all in the spiritual world have a spiritual language, which has nothing in common with any natural language; and that every man after death comes of himself into that language. I once also have experienced, that the very sound of spiritual language, differs so much from the sound of natural language, that a spiritual sound, however loud, cannot be heard at all by a natural man, nor a natural sound by a spiritual man. Afterwards I asked him and the bystanders to go in among their companions, and write some sentence upon paper, and come out with that paper to me, and read it. They did so, and returned with the paper in their hand; but when they would read, they could not; since that writing consisted only of some alphabetical letters with curvatures above, each of which signified some sense of a thing. Because every letter in the alphabet signifies there some sense, it is manifest whence it is, that the Lord is called the *Alpha* and the *Omega*. When they had gone in again and again, and written and returned, they found that that writing involved and comprehended innumerable things, which any natural writing could never express; and it was said that this is so, because the spiritual man thinks things incomprehensible and ineffable to the natural man; and that these cannot be brought into other writing, and into other language. Then, because those standing by were not willing to comprehend that spiritual thought so far exceeded natural thought, that it is respectively ineffable, I said to them, "Make the experiment; enter into your spiritual society, and think of some thing, and retain it, and return and express it before me." And they entered in, thought, retained, and came out; and when they would express the thing thought of, they could not; for they did not find any idea of natural thought adequate to any idea of purely spiritual thought, and so not any words expressing it; for the ideas of thought become words of speech. And afterwards they went in again, and returned, and confirmed themselves, that spiritual ideas were supernatural, inexpressible, ineffable and incomprehensible to the natural man; and because they are so super-eminent, they said, that spiritual ideas or thoughts, in respect to natural, were ideas of ideas, and thoughts of thoughts; and that by them therefore were expressed qualities of qualities, and affections of affections; consequently, that spiritual thoughts were the beginnings and origins of natural thoughts. Thence also it was manifest, that spiritual wisdom was the wisdom of wisdom, thus inexpressible to any wise man in the natural world. Then it was said from the superior heaven, that there is a wisdom still more interior or superior, which is called celestial, whose relation to spiritual wisdom, is like the relation of this to natural; and that these flow in, in order, according to the heavens, from the divine wisdom of the Lord, which is infinite. To this the man speaking with me said, "I see this, because I have perceived, that one natural idea is the continent of many spiritual ideas, and also that one spiritual idea is the continent of many celestial ideas. From this, also, follows this consequence, that a thing divided does not become more and more simple, but more and more multiple, because it draws nearer and nearer to the Infinite, in whom are all things infinitely." These things being done, I said to the by-standers, "You see, from these three experimental proofs, what the distinction is between spiritual and natural, and also the cause why the natural man does not appear to the spiritual, nor the spiritual man to the natural, although each is in a perfect human form, and from this form it seems to him as if the one might see the other; but the interior things, which are of the mind, are what make that form, and the mind of spirits and angels is formed from spiritual things, and the mind of men, as long as they live in the world, from natural things After this, a voice was heard from the superior heaven, saying, to one who stood by, "Ascend hither." And he ascended and returned and said, that "The angels did not before know the differences between the spiritual and the natural, because no opportunity of comparison had been before given, with any man, who was in both worlds at the same time; and those differences cannot be known without comparison and relation."

Before we separated, we conversed again on this subject; and I said, that "These distinctions exist from nothing else, than because you, in the spiritual world, are substantial and not material; and substantial things are the beginnings of material things. What is matter, but an aggregation of substances? You, therefore, are in principles, and thus in singulars; but we are in things derived and composed; you are in particulars, but we in generals; and as generals cannot enter into particulars, so neither can natural things, which are material, enter into spiritual things, which are substantial; just as the cable of a ship cannot enter or be drawn through the eye of a sewing needle, or as a nerve cannot be inserted into one of the fibres of which it consists. This, now, is the cause that the natural man cannot think those things which the spiritual man thinks, and thence cannot speak them. Wherefore Paul calls those things, which he heard from the third heaven, ineffable. Add to this that to think spiritually is to think without time and space, and that to think naturally is to think with time and space; for something from time and space adheres to every idea of natural thought, but not to any spiritual idea. The cause is, that the spiritual world is not in space and time, as the natural world is, but it is in the appearance of these two; in this also thoughts and perceptions differ: wherefore, you can think concerning the essence and omnipresence of God from eternity, that is, concerning God before the creation of the world; because you think concerning the essence of God without time, and concerning his omnipresence without space, and thus you comprehend such things as transcend the natural ideas of man." I then related, that I once thought concerning the essence and omnipresence of God from eternity, that is, concerning God before the creation of the world; and that, because I could not yet remove spaces and times from the ideas of my thought, I became anxious, since the idea of nature entered instead of God; but it was said to me, "Remove the ideas of space and time, and you will see." And it was given me to remove them, and I saw; and from that time I have been able to think of God from eternity, and not at all of nature from eternity, because God is in all time without time, and in all space without space; but nature in all time is in time, and in all space is in space; and nature with its time and space could not but begin, but not God, who is without time and space; wherefore nature is from God, not from eternity, but in time together with its time and space.

281. Fifth Relation. Since it has been given me by the Lord, to be at the same time in the spiritual world and in the natural world, and thence to speak with angels as with men, and thereby to know the states of those, who after death flow into that hitherto unknown world; for I have spoken with all my relations and friends, and likewise with kings and generals, as also with the learned, who have deceased, and this now continually for twenty-seven years; therefore I am able to describe, from lively experience, the states of men after death, both of those who have lived well and of those who have lived ill. But here I shall only relate some things concerning the state of those who have confirmed themselves from the Word in falses of doctrine, who are those, in particular, who have done it in favor of justification by faith alone. The successive states of these are as now follows: I. As soon as they are deceased, and revive as to the spirit, which takes place commonly the third day after the heart has ceased to beat, they appear to themselves in a like body as before in the world, so much so that they do not know otherwise than that they are still living in the former world; nevertheless not in a material body, but in a substantial body, which, to their senses appears like material, although it is not. II. After some days, they see that they are in a world where various societies are instituted, which world is called THE WORLD OF SPIRITS, and is in the middle between heaven and hell. All the societies there, which are innumerable, are wonderfully arranged in order, according to natural affections, good and evil. The societies arranged according to good natural affections, communicate with heaven, and the societies arranged according to evil affections, communicate with hell. III. A novitiate spirit, or spiritual man, is led about and brought into various societies, as well good as evil, and is explored whether he is affected with goods and truths, and in what manner, or whether he is affected with evils and falses, and in what manner. IV. If he is affected with goods and truths, he is led away from evil societies, and is led into good societies, and also into various ones, until he comes into a society corresponding to his own natural affection, and there he enjoys the good corresponding to that affection, and this until he puts off the natural affection and puts on the spiritual, and then he is elevated into heaven; but this is done with

those who have in the world lived the life of charity, and thus also the life of faith; which is, that they have believed in the Lord, and shunned evils as sins. V. But those who have confirmed themselves in falses by rational things, especially by the Word, and so have lived no other than a merely natural, thus an evil life, (for falses accompany evils and evils adhere to falses,) these, because they are not affected with goods and truths, but with evils and falses, are led away from good societies, and are led into evil societies, and also into various ones, until they come into some one corresponding to the concupiscences of their own love. VI. But, because in the world they had feigned good affections in externals, although in their internals there were nothing but evil affections or concupiscences, they are kept by turns in externals; and those who in the world had been over bodies of men, are appointed over societies here and there in the world of spirits, greater or less, according to the magnitude of the duties which they had previously fulfilled. But, because they neither love what is true, nor love what is just, nor can be enlightened so that they may know what is true and just, therefore, after some days, they are deposed. I have seen such transferred from one society into another, and an administration given to them in each, but after a short time as often deposed. VII. After frequent abdications, some from weariness do not wish, and some from fear of the loss of fame, do not dare, to seek any more for offices; wherefore they go away and sit down sorrowful; and then they are led away into a desert, where are cottages, which they enter, and there some work is given them to do; and as they do it, they receive food, and if they do not do it, they are hungry and do not receive any; wherefore necessity compels them. The food there is similar to the food in our world, but it is from a spiritual origin, and is given from heaven by the Lord to all, according to the uses which they do; to the idle, because they are useless, it is not given. VIII. After some time, they scorn their work, and then go out of the cottages; and if they were priests, they wish to build; and then instantly appear piles of hewn stone, bricks, beams, boards, and also heaps of reeds and rushes, of clay, lime and bitumen; when they see which, the lust of building is enkindled, and they begin to build a house, by taking now a stone, now a timber, now a reed, now mortar; and they put one upon another, without order, though in their view with order; but what they build in the day time, falls down in the night; yet the following day they gather from the fallen rubbish, and build again, and this even till they are tired of building; this is done from correspondence, which is, that they had heaped up texts from the Word for confirming the falses of faith, and their falses no otherwise build up the church. IX. Afterwards they go away through weariness, and sit down solitary and idle; and because food is not given from heaven to the idle, as was said, they begin to be hungry, and to think of nothing else than how they shall get food and appease their hunger. When they are in this state, some come to them, of whom they ask alms; and they say, "Why do you sit thus idle? Come with us into our houses, and we will give you work to do, and will feed you." And then they get up joyfully, and go along with them into their houses, and there to each is given his work, and for the work food is given. But, because all who have confirmed themselves in falses of faith, cannot do works of good use, but works of evil use, neither do them faithfully but fraudulently, as also unwillingly, therefore they leave their works, and only love to converse, to talk, to walk, and to sleep; and because they cannot then any longer be induced by their masters to work therefore they are dismissed as useless X. When they are dismissed, their eyes are opened, and they see a way leading to a certain cavern; when they come to which, a door is opened, and they enter, and ask whether there is food there; and when it is answered, that there is food there, they request to be permitted to remain there, and it is said, that it is permitted; and they are led in, and the door is shut after them. And then the overseer of that cavern comes and says to them, "You cannot go out any more; see your companions, they all labor, and as they labor, food is given them from heaven; I tell you this that you may know." And also their companions say, "Our overseer knows for what work every one is fit, and such he enjoins on each daily; and on the day that you perform it, food is given to you; and if not, neither food nor clothing is given; and if any one does evil to another, he is thrown to a corner of the cavern into a kind of bed of cursed dust, where he is miserably tortured; and this even until the overseer sees in him a sign of penitence, and then he is released, and it is commanded him to do his work." And it is also said to him, that every one is permitted, after his work, to walk, to converse, and afterwards to sleep; and he is led along farther into the cavern, where are harlots, some one of whom each is permitted to take to himself, and to call her his woman; but it is forbidden under a penalty to commit whoredom promiscuously. Of such caverns, which are nothing but eternal work-houses, hell consists. It has been given me to enter into some, and see, in order that I might make it known; and they were all seen as vile; neither did one of them know whom, or in what employment, he had been in the world; but the angel, who was with me, said to me, that this had been in the world a servant, this a soldier, this an officer, this a priest, this in dignity, this in opulence; and yet they all know no otherwise, than that they had been slaves and like companions; and this, because they had been inwardly alike, although outwardly unlike; and the interiors consociate all in the spiritual world.

With respect to the hells in general, they consist merely of such caverns or work-houses, but different where satans are from where devils are: those are called satans, who have been in falses and thence in evils, and those devils, who have been in evils and thence in falses. Satans appear in the light of heaven livid like corpses, and some black like mummies; but devils appear, in the light of heaven, darkly ignited, and some black like soot; but all, as to their faces and bodies, monstrous: but in their own light, which is like the light from ignited coals, not as monsters, but as men; this is given them, that they may be consociated.

CHAPTER V.

THE CATECHISM OR DECALOGUE EXPLAINED AS TO ITS EXTERNAL AND INTERNAL SENSE.

282. THERE is not a nation in the whole world which does not know, that it is evil to kill, to commit adultery, to steal, and to testify falsely; and also, unless these evils were guarded against by laws, that kingdom, republic, and any established society whatever, would be done with. Who, then, can suppose, that the Israelitish nation was so stupid above others, that it did not know that those things were evils? On which account one may wonder that those laws, universally known in the world, were promulgated with so great a miracle from mount Sinai by Jehovah himself. But hear; they were promulgated with so great a miracle, that they might know, that those laws were not only civil and moral laws, but also divine laws; and that to do contrary to them, was not only to do evil against the neighbor, that is, a fellow citizen and society, but was also to sin against God. Wherefore those laws, by promulgation from mount Sinai by Jehovah, were made also laws of religion. It is evident, that whatever Jehovah commands, He commands, that it may be of religion, and thus that it is to be done for the sake of salvation. But before the commandments are explained, something is to be premised concerning their holiness, that it may be manifest that religion is in them.

283. THAT THE DECALOGUE WAS HOLINESS ITSELF IN THE ISRAELITISH CHURCH.

The commandments of the decalogue, because they were the first-fruits of the Word, and thence the first-fruits of the church about to be instituted with the Israelitish nation, and because they were, in a short summary, an assemblage of all things of religion, by which conjunction of God with man and of man with God is given, therefore they were so holy, that nothing is holier. That they were most holy, is evidently manifest from these things following: That the Lord Jehovah himself descended upon mount Sinai in fire and with angels, and thence promulgated them with a living voice, and that the mountain was hedged around, lest any should draw near and die. That neither the priests nor the elders approached, but Moses alone. That those commandments were written upon two tables of stone, by the finger of God. That when Moses brought down those tables the second time, his face beamed. That the tables were afterwards laid up in the ark, and the latter inmostly in the tabernacle, and over it was set the propitiatory, and upon this were placed cherubs of gold; that this inmost in the tabernacle, where the ark was, was called the holy of holies. That without the veil, within which that ark was, were arranged many things, which represented the holy things of heaven and the church, which were the table overlaid with gold, upon which was the bread of faces; the golden altar, upon which incense was burned; and the golden candlestick with seven lamps; also the curtains round about, of fine linen, purple and scarlet. The holiness of the whole of this tabernacle was from nothing else, than from the law which was in the ark

On account of the holiness of the tabernacle, from the law in the ark, all the Israelitish people by command encamped around it, in order, according to the tribes, and marched in order after it; and then a cloud was over it by day, and a fire by night. On account of the holiness of that law, and the presence of Jehovah in it, Jehovah spoke with Moses upon the propitiatory between the cherubs, and the ark was called *Jehovah there.* That it was not lawful for Aaron to enter within the veil, except with sacrifices and incense, lest he should die. On account of the presence of Jehovah in that law and around it, miracles also were done by the ark in which that law was; as that the waters of the Jordan were divided; and, while the ark rested in the middle of it, the people passed over on dry ground. That by its being carried around, the walls of Jericho fell down. That Dagon, the god of the Philistines, first fell on his face before it, and afterwards, being severed from the head with the two palms of the hands, lay upon the threshold of the temple. That on account of it, the Bethshemites were smitten, to several thousands. That Uzzah, because he touched it, died. That this ark was introduced by David into Zion, with a sacrifice and jubilations; and afterwards by Solomon into the temple at Jerusalem, where it made its secret recess, besides many other things; from which it is manifest, that the decalogue was holiness itself in the Israelitish church.

284. The things which are adduced above concerning the promulgation, holiness and power of that law, are found in these passages in the Word: *That Jehovah descended upon mount Sinai in fire, and that then the mountain smoked and trembled, and that there were thunderings, lightnings, a heavy cloud, and the voice of a trumpet,* Exod. xix. 16 to 18. Deut. iv. 11; v. 19 to 23. *That the people, before the descent of Jehovah, prepared and sanctified themselves for three days,* Exod. xix. 10, 11, 15. *That the mountain was hedged around, in order that no one should approach to the bottom of it, and come near lest he die; and that the priests might not, but Moses alone,* xix. 12, 13, 20 to 23; xxiv. 1, 2. *The law promulgated from mount Sinai,* xx. 2 to 14. Deut. v. 6 to 18. *That the law was written upon two tables of stone, and that it was written by the finger of God,* Exod. xxxi. 18; xxxii. 15, 16. Deut. ix. 10. *That when Moses brought those tables down from the mountain the second time, his face beamed so that he covered his face with a veil, while he talked with the people,* Exod. xxxiv. 29 to 35. *That the tables were laid up in the ark,* xxv. 16; xl. 20; Deut. x. 5; 1 Kings viii. 9. *That over the ark was given the propitiatory, and that upon this were placed cherubs of gold,* Exod. xxv. 17 to 21. *That the ark, with the propitiatory and the cherubs, was put into the tabernacle; and that it made the first, and thus the inmost of it; and that the table, overlaid with gold, upon which was the bread of faces and the altar of gold for incense, and the candlestick with lamps of gold, made the external of the tabernacle: and the ten curtains of fine linen, purple and scarlet, the most external of it,* xxv. 1 to the end; xxvi. 1 to the end; xl. 17 to 28. *That the place where the ark was, was called the holy of holies,* xxvi. 33. *That the whole people of Israel encamped around the tabernacle, in order, according to the tribes, and marched in order after it,* Num. ii. 1 to the end. *That there was then over the tabernacle, a cloud by day, and a fire by night,* Exod. xl. 38. Num. ix. 15, 16 to the end; xiv. 14. Deut. i. 33. *That Jehovah spoke with Moses over the ark between the cherubs,* Exod. xxv. 22. Num. vii. 89. *That the ark, from the law in it, was called* Jehovah there; *for Moses said, when the ark went forward,* Arise, Jehovah; *and when it rested,* Return, Jehovah, Num. x. 35, 36, &c. 2 Sam. xi. 2. Ps. cxxxii. 7, 8. *That on account of the holiness of that law, it was not lawful for Aaron to enter within the veil, except with sacrifices and incense,* Lev. xvi. 2 to 14, and the following

verses. *That from the presence of the Lord's power in the law which was in the ark, the waters of the Jordan were separated; and whilst it rested in the midst, the people passed over on dry ground*, Josh. iii. 1 to 17; iv. 5 to 20. *That at carrying around the ark, the walls of Jericho fell down*, Josh. vi. 1 to 20. *That Dagon, the god of the Philistines, fell down upon the ground, before the ark, and afterwards lay upon the threshold of the temple, severed from the head, and the palms of the hands being cut off*, 1 Sam. v. *That the Bethshemites, on account of the ark, were smitten, to several thousands*, v. and vi. *That Uzzah, because he touched the ark, died*, 2 Sam. vi. 7. *That the ark was introduced into Zion by David, with sacrifices and jubilations*, vi. 1 to 19. *That the ark was introduced by Solomon into the temple of Jerusalem, where it made the secret recess*, 1 Kings vi. 19, and the following verses; viii. 3 to 9.

285. Since through that law there is conjunction of the Lord with man and of man with the Lord, it is therefore called THE COVENANT, and THE TESTIMONY; *the covenant*, because it conjoins, and *the testimony*, because it confirms the articles of the covenant; for *covenant*, in the Word, signifies conjunction, and *testimony*, the confirmation and attestation of its articles. On this account those tables were two, one for God, and the other for man. Conjunction is effected by the Lord, but only when man does the things which are written in his table; for the Lord is continually present, and wishes to enter; but man, from the freedom which he has from the Lord, must open; for He says, *Behold I stand at the door and knock; if any one hear my voice, and open the door, I will go in to him, and sup with him, and he with Me*, Rev. iii. 20. That the tables of stone, on which the law was written, were called THE TABLES OF THE COVENANT, and that the ark was from them called THE ARK OF THE COVENANT, and the law itself THE COVENANT, may be seen, Num. x. 33; Deut. iv. 13 23; v. 2, 3; ix 9 Josh. iii. 11; 1 Kings viii. 19, 21; Rev. ix 19; and elsewhere. Since *covenant* signifies conjunction, therefore it is said concerning the Lord, *That He shall be for* A COVENANT *to the people*, Isaiah xlii. 6; xlix. 9: and He is called THE ANGEL OF THE COVENANT, Mal. iii. 1; and his blood, THE BLOOD OF THE COVENANT, Matt. xxvi. 28; Zech. ix. 11; Exod. xxiv. 4 to 10: and therefore the Word is called THE OLD COVENANT AND THE NEW COVENANT; for covenants are made for the sake of love, friendship, consociation and conjunction.

286. So great holiness and so great power were in that law, because it was a summary of all things of religion; for it was written upon two tables, one of which contains, in a summary, all things which regard God; and the other, in a summary, all things which regard man: therefore the commandments of that law are called THE TEN WORDS, Ex. xxxiv. 28: Deut. iv. 13; ix. 4. They were so called, because *ten* signifies all, and *words* signify truths; for there were more than ten words. That *ten* signifies all, and that *tithes* were instituted on account of that signification, may be seen in the APOCALYPSE REVEALED, n. 101; and that that law is a summary of all things of religion, will be seen in what follows.

287. THAT THE DECALOGUE, IN THE SENSE OF THE LETTER, CONTAINS THE GENERAL PRECEPTS OF DOCTRINE AND LIFE; BUT, IN THE SPIRITUAL AND CELESTIAL SENSE, ALL UNIVERSALLY.

It is known, that the decalogue is called, in the Word, by way of eminence, THE LAW, because it contains all things which are of doctrine and life; for it contains not only all things which regard God, but also all which regard man; wherefore that law was written upon two tables, one of which treats of God, the other of man. It is also known, that all things of doctrine and life have reference to love to God and love towards the neighbor; all things of these loves are contained in the decalogue

That the whole Word teaches nothing else, is evident from these words of the Lord: JESUS *said, Thou shalt love the Lord thy God from thy whole heart, and in thy whole soul, and in thy whole mind; and the neighbor as thyself; on these two commandments hang the law and the prophets,* Matt. xxii. 37 to 40. The law and the prophets signify the whole Word. And again: *A certain lawyer, tempting Jesus, said, Master, what shall I do, that I may inherit eternal life? And Jesus said to him, What is written in the law? How readest thou? And he, answering, said, Thou shalt love the Lord thy God from thy whole heart, and from thy whole soul, and from thy whole strength, and from thy whole mind; and the neighbor as thyself. And Jesus said,* DO THIS, AND THOU SHALT LIVE, Luke x. 25 to 28. Now, because love to God and love towards the neighbor are all things of the Word; and the decalogue, in the first table, contains in a summary all things of love to God; and in the second table, all things of love towards the neighbor; it follows, that it contains all things which are of doctrine and life. From a sight of the two tables, it is manifest, that they were so conjoined, that God from his table may look to man, and that man from his may look to God, reciprocally; and thus that there is a reciprocal looking, which is such, that God, on his part, never ceases to look at man, and to work such things as are of his salvation; and if man receives and does those things which are in his table, reciprocal conjunction is effected, and then it is done according to the words of the Lord to the lawyer, *Do this, and thou shalt live.*

288. In the Word, the law is often mentioned; and it shall be said what is meant by it in a strict sense, and what is meant by it in a wider sense, and what in the widest sense. In *a strict sense*, by the *law* is meant the decalogue; in *a wider sense*, are meant the statutes given by Moses to the sons of Israel; and in *the widest*, is meant the whole Word. THAT BY THE LAW, IN A STRICT SENSE, IS MEANT THE DECALOGUE, is known; BUT THAT BY THE LAW, IN A WIDER SENSE, ARE MEANT THE STATUTES GIVEN BY MOSES TO THE SONS OF ISRAEL, is evident from the statutes singly in Exodus, in that they are called the *law;* as, *This is the law of the sacrifice,* Lev. vii. 1. *This is the law of the sacrifice of peace-offerings,* vii. 7, 11. *This is the law of the bread-offering,* vi. 7, and the following verses. *This is the law for the whole burnt-offering, for the bread-offering, for the sacrifices of sin and trespass, and for consecrations,* vii. 37. *This is the law of the beast and of the bird,* xi. 46, and the following verses. *This is the law of one bringing forth, for a son and a daughter,* xii. 7. *This is the law of leprosy,* xiii 59; xiv. 2, 32, 54, 57. *This is the law of one affected with the flux,* xv. 31. *This is the law of jealousy,* Num. v. 29, 30. *This is the law of the Nazarite,* vi. 13, 21. *This is the law of cleansing,* xix. 14. *This is the law concerning the red heifer,* xix. 2. *The law for the king,* Deut. xvii. 15 to 19. Yea, *the whole book of Moses is called the law,* xxxi. 9, 11, 12, 26; besides also in the New Testament, as Luke ii. 22; xxiv. 44; John i. 46; vii. 22, 23; viii. 5, and in other places. That these statutes are meant by the works of the law, by Paul, where he says, that *man is justified by faith, without the works of the law,* Rom. iii. 28, is plainly manifest from what there follows; and also from his words to Peter, whom he censured for Judaizing, where he says, three times in one verse, that *no one is justified by the works of the law,* Gal. ii. 14 to 16. THAT BY THE LAW, IN THE WIDEST SENSE, IS MEANT THE WHOLE WORD, is manifest from these passages: *Jesus said, Is it not written in* YOUR LAW, *Ye are gods,* John x. 34. This is written, Psalm lxxxii. 6. *The multitude answered, We have heard from* THE LAW, *that Christ abideth forever,* John xii. 34. This is written, Psalm lxxxix. 29; cx. 4; Dan. vii. 14. *That the Word written* IN THEIR LAW *might be fulfilled, They hated Me without cause,* John xv. 25 This is

written, Psalm xxxv. 19. *The Pharisees said, Hath any one of the rulers believed on Him? But the multitude which knoweth not the* LAW, John vii. 48, 49. *It is easier for heaven and earth to pass away, than for* ONE TITTLE OF THE LAW *to fail*, Luke xvii. 17. By *the law* there, is meant the whole Sacred Scripture; besides in a thousand places in David.

289. That the decalogue, in the spiritual and celestial sense, contains, universally, all the precepts of doctrine and of life, thus all things of faith and charity, is because the Word, in the sense of the letter, in every and each thing of it, or in the whole and in every part, contains two interior senses; one which is called *spiritual*, and another which is called *celestial;* and because, in these senses, divine truth is in its light, and divine goodness in its heat. Now, because the Word, in the whole and in every part, is such, it is necessary that the ten commandments of the decalogue be explained according to those three senses, which are called *natural*, *spiritual*, and *celestial.* That the Word is such, may be evident from the things which have been demonstrated above, in the chapter concerning THE SACRED SCRIPTURE, or THE WORD, n. 193 to 208.

290. No one, unless he knows what the Word is, can get at any idea, that there is infinity in every part of it; that is, that it contains innumerable things, which not even the angels can draw out. Every thing there may be likened to a seed, which may grow up from the ground into a great tree, and produce abundance of seeds, from which again may be similar trees, which together make a garden; and from the seeds of this, other gardens; and thus to infinity. Such is the Word of the Lord, in every part, and such especially is the decalogue; for this, because it teaches love to God and love towards the neighbor, is a short summary of the whole Word. That the Word is such, the Lord also explains by a similitude, thus: *The kingdom of God is like a grain of mustard-seed, which one, taking, sowed in his field which is less than all seeds, but when it hath grown up, it is greater than the herbs, and becometh a tree, so that the winged tribes of heaven come and nest in its branches*, Matt. xiii. 31, 32; Mark iv. 31, 32; Luke xiii. 18, 19. Compare also Ezekiel xvii. 2 to 8. That there is such an infinity of spiritual seeds, or truths, in the Word, may be evident from the wisdom of the angels which is all from the Word; this increases with them to eternity, and the wiser they become, the more clearly they see that wisdom is without end, and perceive that themselves are only in its entrance, and that they cannot, as to the minutest particular, attain to the divine wisdom of the Lord, which they call an abyss. Now, since the Word is from this abyss, because from the Lord, it is manifest, that in all parts of it there is a kind of infinity.

THE FIRST COMMANDMENT.

There shall not be to thee another God before my faces.

291. These are the words of the first commandment, Exod. xx. 3; Deut. v. 7; by which, in THE NATURAL SENSE, which is the sense of the letter, is first of all meant, that idols are not to be worshipped; for it follows, *Thou shalt not make to thee a carving, or any figure, which is in the heavens above, and which is in the earth beneath, and which is in the waters under the earth; thou shalt not bow down thyself to them, and shalt not worship them, because* I, JEHOVAH, AM THY GOD, A JEALOUS GOD, Exod xx. 3, 4, 5, 6. That by this commandment it is first of all meant, that idols are not to be worshipped, was because, before this time, and after it, even to the coming of the Lord, there was idolatrous worship in a great part of Asia: the cause of that worship was, that all the churches, before the Lord, were representative and typical; and the types and representations were such, that divine things were set forth under various

figures and images, which the people, when their significations were obliterated, began to worship for gods. That the Israelitish nation also was in such worship when in Egypt, may be evident from the golden calf which they worshipped in the wilderness instead of Jehovah; and that afterwards they were not alienated from that worship, is evident from many places in the Word, both historical and prophetical.

292. By this commandment, *There shall not be to thee another God before my faces*, in the natural sense, is also meant, that no man, dead or alive, is to be worshipped as a god; which also was done in Asia and around it, in various places. Many gods of the nations were no other; as Baal, Ashtaroth, Chemosh, Milcom, Beëlzebub; and at Athens and Rome, Saturn, Jupiter, Neptune, Pluto, Apollo, Pallas, &c.; some of whom they worshipped first as saints, afterwards as divinities, and lastly as gods. That they also worshipped living men as gods, is evident from the edict of Darius the Mede, that no one, within thirty days, should ask any thing of God, but of the king alone; if otherwise, he should be cast into a den of lions, Dan. vi. 8 to the end.

293. In the natural sense, which is the sense of the letter, is also meant by this commandment, that not any one, except God, and that not any thing, except that which proceeds from God, is to be loved above all things, which is also according to the words of the Lord, Matt. xxii. 35 to 37; Luke x. 25 to 28; for he who and that which is loved above all things, is to the lover a god and divine; as, whosoever loves himself above all things, or also the world, to him himself or the world is his god; which is the cause, that the same do not in heart acknowledge any god; they therefore are conjoined with their like in hell, where are collected all who have loved themselves and the world above all things.

294. THE SPIRITUAL SENSE of this commandment is, that no other God than the Lord Jesus Christ is to be worshipped, because He is Jehovah, who came into the world, and made redemption, without which not any man, nor any angel, could have been saved. That besides him there is no other God, is evident from these passages in the Word: *It shall be said in that day, Behold, this is our God, whom we have expected that he should deliver us; this is Jehovah, whom we have expected; let us exult and be glad in his salvation*, Isaiah xxv. 9. *The voice of one crying in the wilderness, Prepare ye a way for Jehovah, make smooth in the desert a path for our God; for the glory of Jehovah shall be revealed, and all flesh shall see together. Behold! the Lord Jehovah cometh in the Mighty One, He shall feed his flock like a shepherd*, xl. 3, 5, 11. *Only in thee is God; besides, there is no God; verily thou art a God concealed, O God of Israel, the* SAVIOR, xlv. 14, 15. *Am not I Jehovah, and there is no God else beside Me? a just God and* A SAVIOR *there is not beside Me!* xlv. 21, 22. *I am Jehovah, and beside me there is no* SAVIOR, xliii. 11; Hosea xiii. 4. *That all flesh may know, that I Jehovah am* THY SAVIOR, *and* THY REDEEMER, Isaiah xlix. 26; lx. 16. *As for our* REDEEMER, *Jehovah of hosts is his name*, xlvii. 4; Jer. l. 34. *Jehovah, my Rock and* MY REDEEMER, Psalm xix. 14. *Thus said Jehovah*, THY REDEEMER, *the Holy One of Israel, I am Jehovah thy God*, Isaiah xlviii. 17; xliii. 24; xlix. 7. *Thus said Jehovah*, THY REDEEMER, *I am Jehovah, that maketh all things, even alone by Myself*, xliv. 24. *Thus said Jehovah, the King of Israel, and his* REDEEMER, *Jehovah of hosts, I am the First and the Last, and beside Me there is no God*, xliv. 6. *Jehovah of hosts is his name, and* THY REDEEMER, *the Holy One of Israel, shall be called the God of the whole earth*, liv. 8. *Abraham doth not know us, Israel doth not acknowledge us; Thou, Jehovah, art our Father*, OUR REDEEMER *from an age is thy name*, lxiii. 16. *A Child is born to us, a Son is given to us, whose name is Wonderful, Counsellor, God, Hero*, FATHER OF ETERNITY, *the Prince of peace*, ix. 6. *Behold the*

days will come, when I shall raise up to David a righteous Branch, who shall reign King, and this is his name, JEHOVAH OUR RIGHTEOUSNESS, Jer. xxiii. 5, 6; xxxiii. 15, 16. *Philip said to Jesus, Show us the Father. Jesus said to him, He who seeth Me, seeth the Father. Believest thou not that I am in the Father, and the Father in Me?* John xiv. 8, 9. *In Jesus Christ all the fulness of the Godhead dwelleth bodily,* Col. ii. 9. *We are in the Truth, in Jesus Christ; This is the true God and eternal life. Little children, keep yourselves from idols,* 1 John v. 20, 21. From these passages it is clearly manifest, that the Lord our Savior is Jehovah Himself, who is at the same time the Creator, Redeemer, and Regenerator. This is the spiritual sense of this commandment.

295. THE CELESTIAL SENSE of this commandment is, that Jehovah the Lord is Infinite, Immense and Eternal; that He is Omnipotent, Omniscient and Omnipresent; that He is the First and the Last, the Beginning and the End; who Was, Is, and Will Be; that He is Love itself, and Wisdom itself, or Good itself and Truth itself; consequently, Life itself; thus the Only One, from whom are all things.

296. All who acknowledge and worship any other God, than the Lord the Savior Jesus Christ, who is Himself Jehovah God in the human form, sin against this first commandment; just so also do those who persuade themselves that there are three divine persons actually existing from eternity. These, as they confirm themselves in that error, become more and more natural and corporeal, and then they cannot comprehend, internally, any divine truth; and if they hear and receive it, still they defile and disguise it with fallacies. They may, therefore, be compared to those who live in the lower story of a house; or in a room under ground, and on that account do not hear any thing that those who are in the second and third story say to each other, because the covering over head prevents the sound from penetrating. The human mind is like a house of three stories, in the lowest of which are those who have confirmed themselves in favor of three Gods from eternity; in the second and third stories are those who acknowledge and believe in one God, under a visible human form, and the Lord God the Savior to be that God. The sensual and corporeal man, because he is merely natural, viewed in himself, is altogether an animal, and only differs from a brute animal, in that he is able to speak and reason; wherefore he is like one living in a menagerie where are beasts of every kind, and where he sometimes acts the lion, and sometimes the bear, and sometimes the tiger, leopard or wolf; yea, he can also act the sheep, but then he laughs in his heart. The merely natural man does not think concerning divine truths, except from the things of the world, thus from the fallacies of the senses; for he cannot elevate his mind above them. Wherefore the doctrine of his faith may be compared to a pudding made of chaff, which he eats as a dainty, or as it was commanded Ezekiel, the prophet, that he should mix wheat, barley, beans, lentiles and spelt, with man's or cow's dung, and make for himself bread and cakes, and thus represent the church, such as it was with the Israelitish nation, Ezek. iv. 9, and the following verses. It is similar with the doctrine of the church, which is founded and built upon three divine persons from eternity, each of whom singly is God. Who would not see the enormity of that faith, if it should be exhibited, such as it is in itself, in a picture before the eyes, as if the three should stand in order by each other, the first distinguished by a sceptre and crown; the second holding in his right hand a book, which is the Word, and in his left, a cross of gold sprinkled with blood; and the third girded with wings, standing upon one foot, in the effort of flying and operating; over which is written, THESE THREE PERSONS, BEING AS MANY GODS, ARE ONE GOD. What wise man, seeing this picture, would not say with himself, Oh, what a fantasy! But he would

say otherwise, if he should see the picture of one divine Person, with rays of heavenly light around the head, with this superscription, THIS IS OUR GOD, AT THE SAME TIME, CREATOR, REDEEMER AND REGENERATOR, THUS THE SAVIOR. Would not that wise man kiss this picture, and carry it home in his bosom, and with the sight of it, delight both his own mind, and the minds of his wife and children and servants?

THE SECOND COMMANDMENT.

Thou shalt not take the Name of Jehovah thy God in vain; because Jehovah will not hold him guiltless, who taketh his name in vain.

297. By taking the name of Jehovah God in vain, in THE NATURAL SENSE, which is the sense of the letter, is meant the name itself, and the abuse of it, in various conversations, especially in falsehoods or lies, and in oaths without cause, and for the purpose of exculpation in evil intentions, which are execrations, and in tricks and incantations. But to swear by God and his holiness, the Word and the Gospel, at coronations, at inaugurations into the priesthood, at inductions into offices of trust, is not to take the name of God in vain, unless the swearer afterwards rejects his engagements as vain. But the name of God, which is itself holy, is to be constantly used in the holy things which are of the church, as in prayers, psalms, and in all worship; and also in preaching, and in writing on ecclesiastical affairs: the reason is, because God is in all things of religion, and when He is rightly invoked, He is present by his name, and hears; in these things the name of God is hallowed. That the name of Jehovah God is in itself holy, is evident from that name, in that the Jews, since their first time, have not dared, and do not dare, to say *Jehovah*, and that, on their account, neither would the evangelists and apostles; wherefore, instead of JEHOVAH, they said LORD; as is evident from various passages, transcribed from the Old Testament into the New; where, instead of JEHOVAH, LORD is named, as Matt. xxii. 35· Luke x. 27; compared with Deut. vi. 5; and in other places. That the name *Jesus* is in like manner holy, is known from the apostle saying, that at that name the knees in the heavens and in the earths are and must be bowed; and moreover, that it can be named by no devil in hell. The names of God, which are not to be taken in vain, are several, as *Jehovah*, *Jehovah God*, *Jehovah of hosts*, *the Holy One of Israel*, *Jesus Christ*, and *the Holy Spirit*.

298. In THE SPIRITUAL SENSE, by the name of God, is meant all that which the church teaches from the Word, and by which the Lord is invoked and worshipped; all those things are the name of God, in the complex; wherefore by taking the name of God in vain, is meant, to take any thing thence in frivolous conversation, falsehoods, lies, execrations, tricks and incantations; for this is also to revile and blaspheme God, thus his name. That the Word, and whatever of the church is thence, and thus all worship, is the name of God, may be evident from these passages: *From the rising of the sun my name shall be invoked*, Isaiah xli. 25. *From the rising of the sun even to its setting, my name shall be great among the nations; and in every place, incense shall be offered to my name. Ye profane my name, when ye say, The table of Jehovah is polluted; and ye snuff at my name, when ye bring the torn, the lame and the sick*, Mal. i. 11, 12, 13. *All people walk in the name of their God, and we will walk in the name of Jehovah, our God*, Mich. iv. 5. *They shall worship Jehovah in one place, where He shall place his name*, Deut. xii. 5, 11, 13, 14, 18; xvi. 2, 6, 11, 15, 16; that is, where his worship is. *Jesus said, Where two or three are gathered together in my name, there I am in the midst of them*, Matt. xviii. 20. *As many as received Him, He gave to them power that they might be sons of God, believing in his name*, John i

12. *He who doth not believe, is already judged, because he hath not believed in the name of the Only-begotten Son of God,* iii. 17. *Believing, they shall have life in his name,* xx. 31. *Jesus said, I have manifested thy name to men; and I have made known to them thy name,* xvii. 26. *The Lord said, I have a few names in Sardis,* Rev. iii. 4; besides in many other places, in which, as in the preceding, by the name of God, is meant the Divine, which proceeds from God, and by which He is worshipped. But, by the name of JESUS CHRIST, is meant all of redemption, and all of his doctrine, and thus all of salvation; by Jesus, all of salvation by redemption, and by Christ, all of salvation by his doctrine.

299. IN THE CELESTIAL SENSE, by *taking the name of God in vain,* is meant that which the Lord said to the Pharisees: *All sin and blasphemy shall be remitted unto man, but the blasphemy of the Spirit shall not be remitted,* Matt. xii. 31. By the *blasphemy of the Spirit,* is meant blasphemy against the divinity of the Lord's Human, and against the holiness of the Word. That the Divine Human of the Lord is meant, by the name of Jehovah God, in the celestial or highest sense, is evident from these words: *Jesus said,* FATHER, GLORIFY THY NAME; *and a voice came out from heaven, saying, I have both glorified, and will glorify again,* John xii. 28. *Whatsoever ye shall ask in my name, this I will do, that the Father may be glorified in the Son; if ye shall ask any thing in my name, I will do it,* xiv. 13, 14. In the Lord's Prayer, by *Hallowed be thy name,* in the celestial sense, no other is signified; and also by *name,* Exod. xxiii. 21; Isaiah lxiii. 16. Since blasphemy of the Spirit is not remitted to man, according to the words, Matt. xii. 31, 32; and this, in the celestial sense, is meant, therefore it is added to this commandment, *Because Jehovah will not hold him guiltless who taketh his name in vain.*

300. That by the name of any one is not meant his name only, but also all his quality, is manifest from names in the spiritual world, where no man retains the name which he received at his baptism, and from his father or ancestors, in the world; but every one there is named according to his quality, and the angels are called according to their moral and spiritual life; these also are they who are meant by these words of the Lord: *Jesus said, I am the good Shepherd; the sheep hear his voice, and He calleth his own sheep by name, and leadeth them out,* John x. 3. And also by these: *I have a few names in Sardis, who have not defiled their garments. Whosoever overcometh, I will write upon him the name of the city, New Jerusalem, and my new name,* Rev iv. 12. Gabriel and Michael are not the names of two persons in heaven, but by those names are meant all in heaven, who are in wisdom concerning the Lord, and worship Him. Also by the name of persons and places in the Word, are not meant persons and places, but the things of the church. In the natural world also, by *name,* is not meant the name only, but, at the same time, the quality of the person, because this adheres to his name; for it is said in common discourse, "He does this for the sake of his name, or for the fame of a name; This man has a great name;" by which is signified, that he is celebrated for such things as are in him, as for ingenuity, erudition, merit, and so forth. Who does not know, that he who defames and calumniates any one, as to his name, defames and calumniates also the actions of his life? They are conjoined in idea, thence the fame of his name perishes. In like manner whoever utters, disrespectfully, the name of a king, a duke or a grandee, casts reproach also upon their majesty and dignity; so also he, who utters the name of any one with a tone of contempt, at the same time vilifies the actions of his life. The case is similar with every person, whose name, that is, whose quality and consequent fame, according to the laws of all kingdoms, it is not allowable to blast and defame.

THE THIRD COMMANDMENT.

Remember the Sabbath Day, that thou keep it holy; six days thou shalt labor and do all thy work; but the seventh day is a Sabbath to Jehovah thy God.

301. That this is the third commandment, may be seen, Exod. xx. 8, 9, 10; and Deut. v. 12, 13. By this in THE NATURAL SENSE, which is the sense of the letter, is meant, that six days are for man and his labors, and the seventh for the Lord, and for man's rest from Him. *Sabbath*, in the original tongue, signifies *rest*. The Sabbath, among the sons of Israel, was the sanctity of sanctities, because it represented the Lord; the six days, his labors and combats with the hells; and the seventh, his victory over them, and thus rest; and because that day was representative of the close of the whole redemption of the Lord, therefore it was holiness itself. But when the Lord came into the world, and thence the representations of Him ceased, that day became a day of instruction in divine things, and thus also a day of rest from labors, and of meditation on such things as are of salvation and eternal life; as also a day of love towards the neighbor. That it became a day of instruction in divine things, is manifest from this, that the Lord on that day taught in the temple and synagogues, Mark vi. 2; Luke iv. 16, 31, 32; xiii. 10; and that he said to the man who was healed, *Take up thy bed and walk;* and to the Pharisees, *That it was lawful for the disciples on the Sabbath day to gather the ears of corn and to eat*, Matt. xii. 1 to 9; Mark ii. 23 to the end; Luke vi. 1 to 6; John v. 9 to 19; by which particulars, in the spiritual sense, is signified, to be instructed in doctrinals. That that day became also a day of love towards the neighbor, is evident from those things which the Lord did and taught on the day of the Sabbath, Matt. xii. 10 to 14; Mark iii. 1 to 9; Luke vi. 6 to 12; xiii. 10 to 18; xiv. 1 to 7; John v. 9 to 19; vii. 22, 23; ix. 14, 16. From these and the former passages, it is manifest why the Lord said, that *He is Lord also of the Sabbath*, Matt. xii. 8; Mark ii. 28 Luke vi. 5; and because He said this it follows that that day was representative of Him.

302. By this commandment, in THE SPIRITUAL SENSE, is signified the reformation and regeneration of man by the Lord; by the *six days of labor*, the combat against the flesh and its concupiscences, and, at the same time, against the evils and falses which are with him from hell; and by the *seventh day*, is signified his conjunction with the Lord, and thereby regeneration. That, as long as that combat continues, man has spiritual labor, but that, when he is regenerated, he has rest, will be evident from those things which will be said hereafter, in the chapter concerning REFORMATION AND REGENERATION, particularly from these things there: I. *That regeneration is effected in a manner analogous to that in which man is conceived, carried in the womb, born and educated.* II. *That the first act of the new generation is called reformation, which is of the understanding; and that its second is called regeneration, which is of the will, and thence of the understanding.* III. *That the internal man first is to be reformed, and by this the external.* IV. *That then a combat arises between the internal and the external man, and that the one that overcomes rules over the other.* V. *That the regenerate man has a new will and a new understanding*, &c. The reason why the reformation and regeneration of man are signified by this commandment, in the spiritual sense, is, because they coincide with the labors and combats of the Lord with the hells, and with the victory over them, and rest then; for the Lord reforms and regenerates man, and renders him spiritual, in the same manner in which He glorified his Human, and made it Divine: this is what is meant by FOLLOWING HIM. That the Lord had combats, and that they are called *labors*, is manifest in Isaiah liii. and lxiii.; and that similar things are called *labors*, in relation to men, lxv 23; Rev. ii. 23.

303. In THE CELESTIAL SENSE, by this commandment, is meant conjunction with the Lord, and then peace, because protection from hell; for by the *Sabbath*, is signified rest, and in this highest sense, peace; wherefore the Lord is called the ***Prince of Peace;*** and also He calls himself *Peace*, as is evident from these passages: *A Child is born to us, a Son is given to us, upon whose shoulders shall be the government, and his name shall be called Wonderful, Counsellor, God, Hero, the Father of eternity,* THE PRINCE OF PEACE; *to the increase of his government and* PEACE *there will be no end*, Isaiah ix. 6, 7. *Jesus said,* PEACE *I leave to you,* MY PEACE *I give to you*, John xiv. 27. *Jesus said, I have spoken these things, that in* ME YE MAY HAVE PEACE, xvi. 33. *How delightful, upon the mountains, are the feet of Him who* BRINGETH GOOD TIDINGS, *who publisheth* PEACE, *saying, Thy King reigneth*, Isaiah lii. 7. *Jehovah will redeem my soul in* PEACE, Psalm lv. 18. THE WORK OF JEHOVAH IS PEACE, THE LABOR OF RIGHTEOUSNESS IS REST, AND SECURITY FOREVER, THAT THEY MAY DWELL IN A HABITATION OF PEACE, AND IN TENTS OF SECURITY, AND IN TRANQUIL RESTING PLACES, Isaiah xxxii. 17, 18. *Jesus said to the seventy whom He sent forth, Into whatsoever house ye enter, first say,* PEACE TO THIS HOUSE; *and if* A SON OF PEACE *be there, your* PEACE *shall rest upon him*, Luke x. 5, 6; Matt. x. 12, 13, 14. *Jehovah will speak* PEACE *to his people;* RIGHTEOUSNESS AND PEACE *shall kiss each other*, Psalm lxxxv. 9, 10. When the Lord appeared to the disciples, He said, PEACE BE WITH YOU, John xx. 19, 21, 26. Moreover, the state of peace, into which those who are regenerated by the Lord are about to come, is treated of in Isaiah lxv. and lxvi., and in other places; and those will come into it who are received into the New Church, which the Lord is at this day instituting. What the peace is in its essence, in which the angels of heaven are, and those who are in the Lord, may be seen in the work concerning HEAVEN AND HELL, n. 284 to 290. From these things also it is manifest, why the Lord calls Him self the *Lord of the Sabbath*, that is of rest and peace.

304. Celestial peace, which is in respect to the hells, that evils and falses may not thence arise and invade, may be compared with natural peace, in many cases, as with peace after wars, when every one lives in security with respect to enemies, and safe in his city, in his own house and in his own farms and gardens. It is as the prophet said, when he speaks naturally concerning celestial peace; *They shall sit every man under his vine, and under his fig-tree, and none shall terrify them*, Micah. iv. 4; Isaiah lxv. 21, 22, 23. It may be compared also with recreations of the mind and with rests, after grievous labors, and with the consolations of mothers after parturition, when their love, called *storge*, manifests its delights. It may also be compared with serenity after tempests, black clouds and thunders; and likewise with spring after a severe winter passed by; and then with the expressions of joy from the tender plants in the fields, and from the blossoms in gardens, plains and woods. It may be compared also with the state of mind with those, who, after storms and dangers upon the sea, reach the port, and set their feet upon the expected land.

THE FOURTH COMMANDMENT.

Honor thy father and thy mother, that thy days may be prolonged, and that it may be well with thee upon the earth.

305. This commandment is so read, Exod. xx. 12, and Deut. v. 16. By *honoring thy father and thy mother*, in THE NATURAL SENSE, which is the sense of the letter, is meant, to honor parents, to obey them, to be attentive to them, and to be grateful to them for benefits, which are, that they feed and clothe their children, and introduce them into the world, that they may act in it as civil and moral persons; and also into heaven, by the precepts of religion; thus they consult for

their temporal prosperity, and also for their eternal felicity; and they do all these things from the love in which they are from the Lord, whose office they perform. In a respective sense, is meant, the honor of guardians from wards, if the parents are dead. In a wider sense, by this commandment, is meant, to honor the king and magistrates, since they provide things necessary for all in common, which parents do in particular. In the widest sense, by this commandment, is meant, that men should love their country, because this nourishes them and protects them; wherefore country [*patria*] is called from father [*pater*]. But honors should be paid by parents to their country, king and magistrates, and implanted by them in their children.

306. In THE SPIRITUAL SENSE, by *honoring father and mother*, is meant, to adore and love God and the church. In this sense, by *father*, is meant God, who is the Father of all; and by *mother*, the church. Infants and angels in the heavens know no other father and no other mother, since they are born there anew of the Lord by the church; wherefore the Lord says, *Call no one your father on the earth; for one is your Father, who is in the heavens*, Matt. xxiii. 9. These things were said for infants and angels in heaven, but not for infants and men on the earth The Lord teaches the same in the common prayer of Christian churches: *Our Father, who art in the heavens, hallowed be thy name.* That by *mother*, in the spiritual sense, is meant the church, is, because, as a mother on the earth feeds her children with natural food, so the church feeds them with spiritual food; wherefore, also, the church is every where in the Word called *mother*, as in Hosea: *Contend with* YOUR MOTHER; *she is not my wife, and I am not her husband*, ii. 2, 5; in Isaiah: *Where is your mother's bill of divorcement, whom I have put away?* l. 1; and Ezek. xvi. 45; xix. 10. And in the evangelists: *Jesus, stretching out his hand to the disciples, said, My mother and my brethren are those who hear the Word of God and do it*, Matt. xii. 48, 49; Mark iii. 33, 34, 35; Luke viii. 21; John xix. 25, 26, 27.

307. IN THE CELESTIAL SENSE, by *father*, is meant our Lord Jesus Christ; and by *mother*, the communion of the saints, by which is meant his church, spread over all the world. That the Lord is Father, is evident from these passages: *A Child is born to us, a Son is given to us, whose name is God, Hero,* THE FATHER OF ETERNITY, *the Prince of peace*, Isaiah ix. 6. *Thou art* OUR FATHER; *Abraham doth not know us, and Israel doth not acknowledge us:* THOU ART OUR FATHER, *our Redeemer; from an age is thy name*, lxiii. 16. Philip said, *Show us the Father. Jesus saith to him,* HE WHO SEETH ME, SEETH THE FATHER; *how, then, sayest thou, Show us* THE FATHER? *Believe Me, that I am in* THE FATHER, *and* THE FATHER *in Me*, John xv. 7 to 11; xii. 45. That by *mother*, in this sense, is meant the church of the Lord, is evident from these passages: *I saw the holy city, New Jerusalem, prepared* AS A BRIDE ADORNED FOR HER HUSBAND, Rev. xxi 2. The angel said unto John, *Come, I will show thee* THE BRIDE, THE LAMB'S WIFE. *And he showed the city, the holy Jerusalem*, xxi. 9, 10. *The time of* THE MARRIAGE OF THE LAMB *hath come, and* HIS WIFE *hath prepared herself. Blessed are those who are called to the* MARRIAGE-SUPPER *of the Lamb*, xix. 7, 9; and besides, Matt. ix. 15; Mark ii. 19, 20; Luke v. 34, 35; John iii. 29; xix. 26, 27. That by *New Jerusalem*, is meant a New Church, which the Lord is now instituting, may be seen in the APOCALYPSE REVEALED, n. 880, 881: this church, and not the former, is wife and mother in this sense. The spiritual offspring, which are born of this marriage, are the goods of charity and the truths of faith; and those who are in these, from the Lord, are called *children of the marriage, children of God*, and *born of Him.*

308. It is to be held, that there continually proceeds from the Lord a divine sphere of celestial love towards all who embrace the doctrine of his

church, and who obey Him, as little children in the world obey father and mother, apply themselves to Him, and wish to be nourished, that is, instructed by Him. From this celestial sphere arises a natural sphere, which is of love towards infants and children, which is most universal, and not only affects men, but also birds and beasts, even to serpents; and not only animate, but also inanimate things. But that the Lord might operate into these, even as into spiritual things, He created the sun, which might be in the natural world as father, and the earth as mother; for the sun is like a common father, and the earth like a common mother, from whose marriage exist all the germinations that adorn the surface of the globe. From the influx of that celestial sphere into the natural world, exist those wonderful progressions of vegetation, from seed to the fruit, and to new seeds. Thence also it is, that there are many kinds of shrubs, which, in the day time, turn, as it were, their faces to the sun, and turn them away when the sun sets; thence also it is, that there are flowers, which, at the rising of the sun, open themselves, and close themselves at his setting; and thence also it is, that the nightingales sing sweetly at the first dawn of the morning, and in like manner after they have been fed by their mother earth. Thus these and those honor their father and their mother. All these things are testimonies, that the Lord, by means of the sun and the earth, in the natural world, provides all things necessary for animate and inanimate things. Wherefore it is said in David, *Praise Jehovah from the heavens; praise Him, sun and moon. Praise Him from the earth, ye whales and abysses; praise Him, ye trees of fruit and all cedars; wild beast, and every beast, reptile, and bird of wing, kings of the earth, and all people, youths and virgins,* Psalm cxlvii. 7 to 12; and in Job: *Ask, I pray, the beasts, and they will teach thee; or the birds of heaven, and they will show thee; or the shrub of the earth, and it will instruct thee; and the fishes of the sea will tell thee. Who knoweth not from all these, that the hand of Jehovah hath done that?* xii. 7, 8, 9. *Ask, and they will teach,* signifies, Look at, attend to, and judge from them, that the Lord Jehovah hath created them.

The Fifth Commandment

Thou shalt not kill.

309. By this commandment, *Thou shalt not kill,* in THE NATURAL SENSE, is meant, not to kill a man, and not to inflict on him any wound of which he may die, and also not to mutilate his body; and moreover not to bring any deadly evil upon his name and fame, since fame and life with many go hand in hand. In a wider natural sense, by murders, are meant enmity, hatred, and revenge, which breathe death; for murder lies concealed within them, like fire in wood under ashes; infernal fire is nothing else; wherefore one is said to be *inflamed with hatred,* and to *burn with revenge.* These are murders in intention, but not in act; and if the fear of the law, and of retaliation and revenge, were taken from them, they would burst forth into act; especially if there be treachery or ferocity in the intention. That hatred is murder, is evident from these words of the Lord; *Ye have heard, that it was said by the ancients, Thou shalt not kill; and whosoever shall kill, shall be obnoxious to the judgment. But I say unto you, that whosoever is angry with his brother rashly, shall be obnoxious to the fire of hell,* Matt. v. 21, 22. The reason is, because all that is of the intention, is also of the will, and thus in itself of the deed.

310. In THE SPIRITUAL SENSE, by murders, are meant all methods of killing and destroying the souls of men, which are various and manifold; as to turn them away from God, religion, and divine worship, by injecting scandals against them, and by advising such things as create aversion and also abhorrence. Such are all the devils and satans in hell, with whom the violators and prostitutors of the sanctities of the

church, in this world, are conjoined. Those who destroy souls by falses, are meant by the king of the abyss, called Abaddon or Apollyon, that is, the *destroyer*, in Rev. ix; and in the prophetic Word by the *slain*, as in these passages; *Jehovah God said, Feed the sheep of the slaughter, which their possessors have slain*, Zech. xi. 4, 5, 7. *We have been slain all the day, we have been accounted as a flock for the slaughter*, Psalm xliv. 22. *Jacob shall cause those who are to come to take root; is he slain, according to the slaughter of those slain by him?* Isaiah xxvii. 6, 7. *The thief cometh not, but that he may steal and kill the sheep; I have come that they may have life and abundance*, John x. 10; besides in other places, as Isaiah xiv. 21; xxvi. 21; xxvii. 9; Jer. iv. 31; xii. 3; Rev. ix. 4; xi. 7. Thence it is, that the devil is called *a murderer from the beginning*, John viii. 44.

311. In THE CELESTIAL SENSE, by *killing*, is meant, to be angry, rashly, with the Lord, to hate Him, and to wish to blot out his name. These are they concerning whom it is said, that they crucify Him; which also they would do, in like manner as did the Jews, if He should come into the world, as he did before. This is meant by *the Lamb standing as it were slain*, Rev. v. 6; xiii. 8; and by *one crucified*, Rev. xi. 8; Heb. vi. 6; Gal. iii. 1.

312. What the internal of man is, unless it be reformed by the Lord, was manifest to me from the devils and satans in hell; for they have it continually in mind to kill the Lord; and because they cannot do this, they are in the endeavor to kill those who are devoted to the Lord; but because they cannot do this, like men in the world, they attempt every method of destroying their souls, that is, of destroying the faith and charity with them. That hatred and revenge with them appear like dark fires and like bright fires; hatred like dark fires, and revenge like bright fires; yet they are not fires, but appearances. The cruelties of their hearts are sometimes seen above them in the air like combats with the angels, and like the death and destruction of them; it is their anger and hatred against heaven from which such direful mockeries arise. Moreover, they also appear at a distance like wild beasts of every kind, as tigers, leopards, wolves, foxes, dogs, crocodiles, and like serpents of every kind; and when they see, in representative forms, gentle beasts, they attack them in fantasy, and attempt to kill them. There came into my sight, as it were, dragons, standing beside women, with whom were infants, which they endeavored, as it were, to devour, according to those things which are related in Revelation xii; which are nothing else than representations of hatred against the Lord and his New Church. That the men in the world, who wish to destroy the church of the Lord, are similar to them, is not apparent to their companions, because the bodies, by which they perform moral duties, absorb and conceal those things; but still they appear to the angels, who look not at their bodies but at their spirits, in like forms with those devils above described. Who could have known such things, unless the Lord had opened the sight of some one, and enabled him to look into the spiritual world? If this had not been done, must not these things, and others of the greatest importance, have been concealed from men forever?

THE SIXTH COMMANDMENT.

Thou shalt not commit adultery.

313. In THE NATURAL SENSE, by this commandment, is meant, not only to commit adultery, but also to will and do obscene things, and thence to think and speak lascivious things. That only to lust is to commit adultery, is evident from these words of the Lord; *Ye have heard that it was said by the ancients, Thou shalt not commit adultery. But I say unto you, that if any one shall look upon a woman, belonging to another, so as to lust after her, he hath already committed adultery with her in his heart*, Matt v. 27, 28. The reason is, because the lust becomes

as the deed, when it is in the will; for allurement enters only into the understanding, but intention into the will, and the intention of lust is the deed. But more may be seen concerning these things in the work CONCERNING CONJUGIAL LOVE, AND CONCERNING SCORTATORY LOVE, published at Amsterdam in the year 1768; which treats *Concerning the Opposition of Conjugial Love and Scortatory*, n. 423 to 443; *Concerning Fornication*, n. 444 to 460; *Concerning Adulteries and their Kinds and Degrees*, n. 473 to 499; *Concerning the Lust of Defloration*, n. 501 to 505; *Concerning the Lust of Varieties*, n. 506 to 510; *Concerning the Lust of Violation*, n. 511, 512; *Concerning the Lust of seducing Innocences*, n. 513, 514; *Concerning the Imputation of each Love, Scortatory and Conjugial*, n. 523 to 531. All these things are meant by this commandment, in the natural sense.

314. In THE SPIRITUAL SENSE, by *committing adultery*, is meant to adulterate the goods of the Word, and to falsify its truths. That these things, also, are meant by committing adultery, has been hitherto unknown, because the spiritual sense of the Word has been hitherto concealed; that no other is signified in the Word, by committing adultery [*mœchari, adulterari*], and whoredom, is very manifest from these passages; *Run about through the streets of Jerusalem, and seek if ye may find a man* WHO DOETH JUDGMENT AND SEEKETH TRUTH. *When I fed them to the full,* THEY COMMITTED WHOREDOM, Jer. v. 1, 7. *I have seen in the prophets of Jerusalem a horrible obstinacy,* IN COMMITTING ADULTERY AND GOING IN FALSEHOOD, xxiii. 14. *They have done folly in Israel,* THEY HAVE COMMITTED WHOREDOM, AND HAVE SPOKEN MY WORD FALSELY, xxix. 23. *They* COMMITTED WHOREDOM *because they forsook Jehovah*, Hosea iv. 7. *I will cut off the soul that hath respect to diviners and soothsayers, to* GO A WHORING *after them*, Lev. xx. 6. *A covenant should not be made with the inhabitants of the land, lest they should* GO A WHORING AFTER THEIR GODS, Exod. xxxiv. 15. Since Babylon, above all others, adulterates and falsifies the Word, therefore she is called THE GREAT WHORE, and these things are said concerning her in the Revelation; *Babylon hath made all nations drink of the wine of the anger of her whoredom*, xiv. 8. *The angel said, I will show thee the judgment of the great Whore, with whom the kings of the earth have committed whoredom*, xvii. 1, 2. *He hath judged the great* WHORE, *who hath corrupted the earth with her whoredom*, xix. 2. Since the Jewish nation had falsified the Word, therefore it was called by the Lord, AN ADULTEROUS GENERATION, Matt. xii. 39; xvi. 4; Mark viii. 38; and THE SEED OF THE ADULTERER, Isaiah lvii. 3; besides in many other places, where, by adulteries and whoredoms, are meant adulterations and falsifications of the Word, as Jer. iii. 6, 8; xiii. 27; Ezek. xvi. 15, 16, 26, 28, 29, 32, 33; xxiii. 2, 3, 5, 7, 11, 14, 16, 17; Hosea v. 3; vi. 10; Nahum iii. 1, 3, 4.

315. In THE CELESTIAL SENSE, by committing adultery, is meant to deny the holiness of the Word, and to profane it. That this is meant, in this sense, follows from the former spiritual sense, which is, to adulterate its goods and to falsify its truths. Those deny and profane the holiness of the Word, who in heart laugh at every thing of the church and of religion; for all things of the church and of religion, in the Christian world, are from the Word.

316. There are various causes which make a man appear not only to others, but also to himself, to be chaste, and yet he is wholly unchaste; for he does not know, that lust, when it is in the will, is the deed, and that it cannot be removed, except by the Lord after repentance. Abstinence from doing does not make one chaste, but abstinence from willing, when he can do, because it is sin, does; as, if any one abstains from adulteries and whoredoms only from fear of the civil law and its penalties; from fear of the loss of fame, and thence of honor from fear of diseases from them; from fear of chidings at home from his wife, and

thence of unquietness of life; from fear of revenge from the husband and relations and of whips from their servants; or from avarice; or from weakness, arising either from disease, or from abuse, or from age, or from any other cause of impotence; yea, if he abstains from them from any natural or moral law, and not, at the same time, from a spiritual law, he is still, inwardly, an adulterer and a whoremonger; for, nevertheless, he believes that they are not sins, and thence does not in his spirit make them unlawful in the sight of God, and thus in spirit he commits them, although not before the world in the body; wherefore, after death, when he becomes a spirit, he speaks openly in favor of them. Moreover, adulterers may be compared with covenant-breakers, who violate engagements; and also with the satyrs and priapuses of the ancients, who wandered in the woods, and cried, "Where are virgins, brides and wives, with whom we may sport?" Adulterers also, in the spiritual world, actually appear like satyrs and priapuses. They may be compared, also, with he-goats which stink; as also with dogs which run hither and thither through the streets, and look about, and smell where dogs are, with which they may wanton; and so forth. Their manly power, when they become husbands, may be compared to the blossoming of tulips in the time of spring, which, after a month of days, drop their blossoms, and wither away.

THE SEVENTH COMMANDMENT.

Thou shalt not steal.

317. In THE NATURAL SENSE, by this commandment, is meant, according to the letter, not to steal, to rob, or to act the pirate, in time of peace; and, in general, not to take away from any one his goods secretly, or under any pretext. It also extends itself to all impostures, illegitimate gains, usuries and exactions; and also to fraudulent practices in paying duties and taxes, and in discharging debts. Workmen offend against this commandment, who do their work unfaithfully and dishonestly; merchants who deceive in merchandise, in weight, measure and accounts; officers who deprive the soldiers of their just wages; judges who judge for friendship, bribes, relationship, affinity, and other causes, by perverting the laws or legal cases, and thus deprive others of their goods, which they rightfully possess.

318. In THE SPIRITUAL SENSE, by *stealing*, is meant to deprive others of the truths of their faith, which is done by false and heretical things. Priests who minister only for the sake of gain, or worldly honor, and teach such things as they see or may see from the Word, are not true, are spiritual thieves, since they take away from the people the means of salvation, which are the truths of faith. These also are called *thieves* in the Word, in these passages: *He who entereth not through the door into the sheepfold, but climbeth up some other way, is a thief and a robber. The thief cometh not but that he may steal, kill and destroy*, John x. 1, 10 *Lay up treasures, not on the earth, but in heaven, where thieves do not come and steal*, Matt. vi. 19, 20. *If thieves come to thee, if overthrowers by night, how wilt thou be cut off! Will they not steal what is enough for them*, Obad. 5. *They will run about in the city, they will run on the wall, they will climb up into the houses, they will enter through the windows*, Joel ii. 9. *They have made a lie, and the thief cometh, and the troop spreadeth itself abroad*, Hosea vii. 1.

319. In THE CELESTIAL SENSE, by *thieves*, are meant those who take away divine power from the Lord, and also those who claim to themselves his merit and righteousness. These, although they adore God, still do not trust Him, but themselves; and also they do not believe in God, but in themselves.

320. Those who teach false and heretical things, and persuade the common people that they are true and orthodox, and yet read the Word, and thence may know what is false and

what is true; and also those who confirm the falses of religion by fallacies, and seduce, may be compared with impostors and impostures of every kind; which, because they are in themselves thefts, in the spiritual sense, may be compared with impostors who coin false money, and gild it, or give it the color of gold, and pass it for pure; and also with those who know how to cut and polish crystals, and harden them dexterously, and sell them for diamonds; as also with those who carry sphinxes or apes, clothed like men, and covered as to their faces, on horses or mules, through cities, and cry, that they are noblemen of ancient ancestry. They are like those who apply painted masks to their living and natural faces, and conceal their beauty. And they are like those who show selenites and pellucid stones, which shine as from gold and silver, and sell them for stones of great value. They may also be likened to those who, by theatrical exhibitions, lead away people from true divine worship, and from temples to play-houses. Those who confirm falses of every kind, esteeming the truth of no value, and who discharge the office of priest only for the sake of gain and honor, and thus are spiritual thieves, may be likened to those thieves who carry keys, with which they can open the doors of all houses; and also to leopards and eagles, which, with sharp eyes, look about to see where is the richest prey.

The Eighth Commandment.

Thou shalt not bear false witness against thy neighbor

321. By *bearing false witness against the neighbor*, or testifying falsely, in THE NATURAL SENSE, is first of all meant, to act as a false witness before a judge, or before others not in a court of justice, against any one who is rashly accused of any evil, and to asseverate this by the name of God or any thing holy, or by himself, and such things of himself as are of the reputation of any one's name. By this commandment, in a wider natural sense, are meant lies of every kind, and politic hypocrisies, which look to a bad end; and also to traduce and defame the neighbor, so that his honor, name and fame, on which the character of the whole man depends, are injured. In the widest natural sense, are meant unfaithfulness, stratagems, and evil purposes against any one, from various origins, as from enmity, hatred, revenge, envy, rivalship, &c.; for these evils conceal within them the testifying of what is false.

322. In THE SPIRITUAL SENSE, by testifying falsely, is meant, to persuade that the false of faith is the true of faith, and that the evil of life is the good of life, and the reverse; but to do this and that from purpose, and not from ignorance, thus to do them after one knows what is true and good, but not before; for the Lord says, *If ye were blind, ye would not have sin; but now ye say, that we see; therefore your sin remaineth*, John ix. 41. This false is meant in the Word by a lie, and the purpose by deceit, in these passages: *We make a league with death, and with hell we make a vision; we have placed our trust in a lie, and have been hid in falsity*, Isaiah xxviii. 15. *They are people of rebellion, lying children; they are not willing to hear the law of Jehovah*, xxx. 9. *From the prophet even to the priest, every one maketh a lie*, Jer. viii. 10. *The inhabitants speak a lie, and as to the tongue, deceit is in their mouth*, Micah. vi. 12. *Thou wilt destroy those who speak a lie; Jehovah abhors a man of deceit*, Psalm v. 6. *They have taught their tongue to speak a lie; their habitation is in the midst of deceit*, Jer. ix. 15. Because by a lie, is meant the false, therefore the Lord says, that *the devil speaketh a lie from his own*, John viii. 14. A lie signifies what is false, and false-speaking, also, in these passages: Jer. ix. 4; xxiii. 14, 32; Ezek. xiii. 15 to 19; xxi. 24; Hosea vii. 1; xii. 1; Nahum iii. 1; Psalm cxx. 2, 3.

323. In THE CELESTIAL SENSE, by testifying falsely, is meant to blas-

pheme the Lord and the Word, and thus to reject the Truth itself from the church; for the Lord is Truth itself, and also the Word. On the other hand, by testifying, in this sense, is meant, to speak the truth; and by testimony, truth itself. Thence also it is, that the decalogue is called the testimony, Exod. xxiv. 16, 21, 22; xxx. 7, 8; xxxii. 15, 16; xl. 20; Levit. xvi. 13; Num. xvii. 19, 22, 25. And because the Lord is the Truth itself, He says concerning Himself, that He testifies. That the Lord is Truth itself, John xiv. 6; Rev. iii. And that He testifies and is witness of Himself, John iii. 11; viii. 13 to 19; xv. 26; xviii. 37, 38.

324. Those who speak falses from deceit or purpose, and pronounce them with a pretended sound of spiritual affection, and especially if they intermingle truths from the Word, which they thus falsify, were called by the ancients, enchanters; concerning whom, see APOCALYPSE REVEALED, n. 462; and also pythons and serpents of the tree of the knowledge of good and evil. These falsifiers, liars and deceivers may be likened to those who speak courteously and kindly with enemies, and, while they are speaking, hold behind them a dagger, with which they kill them. And they may be compared to those who tinge their swords with poison, and thus attack their enemies; and to those who mingle wolf's-bane with water, and virulent poison with wine and sweetmeats. They may be compared, also, to handsome and alluring harlots, infected with a malignant disease; and also to shrubs full of prickles, which, applied to the nostrils, hurt the smelling fibrils; as also to sweetened poison; and also to dung, which, being dried in the time of autumn, spreads a fragrant odor. Such are in the Word described by leopards; see APOCALYPSE REVEALED, n. 572.

THE NINTH AND TENTH COMMANDMENTS.

Thou shalt not covet thy neighbor's house; thou shalt not covet thy neighbor's wife, nor his servant, nor his maid, nor his ox, nor his ass, nor any thing that is thy neighbor's.

325. In the Catechism which is at this day in use, these are distinguished into two commandments; into one, which makes THE NINTH, which is, *Thou shalt not covet thy neighbor's house;* and into another, which makes THE TENTH, which is, *Thou shalt not covet thy neighbor's wife, nor his servant, nor his maid, nor his ox, nor his ass, nor any thing that is thy neighbor's.* Because these two commandments make one thing, and in Exod. xx. 14, and Deut. v. 18, one verse, I have undertaken to treat of them both together; but not because I wish that they may be joined together into one commandment, but distinguished into two, as before; since those commandments are called TEN WORDS, Exod. xxxiv. 28; Deut. iv. 13; x. 4.

326. These two commandments look to those commandments which precede, and they teach and enjoin that evils should not be done, as also that they should not be lusted for; consequently, that they are not only of the external man, but also of the internal; for he who does not do evils, and yet lusts to do them, still does them. For the Lord says, *If any one lusteth after another's wife, he hath already committed adultery with her in his heart,* Matt. v. 27, 28. And the external man does not become internal, or does not act as one with the internal, until lusts are removed. This also the Lord teaches, saying, *Wo unto you, scribes and Pharisees, because ye cleanse the outside of the cup and the platter, but the insides are full of rapine and intemperance. Blind Pharisee, cleanse first the inside of the cup and the platter, that the outside may be clean also,* Matt. xxiii. 25, 26; and, moreover, in that whole chapter, from the beginning to the end. The internals, which are pharisaical, are lusts for those things which are commanded not to be done, in the first, second, fifth,

sixth, seventh and eighth commandments. It is known, that the Lord, in the world, taught the internal things of the church; and the internal things of the church are, not to lust for evils; and thus He taught, that the internal and the external man make one. This is to be born again, concerning which the Lord spoke to Nicodemus, John iii.; and no one can be born again, or be regenerated, except by the Lord. That these two commandments may look to all those which precede, that they should not be lusted for, therefore *house* is first named, afterwards *wife*, and then *servant*, *maid*, *ox* and *ass;* and lastly, *all that is the neighbor's;* for the house involves all the things which follow; for in it are the husband, wife, servant, maid, ox and ass. The wife, who is afterwards named, then involves those things which follow; for she is mistress, as the husband is master, in the house; the servant and maid are under them, and the oxen and asses under these; and lastly, all things which are below or without, by its being said, *all that is thy neighbor's;* from which it is manifest, that all the preceding are looked to in these two commandments, in general and in particular, in a wide and in a strict sense.

327. In THE SPIRITUAL SENSE, by these commandments, are prohibited all lusts which are contrary to the spirit, thus which are contrary to the spiritual things of the church, which refer themselves, principally, to faith and charity; because, unless lusts were subdued, the flesh would rush, according to its liberty, into all wickedness; for it is known from Paul, that *the flesh lusteth against the spirit, and the spirit against the flesh*, Gal. v. 17; and from James: *Every one is tempted by his own lust, when he is enticed; then lust, after it hath conceived, bringeth forth sin, and sin, when it is finished, bringeth forth death*, James i. 14, 15; and also from Peter: *The Lord reserveth the unrighteous unto the day of judgment, to be punished; especially those who walk after the flesh in lust*, 2 Pet. ii. 9, 10. In fine, these two commandments understood in the spiritual sense, look to all those things which have been before adduced in the spiritual sense, that they should not be lusted for; in like manner, to all the things which have been before adduced in THE CELESTIAL SENSE; but to repeat them is unnecessary.

328. The lusts of the flesh, of the eyes, and of the other senses, separate from the lusts, that is, the affections, desires and delights of the spirit, are altogether similar to the lusts of beasts, wherefore they are in themselves bestial; but the affections of the spirit are such as the angels have, and thence they may be called truly human. Wherefore, as far as any one indulges the lusts of the flesh, so far he is a beast and a wild beast; but as far as he sacrifices to the desires of the spirit, so far he is a man and an ange. The lusts of the flesh may be compared with dried and parched grapes, and with wild grapes; but the affections of the spirit, with juicy and delicious grapes, and also with the taste of the wine pressed out of them. The lusts of the flesh may be compared with stables, in which are asses, he-goats and hogs; and the affections of the spirit, with stables in which are noble horses, and also sheep and lambs: they differ also like an ass and a horse, a he-goat and a sheep, and a hog and a lamb; in general, like dross and gold, like lime and silver, and like a coral and a ruby, &c. Lust and deed cohere like blood and flesh, and like flame and oil; for the lust is in the deed, like the air from the lungs, while one is breathing and speaking, and like wind in the sail, while the vessel continues sailing, and like water in a wheel, from which are the motion and action of a machine.

329. THAT THE TEN PRECEPTS OF THE DECALOGUE CONTAIN ALL THINGS WHICH ARE OF LOVE TO GOD, AND ALL THINGS WHICH ARE OF LOVE TOWARD THE NEIGHBOR.

In eight precepts of the decalogue, in the first, second, fifth, sixth, seventh, eighth, ninth and tenth, there is not any thing said which is of love to God and of love towards the neighbor; for it is not said that God should be loved, nor that the name of God should be hallowed, nor that the neighbor should be loved, so not that we should deal sincerely and uprightly with him; but only, that Thou shalt have no other God before my faces; Thou shalt not take the name of God in vain; Thou shalt not kill; Thou shalt not commit adultery; Thou shalt not steal; Thou shalt not testify falsely; Thou shalt not covet those things which are thy neighbor's. Thus, in general, that evil should not be willed, thought or done against God, nor against the neighbor. But the reason, why such things as are directly of love and charity are not commanded, but only such things as are opposite to them, that they should not be done, is, because as far as man shuns evils as sins, so far he wills the goods which are of love and charity. That the first thing of love to God and of love towards the neighbor, is, not to do evil, and that the second thing of them is, to do good, will be seen in the chapter concerning Charity. There are two loves opposite to each other, the love of willing and doing good, and the love of willing and doing evil; the latter love is infernal, and the former heavenly; for all hell is in the love of doing evil, and all heaven in the love of doing good. Now, because man is born into evils of every kind, thence from birth he inclines to those things which are of hell, and because he cannot come into heaven, unless he be born again, that is, regenerated, it is necessary, that the evils which are of hell should first be removed, before he can will the goods which are of heaven; for no one can be adopted by the Lord, before he is separated from the devil. But how evils are removed, and man brought to do goods, will be demonstrated in the two chapters, one concerning Repentance, and the other concerning Reformation and Regeneration. That evils must first be removed, before the goods, which man does, become good in the sight of God, the Lord teaches in Isaiah: *Wash you, purify you, remove the wickedness of your works from before my eyes; learn to do good; then, if your sins have been as scarlet, they shall become white as snow; if they have been red like crimson, they shall be as wool,* i. 16, 17, 18. Similar to this is this in Jeremiah: *Stand in the gate of the house of Jehovah, and proclaim there this word: Thus said Jehovah of hosts, the God of Israel, Make your ways and your works good; trust not yourselves upon the words of a lie, by saying, The temple of Jehovah, the temple of Jehovah, the temple of Jehovah is here* (that is, the church); *after stealing, killing, committing adultery, and swearing by a lie, will ye come and stand before Me in this house, upon which my name is named, and say, We are delivered, while ye do all these abominations? Hath this house become a den of robbers? Behold, I also have seen, saith Jehovah,* vii. 2, 3, 4, 9, 10, 11. That before washing, or purification from evils, prayers to God are not heard, is also taught in Isaiah: *Jehovah saith, Ah sinful nation, a people heavy with iniquity; they have turned themselves away backward. Wherefore, when ye spread out your hands, I hide my eyes from you; yea, if ye multiply prayer, I do not hear,* i. 4, 15. That love and charity follow him who does the commandments of the decalogue by shunning evils, is evident from these words of the Lord in John: *Jesus said, He that hath my commandments, and doeth them, he it is that loveth Me; and he that loveth Me, will be loved by my Father, and I will love him, and will manifest Myself to him; and We will make an abode with him,* xiv. 21, 23. By *commandments,* there, are meant, particularly, the commandments of the decalogue, which are, that evils should not be done, nor lusted for; and that thus the love of man to God, and the love of God towards man, follow as the good after evil is removed.

330. It was said, that as far as man shuns evils, so far he wills goods; the

reason is, because evils and goods are opposites, for evils are from hell, and goods from heaven; wherefore, as far as hell, that is, evil, is removed, so far heaven approaches, and man looks to good. That it is so, is very manifest from eight commandments of the decalogue, seen thus; as, I. As far as any one does not worship other gods, so far he worships the true God. II. As far as any one does not take the name of God in vain, so far he loves those things which are from God. III. As far as any one is not willing to kill, and to act from hatred and revenge, so far he wishes well to the neighbor. IV. As far as any one is not willing to commit adultery, so far he is willing to live chastely with a wife. V. As far as any one is not willing to steal, so far he practises sincerity. VI. As far as any one is not willing to testify falsely, so far he is willing to think and speak truth. VII. and VIII. As far as any one does not covet those things which are the neighbor's, so far he is willing that the neighbor should enjoy his own. Hence it is evident, that the commandments of the decalogue contain all things which are of love to God, and of love towards the neighbor; wherefore Paul says, *He that loveth another, hath fulfilled the law; for this, Thou shalt not commit adultery, Thou shalt not kill, Thou shalt not steal, Thou shalt not be a false witness, Thou shalt not covet, and if there be any other commandment, it is comprehended in this word, Thou shalt love thy neighbor as thyself. Charity worketh no evil to the neighbor; therefore charity is the fulfilment of the law,* Rom. xiii. 8, 9, 10. To these should be added two canons for the use of the New Church. I. That no one can shun evils as sins, and do goods, which are good in the sight of God, from himself; but that, as far as any one shuns evils as sins, so far he does good, not from himself, but from the Lord. II. That man ought to shun evils as sins, and to fight against them, as from himself; and that if any one shuns evil from any other cause whatever, than because they are sins, he does not shun them, but only causes them not to appear before the world.

331. The reason that evil and good cannot be together, and that as far as evil is removed, good is looked to and felt, is because, in the spiritual world, there is exhaled from every one the sphere of his love, which spreads itself round about, and affects, and causes sympathies and antipathies; by these spheres, the good are separated from the evil. That evil must be removed, before good is known, perceived and loved, may be compared with many things in the natural world, as with these: No one can go to another, who keeps a leopard and a panther in his chamber, and because he gives them food to eat lives securely with them, unless he first removes those wild beasts. What person, invited to the table of a king and a queen, would not first wash his face and hands, before he comes to them? And who enters into the bed-chamber with his bride, after the wedding, unless he have before washed himself all over, and clothed himself with the wedding garment? Who does not purify metallic ores by fire, and separate them from the dross, before he obtains pure gold and silver? Who does not separate the tares from the wheat, before he carries it into the granary? And who does not thresh his barley to separate the grain from the bearded ears, before he gathers it into the house? Who does not prepare his meat by boiling, before it becomes eatable, and is set upon the table? Who does not shake off the worms from the leaves of the trees in the garden, lest the leaves should be consumed, and thus the fruit should perish? Who does not dislike dirt in houses and in courts, and remove it from them, especially when a prince is expected, or a bride, the daughter of a prince? Who loves a virgin, and intends marriage with her, who is infected with malignant diseases, or covered with pimples and blotches, however she may paint her face, dress herself splendidly, and endeavor to infuse enticements of love by

the charms of her conversation? That man ought to purify himself from evils, and not wait that the Lord may do this immediately, is, comparatively, as if a servant, whose face and clothes are daubed with soot and dung, should come up to his master, and say, "Wash me, sir." Would not the master say to him, "You foolish servant, what do you say? See, there is water, soap and a towel. Have you not hands and power to use them? Wash yourself." And the Lord God might say, "The means of purification are from Me, and also your will and your power are from Me; wherefore use these my gifts and talents as your own, and you will be purified," &c. That the external man should be cleansed, but by the internal, the Lord teaches in Matt. xxiii., from the beginning to the end.

---

332. To the above shall be added FOUR RELATIONS. FIRST. Once I heard vociferations, which bubbled up, as it were, from below, through the waters; one at the left hand, "O HOW JUST!" another at the right hand, "O HOW LEARNED!" and a third from behind, "O HOW WISE!" And because it fell into my thought, whether there are also in hell those who are just, learned and wise, I was affected with a desire of seeing whether such are there; and it was said to me from heaven, "You shall see and hear." And I went out of the house in spirit, and saw before me an opening; thither I went, and looked down, and behold a ladder; by this I descended; and when I was below, I saw a champaign country covered over with shrubs, with thorns and nettles intermixed; and I asked whether hell was here; they said, "It is the lower earth, which is next above hell." And then I proceeded according to the exclamations, in order: to the first, "O HOW JUST!" and I saw a company of those who, in the world, had been judges of friendship and bribes; then to the second exclamation, "O HOW LEARNED!" and I saw a company of those who in the world had been reasoners; and to the third exclamation, "O HOW WISE!" and I saw a company of those who in the world had been confirmers. But I turned from these to the first, where were the judges of friendship and bribes, and who were proclaimed just. And I saw at the side, as it were, an amphitheatre, built of brick and covered with black tiles; and it was said to me, that there was their TRIBUNAL. There were three entrances into it on the north side, and three on the west side, and none on the south and east sides—a token that their judgments were not judgments of justice, but judgments of will. In the midst of the amphitheatre, there was seen a fire-place, into which the servants, who tended the fire, threw torches made of sulphur and bitumen; the light from which, darting forth to the plastered walls, formed pictured images of birds of the evening and of night; but that fire-place, and the vibrations of light thence into the forms of those images, were representations of their judgments, in that they could disguise the things of every question, and induce upon them appearances according to favor. After half an hour, I saw old and young men entering, in gowns and robes, who, laying aside their caps, placed themselves on seats at the tables to sit in judgment. And I heard and perceived how dexterously and ingeniously, from the aspect of friendship, they warped and changed judgments into appearances of justice, and this so far, that they themselves did not see what was unjust otherwise than as just, and, reciprocally, what was just otherwise than as unjust. Such persuasions concerning them appeared from their faces, and were heard from the sound of their speech. Then illustration from heaven was given me, from which I perceived the things one by one, whether they were of right or not of right; and I saw how industriously they covered what was unjust, and induced upon it the appearance of what was just; and from the laws they selected one which favored, to which they bent the point in question, and the rest, by artful reason

ings, they removed to the side. After the judgment, the sentences were carried out to their clients, friends and favorers; and these, in order to return the favor to them, for a long way exclaimed, "O HOW JUST! O HOW JUST!" After this, I conversed with the angels of heaven concerning them, and told them some of the things seen and heard; and the angels said, that "such judges appear to others as if endued with the greatest acuteness of understanding, when yet they do not see any thing at all of what is just and equitable. If you take away friendship for any one, they sit in judgment like statues, and only say, 'I accede; I agree with this or that man.' The reason is, because all their judgments are judgments previously formed, and a judgment previously formed with favor follows the cause from the beginning to the end of it; hence they see nothing else than what is of their friend; at all that which is against him, they turn aside their eyes, and look from the corners of them; and if they take it up again, they involve it in reasonings, as a spider does the captives in her web, and consume it. Thence it is, that if they do not follow the web of their previous judgment, they see nothing of right. They have been explored to ascertain whether they were able to see, and they were found to be unable. The inhabitants of your world will wonder that it is so; but tell them, that this is a truth explored by the angels of heaven. Since they see nothing of what is just, we in heaven do not look upon them as men, but as monstrous images of man, of which those things which are of friendship make the heads, those things which are of injustice, the breasts, those things which are of confirmation, the hands and feet, and those things which are of justice, the soles of the feet, which, if they do not favor a friend, they supplant and trample under feet. But you shall see what they are, viewed in themselves, for their end is near at hand;" and lo, then suddenly the ground opened, and the tables fell upon tables, and they, together with the whole amphitheatre, were swallowed up and cast into caverns, and imprisoned. And then it was said to me, "Do you wish to see them there?" And lo, they were seen, as to the face, as if from polished steel, and as to the body from the neck to the loins, like graven images clothed with leopards' skins, and as to the feet, like serpents; and I saw the law-books, which they had laid up on the tables, turned into playing-cards; and now, instead of sitting as judges, the employment given to them is, that they should make vermilion into paint, with which they daub the faces of harlots, and thus turn them into beauties. After these things were seen, I wished to go to the two other companies, to the one where were merely reasoners, and to the other where were merely confirmers. But it was said to me, "Rest a little while; angels from the society next above them shall be given you as companions; by these, light will be given to you from the Lord, and you will see wonderful things."

333. SECOND RELATION. After some time, I heard again from the lower earth the same words as before, O HOW LEARNED! O HOW LEARNED! And I looked around to see who were present; and lo, there were angels, who were in the heaven immediately above those who cried, O HOW LEARNED! And I conversed with them concerning the cry, and they said that "those were the learned, who only reason, WHETHER IT BE OR BE NOT, and rarely think THAT IT IS SO: wherefore they are like winds which blow and pass away; and like bark around trees, which are without pith; and like shells around almonds without meat; and like the rind around fruit without the pulp; for their minds are without interior judgment, and only united with the senses of the body; wherefore, if the senses themselves do not judge, they are able to conclude nothing; in a word, they are merely sensual, and by us they are called REASONERS. They are called reasoners because they never conclude anything, but take up whatever they hear, and dispute whether it be, by continually contradicting. They love nothing more

than to attack truths, and thus to pull them to pieces by discussing them. These are they, who believe themselves to be learned above all in the world. On hearing these words, I requested the angels to lead me to them, and they led me to a cave, from which went steps to the lower earth; and we descended and followed the cry, "O HOW LEARNED!" and lo! there were several hundreds standing in one place, beating the ground. Wondering at this, I asked, "Why do they stand thus, and beat the ground with their feet?" and added, "They can thus excavate the ground with their feet." At this the angels smiled, and said, "It appears that they thus stand, because they think nothing concerning any thing, that it is so, but only, whether it is so, and dispute; and when the thought proceeds no farther, they appear only to tread and stamp upon one spot, and not to proceed." And the angels said, "Those who flow out of the natural world into this, and hear that they are in another world, gather themselves into companies, in many places, and ask, 'Where is heaven, and where is hell?' as also, 'Where is God?' and after they have been instructed, they still begin to reason, to dispute, and to debate, WHETHER THERE IS A GOD. They do this, because there are, at this day, so many naturalists in the natural world, and these, among themselves and with others, when the conversation is concerning religion, propose this for discussion, and this proposition and discussion are seldom terminated in the affirmative of faith, that there is a God; and these afterwards consociate themselves more and more with the evil; and this is done, because no one can do any good from the love of good, except from God." Afterwards, I was led down to the assembly; and lo! there appeared to me men, not unhandsome in the face, and in clothes of ornament; and the angels said, "They appear such in their own light; but if light out of heaven flows in, the faces are changed, and also the clothes." And it was done so, and then they appeared with dark faces, clothed in black sacks; but this light being withdrawn, they were seen as before. Then I spoke with some of the assembly, and said, "I heard the cry of the crowd around you, 'O HOW LEARNED!' wherefore, let us converse with you on things which are of the deepest learning." And they replied, "Say whatever you please, and we will satisfy you." And I asked, "What is the religion by which man is saved?" And they said, "We will divide this question into several; and, until we have concluded these, we cannot give an answer. And the discussion shall be, 1. Whether religion be any thing. 2. Whether salvation be or not. 3. Whether one religion effect more than another. 4. Whether there be a heaven and a hell. 5. Whether there be eternal life after death; besides many more." And I asked concerning the first, *Whether religion be any thing*. And they began to canvass this with abundance of arguments; and I requested that they would refer it to the assembly; and they referred it; and the common answer was, that "This proposition needs so much investigation, that it cannot be finished in an evening." And I asked, "Can it be finished by you within a year?" And one said, "It cannot within a hundred years." And I said, "In the mean time, you are without religion; and because salvation thence depends, you are without the idea, faith and hope of salvation." And he replied, "Should it not be demonstrated first, whether religion is, and what it is, and whether it is any thing? If it is, it will be also for the wise; if it is not, it will be only for the common people. It is known, that religion is called a bond; but it is asked, for whom? If only for the common people, it is not in itself any thing; if also for the wise, it is." On hearing these words, I said, "You are any thing rather than learned, because you cannot think any thing else, than whether it be, and turn this both ways. Can any one be learned, unless he know something for certain, and proceed into it, as a man proceeds from step to step, and successively into wisdom? Otherwise, you do not touch truths, even with the finger-nail; but you remove them more and more out of sight. Wherefore, to reason only whether it be, is to reason from a hat which is never put on, or from a shoe which is not tried on; what thence follows, but that you know not whether any thing exist, or whether it be any thing but an idea; and so whether salvation be given, whether eternal life after death, whether one religion be better than another, whether there be a heaven and a hell. You cannot think any thing concerning these things, so long as you halt at the first step, and beat the sand there, and do not set one foot before the other, and go forward. Take heed to yourselves, lest your minds, while they stand thus on the outside, without judgment, should inwardly grow hard, and become pillars of salt." On saying these words, I departed, and they from indignation threw stones after me; and then they appeared to me like graven images, in which there is nothing of human reason. And I asked the angels concerning their lot; and they said, that the lowest of them are let down into the deep, and there into the desert, and are compelled to carry packs; and then, because they cannot produce any thing from reason, they prate and speak vain things; and there, at a distance, they appear like asses carrying burdens.

334. Third Relation. After this, one of the angels said, "Follow me to the place where they cried, 'O how wise!'" And he said, "You will see prodigies of men; you will see faces and bodies, which are of a man, and yet they are not men." And I said, "Are they beasts, then?" He replied, "They are not beasts, but men-beasts; for they are such as cannot see at all, whether truth be truth or not; and yet they can make whatever they please appear like truth; such with us are called Confirmers." And we followed the cry, and came to the place; and lo! a company of men, and around the company a crowd, and in the crowd some of noble descent, who, when they heard that they confirmed all things that they said, and favored them with so manifest consent, turned themselves about, and said, "O how wise!" But the angel said to me, "Let us not go to them but let us call out one from the company; and we called one out, and retired with him, and spoke various things, and he confirmed them one by one, so that at length they appeared as true. And we asked him whether he could also confirm the contrary; he said that he could as well as the former. Then he said, openly and from the heart, "What is truth? Is there any truth given in the nature of things, but what man makes true? Say whatever you please, and I will make it to be true." And I said, "Make this true, That faith is the all of the church." And he did it so dexterously and ingeniously, that the learned, who stood around, admired and applauded him. Afterwards, I requested that he would make it true that charity was the all of the church; and he did; and afterwards, that charity is nothing of the church. And he clothed and adorned both with appearances, so that the by-standers looked at each other, and said, "Is not this a wise man?" And I said, "Do you not know, that charity is to live well, and that faith is to believe well? Does not he who lives well, also believe well? And thus, that faith is of charity, and charity of faith? Do you not see that this is true?" He replied, "I will make it true, and I shall see." And he did, and said, "Now I see." But presently he made the contrary of that to be true, and then said, "I see also that this is true." At this we smiled, and said, "Are they not contraries? How can two contraries be seen true?" Being indignant at this, he replied, "You err; they are both true, since nothing else is true, but what man makes true." There stood near a certain one, who, in the world, had been an ambassador of the first rank. He wondered at this, and said, "I acknowledge that there is something similar in the world; but still you are insane. Make it to be true-

if you can, that darkness is light, and light, darkness." And he replied, "I shall do this easily. What are light and darkness, but states of the eye? Is not light changed into shade, when the eye comes from a sunny place, as also when a man fixes his eye intensely on the sun? Who does not know, that the state of the eye is then changed, and that thence light appears like shade; and on the other hand, when the state of the eye returns, that that shade appears like light? Does not an owl see the darkness of night as the light of day, and the light of day as the darkness of night, and then the sun itself altogether as an opaque and dusky globe? If any one had eyes like an owl, what would he call light, and what darkness? What then is light, but a state of the eye? And if it be only a state of the eye, is not light darkness, and darkness light? Wherefore the one is true, and the other is true." But, because this confirmation confounded some, I said, "I perceive that that confirmer does not know, that there is given true light and fatuous light: and that both those lights appear as if they were lights, but still fatuous light in itself is not light; but, in respect to true light, it is darkness. An owl is in fatuous light, for there is within its eyes the desire of pursuing and devouring birds; and this light makes its eyes see in time of night, just as cats do, whose eyes in cellars appear like candles; it is the fatuous light, arising from the desire of pursuing and devouring mice, which produces that within in their eyes; thence it is manifest, that the light of the sun is true light, and that the light of lust is fatuous light." After this, the ambassador requested the confirmer, that he would make this as if true: "That a crow is white and not black." And he replied, "This, also, I shall do easily." And he said, "Take a needle or a knife, and open the quills and feathers of a crow; then remove the quills and feathers, and look at the crow's skin; is it not white? What is the black which is around but a shade, from which we should not judge concerning the color of the crow? That black is only a shade, consult those who are skilled in the science of optics, and they will say, 'Grind either a black stone or glass into fine powder, and you will see that the powder is white.'" But the ambassador replied, "Does not the crow appear black to the sight?" But the confirmer replied, "Will you, who are a man, think any thing from appearance? You may, indeed, speak from appearance, that a crow is black, but you cannot think that; as, for example, you may speak from appearance, that the sun rises and sets; but, because you are a man, you cannot think that, because the sun stands unmoved, and the earth goes forward. It is similar with the crow. Appearance is appearance. Say what you will, a crow is all over white; it also grows white, when it grows old; this I have seen." After this, the bystanders looked at me; wherefore I said, that it is true that the quills and feathers of a crow inwardly partake of whiteness, and also its skin but this is the case not only with crows, but also with all the birds in the universe; and every man distinguishes birds by the appearance of their color; if this were not done, we might say concerning every bird, that it is white, which is absurd and ridiculous. Afterwards, the ambassador asked, whether he could make it true, That you are insane. And he said, "I can, but I will not; who is not insane?" Then they requested him, that he would say from the heart, whether he was jesting, or whether he believed that there is not any thing true, except what man makes true And he said, "I swear that I believe it." After this, that universal confirmer was sent to the angels, who explored him as to his quality; and after the exploration, they said, that he did not possess a grain of understanding, because all that which is above the rational, with him, was closed; and only that which is below the rational, was open; above the rational is spiritual light, and below the rational is natural light, and this light with man is such, that he can confirm what ever he pleases; but if spiritual light does not flow into natural light, man does not see whether any truth is truth, nor thence that any thing false is false; to see this and that, is from spiritual light in natural light, and spiritual light is from the God of heaven, who is the Lord; wherefore, that universal confirmer is not a man nor a beast, but a man-beast. I asked the angels concerning the lot of such, whether they can be together with the living, because the life of man is from spiritual light, and from this is his understanding. And they said, that "Such, when they are alone, cannot think any thing, and thence speak; but that they stand mute like automatons, and, as it were, in a deep sleep; but that they are awaked as soon as they hear any thing;" and they added, that "Those become such, who are inwardly evil; into this, spiritual light cannot flow from above, but only something spiritual through the world, whence they have the faculty of confirming." These things being said, I heard a voice from the angels who explored him, saying, "Make a universal conclusion from what has been heard." And I made this, *That it is not the part of an intelligent man to be able to confirm whatever he pleases; but that it is the part of an intelligent man to be able to see that the true is true, and that the false is false, and to confirm it.* After this, I looked at the company where the confirmers were standing, and the crowd around them were crying, "O HOW WISE!" and lo! a dark cloud covered them, and, in the cloud, owls and bats were flying. And it was said to me, "The owls and bats, flying in that cloud, are correspondences, and thence appearances of their thoughts; since confirmations of falsities, so that they appear like truths, are represented in this world under the forms of birds of night, whose eyes are illuminated within by a fatuous light, from which they see objects in darkness, as in the light: such fatuous spiritual light have those, who confirm falses until they appear as truths, and afterwards are believed to be truths. All those are in vision from behind, and not in any vision from before.

335. FOURTH RELATION. Once, at the dawn of day, when I awaked from sleep, I saw before my eyes, as it were, spectres in various shapes; and afterwards, when it was morning, I saw fatuous lights, in divers forms; some like sheets of paper full of writing, which, being folded together again and again, at length appeared like falling stars, which in their descent vanished in the air; and some like open books, some of which shone like little moons, and some burnt like candles; amongst these, were books which raised themselves up on high, and were lost in the height, and others which fell down to the earth, and were dissolved there into dust. From these appearances, I conjectured, that below those meteors there stood those who were disputing about imaginary things, which they esteemed of great moment; for, in the spiritual world, such phenomena appear in the atmospheres, from the reasonings of those standing below; and presently the sight of my spirit was opened to me, and I observed a number of spirits, whose heads were encircled with leaves of laurel, and who were clothed in gowns adorned with flowers, which signified that they were spirits, who, in the natural world, had been renowned for the fame of erudition; and because I was in the spirit, I drew near and mingled myself with the company; and then I heard that they were disputing sharply and warmly among themselves, concerning CONNATE IDEAS; whether there are any in men from birth, as in beasts. Those who denied, turned themselves away from those who affirmed, and at length they stood separated from each other, like the phalanxes of two armies about to fight with swords; but because they had no swords, they fought with the sharp points of words. But then, on a sudden, a certain angelic spirit stood up in the midst of them, and, speaking with a loud voice, he said, "I heard at a distance, not far from you, that

you are ardently engaged, on both sides, in a dispute about connate ideas, whether men have any, like the beasts; but I tell you, THAT MEN HAVE NOT ANY CONNATE IDEAS, AND THAT BEASTS HAVE NOT ANY IDEAS; wherefore, you are quarrelling about nothing, or, as it is said, about goat's wool, or about the beard of this age." On hearing these words, they were very angry, and exclaimed, "Cast him out; he talks contrary to common sense." But when they were in the effort of casting him out, they saw him encircled with heavenly light, through which they could not rush; for he was an angelic spirit; wherefore they retired, and removed themselves a little from him. And after that light was withdrawn, he said to them, "Why are you angry? Hear first, and collect the reasons which I shall offer, and make a conclusion from them yourselves; and I foresee, that those who excel in judgment will accede, and will calm the tempests which have arisen in your minds." To these words, they said, yet with an indignant tone, "Speak, then, and we will hear." And then, beginning to speak, he said, "You believe that beasts have connate ideas, and you have concluded it from this, that their actions appear as if from thought; and yet they have no thought at all, and ideas are not predicable, except of that; and it is the character of thought that they do so or so, for the sake of this or that. Consider, therefore, whether the spider, which weaves her web most curiously, thinks in her little head, 'I will extend the threads in this order, and will tie them together with transverse threads, lest my web should be torn to pieces by the rude vibration of the air; and at the first terminations of the threads, which will make the middle, I will prepare a seat for myself, in which I shall perceive whatever falls in, so that I may run thither; as, if a fly should come, that it may get entangled, and I will quickly seize it, and tie it, and it shall serve me for food.' Again, does the bee think in its little head, 'I will fly abroad; I know where the flowery fields are; and there I will gather wax from these flowers, and suck honey from those; and of the wax I will build little cells contiguous in a series, in such a manner, that I and my companions may freely go in and out, as through streets; and afterwards we will lay up honey in them abundantly, so that there may be enough, also, for the coming winter, that we may not die;' besides other wonderful things, in which they not only emulate, but in some cases excel, the political and economical prudence of men. (See above, n. 12.) Moreover, does the humble-bee think in its little head, 'I and my companions will build a little house of fine papyrus, the walls of which, within, we will wind about in the form of a labyrinth, and in the centre we will prepare, as it were, a forum, into which there shall be an entrance, and out of which there shall be a passage; and this of such workmanship, that no other living creature, except what is of our family, shall find the way to the inmost place, where we assemble.' Again, does the silk-worm, while a worm, think in its little head, 'Now it is time that I should prepare myself for spinning silk, and for the end, that, when it is spun, I may fly abroad, and sport with my companions in the air into which I could not rise before, and provide for myself a progeny?' Do other worms think, in like manner, when they crawl through the walls of houses, and become nymphs, aurelias, chrysalises and at last butterflies? Does a fly have any idea of meeting with another fly, that it happens here, and not there? The case is the same with animals of a larger body, as it is with those little animals, as with birds and winged creatures of every kind, when they come together, and also when they prepare nests, and lay eggs in them, sit upon them, and hatch their young, procure food for them, take care of them until they fly abroad, and then drive them away from their nests, as if they were not their offspring; besides innumerable other things. The case is similar, also, with the beasts of the earth, with serpents and with fishes

Which of you cannot see, from the things above mentioned, that their spontaneous actions do not flow from any thought, of which alone an idea is predicable? The error, that beasts have ideas, flows from no other source, than from the persuasion, that they think, as well as men, and that speech only makes the distinction." After this, the angelic spirit looked around, and because he saw them still hesitating, whether beasts have thought or not, he continued the discourse, and said; "I perceive, that, from the actions of brute animals, similar to those of men, there still clings to you a visionary idea concerning their thought; wherefore I will tell whence their actions are. Every beast, every bird, every fish, reptile and insect, for instance, has its own natural, sensual and corporeal love, the habitations of which are their heads, and in them the brains; through these, the spiritual world flows into the senses of their body immediately, and thereby determines the actions; which is the reason why the senses of their body are much more exquisite than those of men. That influx from the spiritual world, is what is called instinct, and it is called instinct because it exists without the medium of thought; there are also given things accessory to instinct, from habit. But their love, by which, from the spiritual world, is produced the determination to actions, is only for nutrition and propagation, but not for any science, intelligence and wisdom, by which love is successively produced with men.

"That neither has man any connate ideas, may evidently appear from this, that he has not any connate thought; and where there is no thought, there is no idea; for the one is of the other, reciprocally. This may be concluded from infants newly born, in that they cannot do any thing but suck and breathe; that they can suck, is not from any thing connate, but from continual suction in the mother's womb; and that they can breathe, is because they live, for this is a universal of life. The very senses of their body are in the greatest obscurity, and from this they emerge successively by means of objects; in like manner, their motions are acquired by habitual exercise. And as they learn successively to lisp out words, and to sound them, at first without any idea, there arises something obscure of fantasy; and as this becomes clear, something obscure of the imagination arises, and thence of thought. According to the formation of this state, ideas exist, which, as was said above, make one with thought; and thought from none grows by instructions. Wherefore men have ideas, yet not connate, but formed; and from these flow their speech and actions." That no other is born with man, than a faculty for knowing, understanding and becoming wise, as also an inclination to love not only those things, but also the neighbor and God, may be seen in a RELATION above, n. 48, and also in a RELATION below. After this, I looked around, and saw near me Leibnitz and Wolfius, who paid close attention to the reasons produced by the angelic spirit; and then Leibnitz acceded and assented; but Wolfius departed, both denying and affirming, for he had not so strong an interior judgment as Leibnitz.

CHAPTER VI.

CONCERNING FAITH.

336. From the wisdom of the ancients flowed forth this dogma, That the universe, and all the particular parts of it, refer themselves to the good and the true; and thus all things of the church, to love or charity and faith, since all that is called good, which flows from love or charity, and all that is called truth, which flows from faith. Now, because charity and faith are distinctly two, but still make one in man, that he may be a man of the church, that is, that the church may be in man, it was therefore a subject of controversy and dispute amongst the ancients, which of those two should be the first, and thus which by right is to be called the first-born. Some of them said that truth, consequently that faith, should have the priority; and some, that good, consequently that charity, should have it. For they saw that man, soon after his birth, learns to speak and think, and by these to be perfected in understanding, which is done by sciences; and thus that he begins to learn and understand what is true, and that by these means he afterwards learns and understands what is good; consequently, that he learns first what faith is, and afterwards what charity is. Those who thus comprehended this thing, thought that the truth of faith was the first-born, and that the good of charity was born afterwards; wherefore they also attributed to faith the preëminence and prerogative of primogeniture. But these overwhelmed their understanding with such a multitude of arguments in favor of faith, that they did not see that faith is not faith unless it be conjoined with charity, and that charity is not charity unless it be conjoined with faith; and thus that they make one, and that if they do not, neither the one nor the other is any thing in the church. That they do absolutely make one, will be demonstrated in what follows. But in this preface I shall, in a few words, explain how, or in what manner, they make one, for this is of importance, that the things which follow may be in some light. Faith, by which is also meant truth, is first in time, but charity, by which is also meant good, is first in end; and that which is first in the end is actually first, because primary, thus also first-born; but that which is first in time, is not first actually, but apparently. But that this may be comprehended, it shall be illustrated by comparisons; as with the building of a temple, as also of a house, and with the making of a garden, and with the preparing of a field. With THE BUILDING OF A TEMPLE; the first thing in time is to lay the foundation, to raise the walls, to put on the roof, and afterwards to put in the altar, and to erect the pulpit, but the first thing in the end is the worship of God in it, for the sake of which those things are done. With THE BUILDING OF A HOUSE; the first thing in time is to build its exterior parts, and also to furnish it with various things which are of necessity; but the first thing in end is a commodious habitation for himself and for the rest who shall be in the house. With THE MAKING OF A GARDEN; the first thing in time is to level the ground, and prepare the soil, and plant trees, and sow such things as will serve for use; but the first thing in end is the enjoyment

of the fruits of them. With THE PREPARING OF A FIELD; the first thing in time is to clear the land, to plough, to harrow, and then to sow the seeds; but the first thing in end is the harvest, thus also use. From these comparisons, every one may conclude which in itself is first; for does not every one, when he wishes to build a temple or a house, as also to make a garden and to cultivate a field, first intend use, and constantly keep and revolve this in his mind, while he procures the means for it. We conclude, therefore, that the truth of faith is first in time, but that the good of charity is first in end; and that this, because it is primary, is therefore actually the first-begotten in the mind. But it is necessary that it should be known what faith is, and what charity is, each in its essence; and this cannot be known, unless faith and charity be divided, each into its proper articles. The articles of faith, therefore, are these: I. *That saving Faith is in the Lord God the Savior Jesus Christ.* II. *That Faith, in the sum, is, that he, who lives well and believes aright, is saved by the Lord.* III. *That man receives Faith by going to the Lord, learning Truths from the Word, and living according to them.* IV. *That abundance of Truths, cohering as in a bundle, exalts and perfects Faith.* V. *That Faith without Charity is not Faith, and that Charity without Faith is not Charity; and that neither lives, except from the Lord.* VI. *That the Lord, Charity and Faith make one, like Life, Will and Understanding in man; and that, if they are divided, each perishes, like a pearl reduced to powder.* VII. *That the Lord is Charity and Faith in man, and that man is Charity and Faith in the Lord.* VIII. *That Charity and Faith are together in good Works.* IX. *That there is a true Faith, a spurious Faith, and a hypocritical Faith.* X. *That there is no Faith with the Evil.* These are now to be explained one by one.

I. THAT SAVING FAITH IS IN THE LORD GOD THE SAVIOR JESUS CHRIST.

337. That saving faith is in God the Savior, is, because He is God and Man; and He in the Father and the Father in Him, and thus one; wherefore, they who go to Him, go to the Father also at the same time, and thus to the one and only God, and there is no saving faith in any other. That we should believe, or have faith, in THE SON OF GOD, the Redeemer and Savior, conceived from Jehovah, and born of the Virgin Mary, named JESUS CHRIST, is evident from the commands, frequently repeated by Him, and afterwards by the apostles. That faith in Him was commanded by Himself, is very manifest from these passages: *Jesus said, This is the will of the Father who sent Me, that every one who seeth the Son,* AND BELIEVETH IN HIM, *should have eternal life; and I should resuscitate him at the last day,* John vi. 40. *He that* BELIEVETH IN THE SON, *hath eternal life; but he that believeth not the Son, shall not see life, but the anger of God abideth on him,* iii. 36. *That every one, who* BELIEVETH IN THE SON, *should not perish, but have eternal life; for God so loved the world, that He gave his only-begotten Son, that* EVERY ONE, WHO BELIEVETH IN HIM, *should not perish, but have eternal life,* iii. 15, 16. *Jesus said, I am the resurrection and the life;* HE THAT BELIEVETH IN ME, *shall never die,* ix. 25, 26. *Verily, verily, I say unto you,* HE THAT BELIEVETH IN ME, *hath eternal life. I am the bread of life,* vi. 47, 48. *I am the bread of life;* HE THAT COMETH TO ME, *shall never hunger, and* HE THAT BELIEVETH IN ME, *shall never thirst,* vi. 35. *Jesus cried, saying, If any one thirst, come to Me and drink;* WHOSOEVER BELIEVETH IN ME, *as the Scripture hath said, out of his belly shall flow rivers of living water,* vii. 37, 38. *They said to Jesus, What shall we do, that we may work the works of God? Jesus answered, This is the work of God,* THAT YE BELIEVE IN HIM, WHOM THE FATHER HATH SENT, vi. 28, 29. *As long as ye have light, believe in the light, that ye may be sons of the light,* xii. 36. HE THAT BELIEVETH IN THE SON OF GOD, *is not*

judged; BUT HE THAT BELIEVETH NOT, *is already judged,* BECAUSE HE HATH NOT BELIEVED *in the name of the only-begotten Son of God,* iii. 18. *These things are written, that ye may believe that Jesus is the Son of God; and that believing, ye may have life in his name,* xx. 31. UNLESS YE BELIEVE THAT I AM, *ye shall die in your sins,* viii. 24. *Jesus said, When the Paraclete, the Spirit of truth, is come, he will convince the world of sin, of righteousness and of judgment; of sin, because they believe not in Me,* xvi. 8.

338. That the faith of the apostles was no other than in the Lord Jesus Christ, is evident from many passages in their epistles, of which I shall adduce only these: *I live no more, but Christ liveth in me; in that, indeed, I now live in the flesh, I live in* THE FAITH, WHICH IS IN THE SON OF GOD, Gal. ii. 20. *Paul testified to the Jews and to the Greeks, repentance towards God, and* FAITH IN OUR LORD JESUS CHRIST, Acts xx. 21. He who brought Paul out, said, *What must I do to be saved? He said,* BELIEVE IN THE LORD JESUS CHRIST; *thus thou shalt be saved, and thy house,* xvi. 30, 31. *He who hath the Son, hath life; but he who hath not the Son of God, hath not life. These things I have written to you, who believe in the name of the Son of God, that ye may know that ye have eternal life, and that ye may believe in the name of the Son of God,* 1 John v. 12, 13. *We, by nature Jews, and not sinners of the Gentiles, since we know that a man is not justified by the works of the law, but by* THE FAITH OF JESUS CHRIST, WE ALSO HAVE BELIEVED IN JESUS CHRIST, Gal. ii. 15, 16. Since their faith was in Jesus Christ, and also is from Him, therefore they called it the *faith of Jesus Christ,* as just above, Gal. ii. 16, and in the following passages: *The righteousness of God, by* THE FAITH OF JESUS CHRIST, *unto all, and upon all, who believe, that He may be justifying him who is* OF THE FAITH OF JESUS, Rom. iii. 22, 26. *That he may have the righteousness which is* FROM THE FAITH OF CHRIST, *the righteousness which is from* THE GOD OF FAITH, Phil. iii. 9. *Who keep the commandments of God, and* THE FAITH OF JESUS CHRIST, Rev. xiv. 12. *By* THE FAITH, WHICH IS IN JESUS CHRIST, 2 Tim. iii. 15. *In* JESUS CHRIST IS FAITH WHICH WORKETH BY CHARITY, Gal. v. 6. From these, it may be evident, what faith was meant by Paul, in the saying at this day common in the church, WE CONCLUDE, THEREFORE, THAT A MAN IS JUSTIFIED BY FAITH, WITHOUT THE WORKS OF THE LAW, Rom. iii. 28; that it was not in God the Father, but in his Son; still less in three Gods in order, in one from whom, in another for the sake of whom, and in a third by whom. The reason why it is believed, in the church, that its tri-personal faith was meant by Paul in that saying, is, because the church, for fourteen centuries, or ever since the NICENE COUNCIL, has acknowledged no other faith, and thence has known no other; believing thus, that this was the only faith, and that there could be no other. Wherefore, wherever faith is read, in the Word of the New Testament, it has been believed, that it was that, and to that they have applied all the things there. Thence the only saving faith, which is in God the Savior, has been lost; and thence, also, so many fallacies have crept into their doctrines, and so many paradoxes, contrary to sound reason; for all the doctrine of the church, which teaches and shows the way to heaven, or to salvation, depends on faith; and because so many fallacies and paradoxes have crept into it, as was said, therefore it was necessary, that they should proclaim the dogma, that the understanding should be kept under obedience to faith. Now, since in the saying of Paul, Rom. iii. 28, by *faith,* is not meant a faith in God the Father, but in his Son, and by the *works of the law* there, are not meant the works of the law of the decalogue, but the works of the Mosaic law for the Jews, as is manifest from what follows there, and also from similar passages in the epistle to the Galatians, ii. 14, 15, the foundation-stone of the faith, at this day, falls,

and moreover, the temple built upon it, like a house sinking into the earth, the top of whose roof only appears.

339. The reason why we should believe, that is, should have faith, in God the Savior Jesus Christ, is, because it is in a visible God, in whom is the invisible; and faith in a visible God, who is Man, and at the same time God, enters into man; for faith, in its essence, is spiritual, but in its form, natural; wherefore, with man, it becomes spiritual-natural; for all the spiritual is received in the natural, that it may be something with man. The bare spiritual enters, indeed, into man, but it is not received; it is like ether, which flows in and flows out, without affecting; for, in order to affect, there must be perception, and thus reception, each in the mind of man; and this is not given with man, except in his natural. But, on the other hand, merely natural faith, or faith destitute of spiritual essence, is not faith, but only persuasion, or science; persuasion resembles faith in externals, but, because in its internals there is nothing spiritual, therefore there is nothing saving. Such is the faith with all those who deny the divinity of the Lord's Human; such was the Arian faith, and such, also, is the Socinian faith, because both reject the Divinity of the Lord. What is faith, without a definite object? Is it not like a look into the universe, which falls, as it were, into an empty void, and perishes? Or it is like a bird, flying above the atmosphere into the ether, where it expires as in a *vacuum*. The habitation of this faith in the mind of man may be compared to the habitation of the winds in the wings of Æolus, and also to the habitation of light in a falling star; it rises like a comet, with a long tail, but it also passes away like a comet, and disappears. In a word, faith in an invisible God is actually blind, because the human mind does not see its God; and the light of this faith, because it is not spiritual-natural, is a fatuous light; and this light is like the light in a glow-worm, and like the light in marshes, or upon sulphureous earth, in the time of night, and like the light in rotten wood. From this light nothing else exists but what is of fantasy, in which what appears is believed to be something, and yet it is not. Faith in an invisible God, shines in no other light, and, especially, when it is thought that God is a spirit, and concerning spirit it is thought as concerning ether; what else thence follows, but that man looks upon God as he looks upon the ether? and thus he seeks Him in the universe, and when he does not find Him there, he believes nature to be the God of the universe. The naturalism reigning at this day, is from this origin. Did not the Lord say, *that no one hath ever heard the voice of the Father, or seen his shape?* John v. 37; and also, *that no one hath ever seen God, and that the only-begotten Son, who is in the bosom of the Father, He hath revealed*, i. 18. *No one hath seen the Father, but He who is with the Father; He hath seen the Father*, vi. 46. Also, *that no one cometh to the Father, but through Him*, xiv. 6; and moreover, *that the man seeth and knoweth the Father, who seeth and knoweth Him*, xiv. 7, and the following verses. But different is the faith in the Lord God the Savior, who, because He is God and Man, may both be approached and seen in thought; it is not an indeterminate faith, but it has a definite object (*terminum a quo et ad quem*), and when once received, it remains; as, when any one has seen an emperor or a king, as often as he recollects him, their image returns. The sight of that faith is as if any one sees a bright cloud, and an angel in the midst of it, who invites the man to him, that he may be elevated into heaven; thus the Lord appears to those who have faith in Him, and approaches to every one, as he knows and acknowledges Him; which is done, as he knows and does his commandments, which are, to shun evils and do goods; and at length He comes into his house, and makes his abode with him, together with the Father who is in Him, according to these words in

John: *Jesus said, He who hath my commandments, and doeth them, he it is that loveth Me; and he that loveth Me, shall be loved by my Father, and I will love him, and will manifest Myself to him; and We will come to him, and make an abode with him,* John xiv. 21, 23. These things were written in the presence of the twelve apostles of the Lord, who, while I was writing them, were sent to me by the Lord.

340. II. THAT FAITH IN THE SUM, IS, THAT HE WHO LIVES WELL, AND BELIEVES ARIGHT, IS SAVED BY THE LORD.

That man was created for eternal life, and that every man may inherit it, provided he lives according to the means of salvation which are prescribed in the Word, every Christian, and every heathen, also, who has religion and sound reason, admits. The means of salvation, indeed, are many; but they all and each of them refer themselves to living well and believing aright, thus to charity and faith, for charity is to live well, and faith is to believe aright. These two general means of salvation are not only prescribed to man in the Word, but they are also commanded; and because they are commanded, it follows, that man can by them provide for himself eternal life, by virtue of the power put in him and given to him by God; and that as far as man uses that power, and at the same time looks to God, so far God corroborates it, and makes all that which is of natural charity to be of spiritual charity, and all that which is of natural faith to be of spiritual faith; thus God makes dead charity and faith, and at the same time man, alive. There are two things which must be together, that it may be said, that man lives well and believes aright; these two things are called, in the church, the internal man and the external man. When the internal man wills well, and the external acts well, then both make one, the external from the internal, and the internal through the external; and so man from God and God through man. But, on the other hand, if the internal man wills evil, and still the external man acts well, then, nevertheless, both act from hell; for his willing is thence, and his doing is hypocritical; and his will, which is internal, lurks inwardly in every hypocritical deed, like a snake in the grass, or like a worm in a flower. The man who not only knows that there is an internal and an external man, but also what they are, and that they can act as one actually, and also act as one apparently, and, moreover, that the internal man lives after death, and the external is buried,—he has in his power the arcana of heaven and also of the world, in abundance; and he who conjoins those two men with himself, to good becomes happy to eternity; but he who divides them, and still more, he who conjoins them to evil, becomes unhappy to eternity.

341. Suppose that the man who lives well and believes aright, is not saved, and that God, of his free will and pleasure, can save and condemn whomsoever he will, the man who perishes may justly accuse God of unmercifulness and severity, and even of cruelty; yea, deny God to be God; and moreover that He has spoken in his Word vain things, and commanded such things as are of no use, or such as are trifles; and further, if the man who lives well and believes aright, is not saved, he may also accuse God of violating his covenant, which he made upon mount Sinai, and wrote with his finger upon the two tables. That God cannot but save those who live according to his commandments, and have faith in Him, is evident from the words of the Lord in John, xiv. 21 to 24: and every one who has religion and sound reason, may confirm himself in this, while he thinks that God, who is constantly with man, and gives him life, and also the faculty of understanding and of loving, cannot but love him, and by love conjoin Himself to him who lives well and believes aright. Is not this inscribed by God upon every man and every creature? Can a father and a mother reject their children, or a bird its young, or a beast its cubs? Even tigers, panthers and serpents cannot do this. To do otherwise would be contrary to

the order in which God is, and according to which He acts; and also contrary to the order into which He created man. Now, as it is impossible for God to condemn any one who lives well and believes aright, so, on the other hand, it is impossible for God to save any one who lives wickedly, and thence believes falses. This other also is contrary to order, and of course contrary to his omnipotence, which cannot proceed otherwise than by the way of justice; and the laws of justice are truths, which cannot be changed; for the Lord says, *It is easier for heaven and earth to pass away, than for one tittle of the law to fail*, Luke xvi. 17. Every one who knows any thing concerning the essence of God, and concerning the free agency of man, may perceive this; as for example, Adam had the liberty of eating from the tree of life, and also from the tree of the knowledge of good and evil: if he had eaten only from the tree or trees of life, would it have been possible for God to drive him out of the garden? I believe it would not. But after he ate of the tree of the knowledge of good and evil, would it have been possible for God to retain him in the garden? I believe again that it would not; and likewise, that God cannot cast into hell any angel who has been received into heaven, nor introduce into heaven any devil who has been condemned. That He cannot, from his divine omnipotence, do either of these, may be seen above in what was said concerning THE DIVINE OMNIPOTENCE, n. 49 to 70.

342. In the preceding lemma, from n. 336 to 339, it was shown, that saving faith is in the Lord God the Savior Jesus Christ. But it is asked, What is the first thing of faith in Him? And it is answered, That it is AN ACKNOWLEDGMENT, THAT HE IS THE SON OF GOD. This was the first thing of faith, which the Lord, when He came into the world, revealed and announced. For unless they had first acknowledged, that He was THE SON OF GOD, and thus GOD OF GOD, in vain would He himself and the apostles afterwards have preached faith in Him. Now because there is something similar at this day, but with those who think from the proprium, that is, from the external or natural man only, saying with themselves, "How can Jehovah God conceive a Son, and how can man be God?" it is necessary, that this first thing of faith be confirmed and established from the Word; wherefore the following passages shall be adduced thence:—*The angel said to Mary, Thou shalt conceive in the womb and shalt bring forth, and shalt call his name* JESUS. *He shall be great, and shall be called* THE SON OF THE MOST HIGH. *And Mary said to the angel, How shall this be done, since I know not a man? The angel answered, The Holy Spirit shall come upon thee, and* THE POWER OF THE MOST HIGH *shall overshadow thee; wherefore* THE HOLY THING *that is born of thee shall be called* THE SON OF GOD, Luke i. 31, 32, 34, 35. *When Jesus was baptized, a voice came from heaven, saying,* THIS IS MY BELOVED SON, *in whom I am well pleased*, Matt. iii. 16, 17; Mark i. 10, 11; Luke iii. 21, 22. And again, *When Jesus was transfigured, a voice also came from heaven, saying,* THIS IS MY BELOVED SON, *in whom I am well pleased; hear Him*, Matt. xvii. 5; Mark ix. 7; Luke ix. 35. *Jesus asked his disciples, Who do men say that I am? Peter answered,* THOU ART THE CHRIST, THE SON OF THE LIVING GOD. *And Jesus said, Blessed art thou, Simon, son of Jonah. I say unto thee, Upon this rock I will build my church*, Matt. xvi. 13, 16, 17, 18. The Lord said that He would build his church upon this rock, namely, upon the truth and confession, that *He is the Son of God;* for *rock* signifies *truth*, and also *the Lord* as to *Divine Truth;* wherefore, with whomsoever there is not a confession of that truth, *that he is the Son of God*, the church is not; and therefore it was said above, that this is the first thing of faith in Jesus Christ, thus faith in its origin. *John the Baptist saw and testified, that He is the* SON OF GOD, John i. 34. Nathanael the disciple said to Jesus, THOU ART THE SON OF GOD, THOU ART THE

KING OF ISRAEL, i. 50. The twelve disciples said, *We have believed that* THOU ART THE CHRIST, THE SON OF THE LIVING GOD, vi. 69. He is called, THE ONLY-BEGOTTEN SON OF GOD, THE ONLY-BEGOTTEN OF THE FATHER, *who is in the bosom of the Father*, i. 14, 18; iii. 16. *Jesus himself confessed, before the high priest, that* HE WAS THE SON OF GOD, Matt. xxvi. 63, 64; xxvii. 43. Mark xiv. 41, 42. Luke xxii. 70. *Those who were in the ship, came and worshipped Jesus, saying*, TRULY THOU ART THE SON OF GOD, Matt. xiv. 33. *The eunuch, who wished to be baptized, said to Philip*, I BELIEVE THAT JESUS CHRIST IS THE SON OF GOD, Acts viii. 37. *Paul, when he was converted, preached Jesus*, THAT HE WAS THE SON OF GOD, ix. 20. *Jesus said, The hour is coming when the dead shall hear the voice of* THE SON OF GOD, *and those who hear, shall live*, John v. 25. *He who doth not believe, is already judged, because he hath not believed in* THE NAME OF THE ONLY-BEGOTTEN SON OF GOD, iii. 18. *These things are written, that ye may believe, that* JESUS IS THE CHRIST, THE SON OF GOD, *and that believing ye may have life in his name*, xx. 31. *These things I have written to you who believe in* THE NAME OF THE SON OF GOD, *that ye may know that ye have eternal life; and that ye may believe in* THE NAME OF THE SON OF GOD, 1 John v. 13. *We know that the* SON OF GOD *hath come, and given us that we may know Him who is true; and we are in Him who is true, in* HIS SON JESUS CHRIST. *This is the true God and eternal life*, v. 20, 21. *Whosoever confesseth, that* JESUS IS THE SON OF GOD, *God abideth in him, and he in God*, v. 5. And also in other places, as Matt. viii. 29; xxvii. 40, 43, 54 Mark i. 1; iii. 11; xv. 39. Luke viii. 28. John ix. 35; x. 36; xi. 4, 27; xix. 7. Rom. i. 4. 2 Cor. i. 19. Gal. ii. 20 Eph. iv. 13. Heb. iv. 14; vi. 6; vii. 3; x. 29. 1 John iii. 8; v. 10. Rev. ii. 18. Besides in many places where He is called by Jehovah, *Son*, and where He himself calls Jehovah God, his *Father;* as in this; *Whatsoever* THE FATHER *doeth, this* THE SON *doeth; as* THE FATHER *raiseth the dead, and quickeneth them, so doth* THE SON. *As* THE FATHER *hath life in Himself, so hath He given to* THE SON *to have life in Himself; that all may honor* THE SON, *even as they honor* THE FATHER, John v. 19 to 27; and in many other places. And also in David; *I will announce concerning the statute, Jehovah hath said to me*, THOU ART MY SON; *this day I have begotten Thee. Kiss* THE SON, *lest He be angry, and ye perish in the way, because his anger will shortly kindle.* BLESSED ARE ALL WHO CONFIDE IN HIM, Psalm ii. 7, 12. Hence now this conclusion is made; That every one, who wishes to be truly a Christian, and to be saved by Christ, ought to believe, that Jesus is the Son of the living God. He who does not believe this, but only that he is the Son of Mary, implants in himself various ideas concerning Him, which are hurtful and destructive of his salvation, concerning which, see above, n. 92, 94, 102; concerning these the like may be said, as concerning the Jews, that, instead of a royal crown, they put upon his head a crown of thorns; and also that they give Him vinegar to drink, and cry, *If thou be the Son of God, come down from the cross;* or as the tempter, the devil, said, *If thou be the Son of God, say that these stones may become bread;* or, *If thou be the Son of God, cast thyself down*, Matt. iv. 3, 6. These profane his church and his temple, and make it a den of robbers. These are they who make the worship of Him like the worship of Mahomet, and do not distinguish between true Christianity, which is the worship of the Lord, and naturalism. They may be compared with those who are carried in a chariot or a coach upon thin ice, and the ice is broken under them, and they are drowned; and both they, and the horses, and the chariot, are covered with freezing water. They may also be likened to those who make a little boat of reeds and canes, and glue it together with pitch, that it may cohere and in it launch out into the deep, but there the pitchy conglutination is dissolved, and they, being suffocated with the waters of the deep, are swallowed up, and buried at the bottom of it.

343. III. That Man receives Faith by going to the Lord, learning Truths from the Word, and living according to them.

Before I begin to demonstrate the Origin of Faith, which is, that we should go to the Lord, learn truths from the Word, and live according to them, it is necessary, that a summary of faith be premised, from which may be had a general notion of faith, in the particular parts; for thus may be more clearly comprehended, not only the things which are said in this chapter concerning Faith, but also those which are said in the following chapters concerning Charity, concerning Free Agency, concerning Repentance, concerning Reformation and Regeneration, and concerning Imputation. For faith enters into all and every part of a theological system, as blood enters into the members of the body, and vivifies them. What the present church teaches concerning faith, is generally known in the Christian world, and particularly in its ecclesiastical order; for books concerning faith only, and concerning faith alone, fill the libraries of the teachers of the church; for scarcely any thing besides that is esteemed at this day properly theological. But before those things, which the present church teaches concerning its faith, are taken up, considered and examined, which will be done in an Appendix, the general things, which the New Church teaches concerning its faith, will be adduced, which are the following:

344. The Esse of the Faith of the New Church is, 1. Confidence in the Lord God the Savior Jesus Christ. 2. Trust that he who lives well, and believes aright, is saved by Him.

The Essence of the Faith of the New Church, is Truth from the Word.

The Existence of the Faith of the New Church, is, 1. Spiritual sight. 2. Agreement of truths 3. Conviction. 4. Acknowledgment inscribed upon the mind.

The States of the Faith of the New Church, are, 1. Infant faith, adolescent faith, adult faith. 2. Faith of genuine truth and faith of the appearances of truth. 3. Faith of memory, faith of reason, faith of light. 4. Natural faith, spiritual faith, celestial faith. 5. Living faith and miraculous faith. 6. Free faith and forced faith.

The form itself of the Faith of the New Church, in the universal idea, and in the particular idea, may be seen above, n. 2 and 3.

345. Since there have been adduced, in a summary, those things which are of spiritual faith, there shall also be adduced, in a summary, those things which are of merely natural faith, which in itself is a persuasion counterfeiting faith, and is a persuasion of the false, and is called heretical faith. Its denominations are, 1. Spurious faith, in which falses are mixed together with truths. 2. Meretricious faith from falsified truths, and adulterous faith from adulterated goods. 3. Bigoted or blind faith, which is that of mystical things, which are believed, although it is not known whether they be true or false; or whether they be above reason or contrary to it. 4. Wandering faith, which is a faith in several gods. 5. Purblind faith, which is a faith in any other God than in the true, and with Christians, in any other than the Lord God the Savior. 6. Hypocritical or Pharisaical faith, which is that of the mouth, and not of the heart. 7. Visionary and preposterous faith, which is an appearance of what is false as true, from ingenious confirmation.

346. It was said above, that faith, as to its existence with man, is spiritual sight. Now, because spiritual sight, which is that of the understanding, and thus of the mind, and natural sight, which is the sight of the eye, and thus of the body, mutually correspond to

each other, therefore, every state of faith may be compared with a state of the eye and its sight; a state of the faith of truth, with every sound state of the sight of the eye, and a state of the faith of the false, with every perverted state of the sight of the eye. But we will compare the correspondences of those two sights of the mind and of the body, as to the perverted states of each. SPURIOUS FAITH, in which falses are mixed together with truths, may be compared with the disease of the eye and thence of the sight, which is called a white spot upon the cornea, rendering the sight obscure. MERETRICIOUS FAITH, which is from falsified truths, and ADULTEROUS FAITH, which is from adulterated goods, may be compared with the disease of the eye and thence of the sight, which is called *glaucoma*, and is a drying up and hardening of the crystalline humor. BIGOTED OR BLIND FAITH, which is of mystical things, which are believed, although it is not known whether they be true or false, or whether they be above reason or contrary to it, may be compared with the disease of the eye which is called *gutta serena* and *amaurosis*, which is a loss of the sight, and yet the eye appears as if it saw perfectly, arising from an obstruction of the optic nerve. WANDERING FAITH, which is in several gods, may be compared with the disease of the eye which is called a *cataract*, which is a loss of the sight, arising from an obstipation between the sclerotic coat and the uvea. PURBLIND FAITH, which is a faith in any other god than in the true, and with Christians than in the Lord God the Savior, may be compared with the disease of the eye which is called *strabism*. HYPOCRITICAL OR PHARISAICAL FAITH, which is of the mouth and not of the heart, may be compared with an atrophy of the eye, and thence a loss of the sight. VISIONARY, and PREPOSTEROUS FAITH, which is an appearance of the false as if it were true from ingenious confirmation, may be compared with the disease of the eye which is called *nyctalopy*, which is seeing in darkness from fatuous light.

347. But with regard to THE FORMATION OF FAITH; it is formed by man's going to the Lord, learning truths from the Word, and living according to them. FIRST, *That faith is formed by man's going to the Lord* is, because faith which is faith, thus which is the faith of salvation, is from the Lord and in the Lord. That it is from the Lord, is evident from his words to the disciples—*Abide in Me and I in you; because without Me, ye cannot do any thing*, John xv. 4, 5. That faith is in the Lord, is manifest from those passages, which in abundance were adduced above, n. 337, 338, which are, *That we should believe in the Son.* Now, because faith is from the Lord, and in the Lord, it may be said that the Lord is faith itself; for the life and essence of it are in the Lord, thus from the Lord. SECONDLY, *That faith is formed by man's learning truths from the Word.* The reason is, because faith in its essence is truth, for all things which enter into faith, are truths; wherefore, faith is no other than a complex of the truths shining in the mind of man; for truths teach, not only that we should believe, but also in whom we should believe, and what we should believe. That truths should be taken from the Word, is, because all truths which conduce to salvation are there, in which there is efficacy, because they were given by the Lord, and thence inscribed upon the whole angelic heaven: wherefore, when man learns truths from the Word, he comes into communion and consociation with the angels, without knowing it. Faith without truths is like seed destitute of the medullary substance, which, when ground, gives only chaff; but faith from truths is like good grain, which, when ground, gives flour. In a word, the essentials of faith are truths; and if they are not in it and compose it, faith is only like the shrill voice of a whistle; but when they are in it and compose it, faith is like the voice of something healthful. THIRDLY, *That faith is formed by man's living*

according to truths, is, because spiritual life is a life according to truths, and truths do not actually live, before they are in deeds; truths abstracted from deeds are of the thought alone, which, if they do not become also of the will, are only in the entrance to man, and so not within in him; for the will is the man himself, and the thought is, as to quantity and quality, so far the man, as it joins to itself the will. He who learns truths and does not do them, is like one who scatters seed about over a field, and does not harrow it in; thence the seeds become swollen by the rains and are spoiled; but he who learns truths and does them, is like one who sows his seed and ploughs it in; whence the seed is by the rain caused to grow into a harvest, and becomes of use for food. The Lord says, *If ye know these things, happy are ye if ye do them*, John xii. 17. And in another place, *That which was sown in good ground, is he who heareth the Word and attendeth, and thence beareth fruit and doeth*, Matt. xiii. 23. Again, *Every one who heareth my words, and doeth them, I will compare to a prudent man, who built his house upon a rock. But every one who heareth my words, but doeth them not, shall be compared to a foolish man, who built his house upon the sand*, Matt. vii. 24, 26. The words of the Lord are all truths.

348. From the things said above, it is manifest, that there are three things by which faith with man is formed; which are, first, *To go to the Lord;* second, *To learn truths from the Word;* and third, *To live according to them.* Now, because there are three things, and one is not another, it follows, that they can be separated; for any one can go to the Lord, and not know truths concerning God and concerning the Lord, except such as are historical; and also any one can know truths from the Word in abundance, and yet not live according to them. But with the man with whom those three things are separated, that is, one without the other, there is not the faith of salvation; but this faith arises, when those three things are conjoined, and the faith is such as the conjunction is. Where those three things are separated there faith is like barren seed, which, being cast into the earth, moulders into dust: but where those three things are conjoined, there faith is like seed in the earth, which grows up into a tree, the fruit of which is according to the conjunction. Where those three things are separated, faith is like an egg in which there is not any thing prolific; but where those three things are conjoined, that faith is like an egg which produces a beautiful bird. Faith with those with whom those three things are separated, may be likened to the eye of a fish or a crab when boiled; but faith with those with whom those three things are conjoined, may be likened to an eye transparent from the crystalline humor, even to the uvea of the pupil and through it. Faith separated is like a picture of dark colors upon a black stone; but faith conjoined is like a picture of beautiful colors upon a pellucid crystal. The light of faith separated may be compared with the light of a firebrand in the hand of a traveller in the time of night; but the light of faith conjoined may be compared to the light of a torch, which, being vibrated, makes plain every step of the way. Faith without truths is like a vine bearing wild grapes; but faith from truths is like a vine bearing clusters of noble wine. Faith in the Lord, destitute of truths, may be compared with a new star appearing in the expanse of heaven, which in time is obscured; but faith in the Lord, with truths, may be compared with a fixed star, which remains perpetually. Truth is the essence of faith; wherefore, such as the truth is, such is the faith, which without truths is vague, but with them is fixed; the faith of truths also in heaven shines like a star.

349. IV. That a copious Store of Truths cohering, as in a Bundle exalts and perfects Faith.

From perception concerning the faith which exists at this day, it can not be known, that faith, in its com prehensive sense, is a complex of truths, and still less, that man can do something to procure faith for himself, when yet faith in its essence is truth, for it is truth in its light; and thus, as truth can be procured, so also can faith. Who cannot, if he will, go to the Lord? Who cannot, if he will, collect truths from the Word? And every truth in the Word and from the Word gives light, and truth in light is faith. The Lord, who is Light itself, flows in with every man, and in him, in whom there are truths from the Word, He causes them to shine, and thus to become of faith; and this is what the Lord says in John; *That they should abide in the Lord, and his words in them*, xv. 7. The words of the Lord are truths. But that it may be comprehended aright, that a copious store of truths cohering, as in a bundle, exalts and perfects faith, the subject should be divided into these propositions; (1.) *That the truths of faith are multiplicable to infinity.* (2.) *That there is a disposition of them into series, thus, as it were, into bundles.* (3.) *That faith is perfected according to their abundance and coherence.* (4.) *That truths, however numerous they are, and however different they appear, make one from the Lord, who is the Word, the God of heaven and earth, the God of all flesh, the God of the vineyard or church, the God of faith, and the Light itself, Truth and eternal Life.*

350. (1.) *That the Truths of Faith are multiplicable to Infinity*, may be evident from the wisdom of the angels of heaven, in that it increases to eternity: the angels also say, that there is no end of wisdom, and wisdom is from no other source than from divine truths, analytically divided into forms, by means of the light flowing in from the Lord. Human intelligence, which is truly intelligence, is also from no other source. The reason why Divine Truth is multiplicable to infinity, is because the Lord is Divine Truth itself, or truth in its infinity, and He attracts all to Himself; but men and angels can follow the vein of attraction only according to their measure, because they are finite, the effort of attraction to infinity still continuing. The Word of the Lord is an abyss of truths, from which is all angelic wisdom; although to a man who does not know any thing concerning its spiritual and celestial sense, it appears no more than as water in a bucket. The multiplication of the truth of faith to infinity, may be compared with the seed of men, from one of which, families may be propagated to ages of ages. The prolification of the truths of faith may also be compared with the prolification of the seed of a field or a garden, which may be propagated to myriads of myriads, and forever. By *seed*, in the Word, no other is meant, than truth; by *field*, doctrine; and by *garden*, wisdom. The human mind is like ground, in which spiritual and natural truths are implanted, as seeds, and they may be multiplied without end; man derives this from the infinity of God, who with his light and his heat, and with the faculty of generating, is in him perpetually.

351. (2.) *That there is a Disposition of the Truths of Faith into Series, thus, as it were, into Bundles.* That it is so, is unknown as yet, and it is unknown, because the spiritual truths, of which the whole Word is composed, on account of the mystical and enigmatical faith, which makes every point of modern theology, could not appear; and, therefore, like storehouses, they have sunk down into the earth. That it may be known what is meant by series and bundles, it shall be explained. The first chapter of this book, which treats concerning God the Creator, is distinguished into series, the first of which is concerning the Unity of God; the second, concerning the *Esse* of God or Jehovah; the third, concerning the Infinity of God; the fourth, concerning the Essence of God, which is Divine Love and Divine Wisdom; the fifth, concerning the Omnipotence of God; and the sixth, concerning Creation; and the articulations of each make the series; they bind together those things which are therein, as

it were into bundles. These series, in general and in particular, thus conjointly and separately, contain truths, which, according to their abundance and coherence, exalt and perfect faith. He who does not know that the human mind is organized, or that it is a spiritual organism, terminating in a natural organism, in which, and according to which, the mind produces its ideas, or thinks, cannot think otherwise than that perceptions, thoughts and ideas are no other than radiations and variations of light, flowing into the head, and exhibiting forms, which man sees and acknowledges as reasons. But this is delirious; for every one knows, that the head is full of brains, and that the brains are organized, and that the mind dwells in them, and that its ideas are fixed therein, and remain as they have been received and confirmed. Is it asked, then, What is that organization? It is answered, that it is an arrangement of all things into series, as it were into bundles, and that the truths, which are of faith, are so arranged in the human mind. That it is so, may be illustrated by the following things: That the brain consists of two substances, one of which is glandular, and is called cortical and cineritious, and the other is fibrillary, and is called medullary. The first substance, which is the glandular, is disposed into clusters, like grapes on a vine; those clusters are its series. The other substance, which is called medullary, consists of perpetual collections of little bundles of fibrils, proceeding from the little glands of the former substance; these collections of little bundles are its series. All the nerves which proceed thence, and descend into the body to perform various functions, are only collections and bundles of fibres; and so are all the muscles, and, in general, all the viscera and organs of the body. The former and the latter are such, because they correspond to the series, into which the organism of the mind is disposed. Moreover, throughout all nature, there is not any thing which is not bundled together into series; every tree, every shrub, herb and plant, yea, every ear of corn and blade of grass, in whole and in part, is so. The universal cause is, because divine truths have such a conformation; for it is read, That all things were created by the Word, that is, by the Divine Truth, and that the world, also, was made by it, John i. 1, and the following verses. Hence it may be seen, that, unless there were such an arrangement of substances in the human mind, man would not have any analytical faculty of reason, which every one has, according to the arrangement, thus according to the abundance of truths cohering, as it were, in a bundle; and the arrangement is according to the use of reason from a free principle.

352. (3.) *That Faith is perfected according to the Abundance and Coherence of Truths*, follows from the things said above, and manifests itself to every one who collects reasons, and sees what multiplied series effect, when they cohere as one, for then one thing strengthens and confirms another, and they together make a form, and, when in action, they present one act. Now, because faith in its essence is truth, it follows that it becomes, according to the abundance and coherence of truths, more and more perfectly spiritual, thus less and less sensual-natural; for it is exalted into a higher region of the mind, whence it sees under it numerous confirmations of itself in the nature of the world. True faith, by a copious store of truths cohering as it were in a bundle, also becomes more luminous, more perceptible, more evident, and more clear; it also becomes more capable of being conjoined with the goods of charity, and thence of being alienated from evils; and successively more removed from the allurements of the eye, and from the concupiscences of the flesh; consequently, more happy in itself; it becomes, especially, more powerful against evils and falses, and thence more and more living and saving.

353. It was said above, that all

truth in heaven shines, and thence that truth shining is faith in essence; wherefore, the beauty and symmetry of faith, from that illustration, when its truths are multiplied, may be compared with various forms, objects and pictures, formed of different colors fitly arranged according to agreements; consequently, with the precious stones of diverse colors in the breastplate of Aaron, which together were called *Urim and Thummim;* likewise with the precious stones of which the foundations of the wall of the New Jerusalem are to be built, concerning which, see Rev. xxi. It may also be compared with the precious stones, of divers colors, in the crown of a king: precious stones also signify truths of faith. A comparison may be made, also, with the beauty of the rainbow, and with the beauty of a flowery field, and also of a garden blossoming at the commencement of spring. The light and glory of faith, from a copious store of truths composing and adorning it, may be compared with the illumination of temples by multiplied chandeliers, of houses by candles, and of streets by lamps. The exaltation of faith, by a copious store of truths, may be illustrated by comparison with the exaltation of sound, and likewise of melody, from many musical instruments in a concert; and also with the exaltation of fragrance, from a collection of sweet-smelling flowers; and also with other things. The power of faith, composed of many truths, against evils and falses, may be compared with the firmness of a temple, in consequence of the stones being well cemented together, and its walls being strengthened by pilasters, and its roof supported by pillars. It may also be compared with an army drawn up in a square column, in which the soldiers stand closely side by side, and thus form one force and act. It may also be compared with the muscles, of which the whole body is composed, which, although they are numerous and situated in different places, still make one power in actions; and also with other things.

354. (4.) *That the Truths of Faith, however numerous they are, and however different they appear, make one from the Lord, who is the Word the God of Heaven and Earth, the God of all Flesh, the God of the Vineyard or the Church, the God of Faith, the Light itself, Truth and eternal Life.*

The truths of faith are various, and to man they appear different; as, for example, some are concerning God the Creator, some concerning the Lord the Redeemer, some concerning the Holy Spirit and the Divine Operation, some concerning Faith and concerning Charity, and others concerning Free Agency, Repentance, Reformation and Regeneration, Imputation, and so forth Still they make one in the Lord, and with man, from the Lord, like many branches in one vine, John xv. 1, and the following verses; for the Lord joins scattered and divided truths together, as into one form, in which they present one view, and exhibit one act. This may be illustrated by comparison with the members, viscera and organs, in one body, which, although they are various, and to the sight of man different, yet still a man, who is the common form of them, perceives them only as one; and when he acts from all, he acts, as it were, from one. It is similar with heaven, which, although it is distinguished into innumerable societies, still appears before the Lord as one; and, as was shown above, as one man. The case is similar also as with a kingdom; which, although it is divided into many governments, provinces and cities, yet still, under a king, who has justice and judgment, it makes one. The reason why it is similar with the truths of faith, from which the church is a church from the Lord, is, because the Lord is the Word, the God of heaven and earth, the God of all flesh, the God of the vineyard or the church, the God of faith, and the Light itself, Truth, and eternal Life. That the Lord is the Word, and thus all the truth of heaven and the church, is evident in John: *The Word was with God, and the Word was God and the Word became flesh,* i 1, 14

That the Lord is the God of heaven and earth, is evident in Matthew: *Jesus said, Unto Me is given all power in heaven and in earth,* xxviii. 18. That the Lord is the God of all flesh, in John: *The Father hath given to the Son power over all flesh,* xvii. 2. That the Lord is the God of the vineyard or the church, in Isaiah: *My beloved had a vineyard,* v. 1, 2; and in John: *I am the Vine, and ye are the branches,* xv. 5. That the Lord is the God of faith, in Paul: *Thou hast the righteousness of the faith of Christ, from the God of faith,* Philip. iii. 9. That the Lord is the Light itself, in John: *He was the true Light, which enlighteneth every man that cometh into the world,* i. 9; and in another place, *Jesus said, I have come a Light into the world, that every one, that believeth in Me, may not abide in darkness,* xii. 46. That the Lord is the Truth itself, in John: *Jesus said, I am the Way, the Truth, and the Life,* xiv. 6. That the Lord is eternal Life, in 1 John: *We know that the Son of God hath come into the world, that we may know the Truth, and we are in the Truth in Jesus Christ; this is the true God and eternal Life,* v. 20, 21. To the above it should be added, that man, on account of his business in the world, can procure for himself only a few truths of faith; but still, if he goes to the Lord, and worships Him alone, he comes into the power of knowing all truths; wherefore, every true worshipper of the Lord, as soon as he hears any truth of faith, which he did not know before, immediately sees, acknowledges and receives it. The reason is, because the Lord is in him, and he in the Lord; consequently, the light of truth is in him, and he in the light of truth; for, as was said above, the Lord is Light itself, and Truth itself. This may be confirmed by this experience. A spirit was seen by me, who, in the company of others, appeared simple, because he acknowledged the Lord alone as the God of heaven and earth, and confirmed this his faith by some truths from the Word. He was taken up into heaven, among the wiser angels; and it was told me, that there he was as wise as they; yea, that he spoke truths in abundance, altogether as from himself, concerning which he did not know any thing before. Similar will be the state of those who are about to come into the Lord's New Church. This is the same state that is described in Jeremiah: *This shall be the covenant which I will make with the house of Israel, after these days; I will give my law in the midst of them, and I will write it upon their heart; and they shall not teach any more every man his companion, and every man his brother, saying, Know the Lord; for all shall know Me, from the least of them even to the greatest of them,* xxxi. 33, 34. That state will also be such as is described in Isaiah: *A Rod shall go forth from the trunk of Jesse; truth shall be the girdle of his loins. Then the wolf shall dwell with the lamb, the leopard shall lie down with the kid; the sucking child shall play on the hole of the viper, and the weaned child shall put its hand on the den of the basilisk, because the earth shall be full of the knowledge of Jehovah, as the waters cover the sea. In that day, the nations shall seek the Root of Jesse, and his rest shall be glory,* xi. 6 to 10.

355. V. That Faith without Charity is not Faith, and that Charity without Faith is not Charity; and that neither lives but from the Lord.

That the church, at this day, should separate faith from charity, by saying that faith alone, without the works of the law, justifies and saves, and that thus charity cannot be conjoined with faith, since faith is from God, and charity, so far as it is actual in works, from man, never came into the mind of any apostle, as is very manifest from their epistles; but this separation and division was introduced into the Christian church, when they divided the one God into three persons, and ascribed to each equal divinity. But that there is no faith without charity, nor any charity without faith, and that neither has any life, except from the Lord, will be illustrated in the fol lowing lemma; here, to prepare the way, it shall be demonstrated, 1. *That man can procure faith for himself.* 2. *That he can procure charity also.* 3. *And likewise the life of both.* 4. *But that still, nothing of faith, nothing of charity, and nothing of the life of either, is from man, but from the Lord alone.*

356. (1.) *That man can procure Faith for himself,* was shown in the third lemma above, from n. 343 to n. 348, by this, That faith, in its essence, is truth; and truths, from the Word, can be procured by any one; and that so far as any one procures them for himself and loves them, so far he procures for himself the elements of faith. To the above this should be added, that unless man could procure faith for himself, all the things that are commanded in the Word concerning faith, would be vain; for it is read there, *That it is the will of the Father, that men should believe in the Son; and that he that believeth in Him, should have eternal life; and that he that doth not believe, should not see life.* It is also read, that *Jesus would send the Paraclete, who should convince the world of sin, because they believe not in Me;* besides many other passages, which were adduced above, n. 337, 338. Moreover, that all the apostles preached faith, and this in the Lord God the Savior Jesus Christ. What would all these and those things avail, if man should stand with his hands hanging down, like a graven image with movable joints, and wait for influx; and then the joints, without being able to apply themselves to receive it, should be excited, from some extrinsic cause, to something not of faith? For modern orthodoxy, in the Christian world separate from the Roman Catholics, teaches thus: *That man, as to what is good, is utterly corrupt and dead; so that, in the nature of man, since the fall, before regeneration, there remains, or is left, not even a spark of spiritual strength, by which he can, of himself, be prepared for the grace of God, or apprehend it, when offered, or, of and by himself, be capable of retaining that grace; or, in spiritual things, understand, believe, embrace, think, will, begin, finish, act, operate, coöperate, or apply, or accommodate himself to grace, or do any thing towards conversion, wholly or by halves, or in the least degree. And that man, in spiritual things, which respect the salvation of the soul, is like the pillar of salt of Lot's wife, and like a stock or a stone without life, which has not the use of eyes, mouth, or any of the senses. That still he has the power of moving from place to place, or he can direct his external members, come to public assemblies, and hear the Word and the Gospel.* These words are in the book of the church of the Evangelical, called Formula Concordiæ, in the edition of Leipsic, 1756, pp. 656, 658, 661, 662, 663, 671, 672, 673; to which book, and thus to which faith, the priests, when they are inaugurated, take oath. The faith of the Reformed is similar. But who, that possesses reason and religion, would not hiss at those things, as absurd and ridiculous? For he might say with himself, "If it were so, for what purpose, then, is the Word, for what purpose is religion, for what purpose is the priesthood, and for what purpose is preaching, but something vain, or sound without sense? Say such things to any judicious pagan, whom you wish to convert, that he is such, as to conversion and faith; would he not look upon Christianity as one looks upon an empty vessel? For, take away from man all power of believing, as of himself, and then what else is he?" But these things will be exhibited in a clearer light, in the chapter concerning Free Agency.

357. (2.) *That Man can procure Charity for himself.*

The case is the same with charity as with faith; for what else does the Word teach, but faith and charity, because these are the two essentials of salvation? For it is read, *Thou shalt love the Lord with all thy heart, and with all thy soul; and the neighbor as thyself,* Matt. xxii. 34 to 39; and Jesus said, *A commandment I give to you, that ye love one another; by this ye shall be known, that ye are my disci-*

ples, that ye love one another, John xiii. 34, 35; see also xv. 9; xvi. 27. Also, that man should bear fruit, like a good tree; and that he who does good, shall be recompensed at the resurrection; besides many similar things. To what purpose are these things, unless man can of himself exercise charity, and in some way procure it for himself? Can he not give alms, help the needy, and do good in his house and in his office? Can he not live according to the commandments of the decalogue? Has he not a soul, from which he can do them, and also a rational mind, from which he can lead himself to act, for this or that end? Can he not think that he should do them, because they are commanded in the Word, and thus by God? This power is not wanting to any man; and it is not wanting, because the Lord gives it to every one; and He gives it as a certain property or possession; for who knows otherwise, when he does charity, than that he does it of himself?

358. (3.) *That Man can also procure for himself the Life of Faith and Charity,* is also a similar thing; for he procures it for himself, when he goes to the Lord, who is Life itself; and access to Him is not prohibited to any man, for He continually invites every man to come to Him; for He said, *He who cometh to Me shall never hunger, and he who believeth in Me shall never thirst; and him that cometh to Me, I will not cast out,* John vi. 35, 37. *Jesus stood and cried, If any one thirst, let him come unto Me and drink,* vii. 37. And in another place: *The kingdom of the heavens is like one who made a wedding for his son, and sent his servants to call those who were invited; and at last he said, Go to the ends of the streets, and whomsoever ye shall find, call to the wedding,* Matt. xxii. 2 to 9. Who does not know, that the invitation or call is universal, as also the grace of reception? The reason why man obtains life by going to the Lord, is, because the Lord is Life itself; not only the life of faith, but also the life of charity. That the Lord is that, and that man has it from the Lord, is evident from these passages: *In the beginning was the Word; in Him was* LIFE, *and the* LIFE *was the light of men,* John i. 1, 4. *As the Father raiseth the dead, and quickeneth, so the Son* QUICKENETH *whom He will,* v. 21. *As the Father hath life in Himself, so hath He given to the Son* TO HAVE LIFE IN HIMSELF, v. 26. *The bread of God is He who came down from heaven, and giveth* LIFE *to the world,* vi. 31. *The words which I speak unto you are spirit and* LIFE, vi. 63. *Jesus said, He that followeth Me, shall have* THE LIGHT OF LIFE, viii. 12. *I have come, that* THEY MAY HAVE LIFE, *and may have abundance,* x. 10. *He who believeth in Me, although he die,* SHALL LIVE, xi. 25. *I am the Way, the Truth, and* THE LIFE, xiv. 6. BECAUSE I LIVE, YE SHALL LIVE ALSO, xiv. 9. *These things are written, that ye may have* LIFE *in his name,* xx. 31. *That He is* ETERNAL LIFE, 1 John v. 21. By life in faith and charity, is meant spiritual life, which is given by the Lord to man in his natural life.

359. (4.) *That yet still Nothing of Faith, and Nothing of Charity, and Nothing of the Life of either, is from Man, but from the Lord alone.*

For it is read, that *A man cannot take any thing, unless it be given to him from heaven,* John iii. 27. And Jesus said, *He that abideth in Me, and I in him, beareth much fruit; because without Me ye cannot do any thing,* xv. 5. But this should be thus understood; that man, of himself, cannot procure for himself any other faith than natural, which is persuasion that it is so, since a man of authority said so, nor any other charity than natural, which is working for favor, for the sake of some remuneration; in which two there is the proprium of man, and not yet life from the Lord. But still, man by both of them prepares himself, that he may be a receptacle of the Lord; and as he prepares himself, so the Lord enters and causes his natural faith to become spiritual faith, and so likewise his charity, and thus both to be living; and these things are done, when man goes to the Lord, as the God of heaven and earth. Man, because he was created an image of God, was created a habitation of God; wherefore the Lord says, *He who hath my commandments and doeth them, he it is that loveth Me; and I will love him, and will come to him, and make an abode with him,* John xiv. 21, 23. And also, *Behold I stand at the door and knock; if any one hear my voice, and open the door, I will go in to him, and will sup with him, and he with Me,* Rev. iii. 20. Hence follows this conclusion; That as man prepares himself, naturally, for receiving the Lord, so the Lord enters, and makes all the things with him inwardly spiritual, and thus living; but, on the other hand, as far as man does not prepare himself, so far he removes the Lord from him, and he does all things from himself, and that which man himself does from himself, has not any thing of life in it. But these things cannot yet be set forth to be seen in any light, before it is treated concerning CHARITY and concerning FREE AGENCY; and they will be seen afterwards in the chapter concerning REFORMATION and REGENERATION.

360. In the foregoing, it was said, that faith in the beginning with man, is natural, and that as man comes to the Lord it becomes spiritual; likewise charity; but no one has yet known the distinction, which there is between natural faith and charity, and spiritual; wherefore this great secret is to be disclosed. There are two worlds, the natural and the spiritual, and in each world there is a sun, and from each sun proceed heat and light; but the heat and light, from the sun of the spiritual world, have life in them: their life is from the Lord, who is in the midst of that sun; but the heat and light, from the sun of the natural world, have nothing of life in them, but they serve the two former for receptacles, as instrumental causes serve their principals, to convey them to men. It should, therefore, be known, that the heat and light from the sun of the spiritual world, being those from which all spiritual things are, are also spiritual, because there is spirit and life in them; but the heat and light from the sun of the natural world are those from which are all natural things, which, viewed in themselves, are without spirit and life. Now, because faith is of light, and charity is of heat, it is manifest, that as far as man is in the light and heat proceeding from the sun of the spiritual world, so far he is in spiritual faith and charity; but that as far as he is in the light and heat proceeding from the sun of the natural world, so far he is in natural faith and charity. Hence it is evident, that, as spiritual light is inwardly in natural light, as in its receptacle, or in its repository, and in like manner, spiritual heat inwardly in natural heat; so also spiritual faith is inwardly, in natural faith, and in like manner, spiritual charity inwardly in natural charity: and this is effected, in the degree in which man advances from the natural world into the spiritual world; and he advances, as he believes in the Lord, who is the Light itself, the Way, the Truth and the Life, as He himself teaches. Since it is so, it is manifest, that, when man is in spiritual faith, then he is also in natural faith; for, as was said, spiritual faith is inwardly in natural faith. Because faith is of light, it follows that, by that insertion, the natural of man becomes, as it were, transparent, and that, as it is conjoined with charity, it becomes beautifully colored; the reason is, because charity is red, and faith is white; charity is red from the flame of spiritual fire, and faith is white or bright from the splendor of the light thence. The contrary happens, if the spiritual be not inwardly in the natural, but the natural inwardly in the spiritual; this is the case with men who reject faith and charity. With these, the internal of their mind in which they are when they think, left to themselves, is infernal, and also they think from hell, although they do not know it; but the external of their mind, from which they speak with their consociates in the world, is, as it were, spiritual, but this

is filled with such unclean things as are in hell; wherefore these are in hell, for they are in an inverted state with respect to the former.

361. When, therefore, it is known, that the spiritual is inwardly in the natural, with those who are in faith in the Lord, and at the same time in charity towards the neighbor, and that thence the natural with them is transparent, it follows, that man is so far wise in spiritual things, and thence also so far in natural things; for he sees inwardly in himself, whenever he thinks, or reads, or hears any thing, whether it be a truth or not; he perceives this from the Lord, from whom spiritual light and heat flow into the higher sphere of his understanding. As far as faith and charity with man become spiritual, so far he is withdrawn from the proprium, and does not regard himself, reward and recompense, but only the delight of perceiving the truths of faith, and of doing the goods of love; and as far as that spirituality is increased, so far that delight becomes blessed; from this is his salvation, which is called eternal life. This state of man may be compared with the most beautiful and delightful things in the world, and also it is compared with them in the Word; as with fruitful trees, and also with the gardens in which they grow; with flowery fields; with precious stones; and with delicious food; and also with weddings and nuptial festivities and rejoicings. But when it is inverted, that is, when the natural is inwardly in the spiritual, and thence man in his internals is a devil, and in his externals like an angel, he may then be compared with a dead person in a coffin made of costly wood and covered with gold; he may also be compared with a skeleton dressed in handsome clothes, like a man, and carried in a magnificent chariot; and also with a corpse in a sepulchre built like the temple of Diana: yea, his internal may be represented by a nest of serpents in a cavern, but his external by butterflies, whose wings are tinged with colors of every kind, but which, nevertheless, glue their filthy eggs to the leaves of useful trees, by which their fruit is consumed: yea, their internal may be compared with a hawk, and their external with a dove; and their faith and charity, with the flying of a hawk over a dove endeavoring to escape, which at length he wearies out, and then flies upon her and devours her.

362. VI. That the Lord, Charity and Faith, make one, like Life, Will, and Understanding in Man; and that if they are divided, each perishes, like a Pearl reduced to Powder.

In the first place, some things will be mentioned, which have been hitherto unknown in the learned world, and thence in the ecclesiastical order; as much unknown as things which have been buried in the ground; when yet they are treasures of wisdom, and unless they are dug up and given to the public, man strives in vain to come into any just knowledge concerning God, concerning faith, concerning charity, and concerning the state of his life, how he should regulate and prepare it for a state of eternal life. Those unknown things are these;—That man is a mere organ of life: That life, with all the things of it, flows in from the God of heaven, who is the Lord: That there are two faculties of life in man, which are called the will and the understanding, and that the will is the receptacle of love, and the understanding the receptacle of wisdom; and thus, also, that the will is the receptacle of charity, and the understanding the receptacle of faith: That all the things which man wills, and all the things which he understands, flow in from without; the goods which are of love and charity, and the truths which are of wisdom and faith, from the Lord; but all the things contrary to those, from hell: That it is provided by the Lord, that man may sensibly perceive in himself as his, those things which flow in from without, and thence produce them of himself as his own, although nothing of them is his: That, nevertheless, those things are imputed to him as his, on account of the freedom in which he is, to will and to think, and on account of the knowledges of good and truth which are given him, from which he can freely choose whatever conduces to his temporal life and to his eternal life. A man who looks at these things which have been advanced, with an oblique eye, or from the corners of his eyes, may conclude from them many things which are of insanity; but a man who looks at them with a direct eye, or with the pupil, may conclude from them many things, which are of wisdom; and that this may be done, and not that, it was necessary to premise the decisions and tenets concerning God and concerning the Divine Trinity, and after them to establish the decisions and tenets concerning Faith and Charity, concerning Free Agency, and concerning Reformation and Regeneration, as also concerning Imputation; and likewise concerning Repentance, concerning Baptism, and concerning the Holy Supper, as means.

363. But that this article of faith, which is, that the Lord, charity and faith make one, like life, will and understanding in man, and that if they are divided, each perishes, like a pearl reduced to powder, may be seen and acknowledged as a truth, it is expedient that it be considered in this order: (1.) *That the Lord, with all his divine love, with all his divine wisdom, thus with all his divine life, flows in with every man.* (2.) *Therefore, with all the essence of faith and charity.* (3.) *But that they are received by man according to his form.* (4.) *And that the man who divides the Lord, charity and faith, is not a form receiving but a form destroying them.*

364. (1.) *That the Lord, with all his Divine Love, with all his Divine Wisdom, thus with all his Divine Life, flows in with every Man.*

In the book of Creation it is read, *That man was created an image of God; and that God breathed into his nostrils the breath of lives*, Gen. i. 27; ii. 7; by which it is described, that man is an organ of life, and not life; for God could not create another like Himself; if he could have done this, there might have been as many gods as men. Neither could He create life, as light cannot be created; but He could create man a form of life, as He created the eye a form of light. God never could and never can divide his essence, for this is one and indivisible. Since, therefore, God alone is life, it follows, indubitably, that God, from his life, vivifies every man; and that man, without that vivification, would be, as to flesh, a mere sponge, and as to bones, a mere skeleton, in whom there would be no more of life than there is in a clock, which is movable from the pendulum, and at the same time the weight or spring. Since such is the case, it follows also, that God flows in with every man, with all his divine life, that is, with all his divine love and his divine wisdom; these two make his divine life, as may be seen above, n. 39, 40; for the Divine cannot be divided. But how God, with all his divine life, flows in, may be perceived by an idea somewhat like that by which it is perceived that the sun of the world, with all its essence, which is heat and light, flows into every tree, and into every shrub and flower, and into every stone, mean as well as precious; and that every object takes its portion from this common influx, and that the sun does not divide its light and its heat, and dispense a part to this and a part to that. It is similar with the sun of heaven, from which the divine love proceeds as heat, and the divine wisdom as light; these two flow into human minds, as the heat and light of the sun of the world into bodies, and vivify them according to the quality of the form, each of which takes from the common influx as much as is necessary. To this is applicable what the Lord says: *Your Father maketh his sun rise upon the evil and the good, and sendeth rain upon the just and the unjust*, Matt. v. 45. The Lord also is omnipresent; and where He is present, there He is with his whole essence, and it is impossible for Him to take some of it away, and thence to give a part to one, and a part to another; but He gives it whole, and affords man an opportunity to take little or much. He says also, that He has an abode with those who do his commandments; and also that the faithful are in him, and He in them. In a word, all things are full of God, and every one takes his portion from that fulness. It is similar with every thing common, as with the atmospheres and oceans; the atmosphere is such in the least parts as in the greatest; it does not dispense a part of itself for the respiration of man, and for the flying of a bird, nor for the sails of a ship, and for the wings of a mill; but each one takes thence its portion, and applies to itself as much as is sufficient. The case is also the same as with a granary full of corn; the owner takes from this his provision every day, and the granary does not distribute it.

365. (2.) *Therefore, that the Lord, with all the Essence of Faith and Charity, flows in with every Man.*

This follows from the former theorem, since the life of divine wisdom is the essence of faith, and the life of divine love is the essence of charity; wherefore, since the Lord is present with those things which are properly his, which are divine wisdom and divine love, He is also present with all the truths which are of faith, and with all the goods which are of charity; for by *faith* is meant all the truth which man from the Lord perceives, thinks and speaks, and by *charity* is meant all the good with which he is affected by the Lord, and which he thence wills and does. It was said above, that the divine love, which proceeds from the Lord as a sun, is perceived by the angels as heat, and that the divine wisdom thence, is perceived as light; but he who does not think beyond appearance, may imagine that that heat is bare heat, and that that light is bare light, such as are the heat and light proceeding from the sun of our world. But the heat and light proceeding from the Lord, as a sun, contain in their bosom all the infinities that are in the Lord; the heat, all the infinities of his love, and the light, all the infinities of his wisdom, and thus also in infinity, all the good which is of charity, and all the truth which is of faith. The reason is, because that sun itself is present every where, in its heat and in its light, and that sun is the nearest circle encompassing the Lord, emanating from his divine love, and at the same time from his divine wisdom; for, as has been several times said above, the Lord is in the midst of that sun. Hence now it is manifest, that nothing can be wanting, but that man may take from the Lord, because He is omnipresent, all the good which is of charity, and all the truth which is of faith. That there are not any of those things wanting, is evident from the love and wisdom of the angels of heaven, which they have from the Lord, in that they are ineffable and incomprehensible to the natural man, and also multiplicable to eternity. That there are infinite things in the light and heat which proceed from the Lord, although they are perceived as simply heat and light, may be illustrated by various things in the natural world, as by these: The sound of man's voice and speech is heard only as simple sound, and yet the angels, when they hear it, perceive in it all the affections of his love, and they also manifest what and of what sort they are. That those things are inwardly concealed in sound, man also may, in some measure, perceive from the sound of one speaking with him, as whether there be in it contempt, or ridicule, or hatred; and also whether there be in it charity, benevolence, or joy, or other affections. Similar things are concealed in the radiance of the eye, when it looks at any one. It may also be illustrated by the fragrancies from a large garden, or by the fragrancies from extensive fields of flowers; the fragrant odor, breathed forth from them, consists of thousands and myriads of various things, and still they are sensibly perceived as one. It is similar with many other things, which, although they outwardly appear uniform, still inwardly they are manifold; sympathies and antipathies are nothing else than exhalations of affections from minds which affect another according to similitudes, and excite aversion according to dissimilitudes. These, although they are innumerable, and are not sensibly perceived by any sense of the body, are yet perceived by the sense of the soul as one; and according to them all conjunctions and consociations in the spiritual world are made. These things have been adduced, that those things may be illustrated, which were said above, concerning spiritual light which proceeds from the Lord, that all things of wisdom, and thence all things of faith, are therein; and that it is that light from which the understanding sees and perceives rational things analytically, as the eye sees and perceives natural things symmetrically.

366. (3.) *That those Things which flow in from the Lord, are received by Man according to his Form.*

By *form*, here, is meant the state of man, as to his love and wisdom together; hence also as to the affections of the goods of his charity, and at the same time, as to the perceptions of the truths of his faith. That God is one, indivisible, and the same from eternity to eternity, not the same simple, but infinite, and that all variableness is in the subject in which He is, was shown above. That the form or state receiving, induces variations, may be evident from the life of infants, of children, of youths, of adults, and of old people. The same life, because the same soul, is in each one from infancy to old age; but as his state is varied according to ages and accommodations, so also life is perceived. The life of God, in all its fulness, is not only with good and pious men, but also with bad and impious men; in like manner, with the angels of heaven and with the spirits of hell; the difference is, that the bad stop up the way and shut the door, that God may not enter into the lower parts of their mind; but the good clear out the way and open the door, and also invite God to enter into the lower parts of their mind, as He dwells in the highest parts of it; and thus they form the state of the will for the influx of love and charity, and the state of the understanding for the influx of wisdom and faith, consequently for the reception of God; but the bad obstruct that influx, by various lusts of the flesh and spiritual defilements, which hinder and stop the passage; but still God resides in the highest parts of them, with all his divine essence, and gives them the faculty of willing good and of understanding truth, which faculty every man has, but which he would not have, unless life from God were in his soul. That the bad also have this faculty, has been given me to know, by much experience. That every one receives life from God, according to his form, may be illustrated by comparisons with vegetables of every kind. Every tree, every shrub, every herb, and every blade of grass, receives the influx of heat and light, according to its form; thus not only those which are of good use, but also those which are of evil use; and the sun, with its heat, does not change their forms, but the forms change its effects in themselves. It is similar with the subjects of the mineral kingdom; each of them, as well the excellent as the mean, receives influx according to the form of the contexture of the parts among themselves; and so one stone receives it differently from another stone, one mineral differently from another mineral, and one metal differently from another metal. Some of them variegate themselves with most beautiful colors, some transmit the light without variegation, and some confuse and suffocate the light in themselves. From these few cases, it may be evident, that, as the sun of the world, with its heat and with its light, is equally present in one object as in another, but that the recipient forms vary its operations; so the Lord, from the sun of heaven, in the midst of which He is, is universally present, with its heat, which in its essence is love, and with its light, which in its essence is wisdom; but that the form of man, which is induced by the states of his life, varies the operations; consequently, that the Lord is not the cause why man is not regenerated and saved, but man himself.

367. (4.) *But that the Man who divides the Lord, Charity and Faith, is not a Form receiving but a Form destroying them.*

For he who separates the Lord from charity and faith, separates life from them, which being separated, charity and faith either do not exist, or they are abortions. That the Lord is life itself, may be seen above, n. 358. He who acknowledges the Lord, and separates charity, acknowledges Him only with the lips: his acknowledgment and confession are only cold, in which there is no faith; for they are destitute of spiritual essence, for charity is the essence of faith. But he who does charity, and does not acknowledge the Lord, that He is the God of heaven and earth, one with the Father, as He himself teaches, does no other charity than merely natural, in which there is not eternal life. The man of the church knows, that all good, which in itself is good, is from God; consequently, from the Lord, who is *the true God and eternal Life*, 1 John v. 20. In like manner, charity, because good and charity are one. That faith, separate from charity, is not faith, is because faith is the light of man's life, and charity is the heat of his life; wherefore, if charity is separated from faith, it is as when heat is separated from light; thence the state of man becomes such as the state of the world is, in the time of winter, when all the things upon the earth die. Charity and faith, that charity may be charity, and faith may be faith, can no more be separated, than the will and the understanding; and if these are separated, the understanding becomes nothing, and presently also the will: the reason why it is similar with charity and faith, is, because charity resides in the will, and faith in the understanding. To separate charity from faith, is like separating essence from form: it is known, in the learned world, that essence without form and form without essence is not any thing; for essence has no quality except from form, nor is form any subsisting entity, except from essence; consequently, there is not any predication concerning either, when separated from the other. Charity also is the essence of faith, and faith is the form of charity; just as it was said above, that good is the essence of truth, and truth the form of good. These two, namely, good and truth, are in each and every thing that exists essentially; wherefore charity, because it is of good, and faith, because it is of truth, may be illustrated by comparisons with many things in the human body, and with many things upon the earth. It agrees by comparison with the respiration of the lungs and the systolic motion of the heart; for charity can no more be separated from faith, than the heart can from the lungs; for, on the cessation of the pulsation of the heart, the respiration of the lungs, immediately ceases; and on the cessation of the respiration of the lungs, there takes place a failure of all the senses, and also a privation of the motion of all the muscles, and shortly afterwards the heart also ceases, and the all of life is dissipated. This comparison agrees, since the heart corresponds to the will, and thence also to charity, and the respiration of the lungs to the understanding, and thence also to faith; for, as was said above, charity resides in the will, and faith in the understanding; nor is any thing else meant in the Word by heart and breath (or spirit). The separation of charity and faith also coincides with the separation of the blood and flesh; for the blood separated from the flesh is gore, and becomes corruption; and the flesh separated from the blood gradually putrifies, and worms are bred in it. Blood also, in the spiritual sense, signifies the truth of wisdom and faith, and flesh the good of love and charity: that blood signifies this, is shown in THE APOCALYPSE REVEALED, n. 379, and that flesh does, n. 832. Charity and faith, that the one and the other may be any thing, can no more be separated than meat and water, or than bread and wine, with man; for meat and bread, taken without water and win , only distend the stomach, and, like undigested masses, destroy it, and become as putrid mire; water and wine, without meat and bread, also distend the stomach, and likewise the vessels and pores, which, thus destitute of nutrition, emaciate the body even to death. This comparison also coincides, since meat and bread, in the spiritual sense, signify the good of love and charity, and water and wine the truth of wisdom and faith; see THE APOCALYPSE REVEALED, n. 50, 316, 778, 932. Charity conjoined to faith, and faith conjoined to charity, may be likened to the face of a handsome virgin, beautiful from the red and white mixed with each other; which similitude also agrees, since love and thence charity, in the spiritual world, is red from the fire of the sun there, and truth and thence faith is white from the light of that sun; wherefore charity separated from faith may be likened to a face inflamed with pimples, and faith separated from charity may be likened to the pallid face of a corpse. Faith separated from charity may also be likened to a palsy in one side, which is called a *hemiplegy*, of which, as it increases, man dies. It may also be likened to the St. Vitus's dance, which befalls man from the bite of the tarantula: like to this the rational faculty becomes; like this it dances with fury, and believes itself to be then alive; and yet it can no more collect reasons into one, and think concerning spiritual truths, than one lying in bed oppressed with the nightmare. These are sufficient for the demonstration of the two theorems of this chapter;—the first, *That faith without charity is not faith, and that charity without faith is not charity, and that neither lives, except from the Lord;* and the second, *That the Lord, charity and faith make one, like life, will, and understanding in man; and that, if they are divided, each perishes like a pearl reduced to powder.*

368. VII. THAT THE LORD IS CHARITY AND FAITH IN MAN, AND THAT MAN IS CHARITY AND FAITH IN THE LORD

That the man of the church is in the Lord, and the Lord in him, is evident from these passages in the Word, *Jesus said*, ABIDE IN ME AND I IN YOU; *I am the Vine, and ye the branches.* HE THAT ABIDETH IN ME, AND I IN HIM, *beareth much fruit*, John xv. 4, 5. *He that eateth my flesh and drinketh my blood*, ABIDETH IN ME AND I IN HIM, vi. 56. *In that day ye shall know, that I am in my Father*, AND YE IN ME, AND I IN YOU, xiv. 20. *Whosoever confesseth that Jesus is the Son of God, God abideth in him and he in God*, 1 John iv. 15 But man himself cannot be in the Lord, but charity and faith, which are with man from the Lord, from which two man is essentially man. But in order that this arcanum may appear in some light before the understanding, it is to be examined in this series: (1.) *That conjunction with God is that by which man has salvation and eternal life.* (2.) *That conjunction with God the Father is not possible, but with the Lord, and through Him with God the Father.* (3.) *That conjunction with the Lord is reciprocal, which is, that the Lord is in man, and man in the Lord.* (4.) *That this reciprocal conjunction is effected by means of charity and faith.* That these things are so, will be manifest from the following explanation.

369. (1.) *That Conjunction with God is that by which Man has Salvation and eternal Life.*

Man was created that he might be conjoined to God; for he was created a native of heaven, and also a native of the world; and so far as he is a native of heaven, he is spiritual, but so far as he is a native of the world, he is natural; and the spiritual man can think concerning God, and perceive such things as are of God, and also can love God, and be affected with those things which are from God; from which it follows, that he can be conjoined to God. That man can think concerning God, and perceive such things as are of God, is beyond all chance of doubt; for he can think concerning the Unity of God, concerning the Esse of God, which is Jehovah concerning the Immensity and Eternity of God, concerning the Divine Love and Divine Wisdom which make the essence of God, concerning the Omnipotence, the Omniscience, and the Omnipresence of God, concerning the Lord the Savior his Son, and concerning Redemption and Mediation; and also concerning the Holy Spirit, and finally concerning the Divine Trinity; all which are of God, yea, are God; and moreover, concerning the operations of God, which are principally faith and charity; besides other things which proceed from these two. That man can not only think concerning God, but also love God, is evident from the two commandments of God himself, which run thus: *Thou shalt love the Lord thy God with thy whole heart, and with thy whole soul; this is the first and great commandment. The second is like it; Thou shalt love thy neighbor as thyself,* Matt. xxii. 37 to 39; Deut. vi. 5. That man can do the commandments of God, and that this is to love God, and to be loved by God, is evident from these words; *Jesus said, He that hath my commandments, and doeth them, he it is that loveth Me; and he that loveth Me, shall be loved by my Father, and I will love him, and will manifest Myself to him,* John xiv. 21. Besides, what else is faith, but conjunction with God by truths which are of the understanding and thence of the thought? and what is love, but conjunction with God by goods which are of the will and thence of the affection! The conjunction of God with man is spiritual conjunction in the natural, and the conjunction of man with God is natural conjunction from the spiritual. For the sake of this conjunction as an end, man was created a native of heaven, and at the same time of the world; as a native of heaven he is spiritual, and as a native of the world he is natural. If therefore man becomes rational-spiritual, and at the same time moral-spiritual, he is conjoined to God, and by conjunction has salvation and eternal life. But if man is only rational-natural, and likewise moral-natural, there is indeed a conjunction of God with him, but not a conjunction of him with God; thence he has spiritual death, which, viewed in itself, is natural life without spiritual; for the spiritual, in which is the life of God, is extinct with him.

370. (2.) *That Conjunction with God the Father is not possible, but with the Lord, and through Him with God the Father.*

This the Scripture teaches, and reason sees. The Scripture teaches, that God the Father was never seen nor heard, and that He cannot be seen or heard; consequently from Himself, such as He is in his esse, and in his essence, He cannot operate any thing with man; for the Lord says, *No one hath seen God, except He that is with the Father, He hath seen the Father,* John vi. 46. *No one knoweth the Father, except the Son, and he to whom the Son willeth to reveal Him,* Matt. xi. 27. *Ye have never heard the voice of the Father, nor seen his shape,* John v. 37. The reason is, because He is in the firsts and the principles of all things, thus most eminently above all the sphere of the human mind; for He is in the firsts and the principles of all things of wisdom and all things of love, with which man has no possible conjunction. Wherefore, if He should come to man, or man to Him, man would be consumed and dissolved, like wood in the focus of a large burning-glass; or, rather, like an image cast into the sun itself; wherefore it was said to Moses, who desired to see God, that *man cannot see Him and live.* Exod. xxxiii. 20. But that God the Father is conjoined through the Lord, is evident from the passages just adduced; that not the Father, but the only-begotten Son, who is in the bosom of the Father, and has seen the Father, has set forth and revealed the things which are of God and from God. And moreover from these: *In that day ye shall know that I am in my Father, and ye in Me, and I in you,* John xiv. 20. *I have given to them the glory which Thou gavest to Me, that they may be one, as We are* one; I in them, and Thou in Me, xvii. 22, 23, 26. *Jesus said, I am the Way, the Truth, and the Life; no one cometh to the Father, but through Me.* And then Philip wished to see the Father; to whom the Lord answered, *He that seeth Me, seeth the Father also; and he that knoweth Me, knoweth the Father also;* xiv. 6, 7, and following verses. And in another place, *He that seeth Me, seeth Him who sent Me,* xii. 45. And moreover He says, *that He is the Door, and that he that entereth through Him, is saved; and that he that climbeth up any other way, is a thief and a robber,* x. 1, 9. And also He says, that *He that abideth not in Me is cast out, and, like a dried branch, is thrown into the fire,* xv. 6. The reason is, because the Lord our Savior is Jehovah the Father himself in the human form; for Jehovah descended and became Man, that He might be able to come to man, and man to Him, and thus conjunction might be made, and by conjunction man might have salvation and eternal life. For when God became Man, and thus also became God-Man, being then accommodated to man, He could come to him, and be conjoined to him, as Man-God, and God-Man. There are three things which follow in order, ACCOMMODATION, APPLICATION, and CONJUNCTION. There must be accommodation, before there can be application, and accommodation and application together, before there can be conjunction. Accommodation on the part of God was, that He became Man. Application on the part of God is perpetual, so far as man applies himself in turn; and as this is done, conjunction also is effected. These three follow and proceed in their order, in all and each of the things, which become one and coëxist.

371. (3.) *That Conjunction with the Lord is reciprocal, which is, that the Lord is in Man, and Man in the Lord.*

That conjunction is reciprocal, the Scripture teaches, and reason also sees. The Lord, concerning his conjunction with his Father, teaches that it is reciprocal; for He says to Philip, *Believest thou not that I am in the Father, and the Father in Me. Believe Me, that I am in the Father, and the Father in Me,* John xiv. 10, 11. *That ye may know and believe that the Father is in Me, and I in the Father,* x. 38. *Jesus said, Father, the hour hath come; glorify thy Son, that thy Son also may glorify Thee,* xvii. 1. *Father, all mine are thine, and all thine are mine,* xvii. 10. The Lord says the same concerning his conjunction with man, namely, that it is reciprocal; for He says, *Abide in Me, and I in you;* HE THAT ABIDETH IN ME, AND I IN HIM, *beareth much fruit,* John xv. 4, 5. *He that eateth my flesh and drinketh my blood,* ABIDETH IN ME AND I IN HIM, vi. 56. *In that day ye shall know that I am in my Father,* AND YE IN ME, AND I IN YOU, xiv. 20. *He that doeth the commandments of Christ* ABIDETH IN HIM, AND HE IN HIM, I John iii. 24; iv. 13. *Whosoever confesseth that Christ is the Son of God,* GOD ABIDETH IN HIM, AND HE IN GOD, iv. 15. *Whosoever heareth my voice, and openeth the door, I will go in to him, and* I WILL SUP WITH HIM, AND HE WITH ME, Rev. iii. 20. From these plain declarations, it is evident, that the conjunction of the Lord and man is reciprocal; and because it is reciprocal, it follows of course that man ought to conjoin himself with the Lord, that the Lord may conjoin himself with him; and that, otherwise, a conjunction would not be effected, but a recession, and thence a separation; yet this not on the part of the Lord, but on the part of man. That there may be this reciprocal conjunction, free choice is given to man, from which he can enter the way to heaven or the way to hell. From this freedom, given to man, flows his reciprocal faculty, which can conjoin itself with the Lord, and which can conjoin itself with the devil. But that liberty, its quality, and the reason why it is given to man, will be illustrated in the following chapters, where we shall treat concerning Free Agency, concerning Repentance, concerning Reformation and Regeneration, and concerning Imputation. It is to be regretted, that the reciprocal conjunction of the Lord and man, although it stands forth so clearly in the Word, is still unknown in the Christian church. That it is unknown, is on account of hypothetical things concerning faith and concerning free agency. The hypothetical things concerning faith, are, that faith is bestowed without man's contributing any thing to procure it, or accommodating and applying himself to receive it, any more than a stock. The hypothetical things concerning free agency, are, that man has not even a grain of free agency in spiritual things. But that the reciprocal conjunction of the Lord and man, on which the salvation of the human race depends, may be no longer concealed and unknown, necessity itself enjoins that it be disclosed, which cannot be done better, than by examples, because these illustrate.

There are two reciprocations by which conjunction is effected; one is ALTERNATE, and the other is MUTUAL. The alternate reciprocation by which conjunction is effected, may be illustrated by the respiration of the lungs. Man draws in the air, and thereby dilates the thorax; and afterwards he emits the air, which was drawn in, and thereby compresses the thorax. That attraction and thence dilatation is effected by means of the incumbency of the air, according to its column; but that emission and consequent compression is effected by means of the ribs, from the strength of the muscles. Such is the reciprocal conjunction of the air and the lungs, on which depends the life of the senses and motions of the whole body; for, when respiration ceases, sensation and motion also cease. The reciprocal conjunction, which is effected by alternate things, may be illustrated also by the conjunction of the heart with the lungs, and of the lungs with the heart. The heart, from its right ventricle, pours the blood into the lungs, and the lungs pour it back into the left ventricle of the heart; thus this reciprocal conjunction is effected, on which the life of the whole body entirely depends. Similar is the conjunction of the blood with the heart, and of the heart with the blood; the blood of the whole body flows through the veins into the heart, and it flows out from the heart through the arteries into the whole body; action and reaction make this conjunction. There is a similar action and reaction, by which conjunction continues, between the embryo and the womb of the mother. But such is not the reciprocal conjunction of the Lord and man, but it is a mutual conjunction, which is not effected by action and reaction, but by coöperations; for the Lord acts, and man receives action from the Lord, and operates as from himself; yea, of himself, from the Lord. This operation of man from the Lord, is imputed to him as his, since he is, from the Lord, continually kept in free agency. The free agency resulting thence is, that he can will and that he can think from the Lord, that is, from the Word; and also that he can will and think from the devil, that is, against the Lord and the Word. The Lord gives to man this freedom, that he may be able to conjoin himself reciprocally, and by conjunction be gifted with eternal life and happiness; for this, without reciprocal conjunction, is not possible. This reciprocal conjunction, which is mutual, may also be illustrated by various things in man, and in the world. Such is the conjunction of the soul and body with every man; such is the conjunction of the will and action, and such is that of the thought and speech; such also is that of the two eyes with each other, of the two ears with each other, and of the two nostrils with each other. That the conjunction of the two eyes is in its own way reciprocal, is manifest from the optic nerve, in which the fibres from both hemispheres of the brain are folded together among themselves, and, thus folded together, they extend to both the eyes; it is similar with the ears and nostrils. Similar is the mutual reciprocal conjunction of light and the eye, of sound and the ear, of smell and the nostril, of taste and the tongue, of touch and the body; for the eye is in the light and the light is in the eye, sound is in the ear and the ear is in the sound, smell is in the nostril and the nostril is in the smell, taste is in the tongue and the tongue is in the taste, and touch is in the body and the body is in the touch. This reciprocal conjunction may also be compared with the conjunction of a horse and a chariot, of an ox and a plough, of a wheel and a machine, of a sail and the wind, of a flute and the air; in short, such is the reciprocal conjunction of the end and the cause, and such is that of the cause and the effect; but to explain each of these cases particularly, I have not leisure, because it is a work of many pages.

372. (4.) *That this reciprocal Conjunction of the Lord and Man is effected by Means of Charity and Faith.* It is known, at this day, that the church makes the body of Christ, and that every one in whom the church is, is in some member of that body, according to Paul, Eph. i. 24; 1 Cor. xii. 27; Rom. xii. 4, 5. But what is the body of Christ, but divine good and divine truth? This is meant by the words of the Lord in John, *He that eateth my flesh and drinketh my blood, abideth in Me, and I in him,* vi. 56. By the flesh of the Lord, as also by bread, is meant the divine good, and by his blood, as also by wine, is meant the divine truth; that these things are meant will be seen in the chapter concerning the HOLY SUPPER. Thence it follows, that, as far as man is in the goods of charity, and in the truths of faith, so far he is in the Lord, and the Lord in him; for conjunction with the Lord is spiritual conjunction, and spiritual conjunction is effected solely by means of charity and faith. That there is a conjunction of the Lord and the church, and thence of the good and the true, in all and every part of the Word, was shown in the chapter concerning THE SACRED SCRIPTURE, n. 248 to 253; and because charity is good, and faith is truth, there is every where in the Word a conjunction of charity and faith. Hence, now, it follows, THAT THE LORD IS CHARITY AND FAITH IN MAN, AND THAT MAN IS CHARITY AND FAITH IN THE LORD, for the Lord is spiritual charity and faith in the natural charity and faith of man, and man is natural charity and faith from the spiritual of the Lord, which, conjoined, make spiritual-natural charity and faith.

373. VIII. THAT CHARITY AND FAITH ARE TOGETHER IN GOOD WORKS.

In every work which proceeds from man, the whole man is, such as he is as to the mind, or such as he is essentially. By the mind is meant the affection of his love and the thought thence; these form his nature, in general his life. If we contemplate works thus, they are, as it were, mirrors of the man. This may be illustrated by the like in the case of beasts and wild beasts; a beast is a beast, and a wild beast is a wild beast, in all their acts. A wolf is a wolf in all his, and a tiger is a tiger in all his; a fox is a fox in all his, and a lion is a lion in all his; in like manner, a sheep and a kid in all theirs. And so likewise is man, but he is such as he is in his internal man; if in this he is like a wolf or like a fox, all his works are internally those of a wolf or a fox; and so also, if he is like a sheep or a lamb. But that he is such in all his works, is not manifest in his external man, because this is easily turned about the internal; but still it is inwardly concealed in this. The Lord says, *A good man, from the good treasure of his heart, bringeth forth good; and an evil man from the evil treasure of his heart, bringeth forth evil,* Luke vi. 45. And also, *Every tree is known from its own fruit; from thorns they do not gather figs, nor from a bramble-bush do they gather grapes,* vi. 44. That man, in each and every thing that proceeds from him, is such as he is in his internal man, manifests itself to the life with him after death; since he then lives an internal man, and no longer an external. That good is in man, and that every work which proceeds from him is good, when the Lord

34

charity and faith reside in his internal man, will be demonstrated in this series: (1.) *That charity is to will well, and that good works are to do well from willing well.* (2.) *That charity and faith are only mental and perishable things, unless, when it can be done, they are determined to works, and coëxist in them.* (3.) *That charity alone does not produce good works, and still less faith alone; but that they are produced by charity and faith together.* But of these, one by one.

374. (1.) *That Charity is to will well, and that good Works are to do well from willing well.*

Charity and works are distinct from each other, like will and action, and like an affection of the mind and an operation of the body; consequently, also, like the internal man and the external; and these are distinct from each other like cause and effect, since the causes of all things are formed in the internal man, and all effects are produced thence in the external; wherefore charity, because it is of the internal man, is to will well, and works, because they are of the external man, are to do well from willing well. But still there is an infinite diversity between the good will of one and of another; for all that is believed or appears to flow from good will or benevolence, which is done by any one in favor of another; but still it is not known whether the good deeds are from charity, still less from what charity, genuine or spurious. That infinite diversity between the good will of one and another, derives its origin from the end, intention, and consequent purpose; these are inwardly concealed in the will of acting well; the quality of every one's will is thence. And the will seeks ways and means of arriving at its ends, which are effects, in the understanding, and therein it puts itself into the light, that it may not only see the reasons, but also the occasions, when and how it is to determine itself to acts, and thus produce its effects, which are works; and at the same time, in the understanding, it puts itself into the power of acting; whence it follows, that works are essentially of the will, formally of the understanding, and actually of the body. Thus charity descends into good works. This may be illustrated by comparison with a tree. Man himself, as to all the things of him, is like a tree. In the seed of this there is concealed, as it were, the end, intention, and purpose of producing fruits; in these the seed corresponds to the will with man, in which, as was said, are those three things. Then the seed, from its interiors, springs out of the earth, and clothes itself with branches, twigs and leaves, and thus prepares for itself means to the ends, which are fruits; in these the tree corresponds to the understanding with man. And, finally, when the time approaches, and opportunity of determination is given, it blossoms and produces fruits; in these the tree corresponds to good works with man; and it is manifest, that the fruit is essentially of the seed, formally of the twigs and leaves, and actually of the wood of the tree. This may also be illustrated by comparison with a temple. Man is a temple of God, according to Paul; 1 Cor. iii. 16, 17; 2 Cor. vi. 16; Ephes. ii. 21, 22. As a temple of God, man has for his end, intention and purpose, salvation and eternal life; in these there is a correspondence with the will, in which are those three things. Afterwards, he derives the doctrinals of faith and charity from parents, masters, and preachers, and, when he becomes capable of judging for himself, from the Word and from doctrinal books, all which are means to the end; in these there is a correspondence with the understanding. Finally, there is made a determination to uses according to the doctrinals as means, which is done by acts of the body, which are called good works. Thus the end, by mediate causes, produces effects, which, essentially, are of the end, formally, of the doctrinals of the church, and actually, of uses. Thus man becomes a temple of God.

375. (2.) *That Charity and Faith are only mental and perishable Things, unless, when it can be done, they are determined to Works, and coëxist in them.*

Has not man a head and a body, which are joined together by the neck? Is there not a mind in the head, which wills and thinks, and power in the body, which performs and executes? If, therefore, man should only will well, or think from charity, and should not do well and perform uses thence, would not man be like a head alone, and thus like a mind alone, which alone without a body cannot subsist? Who does not see, thence, that charity and faith are not charity and faith, when they are only in the head and its mind, and not in the body? For they are then like birds flying in the air, without any rest upon the earth; and, also, like birds impregnated with eggs, without nests, from which the eggs would drop into the air or upon the branch of some tree, and fall down to the ground and be broken. There is not any thing in the mind, to which something in the body does not correspond; and this, which corresponds, may be called the embodying of that; wherefore charity and faith, whilst they are only in the mind, are not incorporated in man, and then they may be likened to an aërial man, who is called a spectre, such as *Fame* was painted by the ancients, with a laurel around the head, and a *cornucopia* in the hand. Those persons, because they are such spectres, and still are able to think, cannot but be disturbed by fantasies, which also is done by reasonings from various sophistical things, scarcely otherwise than fenny bulrushes are disturbed by the wind, under which shells lie at the bottom, and frogs croak on the surface. Who cannot see that such things take place, when they only know some things from the Word concerning charity and faith, and do not do them? The Lord also says, EVERY ONE WHO HEARETH MY WORDS AND DOETH THEM, *I will compare to a prudent man, who built his house upon a rock. But* EVERY ONE WHO HEARETH MY WORDS AND DOETH THEM NOT, *shall be compared to a foolish man, who built his house upon the sand, or upon the ground without a foundation,* Matt. vii. 24, 26; Luke vi. 47, 48, 49. Charity and faith, with the factitious ideas of them, while man does not practise them, may be compared also with butterflies in the air, at which, when seen, a sparrow flies and devours them. The Lord also says, *A sower went forth to sow; and some fell upon the hard road, and the birds came and ate it up,* Matt. xiii. 3, 4.

376. That charity and faith conduce nothing to man, while they inhere only in one hemisphere of his body, that is, in his head, and are not grounded in works, is evident from a thousand passages in the Word, of which I sha'l adduce only these: *Every tree which* DOTH NOT BEAR GOOD FRUIT, *is cut down, and cast into the fire,* Matt. vii. 19, 20, 21. *That which was sown into good ground, is he that heareth the Word and attendeth, and beareth fruit and doeth. When Jesus said these things, He cried aloud, saying, He that hath ears to hear, let him hear,* Matt. xiii. 9 to 23. *Jesus said, My mother and my brethren are these who hear the Word of God and* DO IT, Luke viii. 21. *We know that God heareth not sinners, but if any one worshippeth God, and* DOETH HIS WILL, *He heareth him,* John ix. 31. *If ye know these things, happy are ye if* YE DO THEM, xiii. 17. *He that hath my commandments, and* DOETH THEM, *he it is that loveth Me, and I will love him, and will manifest Myself to him; and I will come to him and make an abode with him,* xiv. 15 to 21. *By this is my Father glorified, that* YE BEAR MUCH FRUIT, xv. 15, 16. *Not the hearers of the law are justified by God, but the doers of the law,* Rom. ii. 13; James i. 22. *God, in the day of anger and just judgment, will render to every one according to his works,* Rom. ii. 5, 8. *We all must appear before the judgment-seat of Christ, that every one may receive* THE THINGS DONE IN THE BODY ACCORDING TO WHAT HE HATH DONE, *whether good or bad,* 2 Cor

v. 10. *The Son of Man is about to come in the glory of his Father, and then* HE WILL RENDER TO EVERY ONE ACCORDING TO HIS DEEDS, Matt. xvi. 27. *I heard a voice from heaven, saying, Blessed are the dead, who die in the Lord from henceforth, saith the Spirit, that they may rest from their labors,* THEIR WORKS FOLLOW WITH THEM, Rev. xiv. 13. *A book was opened, which is the book of life, and the dead were judged according to those things which were written in the book,* ALL ACCORDING TO THEIR WORKS, xx. 12, 13. *Behold, I come quickly, and my reward is with Me, that I may give to every one* ACCORDING TO HIS WORKS, Rev. xxii. 12. *Jehovah, whose eyes are open upon all the ways of men, to give to every one* ACCORDING TO HIS WAYS, AND ACCORDING TO THE FRUIT OF HIS WORKS, Jerem. xxxi. 19. *I will visit according to his ways, and I will* RENDER TO HIM HIS WORKS, Hosea iv. 9. *Jehovah dealeth with us according to our ways,* AND ACCORDING TO OUR WORKS, Zech. i. 6: besides in a thousand other passages. Whence it may be evident, that charity and faith are not charity and faith, before they are in works, and that, if they are only above works, in the expanse, or in the mind, they are like images of a tabernacle or of a temple in the air, which are nothing but meteors, and disappear of themselves; and that they are like pictures upon paper, which moths consume; as also that they are like habitations upon the house top where there is no bed, and not in the house. Hence, now, it may be seen, that charity and faith are perishable things, while they are only mental, unless, when it can be done, they are determined to works, and coëxist in them.

377. (3.) *That Charity alone does not produce good Works, still less Faith alone, but Charity and Faith together.*

The reason is, because charity without faith is not charity, neither is faith without charity faith, as was shown above, n. 355 to 358; wherefore, charity alone is not given, nor faith alone; thence it cannot be said, that charity by itself produces any good works, nor that faith by itself does. The case here is similar to that of the will and the understanding. A solitary will does not exist, wherefore it does not produce any thing; neither does a solitary understanding exist, and hence does not produce any thing; but all production is effected by both together, and it is effected by the understanding from the will. That it is similar, is, because the will is the habitation of charity, and the understanding is the habitation of faith. It is said, *Still less does faith alone;* it is because faith is truth, and the operation of it is to do truths, and these illuminate charity and its exercises. That they illuminate, the Lord teaches by saying, *He who doeth the truth, cometh to the light, that his works may be manifested, since they are done in God,* John iii Wherefore, when man does good works according to truths, he does them in the light, that is, intelligently and wisely. The conjunction of charity and faith is like the marriage of husband and wife. All natural offspring are born from the husband as father, and from the wife as mother; in like manner, all spiritual offspring, which are the knowledges of good and truth, are born from charity as father, and from faith as mother. From this the generation of spiritual families may be known. In the Word, also, in the spiritual sense, by husband and father is signified the good of charity, and by wife and mother the truth of faith. Hence also it is manifest, that not charity alone nor faith alone can produce good works, as neither a husband alone, nor a wife alone, can produce any offspring. The truths of faith not only illuminate charity, but they also qualify it, and, moreover, nourish it, wherefore, a man who has charity and not the truths of faith, is like one walking in a garden in the time of night, who plucks fruit from the trees, and knows not whether it be of good use, or of bad use. Since the truths of faith not only illuminate charity, but also qualify it, as was said, it follows, that charity, without the truths of faith, is like fruit without juice, like a parched fig, and like a grape after the wine is pressed out of it; since truths nourish faith, as was also said, it follows, that, if charity is without the truths of faith, it has no other nourishment than man has from eating burnt bread, and at the same time drinking dirty water from some pond.

378. IX. THAT THERE IS A TRUE FAITH, A SPURIOUS FAITH, AND A HYPOCRITICAL FAITH.

The Christian church, in its infancy, began to be infested and rent asunder by schisms and heresies, and in process of time to be lacerated and mangled, scarcely otherwise than as it is read concerning the man who went down from Jerusalem to Jericho, and was surrounded by robbers, who, after they had stripped him and beaten him, left him half dead, Luke x. 30. Whence it has come to pass, as it is read concerning that church in Daniel; *At length upon the bird of abominations shall be desolation, and even to consummation and decision, it shall drop upon the devastation*, ix. 27. And according to these words of the Lord; *Then shall the end come, when ye shall see the abomination of desolation foretold by the prophet Daniel*, Matt. xxiv. 14, 15. Its condition may be compared with a ship laden with merchandise of the greatest value, which, as soon as it had got out of the harbor, was immediately tossed about by tempests, and presently, being wrecked in the sea, sunk to the bottom, and then its merchandise is partly corrupted by the water, and partly torn to pieces by fishes. That the Christian church, from its infancy, was so vexed and torn, is evident from ecclesiastical history; e. g., in the very time of the apostles, by SIMON, who was by birth a Samaritan, and by trade a sorcerer, of whom in the Acts of the Apostles, viii. 9, and following verses; and also by HYMENEUS and PHILETUS, who are mentioned by Paul in the epistle to Timothy; as also by NICOLAUS, from whom the Nicolaitans were so called, who are mentioned in Rev. ii. 6, and Acts vi. 5; besides by CERINTHUS. After the times of the apostles, many others rose up, as the MARCIONITES, NOETIANS, VALENTINIANS, ENCRATITES CATAPHRYGIANS, QUARTO-DECIMANS ALOGIANS, CATHARIANS, ORIGENISTS or ADAMITES, SABELLIANS, SAMOSATENES, MANICHÆANS, MELETIANS, and lastly ARIANS. After the times of these, also, troops of heresiarchs invaded the church, as the DONATISTS, PHOTINIANS, ACATIANS or SEMIARIANS, EUNOMIANS, MACEDONIANS, NESTORIANS, PREDESTINARIANS, PAPAEI, ZUINGLIANS, ANABAPTISTS, SCHWENCKFELDIANS, SYNERGISTS, SOCINIANS, ANTITRINITARIANS, QUAKERS, MORAVIANS, besides many others; and at length over these have prevailed LUTHER, MELANCTHON and CALVIN, whose dogmas reign at this day. The causes of so many divisions and seditions in the church are principally three; FIRST, That the Divine Trinity was not understood; SECOND, That there was no just knowledge of the Lord; THIRD, That the passion of the cross was taken for redemption itself. When these three things are unknown, which yet are the very essentials of the faith from which the church is and is called a church, it cannot be otherwise than that all the things of the church should be diverted into the wrong course, and at length into the opposite, and when there, should still believe that it is in the true faith in God, and in the faith of all the truths of God. It is similar with these, as with those who cover their eyes with a handkerchief, and thus in their own fancy walk in a straight line, and yet, step after step, they deviate from it, and at length turn into the opposite direction, where there is a cavern, into which they fall. But the man of the church cannot be led back from his wandering, into the way of truth, except by knowing what is true faith, what is spurious faith, and what is hypocritical faith; wherefore it shall be demonstrated, (1.) *That there is only one true faith, and that it is in the Lord God the Savior Jesus Christ, and that it is with those who believe Him to be the Son of God, the God of heaven and earth, and one with the Father*

(2.) *That spurious faith is every faith which recedes from the true, which is the only one, and that it is with those who climb up some other way, and regard the Lord not as God, but only as a Man.* (3.) *That hypocritical faith is no faith.*

379. (1.) *That there is only one true faith, and that it is in the Lord God the Savior Jesus Christ, and that it is with those who believe Him to be the Son of God, the God of Heaven and Earth, and one with the Father.*

That there is only one true faith, is, because faith is truth, and truth cannot be broken and bisected so that a part of it may look to the left hand, and a part to the right, and remain its truth. Faith, in a general sense, consists of innumerable truths, for it is the complex of them; but those innumerable truths make, as it were, one body, and in that body are the truths which make its members; some make the members which depend on the breast, as the arms and hands; some, those which depend on the loins, as the feet and the soles of the feet; but interior truths make the head, and the truths proximately proceeding thence make the sensories, which are in the face. The reason why interior truths make the head, is, because, when interior is named, superior also is understood; for in the spiritual world, all interior things are also superior; it is so with the three heavens there. The soul and life of this body and of all its members, is the Lord God the Savior; thence it is, that the church is called by Paul the body of Christ, and that the men of the church, according to the states of charity and faith with them, make its members. That there is only one true faith, Paul also teaches thus; *There is one body and one spirit, one Lord,* ONE FAITH, *one baptism, one God. He gave the work of the ministry for the edification of* THE BODY OF CHRIST, *until we all come into* THE UNITY OF THE FAITH, *and the knowledge of the Son of God, and into a life perfected according to the measure of the age of the fulness of Christ,* Ephes. iv. 4, 5, 6, 12, 13. That the true faith, which is the only one, is in the Lord God the Savior Jesus Christ, was fully shown above, n. 337, 338, 339. But the reason why the true faith is with those who believe the Lord to be the Son of God, is, because they also believe that He is God; and faith is not faith unless it be in God. That this article of faith is the primary thing of all the truths which enter into faith and form it, is evident from the words of the Lord to Peter, when he said, THOU ART THE CHRIST, THE SON OF THE LIVING GOD; *Blessed art thou, Simon. I say unto thee, upon this rock I will build my church, and the gates of hell shall not prevail against it,* Matt. xvi. 16, 17. By rock, here, as elsewhere in the Word, is meant the Lord as to Divine Truth, and also divine truth from the Lord. That this truth is the primary thing, and like a diadem upon the head, and like a sceptre in the hand of the body of Christ, is evident from the words of the Lord, That upon that rock He would build his church, and that the gates of hell should not prevail against it. That this article of faith is such, is evident, also, from these words in John: *Whosoever confesseth that Jesus is the Son of God, God abideth in him, and he in God,* 1 John iv. 15. Besides this characteristic of their being in the true faith, which is the only faith, there is also another, *That they believe the Lord to be the God of heaven and earth.* This follows from the former, That He is the Son of God; and from these declarations, *That in Him is all the fulness of the Godhead,* Colos. ii. 9. *That He is the God of heaven and earth,* Matt. xxviii. 18. *That all things of the Father are His,* John iii. 35; xvi. 15. The third sign, that those who believe in the Lord are interiorly in faith in Him, thus in the true faith, which is the only one, is, that they believe, *That the Lord is one with the Father.* That He is one with the Father, and that He is the Father himself in the Human, was fully shown in the chapter concerning the Lord and Redemption, and is very evident from the words of the Lord himself; *That the*

Father and He are one, John x. 30. *That the Father is in Him, and He in the Father*, x. 38; xiv. 10, 11. That He said to the disciples, *That henceforth they have seen and known the Father;* and that he looked at Philip and said, *That now he seeth and knoweth the Father*, John xiv. 7, and following verses. The reason why these three are characteristic testimonies that they are in faith in the Lord, thus in the true faith, which is the only one, is, because all those who go to the Lord, are in faith in Him; for true faith is internal, and at the same time external. Those with whom those three precious characteristics of faith are, are in the internals of that faith, as well as in its externals; thus it is not only a treasure in their heart, but also a jewel in their mouth. But it is otherwise with those who do not acknowledge Him the God of heaven and earth, and not one with the Father; these interiorly look also to other Gods, who have like power, but that it is to be exercised by the Son, either as a Vicar, or as one who, on account of redemption, deserved to reign over those whom He redeemed. But these break the true faith to pieces, by a division of the unity of God, and when it is broken to pieces, it is no longer faith, but only the spectre of faith, which, being seen naturally, appears like a certain image of it, but being seen spiritually, it becomes a chimera. Who can deny but that true faith is in one God, who is the God of heaven and earth; consequently, in God the Father in the human form, thus in the Lord? These three characters, evidences and marks, that faith in the Lord is faith itself, are like touchstones, by which gold and silver are known. They are, also, like stones and hands in the highways, which show the way to the temple, where the one and the true God is worshipped. And they are like lamps upon rocks in the sea, from which those who sail in the night know where they are, and by what wind to direct the ships. The first character of faith, which is, that the Lord is the Son of the living God, is like the morning star, to all who enter into His church.

380. (2.) *That spurious Faith is every Faith which recedes from the true, which is the only one, and that it is with those who climb up some other way, and regard the Lord not as God, but only as a Man.*

That spurious faith is every faith which recedes from the true, which is the only one, is manifest of itself; for when one only is true, it follows that that which recedes is not true. All the good and truth of the church are propagated from the marriage of the Lord and the church; thus all that is essentially charity and essentially faith, is from that marriage; but whatever of those two is not from that, is not from a legitimate, but from an illegitimate bed; thus either from a polygamical bed or marriage, or from adultery. Every faith which acknowledges the Lord, and adopts the falses of heresies, is from a polygamical marriage; and the faith is from adultery, which acknowledges three Lords of one church, for it is either like a female who is a harlot, or like a woman who is married to one man and passes nights with two others, and when she lies with them, she calls each of them her husband. Thence it is, that such faith is called spurious. These the Lord, in many places, calls adulterers; and also He means these by thieves and robbers in John; *Verily I say unto you, he that goeth not in through the door into the sheep-fold, but climbeth up some other way, is a thief and a robber. I am the Door; if any one enter through Me, he shall be saved*, x. 1, 9. To enter into the sheep-fold is to enter into the church, and also into heaven; that it is also into heaven, is, because they make one, and nothing else makes heaven but the church there; wherefore, as the Lord is the Bridegroom and Husband of the church, so also He is the Bridegroom and Husband of heaven. It may be discovered and known, whether faith be a legitimate offspring, or whether it be a spurious offspring, from the three marks of it, mentioned above, which are, The acknowledgment of the Lord as the Son of God; The acknowledgment of Him as the God of heaven and earth; and The acknowledgment, that He is one with the Father. As far, therefore, as any faith recedes from these its essentials, so far it is spurious. A spurious and at the same time an adulterous faith is with those who regard the Lord not as God, but only as a man. That it is so, is very manifest from the two abominable heresies, the ARIAN and SOCINIAN, which were anathematized in the Christian church, and excommunicated from it; and that, because they deny the divinity of the Lord, and climb up some other way. But I fear that those abominations lie concealed in the general spirit of the men of the church at this day. This is wonderful, that the more any one thinks himself superior to others in learning and judgment, the more readily he embraces and appropriates to himself ideas concerning the Lord, that He is a man, and not God; and that, because He is a man, He cannot be God; and he who appropriates to himself those ideas, introduces himself into the company of Arians and Socinians, who in the spiritual world are in hell. The reason why the general spirit of the men of the church at this day is such, is, because there is with every man an associate spirit; for man without that cannot think analytically, rationally and spiritually; thus he would not be a man, but a brute; and every man attaches to himself a spirit similar to the affection of his will, and thence the perception of his understanding. He who brings himself into good affections, by truths from the Word, and by a life according to them, has joined to him an angel from heaven; but he who brings himself into evil affections, by confirmations of falsities, and by an evil life, has joined to him a spirit from hell; and when the spirit is joined, man enters more and more into a fraternity, as it were, with satans, and then confirms himself, more and more, in falses against the truths in the Word, and in the Arian and Socinian abomination against the Lord. The reason is, because no satan can bear to hear any truth from the Word, nor Jesus named; and, if they do hear these things, they become like furies and run hither and thither, and blaspheme. And then, if light from heaven flows in, they cast themselves headlong into caverns and into their thick darkness, in which they have such light as owls have in the dark, and such as cats have in cellars, when they are hunting after mice. All become such after death, who in heart and faith deny the divinity of the Lord, and the holiness of the Word; their internal man is such, howsoever the external may act the hypocrite, and pretend to be a Christian. That it is so, I know, because I have seen and heard. All who honor the Lord, as a Redeemer and Savior, only with the mouth and lips, but in heart and spirit look upon Him as a mere man, while they speak and teach those things, their cheek is like a bladder of honey, but their heart is like a bladder of gall; their words are like cakes of sugar, but their thoughts are like emulsions of poison; and they are like cakes in the hollow of which are serpents. If they are priests, they are like pirates at sea, who hang out the flag of a kingdom of peace, but when a ship approaches them as friends, they raise a piratical flag, in the place of the former, and carry away the ship with its crew into captivity. They are also like serpents of the tree of knowledge of good and evil, which come up like angels of light, holding in their hand apples thence, painted with yellow colors, as if they were plucked from the tree of life; and they reach them out and say, *God doth know, in the day that ye eat of them, your eyes will be opened, and ye will be like God, knowing good and evil*, Gen. iii. 5. And when they have eaten, they follow the serpent into hell, and dwell with him; around that hell are the satans who have eaten of the apples of Arius and Socinus. They are also meant by him who entered having not on a wedding garment, who was cast into outer darkness, Matt. xxvi. 11, 12, 13. The wedding garment is faith in the Lord, as the Son of God, the God of heaven and earth, and one with the Father. Those who honor the Lord only with the mouth and lips, but in heart and spirit look upon Him as a mere man, if they open their thoughts and persuade others, are spiritual murderers, and the worst of them spiritual cannibals; for man has life from love and faith towards the Lord; and if this essential of faith and love, that the Lord is God-Man and Man-God, be removed, his life becomes death; thus, therefore, the man is killed and devoured, as a lamb by a wolf.

381. (3.) *That hypocritical Faith is no Faith.*

Man becomes a hypocrite, whilst he thinks much about himself, and prefers himself to others; for thus he determines and infuses the thoughts and affections of his mind into his body, and conjoins them with its senses; thence he becomes a natural, sensual and corporeal man, and then his mind cannot be withdrawn from the flesh, with which it coheres, and elevated to God, and see any thing of God in the light of heaven, that is, not any thing spiritual; and because he is a carnal man, the spiritual things which enter, which is done through the hearing into the understanding, appear to him no otherwise than spectres, or motes in the air, yea, like flies about the head of a horse running and sweating; wherefore in heart he ridicules them; for it is known, that the natural man regards the things of the spirit, or spiritual things, as foolishness. A hypocrite, among natural men, is to the lowest degree natural, for he is sensual; for his mind is closely connected with the senses of his body, and thence he does not love to think any thing else than what his senses suggest; and the senses, because they are in nature, compel the mind to think concerning every thing from nature, thus also concerning all the things of faith. If that hypocrite becomes a preacher, he retains in his memory such things as are said concerning faith, in the age of childhood and youth; but because there is inwardly in them nothing spiritual, but only what is merely natural, when he produces them in public, they are only inanimate expressions; that they sound as if animated, is from the delights of the love of self and the world, from which they are trumpeted forth according to his eloquence, and soothe the ears, much like the harmonies of music. A hypocritical preacher, after the sermon, when he returns home, laughs at all the things which are concerning faith, and which he had brought forth from the Word before the congregation, and perhaps says with himself, "I have cast a net into the lake, and have caught turbots and shell-fish;" for as such, in his imagination, appear all who are in true faith. A hypocrite is like a carved image having a double head, one within the other; the inner head coheres with the trunk or body, and the outer one, which is movable about the inner, is painted in front with proper colors like a human face, not unlike the wooden heads which are exposed to view at barbers' shops. He is also like a boat, which a sailor, by application of the sail, can direct at pleasure, either with the wind or against the wind; his trimming in favor of every one who indulges the delights of the flesh and its senses is such a managing of the sail. Ministers who are hypocrites, are perfect comedians, buffoons and stage-players, who can represent the persons of kings, dukes, primates and bishops; and presently, when they put off their theatrical garments, go into brothels and cohabit with harlots. They are also like doors hanging on round hinges, which can be turned both ways; such is their mind, for it can be opened towards hell and towards heaven, and when it is opened towards the one, it is shut towards the other; for, what is wonderful, when they are ministering holy things, and teaching from the Word, they know no other than that they believe those things, for the door towards hell is then shut; but presently, when they return home, they do not believe any thing, for then the door towards heaven is shut. With consummate hypocrites there is intestine enmity against truly spiritual men, for it is such as that of satans against the angels of heaven. That it is so is not sensibly perceived by them whilst they live in the world, but it manifests itself after death, when their external, by which they counterfeited the spiritual man, is taken away; since it is their internal man which is such a satan. But I will tell how spiritual hypocrites, who are those *who go in sheep's clothing, and inwardly are ravening wolves,* Matt. vii. 15, appear to the angels of heaven; they appear like soothsayers, walking on the palms of their hands and praying, who with the mouth from the heart cry to demons and kiss them; but strike their shoes together in the air, and thus sound to God; but when they stand upon their feet, they appear as to the eyes like leopards, as to the gait like wolves, as to the mouth like a fox, as to the teeth like crocodiles, and as to faith like vultures.

382. X. That there is no Faith with the Evil.

All those are evil who deny the creation of the world by God, and thus God; for they are atheistical naturalists. The reason why all those are evil, is, because all good, which is not only naturally but also spiritually good, is from God; wherefore, those who deny God are not willing, and therefore are not able, to receive any good from any other source than from their proprium, and the proprium of man is the lust of his flesh; and whatever proceeds from this is spiritually evil, however naturally good it appears. These are theoretically evil; but those are practically evil who despise the divine commandments, which are summarily expressed in the decalogue, and live like lawless people. These also in heart deny God, although many of them confess God with the mouth, because God and his commandments make one; wherefore the ten commandments of the decalogue were called Jehovah there, Num. x. 35, 36; Psalm cxxxii. 7, 8. But that it may be more manifest that the evil have no faith, a conclusion will be made from these two problems: (1.) *That the evil have no faith, because evil is of hell, and faith is of heaven.* (2.) *That all those in Christendom have no faith who reprobate the Lord and the Word, although they live morally, and speak, teach and write rationally, even concerning faith.* But of these one by one.

383. (1.) *That the Evil have no Faith, because Evil is of Hell, and Faith is of Heaven.*

That evil is of hell, is, because all evil is thence; that faith is of heaven, is, because all the truth which is of faith is from heaven. Man, whilst he lives in the world, is held and walks in the middle between heaven and hell, and is there in spiritual equilibrium, which is his free agency; hell is under his feet, and heaven is over his head; and whatever ascends from hell is evil and false, but whatever descends from heaven is good and true. Man, since he is in the middle between those two opposites, and at the same time in spiritual equilibrium, can choose, adopt and appropriate to himself one or the other, freely; if the evil and false, he conjoins himself with hell, but if the good and true, he conjoins himself with heaven. Hence it is manifest, not only that evil is of hell, and faith of heaven, but also that those two cannot be together in one subject or man; for if they were together, man would be distracted, as if he were bound around with two ropes, and drawn by one upwards, and by the other downwards, and thus he would become, as it were, dangling in the air. And it would be as if he should fly, like a blackbird, now upwards, and now downwards; and when upwards, should worship God, and when downwards, should worship the devil; that this is profane, every one sees. That *no one can serve two masters, but must hate one and love the other,* the Lord teaches in Matthew vi. 24. That where evil is there is no faith, may be illustrated by various comparisons, as by these: Evil is like fire (infernal fire is nothing else than the love of evil), and consumes faith like stubble, and reduces it and all that belongs to it to ashes

Evil dwells in darkness, and faith in light; and evil extinguishes faith by falses, as darkness extinguishes the light. Evil is black, like ink, and faith is white, like snow, and clear, like water; and evil blackens faith, as ink does snow and water. Moreover, evil and the truth of faith cannot be conjoined otherwise than as a stinking with an aromatic substance, as urine with delicious wine; and they cannot be together any more than a putrid carcass with a living man in one bed; and they cannot dwell together any more than a wolf in a sheep-fold, and a hawk in a dove-cote, and a fox in a hen-coop.

384. (2.) *That all those in Christendom have no Faith, who reprobate the Lord and the Word, although they live morally, and speak, teach and write rationally, even concerning Faith.*

This follows as a conclusion from all that precedes; for it has been shown, that the faith which is the true and only one, is in the Lord and from the Lord, and that a faith which is not in Him and from Him, is not spiritual faith but natural; and merely natural faith has not in it the essence of faith. Moreover, faith is from the Word; it is not from any other source, because the Word is from the Lord, and thence the Lord himself is in the Word; wherefore He says, that *He is the Word*, John i. 1, 2. Thence it follows, that those who reprobate the Word also reprobate the Lord, for they cohere as one; and also that those who reprobate the one or the other, likewise reprobate the church, because the church is from the Lord through the Word; and further, that those who reprobate the church are out of heaven, for the church introduces into heaven, and those who are out of heaven are among the damned, and these have no faith. The reason why those who reprobate the Lord and the Word have no faith, although they live morally, and speak, teach and write rationally, even concerning faith, is, because their moral life is not spiritual, but natural, and also their rational mind is not spiritual, but natural; and merely natural morality and rationality are in themselves dead; wherefore they, like the dead, have no faith. A man who is merely natural and dead, as to faith, can indeed speak and teach concerning faith, concerning charity, and concerning God, but not from faith, from charity, and from God. That those alone have faith who believe in the Lord, and that others have not faith, is evident from these passages; *He that believeth in the Son, is not judged, but he that believeth not the Son, is now judged, because he hath not believed in the name of the only-begotten Son of God*, John iii. 18. *He that believeth in the Son, hath eternal life, but he that believeth not the Son, shall not see life, but the anger of God abideth on him*, iii. 36. *Jesus said, When the Spirit of truth is come, it will reprove the world of sin, because they believe not in Me*, xvi. 8, 9; and to the Jews, *Unless ye believe that I am, ye shall die in your sins*, viii. 24. Wherefore David says, *I will announce concerning the statute; Jehovah said, Thou art my Son; this day I have begotten Thee. Kiss the Son, lest he be angry, and ye perish in the way. Blessed are all who confide in Him*, Psalm ii. 7, 12. That in the consummation of the age, which is the last time of the church, there would be no faith, because none in the Lord as the Son of God, the God of heaven and earth, and one with the Father, the Lord foretold in the Evangelists, saying, *That there would be the abomination of desolation and affliction, such as hath not been, and will not be. And that the sun will be darkened, and the moon will not give her light, and the stars will fall from heaven*, Matt. xxiv. 15, 21, 29. And in the Revelation, *That Satan, being loosed from his prison, will go forth to seduce the nations, which are in the four corners of the earth, whose number is as the sand of the sea*, xx. 8. And because the Lord foresaw this, He also said, NEVERTHELESS, WHEN THE SON OF MAN COMETH, WILL HE FIND FAITH UPON THE EARTH, Luke xviii. 8

385. To the above will be adjoined these RELATIONS. FIRST. Once, a certain angel said to me, "You wish to see clearly what FAITH and CHARITY are; thus, what faith separate from charity is, and what faith conjoined to charity is; and I will demonstrate them to the eye." I replied, "Do so." And he said, "Instead of faith and charity, think of light and heat and you will see clearly. Faith in its essence is the truth which is of wisdom, and charity in its essence is the affection of love; and the truth of wisdom in heaven is light, and the affection of love in heaven is heat. The light and heat in which the angels are, are in their essence nothing else. Thence you can see clearly what faith separate from charity is, and what faith conjoined to charity is. Faith separate from charity is like the light in winter, and faith conjoined to charity is like the light in spring. The light of winter, which is light separate from heat, because it is conjoined to cold, strips the trees entirely naked, even of leaves, kills the grass, hardens the earth, and congeals the water; but the light of spring, which is light conjoined to heat, causes the trees to vegetate, first into leaves, then into blossoms, and at last into fruits; it opens and softens the earth, that it may produce grass, herbs, flowers and shrubs; and also it melts the ice, that waters may flow from the fountains. Just so it is with faith and charity. Faith separate from charity mortifies or deadens all things, and faith conjoined to charity vivifies or enlivens all things. This *vivification* and that *mortification* may be seen to the life in our spiritual world, because here faith is light, and charity heat; for where faith is conjoined to charity, there are paradisiacal gardens, flower-beds and grass-plots, in their beauty according to conjunction; but where faith separate from charity is, there is not even a blade of grass, and where there is any thing green, it is from briers and brambles." There were then not far off some of the clergy, whom the angel called *justifiers and sanctifiers of men by faith alone*, and also, *dealers in mysteries*. We said these same things to them, and also demonstrated them, so that they might see that it is so; and when we asked whether it was not so, they turned themselves away, and said, "We did not hear." But we cried to them, saying, "Hear now, then." But then they put both hands before their ears and exclaimed, "We do not wish to hear."

After hearing these things, I spoke with the angel concerning solitary faith, and said, that by lively experience it was given me to know, that that faith is like the light of winter; and I told him, that, for several years, spirits of various kinds of faith had passed by me, and that as often as those who separated faith from charity came near, such a cold seized my feet, and afterwards my loins, and at last my breast, that I scarcely knew but that all the vital principle of my body was about to be extinguished, which also would have happened, unless the Lord had driven away those spirits and liberated me. This seemed to me wonderful, that those spirits did not feel any cold in themselves; this they confessed; wherefore I compared them with fishes under the ice, which also do not feel any cold, since their life, and thence their nature, is in itself cold. I perceived, then, that that cold emanated from the fatuous light of their faith, in like manner as is done from marshy and sulphureous places at times in the middle of winter, after the sun has set. such fatuous and cold light travellers often see. They may be compared to mountains of mere ice, torn from their places in northern climates, which are wafted in the ocean here and there, concerning which I have heard it related, that, on their approach, all who are on board begin to shiver from the cold. Wherefore, companies of those who are in faith separate from charity, may be likened to those mountains, and, if you please, may also be called so. It is known, from the Word, that faith without charity is dead; but I will tell whence the death of it is: its death is from cold, from which that faith expires, like a bird in a severe frost, which first dies as to seeing, then at the same time as to flying, and at last as to breathing; and then it falls down headlong from the branch into the snow, and is there buried.

386. SECOND RELATION. One morning, being awaked from sleep, I saw two angels descending from heaven, one from the south of heaven, and the other from the east of heaven, both in chariots, to which were attached white horses. The chariot in which the angel from the south of heaven was carried, shone as from silver, and the chariot in which the angel from the east of heaven was carried, shone as from gold, and the reins which they held in their hands, glittered as from the flamy light of the morning. Thus those two angels seemed to me, at a distance; but when they came near, they did not appear in a chariot, but in their angelic form, which is human. He who came from the east of heaven, was dressed in garments of shining purple, and he who came from the south of heaven, in garments of violet blue. When they were under the heavens, in the lower regions, they ran one to the other, as if they were striving to see which would be first, and mutually embraced and kissed each other. I heard that those two angels, while they lived in the world, were joined together in an interior friendship; but now, one was in the eastern heaven, and the other in the southern heaven: in the eastern heaven are those who are in love from the Lord, but in the southern heaven are those who are in wisdom from the Lord. When they had conversed together for some time concerning the magnificent things in their heavens, this came into their discourse, "Whether heaven in its essence be love, or whether it be wisdom." They agreed immediately that one is of the other; but the question, which was the original, they discussed. The angel who was from the heaven of wisdom, asked the other, "What is love?" And he replied, "That love originating from the Lord, as a sun, is the heat of the life of angels and men, thus the *esse* of their life; and that the derivations of love are called affections, and that by these are produced perceptions, and thus thoughts; whence it flows, that wisdom in its origin is love; consequently, that thought in its origin is the affection of that love; and that it may be seen from the derivations viewed in their order, that thought is nothing else than the form of affection; and that this is not known, because thoughts are in light, but affections in heat; and that, therefore, one reflects upon thoughts, but not upon affections. That thought is nothing else than the form of the affection of some love, may also be illustrated by speech, in that this is nothing else than the form of sound; it is also similar, because sound corresponds to affection, and speech to thought; wherefore affection sounds, and thought speaks. This also may be made perspicuous, when it is said, Take away sound from speech, and is any thing of speech given? In like manner, take away affection from thought, and is any thing of thought given? Thence, now, it is manifest, that love is the all of wisdom; hence, that the essence of the heavens is love, and that their existence is wisdom; or, what is the same, that the heavens are from the divine love, and that they exist from the divine love by the divine wisdom. Wherefore, as was said before, one is of the other." There was with me a novitiate spirit, who, hearing this, asked, whether it is similar with charity and faith, because charity is of affection, and faith is of thought. And the angel replied, "It is altogether similar; faith is no other than the form of charity, just as speech is the form of sound; faith also is formed by charity, as speech is formed by sound. We in heaven know also the mode of formation, but there is not leisure to explain it here." He added, "By faith I understand spiritual faith, in which alone there is life and spirit from the Lord by charity; for this is spiritual, and by it faith becomes so. Wherefore faith without charity is merely natural faith, and this faith is dead; it

also conjoins itself with merely natural affection, which is no other than concupiscence. The angels spoke concerning these things spiritually; and spiritual speech embraces thousands of things which natural speech cannot express; and, what is wonderful, which cannot even fall into the ideas of natural thought." After the angels had conversed on this and that, they departed; and when they returned each to his own heaven, there appeared stars around their heads; and when they were removed to a distance from me, they seemed again in chariots, as before.

387. THIRD RELATION. After those two angels were out of my sight, I saw at the right side a garden, where were olives, fig-trees, laurels, and palms, placed in order according to correspondences. I looked thither, and saw angels and spirits walking and talking together among the trees. And then one of the angelic spirits looked at me, (those are called angelic spirits, who are in the world of spirits preparing for heaven); he came from that garden to me, and said, "Will you come with me into our paradise, and you shall hear and see wonderful things?" And I went with him. And then he said to me, "These, whom you see (for there were many), are all in the love of truth, and thence in the light of wisdom. There is also a palace here, which we call THE TEMPLE OF WISDOM; but no one can see it, who believes himself to be very wise, still less can he who believes himself to be wise enough, and, least of all, he who believes himself to be wise from himself; the reason is, because those are not in the reception of the light of heaven, from the love of genuine wisdom. Genuine wisdom is, that a man sees, from the light of heaven, that what he knows, understands and comprehends (*sapit*), is as little, compared with what he does not know, understand and comprehend, as a drop of water is to the ocean; consequently, scarcely any thing. Every one who is in this paradisiacal garden, and, from perception and sight in himself, acknowledges that he has respectively so little wisdom, sees that TEMPLE OF WISDOM, for interior light in the mind of man enables him to see it, but not his exterior light without that. Now, because I have often thought that, and from science, and then from perception, and at last from interior light, have acknowledged that man has so little wisdom, lo, it was given me to see that temple. It was, as to form, admirable; it was very elevated above the ground, quadrangular, the walls were of crystal, the roof of transparent jasper, elegantly arched; the foundation of various precious stones; the steps by which they ascended into it were of polished alabaster; at the sides of the steps there appeared, as it were, lions with whelps. And then I asked whether I might enter, and it was said that I might; wherefore I ascended, and when I entered I saw, as it were, cherubs flying under the roof, but presently vanishing. The floor upon which we walked was of cedar, and the whole temple, from the transparence of the roof and walls, was built to a form of light. The angelic spirit entered with me, and I related to him what I had heard from the two angels concerning LOVE and WISDOM, and concerning charity and faith; and then he said, "Did they not speak also concerning a third?" And I said, "What third?" He replied, "It is THE GOOD OF USE. Love and wisdom, without the good of use, are not any thing; they are only ideal entities, nor do they become real, before they are in use; for love, wisdom and use are three things which cannot be separated; if they are separated, neither is any thing. Love is not any thing without wisdom, but in wisdom it is formed to something; this something, to which it is formed, is use; wherefore, when love by wisdom is in use, then it really is, because it actually exists. They are just like end, cause and effect; the end is not any thing unless by the cause it be in the effect; if one be loosed from those three, the whole is loosed, and becomes as nothing. It is similar with charity, faith and works. Charity without faith is not any thing, neither is faith without

charity, nor charity and faith without works; but in works they are something, and such a something as the use of the works is. It is similar with affection, thought, and operation, and it is similar with will, understanding, and action; for the will without the understanding is like the eye without sight; and both without action are like a mind without a body; that it is so, may be clearly seen in this temple, because the light in which we are here is a light enlightening the interiors of the mind. Geometry also teaches that there is nothing complete and perfect, unless it be a trine; for a line is not any thing, unless it become an area, nor is an area any thing, unless it become a body; wherefore one must be drawn into another, that they may exist, and they coëxist in the third. As it is in this, it is also in all created things, each of which is terminated in a third. Thence now it is, that in the Word the number three signifies what is complete and perfect. Since it is so, I could not but wonder that some profess faith alone, some charity alone, and some works alone, when yet one without another, or any two together, without the third, is not any thing." But then I asked, "Cannot a man have charity and faith, and still not works? Cannot a man be in affection and thought concerning something, and yet not in the operation of it?" And the angel answered me, "He can only ideally, but not really; he will still be in the endeavor or will to operate, and will or endeavor is in itself an act, because it is a continual striving to act, which becomes, by determination, an act in externals: wherefore, endeavor and will, as an internal act, is accepted by every wise man, because it is accepted by God, altogether as an external act, provided it do not fail when opportunity is given."

388. FOURTH RELATION. I spoke with some who, in the Revelation, are meant by the dragon; and one of them said, "Come with me, and I will show you the delights of our eyes and hearts." And he led me through a dark woods to the top of a hill from which I could see the delights of the dragons; and I saw an amphitheatre built in the form of a circus, with rows of benches round about, raised one above another, upon which the spectators sat. Those who sat upon the lowest benches, appeared to me at a distance like satyrs and priapuses, some with a covering over the parts which should be concealed, and some naked without that. On the benches above them sat whoremongers and harlots; such they appeared to me from their gestures. And then the dragon said to me, "Now you will see our sport." And I saw let into the area of the circus, as it were, bullocks, rams, sheep, kids and lambs; and after those were let in, the gate was opened, and there rushed in, as it were, young lions, panthers, tigers and wolves, and with fury they attacked the flock, tore them in pieces and killed them. But the satyrs, after that bloody slaughter, scattered sand upon the place where the slaughter was made. Then said the dragon to me, "These are our sports, which delight our minds." And I replied, "Begone, demon; after some time you will see this amphitheatre converted into a lake of fire and sulphur." At these words, he laughed and went away. And afterwards I thought with myself, why such things are permitted by the Lord; and I received an answer in my heart, that they are permitted as long as they are in the world of spirits, but when their time in that world has passed, such theatrical scenes are turned into infernal horrors. All those things which were seen were induced by the dragon by fantasies; wherefore there were no bullocks, rams, sheep, kids and lambs, but they made the genuine goods and truths of the church, which they hated, appear so. The lions, panthers, tigers and wolves were appearances of the lusts with those who seemed like satyrs and priapuses. Those without a covering about the parts which should be concealed were those who believed that evils do not appear in the sight of God; and those with a covering were those who believed that they do appear, but do not

condemn, provided they are in faith. The whoremongers and harlots were falsifiers of the truths of the Word; for whoredom signifies falsification of the truth. In the spiritual world, all things appear at a distance, according to correspondences; which, when they appear in forms, are called representations of spiritual things in objects similar to natural.

Afterwards, I saw them going out of the woods, the dragon in the midst of the satyrs and priapuses, and the waiters and drudges, who were whoremongers and harlots, behind them. Their number was increased on the way, and then I heard what they spoke one to another. They said, that they saw in a meadow a flock of sheep with lambs, and that this was a sign that one of the Jerusalem cities, where charity is the primary thing, was near. And they said, "Let us go and take that city, and cast out the inhabitants, and plunder their goods." They came to it, but there was a wall around it, and guardian angels upon the wall. And then they said, "Let us take it by stratagem; let us send some one skilled in muttering, who can make black white, and white black, and disguise the reality of every object. And there was found one skilled in the art of metaphysics, who could turn the ideas of things into ideas of terms, and conceal the things themselves under formulas, and thus fly away like a hawk with the prey under his wings. He was instructed how he should speak with the inhabitants of the city, "That they were consociates with them in religion, and should be admitted." So, coming to the gate, he knocked; and when it was opened, he said that he wished to speak with the wisest man of that city; and he entered, and was led to a certain one, and then he spoke to him, saying, "My brethren are out of the city, and they request that they may be received. They are consociates with you in religion. You and we make faith and charity the two essentials of religion; the only difference is, that you say that charity is the primary one, and faith is thence; and we say that faith is the primary one, and charity is thence. Of what consequence is it, if one or the other be called the primary, when both are believed?" The wise man of the city replied, "Let us not talk on this subject alone, but in the presence of several, who may be witnesses and judges; or else no decision is made." And presently they were sent for, to whom the dragonist spoke the same things as before. And then the wise man of the city replied, "You said, that it is the same thing whether charity or faith be taken as the primary thing of the church, provided they both make the church and its religion; and yet the difference between them is like that between prior and posterior, between cause and effect, between the principal and the instrumental, and between the essential and the formal; I say such things, because I perceive that you are expert in the art of metaphysics, which art we call muttering, and some call it incantation. But let us leave those terms; the difference is as between that which is above, and that which is below; yea, if you will believe it, the difference is as between the minds of those who dwell in the higher regions, and the minds of those who dwell in the lower regions, in this world; for that which is primary makes the head and the breast, and that which is thence makes the feet and the soles of the feet. But let us agree, in the first place, what charity is, and what faith is; that charity is the affection of the love of doing good to the neighbor for the sake of God, salvation and eternal life, and that faith is thought from trust concerning God, salvation and eternal life. But the emissary said, "I grant that this is faith, and also I grant that charity is that affection for the sake of God, because for the sake of his command, but not for the sake of salvation and eternal life." After this agreement and disagreement, the wise man of the city said, "Is not affection or dilection the primary, and thought thence?" But the emissary of the dragon said, "I deny this." But he received for answer, "You cannot deny it Does not man think from some dilection? Take away dilection, can he think any thing? It is just as if you should take away sound from speech. If you should take away sound, could you speak any thing? Sound also is of some affection of love, and speech is of thought, for love sounds and thought speaks. It is also like flame and light; if you take away flame, does not the light perish? It is similar with charity, because this is of love, and with faith, because this is of thought. Can you not thus conceive that the primary is all in the secondary, just like flame and light? Whence it is manifest, that if you do not make that primary which is the primary, you are not in the other; wherefore, if you put faith, which is in the second place, in the first, you would not appear otherwise in heaven than like an inverted man, whose feet stand upwards and his head downwards; or like a soothsayer, who, with his body inverted, walks upon the palms of his hands. Since you appear so in heaven, what then are your good works, which are charity in act, but such as that soothsayer would do with his feet, because he cannot with his hands? Thence it is that your charity is natural and not spiritual, because it is inverted." The emissary understood this, for every devil can understand what is true when he hears it, but he cannot retain it, because the affection of evil, which in itself is the lust of the flesh, when it returns, casts out the thought of truth. And afterwards the wise man of the city showed at large what faith is, when it is received as the primary thing; that it is merely natural, and that it is persuasion without any spiritual life; consequently, that it is not faith. And "I can almost say that in your faith there is no more spirituality than in thought concerning the mogul's kingdom, concerning the diamond mines there, and concerning the treasure and palace of that emperor." On hearing these words, the dragonist went away angry, and related them to his companions out of the city; and when they heard that it was said that charity is the affection of the love of doing good to the neighbor for the sake of salvation and eternal life, they all exclaimed, "This is a lie!" and the dragon himself, "Oh, horrible! are not all the works which are works of charity for the sake of salvation, meritorious?" Then they said to each other, "Let us call together still more of our companions, and let us besiege this city, and cast out those charities." But when they attempted to do this, behold, there appeared, as it were, fire from heaven, which consumed them; but the fire from heaven was the appearance of anger and hatred against those who were in the city, since they cast down faith from the first place to the second, yea, to the lowest under charity, because they said that it was not faith. The reason why they appeared to be consumed, as by fire, was because hell was opened under their feet, and they were swallowed up. Things similar to these happened in many places on the day of the last judgment, which also is meant by this in the Revelation; *The dragon will go forth to seduce the nations which are in the four corners of the earth, that he may gather them together for war; and they went up on the surface of the earth, and encompassed the camp of the saints and the beloved city; but fire came down from God out of heaven and consumed them*, xx. 8, 9.

389. Fifth Relation. Once a paper was seen sent down from heaven to a society in the world of spirits, where were two prelates of the church, with canons and presbyters under them. In that paper there was an exhortation that they should acknowledge the Lord Jesus Christ as the God of heaven and earth, as He himself taught, Matt. xxviii. 18; and that they should recede from the doctrine concerning faith justifying without the works of the law, because it is erroneous. That paper was read and copied by many, and concerning those things which were in it, many thought and spoke from judgment. But after they received it, they said among themselves, "Let us hear the prelates." And they were heard, but they spoke against it and

disapproved of it. The prelates of that society were hard in heart, from the falses imbued in the former world; wherefore, after a short consultation among themselves, they sent the paper back to heaven, whence it came; whereupon, after some murmuring, most of the laity receded from their former opinion, and then the light of their judgment in spiritual things, which before shone bright, was suddenly extinguished. After they were admonished again, but in vain, I saw that society sinking down, but how deep I did not see; so it was removed from the sight of those who worship only the Lord, and hold in aversion the doctrine of justification by faith alone. But after some days, I saw almost a hundred ascending from the lower earth, to which that little society sunk down, who came to me, and one of them spoke and said, "Hear a wonderful thing. When we had sunk down, the place appeared to us like a pond, but presently like dry land, and afterwards like a little city, in which many had each his own house. The next day we consulted among ourselves what should be done; many said that it was best to go to those two prelates of the church and reprove them mildly, because they had sent the paper back to heaven, from which it was sent down, and on account of that this had happened to us. They also chose some, who went to the prelates (and he who spoke with me said that he was one of them), and then one among us, who excelled in wisdom, spoke to the prelates thus: 'We believed that we, above others, had the church among us and religion, because we heard it said that we were in the greatest light of the gospel; but there was given to some of us illustration from heaven, and in the illustration a perception that at this day there is no longer any church in the Christian world, because there is no religion.' The prelates said, 'What do you say? Is not the church where the Word is, where Christ the Savior is known, and where the sacraments are?' To this our speaker replied, 'Those things are of the church, for they make the church but they do not make it without man, but within him.' Moreover, he said, 'Can the church be, where three Gods are worshipped? Can the church be, where its whole doctrine is founded upon one single saying of Paul, falsely understood, and thence not upon the Word? Can the church be, whilst the Savior of the world, who is the very God of the church, is not approached or addressed? Who can deny that religion is to shun evil and do good? Is it any religion, that faith alone saves, and not charity at the same time? Is there religion where it is taught that the charity proceeding from man is nothing but moral and civil charity? Who does not see that in that charity there is not any thing of religion? Is there in faith alone any thing of deed or work, when yet religion consists in doing? Is there a nation in all the world which excludes every thing saving from the goods of charity, which are good works, when yet all of religion consists in good, and all of the church in doctrine, which teaches truths, and by truths goods? What glory we should have had, if we had accepted those things which the paper sent down from heaven brought in its bosom!' Then the prelates said, 'You speak too loftily. Is not *faith in act*, which is faith fully justifying and saving, the church? And is not *faith in state*, which is faith proceeding and perfecting, religion? Apprehend this, children.' But then our wise companion said, 'Hear, O fathers; does not man conceive *faith in act* as a log, according to your dogma? Can a log be vivified into a church? Is not *faith in state*, according to your idea, a continuation and progression of *faith in act?* And since, according to your dogma, every thing saving is in faith, and not any thing in the good of charity from man, where then is religion?' Then the prelates said, 'You speak so, friend, because you do not know the mysteries of justification by faith alone; and he who does not know them, does not know the way of salvation internally: your way is external and plebeian. Go in that way, if you will, but only know that all good is from God, and nothing from man, and that thus man can do nothing, in spiritual things, from himself. How, then, can man do the good, which is spiritual good, from himself?' To this our speaker, being very indignant, replied, 'I know your mysteries of justification better than you do, and I plainly tell you, that inwardly in your mysteries I have seen nothing but spectres. Is not religion to acknowledge God, and to hate and shun the devil? Is not God good itself, and the devil evil itself? Who, in the whole world, that has any religion, does not know this? And is not doing good acknowledging and loving God, because this is of God and from God? And is not shunning and hating the devil, not to do evil, because this is of the devil and from the devil? Does your *faith in act*, which you call fully justifying and saving faith, or, what is the same, your act of justification by faith alone, teach you to do any good, which is of God and from God? And does it teach you to shun any evil, which is of the devil and from the devil? No, not at all; because you maintain that there is nothing of salvation in either. What is your *faith in state*, which you call faith proceeding and perfecting, but the same with *faith in act?* How can this be perfected, since you exclude all good from man, as from himself, by saying, in your mysteries, How can man be saved by any good from himself, when salvation is a free gift? And what good comes from man, but that which is meritorious? and yet all merit belongs to Christ. Wherefore, to do good for the sake of salvation, would be to attribute to one's self what belongs to Christ alone; thus also it would be to wish to justify and save one's self. Again, how can any one perform what is good, when the Holy Spirit performs all, without any help of man? What need, then, is there of any accessory good from man, since all the good from man, in itself, is not good? besides many other things. Are not these your mysteries? But, in my eyes, they are mere subtleties and artifices, contrived for the purpose of removing good works, which are the goods of charity, in order to establish your faith alone; and because you do this, you regard man, as to that, and in general, as to all spiritual things, which are those of the church and religion, as a log, or as a lifeless image, and not as a man, created in the image of God, to whom was given, and continually is given, the faculty of understanding and willing, of believing and loving, and of speaking and doing, altogether as from himself, especially in spiritual things, because man is man from them. If man, in spiritual things, did not think and operate as from himself, what then is the Word; what then is the church and religion, and what then is worship? You know that to do good to the neighbor from love is charity, but you do not know what charity is, when yet charity is the soul and essence of faith; and because charity is both of those, what then is faith, removed from charity, but dead? and dead faith is nothing but a spectre. I call it a spectre, since James calls faith, without good works, not only dead, but also devilish.' Then one of those prelates, when he heard his faith called dead, devilish, and a spectre, became so angry, that he pulled off the cap from his head, and threw it upon the table, saying, 'I will not take that up again until I have punished the enemies of the faith of our church;' and he shook his head, muttering and saying, "THAT JAMES! THAT JAMES!" On the front of the cap there was a thin plate, on which was engraved, FAITH ALONE JUSTIFYING. And suddenly there appeared a monster rising out of the earth, with seven heads, which had feet like a bear, a body like a leopard, and a mouth like a lion, altogether similar to the beast which is described Rev. xiii. 1, 2, an image of which was made and worshipped, verses 14, 15. This spectre took the cap from the table, and made it wide at the bottom, and put it on his seven heads; which being done, the earth opened under his feet, and he sunk down. On seeing this, the prelate exclaimed, 'VIOLENCE! VIOLENCE!' Then we went away from them; and lo, there were steps before our eyes, by which we ascended and returned above the earth and into the sight of heaven, where we were before." These things were related to me by that spirit, who, with a hundred others, had ascended from the lower earth.

390. SIXTH RELATION. In the northern region of the spiritual world, I heard, as it were, a roaring of waters; wherefore I went up thither, and when I was near, the roaring ceased, and I heard a noise as from an assembled multitude, and then there was seen a house full of holes, surrounded with a mound, from which that noise was heard. I went to it, and there was a doorkeeper there, whom I asked who were there. He said, "That they were the wise of the wise, who among themselves conclude supernatural things." (He spoke thus from his simple faith.) And I said, "May I go in?" He said, "You may, only you must not talk any, since I have leave to admit gentiles, who stand with me at the door." Wherefore I entered; and, behold, there was a circus, and in the middle of it a pulpit, and a company of wise men, so called, were canvassing the mysteries of their faith; and then the question or proposition subjected to discussion was, "Whether the good which a man does in THE STATE OF JUSTIFICATION by faith, or in its progression after THE ACT, be the good of religion or not." They said, unanimously, that, by the good of religion, is meant the good which contributes to salvation. The discussion was vehement, but those prevailed who said that the goods which a man does in the state or progression of faith are only moral goods, which conduce to prosperity in the world, but contribute nothing to salvation; to this faith only contributes, and they confirmed it thus: "How can any voluntary good of man be conjoined with free grace? Is not salvation of free grace? How can any good from man be conjoined with the merit of Christ? Is not salvation solely by that? And how can the operation of man be conjoined with the operation of the Holy Spirit? Does He not do all without the help of man? Are not those three things alone conducive to salvation in the act of justification by faith, and do not those three continue alone conducive to salvation in the state or progression of it? Wherefore the accessory good from man can in no wise be called the good of religion, which, as was said, contributes to salvation; but, if any one does it for the sake of salvation, since the will of man is in it, and this cannot but regard it as merit, it should rather be called the evil of religion. There were two gentiles standing by the doorkeeper in the porch; and they heard these things, and said one to the other, "These people have not any religion. Who does not see, that to do good to the neighbor for the sake of God, thus with God and from God, is what is called religion?" And the other said, "Their faith has infatuated them." And then they asked the doorkeeper, "Who are those?" The doorkeeper said, "They are wise Christians." And they replied, "You prate, you lie; they are puppet-players, they talk so." And I went away. It was from the divine auspices of the Lord that I went to that house, and that they then deliberated concerning those things, and that it happened as it is described.

391. SEVENTH RELATION. What a desolation of truth and theological leanness there are at this day in the Christian world, was made known to me from conversing with many of the laity and with many of the clergy in the spiritual world. With the latter there is such a spiritual indigence, that they scarcely know any thing else than that there is a trinity—the Father, Son and Holy Spirit; and that faith alone saves; and concerning the Lord Christ, only the historical things concerning Him in the Evangelists; but as to the other things which the Word of both Testaments teaches concerning Him, as that the Father and He are one; that He is in the Father and the Father in Him; that He has all power in heaven and in earth; that it is the will of the Father

that they should believe in the Son, and that he that believeth in Him hath eternal life; besides many other things; these are as unknown and as hidden from them as those things which are at the bottom of the ocean; yea, as those which lie in the centre of the earth; and when those things are produced from the Word and read, they stand as if they heard and did not hear; and they enter into their ears no deeper than the whistling of the wind, or the beating of a drum. The angels, who are at times sent forth by the Lord to visit the Christian societies which are in the world of spirits, thus under heaven, lament exceedingly, saying, "That there is almost as much dulness, and thence darkness, in the things of salvation, as in a speaking parrot; they say also that the learned among them understand, in spiritual and divine things, no more than statues. An angel once related to me the conversation which he had with two of the clergy, one who was in faith separate from charity, another who was in faith not separate. With the one who was in faith separate from charity he spoke thus: "Friend, who are you?" He replied, "I am a Reformed Christian." "What is your doctrine, and thence religion?" He replied, "It is faith." He said, "What is your faith?" He replied, "My faith is, that God the Father sent the Son to take upon Him the damnation of the human race, and that we are saved by that." He then questioned him, by saying, "What more do you know concerning salvation?" He replied, "Salvation is effected by faith alone." He said, further, "What do you know concerning redemption?" He replied, "It was made by the passion of the cross, and the merit of it is imputed by means of that faith." Again, "What do you know concerning regeneration?" He answered, "It is effected by that faith." "Tell what you know concerning love and charity." He replied, "They are tha faith." "Tell what you think concerning the precepts of the decalogue, and concerning the other things in the Word." He replied, "They are in that faith." Then he said, "You will therefore do nothing." He replied, "What shall I do? I cannot do good, which is good, from myself." He said, "Can you have faith from yourself?" He replied, "I do not inquire into this, I shall have faith." At length he said, "Do you know any thing at all more concerning salvation?" He replied, "What more, since salvation is by that faith alone?" But then the angel said, "You answer like one who plays with one note of a harp; I hear nothing but faith; if you know that, and do not know any thing besides, you know nothing. Go and see your companions.' He went and found them in a desert where there was no grass, and he asked why it was so; and it was said, "Because they have nothing of the church."

With him who was in faith conjoined to charity, the angel spoke thus: "Friend, who are you?" He replied, "I am a Reformed Christian." "What is your doctrine, and thence religion?' He replied, "Faith and charity." He said, "These are two things." He replied, "They cannot be separated" He said, "What is faith?" He replied, "To believe what the Word teaches." He said, "What is charity?" He answered, "To do what the Word teaches." He said, "Have you only believed those things, or have you also done them?" He replied, "I have also done them." The angel of heaven then looked at him and said, "My friend, come with me and dwell with us."

CHAPTER VII.

CONCERNING CHARITY, OR LOVE TOWARDS THE NEIGHBOR, AND CONCERNING GOOD WORKS.

392. Having treated concerning Faith, we now proceed to treat concerning Charity, because faith and charity are conjoined like truth and good, and these two like light and heat in the time of spring. This is said, because spiritual light, which is the light which proceeds from the sun of the spiritual world, in its essence is truth; wherefore truth, in that world, wheresoever it appears, shines with splendor according to its purity; and spiritual heat, which also proceeds from that sun, in its essence is good. These things are said, since it is similar with charity and faith as it is with the good and the true; for charity is the complex of all things of good which a man does to the neighbor, and faith is the complex of all things of truth which a man thinks concerning God and concerning things divine. Since, therefore, the truth of faith is spiritual light, and the good of charity is spiritual heat, it follows that it is similar with these two as it is with the two things of the same name in the natural world; namely, that from their conjunction all things upon the earth flourish, so likewise from their conjunction all things in the human mind flourish; but with this distinction, that natural heat and light cause the things upon the earth to flourish, but that spiritual heat and light cause the things in the human mind to flourish, and that this flourishing, because it is spiritual, is wisdom and intelligence. There is also a correspondence between them; wherefore the human mind, in which charity is conjoined to faith, and faith to charity, is in the Word likened to a garden, and is also meant by the garden of Eden; that it is so, has been fully shown in the Arcana Cœlestia, published at London. Moreover, it is to be known, that unless charity should be treated of, after faith has been treated of, it could not be comprehended what faith is; since, as it was said and shown in the preceding chapter, *Faith without charity is not faith, and charity without faith is not charity; and neither of them lives except from the Lord*, n. 355 to 361. And also, *That the Lord, charity and faith make one, like life, will and understanding; and that if they are divided, each perishes, like a pearl reduced to powder*, n. 362 to 367. And moreover, *That charity and faith are together in good works*, n. 373 and the following.

393. It is a constant truth, that charity and faith cannot be separated, and still man have spiritual life, and thence salvation. That it is so, falls of itself into the understanding of every man, even when not cultivated and enriched with the treasures of learning. Who does not see, from some interior perception, and thence assent from the understanding, when he hears any one say, *That whosoever lives well and believes aright, is saved?* And who does not reject it from the understanding, as a lump of dirt falling into the eye, when he hears, *That whosoever believes aright, and does not live well, is also saved?* Since, from an interior perception, it then falls immediately into the thought, how can any one believe aright, when he does not live well? And what, then, is believing but a painted figure of faith, and not a living image of it? In like manner, if any one should hear, *That whosoever lives*

well, although he does not believe, is saved, does not the understanding, while it revolves this, or turns it over and over, see, perceive and think, that this does not cohere, since to live well is from God; for all good, which in itself is good, is from God? What, then, is it to live well, and not to believe, but like clay in the hand of the potter, which is not capable of being formed into any vessel of use in the spiritual kingdom, but only in a natural kingdom? And besides, who does not see a contradiction in those two things, namely, in this, *That he is saved who believes, and does not live well;* and in this, *That he is saved who lives well, and does not believe?* Now, because to live well, which is of charity, is at this day known, and is not known (it is known what it is to live well naturally, and it is not known what it is to live well spiritually); therefore we shall treat concerning this, because it is of charity; which will be done distinctly in a series by articles.

394. I. That there are three universal Loves, the Love of Heaven, the Love of the World, and the Love of Self.

An exordium is made from these three loves, because they are the universal and fundamental of all, and because charity has something in common with each of them; for by THE LOVE OF HEAVEN is meant love to the Lord, and also love towards the neighbor; and because each of these regards use as the end, it may be called the love of uses. THE LOVE OF THE WORLD is not only the love of wealth and possessions, but also the love of all the things which the world affords, and which delight the senses of the body; as beauty the eyes, harmony the ears, fragrance the nostrils, delicacies the tongue, softness the skin; and, moreover, decent clothes, commodious habitations and social parties, thus all the delights from these and from many other objects. THE LOVE OF SELF is not only the love of honor, glory, fame and eminence, but also the love of meriting and procuring offices, and thus of reigning over others. The reason why charity has something in common with each of those three loves, is, because charity, viewed in itself, is the love of uses; for charity wills to do good to the neighbor, and good is the same with use, and each of those loves regards uses as its ends; the love of heaven spiritual uses; the love of the world natural uses, which may be called civil uses; and the love of self corporeal uses, which also may be called domestic uses, for one's self and his own.

395. That those three loves are in every man, from creation, and thence by nativity, and that when they are rightly subordinated they perfect man, and when not rightly subordinated they pervert him, will be demonstrated in the following article; here it is proper only to observe, that those three loves are then rightly subordinated, when the love of heaven makes the head, the love of the world the breast and belly, and the love of self the feet and soles of the feet. The human mind is distinguished into three regions, as has been several times said above; from the highest region man regards God, from the second or middle, the world, and from the third or lowest, himself. The mind, because it is such, can be elevated and can elevate itself upwards, because to God and heaven; it can be diffused and can diffuse itself to the sides in all directions, because into the world and its nature; and it can be lowered and can lower itself downwards, because to the earth and to hell. In these respects the sight of the body emulates the sight of the mind; that also is capable of looking upwards, of looking around, and of looking downwards. The human mind is like a house of three stories, between which there is a communication by means of stairs, in the highest of which dwell angels from heaven, in the middle, men from the world, and in the lowest, *genii* or evil spirits. The man in whom those three loves are rightly subordinated can ascend and descend at pleasure; and when he ascends to the highest story, he is there in company with the angels, as an angel; and

when he descends thence to the middle, he is there in company with men, as a man-angel; and when from this he descends farther, he is in company with *genii*, as a man of the world, and instructs, reproves and tames them. In the man in whom those three loves are rightly subordinated, they are also arranged together in such a manner, that the highest love, which is the love of heaven, is inwardly in the second, which is the love of the world, and by this in the third or lowest, which is the love of self; and the love which is within directs that which is without, at its pleasure; wherefore, if the love of heaven is inwardly in the love of the world, and by this in the love of self, man does uses in each, from the God of heaven. Those three loves in operating are like will, understanding and action. The will flows into the understanding, and there provides for itself means by which it produces action. But more will be seen concerning these in the following article, where it will be demonstrated, that those three loves, if they are rightly subordinated, perfect man; but if they are not rightly subordinated, they pervert and invert him.

396. But in order that those things which follow in this chapter, and in the succeeding ones, concerning Free-Agency, and concerning Reformation and Regeneration, &c., may be set forth in the light of reason, to be clearly seen, it is necessary that some things be premised concerning THE WILL AND THE UNDERSTANDING; concerning GOOD AND TRUTH; concerning LOVE IN GENERAL; concerning THE LOVE OF THE WORLD, AND THE LOVE OF SELF IN PARTICULAR; concerning THE EXTERNAL AND THE INTERNAL MAN; and concerning THE MERELY NATURAL AND SENSUAL MAN. These things shall be laid open, lest the rational sight of man, in contemplating those things which follow hereafter, should be, as it were, in a thick cloud, and in that should, as it were, run through the streets of a city, until he knows not the way home. For what is theological science without understanding, and this illustrated when the Word is read, but as a lamp in the hand without a lighted candle, such as there was in the hands of the five foolish virgins, who had no oil. Concerning each, therefore, in its order.

397. (1.) *Concerning the Will and the Understanding.*

1. Man has two faculties which make his life; one is called the will, and the other the understanding; they are distinct from each other, but so created that they may be one, and when they are one, they are called the mind. Wherefore they are the human mind, and all the life of man is there, in its principles, and thence in the body. 2. As all things in the universe, which are according to order, refer themselves to good and truth, so all the things with man to the will and the understanding; for the good with man is of his will, and the truth with him is of his understanding; for these two faculties, or these two lives of man, are their receptacles and subjects; the will is the receptacle and subject of all of the good, and the understanding is the receptacle and subject of all of the true. The good and the truth with man are not any where else; and because the good and the truth with man are not any where else, thence also love and faith are not any where else, since love is of good, and good is of love, and faith is of truth, and truth is of faith. 3. The will and the understanding also make the spirit of man; for his wisdom and intelligence, and likewise his love and charity, reside there, and in general his life; the body is only obedience. 4. There is nothing which it is more important to know, than how the will and the understanding make one mind; they make one mind as good and truth make one, for there is a similar marriage between the will and the understanding as there is between good and truth; what that marriage is, will be evident from those things which will presently be adduced concerning the good and the true; namely, that as good is the very *esse* of a thing, and truth is the *existere* of a thing thence, so the will

with man is the very *esse* of his life, and the understanding the *existere* of life thence; for the good which is of the will, forms itself in the understanding, and exhibits itself to be seen.

398. (2.) *Concerning Good and Truth.*

1. All things in the universe which are in divine order, refer themselves to good and truth. There is nothing in heaven, and nothing in the world, which does not refer itself to those two; the reason is, because they both, good as well as truth, proceed from God, from whom are all things. 2. Thence it is manifest, that it is necessary for man to know what good is, and what truth is, and how the one has respect to the other, and how one is conjoined to the other. But it is especially necessary for the man of the church; for, as all the things of heaven refer themselves to good and truth, so likewise do all the things of the church, because the good and the truth of heaven are also the good and the truth of the church. 3. It is according to divine order, that good and truth should be conjoined, and not separated, so that they may be one and not two, for they proceed together from God, and they are conjoined in heaven, and therefore they will be conjoined in the church. The conjunction of good and truth is called in heaven the heavenly marriage, for all who are there are in this marriage. Thence it is that in the Word heaven is compared to a marriage, and that the Lord is called a Bridegroom and Husband, and heaven and likewise the church, the bride and wife. The reason why heaven and the church are so called, is, because all who are there receive the divine good in the truth. 4. All the intelligence and wisdom, which the angels have, is from that marriage, and not any from the good separate from the truth, nor from the truth separate from the good; the case is similar with the men of the church. 5. Since the conjunction of good and truth is like a marriage, it is manifest that good loves the truth, and, reciprocally, the truth loves good and that one desires to be conjoined with the other. The man of the church, who has no such love and such desire, is not in the heavenly marriage;' consequently, the church is not as yet in him, since the conjunction of good and the truth makes the church. 6. There are many kinds of good; in general, there is spiritual good and natural good, and both are conjoined in genuine moral good. As goods are, so are truths; because truths are of good and are the forms of good. 7. As it is with good and the truth so it is, as an opposite, with evil and the false; for, as all things in the universe which are according to divine order refer themselves to good and the true, so all the things which are contrary to divine order refer themselves to evil and the false. And as good loves to be conjoined to the truth' and the truth to good, so evil loves to be conjoined to the false and the false to evil. And, also, as all intelligence and wisdom are born from the conjunction of good and the truth, so all insanity and folly are from the conjunction of evil and the false. The conjunction of evil and the false, viewed interiorly, is not a marriage, but adultery. 8. From this, that evil and the false are opposite to good and the truth, it is manifest that the truth cannot be conjoined to evil, nor good to the false of evil; if the truth be adjoined to evil, it becomes no longer true, but false, because it is falsified; and if good be adjoined to the false of evil, it becomes no longer good, but evil, because it is adulterated. But the false, not of evil, may be conjoined to good. 9. No one who is in evil and the false thence from confirmation and life, can know what are good and truth, since he believes his evil to be good, and thence he believes his false to be true; but every one who is in good and the truth thence, from confirmation and life, may know what is evil and false; the reason is, because all the good and its truth are, in their essence, heavenly, but all evil and the false

thence are, in their essence, infernal; and every thing heavenly is in the light, and every thing infernal, in darkness.

399. (3.) *Concerning Love in general.*

1. The very life of man is his love; and as the love is, such is the life, yea, such is the whole man; but it is the ruling or reigning love which makes the man. This love has several loves subordinate to it, which are derivations. These appear in various forms, but still they are every one of them in the ruling love, and with that they make one kingdom. The ruling love is, as it were, their king and head; it directs them, and by them, as by mediate ends, it regards and intends its own end, which is the primary and last of all; and this both directly and indirectly. 2. That which is of the ruling love is what is loved above all things. That which a man loves above all things, is continually present in his thought, because in his will, and makes his veriest life. As, for example, he who loves riches, whether money or possessions, above all things, continually revolves in his mind how he may procure them for himself; he inwardly rejoices when he gains; he inwardly grieves when he loses; his heart is in them. He who loves himself above all things, remembers himself in every thing; he thinks of himself, he speaks of himself, he acts for the sake of himself, for his life is the life of self. 3. A man has for an end what he loves above all things; that he regards in each and every thing; it is in his will, like the latent current of a river, which draws and carries him away, even when he is doing something else, for it is that which animates him. Such is that which one explores in another, and also sees, and by it he either leads him, or acts with him. 4. A man is altogether such as the ruling principle of his life is; by this he is distinguished from others; according to this, his heaven is made, if he is good, and his hell, if he is evil; it is his very will, his proprium, and his nature; for it is the very *esse* of his life. This, after death, cannot be changed, because it is the man himself. 5. All the delight, pleasure and happiness of every one, are from his ruling love, and according to it; for that which a man loves, he calls delightful, because he feels it; but that which he thinks and does not love, he may also call delightful, but it is not the delight of his life. The delight of the love is what is good to a man, and the opposite is what is evil to him. 6. There are two loves, from which, as from their very fountains, all goods and truths exist; and there are two loves from which all evils and falses exist. The two loves from which are all goods and truths, are love to the Lord, and love towards the neighbor; but the two loves from which are all evils and falses, are the love of self, and the love of the world. These two loves, when they rule, are entirely opposite to those two loves. 7. The two loves, which, as was said, are love to the Lord and love towards the neighbor, make heaven with man, for those reign in heaven; and because they make heaven with man, they also make the church with him. The two loves from which are all evils and falses, which, as was said, are the love of self and the love of the world, make hell with man; for those reign in hell; consequently, they also destroy the church with him. 8. The two loves from which are all goods and truths, which, as was said, are the loves of heaven, open and form the internal spiritual man, for they reside there; but the two loves from which are all evils and falses, which, as was said, are the loves of hell, when they rule, shut up and destroy the internal spiritual man, and make man natural and sensual, according to the degree and quality of their dominion.

400. (4.) *Concerning the Love of Self, and the Love of the World in particular.*

1. The love of self is, to wish well to one's self alone, and not to others except for the sake of self, not even to the church, to one's country, to any human society, or to a fellow citizen; as also to do good to them only for the

sake of one's own fame, honor and glory; and unless it sees these in the good which it does them, it says in heart, "What matters it? Why should I do this? What good will it be to me?" And thus he omits it. Whence it is manifest that he who is in the love of self does not love the church, nor his country, nor society, nor his fellow citizen, nor any thing truly good, but only himself and his own. 2. A man is in the love of self, when, in those things which he thinks and does, he does not regard the neighbor, thus not the public, still less the Lord, but only himself and his own; consequently, when he does all things for the sake of himself and his own, and if for the sake of the public, it is only that it may appear, and if for the neighbor, it is only that he may favor him. 3. It is said, *for the sake of himself and his own;* for he who loves himself, also loves his own, which are, in particular, his children and grandchildren, and, in general, all who make one with him, whom he calls his own; to love these and those is also to love himself, for he regards them, as it were, in himself, and himself in them. Among those whom he calls his own, are likewise all who praise, honor and worship him; others, indeed, he looks upon with the eyes of his body, as men, but with the eyes of his spirit, scarcely otherwise than as phantoms. 4. That man is in the love of self, who despises his neighbor in comparison with himself, who esteems him an enemy if he does not favor him, if he does not venerate and worship him. He is still more in the love of self, who, for that reason, hates and persecutes his neighbor; and still more, who, for that reason, burns with revenge against him, and desires his destruction. Such at length love to exercise cruelty. 5. From a comparison with heavenly love, it may be evident what the love of self is. Heavenly love is to love the uses for the sake of uses, or the goods for he sake of goods, which a man performs for the church, for his country, for human society, and for a fellow citizen; but he who loves those things for the sake of himself, loves them only as he loves domestics, because they serve him. Thence it follows, that he who is in the love of self, wishes that the church, his country, human societies, and his fellow citizens should serve him, and not he them; he places himself above them, and them below himself. 6. Further, as far as any one is in heavenly love, which is to love uses and goods, and to be affected with delight of heart in the performance of them, so far he is led by the Lord; because that is the love in which He is, and which is from Him; but as far as any one is in the love of self, so far he is led by himself, and so far he is led by his proprium, and the proprium of man is nothing but evil; for it is his hereditary evil, which is to love himself in preference to God, and the world in preference to heaven. 7. The love of self also is such that, as far as the reins are given to it, that is, as far as external bonds, which are fears for the law and its penalties, and for the loss of fame, honor, gain, office, and life, are removed, so far it rages, even to such a degree that it wishes to rule not only over all the world, but also over heaven, yea, over God himself; it has nowhere any bound or end. This lurks in every one who is in the love of self, although it is not manifest to the world, where the said reins and bonds restrain it; and every such one, where an insuperable obstacle occurs, stops there until it becomes superable; hence it is, that a man who is in such love, does not know that such a vast, unbounded desire lurks within him. That it is so, however, every one may see in potentates and kings, who, not being subject to such reins, bonds and insuperable obstacles, rush forth and subjugate provinces and kingdoms, as far as they succeed, and aspire after unlimited power and glory; and still more in those who extend their dominion to heaven, and transfer to themselves all the divine power of the Lord; these continually desire more. 8. There are two kinds of dominion, one of love towards the neighbor, and the other of the love of self. These two dominions are opposite to each other. He who exercises dominion from love towards the neighbor, wills good to all, and loves nothing more than to perform uses, thus to serve others, for to serve others, is to do good to others from good will, and to perform uses; this is his love, and this is the delight of his heart; he, also, the more he is exalted to dignities, is the more delighted, not on account of the dignities, but on account of the uses which he is then able to perform in greater abundance, and in a larger sphere; such is the dominion in the heavens. But he who exercises dominion from the love of self, wills good to none, but only to himself and his own; the uses which he performs are for the sake of his own honor and glory, which are to him the only uses; his end in serving others is, that he may be served, honored, and exercise dominion; he seeks dignities, not for the sake of the good which he may perform, but that he may be in eminence and glory, and thence in the delight of his heart. 9. The love of dominion or of ruling remains also with every one after the life in the world; but those who have ruled from love towards the neighbor, are also intrusted with the office of ruling in the heavens, and then they do not rule, but the uses and goods which they love, and when uses and goods rule, the Lord rules. But those who, in the world, ruled from the love of self, after the life in the world, are deprived of authority, and are reduced to servitude. Hence now it is known who are in the love of self; it matters not how they appear in the external form, whether elated or submissive, for such things are in the internal man, and the internal man is by most people concealed, and the external is taught to counterfeit those things which are of the love of the public and of the neighbor, thus contrary things; and this also for the sake of self, for they know that the love of the public and of the neighbor interiorly affects all, and that they are so far esteemed; that it does affect, is because heaven flows into that love. 10. The evils which are with those who are in the love of self, are, in general, contempt of others, envy, enmity against those who do not favor them, hostility thence, hatred of various kinds, revenge, cunning, deceit, unmercifulness and cruelty; and where such evils are, there is also a contempt of God and of divine things, which are the truths and goods of the church; if they honor these, it is only with the mouth, and not with the heart. And because such evils are thence, there are also similar falses, for falses are from evils. 11. But THE LOVE OF THE WORLD is, to wish to appropriate to one's self, by any arts whatever, the wealth of others, and to set the heart upon riches, and to suffer the world to draw it back and lead it away from spiritual love, which is love towards the neighbor, thus from heaven. Those are in the love of the world who desire to appropriate to themselves the goods of others by various arts, especially by cunning and deceit, esteeming the good of the neighbor of no account. Those who are in that love covet the goods of others, and, so far as they do not fear the laws, and the loss of fame on account of gain, they deprive them, yea, rob them, of their goods. 12. But the love of the world is not opposed to heavenly love to such a degree as the love of self is, since there are not so great evils concealed in it. 13. That love is manifold; it is the love of wealth, that they may be exalted to honors; it is the love of honors and dignities, that they may gain wealth; it is the love of wealth for the sake of various uses by which they are delighted in the world; it is the love of wealth for the sake of wealth alone; such is the love of misers; and thus in other instances. The end for which wealth is desired is called use, and the end or use is that from which the love derives its quality; for the love is such as the end in view is; other things serve it as means. 14. In a word, the love of self and the love of the world are altogether opposite to love to the Lord and love towards the neighbor; wherefore the love of self and the love of the world, as they have been described above, are infernal loves; they also reign in hell, and likewise make hell with man; but love to the Lord and love towards the neighbor are heavenly loves; they also reign in heaven, and likewise make heaven with man.

401. (5.) *Concerning the Internal and the External Man.*

Man is so created, that he is at the same time in the spiritual world and in the natural world. The spiritual world is where angels are, and the natural world where men are. And because man is so created, therefore there is given to him an internal and an external; an internal, by which he is in the spiritual world, and an external, by which he is in the natural world. His internal is what is called the internal man, and his external what is called the external man. 2. Every man has an internal and an external, but it is different with the good from what it is with the evil. The internal with the good is in heaven and its light, and the external in the world and its light, and this light with them is illuminated by the light of heaven; and thus, with them, the internal and the external act as one, like cause and effect, or like prior and posterior. But with the evil the internal is in hell and in its light, which light, with respect to the light of heaven, is thick darkness, and their external may be in light similar to that in which the good are; wherefore it is inverted. Thence it is that the evil can speak and teach concerning faith, concerning charity, and concerning God, but not like the good, from faith, charity and God. 3. The internal man is what is called the spiritual man, because it is in the light of heaven, which light is spiritual; and the external man is what is called the natural man, because it is in the light of the world, which light is natural. The man whose internal is in the light of heaven, and whose external is in the light of the world, is a spiritual man as to both, for spiritual light from within illuminates the natural light and makes it as its own; but the case is reversed with the evil. 4. The internal spiritual man, viewed in itself, is an angel of heaven, and also, while it lives in the body, is in society with angels, although it does not know it, and after its separation from the body, it comes among the angels. But the internal man, with the evil, is a satan, and also while it lives in the body, it is in society with them, and likewise after its separation from the body it comes among them. 5. The interiors of the mind with those who are spiritual men are actually elevated towards heaven, for they regard that first of all; but the interiors of the mind with those who are merely natural are turned away from heaven, and turned to the world, because they regard this first of all. 6. Those who entertain only a general idea concerning the internal and the external man, believe that the internal man is that which thinks and which wills, and the external that which speaks and which acts; since to think and to will are internal, and to speak and to act are external. But it should be known that when a man thinks and wills well concerning the Lord, and concerning those things which are of the Lord, and likewise concerning the neighbor, and concerning those things which are of the neighbor, he then thinks and wills from a spiritual internal, because from the faith of truth and from the love of good; but that when a man thinks ill concerning them, and wills evil to them, he then thinks and wills from an infernal internal, because from the faith of the false, and from the love of evil. In a word, as far as a man is in love to the Lord and in love to the neighbor, so far he is in a spiritual internal, and from it he thinks and wills, and likewise from it he speaks and acts; but as far as a man is in the love of self and in the love of the world, so far he thinks and wills from hell, although he speaks and acts otherwise 7. It is so provided and ordered by the Lord, that, as far as a man thinks and wills from heaven, so far the spiritual man is opened and formed; the opening is into heaven, even to the Lord, and the forming is to those things which are of heaven. But, on the other hand, as far as a man thinks and wills, not from heaven, but from the world, so far the internal spiritual man is closed, and the external is opened and formed; the opening is into the world, and the forming is to those things which are of hell. 8. Those with whom the internal spiritual man is opened into heaven to the Lord, are in the light of heaven and in illumination from the Lord, and thence intelligence and wisdom; these see truth from the light of truth, and perceive good from the love of good. But those with whom the internal spiritual man is closed, do not know what the internal man is, neither do they believe the Word, nor a life after death, nor those things which are of heaven and the church; and because they are only in natural light, they believe nature to be from itself and not from God; they see the false as true, and perceive evil as good. 9. The internal and external of which we have treated are the internal and external of the spirit of man; his body is only an external superadded, within which they exist; for the body does nothing of itself, but from the spirit which is in it. It should be known that the spirit of man, after its separation from the body, equally thinks and wills, and speaks and acts; to think and will are its internal, and to speak and do are then its external.

402. (6.) *Concerning the merely Natural and Sensual Man.*

Since few know who are meant by sensual men, and what they are, and yet it is important to know, they will therefore be described. 1. He is called a sensual man who judges all things by the senses of the body, and who believes nothing but what he can see with the eyes and touch with the hands, saying, These things are something, and rejecting the rest. Wherefore, a sensual man is, in the lowest degree, a natural man. 2. That the interiors of his mind, which see from the light of heaven, are closed, so that he sees there nothing of the truth which is of heaven and the church, since he thinks in the outermost things, and not interiorly from any spiritual light. 3. And since he is in gross natural light, he is inwardly against those things which are of heaven and the church, and yet outwardly he can speak in favor of them ardently, according to the dominion attainable by means of them. 4. That sensual men reason keenly and shrewdly, because their thought is so near the speech that it is almost in it, and, as it were, in the lips; and because they place all intelligence in the speech from memory alone. 5. That some of them can confirm whatever they please, and falses dexterously; and that after confirmation they believe them to be true; but that they reason and confirm from the fallacies of the senses, by which the common people are captivated and persuaded. 6. That sensual men are cunning and malicious above all others. 7. That the interiors of their mind are foul and filthy, since by them they communicate with the hells. 8. That those who are in the hells are sensual; and the more sensual they are, the deeper they are in hell; and that the sphere of infernal spirits conjoins itself with the sensual things of man from behind. 9. Since sensual men do not see any genuine truth in the light, but reason and dispute about every thing whether it be so, and these disputations are heard at a distance from them like gnashings of the teeth, which, viewed in themselves, are collisions of falses among themselves, and also of the false and the true, it is manifest what is signified by GNASHING OF THE TEETH in the Word; the reason is, because reasoning from the fallacies of the senses corresponds to the teeth. 10. That men of science and erudition, who have deeply confirmed themselves in falses, and especially against the truths of the Word, are sensual above all others, although to the world they do not appear such. That heretical things have flowed chiefly from such as were sensual. 11. That the hypocritical, the deceitful, the voluptuous, the adulterous and the covetous are, for the most part, sensual. 12. That those who reasoned from sensual things alone, and against the genuine truths of the Word, and thence of the church, were called by the ancients, serpents of the tree of the knowledge of good and evil

Since by sensual things are meant the things presented to the senses of the body, and imbibed through those senses, it follows, 13. That man, by sensual things, communicates with the world, and by the rational things above them, with heaven. 14. That sensual things furnish such things from the natural world as serve for the interiors of the mind in the spiritual world. 15. That there are sensual things which furnish the understanding, and that these are the various things which are called physical; and that there are sensual things which furnish the will, and that these are the delights of the senses and of the body. 16. That unless the thought be elevated above sensual things, man has little wisdom; that a wise man thinks above sensual things; and that when the thought is elevated above sensual things, he comes into clearer light, and at length into the light of heaven; thence man has perception of truth, which is properly intelligence. 17. That elevation of the mind above sensual things, and abstraction from them, was known to the ancients. 18. That if sensual things are in the last place, a way is opened by them for the understanding, and truths are polished by the mode of extraction; but that if sensual things are in the first place, that way is closed by them, and man does not see truths except as in a thick cloud, or as in the night. 19. That sensual things, with a wise man, are in the last place, and subject to the interiors; but that, with a foolish man, they are in the first place, and have dominion. These are they who are properly called sensual. 20. That with man there are sensual things in common with beasts, and that there are sensual things not in common with them. That as far as any one thinks above sensual things, so far he is a man; but that no one can think above sensual things, and see the truths of the church, unless he acknowledge God and live according to his commandments; for God elevates and illustrates.

403. II. THAT THOSE THREE LOVES, WHEN THEY ARE RIGHTLY SUBORDINATED, PERFECT MAN; BUT WHEN THEY ARE NOT RIGHTLY SUBORDINATED, THEY PERVERT AND INVERT HIM.

In the first place, something will be said concerning the subordination of those three universal loves, which are the love of heaven, the love of the world, and the love of self; and afterwards concerning the influx and insertion of one into the other; and lastly, concerning the state of man according to subordination. Those three loves, in relation to each other, are like the three regions of the body, the highest of which is the head; the middle is the breast with the belly; and the knees, the feet, and the soles of the feet, make the third. When the love of heaven makes the head, the love of the world the breast with the belly, and the love of self the feet with the soles of the feet, then man is in a perfect state, according to creation; since then the two inferior loves are subservient to the highest, as the body and all its parts to the head. When, therefore, the love of heaven makes the head, it then flows into the love of the world, which is principally the love of riches, and by these it does uses, and mediately through this into the love of self, which is principally the love of dignities, and by these it does uses; so those three loves breathe uses from the influx of one into the other. Who does not comprehend, that when man, from spiritual love, which is from the Lord, and is what is meant by the love of heaven, wills to do uses, the natural man does them by his riches and by his other goods, and the sensual man in his own function, and that it is his honor to produce them? Who also does not comprehend, that all the works which a man does with his body, are done according to the state of his mind in the head, and that, if the mind is in the love of uses, the body, by means of its members, effects them? And this is done, because the will and the understanding, in their principles, are in the head, and in their derivatives, in the body, like will in deeds, and thought in speech; and, comparatively, as the prolific principle of the seed is in the whole and every part of a tree, by which it produces fruits, which are its uses; and it is like fire and light within a crystal vessel, which from them becomes hot and transparent. And also the spiritual sight in the mind, and at the same time the natural sight in the body, with him in whom those three loves are justly and rightly subordinated, from the light which flows in through heaven from the Lord, may be likened to an African apple, which is transparent even to the middle, where is the repository of the seeds. Something similar is meant by these words of the Lord: *The light of the body is the eye; if the eye be single* (that is, good), *the whole body is lucid,* Matt. vi. 22; Luke xi. 34. No man of sound reason can condemn riches, for they are in the body of the community, like the blood in man; nor can he condemn the honors annexed to offices or functions, for they are the hands of the king and the pillars of society, provided their natural and sensual loves are subordinate to spiritual love. There are also administrations in heaven, and dignities annexed to them; but those who are employed in them love nothing more than to do uses, because they are spiritual.

404. But a man puts on an entirely different state, if the love of the world or of riches makes the head, that is, if that is the reigning love; for the love of heaven is banished from the head and removed to the body. The man who is in this state prefers the world to heaven; he worships God, indeed, but from merely natural love, which places merit in all worship; and also he does good to the neighbor, but for the sake of rewards. The things which are of heaven are to them as coverings, in which they go shining before the eyes of men, but dusky before the eyes of angels; for when the love of the world possesses the internal man, and the love of heaven the external, then the former darkens all the things of the church, and hides them as under a veil. But this love is in much variety; more pernicious in the degree in which it inclines to avarice; in this the love of heaven grows black; in like manner, if it inclines to pride and eminence above others, from the love of self; but it is otherwise if it inclines to prodigality; it is less noxious if for an end it regards the splendid things of the world, as palaces, decorations, fine clothes, domestics, horses and chariots in high style, besides other such things; the quality of every love is predicated from the end which it regards and intends. This love may be likened to a crystal of a blackish hue, which suffocates the light, and variegates it only into dark and faint colors. And it is like a mist and a cloud, which intercept the rays of the sun. It is also like new, unfermented wine, which tastes sweet, but troubles the stomach. Such a man, viewed from heaven, appears like a hunch-backed man, walking with his head bowed down looking to the earth; and when he raises it to heaven, he writhes back the muscles, and soon afterwards relapses into his stooping posture. These were called, by the ancients in the church, *Mammons,* and by the Greeks, *Plutos.*

405. But if the love of self, or the love of ruling, makes the head, then the love of heaven passes through the body to the feet; and as far as that love increases, so far the love of heaven descends through the ankles to the soles of the feet; and if it still increases, it passes through the shoes, and is trampled under foot. There is a love of ruling from the love of the neighbor, and there is a love of ruling from the love of self. Those who are in the love of ruling from the love of the neighbor, seek after dominion, for the purpose of performing uses to the public and to individuals; and to these the office of ruling is intrusted also in the heavens. Emperors, kings and dukes, who are born and educated for ruling, if they humble themselves before God, are sometimes less in that love than those who are of mean extraction, and from pride seek after eminent stations above others. But to those who are in the love of ruling from the love of self, the love of heaven is as a seat, upon

which, for the sake of the common people, they place their feet, which yet, when the common people do not appear, they throw into a corner or out of doors; the reason is, because they love themselves alone, and thence immerse their wills and the thoughts of their mind into the proprium, which, viewed in itself, is hereditary evil; and this is diametrically opposite to the love of heaven. The evils appertaining to those who are in the love of ruling from the love of self, are in general these: contempt of others, envy, enmity against those who do not favor them, hostility thence, hatred, revenge, unmercifulness, tyranny, and cruelty; and where such evils are, there also is contempt of God and of divine things, which are the truths and goods of the church; which if they honor, it is only with the mouth, that they may not be defamed by the ecclesiastical order, and censured by others. But this love assumes one form with the clergy, and another with the laity; with the clergy this love mounts aloft, when the reins are given to it, until they wish to be gods, but with the laity, until they wish to be kings; the fantasy of that love raises their minds to such an extravagant pitch. Since the love of heaven, with a perfect man, holds the highest place, and makes, as it were, the head of the rest which succeed, and the love of the world is below that, and is as the breast is under the head, and the love of self is below this, as the feet are, it follows that, if this should make the head, it would entirely invert the man; and then he would appear to the angels like one lying with the head bowed to the earth, and the back to heaven; when he is in worship, he would appear to dance upon his hands and feet, like the cub of a panther. And, moreover, they appear under various forms of beasts with two heads, one above, having a bestial face, another below, having a human face, which by the higher one would be continually thrust forwards and compelled to kiss the earth. All these are sensual men, and such as were described above, n. 402.

406. III. That every Man, individually, is the Neighbor, that is to be loved, but according to the Quality of his Good.

Man is not born for the sake of himself, but for the sake of others, that is, that he may not live for himself alone, but for others; otherwise there would not be any coherent society, and in it any good. It is a common saying, that every one is neighbor to himself; but the doctrine of charity teaches how this is to be understood, namely; every one should procure for himself the necessaries of life, as food, clothing, a habitation, and other things, which, in the civil life in which he is, are necessarily required; and these not only for himself, but also for his family, and not only for the present time, but also for the future; for unless one procures the necessaries of life, he is not in a state of exercising charity, for he is in want of all things. But how every one ought to be neighbor to himself, may be evident from this similitude. Every one ought to provide his body with food; this will be the first thing; but to the end that there may be a sound mind in a sound body. And every one ought to provide his mind with its food, namely, with such things as are of intelligence and judgment; but to the end that he may thence be in a state to serve his fellow citizen, society, country, the church, and thus the Lord. He who does this, provides well for himself to eternity. Thence it is manifest, what is first in time, and what is first in end, and that that which is first in end, is that to which all have respect. This also is like the case of one who builds a house; he first lays the foundation, but the foundation will be for the house, and the house for a habitation. He who believes that he is neighbor to himself, in the first place, or primarily, is like him who regards the foundation as the end, not a habitation; when yet a habitation is itself the first and last end, and the house with the foundation is only a means to the end.

407. It shall be told what it is to love the neighbor. To love the neigh-

bor, is not only to will and do good to a relation, a friend, and a good man, but also to a stranger, an enemy, and a bad man. But charity is exercised towards these and those in different ways; towards a relation and friend, by direct acts of kindness, but towards an enemy and a bad man, by indirect acts of kindness, which are done by exhortations, discipline and punishments, and thus corrections. This may be illustrated thus: A judge who, according to law and justice, punishes a malefactor, loves the neighbor; for thus he corrects him, and consults for the citizens, that he may not do mischief to them. Every one knows that a father, who chastises his children when they do amiss, loves them; and, on the other hand, that he who does not chastise them for so doing, loves their evils; of which charity cannot be predicated. Further, if any one repels an insulting enemy, and for protection whips him, or delivers him to the judge, that thus he may avert harm from himself, yet with a disposition to become his friend, he acts from a principle of charity. Wars which have for their end the protection of one's country or the church, are not contrary to charity; the end for which they are undertaken shows whether they are charity or not.

408. Since, therefore, charity, in its origin, is good will, and good will resides in the internal man, it is manifest, that when any one, who has charity, resists an enemy, punishes a criminal, or chastises the evil, he does this by means of the external man; wherefore, after he has done it, he returns into charity, which is in the internal man, and then, as far as it is possible and profitable, he wishes him well, and from wishing well, does him good. Those who have genuine charity, have a zeal for what is good, and that zeal in the external man may be seen like anger and flaming fire, but it is extinguished and appeased as soon as the adversary repents. It is otherwise with those who have no charity; their zeal is anger and hatred, for from these their internal is heated and inflamed.

409. Before the Lord came into the world, scarcely any one knew what the internal man was, or what charity was; wherefore, in so many places, He taught dilection, that is, charity; and this makes the distinction between the Old and New Testament or Covenant. That we should, from charity, do good to an adversary and an enemy, the Lord taught in Matthew: *Ye have heard that it was said to the ancients, Thou shalt love thy neighbor, and hate thine enemy. But I say unto you, Love your enemies, bless those who curse you, do good to those who hate you, and pray for those who injure and persecute you; that ye may be sons of your Father who is in the heavens*, v. 43, 44, 45. *And when Peter asked how often he should forgive one sinning against him, whether till seven times, He answered, I say not unto thee till seven times, but even till seventy times seven times*, xviii. 21, 22. And I have heard from heaven, that the Lord remits to every one his sins, and never avenges, and does not even impute them, because He is Love itself and Good itself, but that still sins are not thereby wiped away, for they are not wiped away except by repentance; for, when He said to Peter that he should forgive even to seventy times seven times, why should not the Lord?

410. Since charity itself resides in the internal man, in which it is to will well, and thence in the external man, in which it is to do good, it follows that the internal man should be loved, and thence the external; consequently, that a man should be loved according to the quality of the good which is in him; wherefore, good itself is essentially the neighbor. This may be illustrated by these considerations: when any one chooses for himself a steward or a servant out of three or four, does he not find out his internal man, and choose a sincere and faithful one, and thence love him; in like manner, a king or a magistrate proceeds, that, out of three or four, he may choose one qualified for the office, and reject him who is unqualified, whatever countenance he may show, or however plausibly he may speak and act. Since

therefore, every man is a neighbor, and there is an infinite variety of men, and every one is to be loved as neighbor according to his good, it is manifest that there are kinds and sorts and also degrees of love towards the neighbor. Now, because the Lord is to be loved above all things, it follows, that the degrees of love towards the neighbor are to be measured according to love to the Lord, thus by how much of the Lord or from the Lord another possesses in himself; for so much good he also possesses, because all good is from the Lord But because these degrees are in the internal man, and this seldom manifests itself in the world, it is enough that the neighbor be loved according to the degrees which one knows; but these after death are clearly perceived, for there the affections of the will, and thence the thoughts of the understanding, make a spiritual sphere around them, which is felt in various ways; but that spiritual sphere is absorbed in the world by the material body, and includes itself in the natural sphere, which then exudes from man. That there are degrees of love towards the neighbor, is evident from the Lord's parable concerning the Samaritan, who showed mercy to him who was wounded by robbers, whom the priest and the Levite, when they saw him, passed by; and when the Lord asked, which of those three seemed to have been a neighbor, it was answered, *He that showed mercy*, Luke xi. 30 to 37.

411. It is read, *Thou shalt love the Lord God above all things, and the neighbor as thyself*, Luke x. 27. To love the neighbor as one's self, is not to despise him in comparison with one's self, and to deal justly with him, and not to bear a bad judgment concerning him. The law of charity, made and given by the Lord himself, is this: *Whatsoever ye would wish that men should do to you, do ye also to them, for this is the law and the prophets*, Matt. vii. 12; Luke vi. 31, 32. Thus those love the neighbor, who are in the love of heaven; but those who are in the love of the world, love the neighbor from the world and for the sake of the world; and those who are in the love of self, love the neighbor from self and for the sake of self.

412. IV. THAT MAN COLLECTIVELY, THAT IS, A SMALLER AND A LARGER SOCIETY, AND THAT MAN IN WHAT IS COMPOSED OF THEM, THAT IS, ONE'S COUNTRY, IS THE NEIGHBOR THAT IS TO BE LOVED.

Those who do not know what the neighbor is, in the genuine sense, imagine that it is no other than man as an individual, and that to perform acts of kindness to him, is to love the neighbor; but neighbor is more extensive, and love towards him extends itself more widely; for it ascends, as men are multiplied. Who cannot comprehend, that to love many men in a congregation, is to love the neighbor more than to love one individual of the congregation? Wherefore, the reason why a smaller or a larger society is the neighbor, is, because that is man collectively; thence it follows, that he who loves a society, loves those of whom the society consists; wherefore, he who wishes well and does good to the society, consults for each of its members. A society is like one man, and those who enter into it compose, as it were, one body, and are distinguished from each other like the members in one body. The Lord, and from Him the angels, when they look down into the earth, see a whole society no otherwise than as one man, and the form of it from their qualities. It has also been given me to see a certain society in heaven, altogether as one man, in a similar stature with a man in the world. That love towards a society is a fuller love to the neighbor than towards a separate or individual man, manifests itself in this, that dignities are dispensed according to the extent of government over societies, and honors annexed to them according to the uses which they perform. For there are offices in the world, higher and lower, in subordination, according to the more and less universal government over societies; and he is a king whose government is most universal; and every one, accord ing to the magnitude of his office and the goods of use which he performs, has recompense, glory, and the love of the community. But the governors of this age may perform uses, and consult for society, and still not love the neighbor as those do who perform uses and consult for the sake of the world and for the sake of themselves, that they may appear, or that they may be esteemed worthy to be promoted to higher dignities: but although these are not discerned in the world, still they are discerned in heaven; wherefore, those who, from love to the neighbor, had performed uses, are appointed also as governors over a heavenly society, and are there in splendor and honor; but still they do not place their heart in these, but in uses. But the others, who had done uses from the love of the world and of self, are rejected.

413. The difference of love towards the neighbor, and its exercise towards man individually and towards man collectively or a society, is like that between the office of a citizen, the office of a magistrate, and the office of a duke; and like that between him who traded with two talents and him who traded with ten, Matt. xxv. 14 to 31. The difference is also like that between the value of a shekel and the value of a talent; and like that between the fruit from a vine and from a vineyard; or from an olive-tree and from an olive-yard, or from a fruit-tree and from an orchard. Love towards the neighbor also ascends more and more interiorly with man, and, as it ascends, he loves a society more than a single man, and his country more than a society. Now, since charity consists in wishing well and thence acting well, it follows that it is to be exercised almost in the same manner towards a society as towards a single man; but in one manner towards a society of good men, and in another towards a society of bad men; towards the latter, charity should be exercised according to natural equity; towards the former, according to spiritual equity; but concerning the former and the latter equity, more will be seen elsewhere.

414. The reason why one's country is a neighbor more than a society, is, because it consists of many societies, and thence the love towards it is more extensive and higher; and besides, tc love one's country is to love the public welfare. The reason why one's country is his neighbor, is, because it is like a parent, for there he was born; it nourished and nourishes him, it protected and protects him from injuries. A man should from love do good to his country, according to its necessities, some of which are natural, and some spiritual; the natural respect civil life and order, and the spiritual, spiritual life and order. That one's country should be loved, not as a man loves himself, but more than himself, is a law inscribed on the human heart; whence is promulgated this, which is professed by every just man, that if its ruin is threatened by an enemy, or by any thing whatever, it is honorable to die for it, and glorious for a soldier to shed his blood for it; this is said, because it is to be loved so much. It should be known, that those who love their country, and from good will do good to it, after death love the kingdom of the Lord, for this is then their country; and those who love the kingdom of the Lord, love the Lord, because the Lord is all in all of his kingdom.

415. V. That the Church is the Neighbor that is to be loved in a higher Degree, and the Kingdom of the Lord in the highest Degree.

Since man was born for eternal life, and is introduced into it by the church, therefore the church is to be loved as a neighbor in a higher degree; for she teaches the means which lead to eternal life, and introduces into it; she leads to it by the truths of doctrine, and introduces by the goods of life. It is not meant that the priesthood should be loved in a higher degree, and from it the church, but that the good and the truth of the church should be loved, and for the sake of these the priesthood; this only serves, and as it serves, it is to be honored. The reason why the church is a neighbor that is to be loved in a higher degree, thus even above one's country, is also because a man by his country is initiated into civil life, but by the church into spiritual life, and this life distinguishes man from merely animal life. Moreover, civil life is temporary, which has an end, and then it is as if it had never been; but spiritual life, because it has no end, is eternal; wherefore, of the latter may be predicated to be (*esse*), and of the former, not to be (*non esse*). The difference is as between finite and infinite, between which there is no ratio; for what is eternal is infinite as to time.

416. The reason why the kingdom of the Lord is the neighbor, that is to be loved in the highest degree, is because by the kingdom of the Lord is meant both the church throughout the whole world, which is called the communion of saints, and also heaven; wherefore he who loves the kingdom of the Lord, loves all in the whole world who acknowledge the Lord and have faith in Him and charity towards the neighbor; and he also loves all in heaven. Those who love the kingdom of the Lord, love the Lord above all things; consequently they are more than others in love to God; for the church in the heavens and in the earth is the body of the Lord, for they are in the Lord and the Lord in them. Therefore, love towards the kingdom of the Lord, is love towards the neighbor in its fulness; for those who love the kingdom of the Lord, not only love the Lord above all things, but they also love the neighbor as themselves; for love to the Lord is a universal love, and thence it is in all and every thing of spiritual life, and also in all and every thing of natural life; for that love resides in the highest things with man, and the highest flow into the lower and vivify them, as the will flows into all things of the intention and thence of action, and the understanding into all things of the thought and thence of the speech. Wherefore the Lord says, *Seek first the kingdom of the heavens and its righteousness;* then *all things will be added to you,* Matt. vi. 33. That the kingdom of the heavens is the kingdom of the Lord, is evident from these words in Daniel; *Behold, as it were,* THE SON OF MAN *was coming with the clouds of the heavens; and to Him was given dominion, glory and a kingdom; and all people, nations and tongues shall worship Him. His dominion is the dominion of an age which will not pass away, and his kingdom one which will not be destroyed,* vii. 13, 14.

417. VI. THAT TO LOVE THE NEIGHBOR, VIEWED IN ITSELF, IS NOT TO LOVE THE PERSON, BUT THE GOOD WHICH IS IN THE PERSON.

Who does not know that man is not man from a human face and from a human body, but from the wisdom of his understanding and from the goodness of his will? The quality of these, ascending, makes him more and more a man. Man, when he is born, is more brutish than any animal; but he becomes a man by instructions and as these are received, his mind is formed, from which and according to which, man is man. There are beasts whose faces are similar to human faces; but they enjoy no faculty of understanding and of acting from understanding, but they act from an instinct which their natural love excites. The distinction is, that a beast sounds the affections of its love, but a man speaks them when brought into thought; and also, that a beast looks with its face downwards to the earth, but a man with an erect face looks to heaven on every side; whence it may be concluded, that man is man so far as he speaks from sound reason, and looks to his abode in heaven; and that he is so far not a man as he speaks from perverted reason, and looks only to his abode in the world. But still these are men, though not in act, but in power; for every man enjoys the faculty of understanding truths and of willing goods; but as far as he is not willing to do goods and understand truths, so far he can in externals counterfeit a man, and act the part of an ape.

418. The reason why good is the neighbor, is, because good is of the will, and the will is the *esse* of the life

of man; the truth of the understanding is also the neighbor; but so far as it proceeds from the good of the will, for the good of the will forms itself in the understanding, and there exhibits itself to be seen in the light of reason. That good is the neighbor, is evident from all experience. Who loves a person, except from the quality of his will and understanding, that is, from what is good and just in him? As, for example, who loves a king, a prince, a duke, a governor, a consul, any magistrate, or any judge, but from the judgment from which they act and speak? Who loves a primate, a minister or canon of the church, but for learning, integrity of life, and zeal for the salvation of souls? Who loves the general of an army, or any officer under him, but for courage, and, at the same time, prudence? Who loves a merchant, but for honesty? or a workman and a servant, but for fidelity? Yea, who loves a tree, but for its fruit? or ground, but for its fertility? or a stone, but for its preciousness? &c. And, what is remarkable, not only the honest man loves what is good and just in another, but also the dishonest man, because with him he is not in any fear of the loss of fame, honor or wealth. But the love of good with a dishonest man, is not love of the neighbor; for a dishonest man does not inwardly love another, only so far as he serves him. But to love the good in another, from good in one's self, is genuine love towards the neighbor, for then the goods mutually kiss each other and join themselves together.

419. The man who loves what is good because it is good, and what is true because it is true, eminently loves the neighbor, because he loves the Lord, who is Good itself and Truth itself; the love of good, and thence of truth, and thus of the neighbor, is from no other source; thus love towards the neighbor is formed from a heavenly origin. Whether it be said, *use* or *good*, it is the same; wherefore, to do uses is to do goods, and according to the quantity and quality of the use in goods, so far the goods are good.

420. VII. That Charity and Good Works are two distinct Things, like willing well and doing well.

With every man, there is an internal and an external; his internal is what is called the internal man, and his external, what is called the external man. But he who does not know what the internal man is, and what the external is, may believe that the internal man is that which thinks and wills, and the external that which speaks and acts: these, indeed, are of the external man, and those, of the internal; but still they do not essentially make the external and the internal man. The mind of man is, indeed, in the common perception, the internal man; but the mind itself is divided into two regions; one region, which is the higher and interior is spiritual, and the other, which is the lower and exterior, is natural. The spiritual mind looks principally into the spiritual world, and has for objects those things which are there, whether they be such as are in heaven, or such as are in hell, for both are in the spiritual world; but the natural mind looks principally into the natural world, and has for objects those things which are there, whether they be good or evil. All the action and the speech of man proceed from the lower region of the mind directly, and from its higher region indirectly; since the lower region of the mind is nearer to the senses of the body, and the higher region is farther from them. This division of the mind is with man, because he was created so as to be spiritual and at the same time natural, and thus a man and not a beast. Hence it is manifest that the man who looks to the world and himself primarily, is an external man, because he is natural, not only in body, but also in mind; and that the man who looks to the things which are of heaven and the church, primarily, is an internal man, because he is spiritual both in mind and in body; the reason why he is so also in body, is, because his actions and speech proceed from the higher mind, which is spiritual, through the lower mind, which is natural; for it is known that effects proceed from the body, and the causes which produce them from the mind, and that the cause is all in the effect. That the human mind is so divided, is very manifest from this, that a man can act the dissembler, flatterer, hypocrite and buffoon, and that he can assent to the words of another, and yet laugh at them; this he does from the higher mind, but that from the lower.

421. Hence it may be seen how it is to be understood that charity and good works are distinct, like willing well and doing well; namely, that they are formally distinct, as the mind which thinks and wills, and the body by which the mind speaks and acts; but that they are essentially distinct, because the mind itself is distinct, the interior region of which is spiritual, and the exterior natural, as was shown above. Wherefore, if works proceed from the spiritual mind, they proceed from its good will which is charity; but if from the natural mind, they proceed from a good will which is not charity, although it may appear like charity in the external form, yet still it is not charity in the internal form; and charity in the external form alone, wears indeed the semblance of charity, but the essence of charity it does not possess. This may be illustrated by comparison with seeds in the earth; from every seed there arises a shoot useful or otherwise according to the quality of the seed. The case is similar with spiritual seed, which is the truth of the church from the Word; from this is formed doctrine, useful if from genuine truths, otherwise if from falsified truths. The case is similar with charity from good will, whether the good will be for the sake of self and the world, or for the sake of the neighbor, in a strict or a wide sense; if for the sake of self and the world, it is spurious charity, but if for the sake of the neighbor, it is genuine charity. But more may be seen concerning these things in the chapter concerning Faith; particularly in the article where it is shown, *That charity is to will well, and that good works are to do well from willing well*, n. 473. *And that charity and faith are only mental and perishable things, unless, when it can be done they are determined to works, and co-exist in them*, n. 375, 376.

422. VIII. That Char ty itself is to act justly and faithfully in the Office, Business and Work in which any one is, and with whomsoever he has any Intercourse.

The reason why charity itself is to act justly and faithfully in the office, business and work in which any one is, is because all the things that a man does so, are of use to society, and use is good; and good, in the sense abstracted from persons, is the neighbor. That not only a single man, but also a smaller society, and one's country itself, is the neighbor, was shown above. As, for example, a king, who sets before his subjects an example in doing well, wishes them to live according to the laws of justice, rewards those who do live so regards every one according to his merit, defends them against injuries and invasions, acts as the father of the kingdom, and consults for the general prosperity of his people—he has charity in his heart, and his deeds are good works. A priest, who teaches truths from the Word, and by them leads to the good of life and thus to heaven, he, because he consults for the souls of the men of his church, eminently exercises charity. A judge, who judges according to justice and law, and not from the influence of a bribe, friendship and relationship consults for society and for each individual man; for society, because it is thereby kept in obedience to the law, and in the fear of transgressing it; and for each individual man, in that justice triumphs over injustice. A merchant, if he acts from sincerity and not from fraud, consults for the neighbor with whom he has business. In like manner a workman and an artist, if he does his work uprightly and honestly, and not fraudulently and deceitfully. The case is similar with others, as with captains of vessels and sailors, and with farmers and servants.

423. The reason why this is charity itself, is, because this may be defined

that it is to do good to the neighbor, daily and continually, and not only to the neighbor individually, but also to the neighbor collectively; and this cannot be done without doing what is good and just in the office, business and work in which any one is, and with whomsoever he has any intercourse, for this he does daily; and when he is not doing it, still it is continually fixed in his mind, and he thinks and intends it. The man who thus exercises charity becomes more and more charity in form; for justice and fidelity form his mind, and their exercises his body; and in course of time from his form he wills and thinks nothing else than such things as are of charity. These at length become like those of whom it is said in the Word, that they have the law written in their hearts. These also do not place merit in works, since they do not think of merit, but of duty, that it becomes a citizen to do so. But a man can by no means act from spiritual justice and fidelity, of himself; for every man hereditarily derives from his parents an inclination to do what is good and just for the sake of self and the world, and no one for the sake of what is good and just; wherefore he only who worships the Lord, and acts from Him while he acts from himself, obtains spiritual charity, and imbues it by exercises.

424. There are many who act justly and faithfully in the execution of their office, and although they thus perform works of charity, still they do not possess any charity in themselves. But there are those with whom the love of self and the world predominates, and not the love of heaven; and if by chance this be present, it is under that, like a slave under his master, and like a common soldier under his captain; and it is like a doorkeeper standing at the door.

425. IX. That the beneficent Acts of Charity are, to give to the Poor, and to help the Needy; but with Prudence.

A distinction is to be made between the duties of charity, and the beneficent acts of charity. By the duties of charity are meant the exercises of charity which proceed immediately from charity itself, and which, as was shown just above, are primarily of the employment in which every one is; but by beneficent acts are meant those helps that are afforded out of his employment. They are called *beneficent acts*, because a man is to do them at his liberty and pleasure, and when they are done they are not regarded by the recipient otherwise than as beneficent acts or favors, and they are dispensed according to the reasons and intentions which the benefactor has in his mind. It is a common opinion, that charity is nothing else than giving to the poor, helping the needy, taking care of widows and orphans, and contributing to the building of hospitals and houses for the accommodation of invalids, strangers and orphans; and especially to the building of temples, and to the ornaments and revenues of them; but many of these things are not the proper constituents of charity, but are things extraneous to it. Those who place charity itself in those beneficent acts, cannot do otherwise than place merit in those works; and although they confess with the mouth that they do not wish them to be merits, still inwardly there lurks the belief of merit. This is very manifest from them after death; then they enumerate their works, and demand salvation as a reward. But it is then inquired, from what origin they are, and thence of what quality; and if it is found that they proceeded from vain glory, or from a desire of fame, or from bare munificence, or from friendship, or from merely natural inclination, or from hypocrisy, they are then judged from that origin; for the quality of the origin is in the works. But genuine charity proceeds from those who are imbued with it from justice and judgment in the works which they do without the expectation of reward as an end, according to the words of the Lord, Luke xiv. 12, 13, 14; these also call such things as have been mentioned above, beneficent acts, as also debts, although they are of charity.

426. It is known that some who

have done those beneficent acts which, before the world, appear as images of charity, think and believe that they have exercised works of charity; and that they regard them as many regard papal indulgences, as things on account of which they are purified from sins; and, as regenerate, are to be gifted with heaven; and yet they do not regard as sins, adultery, hatred, revenge, fraud, and, in general, the concupiscences of the flesh, which they indulge at their pleasure. But, then, what else are those good works, than painted images of angels in company with devils, or boxes of *lapis lazuli*, in which are hydras? But the case is quite otherwise, if those beneficent acts are done by those who shun the above-mentioned evils as enemies of charity. Nevertheless, those beneficent acts are in many respects advantageous, particularly giving to poor people and beggars; for thereby boys and girls, servants and maids, and, in general, all the simple, are initiated into charity, for they are its externals, by which they become accustomed to the offices of charity; for they are the rudiments of it, and are then like unripe fruits; but with those who are afterwards perfected in just knowledges respecting charity and faith, they become like ripe fruits; and then they regard those former works done from simplicity of heart, no otherwise than debts.

427. The reason that those beneficent acts are at this day believed to be the proper deeds of charity, which in the Word are meant by good works, is, because charity is often described in the Word by giving to the poor, helping the needy, providing for widows and orphans; but hitherto it has been unknown that the Word, in the letter, mentions only such things as are external, yea, such as are the most external things of worship; and that spiritual things, which are internal, are meant by them; as may be seen above, in the chapter concerning THE SACRED SCRIPTURE, n. 173 to 209; whence it is manifest, that by those called poor, needy, widows and orphans, not those are there meant, but those who are spiritually such. That by the poor are meant those who are not in the knowledges of what is good and true, may be seen in THE APOCALYPSE REVEALED, n. 209; that by widows, those who are without truths, and still desire truths, n. 764, &c.

428. Those who are from nativity pitiful, and do not make their natural pity spiritual by deeds of genuine charity, believe that it is charity to give to every poor person, and to help every needy person, and they do not first inquire whether that poor and needy person be good or bad, for they say that this is not necessary, since God looks only at the help and alms. But these after death are well distinguished and separated from those who did the beneficent acts of charity from prudence; for those who did them from that blind idea of charity, then do good equally to the bad and the good; and thereby the bad do evils, and by them hurt the good; wherefore, those benefactors are the occasion of hurting even the good. For to do a beneficent act to a mischievous man, is like giving bread to the devil, which he turns into poison; for all the bread in the hand of the devil is poison; and if it is not, he turns it into poison, which he does by using good deeds to allure to evil. And it is like handing a sword to an enemy, that he may kill some one; and it is like giving a shepherd's crook to a man-wolf, that he may lead the sheep to the pasture, when yet, as soon as he has got it, he drives the sheep from the pasture into the wilderness, and there kills them; and it is like giving an office to a robber, who only cares and watches for plunder, according to the excellence and abundance of which, he dispenses laws and executes judgments.

429. X. THAT THERE ARE DEBTS OF CHARITY; SOME PUBLIC, SOME DOMESTIC, AND SOME PRIVATE.

The beneficent acts of charity and the debts of charity are distinct from each other, like the things which are done from liberty and those which are done from necessity. But still, by the debts of charity, are not here meant the debts of offices in a kingdom and a republic—as of a minister, that he should minister, of a judge, that he should judge, &c.—but the debts of every one, in whatever office he is, are meant. Wherefore they are from a different origin, and flow from another will; and so they are done from charity, by those who are in charity, and, on the other hand, from no charity, by those who are in no charity.

430. THE PUBLIC DEBTS OF CHARITY are, especially, duties and taxes, which should not be mixed together with the debts of offices. Those who are spiritual pay them with one disposition of heart, and those who are merely natural, with another. The spiritual pay them from good will, because they are collected for the preservation of their country, and for the protection of it and the church, and for the services performed by officers and rulers, to whom salaries and wages are to be paid from the public treasury. Wherefore those to whom their country and also the church are the neighbor, pay them voluntarily and cheerfully, and esteem it as iniquity to deceive and defraud; but those to whom their country and the church are not the neighbor, pay them unwillingly and reluctantly, and whenever opportunity is given, they defraud and cheat, for with them their own house and their own flesh is the neighbor.

431. THE DOMESTIC DEBTS OF CHARITY are those of a husband towards his wife, and of a wife towards her husband; also those of a father and a mother towards their children, and of children towards their father and mother, as also those of a master and a mistress towards their servants and maids, and of the latter towards the former. These debts, because they relate to education and administration in the house, are so many, that if they should be enumerated they would fill a volume. Every man is brought to these debts from a love different from that which brings him to the debts of his office; to those of a husband towards his wife, and of a wife towards her husband, from conjugial love and according to it; of a father and a mother towards their children, from a love implanted in every one, which is called *storge* or parental affection; and of children towards their parents, from another love, and according to it, which closely conjoins itself with obedience from debt. But the debts of a master and a mistress towards their servants and maids partake of the love of reigning, and this according to the state of each one's mind. But conjugial love and love towards children, with their debts and the discharge of them, do not produce love towards the neighbor, like the discharge of debts in offices; for the love called *storge* exists with the bad equally as with the good, and sometimes it is stronger with the bad; and also it exists with beasts and birds, with which no charity can be formed; that it is with bears, tigers and serpents equally as with sheep and goats, and with owls equally as with doves, is known. As to what particularly regards the debts of parents towards children, the debts with those who are in charity are inwardly different from the debts with those who are not in charity, but outwardly they appear similar. With those who are in charity, that love is conjoined with love towards the neighbor and with love to God; for by them children are loved according to their morals, virtues, desires and talents for serving the public; but with those who are not in charity, there is no conjunction of charity with the love called *storge;* wherefore many of them love bad, immoral and crafty children even more than those who are good moral and prudent; thus those who are not useful to the public more than those who are useful.

432. THE PRIVATE DEBTS OF CHARITY are also many, such as paying wages to workmen, paying interest and rents, performing contracts, keeping pledges, and other such like things; of which some are debts by virtue of the statute law, some of the civil law, and some of the moral law. These also are discharged in one state of mind by those who are in charity, and in another by those who are not in charity; by those who are in charity

they are performed justly and faithfully; for it is a precept of charity that every one should act justly and faithfully with all with whom he is in any business and intercourse, of which above, n. 422, and the following; but those same things are performed altogether differently by those who are not in charity.

433. XI. THAT THE RECREATIONS OF CHARITY ARE DINNERS, SUPPERS, AND PARTIES.

It is known that dinners and suppers are in use every where, and that they are made for various purposes, and that with many they are for the sake of friendship, for the sake of relationship, for the sake of gladness, and for the sake of gain and recompense; and that they are bribes to draw over to a party; and that with grandees they are also for the sake of honor, and in the palaces of kings for the sake of splendor. But dinners and suppers of charity are with those only who are in mutual love from a similar faith. In the primitive church, among Christians, dinners and suppers were for the sake of no other end, and they were called FEASTS, instituted both for promoting joy of the heart and also mutual conjunction. SUPPERS with them signified consociations and conjunctions, in the first state of the establishment of the church; for the evening, in which they were made, signified that: but DINNERS, in the second state, when the church was established; for the morning and the day signified that. At table they had conversations upon various subjects, as well domestic as civil, but particularly upon such things as were of the church; and because they were feasts of charity, on whatsoever subject they spoke, charity with its joys and delights was in their speech. The spiritual sphere reigning in those feasts, was a sphere of love to the Lord and of love towards the neighbor, which exhilarated the mind of every one, softened the sound of every speech, and brought festivity from the heart into all the senses; for from every man there emanates a spiritual sphere, which is of the affection of his love, and thence of his thought, and it inwardly affects those who are in his company, especially at feasts; it emanates through the face as well as by respiration. Since by dinners and suppers, or by feasts, such consociations of minds were signified, therefore they are so often mentioned in the Word; and by them there nothing else is meant in the spiritual sense; and in the highest sense, by the paschal supper amongst the sons of Israel, as also by the banquets at the other feasts; as also by eating together of the sacrifices at the tabernacle. Conjunction itself was then represented by breaking the bread and distributing it, and by drinking from the same cup and handing it to another.

434. As to social parties, they were in the primitive church amongst such as called themselves brethren in Christ; wherefore they were social meetings of charity, because they were a spiritual fraternity. They were also consolations for the adversities of the church, exultations for its increase, and also recreations of the mind after studies and labors, and at the same time conversations on various subjects; and because they flowed from spiritual love, as from a fountain, they were rational and moral from a spiritual origin. There are given at this day parties of friendship, which regard as their end the pleasures of conversation, the exhilaration of the mind, and thence they are for the expansion of the soul and the liberation of the imprisoned thoughts, and thus for the refreshment of the sensual parts of the body, and the restoration of their state. But as yet there are not given any parties of charity; for the Lord says, *In the consummation of the age*, that is, in the end of the church, *iniquity will be multiplied, and charity will grow cold*, Matt. xxiv. 12. The reason is, because the church had not yet acknowledged the Lord God the Savior, as the God of heaven and earth, and approached Him immediately, from whom alone genuine charity proceeds and flows in. But the parties, where a friendship emulating charity does

not join minds together, are no other than counterfeits of friendship, and false attestations of mutual love, alluring insinuations into favor, and indulgences of the delights of the body, especially of sensual gratifications, by which others are carried, as a ship by sails and favorable winds, while sycophants and hypocrites stand at the stern and hold the rudder in their hand.

435. XII. THAT THE FIRST THING OF CHARITY IS TO PUT AWAY EVILS, AND THE SECOND THING OF IT IS TO DO GOODS WHICH ARE OF USE TO THE NEIGHBOR.

In the doctrine of charity this holds the first place, that the first thing of charity is not to do evil to the neighbor, and the second, to do good to him; this tenet is as a door to the doctrine of charity. It is known that evil resides in the will of every man, from nativity, and because all evil regards man near itself and at distance from itself, and also society and one's country, it follows that hereditary evil is evil against the neighbor in every degree. Man may see from reason itself, that as far as the evil residing in the will is not removed, so far the good which he does is impregnated with that evil; for then evil is inwardly in the good, like a nut in the shell, and like marrow in the bone; wherefore, although the good which is done by such a man appears as good, still, inwardly, it is not good; for it is like a bright shell within which there is a nut eaten by worms, and it is like a white almond, within which there is rottenness, from which rotten veins extend even to the surface. To will evil and to do good are in themselves opposites; for evil is of hatred against the neighbor, and good is of love towards the neighbor; or evil is the neighbor's enemy, and good is his friend. Those two cannot exist in one mind, that is, evil in the internal man, and good in the external man; if they do, the good in the external man is like a wound superficially healed, in which inwardly there is rotten matter. Man is then like a tree whose root is decayed, and yet it produces fruit which outwardly appears like agreeable and useful fruit, but inwardly it is disagreeable and useless. He is also like the dross of metals, which, when polished on the surface and beautifully colored, are sold for precious stones. In a word, such are like the eggs of an owl, which are believed to be the eggs of a dove. Let every man know that the good which a man does with the body proceeds from his spirit, or from the internal man; the internal man is his spirit, which lives after death; wherefore, when a man casts off the body which made his external man, then whosoever is in evils and delights himself in them, he abhors good, as offensive to his life. That man cannot do good, which is good, before evil is removed, the Lord teaches in many places: *They do not gather grapes from thorns, or figs from thistles. A corrupt tree cannot produce good fruit*, Matt. vii. 16, 17, 18. *Wo to you, scribes and Pharisees; ye cleanse the outside of the cup and of the platter, but the insides are full of rapine and excess. Blind Pharisee, cleanse first the inside of the cup and of the platter, that the outside may be clean also*, xxiii. 25, 26. And in Isaiah; *Wash yourselves; put away the evil of your works; cease to do evil; learn to do good; seek judgment. Then, if your sins be as scarlet, they shall become white like snow; if they be red as crimson, they shall be like wool*, i. 16, 17, 18.

436. This may be further illustrated by these comparisons: one cannot go to another who keeps a leopard and a panther in his chamber, and because he gives them food to eat lives securely with them, unless he first remove those wild beasts. Who, when invited to the table of a king and queen, would not first wash his face and hands before he goes to it? Who does not purify metallic ore by fire, and separate it from the dross, before he obtains pure gold and silver? Who does not separate the tares from the wheat, before he brings it into the barn? Who does not cook raw meat by boiling, before it becomes eatable and is set upon the table? Who does not shake off the worms from the leaves of a tree in the garden

lest the leaves should be consumed, and thus the fruit should perish? Who loves a virgin, and intends marriage with her, who is infected with a malignant disease, and covered with pimples and sores, however she paints her face, dresses herself splendidly, and studies to infuse the incentives of love by the charms of her conversation? That man ought to purify himself from evils is, comparatively, as if a servant, having his face and clothes bedaubed with soot or dung, should go to his master and say, "Wash me, sir." Would not the master say to him, "You foolish servant, what do you say? Behold, there is water, soap and a towel; have you not hands, and power in them? wash yourself." And the Lord God would say, "The means of purification are from Me, and also your will and power are from Me; use those my gifts and talents as your own, and you will be purified."

437. It is believed at this day, that charity is only to do good, and that then one does not do evil; consequently, that the first thing of charity is to do good, and the second not to do evil. But it is altogether the reverse; the first thing of charity is to put away evil, and the second is to do good; for it is a universal law in the spiritual world, and thence also in the natural world, that as far as any one does not will evil, so far he wills good; thus as far as he turns himself away from hell, whence all evil ascends, so far he turns himself towards heaven, whence all good descends; hence also that as far as any one rejects the devil, so far he is accepted by the Lord. No one can stand between both, with a versatile neck, and at the same time pray to the one and to the other; for these are they concerning whom the Lord says these words: *I know thy works, that thou art neither cold nor hot; I would thou wert cold or hot; but because thou art lukewarm, and neither cold nor hot, I will spew thee out of my mouth*, Rev. iii. 15, 16. Who can fly about with his troop between two armies, and favor both? Who can be in evil against his neighbor, and at the same time in good towards him? Does not the evil then hide itself in the good? And, although the evil which hides itself does not appear in acts, still it manifests itself in many things, if they are duly reflected upon. The Lord says, *No servant can serve two masters; ye cannot serve God and mammon*, Luke xvi. 13.

438. But no one can, by his own power and his own strength, purify himself from evils; yet still it cannot be done without the power and strength of man, as his own. Unless it were so, no one could fight against the flesh and its concupiscences, which yet is enjoined upon every one; yea, he would not think of that conflict, and so would give up his mind to evils of every kind, and would only be restrained from them as to the deeds, by the laws of justice made in the world and their punishments; and thus he would be inwardly like a tiger, a leopard and a serpent, which never reflect on the cruel delights of their loves. Hence it is manifest that man, who is more rational than wild beasts, ought to resist evils from the power and strength given him by the Lord, which in every sense appear to him as his own; and this appearance is given to every man by the Lord, for the sake of regeneration, imputation, conjunction, and salvation.

439. XIII. That Man, in the Exercises of Charity, does not place Merit in Works, while he believes that all Good is from the Lord.

To place merit in works which are done for the sake of salvation is hurtful, for therein are concealed evils, concerning which the doer knows nothing. There is concealed a denial of the influx and operation of God with man; trust in one's own power in the things of salvation, faith in one's self and not in God, a justification of one's self, salvation by one's own strength, annihilation of the divine grace and mercy the rejection of reformation and regeneration by divine means, and particularly derogation from the merit and righteousness of the Lord God the Savior, which they claim to themselves; besides a continual looking for reward, which they regard as the first and last end, a suffocation and extinction of love to the Lord and love towards the neighbor, a total ignorance and imperceptibility of the delight of heavenly love, which is without merit, and a sensation only of the love of self. For those who put reward in the first place, and salvation in the second, thus this for the sake of that, invert order, and immerse the interior desires of their mind in their proprium, and in the body defile them with the delights of their flesh. Thence it is that the good of merit appears to the angels like rust, and the good not of merit like purple. That good should be done without the end of reward, the Lord teaches in Luke: *If ye do good to those who do good to you, what thank have ye? Rather love your enemies, and do good; and lend, hoping for nothing thence; then your reward will be great, and ye will be sons of the Most High; for He is kind to the unthankful and the evil*, vi. 33 to 36. That man cannot do good, which in itself is good, except from the Lord, in John; *Abide in Me and I in you; as the branch cannot bear fruit of itself, unless it abide in the vine, so neither can ye, unless ye abide in Me; because without Me ye cannot do any thing*, xv. 4, 5. And in another place; *A man cannot take any thing, unless it be given to him from heaven*, iii. 27.

440. But for men to think that they may come into heaven, and that good should be done for that reason, is not to regard reward as an end, and to place merit in works; for those also think that, who love the neighbor as themselves, and God above all things; for these think thus from faith in the words of the Lord, *That their reward will be great in the heavens*, Matt. v. 11, 12, vi. 1, x. 41, 42; Luke vi. 23, 25, xiv. 12, 13, 14; John iv. 36. *That those who have done good will possess, as an inheritance, the kingdom prepared from the foundation of the world*, Matt. xxv. 34. *That every one will be rewarded according to his works*, Matt. xvi. 27; John v. 29; Rev. xiv. 13, xx. 12, 13; Jerem. xxv. 14, xxxii. 19; Hosea iv. 9; Zech. i. 6; and other places. These are not in the confident expectation of reward from merit, but in the faith of the promise from grace. With these the delight of doing good to the neighbor is a reward; this delight the angels have in heaven, and it is a spiritual delight which is eternal, and immensely exceeds every natural delight. Those who are in that delight do not wish to hear of merit, for they love to do good, and perceive blessedness in it; but they are sorry if it is believed that they do it for the sake of retribution; they are like those who do good to friends for the sake of friendship, to a brother because he is a brother, to wife and children because they are wife and children, to their country because it is their country; thus from friendship and love. Those who do good to others also say and persuade that they do it not for the sake of themselves, but for the sake of them.

441. It is quite otherwise with those who regard reward in works as the end itself; these are like those who enter into friendship for the sake of gain, and also send gifts, perform kind offices, testify love as from the heart, and when they do not obtain the things hoped for, they turn themselves away, renounce friendship, and attach themselves to his enemies and haters. And they are like nurses who suckle infants only for wages, and in the sight of the parents they kiss and fondle them; but as soon as they are not fed delicately, and remunerated exactly according to their wish, they cast away the infants, treat them cruelly, and beat them, laughing at their cries. They are also like those who regard their country from the love of self and the world, and say that they are willing to spend their goods and their lives for it; and yet, if they do not get honors and riches as rewards, they speak evil of it, and join themselves to its enemies. They are likewise like shepherds who feed sheep only for the sake of wages, which if they do not receive at the proper time, they drive the flock with their staff from the pasture into the wilderness. Similar to these are priests who dis-

charge the duties of their ministry only for the sake of the emoluments annexed to them; that these care little for the salvation of the souls over whom they are appointed leaders is manifest. It is similar with magistrates who look only to the dignity of their office or function, and to the revenues of it; when they do good, it is not for the sake of the public, but for the sake of the delight of the love of self and the world, which they regard as the only good. It is similar with others; for the end in view is every thing, and the mediate causes, which are of the office, if they do not promote the end, are renounced. The case is similar with those who claim recompense for their merit in the things of salvation. These after death demand heaven with great confidence; but after they are found to possess nothing of love to God, and nothing of love towards the neighbor, they are sent back to those who may instruct them concerning charity and faith; and if they reject the doctrinals of these, they are sent away to those of a similar character, amongst whom are some who are angry with God, because they do not obtain rewards; and they call faith an imaginary entity. These are they who in the Word are meant by hirelings, to whom services of the lowest kind in the courts of the temple were allotted; they appear at a distance as if splitting wood.

442. It should be well known that charity and faith in the Lord are closely conjoined; thence charity is such as faith is. *That the Lord, charity and faith make one, like life, will and understanding; and that, if they are divided, each perishes like a pearl reduced to powder*, may be seen above, n. 362 and the following. And *that charity and faith are together in good works*, n. 373 to 377. Thence it follows that charity is such as faith is, and that works are such as faith and charity together are. Now, if the faith is, that all the good which man does, as of himself, is from the Lord, man is then the instrumental cause of it, and the Lord the principal cause; which two causes appear to man together, when yet the principal cause is all in all of the instrumental cause. Thence it follows, that if a man believes that all good which in itself is good is from the Lord, he does not place merit in works; and in that degree in which this faith with man is perfected, the fantasy concerning merit is removed from him by the Lord. A man in this state performs exercises of charity in abundance, and at length perceives the spiritual delight of charity, and then he begins to abhor merit as noxious to his life. Merit is easily wiped away by the Lord with those who imbue charity, by acting justly and faithfully in the work, business and office in which they are, and with whomsoever they have any intercourse, concerning which see above, n. 422, 423, 424; but merit is removed with difficulty from those who believe that charity is procured by giving alms and helping the needy; for these, while they are doing those works, in their mind, first openly, and then tacitly, wish for recompense and attract merit.

443. XIV. That a Moral Life, when it is at the same time Spiritual, is Charity.

Every man learns from parents and masters to live morally, that is, to act in a civil capacity, and to perform the offices of honesty, which refer themselves to the various virtues, which are the essentials of honesty, and to produce them by its formal manifestations, which are called the decencies or proprieties of life; and as he advances in age, he learns to superadd rational endowments, and to perfect the moral things of life by them; for moral life, with children, even to the first stage of manhood, is natural, which afterwards becomes more and more rational. He who reflects well may see, that a moral life is the same with the life of charity that this is to act well with the neighbor, and to regulate one's self so as not to be contaminated with evils, follows from those things which were shown above, n. 435 to 438. But still, in the first period of the life of man, moral life is the life of charity in the extremes, that is, only the outward and superficial part of it, and not its inward part. For there are four periods of life through which a man passes from infancy to old age. THE FIRST is that in which he acts from others, according to instructions; THE SECOND is that in which he acts from himself, according to the direction of the understanding; THE THIRD is that in which the will acts into the understanding, and the understanding modifies it; THE FOURTH is that in which he acts from a confirmed principle and from purpose. But these periods of life are periods of the life of the spirit of man, and not in like manner of his body; for this can act morally and speak rationally, and yet his spirit can will and think the contrary. That the natural man is such, is very manifest from dissemblers, flatterers, liars and hypocrites; that these have a double mind, or that their mind is divided into two discordant parts, is evident. It is otherwise with those who will well and think rationally, and thence act well and speak rationally; these are they who are meant in the Word by *the simple in spirit;* they are called simple, because they are not double, or have not a double spirit. Hence it may be seen, what is properly meant by the external and the internal man; and that no one can conclude from the morality of the external man to the morality of the internal, since this may be in the opposite state, and may hide itself, as a tortoise hides its head in its shell, and as a serpent hides its head in its folds; for such a moral man, so called, is like a robber in a city and in a forest, who in the city acts the part of a moral man, but in the forest the part of a robber. It is altogether otherwise with those who are inwardly moral, or moral as to the spirit, which they become by regeneration by the Lord; these are they who are meant by the spiritual moral.

444 The reason why a moral life, when it is at the same time spiritual, is a life of charity, is because the exercises of a moral life and of charity are the same: for charity is to will well to the neighbor, and thence to act well with him; this also is of moral life. The spiritual law is this of the Lord; *All things whatsoever ye would that men should do to you, so also do ye to them; this is the law and the prophets*, Matt. vii. 12. This same law is the universal law of moral life. But to enumerate all the works of charity, and compare them with the works of a moral life, is a work of many pages; let only six precepts of the second table of the law of the decalogue be for illustration. That these are precepts of moral life is manifest to every one, and that they contain all the things which are of love towards the neighbor, may be seen above, n. 329, 330, 331. That charity fulfils all those, is evident from these words in Paul: *Love ye one another; for he that loveth another hath fulfilled the law. For this, Thou shalt not commit adultery, Thou shalt not kill, Thou shalt not steal, Thou shalt not bear false witness, Thou shalt not covet, and if there be any other commandment, it is comprehended in this saying, Thou shalt love thy neighbor as thyself. Charity doeth no evil to the neighbor; charity is the fulfilment of the law*, Rom. xiii. 8, 9, 10. He who thinks from the external man only, cannot but wonder that the seven precepts of the second table were promulgated by Jehovah upon mount Sinai with so great a miracle; when yet those same precepts, in all the kingdoms upon earth, consequently also in Egypt, whence the sons of Israel lately came, were precepts of the law of civil justice; for no kingdom subsists without them. But the reason why they were promulgated by Jehovah, and moreover written upon tables of stone with his finger, was, that they might be not only precepts of civil society, and thus of natural moral life, but also precepts of heavenly society, and thus of spiritual moral life; so that to do contrary to them would be not only to do contrary to men, but also contrary to God.

445. If moral life be viewed in its essence, it may be seen that it is a life according to human and divine laws at

the same time; wherefore, he who lives according to those two laws as one, is a truly moral man, and his life is charity. Every one can comprehend, if he will, from external moral life, what charity is; only transcribe the external moral life, such as it is in the intercourse of civil society, into the internal man, that it may be, in the will and thought of this, similar and conformable to the acts in the external, and you will see charity in its type.

446. XV. That Friendship of Love contracted with a Man, of whatsoever Quality he is, as to the Spirit, is detrimental after Death.

By friendship of love is meant interior friendship, which is such, that not only the external man of the person is loved, but also the internal, and this without examining what he is as to the internal, or the spirit, that is, as to the affections of the mind; whether they be of love towards the neighbor and of love to God, thus capable of being consociated with the angels of heaven; or whether they be of love contrary to the neighbor, and of love contrary to God, thus capable of being consociated with devils. Such friendship with many is contracted from various causes, and for the sake of various ends. This is distinguished from external friendship, which is of the person alone, and is formed for the sake of various delights of the body and the senses, and for the sake of various kinds of intercourse. This friendship may be formed with any one, even with a buffoon who jests at the table of a duke. This is called simply friendship, but that, the friendship of love, because friendship is natural conjunction, but love is spiritual conjunction.

447. That the friendship of love is detrimental after death, may be evident from the state of heaven, from the state of hell, and from the state of the spirit of man respectively. As to the state of heaven; it is distinguished into innumerable societies, according to all the varieties of the affections of the love of good; hell also is divided into societies, according to all the varieties of the affections of the love of evil; and man, after death, who then is a spirit, according to his life in the world, is presently assigned to the society where his reigning love is; to some heavenly society, if love to God and love towards the neighbor had made the head of his loves; and to some infernal society, if the love of self and the world had made the head of his loves. Presently after his entrance into the spiritual world (which is made by death and the rejection of the material body into the sepulchre), man is for some time being prepared for his society to which he has been assigned, and the preparation is made by the rejection of the loves which do not agree with his principal love, wherefore one is then separated from another, friends from friends, clients from patrons, and also parents from children, and brother from brother; and each of them is joined to his like, with whom he is to live a life in common with them and properly his own to eternity. But, at the first time of the preparation, they meet together and converse in a friendly manner, as in the world; but by degrees they are separated, which is done insensibly.

448. But those who in the world had contracted friendships of love one with another, cannot, like others, be separated according to order, and assigned to the society corresponding to their life; for they are inwardly, as to the spirit, tied, nor can they be torn asunder, because they are like branches ingrafted into branches; wherefore, if one, as to his interiors, is in heaven, and another, as to his interiors, in hell, they cohere scarcely otherwise than as a sheep tied to a wolf, or as a goose to a fox, or as a dove to a hawk; and he whose interiors are in hell breathes his infernal influences into him whose interiors are in heaven; for among the knowledges which are in heaven, this also is one, that evils may be inspired into the good, but not goods into the evil. The reason is, because every one, by birth, is in evils; thence the interiors of the good, who thus cohere with the evil, are shut up, and both

are thrust down into hell, where the good suffer hard things; but at length, after a certain space of time, they are taken out, and then they first begin to be prepared for heaven. It has been given me to see such tyings, particularly between brothers and relations, and also between patrons and clients, and of many with flatterers, who possessed contrary affections and diverse dispositions; and I have seen some, like kids with leopards, and them then kissing each other and swearing to the former friendship. And I then perceived the good sucking in the delights of the evil, and both holding each other by the hand, entering together into caverns, where troops of the evil were seen in hideous forms; but to themselves, from the illusion of fantasy, they appeared in beautiful forms. But after a while, I heard from the good, lamentations of fear as for snares, and from the evil, exultations as of enemies over their spoil; besides other sad scenes. I heard that the good, when they were taken out, were prepared for heaven, by means of reformation, but with more difficulty than others.

449. The case is altogether otherwise with those who love the good in another, that is, who love justice, judgment, sincerity, benevolence from charity, especially who love faith and love to the Lord; those, because they love the things which are within a man abstracted from those which are without him, if they do not observe the same qualities in the person after death, immediately break off friendship, and are associated by the Lord with those who are in similar good. It may be said that no one can explore the interiors of the mind of those with whom he is associated and connected: but this is not necessary; only let him be cautious of forming a friendship of love with every one; external friendship, for the sake of various uses, is not hurtful.

450. XVI. That there is spurious Charity, hypocritical Charity, and dead Charity.

There is no genuine charity, which is living, unless it makes one with faith, and unless they both together look to the Lord; for these three, the Lord, charity and faith, are the three essentials of salvation, and when they make one, charity is charity, and faith is faith, and the Lord is in them, and they in the Lord; see above, n. 363 to 367, 368 to 372; but when those three are not conjoined, charity is either spurious, or hypocritical, or dead. There have been diverse heresies in Christendom, since the foundation of the Christian church, and also there are at this day, in each of which these three essentials, which are God, charity and faith, were and are acknowledged; for without those three, there is no religion. As it respects charity in particular, it may be adjoined to any heretical faith, as to the faith of Socinians, to the faith of enthusiasts, to the faith of Jews, yea, to the faith of idolaters; and by all it may be believed that it is charity, since, in the external form, it appears similar; but still it changes its quality, according to the faith to which it is adjoined or conjoined; that it is so, may be seen in the chapter concerning faith.

451. All charity which is not conjoined to faith in one God, in whom there is a Divine Trinity, is spurious; as the charity of the church at this day, whose faith is in three persons of the same divinity, in successive order, in the Father, Son, and Holy Spirit; and because in three persons, each of whom is a God subsisting by himself, therefore in three Gods; to which faith charity may be adjoined, as also has been done by the asserters of that faith, but it never can be conjoined; and the charity only adjoined to faith, is merely natural, and not spiritual, wherefore it is spurious charity. It is similar with the charity of many other heresies, as of those who deny a Divine Trinity, and so address God the Father alone, or the Holy Spirit alone, or both, without God the Savior; to the faith of these charity cannot be conjoined, and if it be conjoined or adjoined, it is spurious. It is said *spurious*, because it is like offspring from an illegitimate

bed, like the son of Hagar by Abraham, who was cast out of the house, Gen. xxi. 9. Such charity is like fruit not naturally belonging to the tree, but fastened to it by a needle; and it is like a chariot to which the horses are fastened only by the reins in the hands of the charioteer, which, when they run, pull the charioteer from the seat, and leave the chariot

452. But HYPOCRITICAL charity is with those who, in temples and houses, bow themselves down almost to the floor before God, pour out long prayers devoutly, wear sanctified faces, kiss images of the cross and the bones of the dead, and now bend their knees at sepulchres, and there mutter with the mouth words of holy veneration for God, and yet in heart think of the worship of themselves, and intend to be adored as divinities. These are similar to those whom the Lord describes in these words; *When thou doest alms, do not sound a trumpet before thee, as the hypocrites do, in the synagogues and in the corners of the streets, that they may have glory of men. And if thou prayest, thou shalt not be like the hypocrites, who love to pray, standing in the synagogues and in the corners of the streets, that they may be seen by men,* Matt. vi. 2, 5. *Wo unto you, scribes and Pharisees, hypocrites; because ye shut up the kingdom of the heavens to men, for ye neither enter, nor permit those to enter who wish to enter. Wo unto you, hypocrites, because ye compass sea and land to make one proselyte, and when he is made, ye make him two-fold more a child of hell than yourselves. Wo unto you, hypocrites, because ye cleanse the outside of the cup and of the platter, but within they are full of rapine and excess,* Matt. xxiii. 13, 15, 25. *Well hath Isaiah prophesied concerning you hypocrites, saying, This people honoreth Me with their lips, but their heart is far from Me,* Mark vii. 6. *Wo unto you* HYPOCRITES, *because ye are like graves which do not appear, so that the men who walk upon them do not know it,* Luke xi. 44; besides other passages. Those are like flesh without blood, like ravens and parrots taught to speak the words of some psalm; and like birds taught to sing the tune of a sacred hymn. The sound of their speech is like the sound of a fowler's pipe.

453. But DEAD charity is with those who have a dead faith, since charity is such as faith is; that they make one, was shown in the chapter concerning FAITH. That the faith of those who are without works is dead, is evident from the Epistle of James, ii. 17, 20. Moreover, those have a dead faith, who do not believe in God, but in living and dead men, and worship idols as holy in themselves, as the gentiles formerly did. The gifts of those who are in this faith, which for the sake of salvation they bestow upon miraculous images, as they call them, and reckon them among the works of charity, are no other than as the gold and silver put into the urns and monuments of the dead; yea, like the little cakes given to Cerberus, and the fare, to Charon, that they may be transported to the Elysian fields. But the charity of those who believe that there is no God, but that nature is instead of God, is not spurious, nor hypocritical, nor dead, but none, because it is not adjoined to any faith; for it cannot be called charity, because the quality of charity is predicated from faith. The charity of these, when viewed from heaven, is like bread made of ashes, or cake made of fish scales, and like fruit made of wax.

454. XVII. THAT THE FRIENDSHIP OF LOVE AMONG THE EVIL IS INTESTINE HATRED TOWARDS EACH OTHER.

It was shown above, that every man has an internal and an external, and that his internal is called the internal man, and his external, the external man; to this it shall be added, that the internal man is in the spiritual world, and the external, in the natural world. The reason why man was created such, is, that he might be associated with spirits and angels in their world, and thence think analytically, and after death be transferred from his own world to another. By the spirit ual world, is meant both heaven and hell. Since the internal man is together with spirits and angels in their world, and the external with men, it is manifest that man may be consociated with the spirits of hell, and also consociated with the angels of heaven; by this faculty and power, man is distinguished from beasts. Man is such in himself, as he is as to his internal man, but not as he is as to the external, because the internal man is his spirit, which acts by the external. The material body, with which his spirit is clothed in the natural world, is an accessory for the sake of procreations, and for the sake of the formation of the internal man; for this is formed in the natural body, as a tree in the earth, and seed in the fruit. More concerning the internal and the external man may be seen above, n. 401.

455. But what an evil man is, as to his internal man, and what a good man is, as to his, may be seen from this short description of hell and heaven; for the internal man, with the evil, is conjoined with the devils in hell; and with the good, it is conjoined with the angels in heaven. Hell is, from its loves, in the delights of all evils, that is, in the delights of hatred, revenge and murder, in the delights of robbery and theft, in the delights of reviling and blaspheming, in the delights of the denial of God and the profanation of the Word. These are concealed in the concupiscences, upon which man does not reflect; by those delights they burn like lighted torches; those are what are meant in the Word by infernal fire. But the delights of heaven are the delights of love towards the neighbor and of love to God. Since the delights of hell are opposite to the delights of heaven, there is a great interstice between them, into which the delights of heaven flow from above, and the delights of hell from beneath; in the middle of this interstice is man, while he lives in the world, in order that he may be in equilibrium, and thus in a state of freedom to turn himself to heaven or to hell. This interstice is what is meant by *the great gulf fixed* between those who are in heaven and those who are in hell, Luke xvi. 26. Hence it may be evident what the friendship of love amongst the evil is; that, as to the external man, it imitates or mimics the gestures and puts on the semblance of morality, for the purpose of spreading its nets and of finding occasions of enjoying the delights of its loves, from which their internal man is enkindled; it is only the fear of the law, and thence of the loss of fame and life, which restrains and prevents the acts; wherefore their friendship is like a spider in sugar, a viper in a loaf of bread, a young crocodile in a cake of honey, and a snake in the grass. Such is the friendship of the evil with every one; but among those who are confirmed in evil, as amongst thieves, robbers, and pirates, that friendship is familiar, whilst they unanimously desire and seek after plunder; for then they kiss each other as brethren, they entertain themselves with feasting, singing and dancing, and conspire together for the destruction of others; yet still each deeply in himself looks at his companion as an enemy looks at an enemy; this also a cunning robber sees and fears in his companion. Hence it is manifest that amongst such there is no friendship, but intestine hatred.

455. Every man, who has not openly attached himself to malefactors, and committed robberies, but has led a civil moral life, for the sake of various uses, as ends, and yet has not bridled the concupiscences residing in the internal man, may believe that his friendship is not such; but that still it is, in various degrees, with all who have rejected faith, and despised the holy things of the church, and reputed them as nothing for them, but only for the common people, has been given me to know for certain, by many examples in the spiritual world. With some of them, the delights of infernal love have been concealed, like fire in burning wood covered over with the bark; with some, like live coals under embers; with some, like little waxen torches, which blaze as soon as fire is put to them and with some, in other ways. Such

is every man who rejects from his heart those things which are of religion; the internal man of these is in hell, and as long as they live in the world, and then are ignorant of it, on account of an apparent morality in externals, they acknowledge none for the neighbor, but themselves and their children; and all others they regard either with contempt, and are then like cats watching for birds in their nests; or with hatred, and are then like wolves, when they see dogs which they may devour. These things are adduced that it may be known what charity is by its opposite.

456. XVIII. CONCERNING THE CONJUNCTION OF LOVE TO GOD, AND LOVE TOWARDS THE NEIGHBOR.

It is known, that the law promulgated from mount Sinai was written upon two tables, and that one of them is concerning God, and the other concerning men; and that they, in the hand of Moses, were one table, on the right side of which it was written concerning God, and on the left side, concerning men; and that thus, when presented to the eyes of men, the writing of both sides might be seen at the same time; thus one side was in sight of the other, like Jehovah speaking with Moses, and Moses with Jehovah, face to face, as it is read. This was done, in order that the tables, thus united, might represent the conjunction of God with men, and the reciprocal conjunction of men with God; for which reason, the law written upon them was called *the Covenant* and *the Testimony;* covenant signifies conjunction, and testimony a life according to the conditions of the covenant. From these two tables, thus united, may be seen the conjunction of love to God and love towards the neighbor. The first table involves all the things which are of love to God, which are, primarily, that we ought to acknowledge One God, the divinity of his Human, and the holiness of the Word; and that He is to be worshipped by the holy things which proceed from Him. That this table involves these things, is evident from the comments upon the precepts of the decalogue, in the fifth chapter The second table involves all those things which are of love towards the neighbor; the five first precepts of it, those things which are of the deed and are called works; and the two last, those things which are of the will, thus those things which are of charity in its origin; for in these it is said, *Thou shalt not covet;* and when a man does not covet those things which are the neighbor's, then he wishes well to him. *That the Ten Precepts of the Decalogue contain all things which are of love to God, and all things which are of love towards the Neighbor,* may be seen above, n. 329, 330, 331; where it was also shown, that there is a conjunction of both tables, with those who are in charity.

457. The case is otherwise with those who are only in the worship of God, and not at the same time in good works from charity; these are like those who break a covenant; and it is still otherwise with those who divide God into three, and worship each separately: and again, it is otherwise with those who do not go to God in his Human; these are they who do not enter through the door, but climb up some other way, John x. 9; and still otherwise with those who deny the divinity of the Lord from confirmation. In all these cases, there is not conjunction with God, and hence no salvation; and the charity of those is no other than spurious, and this does not conjoin face to face, but side to side, or back to back. How conjunction is effected shall also be told in a few words. God flows in with every man with an acknowledgment of Him into the knowledges concerning Him, and at the same time He flows in with his love towards men. The man who only receives the former and not the latter, receives that influx in the understanding and not in the will, and remains in knowledges without an interior acknowledgment of God, and his state is like that of a garden in the time of winter; but the man who receives both the former and the latter, receives the influx in the will, and thence in the understanding,

thus in the whole mind; and he has an interior acknowledgment of God, which vivifies his knowledges concerning God, and his state is like that of a garden in the time of spring. The reason why conjunction is effected by charity, is, because God loves every man; and, because He cannot do good to him immediately, but mediately by men, therefore He inspires his love into them, as He inspires into parents love towards their children; and the man who receives it is conjoined to God, and loves the neighbor from the love of God; with him the love of God is inwardly in the love of man towards the neighbor, which produces the will and the power with him. And because a man does nothing of good, unless it appear to him as if the power, the will and the deed were from himself, therefore this is given to him; and when he does good freely, as from himself, it is imputed to him and accepted, as that reciprocal operation by which conjunction is effected. This is like the active and the passive, and the coöperation of the latter, which is effected from the active in the passive; it is also like the will in actions, and the thought in speech, and the soul from the inmost operating into both; it is also like the effort in motion, and likewise like the prolific principle of a seed, which from within acts in the juices, by which the tree grows even to fruits, and by fruits, produces new seeds; it is also like light in precious stones, which is reflected according to the textures of the parts, whence are various colors as if they were of the stones, when yet they are of the light.

458. Hence it is manifest, whence and what is the conjunction of love to God and love towards the neighbor; that there is an influx of the love of God towards men; and that the reception of it by man, and coöperation with him, is love towards the neighbor. In short, conjunction is according to these words of the Lord; *In that day ye shall know that I am in my Father, and ye in Me, and I in you*, John xiv. 20; and according to these; *He that hath my commandments and doeth them, he it is that loveth Me; and I will love him, and will manifest Myself to him; and I will make an abode with him*, 21, 22, 23. The commandments of the Lord all refer themselves to love towards the neighbor, which, in the sum, are not to do him evil, but to do him good That those love God, and God loves them, is according to those words of the Lord. Since those two loves are so conjoined, John says, *He that keepeth the commandments of Jesus Christ, abideth in Him, and He in him. If any one say, I love God, but hateth his brother, he is a liar; for he that loveth not his brother, whom he seeth, how can he love God, whom he doth not see? This commandment we have from Him, that he that loveth God, love his brother also,* 1 John iii. 24; iv. 20, 21.

---

459. To the above will be added these Relations. First; I saw at a distance five gymnasiums, which were encompassed with various light; the first, with flammeous light, the second with yellow light, the third with a white light, the fourth with a light half way between that of noon and evening, the fifth scarcely appeared, for it stood as it were in the shade of the evening. And I saw in the ways some upon horses, some in chariots, and some walking, and some running and hastening, and these to the first gymnasium, which was covered with flammeous light. On seeing them, I was seized and impelled by a strong desire of going thither, and hearing what was there canvassed; wherefore, I quickly girded myself, and associated myself with those hastening to the first gymnasium, and entered together with them. And lo, there was a great assembly of people, part of whom turned to the right hand, and part to the left, to sit upon the benches which were along the walls. In front I saw a low pulpit, in which stood one who officiated as president; he had a staff in his hand, a cap on his head, and a vesture tinged with the flammeous light of the gymnasium. After they were gathered together, he lifted up his voice and said, "Brethren, canvass on this occasion, What is Charity? Each of

you may know that charity is spiritual in its essence, and natural in its exercises." And immediately one arose from the first bench on the left hand, upon which those sat who were reputed wise, and, beginning to speak, he said, "My opinion is, THAT MORALITY INSPIRED BY FAITH IS CHARITY;" and he confirmed it thus: "Who does not know, that charity follows faith, as a waiting maid her mistress; and that a man who has faith, does the law, and thus charity, so spontaneously, that he does not know that it is the law and charity that he lives, since, if he should know it, and should do so, and at the same time should think of salvation on account of it, he would defile holy faith with his proprium, and so would weaken its efficacy? Is not this according to the dogma of our church?" And he looked at those sitting at the sides, among whom there were canons, and they assented. "But what is spontaneous charity, but the morality into which every one is initiated from his infancy, which therefore in itself is natural, but which, when faith is inspired into it, becomes spiritual? Who distinguishes men from their moral life, whether they have faith or not, for every one lives morally? But God alone, who puts in and seals faith, knows and distinguishes. Wherefore I assert, that charity is morality inspired by faith; and that this morality, from the faith in its bosom, is saving; but no other morality is conducive to salvation, because it is meritorious. All, therefore, lose their labor, who mix charity and faith together, that is, who conjoin them from within, instead of adjoining them from without; for to mix them together, and to conjoin them, would be like letting the servant, who stands behind, get into the chariot with a primate, or like introducing a door-keeper into the dining room to sit at the table with a grandee." After this arose one from the first bench on the right hand, and he spoke and said, "My opinion is, THAT PIETY INSPIRED BY PITY IS CHARITY; and I confirm it by these considerations, that nothing else can propitiate God more than piety from an humble heart, and piety prays continually that God would give faith and charity; and the Lord says, *Ask and it shall be given to you*, Matt. vii. 7; and because it is given, they are both in it. I say that piety inspired by pity is charity: for all devout piety pities; for piety moves the heart of a man to groan, and what else is this but pity? This, indeed, recedes after prayer, but still it returns with it, and when it returns, piety is in it, and thus in charity. Our priests ascribe every thing that promotes salvation to faith, and not any thing to charity; what then remains, but piety praying pitifully for both? When I read the Word, I could not see otherwise, that faith and charity were two means of salvation; but when I consulted the ministers of the church, I heard that faith was the only means, and charity not any thing; and then I seemed to myself as if in the sea, upon a ship floating between two rocks; and when I feared the wreck of it, I betook myself to a boat, and sailed away; my boat was piety. And besides, piety is profitable for all things." After him arose one from the second bench on the right, and he spoke and said, "My opinion is, THAT CHARITY IS, TO DO GOOD TO EVERY ONE, TO THE VIRTUOUS AS WELL AS THE VICIOUS; and I confirm it by these considerations. What is charity but goodness of heart, and a good heart wishes well to all, to the virtuous and also to the vicious. And the Lord says, that we should do good even to our enemies. If, therefore, you take away charity from any one, does not charity then become, as to that particular instance, none, and so like a man hopping upon one foot, the other being cut off? A vicious man is a man, as well as a virtuous man, and charity regards man as man; if he be a vicious man, what is this to me? It is with charity as it is with the heat of the sun; this vivifies beasts, the fierce as well as the gentle, wolves as well as sheep; and it causes trees to grow, the bad as well as the good, and thorns as well as vines." Having said these words, he took in his hand a fresh grape and said, "It is with charity as with this grape; if you divide it, all that is in it flows out." And he divided it, and what was in it did flow out. After he had declared his opinion, another arose from the second bench on the left, and said," My opinion is, THAT CHARITY IS, TO BE SERVICEABLE, IN EVERY WAY, TO ONE'S RELATIONS AND FRIENDS; which I confirm thus. Who does not know that charity begins from one's self; for every one is neighbor to himself? Wherefore, charity proceeds from itself by the degrees of nearness, first to brothers and sisters, and from these to other relations and connections, and thus the progression of charity is terminated by itself. Those who are without are strangers, and strangers are not inwardly acknowledged; thus by the internal man they are alienated or treated as strangers. But kindred and relations are conjoined by nature, and friends by custom, which is a second nature, and thus they become the neighbor; and charity unites to itself another, from within, and so from without; and those who are not united from within, should only be called companions. Do not all birds know their relations, not by their feathers, but by their sound, and when they are near, from the sphere of life exhaled from their bodies? This affection of kindred, and thence conjunction, with birds, is called instinct; but the same with men, when it is for their own, is truly the instinct of human nature. What makes homogeneity, but blood? This the mind of man, which also is his spirit, feels, and as it were smells; in this homogeneity and consequent sympathy, consists the essence of charity. But, on the contrary, heterogeneity, from which also exists antipathy, is, as it were, not blood, and thence not charity: and because custom is a second nature, and this also makes homogeneity, it follows that charity is also to do good to friends. Any one who comes from the sea into any port, and hears that it is a foreign country, inhabited by those with whose language, manners and customs he is not acquainted, is, as it were, out of himself, and feels nothing of the delight of love towards them; but if he hears that it is his own country, the language, manners and customs of whose inhabitants he knows, he is, as it were, within himself, and feels the delight of love, which also is the delight of charity." Afterwards one arose from the third bench on the right, and spoke with a loud voice, saying, "My opinion is, THAT CHARITY IS, TO GIVE ALMS TO THE POOR, AND TO HELP THE NEEDY. This certainly is charity, for this the Divine Word teaches, whose dictate does not admit of contradiction What is it to give to the rich and the opulent, but vain-glory, in which there is no charity, but the prospect of remuneration; and in this there can be no genuine affection of love towards the neighbor, but a spurious affection, which avails on earth and not in the heavens; wherefore want and need should be relieved, because, into this the idea of retribution does not enter. In the city of my residence, where I knew who were virtuous and who were vicious, I saw that all the virtuous, on seeing a poor man in the street, would stop and give alms; but all the vicious, on seeing a poor man at their side, would pass by as if they were blind and deaf, as to seeing and hearing him; and who does not know, that the virtuous have charity, and that the vicious have not? He who gives to the poor, and helps the needy, is like a shepherd who leads the hungry and thirsty sheep to pasture and to water; but he who gives only to the rich and affluent, is like one, who worships *deasters*, and urges food and wine upon those who eat and drink to excess." After him arose one from the third bench on the left, and, speaking, he said, "My opinion is, THAT CHARITY IS TO BUILD HOSPITALS AND HOUSES FOR THE ACCOMMODATION OF INVALIDS, ORPHANS AND STRANGERS, AND TO SUPPORT THEM BY GIFTS. This I confirm by this consideration, that such beneficent acts and aids are public, and exceed by many degrees those which are private; thence charity becomes more opulent and replete with goods, which goods are manifold in number, and the recompense expected from the promises of the Word becomes more abundant; for as any one prepares the ground and sows, so he reaps. Is not this to give to the poor, and to help the needy, in an eminent degree? Who does not thence obtain glory from the world, and at the same time praises, with the humble voice of gratitude, from those who are thus supported? Does not this elevate the heart, and at the same time the affection which is called charity, even to its highest pitch? The rich, who do not walk in the streets, but ride in coaches, cannot take notice of those who sit at the sides of the streets, near the walls of the houses, and give them little pieces of money, but they contribute large sums for such objects as are useful to many, at the same time; but the poorer people, who walk in the streets, and have not such means, do otherwise." On hearing these words, another upon the same bench suddenly drowned his voice by a louder sound, and said; "Still the rich should not prefer the munificence and excellence of their charity, to the pittance which one poor man gives to another; for we know that every one, who acts, acts according to the dignity of his person; a king, a general, a captain, and a sergeant, each, respectively, according to his dignity; for charity, viewed in itself, is not estimated according to the excellence of the person, and thence of the gift, but according to the fulness of the affection which does it: and that thus a common servant, when he gives one little piece of money, may give from fuller charity than a grandee, who gives or bequeaths a treasure; which also is according to these words; *Jesus seeth the rich casting their gifts into the treasury; He seeth also a poor widow casting in thither two mites. He said, Verily I say unto you, that this poor widow hath cast in more than all,*" Luke xxi. 1, 2, 3. After these arose one from the fourth bench on the left, and he spoke and said, "My opinion is, That Charity is to endow Churches, and to do Good to their Ministers. This I confirm by the consideration, that whoever does those things, revolves in his mind a holy thing, and from that holy thing there he acts, which also sanctifies his gifts; this charity requires, because it in itself is holy. Is not all the worship in churches holy? For the Lord says, *Where two or three are gathered together in my name, I am in the midst of them;* and the priests, his servants, minister to him. Thence I conclude, that the gifts which are bestowed on ministers and on churches are superior to the gifts which are bestowed on other persons and on other objects. And besides, to the minister is given the power of blessing, by which also he sanctifies them; and afterwards nothing more expands and exhilarates the mind, than to see one's gifts as so many sanctuaries." Afterwards arose one from the fourth bench on the right, and spoke thus: "My opinion is, That the old Christian Brotherhood is Charity. And this I confirm by this consideration, that every church that worships the true God, begins from charity, in like manner as the old Christian church; which, because charity unites minds, and makes one out of many, therefore they called each other brethren, but in Jesus Christ, their God. But because they were surrounded by barbarous nations, of whom they were afraid, they made a common stock of their goods, which they enjoyed together in harmony; and in their social meetings, every day, they conversed concerning the Lord God their Savior Jesus Christ, and at the dinners and suppers, concerning charity; hence their brotherhood. But after their times, when schisms began to arise, and at last the wicked heresy of Arius, which, with many, took away the idea of the divinity of the Lord's Human, charity decayed, and the brotherhood was dispersed. It is true, that all who in truth worship the Lord, and do his commandments, are brethren, Matt. xxiii. 8, but brethren in spirit; yet because, at this day, no one is known, what he is in the spirit, it is not necessary that they should call each other brethren. A brotherhood of faith alone, and still less of faith in any other God than in the Lord God the Savior, is not a brotherhood, because charity, which makes it, is not in that faith. Wherefore I conclude that the old Christian brotherhood was charity; but this was, and is not; but I prophesy that it is about to be." When he said this, a flammeous light shone through the window on the east, and tinged his cheeks; on seeing which, the assembly were astonished. At last there arose one from the fifth bench on the left, and requested that he might be allowed to add something to what the last had said, and after his request was granted, he said, "My opinion is, THAT CHARITY IS TO FORGIVE EVERY ONE HIS TRESPASSES. This opinion I have received from a form of speaking used by those who come to the holy supper; for some then say to their friends, 'Forgive me whatever I have done amiss,' supposing thus that they have fulfilled all the duties of charity. But I have thought with myself, that this is only a painted figure of charity, and not the real form of its essence; for those say this who do not forgive, and also those who do not make any effort to obtain charity; and these are not amongst those in the prayer, which the Lord himself taught, *Father, forgive us our trespasses, as we forgive those who trespass against us.* For trespasses are like ulcers, which must be opened and healed, or else corrupted matter is collected in them, which corrupts the neighboring parts, and creeps about like a serpent, and turns the blood in all parts of the body into corruption. It is similar with trespasses against the neighbor; these remain and consume us, unless they are removed by repentance, and by a life according to the commandments of the Lord. And those who, without repentance, only pray to God, that He would forgive them their sins, are like the citizens of a city, infected with a contagious disease, who go to the consul and say, 'Heal us, sir.' To whom the consul would say, 'How can I heal you? Go to a physician, and learn the medicines proper for you, and buy them of an apothecary, and take them, and you will be healed.' And the Lord will say to those who pray for the forgiveness of sins without actual repentance, 'Open the Word and read that, which I have spoken in Isaiah: *Ah, sinful nation, heavy with iniquity; wherefore, when ye spread forth your hands, I hide my eyes from you; although ye multiply prayers, I do not hear. Wash yourselves; remove the evil of your works from before mine eyes; cease to do evil; learn to do good; and then your sins shall be removed and forgiven,*'" i. 4, 15, 16, 17, 18. When this was done, I stretched forth my hand, and requested that I might be allowed, although I was a stranger, to declare my opinion also; which request the president proposed, and after it was granted, I spoke as follows: "My opinion is, THAT CHARITY IS, TO ACT FROM THE LOVE OF JUSTICE WITH JUDGMENT, IN EVERY WORK AND OFFICE, BUT FROM A LOVE FROM NO OTHER SOURCE, THAN FROM THE LORD GOD THE SAVIOR. All the things that I have heard from those who sit upon the benches on the right side and on the left, are renowned instances of charity; but, as the president of this assembly premised, charity is spiritual in its origin and natural in its derivation; and natural charity, if it is inwardly spiritual, appears to the angels transparent, like a diamond; but if it is not inwardly spiritual, and thence merely natural, it appears to the angels like a pearl similar to the eye of a boiled fish. It is not mine to say whether the renowned instances of charity, which you have set forth in order, are inspired by spiritual charity, or not; but it is mine to say here, what the spiritual which ought to be in them, must be, that they may be the natural forms of spiritual charity. Their spiritual principle is this, that they be done from the love of justice with judgment, that is, that a man in the exercises of charity should see plainly whether he acts from justice, and he sees this from judgment. For a man may do evil by good deeds; and also, by such acts as appear to be evil, he may do good; as, for example, he does evil by good deeds, who gives to a poor robber money to buy him a sword, although he does not say this when he asks for it; or if he takes him out of prison, and shows him the way to the woods, and says with himself, 'It is not my fault that he practises robbery; I have afforded assistance to a man.' Take also another example; he who feeds an idler, and keeps him from being compelled to labor, and says to him, 'Go into a chamber in my house, and lie down upon the bed; why will you fatigue yourself?' That man favors idleness; as also he who promotes relations and friends of a dishonest disposition to offices of honor, in which they can do many kinds of mischief. Who does not see that such works of charity are not from any love of justice with judgment? Also, on the other hand, that a man may do good by such acts as appear to be evil; as, for example, a judge who acquits a criminal because he sheds tears, and utters words of piety, and prays that he would forgive him, because he is his neighbor; when yet the judge performs a work of charity when he imposes a punishment on him according to the law; for thus he prevents him from doing further mischief, and from being a nuisance to society, which is his neighbor in a higher degree, and he prevents the scandal of a partial judgment. Who does not know also, that it is good for servants if they are chastised by their masters, and for children if they are chastised by their parents, on account of offences? The case is similar with those in hell, all of whom have a love of doing evil, in that they are kept shut up in prison, and when they do evils they are punished; which the Lord permits for the sake of amendment. This is done, because the Lord is justice itself, and whatever He does, He does from judgment itself. Hence it may be clearly seen, whence it is, that, as was said above, charity becomes spiritual from the love of justice with judgment, but from love from no other source than from the Lord God the Savior. The reason is, because all the good of charity is from the Lord; for He says, *He that abideth in Me, and I in him, beareth much fruit; because without Me, ye cannot do any thing*, John xv. 4; and *that He hath all power in heaven and in earth*, Matt. xxviii. 18. And there is no love of justice with judgment from any other source, than from the God of heaven who is justice itself, and from whom man has all judgment, Jer. xxiii. 5; xxxiii. 15. Hence is made this conclusion, that all those things that have been said from the benches on the right and on the left, concerning charity, which are, That charity is morality inspired by faith; That it is piety inspired by pity; That it is to do good to the good as well as to the evil; That it is to be every way serviceable to relations and friends; That it is to give to the poor, and to help the needy; That it is to build hospitals, and to support them by gifts; That it is to endow churches, and to do good to their ministers; That it is the old Christian brotherhood; That it is to forgive every one his trespasses;—all these are excellent instances of charity, when they are done from the love of justice with judgment; otherwise they are not charity, but are only like streams separated from their fountain, and like branches plucked from their tree; since genuine charity is to believe in the Lord, and to act justly and uprightly in every work and office. Whoever, therefore, from the Lord, loves justice, and does it with judgment, he is charity in its image and likeness." After these things were said, a silence was made, such as is made by those who see and acknowledge something in the internal man, that it is so, but not as yet in the external; this I observed from their faces. But suddenly I was then taken away from their sight, for I reëntered from the spirit into my material body; for the natural man, because he is clothed with a material body, does not appear to any spiritual man, that is, to a spirit and an angel; neither does any spiritual man appear to the natural man

460. Second Relation. Once, when I looked around in the spiritual world, I heard, as it were, a gnashing of teeth, and also, as it were, a knocking, and intermixed with them, as it were, a jarring sound; and I asked what they were; and the angels who were with me said, "They are colleges, which by us are called inns, where they dispute one with another. Their disputations are heard thus at a distance, but near they are heard only as disputations." I went up and saw little houses built of rushes, cemented together with clay, and I wished to look in through a window, but there was none; for it was not lawful to enter through the door, because thus light would flow in from heaven and confound. But then, on a sudden, a window was made on the right side, and then I heard them complaining that they were in darkness; but presently a window was made on the left side, the window on the right side being shut, and then by degrees the darkness was dispersed, and they seemed to themselves in their light. And after this, it was given me to enter through the door and hear. There was a table in the middle, and benches round about; yet they all seemed to me to stand upon the benches, and to dispute sharply among themselves concerning Faith and Charity; on one side, that faith was the essential of the church, and on the other, that charity was. Those who made faith the essential, said, "Do we not deal with God by faith, and with men by charity? Is not, then, faith heavenly, and charity earthly? Are we not saved by what is heavenly, and not by what is earthly? Also cannot God give faith from heaven, because it is heavenly? And is not man to give himself charity, because this is earthly? And that which a man gives himself is not of the church, and therefore does not save. Can any one, then, be justified before God by works, which are called the works of charity? Believe us, that by faith alone we are not only justified, but also sanctified, if faith be not defiled with the things of merit, which are from the works of charity;" besides other things. But those who made charity the essential of the church, sharply refuted those things, by saying "That charity saves, and not faith. Does not God hold all dear, and will good to all? How can God do this except through men? Does God only give to speak with men the things which are of faith, and does He not give to do to men the things which are of charity? Do you not see, that you spoke absurdly concerning charity, that it is earthly? Charity is heavenly, and because you do not do the good of charity, your faith is earthly. How do you receive your faith, but as a stock or a stone? You say, 'By the hearing of the Word.' But how can the Word, only heard, operate? and how can it operate upon a stock or a stone? Perhaps you are vivified, while you are altogether unconscious of it; but what is that vivification, except that you can say that faith alone justifies and saves? But what faith is, and what saving faith is, you do not know." But then arose one, who was called by the angel that spoke with me, a *syncretist*. He took off his hood and laid it upon the table; but suddenly he put it on his head again, because he was bald. He said, "Hear; you are all wrong; it is true that faith is spiritual, and charity moral, but still they are conjoined, and they are conjoined by the Word, and then by the Holy Spirit, and by the effect, which indeed may be called obedience, but in which man has not any part, because when faith is brought in, man knows no more than a statue. I have long thought with myself concerning these things, and have at length found out, that man can receive faith from God, which is spiritual, but that he cannot be moved by God to charity which is spiritual, more than a stock." When these things were said, those who were in faith alone clapped, but those who were in charity hissed; and the latter from indignation said, "Hear, friends; do you not know that there is a spiritual moral life, and that there is a merely natural moral life; the spiritual

moral life is with those who do good from God, and still as from themselves, and the merely natural moral life is with those who do good from hell, and yet still as from themselves.

It was said that the disputation was heard as a gnashing of teeth, and a knocking, with which was intermixed a jarring sound. The disputation heard as the gnashing of teeth was from those who made faith the only essential of the church, and the knocking was from those who made charity the only essential of the church, and the jarring sound intermixed was from the syncretist. The reason why their sounds were thus heard at a distance, was, because they all had disputed in the world, and had not shunned any evil, and therefore had not done any good from a spiritual origin; and they were also entirely ignorant, that all of faith is truth, and all of charity is good, and that truth without good is not truth in spirit, and that good without truth is not good in spirit, and that thus one makes the other.

461. Third Relation. I was once conveyed to the southern region in the spiritual world, and into a certain paradise there, and I saw that this excelled the rest that I had hitherto surveyed; the reason was, because a garden signifies intelligence; and all who are superior to others in intelligence are transferred to the south; the garden of Eden, in which Adam with his wife was, signifies nothing else; wherefore their being expelled from it involves that they were deprived of intelligence, and thus also of integrity of life. As I was walking in this southern paradise, I observed some sitting under a certain laurel-tree eating figs. I went to them and asked them for some figs, and they gave me some; and lo, the figs in my hand became grapes; and when I was wondering at this, an angelic spirit, who stood by me, said to me, "The figs in your hand have become grapes, because figs from correspondence signify the goods of charity, and thence of faith, in the natural or external man; but grapes the goods of charity, and thence of faith, in the spiritual or internal man; and because you love spiritual things, therefore it has so happened to you; for, in our world, all things are done, and exist, and also are changed, according to correspondences." Then, instantly, there came upon me a desire of knowing how man can do good from God, and yet altogether as from himself; wherefore I asked those who were eating figs how they comprehend it. They said that they could not comprehend it otherwise than that God works it, inwardly, in man and by man, when he is ignorant of it; since if man should be conscious of it, and should thus do it, he would do only apparent good, which inwardly is evil; for all that proceeds from man proceeds from his proprium, and this from nativity is evil; how, then, can good from God, and evil from man, be conjoined, and thus conjointly proceed into act? And the proprium of man in the things of salvation continually breathes merit, and as far as it does this, it takes away from the Lord his merit, which is the highest injustice and impiety. In a word, if the good which God works in man should flow into the willing of man, and thence into his doing, that good would be utterly defiled and also profaned, which, however, God never permits. Man, indeed, can do good and think that it is from God, and call it the good of God through him; but still that it is, we do not comprehend. But then I opened my mind and said, "You do not comprehend it, because you think from appearance; and thought from appearance, when confirmed, is fallacy. The appearance and fallacy thence are in consequence of your believing that all the things that a man wills and thinks, and thence does and speaks, are in himself, and consequently from himself, when yet nothing of them is in himself except the state of receiving what flows in. Man is not life in himself, but he is an organ receptive of life; the Lord is life in Himself, as He also says in John; *As the Father hath life in Himself, so also hath He given to the Son to have life in Himself*, v. 26; besides in other places, as John xi. 25; xiv. 6

9. There are two things which make life, love and wisdom; or, what is the same, the good of love and the truth of wisdom; these flow in from God, and are received by man as if they were his; and because they are felt thus, they also proceed from man as his. Their being thus felt by man is given by the Lord, that that which flows in may affect him, and thus may be received and remain. But, because all evil also flows in, not from God, but from hell, and this is received with delight, because man is born such an organ, therefore no more of good is received from God, than there is of evil removed by man as by himself, which is done by repentance, and at the same time by faith in the Lord. That love and wisdom, charity and faith, or, more generally speaking, the good of love and charity and the truth of wisdom and faith, flow in, and that the things which flow in appear in man altogether as his, and thence proceed as his, may be seen manifestly from the senses of seeing, hearing, smelling, tasting and touching: all the things which are felt in the organs of those senses flow in from without, and are felt in them: in like manner, in the organs of the internal senses, with the difference only, that spiritual things, which do not appear, flow into these, but natural things, which do appear, flow into the former. In a word, man is an organ receptive of life from God; consequently he is receptive of good, so far as he desists from evil. The power to desist from evil the Lord gives to every man, because He gives him to will and to understand; and whatsoever man does from the will according to the understanding, or, what is the same, whatever he does from the freedom of the will according to the reason of the understanding, this remains; by it the Lord leads man into a state of conjunction with Himself, and in this reforms, regenerates, and saves him. The life which flows in is life proceeding from the Lord, which life also is called the Spirit of God; in the Word, the Holy Spirit, concerning which also it is said that it enlightens and enlivens, yea, that it operates in him; but this life is varied and modified according to the organization induced by love. You may also know that all the good of love and charity, and all the truth of wisdom and faith, flow in, and are not in man, from this, that whosoever thinks that such a thing is in man from creation, must finally think that God infused Himself into man, and thus that men were in part gods; and yet those who think this from faith become devils, and with us stink like carrion. Besides, what is the action of man, but the mind acting? for what the mind wills and thinks, this it acts and speaks by the body, its organ; wherefore, when the mind is led by the Lord, the action and speech are also led, and the action and speech are led by the Lord, when man believes in Him. Unless it were so, say, if you can, why the Lord in his Word has, in thousands of places, commanded that man should love his neighbor; that he should perform the goods of charity, and produce fruits as a tree, and should do the commandments; and this and that, that he may be saved. And also, why did He say that man should be judged according to his deeds or works; he who does goods to heaven and life, and he who does evils to hell and death? How could the Lord have spoken such things, if all that proceeds from man were meritorious, and thence evil? You may know, therefore, that if the mind be charity, the action also is charity; but if the mind be faith alone, which also is faith separate from spiritual charity, the action also is that faith." On hearing this, those who sat under the laurel-tree said, "We comprehend that you have spoken justly, but still we do not comprehend." To whom I replied, "You comprehend that I have spoken justly, from the common perception which man has from the influx of light from heaven, when he hears any truth, but you do not comprehend, from the peculiar perception which man has from the influx of light from the world. Those two perceptions, namely, the internal and the external, or the spiritual and the natural, make one with the

wise; you also can make them one, if you look to the Lord and remove evils. Because they understood this, I plucked some twigs from a certain vine, and handed to them, and said, "Do you believe that this is from me, or from the Lord?" And they said, "That it was of me from the Lord." And lo, the twigs in their hands put forth grapes. But when I retired, I saw a table of cedar, upon which there was a book, under a green olive-tree, the trunk of which was bound around with a vine. I looked at it, and behold, it was a book written by me, called ARCANA CŒLESTIA. And I said, that in that book it is fully shown that man is an organ receptive of life, and not life; and that this cannot be created, and thus created be in man, any more than light in the eye.

462. FOURTH RELATION. I looked towards the sea-coast in the spiritual world, and I saw a spacious dock-yard. I went to it, and looked into it, and behold, there were vessels there, large and small, and in them merchandise of every kind, and upon the decks were sitting boys and girls distributing it to those who wished for it. And they said, "We expect to see our beautiful turtles, which will soon rise up out of the sea to us." And lo, I saw little and great turtles, upon the shells and scales of which there sat young turtles, which were looking to the islands round about. The turtles, the fathers, had two heads; one great one, covered over with a shell similar to the shell of their bodies, whence they shone; and another little one, such as turtles have, which they drew back into the fore part of the body, and also inserted in a secret way into the greater head. But I kept my eyes upon the great shining head, and saw that this had a face like a man, and talked with the boys and girls upon the decks, and licked their hands, and then the boys and girls stroked them, and gave them food and dainties, and also precious things, as silk for clothes, almug wood for tables, purple for decorations, and SCARLET FOR COLORING. On seeing these things, I desired to know what they represented, because I knew that all the things that appear in the spiritual world are correspondences, and represent spiritual things, which are of affection and thence of thought. And then they spoke with me from heaven and said, "You know yourself what the dock represents, and also what the vessels, as also what the boys and girls upon them; but you do not know what the turtles represent." And they said, "The turtles represent those of the clergy there, who entirely separate faith from charity and its good works, affirming with themselves that there is plainly no conjunction; but that the Holy Spirit, by faith in God the Father, for the sake of the Son's merit, enters into man and purifies his interiors even to his own will, of which they make, as it were, an oval plane; and that, when the operation of the Holy Spirit approaches to that plane, on the left side of it, it turns itself away around it, and does not touch it at all, and that thus the interior or higher part of the mental powers of man is for God, and that the exterior or lower part is for man; and thus that not any thing that man does, appears before God, neither the good nor the evil; not the good, because this is meritorious, and not the evil, because this is evil; since if they appeared before God, man would perish from both; and because it is so, that it is allowable for man to will, think, speak and do whatever he likes, provided he takes heed to himself before the world." I asked, whether they also assert that it is allowable to think concerning God, that He is not omnipresent and omniscient. They said from heaven, that this also is allowable for them, because God, with him who has got faith, and is purified and justified by it, does not look at any thing of his thought and will, and that he still retains in the inner bosom, or higher region of his mind or mental powers, the faith which he had received in the act of it, and that this act may some time return, when man is ignorant of it. These things are what the little head represents, which they draw into the fore part of the body, and also insert into

the great head, when they speak with the laity; for they do not speak with them from the little head, but from the great one, which in front appears endued, as it were, with a human face; and they speak with them from the Word, concerning love, concerning charity, concerning good works, concerning the commandments of the decalogue, concerning repentance; and they take from the Word almost all the things that are there concerning them; but then they insert the little head into the great one, from which they think inwardly with themselves that all those things should not be done for the sake of God and salvation, but only for the sake of the public and private good. But because they speak concerning those things from the Word, especially concerning the Gospel, the operation of the Holy Spirit and salvation, sweetly and elegantly, therefore they appear to the hearers like beautiful men, and wiser than all others in the world: wherefore you also saw that dainties and precious things were given to them by the boys and girls sitting upon the decks of the vessels. These, therefore, are those whom you saw represented as turtles. In your world, they are scarcely distinguished from others, only by this, that they believe themselves wiser than all, and laugh at others, even those who are in similar doctrine as to faith, but not in those secrets. They carry with them in their clothes some little sign by which they make themselves distinguished from others. The one who spoke with me said, "I shall not tell you what they think concerning the other things of faith, as what concerning election, concerning free agency, concerning baptism, and concerning the holy supper, which are such things as they do not divulge, but we in heaven know them. But because they are such in the world, and after death it is not allowable for any one to speak otherwise than he thinks, therefore, because they cannot then speak otherwise than from the insanities of their own thoughts, they are reputed as insane, and are cast out of the societies, and at length are let down into the pit of the abyss mentioned in Rev. ix. 2 and they become corporeal spirits, and appear like the mummies of the Egyptians; for a hardness is induced upon the interiors of their minds, because in the world also they interposed a hedge. There is an infernal society of them near to the infernal society of the Machiavelians, and they enter every where from one to the other, and call each other companions; but they go out because there is a diversity arising from this, that there was with the former something religious concerning the act of justification by faith, but not any with the Machiavelians.

After I had seen them cast out from the societies, and collected, that they might be cast down, I saw a vessel in the air, flying with seven sails, and in it officers and sailors clad in purple garments, having upon their caps magnificent laurels, exclaiming, "Lo, we are in heaven; we are doctors, clothed in purple and decked with laurels above all, because we are the heads of the wise of all the clergy in Europe." I wondered what this was; and it was said to me, that they were images of pride, and ideal thoughts which are called fantasies, from those who before seemed like turtles, and now like insane persons cast out from the societies and collected together, and were standing together in one place. And then I desired to speak with them, and went to the place where they stood, and saluted them and said, "Are you those who have separated the internals of men from their externals, and the operation of the Holy Spirit as in faith, from its cooperation with man out of faith, and so have separated God from man? Have you not thus not only removed charity itself and its works from faith, as many other teachers amongst the clergy have done, but also faith itself, as to its manifestation before God from man? But I ask, Do you wish that I should speak with you concerning this subject from reason, or from the Sacred Scripture?" They said, "Speak first from reason." And I spoke, saying, "How can the internal and the external with man be separated? Who does not, or may not see, from common perception, that all the interiors of man proceed and are continued to the exteriors and even to his extremes, that they may produce their effects and perform their works? Are not internal things for the sake of the external, that they may terminate and subsist in them, and thus exist, scarcely otherwise than as a pillar on its pedestal? You can see, that, unless there were a continuation, and thus conjunction, the extremes would be dissolved and dissipated like bubbles in the air. Who can deny that the interior operations of God with man are myriads of myriads, concerning which man knows nothing? And of what use is it for him to know them, if he only knows the extremes, in which, with his thought and will, he is together with God. But this shall be illustrated by an example. Does man know the interior operations of his speech; as how the lungs draw in the air, and with it fill the vesicles, the bronchiæ and the lobes; how they send forth that air into the trachea, and there turn it into sound; how the sound is modified in the glottis by help of the larynx; and how the tongue then articulates it, and the lips complete the articulation, that it may become speech? Are not all these interior operations, concerning which man knows nothing, for the sake of the extreme, that man may be able to speak? Remove or separate one of those internal things from its connection with the extremes, would man have been able to speak any more than a stock? Let there be another example. The two hands are ultimate things of man: are there not interior things, which are continued thither from the head, through the neck, also through the breast, the shoulders, the arms and the fore arms; and are there not innumerable muscular textures, innumerable phalanxes of moving fibres, innumerable bundles of nerves and blood-vessels, and many ginglymuses of the bones with their ligaments and membranes? Does man know any thing concerning them? And yet his hands operate from all and each of them. Suppose that those interior things should turn themselves back about the elbow, to the left or to the right, and should not enter by continuity, would not the hand fall off from the arm, and putrify like something inanimate torn asunder? Yea, if you will believe, it would be as with the body, if a man were beheaded. Just so it would be with the human mind and its two lives, the will and the understanding, if the divine operations which are of faith and charity should stop in the middle of the way, and not extend by continuity even to man; man, indeed, would then be not only a brute but a rotten log. These things are according to reason. Now, if you will hear, the same are also according to the Sacred Scripture. Does not the Lord say, *Abide in Me, and I in you; I am the Vine, and ye the branches. He that abideth in Me, and I in him, beareth much fruit*, John xv. 4, 5. Are not fruits the good works which the Lord does through man, and man of himself from the Lord? The Lord also says, that *He stands at the door and knocks, and that to him who opens, He goes in and sups with him, and he with Him*, Rev. iii. 20. Does not the Lord give pounds and talents that man may trade with them, and gain? and as he gains, does He not give eternal life? Matt. xxv. 14 to 34; Luke xix. 13 to 26. Also, that He gives wages to every one according to the labor in his vineyard, Matt. xx. 1 to 17. But these are a few; pages may be filled from the Word concerning this, that man should produce fruits like a tree, should work according to the commandments, should love God and the neighbor, &c. But I know that your own intelligence cannot have any thing, such as it is in itself, in common with the things which are from the Word, which although you speak, still your ideas pervert them; and you cannot do otherwise, because you remove all things of God from man, as to communication and thence conjunction; what, then, remains, but to remove also all things of worship?" Afterwards they appeared to me in the light of heaven, which discloses and manifests what every one is; and then they did not appear, as before, in a vessel in the air, as if in heaven, nor dressed in purple as to clothes, nor crowned with laurels as to the head; but in a sandy place, in garments of rags, and girded with nets like those of fishermen, about the loins, through which their nakedness appeared; and then they were let down into a society which was contiguous to the Machiavelians.

CHAPTER VIII.

CONCERNING FREE AGENCY.

463. Before I proceed to deliver the doctrinal of the New Church concerning Free Agency, it is necessary that those things be premised, which the present church delivers in its dogmatical books concerning it; since, unless this be done, a man who has sound reason and religion may believe that it is not worth while to write any thing new concerning it; for he might say, "Who does not know that man has free agency in spiritual things? Otherwise, what reason would there be that priests should preach, that men should believe in God, that they should turn themselves about, that they should live according to the precepts in the Word, that they should fight against the concupiscences of their flesh, and that they should make themselves new creatures; besides many such like things? Wherefore he cannot think with himself otherwise than that those things would be only words of wind, if there were not any free agency in the things of salvation, and that to deny it would be madness, because contrary to common sense. But that still the present church goes against it, and casts it out of its temples, may be evident from the book called Formula Concordiæ, to which the Evangelical swear, from these things there, which follow. That there is the same doctrine, and thence faith, concerning free agency, with the Reformed, thus the same in the whole Christian world, therefore in Germany, Sweden, Denmark, England and Holland, is evident from their dogmatical books. These things, therefore, were taken from the Formula Concordiæ, of the Leipsic edition, in the year 1756.

464. "I. The doctors of the Augsburg Confession assert, that man, from the fall of his first parents, was so entirely corrupted, that, in spiritual things which relate to our conversion and salvation, he is by nature blind; that he neither understands, nor can understand, the Word of God when preached, but esteems it as a foolish thing, and never of himself approaches to God, but rather is an enemy of God, and remains so, until, by the power of the Holy Ghost, through the Word preached and heard, he is, of mere grace, without any coöperation on his part, converted, gifted with faith, regenerated and renewed; page 656. II. We believe that the understanding, heart and will of a man not born again, in spiritual and divine things, of their own natural powers, cannot at all understand, believe, embrace, think, will, begin, finish, act, operate, and coöperate; but that man is altogether corrupt and dead to good; so that, in the nature of man, since the fall, before regeneration, there is not remaining a single spark of spiritual strength, by which he can prepare himself for the grace of God, or apprehend it when offered, or accommodate himself, and of himself be capable of receiving it; or can, by his own strength, contribute any thing to his conversion, either in the whole, or by halves, or in the least part, act, operate, or coöperate of himself, or as of himself; but that man is the servant of sin and the slave of Satan, by whom he is actuated; thence, therefore, his natural free agency, by reason of his corrupted powers and his depraved nature, is active and efficacious only to those things which displease and offend God; p. 656. III. That man is industrious and ingenious in civil and natural things, but in spiritual and divine

things, which relate to the salvation of the soul, he is like a stock, a stone, the pillar of salt, Lot's wife, which have not the use of eyes, mouth or of any of the senses; p. 661. IV. That man has still a locomotive power, can govern his external members, hear the gospel, and in some manner meditate, but that still in his secret thoughts he despises it as a foolish thing, neither can he believe, and in this respect he is worse than a stock, unless the Holy Ghost in him be efficacious and enkindle and operate in him faith and other virtues approved by God, and obedience; p. 662. V. With some reason it may be said that man is not a stone or a stock; a stone or a stock does not resist nor understand or feel what is done with it, as man by his will resists God, until he is converted to God; and yet it is true that man, before conversion, is a rational creature, that has an understanding, but not in divine things, and a will, but not that he may will any good conducive to salvation; but yet he can contribute nothing to his conversion, and in this respect he is worse than a stock or a stone; p. 672, 673. VI. That the whole of conversion is the operation, gift and work of the Holy Ghost alone, who operates and effects it, by his virtue and power through the Word, in the understanding, heart and will of man, as in a passive subject, when man does not act at all, but is only acted upon; that yet it is not done in the same manner as a statue is formed out of stone, or a seal impressed upon wax, because the wax has neither knowledge nor will; p. 681. VII. It is according to the sayings of some fathers and modern doctors, *That God draws but the willing*, thus that the will of man does something in conversion; but these are not according to the sacred words, for they confirm a false opinion concerning the powers of the human will in conversion; p. 582. VIII. That in the outward things of the world, there is still left to man something of understanding, powers and faculties, although these miserable remains are very weak · and even these themselves, small as they are, are infected and contaminated with poison by hereditary disease, so that they are of no account in the sight of God; p. 641. IX. That man in conversion, by which from a child of wrath he becomes a child of grace, does not coöperate with the Holy Ghost, for the conversion of man is solely and exclusively his work; p. 219, 519 and the following, 663 and the following; appen. p. 143. That yet a man born again by virtue of the Holy Ghost, can coöperate, although much infirmity still accompanies; and that he operates well, so far and so long as he is led, guided and governed by the Holy Ghost; but still he does not coöperate with the Holy Ghost, as two horses together draw a chariot; p. 674. X. Original sin is not a certain fault which is perpetrated in act, but it is fixed most deeply in the nature, substance and essence of man, which is the source of all actual sins, such as depraved thoughts, words, and evil works; p. 577. That hereditary disease, by which the whole nature was corrupted, is a horrible sin, and indeed the beginning and head of all sins, from which, as the root and source, all transgressions proceed; p. 640. That the whole nature, by that sin, as by a spiritual leprosy, is, even in the inmost bowels and deepest recesses of the heart, wholly infected and corrupted in the sight of God; and on account of this corruption, the person of man is accused and condemned by the law of God; so that by nature we are children of wrath, slaves of death and damnation, unless, by the benefit of Christ's merit, we are delivered and saved from these evils; p. 639. That hence there is a total want or privation of original righteousness or the image of God, created with him in paradise, and that thence is the impotence, unfitness, and stupidity, by which man is altogether unfit for all divine or spiritual things. That instead of the image of God lost in man, there is an inmost, most vile, most deep, inscrutable, inexpressible corruption of the whole nature, and of all the powers, especially of the higher and principal faculties of the soul, in the mind, understanding, heart and will; p. 640."

465. These are the precepts, dogmas and decrees of the present church concerning man's free agency in spiritual and in natural things, as also concerning original sin. These have been adduced, in order that the precepts, dogmas and decrees of the New Church concerning those things, may more evidently appear; for from the two forms thus placed together, the truth appears in the light; as is done in pictures, in which an ugly face is placed at the side of a beautiful face, from which, seen together, the beauty of the one and the ugliness of the other, are clearly exhibited to the eye. The decrees of the New Church are these which follow.

466. I. THAT TWO TREES WERE PLACED IN THE GARDEN OF EDEN, ONE OF LIFE, AND THE OTHER OF THE KNOWLEDGE OF GOOD AND EVIL, SIGNIFIES THAT FREE AGENCY IN SPIRITUAL THINGS WAS GIVEN TO MAN.

It has been believed by many, that by Adam and Eve, in the book of Moses, are not meant the man and woman first created; and to confirm it, they have adduced arguments concerning the Preadamites, from computations and chronologies among some nations; and also from the saying of Cain, the first-born of Adam, to Jehovah; *I shall be a fugitive and vagabond in the earth, so that whoever findeth me will kill me. Wherefore Jehovah set a mark upon Cain, that whoever should find him, might not kill him,* Gen. iv. 14, 15. *And after he had gone out from the face of Jehovah, he dwelt in the land of Nod, and built a city,* 16, 17; consequently, that the earth was inhabited before Adam. But that by Adam and his wife is meant the most ancient church in this earth, has been abundantly demonstrated in the ARCANA CŒLESTIA, published by me at London; and there also, that by the garden of Eden, is meant the wisdom of the men of that church; and by the tree of life, the Lord in man, and man in the Lord; and by the tree of the knowledge of good and evil, man not in the Lord, but in his proprium, as he is who believes that he does all things from himself, even good; and that by eating from this tree is meant the appropriation of evil.

467. In the Word, by the garden of Eden, is not meant any garden, but intelligence; nor by tree, any tree, but man. That the garden of Eden signifies intelligence and wisdom, may be evident from these passages; IN THY INTELLIGENCE AND WISDOM *thou hadst made for thyself riches; thou hast been in* EDEN, THE GARDEN OF GOD; and in what follows there, *Full of* WISDOM, *thou hast been in* EDEN, THE GARDEN OF GOD; *every precious stone thy covering,* Ezek. xxviii. 4, 12, 13. These things are concerning the prince and concerning the king of Tyre, of whom wisdom is predicated, because by Tyre, in the Word, is signified the church as to the knowledges of truth and good, by which is wisdom; by the precious stones which were his covering, are also signified the knowledges of truth and good; for the prince and the king of Tyre were not in the garden of Eden. And elsewhere, in Ezekiel; *Ashur, a cedar in Lebanon; the cedars did not hide him in* THE GARDEN OF GOD; *no tree in* THE GARDEN OF GOD *was equal to him in beauty. All* THE TREES OF EDEN, IN THE GARDEN OF GOD, *emulated him,* xxxi. 1, 8. And further; *To whom hast thou become like, thus in glory and in greatness, among* THE TREES OF EDEN, verse 18. This is said concerning Ashur, because by him, in the Word, is signified rationality and thence intelligence. In Isaiah; *Jehovah will comfort Zion; He will turn her desert into* EDEN, *and her wilderness into* THE GARDEN OF JEHOVAH, li. 3. Zion there is the church, and Eden and the garden of Jehovah, is wisdom and intelligence. In the Revelation; *To him that overcometh, I will give to eat of* THE TREE OF LIFE, *which is in* THE MIDST OF THE PARADISE OF GOD, iii. 7. *In the midst of the street and of the river on each side shall be the tree of life,* xxii. 2. From these it is clearly manifest, that by the garden in Eden, in which Adam is

said to have been placed, is meant intelligence and wisdom, because similar things are said concerning Tyre, Ashur and Zion. By garden is signified intelligence also in other places in the Word, as Isaiah lviii. 11, lxi. 11; Jer. xxxi. 12; Amos ix. 14; Numbers xxiv. 6. This spiritual meaning of garden derives its cause from the representations in the spiritual world; there paradises appear where angels in intelligence and wisdom are. The intelligence itself and wisdom which they have from the Lord, exhibit such things around them; and this is done from correspondence, for all the things which exist in the spiritual world are correspondences.

468. That tree signifies man, is evident from these passages in the Word; *All the trees of the field shall know that I Jehovah humble the high tree, exalt the low tree, and dry the green tree, and make the dry tree flourish*, Ezek. xvii. 24. *Blessed is he whose delight is in the law; he will be like a tree planted by rivers of waters, which will produce its fruit in its season*, Psalms i. 1, 3, Jer. xvii. 8. *Praise Jehovah, ye trees of fruit*, Psalms cxlviii. 9. *The trees of Jehovah are filled full*, civ. 16. *The axe lieth at the root of the tree; every tree not producing good fruit shall be cut down*, Matt. iii. 10; vii. 16 to 21. *Either make the tree good, and the fruit good, or make the tree corrupt; for the tree is known from the fruit*, Matt. xii. 33, Luke vi. 43, 44. *I will kindle a fire, which shall devour every green tree and every dry tree*, Ezek. xx. 47. Since tree signifies man, therefore it was a statute, *That the fruit of a tree serviceable for food in the land of Canaan should be accounted uncircumcised.* Lev. xix. 23, 24. Since olive-tree signifies a man of the celestial church, it is said concerning *the two witnesses who prophesied, That they were two olive-trees standing by the Lord of the whole earth*, Rev. xi. 4; also Zech. iv. 3, 11, 12. And in David; *I am a green olive-tree in the house of God*, Psalms lii. 8. And in Jeremiah; *The Lord called thy name a green olive-tree, beautiful with fruit*, xi. 16, 17; besides many other passages, which, on account of their abundance, are not here brought forward.

469. Every one at this day, who has interior wisdom, may perceive or conjecture, that those things which are written concerning Adam and his wife, involve spiritual things, which no one has hitherto known, because the spiritual sense of the Word has never till now been laid open. Who cannot see afar off, that Jehovah would not have placed two trees in the garden, and one for a stumbling-block, except for the sake of some spiritual representation? And that, because they both ate of a certain tree, they were cursed; and that that curse adheres to every man after them, thus that the whole human race, on account of the fault of one man, in which there was not any evil of the concupiscence of the flesh and iniquity of heart, was condemned; does this square with the divine justice? Especially, why did not Jehovah withhold him from eating, when, being present, He saw it? And why did he not cast the serpent down into hell before he persuaded? But, my friend, God did not do this, since thus He would have taken away free agency from man; from which, however, man is man, and not a beast. When this is known, it appears in evidence, that by those two trees, one for life and the other for death, was represented man's free agency in spiritual things. Besides, hereditary evil is not thence, but from parents, by whom the inclination to evil, in which they themselves were, is communicated to their children That it is so, is clearly seen by any one who attentively observes the manners, minds and faces of the children, yea, of the families, from one father; but still it depends upon each one in the family, whether he will accede or recede, since every one is left to his own choice. But what, in particular, the tree of life signifies, and the tree of the knowledge of good and evil, has been fully explained in a RELATION above, n. 48, which may be seen.

470. II. THAT MAN IS NOT LIFE

BUT A RECEPTACLE OF LIFE FROM GOD.

It is commonly believed, that life is in man his, so that he is not only a receptacle of life, but also life. That it is commonly so believed, is from appearance, because he lives, that is, feels, thinks, speaks and acts altogether as from himself. Wherefore this, that man is a receptacle of life, and not life, cannot but seem as something unheard of, or as a paradox adverse to sensual thought, because to appearance. The cause of this fallacious belief, that man is also life, consequently that life was created inherent in him, and afterwards produced in man by natural generation, I have deduced from appearance; but the cause of the fallacy from appearance is, that most at this day are natural, and few spiritual, and the natural man judges from appearances, and thence fallacies, and these are diametrically opposite to this truth, that man is only a receptacle of life, and not life. That man is not life, but only a receptacle of life from God, is evident from these clear testimonies, that all things which are created are in themselves finite; and that man, because he is finite, could not have been created but from finite things; wherefore in the book of Creation it is said, that Adam was made of the earth and its dust, from which also he was named, for Adam signifies the ground of the earth; and every man actually consists only of such things as are in the earth, and from the earth, in the atmospheres: those things which are in the atmospheres from the earth man sucks in through the lungs, and through the pores of the whole body, and the grosser parts by food made of things from the earth. But as to what concerns the spirit of man, that also is created from finite things. What is the spirit of man, but a receptacle of the life of the mind? The finite things, from which that is, are the spiritual substances, which are in the spiritual world, and also are brought together into our earth, and therein concealed. Unless these were together with material things in the earth, no seed could be impregnated from the inmost parts, and thence grow wonderfully, without any deviation, from the first stamen even to the fruit and to new seeds; nor would any worms be procreated from the effluvia from the earth and from the exhalation of vapors from vegetables, by which the atmospheres are impregnated. Who can from reason think, that the Infinite can create any thing else than finite; and that man, because he is finite, is any thing else than a form, which the Infinite can vivify from the life in itself? And this is meant by these Words; *Jehovah formed man, the dust of the earth, and breathed into his nostrils the breath of lives*, Gen. ii. 7 God, because He is infinite, is life in Himself; this He cannot create and thus transcribe into man, for this would be to make him God; that this was done, was an insanity of the serpent or devil, and from him of Eve and Adam; for the serpent said, *In the day that ye eat of the fruit of this tree, your eyes will be opened, and ye will be as God*, Gen. iii. 5. That this direful persuasion, that God transfused and transcribed himself into men, was entertained by the men of the most ancient church, at its end, when it was consummated, I have heard from their mouth; and these, on account of that horrible belief, that thus they were gods, lie deeply concealed in a cavern, to which no one can approach, without being seized with an inward dizziness, so that he falls down. That by Adam and his wife is understood and described the most ancient church, was made known in the preceding article.

471. Who does not see, if he can think from reason, elevated above the sensual things of the body, that life is not creatable? For what is life, but the inmost activity of love and wisdom, which are in God, and are God, which life also may be called the very living force? He who sees this, can also see that that life cannot be transcribed into any man, except together with love and wisdom. Who denies, or can deny, that all the good of love and all the truth of wisdom are solely from God; and that, as far as man receives them

from God, so far he lives from God, and is said to be born of God, that is, regenerated. And, on the other hand, as far as any does not receive love and wisdom, or, what is similar, charity and faith, so far he does not receive life, which in itself is life, from God, but from hell, which is no other life than inverted life, which is called spiritual death.

472. From the things said above, it may be perceived and concluded that the following things are not creatable, viz: 1. that the infinite is not; 2. that love and wisdom are not; 3. and thence life is not; 4. nor light and heat; 5. yea, neither activity itself viewed in itself; but that organs receiving them are creatable and created. These things may be illustrated by these comparisons;—that light is not creatable, but its organ, which is the eye; that sound, which is an activity of the atmosphere, is not creatable, but its organ, which is the ear; that neither is heat, which is the primary active principle, for receiving which, all the things which are in the three kingdoms of nature were created, which according to reception do not act, but are acted upon. It is from creation, that where there are things active, there are also things passive, and that those two join themselves together as into one. If the active were creatable, as the passive, there would have been no need of the sun, and of heat and light thence, but all created things might subsist without them: when yet, if those should be removed, the created universe would fall into chaos. The sun of the world itself consists of created substances, the activity of which produces fire. These things are adduced for the sake of illustration. It would be similar with man, if spiritual light, which in its essence is wisdom, and spiritual heat, which in its essence is love, should not flow into man and be received by man. The whole man is nothing else than a form organized for the reception of those two, as well from the natural world as from the spiritual world, for they correspond to each other. If it were denied that man is a form receptive of love and wisdom from God, influx would also be denied, and thus that all good is from God; and likewise conjunction with God would be denied, and thence it would be an empty word, that man may be a habitation and temple of God.

473. But that man does not know this from any light of reason, is because fallacies from the believed appearances of the external senses of the body overshadow that light. That man feels no otherwise than that he lives from his own life, is because the instrumental feels the principal as its own, and cannot, therefore, distinguish them; for the principal cause and the instrumental cause act together as one cause, according to a maxim known in the learned world. The principal cause is life, and the instrumental cause is the mind of man. It appears as if beasts also possessed life created in themselves, but this is a similar fallacy; for they are organs created for receiving light and heat from the natural world, and at the same time from the spiritual world; for every species is a form of some natural love, and receives light and heat from the spiritual world mediately through heaven or hell, gentle beasts through heaven, and ferocious ones through hell. Man alone receives light and heat, that is, wisdom and love, immediately from the Lord; this is the difference.

474. That the Lord is Life in Himself, thus Life itself, He teaches in John; *The Word was with God, and God was the Word. In Him was Life, and the Life was the light of men*, John i. 1, 4. And also, *As the Father hath Life in Himself, so He hath given to the Son to have Life in Himself*, v. 26 And again, *I am the Way, the Truth and the Life*, xiv. 6. And again, *He that followeth Me shall have the light of Life*, viii. 12.

475. III. That Man, while he lives in the World, is held in the middle between Heaven and Hell, and there in spiritual Equilibrium, which is Free Agency.

That it may be known what free agency is, and of what quality, it is necessary that it should be known whence it is; from a knowledge of its origin, especially, it is known not only that it is, but also what it is. Its origin is from the spiritual world, where the mind of man is held by the Lord The mind of man is his spirit, which lives after death; and his spirit is continually in consociation with its like in that world; and his spirit, by the material body with which it is encompassed, is with men in the natural world. That man does not know that he is in the midst of spirits as to his mind, is because those spirits with whom he is in consociation in the spiritual world, think and speak spiritually, but the spirit of man, while it is in the material body, naturally; and spiritual thought and speech cannot be understood nor perceived by the natural man, nor the reverse; thence it is, that neither can they be seen. But when the spirit of a man is in society with spirits in their world, then it is also in spiritual thought and speech with them, because his mind is inwardly spiritual, but outwardly natural; wherefore, by its interiors, it communicates with them, but by its exteriors, with men. By this communication, man perceives things, and thinks them analytically; if man had not this, he would not think any more nor any otherwise than a beast; as also, if all commerce with spirits should be taken away from him, he would die in an instant. But that it may be comprehended how man can be held in the middle between heaven and hell, and thereby in spiritual equilibrium, whence he has free agency, it shall be told in a few words. The spiritual world consists of heaven and hell, heaven is over the head, and hell there under the feet; yet still not in the middle of the globe inhabited by men, but under the earths of that world, which also are of a spiritual origin, and thence not in what is extended, but in the appearance of what is extended. Between heaven and hell there is a great interstice, which appears to those who are there like an entire orb. Into this interstice evil from hell is exhaled in all abundance; and on the other hand, good from heaven flows in thither also in all abundance. It is this interstice, of which Abraham said to the rich man in hell, *Between us and you there is a great gulf fixed, so that those who would pass over from hence to you cannot; neither can those who are there pass over to us*, Luke xvi. 26. Every man, as to his spirit, is in the middle of this interstice, solely in order that he may be in free agency. This interstice, because it is so great, and appears to those who are there as a great orb, is called THE WORLD OF SPIRITS; it is also full of spirits, because every man after death first comes thither, and is there prepared either for heaven or for hell; he is there among them in consociation, as before among men in the former world. There is no purgatory there; this is a fable invented by the Roman Catholics. But that world has been particularly treated of in the work concerning HEAVEN AND HELL, published at London, in the year 1758, n. 536 to 603.

476. Every man, from infancy even to old age, changes places or situations in this world. When an INFANT, he is held in the eastern quarter toward the north there; and when a child, as he learns the rudiments of religion, he successively recedes from the north to the south; when a youth, as he begins to think from his own mind, he is carried towards the south; and afterwards, when he has come to the exercise of his own judgment and his own right, according to his advancement in such things as inwardly have respect to God and love towards the neighbor, into the south to the east. But if he favors evil, and imbibes it, he advances towards the west; for all in the spiritual world dwell according to quarters; in the EAST, those who are in good from the Lord, for there is the sun, in the midst of which is the Lord; in the NORTH, those who are in ignorance; in the SOUTH, those who are in intelligence; and in the WEST, those who are in evil. Man himself is not held, as to his body, in that interstice or middle region, but as to his spirit; and as this changes state by coming to good or to evil, so it

is transferred to places or situations in this or that quarter, and there comes into consociation with the inhabitants. But it is to be known, that the Lord does not transfer man hither or thither, but man himself in different ways. If he chooses good, then man, together with the Lord, or rather the Lord, together with man, transfers his spirit towards the east; but if man chooses evil, then man, together with the devil, or rather the devil, together with man, transfers his spirit towards the west. It is to be observed, that when heaven is here mentioned, the Lord also is meant, because the Lord is the all in all of heaven; and when the devil is mentioned, hell is meant, because all there are devils.

477. That man is held in this great interstice, and there continually in the middle of it, is solely in order that he may be in free agency in spiritual things; for this equilibrium is a spiritual equilibrium, because it is between heaven and hell, thus between good and evil. All who are in that great interstice, as to their interiors, are conjoined either with the angels of heaven, or with the devils of hell; but at this day, either with the angels of Michael, or with the angels of the dragon. Every man, after death, betakes himself to his own in that interstice, and associates himself with those who are in a similar love, for love conjoins every one there with his like, and causes him to respire freely, and to be in the state of his past life. But then the externals, which do not make one with the internals, are successively put off; which being done, the good are elevated into heaven, and the evil betake themselves to hell, each to those with whom, as to the reigning love, he makes one.

478. But this spiritual equilibrium, which is free agency, may be illustrated by natural equilibriums. It is like the equilibrium of a man bound around the body, or at the arms, between two men of the same strength, one of whom draws the middle man to the right, and the other to the left; that then the man in the middle can turn himself either way, as if not acted upon by any force; and if he betakes himself to the right hand, he draws the man at the left hand to himself with violence, so that the man at the left hand falls to the earth. So it would be if any one, ever so weak, should be bound between three men on the right hand and as many on the left, of the same power; and so also if between camels or horses. Spiritual equilibrium, which is free agency, may be compared with a balance, in each scale of which are placed equal weights; if then a little be added to the scale of one side, the tongue of the balance above vibrates: it is similar also with a bar or with a large beam placed upon its roller. All and each of the things which are within man, as the heart, the lungs, the stomach, the liver, the pancreas, the spleen, the intestines, and the rest, are in such equilibrium; thence it is that every one in the greatest quietness can perform its functions. It is so with all the muscles; without such an equilibrium of these, all action and reaction would cease, and man would no longer act as man. Since, therefore, all the things that are in the body are in such equilibrium, all the things that are in the brain are also in the like; consequently all the things that are in the mind there, which refer themselves to the will and the understanding. Beasts, birds, fishes and insects, also have freedom, but these are carried away by the senses of their body, at the suggestion of appetite and pleasure. Man would not be unlike these, if he had the liberty of doing, as he has the liberty of thinking; he likewise would be carried away only by the senses of his body, at the suggestion of lust and pleasure. The case is otherwise with him who imbibes the spiritual things of the church, and restrains his free agency by them; he is withdrawn by the Lord from lusts and evil pleasures, and the connate desires of them, and acquires an affection for good, and an aversion to evil; he is then transferred by the Lord nearer to the east, and at the same time to the south, in the spiritual world, and is put in celestial freedom, which is truly freedom.

479. IV. THAT FROM THE PERMISSION OF EVIL, IN WHICH THE INTERNAL MAN OF EVERY ONE IS, IT IS EVIDENTLY MANIFEST THAT MAN HAS FREE AGENCY IN SPIRITUAL THINGS.

That man has free agency in spiritual things, is to be confirmed, first from general things, and afterwards from particular things, which every one at the first hearing will acknowledge. THE GENERAL THINGS are these: 1. That the wisest of mankind, Adam and his wife, suffered themselves to be seduced by the serpent. 2. That their first son, Cain, killed his brother Abel; and Jehovah God did not withdraw them by speaking with them, but only by cursing them after the deeds. 3. That the Israelitish nation, in the desert, worshipped a golden calf; when yet Jehovah saw this, from mount Sinai, and did not guard against it. 4. That David numbered the people, and therefore a pestilence was sent, by which so many thousands of men perished; and that God, not before, but after the deed, sent to him the prophet Gad, and denounced punishment. 5. That Solomon was permitted to institute idolatrous worship. 6. And many kings after him, to profane the temple and the holy things of the church. 7. And at length, that that nation was permitted to crucify the Lord. That Mahomet was permitted to institute a species of religion in many things not conformable to the Sacred Scripture. 8. That the Christian religion is divided into many sects, and each into heresies. 9. That there are so many impious people in Christendom, and also glorying in impiety; as also machinations and stratagems, even against the pious, just and sincere. 10. That injustice sometimes triumphs over justice in judgments and business. 11. That the impious also are exalted to honors, and become grandees and primates. 12. That wars are permitted, and then the destruction of so many men, and the plundering of so many cities, nations and families; besides many other things. Can any one deduce such things from any other source, than from the free agency with every man? The permission known in the whole world, is from no other origin. That the laws of permission are also laws of Divine Providence, may be seen in the work concerning THE DIVINE PROVIDENCE, printed at Amsterdam, in the year 1765, n. 234 to 274, where the things above adduced also are explained.

480. THE PARTICULAR THINGS, showing that there is free agency in spiritual things equally as in natural, are innumerable. Let every one, if he will, consult himself, whether he cannot think seventy times in a day, or three hundred times in a week, concerning God, concerning the Lord, concerning the Holy Spirit, and concerning divine things, which are called the Spiritual things of the church; whether he then feels any thing forced, if he be carried to it from any pleasure, yea, if from any lust, and this whether he have faith, or whether he have not faith. Try, also, in whatever state you may be, whether you can think any thing without free agency, as well in your conversation as in your prayers to God, then in preaching, and also in hearing; does not free agency carry every point in those things? Yea, that without free agency in every thing, yea, in the least things, you would not respire any more than a statue; for respiration follows thought, and thence speech, at every step. I say, not any more than a statue, and not any more than a beast, for a beast respires from natural free agency, but man from free agency in natural things, and at the same time in spiritual; for man is not born like a beast. A beast is born, with all the ideas, attendants of its natural love, into such things as are of nutrition and prolification; but man, without connate ideas, only into the faculty of knowing, understanding and being wise, and into the inclination to love himself and the world, and also the neighbor and God. Wherefore it is said, that if free agency should be taken away from him in every thing that he wills and thinks, he would not respire any more than a statue; and it is not said, not any more than a beast.

481. That man has free agency in natural things, is not denied; but man has this from his free agency in spiritual things; for the Lord from above, or from within, flows into every man with the divine good and the divine truth, as was before shown, and thereby inspires life into man, distinct from the life of beasts, and gives him the ability to will to receive those things, and to act from them; and this He never takes away from any one. Thence it follows, that it is the perpetual will of the Lord, that man should receive truth and do good, and thus become spiritual, for which he was born; and to become spiritual without free agency in spiritual things, is as impossible as it is to thrust a camel through the eye of a sewing needle, or as to touch with the hand a star in heaven. That ability to understand the truth, and to will it, is given to every man, and also to the devils, and is never taken away, has been shown to me by lively experience. One of those who were in hell was once taken up into the world of spirits, and there, being asked by angels from heaven, whether he could understand the things which they were speaking with him (they were spiritual divine things), he answered, that he did understand them; and being asked, why he did not receive such like things, he said that he did not love them, and thence did not will them. Again, it was said to him, that he could will them. He wondered at this, and said, that he could not; wherefore the angels inspired into his understanding the glory of fame with its delight, which he, having received, also willed and likewise loved those things. But presently he was let back into his former state, in which he was a robber, an adulterer and a reviler of his neighbor; and then, because he did not will, he neither any longer understood those things. Hence it is manifest that man is man from free agency in spiritual things, and without it man would be a stock, a stone, or a statue,—Lot's wife.

482. That man would not have any free agency in civil, moral and natural things, if he had no free agency in spiritual things, is evident from this, that spiritual things, which are called theological, reside in the highest region of man's mind, as the soul in the body. That they reside there, is because there is the door through which the Lord enters to man; under those are civil, moral and natural things, which in man receive all their life from the spiritual things which sit above them; and because life from the highest things flows in from the Lord, and the life of man is to be able freely to think, to will, and thence to speak and to do, it follows, that thence, and from no other source, is free agency in political and natural things. From that spiritual freedom, man has the perception of what is good and true, and just and right, in civil things, which perception is understanding itself in its essence. The free agency of man in spiritual things is, comparatively, like air in the lungs, which is inspired, detained and expired, according to all the changes of thought; and without it, it would be worse for him than it is for one who is afflicted with the night-mare, with the quinsy, or with the asthma. And it would be like the blood in the heart, which if it should begin to be deficient, the heart would first palpitate, and after convulsions, it would entirely cease to beat. And it would also be like a body moved, which is carried as long as the effort is in it, and they both cease together. So, also, it is with the free agency in which the will of man is; both together, free agency and will, may be called the living effort in man; for when the will ceases, action ceases, and when free agency ceases, the will ceases. If spiritual freedom were taken away from man, it would be, comparatively, as if the wheels were taken away from machines, the wings from wind-mills, and the sails from ships: yea, it would be as with a man who yields up the spirit when he dies; for the life of man's spirit consists in his free agency in spiritual things. The ange.s groan when it is only said, that this free

agency is at this day denied by many ministers of the church, and the denial of it they call madness upon madness.

483. V. That without Free Agency in spiritual Things, the Word would not be of any Use; consequently, the Church would not be any Thing.

It is known in all the Christian world, that the Word is, in a wide sense, the law, or book of laws, according to which man is to live, that he may obtain eternal life: and what is said there more frequently, than that man should do good, and not evil; and that he should believe in God, and not in idols? And it is full of commands and exhortations to those things, and of blessings and promises of rewards for those who do, and of curses and threatenings for those who do not. To what purpose would all these things be, if man had no free agency in spiritual things, that is, in such things as concern salvation and eternal life? Would they not be vain things, which would serve for no use? And if man should persist in the idea that he has no power and no liberty in spiritual things, thus abstractly from any power of the will in them, would the Sacred Scripture then appear to him otherwise than as blank paper without a single syllable; or like paper upon which a whole bottle of ink has been cast; or like dots and points alone, without letters, thus as an empty volume? It would not, indeed, be necessary to confirm this from the Word; but, because the churches at this day have plunged themselves into emptiness of mind in spiritual things, and to confirm it have produced some passages thence, which they have falsely interpreted, it is necessary to adduce some, which command man to do and to believe, which are these: *The kingdom of God shall be taken from you, and given to a nation producing the fruits of it*, Matt. xxi. 43. *Produce fruits worthy of repentance. Now the axe lies at the root of the tree; every tree, therefore, not producing good fruit, is cut down and cast into the fire*, Luke iii. 8, 9. *Jesus said, Why call ye Me Lord, Lord and do not the things which I say? Every one that cometh to Me and heareth my sayings, and doeth them, is like a man building a house upon a rock; but he that heareth and doeth not, like a man building a house upon the ground without a foundation*, vi. 46 to 49. *Jesus said, My mother and my brethren are these, who hear the Word of God and do it*, viii. 21. *We know that God heareth not sinners; but if any one worshippeth God, and doeth his will, him He heareth*, John ix. 31. *If ye know these things, happy are ye if ye do them*, xiii. 17. *He that hath my commandments, and doeth them, he it is that loveth Me, and I will love him*, xiv. 15. *In this is my Father glorified, that ye bear much fruit*, xv. 8. *Ye are my friends, if ye do whatsoever I command you. I have chosen you that ye may bear much fruit, and that your fruit may remain*, xv. 14, 16. *Make the tree good; the tree is known from the fruit*, Matt. xiii. 12. *Produce fruits worthy of repentance*, iii. 12. *That which was sown into good ground, is he that heareth the Word, and beareth fruit*, xiii. 23. *He that reapeth receiveth wages, and gathereth fruit unto eternal life*, John iv. 36. *Wash yourselves, make yourselves clean, remove the evil of your works, learn to do good*, Isaiah i. 16, 17. *The Son of man is about to come in the glory of his Father; and then He will render to every one according to his deeds*, Matt. xvi. 27. *Those who have done goods will come forth into the resurrection of life*, John v. 29. *Their works follow with them*, Rev. xx. 12, 13. *Behold, I come quickly, and my reward is with Me, that I may give to every one according to his work*, xxii. 12. *Jehovah, whose eyes are open to give to every one according to his ways, according to our works He dealeth with us*, Zech. i. 6. The Lord also teaches the same in parables, many of which involve, that those who do goods are accepted, and those who do evils are rejected; as in the parable concerning the husbandmen in the vineyard, Matt. xxi. 33 to 44. Concerning the talents and pounds with which they should trade, xxv. 14 to 31; Luke xix. 13 to 25. In like manner concerning FAITH: Jesus said, *He that believeth in Me shall never die*, but shall live, John xi. 25, 26. *This is the will of the Father, that every one that believeth in the Son should have eternal life*, vi. 40. *He that believeth in the Son, hath eternal life; but he that believeth not the Son, shall not see life, but the anger of God abideth on him*, iii. 36. *God so loved the world, that He gave his only begotten Son, that every one that believeth in Him, might not perish, but have eternal life*, iii. 15, 16. And further, *Thou shalt love the Lord thy God from thy whole heart, and in thy whole soul, and in thy whole mind; and thou shalt love the neighbor as thyself: on these two commandments hang the law and the prophets*, Matt. xxvi. 35 to 38. But these are a very few from the Word, and as some cups of water from the sea.

484. Who does not see emptiness, I will not say foolishness, in those things which were adduced above, n. 462, from the ecclesiastical book called FORMULA CONCORDIÆ, after he has read these and some other passages here and there in the Word? Would he not think with himself, If it were as it is there taught, that man has no free agency in spiritual things, what would religion be, which is to do good, but a vain word? And what is the church, without religion, but as the bark around wood, which does not serve for any other use than that it may be burned? And moreover, he would think, If there be no church, because no religion, what then are heaven and hell, but fables of the ministers and prelates of the church, to inveigle the common people, and elevate themselves to superior honors? Thence is that detestable saying, in the mouth of many, Who can do good of himself? and, Who can acquire faith of himself? And thence they omit them, and live like pagans.

But, my friend, shun evil, and do good, and believe in the Lord from your whole heart, and in your whole soul, and the Lord will love you, and will give love to do, and faith to believe; and then from love you will do good, and from faith, which is trust, you will believe; and if you persevere thus, a reciprocal conjunction will be effected, and this perpetual, which is salvation itself and eternal life. If man from the strength given should not do good, and from his own mind believe in the Lord, what would man be, but a wilderness and a desert; and altogether like dry ground, which does not receive the rain, but repels it; or like a sandy plain, where are sheep which have no pasture? And he would be like a fountain dried up; or like stagnant water, the course being obstructed; or like a habitation where there is no corn nor any water, from which place one must flee immediately, and seek a habitable abode elsewhere, or else die of hunger and thirst.

485. VI. THAT WITHOUT FREE AGENCY IN SPIRITUAL THINGS, THERE WOULD NOT BE ANY THING OF MAN, BY WHICH HE COULD RECIPROCALLY CONJOIN HIMSELF TO THE LORD, AND THENCE NO IMPUTATION, BUT MERE PREDESTINATION, WHICH IS DETESTABLE.

That without free agency in spiritual things, there would not be charity nor faith with any man, still less conjunction of those two, was fully shown in the chapter concerning Faith. Hence it follows, that without free agency in spiritual things, there would not be any thing of man by which the Lord might conjoin Himself to him; and yet without reciprocal conjunction, no reformation and regeneration, and thence no salvation, can be given That without reciprocal conjunction of man with the Lord, and of the Lord with man, there would not be any imputation, is an irrefragable consequence The conclusions which follow from the confirmation, that there is no imputation of good and evil without free agency in spiritual things, are many; and in the last part of this work, where the heresies, paradoxes and contradictions, flowing from the faith at this day, imputative of the merit and righteousness of the Lord God the Savior, are to be treated of, those enormous conclusions are to be laid open.

486. Predestination is a *fœtus* of the faith of the present church, because it is derived from the faith of an absolute impotency and no agency in spiritual things; from that and also from the conversion of man, as it were inanimate, that he is like a stock, and that afterwards he does not know, from any consciousness, whether he be a stock vivified by grace or not; for it is said, that election is from the mere grace of God, exclusive of the action of man, whether it proceed from the powers of nature or of reason; and that election is made where and when God wills, thus from mere good pleasure. The works which follow faith, as evidences, are, before the reflecting sight, similar to the works of the flesh; and the spirit, which operates them, does not manifest from what origin they are, but makes them of grace or good pleasure, like the faith itself. Hence it is manifest, that the dogma of the present church concerning predestination, proceeded thence, as a shoot from the seed; and I may say, that it flowed as a consequence scarcely avoidable from that faith; which was done first among the PREDESTINARIANS, then by GODOSCHALCUS, afterwards by CALVIN and his followers, and at last was firmly established by the SYNOD OF DORT; and thence, as the palladium of religion, or rather as the head of Gorgon or Medusa engraved upon the shield of Pallas, it was brought by the SUPRALAPSARIANS and INFRALAPSARIANS into their church. But what could have been devised more pernicious, or what could have been believed concerning God more cruel, than that some of the human race were predestined to damnation? For it would be a cruel faith, that the Lord, who is Love itself and Mercy itself, wills that a multitude of men should be born for hell, or that myriads of myriads should be born accursed, that is, should be born devils and satans, and that from his divine wisdom, which is infinite, He did not, and does not, provide that those who live well and acknowledge a God, should not be cast into eternal fire and torment. Still the Lord is the Creator and Savior of all, and He alone leads all, and wills the death of none What more horrible, then, can be believed and conceived, than that a multitude of nations and people, under his auspices and under his inspection, should be, by predestination, delivered to the devil as a prey, and should glut his maw? But this is a *fœtus* of the faith of the present church; but the faith of the New Church abhors it as a monster.

487. Since I thought that such a frantic thing could never have been decreed, still less declared and published to the world by any Christian, which yet was done by so many chosen from the clergy, at the Synod of Dort in Holland, and afterwards was neatly written and published; therefore, that I might not doubt, some of those who were members of that Synod were called to me. When they were seen to stand by me, I said, "Can any one, of any sound reason, conclude predestination? Can it be otherwise, than that cruel ideas concerning God should flow thence, and shocking ideas concerning religion? Can he who has, by confirmations, engraved predestination on his heart, think any thing concerning all the things of the church, but that they are vain? In like manner concerning the Word? And concerning God, because He has predestined so many myriads of men to hell, but as concerning a tyrant?" When I had said these things, they looked at me with a satanic look, saying, "We were among those chosen at the Synod of Dort, and then, and still more afterwards, confirmed ourselves in many things concerning God, concerning the Word and concerning religion, which we durst not publish; but when we spoke and taught concerning that, we wove and twisted a web of threads of various colors, and strewed upon it feathers borrowed from the wings of peacocks." But, because they now wished to do so, the angels, by the power given to them from the Lord, closed up the externals of their mind, and opened its internals with them, and from these they were forced to speak; and then they said,

'Our faith, which we formed by conclusions, one following from another, was, and still is, this: 1. That there is no Word of Jehovah God, but some windy thing breathed out of the mouth of the prophets: this we have thought, because the Word predestinates all to heaven, and that only man is in fault, if he does not walk the ways which lead thither. 2. That there is religion, because there ought to be; but that it is like a tempest bearing a fragrant odor for the vulgar; that it is, therefore, to be taught by ministers, both small and great, and that too from the Word, because this is received: this we have thought, because, where predestination is, there religion is nothing. 3. That the civil laws of justice are religion; but that predestination is not according to a life from them, but from the mere good pleasure of God, as with a king of absolute power from the face alone being seen. 4. That all things that the church teaches, except THAT THERE IS A GOD, are to be exploded as vanities, and rejected as chaff. 5. That the spiritual things, which are vaunted, are no more than ethereal things under the sun, which, if they penetrate deeply into a man, induce upon him a dizziness and stupor, and make him a detestable monster in the sight of God." 6. Being questioned concerning the faith from which they deduced predestination, whether they believed it to be spiritual, they said, "It is made according to that faith, but that when it is given, they are like stocks, from which indeed they are vivified, but not spiritually." After they had uttered these horrible things, they wished to go back, but I said to them, "Stay yet a little while, and I will read to you from Isaiah;" and I read these words, *Rejoice not, whole Philistia, that the rod smiting thee is broken; for out of the root of the serpent came forth a basilisk, whose fruit shall be a venomous flying serpent*, xiv. 29. And I explained it by the spiritual sense; that by *Philistia* is meant the church separate from charity; that by *the basilisk, which came forth out of the root of the serpent*, is meant its doctrine concerning three Gods, and concerning imputative faith applied to each singly; and that by *its fruit, which is a venomous flying serpent*, is meant, no imputation of good and evil, but immediate mercy, whether man has lived well or ill. When they had heard this, they said, "This may be; but take from that volume which you call the Holy Word, something respecting predestination." And I opened, and in the same prophet I found this, which was opposite; *They laid the eggs of an asp, and wove spiders' webs; he that eateth of their eggs dieth, and when any one crusheth, a viper is hatched*, lix. 5. When they had heard these words, they could not bear the explanation; but some of those who had been called to me (there were five) hastened into a cave, around which appeared a dusky fire; a sign that they had not faith nor charity. Hence it is manifest, that that synodical decree concerning predestination, is not only an insane heresy, but also a cruel heresy: wherefore it should be eradicated from the brain, so that not even a trace of it may be left.

488. The horrible faith, that God predestinates men to hell, may be compared with the savageness of parents among some barbarous nations, who cast out their sucking children and infants into the streets; and with the savageness of some enemies, who throw men that are slain into the woods to be devoured by wild beasts. It may also be compared with the cruelty of a tyrant, who divides the people subject to him into companies, and delivers some of them to executioners, throws some into the depth of the sea, and some into the fire. It may be compared also with the outrageousness of certain wild beasts, which devour their young; and also it may be compared with the madness of dogs, which fly at their own images seen in a looking-glass.

489. VII. THAT WITHOUT FREE AGENCY IN SPIRITUAL THINGS, GOD WOULD BE THE CAUSE OF EVIL, AND THUS THERE WOULD BE NO IMPUTATION.

That God is the cause of evil, follows from the present faith, which was first devised by those who constituted the council in the city of Nice. There was forged and produced the heresy, as yet persisting, that there were three divine persons from eternity, and each one a God by himself. When this egg was hatched, its favorers could not do otherwise than address each person separately as God. They compiled a faith imputative of the merit or righteousness of the Lord God the Savior; and that no man might enter into merit with the Lord, they took away from man all free agency in spiritual things, and imposed on him extreme impotence, as to that faith; and because they deduced every thing spiritual of the church from that faith alone, they declared a like impotence, as to every thing which the church teaches concerning salvation. Thence sprung direful heresies, one after another, founded upon that faith and the impotence of man in spiritual things, and also that most pernicious one concerning predestination, which was treated of in the preceding article; all which involve that God is the cause of evil, or that God created both good and evil. But, my friend, trust not any council, but trust the Word of the Lord, which is above councils. What have not the Roman Catholic councils devised? and what has not the council of Dort, whence predestination, that horrid viper, was drawn forth? It may be thought, that the free agency given to man in spiritual things, was the mediate cause of evil; consequently, that if such free agency had not been given to him, he could not have transgressed. But, my friend, stop here and consider, whether any man could have been so created as to be a man, without free agency in spiritual things. If that were taken away from him, he would no longer be a man, but only a statue. What is free agency, but to be able to will and do, and to think and speak, in all appearance, as from one's self? Since this was given to man, that he might live a man, therefore two trees were placed in the garden of Eden, the tree of life, and the tree of the knowledge of good and evil; by which is signified, that from the freedom given to him, he could eat of the fruit of the tree of life, and of the fruit of the tree of knowledge of good and evil.

490. That every thing that God created was good, is manifest from the first chapter of Genesis, where it is said, verses 10, 12, 18, 21, 25, *God saw that it was good;* and at length, verse 31, *God saw all that He had made, and behold, it was very good;* and also from the primeval state of man in paradise. But that evil arose from man, is manifest from the state of Adam at or after the fall, in that he was driven out of paradise. Hence it is manifest, that unless free agency in spiritual things had been given to man, God himself would have been the cause of evil, and not man, and thus that God must have created both good and evil; that He also created evil is horrible to think. That God did not create evil, because He endued man with free agency in spiritual things, and that He never inspires him with any evil, is because He is good itself, and in this God is omnipresent, and continually urges and entreats that He may be received; and if He is not received, still He does not recede; for if He should recede, man would die in an instant; yea, he would fall into nonentity; for the life of man, and the subsistence of all things of which it consists, is from God. The reason that God did not create evil, but that man introduced it, is, because man turns the good, which continually flows in from God, into evil, by turning himself away from God and turning himself to himself; and when this is done, there remains the delight of good, and this then becomes the delight of evil; for without a delight remaining, as similar, man would not live; for delight makes the life of his love. But still those delights are diametrically opposite to each other; yet man does not know this, while he lives in the world; but after death he will know it, and also manifestly perceive it; for then the delight of good is turned into celestial blessedness, but the delight of the love of evil, into infernal horrors. From the things above adduced, it is evident, that every man is

predestinated to heaven, and no one to hell; but that man consigns himself to hell, by the abuse of his free agency in spiritual things, by which he embraces such things as arise from hell; for, as was said above, every man is held in the middle region between heaven and hell, that he may be in equilibrium between good and evil, and thence in free agency in spiritual things.

491. That God has given freedom not only to man, but also to every beast, yea, also what is analogous to it to inanimate things, to each a capacity for receiving it according to its nature, as also that He provides good for them all, but that the objects turn it into evil, may be illustrated by comparisons. The atmosphere gives to every man the power of breathing; in like manner to every tame and wild beast; and also to every bird, to the owl as well as to the dove, and likewise the power of flying; and yet the atmosphere is not the cause of that power's being received by those of contrary genius and disposition. The ocean gives a habitation in itself, and also affords sustenance, to every fish; but it does not cause one there to devour another, nor the crocodile to turn its food into poison with which it kills man. The sun dispenses to all light and heat, but the objects, which are the various vegetables of the earth, receive them in different ways; a good tree and a good shrub in one way, and a thorn and a bramble in another, or a harmless herb differently from a poisonous one. The rain falls from the higher region of the atmosphere every where into the earth, and the earth furnishes water thence to every shrub, herb, and blade of grass, and each of them applies it to itself according to its need. This is what is called analogous to free agency, because they imbibe it freely through the little mouths, pores, and holes, which stand open in the time of heat, and the earth only supplies both moisture and elements; and the shrubs, according to something similar to thirst and hunger, attract them. It is similar with men, in that the Lord with every man flows in with spiritual heat, which in its essence is the good of love, and with spiritual light, which in its essence is the truth of wisdom; but man receives them according to his turning either to God, or to himself. Wherefore the Lord says, when He teaches concerning love towards the neighbor, *That ye may be children of the Father, who maketh the sun rise upon the evil and the good, and sendeth rain upon the just and the unjust*, Matt. v. 45. And in another place, *That He willeth the salvation of all.*

492. To the above I shall add this relation. I have several times heard expressions sent down from heaven concerning the good of charity, which passed through the world of spirits, and penetrated into hell, even to the bottom of it; and that those expressions, in their progress, were turned into such things as were entirely opposite to the good of charity, and at length into those which were of hatred towards the neighbor; a proof that all that proceeds from the Lord is good, and that by the spirits in hell, it is turned into evil. The like was done with some truths of faith, which, in proceeding, were turned into falses opposite to the truths; for the recipient form itself turns the things which fall into it into whatever is agreeable to itself.

493. VIII. That every spiritual Thing of the Church, which enters in Freedom, and is received in a State of Freedom, remains; but not the reverse.

That that remains with man, which is received by him in a state of freedom, is because freedom is of his will; and because it is of the will, it is also of his love: that the will is the receptacle of love, has been shown elsewhere. That all that which is of the love, is free, and that this also is of the will, every one understands, when it is said *I will this because I love it;* and the reverse, *Because I love this, I also will it.* But the will of man is two-fold, interior and exterior, or of the internal and the external man; wherefore a man who is a sycophant, can act and speak before the world in one manner, and with his familiar associates in another. Before the world, he acts and speaks from the will of his external man, and with his familiar associates, from the will of the internal; but here is meant the will of the internal man, where his reigning love is. From these few things it is evident, that the interior will is the man himself, for there is the *esse* and the essence of his life; the understanding is its form, by which the will renders its love visible. All that a man loves, and from love wills, is free; for whatever proceeds from the love of the internal will, is the delight of his life; and because the same is the *esse* of his life, it is also his proprium, which is the cause, that that which is received in a free state of this will remains, for it adds itself to the proprium. The contrary is the case if any thing is introduced not in a state of freedom: this is not thus received: but of this in what follows.

494. It is well to be known that the spiritual things of the Word and of the church, which a man imbibes from love, and the understanding confirms, remain with the man, but not so civil and political things; because spiritual things ascend to the highest region of the mind, and there form themselves. The reason is, because there is the entrance of the Lord with divine truths and goods into man, and as it were the temple in which He is. But civil and political things, because they are of the world, occupy the lower parts of the mind, and some there are like little buildings out of the temple, and some like porches through which they enter. That the spiritual things of the church dwell in the highest region of the mind, is also because they properly belong to the soul, and have respect to its eternal life; and the soul is in the highest, and its nourishment is from no other food than spiritual; wherefore the Lord calls Himself Bread, for He says, *I am the living Bread, which came down from heaven; if any one eat of this Bread, he shall live for ever*, John vi. 51. In that region also resides man's love, which makes his blessedness after death; and there also principally resides his free agency in spiritual things: from this all the freedom which man has in natural things descends; and because its origin is there, it communicates it to all free determinations in natural things, and by them the love reigning in the highest takes to itself every thing that conduces to itself. The communication is like that of the vein of a fountain with its waters thence; and like the prolific principle of the seed with the whole and every part of the tree, especially with the fruit, in which it renews itself. But if any one denies free agency in spiritual things, and thence rejects it, he makes for himself another fountain, and opens a way to it, and changes spiritual freedom into merely natural freedom, and at length into infernal. This freedom also is like the prolific principle of seed, which also passes freely through the trunk and branches into the fruit, which from its source is inwardly rotten.

495. All freedom, which is from the Lord, is real freedom, but that which is from hell and thence with man, is servitude; but still it cannot be otherwise than that spiritual freedom should appear to him who is in infernal freedom, as servitude, because they are opposites. But yet all who are in spiritual freedom, not only know, but also perceive, that infernal freedom is servitude; wherefore the angels loathe it as the stench of dead bodies, but the infernals regale themselves with it as with a fragrant odor. It is known from the Word, that worship from freedom is truly worship, and that what is spontaneous pleases the Lord; wherefore it is said in David, *I will sacrifice a voluntary thing to God*, Psalm liv. 6; and in another place, *The spontaneous ones of the people are gathered together, the people of the God of Abraham*, xlvii. 9. Thence with the sons of Israel there were spontaneous sacrifices; their sacred worship consisted principally in sacrifices. On account of God's complacency in spontaneous things, it was commanded, *That every man, whom his heart impelled, and every one*

whose spontaneous spirit moved him, should bring an offering to Jehovah for the work of the tent, Ex. xxxv. 5, 21, 29. And the Lord says, *If ye abide in my Word, ye are truly my disciples, and ye shall know the truth, and the truth maketh you free. If the Son, therefore, maketh you free, ye will be truly free. But every one that doeth sin, is a servant of sin*, John viii. 31 to 35.

496. That that which is received in a state of freedom remains, is because the will of man adopts and appropriates it to itself, and because it enters into its love, and the love acknowledges it as its own and forms itself by it. But this shall be illustrated by comparisons; but because these are taken from natural things, heat will be instead of love. It is known, that by heat, and according to the degree of it, the pores are opened in every vegetable, and that, as they are opened, the vegetable returns inwardly into the form of its own nature, and spontaneously receives its nutriment, and retains what is agreeable, and grows. The case is similar with a beast; every thing that this chooses and eats, from the love of nutrition which is called appetite, this adds itself to its body, and thus remains: that that which is agreeable continually adds itself to the body, is because all the things that compose the body are perpetually renewed. That it is so is known, but to few. Heat, likewise, with beasts, opens also all things of their body, and makes their natural love act freely; thence it is that in the time of spring and summer, they come and return to the instinct of prolification, and also of the education of their offspring; which is done in the greatest freedom, because it is of the reigning love implanted in them by creation, for the sake of preserving the universe in the state created. That the freedom of love may be illustrated by the freedom which heat induces, is because love produces heat; which is evident from its effects, as that man is enkindled, made warm and inflamed, as love is exalted into zeal, or into the heat of anger. The heat of the blood, or the vital heat of men, and of animals in general, is from no other source. It is from this correspondence, that the things of the body are by heat adapted to receive freely those things to which the love aspires. All the things that are inwardly in man, are in such equilibrium and thence freedom; in such freedom the heart impels its blood equally upwards and downwards, the mesentery its chyle, the liver separates, the kidneys secrete, and the glands purify the blood, &c. If the equilibrium should suffer, the member would be diseased, and would be affected with a palsy or an ataxy. Equilibrium and freedom here are one. In the created universe there is no substance which does not tend to an equilibrium, that it may be in freedom.

497. IX. That the Will and the Understanding of Man are in this Free Agency; but that the doing of Evil in each World, the Spiritual and the Natural, is restrained by Laws, since, otherwise, Society would perish in both.

That every man is in free agency in spiritual things, he may know from the observation only of his own thought. Who cannot, from freedom, think concerning God, concerning the Trinity, concerning charity and the neighbor, concerning faith and its operation, concerning the Word and all the things which are thence; and after he has learned the things of theology, concerning each of them? And who cannot think with those things, or against them? yea, conclude, teach and write? If this freedom should for one moment be taken away from man, would not his thought stop, his tongue be dumb, and his hand be motionless? Wherefore, my friend, you can, if you please, by the observation only of your own thought, renounce and reject that absurd and pernicious heresy, which, at this day, has induced in Christendom a lethargy upon the heavenly doctrine concerning charity and faith, and thence concerning salvation and eternal life. These are the reasons why that free agency resides in the will and understanding of man: 1. Because these two faculties are first to be instructed and reformed, and by them the two faculties of the external man, which make him speak and act. 2. That those two faculties of the internal man constitute his spirit, which lives after death, and not under any other law than the divine, the primary thing of which is, that man should think of the law, do it, and obey it from himself, although from the Lord. 3. Because man, as to his spirit, is in the midst between heaven and hell, thus between good and evil, and thence in equilibrium, he has thence free agency in spiritual things; concerning which equilibrium, see above, n. 445, and the following; but whilst he lives in the world, he is, as to his spirit, in equilibrium between heaven and the world; and man then is almost ignorant, that as far as he recedes from heaven and accedes to the world, so far he accedes to hell; of this, man is ignorant, and yet is not ignorant, in order that, as to this also, he may be in freedom, and be reformed. 4. Because those two, the will and the understanding, are the two receptacles of the Lord—the will the receptacle of love and charity, the understanding the receptacle of wisdom and faith; and the Lord operates each of these, while man is in perfect freedom, that there may be mutual and reciprocal conjunction, by which is salvation. 5. Because all the judgment which is done to man after death, is according to the use which he makes of his free agency in spiritual things.

498. Hence results this, that free agency itself, in spiritual things, resides in the soul of man, in all perfection; and thence, as a vein into a fountain, it flows into his mind, into the two parts of it, which are the will and the understanding, and through these into the senses of the body, and into the speech and actions. For there are three degrees of life with man, the soul, the mind, and the sensual body; all that which is in a higher degree in perfection, is above that which is in a lower degree. This freedom of man is that by which, in which, and with which the Lord is present in man; and He continually urges the reception of Himself, but never removes and takes away freedom; since, as was said above, all that which is done by man in spiritual things, not in freedom, does not remain; wherefore it may be said, that this freedom of man is that in which the Lord dwells with him in his soul. But that the doing of evil in both worlds, the spiritual and the natural, is restrained by laws, since otherwise society would nowhere subsist, is manifest without explanation. But still it shall be illustrated, that, without those external bonds, not only society would not subsist, but also the whole human race would perish. For man is captivated by two loves, which are the love of ruling over all, and the love of possessing the wealth of all: these loves, if the reins be given to them, rush on to infinity. The hereditary evils into which man is born, arose principally from those two loves; nor was that of Adam any other than that he wished to become as God, which evil the serpent infused into him, as it is read; wherefore in his curse it is said, that the earth should bring forth to him the thorn and the thistle, Gen. iii. 5, 18; by which is meant all evil and the false thence. All who are enslaved by those loves, look upon themselves alone as the only one in whom and for whom all others are: such have no pity, no fear of God, no love of the neighbor; and thence they are full of unmercifulness, savageness, and cruelty, and of infernal covetousness and desire of robbing and plundering, and of craft and cunning in effecting those things. Such things are not innate in the beasts of the earth; these kill and devour others from no other love than that of satisfying their appetite, and of defending themselves; wherefore an evil man, viewed as to those loves, is more savage, more ferocious, and worse than any beast. That man inwardly is such, manifests itself in seditious tumults, in which the bonds of the law are loosed; and also in massacres and robberies, when the liberty of exercising fury upon the vanquished and besieged is

sounded, from which scarcely one abstains, before the drum is heard, that they must desist. Hence it is manifest, that, if no fear of punishments from the laws restrained men, not only society, but the whole human race, would be destroyed. But all these things are removed only by the true use of free agency in spiritual things, which is to apply the mind to think earnestly concerning the state of life after death.

499. But this shall be further illustrated by comparisons; by these, that unless there were some free agency in all created things, both animate and inanimate, there could not have been any creation. For without free agency in natural things, as to beasts, there would not be any power of choosing food conducive to their nourishment, nor any power of procreating and preserving their offspring, thus no beast. If the fishes of the sea, and the shell-fish of its bottom, had not such freedom, there would be no fish or shell-fish. In like manner, unless it were in every little insect, there would be no silkworm, from which silk could be produced, no bee, from which honey and wax could be derived, nor any butterfly, which sports with its partner in the air, and nourishes itself with the juices in flowers, and represents the happy state of man in the heavenly aura, after he has, like the worm, laid aside his earthly covering. Unless there were something analogous to free agency in the soil of the earth, in the seed cast into it, and in all the parts of the tree thence produced, and in its fruits, and again in the new seeds, there would not be any vegetable. If there were not something analogous to free agency in every metal, and in every stone, precious and common, there would not be a metal nor a stone, yea, not even a particle of sand; for this freely imbibes the ether, exhales its native properties, rejects what is obsolete, and renews itself with fresh substances; thence there is a magnetical sphere around the magnet, a sphere of iron around iron, of copper around copper, of silver around silver of gold around gold, of stone around stone, of nitre around nitre, of sulphur around sulphur, and a various sphere around every particle of the dust of earth, from which sphere the inmost of every seed is impregnated, and the prolific principle vegetates; for without such an exhalation from every particle of the dust of the earth, there would not be any beginning of germination, and thence continuance of it. In what other way could the earth, with dust and water, penetrate into the inmost centre of the seed sown, than by what is exhaled from it? as into *a grain of mustard seed, which is less than all the seeds; but when it hath grown up, it is greater than the herbs, and becometh a great tree*, Matt. xiv. 32; Mark iv. 30, 31, 32. Since, therefore, freedom has been given to all created subjects, to each according to its nature, why not free agency to man, according to his nature, which is, that he may be spiritual? Thence it is, that free agency in spiritual things is given to man from the womb even to the end of his life in the world, and afterwards to eternity.

500. X. THAT IF MEN HAD NOT FREE AGENCY IN SPIRITUAL THINGS, ALL IN THE WHOLE WORLD MIGHT BE BROUGHT WITHIN ONE DAY TO BELIEVE IN THE LORD; BUT THE REASON THAT THIS CANNOT BE DONE, IS BECAUSE THAT WHICH IS NOT RECEIVED BY MAN IN FREE AGENCY DOES NOT REMAIN.

That God, without having given to men free agency in spiritual things, could bring all in the whole world, within one day, to believe in Himself, follows as true from not understanding the divine omnipotence. Those who do not understand the divine omnipotence, may imagine, either that there is no order, or that God can do contrary to order as well as according to it; when yet, without order, there could have been no creation. The primary thing of order is, that man should be an image of God; consequently, that he should be perfected in love and wisdom, and thus more and more become that image. To effect this, God is continually operating with man; but without free agency in spiritual things by which man can turn himself to God, and reciprocally conjoin himself to Him, it would be in vain, because impossible; for order is that from which and according to which the whole world, with all and every part of it, was created; and because from it and according to it all creation was made, therefore God is called order itself. Wherefore, it is the same whether you say, *to do contrary to divine order*, or say, *to do contrary to God;* yea, God himself cannot do contrary to his own divine order, since this would be to do contrary to Himself. Wherefore he leads every man according to Himself, or according to order, and the wandering and backsliding into it, and the disobedient to it. If man could have been created without free agency in spiritual things, what then would be easier for Almighty God, than to bring all in the whole world to believe in the Lord? Could He not have brought this faith into every one, both immediately and mediately; immediately by his absolute power, and its irresistible operation, which is continual, that man may be saved; or mediately, by torments injected into his conscience, by mortal convulsions of the body, and grievous threats of death, if he did not receive it; and besides, by opening hell, and thence by the presence of devils holding in their hands terrible torches; or by calling out thence the dead whom they had known, under the image of frightful spectres? But to these things it is answered from the words of Abraham to the rich man in hell; *If they hear not Moses and the prophets, neither will they be persuaded if one should rise from the dead,* Luke xvi. 31.

501. It is asked at this day, why miracles are not done, as formerly; for it is believed that if they were done, every one would, in heart, acknowledge. But the reason that miracles are not done at this day, as before, is because miracles force, and take away free agency in spiritual things, and from spiritual make man natural. Every one in the Christian world, since the coming of the Lord, may become spiritual, and he is made spiritual solely by Him through the Word; but the faculty for this would be lost, if man were brought by miracles to believe, since these, as was said above, force and take away from him free agency in spiritual things; and every thing forced in such things, brings itself into the natural man, and shuts up, as with a door, the spiritual, which is truly the internal man, and deprives this of all power of seeing any truth in the light; wherefore afterwards he reasons concerning spiritual things from the natural man alone, which sees every thing truly spiritual upside down. But the reason that miracles were done, before the coming of the Lord, was, because then the men of the church were natural, to whom spiritual things, which are the internals of the church, could not be opened; for if they had been opened, they would have profaned them. Wherefore also all their worship consisted in rituals, which represented and signified the internal things of the church; and they could not be brought to perform those rightly, except by miracles; and that they could not even by miracles, because in those representatives there was a spiritual internal, is manifest from the sons of Israel in the wilderness, who, although they had seen so many miracles in Egypt, and afterwards that greatest one upon mount Sinai, still, after a month of days, when Moses was absent, they danced around a golden calf, and cried that that had brought them forth out of Egypt. Very similar things were done by them in the land of Canaan, although they saw the excellent miracles done by Elijah and Elisha, and at last those truly divine by the Lord. Miracles are not done at this day, especially for this reason, because the church has taken away all free agency from man; and it has taken it away by this, that it has decreed that man can contribute nothing at all towards receiving faith, nor any thing to conversion, and in general to salvation (see above, n. 464). The man who believes these things, becomes more and more natural, and the natural man, as was said above, beholds every thing spiritual upside down, and thence thinks against it The higher region of man's mind

where free agency in spiritual things primarily resides, would be closed up, and spiritual things, which have been, as it were, confirmed by miracles, would occupy the lower region of the mind, which is merely natural; thus above this there would remain falses concerning faith, conversion and salvation. Thence it would be, that satans would dwell above and angels below, like vultures over hens. Then after some time the satans would break the barrier and rush with fury into the spiritual things which are placed below, and would not only deny, but also blaspheme and profane them; thence the latter state of the man would become much worse than the first.

502. The man, who, by falses concerning the spiritual things of the church, has become natural, cannot think otherwise concerning the divine omnipotence, than that it is above order, thus concerning divine omnipotence without order; wherefore he would fall into these wild queries: Why the coming of the Lord into the world, and why thus redemption, when God from his omnipotence could have effected the same from heaven as upon the earth? Why should He not by redemption have saved the whole human race without exception? And why should the devil afterwards be able to prevail over the Redeemer in man? Why is there a hell? Could not and cannot God from his omnipotence destroy it, or bring all out thence and make them angels of heaven? Why the last judgment? Can He not transfer all the goats from the left hand to the right, and make them sheep? Why did He cast down the angels of the dragon, and the dragon himself, from heaven, and not change them into angels of Michael? Why does He not give faith to these and those, and impute the Son's righteousness, and thus remit their sins, and justify and sanctify them? Why does He not make the beasts of the earth, the birds of the air, and the fishes of the sea, speak, and give them intelligence, and introduce them together with men into heaven? Why did he not, or why does He not, make the whole world a paradise, in which there should be no tree of the knowledge of good and evil, nor any serpent; but where all the hills should flow with generous wines, and produce gold and silver, each in its native state; and that all might live there in jubilees and songs, and thus in perpetual festivities and joys, as images of God? Would not these things be worthy of an omnipotent God? Besides other similar things. But, my friend, all those things are vain and frivolous. The divine omnipotence is not without order. God himself is order; and because all things were created from God they were created also from order, in order, and to order. There is an order into which man was made, which is, that his happiness or his misery should depend on his free agency in spiritual things; for, as was said above, man could not have been created without free agency, nor even a beast, bird, or fish; but beasts are in natural free agency only, but man in natural free agency, and at the same time spiritual.

---

503. To the above will be added these Relations. First. I heard that there was a meeting appointed, in which they were to deliberate concerning man's free agency in spiritual things: this was in the spiritual world. The learned from every quarter, who, in the world, in which they before lived, had thought concerning it, were present; and many of those who had been in councils and conventicles both before the Nicene council and after it. They were assembled in a round temple similar to the temple at Rome, which is called the Pantheon, which before had been consecrated to the worship of all the gods, and afterwards dedicated to the worship of all the holy martyrs, from the papal chair. In this temple, at the walls also there were, as it were, altars, but at each of them seats, upon which those who were assembled placed themselves, and leaned with their elbows upon the altars as upon so many tables. There was no one appointed president to act the primate among them; but each one.

as his inclination prompted him, rushed forth into the midst, and from his breast uttered and declared his opinion; and, what I wondered at, all who were in that assembly were full of confirmations for the plenary impotence of man in spiritual things; thus they ridiculed the idea of free agency in those things. When they were assembled, lo, suddenly one rushed forth into the midst, and with a loud voice breathed out this: "Man has not any more free agency in spiritual things, than Lot's wife had, after she was turned into a pillar of salt; for, if man had any more free agency, surely he might of himself claim to himself the faith of our church, which is, that God the Father, of entire freedom and good pleasure, gives it gratuitously to whom He wills and when He wills. God would by no means have this good pleasure and sovereign power, if man, from any freedom or good pleasure, could also claim it to himself; for thus our faith, which is a star shining before us by day and by night, would be dissipated, like a star falling into the air." After him, another burst forth from his seat, and said, "Man has no more free agency in spiritual things, than a beast, yea, than a dog; since, if man had it, he might do good from himself, when yet all good is from God; and man can take nothing to himself, which is not given to him from heaven." After him, one leaped out of his seat, and in the midst lifted up his voice, saying, that "Man has no more free agency in spiritual things, even in seeing them clearly, than an owl has in the day time; yea, no more than a chicken yet concealed in the egg. He is in those things entirely blind, like a mole; for if he were quick-sighted in seeing the things, which are of faith, salvation and eternal life, he might believe that he could regenerate and save himself, and also would attempt it, and thus would profane his thoughts and deeds with merits and merits." Again, another ran out into the midst, and uttered this speech: "He who imagines that he can will and understand any thing in spiritual things, since the fall of Adam, is insane, and becomes a maniac; since, in that case, he would believe himself a little god or deity, possessing a part of the divine power in his own right." After him, another hastened into the midst, carrying under his arm a book, to the orthodoxy of which, as he called it, the Evangelical at this day swear, called FORMULA CONCORDIÆ; and he opened it, and read thence the following: *That man is altogether corrupt and dead to what is good, so that in man's nature, since the fall, before regeneration, there is not even a spark of spiritual strength left or remaining, by which he can be prepared for the grace of God, or can apprehend it when offered, or of himself and by himself be capable of receiving it; or, in spiritual things, understand, believe, embrace, think, will, begin, finish, act, operate, coöperate, or apply or accommodate himself to grace or of himself contribute any thing to conversion, either by halves, or in the least part. And that man, in spiritual things, which have respect to the salvation of the soul, is like the pillar of salt, Lot's wife, and like a stock or a stone without life, which have not the use of eyes, mouth, or any of the senses. That still he has a locomotive power, or can govern the external members, go to public assemblies, and hear the Word and the Gospel.* These things are read in my edition, p. 656, 658, 661, 662, 663, 671, 672, 673. After this, they all concurred and together exclaimed, "This is truly orthodox." I stood by and heard all attentively; and because I became warm in my spirit, I asked with a loud voice, "If, in spiritual things, you make man a pillar of salt, a beast, blind and insane, what, then, are the things of your theology? Are they not all and each of them spiritual?" To this, after some silence, they replied, "In all our theology, there is not any thing at all spiritual, which reason comprehends. Our faith there only is spiritual; but this we have carefully shut up, and, that no one may look into it, we have taken care that no spiritual ray may proceed thence, and appear before the understanding; and besides, man does not contribute a particle to it, from his own agency. Charity also we have removed from every thing spiritual; and we have made it merely natural; likewise the decalogue. Concerning justification, the remission of sins, regeneration and thence salvation, we do not deliver any thing spiritual; we say that faith produces them, but how, we do not know. Instead of repentance, we have taken contrition; and lest this should be believed to be spiritual, we have removed it from faith, entirely. Concerning redemption, we have not adopted any other than purely natural ideas, which are, that God the Father concluded the human race under damnation, and that his Son took that damnation upon himself, and suffered himself to be suspended upon the cross, and that thus he brought over his Father to compassion; besides many similar things, in which you will not find any thing spiritual, but all merely natural." But then, in the warmth before conceived, I continued by saying, 'If man had no free agency in spiritual things, what then would man be but a brute? Is not man distinguished by that above the brute beasts? What would the church be without that, but the black face of a fuller, in whose eyes there is a white spot? What would the Word be without that, but an empty volume? What is more frequently said and commanded there, than that man should love God, and that he should love the neighbor, and also that he should believe, and that he has salvation and life according as he loves and believes? Who is there that has not the faculty of understanding and doing those things which are commanded in the Word and in the decalogue? Tell any rustic, whose mind is not closed up by the fallacies in theology, that he cannot, any more than a stock or a stone, understand and will, in the things of faith and charity and thence of salvation, and cannot even apply and accommodate himself to them; would he not then laugh out, and say, 'What is more silly?' What then have I to do with the priest and his preaching? What then is a temple more than a stable? And what then is worship more than ploughing? Oh what madness to talk so! It is folly upon folly. Who denies that all good is from God? Is it not given to man to do good of himself from God, and also to believe?'" When they had heard this, they all cried, "We have spoken from the orthodox, like the orthodox, but you from the rustics, like a rustic." But then suddenly a thunder-bolt fell from heaven, and that it might not consume them, they burst forth in troops, and fled thence, each to his own home.

504. Second Relation. I was in the interior spiritual sight, in which the angels of the higher heaven are, but then in the world of spirits; and I saw two spirits not far from me, yet at a distance from each other; and I perceived that one of them loved what is good and true, and thereby was conjoined to heaven, and that the other loved what is evil and false, and thereby was conjoined to hell. I went up and called them together; and from their tones and answers, I gathered that one as well as the other could perceive truths, acknowledge them when perceived, thus think from the understanding, and likewise determine the things of the understanding as he pleased, and the things of the will as he liked; consequently that both were in similar free agency as to rational things. And besides, I observed, that from that freedom in their minds, there appeared something lucid, from the first sight, which was that of perception, to the last sight, which was that of the eye. But when he who loved what is evil and false thought, when left to himself, I observed that a smoke, as it were, ascended from hell, and extinguished the lucidity which was above the memory, whence he had thick darkness there like that of midnight; and also that that smoke, being set on fire, burned like a flame, which illuminated the region of the mind, which was below the memory, from which he thought enormous falses from the evils of self-love. But with the other, who loved what is good and true, when he was left to himself, I saw, as it were, a gentle flame flowing down

from heaven, which illuminated the region of his mind above the memory, and also the region below it even to the eye; and that the light from that flame shone more and more, as he perceived and thought truth from the love of good. From seeing these things, it was manifest to me, that every man, as well the evil as the good, had spiritual free agency; but that hell sometimes extinguishes it with the evil, and that heaven exalts and enkindles it with the good. After this, I spoke with each of them, and first with him who loved what is evil and false; and after some things respecting his lot, when I mentioned free agency, he grew warm, and said, "Ah, what madness it is to believe that man has free agency in spiritual things! Can any man take faith to himself, or do good of himself? Does not the priesthood teach at this day from the Word, that no one can take any thing, unless it be given from heaven? And the Lord Christ said to his disciples, 'Without Me ye cannot do any thing.' To which I add this, that no one can move a foot or a hand to do any good, or move the tongue to speak any truth from good. Wherefore the church, from her wise ones, has concluded, that man cannot will, understand and think any thing spiritual, and cannot even accommodate himself to will, understand and think it, more than a statue, a stock and a stone; and that therefore faith is inspired by God, who alone has most free and unlimited power, of his good pleasure; which faith, without our labor and power, through the operation of the Holy Ghost, produces all the things which the unlearned ascribe to man." Then I spoke with the other, who loved what is good and true; and after some things respecting his lot, when I mentioned free agency, he said, "What madness it is to deny free agency in spiritual things! Who cannot will and do good, and think and speak truth of himself from the Word, thus from the Lord, who is the Word? For He said, 'Make the fruits good, and believe in the light, and also love one another, and love God;' and also, 'He that heareth and doeth my commandments, he loveth Me, and I will love him;' besides thousands of similar things in the whole Word. Of what use, therefore, would the Word be, if man had no power at all to will and think, and thence to do and speak what is there commanded? Without that power with man, what would religion and the church be, but like a vessel wrecked, which lies at the bottom of the sea, upon the top of whose mast the pilot stands and cries, 'I cannot do any thing,' and sees the rest of the sailors hoist the sails and escape in boats? Was there not given to Adam the freedom of eating from the tree of life, and also from the tree of the knowledge of good and evil? And because, from his freedom, he ate from this tree, smoke from the serpent, that is, hell, entered his mind, on account of which he was cast out of paradise and cursed. And yet he did not lose free agency, for it is read, that the way to the tree of life was guarded by a cherub; and unless this had been done, he could still have willed to eat from it." These things being said, the other, who loved what is evil and false, said, "The things which I have heard I leave; I retain with me what I have declared. But who does not know, that God alone is alive, and thence active, and that man is of himself dead, and thence merely passive? How can such a one, who in himself is dead and merely passive, take to himself any thing alive and active?" To this I replied, "Man is an organ of life, and God alone is life; and God infuses his life into the organ and every part of it, as the sun infuses its heat into a tree and every part of it; and God gives to man to feel that life in himself, as his own, and God wills that man should feel so, in order that he may live as of himself, according to the laws of order, which are as many as there are precepts in the Word, and dispose himself for receiving the love of God. But still God continually holds, with his finger, the perpendicular over the balance, and moderates, but never violates free agency by forcing. A tree cannot receive any thing, which the heat of the sun introduces through the root, unless it acquire warmth and heat as to each one of its fibres; nor can the elements rise up through the root, unless each of its fibres, from the heat received, also give out heat, and thus contribute to the passage. So also does man from the heat of life received from God. But he, differently from a tree, feels that as his own, although it is not his; but as far as he believes that it is his, and not God's, so far he receives the light of life, but not the heat of love from God, but the heat of love from hell; which, because it is gross, stops and closes up the purer little branches of the organ, as the impure blood does the capillary vessels of the body; thus man makes himself from spiritual merely natural. Man has free agency from this, that he feels life in himself as his own, and that God leaves man to feel thus, that conjunction may be effected, which is not possible unless it be reciprocal; and it becomes reciprocal while man from freedom acts altogether as from himself. If God had not left that to man, man would not be man, nor would he have eternal life; for reciprocal conjunction with God causes man to be man and not a beast, and also causes him to live after death to eternity; free agency in spiritual things effects this." Having heard this, that evil spirit removed himself to a distance; and then I saw a flying serpent, which is called a *prester*, upon a certain tree, which presented the fruit thence to a certain one; and then in the spirit I came up to the place, and there, instead of the serpent, appeared a monstrous man, whose face was so covered over with beard, that nothing of it was visible, except the nose; and instead of a tree there was a fire-brand, at which he stood, into whose mind smoke before entered, and who afterwards rejected free agency in spiritual things. And suddenly a similar smoke came out from the fire-brand and encompassed them both; and because they were thus withdrawn from my sight, I departed; but the other, who loved what is good and true, and asserted that man has free agency in spiritual things, accompanied me home.

505. THIRD RELATION. I once heard a noise as of two mill-stones rubbing against each other. I went to the sound, and it ceased; and I saw a narrow gate leading obliquely downwards to a certain vaulted house, in which were many chambers, in which were little cells, in each of which sat two persons, who were collecting from the Word confirmations in favor of justification by faith alone: one was collecting and the other was writing, and this by turns. I went up to one cell, which was near the door, and asked, "What are you collecting and writing?" They said, "Concerning THE ACT OF JUSTIFICATION, or concerning FAITH IN ACT, which is itself justifying, vivifying and saving faith, and the head of the doctrines of the church in our Christendom." And then I said to him, "Tell me some sign of that act, when that faith is introduced into the heart and into the soul of man." He replied, "The sign of that act is in the moment when a man is pierced with anguish on account of his condemnation, and when, in that contrition, he thinks of Christ, that He took away the condemnation of the law, and lays hold of this his merit with confidence, and with this in his thought goes to God the Father and prays." Then said I, "Thus the act is made, and this is the moment." And I asked, "How shall I comprehend what is said concerning this act, that man contributes nothing towards it, any more than he would if he were a stock or a stone; and that man, as to that act, has no power to begin, will, understand, think, operate, coöperate, apply and accommodate himself? Tell me how this coheres with wha you said, that the act then happens when man is thinking concerning the justice of the law, concerning its condemnation removed by Christ, concerning the confidence in which he lays hold of this his merit, and in thought concerning this goes to God the Father

and prays. Are not all these things done by man?" But he said, "They are not done by man actively, but passively" And I replied, "How can any one think, have confidence, and pray passively? Take away from man what is active and coöperative, then do you not also take away what is receptive, thus all, and with all the act itself? What, then, does your act become, but purely ideal, which is called an imaginary entity? I hope that you do not believe, with some, that such act is given only with the predestinated, who know nothing at all about the infusion of faith into themselves. These can play at dice, and thereby inquire whether faith has been infused into them, or not. Wherefore, my friend, believe that man, as to charity and faith, operates of himself from the Lord, and that without this operation, your act of faith, which you called the head of all the doctrines of the church in Christendom, is nothing else than the statue of Lot's wife, tinkling from mere salt, when touched with a scribe's pen, or his finger nail, Luke xvii. 32. This I said, because you make yourselves, as to that act, similar to statues." When I had said this, he took a candlestick, intending to throw it with all his might into my face, and the candle then suddenly being extinguished, he threw it at the forehead of his companion; and I went away laughing.

506. FOURTH RELATION. There were seen in the spiritual world two flocks, one was of GOATS, and the other of SHEEP. I wondered who they were, for I knew that the animals seen in the spiritual world are not animals, but that they are correspondences of the affections and of the thoughts thence, of those who are there. Wherefore I went up nearer, and as I went up, the likenesses of animals disappeared, and instead of them were seen men. And it was made manifest, that those who made the flock of goats, were those who confirmed themselves in the doctrine of justification by faith alone; and those who made the flock of sheep, those who believed that charity and faith are one, even as good and truth are one. And then I spoke with those who appeared like goats, and said, "Why are you thus assembled?" Most of them were of the clergy, who gloried in the fame of their erudition, because they knew the secrets of justification by faith alone. They said that they were assembled that they might sit as a council, because they had heard that the saying of Paul, Rom. iii. 28, *That man is justified by faith, without the works of the law*, was not rightly understood; since by faith there, he did not mean the faith of the present church, which is in three divine persons from eternity, but a faith in the Lord God the Savior Jesus Christ; and by the works of the law, he did not mean the works of the law of the decalogue, but the works of the Mosaic law, which was for the Jews; and that thus, by a wrong interpretation, they had concluded, from those few words, two enormous falsities, which are, that they meant the faith of the present church, and the works of the law of the decalogue. That Paul did not mean these, but the works of the Mosaic law, which were for the Jews, is clearly evident from his own words to Peter, whom he blamed for Judaizing, when yet he knew, *that no one is justified by the works of the law, but by the faith of Jesus Christ*, Gal. ii. 16. By the faith of Jesus Christ, is meant faith in Him and from Him (see above, n. 338). And, because by the works of the law, he meant the works of the Mosaic law, therefore he distinguished between the law of faith and the law of works, and between the Jews and the Gentiles, or the circumcision and the uncircumcision; and by the circumcision is signified Judaism, as every where else; and he also closes those sayings by these words; *Do we then abrogate the law by faith? Not at all; but we establish the law.* All these things he says in one series, Rom. iii. 27, 28, 29, 30, 31. And also he says in the chapter which precedes, *Not the hearers of the law will be justified by God, but the doers of the law will be justified*, Rom. ii. 13. And also, *That God will render to*

every one according to his works, ii. 6. And again, *We must all appear before the judgment seat of Christ, that every one may receive the things which he hath done in the body, whether good or bad*, 2 Cor. v. 10; besides many other things in his epistles; from which it is manifest, that Paul rejected faith without good works, as well as James, ii. 17 to 26. That the works of the Mosaic law, which were for the Jews, were meant by Paul, we have been still more confirmed from this, that all the statutes for the Jews are called in Moses *the Law*, thus the works of the law; which we saw from these passages: *This is the law of the sacrifice of peace-offerings*, Lev. vii. 11. *This is the law for the burnt-offering, for the meat-offering, for the sacrifice of sin and trespass, for consecrations*, vii. 37. *This is the law of the beast and the bird*, xi. 46, and the following verses. *This is the law of one bringing forth, for a son or a daughter*, xii. 7. *This is the law of leprosy*, xiii. 59; xiv. 2, 32, 54, 57. *This is the law of him that hath an issue*, xv. 32. *This is the law of jealousy*, Num. v. 29, 30. *This is the law of the Nazarite*, vi. 13, 21. *This is the law when a man dieth in a tent*, xix. 14. *This is the law concerning the red heifer*, xix. 2. *The law for the king*, Deut. xvii. 15 to 19. Yea, the whole book of Moses is called *the book of the Law*, xxxi. 9, 11, 12, 26; and also Luke ii. 22; xxiv. 24; John i. 46; vii. 22, 23; viii. 5. To this also they added, that they had seen in Paul, that the law of the decalogue is the rule of life, and that it is fulfilled by charity, Rom. xiii. 8, 9, 10, 11; and also that he says, *That there are three things, faith, hope, and charity; and that the greatest of these is charity*, 1 Cor. xiii. 13; thus not faith. They said, that on account of these things, they had been called together. But lest I should disturb them, I retired; and then again, at a distance, they seemed like goats, and sometimes as lying down, and sometimes as standing up; but they turned themselves away from the flock of sheep. They appeared as if lying down when they were deliberating, and as if standing up when they were concluding. But I kept my sight fixed upon their horns, and I wondered that the horns in their foreheads should appear, now, as if projecting forwards and upwards, now as if turning backwards, and at length as if turned entirely back. And then suddenly they turned themselves about to the flock of sheep, but still they appeared as goats. Wherefore I again went up and asked, "What now?" They said that they had concluded that faith alone produces the goods of charity, as a tree produces fruit. But then thunder was heard and lightning was seen from above; and presently an angel appeared standing between those two flocks, and he cried to the flock of sheep, "Do not hearken; they have not receded from their former faith, which is, that faith alone justifies and saves, and that actual charity does not at all. Neither is faith a tree, but man is a tree. But repent, and look to the Lord, and you will have faith: the faith before that is not a faith in which there is any thing living." Then the goats, which had horns turned backwards, wished to come to the sheep; but the angel, standing between them, divided the sheep into two flocks, and said to those on the left hand, "Join yourselves to the goats; but I tell you that a wolf is coming, which will seize them and you with them."

But after the two flocks of sheep were separated, and those on the left hand had heard the threatening words of the angels, they looked at each other and said, "Let us speak with our old consociates." And then the flock on the left hand spoke to that on the right, saying, "Why have you gone away from our pastors? Are not faith and charity one, as the tree and the fruit are one? For the tree is continued through the branches into the fruit. Break off any of the branches, through which the tree by continuity flows into the fruit, and would not the fruit perish, and, together with the fruit, all the seed of any tree about to arise anew? Ask our priests whether it is not so." And then they asked; and they looked around to the rest, who winked with their eyelids that they should say that they spoke well; and after this they answered, "You have spoken well; but as to what concerns the continuation of faith into good works, we know many secrets, but this is not the place to publish them; in the bond or thread of faith and charity, there are many little knots, which we priests only are able to untie." And then one of the priests, who was among the sheep on the right hand, rose up and said, "They answered to you, that it is so; but to their own, that it is not so; for they think otherwise." Wherefore they asked, 'How then do they think? Do they not think as they teach?" He said, "No; they think that all the good of charity, which is called good work, which is done by man for the sake of salvation and eternal life, is not in the least degree good, because man by work from himself, wishes to save himself by claiming to himself the righteousness and merit of the one Savior; and that it is so with every good work in which man feels his own will; wherefore they assert, that there is no conjunction at all of faith and charity, and that faith is not even retained and preserved by good works." But some of the flock on the left hand said, "You speak lies against them; do they not openly preach to us charity and its works, which they call the works of faith?" And he replied, "You do not understand their preachings; only the clergy who are present attend and understand. They think only of moral charity, and its civil and political goods, which they call those of faith, and they are not so at all; for a man who is an atheist, can do them in like manner, and under the same form; wherefore they unanimously say, that no one is saved by any works, but by faith alone. But this shall be illustrated by comparisons. An apple-tree produces apples; but if a man does goods for the sake of salvation, as that tree produces apples by continuity, then those apples are inwardly rotten and full of worms. They say also, that a vine produces grapes; but if a man should do spiritual goods, as a vine produces grapes, he would produce wild grapes." But then they asked, "What are their goods of charity, or the works which are the fruits of faith?" He replied, "That perhaps they are inconspicuous somewhere near faith, to which, however, they do not cohere; they are like the shadow which follows behind a man when he looks to the sun; which shadow he does not observe, unless he turns himself about. Yea, I may say that they are like the tails of horses, which at this day are in many places cut off; for it is said, What is the use of them? they are good for nothing; if they adhere to the horse, they are apt to be defiled." Having heard this, some one of the flock of sheep on the left said with indignation, "There is certainly some conjunction, or else how can they be called the works of faith? Perhaps the goods of charity may be insinuated by God into the voluntary works of man by some influx, as by some affection, aspiration, inspiration, incitement and excitement of the will, tacit perception in the thought, and thence exhortation, contrition, and thus conscience, and thence an impulse to action and obedience of the decalogue and the Word, as an infant, or as a wise man, or by some other means similar to those; how otherwise can they be called the fruits of faith?" To this the priest replied, "No, it is not so; and if they say that it is done by any such means, still they stuff it in their sermons with expressions from which it results that it is not from faith. Some, however, teach such things; but only as SIGNS OF FAITH, BUT NOT AS THE BONDS OF IT WITH CHARITY. Yet some have thought of conjunction by the Word." And then they said, "Is there not thus a conjunction?" But he replied, "They do not think this, but only by hearing of the Word; for they assert, that every thing rational and every thing voluntary of man, in the things of faith, is impure and meritorious, since man, in spiritual things, is not any more able to understand, will, operate and coöperate, than a log." But one, when he heard that man is believed to be such, in all the things which are of faith and salvation, said, "I heard a certain one say, 'I have planted a vineyard; now I will drink wine even to intoxication.' But another asked, 'Will you drink the wine out of your cup, by your right hand.' And he said, 'No, but out of an invisible cup, by an invisible hand.' And the other replied, 'Certainly, then, you will not be intoxicated.'" Presently the same man said, "But hear me, I pray; I tell you, drink wine from the Word understood. Do you not know, that the Lord is the Word? Is not the Word from the Lord? Thus, is He not in it? If, therefore, you do good from the Word, do you not do it from the Lord, from his own mouth and will? If, then, you look to the Lord, He also will lead and teach you, and you will do it of yourselves from the Lord. Who, that does any thing from a king, from his mouth and command, can say, I do this from my own mouth or command, and from my own will?" After this, he turned himself to the clergy and said, "Ministers of God, do not seduce the flock." Having heard this, the greatest part of the flock on the left hand went away, and united themselves to the flock on the right. Then some of the clergy said, "We have heard what we never heard before. We are pastors; we will not leave the sheep." And they went away together with them. And they said, "This man has spoken a true word. Who, that does any thing from the Word, thus from the Lord, his mouth and will, can say, 'I do this from myself?' Who, that does any thing from a king, his mouth and will, says, 'I do this from myself?' We see now the Divine Providence, why a conjunction of faith and good works has not been found, which is acknowledged by an ecclesiastical society. It could not be found, because it could not be given; for there was not a faith in the Lord, who is the Word, and thence there was not a faith from the Word." But the rest of the priests, who were of the flock of the goats, went away, and waved their hats and cried, "Faith alone, faith alone, shall live still."

507. Fifth Relation. I was in conversation with angels, and at last concerning the concupiscence of evil, in which every man is from his nativity. One said, that in the world where he is, those who are in the concupiscence of evil, appear to us angels, as idiots, but to themselves there as supremely wise. Wherefore, that they may be drawn out of their infatuation, they are by turns let into it, and by turns into the rational faculty, which with them is in externals; and in this state they see, acknowledge and confess their insanity; but still they earnestly desire to return from their rational state into their insane state, and also they let themselves into it, as from a forced and undelightful into a free and delightful state: thus concupiscence inwardly delights them, and not intelligence. There are three universal loves, of which every man, from creation, is composed; the love of the neighbor, which also is the love of doing uses—this love is spiritual; the love of the world, which also is the love of possessing wealth—this love is material; and the love of self, which also is the love of ruling over others—and this love is corporeal. Man is truly man, while the love of the neighbor, or the love of doing uses, makes the head, and the love of the world, or the love of possessing wealth, makes the breast and belly, and the love of self, or the love of ruling, makes the feet and the soles of the feet; but if the love of the world makes the head, man is not man otherwise than as a hunch-backed one; but if the love of self makes the head, he is not like a man standing upon the feet, but as on the palms of the hands, with the head downwards and the buttocks upwards. When the love of doing uses makes the head, and the two other loves make in order the body and the feet, that man appears in heaven of an angelic face, with a beautiful rainbow around his head; but if the love of the world, or of wealth, makes the head he appears from heaven of a pallid face,

like a corpse, with a yellow circle around his head; but if the love of self, or of ruling over others, makes the head, he appears from heaven of a dusky fiery face, with a white circle around his head. At this I asked, "What do the circles around the heads represent?" They replied, "They represent intelligence. The white circle around the head of a dusky fiery face, represents that his intelligence is in externals, or around him, but insanity in his internals, or in him; also a man who is such, is wise when in the body, but insane while in the spirit; and no man is wise in spirit but from the Lord, which is the case when he is born and created anew by Him." When these things were said, the earth opened to the left, and through the opening I saw a devil rising up, of a dusky fiery face, with a white circle around his head, and I asked, "Who are you?" He said, "I am Lucifer, son of the morning; and because I made myself like the Most High, I was cast down, as I am described, Isaiah xiv.;" yet he was not Lucifer, but he believed himself to be him. And I said, "Since you were cast down, why can you not rise again out of hell?" He replied, "I am there a devil, but here I am an angel of light. Do you not see my head girded with a white girdle? And also, if you wish, you shall see that I am moral among the moral, and rational among the rational, yea, spiritual among the spiritual. I could also preach." I asked, "How did you preach?" He said, "Against defrauders, against adulterers, and against all infernal loves; yea, then I called myself, Lucifer, a devil, and cursed myself as such, and on that account was extolled with praises to heaven. Thence it is, that I was called son of the morning. And what I myself wondered at, when I was in the pulpit, I thought no otherwise than that I was speaking rightly and truly; but the cause was discovered to me, which was, that I was in externals, and these were then separate from my internals; and although this was discovered to me, still I could not change myself, because I had exalted myself above the Most High, and lifted up myself against Him." Then I asked, "How could you speak thus, since you are yourself a defrauder and an adulterer." He replied, "I am one thing while I am in externals, or in the body, and another, while in internals, or in the spirit; in the body I am an angel, but in the spirit, a devil; for in the body I am in the understanding, but in the spirit I am in the will; and the understanding carries me upwards, but the will carries me downwards; and while I am in the understanding, a white girdle encompasses my head, but while the understanding subjects itself completely to the will, and becomes its slave, which is our last condition, then the girdle grows black and disappears; and when this is done, I can no more ascend into this light.' But suddenly, as he saw the angels with me, he was inflamed in the face and voice, and became black, even as to the girdle around his head; and through the opening, through which he rose, he slid down into hell. Those who were present, from seeing and hearing these things, made this conclusion: That man is such as his will is, and not such as his understanding is, since the will easily carries away the understanding over to its side, and enslaves it. Then I asked the angels, "Whence have the devils rationality?" And they said, "It is from the glory of the love of self; for the love of self is encompassed with glory; for this is the splendor of its fire, and that glory elevates the understanding almost into the light of heaven. For the understanding with every man is capable of being elevated according to knowledges; but the will, only by a life according to the truths of the church and of reason. Thence it is, that atheists themselves, who are in the glory of fame from the love of self, and thence in the pride of their own intelligence, enjoy a sublimer rationality than many others; but then when they are in the thought of the understanding, but not when in the love of the will; and the love of the will possesses the internal man, but the thought of the understanding the external." Further, the angel told the reason why man is composed of the three loves, namely, the love of use, the love of the world, and the love of self. The reason is, that man may think from God, although altogether as from himself. He said, that the highest things in man's mind are turned upwards to God, the middle things there, outwards to the world, and the lowest things there, downwards into the body; and because these are turned downwards, man thinks altogether as of himself, when yet from God.

508. SIXTH RELATION. One day, there appeared to me a magnificent temple, of a square form, the roof of which was like a crown, arched above and elevated round about. The walls of it were continuous windows of crystals, the gate of the substance of pearl; within, on the south side, towards the west, there was a pulpit, on which, at the right, lay the Word open, girded with a sphere of light, the splendor of which surrounded and illuminated the whole pulpit. In the middle of the temple was the sacred recess, before which was a veil, but now removed, where stood a cherub of gold with a sword in his hand, vibrating hither and thither. When I had viewed these things, it flowed into my meditation, what each of them signified; namely, That that temple signified the New Church; the gate of the substance of pearl, entrance into it; the windows of crystals, the truths which illustrate it; the pulpit, the priesthood and preaching; the Word upon it open, and illuminating the higher part of the pulpit, the internal sense of it, which is spiritual, revealed; the sacred recess in the middle of the temple, the conjunction of that church with the angelic heaven; the cherub of gold therein, the Word in the sense of the letter; the sword vibrating in his hand, signified that this sense may be turned hither and thither, provided this is done in application to some truth; that the veil before the cherub was removed, signified that now the Word was laid open Afterwards, when I came up nearer, I saw these words written on the gate, NOW IT IS LAWFUL; which signified, that now it is lawful to enter intellectually into the secrets of faith. From seeing this writing, it fell into my thought, that it is very dangerous to enter by the understanding into the dogmas of faith, which are formed from man's own intelligence and thence of falses, and still more to confirm them from the Word: thence the understanding is closed above, and by degrees below, to such a degree, that theological things are not only loathed, but also obliterated, as the writing on paper is by worms, and the nap on cloth by moths; the understanding remaining only in political things, which have respect to one's life in the dominion where he is, and in civil things which belong to his employment, and in domestic things which belong to his house; and in these and those he continually kisses nature, and loves her from the allurements of her pleasures, as an idolater does the golden image in his bosom. Now, because the dogmas in the Christian churches at this day are formed not from the Word but from man's own intelligence, and thence from falses, and also confirmed by some things from the Word; therefore, by the divine providence of the Lord, the Word with the Roman Catholics was taken away from the laity, and with the Protestants it is open, but still shut by their common saying, that the understanding is to be kept under obedience to their faith. But in the New Church it is reversed; in this it is lawful by the understanding to enter and penetrate into all the secrets of it, and also to confirm them by the Word; the reason is, because its doctrinals are truths continuous from the Lord, laid open by the Word; and confirmations of them by rational things cause the understanding to be opened above more and more, and thus to be elevated into the light in which the angels of heaven are; and that light in its essence is truth, and in this light the acknowledgment of the Lord, as the God of heaven and earth, shines in its

glory. This is meant by the writing upon the gate of the temple, NOW IT IS LAWFUL; and also by the circumstance that the veil of the sacred recess before the cherub was removed; for it is a canon of the New Church, that falsities close up the understanding, and that truths open it. After these things, I saw, as it were, an infant over head, holding in his hand a paper; he, as he approached me, increased to the stature of a middling sized man; he was an angel of the third heaven, where all at a distance appear as infants. While he was with me, he handed to me the paper; but because it was written with circular letters, such as are in that heaven, I returned it, and requested that they would themselves explain the sense of the words there in expressions adapted to the ideas of my thought. And he replied, "This is written there, ENTER HEREAFTER INTO THE MYSTERIES OF THE WORD, WHICH HAS BEEN HITHERTO CLOSED UP; FOR ITS TRUTHS, ONE AND ALL, ARE SO MANY MIRRORS OF THE LORD.'

CHAPTER IX.

CONCERNING REPENTANCE.

509. After treating of Faith, Charity, and Free Agency, it follows next in course to treat of Repentance; since true faith and genuine charity are not attainable without repentance, and no one can repent without free agency. The reason also why repentance is here treated of, is because the next chapter treats of Regeneration, and no one can be regenerated, before the more grievous evils, which make man detestable in the sight of God, are removed, and these are removed by repentance. What is an unregenerate man, but an impenitent man? And what is an impenitent man, but as one who is in a lethargy, and knows nothing about sin, and so cherishes it in his bosom, and daily kisses it, as an adulterer a harlot in his bed. But that it may be known what repentance is, and what it effects, the discussion of it must be divided into articles.

510. I. That Repentance is the first Thing of the Church with Man.

The communion which is called the church consists of all such persons as have the church in them; and the church with man enters when he is being regenerated; and every one is regenerated by abstaining from the evils of sin, and fleeing from them like one when he sees infernal troops with torches about to attack him and cast him upon a funeral pile. There are many things which prepare man for the church, as he advances in the first stages of life, and which introduce him into the church; but the things which effect the church in man, are acts of repentance. Acts of repentance are such as cause that man should not will, and thence should not do, the evils which are sins against God; for before this is done, man stands out of regeneration; and then, if any thought should enter concerning eternal salvation, he turns himself to it, but presently turns himself from it; for it does not enter further into man than into the ideas of his thought, and thence it goes out into the words of speech, and perhaps also into some gestures conformable to the speech. But when it enters into the will, then it is in man; for the will is the man himself, because his love dwells there; and the thought is out of man, unless it proceeds from his will; if it does, then the will and the thought act as one, and together make the man. Hence it follows, that repentance, in order to be repentance, and efficient in man, must be of the will and thence of the thought, and not of the thought alone; consequently that it must be actual, and not merely oral. That repentance is the first thing of the church, is manifestly evident from the Word. John the Baptist, who was sent before to prepare men for the church, which the Lord was about to institute, when he baptized, at the same time preached repentance; wherefore his baptism was called the baptism of repentance, because by baptism was signified spiritual washing, which is a cleansing from sins. This John did in the Jordan, because the Jordan signifies introduction into the church, for it was the first boundary of the land of Canaan, where the church was. The Lord himself also preached repentance for the remission of sins, by which He taught, that repentance is the first thing of the church and that so far as man does it, his sins are removed, and that so far as these are removed, they are remitted. And besides, the Lord commanded the twelve Apostles, and also the seventy whom he sent forth, that they should preach repentance; from which it is manifest, that the first thing of the church is repentance.

511. That the church is not in man, before his sins are removed, every one may conclude from reason, and it may be illustrated by these comparisons:—Who can introduce sheep, kids and lambs into plains and woods, where are wild beasts of every kind, before he has driven out the wild beasts? And who can prepare for a garden a piece of land, covered over with thorns, briers and nettles, before he has rooted out those noxious plants? Who can introduce a form of administration of justice from judgment into a city possessed by enemies, and establish a civil government, before he has expelled the enemies? The case is similar with the evils in man, which are like wild beasts, like briers and thorns, and like enemies, with which the church cannot dwell together, any more than one can dwell in a den where are tigers and leopards; nor any more than one can lie in a bed, upon which poisonous herbs have been strewed and put into the pillows; nor any more than one can sleep at night in a temple, under the floor of which are sepulchres in which are dead bodies: would not spectres infest him there like furies?

512. II. That Contrition, of which it is at this Day said, that it precedes Faith, and is followed by the Consolation of the Gospel, is not Repentance.

In the reformed Christian world, mention is made of a certain kind of anxiety, grief and terror, which they call CONTRITION, and which, with those who are to be regenerated, precedes their faith and is followed by the consolation of the gospel. They say that this contrition arises in them from fear of the just anger of God, and thence eternal damnation, to every one, on account of the sin of Adam, and thence an inherent propensity to evils; and that without that contrition the faith which is imputative of the merit and righteousness of the Lord the Savior, is not given; and that those who have obtained this faith receive the consolation of the gospel, which is, that they are justified, that is, renewed, regenerated and sanctified, without any coöperation of their own; and that thus they are transferred from damnation to eternal blessedness, which is eternal life. But concerning this contrition, it is to be considered, (1.) *Whether it be repentance.* (2.) *Whether it be of any moment.* (3.) *Whether it be given.*

513. WHETHER THAT CONTRITION BE REPENTANCE OR NOT, may be concluded from the description of repentance in what follows, that it is not attainable, unless a man know, not only in general, but also in particular, that he is a sinner; which no one can know, unless he examine himself, see the evils in himself, and condemn himself on account of them. But that contrition, which is said to be necessary to faith, has nothing in common with those things; for it is only the thought and thence confession, that he was born into the sin of Adam, and into a propensity to the evils thence originating, and that, therefore, he incurs the anger of God, and thence, by desert, damnation, the curse and eternal death; from which it is manifest, that this contrition is not repentance.

514. Another point is, since that contrition is not repentance, WHETHER IT BE OF ANY MOMENT. It is said that it contributes to faith, as what precedes to what follows, but that still it does not enter faith and conjoin itself with it by mixing itself with it. But what else is the faith which follows, than that God the Father imputes the righteousness of his Son, and then declares man, not conscious of any sin, righteous, new, and holy, and thus clothes him with a robe washed and made white by the blood of the Lamb? And when he walks in this robe, what then are the evils of his life, but like sulphurous stones thrown into the bottom of the sea? And what then is the sin of Adam, but some such thing, which is

either covered or removed, or taken away by the imputed righteousness of Christ? When a man, from that faith, walks in the righteousness, and at the same time in the innocence, of God the Savior, to what purpose does that contrition then serve, but for confidence that he is in Abraham's bosom, and thence he beholds those who are not contrite before faith, as miserable in hell, or as dead? For it is said, that a living faith is not in those who have no contrition. Wherefore it may be said, that if they have immersed themselves, or do immerse themselves, in damnable evils, they do not attend to them, and are not sensible of them, any more than pigs lying in the mud are sensible of the stench in the ditches. Hence it is manifest, that that contrition, since it is not repentance, is not any thing.

515. The third point which was to be considered, is, WHETHER THAT CONTRITION WITHOUT REPENTANCE BE GIVEN. In the spiritual world, I have asked many who have confirmed in themselves the faith imputative of the merit of Christ, whether they had any contrition, and they have answered, Why contrition, when from childhood we have believed for certain that Christ, by his passion, has taken away all our sins? Contrition does not square with this faith; for contrition is to cast themselves into hell, and to torture the conscience; when yet they know that they are redeemed, and so rescued from hell, and thence secure from harm. To this they added, that the statute of contrition was only a figment, which was accepted instead of the repentance which is so often mentioned in the Word, and also enjoined; that, perhaps, there may be some emotion of mind with the simple who know but little about the gospel, when they hear or think about the torments in hell. And they said, that the consolation of the gospel, impressed on them from their earliest youth, had removed that contrition, so that they in heart laughed at it, when it was named; that hell could not terrify them any more than the fire of Vesuvius and Ætna can those who dwell in Warsaw and Vienna; nor any more than the basilisks and vipers in the deserts of Arabia, or the tigers and lions in the forests of Tartary, can terrify those who are in safety, tranquillity and quietness in some city of Europe; and that the anger of God excited in them no more terror and contrition, than the anger of the king of Persia did in those who are in Pennsylvania. From these things, and from reasons deduced from their traditions, I am confirmed, that contrition, unless it be repentance, such as is described in what follows, becomes nothing else than a sport of the fancy The reason, also, why the Reformed took up contrition instead of repentance, was that they might be torn away from the Roman Catholics, who urge repentance, and at the same time charity; and after they had confirmed justification by faith alone, they alleged the reason, that by repentance, as by charity, something of man, which savors of merit, would enter into his faith and blacken it.

516. III. THAT THE ORAL CONFESSION ALONE, THAT ONE IS A SINNER, IS NOT REPENTANCE.

Concerning this oral confession, the Reformed, who are attached to the Augsburg Confession, thus teach: "No one can ever know his own sins, wherefore they cannot be enumerated; they are also interior and hidden; wherefore the confession would be false, uncertain, imperfect and mutilated; but he who confesses himself to be altogether mere sin, comprehends all sins, excludes none, and forgets none. But, still, the enumeration of sins, although it is not necessary, is not to be taken away, on account of tender and timid consciences; but this is only a puerile and common form of confession for the more simple and ignorant." FORMULA CONCORDIÆ, pages 327, 331, 380. But this confession was accepted instead of actual repentance, by the Reformed, after they had separated themselves from the Roman Catholics, because it is founded on their imputative faith, which alone, without charity, and thus also without repentance, produces remission of sins, and regenerates man; and also upon this, which is an inseparable appendage to that faith, that there is no coöperation of man with the Holy Spirit in the act of justification; and upon this, that no one has free agency in spiritual things; and again upon this, that every thing is of immediate mercy, and nothing at all of that which becomes mediate by man and through him.

517. Among the many reasons why the oral confession that one is a sinner is not repentance, is this; that every man can say this, even a wicked man, and also a devil, and this with much external devotion, when he thinks of the torments in hell, threatening him and present to him. But who does not see that this is not from any internal devotion, consequently that it is imaginative, and thence from the lungs, but not voluntary from within, and thence from the heart? For a wicked man and a devil still burn inwardly with the lusts of the love of doing evil, by which they are carried like mills driven by tempests; wherefore, such an exclamation is nothing else than a contrivance to deceive God or impose upon the simple for the sake of deliverance. For what is easier, than to force the lips to vociferate, and to accommodate the breath of the mouth to it, and to raise the eyes and lift the hands upwards? This is the same that the Lord says in Mark; "*Well hath Isaiah prophesied concerning you, hypocrites; This people honoreth me with their lips, but their heart is far from me*, vii. 6. And in Matthew; *Wo to you, scribes and Pharisees, because ye make clean the outside of the cup and of the platter, but the insides are full of rapine and excess. Blind Pharisee, cleanse first the inside of the cup and of the platter, that the outside also may be made clean*, xxiii. 25, 26; and more in the same chapter.

518. In the like hypocritical worship are those who have confirmed in themselves the faith of this day, that the Lord, by the passion of the cross, took away all the sins of the world; and thereby they understand the sins of every one, who only prays the forms respecting propitiation and mediation Some of these can, in pulpits, with a loud voice, and, as it were, an ardent zeal, pour forth many holy things concerning repentance and concerning charity, and they think both of no avail to salvation; for they mean no other repentance than oral confession, and no other charity than forensic; but they do that to gain the favor of the people. These are they who are meant by these words of the Lord; *Many will say to me in that day, Lord, Lord, have we not prophesied by thy name; and in thy name done many mighty works? But then I shall confess to them, I know you not; depart from Me, ye workers of iniquity*, Matt. vii. 22, 23. Once, in the spiritual world, I heard a certain one praying thus: "I am full of the scab, leprous and filthy from my mother's womb. There is nothing sound in me, from the head to the sole of the foot. I am not worthy to lift up my eyes to God. I am deserving of death and eternal damnation. Have mercy on me for the sake of thy Son. Purify me, by his blood. The salvation of all is in thy good pleasure. I implore mercy." Those who stood by him and heard these words asked, "Whence do you know that you are such?" He replied, "I know because I have heard." But then he was sent to the examining angels, in whose presence he spoke similar things; and they, having made an examination, reported, that he had spoken truths concerning himself, but that still he did not know one evil in himself, because he had never examined himself, and had believed that evils, after an oral confession, are no longer evils in the sight of God, both because God turns away his eyes from them, and because He is propitiated; and that, therefore, he had not repented of any, although he was a deliberate adulterer, a robber, a deceitful detracter, and a burning revenger; and that he was such in will and heart, and thence would be such in words and deeds, unless the fear of the law and of the loss of fame restrained him. After

it was found out that he was such, he was judged and cast off to the hypocrites in hell.

519. What those are may be illustrated by comparisons. They are like temples in which are assembled only spirits of the dragon, and those who are meant by locusts in the Revelation; and they are like the pulpits there, where the Word is not, because it is buried under feet. They are like the walls of houses plastered, and the plastering beautifully colored, within which owls and direful birds of night fly about, the windows being open. They are like whitened sepulchres, in which are bones of the dead. They are like coins made of the lees of oil, or dried dung, and covered over with gold. They are like the bark and rind around rotten wood; and they are like the garments of the sons of Aaron about a leprous body: yea, they are like ulcers, within which there is corrupted matter, covered over with a thin skin, which are believed to be healed. Who does not know, that a holy external and a profane internal do not agree together? Such, also, more than others, are afraid to explore themselves; wherefore they have no more perception of the vicious things within them, than of the noisome and loathsome things in the stomach and in the bowels, before they are cast out into the draught. But it is to be held, that those who have been hitherto spoken of are not to be confounded with those who act well and believe well; nor with those who repent of some sins, and from a like oral confession, while in worship, and still more in spiritual temptation, speak with themselves, or pray; for that general confession both precedes and follows reformation and regeneration.

520. IV. That Man is born to Evils of every Kind, and that, unless he remove them in part by Repentance, he remains in them, and he who remains in them cannot be saved.

That every man is born to evils, thus that from his mother's womb he is nothing but evil, is known in the church; and it became known in consequence of its being taught by councils and by the prelates of churches, that the sin of Adam was transmitted to all his posterity; and that this is the only thing, on account of which every man after him was condemned together with him; and that this is what is inherent in every man from his birth. Besides, many other things which the churches teach are founded upon this assertion; as that the laver of regeneration, which is called baptism, was instituted by the Lord that this sin might be removed; and that this was the cause of the Lord's coming; and that faith in his merit is the means by which it is removed; besides many other things, which the churches have founded upon this assertion. But that there is no hereditary evil from that origin, may be evident from those things which were shown above, n. 466, and the following; that Adam was not the first of men, but that by Adam and his wife, the first church on this globe is representatively described; and by the garden of Eden, the wisdom of that church; and by the tree of life, its looking to the Lord who was to come; and by the tree of the knowledge of good and evil, its looking to self, and not to the Lord. That this church was representatively described by the first chapters of Genesis, has been evinced from many parallel passages from the Word, in the Arcana Cœlestia, published at London. From these things being understood and assumed, the opinion hitherto entertained, that the evil innate in man from his parents is thence, falls to the ground; when yet it does not derive its origin thence, but from another source. That the tree of life, and the tree of the knowledge of good and evil, are with every man; and that their being said to be placed in a certain garden signified the liberty and ability of turning one's self to the Lord, and of turning one's self away from Him, has been fully demonstrated in the chapter concerning Free Agency.

521. But, my friend, hereditary evil is from no other source than from parents; not indeed the evil itself

which a man actually commits, but an inclination to it. That it is so, every one will acknowledge, if he only joins reason to experience. Who does not know that children are born into a common likeness of their parents, as to their faces, and manners, and dispositions? And also that grandchildren and great-grandchildren are born into those of their grandfathers and great-grandfathers, and that thence families, and also nations, are distinguished from each other by many, as Africans from Europeans, Neapolitans from Germans, Englishmen from Frenchmen, and so forth? And who does not know a Jew from his face, eyes, speech and gestures? And if you could feel the sphere of life diffusing itself from the native disposition of every one, you might also be convinced of the likeness of their dispositions and minds. Hence it follows, that man is not born into evils themselves, but only into an inclination to evils, yet with a greater or less bias to particular ones. Wherefore, after death, no one is judged from any hereditary evil, but from the actual ones, which he himself has committed. This also is evident from this statute of the Lord: *The father shall not die for the son, and the son shall not die for the father; every one shall die for his own sin*, Deut. xxiv. 16. This was made certain to me, in the spiritual world, from the infants which die, in that they only incline to evils, so that they will, but still they do not do them, for they are educated under the auspices of the Lord, and saved. The above-mentioned inclination and bias to evils, transmitted from parents to their children and posterity, is broken only by a new birth from the Lord, which is called regeneration: without this, that inclination not only remains uninterrupted, but also increases from successive parents, and becomes more prone to evils, and at length to every kind of them. Thence it is, that the Jews are still images of their father Judah, who took to wife a Canaanitess, and by adultery with his daughter-in-law Tamar, begot the three races of them. Wherefore this hereditary disposition, in process of time, has increased with them to such a degree, that they cannot, with a faith of the heart, embrace the Christian religion. It is said, that they cannot, because the interior will of their mind is averse to it, and this will causes the inability.

522. That every evil, unless it be removed, remains with man; and that man, if he remain in his evils, cannot be saved, follow of themselves. That no evil can be removed but by the Lord, with those who believe in Him and love the neighbor, may be very evident from what has been said above, particularly from these things in the chapter concerning Faith; *That the Lord, charity and faith make one, like life, will and understanding; and if they are divided, each perishes like a pearl reduced to powder*. And from these there, *That the Lord is charity and faith in man, and that man is charity and faith in the Lord*. But is it asked, How can man enter into that union? It is answered, that he cannot, unless he remove his evils, in part, by repentance. It is said, that man removes them, because the Lord does not do it immediately without the coöperation of man, which also was fully shown in the same chapter, and in the following one concerning Free Agency.

523. It is affirmed that no one can fulfil the law, especially since he who offends against one precept of the decalogue, offends against all. But this form of speaking is not just as it sounds; for it is to be understood in this manner, that he, who, from purpose or confirmation, acts against one precept, acts against the rest, since to act from purpose and confirmation, is utterly to deny that it is sin; and if it is said that it is sin, to reject it as of no moment: and he who thus denies and rejects sin, makes light of every thing that is called sin. Those who are not willing to hear any thing about repentance, come into this purpose; but, on the other hand, those who by repentance have removed some evils, which are sins, come into the purpose of believing in the Lord and loving the neighbor: these are held by the Lord

in the purpose of abstaining from more sins; wherefore, if they sin from ignorance, or from some very powerful lust, it is not imputed to them, because they did not propose it to themselves, nor do they confirm it in themselves. This may be confirmed by these facts. In the spiritual world I have met with many, who in the natural world lived like others, in clothing themselves splendidly, feasting sumptuously, trading with interest like others, seeing theatrical exhibitions, joking about lovers as if from lust, besides other similar things; and yet the angels charged those things to some, as evils of sin, and to some they did not charge them as evils, and these they declared innocent, but those guilty. To the question, Why so? when yet they did the like things, they replied; that they regard all from the purpose, intention, and end, and distinguish according to these; and that, therefore, those whom the end either excuses or condemns, they themselves excuse or condemn, since all in heaven have the end of good, and all in hell the end of evil.

524. But these things shall be illustrated by comparisons. When sins are retained in an impenitent man, they may be compared with various diseases in him, of which, unless medicines be applied to them, and their malignity thereby removed, the man dies; particularly with the disease called gangrene, which, unless it be cured in season, spreads itself around and brings on inevitable death; in like manner with impostumes and abscesses, unless they be uncovered and opened; for thence collections of putrid matter would be spread into the neighboring parts, and thence into the adjacent viscera, and at last into the heart, whence death would ensue. They may also be compared with tigers, leopards, lions, wolves and foxes, which, unless they be kept in dens, or tied with chains or ropes, would attack the flock and herd, and the fox, the hens, and kill them; and also with venomous serpents, which, unless they are held down and confined by poles, or deprived of their teeth, wou'd inflict upon man deadly wounds. The whole flock, if it were left in plains where there are poisonous herbs, would perish, unless it were led away thence by the shepherd into wholesome pastures. The silk-worm, too, would perish, and thus all the silk, unless other worms were shaken off from the leaves of its tree. It may be compared also with corn in barns or houses, which would become musty and rancid, and thus unfit for use, unless the air were suffered to pass freely through it, and preserve it from damage. Fire, unless it were extinguished at its first breaking out, would consume a whole city or forest. A garden would be covered all over with brambles, thistles and briers, unless they were rooted up. Skilful gardeners know, that a bad tree, from the seed and root, brings its bad juices into the stock of a good tree, engrafted or inoculated into it, and that the bad juices, which enter from beneath, are turned into good juices, and produce good fruit. The like is done to man by the removal of evil by means of repentance, for by this, man is engrafted into the Lord, as a branch into a vine, and bears good fruit, John xv. 4, 5, 6.

525. V. That the Knowledge of Sin, and the Searching out of some one Sin in one's self, begins Repentance.

No one in the Christian world can be without the knowledge of sin; for every one there is taught, from his infancy, what evil is, and from his childhood, what is the evil of sin. All young people learn this from their parents and masters, and also from the decalogue, which is the first book for all in Christendom; and in their progress afterwards, from preaching in temples, and from instruction at home, and in fulness from the Word; and besides, from the civil laws of justice, which teach the same things as the decalogue and the other parts of the Word. For the evil of sin is nothing else than evil against the neighbor; and evil against the neighbor is also evil against God, which is sin. But the knowledge of sin does not effect any thing unless a man explores the acts of his life, and sees whether he has done any such thing, in secret or in public; previous to this it is all only science, and then all that the preacher brings forth is only something sounding in his left ear, from which it passes through to his right and flies away; and at last it becomes only something of thought and something devout from the lungs, and with many something imaginary and chimerical. But the case is quite different, if a man, according to his knowledge of what sin is, explores himself, and finds some sin in himself, and says with himself, This evil is a sin, and abstains from it through fear of eternal punishment; then, for the first time, instructive and oratorial preaching in temples, is received with both ears and admitted into the heart, and the man, from a pagan, becomes a Christian.

526. What can be more known in the whole Christian world, than that a man ought to examine himself? For every where in the empires and kingdoms, which are devoted either to the Roman Catholic or the Evangelical religion, they are taught and admonished, before coming to the holy supper, that a man should examine himself, and know and acknowledge his sins, and begin to live otherwise; and this with horrible threatenings in the dominions of England, where, from the preparatory service before communion, these words are read and proclaimed by the priest from the altar: "The way and means," to become a worthy partaker of the holy supper, "is, First, to examine your lives and conversations by the rule of God's commandments; and whereinsoever ye shall perceive yourselves to have offended, either by will, word, or deed, there to bewail your own sinfulness, and to confess yourselves to Almighty God, with full purpose of amendment of life. And if ye shall perceive your offences to be such as are not only against God, but also against your neighbors, then ye shall reconcile yourselves unto them, being ready to make restitution and satisfaction according to the uttermost of your powers, for all injuries and wrongs done by you to any other; and being likewise ready to forgive others that have offended you, as ye would have forgiveness of your offences at God's hand; for otherwise the receiving of the holy communion doth nothing else but increase your damnation. Therefore, if any of you be a blasphemer of God, a hinderer or slanderer of his Word, an adulterer, or be in malice, or envy, or in any other grievous crime; repent ye of your sins, or else come not to that holy table; lest, after the taking of that holy sacrament, the devil enter into you, as he entered into Judas, and fill you full of all iniquities, and bring you to destruction both of body and soul."

527. But still there are some who cannot examine themselves, as infants, boys and girls, before they arrive at an age when they become capable of self-examination; in like manner, the simple, who are incapable of reflection; and also all who have not the fear of God; besides these some who are diseased in mind and body; and moreover those, who, being confirmed in the doctrine of justification by faith alone imputative of the merit of Christ, have persuaded themselves that by examination and thence repentance, something of man would enter, which would destroy faith, and thus throw salvation out of its only focus, and throw it away. These and those make use only of oral confession, which has been shown above, in this chapter, not to be repentance. But those who know what sin is, and especially those who know many things from the Word, and teach them, and do not explore themselves, and thence see no sin in themselves, may be likened to those who scrape together riches and lay them up in coffers and chests, without any other use of them, than to look at them and count them; and like those who collect in treasuries jewels of gold and silver, and shut them up in cellars, solely for the sake of opulence; who are like the trader that hid his talent under the ground, and like him that hid his

pound in a napkin, Matt. xxv. 25; Luke xix. 20. They are also like hard and stony ways, on which seed falls, Matt. xiii. 4; and also like fig-trees luxuriant in leaves, and bearing no fruit, Mark xi. 12. And they are hearts of adamant, which do not become hearts of flesh, Zech. vii. 12. They are like *partridges, which sit and do not hatch. They get riches, but not with judgment; in the midst of their days they leave them, and in their end they become fools,* Jer. xvii. 11. They are like the five virgins who had lamps and not oil, Matt. xxv. 1 to 12. Those who derive from the Word many things concerning charity and concerning repentance, and know precepts in abundance, and do not live according to them, may be compared with voracious eaters, who stuff their mouths with food, and, without chewing it with their teeth, let it down into the stomach, where it remains undigested, and being thence pressed out, it vitiates the chyle, and brings on lingering diseases, of which at last they die miserably. Such, because they are without spiritual heat, however they may be in light, may be called winters, frozen countries, arctic climates, yea, heaps of snow and ice.

528. VI. That actual Repentance is, to examine one's self to know and acknowledge one's Sins, to make Supplication to the Lord, and to begin a new Life.

That repentance must surely be performed, and that the salvation of man depends upon it, is evident from many passages and plain declarations of the Lord in the Word; of which these at present will be adduced. *John preached the baptism of repentance, and said, Bring forth fruits worthy of repentance,* Luke iii. 3, 8; Mark i. 9. *Jesus began to preach and say, Repent ye,* Matt. iv. 17. *And He said, Because the kingdom of God is at hand, repent ye,* Mark i. 14, 15. *Again, Unless ye repent, ye will all perish,* Luke xiii. 5. *Jesus instructed his disciples, that repentance and remission of sins should be preached in his name, to all nations,* xxiv. 47; Mark vi. 12. Wherefore *Peter preached repentance and baptism in the name of Jesus Christ, for the remission of sins,* Acts ii. 38. And also he said, *Repent ye, and turn yourselves about, that your sins may be blotted out,* iii. 19. *Paul preached to all every where, that they should repent,* xvii. 30. *Paul also announced in Damascus, in Jerusalem, through the whole region of Judea, and to the Gentiles, that they should repent, and turn themselves to God; and that they should do works worthy of repentance,* xxvi. 20. *And also he testified, both to the Jews and to the Greeks, repentance towards God, and faith in the Lord Jesus Christ,* xx. 21. The Lord said to the church of Ephesus, *I have against thee, that thou hast left the first charity; repent, or else I will remove thy candlestick out of its place, unless thou repent,* Rev. ii. 2, 4, 5. To the church in Pergamus, *I know thy works; repent,* ii. 16. To the church in Thyatira, *I will give her up to affliction, if she do not repent of her works,* ii. 19, 20, 23. To the church of the Laodiceans, *I know thy works; be zealous and repent,* iii. 15, 19. *There is joy in heaven over one sinner that repenteth,* Luke xv. 7; besides in other places. Hence it is evident, that repentance must by all means be performed; but what, and in what manner, will be made manifest in what follows.

529. Who cannot understand from the reason given to him, that it is not repentance for one merely to confess with the mouth, that he is a sinner, and to utter many things about it, like the hypocrite, who was mentioned above, n. 518? For what is easier for a man, when he is in anguish and in agony, than to breathe out from the lungs, and to pour forth thence, through the lips, sighs and groans, and also to beat the breast, and make himself guilty of all sins, when yet he is conscious of no one in himself? Does the diabolical crew which is in his loves go out together with his sighs? Do they not rather hiss at them and remain in him, as before, as in their own house? Hence it is manifest that such repentance was not meant in the Word, but

repentance from evil works, as it is said.

530. Is it asked, then, How is repentance to be performed? It is answered, Actually; and this is, for one to examine himself, to know and acknowledge his sins, to make supplication to the Lord, and begin a new life. That there can be no repentance without examination, was shown in the article which precedes. But for what purpose is examination, but that one may know his sins? And for what purpose is that knowledge, but that he may acknowledge that they are in him? And for what purpose are those three, but that he may confess them before the Lord, and make supplication for help, and from this begin a new life, which is the end that was to be attained? This is actual repentance. Every man, after the first stage of life, and more and more as he comes to the exercise of his right and his reason, may know from baptism, by the washing of which is meant regeneration, that he ought to proceed and do thus; for at his baptism, his sponsors promise for him, that he shall renounce the devil and all his works. The like is manifest from the holy supper, before the worthy celebration of which, all are admonished to repent of their sins, turn themselves to God, and begin a new life. And it is also manifest from the decalogue, or catechism, which is in the hands of all Christians, where, in six precepts of the decalogue, nothing else is commanded, but that men should not do evils; and unless man removes evils by repentance, he cannot love his neighbor, and still less God; when yet, on these two commandments hang the law and the prophets; that is, the Word, and, consequently, salvation. If actual repentance be performed at stated times; for instance, as often as a man prepares himself for the communion of the holy supper; and if he afterwards abstain from one or more sins, which he then discovers in himself, it is sufficient to initiate him into actual repentance; and when he is in that, he is in the way to heaven; for then man begins from natural to become spiritual, and to be born anew of the Lord.

531. This may be illustrated by the following comparisons. Man, before repentance, is like a desert, in which there are terrible wild beasts, dragons, owls, screech owls, vipers, venomous serpents; and in the thickets there, *ochim* and *ziim*, and satyrs dance: but when these are cast out by the industry and labor of man, that desert may be ploughed and cultivated for fields, and in them may be sown first oats, beans and flax, and afterwards barley and wheat. And also it may be compared with the wickedness which reigns abundantly among men: unless the wicked were chastised and punished according to the laws, with stripes or death, no city and no kingdom could subsist. Man is like a society in the least form: unless he dealt with himself in a spiritual manner, as the wicked are dealt with in a great society in a natural manner, he, after death, would be chastised and punished; and this until, through fear of punishment, he does not do evil, although he can never be reduced to do good from the love of good.

532. VII. That true Repentance is, to explore not only the Acts of one's Life, but also the Intentions of his Will.

That true repentance is, to explore not only the acts of one's life, but also the intentions of his will, is because the understanding and the will make the acts; for man speaks from thought and acts from will; wherefore speech is thought speaking, and action is will acting; and because the words and actions are thence, it follows indubitably that those two are what sin, when the body sins. And also a man can repent of the evils which he has done with the body, and still think and will evil; but this is like cutting off the trunk of a bad tree and leaving its root in the ground, from which the same bad tree grows up and spreads itself around. But it is otherwise, when the root also is pulled up; and this is done in man, when he at the same time explores the intentions of his will, and removes evils by repentance. A man explores the intentions of his will, while he explores his thoughts, for the intentions manifest themselves in them; as while he thinks, wills and intends, revenge, adultery, theft, false witness, and the desires for those things, and also blasphemy against God, the holy Word and the church, and so forth: if he still applies his attention to it, and considers whether he would do those things, if the fear of the law and of fame did not oppose, and then, after such scrutiny, thinks that he will not do them, because they are sins, he performs true and interior repentance; and still more when he is in the delight of those evils and at the same time in the liberty of doing them, and then resists and abstains. He who repeatedly exercises this, finds the delights of evils, when they return, undelightful, and at length condemns them to hell. This is what is meant by these words of the Lord; *Whosoever will find his life, shall lose it; and whosoever shall lose his life, for my sake, shall find it*, Matt. x. 39. He who removes the evils of his will by repentance, is like him who seasonably pulls up the tares sown in his field by the devil, whence the seeds implanted by the Lord God the Savior find a free soil and grow up into a harvest, Matt. xiii. 25 to 31.

533. There are two loves, which for a long time have been rooted in the human race, the love of ruling over all, and the love of possessing the goods of all. The former love, if it have the reins freely, rushes on even so far that it would be the God of heaven; and the latter love, if it have the reins freely, rushes on so far that it would be the God of the world. To these two loves, all the other evil loves, which are hosts, are subordinate. But it is very difficult to explore those two, because they reside most interiorly, and hide themselves; for they are like vipers concealed in a rock full of holes, which retain their poison, that, when any one lies down upon that rock, they may inflict deadly wounds, and draw themselves back. They are also like the sirens of the ancients, who allured men by singing, and thereby killed them. Those two loves also adorn themselves with shining gowns and coats, as the devil from magical fantasy does among his own, and among others whom he wishes to mock. But it is well to be known, that those two loves may reign more with the little than with the great, more with the poor than with the rich, and more with subjects than with kings; for these are born to dominion and to wealth, which at length they look upon no otherwise than as another looks upon his household and possessions, whether he be a governor, a general, a captain of a vessel, yea, even a poor husbandman. But the case is different with kings who aspire to dominion over the kingdoms of others. The reason that the intentions of the will are to be explored, is, because the love resides in the will, for the will is the receptacle of it, as was shown above. Every love thence breathes forth its delights into the perceptions and thoughts of the understanding; for these do nothing from themselves, but from the will, for they favor it, and consent to and confirm all the things which are of its love: wherefore the will is the house itself, in which man dwells, and the understanding is the entry, through which he goes out and comes in. Thence it is, that it was said, that the intentions of the will should be explored; and when they are explored and removed, man is elevated from the natural will, in which hereditary and actual evils reside, into a spiritual will, by which the Lord reforms and regenerates the natural, and by means of this, the sensual and voluntary things of the body, thus the whole man.

534. Those who do not explore themselves, are in comparison like sick people, in whom the blood, in consequence of obstruction in the smallest vessels, is vitiated, whence atrophy, sleepiness of the limbs, and acute chronic diseases, arising from the thickness, tenacity, acrimony and acidity of the humors, and thence of the blood; but those who do explore themselves also as to the intentions of the will, in comparison, are like those who are cured of those diseases, and return into the life

in which they were when young. Those who rightly explore themselves, are like ships from Ophir, laden with gold, silver and precious things; but before they have explored themselves, they are like ships loaded with filth, in which are carried off the dirt and dung of the streets. Those who explore themselves interiorly, become like mines, all the sides of which glitter with the ores of noble metal; but before, they are like stinking bogs, in which are water-snakes and venomous serpents which glitter with their scales, and noxious insects which shine with their wings. Those who do not explore themselves, are like the dry bones in the valley; but after they have explored themselves, they are like the same bones, upon which the Lord Jehovah gave sinews, brought on flesh, and covered with skin, and into which He put breath, and they lived, Ezek. xxxvii. 1 to 14.

535. VIII. That those also perform Repentance who do not explore Themselves, but still desist from Evils, because they are Sins; and that this Repentance is done by those who do the Works of Charity from Religion.

Since actual repentance, which is to explore one's self, to know and acknowledge his sins, to make supplication to the Lord, and to begin a new life, is very difficult in the Reformed Christian world, for several reasons, of which in the last article in this chapter, therefore an easier kind of repentance will be proposed; which is, that, when any one revolves evil in his mind and intends it, he should say to himself, "I think of this and I intend it; but because it is a sin, I will not do it." By this the temptation injected from hell is broken, and its further entrance is prevented. It is wonderful, that every one can chide another, who intends evil, and say, "Do not do this, because it is a sin;" and yet with difficulty can say it to himself: the reason is, because this moves the will, but that only the thought next to the hearing. It was inquired in the spiritual world, who could do this other; and they were found as few as the doves in a spacious desert. Some said that they could indeed do that, but that they could not explore themselves and confess their sins before God. But still all those who do good from religion, avoid actual evils; and yet how very seldom they reflect on the interior things which are of the will, believing that they are not in evils, because they are in good; yea, that the good covers the evil. But, my friend, the first thing of charity is, to shun evils; this the Word teaches, and also the decalogue, baptism, the holy supper, and also reason; for how can any one shun evils and put them away from him, without some self-inspection? And how can good become good, unless it be inwardly purified? I know that the pious, and also those of sound reason, while they read this, will assent and see it as genuine truth, but that still few will do so.

536. But still all who do good from religion, not only Christians, but also pagans, are accepted by the Lord, and are adopted after death; for the Lord said, *I was hungry, and ye gave Me to eat; I was thirsty, and ye gave Me drink; I was a stranger, and ye took Me in; naked, and ye clothed Me; I was sick, and ye visited Me; I was in prison, and ye came to Me. And He said, Inasmuch as ye have done it to one of my least brethren, ye have done it to Me. Come, ye blessed, possess, as an inheritance, the kingdom prepared for you from the foundation of the world*, Matt. xxv. 31 to the end. To the above I shall add this news. All those who do good from religion, after death reject the doctrine of the present church concerning three divine persons from eternity, and also its faith applied to those three in order, and turn themselves to the Lord God the Savior, and receive with pleasure those things which are of the New Church. But the rest, who have not exercised charity from religion, are hearts of adamant, thus hard. These first go to three Gods, afterwards to the Father only, and at last to none. The Lord God the Savior they regard as only the Son of Mary by her marriage with Joseph,

and not as the Son of God; and then all the things of the New Church, good and true, they shake off, and presently join themselves to the spirits of the dragon, and are driven away with them into deserts or into caverns, which are in the outermost bounds of what is called the Christian world; and after a time, because they are separated from the new heaven, they rush into villanous deeds, and are therefore let down into hell. Such is the lot of those who do not perform the works of charity from religion, in consequence of a belief that no one can do good from himself, unless it be meritorious; and thence they omit those works, and herd together with the goats, who are condemned, and cast into eternal fire, prepared for the devil and his angels, because they did not the things that the sheep did, Matt. xxv. 41 and the following verses. It is not said there that they did evils, but that they did not do goods, and those who do not do good from religion, do evil; *Since no one can serve two lords, but he will hate one and love the other; or he will cleave to one and neglect the other*, Matt. vi. 24. Jehovah says by Isaiah, *Wash yourselves, make yourselves clean; remove the evil of your works from before my eyes; cease to do evil; learn to do good: and then, though your sins be as scarlet, they shall become white as snow; though they be red like crimson, they shall be like wool*, i. 16, 17, 18. And to Jeremiah, *Stand in the gate of the house of Jehovah, and proclaim there this word; Thus said Jehovah of hosts, the God of Israel, Make your ways and your works good, and trust ye not in the words of a lie, by saying, The temple of Jehovah, the temple of Jehovah is here* (that is, the church); *after stealing, killing, and swearing by a lie, will ye then come and stand in this house, upon which my name is named, and say, We are delivered, while ye do all those abominations? Is this house become a den of robbers? Behold, I also have seen, saith Jehovah*, vii. 2, 3, 4, 9, 10, 11.

537. It is to be known, that those who do good from natural goodness only, and not at the same time from religion, are not accepted after death, because there is only natural good in their charity, and not at the same time spiritual; and the spiritual is what conjoins the Lord to man, and not the natural without it. Natural goodness is of the flesh alone, born of parents, but spiritual goodness is of the spirit, born anew of the Lord. Those who do the goods of charity from religion and thence not evils, before they have received the doctrine of the New Church concerning the Lord, may be likened to trees that bear good fruits, although few; and also to trees that bear noble fruit of small size, which, nevertheless, are carefully preserved in gardens. And also they may be likened to olive-trees and fig-trees, in forests, and also to fragrant herbs and balsamic plants upon hills. They are like little chapels or houses of God, in which pious worship is performed; for they are the sheep on the right hand, and the rams, which the he-goats attack, according to Daniel, viii. 2 to 14. In heaven they are clothed with garments of a red color, and after they have been initiated into the goods of the New Church, they are clothed with garments of a purple color; which, as they receive truths also, become beautifully tinged with yellow.

538. IX. THAT CONFESSION OUGHT TO BE MADE BEFORE THE LORD GOD THE SAVIOR, AND THEN SUPPLICATION FOR HELP AND POWER TO RESIST EVILS.

The reason that the Lord God the Savior is to be addressed, is, because He is the God of heaven and earth, the Redeemer and Savior, who has omnipotence, omniscience, omnipresence, mercy itself, and at the same time righteousness; and because man is his creature and the church his fold; and He has many times commanded, in the new covenant, that men should address, worship and adore Him. That he alone should be addressed, He enjoined by these words in John; *Verily, verily I say to you, he that entereth not through the door into the sheepfold, but climbeth up some other way, he is a thief and a robber; but he that goeth in through the door, is the shepherd of the sheep. I am the Door; If any one enter through Me, he shall be saved and shall find pasture. The thief cometh not but that he may steal, kill and destroy. I have come that they may have life and abundance. I am the good Shepherd*, x. 1, 2, 9, 10, 11. That man ought not to climb up any other way, is, that he should not to God the Father, because He is invisible, and thence inaccessible, and incapable of conjunction; and therefore He came into the world, and made himself visible, accessible, and capable of conjunction, which was solely for the end that man might be saved; for unless God be approached in thought as Man, all idea concerning God is lost; it falls like the sight into the universe, thus into empty nothing, or into nature, or into some objects within nature. That God himself, who from eternity is One, came into the world, is clearly manifest from the nativity of the Lord the Savior, in that He was conceived from the power of the Most High by the Holy Spirit, and that thence his Human was born of the Virgin Mary; whence it follows, that his soul was the Divine Itself, which is called the Father, for God is indivisible, and that the Human born thence, is the Human of God the Father, which is called the Son of God, Luke i. 32, 34, 35. Hence it follows again, that whilst the Lord God the Savior is addressed, God the Father is addressed also. Wherefore He answered Philip, when he requested that He would show the Father: *He that seeth Me, seeth the Father; how then sayest thou, Show us the Father? Believest thou not, that I am in the Father and the Father in Me. Believe Me, that I am in the Father and the Father in Me*, John xiv. 6 to 11. But more may be seen concerning this subject in the chapters concerning God, the Lord, the Holy Spirit, and concerning the Trinity.

559. There are two duties, which it is incumbent on man to do after examination, which are supplication and confession. SUPPLICATION will be, that the Lord would show mercy, give power to resist the evils of which he has repented, and supply inclination and affection to do good, *Since man without Him cannot do any thing*, John xv. 5. CONFESSION will be, that he sees, knows and acknowledges his evils, and finds himself a miserable sinner. There is no need of enumerating sins before the Lord, nor of supplicating for their remission. The reason that there is no need of enumerating the sins, is because the man has searched and seen them in himself, and thence they are present to the Lord, because they are present to himself. The Lord also led him in searching, and opened them, and inspired him with sorrow, and together with this the endeavor to desist from them and begin a new life. There are these two reasons why supplication for the remission of sins need not be made before the Lord: first, because sins are not abolished but removed; and they are removed, as man afterwards desists from them and enters upon a new life; for there are innumerable concupiscences, involved in every evil, which cannot be removed in a moment, but successively, as man suffers himself to be reformed and regenerated. The other reason is, that the Lord, because He is Mercy itself, remits to all their sins, nor imputes one to any; for He says, *They know not what they do;* (but still they are not therefore taken away;) for He said to Peter, when he asked how often he should forgive his brother his trespasses, whether till seven times? *I say not to thee, till seven times, but until seventy times seven*, Matt. xviii. 21, 22; why should not the Lord? But still it is not hurtful for any one whose conscience is burdened, to enumerate his sins before a minister of the church, for the sake of absolution and alleviation; because he is thus introduced into the habit of examining himself, and of reflecting upon his daily evils. But this confession is natural; but that above described is spiritual.

560. To adore any vicar upon earth, or to invoke any saint, as God, is of no more avail in heaven than to make

supplication to the sun, moon and stars, and to ask a diviner for an answer, and to believe his word, which is vain. This would be also like worshipping a temple, and not God in the temple. And it would be like supplicating the servant of a king, who carries in his hand his sceptre and crown, for the honors of glory, and not the king himself. And this would be as useless as, abstractedly from the subjects, to kiss the splendor of purple, the glory, light and golden rays of the sun, and a mere name. Let those who do such things, consider these words in John: *We abide in the truth, in Jesus Christ. This is the true God and eternal life. Little children, keep yourselves from idols*, 1 John v. 20, 21.

561. X. THAT ACTUAL REPENTANCE IS EASY WITH THOSE WHO HAVE DONE IT SEVERAL TIMES, BUT EXTREMELY DIFFICULT TO THOSE WHO HAVE NOT DONE IT.

Actual repentance is, to examine one's self, to know his sins, to confess himself before the Lord, and thus to begin a new life; it is that according to the description of it in the foregoing pages. To those in the Reformed Christian world, by which are meant all who are separated from the Roman Catholic church, and also to those of that church who have not performed any actual repentance, this actual repentance is extremely difficult. The reason is, because some are not willing, and some are afraid, and disuse renders man inveterate, and induces unwillingness, and at length consent from the reasonings of the understanding, and with some, sorrow, dread and terror on account of it. The principal cause, that actual repentance is so extremely difficult in the Reformed Christian world, is their faith, that repentance and charity contribute nothing to salvation, but faith alone; from the imputation of which, follow the remission of sins, justification, renovation, regeneration, sanctification, and eternal salvation, without man's cooperating of himself or as of himself; this their dogmatists call a useless thing, and opposite, repugnant, and injurious to the merit of Christ: and this is implanted in the common people although they are ignorant of the mystical things of that faith, by these words merely, that "Faith alone saves; and Who can do good of him self?" Thence it is, that, with the Reformed, repentance is like a bird's nest with the young ones, forsaken by the birds, which were taken by the fowler and killed. To this cause another is added, that a Reformed man, so called, as to his spirit, in the spiritual world, is among no others than his like, who put such things into the ideas of his thoughts, and lead him away from the track to self-inspection and examination.

562. I have asked many of the Reformed, in the spiritual world, why they did not perform actual repentance, when yet this was enjoined upon them both in the Word and at their baptism, and also before the holy communion in all their churches; and they have answered various things. SOME, "That contrition is sufficient, and then the oral confession that he is a sinner." SOME, "That such repentance, because it is performed by man operating from his own will, does not coincide with the faith universally received." SOME, "Who can explore himself, when he knows that he is mere sin? This would be like casting a net into a lake full of mud, from the bottom to the top, in which are noxious worms." SOME, "Who can so thoroughly inspect himself as to see in himself the sin of Adam, from which all his actual evils have flowed? Are not these, together with that, washed away by the waters of baptism, and wiped off and covered over by the merit of Christ? What then is repentance, but an imposition which grievously troubles the conscientious? Are we not by the gospel under grace, and not under the hard law of that repentance?" Besides other things. SOME said, "That whenever they intended to examine themselves, a dread and terror would seize them, as if they saw a monster by the side of their bed at the dawn of day." Hence were made known the causes

why actual repentance, in the Reformed Christian world, is as it were out of use and rejected. And I asked, in their presence, some who were attached to the Roman Catholic religion, concerning their actual confession before their ministers, whether it was difficult. And they replied, that, after they were initiated into it, they were not afraid of recounting their sins before a confessor who was not severe, and that they collected them together with a kind of pleasure, and cheerfully told the lighter ones, but the more grievous ones somewhat timidly; and that, from custom, they freely returned every year to their appointed confession, and after absolution to festivity; and also that they look upon all as impure, who are not willing to lay open the defilements of their hearts. After hearing these things, the Reformed, who were present, fled away, some laughing and sneering, some wondering and yet commending. Afterwards there came up some who were attached to the same church, but who, residing in countries amongst the Reformed, according to the usual practice there, did not make a particular confession, as their brethren elsewhere did, but only a general one before their leader; these said that they could not search, find out and make known their actual evils and the secrets of their thoughts, and that they felt it as repugnant and terrible, as it would be to pass over a ditch to a rampart, where an armed soldier stands and cries, "Do not come here." Hence now it is manifest, that actual repentance is easy to those who have several times done it, but extremely difficult to those who have not done it.

563. It is known that custom makes a second nature, and that thence that is easy for one which is difficult for another; thus also to explore one's self, and to confess the evils that are discovered. What is easier for a laborer, a porter, or a husbandman, than to work with his hands from morning till evening, when yet a gentleman or a delicate man could not do it for half an hour without fatigue and sweat? It is easy for a footman with light shoes to take a journey of many miles, while one who is accustomed to ride in a coach, can with difficulty run slowly from one street to another. Every workman, who is diligent at his work, performs it with ease and pleasure, and when he goes away from it he desires to return; when another, who knows how to do the same work, but is slothful, can scarcely be forced to it. It is just so in every employment and in every study. What is easier, for any one studious of piety, than to pray to God? and what is more difficult for one who is addicted to impiety? and the reverse? What priest, when he preaches for the first time before a king, is not afraid? but when he is accustomed to it, he goes through it without fear. What is easier for a man-angel than to lift up his eyes to heaven, and for a man-devil, than to cast down his eyes to hell? but if he be a hypocrite, he likewise can look up to heaven, but his heart is the other way. The end regarded, and the habit thence, imbues every one.

564. XI. That he who has never performed Repentance, or has not looked into and examined himself, at length does not know what damnable Evil is, and what saving Good is.

Since few, in the Reformed Christian world, perform repentance, it is therefore added, that he who has not looked into and examined himself, at length does not know what damnable evil is, and what saving good is; for he has no religion, from which he can know this. For the evil which a man does not see, know and acknowledge, remains; and that which remains, is rooted more and more, until it obstructs the interiors of his mind; whence man becomes first natural, then sensual, and at last corporeal, and neither this nor that knows any evil which condemns, nor good which saves. He becomes like a tree upon a hard rock, which spreads its roots among the holes of the rock, and at length, because moisture fails, it withers away. Every man, properly educated, is rational and moral; but there are two ways to rationality, one from the world, the other from heaven. He who is made rational and moral from the world, and not from heaven also, is rational and moral only with the mouth and gesture, and inwardly he is a beast, yea, a wild beast, because he acts as one with those who are in hell, where all such are. But he who is rational and moral from heaven also, is truly rational and moral, because he is so at the same time with the spirit, mouth and body; for the spiritual is inwardly in these two as a soul, which actuates the natural, sensual and corporeal; he also acts as one with those who are in heaven. Wherefore, there is a spiritual-rational and moral man, and also a merely natural-rational and moral man; and one is not distinguished from the other in the world, especially if he acquires hypocrisy by exercise; but by the angels in heaven, they are distinguished as well as doves from owls, and as sheep from tigers. The merely natural man can see evils and goods in others, and also can reprove them, but because he never looked into and examined himself, he does not see any evil in himself; and if any is laid open by another, he covers it over by means of his rational faculty, as a serpent covers its head with dust, and immerses himself in it, as a hornet immerses itself in dung. This is done by the delight of evil, which surrounds him, as a thick cloud surrounds a bog, and absorbs and suffocates the rays of light. The delight of hell is nothing else; this is exhaled thence, and it flows into every man, but into the soles of the feet, the back, and the hinder part of the head; but if it is received by the head in the fore part, and by the body in the breast, the man is then enslaved to hell; the reason is, because the *cerebrum* of man is dedicated to the understanding and to the wisdom there, but the *cerebellum* to the will and to its love; thence it is, that there are two spheres of the brain. But that infernal delight is amended, reformed and inverted, solely by the spiritual-rational and moral.

565. There follows now some description of the merely natural-rational and moral man, who, viewed in himself, is sensual, and if he goes on, he becomes corporeal or carnal; but this description will be given in a sketch divided into parts. The sensual is the ultimate of the mind of man, adhering to, and cohering with, the five senses of his body. He is called a sensual man who judges all things from the senses of the body, and who believes only what he can see with the eyes and touch with the hands, saying these are something, and rejecting every thing else. The interiors of his mind, which see from the light of heaven, are closed, so that he sees nothing of the truth which is of heaven and the church. Such a man thinks in the outermost things, and not inwardly from any spiritual light, because he is in gross natural light; thence it is, that he is inwardly opposed to those things which are of heaven and the church, although outwardly he can speak in favor of them, ardently according to the hope of obtaining power and opulence by them. That men of learning and erudition, who have confirmed themselves deeply in falses, and especially those who have confirmed themselves against the truths of the Word, are more sensual than others. That sensual men reason acutely and ingeniously, because their thought is near the speech, so as to be almost in it, and as it were in their lips, and because they place all intelligence in the speech merely from the memory; and also that they can confirm falses dexterously, and that after confirmation they believe them to be true; but that they reason and confirm from the fallacies of the senses, by which the common people are captivated and persuaded. That sensual men are cunning and malicious above all others. That the covetous, the adulterous and the deceitful, are most of all sensual, although they appear before the world as ingenious. That the interiors of their mind are foul and filthy; that by these they communicate with the hells; that in the Word they are called dead. That those who are in the hells are sensual, and the

more so, the deeper they are; that the sphere of infernal spirits conjoins itself with the sensual of man from behind; and that, in the light of heaven, the hinder part of their head appears hollow. That those who reasoned from sensual things alone, were called by the ancients, serpents of the tree of knowledge. That sensual things ought to be in the last place, and not in the first; and that, with a wise and intelligent man, they are in the last place and subject to the interiors; but that with an unwise man, they are in the first place and predominate. If sensual things are in the last place, that a way is opened through them to the understanding, and truths are refined by the mode of extraction. That sensual things stand forth next to the world, and admit the things which come from the world, and as it were sift them. That man by sensual things communicates with the world, and by rational things with heaven. That sensual things supply those things which are subservient to the interiors of the mind. That there are sensual things which supply the understanding, and also which supply the will. That unless the thought is elevated above sensual things, man has but little wisdom; that man, when his thought is elevated above sensual things, comes into clearer light, and at length into heavenly light, and then perceives such things as flow down from heaven. That the ultimate of the understanding is what relates to natural science, and that the ultimate of the will is what relates to sensual delight.

566. Man, as to the natural man, is like a beast, and he acquires the image of a beast by life; wherefore, around such, in the spiritual world, beasts of every kind appear, which are correspondences. For the natural of man, viewed in itself, is merely animal, but because the spiritual is superadded to it, it can be made man; and if it is not made so, from the faculty which it has, it can counterfeit the man, but still it is a talking beast, for he speaks from the natural-rational, but thinks from spiritual madness, and acts from the natural-moral, but loves from a perpetual lust: his actions, viewed by the spiritual-rational man, are scarcely any thing else than, as it were, the dancing of one who has been bitten by a tarantula, and is called St. Vitus's dance. Who does not know that a hypocrite can talk about God, a robber about sincerity, an adulterer about chastity, &c.? But unless man had the power of shutting and opening the door between his thoughts and words, and between his intentions and actions, and for a door-keeper there, prudence or cunning, he would rush more furiously than any beast into wicked and cruel deeds. But that door is opened to every one after death, and then he appears such as he was; but he is held in bonds by punishments and guards in hell. Wherefore, kind reader, look into yourself, and search out one or more of the evils in you, and remove it from religious principle; if you remove them from any other purpose or end, you only remove them so that they do not appear before the world

---

567. To the above the following Relations will be added. First. I was suddenly seized with a disease almost mortal; my head ached all over; a pestilential smoke was sent upon me from the Jerusalem, which is called Sodom and Egypt, Rev. xi. 8; I was half dead with severe pain; I expected my last end. Thus I lay in my bed for three days and a half. My spirit became such, and from it my body. And then I heard around me the voices of those who said, "Lo, he lies dead in the street of our city, who preached repentance for the remission of sins, and Christ only man." And they asked some of the clergy, whether he was worthy of burial. They said, "No, let him lie, and be seen for a spectacle." And they went away and came back, and mocked. Of a truth, it thus happened to me, while the eleventh chapter of the Revelation was being explained. Then were heard harsh speeches of mockers, especially these,

"How can repentance be performed without faith? How can Christ, a man, be adored as God? Since we are saved freely without any merit of our own, what need, then, is there of any thing but merely the faith that God the Father sent the Son to take away the condemnation of the law, to impute to us his merit, and thus to justify us in his sight, and absolve us from sins by the declaration of a priest, and then give us the Holy Ghost to produce in us all good? Are not these things according to the Scripture, and also according to reason?" At these words, the company standing by clapped their hands. I heard these things, and was not able to reply, because I lay almost dead. But after three days and a half, my spirit recovered, and as to it I went out of the street into the city and said again, "Repent and believe in Christ, and your sins will be remitted to you, and you will be saved; and if not, you will perish. Did not the Lord himself preach repentance for the remission of sins, and that men should believe in Him? Did He not command the disciples, that they should preach the same? Does not a careless security follow the dogma of your faith?" But they said, "How you prate. Has not the Son made satisfaction? And does not the Father impute it, and justify us, who have believed this? We are thus led by the spirit of grace; what sin then is there in us? what then has death to do with us? Do you comprehend this gospel, O preacher of sin and repentance?" But then a voice came forth out of heaven, saying, "What is the faith of an impenitent man, but a dead faith? The end is come, the end is come upon you, who are secure, unblamable in your own eyes, justified in your faith, O satans." And then suddenly a gulf was opened in the midst of the city, and it enlarged itself, and house fell upon house, and they were swallowed up; and presently water bubbled up from the wide whirlpool, and overflowed the waste.

When they were thus sunk and apparently overflowed, I desired to know their condition in the deep; and it was said to me from heaven, "You shall see and hear." And the waters, with which they seemed to be overflowed, disappeared before my eyes, because waters in the spiritual world are correspondences, and thence they appear around those who are in falses. And then they appeared to me on a sandy bottom, where heaps of stones were collected, among which they were running and lamenting that they had been cast out of their great city. And they screamed and cried, "Why is this to us? Are we not by our faith clean, pure, just and holy? Are we not by our faith cleansed, purified, justified and sanctified?" And others, "Are we not by our faith made such that we appear, are seen and reputed before God the Father, and declared before the angels, clean, pure, just and holy? Are we not reconciled, propitiated, expiated, and thus freed, washed and wiped from sins? Is not the condemnation of the law taken away by Christ? Why, then, are we cast into this place, as condemned? We heard from a bold preacher of sin, in our great city, *Believe in Christ, and repent?* Did we not believe in Christ, when we believed in his merit? And did we not repent, when we confessed that we were sinners? Why, then, has this happened to us?" But then was heard a voice to them from the side, "Do you know any sin in which you are? Have you ever explored yourselves? Have you in consequence shunned any evil as a sin against God? And he who has not shunned it, is in it. Is not sin the devil? Wherefore you are those of whom the Lord says, *Then ye will begin to say, We have eaten and drunk in thy presence, and Thou hast taught in our streets. But He will say, I tell you, I know you not, whence ye are; Depart from Me, all ye workers of iniquity,* Luke xiii. 26, 27, and also Matt. vii. 22, 23. Depart, therefore, each to his own place. You see the openings into the caverns; enter thither, and work will be given there for each of you to do, and then food according to your work; if not still hunger will compel you to enter."

Afterwards a voice came from heaven to some on the earth, who were out of that great city, who also are mentioned Rev. xi. 13, saying aloud, "Beware, beware of associating yourselves with such persons. Can you not understand that the evils which are called sins and iniquities render man unclean and impure? How can man be cleansed and purified from them, but by actual repentance, and by faith in the Lord Jesus Christ? Actual repentance is to explore one's self, to know and acknowledge his sins, to make himself guilty, to confess them before the Lord, to implore help and the power of resisting them, and thus to desist from them and lead a new life; and all these things as of yourselves. Do so once or twice a year, when you come to the holy communion: and afterwards when the sins of which you have made yourselves guilty recur, then say to yourselves, 'We will not do them, because they are sins against God;' this is actual repentance. Who does not understand, that he who does not search out and see his sins, remains in them? For all evil is from nativity delightful; for it is delightful to revenge, to commit whoredom, to defraud, to blaspheme, especially to rule from the love of self. Does not the delight cause them not to be seen? And if by chance it is said that they are sins, do you not from their delight excuse them? Yea, do you not strive to prove by falses that they are not sins, and thus remain in them, and do them more than before, and this even until you do not know what sin is, yea, whether there be any sin? The case is otherwise with every one who has actually performed repentance; his evils, which he has discovered and acknowledged, he calls sins, and therefore begins to shun and avoid them, and at length to feel their delight undelightful; and, as far as this is the case, he sees and loves what is good, and at length feels the delight of this, which is the delight of the angels of heaven. In a word, so far as any one rejects the devil to the back, he is adopted by the Lord, and by Him is taught, led, withheld from evil and held in good; this is the way, and there is no other, from hell to heaven." It is strange that the Reformed have a certain innate repugnance, abhorrence and aversion to actual repentance, which is so great that they cannot force themselves to explore themselves and see their sins, and confess them before God; it is as if a horror seized them, when they intend it. I have asked a good many in the spiritual world about it, and they all said, that this was beyond their power. When they heard that the Papists still do this, that is, that they explore themselves and openly confess their sins before a monk, they wondered very much; and still more that the Reformed cannot do it in secret before God, although it is equally enjoined upon them, before they come to the holy supper. And some there inquired why this should be; and they found that faith alone had induced such a state of impenitence and such a heart. And then it was given them to see, that those of the Papists who adore Christ and do not invoke saints are saved.

After this there was heard, as it were, thunder, and a voice speaking from heaven, saying, "We wonder. Say to the company of Protestants, 'Believe in Christ, and perform repentance, and you will be saved.'" And I said so. And moreover I said, "Is not Baptism a sacrament of repentance, and thence an introduction into the church? What else do the sponsors promise for the child that is to be baptized, but that he will renounce the devil and his works? Is not the Holy Supper a sacrament of repentance, and thence an introduction into heaven? Is it not said to the communicants, that they must by all means perform the work of repentance before they come to it? Is not the Catechism the universal doctrine of the Christian church teaching repentance? Is it not said there, in six precepts of the second table, Thou shalt not do this and that evil; and not, Thou shalt do this and that good? Thence you may know, that, as far as any one renounces and avoids evil, so far he desires and loves good; and that, before, he does not know what good is; yea, nor what evil is."

568. SECOND RELATION. What wise and pious man does not wish to know the condition of his life after death? Wherefore I will manifest the general things, that he may know. Every man, after death, when he feels that he still lives, and that he is in another world, and hears that heaven is above him, where are eternal joys, and that hell is below him, where are eternal sorrows, is first let again into his externals, in which he was in the former world; and then he believes that he shall certainly come into heaven, and he speaks intelligently and acts prudently. And some say, "We have lived morally; we have followed honest pursuits; we have not intentionally done evil." Others say, "We have frequented temples; we have heard masses; we have kissed holy images; we have uttered prayers on our knees." And some say, "We have given to the poor; we have helped the needy; we have read books of piety, and also the Word;" besides many other things. And after they have said these things, the angels stand by them and say, "All those things, which you have mentioned, you did in externals, but you do not know yet what you are in internals. Now you are spirits in a substantial body, and the spirit is your internal man; it is this in you which thinks what it wills, and wills what it loves, and this is the delight of its life. Every man from infancy begins life from externals, and learns to act morally and to speak intelligently; and when he has got an idea of heaven and of the blessedness there, he begins to pray, to frequent temples, and to perform the solemnities of worship; and still, when evils flow from their native fountain, he hides them in the bosom of his mind, and also ingeniously veils them over by reasonings from fallacies, even till he does not know that evil is evil. And then, because the evils are veiled over, and covered as it were with dust, he thinks no more about them, than merely to take care that they do not appear before the world. Thus he only studies to lead a moral life in externals, and so becomes a double man; he becomes a sheep in externals, and a wolf in internals; and as it were a golden box in which there is poison; and he becomes like a person having a foul breath holding something fragrant in his mouth, that it may not be perceived by the bystanders; and like the skin of a mouse, which is scented with balsam. You said that you had lived morally, and that you had followed the pursuits of piety. But I ask whether you have ever explored your internal man, and perceived any desires of revenging even to death, and of indulging lust even to adultery, of defrauding even to theft, and of lying even to false testimony. In four precepts of the decalogue it is said, Thou shalt not do these things; and in the two last, Thou shalt not covet them. Do you believe that your internal man, in these things, was like your external? If you do believe this, perhaps you are deceived." But to this they replied, "What is the internal man? Is not this and the external the same one? We have heard from our ministers, that the internal man is nothing else than faith, and that the piety of the mouth and the morality of the life are the sign of it, because the operation of it." To which the angels replied, "Saving faith is in the internal man, and so is charity; and thence are Christian faithfulness and morality in the external; but if the above-mentioned lusts remain in the internal man, thus in the will, and thence in the thought—consequently, if you inwardly love them, and yet in externals act and speak otherwise—then evil with you is above good, and good is below evil; wherefore, howsoever you speak as from understanding, and act as from love, within there is evil, and this thus veiled over; and then you are like cunning apes, which perform actions similar to those of men, but their heart is far from them. But what your internal man is, of which you know nothing, because you have not explored yourselves and afterwards performed repentance, you will see after a while, when you are stripped of the external man

and let into the internal; and when this is done, you will no longer be acknowledged by your associates, nor by yourselves. I have seen moral-evil men then like wild beasts, looking upon the neighbor with cruel eyes, burning with deadly hatred, and blaspheming God, whom in the external man they adored." Having heard this, they retired; and the angels then said, "You will see the condition of your life hereafter; for in a short time your external man will be taken from you, and you will enter into the internal, which is now your spirit."

569. THIRD RELATION. Every love with man exhales a delight, by which it makes itself felt, and it exhales it first into the spirit and thence into the body; and the delight of one's love, together with the pleasantness of his thought, makes his life. Those delights and pleasures are felt but slightly by man, while he lives in the natural body, because this body absorbs and blunts them; but after death, when the material body is taken away, and thus the covering or clothing of the spirit is removed, then the delights of his love and the pleasures of his thought are fully felt and perceived; and, what is wonderful, sometimes as odors. Thence it is, that all in the spiritual world are consociated according to their loves; in heaven according to theirs, in hell according to theirs. The odors into which the delights of the loves in heaven are turned, are all perceived like such fragrances, sweet smells, pleasant exhalations, and delightful perceptions, as are perceived in gardens, flower-beds, fields and woods in mornings in the time of spring. But the odors into which the delights of those loves which are in hell, are turned, are perceived as noisome, fetid and putrid stenches, such as from privies, dead bodies, pond holes filled with filth and dung; and, what is wonderful, the devils and satans there perceive them as balsams, spices and frankincense, which refresh their nostrils and hearts. In the natural world, also, it is given to beasts, birds and worms to be consociated according to odors, but not to men then until they have cast off their bodies, as slough. Thence it is, that heaven is arranged in the most distinct order, according to all the varieties of the love of good; and hell as an opposite, according to all the varieties of the love of evil. It is on account of this opposition, that there is between heaven and hell a gulf which cannot be passed; for those who are in heaven cannot endure any odor of hell, for it excites sickness of the stomach and vomiting, and threatens those who inhale it with fainting. The like happens to those who are in hell, if they climb up over the middle of that gulf. Once I saw a certain devil, appearing at a distance like a leopard, who, some days before, was seen among the angels of the last heaven, and was skilled in the art of making himself an angel of light, passing the middle of the gulf, and standing between two olive-trees, and not perceiving any odor offensive to his life. The reason was, because angels were not present; but as soon as they came, he was seized with convulsions, and fell down, all his limbs being contracted; and then he appeared like a great serpent writhing himself into folds, and at length tumbling himself down through a chasm; and he was taken up by his associates and carried away into a cavern, where, from the stinking odor of his delight, he revived. Once also I saw a certain satan punished by his associates. I asked the cause; and it was said, that he, having stopped up his nostrils, went to those who were in the odor of heaven, and that he returned, and brought with him that odor upon his clothes. It has happened several times, that a stench, as of a dead body, from some open cavern of hell, has grazed my nostrils, and excited vomiting. Hence it may be evident whence it is, that, in the Word, smelling signifies perception; for it is often said, that Jehovah smelled a grateful odor from the burnt-offerings; and also that the oil of anointing, and the frankincense, were made of fragrant things: and on the other hand, that a charge was given to the sons of Israel, that the unclean things of their camp should be carried out of the camp; and

that they should dig down, and cover up their excrements, Deut. xxiii. 14, 15. The reason was, because the camp of Israel represented heaven, and the desert out of the camp represented hell.

570. FOURTH RELATION. Once I spoke with a novitiate spirit, who, while he was in the world, meditated much about heaven and hell. By novitiate spirits are meant men lately deceased, who, because they are then spiritual men, are called spirits. He, as soon as he entered into the spiritual world, began to meditate in like manner about heaven and hell; and he seemed to himself, when meditating about heaven, to be in gladness, and when about hell, to be in sadness. When he perceived himself to be in the spiritual world, he immediately inquired, where heaven was, and where hell was; and also, what the one was, and what the other was. And they replied, "Heaven is over your head, and hell is under your feet; for you are now in the world of spirits, which is in the middle between heaven and hell. But what heaven is, and what hell is, we cannot describe in a few words." And then, because he was inflamed with the desire of knowing, he threw himself upon his knees and prayed devoutly to God, that he might be instructed. And lo, an angel appeared at his right hand, and lifted him up and said, "You prayed that you might be instructed concerning heaven and hell. INQUIRE AND LEARN WHAT DELIGHT IS, AND YOU WILL KNOW." And the angel, having said these words, was taken up. Then the novitiate spirit said with himself, "What does this mean? *Inquire and learn what delight is, and you will know what heaven and hell are.*" Then, departing from that place, he wandered about, and, addressing every one that he met, he said, "Tell me, I pray, if you please, what delight is." And some said, "Why, what a question this is! Who does not know what delight is? Is it not joy and gladness? Wherefore delight is delight, one just like another; we know no distinction." Others said, that delight was a laughter of the mind; for while the mind laughs, the face is cheerful, the speech jovial, the gestures playful, and the whole man in delight. But some said, "Delight is nothing else than to feast and to eat dainties, and to drink and to be intoxicated with generous wine, and then to tell stories about various things, especially about the sports of Venus and Cupid." The novitiate spirit, hearing these things, said to himself with indignation, "These answers are clownish and not civil; these delights are not heaven nor hell. I wish I could meet with the wise." And he went away from them, and asked where the wise were. And then he was seen by a certain angelic spirit, who said, "I perceive that you are inflamed with a desire of knowing that which is the universal of heaven and the universal of hell; and because this is delight, I will conduct you to the top of a hill, where those who examine effects, and those who investigate causes, and those who explore ends, meet together every day. Those there who examine effects are called spirits of sciences, and abstractly, sciences; and those who investigate causes are called spirits of intelligence, and abstractly, intelligences; and those who explore ends are called spirits of wisdom, and abstractly, wisdoms. Directly over them, in heaven, are angels who from ends see causes, and from causes effects; from these angels, those three companies have illustration." Then, taking the novitiate spirit by the hand, he led him to the top of the hill, and to the company which was of those who explore ends, and are called wisdoms. To these he said, "Pardon me for coming up to you: the reason is, because I have from my childhood meditated about heaven and hell; and I lately came into this world, and some who were then associated with me, said that here heaven is over my head, and hell is under my feet; but they did not say what is the quality of the one and the other; wherefore, becoming anxious, by constant thought concerning them, I prayed to God; and then an angel stood by me and said, INQUIRE AND LEARN WHAT DELIGHT IS, AND YOU WILL

KNOW. I have inquired, but hitherto in vain. I ask, therefore, that you would teach me, if you please, what delight is." To this the wisdoms replied, "Delight is the all of life to all in heaven, and the all of life to all in hell. Those who are in heaven, have the delight of what is good and true, but those who are in hell have the delight of what is evil and false; for all delight is of love, and love is the *esse* of the life of man; wherefore, as man is man according to the quality of his love, so he is man according to the quality of his delight. The activity of love makes the sense of delight; the activity of it in heaven is with wisd , and the activity of it in hell is with insanity; each in its subjects exhibits delight. But the heavens and the hells are in opposite delights; the heavens being in the love of good, and thence in the delight of doing good; but the hells, in the love of evil, and thence in the delight of doing evil. If, therefore, you know what delight is, you will know what heaven and hell are. But inquire and learn further what delight is, from those who investigate causes, and are called intelligences; they are to the right from this." And he departed and went to them, and told the cause of his coming, and requested that they would instruct him about delight. And being pleased with the question, they said, "It is true that he who knows delight, knows what heaven and hell are. The will, from which man is man, is not moved even a single atom, except by delight; for the will, viewed in itself, is only an affection of some love, thus of delight; for it is some pleasure, and thence satisfaction, which causes it to will; and because the will impels the understanding to think, there is not given the least of thought but from the influent delight of the will. The reason that it is so, is because the Lord, by influx from Himself, actuates all things of the soul and all things of the mind with angels, spirits and men; and He actuates by an influx of love and wisdom, and this influx is the very activity from which all delight is, which in its origin is called blessed, prosperous and happy, and in its derivation, delightful, agreeable and pleasant; and in a universal sense, good. But infernal spirits invert all things with them: thus they turn the good into evil, and the true into false, delight still remaining, for unless delight remained, they would not have will, nor sensation, thus not life. Hence it is manifest, what and whence is the delight of hell, and also what and whence is the delight of heaven." After he had heard this, he was conducted to the third company, where were those who examine effects, and are called sciences. And these said, "Descend to the earth below, and ascend to the earth above; in these you will perceive and feel the delights both of heaven and of hell." But lo, at a distance from them, the earth then opened, and through the opening three devils ascended, appearing ignited from the delight of their love; and because the angels who were consociated with the novitiate spirit, perceived that those three providentially ascended from hell, they cried to the devils, "Do not come any nearer, but from the place where you are, tell something concerning your delights." And they replied, "Know that every one, whether he be called good or evil, is in his own delight; the good, so called, in his, and the evil, so called, in his." And the angels asked, "What is your delight?" They said that it was the delight of committing whoredom, of revenging, of defrauding, and of blaspheming. And again they asked, "What is the quality of those delights of yours?" They said, that they were perceived by others as fetid smells from dunghills, as putrid smells from dead bodies, and as noisome smells from stagnant urine. And they asked, "Are those things delightful to you?" They said, "They are most delightful." Then said they, "You are like the unclean beasts that live in them." And they replied, "If we are, we are; but such things are the delight of our nostrils." And they asked, "What more?" They said, "It is lawful for every one to be in his own delight, even the most unclean, as they call it, provided he do not infest good spirits and angels; but because, from our delight, we could not do otherwise than infest them, we were cast into workhouses, where we suffer hard things. The hindering and withdrawing of our delights there are what are called the torments of hell; there is also interior pain." And they asked, "Why did you infest the good?" They said that "They could not do otherwise. It is as if fury seized us, when we see any angel, and feel the divine sphere of the Lord around him." To which we said, "Then you are also like wild beasts." And presently, when they saw the novitiate spirit with the angels, fury came upon the devils, which appeared like the fire of hatred; wherefore, lest they should do harm, they were cast back into hell. After this the angels appeared, who from ends saw causes, and through causes effects, who were in heaven over those three companies; and they were seen in a bright light, which, rolling itself down by spiral flexures, brought with it a round garland of flowers, and placed it upon the head of the novitiate spirit, and then a voice came to him thence, "This laurel is given to you for this reason, because from childhood you have meditated about heaven and hell."

CHAPTER X.

CONCERNING REFORMATION AND REGENERATION.

571. After Repentance has been treated of, Reformation and Regeneration are next to be treated of in their order, because these follow repentance, and by repentance they are gradually promoted. There are two states which man is to enter and undergo, while from natural he becomes spiritual; the first state is called Reformation, and the other Regeneration. A man in the first state looks from his natural to the spiritual, and desires this; in the other state, he becomes spiritual-natural. The first state is formed by the truths which will be of faith, by which he looks to charity; the other state is formed by the goods of charity, and from these he enters into the truths of faith; or, what is the same, the first state is of thought from the understanding, but the other is of love from the will. When this state begins and advances, a change is effected in the mind; for a turn is made, because then the love of the will flows into the understanding, and impels and leads it to think in accordance and agreement with its love; wherefore, as far as the good of love then acts the first part, and the truths of faith the second, so far the man is spiritual, and is a new creature; and then he acts from charity, and speaks from faith, and feels the good of charity, and perceives the truth of faith, and is then in the Lord and in peace, and thus regenerated. The man who in the world has begun the first state, after death can be introduced into the other; but he who has not entered into the first state in the world, cannot, after death, be introduced into the other, thus cannot be regenerated. These two states may be compared with the progression of light and heat in the days in the time of spring; the first with the dawning of the day or the time of cock-crowing; the other with the morning and the time of sunrising; and the progression of this state, with the progression of the day to noon, and thus into light and heat. It may be compared also with a crop of corn, which is first an herb, then it grows into prickly heads and ears of corn, and afterwards in these the grain is formed; and also with a tree, which first from the seed grows out of the earth; afterwards it becomes a stalk, from which branches shoot forth, and these are adorned with leaves, and then it blossoms, and in the inmost of the flowers it begins fruits, which, as they ripen, produce new seeds, like new races. The first state, which is that of reformation, may be compared also with the state of a silk-worm, when it draws out of itself and unfolds the threads of silk; and, after its industrious labor, flies away into the air, and nourishes itself, not as before from leaves, but from the juices in flowers.

572. I. That a Man, unless he is born again, and as it were created anew, cannot enter into the Kingdom of God.

That a man, unless he is born again, cannot enter into the kingdom of God, is the doctrine of the Lord in John, where are these words: *Jesus said to Nicodemus, Verily, verily, I say unto thee, unless a man be born again, he cannot see the kingdom of God.* And again; *Verily, verily, I say unto thee, unless a man be born of water and spirit, he cannot enter into the kingdom of God. That which is born of flesh is flesh; and that which is born of spirit is spirit,* iii. 3, 5 6

By the kingdom of God, is meant both heaven and the church; for the kingdom of God on earth is the church. In like manner in other places, where the kingdom of God is named, as Matt. xi. 11; xii. 28; xxi. 43; Luke iv. 43; vi. 20; viii. 1, 10; ix. 11, 60, 62; xvii. 21; and elsewhere. To be *born by water and spirit* signifies, by the truths of faith and a life according to them. That *water* signifies truths, may be seen in the APOCALYPSE REVEALED, n. 50, 614, 615, 685, 932. That *spirit* signifies a life according to divine truths, is manifest from the words of the Lord in John vi. 63. By *Verily, verily* (or *Amen, amen*), is signified that it is truth; and because the Lord was Truth itself, therefore He said that so often. He is called also, *the Amen*, Rev. iii. 14. The regenerate are called in the Word *sons of God*, and *born of God*, and regeneration is described by *a new heart* and *a new spirit*.

573. Since to be created also signifies to be regenerated, therefore it is said, *who is born again, and as it were created anew*. That to be created signifies this in the Word, is evident from these passages: CREATE *for me a clean heart, O God, and renew a firm spirit in the midst of me*, Psalm li. 10. *Thou openest thy hand, they are satisfied with good; Thou sendest forth thy spirit, they are* CREATED, civ. 28, 30. *The people that shall be* CREATED *will praise Jah*, cii. 18. *Behold I am about to* CREATE *Jerusalem an exultation*, Isaiah lxv. 18. *Thus said Jehovah, thy* CREATOR, *O Jacob, thy Former, O Israel, I have redeemed thee; every one called by my name, for my glory I have* CREATED *him*, xliii. 1, 7. *That they may see, know, attend, and understand, that the Holy One of Israel hath* CREATED *this*, xli. 19: besides in other places; and where the Lord is called Creator, Former and Maker. Thence it is made manifest, what is meant by these words of the Lord to the disciples; *Going into all the world, preach the gospel to every* CREATURE, Mark xvi. 15. By *creatures* are meant all who can be regenerated; and also in Rev. iii. 14; 2 Cor. v. 16, 17.

574. That man is to be regenerated, is manifest from all reason; for he is born into evils of every kind from parents, and these reside in his natural man, which of itself is diametrically opposite to the spiritual man; and yet he is born for heaven, and he does not come to heaven, unless he become spiritual, which is done solely by regeneration. Thence it necessarily follows, that the natural man with its lusts is to be subdued, subjugated and inverted; and that otherwise man cannot approach a single step towards heaven, but lets himself down more and more into hell. Who does not see this, who believes that he is born into evils of every kind, and acknowledges that there are good and evil, and that one is contrary to the other; and if he believes a life after death, and hell and heaven, and that evils make hell, and goods heaven. The natural man, viewed in himself, as to his nature, differs not at all from the nature of beasts; he is likewise a wild beast, but he is such as to the will; but he differs from beasts as to the understanding; this can be elevated above the lusts of the will, and not only see them, but also moderate them. Thence it is that man can think from understanding, and speak from thought, which beasts cannot do. What man is from birth, and what he would be if he were not regenerated, may be seen from savage beasts of every kind; that he would be a tiger, a panther, a leopard, a wild boar, a scorpion, a tarantula, a viper, a crocodile, &c.; wherefore, unless he were transformed by regeneration into a sheep, what else would he be than a devil among the devils in hell? And then, if the laws of civil government did not restrain such, would they not, from innate ferocity, rush one upon another, and kill each other, or strip each other even to the skin? How many are there of the human race, who were not born satyrs and priapuses or four-footed lizards? And which of these or those, unless he be regenerated, does not become an ape? The

external morality, which is acquired for the sake of covering his internals, does this.

575. What an unregenerate man is, may be further described by these comparisons and similitudes in Isaiah: *The cormorant and the bittern shall possess it, and the owl and the raven shall dwell there. He shall stretch out over it the line of emptiness, and the plumb-line of desolation; and the thorn shall come upon its altars, the thistle and the bramble in its fortresses, and it shall become a habitation of dragons, a court for the daughters of the owl. And the ziim shall meet with the ijim, and the satyr shall encounter his companion; yea, the lilith shall rest there; the black-bird shall build her nest there, and lay, and sit, and hatch in its shade. Yea, the kites shall be gathered together there, one with his companion*, xxxiv. 11, 13, 14, 15.

576. II. That the new Generation or Creation is effected by the Lord alone by Charity and Faith, as the two Means, with the Coöperation of Man.

That regeneration is effected by the Lord alone, by charity and faith, follows from what was demonstrated in the chapters concerning Faith and concerning Charity, and particularly from this there; *That the Lord, charity and faith make one, like life, will and understanding; and that if they are divided, each of them perishes, like a pearl reduced to powder.* These two, charity and faith, are called means, because they conjoin man with the Lord, and cause charity to be charity, and faith to be faith; and this cannot be done unless man also have a part in regeneration; wherefore it is said, *with the coöperation of man.* In the chapters which precede, the coöperation of man with the Lord has occasionally been mentioned; but because the human mind is such, that it does not perceive it otherwise than that man effects it from his own power, therefore it shall be again illustrated. In all motion, and thence in all action, there is an active and a passive; that is, there is something active which acts, and something passive which acts from the active, thence from both one action is produced; comparatively as a mill moved by a wheel, a coach drawn by a horse, motion produced by an effort, an effect by a cause, a dead force acted upon by a living force; in general as the instrumental by the principal; that these two together make one action every one knows. As to charity and faith, the Lord acts, and man acts from the Lord, for the active of the Lord is in the passive of man; wherefore the power of acting well is from the Lord, and thence the will of acting is as it were man's, because he is in free agency; from which he can act together with the Lord, and thus conjoin himself, and he can act from the power of hell, which is without, and thus separate himself. The action of man, concordant with the action of the Lord, is what is here meant by coöperation; that this may be more clearly perceived, it will be illustrated still more by comparisons below.

577. From these things this also follows, that the Lord is continually in the act of regenerating man, because He is continually in the act of saving him; and no one can be saved, unless he be regenerated, according to the Lord's own words in John, *That he who is not born again, cannot see the kingdom of God*, iii. 3, 5, 6. Regeneration, therefore, is the means of salvation, and charity and faith are the means of regeneration. That regeneration follows the faith of the present church, which is without the coöperation of man, is a vanity of vanities. Action and coöperation, such as have been described, may be seen in every thing which is in any activity and mobility. Such is the action and coöperation of the heart and its artery; the heart acts, and the artery, from its coverings or coats, coöperates; thence is circulation. The case is similar with the lungs; the air acts from its incumbency according to the height of its atmosphere, and the ribs with the lungs first coöperate, and presently afterwards the lungs with the ribs; thence is the respiration of every mem-

brane in the body: thus the meninges of the brain, the pleura, the peritonæum, the diaphragm, and the other membranes which cover the viscera, and which inwardly compose them, act and are acted upon, and thus coöperate, for they are elastic; thence their existence and subsistence. The case is similar in every fibre and nerve, and in every muscle, yea in every cartilage; that in each of these there is action and coöperation is known. There is such coöperation also in every sense, for the organs of sense, like the organs of motion of the body, consist of fibres, membranes and muscles; but to describe the coöperation of each is needless, for it is known that light acts in the eye, sound in the ear, odor in the nostril, taste in the tongue, and that the organs adapt themselves to them, whence is sensation. Who cannot thence perceive, that unless there were such action and cöoperation with the influent life in the spiritual organism of the brain, thought and will could not exist? For life from the Lord flows into that spiritual organism, and because this coöperates, that which is thought is perceived, and also that which is there weighed, concluded and determined into act. If life alone acted, and man did not coöperate as of himself, he would not be able to think any more than a stock, or than a temple when the minister is preaching; this indeed, from the repercussion of the sound from its doors, may feel as it were an echo, but nothing of the sermon. Such would man be, unless he coöperated with the Lord, as to charity and faith.

578. It may be illustrated also by comparisons, what man would be, if he did not cöoperate with the Lord: when he perceives and feels any spiritual thing of heaven and the church, it would be as if something disagreeable or discordant flowed in, and as stench into the nose, discord into the ear, deformity into the eye, and something nasty into the tongue. If the delight of charity and the pleasantness of faith should flow into the spiritual organism of the mind of those who are in the delight of evil and the false, these, if those delights and pleasantnesses should be intruded, would be distressed and tormented, and at length would fall into a swoon; that organism, because it consists of perpetual spiral lines, would with such persons involve itself into spires, and would be tortured like a serpent upon a heap of ants. That it is so, has been made evident to me from much experience in the spiritual world.

579. III. That, because all have been redeemed, all can be regenerated, every one according to his State.

That these things may be understood, something is to be premised concerning redemption. The Lord came into the world principally for these two purposes, that He might remove hell from angel and man, and that He might glorify his Human. For before the coming of the Lord, hell had grown up so as to infest the angels of heaven, and, by interposition between heaven and the world, to intercept the communication of the Lord with the men of the earth; whence no divine truth and good could pass through from the Lord to men; thence a total damnation threatened the whole human race, nor could even the angels of heaven have long subsisted in their integrity. Therefore, that hell might be removed, and thus that impending damnation be taken away, the Lord came into the world and removed hell and subjugated it, and thus opened heaven; so that afterwards He could be present with the men of the earth, and save those who would live according to his commandments, consequently regenerate and save them; for those are saved who are regenerated. Thus this is understood, *That because all have been redeemed, all can be regenerated;* and because regeneration and salvation make one, that all can be saved. This, therefore, which the church teaches, that without the coming of the Lord no one could have been saved, is to be thus understood, that no one without the coming of the Lord could have been regenerated

As to the other end for which the Lord came into the world, which is, That He might glorify his Human, it was because He thus became Redeemer, Regenerator and Savior to eternity; for it is not to be believed, that by the redemption once wrought in the world, all after it were redeemed, but that He continually redeems those who believe in Him and do his words. But more may be seen concerning these things, in the chapter concerning REDEMPTION.

580. That every one can be regenerated, each according to his state, is because the simple and the learned are to be regenerated differently; and also those who are engaged in different studies and in different offices; those who are inquisitive about the externals of the Word, differently from those who are inquisitive about its internals; those who from parents are in natural good, differently from those who are in evil; those who from infancy have brought themselves into the vanities of the world, differently from those who have sooner or later removed themselves from them; in a word, those who constitute the external church, differently from those who constitute the internal. This variety is infinite, like that of faces and dispositions; but still every one, according to his state, may be regenerated and saved. That it is so, may be evident from the heavens into which all the regenerate come, in that they are three, the highest, the middle, and the last; and into the highest those come, who by regeneration receive love to the Lord; into the middle, those who receive love towards the neighbor; into the last, those who only practise external charity, and at the same time acknowledge the Lord as God, the Redeemer and Savior. All these are saved, but in various ways. That all may be regenerated, and thus saved, is because the Lord with his divine good and truth is present with every man; thence is the life of every one, and thence is the faculty of understanding and willing, and these have free agency in spiritual things. These things are wanting to no man; and also means are given; to Christians, in the Word; and to the Gentiles, in each one's religion, which teaches that there is a God, and precepts concerning good and evil. Hence this follows, that every one may be saved; consequently that the Lord is not in the fault, but man, if he is not saved; and man is in the fault because he does not coöperate.

581. That redemption and the passion of the cross are two distinct things, and not at all to be confounded, and that the Lord by both put himself into the power of regenerating and saving men, was shown in the chapter concerning REDEMPTION. From the received faith of the present church concerning the passion of the cross, that it was redemption itself, have arisen legions of horrible falsities concerning God, concerning Faith, concerning Charity, and concerning the other things which necessarily depend on those three; as concerning God, that He concluded the condemnation of the human race, and that He was willing to be brought back to mercy by the condemnation laid upon the Son, or taken by the Son upon Himself; and that those only are saved to whom the merit of Christ is given either by foreknowledge or predestination. From that fallacy this tenet also of that faith was hatched, that those who have been gifted with that faith, were regenerated all at once, without their coöperating at all; yea, that they were thus absolved from the condemnation of the law, and that they are no more under the law, but under grace; and this, although the Lord said that He took not away even a tittle of the law, Matt. v. 18, 19; Luke xvi. 17; and also commanded the disciples that they should preach repentance for the remission of sins, xxiv. 47; Mark vi. 12; and also He said, *The kingdom of God is at hand; repent and believe the gospel,* Mark i. 15. By *the gospel* is meant, that they could be regenerated, and thus saved; which could not have been done, unless the Lord had performed redemption, that is, unless He had taken away power from hell by combats against it and by victories over it, and

unless He had glorified his Human, that is, made it Divine.

582. Tell me from rational thought, what the whole human race would be, if the faith of the present church should continue, which is, That they were redeemed solely by the passion of the cross; and that those who have been gifted with that merit of the Lord, are not under the condemnation of the law; and also that that faith, concerning which man never knows whether it is in him or not, remits sins and regenerates; and that the coöperation of man in the act of it, which is while it is given and enters, would destroy that faith, and with it would take away salvation, since he would mix his own merit with the merit of Christ: tell me, I say, from rational thought, whether the whole Word, where is principally taught regeneration by spiritual washing from evils, and by exercises of charity, would not thus have been rejected? What then is the decalogue, the principle of reformation, more than the paper which is sold at the shops of hucksters, and is formed into wrappers around spices? What then is religion but a man's lamentation that he is a sinner, and supplication that God the Father would have mercy for the sake of his Son's passion? Thus something of the mouth only from the lungs, and nothing of deed from the heart. And what then is redemption, but a papal indulgence, or more than the flogging of one monk for the whole company, as is done. If that faith alone regenerated man, and not repentance and charity, what then is the internal man, which is his spirit that lives after death, but like a city set on fire, the rubbish of which makes the external man? or like a field or a plain laid waste by palmer-worms and locusts? Such a man appears before the angels just as if he cherished a serpent in his bosom, and put his garment over it that it might not appear; and also like one who sleeps as a sheep with a wolf; or like one who lies down, under a beautiful coverlet, in a shirt woven of spiders' webs. And what then is the life after death, when all are distinguished according to the distinctions of regeneration in heaven, and according to the distinctions of its rejection in hell, but a carnal life, thus like the life of a fish or a crab?

583. IV. THAT REGENERATION IS EFFECTED, COMPARATIVELY, AS MAN IS CONCEIVED, CARRIED IN THE WOMB, BORN AND EDUCATED.

There is with man a perpetual correspondence between those things which are done naturally and those which are done spiritually; or those which are done in the body and those which are done in the spirit. The reason is, because man is born spiritual as to the soul, and is clothed with a natural which constitutes his material body; wherefore, when this is put off, his soul, clothed with a spiritual body, comes into a world where all things are spiritual, and is there associated with its like. Now, because the spiritual body is to be formed in the material body, and is formed by the truths and goods which flow in from the Lord through the spiritual world, and are received by man inwardly in such things of him as are from the natural world, which are called civil and moral, it is manifest how its formation is effected. And because, as was said, there is a perpetual correspondence, with man, between those things which are done naturally and those which are done spiritually, it follows that there is, as it were, a conception, carrying in the womb, birth and education. It is from that cause, that in the Word by natural births are meant spiritual births, which are of good and truth; for whatever is extant in the sense of the letter of the Word, which is natural, involves and signifies that which is spiritual. That in all and every part of the sense of the letter of the Word, there is a spiritual sense, was fully shown in the chapter concerning the SACRED SCRIPTURE. That the natural births named in the Word, involve spiritual births, manifestly appears from these passages there: *We have conceived, we have been in travail, we have as it were brought forth, we have not wrought salvation*, Isaiah xxvi. 18

At the presence of the Lord the earth bringeth forth, Psalm cxiv. 7. *Hath the earth brought forth in one day? Shall I break and not beget? Shall I cause to bring forth, and not have shut up?* Isaiah lxvi. 7 to 10. *Sin is in travail, and will not be able to bring forth*, Ezek. xxx. 15, 16. *The pangs of a travailing woman shall come upon Ephraim; he is an unwise son, because he doth not stay his time in the womb of sons*, Hosea xiii. 13; and likewise in many other places. Since natural generations in the Word signify spiritual ones, and these are from the Lord, thence he is called the Former, and Drawer-forth from the womb, which is manifest from these passages: *Jehovah, thy Maker and Former from the womb*, Isaiah xliv. 2. *He that drew me out from the womb*, Psalm xxii. 9. *I have been laid upon Thee from the womb, Thou drewest me out from the bowels of my mother*, Psalm lxxi. 6. *Hearken ye to Me, who have been borne from the womb, carried from the belly*, Isaiah xlvi. 3; besides in other places. Thence it is, that the Lord is called *Father*, as Isaiah ix. 6; lxiii. 16; John x. 30; xiv. 8, 9; and that those who are in goods and truths from Him, are called *sons and born of God*, and among themselves *brethren*, Matt. xxiii. 8; and also that the church is called *Mother*, Hosea ii. 2, 5; Ezek. xvi. 45.

584. Hence now it is manifest, that there is a correspondence between natural generations and spiritual generations; and because there is a correspondence, it follows that conception, carrying in the womb, birth and education may not only be predicated of the new generation, but also that they actually are; but what they are, is exhibited to view in their order in this article concerning Regeneration. Here only, that the seed of man is conceived inwardly in the understanding, and is formed in the will, and thence is transferred into the testicle, where it clothes itself with a natural covering; and thus it is conveyed into the womb, and comes into the world. Moreover, there is a correspondence of the regeneration of man with all the things that are in the vegetable kingdom; wherefore also in the Word man is described by a tree, his truth by the seed, and his good by the fruit. That a bad tree may be as it were born anew, and afterwards bear good fruit, is evident from engraftings and inoculations, in that then, although the same juice ascends from the root through the trunk even to that which is engrafted or inoculated, still it is turned into good juice and makes a good tree. The case is similar in the church with those who are engrafted into the Lord, as He teaches in these words; *I am the Vine, ye the branches. He that abideth in Me, and I in him, the same beareth much fruit. Unless a man abide in Me, he is cast away as a branch, and, being dried, is cast into the fire*, John xv. 5, 6.

585. That the vegetations not only of trees, but also of all shrubs, correspond to the prolifications of men, has been taught by many of the learned; wherefore I shall add something concerning these, in the place of a conclusion. In trees and in all other subjects of the vegetable kingdom, there are not two sexes, the male and the female, but every one there is male: the earth alone, or the ground, is the common mother, thus as it were the female; for this receives the seeds of all plants, opens them, carries them as it were in the womb, and then nourishes them, and brings them forth, that is, brings them into open day, and afterwards clothes them and sustains them. The earth, when she first opens the seed, begins from the root, which is like a heart; from that it emits and transmits juice, like blood, and thus makes as it were a body furnished with members; the body is the stalk itself, and the branches and their twigs are its members. The leaves which it puts forth immediately after birth are in the place of lungs; for as the heart without the lungs does not produce sense and motion, and by these vivify man, so the root does not cause the tree or shrub to vegetate without the leaves. The flowers which precede the fruit, are the means of decanting

the juice, its blood, and of separating the grosser parts of it from the purer, and of forming for the influx of these in their bosom a new little stalk, through which the decanted juice may flow in, and thus begin and successively form the fruit, which may be compared to a testicle in which the seeds are perfected. The vegetative soul, which reigns most inwardly in every particle of the juice, or its prolific essence, is from no other source than from the heat of the spiritual world, which, because it is from the spiritual sun there, does not breathe after any thing else than generation, and by this the continuation of creation; and because it essentially breathes after the generation of man, therefore, whatsoever it generates, it induces upon it a certain likeness of man. Lest any one should wonder that it was said, that the subjects of the vegetable kingdom are only male, and that the earth alone, or the ground, is as a common mother, or as the female, this shall be illustrated by the like in bees. These, according to the observation and testimony of SWAMMERDAM, in his BOOKS OF NATURE, have only one common mother, from whom all the offspring of the whole hive are produced. Since these little animals have only one common mother, why should not all plants? That the earth is a common mother, may be illustrated also spiritually; and it is illustrated by this, that the earth in the Word signifies the church, and the church is the common mother, as she is also called in the Word. That the earth signifies the church, consult the APOCALYPSE REVEALED, n. 285, 902, where it is shown. But that the earth, or ground, can enter into the inmost of the seed, even to its prolific principle, and draw this out and carry it around, is because every particle of dust or pollen exhales from its essence something fine, like an effluvium, which penetrates; this is done from the active force of the heat from the spiritual world.

586. That man can be regenerated only successively, may be illustrated by all and each of the things that exist in the natural world. A tree cannot grow into a tree in one day; but it grows first from the seed, afterwards from the root, then from the shoot, from which is formed the stalk, and from this proceed branches with leaves, and at last flowers and fruits. Neither does wheat or barley rise into a harvest in one day. A house is not built in one day; neither does man attain to his stature in one day, much less to wisdom; nor is the church instituted and perfected in one day; nor is there any progression to an end, unless there be a beginning as a starting point. Those who conceive otherwise of regeneration, do not know any thing concerning charity and faith, and concerning the growth of each according to the coöperation of man with the Lord. Hence it is manifest, that regeneration is effected, comparatively, as man is conceived, carried in the womb, born and educated.

587. V. THAT THE FIRST ACT OF THE NEW GENERATION IS CALLED REFORMATION, WHICH IS OF THE UNDERSTANDING, AND THAT THE SECOND ACT IS CALLED REGENERATION, WHICH IS OF THE WILL, AND THENCE OF THE UNDERSTANDING.

Since reformation and regeneration are treated of here and in the following articles, and reformation is ascribed to the understanding, and regeneration to the will, it is necessary that the distinctions should be known which are between the understanding and the will, and these have been described above, n. 397; wherefore it is advised, that that be first read, and afterwards what is in this article. That the evils into which man is born, are generated in the will of the natural man, and that the will brings the understanding to favor itself by thinking in agreement, was also there shown; wherefore, that man may be regenerated, it is necessary that this should be done by the understanding, as by a mediate cause, and this is done by the information which the understanding receives, first from parents and masters, afterwards from the reading of the Word, from preaching, books and conversation. Those things which the understanding thence receives, are called truths wherefore it is the same, whether it be said, that reformation is effected by the understanding, or whether it be said, that it is effected by the truths which the understanding receives; for truths teach man in whom and what he should believe, and also what he should do, and thus what he should will; for whatever any one does, he does it from the will according to the understanding. Since, therefore, the will itself of man is evil from nativity, and because the understanding teaches what is evil and good, and he is able to will the one, and not to will the other, it follows that man is to be reformed by the understanding. But as long as any one sees, and acknowledges in his mind, that evil is evil, and good good, and thinks that good is to be chosen, so long that state is called *reformation;* but when he wills to shun evil and do good, the state of *regeneration* begins.

588. For this end there is given to man the faculty of elevating the understanding almost into the light in which the angels of heaven are, that he may see what he ought to will and thence to do, in order that he may be prosperous in the world in time, and blessed after death to eternity. He becomes prosperous and blessed, if he procures for himself wisdom, and keeps his will in obedience to it; but unprosperous and unhappy, if he puts his understanding under obedience to the will; the reason is, because the will from nativity inclines to evils, even to enormous ones; wherefore, unless it were restrained by the understanding, man, left to the freedom of his own will, would rush into wicked deeds, and, from his innate savage nature, would plunder and massacre, for his own sake, all who do not favor him and indulge his inordinate desires. Moreover, unless the understanding could be perfected separately, and the will by it, man would not be man, but a beast; for without that separation, and without the ascent of the understanding above the will, he would not be able to think, and from thought to speak, but only to sound his affection; nor would he be able to act from reason, but from instinct; still less could he know those things which are of God, and by them God, and thus be conjoined to Him and live to eternity. For man thinks and wills as of himself, and this, *as of himself,* is the reciprocal of conjunction; for conjunction without a reciprocal, is not possible; as there can be no conjunction of what is active with what is passive without adaptation or application. God alone acts, and man suffers himself to be acted upon, and coöperates in all appearance as from himself, although inwardly from God. But from these things, rightly perceived, it may be seen what the love of man's will is, if it be elevated by the understanding, and also what it is, if it be not elevated; thus what man is.

589. It is to be known that the faculty of elevating the understanding even to the intelligence in which the angels of heaven are, is from creation inherent in every man, in the bad as well as the good; yea, also in every devil in hell, for all who are in hell were men; this has often been shown to me by lively experience. But that they are not in intelligence, but in insanity, in spiritual things, is because they do not will good, but evil; and thence they are averse to know and understand truths, for truths are in favor of good and against evil. Hence also it is manifest, that the first thing of the new generation, is the reception of truths in the understanding, and that the second is, that he wills to do according to truths, and at length to do them. But yet no one can be said to be reformed by the mere knowledges of truths; for man, from the faculty of elevating the understanding above the love of the will, can apprehend them and also speak, teach and preach them but he is reformed who is in the affection of truth for the sake of truth; for this affection conjoins itself with the will, and, if it goes on, conjoins the will to the understanding, and then regeneration begins. But how regeneration progresses and is perfected, wil be told in what follows.

590. But what the man is, whose understanding is elevated, and the love

of the will not elevated by it, will be illustrated by comparisons. He is like an eagle flying on high, but as soon as he sees food below, such as hens, young swans, yea, lambs, in a moment he descends and devours them. He is also like an adulterer, who keeps a harlot concealed below in the cellar, and by turns ascends to the highest story of the house, and, with those who stay there, in the presence of his wife, he speaks wisely concerning chastity; and by and by he suddenly retires from the company and indulges his lasciviousness below with the harlot. He is also like the flies of a bog, which fly in a column over the head of a running horse, which, when the horse stops, descend and immerse themselves in their bog. Such is the man who is in elevation as to the understanding, but the love of the will sinks below to the foot, immersed in the unclean things of nature and the libidinous things of the senses. But because they shine as from wisdom, as to the understanding, and the will is contrary to it, they may be likened also to serpents, which shine with scales, and to Spanish flies, which glitter as from gold, and also to the *ignis fatuus* in marshes, and to shining rotten wood, and to phosphorus. There are among them those, who can counterfeit angels of light, both among men in the world, and after death among the angels of heaven: but these, after a short examination, are deprived of their garments, and cast down naked. The like, however, cannot be done in the world, because there their spirit is not open, but covered over with a mask, like that of actors on the theatre. The reason that they can counterfeit angels of light, and also a proof of it, is that they can elevate the understanding almost to angelic wisdom, above the love of the will, as was said. Now, because the internal and the external of man can thus go contrary ways, and because the body is cast away, and the spirit remains, it is evident that a dusky spirit may dwell under a white face, and a fiery one under a smooth mouth. Wherefore, my friend, know a man not from his mouth, but from his heart, that is, not from his speech, but from his deeds; for the Lord says, *Beware of false prophets, who come to you in sheep's clothing, but inwardly they are ravening wolves. From their fruits ye shall know them*, Matt. vii. 15, 16.

591. VI. THAT THE INTERNAL MAN IS FIRST TO BE REFORMED, AND BY THIS THE EXTERNAL, AND THAT MAN IS THUS REGENERATED.

That the internal man is first to be regenerated, and by it the external, is commonly said in the church at this day; but by the internal man nothing else is thought of, than faith, which is, that God the Father imputes the merit and righteousness of his Son, and sends the Holy Spirit. This faith, they believe, makes the internal man, and that from it flows the external, which is the natural moral man, and that this is an appendage of that; comparatively, like the tail of a horse or an ox, or like the tail of a peacock or bird of paradise, which is continued to the soles of its feet without cohering. For it is said that charity follows that faith, but if charity from the will of man enters, that faith perishes. But because no other internal man is acknowledged in the church at this day, there is not any internal man, for no one knows whether that faith be given to him, or not; that also it cannot be given, and thence is imaginary, was shown above Thence it follows, that, at this day, with those who have confirmed themselves in that faith, there is no other internal man, than that natural man, which from nativity overflows with evils in all abundance. It is added also, that regeneration and sanctification follow that faith of themselves, and that the coöperation of man, by which alone regeneration is effected, is to be excluded. Thence it is, that regeneration is not knowable in the present church; when yet the Lord says that he who is not regenerated cannot see the kingdom of God.

592. But the internal and the external man of the New Church are altogether different; the internal man is of his will, from which he thinks when he is left to himself, as is the case at

home but the external man is his action and speech, which proceed from him in company, thus abroad; consequently the internal man is charity, because this is of the will, and at the same time faith, which is of the thought. Both of these, before regeneration, make the natural man, which is thus divided into internal and external; this is manifest from this, that it is not lawful for a man to act and speak in company or abroad, as when he is left to himself or at home. The cause of this division is, that the civil laws prescribe punishments for those who do ill, and rewards for those who do well; and thus they force themselves to separate the internal man from the external; for no one wishes to be punished, and every one wishes to be rewarded, which is done by riches and honors; both of these man does not attain, if he does not live according to those laws. Thence it is that there is morality and benevolence in externals with those who have no morality and benevolence in internals; all hypocrisy, flattery and insincerity are from this origin.

593. As to the division of the natural man into two forms, it is an actual division, both of the will and of the thought there; for all the action of man proceeds from his will, and all speech from his thought; wherefore another will is formed by man below the former, and also another thought, but still both of these constitute the natural man. This will, which is formed by man, may be called the corporeal will, because it impels the body to conduct itself morally; and that thought may be called pulmonary thought, because it impels the tongue and lips to speak such things as are of the understanding. This thought and that will together may be compared to the thin skin which inwardly adheres to the bark of a tree, and to the membrane which adheres to the shell of an egg, within which is the internal natural man, which, if evil, may be compared to the wood of a rotten tree, around which the said bark with its thin skin appears entire; and also to a rotten egg within a white shell. But what the internal natural man is from nativity shall be told; his will inclines to evils of every kind, and the thought thence to falses also of every kind; this internal man, therefore, is what is to be regenerated; for, unless this be regenerated, there is nothing but hatred against all things which are of charity, and thence wrath against all things that are of faith. Thence it follows, that the internal natural man is first to be regenerated, and by it the external, for this is according to order; but to regenerate the internal by the external is contrary to order; for the internal is as a soul in the external, not only in general, but also in every particular; consequently it is in every single thing that he speaks, without the man's knowing it. Thence it is, that the angels perceive from one action of a man what his will is, and from one expression of his what his thought is, whether it be infernal or heavenly. Thence they know the whole man; from the sound they perceive the affection of his thought, and from the gesture or form of action, the love of his will; they perceive them, however he may counterfeit the Christian and the moral citizen.

594. The regeneration of man is described in Ezekiel by the dry bones, upon which were brought sinews, afterwards flesh, and skin, and at last breath was breathed into them, by which they revived; xxxvii. 1 to 14. That regeneration was represented by them, is clearly manifest from these words there; *These bones are the whole house of Israel*, verse 11. It is also compared there with sepulchres, for it is read, that *He would open the sepulchres, and cause the bones to ascend thence, and put spirit in them, and place them upon the land of Israel*, verses 12, 13, 14. By the land of Israel, there and elsewhere, is meant the church. The reason why a representation of regeneration was made by bones and sepulchres, is because the unregenerate man is called dead, and the regenerate alive; for in the latter there is spiritual life, but in the former spiritual death.

595. In every created thing in the world, whether living or dead, there is an internal and an external; one is not where the other is not, as no effect is without a cause; and every created thing is estimated according to its internal goodness, and is disesteemed from its internal vileness; and so is external goodness in which there is internal vileness. Every wise man in the world, and every angel in heaven, thus judges. But what the unregenerate man is, and what the regenerate is, may be illustrated by comparisons. The unregenerate man, who counterfeits the moral citizen and the Christian man, may be compared to a dead body, which is wrapped up in aromatics, and which still spreads a stench, by which it infects the aromatics and insinuates itself into the nostrils and injures the brain. And also he may be compared with a mummy covered with gold, or placed in a silver coffin, on looking into which an ugly black corpse comes to view. He may be compared with bones or skeletons in a sepulchre built of *lapis lazuli*, and adorned with other precious things. He may be compared also to the rich man, who was clothed with purple and fine linen, whose internal, nevertheless, was infernal, Luke xvi. He may further be compared to poison of a taste like that of sugar; to hemlock when in bloom; to fruits in shining shells, the kernels of which have been eaten out by worms; and also to an ulcer covered over with a plaster, and afterwards with a thin skin, in which there is nothing but corrupted matter. The internal may be estimated from the external in the world, but only by those who have not a good internal and who therefore judge from appearance. But it is otherwise in heaven; for when the body, versatile about the spirit and flexible from evil to good, is separated by death, then the internal remains, for this makes his spirit; and then it appears at a distance like a serpent that has cast its skin, or like rotten wood stripped of the bark in which it shone But it is otherwise with a regenerate man; his internal is good, and his external similar to the external of another; the external of this differs from that of the former, as heaven from hell, since there is a soul of good in it. And it is of no consequence whether he be a grandee, and live in a palace, and walk in state surrounded by guards, or whether he live in a cottage, and be served by a boy; yea, whether he be a primate, arrayed in a robe of purple, and wear a cap of two degrees, or whether he be the shepherd of a few sheep in the woods, and be dressed in a rustic loose gown, and covered as to the head with a hood. Gold is still gold, whether it glitter by being placed near the fire, or become dusky as to the surface by exposure to the smoke; and also whether it be cast into a beautiful form as of an infant, or into an ugly form as of a mouse. The mice made of gold, and placed near the ark, also were accepted, and they appeased; 1 Sam. vi. 3, 4, 5, and the following verses; for gold signifies internal good. A diamond and a ruby, in whatever matrix, calcareous or clayey, when taken out, are estimated in the same manner, from their internal goodness, as those in the necklace of a queen, &c. Hence it is manifest, that the external is estimated from the internal, and not the reverse.

596. VII. THAT WHEN THIS TAKES PLACE, A COMBAT ARISES BETWEEN THE INTERNAL AND THE EXTERNAL MAN, AND THEN THAT WHICH CONQUERS RULES OVER THE OTHER.

The reason that a combat then arises, is because the internal man has been reformed by truths, and from these it sees what is evil and false, and these are still in the external or natural man. Wherefore, there first arises a dissension between the new will which is above, and the old will which is below; and because it is between the wills, it is also between the delights of both; for it is known that the flesh is contrary to the spirit, and the spirit to the flesh, and that the flesh with its lusts must be subdued, before the spirit can act and the man become new. After this dissension of the wills, a combat arises, which is what is called spiritual temptation; but this temptation or combat is not waged between goods and evils, but between the truths of good and the falses of evil; for good of itself cannot fight, but it fights by truths; neither can evil fight of itself, but by its falses; as the will cannot fight of itself, but by the understanding, where its truths are. Man feels that combat no otherwise than in himself, and as remorse of conscience; but yet it is the Lord and the devil, that is, hell, that fight in man, and they fight for dominion over man, or which shall possess him. The devil, or hell, assaults man and calls forth his evils, and the Lord defends him and calls forth his goods. But although that combat is fought in the spiritual world, yet still it is fought in man between the truths of good and the falses of evil which are in him; wherefore man should fight altogether as from himself, for he is in free agency to act for the Lord and also to act for the devil; he is for the Lord, if he remains in truths from good, and for the devil, if in falses from evil. Hence it follows, that that which conquers, whether the internal man or the external, rules over the other; just like two enemies, that contend which shall be the master of the other's kingdom; he who conquers takes the kingdom and puts all there under obedience to him. Here, therefore, if the internal man conquers, he commands and subjugates all the evils of the external man, and then regeneration is continued; but if the external man conquers, he commands and dissipates all the goods of the internal man, and then regeneration perishes.

597. It is, indeed, known at this day, that there are temptations, but scarcely any one knows whence they are, and what they are, and what good they produce; whence and what they are, was shown just above, and also what good they produce, namely, that when the internal man conquers, the external is subjugated; which being subjugated, lusts are dispersed, and in their place affections of good and truth are implanted, and are so arranged that the goods and truths which man wills and thinks, he may also do them and speak them from the heart. Besides this, by victory over the external man, man becomes spiritual, and then he is by the Lord associated with the angels of heaven, who all are spiritual. The reason why temptations have been hitherto unknown, and why scarcely any one has known whence and what they are, is because the church hitherto has not been in truths; no one is in truths, but he who goes immediately to the Lord, and rejects the former faith and embraces the new. Thence it is, that no one has been admitted into any spiritual temptation for ages, even from the age when the Nicene synod introduced the faith of three Gods; for if any one had been admitted, he would have fallen immediately, and thus would have precipitated himself deeper into hell. The contrition which is said to precede the present faith, is not temptation; I have asked a good many about it, and they have said that it was a word and nothing else; unless perhaps it might be some timid thought about the fire of hell with the simple.

598. Man, after temptation has passed, is, as to the internal man, in heaven, and by the external in the world; wherefore by temptations in man the conjunction of heaven and the world is effected, and then the Lord with him, according to order, governs his world from heaven. The contrary takes place, if man remains natural; then he desires to govern heaven from the world. Such every one becomes, who is in the love of ruling from the love of self; if he be inwardly explored, he does not believe in any God, but in himself; and after death he believes him to be God who is preëminent in power over others. Such insanity there is in hell, which has become so profound, that some say that they are God the Father, some God the Son, and some God the Holy Ghost; and among the Jews, some that they are the Messiah. Thence it is manifest what man becomes after death, if the natural man is not regenerated; consequently what he would become in his fantasy if a new church were not instituted by the Lord, in which genuine truths are

taught. This is what is meant by these words of the Lord; *In the consummation of the age*, that is, in the end of the present church, *there shall be such affliction as has not been from the beginning of the world, neither shall be. Wherefore unless those days should be shortened, no flesh could be saved*, Matt. xxiv. 21, 22.

599. In the combats or temptations of men, the Lord performs a particular redemption, as He did a general one, when He was in the world. The Lord in the world, by combats and temptations, glorified his Human, that is, made it Divine; in like manner now, with every individual man, when he is in temptations, He fights for him in them, and overcomes the infernal spirits which infest him, and glorifies him after temptation, that is, renders him spiritual. The Lord, after his universal redemption, reduced all things in heaven and in hell into order; in like manner He does with man, that is, He reduces into order all things which are of heaven and t e world with him. The Lord after redemption instituted a new church; in like manner He also institutes those things which are of the church with man, and makes him a church in particular. The Lord after redemption gave peace to those who believed in Him, for He said, *My peace I leave with you my peace I give to you; not as the world giveth, give I to you*, John xiv. 27. In like manner He gives to man after temptation to feel peace, that is, gladness of mind, and consolation. Hence it is manifest, that the Lord is a Redeemer to eternity.

600. The internal man being regenerated, and the external at the same time not regenerated, may be compared to a bird flying in the air without a seat on dry ground, but only in a bog where it is infested by serpents and frogs, wherefore it flies away and dies. It may be compared also to a swan swimming in the midst of the sea, which is not able to reach the shore and build a nest; wherefore the eggs which she lays are immersed in the water, where they are devoured by fishes. It may be compared also to a soldier upon a wall, who, when the wal is undermined under his feet, falls down and expires in the ruins. It may be compared also with a beautiful tree transplanted into a filthy soil, where worms in a troop eat up the root, from which it withers and perishes. It may be compared also to a house without a foundation, and also to a column without a pedestal. Such is the internal man, when it only is reformed, and not the external at the same time; for it has no ultimate for doing good.

601. VIII. That the Regenerate Man has a new Will and a new Understanding.

That the regenerate man is a renewed or new man, the church at this day knows, both from the Word and from reason. From the Word, from these passages: *Make to yourselves a new heart and a new spirit; why will ye die, O house of Israel*, Ezek. xviii. 31. *I will give you a new heart, and a new spirit in the midst of you; and I will remove the heart of stone out of your flesh, and I will give you a heart of flesh; and I will give my spirit in the midst of you*, xxxvi. 26, 27. *Henceforth we know no one according to the flesh; wherefore, if any one be in Christ, he is a new creature*, 2 Cor. v. 6, 7. By *a new heart* there, is meant a new will, and by *a new spirit*, a new understanding; for heart, in the Word, signifies the will, and spirit, when it is joined with heart, the understanding. From Reason: That the regenerate man has a new will and a new understanding, is because these two faculties make man, and these are what are regenerated. Wherefore every man is such as he is as to those faculties; he is a bad man, whose will is bad, and still worse if the understanding favors it; but he is a good man, whose will is good, and still better if the understanding favors it. Religion alone renews and regenerates man, for this occupies the highest seat in the human mind, and sees under it the civil things which are of the world, and also it ascends through them, as the pure juice ascends through a tree even to its top, and from that height it looks around upon natural things, like one who from a tower or a mountain looks around upon the plains below.

602. But it should be known, that man, as to the understanding, may rise almost into the light in which the angels of heaven are; but if he does not also rise as to the will, he is still an old and not a new man. But how the understanding elevates the will to higher and higher degrees with itself, was before shown; wherefore regeneration is predicated primarily of the will, and secondarily of the understanding; for the understanding with man is like the light in the world, and the will like the heat there; that light without heat does not produce life and vegetation, but light joined with heat, is known. The understanding also, as to the lower region in the mind, is also actually in the light of the world, and as to the higher region, in the light of heaven; wherefore, unless the will be elevated from the lower region to the higher, and conjoined there to the understanding, it remains in the world; and then the understanding flies upwards and downwards, but every night to the will below, and there it lies, and they join themselves together, like a man and a harlot, and produce a two-headed offspring. Hence also it is manifest, that unless man has a new will and a new understanding, he is not regenerated.

603. The human mind is distinguished into three regions; the lowest is called natural, the middle spiritual, and the highest celestial; man by regeneration is elevated from the lowest region which is natural, into the next higher which is spiritual, and by this into the celestial. That there are three regions of the mind, will be demonstrated in the following article. Thence it is, that the unregenerate man is called natural, and the regenerate spiritual; whence it is manifest that the mind of the regenerate man is elevated into the spiritual region, and there, from a higher station, sees those things which are passing in the lower or natural mind. That there is a higher and a lower region in the human mind, every one may see and acknowledge from a slight attention to his own thoughts; for he sees what he thinks, wherefore he says that he was thinking or is thinking this or that; this could not be, unless there were an interior thought, which is called perception, which looks into the lower, which is called thought. A judge, when he has heard or read the cases brought together in a long series by an advocate, collects them into one view in the higher region of his mind, thus into a universal idea, and afterwards looks down thence into the lower region, which is of the natural thought, and there disposes the arguments in order, and according to the higher pronounces sentence and judges. Who does not know that a man can think and conclude in a moment or two, what he cannot by the lower thought express in the space of an hour? These things are adduced that it may be known, that the human mind is distinguished into lower and higher regions.

604. As to the new will, this is above the old will in the spiritual region, and in like manner the new understanding, this with that and that with this; in that region they join themselves together, and conjointly look into the old or natural will and understanding, and dispose all things there to compliance and obedience. Who cannot see, that, if there were only one region in the human mind, and evils and goods, and falses and truths were put there and mixed together, a conflict would ensue, just as if wolves and sheep, tigers and calves, hawks and doves were put together into one den? And what then would be done there? Would there not be a cruel butchery? Would not the savage animals tear in pieces the gentle ones? Wherefore it is provided that goods with their truths should be collected into the higher region, that they may be able to subsist in safety, and repel assault, and also by chains and other means subjugate and afterwards disperse evils with their falses. This, therefore, is what was said in the former article, that the Lord

through heaven governs those things which are of the world with the regenerate man. The higher or spiritual region of the human mind is also heaven in miniature, and the lower or natural region is the world in miniature; wherefore man was called by the ancients a *microcosm*, or little world, and also he may be called a *microüranos*, or little heaven.

605. That a man who is regenerated, that is, renewed as to the will and understanding, is in the heat of heaven, that is, in its love, and at the same time in the light of heaven, that is, in its wisdom; and, on the other hand, that a man who is not regenerated, is in the heat of hell, that is, in its love, and at the same time in the darkness of hell, that is, in its insanity, is at this day known and yet unknown. The reason is, because the church which is at this day, has made regeneration an appendage of its faith, into which reason is not to be admitted; consequently not into any thing which is of this appendage, which, as was said, is regeneration and renovation: these, with the faith itself, are to them like a house, whose doors and windows are shut; wherefore it is not known what is within that house, whether it be entirely empty, or whether it be full of genii from hell, or of angels from heaven. It is to be added, that a fallacy has confused this, which is, that any man may by the understanding ascend almost into the light of heaven, and thence from intelligence think and speak concerning spiritual things, whatever may be the love of his will. From the ignorance of this truth, every thing that concerns regeneration and renovation has become unknown.

606. Hence these things may be concluded, that an unregenerate man is like one who sees apparitions in the night, and believes them to be men; and then, when he is being regenerated, like the same one who sees those things, which he saw in the night, at the dawn of day, that they were mockeries; and afterwards, when he has become regenerated, and is in the day, that they were the effects of delirium. The unregenerate man is like one who is dreaming, and the regenerate man like one who is awake; in the Word. also, natural life is likened to sleep, and spiritual life to wakefulness. The unregenerate man is meant by the foolish virgins, who had lamps and not oil; and the regenerate man, by the prudent virgins, who had lamps and at the same time oil. By lamps are meant such things as are of the understanding, and by oil such as are of love. The regenerate are like the lamps of the candlestick in the tabernacle, and they are like the bread of faces with frankincense upon it there; and they are those who will glitter like the brightness of the expanse, and who will shine like the stars for ever and ever, Dan. xii. 3 An unregenerate man is like one who is in the garden of Eden, and eats of the tree of the knowledge of good and evil, and is therefore cast out of the garden; yea, he is that very tree; but a regenerate man is like one who is in that garden, and eats of the tree of life. That it is given to eat of it, is evident from these words in the Revelation; *To him that overcometh, I will give to eat of the tree of life, which is in the midst of the paradise of God*, ii. 7. By the garden of Eden, is meant intelligence in spiritual things from the love of truth. See the APOLCALYPSE REVEALED, n. 90. In a word, an unregenerate man is a son of the evil one, and a regenerate man is a son of the kingdom, Matt. xiii. 38. The son of the evil one there, is a son of the devil, and the son of the kingdom there, is a son of the Lord.

607. IX. THAT A REGENERATE MAN IS IN COMMUNION WITH THE ANGELS OF HEAVEN, AND AN UNREGENERATE MAN IN COMMUNION WITH THE SPIRITS OF HELL.

The reason that every man is in communion, that is, in consociation, with angels of heaven, or with spirits of hell, is, because he is born that he may become spiritual, and this is not possible, unless he be in some conjunction with those who are spiritual. That man is in both worlds, the natural and the spiritual, as to the mind, is shown in the book concerning HEAVEN AND HELL. But neither man, nor angel or spirit, knows concerning this conjunction, because a man, while he lives in the world, is in a natural state, and an angel and a spirit in a spiritual state; and on account of the distinction between natural and spiritual, one does not appear to the other; this distinction, what it is, has been described in the book concerning CONJUGIAL LOVE, in a RELATION there, n. 326 to 329 [*see also above, n.* 280]; from which it is manifest, that they are not conjoined as to thoughts, but as to affections, and upon these scarcely any one reflects, because they are not in the light in which the understanding is and thence its thought, but in the heat in which the will is and thence the affection of his love. The conjunction, by the affections of love, between men, and angels and spirits, is so close, that, if it were severed, and hence they were separated, men would instantly fall into a swoon, and if it should not be restored, and they conjoined, men would expire. By what was said, that man by regeneration becomes spiritual, it is not meant that he becomes as spiritual as an angel is in himself; but that he becomes spiritual-natural, that is, that there is a spiritual within his natural, just as thought is in the speech, and as will in the action; for when one ceases, the other ceases. In like manner, the spirit of man is in every thing that is done in the body, and this is what impels the natural to do what it does; the natural, viewed in itself, is only passive, or a dead force, but the spiritual is active, or a living force; the passive, or the dead force, cannot act of itself, but it must be acted upon by the active, or the living force. Since man lives continually in communion with the inhabitants of the spiritual world, therefore also, when he goes out of the natural world, he is immediately introduced among his like, with whom he had been in the world; thence it is, that every one after death seems to himself as if he were still living in the world, for then he comes into consociation with his like, as to the affections of his will, whom he then acknowledges, as kindred and relations acknowledge each other in the world; and this is what is said in the Word concerning those who die, that they were collected and gathered to their own. Hence now it may be evident that the regenerate man is in communion with the angels of heaven, and the unregenerate with the spirits of hell.

608. It is to be known, that there are three heavens, and those distinguished from each other according to the three degrees of love and wisdom, and that man, according to regeneration, is in communion with angels from those three heavens; and, because it is so, that the human mind is distinguished into three degrees or regions, according to the heavens. But concerning these three heavens, and the distinction of them according to the three degrees of love and wisdom, see in the book concerning HEAVEN and HELL, n. 29 and the following; and also in the little treatise concerning THE INTERCOURSE BETWEEN THE SOUL AND THE BODY, n. 16, 17. Here it is only to be illustrated by some similitude what those three degrees are, according to which those heavens are distinguished; they are like the head, body and feet in man; the highest heaven makes the head, the middle makes the body, and the last makes the feet, for the whole heaven is in the sight of the Lord as one man. That it is so, has been disclosed to me by ocular demonstration; for it has been given me to see one society of heaven, which consisted of a myriad, as together one man; why not the whole heaven in the sight of the Lord? Concerning this lively experience, see in the book concerning HEAVEN AND HELL, n. 59 and the following. Hence also it is manifest, how this, which is known in the Christian world, is to be understood, That the church makes the body of Christ, and that Christ is the life of that body. By that, this also may be illustrated, that the Lord is the all in all of heaven, for He is the life in that body. In like manner the Lord is the church with those who acknowledge Him for the God of heaven and earth, and believe in Him. That He

is the God of heaven and earth, He teaches in Matt. xxviii. 18; and that men should believe in Him, John iii. 15, 36; vi. 40; xi. 25, 26.

609. Those three degrees in which the heavens are, consequently in which the human mind is, may be, in some degree, illustrated by comparisons with material things in the world: those three degrees are in excellence like gold, silver and copper, with which metals also a comparison is made in Nebuchadnezzar's statue, Dan. ii. 31, and the following verses. Those three degrees also are distinguished from each other, in purity and goodness, like a ruby, a sapphire and an agate, and also like an olive-tree, a vine and a fig-tree, &c. Also gold, a ruby and an olive-tree, in the Word, signify celestial good, which is the good of the highest heaven; and silver, a sapphire and a vine signify spiritual good, which is the good of the middle heaven; and copper, an agate and a fig-tree, natural good, which is the good of the last heaven; that there are three degrees, the celestial, the spiritual and the natural, was said above.

610. To what has been said above, this shall be added; that the regeneration of man is not effected in a moment, but successively, from the beginning to the end of life in the world, and that after this, it is continued and perfected; and because man is reformed by combats and victories over the evils of his flesh, therefore the Son of man says to each of the seven churches, that He will give gifts to him that overcomes;—as, to the church of Ephesus; *To him that overcometh, I will give to eat of the tree of life*, Rev. ii. 7;—to the church of Smyrna; *He that overcometh shall not suffer harm in the second death*, ii. 11;—to the church in Pergamos; *To him that overcometh, I will give to eat of the hidden manna*, ii. 17;—to the church in Thyatira; *To him that overcometh, I will give power over the nations*, ii. 25;—to the church in Sardis; *He that overcometh shall be clothed in white garments*, iii. 5;—to the church in Philadelphia; *Him that overcometh, I will make a pillar in the temple of God*, iii. 12;—to the church of the Laodiceans; *To him that overcometh, I will give to sit with Me on my throne* iii. 21. Lastly, this shall be added: that as far as man is regenerated, or as far as regeneration is perfected in him, so far he does not attribute any thing of good and truth, that is, of charity and faith, to himself, but to the Lord; for the truths which he successively imbibes, manifestly teach that.

611. X. THAT AS FAR AS MAN IS REGENERATED SO FAR SINS ARE REMOVED, AND THAT THIS REMOVAL IS THE REMISSION OF SINS

That as far as man is regenerated, so far sins are removed, is, because regeneration is to restrain the flesh that it may not rule, and to subdue the old man with his lusts, that he may not rise up and destroy the intellectual, which being destroyed, man is no longer capable of being reformed; which reformation cannot be effected, unless the spirit of man, which is above the flesh, be instructed and perfected. Who that has yet a sound understanding, cannot conclude from those things, that such things cannot be effected in one moment, but successively, as man is conceived, carried in the womb, born and educated, according to what was shown above? For those things which are of the flesh, or of the old man, are inherent from nativity, and they build the first house of his mind, in which lusts dwell, like wild beasts in their dens, and they live first in the outer courts, and go down by turns as it were into the rooms of that house under ground, and afterwards ascend by stairs, and form to themselves chambers; which takes place successively as the infant grows, becomes a child, and afterwards a young man, and then begins to think from his own understanding and to act from his own will. Who does not see, that this house, thus far built in the mind, in which lusts, like *ochim*, *ghoim* and satyrs, dance hand in hand, cannot be destroyed in one moment, and a new house built up in its place? Must not the lusts, which hold each other by the hand and sport, first be removed, and new desires, which are those of good and truth, be introduced instead of the desires which are those of what is evil and false? That these things cannot be done in a moment, every wise man may see from this alone; that every evil is composed of innumerable lusts, and that it is like fruit, which, within the surface, is full of worms with white bodies and black heads; and that evils are numerous, and joined together like the offspring of a spider when first hatched; wherefore, unless one evil is drawn out after another, and this until their connection is broken, man cannot become new. These things are adduced in order that it may be known, that as far as any one is regenerated, so far sins are removed.

612. Man from nativity inclines to evils of every kind, and from inclination he lusts after them, and as far as he is in freedom, he also does them; for from nativity he desires to rule over others and to possess the goods of others, which two destroy all love towards the neighbor; and then he hates every one that opposes him, and from hatred breathes revenge, which inwardly cherishes murder. Thence also it is, that he makes light of adulteries, and depredations, which are clandestine thefts, and blasphemy, which also is false witness; and he who makes light of these and those, is in heart an atheist. Such is man from nativity; whence it is manifest, that from nativity he is a hell in miniature. Now, because man, as to the interiors of his mind, is born spiritual, differently from the beasts, consequently is born for heaven, and yet his natural or external man is, as was said, a hell in miniature, it follows that heaven cannot be implanted in hell, unless this be removed.

613. He who knows how heaven and hell are related to each other, and how the one is removed from the other, may know how man is regenerated. That this may be understood, it shall be made manifest in a summary, that all who are in heaven look to the Lord face to face, and all who are in hell turn the face away from the Lord; wherefore, when hell is looked into from heaven, they appear only as to the hinder part of the head and the back; yea, they also appear as if inverted, like antipodes, with their feet upwards and heads downwards, and this although they walk upon their feet and turn around their faces; for it is the opposite direction of the interiors of their mind which produces that sight. These wonderful things I relate from my own observation. Hence it was discovered to me, how regeneration is effected, and that it is effected as hell is removed and thus separated from heaven; for, as was said above, man, as to the first nature, which he derives from nativity, is a hell in miniature, and as to the other nature, which he derives from a second nativity, he is a heaven in miniature. Hence it follows that evils are removed and separated, as heaven and hell are in a great effigy; and that evils, as they are removed, turn themselves from the Lord, and successively invert themselves; and that this is done in that degree in which heaven is implanted, that is, as man is made new. To this it shall be added, for the sake of illustration, that every evil with man has conjunction with such in hell as are in the like evil; and, on the other hand, that every good with man has conjunction with such in heaven as are in the like good.

614. From what has been adduced it may be evident, that the remission of sins is not an extirpation of them, and a wiping of them away, but that it is a removal and thus a separation of them; and also that every evil which a man has actually appropriated to himself remains; and because the remission of sins is the removal and separation of them, it follows that man is withheld from evil and held in good, and that this is what is given to man by regeneration. Once I heard a certain one in the last heaven say, that he was free from sins, because they were wiped away; he added, by the blood of Christ; but because he was in heaven, and from ignorance in that error, he was let into his own sins, which, as they returned, he acknowledged, whence he received a new faith, which was, that every man, as well as every

angel, is of the Lord withheld from evils and held in goods. Hence it is manifest what the remission of sins is; that it is not instantaneous, but that it follows regeneration according to its progress. The removal of sins, which is called their remission, may be compared with the casting of filth out of the camp of the sons of Israel into the desert which was around it, for their camp represented heaven, and the desert hell. It may be compared also with the removal of the nations from the sons of Israel in the land of Canaan, and of the Jebusites from Jerusalem, which were not cast out, but separated. It may be compared with Dagon, the god of the Philistines, which, when the ark was introduced, first lay upon his face on the earth, and afterwards, with his head and the palms of his hands cut off, upon the threshold; thus not cast out, but removed. It may be compared with the demons sent by the Lord into the swine, which afterwards immersed themselves in the sea; by the *sea* here, and elsewhere in the Word, is signified hell. It may be compared also with the dragon's crew, which, being separated from heaven, first invaded the earth, and afterwards was cast down into hell. It may be compared also to a forest where are many sorts of wild beasts, which being cut down, the wild beasts flee into the thickets round about; and then the land in the midst, being cleared up, is cultivated into a field.

615. XI. That Regeneration cannot be effected without Free Agency in Spiritual Things.

Who except the stupid cannot see, that man, without free agency in spiritual things, cannot be regenerated? Can he without it go to the Lord, and acknowledge Him as the Redeemer and Savior, and as the God of heaven and earth, as He teaches, Matt. xxviii. 18? Who, without that free agency, can believe, that is, from faith look to and worship Him, and apply himself to receive the means and benefits of salvation from Him, and coöperate to receive them from him? Who, without free agency, can do any good to the neighbor, and exercise charity, and bring into his thought and will many other things which are of faith and charity, and bring them out and put them forth into act? Otherwise, what is regeneration, but a mere word, dropped from the mouth of the Lord, John iii., which either stops in the ear, or, falling into the mouth from the thought next to the speech, is made an articulate sound of only twelve letters, which sound cannot by any sense be elevated into any higher region of the mind, but falls into the air, where it is dissipated?

616. Say, if you can, whether there can be any blinder stupidity concerning regeneration, than there is with those who confirm themselves in the present faith, which is, that faith is infused into man when he is like a stock or a stone, and that then, when it is infused, it is followed by justification, which is the remission of sins, regeneration and many other gifts; and that the operation of man is to be entirely excluded, in order that it may not do any violence to the merit of Christ. And, that this dogma might be more firmly established, they have taken away from man all free agency in spiritual things, by inducing absolute impotence in them; and then as if God only operated on his part, and no power were given to man of coöperating on his, and thus of conjoining himself. What then is man, as to regeneration, but as one bound, as to his hands and feet, like those who are bound in vessels called galleys, who would be punished and condemned to death, as they would if they should free themselves from manacles and fetters, that is, if from free agency he should do good to the neighbor, and of himself believe in God, for the sake of salvation? What would a man be, who is confirmed in such things, and yet is in a pious desire for heaven, but like a phantom standing in vision to see whether that faith with its benefits has been infused into him; or, if not, whether it may be infused; consequently, whether God the Father has had mercy on him, or whether his Son has interceded, or whether the Holy Ghost, being elsewhere occupied,

does not operate; and at length, from entire ignorance concerning this, he would go away and comfort himself by this, that "Perhaps that grace may be in the morality of my life, in which I am and remain as before, and thus that in me may be holy, but in those who have not obtained that faith, profane; wherefore, that holiness may remain in my morality, I will take care hereafter that I do not operate of myself either faith or charity." Such a phantom, or, if you please, such a pillar of salt, every one becomes, who thinks about regeneration without free agency in spiritual things.

617. A man who believes regeneration to take place without any free agency in spiritual things, thus without coöperation, becomes as to all the truths of the church as cold as a stone; or, if warm, he is like a brand lighted in the fire, which burns from the combustibles in it, because he is warm from lusts. He is comparatively like a palace which sinks down into the earth even to its roof, and is overflowed with muddy waters, and after this the occupant dwells upon the bare roof, and there makes for himself a tent of marshy reeds, and at length the roof also sinks down, and he is drowned. He is also like a ship, in which are precious commodities of every kind taken from the Word as a treasury; which are either devoured by mice and moths, or thrown out by the sailors into the sea, and thus the merchants are defrauded of their goods. The learned, or those who are enriched from the mysteries of that faith, are like pedlers in shops who sell statues of idols, fruits and flowers made of wax, shells, vipers in phials, and other such things. Those who, from no spiritual power applied and given to man by the Lord, are not willing to look upwards, are actually like beasts which look with the head downwards, and only seek for pasture in the woods; and if they come into gardens, they are like worms which consume the leaves of trees; and if they see fruits with their eyes, and especially if they feel them with their hands, they fill them with worms; and at length they become like scaly serpents, whose fallacies sound and glitter like their scales.

618. XII. That Regeneration cannot be effected without Truths, by which Faith is formed, and with which Charity conjoins itself.

There are three things by which man is regenerated—the Lord, faith and charity; these three would lie concealed, like the most precious things buried in the earth, if divine truths from the Word did not disclose them; yea, they would lie concealed before those who deny coöperation, even if they should read the Word a hundred or a thousand times, although they stand forth there in clear light. As to what respects the Lord; who, that is confirmed in the present faith, sees with an open eye these things there; that He and the Father are one; that He is the God of heaven and earth; and that it is the will of the Father, that they should believe in the Son; besides many similar things concerning the Lord in both covenants? The reason is, because they are not in truths, and thence not in the light from which things of this kind can be seen; and if light were given, still falses would extinguish it, and then those things would be passed by, as things that are covered over with blots, or as subterranean ditches, which are trampled on and walked over. These things have been said, that it may be known, that, without truths, this primary thing of regeneration is not seen. As to what respects faith, that neither can exist without truths, for faith and truth make one thing; for the good of faith is as a soul, and truths make its body; wherefore, to say that one believes or has faith, without knowing any truths of it, is like drawing the soul out of the body, and speaking with it when thus invisible. Besides, all truths which make the body of faith, send forth light from themselves, and illustrate and set forth its face to be seen. The case is similar with charity; this sends forth from itself heat, with which the light of truth conjoins itself, as heat with light in the time of spring in the world.

from the conjunction of which the animals and vegetables of the earth return to their prolification. The case is similar with spiritual light and heat; these in like manner conjoin themselves in man, while he is in the truths of faith and at the same time in the goods of charity; for, as was said above, in the chapter concerning faith, from each of the truths of faith light flows forth, which illustrates, and from each of the goods of charity heat flows forth, which enkindles; and also, that spiritual light in its essence is intelligence, and that spiritual heat in its essence is love; and that the Lord alone conjoins those two in man, when He regenerates him. For the Lord said, *The words which I speak, are spirit and life*, John vi. 63. *Believe in the light, that ye may be sons of the light. I am come a light into the world*, xii. 36. The Lord is the sun in the spiritual world; thence is all spiritual light and heat; and that light illustrates, and that heat enkindles, and by the conjunction of both, He vivifies and regenerates man.

619. Hence it may be evident, that without truths there is no knowledge of the Lord, and also that without truths there is no faith, and thus no charity; consequently that without truths there is no theology, and where this is not, there is no church. Such is the company of people at this day, who call themselves Christians, and say that they are in the light of the gospel, when yet they are in thick darkness itself; for truths lie concealed under falses, like gold, silver and precious stones buried among the bones in the valley of Hinnom. That it is so, was clearly manifest to me from the spheres in the spiritual world, which flow forth from modern Christendom, and spread themselves around. One sphere is concerning the Lord; this exhales and pours itself forth from the southern quarter, where the learned of the clergy and the erudite of the laity are. This sphere, wherever it goes, enters the ideas, and with many it takes away faith concerning the divinity of the Lord's Human; with many it weakens it, and with many it makes it foolishness; the reason is, because it brings in at the same time the faith of three Gods, and thus it is confused. Another sphere which takes away faith, is as a black cloud in the time of winter, which brings on darkness, turns the rain into snow, strips the trees bare, freezes the waters, and takes all pasture away from the sheep; this sphere, conjoined to the former, insinuates as it were a lethargy concerning the one God, and concerning regeneration, and concerning the things which bring salvation. The third sphere is of the conjunction of faith and charity, which is so strong that it cannot be resisted, but at this day it is abominable, and infects like a pestilence whomsoever it breathes upon, and rends every bond between those two means of salvation established from the creation of the world, and renewed by the Lord. This sphere also invades men in the natural world, and extinguishes the nuptial torches at the marriage between truths and goods. I have felt this sphere; and at the time when I was thinking of the conjunction of faith and charity, it interposed itself between them, and violently endeavored to separate them. The angels complain much of these spheres, and pray to the Lord that they may be dissipated; but they have received answer that they cannot be dissipated, whilst the dragon is upon the earth, since they are from the spirits of the dragon; for it is said of the dragon, that he was cast forth into the earth, and then thus; *Therefore rejoice, ye heavens; and wo to those who inhabit the earth*, Rev. xii. Those three spheres are like atmospheres driven by a tempest arising from the breathing holes of the dragons, which, because they are spiritual, invade minds and force them. The spheres of spiritual truths there are as yet few, being only in the new heaven, and with those under heaven who are separated from the spirits of the dragon; which is the cause that those truths are at this day as invisible to men in the world, as ships in the eastern ocean are to pilots and captains of vessels who are sailing in the western ocean.

620. That regeneration cannot be

effected without truths by which faith is formed, may be illustrated by these comparisons. It cannot be effected any more than the human mind can exist without understanding, for the understanding is formed by truths, and therefore it teaches what is to be believed, and what is to be done, and what regeneration is, and how it is effected. Regeneration without truths can no more be effected than the vivification of animals and the vegetation of trees without light from the sun; for unless the sun gave light at the same time that it gives heat, the sun would become as it is described in the Revelation, like sackcloth of hair, vi. 12; and darkened, Joel ii. 10; and thus mere darkness would be on the earth, iii. 15. Just so it would be with man without truths which send forth light from themselves; for the sun, from which the light of truth flows, is the Lord in the spiritual world; unless spiritual light flowed thence into human minds, the church would be in mere darkness, or in the shade, from a perpetual eclipse. Regeneration, which is effected by faith and charity, without truths which teach and lead, would be like sailing on a great ocean without a rudder or without a mariner's compass and charts; and it would be like riding on horse-back in a thick forest in the time of night. The internal sight of the mind with those who are not in truths, but in falses, and believe these to be truths, may be compared with the sight of those with whom the optic nerves are obstructed, and the eye still appears whole and seeing, although it sees nothing; which blindness is called by physicians *amaurosis* and *gutta serena*. For with them the rational or intellectual is obstructed above, and opened only below; whence the rational light becomes like the light of the eye, and thence all judgments are only imaginary, and formed from mere fallacies; and then men would be like astrologers standing in the market-places with long telescopes and uttering vain prophecies. Such would all become who study theology, unless genuine truths from the Word were opened by the Lord.

---

621. To the above will be added these RELATIONS. FIRST. I saw a company of spirits all on their knees praying to God, that He would send to them angels with whom they might speak mouth to mouth, and to whom they might open the thoughts of their hearts. And when they rose up, three angels in fine linen were seen standing in their sight; they said, "The Lord Jesus Christ has heard your prayers, and therefore has sent us to you; open to us the thoughts of your hearts." And they answered, "The priests have told us, that in theological subjects, the understanding does not avail, but faith, and that intellectual faith is not profitable in those things, because this savors of man, and is derived from him, and not from God. We are Englishmen, and we have heard a great many things from our sacred ministry which we believed; but when we spoke with some who also called themselves Reformed, and others who called themselves Roman Catholics, and moreover with sectaries, they all appeared learned, and yet in many things they did not agree one with another, and still they all said, BELIEVE US; and some, WE ARE MINISTERS OF GOD, AND WE KNOW. But because we knew that divine truths, which are called truths of faith, and are of the church, are not derived by any one from his native soil, nor by inheritance, but out of heaven from God; and because they show the way to heaven, and enter life together with the good of charity, and thus lead to eternal life, we became anxious, and on our knees prayed to God." Then answered the angels, "Read the Word and believe in the Lord, and you will see truths which will be of your faith and life. All in the Christian world derive their doctrinals from the Word, as from the only fountain." But two of the company said, "We have read it, but did not understand it." And the angels replied, "You did not go to

the Lord, who is the Word, and also you had previously confirmed yourselves in falses." And the angels said further, "What is faith without light? And what is thinking without understanding? This is not human. Crows and magpies also can learn to speak without understanding. We can assure you that every man, whose soul desires it, can see the truths of the Word in light. There is no animal that does not know the food of its life, when it sees it; and man is a rational and spiritual animal, and he sees the food of his life, not indeed of his body but of his soul, which is the truth of faith, if he hungers for it and asks it of the Lord. Whatever also is not received by the understanding, this is not fixed in the memory, as to the thing, but only as to the words; wherefore, when we have looked down from heaven into the world, we have not seen any thing, but only have heard sounds most of them unharmonious. But we will mention some things which the learned of the clergy have removed from the understanding, not knowing that there are two ways to the understanding, one from the world, and the other from heaven; and that the Lord withdraws the understanding from the world, when He illustrates it. But if the understanding is closed from religion, the way to it from heaven is closed, and then man sees no more in the Word than if he were blind; we have seen a good many such fall into pits, from which they did not rise. Let examples be for illustration. Can you not understand what charity is, and what faith is? That charity is to act well with the neighbor, and that faith is to think aright concerning God and concerning the essentials of the church; and thence that he who acts well and thinks aright, that is, he who lives well and believes aright, is saved?" To this they said that they understood it. Moreover the angels said, "That actual repentance from sins must be performed in order that man may be saved; and that unless man performs actual repentance he remains in the sins in which he was born; and that to perform actual repentance, is, not to will evils because they are contrary to God; and to examine one's self once or twice in a year, to see his evils, to confess them before the Lord, to implore help, to desist from them, and to enter a new life; and as far as he does this, and believes in the Lord, so far sins are remitted." Then some of the company said, "We understand this, and thus also what the remission of sins is." And then they requested the angels that they would inform them further; and indeed now concerning God, concerning the Immortality of the Soul, concerning Regeneration, and concerning Baptism. To this the angels replied, "We shall not say any thing but what you understand, otherwise our discourse falls like rain upon the sand, or upon the reeds there, which, although they be watered from heaven, still wither and perish." And they said concerning GOD, "All who come into heaven obtain a place there, and thence eternal joy, according to the idea of God, because this idea reigns universally in all things of worship. An idea concerning God as a spirit, when spirit is believed to be like ether or wind, is an empty idea; but an idea concerning God as man is a just idea; for God is Divine Love and Divine Wisdom with all their qualities, and the subject of these is man, and not ether or wind. The idea of God in heaven is the idea of the Lord the Savior. He is the God of heaven and earth, as He taught. Let your idea of God be like ours, and we shall be consociated." When they said these words their faces shone. Concerning the IMMORTALITY OF THE SOUL, they said, "Man lives to eternity, because he can be conjoined to God by love and faith; every one has this ability; that this ability makes the immortality of the soul, you can understand, if you think concerning it a little more deeply." Concerning REGENERATION; "Who does not see that every man has liberty to think about God, or not to think about Him, provided he has been instructed that there is a God? Thus every man has liberty in spiritual things equally as in civil and natural things. The Lord gives this continually to all; wherefore man becomes guilty if he does not think. Man is man from having this ability, but a beast is a beast from not having it; wherefore man can, as of himself, reform and regenerate himself, provided he in heart acknowledge that it is from the Lord. Every one who performs actual repentance, and believes in the Lord, is reformed and regenerated; man is to do both as of himself, but the AS OF HIMSELF, is from the Lord. It is true that man of himself cannot contribute any thing at all to it, but yet you were not created statues, but you were created men, that you may do it from the Lord as from yourselves. This is the only reciprocal of love and faith, which the Lord absolutely wills to be done to Him by man. In a word, do of yourselves, and believe that it is from the Lord; thus do as of yourselves." But then they asked, "Whether to do as of himself, is inherent in man from creation." The angel replied, "It is not inherent, because to act of himself is of God alone; but it is given continually, that is, adjoined continually; and then as far as man does good and believes truth, as of himself, he is an angel of heaven; but as far as he does evil, and thence believes what is false, which also is as of himself, so far he is a spirit of hell. You wonder that this also is as of himself, but still you see it, when you pray that you may be preserved from the devil, lest he should seduce you, lest he should enter into you, as into Judas, should fill you with all iniquity, and destroy both soul and body. But every one becomes guilty, who believes that he does of himself, whether it be good or whether it be evil; but he does not become guilty, who believes that he does as of himself; for if he believes that good is from himself, he claims to himself that which belongs to God; and if he believes that evil is from himself, he attributes to himself that which belongs to the devil." Concerning BAPTISM they said, "That it is a spiritual washing, which is reformation and regeneration; and that an infant is reformed and regenerated, when, having become an adult, he does those things which the sponsors promised for him, which are two, repentance and faith in God. For, *first*, they promise that he shall renounce the devil, and all his works; *secondly*, that he shall believe in God. All infants in heaven are initiated into those two, but to them the devil is hell, and God is the Lord. Moreover, baptism is a sign before the angels that the man is of the church." Having heard this, some of the company said, "We understand this." But then a voice was heard at the side, crying, "We do not understand;" and another voice, "We do not wish to understand." And inquiry was made from whom those voices came· and it was discovered that they came from those who had confirmed in themselves the falses of faith, and who wished to be believed as oracles, and thus to be adored. The angels said, "Do not wonder; there are a great many such at this day; they appear to us from heaven like graven images made with such art, that they can move their lips, and sound like organs, and they do not know whether the breath from which they sound be from hell or from heaven, because they do not know whether it be false or true. They reason and reason, and also confirm and confirm, and they do not see any thing, whether it be so. But you must know that human ingenuity can confirm whatever it will, so that it may appear as if it were so; wherefore heretics can do this, the wicked can do it, yea, atheists can confirm their doctrine that there is no God, but nature alone." After this that company of Englishmen, inflamed with the desire of becoming wise, said to the angels, "They say things so various concerning the HOLY SUPPER, tell us what is the truth." The angels replied, "The truth is, that the man who looks to the Lord, and performs actual repentance, by that most holy medium is conjoined to the Lord, and introduced into heaven." But some of the company said, "This is a mystery." And the angels replied

"It is a mystery, but still such that it may be understood. The bread and wine do not effect this, nor is there any thing holy from them; but material bread and spiritual bread correspond to each other, and material wine and spiritual wine; and spiritual bread is the holy of love, and spiritual wine is the holy of faith, both from the Lord, and both the Lord. Hence the conjunction of the Lord with man, and of man with the Lord, not with bread and wine, but with the love and faith of the man who has performed actual repentance; and conjunction with the Lord is also an introduction into heaven." And after the angels had taught them something concerning correspondence, some of the company said, "Now, for the first time, we can also understand this." And when they said this, lo, a flame with light descending from heaven consociated them with the angels, and they loved each other.

622. Second Relation. All who have been prepared for heaven, which is done in the world of spirits, which is in the middle between heaven and hell, after the time has elapsed, long and sigh for heaven; and presently their eyes are opened, and they see a way which leads to some society in heaven; this way they enter and ascend; and in the ascent there is a gate and a keeper there; he opens the gate, and thus they enter. Then an examiner meets them, who says to them, from the governor, that they may enter farther and inquire whether there are any houses any where which they recognize as theirs, for there is a new house for every novitiate angel; and if they find one, they tell of it and stay there; but if they do not find any, they return and say that they did not see any. And then examination is made by some wise one, whether the light which is in them agrees with the light which is in the society, and especially whether the heat does; for the light of heaven in its essence is divine truth, and the heat of heaven in its essence is divine good, both proceeding from the Lord as the sun there. If other light and other heat than the light and heat of that society are in them, that is, if other good and truth, they are not received; wherefore they depart thence, and go in the ways that are open from one society to another in heaven, and this until they find a society altogether agreeable to their affections, and there their habitation is made for ever; for there they are among their own, as among relations and friends, whom, because they are in similar affection, they love from the heart; and there they are in the full enjoyment of their life, and in the highest delight of their heart from peace of soul; for there is in the heat and light of heaven an ineffable delight, which is communicated. Thus it is with those who become angels. But those who are in evils and falses, are by permission allowed to ascend into heaven; but when they enter, they begin to draw their breath, and to respire with difficulty; and presently their sight is obscured, and their understanding is darkened, and their thought ceases, and death seems to stare them in the face, and thus they stand like stocks; and then the heart begins to beat, the breast to be straitened, and the mind to be seized with anguish, and to be tortured more and more, and in that state they twist themselves about like snakes brought near the fire; wherefore they roll themselves away, and cast themselves down over a precipice, which then appears, nor do they rest till they are in hell with their like, where they can breathe, and where their heart vibrates freely. Afterwards they hate heaven, and reject the Word, and in heart blaspheme the Lord, believing that their pains and torments in heaven were from Him. From these few things it may be seen, what is the condition of those who despise the truths which are of faith, which yet make the light in which the angels of heaven are, and who despise the goods which are of love and charity, which yet make the heat of life, in which the angels of heaven are. Hence also it may be seen how much they err who believe that every one can enjoy the blessedness of heaven, provided he be admitted

into heaven; for there is a belief at this day, that to be received into heaven is from mercy alone, and that reception into heaven, is like one's coming into a house in the world, where there is a wedding, and then, at the same time, into the joy and gladness there. But they should know, that, in the spiritual world, there is a communication of the affections of love and of the thoughts thence, since man is then a spirit, and the life of the spirit is the affection of love and the thought thence; and that homogeneous affection conjoins, and heterogeneous affection separates, and that what is heterogeneous tortures a devil in heaven, and an angel in hell; therefore they are separated just according to the diversities, varieties and differences of the affections which are of love.

623. Third Relation. Once it was given me to see three hundred of the clergy and laity together, all learned and erudite, because they knew how to confirm faith alone even to justification, and some still farther; and because there was with them a belief that there is admission to heaven from favor only, permission was given them to ascend into one society of heaven, which, however, was not among the higher ones; and when they ascended, they seemed at a distance like calves. And when they entered heaven, they were received by the angels civilly; but when they began to converse with them, they were seized with tremor, afterwards with horror, and at last with torture as it were of death; and then they cast themselves down headlong, and in their descent they seemed like dead horses. That they appeared like calves in their ascent, was because the natural affection of seeing and knowing, leaping, often appears from correspondence like a calf; and that, in their descent, they appeared like dead horses, was because the understanding of truth appears from correspondence like a horse, and no understanding of the truth which is of the church, like a dead horse.

There were boys below, who saw them descending, and in their descent appearing like dead horses; and then they turned away their faces, and said to their master, who was with them, "What is this monstrous thing? We saw men, and now, instead of them dead horses; and because we could not look at them, we turned away our faces. Master, let us not stay in this place, but let us go away;" and they went away. And then the master instructed them in the way, what a dead horse signifies, saying, "A horse signifies the understanding of truth from the Word. All the horses that you have seen signified that; for when any one goes meditating from the Word, then his meditation at a distance appears like a horse, generous and lively, as he meditates spiritually; on the contrary, mean and dead, as he meditates materially." Then the boys asked, "What is it to meditate spiritually and materially from the Word?" And the master replied, "I will illustrate this by examples. Does not every one, while he is devoutly reading the Word, think inwardly in himself about God, about the neighbor, and about heaven? Every one who thinks about God only from person, and not from essence, thinks materially; and also he who thinks about the neighbor only from the external form, and not from quality, thinks materially; and he who thinks about heaven only from place, and not from love and wisdom, from which heaven is heaven, he also thinks materially." But the boys said, "We have thought about God from person, about the neighbor from form, that he is a man, and about heaven from place, that it is above us; did we, therefore, when we read the Word, appear to any one like dead horses?" The master said, "No; you are yet boys, and you cannot do otherwise. But I have perceived in you an affection of knowing and understanding; and because this is spiritual, you have also thought spiritually, for some spiritual thought is concealed within your material, of which you are yet ignorant. But I will return to the former things which I said; that he who thinks materially while he reads the Word, or meditates from the Word appears at a distance like a dead horse but he who thinks spiritually appears like a live horse; and that he thinks materially concerning God, who thinks only from person, and not from essence. For there are many attributes of the Divine Essence, as omnipotence, omniscience, omnipresence, eternity, love, wisdom, mercy and grace, and others; and there are attributes proceeding from the Divine Essence, which are creation and preservation, redemption and salvation, illustration and instruction. Every one who thinks concerning God from person, makes three Gods, saying, that one God is the Creator and Preserver, and another the Redeemer and Savior, and a third, the Illustrator and Instructer; but every one who thinks concerning God from essence, makes one God, saying, God created us, and the same has redeemed and saves, and also illustrates and instructs us. Hence the reason why those who think concerning the trinity of God from person, and thus materially, cannot, from the ideas of their thought, which is material, do otherwise than make three of one God; but still, contrary to their thought, they are obliged to say that there is a union of those three by essence, because, as it were through a latticed window, they also have thought concerning God from essence. Wherefore, my scholars, think from essence, and from this concerning person; for to think from person concerning essence, is to think materially also concerning essence; but to think from essence concerning person, is to think spiritually also concerning person. The ancient Gentiles, because they thought materially concerning God, and thus also concerning the attributes of God, not only made three Gods, but many more, even to a hundred; for of each attribute they made a God. You should know that the material does not enter into the spiritual, but the spiritual into the material. The case is similar with thinking concerning the neighbor from his external form, and not from his quality; as also with thinking concerning heaven from place, and not from love and wisdom, from which heaven is. The case is similar with all and every thing that is in the Word; wherefore he who cherishes a material idea concerning God, and also concerning the neighbor, and concerning heaven, cannot understand any thing there; the Word is to him a dead letter, and he himself appears at a distance, while he is reading it, or meditating from it, like a dead horse. Those whom you saw descending from heaven, appearing before your eyes like dead horses, were those, who had shut up the rational sight, as to theological things, or the spiritual things of the church with themselves and with others, by the peculiar dogma, 'that the understanding is to be kept under obedience to their faith;' not thinking that the understanding, shut up by religion, is as blind as a mole, and in it has mere thick darkness, and such thick darkness as rejects from itself all spiritual light, stops the influx of it from the Lord and from heaven, and puts before it an obstruction in the corporeal sensual, far below the rational in the things of faith; that is, it puts it near the nose, and fixes it in its cartilage, on account of which it cannot afterwards even smell the odor of spiritual things; whence some have become such, that, as soon as they perceive the odor of spiritual things, they fall into a swoon; by odor I mean perception. These are they who make God three; they say indeed from essence that God is one, but still, when they pray according to their faith, which is, that God the Father has mercy for the sake of the Son, and sends the Holy Ghost, they manifestly make three Gods. They cannot do otherwise; for they pray to one, that he would have mercy for the sake of another, and send a third." And then their master taught them concerning the Lord, that He is the one God, in whom is a Divine Trinity.

624. Fourth Relation. In the middle of the night, being awaked from sleep, I saw, at some height towards the east, an angel holding in his right hand a paper, which from the sun appeared in a bright whiteness, in the middle of which there was a writing from golden

letters; and I saw written, THE MARRIAGE OF THE GOOD AND THE TRUE. From the writing there issued a bright radiance, which went off into a broad circle around the paper; that circle or border appeared then as the light of the morning appears in the time of spring. After this I saw the angel, with the paper in his hand, descending, and as he descended, the paper appeared less and less lucid, and the writing, which was THE MARRIAGE OF THE GOOD AND THE TRUE, converted from a golden color into a silver, and then into a copper, afterwards into an iron, and finally into a ferruginous and rusty color; and at last the angel was seen to enter into a dark cloud, and through the cloud upon the earth; and there that paper, although it was still held in the angel's hand, was not seen. This was in the world of spirits, into which all men after death first come together. And then the angel spoke to me, saying, "Ask those who come hither whether they see me, or any thing in my hand." There came a multitude, a company from the east, a company from the south, a company from the west, a company from the north; and I asked those who came from the east and south, who were such as in the world were devoted to learning, whether they saw any one with me, or any thing in his hand. They all said that they saw nothing at all. Then I asked those who came from the west and the north, who were such as had believed in the words of the learned in the world. These said that they neither saw any thing. But yet the last of these, who in the world had been in simple faith from charity, or in some truth from good, after the former had gone away, said that they saw a man with a paper, a man in a handsome dress, and a paper upon which letters were written; and when they viewed it more closely, they said that they read, THE MARRIAGE OF THE GOOD AND THE TRUE. And they spoke to the angel, requesting that he would tell what this meant. And he said, 'That all things that are in the whole heaven, and all that are in the whole world, are from creation nothing but a marriage of the good and the true; since all and every thing, as wel those which live and breathe, as those which do not live and breathe, were created from the marriage of the good and the true, and into it; there is not any thing created into truth alone, nor any thing into good alone; this or that alone is not any thing; but by marriage they exist and become something, such as is the marriage. In the Lord God the Creator, there is Divine Good and Divine Truth in their substance itself; the *esse* of substance itself is the Divine Good, and the *existere* of substance itself is the Divine Truth; and also they are in their union itself, for in Him they infinitely make one. Since those two in God himself, the Creator, are one, therefore also they are one in all and every thing created by Him; by this also the Creator is conjoined, in an eternal covenant, like that of marriage, with all the things created by Him. Further, the angel said, that the Sacred Scripture, which was dictated by the Lord, is, in general and in particular, a marriage of the good and the true (see above, n. 248 to 253); and because the church, which is formed by truths of doctrine, and religion, which is formed by goods of life according to truths of doctrine, with Christians are solely from the Sacred Scripture, it may be evident that the church also, in general and in particular, is a marriage of the good and the true." The same that was said above concerning the marriage of the good and the true, was said also concerning the MARRIAGE OF CHARITY AND FAITH, since good is of charity, and truth is of faith. After these things were said, the angel raised himself from the earth, and, passing through the cloud, ascended into heaven; and then the paper, according to the degrees of ascent, shone as before; and behold, then the circle, which before appeared like the light of the morning, descended and dispelled the cloud which brought darkness on the earth, and a bright sun-shine ensued

625 Fifth Relation. Once, when I was meditating on the second coming of the Lord, suddenly there appeared a beam of light, powerfully striking upon my eyes; wherefore I looked up, and lo, the whole heaven above me appeared luminous, and from the east to the west there was heard in a long series a Glorification; and an angel stood by and said, "That glorification is a glorification of the Lord, on account of his coming, and it is made by the angels of the eastern and western heaven." From the southern and northern heaven, nothing was heard but a soft murmur. And because the angel heard all, he said to me, first, that those glorifications and celebrations of the Lord were made from the Word. And presently he said, "Now they are glorifying and celebrating the Lord, particularly by these words, which are in the prophet Daniel: *Thou sawest iron mixed with miry clay, but they shall not cohere. And in those days will the God of heaven set up a kingdom, which shall never be destroyed; it shall break up and consume all those kingdoms, but it shall stand for ever*, ii. 43, 44." After this I heard, as it were, the voice of singing; and farther in the east I saw a coruscation of light brighter than the former; and I asked the angel, "What are they glorifying there?" He said, "By these words in Daniel: *I was seeing in the visions of the night, and behold the Son of Man was coming with the clouds of heaven; and to Him was given dominion, and a kingdom, and all people and nations shall worship Him. His dominion is the dominion of an age which shall not pass away, and his kingdom that which shall not be destroyed*, vii. 13, 14. Moreover, they are celebrating the Lord from these words in the Revelation: *To Jesus Christ be glory and strength. Behold, He cometh with clouds. He is the Alpha and the Omega, the Beginning and the End, the First and the Last; who is, who was, and who is to come, the Almighty. I John heard this from* the Son of Man, *out of the midst of the seven candlesticks*, Rev. i. 5, 6, 7, 10, 11, 12, 13 xxii. 13, also from Matt. xxiv. 30, 31.' I looked again into the eastern heaven, and a light shone on the right side, and it entered into the southern expanse, and I heard a sweet sound; and I asked the angel, "What of the Lord are they glorifying there?" He said, "By these words in the Revelation: *I saw a new heaven and a new earth; and I saw the holy city, New Jerusalem, coming down from God out of heaven, prepared as a Bride for her Husband. And I heard a great voice out of heaven, saying, Behold the tabernacle of God with Men, and He will dwell with them. And the angel spoke with me and said, Come, I will show thee* the Bride, the Lamb's Wife. *And he carried me away in the spirit on to a great mountain, and showed me the holy city Jerusalem*, Rev. xxi. 1, 2, 3, 9, 10. Also by these words: *I Jesus am the bright and morning Star; and the Spirit and the* Bride *say*, Come. *And He said*, I come quickly. *Amen; even so*, come Lord Jesus, xxii. 16, 17, 20." After these and many more, there was heard a general glorification from the east to the west of heaven, and also from the south to the north: and I asked the angel, "What now?" And he said, "They are these words from the prophets: *All flesh shall know that* I Jehovah am thy Savior and thy Redeemer, Isaiah xlix. 26. *Thus said Jehovah, the King of Israel*, and his Redeemer, Jehovah of hosts, I am the First and the Last, and beside Me there is no God, xliv. 6. *It shall be said in that day*, Lo, this is our God, *whom we have expected to deliver us;* This is Jehovah, whom we have expected, xxv. 9. *The voice of one crying in the desert, Prepare ye a way for Jehovah.* Behold the Lord Jehovih cometh in the Mighty One. *He will feed his flock like a* Shepherd, xl. 3, 5, 10, 11. *A Child is born to us, a Son is given to us, whose name is Wonderful, Counsellor, God, Hero*, the Father of eternity, the Prince of peace, ix 6. *Behold the days will come, and I*

shall raise unto David a righteous Branch, who shall reign a King; and this is his name, JEHOVAH OUR RIGHTEOUSNESS, Jer. xxiii. 5, 6; xxxiii. 15, 16. *Jehovah of Hosts is his name,* AND THY REDEEMER, THE HOLY ONE OF ISRAEL, THE GOD OF THE WHOLE EARTH, SHALL HE BE CALLED, Isaiah, liv. 5. IN THAT DAY JEHOVAH SHALL BE FOR A KING OVER THE WHOLE EARTH; IN THAT DAY THERE SHALL BE ONE JEHOVAH, AND HIS NAME ONE, Zech. xiv. 9." Having heard and understood these things, my heart exulted, and I went home with joy, and there I returned from the state of the spirit into the state of the body, in which I wrote down these things which were seen and heard.

CHAPTER XI.

CONCERNING IMPUTATION.

626. I THAT THE FAITH OF THE PRESENT CHURCH, WHICH ALONE IS SAID TO JUSTIFY, AND IMPUTATION, MAKE ONE.

That the faith of the present church, which alone is said to justify, is imputation, or that faith and imputation, in the present church, make one, is because one is of the other, or one enters into the other, mutually and reciprocally, and causes it to be; for if faith is spoken of, and imputation is not added, faith is merely a sound; and if imputation is spoken of, and faith is not added, it is also merely a sound; but if those two are spoken of conjointly, something articulate is produced, but as yet without a meaning. Wherefore, that the understanding may perceive something, a third must necessarily be added, which is, the merit of Christ; thence a sentence is made, which a man can speak with some reason; for the faith of the present church is, that God the Father imputes the righteousness of his Son, and sends the Holy Ghost to operate the effects of it.

627. These three, therefore—faith, imputation, and the merit of Christ—in the present church, are one, and may be called a triune; for if one of those three were taken away, the present theology would become not any thing, for it depends on those three perceived as one, just as a long chain depends on a fixed hook; so that if either faith, or imputation, or the merit of Christ, were taken away, all that is said concerning justification, concerning the remission of sins, concerning vivification, renovation, regeneration, sanctification, and concerning the gospel, concerning free agency, concerning charity and good works, yea, concerning eternal life, would become like desolate cities, or like the rubbish of a temple; and faith itself, which stands in front, would not be any thing, and thus the whole church would be a desert and a desolation. Hence it is manifest on what pillar the house of God at this day is founded; and if this were pulled away, the house would fall, like that in which the lords of the Philistines, together with three thousand of the people, were sporting, who then died and were slain, when Samson pulled away the two pillars of the house; Judges xvi. 20. This is said, because it was shown in what precedes, and is to be shown in the appendix, that that faith is not Christian, because it differs from the Word, and that the imputation of that faith is vain, because the merit of Christ is not imputable.

628. II. THAT THE IMPUTATION WHICH IS OF THE PRESENT FAITH, IS TWO-FOLD, ONE PART OF THE MERIT OF CHRIST, AND THE OTHER OF SALVATION THENCE. It is taught in the whole Christian church, that justification, and thence salvation, are effected by God the Father by means of the imputation of the merit of Christ his Son; and that imputation is made from grace, WHEN AND WHERE HE WILLS, thus arbitrarily; and that those to whom the merit of Christ is imputed, are adopted into the number of the sons of God: and because the leaders of the church have not moved on a step beyond that imputation, or elevated their minds above it, from having decreed that the election of God is merely arbitrary, they have fallen into enormous and fanatical errors, and at length into the detestable one concerning predestination, and also into this abominable one, that God

does not attend to the deeds of a man's life, but only to the faith inscribed on the interiors of his mind; wherefore, unless the error concerning imputation should be abolished, atheism would invade the whole of Christendom, and then the king of the abyss would reign over them, whose *name in Hebrew is Abaddon, but in Greek he hath the name Apollyon*, Rev. ix. 11. By *Abaddon* and *Apollyon* is signified a destroyer of the church by falses; and by the *abyss* is signified where those falses are; see the APOCALYPSE REVEALED, n. 421, 440, 442. Whence it is manifest, that that false principle, and the falses thence following in an extended series, are the things over which that destroyer reigns; for, as was said above, the whole theological system at this day depends on that imputation, as a long chain on a fixed hook, and as man with all his members on the head: and because that imputation every where reigns, it is as Isaiah says; *The Lord will cut off from Israel head and tail; he that is honored is the head, and the teacher of falsehood the tail*, ix. 14, 15.

629. It is said, that the imputation taught by the present faith, is twofold, but not so twofold as God and mercy towards all, but as God and mercy towards some; or not as a parent and his love towards all his offspring, but as a parent and his love towards one or another of his offspring; or not as the divine law and its command to all, but as the divine law and its command to a few. Wherefore one doubleness is extended and undivided, and the other is restricted and divided, and this is doubleness, but that is unity; for it is taught that the imputation of the merit of Christ is from an arbitrary election, and that to these there is imputation of salvation, thus that some are adopted and the rest rejected; which would be as if God should elevate some into Abraham's bosom, and deliver some to the devil as food, when yet, the truth is, the Lord rejects and delivers up no one, but man himself.

630. It is added, that the imputation at this day takes away from man all power from any free agency in spiritual things, and does not leave him even so much that he can shake off fire from his clothes, keep his body from harm, or extinguish his house, when on fire, by water, and rescue his family; when yet the Word, from beginning to end, teaches that every one should shun evils, because they are of the devil and from the devil, and do goods, because they are of God and from God, and that he is to do them from himself, the Lord operating. But the imputation at this day proscribes the power for so doing, as destructive to faith and thence to salvation, for this reason, lest something of man should enter the imputation, and thus the merit of Christ; from which being established, this satanical tenet has flowed forth, that man is absolutely destitute of power in spiritual things, which is like saying, "Walk on," although you have no feet, not even one; "Wash yourself," and yet both your hands are cut off; or, "Do good, but sleep;" or, "Feed yourself," but without a tongue. It is also like having a will given which is not a will. Cannot one say, "I cannot, any more than the statue of Lot's wife; nor any more than Dagon, the god of the Philistines, when the ark of God was introduced into his temple; I am afraid that I should fare as he did when his head was broken off, and the palms of his hands thrown upon the threshold, 1 Sam. v. 4; nor more than Beelzebub, the god of Ekron, who, from the signification of his name, can only drive away flies." That such impotence in spiritual things is believed at this day, may be seen from what was collected above concerning FREE AGENCY, n. 464.

631. As to what concerns the first part of that twofold imputation concerning the salvation of man, which is, the imputation of the merit of Christ arbitrarily, and thence the imputation of salvation, the doctors differ: some teach that that imputation is absolute from free power, and is made to those whose external or internal form is well pleasing; or that the imputation is made from foreknowledge to those in

whom grace is infused and that faith can be applied; but still those two opinions aim at one mark, and are like the two eyes, which have for their object one stone, or like the two ears, which have for their object one song. At first sight it appears as if they went away from each other, but still in the end they unite and play together: for since on both sides entire impotency in spiritual things is taught, and every thing of man is excluded from faith, it follows that the grace receptive of faith, infused arbitrarily or of foreknowledge, is a similar election: for if that grace, which is called preventing grace, were universal, man's application, from some power of his own, must be added, which yet is rejected as a leprosy. Thence it is, that no one knows whether that faith has been given to him of grace, any more than a stock or a stone, such as he was when it was infused; for there is no sign testifying it, when charity, piety, the desire of a new life, and the free faculty of doing good as well as evil, are denied to man: the signs which are mentioned as testifying that faith in man, are all ludicrous, and not different from the auguries of the ancients from the flying of birds, or the prognostications of astrologers from the stars, or of players from dice. Things of this kind, and those still more ludicrous, follow from the imputed righteousness of the Lord, which, together with the faith which is called that righteousness, is infused into a man who is elected.

632. III. That the Faith which is imputative of the Merit and Righteousness of Christ the Redeemer, first arose from the Decrees of the Nicene Synod concerning three Divine Persons from Eternity, which Faith, from that Time to the present, has been received by the whole Christian World.

As it respects the Nicene synod itself, the emperor Constantine the Great, by the advice of Alexander, bishop of Alexandria, held it in his palace at Nice, a city of Bithynia; where all the bishops in Asia, Africa and Europe were called together, that they might from the Sacred Scriptures refute and condemn the heresy of Arius, a presbyter of Alexandria, who denied the divinity of Jesus Christ. This was done in the year of Christ 325. That those called together concluded that there were from eternity three divine persons, the Father, the Son, and the Holy Ghost, may be very evident from the two creeds, called the Nicene and Athanasian. In the Nicene it is read, *I believe in one God, the Father Almighty, Maker of heaven and earth; and in one Lord, Jesus Christ, the Son of God, the Only-begotten of the Father, born before all ages, God of God, of the same substance with the Father, who came down from heaven, and became incarnate by the Holy Ghost from the virgin Mary; and in the Holy Ghost, the Lord and Giver of life, who proceeds from the Father and the Son, who, together with the Father and the Son, is worshipped and glorified.* In the Athanasian Creed are these words: *The Catholic faith is this, That we worship one God in trinity, and the trinity in unity, neither confounding the persons, nor dividing the substance But whereas we are compelled by the Christian verity to confess each person singly to be God and Lord, so we are forbidden by the Catholic religion to say three Gods or three Lords:* that is, it is lawful to confess three Gods and three Lords, but not to say it; and this is not lawful because religion forbids, but that is because the truth dictates it. This Athanasian Creed was written, soon after the council of Nice was held, by one or more of those who had been present at the council, and also it was received as ecumenical or Catholic. Thence it is manifest, that it was then decreed, that three divine persons from eternity are to be acknowledged; and, although each person singly by himself be God, that still they are not to be called three Gods and Lords, but one.

633. That the faith of three divine persons has been received from that time, and confirmed and preached by all bishops, prelates, rulers of the church,

and presbyters, even to the present time, is known in the Christian world: and because there has emanated thence a mental persuasion of three Gods, no other faith could be devised, than that which might be applied to those three in their order; which is, that God the Father is to be approached and implored to impute the righteousness of his Son, or to show mercy on account of the Son's passion of the cross, and to send the Holy Ghost to work the mediate and ultimate effects of salvation. This faith is a fetus born of those two creeds: but when the swaddling clothes are taken off, there comes to view not one, but three; at first joined together, as it were in an embrace, but presently separated; for they decree, that essence joins them together, but the properties, which are creation, redemption and operation, or imputation, imputed righteousness, and effectual application, separate them; which is the cause, that although they have made up one God out of three, yet still out of three persons they have not made one, lest the idea of three Gods should be obliterated: for while each person singly is believed to be God, as it is said in the creed, if then consequently the three persons should be made one, the whole house, founded, as it were, upon three pillars, would fall down in a heap. The reason why that synod introduced three divine persons from eternity, was because they did not rightly search the Word, and thence they did not find any other asylum against the Arians; but the reason why they brought together into one God those three persons, each of whom is a God by himself, was because they were afraid of being censured and reproached by every rational religious man in the three parts of the world for a faith of three Gods. The reason that they taught a faith applied to the three in order, was because no other could flow from that principle: to this it may be added, that if one of those three were omitted, a third would not be sent, and thus all the operation of divine grace would come to nothing.

634. But the truth shall be declared: When a faith in three Gods was introduced into the Christian churches, which was done at the Nicene synod, all the good of charity and all the truth of faith were exiled; for those two can never consist with the mental worship of three Gods, and at the same time with the oral worship of one God; for the mind denies what the mouth speaks, and the mouth denies what the mind thinks; thence it comes to pass, that there is neither a faith of three Gods, nor a faith of one. Hence it is manifest, that the Christian temple has, since that time, not only been shattered, but also has fallen in ruins; and that, since that time, the pit of the abyss has been open, from which smoke as of a great furnace has ascended, and the sun has been darkened, and the air, and from which locusts came forth into the earth, Rev. ix. 2, 3. See the explanation of those things in the APOCALYPSE REVEALED. Yea, from that time the desolation foretold by Daniel began and has increased, Matt. xxiv. 15; and to that faith, and the imputation of it, the eagles have been gathered together, verse 28 of the same chapter; by *eagles* there are meant leaders of the church, who are, as it were, lynx-eyed. If it is said, that the council, in which so many bishops and laurelled men sat, decreed that, by their unanimous suffrages, what confidence is to be put in councils, when Roman Catholic councils have also, by their unanimous suffrages, decreed the vicarship of the pope, the invocation of saints, the veneration of images and bones, the division of the holy eucharist, purgatory, indulgences, &c.? What confidence is to be put in councils, when that of Dort also, by their unanimous suffrages, decreed a detestable predestination, and extolled it as the palladium of religion. But, my reader, do not trust to councils, but to the Holy Word, and go to the Lord, and you will be enlightened; for He is the Word, that is, the Divine Truth itself there.

635. Finally, this arcanum shall be disclosed. In seven chapters in the Revelation the consummation of the present church is described, in like

manner as the devastation of Egypt is described, and both by similar plagues, each of which spiritually signifies some false, which promoted its devastation even to destruction; wherefore also this church, which has at this day been destroyed, is called Egypt, spiritually understood, Rev. xi. 8. The plagues in Egypt were these: That the waters were turned into blood, whence every fish died, and the river stank, Exod. vii. In like manner it is said in Rev. viii. 8; xvi. 3. By *blood* is signified divine truth falsified; see the Apocalypse Revealed n. 379, 404, 681, 687, 688; and by the fishes which then died, the truths in the natural man also dead, n. 290, 405. In the land of Egypt frogs were produced, Exod. viii. Something concerning frogs also is said in Rev. xvi. 13. By *frogs* are signified reasonings from the desire of falsifying truths. See Apoc. Rev. n. 702. In Egypt noxious ulcers came upon man and beast, Exod. ix. In like manner, in Rev. xvi. 2. By *ulcers* are signified interior evils and falses destructive of the good and truth in the church. See Apoc. Rev. n. 678. In Egypt there was hail mingled with fire, Exod. ix. In like manner in Rev. viii. 7; xvi. 21. *Hail* signifies the infernal false. See Apoc. Rev. n. 399, 714. Upon Egypt was sent the locust, Exod. x. In like manner in Rev. ix. 1 to 11. *Locusts* signify falses in the outermost things. See Apoc. Rev. n. 424, 430. Upon Egypt a grievous darkness was brought, Exod. x. In like manner in Rev. viii. 12. *Darkness* signifies falses arising either from ignorance, or from falses of religion, or from evils of life. See Apoc. Rev. n. 110, 413, 695. That at length the Egyptians perished in the Red sea, Exod. xiv.; but in the Revelation, the dragon and the false prophet, in the lake of fire and brimstone, xix. 20; xx. 10. Both *the Red sea* and that *lake* signify hell. The reason why similar things are said concerning Egypt, and concerning the church, whose consummation and end are described in the Revelation, is because by *Egypt* is meant a church, which in its beginning was excellent; wherefore Egypt, before its church was devastated, is compared to the garden of Eden, and the garden of Jehovah, Gen. xiii. 10; Ezek. xxxi. 8; and also it is called the corner-stone of the tribes, the son of the wise, and of the kings of antiquity, Isaiah xix. 11, 13. More may be seen concerning Egypt in its primeval state, and in its devastated state, in the Apocalypse Revealed, n. 503.

636. IV. That the Faith imputative of the Merit of Christ was not known in the Apostolic Church, which preceded, and is no where meant in the Word.

The church which preceded the Nicene synod, was called the Apostolic church; that this was large, and propagated into the three parts of the world, Asia, Africa and Europe, is evident not only from Constantine the Great, and his monarchy over not only many kingdoms of Europe, afterwards divided, but also over the nearer ones out of Europe, in that he was a Christian, and a zealot for religion; wherefore, as was said above, he called together the bishops from Asia, Africa and Europe to his palace at Nice, a city of Bithynia, that he might cast the scandals of Arius out of his empire. This was done from the divine providence of the Lord, since, if the divinity of the Lord is denied, the Christian church dies, and becomes like a sepulchre adorned with this epitaph, "*Here lies.*" The church which was before this time was called Apostolic, and the eminent writers of that church were called fathers, and true Christians at their side, brethren. That this church did not acknowledge three divine persons, and thence neither a Son of God from eternity, but only the Son of God born in time, is evident from the creed which from their church was called Apostolic, where these words are read: *I believe in God the Father Almighty, Creator of heaven and earth; and in Jesus Christ, his only Son our Lord, who was conceived by the Holy Ghost, born of the virgin Mary. I believe in the Holy Ghost; the holy Catholic church; the communion of saints.* Whence it is manifest that they did not acknowledge any other Son of God than that conceived by the Holy Spirit, and born of the virgin Mary, and not at all any Son of God born from eternity. This creed, like the two others, has been acknowledged as the genuine Catholic, by the whole Christian church to the present day.

637. That in that primeval time, all in that Christian world acknowledged that the Lord Jesus Christ was God, to whom is given all power in heaven and in earth, and power over all flesh, according to his own words, Matt. xxviii. 18; John xvii. 2; and that they believed in Him according to his command from God the Father, John iii. 15, 16, 36; vi. 40; xi. 25, 26. The same is also very manifest from the convocation of all the bishops by the emperor Constantine the Great, for the purpose of convicting and condemning, from the Sacred Scriptures, Arius and his followers, who denied the divinity of the Lord the Savior, born of the virgin Mary. This, indeed, was done; but they, in order to avoid a wolf, fell upon a lion; or, as it is said in the proverb, *Wishing to avoid Charybdis, he fell upon Scylla;* by feigning a Son of God from eternity, who descended and assumed the Human, believing that thus they should vindicate and restore divinity to the Lord; not knowing that God himself, the Creator of the universe, descended, that He might become Redeemer, and thus Creator anew, according to these manifest declarations in the Old Testament: Isaiah xxv. 9; xl. 3, 5, 10, 11; xliii. 24; xliv. 6, 24; xlvii. 4; xlviii. 17; xlix. 7, 26; lx. 16; lxiii. 16; Jer. l. 34; Hos. xiii. 4; Psalm xix. 15: to these add John ix. 15.

638. That Apostolic church, because it worshipped the Lord God Jesus Christ, and at the same time God the Father in Him, may be likened to the garden of God; and Arius, who then arose, to the serpent sent from hell; and the Nicene council, to Adam's wife, who presented the fruit to her husband and persuaded; after the eating of which, they appeared to themselves naked, and covered their nakedness with leaves of the fig-tree; by their *nakedness* is meant the innocence in which they were before; and by *leaves of the fig-tree,* the truths of the natural man, which were successively falsified. That primitive church may be compared also to the dawning of the day and the morning, from which the day proceeded to the tenth hour; but then a thick cloud intervened, under which the day proceeded to the evening, and after this into the night, in which the moon arose, for some, from the light of which some saw something from the Word; and the rest went on into the thick darkness of night, so far, that they saw nothing of divinity in the Lord's humanity; although Paul says, that *in Jesus Christ all the fulness of the Godhead dwelleth bodily,* Coloss. ii. 9; and John, that *The Son of God sent into the world is the true God and eternal life,* 1 John v. 20. The primitive or Apostolic church never could have conceived that a church could succeed, which would worship several Gods with the heart, and one with the mouth, which would separate charity from faith, the remission of sins from repentance and the desire of a new life, and which would introduce a total impotence in spiritual things; and least of all that any Arius should lift up his head, and when he had died should rise again and rule secretly even to the end.

639. That no faith imputative of the merit of Christ was meant in the Word, is clearly manifest from this, that that faith was not known in the church before the Nicene synod introduced three divine persons from eternity; and when this faith was introduced, and had pervaded the whole Christian world, all other faith was rejected into darkness; wherefore, whoever then reads the Word, and sees faith, imputation and the merit of Christ, falls of himself into that which he had believed the only thing; like one who sees the writing of one page, and stops there, and does not turn it over and see any thing else; or like one who persuades himself that this is true, although it is false, and confirms it alone; then he sees the false as true, and the true as

false; he would afterwards press his teeth together, and hiss with his mouth at every one who opposes it, and would say, "You are not intelligent." His mind is wholly in it, covered over with a hard shell, which rejects as heterodox every thing that is not consonant to his orthodoxy so called; for his memory is like a tablet on which only this ruling theological tenet is written; if any thing else enters, it has no place where it could be inserted; wherefore it casts it out, as the mouth does froth. For example, say to a confirmed naturalist, who either believes that nature created herself, or that God existed after nature, or that nature and God are one, that it is altogether contrary; would he not look upon you either as deluded by the fables of presbyters, or as simple, or as dull, or as a dunce? The case is similar with all things that persuasion and confirmation fix, which at last appear like painted tapestry fastened with many nails to a wall glued together of decayed little stones.

640. V. That the Imputation of the Merit and Righteousness of Christ is impossible.

That it may be known that the imputation of the merit and righteousness of Jesus Christ is impossible, it is necessary to know what his merit and righteousness are. The merit of our Lord the Savior is redemption, and what this was, may be seen above in its chapter, n. 114 to 133; which is there described to have been a subjugation of the hells, the establishment of order in the heavens, and afterwards the institution of a church; and thus that redemption was a work purely divine. It was also shown there, that by redemption the Lord took to himself the power of regenerating and saving the men who believe in Him and do his commandments, and that without that redemption no flesh could have been saved. Since, now, redemption was a work purely divine, and of the Lord alone, and that is his merit, it follows that this cannot be applied, ascribed and imputed to any man, any more than the creation and preservation of the universe. Redemption also was a certain creation of the angelic heaven anew, and also of the church. That the church at this day attributes that merit of the Lord the Redeemer to those who by grace obtained faith, is manifest from their dogmas, among which this is the principal; for it is said by the dignitaries of this church, and by their dependants, as well in the Roman Catholic church, as in the churches of the Reformed, that by the imputation of the merit of Christ, those who have obtained faith are not only reputed just and holy, but that they are so; and that their sins are not sins in the sight of God, because they are remitted, and they themselves are justified, that is, reconciled, renewed, regenerated, sanctified and enrolled in heaven. That the universal Christian church at this day teaches those same things, is manifestly evident from the council of Trent, the Augustan and Augsburg confessions, and from the commentaries attached to them, and also received. From the things above said and transferred into that faith, what else flows, than that the possession of that faith is that merit and that righteousness of the Lord? consequently that the possessor of it is Christ in another person? For it is said that Christ himself is righteousness, and that that faith is righteousness, and that imputation, by which also is meant ascription and application, causes them not only to be reputed just and holy, but to be so. Add only Transcription to imputation, application and ascription, and you will be a vicarious pope.

641. Since, therefore, the merit and righteousness of the Lord are purely divine, and since things purely divine are such that, if they were applied and ascribed, man would die in an instant, and, like a fire-brand thrown into the naked sun, would be so consumed that scarcely any spark would remain of him; therefore the Lord with his Divine approaches to angels and to men by light tempered and moderated according to the faculty and quality of each, thus by what is adequate and accommodated; in like manner He approaches by heat. In the spiritual

world there is a sun, in the midst of which is the Lord; from that sun He flows in by light and heat into the whole spiritual world, and into all who are there; all the light and all the heat there are thence. The Lord from that sun flows in with the same light and the same heat also into the souls and minds of men; that heat in its essence is his divine love, and that light in its essence is his divine wisdom; this light and that heat the Lord adapts to the faculty and quality of the recipient angel and man, which is done by means of spiritual *auras* or atmospheres which convey and transfer them: the Divine itself, immediately encompassing the Lord, makes that sun. This sun is distant from the angels, as the sun of the natural world is from men, in order that it may not touch them with its naked rays, and thus immediately; for thus they would be consumed like a firebrand thrown into the naked sun, as was said. Hence it may be evident, that the merit and righteousness of the Lord, because they are purely divine, cannot possibly be introduced by imputation into any angel or man; yea, if any drop of it, without being thus moderated, as was said, should touch them, they would instantly be tortured like those laboring with death, struggling with their feet, staring with their eyes, and they would expire. This was made known in the Israelitish church by this, that no one could see God and live. The sun of the spiritual world, such as it is since Jehovah God assumed the Human, and added to it redemption and new righteousness, is also described by these words in Isaiah: *The light of the sun shall be seven-fold, as the light of seven days, in the day when Jehovah shall bind up the breach of his people*, xxx. 26; in which chapter, from the beginning to the end, the coming of the Lord is treated of. It is also described, what the case would be if the Lord should descend and approach to any wicked man, by these words in the Revelation: *They hid themselves in the caves and in the rocks of the mountains, and said to the mountains and to the rocks, Hide us from the face of Him that sitteth upon the throne, and from the anger of the Lamb*, vi. 15; it is said, *the anger of the Lamb*, because the terror and torment appear so to them, when the Lord approaches. This again may be evidently concluded from this, that if any wicked person is introduced into heaven, where charity and faith in the Lord reign, his eyes are seized with darkness, his mind with dizziness and insanity, his body with pain and torment, and he becomes as it were lifeless. What then, if the Lord himself with his divine merit, which is redemption, and with his divine righteousness, should enter man? The apostle John himself could not sustain the presence of the Lord; for it is read, that *when he saw the Son of Man in the midst of the seven candlesticks, he fell at his feet as dead*, Rev. i. 17.

642. It is said in the decrees of the councils, and in the articles of the confessions to which the Reformed swear, that God, by the merit of Christ being infused, justifies the wicked; when yet the good of any angel cannot even be communicated, still less conjoined, to a wicked man, without being rejected and rebounding, like an elastic ball thrown against the wall, or absorbed, like a diamond sent into a bog; yea, if any thing truly good were thrust in, it would be as if a pearl were tied to a swine's snout. For who does not know, that clemency cannot be injected into unmercifulness, innocence into revenge, love into hatred, concord into discord; which would be like mixing together heaven and hell. A man not born again is, as to his spirit, like a panther, or like an owl, and may be likened to a brier and a nettle; but a man born again is like a sheep, or like a dove, and may be likened to an olive-tree or a vine. Think, I pray, if you please, how can a man-panther be converted into a man-sheep, or an owl into a dove, or a brier into an olive-tree, or a nettle into a vine, by any imputation ascription, or application of divine righteousness, which would rather condemn than justify him. In order that the conversion may be effected, must not the savageness of the panther and

the owl, and the noxiousness of the brier and the nettle be taken away, and that which is truly human and harmless be implanted in their place? How this is done, the Lord also teaches in John xv. 1 to 7.

643. VI. THAT THERE IS IMPUTATION, BUT OF GOOD AND OF EVIL, AND AT THE SAME TIME OF FAITH.

That it is the imputation of good and evil which is meant in the Word, when it is named, is evident from innumerable passages there, which indeed have been, in part, adduced before; but that every one may be certain, that there is no other imputation, some things here also shall be adduced from the Word; which are, *The Son of Man is about to come, and then He will render to every one according to his deeds*, Matt. xvi. 27. *Those who have done goods shall come forth to the resurrection of life, but those who have done evils to the resurrection of judgment*, John v. 29. *A book was opened, which is the book of life, and they were all judged according to their works*, Rev. xx. 12, 13. *Behold, I come quickly, and my reward is with Me, that I may give to every one according to his work*, xxii. 12. *I will visit according to his ways. I will reward him according to his works*, Hosea iv. 9; Zech. i. 6; Jer. xxv. 14; xxxii. 19. *God, in the day of his anger and just judgment, will render to every one according to his works*, Rom. ii. 5, 6. *We all must appear before the judgment seat of Christ, that every one may receive the things which he hath done in the body, according to what he hath done, whether good or evil*, 2 Cor. v. 10. There was no other law of imputation at the beginning of the church, nor is there to be any other at the end of it. That there was no other at the beginning of the church, is manifest from Adam and his wife; that because they did evil, in eating from the tree of the knowledge of good and evil, they were condemned, Gen. ii. and iii.; and that there is to be no other at the end of the church, is manifest from these words of the Lord: *When the Son of Man shall come in the glory of his Father, then He will sit upon the throne of his glory. And He will say to the sheep on his right hand, Come, ye blessed, and possess, as an inheritance, the kingdom prepared for you from the foundation of the world. For I was hungry, and ye gave Me to eat; I was thirsty, and ye gave Me to drink; I was a stranger, and ye took Me in; I was naked, and ye clothed Me; I was sick, and ye visited Me; I was in prison, and ye came to Me.* But to the goats on his left hand, because they did not do goods, He said, *Depart from Me, ye cursed, into everlasting fire prepared for the devil and his angels*, Matt. xxv. 33, and following verses. Hence every one, with open eyes, may see that there is an imputation of good and of evil. That there is also an imputation of faith, is because charity, which is of good, and faith, which is of truth, are together in good works; and that unless they are together, the works are not good, may be seen above, n. 373 to 377; wherefore James says, *Was not Abraham our father justified by works when he offered his son upon the altar? Seest thou not that faith cooperated with works, and by the works the faith was known to be perfect? And the Scripture was fulfilled, which saith Abraham believed God, and it was imputed to him for righteousness*, James ii. 21, 22, 23.

644. The cause that the leaders of the Christian churches, and thence their subalterns, by imputation in the Word, have understood an imputation of the faith on which the righteousness and merit of Christ are inscribed, and thus ascribed to man, is because, for fourteen centuries, that is, since the time of the Nicene synod, they have not been willing to know of any other faith; wherefore that alone was fixed in their memory, and thence in their mind, as if it were organized; which from that time borrowed a light such as there is from fire in the time of night, from which light that faith was seen as the very theological truth, on which all the rest depend in a connected series, which would fall to pieces, if that head, or that pillar, were moved away

Wherefore, if they had thought of any other faith than that imputative faith, when they read the Word, that light, together with every thing of their theology, would have been extinguished, and darkness would have arisen, by which the whole Christian church would have vanished; wherefore that was left *as a stump of roots in the earth, when the tree was cut down and destroyed, until seven times should pass over it,* Dan. iv. 20. Who among the confirmed leaders of the church at this day, when that faith is attacked, does not stop his ears as with cotton, on hearing any thing against it? But, my reader, open your ears and read the Word, and you will clearly perceive another faith and another imputation, than what you had before persuaded yourself to believe.

645. It is wonderful, that although the Word, from the beginning to the end, is full of testimonies and confirmations, that to every one his good or evil is imputed, still the dogmatical teachers of the Christian religion have stopped up their ears as with wax, and anointed their eyes as with eye-salve, so that they have not heard or seen, nor do they hear or see, any other imputation, than that of their faith above mentioned: and yet that faith may be rightly compared with the disease of the eye which is called GUTTA SERENA, yea, it ought to be named so, which is an absolute blindness of the eye arising from an obstruction of the optic nerve, and yet the eye appears as if it saw perfectly. In like manner, those who are in that faith go as with open eyes, and appear to others as if they saw all things, when yet they see nothing; since man knows nothing about that faith when it enters, for he is then like a stock; neither does he know afterwards whether it is in him, nor does he know whether there is any thing in it; and afterwards they also, as with clear eyes, see that faith begetting and bringing forth the noble offspring of justification, namely, the remission of sins, vivification, renovation, regeneration and sanctification, when yet they neither have seen nor can see a sign of any of them.

646. That good which is charity, and evil which is iniquity, are imputed after death, has been made evident to me by all my experience concerning the condition of those who pass from this world into the other. Every one after he has been there some days, is examined as to what he is, thus as to what he was in the former world as to religion; which being done, the examiners report this to heaven, and then he is transferred to those who are like him, thus to his own; thus imputation is effected. That there is an imputation of good to all who are in heaven, and an imputation of evil to all who are in hell, was manifest to me from the arrangement of both by the Lord. All heaven is arranged into societies according to all the varieties of the love of good, and all hell according to all the varieties of the love of evil. In like manner the church on earth is arranged by the Lord, for this corresponds to heaven; its religion is good. Moreover, ask any men you please, who are endued with religion, and at the same time with reason, whether they be of this or of the two other parts of the world, who they believe will go to heaven, and who to hell, and they will answer unanimously, that those who do good will go to heaven, and those who do evil to hell. Besides, who does not know, that every true man loves a man, a company of men, a state, and a kingdom, from their good; yea, not only men, but also beasts, and even inanimate things, as houses, possessions, fields, gardens, trees, woods, and lands, yea, metals and stones, from their goodness and use; good and use are one. Why should not the Lord love man and the church from good?

647. VII. THAT THE FAITH AND IMPUTATION OF THE NEW CHURCH CANNOT BE TOGETHER WITH THE FAITH AND IMPUTATION OF THE FORMER CHURCH; AND THAT IF THEY ARE TOGETHER, SUCH A COLLISION AND CONFLICT ENSUE, THAT EVERY THING OF THE CHURCH WITH MAN PERISHES.

The reason why the faith and imputation of the New Church cannot be together with the faith and imputation of the former or still subsisting church, is because they do not agree in one third, nor even in one tenth; for the faith of the former church teaches that there existed from eternity three divine persons, each of whom, singly or by himself, was God, also as many Creators; but the faith of the New Church is, that there was from eternity only one Divine Person, thus one God, and that beside Him there is no other God. Wherefore the faith of the former church taught a Divine Trinity divided into three persons, but the faith of the New Church teaches a Divine Trinity united in one person. The faith of the former church was in a God who is invisible, inaccessible, and incapable of conjunction; the idea of whom was like that of spirit, which is like that of ether or wind: but the faith of the New Church is in a God who is visible, accessible, and capable of conjunction, in whom, as the soul in the body, is the God invisible, inaccessible, and incapable of conjunction; the idea of whom is that of a man, because the one God, who was from eternity, became Man in time. The faith of the former church attributes all power to an invisible God, and denies it to the visible God; for it teaches that God the Father imputes faith, and by it gives eternal life; and that the visible only intercedes; and that both, or, according to the Greek church, God the Father, gives to the Holy Ghost (who is the third in order, a God by himself) all power of working the effects of that faith: but the faith of the New Church attributes to the visible God, in whom is the invisible, all power of imputing and also of working the effects of salvation. The faith of the former church is primarily in God the Creator, and not at the same time in Him as Redeemer and Savior; but the faith of the New Church is in one God, who at the same time is Creator, Redeemer and Savior. The faith of the former church is, that when faith is given and imputed, repentance, remission of sins, renovation, regeneration, sanctification and salvation follow it of themselves, without any thing of man being mixed or conjoined with them; but the faith of the New Church teaches repentance, reformation, regeneration, and thus remission of sins, with man's coöperation. The faith of the former church teaches the imputation of Christ's merit, which the faith given embraces; but the faith of the New Church teaches an imputation of good and of evil, and at the same time of faith; and that this imputation is according to the Sacred Scripture, but that contrary to it. The former church teaches the giving of faith in which is the merit of Christ, when man is like a stock and a stone, and also it teaches a total impotence in spiritual things; but the New Church teaches altogether another faith, which is not in the merit of Christ, but in Jesus Christ himself as God, Redeemer and Savior, and free agency both for applying one's self to reception and for coöperating. The former church adjoins charity to its faith, as an appendage, but not as saving, and thus it makes religion; but the New Church conjoins faith in the Lord and charity towards the neighbor, as two inseparable things, and thus it makes religion: besides many other discordances.

648. From this brief review of their discordances or disagreements, it is manifest that the faith and imputation of the New Church cannot possibly be together with the faith and imputation of the former or still subsisting church. And because there is such a discord and disagreement between the faith and imputation of the two churches, there is a complete heterogeneity; wherefore, if they were together in the mind of a man, such a collision and conflict would ensue, that every thing of the church would perish, and man, in spiritual things, would fall either into a delirium or into a swoon, whence he would not know what the church is, and whether there be any church Would he then know any thing about

God, any thing about faith, and any thing about charity? The faith of the former church, because it excludes every thing of light from reason, may be likened to an owl; but the faith of the New Church may be likened to a dove, which flies in the day time, and sees from the light of heaven; wherefore their conjunction in one mind would be like the conjunction of an owl and a dove in one nest, where the owl would lay her eggs and the dove hers, and, after sitting, the young ones would be hatched, and then the owl would tear the dove's young ones in pieces, and give them to her own young ones for food; for the owl is a voracious bird. Because the faith of the former church is described in Rev. xii. by the dragon, and the faith of the New Church by the woman encompassed with the sun, upon whose head was a crown of twelve stars, it may be concluded from the comparison what would be the state of a man's mind, if they should be together in one house; namely, that the dragon would stand by the woman about to bring forth, with the intention of devouring her child; and that after she flew away into the desert, he would pursue her, and cast water as a flood upon her, that she might be swallowed up.

649. The like would happen, if any one should embrace the faith of the New Church, and retain the faith of the former church concerning the imputation of the Lord's merit and righteousness; for from this, as their root, all the dogmas of the former church, as shoots, have sprung up. If this should be the case, it would be comparatively as if one should rescue himself from five horns of the dragon, and entangle himself in his remaining five; or as if one should escape from a wolf, and fall upon a tiger: or as if one, coming out of a pit where there was no water, should fall into a pit where there was water, and be drowned. For thus he would easily return into all things of the former faith; and what these are, has been explained above: and then into this damnable error, that he might impute and apply to himself the very divine things of the Lord, which are redemption and righteousness, which may be adored and not applied; for if man should impute and apply them to himself, he would be consumed, as if he were cast into the naked sun, from the light and heat of which, however, he sees, and, as to the body, lives. That the merit of the Lord is redemption, and that his redemption and his righteousness are two divine things, which cannot be conjoined to man, was shown above. Let every one, therefore, beware of transcribing the imputation of the former church into the imputation of the New, since tragical things would thence arise, which might hinder his salvation.

650. VIII. That the Lord imputes Good to every Man, and that Hell imputes Evil to every Man.

That the Lord imputes good to man and not any evil, and that the devil, by which is meant hell, imputes evil to man, and not any good, is new in the church; the reason that it is new, is because it is read in the Word many times, that God is angry, that He avenges, hates, condemns, punishes, casts into hell, tempts; which all are of evil, and thence evils. But that the sense of the letter of the Word is composed of such things as are called appearances and correspondences, in order that there may be a conjunction of the external church with its internal, thus of the world with heaven, was shown in the chapter concerning the Sacred Scripture; and there also, that when such things in the Word are read, the appearances of truth themselves, while they are passing from man to heaven, are turned into genuine truths, which are, that the Lord never is angry, never avenges, hates, condemns, punishes, casts into hell, tempts; consequently, that He does evil to no man. This change and turning I have often observed in the spiritual world.

651. Reason itself assents to this, that the Lord cannot do evil to any man, and consequently cannot impute it to him; for He is Love itself, Mercy itself, thus Good itself, and these are of his Divine Essence: wherefore to

attribute evil, or any thing of evil, to the Lord, would be contrary to his Divine Essence, and thus contradictory; and this would be as inexpressibly wicked, as it is to conjoin the Lord and the devil, or heaven and hell, when yet *between them there is a great gulf fixed, so that those who would pass from this to that, or from that to this, cannot*, Luke xvi. 26. Not even an angel of heaven can do evil to any one, because the essence of good from the Lord is in him; and, on the other hand, a spirit of hell cannot but do evil to another, because the nature of evil from the devil is in him; the essence or nature which any one has appropriated to himself in the world, cannot be changed after death. Think, I pray, what the Lord would be, if He looked upon the evil from anger, and upon the good from clemency (the evil are myriads of myriads, and the good are myriads of myriads in number). If He saved these from grace, and condemned those from vengeance; or looked upon these and those with an eye so different, gentle and severe, or mild and stern, what then would be the character of the Lord God? Who that is instructed by preaching in temples does not know, that all good which is in itself good is from God; and, on the other hand, that all evil which is in itself evil, is from the devil? If, therefore, any man should receive both good and evil, good from the Lord, and evil from the devil, both of them in the will, would he not become neither cold nor hot, but lukewarm, which would be spewed out, according to the words of the Lord in Rev. iii. 15, 16.

652. That the Lord imputes good to every man, and not evil to any one, consequently that He does not judge any one to hell, but elevates all, so far as man follows, to heaven, is evident from these his words: *Jesus said, When I am lifted up from the earth, I will draw all to myself*, John xii. 32. *God sent not his Son into the world to judge the world, but that the world might be saved by Him. He that believeth in Him is not judged; but he that believeth not, is already judged*, iii. 18. *If any one hear my words and yet believe not, I judge him not; for I came not to judge the world, but to save the world. He that despiseth Me, and receiveth not my words, hath one that judgeth him; the Word which I have spoken shall judge him at the last day*, xii. 47, 48. *Jesus said, I judge no one*, viii. 15. By *judgment* here and elsewhere in the Word, is meant judgment to hell, which is condemnation; but resurrection to life, and not judgment, is predicated of salvation, John v. 24, 29; iii. 18. By *the Word* which will judge, is meant the truth, and it is a truth that all evil is from hell, and thus that evil and hell are one; wherefore, when an evil person is elevated by the Lord towards heaven, then his evil draws him down, and because he loves evil, he follows of his own accord. It is also a truth in the Word, that good is heaven; wherefore when a good person is elevated by the Lord towards heaven, he ascends as of his own accord, and is introduced; these are said to be written in the book of life, Dan. xii. 1; Rev. xii. 8, 12, 23; xvii. 8; xxi. 6. There is actually a sphere elevating all to heaven, which continually proceeds from the Lord, and fills all the spiritual world and all the natural world; and it is like a strong current in the ocean which secretly draws the ship. All those who believe in the Lord, and live according to his commandments, enter that sphere or current, and are elevated; but those who do not believe, are not willing to enter, but remove themselves to the sides, and there are carried away by a stream which leads to hell.

653. Who does not know that a lamb cannot act otherwise than as a lamb, and a sheep not otherwise than as a sheep; and, on the other hand, that a wolf cannot act otherwise than as a wolf, and a tiger than as a tiger? If those beasts were mixed together, would not the wolf devour the lamb, and the tiger the sheep? Wherefore there are shepherds for guards. Who does not know that a fountain of sweet water cannot send forth from its vein bitter waters; and that a good tree cannot

produce bad fruit; and that a vine cannot prick like a thorn, the flower of a lily gall like a brier, and a hyacinth sting like a thistle; and the reverse? Wherefore those noxious plants are rooted up out of fields, vineyards and gardens, and, being collected into heaps, they are cast into the fire. The like is done with the evil who flow into the spiritual world, according to the words of the Lord, Matt. xiii. 30; John xv. 6. The Lord also said to the Jews, *O offspring of vipers, how can ye speak good things, when ye are evil? A good man, from the good treasure of his heart, sends forth good things; and an evil man, from the evil treasure, sends forth evil things*, Matt. xii. 34, 35.

654. IX. THAT FAITH, WITH WHATSOEVER IT CONJOINS ITSELF, MAKES A SENTENCE: IF TRUE FAITH CONJOINS ITSELF WITH GOOD, A SENTENCE IS MADE FOR ETERNAL LIFE; BUT IF FAITH CONJOINS ITSELF WITH EVIL, A SENTENCE IS MADE FOR ETERNAL DEATH.

The works of charity which are done by a Christian, and those which are done by a heathen, in the external form appear similar; for one as well as the other does the goods of civility and morality to a companion, which are in some degree similar to the goods of love towards the neighbor; yea, he can give to the poor, help the needy, and hear sermons in temples; but who can thence judge, whether those external goods are similar in the internal form, or whether the natural are also spiritual? Concerning this, it can be concluded only from faith, for faith qualifies them; for faith causes God to be in them, and conjoins them with itself in the internal man; thence natural goods become inwardly spiritual. That it is so, may be more clearly seen from what was said in the chapter concerning FAITH, where the following things are demonstrated: *That Faith is not living before it is conjoined to Charity. That Charity is made spiritual by Faith, and Faith by Charity. That Faith without Charity, because it is not spiritual, is not Faith; and that Charity without Faith, because it is not living, is not Charity. That Faith and Charity apply and conjoin themselves to each other reciprocally. That the Lord, Charity and Faith make one, like life, will and understanding; but if they are divided, each perishes, like a pearl reduced to powder.*

655. From the things adduced, it may be seen, that faith in the one and true God causes good to be good also in the internal form; and, on the other hand, that faith in a false god causes good to be good only in the external form, which is not good in itself; as the faith of the Gentiles formerly in Jupiter, Juno and Apollo; of the Philistines in Dagon; and of others in Baal and Baal-peor; and of Balaam the magician in his god; and of the Egyptians in many. It is altogether different with faith in the Lord, who is *the true God and eternal Life*, according to John, 1 Epist. v. 20; *and in whom all the fulness of the Godhead dwelleth bodily*, according to Paul, Coloss. ii. 9. What is faith in God but the sight of Him, and thence His presence, and at the same time a confidence that He helps? And what is true faith but that, and at the same time a confidence that all good is from Him, and makes one's good to be saving? Wherefore if this faith conjoin itself with good, a sentence is made for eternal life; altogether otherwise if it do not conjoin itself with good, and especially if it conjoin itself with evil.

656. What the conjunction of charity and faith is, with those who believe in three gods, and yet say that they believe in one, was shown above, namely, that charity conjoins itself with faith only in the external natural man; the reason is, because his mind is in the idea of three gods, and his mouth in the confession of one God; wherefore if the mind at that moment should infuse itself into the confession of the mouth it would expunge the enunciation of one God, and would open the lips and force out its three gods!

657. That evil and faith in the one and true God cannot be together, every one may see from reason, for evil is against God, and faith is for God; and

evil is of the will, and faith is of the thought, and the will flows into the understanding and causes it to think, but not conversely; the understanding only teaches what is to be willed and to be done. Wherefore the good which such a man does, is in itself evil; it is like a shining bone, the marrow of which is rotten; it is like an actor upon the stage, who personates a grandee; and it is like the handsome face of an antiquated harlot; and it is like a butterfly, flying with silver wings, which lays little eggs on the leaves of a good tree, from which all its fruit perishes; it is like fragrant smoke from a poisonous herb; yea, it is like a moral robber and a pious sycophant. Wherefore the good of such a man, which in itself is evil, is in a chamber within; but his faith, walking in the porch and reasoning, is a mere chimera, a spectre and a bubble. Hence the truth of the proposition is manifest, that faith makes sentence concerning the good and the evil which is conjoined to it.

658. X. That Thought is imputed to no one, but Will.

Every man of erudition knows that there are two faculties or parts of the mind, the will and the understanding; but few know how to distinguish them accurately, and to survey their properties separately, and afterwards to conjoin them. Those who cannot do this, cannot get for themselves any other than a very obscure notion concerning the mind; wherefore, unless the properties of each by itself be first described, this will not be comprehended, *That thought is imputed to no one, but will.* The properties of both, in a summary, are these: 1. That love itself, and the things which are of love, reside in the will; and that science, intelligence and wisdom reside in the understanding; and that the will inspires its love into these, and produces favor and assent: thence it is, that as the love is, and the intelligence thence, such is the man. 2. From this it also follows, that all good, and also all evil, is of the will; for whatever proceeds from the love, is called good, although it be evil; for delight, which makes the life of love, produces this; the will by this delight enters the understanding, and produces consent. 3. The will, therefore, is the *esse* or the essence of the life of man, but the understanding is the *existere* or the existence thence; and because essence is not any thing unless it be in a certain form, so the will is not any thing unless it be in the understanding; wherefore the will forms itself in the understanding, and thus comes forth into the light. 4. Love in the will is the end, and in the understanding it seeks and finds causes by which it may promote itself to the effect; and because the end is the purpose, and this intends, purpose also is of the will, and through the intention it enters the understanding and causes it to consider and revolve the means, and to conclude such as tend to effects. 5. All the *proprium* of man is in the will, and this is evil from his first nativity, and becomes good by a second; the first nativity is from parents, but the other is from the Lord. From these few things it may be seen, that there is one property of the will, and another of the understanding, and that from creation they are joined together, like *esse* and *existere;* consequently that man is man primarily from the will, and secondarily from the understanding. Thence it is that will is imputed to man, but not thought; consequently evil and good, because these, as was said, reside in the will, and thence in the thought of the understanding.

659. The reason that no evil is imputed to man, which he thinks, is because man is so created that he can understand and thence think good or evil, good from the Lord and evil from hell; for he is in the midst, and in the faculty of choosing one or the other, from free agency in spiritual things, which has been treated of in its chapter; and because he is in the faculty of choosing from freedom, he can will and not will, and what he wills is received by the will and appropriated, but what he does not will is not received and thus is not appropriated All the evils to which a man inclines from nativity, a e inscribed on the will

of his natural man; those, as far as he takes from them, flow into the thoughts; in like manner goods with truths from above flow into them from the Lord, and there they are poised like weights in the scales of a balance: if then a man adopt evils, they are received by the old will, and add themselves to those; but if he adopt goods with truths, there is formed by the Lord a new will and a new understanding above the old, and there the Lord successively implants goods by means of truths, and by them He subjugates the evils which are below, and removes them, and disposes all things in order. Hence also it is manifest, that the thought is a purificatory and excretory of the evils inherited from parents; wherefore if the evils which man thinks were imputed, reformation and regeneration could not be effected.

660. Since good is of the will, and truth is of the understanding, and many things in the world correspond to good, as fruits and uses, and imputation itself to estimation and price, it follows, that the things which are here said concerning imputation may be compared with all created things; for, as was shown before, here and there, all things in the universe refer themselves to good and truth, and, on the contrary, to what is evil and false. A comparison, therefore, may be made with the church, in that it is estimated from charity and faith, and not from the rituals which are adjoined. A comparison may be made also with a minister of the church, in that he is estimated from his will and love, and at the same time from his understanding in spiritual things, and not from his affability and dress. There is also a comparison given with worship, and with the temple in which it is performed: worship itself is performed in the will and in the understanding, as in its temple; and the temple is called holy, not from itself, but from the Divine which is there taught. And also a comparison is given with a government, which is loved when good reigns and at the same time truth, but not when truth reigns and not good. Who judges of a king by his guards, horses and chariots, and not from the royalty which they know to be in him? Royalty consists of the love and prudence of governing. Who, in a triumph, does not look at the conqueror, and from him to the pomp, and not from the pomp to the conqueror; consequently from the essential to the formal, and not from the formal to the essential? Will is the essential, and thought is the formal, and no one can impute to the formal except what it derives from the essential, consequently to the latter, and not to the former.

---

661. To the above I shall add these Relations. First. In a higher northern quarter, near to the east in the spiritual world, there are places of instruction for boys, some for youths, and some for men, and some for old men. All who have died infants are sent to these places, and are educated in heaven; and also all are sent thither, who newly come from the world, and desire knowledges concerning heaven and hell. That tract is near the east, that all may be instructed by influx from the Lord; for the Lord is east, because He is in the sun there, which from Him is pure love. Thence the heat from that sun in its essence is love, and the light from it in its essence is wisdom; these are inspired into them by the Lord from that sun, and they are inspired according to reception, and the reception is according to the love of becoming wise. After the times of instruction, those are sent forth thence, who have become intelligent, and they are called disciples of the Lord; they are sent forth thence first to the west, and, those who do not continue there, to the south, and some through the south to the east, and are introduced into societies, where their mansions will be. Once, when I was meditating about heaven and hell, I began to desire universal knowledge concerning the state of both, knowing that he who knows the universals can afterwards comprehend the particulars,

because these are in those, as the parts are in a whole. In this desire I looked towards that tract, in the northern quarter near to the east, where the places of instruction were, and, by a way then opened to me, I went thither, and entered into a college where the young men were; and I went there to the head teachers, who were instructing, and asked them whether they knew the universals concerning heaven and hell. And they replied "That they knew something, not much; but if we look towards the east to the Lord, we shall be illustrated and shall know." And they did so, and said, "The universals of hell are three, but these are diametrically opposite to the universals of heaven. The universals of hell are these three loves—the love of ruling from the love of self, the love of possessing the goods of others from the love of the world, and scortatory love. The universals of heaven opposite to those, are these three loves—the love of ruling from the love of use, the love of possessing the goods of the world from the love of doing uses by them, and truly conjugial love." When they had said these things, after wishing them peace, I departed and returned home. When I was at home, it was said to me from heaven, "Survey those three universals above and below, and afterwards we shall see them on your hand; it was said *on the hand*, because every thing that a man surveys with the understanding, appears to the angels as if inscribed on the hands. Wherefore it is said in the Revelation, that *they received a mark upon the forehead and upon the hand*, xiii. 16; xiv. 9; xx. 4.

After this I surveyed the first universal love of hell, which was the love of ruling from the love of self; and afterwards the universal love of heaven corresponding to it, which was the love of ruling from the love of uses; for it was not lawful for me to survey one love without the other, because the understanding does not perceive one love without the other, for they are opposite: wherefore, that both may be perceived, they must be set in opposition one against the other; for a fair and beautiful face appears more conspicuous when an ugly and deformed face is opposed to it. When I was canvassing the love of ruling from the love of self, it was given me to perceive that this love was supremely infernal, and thence with those who are in the deepest hell; and that the love of ruling from the love of uses was supremely heavenly, and thence with those who are in the highest heaven. That the love of ruling from the love of self is supremely infernal, is because to rule from the love of self is from *proprium*, and the *proprium* of man from nativity is evil itself, and evil itself is diametrically opposed to the Lord; wherefore, the more men advance into that evil, the more they deny God and the holy things of the church, and adore themselves and nature. Let those who are in that evil only explore it in themselves, and they will see. This love also is such, that, so far as the reins are given to it, which is the case when no impossibility stands in the way, it rushes on from one degree to another, and even to the highest; and there it is not terminated, but if a higher degree is not given, it grieves and groans. This love with statesmen ascends so far, that they wish to be kings, and emperors, and, if possible, to rule over all things of the world, and to be called kings of kings, and emperors of emperors; but the same love with clergymen ascends so far, that they wish to be gods, and, as far as possible, to rule over all things of heaven, and to be called gods. That these and those in heart do not acknowledge any God, will be seen in what follows. But, on the other hand, those who wish to rule from the love of uses, do not wish to rule from themselves, but from the Lord, since the love of uses is from the Lord, and is the Lord himself; these look upon dignities only as means for doing uses, which they place far above dignities, but the former place dignities far above uses.

When I was meditating on these things, it was said to me by an angel from the Lord, "Now, now, you will see and from sight be confirmed, what that infernal love is." And then on a sudden the earth opened itself on the left hand, and I saw a devil ascending from hell, who had on his head a square cap pressed down over the forehead even to the eyes; his face full of pimples as of a burning fever; his eyes fierce, his breast swelling into a rhombus; from his mouth he belched forth smoke like a furnace; his loins were completely ignited; instead of feet he had long ankles without flesh, and from his body there was exhaled a foul and stinking heat. On seeing him I was terrified, and cried to him, "Do not come here; tell whence you are." And he replied, with a hoarse voice, "I am from the lower regions, and there in a society with two hundred, which is the most supereminent of all societies. There we all are emperors of emperors, kings of kings, dukes of dukes, and princes of princes; no one there is barely an emperor, nor barely a king, a duke and a prince. We sit there upon thrones of thrones, and thence send forth mandates into all the world and beyond." Then I said to him, "Do you not see that you are insane from the fantasy of supereminence?" And he answered, "How can you talk so! because we absolutely seem to ourselves, and also are acknowledged by our companions, as such." On hearing this, I did not wish to say again, "You are insane," because he was insane from fantasy. And it was given me to know that that devil, when he lived in the world, was only the steward of a certain house; and that then he was so elated in spirit, that he despised all the human race in comparison with himself, and indulged the fantasy that he was of more dignity than a king, and even than an emperor; in consequence of which pride, he had denied God, and accounted all the holy things of the church as of no importance for him, but as something for the stupid common people. At length I asked him, "How long do you two hundred there, thus glory among yourselves?" He said, "For ever; but that those of us who torture others on account of denying supereminence, sink down; for it is lawful for us to glory, but not to do evil to any one. I asked again, "Do you know what is the condition of those who sink down?" He said, "They sink down into a certain prison, where they are called viler than the vile, or the most vile, and where they labor." Then I said to that devil, "Beware, then, lest you also sink down."

After this the earth again opened itself, but to the right; and I saw another devil rising up, upon whose head there was, as it were, a mitre encompassed with folds as of a snake, the head of which rose up from the top; his face was leprous from the forehead to the chin, and also both of his hands; his loins were naked and black as soot, through which appeared a dusky fire as of a fire hearth; and the ankles of his feet were like two vipers. The former devil, seeing this, cast himself upon his knees and adored him. I asked, "Why so?" He said, "He is the god of heaven and earth, and he is omnipotent." And then I asked him, "What do you say to this?" He answered, "What shall I say? I have all power over heaven and hell; the lot of all souls is in my hand." And I again asked, "How can he who is emperor of emperors, submit himself thus, and you receive adoration?" He answered, "He is still my slave. What is an emperor in the sight of God? In my hand is the thunderbolt of excommunication." And then I said to him, "How can you be so insane? You were in the world only a priest; and because you labored under the fantasy that you had the keys, and thence the power of binding and loosing, you worked up your spirit to this degree of madness, that you now believe that you are God himself." At this being indignant, he swore that he was, "and that the Lord had not any power in heaven, because He has transferred it all to us. We have only to give command, and heaven and hell obey with reverence. If we send any one to hell, the devils immediately receive him, and so do the angels him whom we send to heaven."

I asked further, "How many are there of you in your society?" He said, "Three hundred, and we all there are gods, but I am the god of gods." After this the earth opened under the feet of both, and they sunk down deep into their hells; and it was given me to see, that, under their hells, there were work-houses, into which those would fall who do harm to others; for to every one in hell is left his fantasy, and also his glorying in it, but it is not lawful to do evil to another. The reason that they are such there, is because man then is in his spirit, and the spirit, after it is separated from the body, comes into the full liberty of acting according to its affections and the thoughts thence. Afterwards it was given to look into their hells; and the hell where the emperors of emperors and kings of kings were, was full of all uncleanness, and they seemed like various wild beasts with fierce-looking eyes: and also in the other hell, where were the gods and the god of gods; and in this there appeared direful birds of night, which are called *ochim* and *ijim*, flying around them; the images of their fantasy thus appeared to me. Hence it was manifest what political self-love is, and what ecclesiastical self-love is; that this is, that they wish to be gods, but that, that they wish to be emperors; and that they thus wish, and also aspire after what they wish for, so far as the reins are given to those loves.

After these sad and horrible things had been seen by me, I looked around and saw two angels not far from me standing and talking together: one was clad in a woollen robe, shining from a bright purple, and a tunic of shining fine linen under it: the other in similar garments of scarlet, with a mitre in which some carbuncles were inserted on the right side. I went up to them and gave the salutation of peace; and with reverence I asked, "Why are you here below?" They answered, "We have let ourselves down from heaven to this place, at the command of the Lord, to speak with you concerning the happy lot of those who wish to rule from the love of uses. We are worshippers of the Lord; I am the prince of a society and the other the high-priest there.' And the prince said that he was the servant of his society, because he served it in doing uses; and the other said that he was the minister of the church there, because in serving them he ministered holy things for the uses of their souls; and that both are in perpetual joys from the eternal happiness which was in them from the Lord; and that every thing in that society was splendid and magnificent; splendid from gold and precious stones, and magnificent from palaces and paradises. "The reason is, because our love of ruling is not from the love of self, but from the love of uses; and because the love of uses is from the Lord, therefore all good uses in the heavens are splendid and refulgent; and because we all in our society are in this love, therefore the atmosphere there appears gilded, from the light there, which partakes of the flammeous of the sun, and the flammeous of the sun corresponds to that love." When they had said this, there appeared also to me a similar sphere around them, and an aromatic odor was perceived from it, which also I mentioned to them; and I requested that they would add something more to what had been said respecting the love of use. And they continued by saying, "The dignities in which we are, we sought for, indeed, but for no other end than that we might be able more fully to do uses and to extend them more widely. And also we are surrounded with honor, and we receive it, not for the sake of ourselves, but for the good of the society; for our brethren and companions, who are of the common people there, scarcely know but that the honors of our dignities are in us, and thence that the uses which we do are from us: but we feel otherwise; we feel that the honors of our dignities are out of us, and that they are like the garments with which we are clothed; but that the uses which we perform are from the love of them within us from the Lord, and this love receives its blessedness from communication with others by uses. And we know by ex perience, that as far as we do uses from the love of them, so far that love increases, and with the love wisdom, from which the communication is made; but that as far as we retain the uses in ourselves, and do not communicate them, so far the blessedness perishes; and then the use becomes like food retained in the stomach, which, not being diffused, does not nourish the body and its parts, but remains undigested, by which sickness of the stomach is occasioned. In a word, the whole heaven is a continent of uses from first to last: what is use but actual love of the neighbor? and what holds the heavens together but this love?" Having heard this, I asked, "How can any one know whether he does uses from the love of self, or from the love of uses? Every man, whether good or bad, does uses, and he does them from some love. Let it be supposed that in the world there is a society composed of mere devils, and a society composed of mere angels; and I am of opinion that the devils in their society, from the fire of self-love and from the splendor of their own glory, would do as many uses as the angels in theirs: who then can know from what love and from what origin the uses are?" To this the two angels replied, "The devils do uses for the sake of themselves, and for the sake of fame, that they may be promoted to honors or may gain riches; but the angels do uses, not for the sake of those things, but for the sake of uses from the love of them. Man cannot distinguish those uses, but the Lord distinguishes them. Every one who believes in the Lord, and shuns evils as sins, does uses from the Lord; but every one who does not believe in the Lord, nor shun evils as sins, does uses from himself and for the sake of himself. This is the distinction between the uses done by devils and the uses done by angels." The two angels, after saying these words, departed, and at a distance they seemed to be carried in a fiery chariot, like Elijah, and taken up into their heaven.

662. Another Relation. After a certain space of time, I entered a certain grove, and there walked about in meditation on those who are in the lust, and thence in the fantasy, of possessing the things which are of the world; and then, at some distance from me, I saw two angels talking together, and by turns looking at me; wherefore I went up nearer. As I approached, they spoke to me and said, "We perceive in ourselves that you are meditating on what we are speaking, or that we are speaking what you are meditating, which is from the reciprocal communication of affections." I asked, therefore, what they were talking about. They said, "About fantasy, about lust, and about intelligence; and now about those who delight themselves with the vision and imagination of possessing all the things in the world." And then I requested that they would express their mind respecting those three—respecting lust, fantasy and intelligence. And, commencing their discourse, they said, "That every one is inwardly in lust from nativity, but outwardly in intelligence from education; and that no one is in intelligence, still less in wisdom, inwardly, thus as to the spirit, but from the Lord; for every one is withheld from the lust of evil, and held in intelligence, according as he looks to the Lord, and is at the same time in conjunction with Him. Without this, man is nothing but lust; but still, in externals, or as to the body, he is in intelligence from education; for man lusts for honors and riches, or eminence and opulence, and these two things he does not obtain, unless he appears moral and spiritual, thus intelligent and wise; and to appear thus he learns from infancy, which is the reason that, as soon as he comes among men, or into company, he inverts his spirit, and removes it from lust, and acts and speaks from the principles of decency and honor, which he has learned from his infancy, and retains in the memory of his body; and he takes the greatest precaution that nothing may come forth from the madness of the lust in which his spirit is. Thence every man, who is not inwardly led by the Lord, is a dissembler, a sycophant

and a hypocrite, and thus an apparent man, and yet not a man; of whom it may be said, that his shell or body is wise, but his kernel or spirit is insane; and that his external is that of a man, and his internal that of a wild beast. Such with the hinder part of the head look upwards, and with the forehead look downwards; thus they walk as if oppressed with heaviness, the head hanging with the face towards the ground. When they put off the body, and become spirits, and are then manumitted, they become each the madness of his own lust; for those who are in the love of self, desire to rule over the universe, yea, to extend the limits of it, in order to enlarge their dominion; they nowhere see an end. Those who are in the love of the world, desire to possess every thing in it, and they are sorrowful and envious, if any treasures are concealed by any; wherefore, lest such should become merely lusts, and thus not men, it is given them, in the spiritual world, to think from the loss of fame, and thus of honor and gain, as also from the fear of the law and its penalty; and it is also given to apply the mind to some study or work, by which they are kept in externals, and thus in a state of intelligence, however delirious and insane they may be inwardly." After this I asked, whether all those who are in lust, are also in its fantasy. They replied, "That those are in the fantasy of their lust, who think inwardly in themselves, and indulge their imagination too much in talking with themselves; for they almost separate their spirit from its connection with the body, and from vision overwhelm the understanding, and foolishly entertain themselves as with the possession of the universe. Into this delirium the man is let after death, who has abstracted his spirit from the body, and has not been willing to recede from the delight of the delirium, by thinking any thing from religion concerning evils and falses, and least of all any thing concerning the unbridled love of self, that it is destructive of love to the Lord, and concerning the unbridled love of the world, that it is destructive of love towards the neighbor.

After this there came upon the two angels, and also upon me, a desire of seeing those who are in the visionary lust or fantasy of possessing all wealth, from the love of the world; and we perceived that that desire was inspired, in order that they might be known. Their abodes were under the ground of our feet, but above hell; wherefore we looked at each other and said, "Let us go." And an opening was seen, and a ladder there; by this we descended. And it was said that they must be approached from the east, lest we should enter into the cloud of their fantasy, and be beclouded as to the understanding, and then, at the same time, as to the sight. And behold, a house was seen, built of reeds, thus full of chinks, standing in the cloud which, like smoke, continually issued through the chinks of the walls on three sides We entered; and there were seen fifty here, and fifty there, sitting upon benches; and, being turned from the east and south, they were looking towards the west and north. Before each one there was a table, and upon the table purses filled full, and around the purses a plenty of gold coin. And we asked, "Are those the riches of all in the world?" They said, "Not of all in the world, but of all in the kingdom." The sound of their voice was like hissing, and they appeared with round faces, which glittered like the shell of a cockle, and the pupil of the eye, in a green plane, as it were sparkled, which was from the light of fantasy. We stood in the midst of them and said, "Do you believe that you possess all the riches in the kingdom?" And they replied, "We do." Then we asked, "Which of you?" They said, "Every one." And we asked "How, every one? there are many of you." They said, "Every one of us knows that all his is mine; it is not lawful for any one to think, still less to say, *Mine is not thine;* but it is lawful to think and to say, *Thine is mine*" The coin on the tables appeared as of pure gold, even in our sight; but when we let in light from the east, they were little grains of gold, which, by their common united fantasy, they had thus magnified. They said that every one that came in must bring with him some gold, which they cut into little pieces and these into little grains, and, by the unanimous power of fantasy, they enlarge them into coins of larger size. And then we said, "Were you not born men of reason? Whence have you this visionary infatuation?" They said, "We know that it is an imaginary vanity; but because it delights the interiors of our minds, we come in here and are delighted as with the possession of all things. But we stay here only a few hours, after which we go out, and then a sound mind returns to us; but still our visionary recreation comes upon us again, and causes us to come in and to go out by turns; thus we are by turns wise and insane. We know also that a hard lot awaits those who, by artifice, defraud others of their goods." We asked, "What lot?" They said, "They are swallowed up and thrust naked into some infernal prison, where they are obliged to labor for clothes and for food, and afterwards for some little pieces of money, which they collect, and in which they place the joy of their heart; but if they do evil to their companions, they must give a part of their money for a fine.

663. Third Relation. Once I was in the midst of angels and heard their discourse; their discourse was concerning intelligence and wisdom, that man does not feel or perceive otherwise than that they both are in himself, and thus that whatever he wills and thinks is from himself; when yet not a particle of them is from man, but only the faculty of receiving them. Among the many things which they mentioned, there was also this, that the tree of the knowledge of good and evil in the garden of Eden signified the faith, that intelligence and wisdom were from man; and that the tree of life signified that intelligence and wisdom were from God; and because Adam, by the persuasion of the serpent, ate of the former tree, thus believing that he should be, or should become, like God, therefore he was driven out of the garden and condemned. While the angels were in this discourse, there came two priests, together with a man who in the world had been an ambassador of a kingdom, and I related to them what I had heard from the angels concerning intelligence and wisdom; on hearing which, those three began to dispute about each of them, and also about prudence, whether they are from God or from man. The dispute was warm; the three believed alike, that they are from man, because sensation itself and thence perception confirm it; but the priests, who then were in theological zeal, insisted that nothing of intelligence and wisdom and thus nothing of prudence was from man, and this they confirmed from these things in the Word; *A man cannot take any thing, unless it be given to him from heaven*, John iii. 27; and from these, Jesus said to the disciples, *Without Me ye cannot do any thing*, xv. 5. But then, because it was perceived by the angels, that, although the priests spoke thus, still in heart they believed the same as the ambassador, therefore the angels said to them, "Put off your garments, and put on the garments of ministers of state, and believe that you are such." And they did so; and then they thought from their interior selves, and spoke from the arguments which they inwardly cherished, which were, that all intelligence and wisdom dwell in man, and that they are his; saying, "Who has ever yet felt, that they flowed in from God?" And they looked each other in the face, and confirmed each other. It is something peculiar in the spiritual, that a spirit thinks himself to be such, as the garment upon him is: the reason is, because the understanding clothes every one there. At that moment there appeared a tree near them, and it was said to them, "It is the tree of the knowledge of good and evil; beware that you do not eat from it." But still, being infatuated with their own intelligence, they burned with the desire of eating from it; and they said

one to another, "Why not? Is not the fruit good?" And they went up and ate. When the ambassador observed this, they went together and became cordial friends; and, holding each other by the hand, they went together the way of their own intelligence, which led towards hell; but still I saw them returning thence, because they were not yet prepared.

664. Fourth Relation. Once I looked into the spiritual world to the right, and observed some of THE ELECT conversing together; and I went up to them, and said, "I saw you at a distance, and around you a sphere of heavenly light, from which I knew that you were of those who in the Word are called *the elect;* wherefore I came up for the sake of hearing on what heavenly subject you are conversing." And they replied, "Why do you call us the elect?" I answered, "Because in the world, where I am in the body, they know no otherwise than that by the elect in the Word are meant those who are elected by God, before they were born or after they were born, and predestinated to heaven; and that to them alone faith is given, as the badge of election, and that the rest are reprobated and left to themselves, that they may go whatever way they please to hell; when yet I know, that no election is made before nativity nor after it, but that all are elected and predestinated, because all are called, to heaven; and that the Lord, after death, elects those who have lived well and believed aright, and elects them after they have been explored. That it is so, has been given me to know from much experience; and because I saw you encircled as to your heads with a sphere of heavenly light, I perceived that you were of the elect, who are being prepared for heaven." To this they replied, "You relate things not heard before. Who does not know, that there is not any man born, who is not called to heaven; and that out of them, after death, those are elected, who had believed in the Lord, and lived according to his commandments; and that to acknowledge any other election, is to accuse the Lord himself not only of inability to save, but also of injustice?'

665. After this a voice was heard out of heaven, from the angels who were immediately above us, saying, "Come up hither, and we will ask one of you, who is still in the natural world as to the body, what they know there about Conscience." And we went up; and after entering, some wise ones came to meet us, and they asked me, "What do they know in your world about conscience?" And I replied, "Let us go down, if you please, and call together, both from the laity and from the clergy, a number of those who are believed to be wise; and we will stand directly under you and question them, and thus you will hear with your ears what they will answer." And it was done so; and one of the elect took a trumpet, and sounded it towards the south, the north, the east and the west; and then, after an hour's time, there came so many that they almost filled up the space of a furlong. And the angels from above arranged them all into four companies, one of which consisted of politicians, another of scholars, the third of physicians, and the fourth of clergymen; to whom, being thus arranged, we said, "Pardon us, that you have been called together; the reason is, because the angels who are directly above us have an ardent desire to know what you thought, in the world in which you were before, concerning conscience, and thence what you still think concerning it, since you still retain the former ideas concerning such things; for it has been related to the angels, that the knowledge concerning conscience is among the knowledges that have been lost in the world." After this we began; and first we turned ourselves to the company which consisted of politicians, and requested that they would say from the heart, if they pleased, what they had thought, and thence what they still thought, concerning Conscience. To this they replied one after another; whose answers, being collected into one, were, "That they knew no other than that conscience was to know in

one's self thus to be conscious, what he has intended, thought, done and spoken." But we said to them, "We did not ask about the etymology of the word *conscience*, but about conscience." And they replied, "What else is conscience, but a pain arising from the fearful anticipation of the losses of honor or of wealth, and also of reputation on account of those two? But that pain is removed by feasts, and by cups of noble wine, and by talk about the sports of Venus and her boy." To this we said, "You are jesting; tell us, if you please, whether any of you has ever felt any anxiety from any other source." They replied, "Why from any other source? is not the whole world like a theatre, upon which every one acts his part, as comedians do upon theirs? We have eluded and circumvented a multitude, each one by his own lust; these by mockeries, these by flatteries, these by knaveries, these by pretended friendship, these by feigned sincerity, and these by other politic artifice and intrigue. We have thence no pain of mind, but on the contrary cheerfulness and gladness, which we silently and yet fully exhale from an expanded breast. We have heard, indeed, from some of our sodality, that anxiety and straitness, as it were, of the heart and breast, and thence, as it were, a contraction of the mind, have at times come upon them; but when they asked the apothecaries about these things, they were instructed that they were from a melancholy humor arising from things undigested in the stomach, or from a disordered state of the spleen; but with respect to some of these, we have heard of their being restored to their former cheerfulness by drugs." After we had heard this, we turned ourselves to the company which consisted of scholars, among whom there were also several skilled in natural philosophy; and, addressing them, we said, "You, who have studied the sciences, and are thence believed to be oracles of wisdom, tell, if you please, what conscience is." And they replied, "Why, what a proposition this is! We have heard, indeed, that there is, with some, sadness, sorrow and anxiety, infesting not only the gastric regions of the body, but also the habitations of the mind; for we believe that the two brains are those habitations, and, because these consist of connected fibres, that there is some acrid humor, which twitches, bites and gnaws the fibres there, and thus so compresses the sphere of the thoughts of the mind, that it cannot be diffused into any agreeable recreations from varieties; thence it comes to pass, that man attends only to one thing, by which the tensibility and elasticity of those fibres are destroyed, whence their obnixity and stiffness, from which arises an irregular motion of the animal spirits, which is called by physicians *ataxy*, and also a defect in their functions, which is called *lipothymy*. In a word, the mind then sits as if it were beset with hostile troops, nor can it turn itself hither and thither any more than a wheel fastened with nails, or than a ship fixed on quicksands. Such straitnesses of the mind, and thence of the breast, arise in those with whom the reigning love suffers loss; for if this is opposed, the fibres of the brain contract themselves, and that contraction prevents the mind from expatiating freely, and enjoying delights in various forms: these persons, when they are in this crisis, are seized, each according to his temperament, with various kinds of fantasy, madness and delirium, and some with brain-sick scruples in religious matters, which they call stings of conscience." After this we turned ourselves to the third company, which consisted of physicians, among whom there were also surgeons and apothecaries; and we said, "You perhaps know what conscience is, whether it is a troublesome pain which seizes both the head and the parenchyma of the heart, and thence the epigastric and hypogastric regions situated below, or something else." And they replied, "Conscience is nothing but such pain; we know the origins of it better than others, for they are contingent diseases, which infest the organic parts of the body, and also the organic parts of the head, consequently also the mind, for this sits in the organs of the brain, like a spider in the centre of the threads of her web, through which she runs back and forth in like manner. These diseases we call organic diseases, and those of them which at times return, chronic diseases. But such pain as is described to us by sick people, as the pain of conscience, is nothing else than a hypochondriac disease, which primarily deprives the spleen, and secondarily the pancreas and mesentery, of their proper functions; thence are derived diseases of the stomach, among which is cacochymy; for a compression is made about the orifice of the stomach, which is called *cardialgy;* from these are derived humors impregnated with black, yellow or green bile, by which the smallest blood-vessels, which are called capillary, are obstructed, whence cachexy, atrophy and symphesis, and likewise a spurious peripneumony from sluggish phlegm, and an ichorous and corrosive lymph in the whole mass of the blood. The same things also flow from the falling of purulent matter into the blood and its serum, from opened empyemas, abscesses, and imposthumes in the body; which blood, when it rises through the carotids into the head, frets, corrodes and consumes the medullaries, corticals and meninges of the brain, and thus excites pains, which are called the pains of conscience." On hearing these things, we said to them, "You speak in the language of Hippocrates and Galen. Those things are Greek to us; we do not understand them. We did not ask about these diseases, but about conscience, which is of the mind alone." And they said, "The diseases of the mind and the diseases of the head are the same; and these ascend from the body, for they cohere like two stories of one house, between which there are stairs for ascending and descending; wherefore we know hat the state of the mind depends inseparably on the state of the body. But those heavinesses or headaches, which we took you to mean by conscience, we have cured, some by plasters and cupping-glasses, some by infusions and emulsions, and some by condiments and by anodynes." When, therefore, we still heard the like things from them, we turned ourselves away from them, and towards the clergymen, and said, "You know what conscience is; tell, therefore, and instruct these who are present." And they replied, "What conscience is, we know and we do not know. We believed that it was the CONTRITION which precedes election, that is, the moment when man is gifted with faith, by which a new heart and a new spirit is made for him and he is regenerated; but we perceived that that contrition happened to few; to some only dread and thence anxiety on account of hell-fire, and scarcely to any on account of sins and thence the just anger of God; but those we confessors healed by the gospel, that Christ, by the passion of the cross, took away condemnation, and thus extinguished hell-fire, and opened heaven to those who are blessed with faith, on which is inscribed the imputation of the merit of the Son of God. Besides, there are conscientious persons of various religions, both true and fanatical, who make for themselves scruples in things of salvation, not only those which are essential, but also those which are formal, and even in those which are indifferent. Wherefore, as we said above, we know that conscience is; but what it is, or what true conscience, which must be altogether spiritual, is, we do not know."

666. All these things, which were said by the four companies, the angels who were above them heard; and they said one to another, "We perceive that no one in Christendom knows what conscience is; wherefore we will send down one from us who may instruct." And then immediately there stood in the midst of them an angel in white raiment, about whose head there appeared a lucid girdle in which were small stars; and, addressing the four companies, he said, "We heard in heaven that you brought forth your sentiments in order concerning CONSCIENCE, and that all supposed that it is a certain pain of mind, which infests the head with heavi-

ness and thence the body, or the body and thence the head; but conscience, viewed in itself, is not any pain, but it is a spiritual willingness to do according to the things which are of religion and faith. Thence it is, that those who enjoy conscience are in the tranquillity of peace and in internal blessedness, when they do according to conscience, and in a certain intranquillity when they do contrary to it. But the pain of mind which you believed to be conscience is not conscience, but it is temptation, which is a combat of the spirit and the flesh; and this, when it is spiritual, derives its source from conscience, but if it is only natural, it derives its origin from the diseases which the physicians just recounted. But what conscience is may be illustrated by examples. A priest, who has a spiritual willingness to teach truths for the end that his flock may be saved, he has conscience; but he who does so for any other reason as an end, has no conscience. A judge, who looks only at justice, and does it with judgment, he has conscience; but he who primarily looks at reward, friendship and favor, has no conscience. Again, every man who has the goods of another in his possession, without the other's knowledge, and thus can gain them without fear of the law, and of the loss of honor and fame, if still he returns them to the other, because they are not his own, he has conscience, for he does what is just for the sake of what is just. Suppose also there be one, who can come to an office, but he knows that another, who also seeks it, would be more useful to society; if he gives place to the other for the good of society, he has a good conscience; and so in other cases. All those who have conscience, speak from the heart whatever they speak, and do from the heart whatever they do; for they have not a divided mind, for they do and speak according to that which they understand and believe to be true and good. Hence it follows, that a more perfect conscience may be given with those who are in the truths of faith more than others, and who are in a clearer perception than others, than with those who are less illustrated, and in obscure perception. The spiritual life itself of man is in a true conscience, for there his faith is conjoined to charity; wherefore to do from conscience is to them to do from their spiritual life, and to do contrary to conscience, is to them to do contrary to their spiritual life. Besides, who does not know, from common discourse, what conscience is? As, when it is said of any one, 'He has a conscience,' is it not then also understood, he is a just man? And, on the other hand, when it is said of any one, 'He has no conscience,' is it not then also understood, he is an unjust man?" When the angel had said these things, he was suddenly taken up into his heaven; and the four companies came together into one, and after they had conversed together some time about the things which the angel had spoken, behold, they were again divided into four companies, but into other ones than before; into one, where were those who comprehended the words of the angel, and assented to them; into another, where were those who did not comprehend, but still favored; into a third, where were those who did not wish to comprehend, saying, "What have we to do with conscience?" into a fourth, where were those who mocked, saying, "What is conscience but a puff?" And I saw them withdrawing from each other, and then the two former companies going off to the right, and the two latter companies to the left, and these descending, but those ascending.

CHAPTER XII.

CONCERNING BAPTISM.

667. THAT WITHOUT KNOWLEDGE CONCERNING THE SPIRITUAL SENSE OF THE WORD, NO ONE CAN KNOW WHAT THE TWO SACRAMENTS, BAPTISM AND THE HOLY SUPPER, INVOLVE AND EFFECT.

That there is a spiritual sense in all and every part of the Word, and that this sense has been hitherto unknown, and that it is at this day opened for the sake of the New Church which is to be instituted by the Lord, was shown in the chapter concerning the SACRED SCRIPTURE. What that sense is, may be seen not only there, but also in the chapter concerning the DECALOGUE, which was also explained according to that sense. Unless that sense had been opened, who would think any thing else concerning the two sacraments, baptism and the holy supper, than according to the natural sense, which is the sense of the letter? And thence any one might say or mutter to himself, "What is baptism but the pouring of water upon the head of an infant? and what is this to salvation?" And also, "What is the holy supper but the taking of bread and wine? and what is this to salvation? And besides, where is there any thing holy in them, except from this, that they have been received and enjoined from the ecclesiastical order as holy and divine, and that in themselves they are nothing more than ceremonies, concerning which the churches say, that when the Word of God comes to those elements, they become sacraments?" I appeal to the laity and also to the clergy, whether they have perceived in spirit and heart any thing else concerning those sacraments; and that they have worshipped them as divine for various causes and reasons; when yet those two sacraments, viewed in the spiritual sense, are the most holy things of worship: that they are such, will be evident from what follows, where their uses will be explained. But because the uses of these sacraments can never come into the mind of any one, unless the spiritual sense disclose and unfold them, it follows that, without that sense, no one can know but that they are ceremonies, which are holy because they were instituted by command.

668. That baptism was commanded, is manifestly evident from the baptism of John in the Jordan, to which all Judea and Jerusalem came, Matt. iii. 5, 6; Mark i. 4, 5; and also that the Lord himself our Savior was baptized by John, Matt. iii. 13 to 17; and moreover that He commanded the disciples, that they should baptize all nations, xxviii. 19. Who does not see, if he is willing to see, that there is something divine in that institution, which has hitherto been concealed, because the spiritual sense of the Word was not before revealed? And this is now revealed, because the Christian church, such as it is in itself, is now first commencing; the former church was Christian only in name, but not in essence and reality.

669. The two sacraments, baptism and the holy supper, are, in the Christian church, like two jewels on the sceptre of a king; but if their uses are not known, they are like two figures of ebony on a staff. Those two sacraments in the Christian church may also be compared with two rubies or carbuncles in the robe of an emperor; but if their uses be unknown, they are like two carnelians or crystals in any gown.

Without the uses of those two sacraments, revealed by means of the spiritual sense, mere conjectures would be spread concerning them, such as are with those who divine from the stars, yea, such as were with those formerly who presaged from the flying of birds or from the entrails of beasts. The uses of those two sacraments may be compared to a temple, which, from its antiquity, has sunk down into the earth, and lies covered with ruins even to its roof, over which the young and the old walk and ride in coaches and on horses, not knowing that any such temple is under their feet and concealed, in which are altars of gold, walls within of silver, and decorations of precious stone; which cannot be dug up and brought forth into the light, except by means of the spiritual sense, which is at this day disclosed for the New Church, on account of its use in the worship of the Lord. Those sacraments also may be compared to a double temple, one of which is below and the other above; and in the lower of which the gospel concerning the new advent of the Lord is preached, and also concerning regeneration and thence salvation by Him. From this temple, around the altar, there is an ascent into the upper temple, in which the holy supper is celebrated, and thence a passage into heaven, where the Lord receives them. They may be compared to the tabernacle, in which, behind the entrance, appeared the table upon which the bread of faces was arranged in order; and also the golden altar for incense, and in the midst the candlestick with the lamps lighted, by which all those things come into view; and at length, for those who suffer themselves to be illuminated, the veil is opened to the holy of holies, where, in the place of the ark, in which the decalogue had been, the Word is laid up, over which was the propitiatory with cherubs of gold. These are representations of those two sacraments with their uses.

670. II. THAT BY THE WASHING WHICH IS CALLED BAPTISM, IS MEANT SPIRITUAL WASHING, WHICH IS PURIFICATION FROM EVILS AND FALSES, AND THUS REGENERATION.

That washings were enjoined upon the sons of Israel, is known from the statutes made by Moses, as that Aaron should wash himself before he put on the garments of the ministry, Lev. xvi. 4, 24; and before he came to the altar to minister, Exod. xxx. 18 to 21; xl. 30, 31; in like manner the Levites, Num. viii. 6, 7; and also others who became unclean by sins; and that they are said to be sanctified by washings, Ex. xix. 14; xl. 12; Lev. viii. 6: wherefore, that they might wash themselves a brazen sea and many lavers were placed near the temple, 1 Kings vii. 23 to 39: yea, that they washed vessels and utensils, as tables, benches, beds, dishes and cups, Lev. xi. 32; xiv. 8, 9; xv. 5 to 12; xvii. 15, 16; Mark vii. 4. But washings and many such like things were commanded and enjoined upon the sons of Israel, because the church instituted with them was a representative church, and this was such, that it prefigured the Christian church which was about to come. Wherefore, when the Lord came into the world, He abrogated the representatives, which all were external, and instituted a church, of which all things should be internal; thus the Lord put away the figures, and revealed the effigies themselves; as one removes a veil or opens a door, and causes the things within not only to be seen, but also to be approached. Of all those things the Lord retained only two, which should contain, in one complex, all things of the internal church; which two things are baptism instead of washings, and the holy supper instead of the lamb, which was sacrificed every day, and fully at the feast of the passover.

671. That the washings above mentioned figured and shadowed forth, that is, represented, spiritual washings, which are purifications from evils and falses, is manifestly evident from these: *When the Lord shall have washed away the filth of the daughters of Zion, and the blood, by the spirit of judgment, and by the spirit of cleansing*, Isaiah iv 4

Though thou wash thyself with nitre, and apply to thyself much soap, still thy iniquity will retain spots, Jer. ii. 22; Job ix. 30, 31. *Wash me from my iniquity, and I shall be whiter than snow*, Psalm li. 2, 7. *Wash thy heart from wickedness, O Jerusalem, that thou mayest be saved*, Jer. iv. 14. *Wash yourselves, make yourselves clean; remove the wickedness of your works from my eyes; cease to do evil*, Isaiah i. 16. That the washing of the spirit of man was meant by the washing of his body, and that the internal things of the church were represented by external things, such as were in the Israelitish church, manifestly appears from these words of the Lord: *The Pharisees and scribes, seeing that his disciples ate bread with unwashed hands, found fault; (for the Pharisees and all the Jews, unless they wash their hands up to the wrist, eat not; beside many other things which they have received to hold, as the washing of cups, and earthen and brazen vessels, and beds;) to whom and to the multitude the Lord said, Hear Me, all of you, and understand; there is nothing out of a man, which, entering into him, can make him unclean; but the things which go out of him make him unclean*, Mark vii. 1, 2, 3, 4, 14, 15; Matt. xv. 2, 11, 17, 18, 19, 20. And in other places; as, *Wo to you, scribes and Pharisees, because you make the outside of the cup and of the platter clean, but the insides are full of rapine and excess. Blind Pharisee, first make the inside of the cup and of the platter clean, that the outside may be made clean also*, Matt. xxiii. 25, 26. From these it is evident, that by the washing which is called baptism, spiritual washing is meant, which is purification from evils and falses.

672. What man of sound reason cannot see, that the washing of the face, of the hands and feet, and of all the limbs, yea, of the whole body in a bath, effects nothing else than that the dirt is washed off, so that, in the sight of men, in the human form they may appear clean? And who cannot understand that no washing enters into the spirit of man and makes this equally clean? For every villain, robber or murderer can wash himself even to neatness: is the disposition of the villain, the robber and the murderer thus wiped away? Does not the internal flow into the external, and work the effects of its will and understanding; but not the external into the internal? for this is contrary to nature, because contrary to order; but that is according to nature, because according to order.

673. Hence it follows, that washings, and baptisms also, unless the internal of man be purified from evils and falses, effect nothing more than the platters and plates cleansed by the Jews; and as it also follows there, than *the sepulchres, which outwardly appear beautiful, but within are full of the bones of the dead, and of all uncleanness*, Matt. xxiii. 25 to 28; which is still more manifest from this, that the hells are full of satans from men as well baptized as not baptized. But what good baptism effects, will be seen in what follows. Wherefore, without its uses and fruits, it conduces no more to salvation, than the triple cap on the pope's head, and the sign of the cross on his shoes, to his pontifical supereminence; nor more than the purple robe about a cardinal to his dignity, or the cloak about a bishop to the true discharge of his ministry; nor more than the throne, crown, sceptre and robe of a king, to his regal power; nor more than the cap of silk upon the head of a laurelled doctor to his intelligence; nor more than the standards before troops of horsemen to their bravery in war. Yea, it may further be said, that it does not purify man any more than the washing of a sheep and a lamb before shearing; for the natural man, separate from the spiritual man, is merely an animal; yea, as was before shown, he is more of a wild beast than the wild beast of the forest. Wherefore, if you are washed with the water of rain, with the water of dew, with the waters of the most excellent fountains, or, as the prophets say, if you are cleansed with nitre, hyssop or soap every day, still

you are not purified from iniquities, except by means of regeneration, concerning which we have treated in the chapters concerning Repentance and concerning Reformation and Regeneration.

674. III. That Baptism was instituted in the Room of Circumcision; because by the Circumcision of the Foreskin, was represented the Circumcision of the Heart, in order that an Internal Church might succeed the External Church, which in all and every Thing figured forth the Internal Church.

It is known in the Christian world, that there is an internal and an external man, and that the external is the same with the natural man, and the internal the same with the spiritual man, because his spirit is in it; and, because the church consists of men, that there is given an internal church and an external church; and, if the successions of churches from ancient times to the present, be traced, it will be seen that the former churches were external churches, that is, that their worship consisted in external things, which represented the internal things of the Christian church, which was founded by the Lord when he was in the world, and now is first being built up by Him. The primary thing which distinguished the Israelitish church from the rest in the Asiatic world, and afterwards from the Christian, was circumcision; and because, as has been said, all the things of the Israelitish church, which were external, figured forth all the things of the Christian church, which are internal, therefore the primary sign of that church was inwardly similar to the sign of the Christian church; for circumcision signified the rejection of the lusts of the flesh, and thus purification from evils; baptism also signifies the like. Whence it is manifest, that baptism was commanded in the room of circumcision, in order both that the Christian church might be distinguished from the Jewish church, and that the internal church might thus be better known; and this is known from the uses of baptism, which will be treated of in what follows.

675. That circumcision was instituted for a sign that the men of the Israelitish church were of the posterity of Abraham, Isaac and Jacob, is evident from these words: *God said to Abraham, This is the covenant with Me, which ye shall observe between Me and you, and thy seed after thee; circumcise every male among you, and ye shall circumcise the flesh of your foreskin, that it may be for a sign of the covenant between Me and you*, Gen. xvii. 10, 11; which covenant, or its sign, was afterwards confirmed by Moses, Lev. xii. 1, 2, 3. And because that church was distinguished from the rest by that sign, therefore, before the sons of Israel passed over the Jordan, it was commanded that they should be circumcised again, Josh. v. The reason was, because the land of Canaan represented the church, and the river Jordan introduction into it. And moreover, that they might remember that sign in the land of Canaan itself, this was commanded: *When ye shall have come into the land, and shall have planted every tree for food, ye shall circumcise the foreskin of its fruit; three years it shall be to you uncircumcised, it shall not be eaten*, Lev. xix. 23. That circumcision represented, and thence signified, the rejection of the lusts of the flesh, and thus purification from evils, the same as baptism, is evident from the passages in the Word where it is said, that they should circumcise the heart, as in these: Moses said, *Circumcise the foreskin of your heart; harden not your neck*, Deut. x. 16. *Jehovah God will circumcise thy heart, and the heart of thy seed, that thou mayest love Jehovah thy God from thy whole heart, and from thy whole soul, that thou mayest live*, xxx. 6. And in Jeremiah: *Circumcise yourselves to Jehovah, that He may remove the foreskins of your heart, ye men of Judah and inhabitants of Jerusalem, lest my anger go forth like fire, on account of the wickedness of your works*, iv. 4. And in Paul: *In Jesus Christ neither circumcision availeth any thing*,

nor uncircumcision, but faith working by charity; and a new creature, Gal. v. 6; vi. 15. From these now it is manifest, that baptism was instituted in the place of circumcision, because, by the circumcision of the flesh, the circumcision of the heart was represented, which also signifies purification from evils; for evils of every kind arise from the flesh, and the foreskin signifies its filthy loves. Since circumcision and the washing of baptism signify the same thing, therefore it is said in Jeremiah, *Circumcise yourselves to Jehovah, that He may remove the foreskins of your heart*, iv. 4; and a little after, *O Jerusalem, wash thy heart from wickedness, that thou mayest be saved*, verse 14. What the circumcision and washing of the heart are, the Lord teaches in Matt. xv. 18, 19.

676. There were many among the sons of Israel, and there are at this day many among the Jews, who believe themselves to have been elected in preference to all others, because they have been circumcised; and among Christians, because they have been baptized; when yet both circumcision and baptism were given only for a sign and for a memorial, that they should be purified from evils, and thus become elect. What is an external without an internal with man, but like a temple without worship, which is not for any use, unless it may serve for a stable? And further, what is an external without an internal, but like a field of mere straw and stalks without any corn? or like a vineyard of mere branches and leaves without any grapes? or like a fig-tree without its fruit, which the Lord cursed? Matt. xxi. 19; or like the lamps in the hands of the foolish virgins without oil? Matt. xxv. 3; yea, what, but like a habitation in a mausoleum, where dead bodies are under the feet, bones about the walls, and nocturnal spectres flying under the roof? or like a coach drawn by leopards, upon which a wolf sits as coachman, and an ideot rides in it? For the external man is not the man, but only the figure of a man; for the internal, which is, to be wise from God, makes the man. So it is with one who is circumcised and baptized, unless he circumcise or wash his heart.

677. IV. That the first Use of Baptism is Introduction into the Christian Church, and at the same Time Insertion among Christians in the Spiritual World.

That baptism is an introduction into the Christian church, is evident from many things, as from these: (1.) That baptism was instituted in the place of circumcision, and that as circumcision was a sign that they were of the Israelitish church, so baptism is a sign that they are of the Christian church, as was shown in the preceding article; and a sign does nothing else than that they may be known, like swaddling clothes of diverse colors put on the infants of two mothers, that they may be distinguished from each other, and may not be changed. (2.) That it is only a sign of introduction into the church, is manifestly evident from the baptizing of infants, who are partakers of no reason at all, and are not as yet more fit for receiving any thing of faith, than young shoots in any tree. (3.) That not only infants are baptized, but also all foreign proselytes who are converted to the Christian religion, both small and great, and this before they have been instructed, merely from the confession that they wish to embrace Christianity, into which they are inaugurated by baptism; which also the apostles did, according to the words of the Lord, that *they should make disciples of all nations, and baptize them*, Matt. xxviii. 19. (4.) That *John baptized all that came to him from Judea and Jerusalem, in the Jordan*, iii. 6; Mark i. 9. The reason why he baptized in the Jordan was, because the entrance into the land of Canaan was through that river; and by the land of Canaan was signified the church, because it was there; and thence, by the Jordan, introduction into it. That that land signified the church, and the Jordan introduction into it, may be seen in the Apocalypse Revealed, n. 285. But this is done on earth; but in the heavens, infants are introduced by baptism into the

Christian heaven, and angels are there assigned to them by the Lord, to take care of them. Wherefore, as soon as infants are baptized, angels are appointed over them, by whom they are kept in a state of receiving faith in the Lord; and as they grow up, and come to the exercise of their own right and their own reason, the guardian angels leave them, and they associate to themselves such spirits as make one with their life and faith. Whence it is manifest, that baptism is an insertion among Christians also in the spiritual world.

678. That not only infants, but also all, are inserted by baptism among Christians in the spiritual world, is because people and nations in that world are distinguished according to their religions; Christians are in the middle, Mahometans around them, idolaters of various kinds behind them, and Jews at the sides. Moreover, all of the same religion are arranged into societies in heaven according to the affections of love to God and towards the neighbor; in hell into congregations according to the affections opposite to those two loves, thus according to the lusts of evil. In the spiritual world, by which we mean both heaven and hell, all things are most distinctly arranged, in the whole and in every part, or in general and in every particular. On the distinct arrangement there, the preservation of the whole universe depends, and this distinction cannot be effected, unless every one, after he is born, be known by some sign, indicating to what religious assembly he belongs; for without the Christian sign, which is baptism, some Mahometan spirit, or some one of the idolaters, might apply himself to Christian infants newly born, and also to children, and infuse into them an inclination for his religion, and thus draw away their mind and alienate them from Christianity, which would be to distort and destroy spiritual order.

679. Every one, who traces effects to causes, may know that the consistence of all things depends on order; and that there are manifold orders, general and particular; and that there is one, which is the most universal of all, and on which the general and particular ones depend in a continued series; and that the most universal one enters into all, as the essence itself into forms; and that thus, and thus only, they make one: this oneness is what causes the preservation of the whole, which otherwise would fall to pieces, and not only relapse into the first chaos, but into nothing. How would it be with man, unless all and every thing in his body were most distinctly arranged, and the whole of them depended on one heart and lungs? What else but a confused something? Could the stomach then exercise its functions, the liver and pancreas theirs, the mesentery and mesocolon theirs, the kidneys and intestines theirs? It is from the order in them and among them, that all and each of them appear before man as one. Without distinct order in the mind or spirit of man, and unless the whole of it depended on the will and understanding, what could it be, but a confused and indigested something? Without that order, would a man be able to think and will any more than his picture on a tablet, or his statue in the house? What would man be without the most orderly influx from heaven, and the reception of it? And what would this influx be, without one most universal, on which the government of the whole and of all its parts depends, thus unless it were from God, and unless in Him and from Him all things existed, lived and moved? These things may be illustrated to the natural man by innumerable things, as by these: What would an empire or kingdom be without order, but a gang of robbers, many of whom being gathered together would slay thousands, and at length a few, these many? What would a state be without order? yea, what would a house be without order? And what would a kingdom, state, or house be, unless some one in each should act as supreme?

680. Besides, what is order without distinction? and what is distinction without indications? and what are indications without signs, by which the qualities are known? For without a knowl

edge of the qualities, order is not known as order. The signs or signatures in empires and in kingdoms are titles of dignities and rights of administration annexed to them; thence are subordinations, by means of which all are arranged together as into one: in this manner a king exercises, according to order, his regal power distributed among many, whence a kingdom becomes a kingdom. The case is similar in very many other things, as in armies: what valor would they have, unless they were distinguished in an orderly manner into phalanxes, these into cohorts, and these into companies; and subordinate leaders were appointed over each, and one over all, who is supreme? And what would those arrangements be, without the signs, which are called standards, to show in what station every one is to be? By such means all act in battles as one, and without them they would rush against the enemy, like troops of dogs, with open mouths, howling and empty fury; and then all without strength would be cut to pieces by the enemy arranged in the proper order of battle; for what can the divided do against the united? By these things is illustrated this first use of baptism, which is a sign in the spiritual world, that he is of Christians, where every one is inserted among societies and congregations there, according to the quality of the Christianity in him or out of him.

681. V. The second Use of Baptism is that the Christian may know and acknowledge the Lord Jesus Christ, the Redeemer and Savior, and follow Him.

This other use of baptism, which is, that one may know the Lord, the Redeemer and Savior Jesus Christ, inseparably follows the first, which is, that there may be introduction into the Christian church, and insertion among Christians in the spiritual world; and what is that first use without this other, but only a name? It is like a subject who attaches himself to a king, and yet disobeys his laws or those of his country, and attaches himself to a foreign king, and serves him; or like a servant who engages himself to some master and receives a livery as his badge, and runs away and in his livery serves another; or like a standard-bearer who goes off with the standard, and cuts it in pieces, and throws the pieces of it either into the air, or under the soldiers' feet, that they may be trampled upon In a word, the name that one is a Christian, that is, that he is of Christ, and not to acknowledge Him and follow Him, that is, to live according to his commandments, is as empty as a shadow, as smoke, and as a blackened picture; for the Lord says, *Why call ye Me Lord, and do not the things that I say?* Luke vi. 46, and the following. *Many will say to Me in that day, Lord, Lord; but then I shall confess to them, I know you not,* Matt. vii. 22, 23.

682. By the name of the Lord Jesus Christ, nothing else is meant in the Word, than an acknowledgment of Him, and a life according to his commandments. The reason why His name signifies those things, you may see in the explanation of the second commandment of the decalogue, *Thou shalt not take the name of God in vain* Nothing else is meant by the name of the Lord in these passages: *Jesus said, Ye will be hated by all nations on account of my name,* Matt. x. 22; xxiv. 9, 10. *Where two or three are gathered together in my name, there am I in the midst of them,* xviii. 20. *As many as received Him, to them He gave power that they might be sons of God, believing in his name,* John i. 12. *Many believed in his name,* ii. 23. *He that believeth not is already judged, because he hath not believed in the name of the only begotten Son of God,* iii. 17, 18. *Believing, they shall have life in his name,* xx. 31. *On account of my name thou hast labored and hast not fainted,* Rev. ii. 3; and elsewhere Who cannot see, that by the name of the Lord, in those passages, is not meant the name only, but the acknowledgment of Him, that He is the Redeemer and Savior, and at the same time obedience, and at length faith in Him? for at baptism an infant receives the

sign of the cross upon the forehead and breast, which is a sign of inauguration into the acknowledgment and worship of the Lord. By name also is meant the quality of any person; the reason is, because, in the spiritual world, every one is named according to his quality; wherefore by the name that one is a Christian, is meant his quality, that he has faith in Christ, and charity towards the neighbor, from Christ. This is meant by name in the Revelation. The Son of Man said, *I have a few names in Sardis, that have not defiled their garments, and they shall walk with Me in white, because they are worthy*, Rev. iii. 4. By walking with the Son of Man in white, is signified to follow the Lord, and to live according to the truths of his Word. The like is meant by name in John: *Jesus said, The sheep hear my voice, and I call my own sheep by name, and lead them out. I go before them, and the sheep follow Me, because they know my voice; but a stranger they do not follow, because they know not the voice of strangers*, x. 3, 4, 5. *By name* is by the quality, in that they are Christians; and to follow Him is to hear his voice, that is, to obey his commands. This name all receive at baptism, for it is in the sign.

683. What is a name without the thing, but a something vain, and a sound, such as rebounds from the trees of a forest, or from arched roofs, which is called an echo? or like the almost inanimate sound from persons dreaming? or like the sound of the wind of the sea, or of a machine, in which there is nothing of use? Yea, what is the name of being a king, a duke, a consul, a bishop, an abbot, a monk, without the office which adheres to the name, but vanity? Thus what is the name of being a Christian, when yet the man lives like a barbarian, and contrary to the precepts of Christ, but like looking at the sign of Satan instead of the sign of Christ, whose name, nevertheless, was interwoven in golden threads at baptism? What are those, who, after they have received the signature of Christ, laugh at his worship, scoff at his name, and profess Him, not as the Son of God, but as the son of Joseph, but rebels and regicides? And what are their speeches, but blasphemies against the Holy Spirit, which cannot be forgiven in this world nor in the future? These, like dogs with open mouths, bite the Word, and tear it to pieces with their teeth. With these, who are opposed to Christ and his worship, *all the tables are full of the vomit of eating*, Isaiah xxviii. 8; xlviii. 26; when yet the Lord Jesus Christ is the Son of the Most High God, Luke i. 32, 35; the Only-begotten, John i. 18; iii. 16; the true God and eternal Life, 1 John v. 20, 21; in whom all the fulness of the Godhead dwelleth bodily, Coloss. ii. 9; and that He is not the son of Joseph, Matt. i. 25; besides in thousands of other places.

684. VI. That the third Use of Baptism, which is the final Use, is, that Man may be regenerated.

This use is the very use for the sake of which baptism was instituted, thus the final use; the reason is, because he who is truly a Christian, knows and acknowledges the Lord the Redeemer Jesus Christ, who, because He is the Redeemer, is also the Regenerator. That redemption and regeneration make one, may be seen in the chapter concerning Reformation and Regeneration, art. iii. And also a Christian possesses the Word, in which the means of regeneration are fully described; and the means there are faith in the Lord, and charity towards the neighbor. This is the same with what is said concerning the Lord, that *He baptizeth with the Holy Spirit and fire*, Matt. iii. 11; Mark i. 9 to 11; Luke iii. 16; John i. 33. By the Holy Spirit is meant the divine truth of faith, and by fire the divine good of love or charity, both proceeding from the Lord. That the divine truth of faith is meant by the Holy Spirit, may be seen in the chapter concerning the Holy Spirit: and that the divine good of love is meant by fire, may be seen in the Apocalypse Revealed, n. 468, 395; and by means of these two, all regeneration is effected by the Lord. The reason that the Lord himself was baptized by John, (Matt. iii. 13 to 17; Mark i. 9; Luke iii. 21, 22,) was not only that He might institute baptism for the future, and go before as an example, but also because He glorified his Human, and made it Divine, as He regenerates man, and makes him spiritual.

685. From what has been said before and now, it may be seen, that the three uses of baptism cohere as one; in like manner as the first cause, the mediate cause, which is the efficient, and the ultimate cause, which is the effect, and the end itself for the sake of which the former were. For the first use is, that one may be named a Christian; the second, following from this, is, that he may know and acknowledge the Lord the Redeemer, Regenerator and Savior; and the third is, that he may be regenerated by Him, and when this is done, he is redeemed and saved. Since these three uses follow in order, and join themselves together in the last, and thence, in the idea of the angels, cohere as one, therefore, when baptism is performed, read in the Word, and named, the angels who are present do not understand baptism, but regeneration; wherefore by these words of the Lord, *Whosoever believeth and is baptized, shall be saved, but whosoever believeth not shall be condemned*, Mark xvi. 16, this is understood by the angels in heaven, that he who acknowledges the Lord and is regenerated is saved. Thence also it is, that baptism is called by Christian churches on earth THE LAVER OF REGENERATION. Let the Christian, therefore, know that whosoever doth not believe in the Lord cannot be regenerated, although he has been baptized; and that baptizing, without faith in the Lord, does nothing at all, may be seen above in this chapter, art. ii. n. 673. That baptism involves purification from evils, and thus regeneration, may be very well known to every Christian; for when the priest, as an infant is baptized, makes with his finger a sign of the cross on the forehead and on the breast, as a memorial of the Lord, he afterwards turns himself to the sponsors, and asks whether he renounces the devil and all his works, and whether he receives faith; to which, instead of the infant, it is answered by the sponsors, "Yes." Renunciation of the devil, that is, of the evils which are from hell, and faith in the Lord, perfect regeneration.

686. It is said in the Word, that the Lord God our Redeemer baptizes with the Holy Spirit and fire: that by this is meant, that the Lord regenerates man by the divine truth of faith, and by the divine good of love or charity, may be seen above in this article, n. 684. Those who have been regenerated by the Holy Spirit, that is, by the divine truth of faith, are in the heavens distinguished from those who have been regenerated by fire, that is, by the divine good of love. Those who have been regenerated by the divine truth of faith, go in heaven in white garments of fine linen, and are called spiritual angels; but those who have been regenerated by the divine good of love, go in purple garments, and are called celestial angels. Those who go clothed in white garments, are meant by these: *They follow the Lamb, clothed in fine linen white and clean*, Rev. xix. 14. *They shall walk with Me in white*, iii. 4; and also vii. 14. *The angels at the Lord's sepulchre, seen in white and shining garments*, (Matt. xxviii. 3; Luke xxiv. 4,) were of this kind; for fine linen signifies *the righteousness of the saints*, Rev. xix. 8, where this is openly said. That garments, in the Word, signify truths, and white and fine linen garments, divine truths, may be seen in the APOC. REVEALED, n. 379, where that is shown. That those who have also been regenerated by the divine good of love are in purple garments, is because purple is the color of love, which it derives from the fire of the sun and its redness, by which is signified love: see the APOCALYPSE REVEALED, n. 468, 725. Since garments signify truths, therefore he who was found among the guests not clothed with wedding garments, was cast out and cast into outer darkness, Matt. xxii. 11, 12, 13.

687. Besides, baptism, like regeneration, is represented, both in heaven and

in the world, by many things. In heaven, as has now been said, by white and purple garments, and besides by the marriage of the church with the Lord; and also by the new heaven and new earth, and the New Jerusalem descending thence, concerning which, He that sat upon the throne said, *Behold I make all things new,* Rev. xxi. 1 to 4, 5; and by the river of living water proceeding from the throne of God and of the Lamb, xxii. 1, 2; and also by the five prudent virgins, who had lamps and oil, and went in with the bridegroom to the wedding, Matt. xxv. 1, 2, 10. One baptized, that is, regenerated, is meant by *creature*, Mark xvi. 15; Rom. viii. 19, 20, 21; and by *a new creature*, 2 Cor. v. 17; Gal. vi. 15: for *creature* is said from *to be created*, by which also is signified to be regenerated: see the Apocalypse Revealed, n. 254. In the world, regeneration is represented by various things, as by the blossomings of all things of the earth in the time of spring, and by their successive growth even to fructifications; in like manner, by the growth of every tree, shrub and flower, from the first month of heat even to the last of it. It is represented also by the progressive ripening of all fruits from the first stamen to full maturity: it is represented then by morning and evening showers and by dews, at the coming of which the flowers open themselves, and at the darkness of night they contract themselves; again, by the fragrances from gardens and fields, and also by the rainbow in the cloud, Gen. ix. 14 to 17; as also by the splendid colors of the morning before sunrise; and, in general, by the continual renovation of all things in bodies, by means of the chyle, and by means of the animal spirit, and thence the blood, the purification of which from useless things, and renovation, and as it were regeneration, is perpetual. If attention be given to the vilest things in the earth, an image of regeneration is presented in the wonderful transformation of silkworms and many other worms into nymphs and butterflies, and in that of others, which in time are furnished with wings. To which we may add things still more trivial; it is represented by the desire of certain birds of immersing themselves in waters for the sake of washing and cleansing themselves, after which they return, like the nightingales, to their songs. In a word, the whole world, from the firsts to the lasts of it, is full of representations and types of regeneration.

688. VII. That by Means of the Baptism of John, a Way was prepared, that Jehovah the Lord might be able to come down into the World and perform Redemption.

It is read in Malachi, *Behold I send my angel, who will prepare the way before Me; and suddenly the Lord whom ye seek will come to his temple, even the Angel of the covenant, whom ye desire. Who will be able to bear the day of his coming, and who will stand when He shall appear?* iii. 1, 2. And again; *Behold I will send to you Elijah the prophet, before the great and terrible day of Jehovah cometh, lest I come and smite the earth with a curse*, iv. 5, 6. And Zachariah the father, prophesying concerning his son John: *Thou child shalt be called the prophet of the Most High; thou shalt go before the face of the Lord, to prepare his ways*, Luke i. 76. And the Lord himself, concerning John: *This is he of whom it is written, Behold I send my angel before my face, who will prepare thy way before Thee*, Luke vii. 27. From these it is evident, that John was that prophet who was sent to prepare the way for Jehovah God, that He might come down into the world, and perform redemption; and that he prepared that way by baptism, and then the annunciation of the coming of the Lord; and that without that preparation, all there would have been smitten with a curse, and would have perished

689. The reason why a way was prepared by the baptism of John was, because, by means of that, as was shown above, they were introduced into the future church of the Lord, and in heaven were inserted among those there, who expected and desired the

Messiah, and thus were guarded by angels, so that devils from hell might not break forth and destroy them. Wherefore it is said in Malachi, *Who will be able to bear the day of his coming?* and, *Lest Jehovah come and smite the earth with a curse*, iii. 2, and iv. 6. In like manner in Isaiah; *Behold the day of Jehovah cometh, cruel, and of indignation, and of wrath, and of anger. I will shake the heaven, and the earth shall tremble out of its place, in the day of the wrath of his anger*, xiii. 6, 9, 13; xxii. 5, 12. Likewise in Jeremiah, that day is called *a day of wasting, of vengeance, and of destruction*, iv. 9; vii. 32; xlvi. 10, 21; xlvii. 4; xlix. 8, 26: in Ezekiel, *a day of anger, of cloud and thick darkness*, xiii. 5; xxx. 2, 3, 9; xxxiv. 11, 12; xxxviii. 14, 16, 18, 19: and also in Amos, v. 13, 18, 20; viii. 3, 9, 13: in Joel, *the great and terrible day of Jehovah, and who will be able to bear it?* ii. 1, 2, 11; iii. 2, 4: and in Zephaniah; *In that day there shall be the voice of a cry; the great day of Jehovah is near, this day a day of wrath, a day of trouble and distress, a day of wasting and devastation. In the day of Jehovah's wrath the whole earth shall be devoured, and He will make a consummation with all the inhabitants of the earth*, i. 7 to 18: besides in other places. From which it is manifest, that unless a way had been prepared for Jehovah coming down into the world, by baptism, the effect of which in heaven was, that the hells were closed, and the Jews preserved from total destruction, [they must have perished]. Jehovah also said to Moses, *In one moment, if I should come up into the midst of thee, I should consume the people*, Exod. xxxiii. 5. That it is so, is clearly manifest from the words of John to the multitudes coming out to be baptized by him: *O generation of vipers, who hath warned you to flee from the wrath to come?* Matt. iii. 7; Luke iii. 7. That John also taught Christ and his coming, when he baptized, may be seen Luke iii. 16; John i. 25, 26, 31, 32, 33; iii. 26. Hence it is manifest how John prepared the way.

690. As to what concerns the baptism of John, it represented the cleansing of the external man; but the baptism which is at this day with Christians, represents the cleansing of the internal man, which is regeneration: wherefore it is read, that John baptized with water, but that the Lord baptizes with the Holy Spirit and fire; and therefore the baptism of John is called *the baptism of repentance*, Matt. iii. 2; Mark i. 4, and the following; Luke iii. 3, 16; John i. 25, 26, 33; Acts i. 22; x. 37; xviii. 25. The Jews who were baptized were merely external men, and the external man cannot become internal without faith in Christ. That those who were baptized with the baptism of John became internal men, when they received faith in Christ, and then were baptized in the name of Jesus, may be seen in the Acts of the Apostles, xix. 3 to 6.

691. Moses said to Jehovah, *Show me thy glory; to whom Jehovah said, Thou canst not see my face, because no man shall see Me and live. And He said, Behold there is a place where thou shalt stand upon a rock, and I will put thee in a hole of the rock, and I will cover thee with my hand, until I shall have passed by; and when I shall have removed my hand, thou shalt see my back parts, but my face shall not be seen*, Exod. xxxiii. 18 to 23. The reason why man cannot see God and live, is, because God is Love itself, and Love itself or the Divine Love, in the spiritual world, appears before the angels as a sun, distant from them as the sun of our world is distant from men. Wherefore, if God, who is in the midst of that sun, should approach near to the angels, they would perish, as men would if the sun of the world should approach to them, for it is equally burning; for which reason there are perpetual temperatives, which modify and moderate the heat of that love, lest it should flow in, as it is in itself, into heaven, for then the angels would be consumed. And therefore, when the Lord exhibits Himself more immediately present in heaven, the wicked who are under heaven begin to lament, to be

tortured, and to become inanimate; wherefore they flee away into caves and clefts of the mountains, crying, *Fall upon us, and hide us from the face of Him that sitteth upon the throne*, Rev. vi. 16; Isaiah ii. 19, 21. The Lord himself does not descend, but an angel with a sphere of love from the Lord around him. I have several times seen the wicked terrified by that descent, as if they saw death itself before their eyes; some who precipitated themselves deeper and deeper into hell, and some driven to madness. Thence it was that the sons of Israel prepared themselves for three days, before the descent of Jehovah the Lord upon mount Sinai; and that the mount was hedged around, lest any one should approach and die, Exod. xix. It was similar with the holiness of Jehovah the Lord in the decalogue, then promulgated and written upon two tables with the finger of God, and afterwards laid up in the ark, over which, in the tabernacle, the mercy-seat was placed, and upon this the cherubs, that no one might touch that holiness immediately with the hand or eye; to which neither could Aaron come but once in a year, after he had expiated himself by sacrifices and incense. Thence it was that the Ekronites and Bethshemites to several thousands died, only because they saw the ark with their eyes, 1 Sam. v. 11, 12; vi. 19: and also Uzzah, because he touched it, 2 Sam. vi. 6, 7. From these few things it has been illustrated, with what a curse and destruction the Jews would have been smitten, unless they had been prepared, by means of the baptism of John, for receiving the Messiah, who was Jehovah God in the human form, and unless He had assumed the Human, and thus revealed Himself; and that they were prepared by this, that in heaven they were enrolled and numbered among those who, in heart, expected and desired the Messiah; whence angels were then sent and made their guardians.

---

692. To the above I shall add these RELATIONS. FIRST. When I was going home from the schoo of wisdom, I saw in the way an angel in a violet-colored garment. He joined himself to my side, and said, "I see that you have come from the school of wisdom, and that you were delighted with the things heard there; and because I perceive that you are not fully in this world, because you are at the same time in the natural world, and are therefore ignorant of our Olympiac gymnasiums, where the ancient sages meet together, and learn of the new comers from your world what changes of state and successions wisdom has undergone and still undergoes; if you please, I will conduct you to a place where several of the ancient sages and their sons, that is, their disciples, dwell." And he conducted me to the confines between the north and east; and when, from an elevated place, I looked forward thither, behold, there appeared a city, and on one side of it two hills, and the one next to the city lower than the other; and he said to me, "That city is called Athenæum, the lower hill Parnassium, and the higher Heliconæum. They are so called, because the ancient wise men in Greece, as Pythagoras, Socrates, Aristippus, Xenophon, with their disciples and scholars, reside in the city and around it." And I inquired about Plato and Aristotle. He said that they and their followers dwelt in another region, because they taught rational things, which are of the understanding; but the former, moral things, which are of life. He said that students were frequently sent away from the city Athenæum to the learned of the Christians, that they might tell what they think at this day concerning God, concerning the creation of the universe, concerning the immortality of the soul, concerning the state of man relative to the state of beasts, and concerning other subjects which are of interior wisdom. And he said that the herald had announced a meeting to-day, an indication that the emissaries had found new comers from the earth, from whom they have heard curious things. And we saw many going out of the city and from the vicinity, some having laurels upon their heads, some

holding palms in their hands, some with books under their arms, and some with pens under the hair of the left temple. We joined them, and went up together with them; and behold, upon the hill an octagonal palace, which they called the Palladium; and we entered, and behold there eight hexangular apartments, in each of which there was a library, and also a table, at which the laurelled ones sat down; and in the Palladium itself were seen seats carved out of stone, upon which the rest seated themselves. And then a door was opened to the left, through which two new comers from the earth were introduced, and after they had been saluted, one of the laurelled ones asked them, "WHAT NEWS FROM THE EARTH?" And they said, "The news is, that they have found in the woods men like beasts, or beasts like men; but that from the face and body they know that they were born men, and in the second or third year of their age lost or left in the woods. They said that they could not express any thing of thought, nor learn to articulate sound into any word; that they did not know the food convenient for them, as beasts do, but that they put wild fruits both clean and unclean into their mouth; beside many other things; from which some of the learned with us conjectured, and some concluded, many things concerning the state of men relative to the state of beasts." On hearing this, some of the ancient sages asked, "What do they conjecture and conclude from them?" And the two new comers answered, "Many things, which, however, may be referred to these: 1. That man, from his nature, and also from nativity, is more stupid, and thence more vile, than any beast, and that he becomes so, if he is not instructed. 2. That he can be instructed, because he has learned to sound articulately, and thence to speak; and that by this means he began to utter thoughts, and this successively more and more, until he could express the laws of society, many of which, however, are impressed upon beasts from nativity. 3. That beasts have rationality as well as men. 4 Wherefore, if beasts could speak they would reason on any subject as ingeniously as men; a proof of which is, that they think from reason and prudence as well as men. 5. That understanding is only a modification of light from the sun, heat coöperating, by means of ether, so that it is only the activity of interior nature, and that this can be exalted so that it may appear as wisdom 6. That it is therefore vain to believe that man lives after death, any more than a beast; except that he may, perhaps, for several days after his decease, from an exhalation of the life of the body, appear as a thick cloud under the form of a ghost, before he is dissipated into nature; scarcely otherwise than as a twig, taken out of the ashes, appears in the likeness of its own form. 7. Consequently that religion, which teaches a life after death, was invented, that the simple may be held inwardly in bondage by its laws, as they are held outwardly by the laws of the state.' To this they added, that the merely ingenious reason thus, but not the intelligent. And they asked, "How do the intelligent?" They said that they had not heard, but that they thought so.

On hearing these things, all who sat at the tables said, "Oh! what times now upon the earth! Alas! what changes has wisdom undergone! Is it not turned into an infatuated ingenuity? The sun is set, and it is under the earth diametrically opposite to its meridian. From the case of those who were left and found in the woods, who may not know that man uninstructed is such? Is he not as he is instructed? Is he not born in ignorance more than the beasts? Must he not learn to walk and to speak? If he did not learn to walk, would he raise himself up on his feet? If he did not learn to speak, would he utter any thing of thought? Is not every man just as he is instructed, insane from falses, and wise from truths? And is not he who is insane from falses, in the full persuasion that he is wiser than one who is wise from truths? Are there not idiots and insane persons, who are no more men than those found in the woods? Are not those who are deprived of memory like these? From all these cases we have concluded, that man, without instruction, is not a man nor a beast, but a form which can receive into itself that which makes a man; and thus that he is not born a man, but that he becomes a man; and that man is born such a form, that he may be an organ receptive of life from God, in order that he may be a subject into which God can put every good, and, by union with himself, make him happy for ever. We perceive, from your discourse, that wisdom at this day is so far extinguished or infatuated, that they know nothing at all concerning the state of the life of men relative to the state of the life of beasts; thence it is, that they do not know the state of the life of man after death. But those who could know this, but are not willing to know it, and thence deny it, as many of you Christians do, we can liken to those found in the woods; not that they became so stupid from want of instruction, but that they have made themselves so stupid by means of the fallacies of the senses, which are the darkness of truths."

But then a certain one, standing in the middle of the Palladium, holding in his hand a palm, said, "Unfold, I pray, this mystery, how man, created a form of God, could be changed into the form of the devil. I know that the angels of heaven are forms of God, and that the angels of hell are forms of the devil; and the two are opposite to each other, these insanities, and those wisdoms. Tell, therefore, how a man, created a form of God, could pass from day into such night as to be able to deny God and eternal life." To this the teachers answered in order, first the Pythagoreans, then the Socratics, and afterwards the rest. But among them there was a certain Platonist: he spoke last, and his opinion prevailed, which was, "That the men of the Saturnian or the golden age knew and acknowledged, that they were forms receptive of life from God, and that, therefore, wisdom was inscribed upon their souls and hearts; and thence, that from the light of truth they saw truth, and by means of truths perceived good from the delight of the love of it. But as the human race, in the following ages, receded from the acknowledgment that all the truth of wisdom, and thence the good of love with them, continually flowed in from God, they ceased to be habitations of God; and then also ceased communion with God, and consociation with angels; for the interiors of their mind were bent out of their direction, which had been elevated upwards to God by God, into a direction more and more oblique outwards into the world, and thus to God by God through the world; and at length turned about into the opposite direction, which is downwards to themselves. And because God cannot be looked at by man interiorly inverted, and thus averted, men separated themselves from God and became forms of hell, and thus of the devil. Hence it follows, that in the first ages they acknowledged, in heart and soul, that they had all the good of love, and thence the truth of wisdom, from God, and also that these were of God in them, and thus that they were mere receptacles of life from God, and thence called images of God, sons of God, and born of God; but that in succeeding ages they did not acknowledge that in heart and soul, but with a certain persuasive faith, and then with an historical faith, and, at last, only with the mouth; and to acknowledge such a thing only with the mouth, is not to acknowledge it, yea, it is to deny it in heart. Hence it may be seen, what sort of wisdom there is at this day on the earth with Christians; although from a written revelation they could be inspired by God, yet they do not know the distinction between man and beast; and thence many believe, that if man lives after death, beasts will live also; or, because a beast does not live after death, that man will not. Has not our spiritual light, which enlightens the sight of the mind, with them become thick darkness? And has not their natural light, which enlightens only the sight of the body, become to them brightness?"

After this, they all turned themselves towards the two new comers, and thanked them for coming and telling the news, and requested that they would relate to their brethren the things which they had heard. And the new comers replied, that they would confirm their brethren in this truth, that, as far as they attribute all the good of charity and truth of faith to the Lord, and not to themselves, so far they are men, and so far they become angels of heaven.

693. Second Relation. After some weeks, I heard a voice from heaven, saying, "Behold, again a meeting in Parnassium; come hither, we will show the way." I went up, and when I was near, I saw a certain one upon Heliconæum with a trumpet, with which he announced and proclaimed the meeting. And I saw them going up from the city Athenæum and its confines, as before; and in the midst of them, three new comers from the world. Those three were from the Christians; one was a priest, another a politician, and the third a philosopher; these they entertained in the way with various conversation, especially concerning the ancient wise men, whom they named. They asked if they should see them. They said that they should, and, if they wished, they might speak to them, since they were affable. They asked about Demosthenes, Diogenes, and Epicurus. They said, "Demosthenes is not here, but with Plato. Diogenes, with his scholars, resides under Heliconæum, because he reputes the things of the world as of no account, and revolves in his mind only heavenly things. Epicurus dwells to the west, on the boundary; nor does he come in to us, because we distinguish between good affections and evil affections, and say that good affections are in agreement with wisdom, and evil affections are contrary to wisdom." When they had ascended the hill Parnassium, some guards there brought water from the fountain there, in crystal cups, and said it was water from the fountain, concerning which the ancients fabled that it was broken through by the hoof of the horse Pegasus, and afterwards consecrated to the nine virgins But by the winged horse Pegasus the ancients understood the understanding of truth, by which is wisdom; by the hoofs of his feet they understood experiments, by which is natural intelligence; and by the nine virgins, they understood knowledges and sciences of every kind. These things are at this day called fables, but they were correspondences, from which the primeval people spoke. The companions said to the three new comers, "Do not wonder; the guards have been instructed to speak thus; and we understand, by drinking water from a fountain, to be instructed concerning truths, and, by means of truths, concerning goods, and thus to be wise." After this they entered the Palladium, and with them the three new comers from the world—the priest, the politician and the philosopher. And then the laurelled ones who sat at the tables asked, "What news from the earth?" And they answered, "This is new, that a certain man affirms that he speaks with angels, and has his sight open into the spiritual world equally as he has it open into the natural world; and he brings thence many new things, among which are these: That man lives a man after death, just as he did before in the world; that he sees, hears, speaks, as before in the world; that he is clothed and adorned as before in the world; that he hungers and thirsts, eats and drinks, as before in the world; that he enjoys conjugial delight as before in the world; that he sleeps and awakes as before in the world; that there are there lands and lakes, mountains and hills, plains and valleys, fountains and rivers, paradises and groves; and also that there are there palaces, and houses, and cities, and villages, as in the natural world; as also that there are writings and books, and that there are employments and tradings, and also precious stones, gold and silver; in a word, that there are all things and every thing that there is in the earth; and those in the heavens are infinitely more perfect, with the difference only, that all the things that are in the spiritual world are from a

spiritual origin, and thence spiritual, because they are from the sun there, which is pure love; and that all the things that are in the natural world are from a natural origin, and thence natural and material, because they are from the sun there, which is pure fire; in a word, that man after death is perfectly man, yea, more perfectly man than before in the world; for before, in the world, he was in a material body, but in this he is in a spiritual body."

After these things were said, the ancient wise men asked, "What do they think about those things upon earth?" The three said, "We know that they are true, because we are here, and have surveyed and explored them all; wherefore we will tell how they talked and reasoned about them upon the earth." And then the PRIEST said, "Those who are of our order, at first, when they heard those things, called them visions, then fictions, afterwards that he may have seen spectres, and at last they hesitated and said, 'Believe if you will; we have hitherto taught that man is not to be in a body after death, before the day of the last judgment.'" And they asked, "Are there not some intelligent ones among them, who can demonstrate and convince them of the truth, that man lives a man after death?" The priest said, "There are those who demonstrate, but they do not convince. Those who demonstrate, say that it is contrary to sound reason to believe that man does not live a man before the day of the last judgment, and that in the mean time he is a soul without a body. What is the soul, and where is it, in the mean time? Is it breath, or something of wind flying about in the air, or an entity hid in the middle of the earth? Where is its location? (*Pu*) Are the souls of Adam and Eve, and of all after them now for six thousand years, or sixty centuries, flying about in the universe, or kept shut up in the centre of the earth, and in expectation of the last judgment? What is more anxious and miserable than such expectation? May not their condition be compared with the condition of those who are bound with chains and fetters in prisons? If such were the condition of men after death, would it not be better to be born an ass than a man? Is it not also contrary to reason to believe, that the soul can be reinvested with its body? Is not the body eaten up by worms, mice and fishes? And can a bony skeleton, burnt up by the sun or reduced to dust, be put into that new body? How will those cadaverous and stinking things be collected and united to the souls? But to such things, when they hear them, they do not answer any thing from reason, but stick to their faith, saying, 'We keep reason under obedience to faith.' To the collecting of all from the sepulchres at the day of the last judgment they say, 'This is the work of omnipotence.' And when they name omnipotence and faith, reason is banished; and I can say, that then sound reason is as nothing, and to some as a spectre; yea, they can say to sound reason, 'You are insane.'" Having heard these things, the wise men of Greece said, "Are not those paradoxes, as contradictions, dissipated by themselves? And yet, at this day, they cannot be dissipated in the world by sound reason. What more paradoxical can be believed, than that wh[illegible]h is told about the last judgment? that then the universe is to be des[illegible]yed, and that then the stars of heaven are to fall down upon the earth, which is smaller than the stars; and that then the bodies of men, whether carcasses or mummies eaten up by men, or floating atoms, are to be reunited to their souls? When we were in the world, we believed in the immortality of the souls of men, from the inductions which reason afforded us, and also we designated places for the blessed, which we called the Elysian fields; and we believed them to be human effigies or shapes, but delicate because spiritual." After these things were said, they turned themselves about to another new comer, who in the world had been a POLITICIAN. He confessed that he had not believed in a life after death, and that he had thought concerning the new things which he heard about it, that they were fictions and inventions. Meditating upon it, I said, "How can souls be bodies? Does not all of the man lie dead in the sepulchre? Is not the eye there? how can he see? Is not the ear there? how can he hear? Whence has he a mouth with which he may speak? If any thing of man lived after death, would it be any thing else than like a spectre? How can a spectre eat and drink, and how can it enjoy conjugial delight? Whence has it clothes, house, food, &c.? And spectres, which are aërial effigies, appear as if they were, and yet they are not. These and the like things I thought in the world, concerning the life of man after death; but now, since I have seen all, and touched all with my hands, I am convinced, by the senses themselves, that I am a man, as in the world, so that I know no other than that I live just as I have lived, with the difference that I have now sounder reason. I have several times been ashamed of my former thoughts." The PHILOSOPHER related similar things respecting himself; but yet with this difference, that he reckoned those new things which he had heard concerning the life after death, among the opinions and hypotheses which he had collected from the ancients and the moderns. On hearing these things, the sages were astonished; and those who were of the Socratic school said, that they perceived, by the news from the earth, that the interiors of human minds have been successively closed up, and that now in the world the faith of the false shines like the truth, and an infatuated ingenuity like wisdom, and that the light of wisdom, since our times, has got down from the interiors of the brain into the mouth, under the nose, where it appears to the eyes as the splendor of the lip, and the speech of the mouth thence, as wisdom. Having heard these things, one of the tyros there said, "And how stupid are the minds of the inhabitants of the earth at this day! O that the disciples of Heraclitus and Democritus, who laugh at every thing, and who weep at every thing, were present, and we should hear great laughter and great weeping." After this meeting was over, they gave to the three new comers from the earth the badges of their authority, which were little copperplates, upon which some hieroglyphics were engraved, with which they departed.

694. THIRD RELATION. Some time after, I looked towards the city Athenæum, concerning which something was said in the foregoing Relation, and I heard thence an unusual cry; there was in it something of laughter, in this something of indignation, and in this something of sadness; but still that cry was not thence discordant, but harmonious, because one was not together with another, but one within another. In the spiritual world, a variety and mixture of affections are distinctly perceived in sound. I asked at a distance, "What is the matter?" And they said that a messenger had come from the place where the new comers from the Christian world first appear, saying, "That he heard from three there, that in the world whence they came, they had believed with the rest there, that the blessed and happy after death would have entire rest from all labors; and because administrations, offices and employments are labors, that they would have rest from them. And because those three have now been brought hither by our emissary, and are standing at the door and waiting, a cry was made; and after consultation they determined that they should not be introduced into the Palladium in Parnassium, as the former had been, but into a large auditory there, that they might tell their news from the Christian world; and some deputies have been sent to introduce them in due form." Because I was in the spirit, and to spirits distances are according to the states of their affections, and because I then had the affection of seeing and hearing them, I seemed to myself present there, and saw them introduced, and heard them speak. The older or wiser in the auditory sat at the sides, and the rest in the middle; and before these there was an elevated place; hither the three new comers, with the messenger, were conducted, in

a formal manner, by the younger ones, through the middle of the auditory. And after silence was made, they were saluted by a certain elder there, and asked, "WHAT NEWS FROM THE EARTH?" And they said, "There are many new things, but tell, I pray, concerning what subject." And the elder answered, "WHAT NEWS FROM THE EARTH CONCERNING OUR WORLD AND CONCERNING HEAVEN?" And they answered, "When we had just come into this world, we heard that there are there and in heaven administrations, offices, employments, tradings, studies, in all the departments of learning, and wonderful pieces of workmanship; and yet we believed that after emigration or translation from the natural world into this spiritual world, we should come into an eternal rest from labors; and what are employments but labors?" To this the elder said, "By eternal rest from labors, did you understand eternal idleness, in which you would be continually sitting and lying down, drawing in delights with your breast, and drinking in joys with your mouth?" To this the three new comers, smiling pleasantly, said, that they supposed some such thing. And then it was answered them, "What have joys and delights and the happiness thence, in common with idleness? From idleness the mind collapses and is not expanded, or the man is deadened and not enlivened. Suppose some one sitting in perfect idleness, with his hands dangling, his eyes cast down or withdrawn, and suppose that he is surrounded with an atmosphere of gladness; would not a lethargy seize both his head and body, and would not the vital expansion of his face fall away; and at length, his fibres being relaxed, would he not totter and totter till he should fall to the earth? What keeps the system of the whole body in expansion and tension, but the intention of the mind? And whence the intention of the mind, but from occupations and employments, when they are engaged in from delight? Wherefore I will tell you some news from heaven, that there are there administrations, offices, courts of justice, superior and inferior, mechanical arts and trades." The three new comers when they heard that there were courts of justice, superior and inferior, in heaven, said, "Why those? Are not all in heaven inspired and led by God, and thence do they not know what is just and right? What need, then, of judges?" And the elder answered, "In this world we are instructed, and we learn what is good and true, and also what is just and equitable, in like manner as in the natural world; and these things we learn, not immediately from God, but mediately through others; and every angel, as well as every man, thinks truth and does good as from himself, and this, according to the state of the angel, is mixed and not pure; and also among the angels there are the simple and the wise, and the wise will judge, while the simple, from simplicity and from ignorance, doubt concerning what is just, or depart from it. But because you are as yet fresh in this world, if it be your good pleasure, follow me into our city, and we will show you every thing." And they went out of the auditory, and some of the elders also accompanied them; and first they went into a large library, which was distinguished into smaller collections according to the sciences. The three new comers, on seeing so many books, were astonished, and said, "Are there books, too, in this world? Whence are the parchment and paper, whence the pens and ink?" To this the elders replied, "We perceive that you believed in the former world, that this world was empty, because spiritual; and that you believed this, is, because you cherished an idea of the spiritual abstracted from the material; and what is abstracted from the material appeared to you as nothing, thus as empty, when yet there is here a plenty of all things. All things here are SUBSTANTIAL, and not material, and material things derive their origin from substantial things. We who are here are spiritual men, because substantial and not material, thence it is, that all the things that are in the natural world are here in their perfection, even books and writings, and many more things." The three new comers, when they heard things SUBSTANTIAL named, thought that it was so, both because they saw written books, and because they heard it said that matter was originally from substance. That they might be still more confirmed concerning this, they were brought to the abodes of the scribes, who were transcribing copies of what had been written by the wise men of the city; and they inspected the writing, and wondered that it should be so neat and handsome. After this they were conducted to the museums, gymnasiums and colleges, and where their schools were, some of which they called the schools of the Heliconides, some the schools of the Parnassides, some the schools of the Atheneides, and some the schools of the virgins of the fountain. They said that these were so called, because virgins signify the affections of sciences, and according to the affection of sciences, every one has intelligence; the schools, so called, were spiritual exercises and trials of skill. Afterwards they were led around in the city to the rulers, administrators, and their subordinate officers, and by these they were led to the wonderful works which are done by the workmen in a spiritual manner. After these things were seen, the elder spoke with them again concerning the eternal rest from labors, into which the blessed and happy come after death; and he said, "Eternal rest is not idleness, since from idleness there is a languor, torpor, stupor, and sleepiness of the mind, and thence of the whole body, and these are death and not life, and still less eternal life in which the angels of heaven are. Wherefore eternal rest is a rest that disperses those things, and causes man to live; and this is nothing else than such as elevates the mind; it is therefore some study and work by which the mind is excited, enlivened and delighted; and this is done according to the use from which, in which, and for which one works. Thence it is that the whole heaven is viewed by the Lord as containing uses, and every angel is an angel according to use; the delight of use carries him along, as a favorable stream does a ship, and causes him to be in eternal peace and in the rest of peace; thus is understood eternal rest from labors. That an angel is alive according to the exertion of the mind from use, appears manifest from this, that every one has conjugial love with its vigor, potency and delights, according to the performance of the genuine use in which he is." After those three new comers were confirmed, that eternal rest was not idleness, but the delight of some work which is for use, there came some virgins with things embroidered and spun, the works of their own hands, and presented these to them. And the virgins, when those novitiate spirits were departing, sung an ode, in which they expressed, with angelic melody, the affection of works of use with its gratifications.

695. FOURTH RELATION. Most people at this day, who believe in a life after death, also believe that in heaven their thoughts will be only devotions, and their words only prayers, and these and those, together with the expressions of the face and the actions of the body, only glorifications of God, and thus their houses only so many houses of worship, or temples, and thus that all will be priests of God. But I can assert, that there the holy things of the church do not occupy the minds and houses, more than in the world, when God is duly worshipped, although more purely and interiorly; but that there the various things which are of civil prudence, and the various things which are of rational learning, are in their excellence. One day I was raised up into heaven, and brought into a society where were the sages who, in ancient times, excelled in learning, by study and meditation upon such things as were of reason, and at the same time of use, and who are now in heaven, because they believed in God, and now in the Lord, and love the neighbor as themselves. Afterwards I was introduced into an assembly of them, and there was asked whence I was. I told them that with the body I was in

the natural world, but with the spirit in your spiritual world. On hearing this, those angels were delighted; and they asked, "What do they, in the world, where you are with the body, know and understand about INFLUX?" And then, after I had recollected what I had learned about it from the discourses and writings of the celebrated, I answered, "That they did not yet know of any influx from the spiritual world into the natural world, but concerning an influx from nature into the things derived from nature, as concerning the influx of heat and light from the sun into animate bodies, as also into trees and shrubs, whence these and those are enlivened; and also of cold into the same, whence they become dead; and, moreover, concerning an influx of light into the eyes, whence is seeing, concerning an influx of sound into the ears, whence is hearing, and concerning an influx of smell into the nostrils, whence is smelling, &c. Beside these, the learned of this age reason differently concerning the influx of the soul into the body, and of this into the soul; and respecting this they are divided into three parties, whether the influx be of the soul into the body, which they call occasional, from the occasion of things falling into the senses of the body; or whether there be an influx of the body into the soul, which they call physical, because objects fall into the senses, and from them into the soul; or whether there be a simultaneous and instantaneous influx into the body, and at the same time into the soul, which they term preëstablished harmony; but yet each thinks concerning his influx, that it is within nature. Some believe that the soul is a particle or drop of ether; some that it is a globule or spark of heat and light; some that it is a certain something concealing itself in the brain. But this and that, which to them is the soul, they call, indeed, spiritual; but by spiritual, they understand the purer natural, for they do not know any thing about the spiritual world and about the influx of this into the natural world; wherefore they remain within the sphere of nature, and in it ascend and descend, and raise themselves into it, like eagles in the air. And those who stop in nature, are like the inhabitants of some island in the sea, who do not know that there is any other country beyond them; and they are like the fishes in a river, which do not know that there is air above their waters. Wherefore, when it is mentioned that there is a world distinct from theirs, where angels and spirits dwell, and that all the influx into men, and also an interior influx into trees, is thence, they stand amazed, as if they heard visionary stories about spectres, or idle tales from astrologers. Beside the philosophers, our people in the world, where I am with the body, do not think and speak of any other influx than of the influx of wine into cups, of the influx of food and drink into the stomach, and of taste into the tongue, and also perhaps of the influx of air into the lungs, &c.; but if they hear any thing about an influx of the spiritual world into the natural, they say, 'Let it flow in, if it does; what advantage is it, and of what use is it to know it?' and they go away, and afterwards, when they speak about what they have heard concerning that influx, they play with it, as some play with cockles between their fingers."

Afterwards I spoke with those angels about the wonderful things which exist from the influx of the spiritual world into the natural, as concerning worms when they become butterflies, and also concerning bees and drones, and the wonderful things respecting silk-worms, and also respecting spiders; and that the inhabitants of the earth ascribe those things to the light and heat of the sun, and thus to nature; and, what I have often wondered at, by means of these things they confirm themselves in favor of nature, and by confirmations in favor of nature, they bring upon their minds sleep and death, and become atheists. After this I related wonderful things respecting vegetables, that they all succeed in just order from a seed even to new seeds; just as if the earth knew how to suit and accommodate its elements to the prolific principle of the seed, and from this to draw forth the germ and expand it into a stalk; and from this to put forth branches and clothe them with leaves, and afterwards adorn them with flowers; and from the interiors of these to initiate and produce fruits, and by them, for the sake of re-production, seeds as an offspring. But these things, because they have become familiar, customary and common, by being continually observed, and constantly recurring, they do not look upon as wonderful, but as mere effects of nature; and this they think solely because they do not know that there is any spiritual world, and that this operates from within, and actuates all and each of the things that exist and are formed in the world of nature, and upon its earth, and operates as the human mind does into the senses and motions of the body; and that all the particular things of nature are as it were coats, sheaths and coverings, which encompass spiritual things, and proximately produce effects corresponding to the end of God the Creator.

696. Fifth Relation. Once I prayed to the Lord that it might be given me to speak with the disciples of Aristotle, and at the same time with the disciples of Descartes, and with the disciples of Leibnitz; in order that I might learn the opinions of their mind concerning the intercourse of the soul and the body. After I had prayed, nine men were present, three Aristotelians, three Cartesians, and three Leibnitzians, and stood around me; the adorers of Aristotle on the left side, the followers of Descartes on the right, and the favorers of Leibnitz behind. At a distance from me, and at intervals from each other, were seen, as it were, three laurelled men; and from the perception which flowed in from heaven, I knew that they were the leaders or founders themselves. Behind Leibnitz there stood one holding in his hand the skirt of his garment, and it was said that it was Wolfius. Those nine men, when they looked at each other, at first saluted and spoke to each other with a friendly voice; but presently after, there arose from below a spirit with a torch in his right hand, and he vibrated it before their faces; thence they became enemies, three against three, and looked at each other with a stern aspect; for the lust of disputing and wrangling seized them. And then the Aristotelians, who also were schoolmen, rose up, saying, "Who does not see that objects flow in through the senses into the soul, as one enters through the door into a room, and that the soul thinks according to the influx? When a lover sees a beautiful virgin or bride, does not his eye sparkle, and carry the love of her to the soul? Does not a miser, when he sees purses in which there is money, burn for them in every sense? and does he not infuse this burning thence into the soul, and excite the desire of possessing them? When any proud man hears praises of himself from another, does he not prick up his ears? and do not these convey them to the soul? Are not the senses of the body like entries, through which alone entrance is made to the soul? Who can conclude, from these and many similar things, otherwise than that influx is from nature, or physical?" To these things the followers of Descartes, holding their fingers under their forehead, and now drawing them back, replied by saying, "Alas! you speak from appearances. Do you not know, that it is not the eye that loves a virgin or a bride, but the soul? and, that the sense of the body does not desire the money in the purse from itself, but from the soul? and also, that the ears eagerly catch hold of the praises of flatterers in no other manner? Is not perception that which causes sensation? And perception is of the soul and not of the organ. Tell, if you can, what else makes the tongue and lips speak, but thought; and wha else makes the hands work, but the will; and thought and will are of the soul. Thus what makes the eye see, and the ears hear, and the other organs feel, attend and advert to their objects, but the soul? From these and many other similar things, every one who is wise above the sensual hings of the

body, concludes that there is not an influx of the body into the soul, but of the soul into the body, which we call occasional influx, and also spiritual." Having heard this, the three men who stood behind the former triads, who were favorers of Leibnitz, lifted up their voice, saying, "We have heard the arguments on both sides, and have compared them, and have perceived that in many things these are stronger than those, and in many things those are stronger than these; wherefore, if it be permitted, we will settle the dispute." And to the question, How? they said, "There is not any influx of the soul into the body, nor of the body nto the soul; but there is a unanimous and instantaneous operation of both together, which a celebrated author has designated by a noble name, calling it preëstablished harmony." After this, the spirit appeared again with a torch in his hand, but now in the left hand; and he vibrated it at the hinder part of heir heads; thence the ideas of them all became confused, and they cried together, "Neither our soul nor our body knows which side we should take; wherefore, let us decide this dispute by lot, and the lot which comes out first we will favor." And they took three pieces of paper, and on one of them they wrote PHYSICAL INFLUX, on another, SPIRITUAL INFLUX, and on the third, PRE-ESTABLISHED HARMONY; and they put these three into the crown of a cap, and chose one to take them out. And this one put in his hand and took hold of that on which was written SPIRITUAL INFLUX; which being seen and read, they all said, yet some with a clear, flowing sound, some with an obscure and stifled one, "Let us favor this, because it came out first." But an angel then suddenly stood by and said, "Do not suppose that the piece of paper in favor of spiritual influx came out by chance, but providentially: for you do not see the truth of it, because you are in confused ideas, but the truth offered itself to the hand, that you might favor it."

697. SIXTH RELATION. Once I saw, not far from me, a meteor: I saw a cloud divided into little clouds, some of which were azure and some dark; and I saw them as if they were dashing against each other. Rays in streaks darted through them, which now seemed sharp like the points of swords, now blunt like broken swords. The streaks sometimes ran out to meet each other; sometimes they drew themselves back within themselves, just like boxers; thus the little clouds of diverse colors appeared as if they were fighting with each other; but they were playing. And because this meteor was seen not far from me, I lifted up my eyes, looked attentively, and saw boys, young men and old men entering into a house, which was built of marble, and underpinned with porphyry. Over this house was that phenomenon. And then, addressing one of those who were entering, I asked, "What is there?" He answered, "It is a gymnasium, where the young are initiated into the various things which are of wisdom." On hearing this, I entered with them. I was in the spirit, that is, in a state like that in which the men of the spiritual world are, who are called spirits and angels. And behold, in that gymnasium, in the front, there was seen a desk, in the middle, benches, at the sides round about, seats, and over the entrance an orchestra. The desk was for the young men who were to answer to the problem then about to be proposed; the benches for the hearers; the seats at the sides for those who had before answered wisely; and the orchestra for the elders who were to be the arbiters and judges. In the middle of the orchestra there was a pulpit, where sat a wise man, whom they called the head-master, who proposed the problems, to which the young men in the desk were to answer. And after they had assembled, the man rose up from the pulpit, and said, "Answer now, I pray, to this problem, and solve it if you can: WHAT IS THE SOUL, AND WHAT IS THE QUALITY OF IT?" On hearing these words, all were astonished and murmured, and some of those who sat upon the benches cried out, "What man, from the age of Saturn even to this

of ours, has been able, by any thought of reason, to see and find out what the soul is, and still less what its quality is? Is not this above the sphere of every one's understanding?" But to this they answered from the orchestra, "It is not above the understanding, but in it and before it; so answer now." And the young men rose up, who were appointed that day to ascend the desk and answer to the problem. There were five who had been explored by the elders, and found to be distinguished for sagacity, and then they were sitting at the sides of the desk on sofas; and afterwards they ascended in the order in which they sat; and each one, when he ascended, put on a tunic of an opaline color, and over it a gown of soft wool, in which flowers were interwoven; and moreover a cap, on the top of which there was a bunch of roses encircled with little sapphires. And I saw the first thus clad ascend, who said, "What the soul is and what its quality is, has not been revealed to any one since the day of creation; it is a secret in the treasures of God alone. But this has been disclosed, that the soul resides in man like a queen; but where her court is, learned interpreters have conjectured; some that it is in the little tubercle between the *cerebrum* and the *cerebellum*, which is called the pineal gland; and in this they have fixed the seat of the soul, because the whole man is governed by those two brains, and that tubercle disposes them. Wherefore, whatever disposes the brains at its nod, the same also disposes the whole man from the head to the heel. And," said he, "this has thence appeared to many in the world as true or probable, but after an age it was rejected as a figment." After he had said this, he took off the gown, tunic and cap, which the second of those who were appointed put on, and went into the desk. His proposition concerning the soul was, "That in the whole heaven and in the whole world, it is unknown what the soul is, and what its quality is. It is known that it is, and that it is in man, but where, it is conjectured. It is certain that it is in the head, since there the understanding thinks and there the will intends; and in the fore part of the head, or in the face, are the five sensories of man. To these and those nothing else gives life but the soul, which resides inwardly in the head; but where its court is there, I should not dare to say; but I agreed once with those who assigned to it a seat in the three ventricles of the *cerebrum;* now, with those who fix it in the *corpora striata* there; now, with those who fix it in the medullary substance of both parts of the brain; now, with those who fix it in the cortical substance; now with those who fix it in the *dura mater;* for there were some plausible arguments from confirmations in favor of each seat. The arguments in favor of the three ventricles of the *cerebrum* were, that they are the receptacles of the animal spirits, and of all the lymphs of the cerebrum. The arguments in favor of the *corpora striata* were, that they make the marrow, through which the nerves go forth, and through which both parts of the brain are continued into the spine, and that from this and from that the fibres emanate, of which the contexture of the whole body is formed. The arguments in favor of the medullary substance of both parts of the brain were, that that is a collection and assemblage of all the fibres which are the initiaments of the whole man. The arguments in favor of the cortical substance were, that these are the first and last ends, and thence the beginnings of all the fibres, and thus of all the senses and motions. The arguments in favor of the *dura mater* were, that that is the common covering of both parts of the brain, and thence, by something continuous, it extends itself over the heart and over the viscera of the body. As for me, I do not decide in favor of one more than another; I pray you to decide and choose what is best." Having said this, he descended from the desk, and handed the tunic, gown and cap to the third, who, mounting the desk, spoke these words: "What have I, a youth, to do with so sublime a theorem? I appeal to the learned sitting here at the sides; I appeal to you wise men in the orchestra yea, I appeal to the angels of the highest heaven, whether any one from his own rational light is able to form to himself any idea concerning the soul. But concerning its seat in man, I, like others, can guess, and I guess that it is in the heart and thence in the blood; and this is my guess, because the heart with its blood rules both the body and the head, for it sends forth the large vessel, called *aorta*, into the whole of the body, and it sends forth the vessels called *carotids* into the whole of the head; thence there is a universal agreement, that the soul from the heart, by means of the blood, sustains, nourishes and vivifies the whole organic system both of the body and the head. In confirmation of this assertion it may be added, that the soul and heart are so often spoken of in the Sacred Scripture; as that, Thou shalt love God from the whole soul, and from the whole heart; and that God creates in man a new soul and a new heart, Deut. vi. 5, x. 12; xi. 13; xxvi. 16; Jer. xxxii. 41; Matt. xxii. 37; Mark xii. 30, 33; Luke x. 27; besides other passages; and it is said openly that the blood is the soul of the flesh, Lev. xvii. 11, 14." On hearing this, some raised their voice, saying, "Learned, learned:" they were of the regular clergy. After this, the fourth, putting on his garments, and going into the desk, said, "I also suspect that there is no one of so subtile and refined a genius, that he can discern what the soul is, and what its quality is: wherefore I think that with him who wishes to pry into it, subtilty is wasted in superfluous things. But even from my childhood, I have continued in the belief of the opinion, in which the ancients were, that the soul of man is in the whole of him, and in every part of this whole; and thus that it is as well in the head and in every part of it, as in the body and in every part of it; and that it was a vain invention of the moderns to designate for it a seat somewhere, and not every where. The soul also is a spiritual substance, of which extension cannot be predicated, nor place, but habitation and impletion. Also, who does not mean life, when he mentions the soul? Is not life in the whole and in every part?" These words many in the auditory favored. After him the fifth rose up and being adorned with the same insignia, he delivered from the desk this "I do not stop to say where the soul is whether it be in some part, or every where in the whole; but from my stock and store I will open my mind concerning this, what the soul is, and what its quality is. The soul is not thought of by any one, but as something pure, which may be likened to ether or air or wind, in which there is a vital principle from the rationality which man has above the beasts. This opinion I have founded upon this, that when man expires, he is said to breathe out, or give up the soul or spirit. Thence also the soul, which lives after death, is believed to be such breath, in which there is a cogitative life, which is called soul: what else can the soul be? But because I heard those from the orchestra say that the problem concerning the soul, what it is, and what its quality is, is not above the understanding, but in it and before it, I beg and pray that you yourselves would disclose this eternal secret." And the elders in the orchestra looked at the head-master, who had proposed that problem, who understood from their nods that they wished that he would descend and teach. And immediately he descended from the pulpit, passed through the auditory, and went into the desk; and there, stretching forth his hand, he said, "Listen, I pray: who does not believe that the soul is the inmost and most subtile essence of man? But what is an essence without a form, but an imaginary entity? Wherefore the soul is a form; but what form shall be told. It is the form of all things of love, and of all things of wisdom. All the things of love are called affections, and all the things of wisdom are called perceptions: these from those and thus with those make one form, in which there are innumerable things, in such order, series and coherence, that they may be called one; and they may be called one, because not any thing can be taken from it, nor any thing added to it, that it may be such. What is the human soul but such a form? Are not all things of love, and all things of wisdom, the essentials of that form? And these with man are in the soul, and from the soul in the head and body. You are called spirits and angels, and you believed in the world that spirits and angels were like winds or ethers, and thus rational and animal minds; and now you see clearly, that you are truly, really and actually men, who in the world lived and thought in a material body; and you knew that the material body did not live and think, but a spiritual substance in that body, and this you called the soul, the form of which you did not know, and yet now you have seen it and do see it. You all are souls, concerning whose immortality you have heard, thought, said and written so much; and because you are forms of love and wisdom from God, you cannot die to eternity. The soul, therefore, is a human form, from which nothing at all can be taken away and to which nothing at all can be added; and it is the inmost form of all the forms of the whole body; and because the forms which are without receive from the inmost both essence and form, therefore you are, as you appear to yourselves and to us, souls. In a word, the soul is the man himself, because it is the inmost man; wherefore its form is fully and perfectly the human form; nevertheless it is not life, but it is the proximate receptacle of life from God, and thus the habitation of God." These words many applauded, but some said, "We will consider." I then went home; and behold, over the gymnasium, instead of the former meteor, there appeared a bright cloud, without streaks or rays fighting with each other; which cloud, penetrating through the roof, entered the room, and illuminated the walls; and I heard that they saw pieces of writing, and amongst others also this: *Jehovah God breathed into man's nostrils the* SOUL OF LIVES *and man became a* LIVING SOUL, Gen. ii 7

CHAPTER XIII.

CONCERNING THE HOLY SUPPER.

698. I. THAT WITHOUT INFORMATION CONCERNING THE CORRESPONDENCES OF NATURAL THINGS WITH SPIRITUAL, NO ONE CAN KNOW THE USES OF THE HOLY SUPPER.

This was in part unfolded in the chapter concerning Baptism, where it was shown; *That without a knowledge of the spiritual sense of the Word, it cannot be known what the two sacraments, Baptism and the Holy Supper, involve and effect;* which may be seen, n. 667 to 669. Here it is said, *That without information concerning the correspondences of natural things with spiritual;* which is the same thing, because the natural sense of the Word is turned into the spiritual, by correspondences, in heaven. Thence it is, that those two senses correspond to each other; wherefore he who knows the correspondences, may know the spiritual sense. But what correspondences are, may be seen in the chapter concerning the SACRED SCRIPTURE, from the beginning to the end; and also in the EXPLANATION OF THE DECALOGUE, from the first commandment to the last; and particularly in the APOCALYPSE REVEALED.

699. Who that is truly a Christian, does not acknowledge that those two sacraments are holy; yea, that they are the most holy things of worship in Christendom? But who knows where their holiness resides, or whence it is? In the institution of the holy supper, from the literal sense, no more is known, than that the flesh of Christ is given for eating, and his blood for drinking; and that, instead of these, bread and wine. Who can thence think otherwise, than that it is holy only on account of the command of the Lord? Wherefore the most sagacious of the church have taught, that while the Word comes to the element, it becomes a sacrament. But because this origin of its holiness does not fall into the understanding, nor appear in the elements or symbols of the sacrament, but only into the memory, therefore some observe it from a confidence that sins are remitted by means of it; some because they believe that it sanctifies; some because it strengthens faith, and thus also promotes salvation. But those who think lightly of it, frequent it merely from custom from childhood; and some, because they see nothing of reason concerning it, neglect it; but the impious turn themselves away from it, and say to themselves, "What is it, but a certain ceremony, on which holiness has been impressed by the clergy? For what is there there but bread and wine? And what is it but a figment, that the body of Christ, which hung upon the cross, and his blood which was then shed, are distributed to the communicants together with the bread and wine?" Besides other things.

700. Such ideas of this most holy sacrament are at this day entertained in all Christendom, solely because they coincide with the sense of the letter of the Word; and the spiritual sense has been hitherto concealed, and not until this day disclosed, in which alone the use of the holy supper is clearly seen in its truth. The reason that this sense is now for the first time disclosed is, because there was before no Christianity, except in name, and with some a kind of shadow of it; for hitherto they have not immediately approached and worshipped the Savior himself, as the one God in whom is the

Divine Trinity, but only mediately; which is not to approach and worship, but only to honor as the cause on account of which man has salvation; which is not the essential cause, but a mediate cause, which is below the essential and out of it. But, because Christianity itself is now first beginning to dawn, and a New Church, which is meant by the New Jerusalem in the Revelation, is now being established by the Lord, in which God the Father, Son and Holy Spirit are acknowledged as one, because in one person, it has pleased the Lord to reveal the spiritual sense of the Word, that this church may come into the very use of the sacraments, baptism and the holy supper; which is done when men see, with the eyes of their spirit, that is, with the understanding, the holiness which is concealed therein, and apply it to themselves,by the means which the Lord has taught in his Word.

701. The holiness of the sacrament which is here treated of, without the spiritual sense of the Word being opened, or, what is the same thing, without the correspondences of natural things with spiritual being revealed, can no more be acknowledged interiorly,than a treasure hid in a field; which field is valued no more than any common one; but when it is discovered that there is a treasure in that field, the field is valued at a great price; and the buyer then appropriates to himself opulence thence; and still more when it is known, that in it there is a treasure more precious than all gold. Without the spiritual sense, that sacrament is like a house shut up full of jewels and treasures, which is passed by as any other house in the street; but because it was built by the clergy, as to the walls, of marble, and overlaid, as to the roof, with plates of gold, the sight of those who pass by is attracted, to view, to praise and to prize. It is otherwise when that house is opened, and leave of entering is given to every one, and the keeper furnishes to some a loan thence, to some a gift thence, to every one according to his dignity. It is said, *a gift thence*, because the precious things there are inexhaustible, and they are continually supplied; so it is with the Word as to its spiritual things, and with the sacraments as to their celestial things. The sacrament, which is here treated of, without its holiness being revealed, which is concealed within, appears like the sand of a river, in which there are little grains of gold in great abundance, which are not conspicuous; but when it is revealed, it is like the gold collected thence and melted into a mass, and this fabricated into beautiful forms. This sacrament, without its holiness being disclosed and seen, is like a box or a chest of beech or poplar, in which lie diamonds, rubies, and many other precious stones, disposed in order in the partitions. Who does not value that box or chest, who knows that such things are concealed within; and the more when he sees them, and also when they are distributed freely? That sacrament, without its correspondences with heaven being revealed, and thus the heavenly things to which it corresponds being seen, is like an angel seen in the world in a common dress, who is honored only according to the dress; it is altogether otherwise, when it is known that he is an angel, and something angelic is heard from his mouth, and wonderful things are seen from his deeds. What the holiness is which is only proclaimed, and what the holiness is which is seen, may be illustrated by this example, seen and heard in the spiritual world. There was read an epistle written by Paul, at the time when he sojourned in the world, but not published, without any one's knowing that it was by Paul. This at first was lightly esteemed by the hearers; but when it was discovered that it was one of Paul's epistles, it was received with joy, and all and each of the things there were adored. Whence it was manifest, that the mere proclaiming of holiness respecting the Word and respecting the sacraments, when it is done by the primates of the clergy, gives an impression, indeed, of holiness; but it is otherwise when the holiness

itself is disclosed and set forth before the eyes to be seen, which is done by the revelation of the spiritual sense: from this, external holiness becomes internal, and the proclamation of it becomes an acknowledgment of it. It is similar with the holiness of the sacrament of the supper.

702. II. THAT FROM CORRESPONDENCES BEING KNOWN, IT MAY BE KNOWN WHAT IS MEANT BY THE FLESH AND BLOOD OF THE LORD, AND THAT THE LIKE IS MEANT BY BREAD AND WINE; NAMELY, THAT BY THE FLESH OF THE LORD, AND BY BREAD, IS MEANT THE DIVINE GOOD OF HIS LOVE, AND ALSO ALL THE GOOD OF CHARITY; AND THAT BY THE BLOOD OF THE LORD, AND BY WINE, IS MEANT THE DIVINE TRUTH OF HIS WISDOM, AND ALSO ALL THE TRUTH OF FAITH; AND BY EATING, APPROPRIATION.

Since the spiritual sense of the Word is at this day disclosed, and together with it correspondences, because these are mediates, therefore there will only be adduced passages from the Word, from which it may be clearly seen, what is meant by flesh and blood, and by bread and wine, in the holy supper. But to these will be premised the institution itself of that sacrament by the Lord; and also his doctrine concerning his flesh and his blood, and concerning bread and wine.

703. THE INSTITUTION OF THE HOLY SUPPER BY THE LORD. *Jesus kept the passover with the disciples; and when the evening was come, He sat down with them. And as they were eating, Jesus, taking* BREAD, *and blessing, broke and gave to the disciples, and said, Take, eat; this is* MY BODY. *And taking the* CUP, *and giving thanks, He gave to them, saying, Drink ye all of it; this is* MY BLOOD, *that of the New Testament, which is shed for many*, Matt. xxvi. 26, 27, 28; Mark xiv. 22, 23, 24; Luke xxii. 19, 20.

THE DOCTRINE OF THE LORD CONCERNING HIS FLESH AND HIS BLOOD, AND CONCERNING BREAD AND WINE. *Work not for the food which perisheth, but for the food which endureth unto eternal life, which the Son of Man will give to you. Verily, verily, I say to you, Moses gave you not the bread from heaven, but my Father giveth you the true bread from heaven; for the bread of God is He that came down from heaven, and giveth life to the world. I am the bread of life; he that cometh to Me, shall never hunger, and he that believeth in Me, shall never thirst. I am the bread which came down from heaven. Verily, verily, I say to you, he that believeth in Me, hath eternal life. I am the bread of life. Your fathers ate manna in the desert, and died; this is the bread which came down from heaven, that any one may eat of it, and live, and not die. I am the living bread which came down from heaven; if any one eat of this bread, he shall live for ever. The bread which I will give, is my flesh, which I will give for the life of the world. Verily, verily, I say to you, unless ye eat the flesh of the Son of Man, and drink his blood, ye will not have life in you He that eateth my flesh, and drinketh my blood, hath eternal life, and I will resuscitate him at the last day; for my flesh is truly meat, and my blood is truly drink. He that eateth my flesh and drinketh my blood, abideth in Me and I in him*, John vi. 27, 32, 33, 35, 41, 47, 48, 49, 50, 51, 53, 54, 55, 56.

704. That by *flesh* there, is not meant flesh, nor by *blood* blood, any one enlightened from heaven may perceive in himself; but that by both is meant, in THE NATURAL SENSE, the passion of the cross, which they should remember; wherefore He said, when He instituted this supper of the last Jewish passover, and the first Christian passover, *Do this in remembrance of Me*, Luke xxii. 19; 1 Cor. xi. 24, 25. In like manner, that by *bread* is not meant bread, nor by *wine* wine, but in the NATURAL SENSE, the same as by flesh and blood, namely, his passion of the cross; for it is read; *Jesus broke bread, and gave to the disciples, and said, This is my body And taking the cup, He gave to them, saying, This is my blood*, Matt. xxvi.; Mark xiv.; Luke xxii. Wherefore also He called the passion of the cross a *cup*, Matt. xiv. 36; John xviii. 11

705. That by these four things, *flesh, blood, bread* and *wine*, are meant the spiritual and celestial things which correspond to them, may be evident from the passages in the Word, where they are named. That by *flesh* in the Word is meant something spiritual and celestial, may be evident from these passages there: *Come, and be gathered together to the* SUPPER OF THE GREAT GOD, *that ye may eat the flesh of kings, and the flesh of captains, and the flesh of mighty ones, and the flesh of horses, and of those who sit upon them, and the flesh of all, free and bond, small and great*, Rev. xix. 17, 18. And in Ezekiel: *Gather yourselves together from every side to* MY SACRIFICE *which I sacrifice for you, a* GREAT SACRIFICE *upon the mountains of Israel, that ye may eat flesh and drink blood; ye shall eat the flesh of the mighty, and drink the blood of the princes of the earth; and ye shall eat fat to satiety, and drink blood even to drunkenness of my sacrifice; and ye shall be satiated at my table, with horse and chariot, with the mighty, and with every man of war. Thus I will give my glory among the nations*, xxxix. 17 to 21. Who does not see, that, in those passages, by *flesh* is not meant flesh, nor by *blood* blood, but the spiritual and celestial things which correspond? Otherwise, what would these be but strange and unmeaning expressions, that they should eat the flesh of kings, of captains, of the mighty, of horses, of those that sit upon them; and that they should be satiated at the table with horse and chariot, the mighty, and every man of war; and that they should drink the blood of the princes of the earth, and blood even to drunkenness? That these things were said concerning the holy supper of the Lord is clearly manifest, for it is called the supper of the great God, and also a great sacrifice. Since all spiritual and celestial things refer themselves solely to good and truth, it follows, that by flesh is meant the good of charity, and by blood, the truth of faith, and, in the highest sense, the Lord as to the Divine Good of love and as to the Divine Truth of wisdom. Spiritual good is also meant by flesh, by these words in Ezekiel: *I will give them one heart, and a new spirit I will give in the midst of you; and I will remove the heart of stone, and will give them a heart of flesh*, xi. 19; xxxvi. 26. By *heart*, in the Word, is signified love; thence by a *heart of flesh*, the love of good. Moreover, that by *flesh* and *blood* are meant good and truth, both spiritual, is still more evident from the signification of bread and wine in what now follows; since the Lord says, that his flesh is bread, and that his blood is wine, which was drunk out of a cup.

706. That by the blood of the Lord is meant the Divine Truth of Himself and the Word, is, because by his flesh spiritually is meant the Divine Good of love; and these two are united in the Lord. It is known that the Lord is the Word; and there are two things to which all things of the Word refer themselves, divine good and divine truth; wherefore if the Word is taken for the Lord, it is manifest that those two things are meant by his flesh and blood. That the divine truth of the Lord, or of the Word, is meant by blood, is evident from many passages; as that blood was called the blood of the covenant, and a covenant is conjunction, and this is effected by the Lord by means of his divine truth, as in Zechariah: *By the blood of thy covenant I will send forth the prisoners out of the pit*, ix. 11. And in Moses: *After Moses had read the book of the law in the ears of the people, he sprinkled half of the blood upon the people, and said,* BEHOLD THE BLOOD OF THE COVENANT *which Jehovah hath made with you upon all these words*, Exod xxiv. 3 to 11. *And Jesus took the cup, and gave it to them, saying, This is my blood, that of the New Covenant*, Matt. xxvi. 27, 28; Mark xiv. 24; Luke xxii. 20. By *the blood of the New Covenant*, or Testament, nothing else is signified but the Word, which is called a Covenant and Testament, Old and New, thus the divine truth there. Since this is signified by blood, therefore the

Lord gave them wine, saying, *This is my blood;* and wine signifies divine truth; wherefore it also is called *the blood of grapes,* Gen. xlix. 11; Deut. xxxii. 14. This is still more manifest from the words of the Lord: *Verily, verily, I say to you, Unless ye eat the flesh of the Son of Man, and drink his blood, ye will not have life in you; for my flesh is truly meat, and my blood is truly drink. He that eateth my flesh, and drinketh my blood, abideth in Me, and I in him,* John vi. 50 to 58. That by blood here is meant the divine truth of the Word is very manifest, because it is said, that he that drinketh hath life in himself, and abideth in the Lord, and the Lord in him. That divine truth effects this, and a life according to it, and that the holy supper confirms it, may be known in the church. Since blood signified the divine truth of the Lord, which also is the divine truth of the Word, and this is the Covenant itself and Testament Old and New, therefore blood was the most holy representative of the church with the sons of Israel, in which all and each of the things were correspondences of natural things with spiritual: as, *That they should take of the paschal blood, and put upon the posts of the door, and on the lintels of the houses, lest the plague should come upon them,* Exod. xii. 7, 13, 22. *That the blood of the burnt-offering should be sprinkled upon the altar, at its foundations, and upon Aaron, his sons and their garments,* xxix. 12, 16, 20, 21; Lev. i. 5, 11, 15; iii. 2, 8, 13; iv. 25, 30, 34; viii. 15, 24; xvii. 6; viii. 8; Deut. xii. 27. Also, *Upon the veil which was over the ark, upon the mercy-seat there, and upon the horns of the altar of incense,* Lev. iv. 6, 7, 17, 18; xvi. 12, 13, 14, 15. The like is signified by the blood of the Lamb in the Revelation: *These have washed their robes, and whitened them in the blood of the Lamb,* vii. 14. And by these there, *War was made in heaven; Michael and his angels fought against the dragon, and overcame him by the blood of the Lamb, and by the word of their testimony,* xii. 7, 11. For it cannot be thought that Michael and his angels overcame the dragon by any thing else than by the divine truth of the Lord in the Word; for the angels in heaven cannot think of any blood, nor do they think of the Lord's passion, but of divine truth, and of his resurrection. Wherefore, when man thinks of the blood of the Lord, the angels perceive the divine truth of his Word, and when he thinks of the passion of the Lord, they perceive his glorification, and then only the resurrection. That it is so, it has been given me to know by much experience. That blood signifies divine truth, is manifest also from these words in David: *God will preserve the souls of the needy; precious shall their blood be in his eyes, and they shall live, and He will give them of the gold of Sheba,* Psalm lxxii. 13, 14, 15, 16. *The blood precious in the eyes of God,* for the divine truth with them; *the gold of Sheba* is the wisdom thence. And in Ezekiel: *Gather yourselves together to the great sacrifice upon the mountains of Israel, that ye may eat flesh and drink blood; ye shall drink the blood of the princes of the earth, and ye shall drink blood even to drunkenness. Thus I will give my glory among the nations,* xxxix. 17 to 21. There the church is treated of, which the Lord was about to institute among the nations. That by *blood* here cannot be meant blood, but the truth from the Word with them, may be seen just above.

707. That the like is meant by BREAD as by flesh, is clearly evident from the words of the Lord: *Jesus, taking* BREAD, *broke and gave, saying, This is my body,* Matt. xxvi.; Mark xiv.; Luke xxii. And also, *The* BREAD *which I will give is my flesh, which I will give for the life of the world,* John vi. 51. And also He says, *That He is the* BREAD OF LIFE; *he that eateth of this* BREAD SHALL LIVE FOR EVER, vi. 48, 51, 58. This bread also is what is meant by the sacrifices, which are called bread in the following passages: *The priest shall burn them upon the altar, the* BREAD OF THE OFFERING MADE BY FIRE TO JEHOVAH, Lev. iii. 11, 16 *The sons of Aaron shall be holy to*

their God; neither shall they profane the name of their God, because they offer the OFFERINGS MADE BY FIRE TO JEHOVAH, THE BREAD OF THEIR GOD. *Thou shalt sanctify him because he offereth the* BREAD OF THY GOD. *A man of the seed of Aaron, in whom there is a blemish, shall not come to offer the* BREAD OF HIS GOD, Lev. xxi. 6, 8, 17, 21. *Command the sons of Israel, and say to them, My offering,* MY BREAD, FOR THE OFFERINGS MADE BY FIRE OF AN ODOR OF REST, *ye shall observe to offer to Me at the set time,* Num. xxviii. 2. *He that hath touched an unclean thing shall not eat of the holy things; but he shall bathe his flesh in water, and afterwards he shall eat of the holy things, because it is his bread,* Lev. xxii. 6, 7. To eat of the holy things, was to eat the flesh of the sacrifices, which here also is called bread; besides in Malachi, i. 7. By the MEAL OFFERINGS in the sacrifices, which were of the flour of wheat, thus bread, nothing else was signified, Lev. ii. 1 to 11; vi. 6 to 14; vii. 9 to 13, and in other places. Nor was any thing else signified by the bread upon the table in the tabernacle, which was called *the bread of faces and the shew bread,* concerning which, Exod. xxv. 30; xl. 23; Lev. xxiv. 5 to 10. That by bread is not meant natural bread, but heavenly bread, is manifest from these passages: *Man liveth not by bread alone, but by every thing that proceedeth out of the mouth of Jehovah man doth live,* Deut. xviii. 2, 3. *I will send hunger into the land; not hunger for bread, nor thirst for water, but for hearing the words of Jehovah,* Amos viii. 11. Moreover, by bread is meant all food, Lev. xxiv. 5 to 9; Exod. xxv. 30; xl. 23; Num. iv. 7; 1 Kings vii. 48. That spiritual food also is meant, is manifest from these words of the Lord; *Work not for the food which perisheth, but for the food which endureth unto eternal life, which the Son of Man will give to you,* John vi. 27.

708. That by WINE the same is meant as by blood, is clearly manifest from the words of the Lord: *Jesus took the* CUP, *saying, This is my blood,* Matt. xxvi.; Mark xiv.; Luke xxii. And also from these: *He washeth his vesture in* WINE, *and his robe in* THE BLOOD OF GRAPES, Gen. xlix. 11. These are concerning the Lord. *Jehovah of hosts will make for all people a feast of* FAT THINGS, *a feast of the lees of wine, or* OF SWEET WINE, Isaiah xxv. 6. These are concerning the sacrament of the holy supper, which was to be instituted by the Lord. In the same: *Every one that thirsteth, come ye to the waters, and he that hath no money, come ye, buy and eat; and buy* WINE *without money,* lv. 1. By the PRODUCE OF THE VINE, which they were about to drink new in the heavenly kingdom, Matt. xxvi. 29; Mark xiv. 22; Luke xxii. 17, 18, nothing else is meant but the truth of the new church and heaven; wherefore, also, the church, in many places in the Word, is called a VINEYARD, as Isaiah v. 1, 2, 4; Matt. xx. 1 to 13: And the Lord calls Himself the TRUE VINE, and those who are ingrafted into Him the BRANCHES, John xv. 1, 5; besides in many other places.

709. Hence, now, it may be evident what is meant by the flesh and blood of the Lord, and by bread and wine, in the threefold sense, natural, spiritual and celestial. Every man in Christendom, imbued with religion, may know, or, if he does not know, may learn, that there is natural nourishment and spiritual nourishment; and that natural nourishment is for the body, but spiritual nourishment for the soul: for Jehovah the Lord says in Moses, *Man doth not live by bread alone, but by every thing that proceedeth out of the mouth of Jehovah doth man live,* Deut. viii. 3. Now, because the body dies, and the soul lives after death, it follows, that spiritual nourishment is for eternal salvation. Who, then, does not see, that those two kinds of nourishment are by no means to be confounded, and that if any one does confound them, he cannot form to himself any other ideas concerning the flesh and blood of the Lord, and concerning bread and wine, than natural and sensual ones, which are material, corporeal and carnal, which suffocate spiritual ideas concerning this most holy sacrament

But if any one is so simple that he cannot think any thing else from the understanding, than what he sees with the eye, I advise him to think with himself, concerning the holy supper, when he takes the bread and wine, and hears them then called the flesh and blood of the Lord, that it is the most holy thing of worship, and to remember the passion of Christ and his love for the salvation of man; for He says, *Do this in remembrance of Me*, Luke xxii. 19. And also, *The Son of Man hath come to give his life a ransom for many*, Matt. xx. 28; Mark x. 4. *I lay down my life for the sheep*, John x. 15, 17; xv. 13.

710. This also may be illustrated by comparisons. Who does not remember and love him, who, from the zeal of love for his country, fights with the enemy even to death, that he may thereby deliver it from the yoke of bondage? And who does not remember and love him, who, when he sees his fellow citizens in extreme want, and their death by distressing famine before their eyes, then, from compassion, brings forth all his silver and gold out of his house and distributes it freely? And who does not remember and love him, who, from love and friendship, takes the only lamb that he possesses, and kills it and sets it before his guests? &c.

711. III. THAT FROM THESE THINGS BEING UNDERSTOOD, IT MAY BE COMPREHENDED THAT THE HOLY SUPPER CONTAINS, UNIVERSALLY AND PARTICULARLY, ALL THINGS OF THE CHURCH AND ALL THINGS OF HEAVEN.

In the preceding article it was shown, that the Lord himself is in the holy supper, and that the flesh and bread are Himself, as to the divine good of love, and that the blood and wine are Himself as to the divine truth of wisdom; wherefore, there are three things which the holy supper involves, namely, the Lord, his divine good, and his divine truth Since, therefore, the holy supper includes and contains these three things, it follows that it also includes and contains the universals of heaven and the church; and because all particulars depend on universals, as the things contained on the things containing them, it follows, also, that the holy supper includes and contains all particulars of heaven and the church. Hence, first, it is evident, that because, by the flesh and blood of the Lord, and in like manner by bread and wine, are meant the divine good and divine truth, both from the Lord, and the Lord, the holy supper contains universally and particularly all things of heaven and the church.

712. It is also known, that the essentials of the church are three, namely, God, charity and faith; and that all things there refer themselves to those three, as to their universals. These are the same with those which were said above; for God, in the holy supper, is the Lord, charity is the divine good, and faith is the divine truth. What else is charity than the good which man does from the Lord? And what else is faith, but the truth which man believes from the Lord? Thence it is, that there are three things in man, as to his internal, namely, the soul or mind, the will and the understanding. These three are the receptacles of those three universals: the soul itself, or mind, is the receptacle of the Lord, for thence it lives; the will is the receptacle of love or good; and the understanding is the receptacle of wisdom or truth; wherefore, all and each of the things in the soul or mind not only refer themselves to those three universals of heaven and the church, but also proceed from them. Name any thing that proceeds from man, in which are not the mind, will and understanding; if one of them were taken away, would man be any thing more than something inanimate? In like manner, there are three things in man, as to his external, to which also all and each of the things refer themselves, and on which they depend; namely, the body, the heart and the lungs; and these three things of the body correspond to the three things of the mind, the heart to the will, and the lungs or respiration to the understanding. That there is such a correspondence has been fully shown in the foregoing pages. Thus now al'

and each of the things in man, as well universally as particularly, were formed as receptacles of those three universals of heaven and the church. The reason is, because man was created an image and likeness of God; consequently, that he may be in the Lord and the Lord in him.

713. On the other hand, there are hree things opposite to those universals, which are the devil, evil and the false. The devil, by which is meant hell, is in opposition to the Lord, evil is in opposition to good, and the false to the truth; these three make one, for where the devil is, there also is evil and the false thence. These three also contain, universally and particularly, all things of hell, and likewise all the things of the world, which are contrary to heaven and the church. But because they are opposites, therefore they are entirely separate, but still they are kept together in connection by a wonderful subjection of all hell under heaven, of evil under good, and of the false under truth; which subjection is treated of in the work concerning HEAVEN AND HELL.

714. That particulars may be kept together in their order and connection, it is necessary that there should be universals from which they exist and in which they subsist; and also it is necessary that the particulars should, in a certain image, relate to their universals; otherwise the whole with the parts would perish. This relation is the cause of the preservation of all things of the universe, from the first day of creation to this time, and hereafter. That all things in the universe refer themselves to good and truth, is known: the reason is, because all things were created by God, from the divine good of love by the divine truth of wisdom. Take whatever thing you will, either an animal, or a shrub, or a stone, those three most universal things are in a certain relation inscribed upon them.

715. Since the divine good and divine truth are the most universal of all the things of heaven and the church, therefore alsc Melchisedek, who represented the Lord, brought forth bread and wine to Abraham, and blessed him. Concerning Melchisedek it is thus read· *Melchisedek, king of Salem, brought forth to Abram bread and wine; ana he was a priest to the most High God; and he blessed him,* Gen. xiv. 18, 19. That Melchisedek represented the Lord is evident from these words in David: *Thou art a priest for ever after the order of Melchisedek,* Psalm cx. 4. That these words are concerning the Lord, may be seen, Heb. v. 6, 8, 10; vi. 20; vii. 1, 10, 11, 15, 17, 21. The reason why he brought forth bread and wine was, because those two include all things of heaven and the church, thus all things of blessing; in like manner as the bread and wine in the holy supper.

716. IV. THAT THE WHOLE OF THE LORD IS IN THE HOLY SUPPER, AND THE WHOLE OF HIS REDEMPTION.

That the whole of the Lord is in the holy supper, as well as to the glorified Human as to the Divine, from which the Human proceeded, is evident from his own express words. That his Human is present in the holy supper is evident from these words: *Jesus took bread, and broke, and gave to the disciples, and said, This is my body. Ana taking the cup, He gave to them, saying, This is my blood,* Matt. xxvi.; Mark xiv.; Luke xxii. And also in John: *I am the bread of life; if any one eat of this bread, he shall live for ever. The bread which I will give is my flesh. Verily, verily, I say to you, He that eateth my flesh, and drinketh my blood, abideth in Me and I in him; and he shall live for ever,* vi. From these words it evidently appears, that the Lord, as to his glorified Human, is in the holy supper. That the whole of the Lord, also, as to His Divine, from which the Human proceeded, is present in the holy supper, is evident from this, that He is the bread which came down from heaven, John vi. He came down from heaven with the Divine, for it is said, *The Word was with God, ana God was the Word. All things were made by Him. And the Word became flesh,* i 1, 3, 14. And further from these: *That the Father and He are one,* x. 30. *That all things of the Father are His,* iii. 35; xvi 15. *That He is in the Father and the Father in Him,* xiv. 10, 11, &c. And further, that his Divine can no more be separated from his Human than the soul from the body. Wherefore, when it is said that the whole of the Lord, as to his Human, is in the Holy Supper, it follows that his Divine, from which it proceeded, is also there at the same time. Now, since his flesh signifies the divine good of his love, and his blood the divine truth of his wisdom, it is manifest that the whole of the Lord, both as to the Divine and as to the glorified Human, is omnipresent in the holy supper; consequently, that it is a spiritual eating.

717. That the whole of the Lord's redemption is present in the holy supper follows, as a consequence, from what has now been said; for where the whole of the Lord is, there also is the whole of his redemption; for He is, as to the Human, the Redeemer; consequently, also, redemption itself: not any thing of redemption can be absent, where He is wholly present. Wherefore, all those who worthily go to the holy communion, become his redeemed ones; and because by redemption are meant deliverance from hell, conjunction with Him and salvation (of which below, in this chapter, and more fully in the chapter concerning Redemption), therefore those fruits are ascribed to man; not, indeed, so far as the Lord wills, because from his divine love He wills to ascribe them all, but as far as man receives; and he who receives, is redeemed in the degree in which he receives. Whence it is evident, that the effects and fruits of the Lord's redemption return to those who worthily approach.

718. With every sound man there is a faculty of receiving wisdom from the Lord, that is, of multiplying the truths from which it is, to eternity; and also of receiving love, that is, of fructifying the goods from which this is, in like manner to eternity. This perpetual fructification of good and thence of love, and that perpetual multiplication of truth and thence of wisdom, is given with the angels, and also it is given with men who become angels; and because the Lord is Love itself and Wisdom itself, it follows that man has the faculty of conjoining himself to the Lord, and the Lord to him, for ever. But still, because man is finite, the Divine itself of the Lord cannot be conjoined to him, but only adjoined; as for illustration, the light of the sun cannot be conjoined to the eye, nor the sound of the air conjoined to the ear, but only adjoined to them, and thus give the faculty of seeing and hearing; for man is not life in himself, as the Lord is, even as to the Human, (John v. 26,) but he is a receptacle of life; and life itself is what is adjoined to man, but is not conjoined. These things are added in order that it may be understood, in what way the whole of the Lord, and the whole of his redemption, is present in the holy supper.

719. V. That the Lord is present and opens Heaven to those who worthily come to the Holy Supper, and that He is also present with those who come unworthily, but that He does not open Heaven to them; consequently, that as Baptism is an Introduction into the Church, so the Holy Supper is an Introduction into Heaven.

Who they are that come to the holy supper worthily, is shown in the two following articles, and at the same time concerning those who come unworthily; for from the one which is affirmed, the other is known from its opposition. That the Lord is present both with the worthy and with the unworthy, is because He is omnipresent, both in heaven and in hell, and also in the world; consequently, with the evil as well as with the good; but with the good, that is, the regenerate, He is present universally and particularly, for the Lord is in them and they in the Lord, and where the Lord is, there is heaven. Heaven also makes the body of the Lord; wherefore, to be in his body, is to be at the same time in heaven. But the presence of the Lord with those who come unworthily, is his universal but not his particular presence; or, what is the same, it is his external but not his internal presence; and his universal or external presence causes man to live as man, and to enjoy the faculty of knowing, of understanding, and of speaking rationally from the understanding; for man is born for heaven, and therefore also spiritual, and not like a beast, only natural. He enjoys also the faculty of willing and of doing those things which the understanding can know, understand, and thence speak rationally; but if the will refuses obedience to the truly rational things of the understanding, which also are intrinsically spiritual, then the man becomes external. Wherefore, with those who only understand what is true and good, the presence of the Lord is universal or external; but with those who also will and do what is true and good, the presence of the Lord is both universal and particular, or both internal and external. Those who only understand and talk about truths and goods are comparatively the foolish virgins, who had lamps but not oil; but those who not only understand and talk about truths and goods, but also will and do them, are the prudent virgins, who were admitted into the wedding, but the former stood at the door and knocked, but were not admitted, Matt. xxv. 1 to 12. Hence it is evident that the Lord is present and opens heaven to those who come worthily to the holy supper; and that He is also present with those who come unworthily, but that he does not open heaven to them.

720. But still it is not to be believed that the Lord shuts heaven to those who come unworthily; this He does not to any man even to the end of his life in the world; but that man shuts it against himself, which he does by the rejection of faith, and by evil of life. But still man is continually kept in a possible state of repentance and conversion; for the Lord is perpetually present, and urges that He may be received; for He says, *I stand at the door and knock; if any one hear my voice, and open the door, I will go in and* SUP WITH HIM AND HE WITH ME. Rev. iii. 20. Wherefore man himself is in the fault, who does not open the door. The case is otherwise after death; then heaven is shut, and is not to be opened to those who, even to the end of life, have come to the holy supper unworthily, for then the interiors of their mind are fixed and established.

721. That baptism is an introduction into the church, was shown in the chapter concerning Baptism; but that the holy supper is an introduction into heaven, is evident from the things above said and perceived. Those two sacraments, baptism and the holy supper, are as it were two gates to eternal life. Every Christian man by baptism, which is the first gate, is admitted and introduced into the things which the church teaches from the Word concerning another life; which all are means by which man may be prepared for and led to heaven. The other gate is the holy supper, through which every man who has suffered himself to be prepared and led by the Lord, is admitted and introduced into heaven. There are no more universal gates. These two may be compared with a prince born for a kingdom, in that he is first introduced into the knowledges which belong to the office of governing, and then follows his coronation and government. They may be compared also with a son born to a great inheritance, who will first learn and imbue himself with such things as pertain to the just disposition of possessions and wealth; the other thing is the possession and administration. They may be compared also with the building of a house, and with its being inhabited; and also with the instruction of a man from infancy even to the age when he comes to the exercise of his own right and judgment, and with his rational and spiritual life afterwards: one period necessarily precedes, that the other may be obtained; for this is not attainable without that. By these things it is illustrated, that baptism and the holy supper are, as it were, two gates, through which man is introduced into eternal life, and that after the first gate, there is a plain, over

which he must run, and that the other is the goal, where is the prize to which he directed his course; for the palm is not given till after the contest, nor the reward till after the combat.

722. VI. That those come to the Holy Supper worthily, who are in Faith in the Lord, and in Charity towards the Neighbor, thus who are regenerate.

That God, charity and faith are the three universals of the church, because they are the universal means of salvation, is known, acknowledged and perceived by every Christian who studies the Word. That *God is to be acknowledged,* in order that any one may have religion, and any thing of the church in him, reason itself, in which there is something spiritual, dictates. Wherefore, he who comes to the holy supper, and does not acknowledge God, profanes it; for he sees with the eye the bread and wine, and tastes them with the tongue; but the mind thinks, What is this but an idle ceremony? And how do they differ from similar things upon my table? Yet I do this lest I should be accused by the priesthood, and thence by the vulgar, of the infamous crime of being an atheist. That, after the acknowledgment of God, *Charity is another means* which causes one to come worthily, is evident both from the Word and from the exhortations read before coming to the communion in the whole Christian world. From the Word: that *the first commandment and precept is, that men should love God above all things, and the neighbor as themselves,* Matt. xxii. 34 to 39; Luke x. 25 to 28. And also Paul says, that *there are three things which contribute to salvation, and that the greatest of them is charity,* 1 Cor. xiii. 13. As also from these, *We know that God heareth not sinners; but if any one worshippeth God and doeth his will, him He heareth,* John ix. 31. *Every tree that produceth not good fruit, is cut down and cast into the fire,* Matt. vii. 19, 20; Luke iii. 8, 9: From the exhortations read before coming to the Holy Supper in the whole Christian world: in those the people are every where seriously admonished to be in charity by reconciliation and repentance; of which I shall here transcribe only these words from the exhortation to communicants in England:—"The way and means," to become a worthy partaker of the holy supper, "is, first, to examine your lives and conversations by the rule of God's commandments; and whereinsoever ye shall perceive yourselves to have offended, either by will, word, or deed, there to bewail your own sinfulness, and to confess yourselves to Almighty God, with full purpose of amendment of life. And if ye shall perceive your offences to be such as are not only against God, but also against your neighbors; then ye shall reconcile yourselves unto them, being ready to make restitution and satisfaction, according to the uttermost of your powers, for all injuries and wrongs done by you to any other; and being likewise ready to forgive others that have offended you, as ye would have forgiveness at God's hand; for otherwise, the receiving of the holy communion doth nothing else but increase your damnation. Therefore, if any of you be a blasphemer of God, a hinderer or slanderer of his Word, an adulterer, or be in malice or envy, or in any other grievous crime, repent ye of your sins, or else come not to that holy table: lest, after the taking of that holy sacrament, the devil enter into you, as he entered into Judas, and fill you full of all iniquities, and bring you to destruction both of body and soul." That *Faith in the Lord is a third means* of the worthy participation of the holy supper, is because charity and faith make one, like heat and light in the time of spring, from which two conjoined, every tree springs forth afresh; in like manner, from spiritual heat, which is charity, and from spiritual light, which is the truth of faith, every man lives. That faith in the Lord does this, is evident from these passages: *He that believeth in Me shall never die, but shall live,* John xi. 25, 26. *This is the will of the Father, that every one that believeth in the Son should have eternal life,* vi. 40. *God so loved the world that He gave his only-begotten Son, that every one that believeth in Him might have eternal life*, iii. 15, 16. *He that believeth in the Son hath eternal life; but he that believeth not the Son shall not see life, but the anger of God abideth on him*, iii. 36. *We are in the truth, in the Son of God, Jesus Christ: this is the true God and eternal life*, 1 John v. 20, 21.

723. It was shown in the chapter concerning REFORMATION AND REGENERATION, that man is regenerated by these three, the Lord, charity and faith, as one; and that one cannot come into heaven, unless he be regenerated; wherefore the Lord can open heaven to no others than the regenerate, and after natural death introduction into it is given to no others. By the regenerate who come worthily, are meant those who are internally in those three essentials of the church and heaven, but not those who are only externally; for these do not confess the Lord with the soul, but only with the tongue; and they do not exercise charity towards the neighbor with the heart, but only with the body. Such are all who work iniquity, according to these words of the Lord: *Then ye will begin to say, Lord, we have eaten and drunk in thy presence; but I shall say to you, I know you not whence ye are; depart from Me, all ye workers of iniquity*, Luke xiii. 26, 27

724. These things, like the former, may be illustrated by various things which agree and also correspond, as by these: That no others are admitted to the table of an emperor or a king, than those who are in high office and dignity; and that these also, before they come, clothe themselves with suitable garments, and adorn themselves with the badges of their office, that they may come acceptably, and be favored. Why not, when they come to the table of the Lord, who is *the Lord of lords and King of kings*, Rev. xvii. 14, to which all are called and invited; but those only who are spiritually worthy, and clothed in honorable apparel, after they rise up from the table, are admitted into the palaces of heaven, and into the joys there, and honored as princes, because they are sons of the greatest King; and afterwards they sit down daily with Abraham, Isaac and Jacob, Matt. viii. 11; by whom is meant the Lord as to the celestial Divine, the spiritual Divine and the natural Divine. Those same things may be compared also with weddings on earth, to which no others are invited than the relations, kindred and friends of the bridegroom and the bride; if any other one enters, he is admitted, indeed, but because he has no place at the table, he retires. It is similar with those who are called to the marriage of the Lord, as bridegroom, with the church, as bride; among whom those are relations, kindred and friends, who derive their lineage by regeneration from the Lord. Moreover, who in the world is initiated into the friendship of another, unless he trusts him with a sincere heart, and does his will? This one, and not others, he reckons among his friends, and intrusts to him his possessions.

725. VII. THAT THOSE WHO COME TO THE HOLY SUPPER WORTHILY, ARE IN THE LORD AND THE LORD IN THEM; CONSEQUENTLY, THAT CONJUNCTION WITH THE LORD IS EFFECTED BY THE HOLY SUPPER.

That those come to the Holy Supper worthily who are in faith in the Lord, and in charity towards the neighbor, and that the truths of faith set forth the presence of the Lord, and the goods of charity, together with faith, conjunction, has been demonstrated above in several chapters; from which it follows, that those who come to the holy supper worthily, are conjoined to the Lord, and those who are conjoined to the Lord are in Him and He in them. That this is the case with those who come worthily, the Lord himself declares in John, in these words: *He that eateth my flesh and drinketh my blood, abideth in Me and I in him*, vi. 56. That this is conjunction with the Lord, He also teaches elsewhere in the same: *Abide in Me and I in you; he that abideth in Me and I in him, the same beareth much fruit*, xv. 4, 5; and Rev. iii. 20. What else is conjunction with the Lord, but being among those who are in his body?

And those constitute his body, who believe in Him and do his will. His will is the exercise of charity according to the truths of faith.

726. That without conjunction with the Lord, eternal life and salvation cannot be given, is because He is both. That He is ETERNAL LIFE, is clearly evident from passages from the Word, and from this in John: *Jesus Christ is the true God, and eternal Life*, 1 John v. 21. That He is SALVATION, is because this and eternal life are one. His name JESUS also signifies salvation, and thence, in the whole Christian world, He is called THE SAVIOR. But still no others come worthily to the holy supper, but those who are interiorly conjoined to the Lord, and those are interiorly conjoined who are regenerate; but who the regenerate are was shown in the chapter concerning REFORMATION AND REGENERATION. Besides, there are many who confess the Lord and who do good to the neighbor; but if they do not do this from love towards the neighbor and from faith in the Lord, they are not regenerate; for they do good to the neighbor only for reasons which regard the world and themselves, but not the neighbor as the neighbor. The works of these are merely natural, which do not inwardly contain in them any thing spiritual; for they confess the Lord only with the mouth and lips, from which the heart is far distant. Love itself towards the neighbor, and faith itself, are from the Lord alone; and both are given to man, while, from his own free choice, he does good to the neighbor, and believes truths rationally, and looks to the Lord, and does these three things on account of the commandments in the Word; then the Lord implants charity and faith in the midst of him, and makes both spiritual. Thus the Lord conjoins man to Himself, and man himself to the Lord; for there is no conjunction, unless it be made reciprocally. But these things have been fully shown in the chapters concerning CHARITY, FAITH, FREE AGENCY AND REGENERATION.

727. It is known that conjunctions and consociations are made in the world by invitations to tables and by feasts, for thereby the person who invites intends something which contributes to some end, which respects agreement or friendship; much more the invitations which have spiritual things for an end. The feasts in the ancient churches were feasts of charity; in like manner in the primitive Christian church, in which they encouraged one another to continue in the worship of the Lord, from a sincere heart. The sons of Israel's eating together of the sacrifices near the tabernacle, signified nothing else than unanimity in the worship of Jehovah; wherefore, the flesh which was eaten was called holy, Jer. xi. 15; Hag. ii. 12; and in many other places, because it was a part of the sacrifice; why not the bread and wine and the paschal flesh, at the supper of the Lord, who offered Himself a sacrifice for the sins of the whole world? Moreover, conjunction with the Lord, by means of the holy supper, may be illustrated by the conjunction of families from one common father; from him descend those who are related by blood, and in order kindred and relations, and they all derive something from the first stock; but they do not thus derive flesh and blood, but from the flesh and blood, thus a soul and thence an inclination to similar things, by which they are conjoined. The conjunction itself also appears generally in the faces and also in the manners, and thence they are called one flesh, as Gen. xxix. 14; xxxvii. 27; 2 Sam. v. 1; xix. 12, 13; and elsewhere. The case is similar with conjunction with the Lord, who is the Father of all the faithful and the blessed; conjunction with Him is effected by means of love and faith, by which two are called one flesh. Thence it is, that He said, *He that eateth my flesh and drinketh my blood, abideth in Me and I in him.* Who does not see that bread and wine does not effect this, but that it is effected by the good of love which is meant by bread, and by the truth of faith which is meant by wine, which are the Lord's own, and from Him alone they proceed and are communicated? All conjunction also is

effected by love; and love is not love without confidence. Those who believe that the bread is flesh, and the wine blood, and cannot elevate the thought further, may remain in that belief, but no otherwise than that the most holy thing, which effects conjunc-'on with the Lord, is what is attributed and appropriated to man as his, although t continually remains the Lord's.

728. VIII. THAT THE HOLY SUPPER IS TO THOSE WHO COME TO IT WORTHILY AS A SIGNING AND SEAL THAT THEY ARE THE SONS OF GOD.

That the holy supper is to those who come to it worthily a signing and seal that they are the sons of God, is because, as was said above, the Lord is then present, and introduces into heaven those who are born of Him, that is, the regenerate. That the holy supper does this, is because the Lord is then present also as to his Human; for it was shown above, that the whole of the Lord is present in the holy supper, and the whole of his redemption; for He says of the bread, *This is my body*, and of the wine, *This is my blood;* consequently, He admits them then into his body; and the church and heaven constitute his body. When man is being regenerated, the Lord is indeed present, and by his divine operation prepares man for heaven; but that he may actually enter, man must actually present himself to the Lord; and because the Lord actually presents Himself to man, man must actually receive Him, not, indeed, as He hung on the cross, but as He is in his glorified Human, in which He is present; and the body of this is divine good, and its blood is divine truth: these are given to man, and by them he is regenerated, and is in the Lord and the Lord in him; for, as was shown above, the eating which is exhibited in the holy supper is a spiritual eating. From these things rightly perceived, it is evident, that the holy supper is a signing and seal that those who come to it worthily are the sons of God.

729. But those who die in infancy or childhood, and thus do not attain such an age that they can worthily come to the holy supper, are introduced by the Lord by means of baptism; for as it was shown in the chapter concerning baptism, *baptism is an introduction into the Christian church, and at the same time an insertion among Christians in the spiritual world;* and the church and heaven there are one; wherefore, for those there, introduction into the church is also into heaven, and these, because they are educated under the auspices of the Lord, are regenerated more and more, and become his children; for they know no other father. But infants and children, born out of the Christian church, are introduced by other means, than by baptism, into the heaven designated for their religion, after the reception of faith in the Lord; but they are not mixed with those who are in the Christian heaven. For there is not any nation in all the world which may not be saved, if they acknowledge a God and live well; for the Lord redeemed them all, and man is born spiritual, by which he has the faculty of receiving the gift of redemption. Those who receive the Lord, that is, have faith in Him, and are not in evils of life, are called SONS OF GOD, AND BORN OF GOD, John i. 12, 13; xi. 52; and also SONS OF THE KINGDOM, Matt. xiii. 38; and likewise HEIRS, xix. 29; xxv. 34. The DISCIPLES of the LORD are also called SONS, ix. 15; and so are ALL THE ANGELS, Job i. 6; ii. 1.

730. It is with the holy supper as with a covenant, which, after the articles are agreed upon, is ratified and sealed up with a seal. That the blood of the Lord is a covenant He himself teaches; for He said, when He took the cup and gave, *Drink ye all of it; this is my blood, that of the New Testament*, Matt. xxvii. 28; Mark xiv. 24; Luke xxii. 20. The New Testament is the New Covenant; wherefore, the Word written by the prophets before the coming of the Lord is called the Old Testament and Covenant; and the Word written by the evangelists and apostles, after his coming, the New Testament or Covenant. That the divine truth of the Word is meant by blood, and likewise by the wine, in the holy supper, may be seen above in ar

ticle ii. n. 706, 708; and the Word is the covenant itself, which the Lord has made with man, and man with the Lord; for the Lord descended as the Word, that is, as the Divine Truth. And because this is his blood, therefore blood, in the Israelitish church, which was representative of the Christian church, was called THE BLOOD OF THE COVENANT, Exod. xxiv. 7, 8; Zech. ix. 11; and the Lord, THE COVENANT OF THE PEOPLE, Isaiah xlii. 6; xlix. 8, Jer. xxxi. 31 to 34; Psalm cxi. 9. It is also according to the order in the world, that a covenant should be signed and sealed in order that there may be any certainty, and that that should follow after deliberate acts. What is a commission or a will, unless it be sealed? What is the decision of a judge, without the sentence subscribed, that the judgment may be established? What is a high office in a kingdom, without a diploma? What is promotion to any office, without confirmation? What is the possession of a house without a purchase, or agreement with the owner? What is a progression to any end, or running to any goal, and thus for a prize, if there is not any end or goal, where one will obtain the prize, and unless the judge has in some manner made his wager sure? But these last things are added only for the sake of illustration, that it may be perceived even by the simple, that the holy supper is as it were a signing, a seal, a ticket, and the witnessing of a commission, even before the angels, that they are the sons of God; and moreover as a key to the house in heaven where they will dwell to eternity.

---

731. Once an angel was seen by me, flying under the eastern heaven, who held a trumpet in his hand and to his mouth, and sounded towards the north, towards the west, and towards the south. He had on a robe which flowed backwards, as he flew, and was girded with a belt of carbuncles and sapphires, as it were, flaming and shining. He flew downwards, and gently alighted on the earth, near the spot where I was. As soon as he touched the earth, erect on his feet, he went hither and thither; and then, seeing me, directed his steps towards me. I was in the spirit, and in it was standing on a hil. in the southern quarter; and when he was near, I spoke to him, and asked, "What is the matter now? I heard the sound of your trumpet, and saw your descent through the air." The angel answered, "I am sent to call together the most celebrated for erudition, the most acute in genius, and the most eminent in reputation for wisdom, that are from the kingdoms of the Christian world on this earth; that they may come together upon this hill, where you are staying, and disclose their minds, what they in the world had thought, understood and tasted of HEAVENLY JOY and of ETERNAL HAPPINESS. The cause of my being sent is this; that some new comers from the world, being admitted into our heavenly society, which is in the east, related that not a single one in the whole Christian world knows what heavenly joy is, and what eternal happiness is, thus what heaven is. At this, my brethren and companions greatly wondered; and they said to me, 'Descend, convoke and assemble the wisest in the world of spirits, into which all mortals are first gathered together after their departure from the natural world, in order that, from the mouth of many, we may be assured whether it is true, that Christians are in such thick darkness and profound ignorance concerning the future life.'" And he said to me, "Wait a while, and you will see companies of the wise flowing hither; the Lord will prepare a house of meeting for them." I waited, and behold, after half an hour, I saw two troops from the north, two from the west, and two from the south; and as they came, they were introduced by the angel of the trumpet into the house prepared, and there occupied the places designated for them according to the quarters. There were six troops or companies; a seventh was from the east, which, on account of the light, was not seen by the rest. After they had assembled, the angel opened the cause of their being called together, and requested that the companies in

order would bring forth their wisdom concerning HEAVENLY JOY and concerning ETERNAL HAPPINESS. And then each company formed itself into a circle, their faces being turned to faces, that they might recall the subject from the ideas entertained in the former world, and might now consider it, and, after consideration and consultation, express their sentiments.

732. After consultation, the FIRST COMPANY, which was from the north, said, "That heavenly joy and eternal happiness were one with the very life of heaven; wherefore, every one who enters heaven, as to life, enters into its festivities, just as one who enters into a wedding enters into its festivities. Is not heaven before our eyes above us, thus in place? And are there not there, and not elsewhere, enjoyments upon enjoyments and pleasures upon pleasures? Into these man is brought, as to every perception of the mind, and as to every sensation of the body, from the fulness of the joys of that place, when he is brought into heaven. Wherefore, heavenly happiness, which is also eternal, is nothing else than admission into heaven, and admission is of divine grace." When they had said this, the OTHER COMPANY from the north, from their wisdom, expressed this opinion: "Heavenly joy and eternal happiness are nothing else than the most delightful intercourse with angels and the sweetest conversations with them, by which their faces are continually kept expanded in gladness, and the mouths of the whole company in pleasant smiles from entertaining and facetious discourse; and what are heavenly joys, but the variations of such things to eternity?" The THIRD COMPANY, which was the first of the wise from the western quarter, from the thoughts of their affections, uttered this: "What else is heavenly joy and eternal happiness, than feasting with Abraham, Isaac and Jacob, upon whose tables there will be rich and delicate food, and generous and noble wines; and after the feasts, sports and dances of virgins and young men, dancing to concerts of vocal and instrumental music, the sweetes songs being sung at intervals; and finally, in the evening, there will be shows of persons masked; and after this feasts again, and thus every day to eternity?" When they had said this, the FOURTH COMPANY, which was the second from the western quarter, declared their sentiments, saying, "We have entertained many ideas concerning heavenly joy and eternal happiness, and we have examined various joys, and compared them one with another, and have concluded that heavenly joys are paradisiacal joys. What is heaven, but a paradise, which extends from the east to the west, and from the south to the north, having in it trees of fruit and flowers of delight, in the midst of which is the magnificent tree of life, around which the blessed will sit, eating fruits of delicate flavor, and adorned with garlands of flowers of the sweetest odor? And as these fruits and flowers, by the genial influences of a perpetual spring, are produced and reproduced every day, with infinite variety; and as the mind is continually renovated by their perpetual growth and bloom, and at the same time by the vernal temperature of the air; it cannot but daily imbibe and respire new joys, and thence be brought back to the bloom of life, and through this to the primitive state, in which Adam and his wife were created, and thus b· sent back into their paradise, which was transferred from earth to heaven." The FIFTH COMPANY, which was the first of the ingenious from the southern quarter, expressed this opinion: "Heavenly joys and eternal happiness are nothing else than supereminent dominions and immense riches, and thence more than royal magnificence, and the most dazzling splendor. That the joys of heaven, and the continual fruition of these joys, which is eternal happiness, are those things, we clearly saw from those in the former world who possessed them; and also from this, that the happy in heaven are to reign with the Lord, and to be kings and princes, because they are the sons of Him who is King of kings, and Lord of lords; and that they are to sit upon thrones, and

that the angels are to minister to them. The magnificence of heaven we clearly saw from this, that the New Jerusalem, by which is described the glory of heaven is to have gates, each of which will be one pearl, and streets of pure gold, and a wall founded upon precious stones; consequently, that every one who is received into heaven, has a palace of his own glittering with gold and precious stones, and a dominion which will pass in order from one to another. And because we know, that there are, in such things, innate joys and inherent happiness, and that the promises of God are irrefragable, we could not deduce the most happy state of heavenly life from any other source." After this, the SIXTH COMPANY, which was the second from the southern quarter, lifted up their voice, and said, "The joy of heaven and its eternal happiness are nothing else than a perpetual glorification of God, a never-ceasing festival, and most blessed worship, with songs and jubilees; and thus a constant elevation of the heart to God, with full confidence of his acceptance of prayers and praises, on account of the divine munificence of their blessedness." Some of the company added, "That this glorification is to be accompanied with magnificent illuminations and with most fragrant incense, and with processions of pomp, the high-priest going before with a great trumpet, the primates and officers of different degrees following him, and after these, men with palms, and women with golden images in their hands."

733. The SEVENTH COMPANY, which, on account of its light, was not seen by the rest, was from the east of heaven: the angels were of the same society as the angel of the trumpet. They, when they heard in heaven, that not a single one in the Christian world knew what heavenly joy and eternal happiness were, said one to another, "Surely this cannot be true: it is impossible that Christians should be in such thick darkness, and in such stupor of mind. Let us also go down and hear whether it be true, and if it be so, it is indeed a prodigy." Then those angels said to the angel of the trumpet, "You know that every man who had desired heaven, and had thought any thing certain concerning the joys there, after death, is introduced into the joys of his imagination; and that, after they have experienced what those joys are, that they are according to the vain ideas of their mind, and according to the deliriums of their fantasy, they are led out of them, and are instructed: this is done to most of those in the world of spirits, who, in the former life, meditated about heaven, and concluded any thing respecting the joys there, even to the desire of them." Having heard this, the angel of the trumpet said to the six companies called together from the wise of the Christian world, "Follow me, and I will introduce you into your joys, thus into heaven."

734. Having said this, the angel went before, and was first attended by the company of those who had persuaded themselves that heavenly joys were only the most pleasant intercourse and the sweetest conversations: these the angel introduced to companies in the northern quarter, who in the former world had entertained no other ideas of the joys of heaven. There was there a spacious house, in which such were gathered together; in the house there were more than fifty apartments, distinguished according to the various kinds of conversation. In some apartments they conversed about such things as they had seen and heard in the public squares and in the streets; in others they conversed about the various amiable qualities of the fair sex, with so much pleasantry that the faces of all in the company were expanded with smiles of mirth; in other apartments they spoke of the news, concerning courts, concerning ministries, concerning state policy, concerning various things which had emanated from privy councils, together with reasonings and conjectures concerning the events; in others concerning trade; in others concerning subjects of literature; in others about such things as are of civil prudence and moral life; in others concerning the affairs of the church and concerning

sects; &c. It was given me to look into that house, and I saw them running about from one apartment to another, seeking for some to sympathize with their affection, and thence to participate of their joy. And in the companies I saw three kinds of persons, some, as it were, panting to speak, some desiring to ask questions, and some eager to hear. The house had four doors, one on each side; and I observed that many were leaving the company and hastening to go out. I followed some to the east door, and saw some sitting near it with sad faces, and I went to them and asked why they sat so sad; and they replied, "The doors of this house are kept shut for those who would go out; and now it is the third day since we entered, and we have exhausted the life of our desire in company and conversation, and we have become so tired of continual talking that we can scarcely bear to hear the noise of their talk. Wherefore, from weariness, we betook ourselves to this door and knocked; but the answer to us is, 'That the doors of this house are not opened for those who would go out, but for those who would come in. Stay and enjoy the joys of heaven.' From which answers we have concluded that we are to remain here to eternity. Thence sadness seized our minds, and now our breast begins to be contracted, and anxiety to arise." Then the angel addressed them, and said, "This state is the death of your joys, which alone you believed to be heavenly; when yet they are only accessory to heavenly joys." And they asked the angel, "What, then, is heavenly joy?" And the angel answered in these few words: "It is the delight of doing something which is of use to one's self and to others; and the delight of use derives its essence from love, and its existence from wisdom. The delight of use arising from love through wisdom, is the life and soul of all heavenly joys. There is in the heavens most pleasant intercourse, which exhilarates the minds of the angels, gladdens their hearts, delights their breasts, and recreates heir bodies; but these are for them after they have performed uses in their offices and in their employments. From these there is a soul and life in all their joys and entertainments; but if you take away that soul or life, the accessory joys gradually become no joys; but first they become indifferent, then, as it were, worthless, and finally sad and anxious." This being said, the door was opened, and those who sat there leaped out, and ran home, each to his office and to his employment; and they were refreshed.

735. After this, the angel addressed those who had formed to themselves the idea concerning the joys of heaven, and concerning eternal happiness, that they would consist in feasting with Abraham, Isaac and Jacob; and, after the feasts, in games and shows, and feasts again, and so to eternity. And he said to them, "Follow me, and I will introduce you into the felicities of your joys." And he led them through a grove into a plain covered over with a floor, upon which were set tables, fifteen on one side and fifteen on the other; and they asked why there were so many tables. And the angel answered, "The first table is Abraham's, the second Isaac's, the third Jacob's; and next to them, in a series, are the tables of the twelve apostles: on the other side are the same number of tables for their wives; the three first tables are for Sarah, Abram's wife, for Rebecca, Isaac's wife, and for Leah and Rachel, Jacob's wives, and the other twelve for the wives of the twelve apostles." After a while, all the tables appeared covered with dishes, and the spaces between them ornamented with little pyramids filled with sauces. The guests stood around them in expectation of seeing the presidents of the tables, who, after a little while, were seen entering in the order of a procession from Abram to the last of the apostles; and presently each one, coming to his table, placed himself on a couch at the head of it; and then they said to those who were standing around, "Take your places also with us;" and the men took their places with those fathers, and the women with their wives

and they ate and drank with joy and with veneration. After dinner, those fathers went out, and then games were introduced, and dances of virgins and young men, and then shows; after which they were again invited to feasting, but with this statement, that the first day they should eat with Abram, the next with Isaac, the third with Jacob, the fourth with Peter, the fifth with James, the sixth with John, the seventh with Paul, and with the rest in order, even to the fifteenth day, when they should again renew their festivities in a similar order, only changing seats; and thus to eternity. After this the angel called together the men of the company, and said to them, "All those whom you saw at the tables were in a like imaginary thought concerning the joys of heaven, and thence of eternal happiness, with you; and in order that they might see the vanity of their ideas, and be led away from them, such festival scenes were appointed and permitted by the Lord. Those chiefs whom you saw at the heads of the tables were personated old men, most of them rustics who had beards, and were proud of their superior opulence, and fancied that they were those ancient fathers. But follow me into the ways that lead from this apartment." And they followed, and saw fifty here and fifty there, who had filled their stomachs with food even to the desire of vomiting: and they ardently desired to return to the proper duties of their homes, some to their offices, some to their trades, and some to their labors. But many were retained by the keepers of the grove, and questioned concerning the days of their feasting, and whether they had yet eaten at the tables with Peter and with Paul: and if they went out before, it would be to their shame, because it is indecent. But most of them answered, "We have exhausted our joys; food has become insipid to us; we have no relish for it; our stomach loathes it, and we cannot bear to taste it; we have spent several days and nights in that luxury, and we earnestly beg that we may be let out." And being let go, with a short breath and quick step they ran home. After this the angel called the men of the company, and in the way he taught them these things respecting heaven "In heaven, as well as in the world there are meats and drinks, there are feasts and repasts: the great ones there have tables, upon which are the richest kinds of food, dainties and delicacies, by which their minds are exhilarated and recreated; and there are also games and shows; there is music, vocal and instrumental; and all those things in the highest perfection. Such things also are joys to them, but not happiness; happiness must be in the joys, and thence from the joys; the happiness in joys causes them to be joys; it gives them their relish, and prevents them from becoming tasteless and loathsome; and this happiness every one has from the use which he performs in his function. There is a certain latent vein in the affection of the will of every angel, which draws his mind to do something; the mind, by this, tranquillizes and satisfies itself; this satisfaction and that tranquillity make a state of mind receptible of the love of use from the Lord; from the reception of this is heavenly happiness, which is the life of those joys which have been before mentioned. Heavenly food, in its essence, is nothing else than love, wisdom and use together; that is, use through wisdom from love; wherefore, food for the body is given to every one in heaven, according to the use which he performs; magnificent to those who are in eminent uses: moderate, but of exquisite relish, to those who are in uses of a middle degree; and mean to those who are in mean uses; but none to the slothful."

736. After this he called to him the company of the wise, so called, who had placed heavenly joys, and from them eternal happiness, in supereminent dominions and inexhaustible treasures, and in more than royal magnificence and splendor; because it is said in the Word, that they were to be kings and princes, and that they were to reign with Christ for ever, and that they were to be ministered to by angels

beside many more things. The angel said to them, "Follow me, and I will introduce you into your joys." And he led them into a portico constructed of columns and pyramids; in the front there was a porch, through which was the entrance into the portico; through this he introduced them; and behold there were seen twenty there, and they were waiting. And then suddenly there came one who personated an angel, and said to them, "The way to heaven is through this portico. Stay a little while, and prepare yourselves, because the older of you are to be kings, and the younger princes." This being said, there appeared near each column a throne, and upon each throne a robe of silk, and upon each robe a sceptre and a crown; and near each pyramid there appeared a seat raised three cubits from the ground, and upon the seat a chain of little links of gold, and the badges of the order of knighthood, tied together at the ends with diamond rings. And then it was said with a loud voice, "Go now, put on your garments, sit down and wait." And forthwith the older ones ran to the thrones, and the younger ones to the seats, and put on their garments, and seated themselves. But then there appeared, as it were, a thick cloud ascending from below, which being drawn to those who sat upon the thrones and seats, they began to swell in the face, to be elevated in the breast, and to be filled with confidence that they were now kings and princes: that cloud was an exhalation of fantasy, with which they were inspired; and suddenly there flew to them young men, as it were, from heaven, and they stood, two behind each throne, and one behind each seat, to minister. And then proclamation was made to them by a herald, "Kings and princes, wait yet a little while; your palaces in heaven are now being prepared; very soon the courtiers, with the guards, will come and introduce you." They waited and waited, until their spirits drooped, and they became weary with desire. After the space of three hours, the heaven was opened over their heads, and the angels looked down, and, pitying them, said, 'Why do you sit thus infatuated, and act parts that do not belong to you? They have played tricks with you, and changed you from men into idols, because you had taken it into your hearts, that you are to reign with Christ as kings and princes, and that then the angels are to minister to you. Have you forgotten the words of the Lord, that in heaven whosoever wishes to be great, let him become a servant? Learn, then, what is meant by being kings and princes, and what by reigning with Christ; that it is to be wise and do uses; for the kingdom of Christ, which is heaven, is a kingdom of uses. For the Lord loves all, and thence wills good to all, and good is use; and because the Lord does good or uses mediately by angels, and in the world by men, therefore, to those who faithfully perform uses, He gives the love of use and its reward, which is internal blessedness; and this is eternal happiness. There are in the heavens, as on earth, supereminent dominions, and the richest treasures; for there are governments and forms of governments, and thus there are greater and less powers and dignities; and those who are in the highest stations have palaces and courts, which, in magnificence and splendor, exceed the palaces and courts of emperors and kings on the earth; and from the number of their courtiers, ministers and guards, and from the magnificent vestures of these, honor and glory surround them. But those highest ones are chosen from those whose hearts are in the public welfare, and only the senses of the body in the amplitude of magnificence for the sake of obedience; and because it is of the public welfare that every one should be of some use in the society, as in a common body, and because all use is from the Lord, and is done by angels and men as if from them, it is manifest that this is to reign with the Lord." These things being heard from heaven, those who had personated kings and princes descended from their thrones and seats, and cast away the sceptres, crowns and robes, and the thick cloud, in which was the aura of fantasy, receded from them, and a bright cloud, in which was the aura of wisdom, encompassed them; from which sanity returned to their minds.

737. After this the angel returned to the house of assembly of the wise from the Christian world, and called to him those who had induced upon themselves a belief, that the joys of heaven and eternal happiness were paradisiacal delights. To these he said, "Follow me, and I will introduce you into paradise, your heaven, that you may commence the beatitudes of your eternal happiness." And he introduced them through a high gate, formed of interwoven boughs and shoots of noble trees. After they had entered, he led them about, through winding ways, from quarter to quarter. It was actually a paradise, at the first entrance into heaven, into which those are sent, who, in the world, had believed that the whole heaven was one paradise, because it is called paradise, and who had impressed on themselves the idea, that after death there is a perfect rest from labors, and that this rest would be nothing else than inhaling the most exquisite delights, walking upon beds of roses, regaling themselves with the most delicate wines, and celebrating festive repasts; and that this life is not given, except in a celestial paradise. Being led by the angel, they saw a great multitude both of old and young men, and boys, and also of women and girls, sitting three and three, and ten and ten, upon beds of roses, wreathing garlands to adorn the heads of the old men, the arms of the young, and the bosoms of the boys; others were pressing the juice out of grapes, cherries and mulberries, into cups, and drinking merrily; others were inhaling with their nostrils the fragrancies exhaled from the flowers, fruits and odoriferous leaves in all directions; others were singing sweet songs, with which they soothed the ears of those present; others were sitting by fountains, and directing the waters of the gushing stream into various forms; others were walking, talking together, and scattering wit and pleasantry; others were going into arbors, that they might lie down upon couches; besides many other paradisiacal pleasures. After these things had been seen, the angel led his companions hither and thither through winding paths and at last to some who were sitting in a most beautiful bed of roses, which was surrounded with olive, orange and citron-trees, who nodding, held their hands under their cheeks, mourning and weeping. The companions of the angel spoke to them, and said, "Why do you sit thus?" And they answered, "It is now the seventh day since we came into this paradise. When we entered, our minds seemed as if elevated into heaven, and let into the inmost happiness of its joys; but after the space of three days, those pleasures began to grow dull, to lose their relish in our minds, and to become imperceptible, and thus none: and when our imaginary joys thus expired we feared the loss of all the enjoyment of our life, and became doubtful about eternal happiness, whether there be any such thing. Afterwards we wandered through streets and uninhabited places in search of the gate through which we entered; but we wandered round and round, and inquired of whomsoever we met; some of whom said, that the gate is not to be found, because this paradisiacal garden is a spacious labyrinth, which is such, that whoever wishes to go out of it, gets farther in: wherefore, you cannot do otherwise than remain here to eternity; you are in the middle of it, where all delights are in their centre." And, moreover, they said to the companions of the angel, "We have now been sitting here for a day and a half, and because we are without hope of finding the way out, we have seated ourselves upon this rose-bed, and we see around us, in abundance, olives grapes, oranges and citrons; but the more we look at them, the more our sight is wearied with seeing, our smell with smelling, and our taste with tasting: this is the cause of the sadness, mourning and weeping in which you see us." On hearing these things, the conducting angel said to them, "This

paradisiacal labyrinth is truly an entrance into heaven. I know the way out of it, and will lead you out." When he had said this, those who were sitting arose, and embraced the angel, and followed him together with his company. And in the way the angel taught them what heavenly joy is, and eternal happiness thence, that they are not external paradisiacal delights, unless with these there are internal paradisiacal delights. External paradisiacal delights are only delights of the senses of the body, but internal paradisiacal delights are delights of the affections of the soul: unless the latter be in the former, there is no heavenly life, because there is no soul in them: and every delight, without its corresponding soul, continually becomes more and more languid and dull, and wearies the mind more than labor. There are every where in the heavens paradisiacal gardens, and from them also the angels have joys, and as far as the delight of the soul is in them, so far those joys are joys to them. On hearing this, they all asked, "What is the delight of the soul, and whence is it?" The angel answered, "The delight of the soul is from love and wisdom from the Lord; and because love is effective, and is effective by means of wisdom, therefore the seat of both is in the effect, and the effect is use. This delight from the Lord flows into the soul, and descends through the higher and lower regions of the mind into all the senses of the body, and fills itself in them; thence joy becomes joy, and it becomes eternal from the eternal source of it. You have seen the things of paradise, and I assure you that there is not any thing there, not even a little leaf, that is not from the marriage of love and wisdom in use: wherefore, if man be in this marriage, he is in a heavenly paradise, thus in heaven."

738. After this the conducting angel returned into the house to those who had firmly persuaded themselves, that heavenly joy and eternal happiness are a perpetual glorification of God, and a festival continuing to eternity, because they had, in the world, believed that they should then see God, and because the life of heaven, from the worship of God, is called a perpetual sabbath. To these the angel said, "Follow me, and I will introduce you into your joy." And he introduced them into a little city, in the middle of which there was a temple, and all the houses were called sacred chapels. In that city they saw a multitude flowing from every corner of the surrounding country, and among them a number of priests, who received those who came, saluted them, and, taking them by the hand, led them to the gates of the temple, and thence into some of the chapels around the temple, and initiated them into the everlasting worship of God; saying that this city was a place of entrance into heaven, and that the temple of this city was an entrance to the most spacious and magnificent temple, that is in heaven, where God is glorified by the angels with prayers and praises to eternity. The statutes here and there are, that they should first enter the temple, and remain there three days and three nights, and that after this initiation they should go into the houses of this city, which are so many chapels consecrated by us, and from chapel to chapel, and, in communion with those who are assembled there, should pray, shout, and rehearse what has been preached. You must by all means beware, lest you should think any thing in yourselves, and speak any thing with your consociates, but what is holy, pious and religious. After this the angel introduced his companions into the temple, which was filled and crowded with many who had been in great dignity in the world, and also with many of the common people; and guards were stationed at the gates, that no one might be allowed to go out, before completing the stay of three days. And the angel said, "To-day is the second day since these entered; observe them, and you will see their glorification of God." And they observed them, and saw most of them asleep, and those who were awake yawning and yawning, and some of them, from a continual elevation of the thoughts to God, without any relapse of them into the body, like

faces severed from the body, for so they appeared to themselves, and thence also to others; some roving with their eyes, from a perpetual withdrawing of them: in a word, all felt a compression of the breast, and weariness of spirit from fatigue, and were turned away from the pulpit, and crying, "Our ears are stunned; finish your discourses; your voice is no longer heard, and the sound of it begins to be intolerable." And then they rose up, and ran in a body to the gates, broke them open, and rushed upon the guards, and drove them away. On seeing this, the priests followed them, and joined themselves to their sides, teaching and teaching, praying, sighing and saying, "Celebrate the festival; glorify God; sanctify yourselves: in this entry of heaven we will initiate you into the eternal glorification of God in the most spacious and magnificent temple, that is in heaven, and thus to the enjoyment of eternal happiness. But these things were not understood by them, and were scarcely heard, on account of the listlessness occasioned by the suspension of their mind for the space of two days, and its detention from domestic and secular affairs. But when they attempted to tear themselves away from the priests, the priests took hold of their arms, and also of their garments, urging them to the chapels where what had been preached was rehearsed; but in vain. And they cried, "Let us alone; we feel as if we should faint away." At these words, lo, there were seen four men in white garments, and wearing mitres: one of them in the world had been an archbishop, and the other three had been bishops, and had now become angels. These called the priests together, and addressing them, said, "We have seen you from heaven with these sheep, how you feed them: you feed them even to insanity. You do not know what is meant by the glorification of God: it is meant, to produce the fruits of love, that is, to do faithfully, sincerely and diligently the work of one's station; for this is of the love of God and of the love of the neighbor, and this is the bond of society and its good: by this God is glorified, and then by worship at stated times Have you not read these words of the Lord? *In this is my Father glorified, that ye bring forth much fruit, and become my disciples*, John xv. 8. You priests can be in the glorification of worship, because this is your office, and thence you have honor, glory and recompense; but still you could not be, any more than they, in that glorification, unless honor, glory and recompense were together with your office." Having said these words, the bishops commanded the keepers of the door to let all in, and let all out; for there are a great many who cannot think of any other heavenly joy than the perpetual worship of God, because they do not know any thing concerning the state of heaven.

739. After this the angel, with his companions, returned to the house of assembly, from which the several companies of the wise had not yet departed; and there he called to him those who believed that heavenly joy and eternal happiness were only an admission into heaven, and admission from divine grace; and that then they should have joy, just as those do in the world, who go into the palaces of kings on days of festivity, or who go by invitation to a wedding. To these the angel said, "Stay here a little while, and I will sound the trumpet, and hither will come those who are renowned for wisdom in the spiritual things of the church." After some hours, there came nine men, each adorned with a laurel as the mark of his fame. These the angel introduced into the house of assembly, in which all those before called together were present. In their presence the angel addressed the nine laurelled ones, and said, "I know that, agreeably to your desire, and according to your idea, it has been given you to ascend into heaven, and that you have returned to this lower or subcelestial earth, with a full knowledge of the state of heaven. Tell us, therefore, how heaven seemed to you." And they answered in order; and the First said, "My idea of heaven, from my earliest childhood even to the end of my life in the world, was, that it was a place of all

blessings, enjoyments, delights, gratifications and pleasures; and that if I were admitted into it, I should be encompassed with an atmosphere of such felicities, and should drink them in with a full breast, like a bridegroom, when he celebrates his nuptials, and when he enters the bride-chamber with the bride. In this idea I ascended into heaven, and passed the first guard, and also the second; but when I came to the third, the captain of the guard accosted me, and said, 'Who are you, friend?' And I answered, 'Is not heaven here? According to my ardent desire I have ascended hither. Admit me, I beseech you.' And he admitted me. And I saw angels in white garments, and they came around me, and examined me, and murmured this: 'Behold here a new guest who is not clothed with the raiment of heaven.' I heard these words, and thought, This appears to me like the case of him of whom the Lord said, that he came into the wedding without a wedding garment. And I said, 'Give me such garments;' but they laughed. And then one ran to me from the court, with the command, 'Strip him naked, cast him out, and throw his clothes after him.' And so I was cast out." The SECOND in order said, "I believed, likewise, that, if I were only admitted into heaven, which is over my head, joys would flow around me, and I should inhale them to eternity. I also obtained what I desired; but the angels, on seeing me, fled away, and said one to another, 'What monster is this? How came this bird of night hither?' And I actually felt a change from being a man, although I was not changed: this was occasioned by my inhaling the heavenly atmosphere. But presently there ran to me one from the court, with the command that two servants should lead me out, and conduct me back by the way of ascent even to my house; and when I was at home, I appeared to others, and also to myself, as a man." The THIRD said, "I always had an idea of heaven from place, and not from love; wherefore, when I came into this world, I desired heaven with great desire; and I saw some ascending, and I followed them, and was admitted, but only for a few steps: and when I wished to regale my mind according to my idea of the joys and blessedness there, from the light of heaven, which was white as snow, the essence of which is said to be wisdom, my mind was seized with stupor, and thence my eyes with thick darkness, and I began to be insane. And presently, from the heat of heaven, which corresponds to the brightness of its light, the essence of which is said to be love, my heart palpitated, I was seized with anxiety, and tortured with inward pain, and I threw myself down flat upon the ground there. While I lay there, an attendant came from the court, with a command that they should carry me gently away into my own light, and into my own heat; into which when I came, my spirit and my heart returned to me." The FOURTH said, "That he also had been in the idea of place, and not in the idea of love, respecting heaven. As soon as I came into the spiritual world, I asked the wise whether it were lawful to ascend into heaven. They said it was lawful for any one; but that they must beware lest they should be cast down. At this I laughed, and ascended, believing, as others do, that all in the whole world were receptible of the joys there in their fulness. But truly, when I was within, I became almost lifeless, and, from the pain and torment in my head and in my body, I prostrated myself upon the ground, and writhed like a serpent put near the fire: and I crept even to the brink of a precipice, and cast myself down there; and afterwards I was taken up by those standing below, and carried into an inn, where soundness returned to me." The OTHER FIVE also told wonderful things respecting their ascents into heaven, and they compared the changes of the states of their life with the state of fishes, when they are raised out of water into air, and with the state of birds in ether. And they said that after those hard lots, they desired heaven no more but only a life in connection with their like wherever they are; and that they knew that, in the world of spirits, where we are, all are before prepared, the good for heaven, and the bad for hell; and that after they are prepared, they see ways open for them to societies of their like, with whom they are to remain to eternity, and that they then enter these ways with delight, because they then are ways of their love. All those who were first called together, hearing these things, also confessed that they neither had entertained any other idea, of heaven than as of a place where, with a full mouth, they should drink in the circumfluent joys to eternity. After this the angel of the trumpet said to them, "You see now that the joys of heaven and eternal happiness are not of any particular place, but that they are of the state of man's life; and the state of heavenly life is from love and wisdom; and because use is the continent of those two, the state of heavenly life is from the conjunction of these in use. It is the same if it be said, charity, faith, and good works, since charity is love, faith is truth from which is wisdom, and good work is use. Moreover, in our spiritual world, there are places as in the natural world, otherwise there would be no habitations and distinct abodes; but still, place there is not place, but an appearance of place, according to the state of love and wisdom, or of charity and faith. Every one who becomes an angel carries within himself his own heaven, because the love of his own heaven; for man from creation is the least effigy, image and type of the great heaven; the human form is nothing else. Wherefore every one comes into the society of heaven, of which he is the form, in a single effigy; therefore, when he enters into that society, he enters into a form corresponding to himself, thus, as it were, from himself into that self, and from that into that in himself, and draws the life of that as his own, and his own as the life of that. Every society is as a whole body, and the angels there are as similar parts from which the whole body coexists. Hence now it follows, that those who are in evils, and thence in falses, have formed in themselves the effigy of hell, and this is tortured in heaven from the influx and violence of the activity of an opposite upon an opposite; for infernal love is opposite to heavenly love, and thence the delights of those two loves clash with each other like enemies, and destroy each other whenever they come together."

740. After this a voice was heard from heaven to the angel of the trumpet: "Select ten from all those who are assembled, and introduce them to us. We have heard from the Lord, that He will prepare them, so that the light and heat, or the love and wisdom, of our heaven may not bring any harm upon them for three days." And ten were selected, and they followed the angel and they ascended by a steep path on to a certain hill, and from this on to a mountain, upon which was the heaven of those angels, which before, at a distance, had appeared to them like an expanse in the clouds. And the gates were opened for them, and after they had passed the third one, the introducing angel ran to the prince of that society or heaven, and announced their arrival. And the prince answered, "Take some of my guard, and carry them back word that their arrival is acceptable to me, and introduce them into my antecourt, and assign to each one his room with his bed-chamber; and take some of my attendants and servants, who may minister to them and serve them at their nod." And so it was done. But when they were introduced by the angel, they asked whether it was allowable to go and see the prince. And the angel answered, "It is now morning, and it is not allowable before noon; all are till then in their offices and employments; but you have been invited to dinner, and then you will sit at the table with our prince. In the mean time I will introduce you into his palace, where you will see magnificent and splendid things."

When they were brought to the palace, they first viewed it from without: it was large, built of porphyry, and had a foundation of jasper; and before the gate were six high columns of *lapis lazuli;* the roof was of plates of gold; the windows high, of the most transparent crystal; their frames also of gold. After this they were introduced within into the palace, and led around from room to room; and they saw ornaments of ineffable beauty, under the roof, decorations of inimitable sculpture. Near the walls were set tables of silver overlaid with gold, upon which were various utensils made of precious stones and of entire gems, in celestial forms, and many more things which no eye on earth had ever seen, and thence neither could any one make himself believe that such things are in heaven. While they were in astonishment at seeing those magnificent things, the angel said, "Do not wonder: these things which you see were not made and fabricated by any angelic hand, but were built by the Maker of the universe, and presented as a gift to our prince; wherefore, architecture is here in its very art, and from this are all the rules of this art in the world." Further, the angel said, "You may suppose that such things fascinate our eyes and infatuate them, so that we should believe them to be the joys of our heaven; but because our hearts are not in them, they are only accessory to the joys of our hearts: therefore, as far as we contemplate them as accessory, and as the workmanship of God, so far we contemplate in them the divine omnipotence and benignity."

741. After this the angel said to them, "It is not yet noon; come with me into the garden of our prince, contiguous to this palace." And they went, and at the entrance he said, "Behold the most magnificent garden in this heavenly society." But they answered, "What do you say? There is no garden here. We see only one tree, and on its branches and on its top, as it were, fruits of gold, and, as it were, leaves of silver, and the edges of them adorned with emeralds; and under that tree infants with their nurses." To this the angel, with an inspired voice, said, "This tree is in the midst of the garden, and it is called by us the tree of our heaven, and by some the tree of life. But proceed and approach, and your eyes will be opened, and you will see the garden." And they did so, and their eyes were opened, and they saw trees full of delicious fruits, entwined with vines full of leaves, the tops of which, with their fruit, bent towards the tree of life in the midst. These trees were set in a continued series, which commenced and proceeded in endless orbs or circles, as of a perpetual spiral: it was a perfect spiral of trees, in which one species followed another continually, according to the excellence of the fruits. The beginning of the circumgyration was at a considerable distance from the tree in the midst, and the intervening space glistened with a beam of light, from which the trees of the circle shone with a splendor which reached successively from the first to the last. The first trees were the most excellent of all, abounding with the richest fruits, called trees of paradise, never seen in any region of the natural world, because they do not and cannot grow there. After these followed trees of oil, after these trees of wine, after these trees of fragrance, and lastly, trees of timber useful for building. Here and there, in this spiral of trees, or in this circle, there were seats formed of the boughs of the trees behind brought together and interwoven with each other, and they were enriched and adorned with their fruits. In that perpetual orb of trees, there were passages which opened into flower-gardens and grass-plots, distinguished into areas and beds. The companions of the angel seeing these things, exclaimed, "Behold heaven in form! Whithersoever we turn our eyes, something of heaven and paradise flows in, which is ineffable." On hearing this, the angel rejoiced, and said, "All the gardens of our heaven are representative forms or types of heavenly beatitudes in their origins; and because the influx of these beatitudes elevated your minds, you exclaimed, *Behold heaven in form!* But those who do not receive that influx, look upon these things of paradise only as they look upon the things of a forest; and all those receive the influx who are in the love of use, but those do not receive it who are in the love of glory

and not from use." Afterwards he explained and taught what each of the things in the garden represented and signified.

742. While they were engaged in these things, there came a messenger from the prince, who invited them to eat bread with him; and then, at the same time, two attendants of the court brought garments of fine linen, and said, "Put on these, because no one is admitted to the table of the prince, unless he is clothed in the garments of heaven." And they prepared themselves, and accompanied their angel, and were introduced into an open gallery, the walk of the palace, and they waited for the prince; and there the angel introduced them to an acquaintance with grandees and moderators, who also were waiting for the prince. And lo, in about an hour the doors were opened, and through a wider one, on the western side, they saw his entrance in the order and pomp of a procession. Before him went his familiar counsellors, after these his privy counsellors, and after these the principal officers of the court; in the midst of these was the prince, and after him courtiers of various ranks, and lastly the guards; all together amounting to a hundred and twenty. The angel, standing before the ten new comers, who then appeared, from their dress, as inhabitants of the place, came up with them to the prince, and reverently presented them. And the prince, without stopping in the procession, said to them, "Come with me to eat bread." And they followed him into the dining room, and saw a table magnificently set; in the middle of it a high pyramid of gold with a hundred little dishes in triple order upon its branches, upon which were sweet cakes and condiments, with other delicacies made of bread and wine; and through the middle of the pyramid there issued, as it were, a fountain overflowing with nectareous wine, the stream of which, from the summit of the pyramid, dispersed itself, and filled the cups. At the sides of this high pyramid were various celestial forms of gold, upon which were dishes and plates filled with food of every kind. The celestial forms upon which the dishes and plates were set, were forms of art from wisdom, which cannot be produced by any art in the world, nor described by any words. The dishes and plates were of silver, having forms sculptured upon them like their supports: the cups were of transparent gems. Such was the furniture of the table.

743. The dress of the prince and his ministers was this: The prince had on a long robe of a purple color, spangled with stars of a silver color wrought with a needle. Under the robe he wore a tunic of shining silk of a blue color: this was open about the breast, where was seen the front part of a belt, with the ensign of his society The ensign was an eagle brooding over her young in the top of a tree: this was of shining gold set round with diamonds. The counsellors were dressed not very differently, but without that ensign: instead of it they had sculptured sapphires hanging from the neck by a golden chain. The courtiers were dressed in gowns of a brown color, in which were wrought flowers around young eagles: the tunics under them were of silk of an opaline color, as also were their breeches and stockings. Such was their dress.

744. The familiar counsellors, and the privy counsellors, and the moderators, stood around the table, and by order of the prince they folded their hands together, and at the same time whispered votive praise to the Lord, and after this the prince beckoned to them, and they seated themselves at the table. And the prince said to the ten strangers, "You also sit down with me: there are your seats." And they sat down; and the courtiers who were before sent by the prince to wait upon them stood behind them. And then the prince said to them, "Take each of you a plate from its stand, and afterwards each a saucer from the pyramid." And they did so; and lo, instantly new plates and saucers appeared set on in the place of them; and their cups were filled with wine from the fountain flow-

ing from the great pyramid; and they began to eat. When they had above half done, the prince addressed the ten invited guests, and said, "I heard, that in the earth, which is under this heaven, you were called together to disclose your thoughts concerning the joys of heaven and the eternal happiness thence, and that you expressed diverse opinions, each according to the delights of the senses of his body. But what are the delights of the senses of the body, without the delights of the soul? It is the soul which fills them with delight. The delights of the soul are in themselves imperceptible beatitudes, but they become more and more perceptible as they descend into the thoughts of the mind, and from these into the sensations of the body. In the thoughts of the mind they are perceived as happinesses, in the sensations of the body as delights, and in the body itself as pleasures: eternal happiness is from the former and the latter together; but from the latter alone that happiness is not eternal, but temporal, which comes to an end and passes away, and sometimes becomes unhappiness. You have seen now that all your joys also are joys of heaven, and more excellent than you could ever have conceived; but still these do not inwardly affect our minds. There are three things which as one flow from the Lord into our souls; these three as one, or this trine, are love, wisdom and use; but love and wisdom do not exist,except ideally, because only in the affection and thought of the mind; but in use really, because at the same time in the act and work of the body; and where they exist really, there they also subsist; and because love and wisdom exist and subsist in use, it is use that affects us; and use is faithfully, sincerely and diligently to perform the works of one's function. The love of use, and thence an application to use, keep the mind from becoming dissipated, and from wandering about and imbibing all the inordinate desires which flow in from the body and from the world through the senses, with allurements, by which the truths of religion and the truths of morality, with their goods, are scattered to all the winds; but application of the mind to use holds and binds them together, and disposes the mind into a form receptive of wisdom from those truths, and then it exterminates the fooleries and mockeries of falsities and vanities. But you will hear more about these things from the wise ones of our society, whom I will send to you in the afternoon." Having said this, the prince arose, and the guests also with him; and he said, "Peace," and commanded the angel, their leader, to conduct them back to their rooms, and show them all the honors of civility, and also to call men of politeness and affability to entertain them with conversation about the various joys of this society.

745. When they returned, it so was done; and those who were called from the city to entertain them with conversation about the various joys of the society, came, and after the usual salutations, they conversed with them, as they walked, very pleasantly. But the angel, their leader, said, "These ten men were invited into this heaven that they might see its joys, and thence receive a new idea concerning eternal happiness: tell, therefore, some of its joys, which affect the senses of the body: afterwards the wise are to come, who will tell some things which render those joys pleasant and happy." On hearing this, those who were called from the city recounted these things: (1.) There are here days of festivity appointed by the prince, that the mind may be relaxed from the fatigue which the desire of emulation had induced upon some. On these days there are concerts of music and songs in the public places; and out of the city games and shows. Then orchestras are raised in the public places, surrounded with lattices formed of thick vines, from which hang clusters of grapes; within which, on three elevations, sit musicians with stringed instruments, and with wind instruments, of tones high and low, soft and loud; and at the sides are men singers and women singers, and they entertain the citizens with the most delightful songs and anthems, choruses and solos, varied by

intervals, as to the kinds. These things continue here, on those days of festivity, from morning to noon, and after this till evening. (2.) Moreover, every morning there are heard, from the houses around the forum, the sweetest songs of virgins and girls, with which the whole city resounds. There is an affection of spiritual love, which is sung every morning, that is, is sounded by modifications or modulations of a musical voice, and that affection is perceived in the singing as if it were itself: it flows into the souls of the hearers, and excites them to a correspondence. Such is heavenly singing. The female singers say that the sound of their singing, as it were, inspires and animates itself from within, and delightfully exalts itself according to its reception by the hearers. This being ended, the windows of the houses of the forum, and at the same time of the houses of the streets, are shut, and also the doors; and the whole city is still, nor is any noise any where heard, nor do any loiterers appear: all then go about the duties of their offices. (3.) At noon the doors are opened, and in the afternoon the windows also, in some places, and sports of boys and girls are seen in the streets, their nurses and masters regulating them, sitting in the porches of the houses. (4.) At the sides of the city, in the outermost parts of it, there are various games of boys and young men; there are games of running, there are games of ball, there are games with the ball called racket; there are contests among the boys to find who are most expert in speaking, acting and perceiving, and for those who are most expert some leaves of laurel are given as a reward; besides many other things, which call forth into exercise the latent talents of the boys. (5.) Moreover, out of the city there are exhibitions of comedians upon theatres, representing the various proprieties and virtues of moral life, among whom there are also actors for the sake of relations." And one of the ten asked, "Why for the sake of relations?" And they answered "No virtue, with its proprieties and graces, can be set forth to the life, except by relatives from the greatest to the least of them. The actors represent the least of them even till they become none; but it is ordained by law, that they should exhibit nothing of the opposite, which is called dishonorable and indecorous, except figuratively, and, as it were, remotely: the reason that it is so ordained, is because nothing that is honorable and good, in any virtue, ever passes, by successive progressions, into what is dishonorable and evil, but to the least degrees of it, even till it perishes; and when it perishes the opposite commences. Wherefore heaven, where all things are honorable and good, has nothing in common with hell, where all things are dishonorable and evil."

746. While they were speaking, a servant came and told them that eight wise ones, by the order of the prince, had come, and wished to enter. On hearing which, the angel went and received them, and introduced them; and presently the wise ones, after the usual and proper civilities, first spoke with them concerning the beginnings and increments of wisdom, with which they intermixed various things respecting its progress, and that wisdom with the angels never ceases and comes to an end, but grows and increases to eternity. On hearing this, the angel of the company said to them, "Our prince at the table spoke with them about the seat of wisdom, that it is in use. Do you also, if you please, speak with them about that." And they said, "Man when first created, was imbued with wisdom and its love, not for the sake of himself, but for the sake of the communication of it with others from himself. Thence it is inscribed upon the wisdom of the wise, that no one should be wise and live for himself alone, but for others at the same time: thence is society, which otherwise would not be To live for others, is to perform uses: uses are the bonds of society, which are as many as there are good uses, and uses are infinite in number. There are spiritual uses, which are of love to God and love towards the neighbor there are moral and civil uses, which

are of the love of the society and state in which a man is, and of the associates and citizens with whom he is; there are natural uses, which are of the love of the world and its necessities; and there are bodily uses, which are of the love of self-preservation for the sake of higher uses. All these uses are inscribed upon man, and they follow in order one after another; and when they are together, one is in another. Those who are in the first uses, which are spiritual, are also in the following, and they are wise: but those who are not in the first, and yet in the second, and thence in the following, are not so wise, but only from external morality and civility, appear as if they were; those who are not in the first and second, but in the third and fourth, are not at all wise, for they are satans, for they love only the world, and themselves for the sake of the world; but those who are only in the fourth, are the least wise of all, for they are devils, because they live for themselves alone, and if for others, it is only for the sake of themselves. Moreover, every love has its delight, for love lives by this, and the delight of the love of uses is heavenly delight, which enters the delights following in order, and, according to the order of the succession, exalts them and makes them eternal. After this they enumerated the heavenly delights proceeding from the love of use, and said that they were myriads of myriads, and that those who are in heaven enter into them. And thus, by discourses of wisdom concerning the love of use, they passed the day with them even till evening.

But towards evening, a footman, clothed in linen, came to the ten strangers, the companions of the angel, and invited them to a wedding to be celebrated the next day; and the strangers were very glad that they were also to see a wedding in heaven. After this they were led to one of the familiar counsellors, and supped with him; and after supper they returned, and retired separately, each one into his bed-chamber, and slept till morning. And then, when they awoke, they heard the singing of virgins and girls from the houses around the forum, of which above. Then was sung the affection of conjugial love; by the sweetness of which, being deeply affected and moved, they perceived a blessed pleasantness infused into their joys, which elevated them and renewed them When it was time, the angel said, "Prepare yourselves, and put on the garments of heaven, which our prince has sent to you." And they put them on, and lo, the garments shone as from a flammeous light; and they asked the angel, "Whence is this?" He answered, "Because you are going to a wedding: with us the garments then shine and become wedding garments."

747. After this the angel led them to the house of the wedding, and the porter opened the door; and presently they were received within the threshold, and saluted by an angel sent from the bridegroom, and introduced, and led to the seats appointed for them; and soon they were invited into a room opposite to the bride-chamber, where they saw, in the middle, a table, on which was placed a magnificent candlestick, with seven branches and sconces of gold; and upon the walls hung lamps of silver, from which, when lighted, the atmosphere appeared as if gilded. And they saw at the sides of the candlestick two tables, upon which loaves of bread were placed in triple order; and at the four corners, tables on which were crystal cups. While they were surveying those things, lo, a door was opened from a room next to the bride-chamber, and they saw six virgins coming out, and after them the bridegroom and the bride, holding each other by the hand, and leading each other to a seat which was placed opposite to the candlestick, on which they seated themselves, the bridegroom on the left hand and the bride on his right, and the six virgins stood by the seat near the bride. The bridegroom had on a robe of glittering purple and a tunic of shining fine linen, with an ephod, upon which was a plate of gold set around with diamonds, and on the plate was engraven a young

eagle, the nuptial ensign of that society of heaven, and a mitre covered the bridegroom's head. But the bride had on a scarlet mantle, and under it an embroidered gown reaching from her neck to her feet, and under her breast a golden girdle, and upon her head a crown of gold with rubies set in it. When they had thus seated themselves, the bridegroom turned himself to the bride, and put on her finger a golden ring; and he took out a pair of bracelets and a collar of pearls, and tied the bracelets on her wrists, and the collar around her neck, and said, "Accept these pledges." And when she accepted them, he kissed her, and said, "Now you are mine;" and he called her his wife. This being done, the guests exclaimed, "A blessing be upon you." Each one exclaimed this by himself, and afterwards all of them together; one who was sent from the prince also exclaimed in his stead; and at that moment the room opposite to the bride-chamber was filled with that aromatic smoke, which was a sign of blessing from heaven. And the servants took the loaves of bread from the two tables near the candlestick, and the cups, now filled with wine, from the tables at the corners of the room, and gave to each of the guests his loaf and his cup, and they ate and drank. After this, the husband and his wife rose up, the six virgins, with silver lamps now lighted in their hands, following them to the threshold; and the married pair entered the bride-chamber, and the door was shut.

748. Afterwards the angel, who was the leader, spoke to the guests concerning his ten companions; that he had by command introduced them, and shown them the magnificent things in the palace of the prince, and the wonders there, and that they had dined at the table with him, and that afterwards they had conversed with our wise ones; and he asked, "May they also have some conversation with you?" And they came up and spoke with them. And one of the wise men that attended the wedding said, "Do you understand what those things signify, which you have seen?" They said that they did not very well. And then they asked him why the bridegroom, now a husband, was in such a dress. He answered that the bridegroom, now a husband, represented the Lord, and the bride, now a wife, represented the church; because a wedding in heaven represents the marriage of the Lord with the church. Thence it is, that there was a mitre on his head, and he had on a robe, a tunic and an ephod, like Aaron; and that there was a crown on the head of the bride, now a wife, and she had on a gown like a queen; but to-morrow they will be dressed differently, because this representation lasts only to-day. They asked again, "Since he represented the Lord, and she the church, why did she sit at his right hand?" The wise one answered, "Because there are two things which make the marriage of the Lord and the church, love and wisdom; and the Lord is love, and the church is wisdom, and wisdom is at the right hand of love; for the man of the church is wise as of himself, and as he becomes wise, he receives love from the Lord. The right hand also signifies power, and love has power by means of wisdom. But, as was said, after the wedding, the representation is changed; for then the husband represents wisdom, and the wife the love of his wisdom; but this love is not the prior love, but it is a secondary love, which the wife has from the Lord, through the wisdom of the husband. The love of the Lord, which is the prior love, is the love of becoming wise, with the husband; wherefore, after the wedding, both together, the husband and his wife, represent the church." They asked again, "Why did not you men stand by the side of the bridegroom, now the husband, as the six virgins stood by the side of the bride, now the wife?" The wise one answered, "The reason is, because we to-day are numbered among the virgins, and the number *six* signifies all and complete." But they said, "What is this?" He answered, "Virgins signify the church, and the church is of both sexes; wherefore we also, as to the church, are virgins. That it is so, is evident from these words in the

Revelation: *These are they who have not been defiled with women, for they are* VIRGINS; *and they follow the Lamb whithersoever He goeth,* xiv. 4. And because virgins signify the church, therefore the Lord *likened it to ten* VIRGINS *invited to a wedding,* Matt. xxv. 1, &c. And because the church is signified by Israel, Zion and Jerusalem, therefore it is so often said in the Word, THE VIRGIN AND DAUGHTER OF ISRAEL, OF ZION AND OF JERUSALEM. The Lord also describes his marriage with the church, in these words in David: THE QUEEN AT THY RIGHT HAND, *in the best gold of Ophir; her clothing is of wrought gold. She shall be brought to the King in* RAIMENT OF NEEDLE-WORK; *the* VIRGINS *her companions shall come after her into the king's palace,* Psalm xlv. 9 to 16." Afterwards they said, "Is it not proper that a priest should be present and minister in these things?" The wise one answered, "This is proper on earth, but not in the heavens, on account of the representation of the Lord himself and the church: this they do not know on earth. But still, with us a priest ministers at betrothings, and hears, receives, confirms and consecrates the consent: consent is the essential of marriage, and the other things which follow are its formalities."

749. After this, the conducting angel came to the six virgins, and told them also about his companions, and requested that they would favor them with their company. And they came up, but when they were near, they suddenly went back, and entered the women's apartment, where were also the virgins their companions. On seeing this, the conducting angel followed them, and asked why they went back so suddenly, without speaking with them. And they answered, "We could not approach." And he said, "Why is this?" And they answered, "We do not know; but we perceived something which repelled and led us back: they must excuse us." And the angel returned to his companions, and told their answer, and added, "I guess that your love of the sex is not chaste. In heaven, we love virgins for their beauty and the elegance of their manners; and we love them intensely, but chastely." At this his companions laughed, and said, "You guess rightly. Who is able to see such beauties near, and not desire something?"

750. After this social entertainment, all who had been invited to the wedding departed, and also those ten men with their angel: it was late in the evening, and they retired to rest. At the dawn of day, they heard a proclamation, TO-DAY IS THE SABBATH; and they arose, and asked the angel what that was for. He answered, "That it was for the worship of God, which returns at stated times, and is proclaimed by the priests. It is performed in our temples, and lasts about two hours. Wherefore, if you like, come with me, and I will introduce you." And they prepared themselves, and accompanied the angel, and entered; and behold, the temple was large, capable of holding about three thousands. It was of a semicircular form: the benches or seats were likewise curved, according to the form of the temple. The pulpit was before them, placed back a little from the centre; the door behind the pulpit, on the left hand. The ten strangers entered with the angel, their guide, and the angel showed them the seats where they should sit, saying to them, "Every one that enters the temple knows his place: this he knows from something within, nor can he sit any where else; if he does, he hears nothing and perceives nothing, and also he disturbs order, which being disturbed, the priest is not inspired."

751. After they had assembled, the priest ascended the pulpit, and preached a sermon full of the spirit of wisdom. The discourse was concerning the holiness of the Sacred Scripture, and concerning the conjunction of the Lord with both worlds, the spiritual and the natural, by means of it. In the illustration in which he was, he fully proved that that Holy Book was dictated by Jehovah the Lord, and that thence He is in it, so that He is the wisdom there; but that the wisdom which is Himself

therein, lies concealed under the sense of the letter, and is not opened except to those who are in the truths of doctrine, and at the same time in the goods of life; and thus in the Lord, and the Lord in them. To the discourse he subjoined a prayer, and descended. As the hearers were going out, the angel requested the priest to speak some words of peace to his ten companions. And he came to them, and they conversed together for half an hour; and he spoke of the Divine Trinity, that it is in Jesus Christ, in whom all the fulness of the Godhead dwelleth bodily, according to the declaration of the apostle Paul; and afterwards of the union of charity and faith; but he said, of the union of charity and truth, because faith is truth.

752. After expressing their thanks, they went home; and there the angel said to them, "This is the third day since your ascent into the society of this heaven, and you were prepared by the Lord to stay here three days; wherefore, it is time for us to be separated: take off, therefore, the garments sent to you by the prince, and put on your own." And when they were in them, they were inspired with a desire of withdrawing; and they withdrew and descended, the angel accompanying them as far as to the place of assembly; and there they rendered thanks to the Lord that He had deigned to bless them with knowledge, and thence with intelligence, concerning heavenly joys, and concerning eternal happiness.

CHAPTER XIV.

CONCERNING THE CONSUMMATION OF THE AGE; CONCERNING THE COMING OF THE LORD; AND CONCERNING THE NEW HEAVEN AND THE NEW CHURCH.

753. I. THAT THE CONSUMMATION OF THE AGE IS THE LAST TIME OR END OF THE CHURCH.

On this earth there have been several churches, and all in the course of time have been consummated; and after their consummation, new ones have existed; and thus even to the present time. The consummation of the church takes place when no divine truth remains, except what is falsified or rejected; and when there is no genuine truth, no genuine good can be given, since all the quality of good is formed by truths; for good is the essence of truth, and truth is the form of good; and without a form quality is not given. Good and truth can no more be separated, than the will and the understanding, or, what is the same thing, than the affection of love and the thought thence: wherefore, when the truth in the church is consummated, the good there is consummated also; and when this is done, then the church has an end, that is, there is a consummation of it.

754. The church is consummated by various things, especially by such as make the false appear as true; and when that appears true, then the good, which in itself is good, and is called spiritual good, is not any more given: the good which is then believed to be good, is only the natural good, which moral life produces. The causes that truth, and together with it good, are consummated, are principally the two natural loves, which are diametrically opposite to the two spiritual loves, which are called the love of self, and the love of the world. The love of self, when it is predominant, is opposed to love to God; and the love of the world, when it is predominant, is opposed to love towards the neighbor. The love of self is, to wish well to one's self alone, and to no other except for the sake of self; likewise the love of the world; and those loves, when they are indulged, spread themselves like a mortification through the body, and successively consume the whole of it That such love has invaded churches, is manifestly evident from Babylon and the description of it, Gen. xi. 1 to 9; Isaiah xiii. xiv. xlvii.; Jer. l.; and in Daniel ii. 31 to 47; iii. 1 to 7, and the following verses; v. vi. 8, to the end; vii. 1 to 14; and in Rev. xvii. and xviii., from the beginning to the end of each; which at length has exalted itself to such a degree, that it has not only transferred to itself the divine power of the Lord, but also it labors with the utmost zeal to bring together into itself all the riches of the world. That similar loves would burst forth from many of the rulers of the churches out of Babylon, unless their power were limited, and thus restrained, may be concluded from indications and appearances not so vain. What else, then, would be the consequence, than that such a man would regard himself as a god, and the world as heaven; and that he would pervert all the truth of the church? For truth itself, which in itself is truth, cannot be known and acknowledged by the merely natural man, nor can it be given to him by God, because it falls into what is inverted, and becomes false. Besides these two loves, there are still several causes of the consummation of good and truth

and thence of the consummation of the church; but these causes are secondary and subordinate to those two.

755. That the consummation of the age is the last time of the church, is evident from the passages in the Word, where it is named, as from these: *I have heard from Jehovah a* CONSUMMATION *and* DECISION *upon all the land,* Isaiah xxviii. 22. *A* CONSUMMATION *is determined, righteousness is overflowed, for the Lord Jehovih of hosts is making a* CONSUMMATION *and* DECISION *in the whole land,* x. 22, 23. *In the fire of the zeal of Jehovah, the whole land shall be devoured, because He will make a speedy* CONSUMMATION *with all the inhabitants of the land,* Zeph. i. 18. By land, in these passages, is signified the church, because the land of Canaan is meant, where the church was. That the church is signified by land, may be seen confirmed from many passages from the Word, in the APOCALYPSE REVEALED, n. 285, 902. *At length, upon the bird of abominations, there shall be* DESOLATION, *and even to* CONSUMMATION *and* DECISION *it shall drop upon the* DEVASTATION, Dan. ix. 27. That these things were said by Daniel concerning the end of the present Christian church, may be seen Matt. xxiv. 15. *The whole land shall be a* WASTE, *yet I will not make a* CONSUMMATION, Jer. iv. 27. *The iniquity of the Amorites is not yet* CONSUMMATED, Gen. xv. 16. *Jehovah said, I will go down and see whether they have made a* CONSUMMATION, *according to the cry which has come to Me,* xviii. 21; concerning Sodom. The last time of the present Christian church is also meant by the Lord, by the consummation of the age, in these passages: The disciples asked Jesus, *What will be the sign of thy coming, and of the* CONSUMMATION OF THE AGE? Matt. xxiv. 3. *In the time of the harvest, I will say to the reapers, Gather first the tares, to be burned; gather the wheat into the barns: thus it shall be in the* CONSUMMATION OF THE AGE, Matt. xiii. 40. *In the* CONSUMMATION OF THE AGE, *the angels will go forth and separate the evil from the midst of the just,* xiii. 49. Jesus said to the disciples, *Lo, I am with you even to the* CONSUMMATION OF THE AGE, xxviii. 20. It is to be known, that vastation, desolation and decision signify the same as consummation; but desolation, the consummation of truth, vastation, the consummation of good, and decision, the full consummation of both; and that the fulness of time, in which the Lord came into the world, and in which He is to come, is also a consummation.

756. The consummation of the age may be illustrated by various things in the natural world; for in it each and every thing that there is upon the earth, becomes old, and is consumed; but by alternate changes, which are called the circles of things. Times, in general, and in particular, run through these circles. In general, the year passes from spring to summer, and through this to autumn, and terminates in winter, and from this returns to spring; but this is a circle of heat. In particular, the day passes from morning to noon, and through this to evening, and terminates in night, and from this returns to morning; but this is a circle of light. Every man also runs through the circle of nature; he begins life from infancy, from which he goes on to youth and manhood, and from this to old age, and dies; just so every bird of the air, and every beast of the earth. Every tree also begins from the germ, proceeds to the full stature, and successively decays until it falls. The case is similar with every shrub, and with every twig, yea, with every leaf and flower, and also with the ground itself, which in time becomes sterile; as also with all stagnant water, which successively becomes putrid. All these are alternate consummations, which are natural and temporary, but still periodical; for when one thing has passed from its beginning to its end, another similar one springs up; thus every thing is born, and decays, and is again born, in order that creation may be continued. That the case is similar with the church, is because man is the church, and in general constitutes it; and one generation follows another, and there is a va-

riety of all minds, and iniquity, being once rooted, as to the inclination to it, is transmitted to posterity, and it is not extirpated, except by regeneration, which is effected by the Lord alone.

757. II. THAT AT THIS DAY IS THE LAST TIME OF THE CHRISTIAN CHURCH, WHICH IS FORETOLD AND DESCRIBED BY THE LORD IN THE EVANGELISTS, AND IN THE REVELATION.

That the consummation of the age signifies the last time of the church, was shown in the preceding article; thence it is manifest what is meant by the consummation of the age, concerning which the Lord spoke in the Evangelists, Matt. xxiv.; Mark xiii.; Luke xxi.; for it is read, *As Jesus sat upon the mount of Olives, the disciples came to Him privately, saying, What is the sign of thy coming, and of the consummation of the age?* Matt. xxiv. 3. And then the Lord began to foretell and describe the consummation, such as it is to be successively, even to his coming: and that then He is to come in the clouds of heaven with virtue and glory, and to gather together his elect, beside many other things, verses 30, 31, which did not come to pass at the destruction of Jerusalem. These things the Lord described there in prophetic language, in which every single word has its weight: what each one there involves has been explained in the ARCANA CŒLESTIA, n. 3353 to 3356, 3486 to 3489, 3650 to 3655, 3751 to 3757, 3898 to 3901, 4057 to 4060, 4229 to 4231, 4332 to 4335, 4422 to 4424.

758. That all those things which the Lord spoke with the disciples, were said concerning the last time of the Christian church, is very manifest from the Revelation, where the like things are foretold concerning the consummation of the age, and concerning his coming; which all are particularly explained in the APOCALYPSE REVEALED, published in the year 1766. Now, because those things which the Lord said concerning the consummation of the age, and concerning his coming, before the disciples, coincide with those which He afterwards revealed in the Revelation by John, concerning the same things, it is clearly manifest, that He meant no other consummation than that of the present Christian church. Besides, it is also prophesied in Daniel concerning the end of this church: wherefore the Lord says, *When ye see the abomination of desolation foretold by the prophet Daniel, standing in the holy place; whoso readeth, let him observe it well,* Matt. xxiv. 15; Dan. ix. 27; in like manner also in the other prophets. That there is at this day such abomination of desolation in the Christian church, will be still more manifest from the Appendix; in which i will be seen, that there is not one genuine truth left in the church, and also that unless a new church be raised up in the place of the present, *no flesh could be saved,* according to the words of the Lord in Matt. xxiv. 22. That the Christian church, such as it is at this day, is consummated and vastated to such a degree, cannot be seen by those on earth, who have confirmed themselves in its falses: the reason is, because a confirmation of the false is a denial of the true; wherefore, it as it were veils the understanding, and thereby prevents the entrance of any thing else, which might pull up the cords and stakes, with which it has built and formed its system, as a strong tent. Add to this, that the natural rational can confirm whatsoever it pleases, thus the false as well as the true, and both, when they are confirmed, appear in similar light; and it is not known whether the light be fatuous, such as is given in a dream, or whether it be true light, such as is given in the day; but it is quite otherwise with the spiritual rational, in which those are who look to the Lord, and from Him are in the love of truth.

759. It is from this, that every church, built up by those who see by confirmations, appears as if it alone were in the light, and that all the rest, which dissent, are in darkness; for those who see by confirmations are not unlike owls, which see light in the shade of night, and in the day time, the sun

and its rays, as thick darkness. Such has been, and such is every church which is in falses, when it has once been founded by leaders appearing to themselves as lynxes, who have formed to themselves a morning light from their own intelligence, and an evening light from the Word. Did not the Jewish church, when it was entirely vastated, which was when our Lord came into the world, proclaim by its scribes and lawyers, that because it had the Word, it alone was in heavenly light? when yet they crucified the Messiah, or Christ, who was the Word itself, and the all in all of it! And what else is proclaimed by the church, which in the prophets and in the Revelation is meant by Babylon, than that she is the queen and mother of all churches, and that the rest, which recede, are spurious offspring, which are to be excommunicated; and this, although she has thrust down the Lord the Savior from the throne and altar, and placed herself thereon? Does not every church, even to the most heretical, when it has once been received, fill all countries and cities with the cry, that it alone is orthodox and ecumenical, and that with it is the gospel, which the angel flying in the midst of heaven announced? Rev. xiv. 6. And who does not hear the echo of their voice from the common people, that it is so? Did the whole synod of Dort see predestination otherwise than as a star falling from heaven upon their heads, and kiss that dogma, as the Philistines did the idol of Dagon, in the temple of Ebenezer at Ashdod, and as the Greeks did the Palladium in the temple of Minerva? For they called it the Palladium of religion; not knowing that a falling star is a meteor from fatuous light, which, when it falls on the brain, can confirm every falsity, which is done by fallacies, so that it is believed to be true light, and decreed to be a fixed star, and at length sworn to be the star of stars. Who speaks more confidently of the certainty of his fantasy than an atheistic naturalist? Does he not laugh most heartily at the divine things of God, the celestial things of heaven, and the spiritual things of the church? What lunatic does not believe his folly to be wisdom, and wisdom to be folly? Who, by the sight of the eye, distinguishes the fatuous light of rotten wood from the light of the moon? Who that loathes balsamic odors, as those who are affected with the *morbus uterinus*, does not repel them from his nostrils, and prefer to them stinking odors? &c. These things are adduced for the sake of illustration, to show that it is not known by natural light alone that the church is consummated, that is, that it is in mere falses, before truth shines forth from heaven in its own light; because the false does not see the true, but the true sees the false; and every man is such, that he can see and comprehend the truth when he hears it; but one who is confirmed in falses, cannot bring it into the understanding so that it may remain, since it does not find any room, and if by chance it enters, the troop of falsities there gathered together, casts it out as heterogeneous.

760. III. This last Time of the Christian Church is the very Night in which former Churches have come to their End.

That on this earth, since its creation, there have been four churches, in general, one of which has succeeded another, may be evident from the Word, both historical and prophetical; especially in Daniel, where those four churches are described by the statue of Nebuchadnezzar seen in a dream, Dan. ii., and afterwards by the four beasts coming up out of the sea, vii The first church, which is to be called the most ancient, existed before the flood, the consummation or end of which is described by the flood. Another church, which is to be called the ancient, was in Asia, and partly in Africa, which was consummated and destroyed by idolatries. The third church was the Israelitish, begun at the promulgation of the decalogue upon mount Sinai, and continued by the Word written by Moses and the prophets, and consummated or ended by the profanation of the Word; the fulness of which was at the time when the

Lord came into the world; wherefore, Him who was the Word they crucified. The fourth church is the Christian, instituted by the Lord, through the evangelists and the apostles. Of this there have been two epochs; one from the time of the Lord to the council of Nice, and the other from that council to the present day. But this, in its progress, has been divided into three parts, the Greek, the Roman Catholic, and the Reformed; but still all these are called Christian. Besides, within each general church, there have been several particular ones, which, although they have receded, have still retained the name from the general one, as the heresies in the Christian.

761. That the last time of the Christian church is the very night in which former churches have come to their end, is evident from the Lord's prediction concerning it in the evangelists, and in Daniel. In the evangelists from these words: *That they should see the abomination of desolation; and that there should be great affliction, such as was not from the beginning of the world until now, nor shall be; and that, unless those days should be shortened, no flesh could be saved;* and finally, *that the sun shall be darkened, and the moon shall not give her light, and the stars shall fall from heaven,* Matt. xxiv. 15, 21, 22, 29. That time is called night also in other places in the evangelists, as in Luke: *In that night there shall be two in one bed; one shall be taken, but the other shall be left,* xvii. 34; and in John: *I must work the works of Him who sent Me; the night is coming when no one will be able to work,* ix. 4. Since all light departs at midnight, and the Lord is the true Light, John i. 4, and the following verses; viii. 12; xii. 35, 36, 46, therefore He said to his disciples, when He ascended into heaven, *I am with you even to the consummation of the age,* Matt. xxviii. 20; and then He departs from them to a new church. That this last time of the church is the very night in which the former churches have come to their end, is evident also in Daniel, from these words: *At length, upon the bird of abominations shall be desolation, and even to the consummation and decision it shall drop upon the devastation,* ix. 27. That this was foretold concerning the end of the Christian church, is clearly manifest from the words of the Lord, Matt. xxiv. 18, and from these in Daniel, concerning the fourth kingdom, or concerning the fourth church, represented by Nebuchadnezzar's image: *Whereas thou sawest iron mixed with miry clay, they shall mix themselves together with the seed of man, but they shall not cohere one with another, as iron does not cohere with clay,* ii. 43. The seed of man is the truth of the Word. And also from these concerning the fourth church, represented by the fourth beast coming up out of the sea: *I was seeing in the visions of the night, and behold, a fourth beast terrible and dreadful; it shall devour all the land, and trample upon it, and lay it waste,* vii. 7, 23; by which is meant, that it would consummate every truth of the church, and that then there will be night, because the truth of the church is light. Many similar things are predicted of this church, in the Revelation, particularly in the sixteenth chapter, where mention is made of the vials of the anger of God poured out upon the earth, by which are signified the falsities which will then overflow and destroy the church; in like manner in many places in the prophets, as in these: *Shall not the day of Jehovah be darkness, and not light? thick darkness, and no brightness?* Amos v. 18, 20; Zeph. i. 15; and also, *In that day, Jehovah will look down upon the land, and behold darkness, and the light shall become dark in its ruins,* Isaiah v. 30; viii. 22. The day of Jehovah is the day of the Lord's coming.

762. That four churches, since the creation of the world, should have existed on this earth, is according to divine order, which is, that there should be a beginning, and an end of it, before a new beginning arises. Thence it is, that every day begins from morning, and advances, and ends in night, and after this it begins anew; and also that

every year begins from spring, and proceeds through summer to autumn, and ends in winter, and after this it begins again. It is that these things may take place, that the sun rises in the east, and thence proceeds through the south to the west, and sets in the north, whence it rises again. It is similar with churches: the first of them, which was the most ancient, was as the morning, the spring and the east; the second, or the ancient, as the day, the summer and the south; the third, as the evening, the autumn and the west; and the fourth, as the night, the winter and the north. From these progressions according to order, the wise ancients concluded the four ages of the world; the first of which they called golden, the second silver, the third copper, and the fourth iron; with which metals also the churches themselves were represented in the image seen by Nebuchadnezzar. Besides, the church appears before the Lord as one man; and this greatest man must pass through his several ages, like an individual man; namely, from infancy to youth, and through this to manhood, and at length to old age, and then, when he dies, he will rise again. The Lord says, *Unless a grain of wheat, falling into the ground, die, it remaineth; but if it die, it beareth much fruit*, John xii. 24.

763. It is according to order, that the first should proceed to its last, in general and in particular, in order that a variety of all things may exist, and by varieties every quality; for the quality is perfected by differences relative to things more or less opposite. Who cannot see that truth receives its quality by means of the false being given, and good by means of evil being given; just as light receives its quality by means of darkness being given, and heat by means of cold being given? What would color be, if only white were given, and not black? The quality of the intermediate colors, from any other source, is but imperfect. What is sense without relation? And what is relation, but to things opposite? Is not the sight of the eye darkened by white alone, and enlivened by a color which inwardly derives something from black, such as the color of green? Is not the ear deafened by one tone continually striking its organs, and excited by modulation which is varied by relations? What is the beautiful without relation to the ugly? Wherefore, that the beauty of a virgin may be exhibited to the life, in some pictures an ugly image is placed at the side. What is the pleasant and prosperous without relation to the unpleasant and unprosperous? Who does not become delirious by the constant contemplation of one idea, unless a variety of such things as tend to the opposite diversify it? It is similar in the spiritual things of the church, the opposites of which refer themselves to the evil and the false, which yet are not from God, but from man, who has free agency, which he can turn to good use or to bad use; comparatively, as it is with darkness and cold, these are not from the sun, but from the earth, which, by its circumvolutions, successively withdraws itself and turns itself, and yet, without the turning and withdrawing of it, there would be no day nor year, and thence not any thing, nor any man upon the earth. I have heard that the churches which are in different goods and truths, provided their goods refer themselves to love to the Lord and their truths to faith in the Lord are like so many jewels in the crown of a king.

764. IV. That after this Night there follows a Morning, and that this is the Coming of the Lord.

Since the successive states of the church, in general and in particular, are described in the Word by the four seasons of the year, which are spring, summer, autumn and winter, and by the four times of the day, which are morning, noon, evening and night, and because the present church in Christendom is the night, it follows, that the morning is at hand, that is, the first of a new church. That the successive states of the church are described in the Word by the four states of the light of the day, is evident from these passages there: *Until the* EVENING *and the* MORNING, *two thousand three hundred, then the holy shall be justified; the vision of the* EVENING *and the* MORNING *is truth*, Dan. viii. 14, 16. *He calleth to me out of Seir, Watchman, watchman, what of the* NIGHT? *The watchman said, The* MORNING *cometh, and also the* NIGHT, Isaiah xxi. 11, 12. *The end is come, the* MORNING *is come upon thee, O inhabitant of the land; behold, the day is coming, the* MORNING *is gone forth*, Ezek. vii. 6, 7, 10. *Jehovah, in the* MORNING, *in the* MORNING, *will give his judgment to the light, neither will He fail*, Zeph. iii. 5. *God is in the midst of her, God will help her, when she looks for the* MORNING, Psalm xlvi. 6. *I waited for Jehovah, my soul waiteth for the Lord, more than those who watch for the* MORNING, *who watch for the* MORNING; *because there is with Him plenteous redemption, and He will redeem Israel*, cxxx. 5 to 8. In these passages, the last time of the church is meant by evening and night, and its first time by morning. The Lord himself also is called Morning in these passages: *The God of Israel said, the Rock of Israel spoke to me; He is as the light of the* MORNING, *a* MORNING *without clouds*, 2 Sam. xxiii. 3, 4. *I am the Root and the Offspring of David, the bright and the* MORNING STAR, Rev. xxii. 16. *From the womb of the* MORNING *thou hast the dew of thy youth*, Psalm cx. 3. These passages are concerning the Lord. Since the Lord is the Morning, therefore, also, He rose from the sepulchre early in the morning, being about to institute a new church, Mark xvi. 2, 9. That the coming of the Lord is to be expected, is manifestly evident from the prediction of it by the Lord in Matthew: *As Jesus sat upon the mount of Olives, the disciples came to Him, saying, Tell us what will be the* SIGN OF THY COMING, *and of the consummation of the age*, xxiv. 3. *After the affliction of those days, the sun will be darkened, and the moon will not give her light, and the stars will fall from heaven, and the powers of the heavens will be shaken; and then shall appear the* SIGN OF THE SON OF MAN; *and they will see the* SON OF MAN COMING IN THE CLOUDS OF HEAVEN, WITH VIRTUE AND GLORY, xxiv. 29, 30; Mark xiii. 26; Luke xxi. 27. *As the days of Noah were, so shall also the* COMING OF THE SON OF MAN BE. *Therefore, be ye also ready, because, in an hour that ye think not*, THE SON OF MAN WILL COME, Matt. xxiv. 37, 39, 44, 46. In Luke: *When the* SON OF MAN COMETH, *will He find faith upon the earth?* xviii. 8. In John: Jesus said concerning John, *If I will that he remain* TILL I COME, xxi. 22, 23. In the Acts of the Apostles: *When they saw Jesus taken up into heaven, two men stood by them, in white apparel, and said, Jesus, who was taken up from you*, WILL SO COME, EVEN AS YE HAVE SEEN HIM GOING INTO HEAVEN, i. 9, 10, 11. In the Revelation: *The Lord God of the holy prophets hath sent his angel to show his servants the things which must be done.* BEHOLD, I COME; *blessed is he who keepeth the commandments of this book. And* BEHOLD I COME, *and my reward is with Me, that I may give to every one according to his work*, xxii. 6, 7, 12. And again; *I Jesus have sent my angel to testify to you these things in the churches. I am the Root and the Offspring of David, the bright and the Morning Star. And the spirit and the bride say*, COME; *and let him that heareth say*, COME; *and let him that is thirsty* COME; *and whosoever will, let him take the water of life freely*, xxii. 16, 17. And again; *He that testifieth these things saith*, YEA, I COME, AMEN. EVEN SO, COME, LORD JESUS. THE GRACE OF THE LORD JESUS CHRIST BE WITH YOU ALL, *Amen*, xxii. 20, 21.

766. The Lord is present with every man, and urges and insists that He may be received; and when man receives Him, which is done when he acknowledges Him for his God, Creator, Redeemer and Savior, it is his first coming, which is called the dawn. From this time, man, as to the understanding, begins to be enlightened in spiritual things, and to progress in wisdom more and more interior; and as he receives that from the Lord, so he proceeds through the morning on to the

day, and this day continues with him into old age, even to death; and after this, he comes into heaven to the Lord himself, and there, although he died an old man, he is restored to the morning of his life, and continues the beginnings of wisdom, implanted in the natural world, to eternity.

767. A man who is in faith in the Lord, and in charity towards the neighbor, is a church in particular: the church in general is composed of those similar. This is wonderful, that every angel beholds the Lord before him, in whatsoever direction his body and face are turned; for the Lord is the sun of the angelic heaven, and it is this which appears before their eyes, when they are in spiritual meditation. The case is similar with a man in the world, in whom the church is, as to the sight of his spirit; but because this is veiled over by the natural sight, which the other senses flatter, the objects of which are such things as are of the body and the world, this state of his spirit is unknown. This aspect of the Lord, in whatsoever direction they are, derives its origin from this, that all truth, from which wisdom and faith are, and all good, by which love and charity are, are from the Lord, and that they are the Lord's with him; and thence every truth of wisdom is a mirror in which the Lord is seen, and every good of love is an image of the Lord; thence is this wonderful appearance. But an evil spirit perpetually turns himself away from the Lord, and continually looks to his own love; and this, too, in whatsoever direction his face and body are turned. The cause is the same, but the case is reversed; for all evil is, in a certain form, an image of his reigning love, and the false thence exhibits that image, as in a mirror. That there is also some such thing implanted in nature, may be concluded from certain plants springing up among the grass, in that they rise above the things with which they are surrounded, that they may look at the sun; and also that some, from the rising to the setting of the sun, turn themselves towards him, that thus they may ripen under his auspices; nor do I doubt but that there is a like tendency and effort in every twig and bough of every tree; but because they have no elastic power of bending and turning about, the act stops. That all whirlpools of water and quicksands of the ocean are spontaneously carried around, according to the common progress of the sun, is obvious to the attentive observer. Why not man, who was created after the image of God, unless by means of his free agency he turned that tendency and effort, implanted by the Creator, into another direction? This also may be likened to a bride, in that she continually carries something of the image of the bridegroom in the sight of her spirit, and sees him in his gifts as in mirrors, and longs for his coming; and when he comes, she receives him with joy, in which the love of her breast exults.

768. V. That the Coming of the Lord is not his Coming to destroy the visible Heaven and the habitable Earth, and to create a New Heaven and a New Earth, as many hitherto, from not understanding the Spiritual Sense of the Word, have supposed.

The opinion at this day prevailing in the churches is, that the Lord, when He shall come to the last judgment, will appear in the clouds of heaven, with angels and the sound of trumpets, and will gather together all who dwell upon the earth, and also those who are deceased, and will separate the evil from the good, as a shepherd separates the goats from the sheep; and that then He will cast the evil or the goats into hell, and raise up the good or the sheep into heaven; and that then also He will create a new visible heaven and a new habitable earth, and upon this send down a city, which will be called the New Jerusalem, the structure of which will be according to the description in Revelation xxi.; namely, of jasper and gold, and the foundations of its wall of every precious stone, and its height, breadth and length equal, each of twelve thousand furlongs; and that all the elect, both those who are living, and those that have died since the beginning of the world, will be gathered together into this city; and that they will then return into their bodies, and enjoy eternal bliss in that magnificent city, as in their heaven. This opinion concerning the coming of the Lord, and concerning the last judgment, is at this day reigning in Christian churches.

769. Concerning the state of souls after death, these things, in general and in particular, are at this day believed; that human souls after death are spirits, of which they cherish an idea as of a breath of wind; and that, because they are such, they are reserved until the day of the last judgment, either in the middle of the earth, where their place is, or in the *Limbo* of the fathers. But in these things they differ: some suppose that they are ethereal or aërial forms, and that thus they are like ghosts and spectres, and that some of them dwell in the air, some in the woods, and some in the waters; but some suppose that the souls of the deceased are transferred to the planets or to the stars, and there abodes are given to them; and some that, after thousands of years, they return into bodies. But most suppose that they are reserved to the time when all the firmament, together with the terraqueous globe, will be destroyed, which will be effected by fire, either bursting forth from the centre of the earth, or cast down from heaven, like a universal lightning; and that then the sepulchres will be opened, and the souls which had been reserved, clothed again with their bodies, and transferred into that holy city Jerusalem, and thus, upon another earth, they will dwell together in purified bodies, some below there, and some above, because the height of the city is to be twelve thousand furlongs, as its length and breadth, Rev. xxi. 16.

770. When any of the clergy or laity are asked whether they firmly believe all those things, as that the antediluvians, together with Adam and Eve, and the postdiluvians, together with Noah and his sons, and also Abraham, Isaac and Jacob, together with all the prophets and apostles, as well as the souls of other men, are still reserved in the middle of the earth, or are flying about in the ether or air; and also whether they believe that souls will be clothed again with their bodies, and become united with them, which yet are carcasses eaten up by worms, mice and fishes, and those of the Egyptians, as mummies, eaten up by men, and some merely skeletons burnt up by the sun, and reduced to powder; and likewise whether they believe that the stars of heaven will then fall upon the earth, which yet is smaller than one of them; are not such things paradoxes, which reason itself dissipates, as it does things that are contradictory? But to these things some answer nothing; some, that those are matters of faith, under obedience to which we keep the understanding; some, that not only these things, but many more that are above reason, are of the divine omnipotence; and when they name faith and omnipotence, reason is banished, and then sound reason either disappears and becomes as nothing, or becomes like a spectre, and is called insanity. They add, "Are not those things according to the Word? Who will not think and speak from that?"

771. That the Word in the letter is written by appearances and correspondences, and that, therefore, there is in every part of it a spiritual sense, in which the truth is in its light, and the sense of the letter in the shade, was shown in the chapter concerning the Sacred Scripture. Lest, therefore, the man of the New Church, like the man of the old church, should wander in the shade, in which the sense of the letter of the Word is, especially concerning heaven and hell, and concerning his life after death, and here concerning the coming of the Lord, it has pleased the Lord to open the sight of my spirit, and thus to let me into the spiritual world, and not only to give me to speak with spirits and angels, and with relations and friends, but with kings and princes, who have departed from the natural world, but also to see the stupendous things of heaven, and the miserable things of hell; and thus that

man does not live in some unknown place of the earth, nor fly about blind and dumb in the air, or in empty space; but that he lives as man in a substantial body, in a much more perfect state, if he comes among the blessed, than before, when he lived in the material body. Therefore, lest man should become more deeply grounded in the opinion concerning the destruction of the visible heaven and the habitable earth, and thus concerning the spiritual world, from ignorance, which is the source of naturalism, and then, at the same time, atheism, which, at this day, among the learned, has begun to take root in the interior rational mind, should, like a mortification in the flesh, spread itself around more widely, even into his external mind, from which he speaks, it has been enjoined upon me by the Lord, to promulgate some of the things seen and heard, both concerning HEAVEN AND HELL, and concerning the LAST JUDGMENT, and also to explain the APOCALYPSE, where the coming of the Lord, and the former heaven, and the new heaven, and the holy Jerusalem, are treated of; from which, when read and understood, any one may see what is meant there by the coming of the Lord, and by the new heaven, and by the New Jerusalem.

772. VI. THAT THIS COMING OF THE LORD, WHICH IS THE SECOND, IS IN ORDER THAT THE EVIL MAY BE SEPARATED FROM THE GOOD, AND THAT THOSE MAY BE SAVED WHO HAVE BELIEVED AND DO BELIEVE IN HIM; AND THAT A NEW ANGELIC HEAVEN MAY BE FORMED FROM THEM, AND A NEW CHURCH ON EARTH; AND THAT WITHOUT IT NO FLESH COULD BE SAVED, Matt. xxiv. 22.

That this second coming of the Lord is not to destroy the visible heaven and the habitable earth, has been shown in the preceding article. That it is not to destroy any thing, but to build up, consequently not to condemn, but to save those who have believed in Him since his first coming, and who will hereafter believe, is evident from these words of the Lord: *God sent not his Son into the world to judge the world, but that the world might be saved through Him. He that believeth in Him is not judged, but he that believeth not is already judged, because he hath not believed in the name of the only begotten Son of God*, John iii. 17. And in another place; *If any one hear my words, and yet believe not, I judge him not; for I came not to judge the world, but to save the world. He that despiseth Me, and receiveth not my words, hath that which judgeth him; the Word which I have spoken, that will judge him*, xii. 47, 48. That the last judgment took place in the spiritual world in the year 1757, was shown in a little work concerning the LAST JUDGMENT, published at London, in the year 1758; and further, in a CONTINUATION CONCERNING IT, published at Amsterdam, 1763; which I testify, because I saw it with my eyes in full wakefulness.

773. That the coming of the Lord is to form a new heaven of those who have believed in Him, and to institute a new church of those who hereafter believe in Him, is because those two things are the ends of his coming. The very end of the creation of the universe was no other, than that an angelic heaven might be formed from men, in which all who believe in God are to live in eternal blessedness; for the Divine Love, which is in God, and essentially is God, cannot intend any thing else, and the Divine Wisdom, which also is in God, and is God, cannot produce any thing else. Since the creation of the universe had for its end an angelic heaven from the human race, and at the same time a church on earth,—for through this man will pass into heaven,—and since the salvation of men, which is effected among men who are born in the world, is thus a continuation of creation,—therefore it is said every where in the Word, *to create;* and by it is meant to form for heaven; as in these passages: CREATE *in me a clean heart, O God, and renew a firm spirit in the midst of me*, Psalm li. 10. *Thou openest thy hand, they are filled with good; Thou sendest forth thy spirit, they are* CREATED, civ. 28, 30. *The people that shall be* CREATED *shall*

praise Jah, cii. 18. *Thus said Jehovah thy* CREATOR, *Jacob, thy* FORMER, *Israel; I have redeemed thee, I have called thee by my name. Every one called by my name, for my glory I have* CREATED *him*, Isaiah xliii. 1, 7. *In the day that thou wast* CREATED, *they were prepared. Thou wast perfect in thy ways in the day that thou wast* CREATED, *until perverseness was found in thee*, Ezek. xxviii. 13, 15. These are concerning the king of Tyre: *That they may see, know, attend and understand, that the hand of Jehovah hath done this, and the Holy One of Israel hath* CREATED *it*, xli. 20. Hence it is evident what is meant by *creating*, in the following passages: *Jehovah, who* CREATETH *the heavens, stretcheth out the earth, giveth soul to the people upon it, and spirit to those who walk in it*, xlii. 5; xlv. 12, 18. *Behold*, I CREATE A NEW HEAVEN AND A NEW EARTH; *rejoice for ever in that which* I CREATE. *Behold*, I AM ABOUT TO CREATE JERUSALEM *an exultation*, lxv. 17, 18.

774. The presence of the Lord is perpetual with every man, both evil and good, for without his presence no man lives; but his coming is only with those who receive Him, who are those who believe in Him and do his commandments. The perpetual presence of the Lord causes man to become rational, and enables him to become spiritual: this is done by the light proceeding from the Lord, as a sun in the spiritual world, which man receives with the understanding; and that light is truth, by which he has rationality. But the coming of the Lord is with those who conjoin heat to that light, that is, love to truth; for the heat proceeding from that same sun is love to God and towards the neighbor. The presence only of the Lord, and the illustration of the understanding thence, may be compared with the presence of solar light in the world; unless this be conjoined with heat, all things become desolate upon earth; but the coming of the Lord may be compared with the coming of heat, which takes place in the time of spring; and because then heat conjoins itself to light, the earth is softened, the seeds spring up and bear fruit. Such is the parallelism between spiritual things, in which the spirit of man is, and natural things, in which his body is.

775. It is the same with the man of the church, in the concrete, or in the compound, as it is with an individual man, or in particular. Man, in the concrete, or compound, is a church among many; and man in an individual or particular capacity, is a church in each one among those many. It is according to divine order that there should be generals and particulars, and that both should be together in every thing, and that particulars should not otherwise exist and subsist; as there would not be any particulars inwardly in man, unless there were generals, by which they are encompassed. The particulars in man are the viscera and the parts of them, and the generals are the coverings, which are not only around the whole man, but also around each of the viscera, and around each part of them. The case is similar in every beast, bird and worm; and likewise in every tree, shrub and seed; nor could sound be given from strings or by the breath, unless there were something most general, from which each part of the modulation derived its general, that it might exist. It is similar also with every sense of the body, as with seeing, hearing, smelling, tasting and touching; and likewise it is similar with all the internal senses, which are of the mind. These things are adduced for the sake of illustration, that it may be known that there are also in the church generals and particulars, and likewise things most general; and that it is thence, that four churches have preceded in order, from which progression the most general thing of the church arose, and successively, the generals and particulars of every one. In man also there are two most general things, from which all his generals and each of his particulars derive their existence. Those two most general things in his body are the heart and lungs, and in his spirit the will and understanding; on these and those all things of his life, both in

general and in particular, depend, which without them would fall to pieces and die. It would be similar with the whole angelic heaven, and with the whole human race, yea, with the whole created world, unless all things in general, and each in particular, depended on God, his love and wisdom.

776. VII. THAT THIS SECOND COMING OF THE LORD IS NOT IN PERSON, BUT THAT IT IS IN THE WORD, WHICH IS FROM HIM, AND IS HIMSELF.

It is read in many places, that the Lord is to come in the clouds of heaven, as Matt. xvii. 5; xxiv. 30; xxvi. 64; Mark xiv. 61, 62; Luke ix. 34, 35; xxi. 27; Rev. i. 7; xiv. 14; Dan. vii. 13. But hitherto no one has known what was meant by the clouds of heaven: they have believed that He would appear in them in person. But that, by the clouds of heaven, is meant the Word in the sense of the letter, and by glory and virtue, in which also He is then to come, Matt. xxiv. 30, is meant the spiritual sense of the Word, has been hitherto concealed, because no one has ever yet even conjectured, that there is in the Word any spiritual sense, such as it is in itself. Now, because the spiritual sense of the Word has been opened to me by the Lord, and it has been given to me to be together with angels and spirits in their world, as one of them, it has been discovered, that by the clouds of heaven is meant the Word in the natural sense, and by glory, the Word in the spiritual sense, and by virtue, the power of the Lord by means of the Word. That the clouds of heaven signify that, may be seen from these passages in the Word: *Not like the God of Jeshurun, riding in heaven, and in magnificence upon the* CLOUDS, Deut. xxxiii. 26, 27. *Sing unto God, praise His name, extol Him that rideth upon the* CLOUDS, Psalm lxviii. 4. *Jehovah riding upon a* SWIFT CLOUD, Isaiah xix. 1. To ride signifies to instruct in divine truths from the Word; for a horse signifies the understanding of the Word: see APOCALYPSE REVEALED, n. 298. Who does not see that God does not ride upon the clouds? Again; *God rode upon cherubs, and made his pavilion the* CLOUDS *of the heavens*, Psalm xviii. 10 to 13. Cherubs also signify the Word: see APOCALYPSE REVEALED, n. 239, 672. *Jehovah bindeth the waters in his* CLOUDS; *He spreadeth out his cloud over his throne*, Job xxvi. 8, 9. *Give strength to Jehovah, strength upon the* CLOUDS, lxviii. 34. *Jehovah hath created upon every habitation of Zion a* CLOUD *by day, for upon all the glory there shall be a covering*, Isaiah iv. 5. The Word, in the sense of the letter, also was represented by the cloud in which Jehovah descended upon mount Sinai, when He promulgated the law: the things of the law which were then promulgated were the first fruits of the Word. For confirmation these things also are to be added. There are clouds in the spiritual world as well as in the natural world, but from another origin. In the spiritual world there are sometimes bright clouds above the angelic heavens, but dark clouds over the hells: the bright clouds over the angelic heavens signify obscurity there, from the literal sense of the Word; but when those clouds are dispersed, they signify that they are in its clear light from the spiritual sense; but the dark clouds over the hells signify the falsification and profanation of the Word. The origin of this signification of clouds in the spiritual world, is, because the light which proceeds from the Lord as a sun there, signifies divine truth; wherefore He is called *the Light*, John i. 9; xii. 35. Thence it is that the Word itself, which is kept in the recesses of the temples there, appears encompassed with a bright light, and the obscurity of it is induced by clouds.

777. That the Lord is the Word, is evident from these words in John: *In the beginning was the Word, and the Word was with God, and God was the Word; and the Word became flesh*, i. 1, 14. That the Word there is the divine truth, is because Christians have divine truth from no other source than from the Word, which is a fountain from which all the churches named from Christ draw living waters in their

fulness, although as in a cloud in which its natural sense is, but in glory and virtue, in which its spiritual and celestial sense is. That there are three senses in the Word,—natural, spiritual and celestial,—one within another, was shown in the chapter concerning the SACRED SCRIPTURE, and in the chapter concerning the DECALOGUE or CATECHISM. Thence it is manifest, that by the Word, in John, is meant the Divine Truth. John also testifies the same in his first epistle: *We know that the Son of God hath come and given us understanding that we may know the* TRUE, *and we are in the* TRUE, *in his Son Jesus Christ*, v. 20. And therefore the Lord so often said, VERILY [AMEN] *I say unto you;* for *amen* in the Hebrew language is truth; and that He is the AMEN, may be seen Rev. iii. 14; and the TRUTH, John xiv. 6. When, also, the learned of this age are asked what they understand by the Word in John i. 1, they say, that they understand the Word in its supereminence; and what else is the Word in its supereminence, than divine truth? Hence it is manifest, that the Lord is also now to appear in the Word. The reason that He is not to appear in person, is because, since his ascension into heaven, He is in the glorified Human; and in this He cannot appear to any man, unless He first open the eyes of his spirit; and these cannot be opened in any one who is in evils, and thence in falses; thus not in any of the goats which he sets at the left hand. Wherefore, when He manifested Himself to the disciples, he first opened their eyes; for it is read, *And their eyes were opened, and they knew Him; but He became invisible to them*, Luke xxiv. 31. The case was similar with the women at the sepulchre after the resurrection; wherefore they at that time also saw angels sitting in the sepulchre and speaking with them, whom no man can see with the material eye. That neither did the apostles, before the Lord's resurrection, see the Lord in the glorified Human, with the eyes of the body, but in the spirit (which appears, after awaking, as if it were in sleep), is evident from his transfiguration before Peter, James and John, in that *their eyes were heavy with sleep*, Luke ix. 32. Wherefore, it is a vain thing to believe that the Lord is to appear in the clouds of heaven in person; but He is to appear in the Word, which is from Him, thus is Himself.

778. Every man is his own love and his own intelligence, and whatever proceeds from him derives its essence from those two essentials or properties of his life; wherefore the angels know a man, what he is essentially, from a short intercourse with him, his love from the sound of his voice, and his intelligence from his speech: the reason is, because there are two universals of the life of every man, the will and the understanding; and the will is the receptacle and habitation of his love, and the understanding is the receptacle and habitation of his intelligence; wherefore all the things that proceed from man, whether it be action or speech, make the man and are the man himself. In like manner, but in a supereminent degree, the Lord is Divine Love and Divine Wisdom, or, what is the same, Divine Good and Divine Truth; for his will is of the divine love, and the divine love is of his will, and his understanding is the divine wisdom, and the divine wisdom is his understanding; the human form is the continent of them; hence it may be conceived how the Lord is the Word. But, on the other hand, he who is against the Word, that is, against the divine truth there, consequently against the Lord and his church, is his own evil and his own false, both as to the mind and as to its effects from the body, which refer themselves to actions and words.

779. VIII. THAT THIS SECOND COMING OF THE LORD IS EFFECTED BY MEANS OF A MAN, BEFORE WHOM HE HAS MANIFESTED HIMSELF, AND WHOM HE HAS FILLED WITH HIS SPIRIT, TO TEACH THE DOCTRINES OF THE NEW CHURCH THROUGH THE WORD FROM HIM.

Since the Lord cannot manifest

Himself in person, as has been shown just above, and yet He has foretold that He would come and establish a New Church, which is the New Jerusalem, it follows, that He is to do it by means of a man, who is able not only to receive the doctrines of this church with his understanding, but also to publish them by the press. That the Lord has manifested Himself before me, his servant, and sent me on this office, and that, after this, He opened the sight of my spirit, and thus let me into the spiritual world, and gave me to see the heavens and the hells, and also to speak with angels and spirits, and this now continually for many years, I testify in truth; and also that, from the first day of that call, I have not received any thing which pertains to the doctrines of that church from any angel, but from the Lord alone, while I read the Word.

780. To the end that the Lord might be constantly present, he has disclosed to me the spiritual sense of his Word, in which divine truth is in its light, and in this He is continually present; for his presence in the Word is only by means of the spiritual sense: through the light of this He passes into the shade in which the sense of the letter is; comparatively as it happens with the light of the sun in the day-time, by the interposition of a cloud. That the sense of the letter of the Word is as a cloud, and the spiritual sense glory, and the Lord himself the sun from which the light proceeds, and that thus the Lord is the Word, has been demonstrated above. That the glory in which He is to come, Matt. xxiv. 30, signifies divine truth in its light, in which the spiritual sense of the Word is, appears clearly from these passages: *The voice of one crying in the desert, Prepare a way for Jehovah; the* GLORY OF JEHOVAH *shall be revealed, and all flesh shall see*, Isaiah xl. 3, 5. *Be thou enlightened, because* THY LIGHT *hath come, and the* GLORY OF JEHOVAH *hath risen upon thee*, ix. 1 to the end. *I will give Thee for a covenant to the people, for the* LIGHT OF THE NATIONS; *and* MY GLORY *I will not give to another*, xlii. 6, 8; xlviii. 11. THY LIGHT *shall break forth as the morning; the* GLORY OF JEHOVAH *shall gather thee up*, lviii 8. *All the earth shall be filled with the* GLORY OF JEHOVAH, Num. xiv. 8; Isaiah vi. 1, 2, 3; lxvi. 18. *In the beginning was the Word; in Him was life, and the life was the* LIGHT OF MEN *He was the* TRUE LIGHT. *And the Word became flesh, and we saw* HIS GLORY, THE GLORY AS OF THE ONLY BEGOTTEN OF THE FATHER, John i. 1, 4, 9, 14 *The heavens shall tell the* GLORY OF GOD, Psalm xix. 1. *The* GLORY OF GOD *shall enlighten the New Jerusalem, and the Lamb shall be its light, and the nations which are saved shall walk in* HIS LIGHT, Rev. xxi. 23, 24, 25; besides in many other places. That glory signifies divine truth in its fulness, is because every thing magnificent in heaven is from the light which proceeds from the Lord, and the light proceeding from Him, as a sun there, in its essence is divine truth.

781. IX. THAT THIS IS MEANT, IN THE REVELATION, BY THE NEW HEAVEN AND NEW EARTH, AND THE NEW JERUSALEM DESCENDING THENCE.

It is read in the Revelation, *I saw a new heaven and a new earth, because the former heaven and the former earth had passed away. And I John saw the holy city, New Jerusalem, coming down from God out of heaven, prepared as a bride adorned for her husband*, xxi. 1, 2. The like also is read in Isaiah; *Behold, I create a new heaven and a new earth; rejoice and exult for ever; and behold, I am to create Jerusalem an exultation and her people a joy*, lxv. 17, 18. It has been shown above, in this chapter, that the Lord is at this day forming a new heaven of the Christians who acknowledged in the world, and were able to acknowledge after their departure out of the world, that He is the God of heaven and earth, according to his vords in Matt. xxviii. 18.

782. That a New Church is meant by the New Jerusalem coming down from God out of heaven, Rev. xxi, is because Jerusalem was the metropolis in the land of Canaan; and there was

the temple, the altar, there sacrifices were offered, and thus divine worship itself performed, to which every male in the land was commanded to come three times in a year; and also because the Lord was in Jerusalem, and taught in his temple, and afterwards glorified his Human there; thence it is, that by Jerusalem is signified the church. That the church is meant by Jerusalem, is very evident from the prophecies in the Old Testament concerning a new church to be instituted by the Lord, in that it is there called Jerusalem. The passages themselves will only be adduced, from which every one endued with interior reason may see that the church is there meant by it. Let these passages only be adduced thence: *Behold, I create a* NEW HEAVEN AND A NEW EARTH; *the former shall not be remembered. Behold, I am to* CREATE JERUSALEM *an exultation, and her people a joy, that I may exult over* JERUSALEM, *and rejoice over my people. Then the wolf and the lamb shall feed together; they shall not do evil in all the mountain of my holiness*, Isaiah lxv. 17, 19, 25. *For Zion's sake I will not hold my peace, and for* JERUSALEM'S *sake I will not rest, until the righteousness thereof go forth as brightness, and the salvation thereof as a lamp that burneth. Then the nations shall see thy righteousness, and all kings thy glory; and thou shalt be called by a new name, which the mouth of Jehovah shall utter. And thou shalt be a crown of glory and a royal diadem in the hand of thy God; Jehovah shall delight in thee, and thy land shall be married. Behold, thy salvation shall come; behold, His reward is with Him. And they shall call them the holy people, the redeemed of Jehovah; and thou shalt be called a city sought for, not forsaken*, lxii. 1 to 4, 11, 12. *Awake, awake, put on thy strength, O Zion; put on the garments of thy beauty, O* JERUSALEM, *the city of holiness; because henceforth there shall no more come into thee the uncircumcised and the unclean. Shake thyself from the dust, arise sit down, O* JERUSALEM. *The people shall know my name in that day, for it is I that speak, behold, I. Jehovah hath comforted his people, He hath redeemed* JERUSALEM, lii. 1, 2, 6, 9. *Shout, O daughter of Zion, rejoice with all thy heart, O daughter of* JERUSALEM; *the King of Israel is in the midst of thee; fear not evil any more. He will rejoice over thee with joy. He will rest in his love, He will exult over thee with shouting. I will give you for a name and for a praise to all the people of the earth*, Zeph. iii. 14 to 17, 20. *Thus said Jehovah, thy Redeemer, saying to* JERUSALEM, *Thou shalt be inhabited*, Isaiah xliv. 24, 26. *Thus said Jehovah, I will return to Zion, and will dwell in the midst of* JERUSALEM; *whence* JERUSALEM *shall be called the city of truth, and the mountain of Jehovah of hosts the mountain of holiness*, Zech. viii. 3, 20 to 23. *Then ye shall know that I Jehovah am thy God, dwelling in Zion, the mountain of holiness; and Jerusalem shall be holiness. And it shall come to pass in that day, the mountains shall drop new wine, and the hills shall flow with milk; and Jerusalem shall remain from generation to generation*, Joel iv. 17 to 21. *In that day, the branch of Jehovah shall be for beauty and glory; and it shall be, that he that is left in Zion, and he that remaineth in* JERUSALEM, *shall be called holy, every one that is written for life in* JERUSALEM, Isaiah iv. 2, 3. *In the end of the days, the mountain of the house of Jehovah shall be established on the top of the mountains; for out of Zion shall go forth doctrine, and the Word of Jehovah out of Jerusalem*, Micah iv. 1, 2. *At that time they shall call Jerusalem the throne of Jehovah, and all the nations shall be gathered together, on account of the name of Jehovah, to Jerusalem; neither shall they go any more after the confirmation of their evil heart*, Jer. iii. 17. *Look upon Zion, the city of our stated feast; let your eyes see Jerusalem a quiet habitation, a tabernacle which shall not be taken down; the stakes of it shall not be removed for ever, and the cords of it shall not be broken*, Isaiah xxxiii. 20; besides other places also, as Isaiah xxiv

23; xxxvii. 32; lxvi. 10 to 14; Zech. xii. 3, 6 to 10; xiv. 8, 11, 12, 21; Mal. iii. 4; Psalm cxxii. 1 to 7; cxxxvii. 5, 6, 7. That by Jerusalem there is meant the church which was to be instituted by the Lord, and not the Jerusalem inhabited by the Jews, is manifest from every part of its description in the passages adduced; as that Jehovah God would create a new heaven and a new earth, and also Jerusalem at the same time; and that this would be a crown of glory and a royal diadem; that it was to be called holiness, the city of truth, the throne of Jehovah, a quiet habitation, a tabernacle that shall not be taken down; that there the wolf and the lamb shall feed together; and it is said, that there the mountains shall drop new wine, and the hills shall flow with milk, and it shall remain from generation to generation; beside many other things; also concerning the people there, that they should be holy, every one written for life; that they should be called the redeemed of Jehovah. Moreover, in all those passages, the coming of the Lord is treated of, especially his second coming, when Jerusalem will be such as it is there described; for before, she was not married, that is, made the bride and wife of the Lamb, as it is said of the New Jerusalem in the Revelation. The former or present church is meant by Jerusalem in Daniel, and the commencement of it is there described by these words: *Know and perceive, from the going forth of the word for restoring and building Jerusalem, even to the Prince Messiah, shall be seven weeks; afterwards, in sixty and two weeks, the street and the trench shall be restored and built, but in troublesome times*, ix. 25. But the end of it is described there by these words: *At length, upon the bird of abominations shall be desolation, and even to the consummation and decision it shall drop upon the devastation*, ix. 27. These last are the things that are meant by these words of the Lord in Matthew: *When ye shall see the abomination of desolation, foretold by the prophet Daniel, standing in the holy place, let him that readeth observe it well*, xxiv. 15. That by Jerusalem, in the passages above adduced, was not meant the Jerusalem inhabited by the Jews, may be evident from the passages in the Word, where it is said of this, that it was entirely ruined, and that it was to be destroyed; as Jer. v. 1; vi. 6, 7; vii. 17, 18, &c.; viii. 6, 7, 8, &c.; ix. 10, 11, 13, &c., xiii. 9, 10, 14; xiv. 16; Lam. i. 8, 9 17; Ezek. iv. 1 to the end; v. 9 to the end; xii. 18, 19; xv. 6, 7, 8; xvi. 1 to 63; xxiii. 1 to 40; Matt. xxiii. 37, 38; Luke xix. 41 to 44; xxi. 20, 21, 22; xxiii. 28, 29, 30; besides in many other places; also where it is called Sodom, Isaiah iii. 9; Jer. xxiii. 14; Ezek. xvi. 46, 48, and in other places.

783. That the church is the Lord's, and that from a spiritual marriage, which is that of the good and the true, the Lord is called Bridegroom and Husband, and the church the bride and wife, is known to Christians from the Word, particularly from these passages. John says concerning the Lord, *He who hath the* BRIDE *is the* BRIDEGROOM; *but the friend of the* BRIDEGROOM, *who standeth and heareth Him, rejoiceth on account of the* BRIDEGROOM'S VOICE, John iii. 29. *Jesus said, While the* BRIDEGROOM *is with them, the* SONS OF THE WEDDING *cannot fast*, Matt. ix. 15; Mark ii. 19, 20; Luke v. 35. *I saw the holy city, New Jerusalem, coming down from God out of heaven, prepared as a* BRIDE ADORNED FOR HER HUSBAND, Rev. xxi. 2. *The angel said to John, Come, and I will show thee the* BRIDE, THE LAMB'S WIFE; *and from the mountain he showed him the holy city Jerusalem*, xxi. 9, 10. *The time of the* LAMB'S WEDDING HATH COME, *and* HIS WIFE *hath prepared herself. Blessed are those who are called to the wedding supper of the Lamb*, xix. 7, 9. *I am the Root and the Offspring of David the bright and the Morning Star:* THE SPIRIT AND THE BRIDE *say, Come and let him that is thirsty come; and whosoever will, let him take of the water of life freely*, Rev. xxii. 16, 17.

784. It is according to divine order

that a new heaven should be formed before a New Church on earth; for the church is internal and external, and the internal church makes one with the church in heaven, thus with heaven; and the internal is to be formed before the external, and afterwards the external by the internal: that it is so, is known among the clergy in the world. As this new heaven, which makes the internal of man, increases, so far the New Jerusalem, that is, the New Church, comes down from that heaven; wherefore, this cannot be done in a moment, but it is done as the falses of the former church are removed; for what is new cannot enter where falses have been ingenerated, unless these are eradicated, which will be done among the clergy, and thus among the laity; for the Lord said, *No one putteth new wine into old bottles, else the bottles break, and the wine runneth out; but they put new wine into new bottles, and both are preserved together*, Matt. ix. 17; Mark ii. 22; Luke. v. 37, 38. That these things cannot be done, except at the consummation of the age, by which is meant the end of the church, is evident from these words of the Lord: *Jesus said, The kingdom of the heavens is like a man that sowed good seed in his field; but while men slept, his enemy came and sowed tares and went away. But when the blade had sprung up, then the tares also appeared. The servants came and said to him, Wilt thou that we go and gather up the tares? But he said to them, No; lest perhaps, in gathering the tares, ye should root up the wheat with them. Let them both grow together till the harvest, and in the time of the harvest, I will say to the reapers, Gather first the tares, and bind them up in bundles for burning; but gather the wheat into my barn. The harvest is the consummation of the age; as tares are gathered and burned in the fire, so shall it be in the consummation of the age*, Matt. xiii. 24 to 30, 39, 40. By wheat there are meant the truths and goods of the New Church, and by tares, the falses and evils of the former. That by the consummation of the age is meant the end of the church, may be seen in the first article of this chapter.

785. That there is in every thing an internal and an external, and that the external depends on the internal, as the body on the soul, is evident from every single thing in the world, when rightly viewed. With man this is manifest: his whole body is from his mind, and thence, in every thing that proceeds from man, there is an internal and an external; in every action of man there is the will of the mind, and in every expression there is the understanding of the mind; in like manner in each of his senses. In every bird and beast, yea, in every insect and worm, there is an internal and an external; and also in every tree, plant and twig; yea, in every stone and particle of dust. Some instances are sufficient to illustrate this, concerning the silkworm, the bee and the dust. The internal of the silkworm is that from which its external is induced to make silk, and afterwards to fly away as a butterfly. The internal of the bee is that from which its external is induced to suck honey out of flowers, and to build cells in wonderful forms. The internal of the small dust of the ground, from which its external is inclined, is its tendency to make seeds vegetate: it exhales from its little bosom something which insinuates itself into the inmost parts of the seed, and produces this; and that internal follows its vegetation even to the new seed. The case is similar in the opposites, in which also there is an internal and an external, as in a spider; the internal of which, from which its external is inclined, is the faculty, and thence the inclination, to weave a curious web, in the middle of which it lies in wait for the flies which fly into it, which it eats. The like is in every other noxious worm, and in every serpent, and also in every wild beast of the forest; likewise in every wicked, cunning and deceitful man.

786. X. That this New Church is the Crown of all the Churches that have hitherto been in the World

It has been shown above, that there have been four churches, in general, since the beginning, in this earth; one before the flood, another after the flood, a third called the Israelitish church, and a fourth the Christian; and because all churches depend on the knowledge and acknowledgment of one God, with whom the man of the church can be conjoined, and all the four churches have not been in that truth, it follows that a church is to succeed those four, which will know and acknowledge one God. The divine love of God had nothing else for an end, when He created the world, than that He might conjoin man to Himself, and Himself to man, and thus dwell with man. That the former churches were not in the truth, is, because the most ancient church, which was before the flood, worshipped an invisible God, with whom there can be no conjunction. The ancient church, which was after the flood, did in like manner. The Israelitish church worshipped Jehovah, who in Himself is an invisible God, Exod. xxxiii. 18 to 23; but under a human form, which Jehovah God put on by means of an angel, in which He appeared to Moses, Abraham, Sarah, Hagar, Gideon, Joshua, and sometimes to the prophets; which human form was representative of the Lord who was to come; and because this was representative, therefore also each and every thing in their church was made representative. That the sacrifices and the rest of their worship represented the Lord, who was to come, and that they were abrogated when he came, is known. But the fourth church, which was called the Christian, did, indeed, acknowledge one God with the mouth, but in three persons, each of whom singly or by himself was God, and thus a trinity divided, and not united in one person; thence the idea of three Gods was fixed in the mind, although in the lips there was a confession of one. And, moreover, the doctors of the church, from their doctrine itself, which they composed after the council of Nice, teach, that men must believe in God the Father, God the Son, and God the Holy Ghost, all invisible, because existing in a similar divine essence before the world was; and yet, as was said above, there can be no conjunction with an invisible God; not as yet knowing that the one God, who is invisible, came into the world and assumed the Human, not only that He might redeem men, but also that He might become visible, and thus capable of being conjoined; for it is read, *The Word was with God, and the* WORD WAS GOD; AND THE WORD BECAME FLESH, John i. 1, 14; and in Isaiah, *A Child is born to us; a Son is given to us, whose name shall be called* GOD, HERO, THE FATHER OF ETERNITY, ix. 6; and in the prophets many times, that Jehovah himself was to come into the world, and to be the Redeemer; which also He became in the Human which He assumed.

787. That this church is the crown of all the churches that have hitherto been in the world, is, because it will worship one visible God, in whom is the invisible God, as the soul is in the body. That thus and no otherwise there can be conjunction of God with man, is because man is natural, and thence thinks naturally; and the conjunction must be in his thought, and thus in the affection of his love, and this is effected when man thinks of God as Man. Conjunction with an invisible God is like conjunction of the sight of the eye with the expanse of the universe, of which it sees no end; and also like sight in the middle of the ocean, which falls into the air and into the sea, and perishes; but conjunction with a visible God is like the sight of a man, in the air or on the sea, spreading out his hands and inviting to his arms; for all conjunction of God with man must also be a reciprocal one of man with God, and this other reciprocal cannot be given, except with a visible God. That God was not visible before He assumed the Human, the Lord himself also teaches in John: *Ye have not heard the voice of the Father, at any time, nor seen his shape*, v. 37; and in Moses: *No one can see God and live*, Exod. xxxiii. 20. But that He is seen through his Human

in John: *No one hath seen God at any time; the only begotten Son, who is in the bosom of the Father, He hath brought Him forth to view*, i. 18; and again: *Jesus said, I am the Way, the Truth and the Life; no one cometh to the Father, except through Me. He that knoweth Me, knoweth the Father, and He that seeth Me, seeth the Father*, xiv. 6, 7, 9. That there is conjunction with the invisible God through Him who is visible, thus through the Lord, He teaches in these passages: *Jesus said, Abide in Me and I in you; he that abideth in Me and I in him, the same beareth much fruit*, John xv. 4, 5. *In that day ye shall know that I am in the Father, and ye in Me, and I in you*, xiv. 20. *I have given to them the glory which Thou gavest to Me, that they may be one, as we are one. I in them and Thou in Me; that the love with which Thou hast loved Me, may be in them, and I in them*, xvii. 21, 22, 23, 26; and also vi. 56. Moreover, that He and the Father are one, and that any one must believe in Him in order to have eternal life. That salvation depends on conjunction with God, has been abundantly shown above.

788. That this church is to succeed the churches which have existed since the beginning of the world, and that it is to endure for ages of ages, and that thus it is to be the crown of all the churches that have been before, was prophesied by Daniel; first, when he told and explained to Nebuchadnezzar his dream concerning the four kingdoms, by which are meant the four churches, represented by the statue seen by him; saying, *In the days of these, the God of heaven shall cause to arise a kingdom, which shall not perish for ages; and it shall consume all those kingdoms, but it shall stand for ages*, Dan. ii. 44; and that this should be done by the stone, which became a great rock, filling the whole earth, 35. By a *rock* in the Word is meant the Lord as to divine truth. And the same prophet elsewhere says; *I was seeing in the visions of the night, and behold, with the clouds of heaven, as it were, the Son of Man; to Him was given dominion, and glory, and a kingdom; and all people, nations and tongues shall worship Him. His dominion is the dominion of an age which will not pass away and his kingdom one which will not perish*, vii. 13, 14. And this he says after he had seen the four beasts coming up out of the sea, verse 3; by which also the four former churches were represented. That these things were prophesied by Daniel concerning this time, is evident from his words, xii. 4, and also from the words of the Lord, Matt. xxiv. 15, 30. The like is said in the Revelation: *The seventh angel sounded; then there came great voices from heaven, saying, The kingdoms of the world are become the kingdom of our Lord and of his Christ, and He shall reign for ages of ages*, xi. 15.

789. Besides, the rest of the prophets have, in many places, predicted concerning this church, what it is to be; from which these few will be adduced. In Zechariah: *There shall be one day which shall be known to Jehovah, not day nor night, because about the time of evening there shall be light. In that day, living waters shall go forth out of Jerusalem; and Jehovah shall be King over all the earth. In that day, Jehovah shall be one, and his name one*, xiv. 7, 8, 9. In Joel: *It shall come to pass in that day, that the mountains shall drop new wine, and the hills shall flow with milk, and Jerusalem shall remain to generation and generation*, iv. 17 to 21. In Jeremiah: *At that time they shall call Jerusalem the throne of Jehovah, and all the gentiles shall be gathered together, on account of the name of Jehovah, to Jerusalem; neither shall they go any more after the confirmation of their evil heart*, iii. 17; Rev. xxi. 24, 26. In Isaiah: *Let thy eyes see Jerusalem a quiet habitation, a tabernacle which shall not be taken down; its stakes shall never be removed, and its cords shall not be broken*, xxxiii. 20. In these passages, by Jerusalem is meant the holy New Jerusalem, described in Rev. xxi., by which is meant the New Church. Again in Isaiah: *There shall go forth a Rod*

out of the stem of Jesse, and righteousness shall be the girdle of his loins, and truth the girdle of his thighs. Wherefore the wolf shall dwell with the lamb, and the leopard with the kid, and the calf and the young lion and the fatling together, and a little child shall lead them. And the cow and the bear shall feed, and the young ones shall lie down together; and the sucking child shall play on the hole of the viper, and the weaned child shall put his hand over the den of the basilisk. They shall not do evil, nor corrupt themselves, in all the mountain of my holiness; for the earth shall be full of the knowledge of Jehovah. It shall come to pass in that day, the nations shall seek the Root of Jesse, which standeth for an ensign of the people, and his rest shall be glorious, xi. 1, 5 to 10. That such things have not as yet existed in the churches, and especially in the last, is known. In Jeremiah: *Behold the days are coming, in which I will make a new covenant. And this shall be the covenant: I will give my law in the midst of them, and will write it on their heart; and I will be to them a God, and they shall be to Me a people; they all shall know Me, from the least of them even to the greatest of them*, xxxi. 31 to 34; Rev. xxi. 3. That these things have not been given hitherto in the churches, is also known: the reason was, because they did not approach a visible God, whom all shall know, and because He is the Word, or the law, which He will put in the midst of them, and write it on their heart. In Isaiah: *For Jerusalem's sake I will not rest, until the righteousness thereof go forth as brightness, and the salvation thereof as a lamp that burneth. And thou shalt be called by a new name, which the mouth of Jehovah shall utter. And thou shalt be a* CROWN OF GLORY AND A DIADEM OF ROYALTY *in the hand of thy God. Jehovah will delight in thee, and thy land shall be* MARRIED. *Behold, thy Salvation shall come; behold, his reward is with Him; and they shall call them the people of holiness, the redeemed of Jehovah; and thou shalt be called a city sought, and not deserted.*

790. What this church is to be, is described at large in the Revelation, where it is treated of the end of the former church, and the rise of the New. This New Church is described by the New Jerusalem, and by its magnificent things, and that it is to be the bride and wife of the Lamb, xix. 7; xxi. 2, 9. Besides, I will take from the Revelation only these words. When the New Jerusalem was seen to descend from heaven, it is said, *Behold the tabernacle of God is with men, and He will dwell with them, and they shall be his people, and He will be with them their God. And the nations that are saved shall walk in his light, and there shall not be night there. I Jesus have sent my angel to testify to you these things in the churches. I am the Root and the Offspring of David, the bright and the morning Star. The Spirit and the Bride say, Come; and let him that heareth say, Come; and let him that is thirsty come; and whosoever will, let him take the water of life freely. Yea, come, Lord Jesus, Amen*, xxi. 3, 4, 25; xxii. 16, 17, 20.

---

791. A MEMORANDUM. After this work was finished, the Lord called together his twelve disciples, who followed Him in the world; and the next day He sent them all out into the whole SPIRITUAL WORLD, to preach the GOSPEL, that the LORD GOD JESUS CHRIST reigns, whose reign will be for ages of ages, according to the prediction by Daniel, vii. 13, 14; and in Rev. xi. 15; *and that they are blessed who come to the wedding-supper of the Lamb*, xix. 9. This was done on the 19th day of June, in the year 1770. This was meant by these words of the Lord: *He will send his angels, and they shall gather together his elect from one end of the heavens even to the other*, Matt. xxiv. 31.

SUPPLEMENT.

CONCERNING THE SPIRITUAL WORLD

THE spiritual world has been treated of in a particular work concerning HEAVEN AND HELL, in which many things of that world are described; and because every man after death comes into that world, the state of men there is also described. Who does not know, or may not know, that man lives after death; both because he is born a man, created an image of God, and because the Lord teaches it in his Word? But what life he is to live, has been hitherto unknown. It has been believed, that then he would be a soul, of which they entertained no other idea than as of ether or air, thus that it is breath or spirit, such as man breathes out of his mouth when he dies, in which, nevertheless, his vitality resides; but that it is without sight such as is of the eye, without hearing such as is of the ear, and without speech such as is of the mouth; when yet man after death is equally a man, and such a man, that he does not know but that he is still in the former world. He walks, runs and sits, as in the former world; he lies down, sleeps and wakes up, as in the former world; he eats and drinks, as in the former world; he enjoys conjugial delight, as in the former world; in a word, he is a man as to all and every particular. Whence it is manifest, that death is not an extinction, but a continuation of life, and that it is only a transition.

793. That man is equally a man after death, although he does not then appear to the eyes of the material body, may be evident from the angels seen by Abraham, Hagar, Gideon, Daniel, and some of the prophets; from the angels seen in the Lord's sepulchre, and afterwards many times by John, concerning whom in the Revelation; and especially from the Lord himself, who showed that he was a man by the touch and by eating; and yet he became invisible to their eyes. Who can be so delirious as not to acknowledge, that, although He was invisible, He was still equally a Man? The reason why they saw Him, was, because then the eyes of their spirit were opened; and when these are opened, the things which are in the spiritual world appear as clearly as those which are in the natural world. The difference between a man in the natural world and a man in the spiritual world is, that the latter is clothed with a substantial body, but the former with a material body, in which inwardly is his substantial body; and a substantial man sees a substantial man as clearly as a material man sees a material man; but a substantial man cannot see a material man, nor a material man a substantial man, on account of the difference between material and substantial, which is such as may be described, but not in a few words.

794. From the things seen for so many years I can relate the following: That there are lands in the spiritual world as well as in the natural world, and that there are also plains and valleys, and mountains and hills, and likewise fountains and rivers; that there are paradises, gardens, groves and woods; that there are cities, and in them palaces and houses; and also that there are writings and books, that there are employments and tradings; and that there are gold, silver and precious stones; in a word, that there are all things whatsoever, that are in the natural world; but those in heaven are immensely more perfect. But

the difference is, that all things that are seen in the spiritual world, are created in a moment by the Lord, as houses, paradises, food and other things; and that they are created for correspondence with the interiors of the angels and spirits, which are their affections and thoughts thence; but that all things that are seen in the natural world exist and grow from seed.

795. Since it is so, and I have daily spoken there with the nations and people of this world, thus not only with those who are in Europe, but also with those who are in Asia and in Africa, thus with those who are of various religions, I shall add, as a conclusion to this work, a short description of the state of some of them. It is to be observed, that the state of every nation and people in general, as well as of each individual in particular, in the spiritual world, is according to the acknowledgment of God and the worship of Him; and that all who in heart acknowledge a God, and after this time, those who acknowledge the Lord Jesus Christ to be God, the Redeemer and Savior, are in heaven; and that those who do not acknowledge Him, are under heaven, and are there instructed; and that those who receive, are raised up into heaven, and that those who do not receive, are cast down into hell. Among these also those come, who, like the Socinians, approached only God the Father; and who, like the Arians, denied the divinity of the Lord's Human; for the Lord said, I AM THE WAY, THE TRUTH, AND THE LIFE; NO ONE COMETH TO THE FATHER, EXCEPT THROUGH ME; and to Philip, who wished to see the Father, THAT HE THAT SEETH AND KNOWETH ME, SEETH AND KNOWETH THE FATHER, John xiv. 6, &c.

---

796. CONCERNING LUTHER, MELANCHTHON AND CALVIN, IN THE SPIRITUAL WORLD.

With these three leaders, who were the reformers of the Christian church, I have often conversed, and have thence been instructed what was the state of their life, from the beginning even to this day. With respect to Luther, from the first time, when he came into the spiritual world, he was a most strenuous asserter and defender of his dogmas; and his zeal for them increased, as the multitude increased, that approved and favored, from the earth. A house was given to him there, such as he had had in the life of the body at Eisleben, and there, in the middle, he erected a seat, a little elevated, on which he sat, and through an open door he admitted hearers, and disposed them in ranks. He put those in the seat nearest to him who were most favorable to his dogmas, and behind them he placed those who were less favorable; and then he spoke right on; and, occasionally, permitted questions to be asked, so that, when he had finished what he had to say, he might begin again from some new topic. From this general favor he at length acquired the power of PERSUASION, which, in the spiritual world, is of such efficacy, that no one is able to resist it, or to speak against what is said. But, because this was a species of the incantation in use among the ancients, he was seriously forbidden to speak from that persuasion any more; and afterwards he taught, as before, from the memory and the understanding. Such persuasion, which is a species of incantation, springs from the love of self, from which, at length, it becomes such, that when any one contradicts, it not only attacks the thing in question, but also the person himself. This was the state of his life until the last judgment, which took place in the spiritual world in the year 1757. The year after, he was transferred from his first house to another, and then, at the same time, into another state; and because he heard that I, who am in the natural world, spoke with those who are in the spiritual world, he, among several others, came to me; and after some questions and answers, he perceived, that there is at this day an end of the former church, and the beginning of the new one, concerning which Daniel prophesied, and which the Lord himself foretold in the evangelists; and that this New Church is meant by the New Jerusalem in the Revelation, and by the everlasting gospel, which the angel flying in the midst of heaven preached to those who dwell upon the earth, xiv. 6. Then he became very indignant and stormed; but as he perceived that the New Heaven, which was made and is being made by those who acknowledge the Lord alone for the God of heaven and earth, according to His words, Matt. xxviii. 18; and as he observed the congregations assembled before him to be daily decreasing, his storming ceased; and then he came nearer to me, and began to speak more familiarly with me. And after he was convinced, that he had taken his principal dogma concerning justification by faith alone, not from the Word, but from his own intelligence, he suffered himself to be instructed concerning the Lord, concerning charity, concerning true faith, concerning free agency, and further concerning redemption; and this solely from the Word. At length, after conviction, he began to favor, and then to confirm himself more and more in the truths of which the New Church is built up. At this time he was with me daily; and then, as often as he recollected those truths, he began to laugh at his former dogmas, as being diametrically opposite to the Word. And I heard him say, "Do not wonder that I seized upon faith alone, as justifying, and excluded charity from its spiritual essence, and also took away from men all free agency in spiritual things, besides many other things, which depend on faith alone, when once received, as hooks on a chain; since my end was, to be torn away from the Roman Catholics, which end I could not otherwise reach and obtain. Wherefore, I do not wonder that I erred, but I do wonder that one delirious man should be able to make so many delirious (and at his side, he looked upon some dogmatical writers, celebrated in their time, faithful followers of his doctrine), that they did not see the oppositions in the Sacred Scripture, when yet they are very manifest." It was said to me, by the exploring angels, that that champion was in a state of conversion before many others, who had confirmed themselves in justification by faith alone, since, in his childhood, before he began to make a reformation, he was imbued with the doctrine of the preëminence of charity; for which reason also, both in his writings and preaching, he taught so excellently concerning charity; whence it came to pass, that the faith of justification, with him, was implanted in his external natural man, but not rooted in his internal spiritual man. But the case is otherwise with those, who, in their childhood, confirm themselves against the spirituality of charity; which also is done of itself, when justification by faith alone is established by confirmations. I have spoken with the prince of Saxony, with whom Luther had been in the world. He told me that he often reproved him; particularly, because he separated charity from faith, and declared this and not that to be saving; when yet the Sacred Scripture not only joins together those two universal means of salvation, but also Paul prefers charity to faith, in saying, *That there are three things, faith, hope and charity, and that the greatest of these is charity*, 1 Cor xiii. 13; but that Luther as often replied, that he could not do otherwise, on account of the Roman Catholics. This prince is among the happy.

797. With respect to MELANCHTHON, it has been given me to know many things concerning his condition, what it was when he first came into the spiritual world, and what it was afterwards, not only from the angels, but also from himself; for I have spoken with him several times, but not so often and so intimately as with Luther. The reason that I have not spoken so often and so intimately, was, because he could not approach me so well, since he applied his attention only to justification by faith alone, but not to charity; and I was surrounded by angelic spirits, who are in charity, and they prevented his

coming to me. I heard, that as soon as he entered the spiritual world, a house was prepared for him, similar to the house in which he lived in the world. This also is the case with most of the new comers; whence they do not know but that they are still in the natural world, and that the time elapsed since death has been only as a sleep. In his chamber, also, there were many similar things, a similar table, a similar desk with drawers, and also a similar library. Wherefore, as soon as he came thither, as if he had just awaked from sleep, he seated himself at the table, and continued to write, and then concerning justification by faith alone, and so for several days; and nothing at all concerning charity. This being perceived by the angels, he was asked by messengers, why he did not write also concerning charity. He replied, that there was nothing of the church in charity, for if that should be received as an essential attribute of the church, man would also claim to himself the merit of justification and thence of salvation, and thus also faith would be deprived of its spiritual essence. When the angels who were over his head perceived this, and the angels who were associated with him, when he was out of his house, heard it, they withdrew; for angels are associated with every new comer, in the beginning. Some weeks after this, the things which were of use to him in his chamber, began to be obscured, and finally to vanish away; and at length, to such a degree, that nothing remained there except the table, paper and ink; and, moreover, his chamber, as to its walls, appeared to be plastered with lime, and the floor to be covered over with a yellow material like brick, and he himself to be in a coarser garment. When he wondered at this, and asked those around him why it was, he received answer,—"Because he had removed charity from the church, which yet is the heart of it." But because he so often contradicted and continued to write concerning faith, as the only essential of the church, and means of salvation, and to remove charity more and more, suddenly he seemed to himself under ground, in a certain work-house, where similar ones were, and when he wished to go out thence, he was retained; and it was told him that no other lot awaits those who have turned charity and good works out of the doors of the church. But since he was one of the reformers of the church, at the command of the Lord he was taken out thence, and sent back to his former chamber, where were only a table, paper and ink; but still, from the ideas confirmed in him, he soiled the paper with the like error; wherefore, he could not be kept from being alternately let down to his captive companions, and alternately released; and when he was released, he appeared clad in a hairy garment, because faith without charity is cold. He told me himself, that there was another chamber adjoining his, on the back side of the house, in which there were three tables, at which three similar to him sat, who also had cast out charity into exile; and that sometimes a fourth table also appeared there upon which monstrous things, in various forms, were seen, by which, however, they were not deterred. He said that he conversed with them, and was by them daily more and more confirmed. But after some time, being struck with fear, he began to write something concerning charity; but what he wrote on the paper one day, he did not see the next; for this is the case with every one there, when he puts any thing upon paper from the external man only, and not at the same time from the internal, thus from compulsion and not from freedom, it is obliterated of itself. But after the new heaven began to be established by the Lord, from the light from this heaven he began to think, that perhaps he might be in error; wherefore, from anxiety on account of his condition, he felt some interior ideas impressed on him concerning charity, in which state he consulted the Word; and then his eyes were opened, and he saw that the whole of it was full of LOVE TO GOD AND LOVE TOWARDS THE NEIGHBOR; thus that it was as the Lord says, that on those two commandments hang the law and the prophets, that is, the whole Word. From this time he was transferred interiorly into the south, towards the west, and thus into another house, from which he spoke with me, saying, that now his writing concerning charity did not vanish as before, but that the next day it appeared obscurely. This I wondered at, that when he walks, his steps are heard, like those who go with iron shoes on a stone pavement. To which it is to be added, that when any new comers from the world enter his chamber, for the sake of seeing him and speaking with him, he would call one of the magical spirits, who were able to induce various beautiful appearances, who then adorned his chamber with decorations and tapestry embroidered with roses, and also, as it were, with a library in the middle: but as soon as they departed, those appearances vanished, and the former plastering of lime and emptiness returned; but this when he was in his former state.

798. Concerning CALVIN, I have heard the following things: I. That when he first came into the spiritual world, he believed no otherwise than that he was still in the world where he was born; and although he heard from the angels, who were associated with him at his first entrance, that he was now in their world, and not in his former world, he said, "I have the same body, the same hands and the like senses." But the angels instructed him that he was now in a substantial body, and that before he was not only in the same, but also in a material body, which invested the substantial; and that the material body had been cast off, while the substantial remained, from which man is man. This at first he understood; but the next day he returned into his former faith, that he was still in the world, where he was born: the reason was, because he was a sensual man, believing nothing but what he derived from the objects of the senses of the body. Thence it was, that he concluded all the dogmas of his faith from his own intelligence, and not from the Word. Whenever he quoted the Word, he did it for the sake of the common people, that they might favor him with their assent. II. That after this first period, having left the angels, he wandered about and inquired where those were, who, in ancient times, believed in PREDESTINATION; and it was said to him, that they were removed from hence, and shut up and concealed; and that there was no way open to them, except on the back side, under ground; but that the disciples of Godoschalchus still go about freely, and sometimes are gathered together in a place, which, in spiritual language, is called ***Pyris.*** And because he desired their company, he was conducted to the assembly, where some of them were standing; and when he came among them, he was in the delight of his heart, and contracted an interior friendship with them. III. But after the followers of Godoschalchus were led away to their brethren in the cavern, he became weary; wherefore he sought here and there for an asylum, and at length was received into a certain society, where were merely simple ones, and among them also religious ones: and when he observed that they did not know, nor were able to comprehend any thing about predestination, he betook himself to one corner of the society, and there lay concealed for a considerable time; neither did he open his mouth concerning any thing of the church: this was provided, that he might recede from his error concerning predestination, and that the companies of those, who, after the synod of Dort, adhered to that destestable heresy, might be filled up, who all were successively sent into the cavern to their companions. IV. At last, when it was asked by the modern predestinarians, where Calvin was, and, on searching for him, he was found in the extreme confines of a certain society, which consisted of simple ones, he was then called forth thence, and led to a certain governor, who had swallowed similar dregs. He therefore received him into his house, and kept him, and this until the new heaven be

gan to be instituted by the Lord; and then, because the governor, his keeper, was cast out, together with all his company, Calvin betook himself to a certain house occupied by harlots, and there remained for some time. V. And because he then enjoyed the liberty of wandering about, and also of coming nearer to the lodgings where I was, it was given me to speak with him; and first concerning the new heaven, which at this day is being formed of those who acknowledge the Lord alone for the God of heaven and earth, according to his words in Matt. xxviii. 18; and that these believe that He and the Father are one, John x. 30; and that He is in the Father and the Father in Him; and that he that seeth and knoweth Him, seeth and knoweth the Father, xiv. 6 to 11; and that thus there is one God in the church, as in heaven. On hearing these things said by me, he was at first silent, as usual; but after a half an hour, he broke silence, and said, "Was not Christ a man, the son of Mary, who was married to Joseph? How can a man be adored as God?" And I said, "Is not Jesus Christ, our Redeemer and Savior, God and Man?" To which he replied, "He is God and Man; but still divinity is not his, but the Father's." And I asked, "Where, then, is Christ?" He said, "He is in the lowest parts of heaven;" which he confirmed, by his humiliation before the Father, and by his suffering Himself to be crucified. To these he added jests against the worship of Him, which then rushed into his memory from the world, which in the sum were, that the worship of Him was nothing else than idolatry; and he wished to add abominable things concerning that worship, but the angels who were with me closed his lips. But I, from the zeal of converting him, said that the Lord our Savior is not only God and Man, but also that in Him, God is Man and Man God; and this I confirmed from Paul, that *in Him dwelleth all the fulness of the Godhead bodily*, Colos. ii. 9; and from John, *that He is the true God and eternal Life*, 1 Epist. v. 20, 21; and also from these words of the Lord himself: *That it is the will of the Father, that every one that believeth in the Son should have eternal life; and that he that believeth not shall not see life, but the anger of God abideth on him*, John iii. 36; vi. 40; and moreover, that the confession of faith, which is called the Athanasian, dictates that in Christ, God and Man are not two, but one; and that they are in one person, like the soul and body in man. On hearing these things, he replied, "What are all these things, which you have brought forward from the Word, but empty sounds? Is not the Word the book of all heresies? And thus it is like a vane upon the top of houses and ships, which is carried about hither and thither according to the wind. It is PREDESTINATION ALONE which establishes all things of religion: this is the habitation of all things of religion, and the tabernacle of the congregation; and the faith, by which justification and salvation are effected, is the sacred recess and sanctuary there. Has any man free agency in spiritual things? Are not all things of salvation gratuitous? Wherefore, the arguments against these things, and thus against predestination, I hear and perceive no otherwise, than as eructations from the stomach, and as *boribogmos;* and because it is so, I have thought with myself, that a temple, where they teach about any thing else, and from the Word, and the congregation then assembled, is like a menagerie, in which sheep and wolves are put together, but the wolves are muzzled by the laws of civil justice, lest they should fall upon the sheep (by the sheep I mean the predestinate) and that the preachings there are then only as sobbings from the breast. But I will give my confession, which is this: There is a God, and He is omnipotent; and there is no salvation for any others than those who are elected and predestinated by God the Father, and every one else is doomed to his lot, that is, to his fate." On hearing these words, in great heat I rejoined, "You talk impiously; begone, you evil spirit. Do you not know, because you are in the spiritual world, that there is a heaven and that there is a hell, and that predestination involves that some were assigned to heaven, and some to hell? Can you thus form to yourself any other idea of God, than as of a tyrant, who admits his clients into the city, and casts out the rest into a place of execution? Wherefore, be ashamed of yourself." Afterwards I read to him what is written in the dogmatical book of the Evangelical, called FORMULA CONCORDIÆ, concerning the erroneous doctrine of the CALVINISTS, concerning the Worship of the Lord, and concerning Predestination. Concerning the WORSHIP OF THE LORD, these things: *That it is damnable idolatry, if the trust and faith of the heart be placed in Christ, not only as to his divine, but also as to his human nature, and the honor of adoration be directed to both.* And concerning PREDESTINATION, these: *That Christ did not die for all men, but only for the elect. That God created the greatest part of men for eternal damnation, and is unwilling that the greatest part should be converted and live. That the elect and regenerate cannot lose faith and the Holy Spirit, although they should commit great crimes and sins of every kind. But that those who are not elected are necessarily damned, and cannot attain to salvation, although they should be baptized a thousand times, and come to the eucharist every day, and besides lead as holy and blameless lives as ever can be done*, p. 837, 838, of the Leipsic edition, published in the year 1756. After reading the above, I asked him whether the things which are written in that book were from his doctrine or not; and he replied, that they were; but that he did not remember whether those very words flowed from his pen, although they did from his mouth. On hearing this, all the servants of the Lord retired from him; and he hastily betook himself to the way leading to a cave, where those were who had confirmed in themselves the execrable dogma of predestination. Afterwards, I spoke with some of those who were imprisoned in that cave, and asked about their condition. And they said that they were forced to labor for victuals, and that they all were enemies one to another; and that every one sought a cause of doing evil to another; and that they also did evil, whenever they found any slight cause, and that this was the delight of their life. Besides, see what is written concerning Predestination, and the Predestinarians, above, n. 485 to 488.

799. I have conversed with many others, as well the followers of those three as with heretics; and it was given me to conclude concerning them all, that as many of them as had lived a life of charity, and especially those who loved truth, because it is truth, in the spiritual world suffer themselves to be instructed, and receive the doctrinals of the New Church; but, on the other hand, those who have confirmed themselves in the falses of religion, and also those who have lived a bad life, do not suffer themselves to be instructed; and that these remove themselves by degrees from the new heaven, and join themselves together with their like, who are in hell, where they confirm themselves more and more against the worship of the Lord, and are so obstinate against it, that they cannot bear to hear the name of Jesus. But the case is opposite in heaven, where all unanimously acknowledge the Lord for the God of heaven.

---

800. CONCERNING THE DUTCH IN THE SPIRITUAL WORLD.

In the work concerning HEAVEN AND HELL, it is related that Christians, with whom the Word is read, and there is a knowledge and acknowledgment of the Lord the Redeemer and Savior, are in the middle of the nations and people of the whole spiritual world; because the greatest spiritual light is with them, and the light is propagated thence, as from a centre, in all directions, even to the farthest circumference, according to what was shown in the chapter concerning the SACRED SCRIPTURE, above, n. 267 to 272. In this middle, occupied by Christians, the

Reformed have places allotted to them, according to their reception of spiritual light from the Lord; and because the Dutch possess that light more deeply and fully inserted in their natural light, and are thence more receptible than others of such things as are of reason, therefore they have obtained habitations in that middle occupied by Christians, in the east and south; in the east, from the faculty of receiving spiritual heat, and in the south, from the faculty of receiving spiritual light. That the quarters in the spiritual world are not like the quarters in the natural world, and that habitations according to quarters are habitations according to the reception of faith and love, and that those are in the east, who excel in love, and those in the south, who excel in intelligence, may be seen in the work concerning HEAVEN AND HELL, n. 141 to 153.

801. The reason why the Dutch are in those quarters of the middle space occupied by Christians, is also because trading is their final love, and money is a mediate subservient love, and that love is spiritual; but when money is the final love, and trading is the mediate subservient love, as it is with the Jews, that love is natural and is derived from avarice. That the love of trading, when it is the final love, is spiritual, is from its use, in that it is conducive to the general good, with which the particular good of the individual indeed coheres, and this appears before that, because the man thinks from his natural man. But still, when trading is the end, it is also that love, and every one is regarded in heaven according to his final love; for the final love is as the ruler of a kingdom, or as the master of a house, and the other loves are as its subjects and servants; and also the final love resides in the highest and inmost regions of the mind, and the mediate loves are below and out of it, and they serve it at its nod. The Dutch are before others in this spiritual love; but the Jews are in an inverted love, wherefore their love of trading is merely natural, in which there is nothing latent from the general good, but only from the particular.

802. The Dutch are fixed in the principles of their religion more firmly than others, neither are they moved away from them; and if they are convinced, that this or that is not according to the truth, still they do not affirm, but turn themselves back and remain unmoved: thus also they remove themselves from the interior intuition of truth, for they keep their rational under obedience. Since they are such, therefore, after death, when they come into the spiritual world, they are prepared in a peculiar manner for receiving the spiritual things of heaven, which are divine truths. They are not taught, because they do not receive, but heaven is described to them, what it is, and then it is given them to ascend thither and see it; and then whatever agrees with their genius is infused into them: thus, being sent down, they return to their own with a full desire of heaven. If they do not then receive this truth, that God is one in person and essence, and that the Lord, the Redeemer and Savior, is that God, and that the Divine Trinity is in Him; and also this truth, that faith and charity, in knowledge and discourse, do not effect any thing, without the life of them, and that they are given by the Lord, when, after examination, men perform actual repentance—if they turn themselves away from those truths, when they are taught, and still think of God, that there are three as to persons, and of religion, only that it is, they are reduced to a state of wretchedness, and their trade is taken away from them, until they see themselves reduced to extremities; and then they are brought to those, who, because they are in divine truths, abound in all things, and with whom trade flourishes; and there the thought is insinuated into them from heaven, whence it is that they are so, and at the same time a reflection upon their faith and upon their life, that they shun evils as sins; they also inquire a little, and perceive an agreement with their own thought and re-

flection, and this is done by turns. At length, they think of themselves, that, in order to get out of their state of wretchedness, they must believe in like manner, and live in like manner; and then, as they receive that faith, and live that life of charity, there is given to them opulence and happiness of life. In this manner those, who, in the world, led any life of charity, are amended by themselves, and prepared for heaven. These afterwards become more constant than others, so that they may be called CONSTANCIES; nor do they suffer themselves to be led away by any reasoning, fallacy, obscurity induced by sophistry, or by preposterous vision from confirmations alone; for they become more clear-sighted than before.

803. The doctors who instruct in their schools study very zealously the mysteries of the present faith, especially those who are called COCCEIANS; and because the dogma of predestination inevitably results from those mysteries, and this too was established by the synod of Dort, it also is inseminated and implanted, as seed taken from the fruit of any tree is planted in a field. Thence it is, that the laity talk much among themselves about predestination, but in different ways: some embrace it with both hands, some only take it with one hand and laugh at it, and some cast it away as a snake; for they are ignorant of the mysteries of faith, from which that viper was hatched. The reason that they are ignorant of these mysteries is because they are intent on their business, and the mysteries of that faith indeed touch their understanding, but do not penetrate into it; wherefore, the dogma of predestination, with the laity, and also with the clergy, is like an image in the human form, placed upon a rock in the sea, with a great shell in its hand, which shines from gold; at the sight of which some captains, as they sail by, let down the sail of the mast, for the sake of honoring and venerating it; some only wink at it with their eyes, and salute it; and some hiss at it, as something ridiculous. It is also like an unknown bird from India placed upon a high tower, which some affirm to be a turtle, some conjecture to be a cock, and some with an oath exclaim Certainly it is an owl.

804. The Dutch are easily distinguished from others, in the spiritual world, because they appear in garments like those which they wore in the natural world, with the distinction, that those appear in finer ones, who have received faith and spiritual life. The reason why they are clothed in the like garments, is, because they remain constantly in the principles of their religion; and all in the spiritual world are clothed according to them; wherefore, those there who are in divine truths have white garments and of fine linen.

805. The cities in which the Dutch live are guarded in a singular manner: all the streets in them are covered with roofs, and there are gates in the streets, so that they may not be seen from the rocks and hills round about: this is done on account of their inherent prudence in concealing their designs, and not divulging their intentions; for such things, in the spiritual world, are drawn forth by inspection. When any one comes for the purpose of exploring their state, and is about to go out, he is led to the gates of the streets, which are shut, and thus is led back and led to others, and this even to the highest degree of vexation, and then he is let out: this is done that he may not return. WIVES, who affect dominion over their husbands, live at one side of the city, and do not meet their husbands, except when they are invited, which is done in a civil manner; and then they also lead them to houses, where consorts live without exercising dominion over each other, and show them how clean and elegant their houses are, and what enjoyment of life they have, and that they have these things from mutual and conjugal love. Those wives who attend to these things, and are affected by them, cease to exercise dominion and live together with their husbands;

and then they have a habitation assigned to them nearer to the middle, and are called angels: the reason is, because truly conjugal love is heavenly love, which is without dominion.

---

806. Concerning the English in the Spiritual World.

There are two states of thought with man, external and internal: man in the external is in the natural world, in the internal he is in the spiritual world. These states make one with the good, but not one with the evil. What man is, as to his internal, seldom appears in the world, since from infancy he has learned to be moral and rational, and loves to appear so; but in the spiritual world it clearly appears what he is, for then man is a spirit, and the spirit is the internal man. Now, because it has been given me to be in that world, and there to see what is the quality of the internal men from one kingdom and from another, I ought, because it is important, to make it manifest.

807. With respect to the English nation, the best of them are in the centre of all Christians, because they have interior intellectual light: this does not appear to any one in the natural world, but it appears conspicuously in the spiritual world: this light they derive from the liberty of speaking and writing, and thereby of thinking: with others, who are not in such liberty, that light, not having any outlet, is obstructed. That light, indeed, is not active of itself, but it is made active by others, especially by men of reputation and authority: as soon as any thing is said by them, that light shines forth. For this reason they have moderators appointed over them, in the spiritual world, and priests are given to them of high reputation and eminent talents, in whose opinions, from this their natural disposition, they acquiesce.

808. There is a similitude of minds among them, in consequence of which they contract a familiarity with friends, who are from their nation, and seldom with others: they also render mutual assistance; and they love sincerity. They are lovers of their country, and zealous for its glory; and they regard foreigners, as one looking through a telescope, from the top of his palace, regards those who dwell or wander about out of the city. The political affairs of their kingdom occupy their minds and possess their hearts, sometimes to such a degree as to withdraw their spirits from studies of sublimer judgment, by which superior intelligence is acquired: these studies, indeed, are zealously prosecuted by those among the young, who attend to such things in the public seminaries; but they pass away like phenomena. But still, by those political affairs, their rationality is made lively, and sparkles with light, of which they form beautiful images; as a crystal prism, turned towards the sun, forms rainbows, and tinges a plane object with brilliant colors.

809. There are two great cities, like London, into which most of the English come after death: it has been given me to see the former city, and also to walk over it. The middle of that city is where the merchants meet in London, which is called the Exchange: there the moderators dwell. Above that middle is the east, below it is the west, on the right side is the south, on the left side is the north. In the eastern quarter those dwell who have preëminently led a life of charity: there are magnificent palaces. In the southern quarter the wise dwell, with whom there are many splendid things. In the northern quarter those dwell who have preëminently loved the liberty of speaking and writing. In the western quarter those dwell who boast of justification by faith alone. On the right there, in this quarter, is the entrance into this city, and also a way out of it: those who live ill are sent out there. The ministers who are in the west, and teach that faith alone, dare not enter the city through the great streets, but through narrow alleys, since no other inhabitants are tolerated in the city itself, than those who are in the faith of charity. I have

heard them complaining of the preachers from the west, that they compose their sermons with such art and eloquence, and introduce into them the strange doctrine of justification by faith, that they do not know whether good ought to be done or not. They preach faith as intrinsic good, and separate this from the good of charity, which they call meritorious, and thus not acceptable to God. But when those who dwell in the eastern and southern quarters of the city hear such sermons, they go out of the temples; and the preachers afterwards are deprived of the priestly office.

810. I heard afterwards several reasons why those preachers are deprived of the priestly office. They said that the principal one was, that they do not make their sermons from the Word, and thus from the Spirit of God, but from their rational light, and thus from their own spirit. They take texts, indeed, from the Word, as preludes; but these they only touch with their lips, and leave them as things not savory, and then choose something savory from their own intelligence, which they roll in the mouth, and turn upon the tongue, as rich dainties, and thus teach. They said, that thence there was no more spirituality in their harangues than there is in the songs of nightingales; and that their allegorical ornaments were like false hair beautifully trimmed and whitened with barley flour, upon a bald head. The mystical things of their sermons, concerning justification by faith alone, they compared to the quails from the sea cast upon the camp of the sons of Israel, of which several thousands of the people died, Num. xi.; but theological doctrine concerning charity and faith together, they compared to the manna from heaven. Once I heard their ministers conversing together about faith alone, and I saw a certain image formed by them, which represented their faith alone: this appeared in their light, which was that of fantasy, like a great giant; but when the light from heaven was let in, it appeared above like a monster, and below like a serpent; on seeing which, they retreated, and it was thrown by the by standers into a pond.

811. The other great city, also called London, is not in the middle of the Christian region, but at a distance from it, to the north: into that those come, after death, who are inwardly evil. In the middle of it, there is an open communication with hell, by which also they are occasionally swallowed up.

812. From those who are from England, in the spiritual world, it has been perceived that they have a twofold theology, one from the doctrine of their faith, and the other from the doctrine of charity. That from the doctrine of faith is held by those who are initiated into the priesthood, and that from the doctrine of charity, by many of the laity, especially those who reside in Scotland and in its confines. With these the Solifidians are afraid to enter the lists, since they fight both from the Word and from reason. This doctrine of charity is held forth in the exhortation, read in the temples every sabbath day, to those who attend the sacrament of the supper; in which it is openly said, that if they are not in charity, and do not shun evils as sins, they cast themselves into eternal damnation; and that otherwise, if they come to the holy communion, the devil will enter into them, as he entered into Judas.

---

813. Concerning the Germans in the Spiritual World.

It is known that the inhabitants of every kingdom divided into several provinces, are not of a like genius; and that they differ from each other, particularly, as the inhabitants of the several climates of the globe differ, generally; but that still a common genius reigns among those who are under one king, and thence under one statute law. With respect to Germany, it is divided into more governments than the kingdoms around it. There is an empire there, under the general authority of which they all are; but still the pr nce of each government enjoys despotic right, in his particular government; for there are there greater and smaller dukedoms, and each duke is as a monarch in his own dukedom. And, moreover, religion there is divided; in some dukedoms they are evangelical, so called; in some they are reformed; and in some they are papists. Since there is such a diversity of governments, and also of religions, it is more difficult to describe the Germans, as to their minds, inclinations and lives, from things seen in the spiritual world, than the nations and people elsewhere; but because a common genius reigns every where among people of the same language, that, from ideas collected together, may in some degree be seen and described.

814. Since the Germans are under a despotic government, in each particular dukedom, therefore they are not in the liberty of speaking and writing, as the Dutch and Britons are; and when the liberty of speaking and writing is restrained, the liberty of thinking, that is, of viewing things in their amplitude, is also at the same time held under restraint. For it is as the cistern of a fountain encompassed around, from which the water therein is elevated even to the orifice of the stream, whence the stream itself no longer jets; thought is like the stream, and speech thence is like the cistern. In a word, influx adapts itself to efflux; and so does the understanding from above to the degree of the liberty of speaking and acting out the thoughts. Wherefore, that noble nation attends little to the things of judgment, but to the things of memory; which is the reason why they are devoted particularly to literary history, and in their books trust to the men of reputation and authority among them, and quote the opinions of these in abundance, and subscribe to some one. This their state is represented in the spiritual world by a man who carries books under his arms; and when any one contends about any matter of judgment, he says, "I will give you an answer;" and immediately he takes out some book under his arm, and reads.

815. From this their state proceed many consequences, and among them this; that they keep the spiritual things of the church inscribed on the memory, and seldom elevate them into the higher understanding, but only let them into the lower understanding, from which they reason concerning them: thus they do altogether differently from free nations: these, as to the spiritual things of the church, which are called theological, are like eagles which raise themselves up to whatever height they please; but the nations which are not free are like swans in a river. And free nations are also like the larger stags with high horns, which run through plains, groves and woods with full license; but nations which are not free are like stags kept in parks, that they may be for the use of the prince. Further, people of freedom are like flying horses, called by the ancients Pegasuses, which fly not only over seas, but also over hills which are called Parnassian, and likewise over the seats of the muses beneath them; but people who are not made free, are like horses of noble breed beautifully caparisoned in the stables of kings. Similar to these are the differences of judgments in the mystical things of theology. The clergy there, when they are pupils, write down maxims from the mouth of the teachers in the public seminaries, and keep them as tokens of their erudition; and when they are inaugurated into the priestly office, or are appointed lecturers in the public schools, they derive their canonical discourses, the latter from the chair, and the former from the pulpit, as much as possible from the maxims of which we have just now spoken. Their priests who do not teach from orthodoxy, generally preach the Holy Spirit and his wonderful operations and excitations of holiness in the heart; but those who teach from the modern orthodoxy concerning faith, appear to the angels as if they were distinguished with a wreath formed of leaves of the beech-tree; but those who, from the Word, teach concerning charity and its works, appear as if they were adorned with a wreath formed of

the odoriferous leaves of the laurel. The evangelical there, in their contentions with the reformed about truths, appear as if they tore their clothes, because clothes signify truths.

816. I asked where the people of Hamburg are found in the spiritual world; and it was said, that they no where appear collected into one society, and still less into any one state, but that they are dispersed and intermixed with the Germans, in various quarters; and when the reason was asked, it was said to be this, that their minds are continually looking abroad, and, as it were, travelling out of their city, and very little within it; for as the state of a man's mind is, in the natural world, such is its state in the spiritual world; for the mind of man is his spirit, or the posthumous man that lives after his departure out of the material body.

---

817. Concerning the Papists in the Spiritual World.

The papists, in the spiritual world, appear around and beneath the Protestants, and they are distinguished by bounds, which they are forbidden to pass; but still the monks, by clandestine arts, procure for themselves a communication, and also send out emissaries through unknown paths, that they may seduce; but they are searched out, and after they have been punished, they are either sent back to their companions, or cast down.

818. Since the last judgment, which took place in the spiritual world, in the year 1757, the state of all, and thus also of them, is so changed, that it is not lawful for them to gather themselves together into companies as before; but for every love, both good and evil, there are appointed ways, which those who come from the world, immediately enter, and go to the societies corresponding to their loves: thus the evil are conveyed to societies which are in hell, and the good to societies which are in heaven: thus precaution is taken, that they may not form to themselves artificial heavens as before. Such societies, in the world of spirits, which is in the middle between heaven and hell, are manifold, for there are as many as there are different kinds and sorts of the affections of the love of good and evil; and in the mean time, before they are either elevated into heaven or cast down into hell, they are in spiritual conjunction with men of the world because that they, also, are in the middle between heaven and hell.

819. The papists have a certain council-house, in the southern quarter, towards the east, in which their prelates meet together and consult about the various matters of their religion, especially how the common people may be kept in blind obedience, and how their own dominion may be extended; but no one is admitted into it, who, in the world, had been a pope, because something like divine authority is fixed in his mind, in consequence of his having arrogated to himself the power of the Lord in the world. Neither is any cardinal permitted to enter into that council-house, and this on account of supereminence: these, however, collect themselves together in a large conclave under them, and after staying there some days, they are removed, but it was not given me to know whither. There is also another place of meeting in the southern quarter, towards the west: the business there is to let the credulous common people into heaven. There they form around themselves several societies, which are in various external delights: in some there are dances, in some concerts of music, in some processions, in some theatres and theatrical exhibitions; in some there are those, who, by fantasies, induce various species of magnificence; in some they only tell fortunes and crack jokes; in some they hold friendly conversation together, in one place about religious affairs, in another about civil affairs, and in another about wanton sports, &c. Into some one of these societies they introduce the credulous, according to the peculiar pleasure of each one, calling it heaven; but after they have been there one or two days, they all grow weary and depart, because those delights are external and not internal: thus also many are led away

from the frivolous things of faith concerning the power of introducing into heaven. As it respects their worship, in particular, it is almost like their worship in the world: it consists in like manner in masses, which are not said in the common language of spirits, but composed of high-sounding words, inspiring external sanctity and trembling, which they do not at all understand.

820. All who come into the spiritual world from the earth, are kept in the confession of faith and in the religion of their country, in the beginning; thus also are the papists; wherefore, they always have some representative pope set over them, whom also they adore in a similar manner as in the world. Seldom any pope in the world, after his departure thence, is set over them: but still he who discharged the office of pope thirty or forty years ago, was appointed over them, because he had cherished in his heart the idea that the Word was more holy than it is believed to be, and that the Lord was to be worshipped. It was given me to speak with him; and he said, that he adored the Lord alone, because He is God, who has all power in heaven and in earth, according to his words, Matt. xxviii. 18; and that invocations of the saints are mockeries; and also that in the world he intended to restore that church, but that he could not, for reasons which he mentioned. I saw him, when that great northern city, in which the papists and the reformed were together, was destroyed, in the day of the last judgment, carried out in a litter and conveyed to a place of safety. At the sides of the great society, in which he acts as pope, there are schools established, to which those go who are in doubt or difficulty respecting religion; and there there are converted monks, who teach them concerning God the Savior Christ, and also concerning the holiness of the Word; and the monks leave it to their option to turn away their minds from the sanctifications introduced into the Roman Catholic church. Those who receive are introduced into a large society, where those are who have receded from the worship of the pope and saints; and when they come into it, they are like those who have been awaked out of a deep sleep; and like those who come from the dreariness of winter to the pleasantness of spring; and like one sailing, when he touches the port; and then they are invited by those who are there to feasts, and noble wine is given them to drink out of crystal cups. And I heard that the angels from heaven send down to the host a plate, upon which there is manna, in like form, and of like taste, as that sent down upon the camp of the sons of Israel in the desert; which plate is carried around to the guests, and to every one is given the liberty of tasting it.

821. All those of the Roman Catholic religion, who, when they find themselves to be alive after death, and in the former world had thought more about God than about the pope, and had done works of charity from a simple heart, after they have been instructed that the Lord himself, the Savior of the world, reigns here, are easily led away from the superstitious things of that religion. To these the transition from popery to Christianity is as easy as it is to enter into a temple through open doors; and as it is to pass by the sentinels in the courts into the palace, when the king commands; and as it is to lift up the countenance and look up to heaven, when voices are heard thence. But, on the other hand, it is as difficult to withdraw those from the superstitious things of that religion, who, in the course of their life in the world, seldom if ever thought about God, and loved that worship only on account of its festivities, as it is to enter into a temple, when the doors are shut; and as it is to pass by the sentinels in the courts into the palace, when the king forbids; and as it is for a snake in the grass to lift up its eyes to heaven. It is wonderful, that none of those who come from the Roman Catholic religion into the spiritual world, see heaven there, where the angels are: there is, as it were, a dark cloud over them, which terminates

their vision; but as soon as any converted one comes to those who are converted, heaven is opened, and sometimes they see angels there in white garments, to whom also they are elevated, after having completed the time of preparation.

---

822. Concerning the Popish Saints in the Spiritual World.

It is known that man has innate or hereditary evil from parents, but it is known to few in what that dwells, in its fulness: it dwells in the love of possessing the goods of all others, and in the love of ruling; for this latter love is such, that as far as the reins are given to it, so far it bursts forth, until it burns with the desire of ruling over all, and at length wishes to be invoked and worshipped as a god. This love is the serpent, which deceived Eve and Adam; for it said to the woman, *God doth know in the day that ye eat of the fruit of that tree, your eyes will be opened*, AND THEN YE WILL BE AS GOD, Gen. iii. 4, 5. As far, therefore, as man, without restraint, rushes into this love, so far he averts himself from God, and turns to himself, and becomes a worshipper of himself; and then he can invoke God with a warm mouth from the love of self, but with a cold heart from contempt of God. And then also the divine things of the church may serve for means; but because the end is dominion, the means are regarded no more than as they are subservient to it. Such a person, if he is exalted to the highest honors, is, in his own imagination, like Atlas bearing the terraqueous globe upon his shoulders, and like Phœbus with his horses carrying the sun around the world.

823. Since man hereditarily is such, therefore all, who, by papal bulls, have been made saints, in the spiritual world are removed from the eyes of others and concealed, and all intercourse with their worshippers is taken away from them: the reason is, lest that most pernicious root of evil should be excited in them, and they should be brought into such fantastic deliriums as there are with demons. Into such deliriums those come, who, while they live in the world, zealously aspire to be made saints after death, that they may be invoked.

824. Many of the Roman Catholic persuasion, especially the monks, when they come into the spiritual world, inquire for the saints, particularly the saint of their order; but they do not find them, at which they wonder; but afterwards they are instructed that they are mixed together, either with those who are in heaven or with those who are in the earth below; and that, in either case, they know nothing of the worship and invocation of themselves, and that those who do know and wish to be invoked, fall into deliriums and talk foolishly. The worship of saints is such an abomination in heaven, that, if they only hear it, they are filled with horror; since, as far as worship is ascribed to any man, so far it is withheld from the Lord; for thus He alone is not worshipped, and if the Lord alone is not worshipped, a discrimination is made, which destroys communion and the happiness of life flowing from it. That I might know what the Roman Catholic saints are, in order that I might make it known, as many as a hundred were brought forth from the earth below, who knew of their canonization. They ascended behind my back, and only a few before my face, and I spoke with one of them, who they said was Xavier. He, while he talked with me, was like a fool; yet he could tell, that in his place, where he was shut up with others, he was not a fool, but that he becomes a fool as often as he thinks that he is a saint, and wishes to be invoked. A like murmur I heard from those who were behind my back. It is otherwise with the saints so called in heaven: these know nothing at all of what is done on earth; nor is it given them to speak with any of the Roman Catholic persuasion, who are in that superstition, lest any idea of that thing should enter into them.

825. From this then state, every one may conclude that invocations of them

are only mockeries; and, moreover, I can assert, that they do not hear their invocations on earth any more than their images do at the sides of the streets, nor any more than the walls of the temple, nor any more than the birds that build their nests in towers. It is said, by their servants on earth, that the saints reign in heaven together with the Lord Jesus Christ; but this is a figment and a falsehood, for they no more reign with the Lord, than an hostler with a king, a porter with a grandee, or a footman with a primate; for John the Baptist said concerning the Lord, *that he was not worthy to unloose the latchet of His shoe*, Mark i. 7; John i. 27: what then are those who are such?

826. There appears sometimes to the people of Paris, who are in the spiritual world, in a society, a certain woman of a common stature, in shining raiment, and of a face as it were holy, and she says that she is GENEVIEVE; but when any begin to adore her, then her face is immediately changed, and also her raiment, and she becomes like an ordinary woman, and reproves them for wishing to adore a woman, who among her companions is in no higher estimation than as a maid servant, wondering that the men of the world should be captivated by such trifles.

827. To the above I shall add this, which is most worthy of attention. Once, MARY THE MOTHER OF THE LORD passed by, and was seen over head in white raiment; and then, stopping a while, she said, that she was the mother of the Lord, and that He was indeed born of her; but that He, being made God, put off all the human from her, and that, therefore, she now adores Him as her God; and that she is unwilling that any one should acknowledge Him for her son, since in Him all is Divine.

---

828. CONCERNING THE MAHOMETANS IN THE SPIRITUAL WORLD.

The Mahometans, in the spiritual world, appear behind the papists in the west, and make, as it were, a circle. The reason that they appear next after the Christians is, because they acknowledge our Lord as the greatest Prophet, the wisest of all, who was sent into the world to teach men, and also as the Son of God. Every one in that world dwells at a distance from the middle, where the Christians are, according to his confession of the Lord and of one God; for that conjoins minds to heaven, and makes the distance from the east, over which the Lord is.

829. Since religion resides in the highest things with man, and from the highest his lower things derive life and light, and because Mahomet is always in their minds in connection with religion, therefore, some Mahomet is always placed in their view; and that they may turn their faces towards the east, over which the Lord is, therefore he is placed beneath the middle, occupied by Christians. It is not Mahomet himself, who wrote the Koran, but another, who fills his place; nor is it always the same; but he is changed. Once, it was one from Saxony, who, being taken by the Algerines, became a Mahometan. He, because he had also been a Christian, was led several times to speak with them of the Lord, that He was not the Son of Joseph, but the Son of God himself. That Mahomet was afterwards succeeded by others. In the place where that representative Mahomet has his seat, there appears a fire, as of a little torch, that he may be known; but that fire is conspicuous only to Mahometans.

830. Mahomet himself, who wrote the Koran, does not at this day come into view. It was told me, that at first he presided over them; but because he wished to rule over all things of their religion, as a god, he was cast out of his seat, which he had under the papists, and sent down to the right side near the south. Once, a certain society of Mahometans was instigated, by malicious persons, to acknowledge Mahomet as a god; and, in order to appease the sedition, Mahomet was raised up from the earth below and shown; and then he was seen by me also. He

appeared similar to corporeal spirits, who have no interior perception, his face verging towards black; and I heard him speak these words, "I am your Mahomet;" and presently he seemed to sink down.

831. The Mahometans are hostile to the Christians, principally on account of the faith of three divine persons, and thence the worship of three Gods, as so many Creators; and to the Roman Catholics, moreover, on account of their bending the knee before images; and thence they call the latter idolaters, and the former fanatics, saying that they make a three-headed God, and that they say one, and mutter three; consequently, that they divide omnipotence, and out of one and of one make three; and that thus they are like Fauns with three horns, one for each God, and at the same time three for one God; and that thus they pray, thus they sing, and thus they preach from the pulpit.

832. Mahometans, like all the nations who acknowledge one God, and love what is just, and do good from religion, have their own heaven, but out of the Christian. But the Mahometan heaven is distinguished into two: in the lower one, they live honestly with several wives, but no others are elevated thence into the upper heaven, than those who give up their concubines and acknowledge the Lord our Savior, and, at the same time, his dominion over heaven and hell. I have heard that it is impossible for them to think that God the Father and our Lord are one, but that it is possible for them to believe that He rules over the heavens and the hells, because He is the Son of God the Father. This faith with them is that by which an ascent into the upper heaven is given to them by the Lord.

833. That the Mahometan religion has been received by more nations than the Christian religion, may be an offence to those who think concerning the Divine Providence, and at the same time believe that none can be saved, except those who are born Christians; but the Mahometan religion is not an offence to those who believe that all things are of the Divine Providence: these inquire, in what it is, and they also find. It is in this, that the Mahometan religion acknowledges the Lord for the greatest Prophet, the wisest of all, and also for the Son of God; but because they have made only the Koran the book of their religion, and thence Mahomet, who wrote it, is fixed in their thoughts, and they offer to him some worship, therefore they think but little concerning our Lord That it may be fully known, that that religion was raised up by the Divine Providence of the Lord, to destroy the idolatries of many nations, it shall be told in some order; but first concerning the origin of idolatries. Before that religion, idolatrous worship was spread abroad into very many kingdoms of the world: the reason was, because the churches, before the coming of the Lord, were all representative churches; such also was the Israelitish church; there the tabernacle, the garments of Aaron, the sacrifices, all things of the temple at Jerusalem, and also the statutes, represented; and among the ancients, the science of correspondences, which also is the science of representations, was the very science of sciences, and was particularly cultivated by the Egyptians; hence their hieroglyphics. From that science they knew what animals of every kind signified, and also what was signified by trees of every kind, as also what by mountains, hills, rivers, fountains, and also what by the sun, moon and stars By that science they also had knowledge of spiritual things, since those things which were represented, being such as are of spiritual wisdom with the angels in heaven, were the origins. Now, because all their worship was representative, consisting of mere correspondences, therefore they had worship on mountains and hills, and also in groves and gardens; and therefore they consecrated fountains, and also made carved horses, oxen, calves, lambs, yea, birds, fishes and serpents, and placed them near the temples and in their courts, and also at home, in order according to the spiritual things

of the church, to which they corresponded, or which they represented and thence signified. After a time, when the science of correspondences was obliterated, posterity began to worship the carved images themselves, as in themselves holy, not knowing that their forefathers did not see any thing holy in them, but only that they represented holy things according to correspondences. Hence arose the idolatries which had filled so many kingdoms of the world. That those idolatries might be extirpated, it was permitted, by the Divine Providence of the Lord, that a new religion, accommodated to the genius of the Orientals, should be introduced, in which there should be also something from both Testaments of the Word, and which should teach that the Lord came into the world, and that He was the greatest Prophet, the wisest of all, and the Son of God. This was done by Mahomet, from whom that religion derived its name. Hence it is manifest, that this religion was raised up of the Divine Providence of the Lord, and accommodated, as was said, to the genius of the Orientals, that it might destroy the idolatries of so many nations, and give some knowledge concerning the Lord, before they should come, as they do after death, into the spiritual world. This religion would not have been received by so many kingdoms, and could not have extirpated the idolatries there, unless it had been made suitable to the ideas of their thoughts, especially unless polygamy had been permitted; because the Orientals, without that permission, would have burned with the filthy lusts of adultery, more than the Europeans, and would have perished.

834. Once it was given me to perceive what is the heat of their polygamical love. I spoke with one who filled the place of Mahomet, and that vicar, after some discourse with him at a distance, sent to me an ebony spoon, and other things, which were indications that they were from him. And then, at the same time, there was opened a communication, from various places, for their polygamical love, which, from some places, was felt like the heat in baths after bathing; from some, like the heat in kitchens, where flesh is being boiled; from some, like the heat in places where fetid esculents are exposed for sale; from some, like tha in the cellars of apothecaries, where emulsions and similar things are prepared; from some, like the heat in stews and brothels; and from some, like that in shops where skins, hides and shoes are sold. There was also in that heat something rancid, austere and burning, from jealousy. But the heat in the Christian heavens, where the delight of their love is felt as an odor, is fragrant as in gardens and vineyards, and as in rose-beds; and in some places, like the odor in shops where spices are sold; and in some, like that in wine-presses and wine-cellars. That the delights of loves, in the spiritual world, are frequently felt as odors, has been shown every where in my Relations after the chapters.

---

835. Concerning the Africans in the Spiritual World; and also something concerning the Gentiles.

The Gentiles, who have not known any thing concerning the Lord, appear in the spiritual world beyond those who have; so much so that the outermost borders are made by no others than those who are altogether idolaters, and in the former world had worshipped the sun and moon. But those who acknowledge one God, and make precepts, such as those in the decalogue, precepts of religion, and thence of life, more immediately communicate with Christians in the middle; for the communication is not so intercepted by Mahometans and papists. The Gentiles also are distinguished according to their genius and capacities of receiving light through the heavens from the Lord; for some of them are interior and some exterior, which they derive partly from climate, partly from parentage, partly from education, and partly from religion The Africans are more interior than the rest.

836. All who acknowledge and worship one God, the Creator of the universe, entertain the idea of a man respecting God: they say that no one can have any other idea of God. When they hear that many entertain an idea concerning God as of ether or of a cloud, they ask where they are; and when it is said that they are among Christians, they deny that it is possible. But it is answered, that they have such an idea from this, that God, in the Word, is called a spirit, and they think no otherwise of spirit, than as of the substance of ether, or of some form of a cloud; not knowing that every spirit and every angel is a man. But still inquiry was made whether their spiritual idea was similar to their natural; and it was found that it was not similar with those who interiorly acknowledge the Lord the Savior for the God of heaven and earth. I heard a certain presbyter say, that no one can have an idea of Divine Human; and I saw him transferred to the Gentiles, to those more and more interior, and also to their heavens, and at length to the Christian heaven; and every where there was given a communication of their interior perception concerning God; and he observed that they had no other idea concerning God, than that of a Divine Man; and that man, who is his image and likeness, could not have been created by any other.

837. Since the Africans are superior to the rest in interior judgment, I have had conversation with them, on subjects of deeper investigation; and lately concerning God; concerning the Lord the Redeemer; and concerning the interior and exterior man; and because they were delighted with that conversation, I shall here mention some things, which they perceived from interior sight, concerning those three subjects. CONCERNING GOD they said, That He surely came down and presented himself to the sight of men, because He is their Creator, Guardian and Guide. and because the human race is his; and that He sees, surveys and provides each and all the things that are in the heavens and in the earth, and their goods as in Himself, and Himself as in them: the reason is, because He is the sun of the angelic heaven, which is seen as high above the spiritual world as the sun of the earth is above the natural world; and He who is the sun, sees, surveys and provides for each and all of the things that are beneath; and because it is his divine love which appears as a sun, it follows that He provides for the greatest and the least such things as are of life, and for men such things as are of love and wisdom; the things which are of love by means of the heat thence, and the things which are of wisdom by means of the light thence. If, therefore, you form to yourselves an idea concerning God, that He is the sun ot the universe, surely from that idea you will see and acknowledge his omnipresence, omniscience and omnipotence.

838. Further, I had conversation with them CONCERNING THE LORD THE SAVIOR. And it was said that God, in his essence, is Divine Love, and that Divine Love is as the purest fire; and because love, viewed in itself, cannot intend any thing else than to become one with another whom it loves, and the Divine Love nothing else than to unite itself to man and man to itself, so that it may be in him, and he in it; and because the Divine Love is as the purest fire, it is manifest that God, because He is such, could not possibly be in man, and cause man to be in Him, for thus He would reduce the whole man to the thinnest vapor. But because God, from his essence, burned with the love of uniting Himself with man, it was necessary that He should veil Himself over with a body accommodated to reception and conjunction; wherefore He came down and assumed the Human, according to the order established by Himself from the creation of the world; which was, that He should be conceived by a virtue propagated from Himself, be carried in the womb, be born, and then grow in wisdom and love, and thus approach to union with his Divine Origin; and that thus God became Man, and Man God

That it is so, the Scripture concerning Him, which is with Christians, and is called the Word, manifestly teaches and testifies; and God himself, who, in his Human, is called Jesus Christ, says, That the Father is in Him and He in the Father; and that he that seeth Him seeth the Father; besides many more things to the same purpose. Reason also sees, that God, whose love is as the purest fire, could not otherwise unite Himself to man and man to Himself. Can the fire of the sun, such as it is in itself, touch man, still less enter into him, unless it veil its rays with atmospheres, and thus, by a tempered heat, present itself accommodated? Can pure ether encompass a man, and still less flow into the *bronchiæ* of his lungs, unless it be thickened with air, and thus adapt itself? A fish cannot live in the air, but in an element suited to its life. Yea, a king on earth cannot, in his own person, or immediately, administer all and each of the things in his kingdom, except by superior and inferior governors, who together constitute his royal body. Nor can the soul of a man make itself visible to another, hold intercourse with him, and communicate tokens of its love, except through the body. How then can God, except through the Human, which is his? On hearing these things, the Africans perceived them better than the rest, because they are more interiorly rational, and each favored them according to his perception.

839. Lastly, we discoursed concerning THE INTERIOR AND EXTERIOR MAN. And it was said, that men who perceive things interiorly, are in the light of truth, which is the light of heaven; and that men who perceive things exteriorly, are in no light of truth, because only in the light of the world; and that thus interior men are in intelligence and wisdom, but exterior men in insanity and preposterous vision; that interior men are spiritual, because they think from the spirit elevated above the body, wherefore they see truths in the light; but that exterior men are sensual-natural, because they think from the fallacies of the senses of the body; wherefore they see truths as in a thick cloud, and when they revolve them in their minds, they see falses as truths; that internal men are like those who stand on a mountain in a plain, or on a tower in a city, or on a beacon in the sea; but external men are like those who stand in a valley under a mountain, or in a vault under a tower, or in a boat under a beacon, who see only the nearest things. And further, internal men are like those who dwell in the second or third story of a house or palace, the walls of which are continued windows of crystal glass, who see through into the city round about to a great extent, and know every little building there; but external men are like those who dwell in the lowest story, the windows of which are made of paper pasted together, who do not see even a single street out of the house, but only the things that are within the house, and these not without a candle or a fire. Internal men also are like eagles which soar on high, and see far and wide all things under them; but, on the other hand, external men are like cocks, which stand on a post, and crow aloud before the hens which walk on the ground. And, moreover, internal men perceive that the things which they know are to the things which they do not know, as the water in an urn is to the water in a lake; but external men do not perceive but that they know all things. The Africans were delighted with this discourse, because, from the interior sight, in which they excel, they acknowledged that it was so.

840. Since the Africans are such, therefore, there is at this day a revelation made to them, which, having commenced, goes from its region around, but not yet to the seas. They despise foreigners coming from Europe, who believe that man is saved by faith alone, and thus by only thinking and speaking, and not at the same time by willing and doing; saying that there is no man that has any worship who does not live according to his religion; and if not, he cannot but become stupid and wicked, because then he does not

receive any thing from heaven. They also call ingenious wickedness stupidity, because there is not any life in it, but death. I have spoken several times with Augustine, who, in the third age, had been bishop at Hippo in Africa. He said that he is there at this day, and inspires into them the worship of the Lord, and that there is hope of the propagation of this new gospel into the neighboring regions there. I heard the joy of the angels at that revelation, because by it there is opened to them a communication with the rational human, hitherto closed up by the universal dogma, that the understanding is to be under obedience to ecclesiastical faith.

---

841. CONCERNING THE JEWS IN THE SPIRITUAL WORLD.

The Jews, before the last judgment, which took place in the year 1757, appeared at the left side of the middle occupied by Christians, in a valley there: after that, they were transferred to the north, and were forbidden to have intercourse with Christians, except those wandering out of the cities. There are in that quarter two great cities, into which the Jews after death are transferred, which, before the judgment, they called Jerusalem, but after that, by another name; because, since the judgment, by Jerusalem is meant the church, as to doctrine, in which the Lord alone is worshipped. Converted Jews are set over them in their cities, who admonish them not to speak reproachfully of Christ, and they punish those who still do it. The streets of their cities are filled up with dirt even to the ankles, and their houses with filthiness, which causes them to smell so offensively that they cannot be approached. Afterwards, I observed that some of that nation also obtained a place of abode in the southern quarter; and when I asked who they were, it was said, that they were those who made little account of the worship of the rest, and hesitated in their minds respecting the Messiah, whether he is ever to come, and also who thought concerning various things in the world from reason, and lived according to it The Jews who are called Portuguese constitute the greatest part of these.

842. There sometimes appears to the Jews an angel above, of a middling stature, with a rod in his hand, and he makes them believe that he is Moses, and exhorts them to desist from the folly of expecting the Messiah even there, because the Messiah is Christ, who governs them and all, and that he knows it, and also knew concerning Him, when he was in the world; on hearing which they retire, and the greatest part of them forget, and a few retain. Those who do retain, are sent into the synagogues, which consist of the converted, and they are instructed; and after they are instructed, new garments are given to them instead of tattered ones; and the Word, neatly written, is given to them; and also a decent habitation in the city. Those who do not receive are cast down, and many into woods and deserts, where they practise robberies among themselves.

843. The Jews trade in that world, as in the former world, with various things, especially with precious stones, which, by unknown ways, they procure for themselves from heaven, where there are precious stones in abundance. The cause of their trading with precious stones, is, because they read the Word in its original language, and esteem the sense of its letter holy; and precious stones correspond to the sense of the letter. That the spiritual origin of those stones is the sense of the letter of the Word, and that thence is their correspondence, may be seen above, in the chapter concerning the SACRED SCRIPTURE, n. 217, 218. They can also make similar ones by art, and induce the fantasy that they are genuine; but these are severely fined by their governors.

844. The Jews are more ignorant than others that they are in the spiritual world, but believe that they are still in the natural world: the reason is, because they are altogether external men, and do not think any thing concerning

religion from within; wherefore also they talk about the Messiah just as they did before; and some say that he will come with David, and, shining with diadems, will go before them, and introduce them into the land of Canaan, and in the way, by lifting up his rod, he will dry up the rivers, which they will pass over; and that the Christians, whom, among themselves, they also call Gentiles, will then take hold of the skirts of their garments, humbly begging that they may be permitted to accompany them; and that they will receive the rich according to their wealth, and that these will serve them. They confirm themselves in these things, by what is read in Zechariah viii. 23, and in Isaiah lxvi. 20; and concerning David, that he is to come and to be their king and shepherd, from Jeremiah xxx. 9, and from Ezekiel xxxiv. 23 to 25, xxxvii. 23 to 26; being altogether unwilling to hear, that by David there, is meant our Lord Jesus Christ; and by Jews there, are meant those who will be of his church.

845. When they are asked whether they firmly believe that they all are to come into the land of Canaan, they say that then all will, and that then the Jews who are deceased are to rise again, and that, from their sepulchres, they are to enter into that land. When it is replied, that they can never come out of sepulchres, since they live themselves after death, they answer, that they are then to descend, and to enter into their bodies, and thus to live. When it is said, that that land cannot contain them all, they answer, that it will then be enlarged. When it is said, that the kingdom of the Messiah, because He is the Son of God, is not to be upon earth, but in heaven, they answer that the land of Canaan will then be heaven. When it is said, that they do not know where Bethlehem Ephratah is, where the Messiah will be born, according to the prediction in Micah v. 2, and in David, Psalm cxxxii. 6, they answer that the mother of the Messiah still is to bring forth there; and some, that where she brings forth, there is Bethlehem. When it is said, How can the Messiah dwell with those who are so bad? and it is confirmed by many passages from Jeremiah, and especially from the song of Moses, Deut. xxxii. that they are the worst, they answer that among the Jews there are both good and bad, and that the bad are there meant. When it is said, that their rise was from a Canaanitess, and from the whoredom of Judah with his daughter-in-law, Gen. xxxviii. they answer that it was not whoredom; but when it is rejoined, that still Judah commanded that she should be brought forth and burned on account of whoredom, they go away to consult; and after consultation, they say, It was only the office of her husband's brother, which neither his second son Onan, nor his third son Selah, performed; and to this they add, that very many of them are of the tribe of Levi, who had the priesthood; it is sufficient that we all are from the loins of Abraham. When it is said to them, that there is inwardly in the Word a spiritual sense, in which Christ or the Messiah is much treated of, they answer that it is not so; but some of them say that inwardly in the Word, or at the bottom of it, there is nothing but gold; besides other like things.

---

846. Once I was raised up, as to my spirit, into the angelic heaven, and into a society there; and then some of the wise there came to me, and said, "What, is there new from the earth?" I said to them, "This is new, that the Lord has revealed secrets, which, in excellence, exceed the secrets hitherto revealed since the beginning of the church." They asked, "What are they?" I said that they were these: I. That in the Word, in all and every part of it, there is a Spiritual Sense corresponding to the natural sense; and that the Word, by means of that sense, is a conjunction of the men of the church with the Lord, and also a consociation with the angels, and that the holiness of the Word resides in that sense. II. That the Correspondences of which the spiritual sense consists, are disclosed. And the angels asked, "Did

not the inhabitants of the world know about correspondences before?" I said that they did not know any thing at all, and that they have been concealed now for thousands of years, that is, ever since the time of Job; and that, with those who lived at that time and before it, the science of correspondences was the science of sciences, from which they had wisdom, because knowledge concerning spiritual things, which are of heaven and the church; but that that science, because it was turned into an idolatrous science, was, by the Divine Providence of the Lord, so obliterated and lost, that no one saw any sign of it; but that still it is now disclosed by the Lord, that there may be effected a conjunction of the men of the church with Him, and a consociation with angels; and these are effected by means of the Word, in which all and each of the things are correspondences. The angels rejoiced greatly that it had pleased the Lord to reveal this great secret, which had been so deeply hidden for thousands of years; and they said that it was done in order that the Christian church, which was founded upon the Word, and now is at its end, may again revive and derive spirit, through heaven, from the Lord. They asked whether it was at this day disclosed, by means of that science, what BAPTISM and what the HOLY SUPPER signify, concerning which they have hitherto thought such various things. And I answered, that it was. III. Further, I said, that a revelation has been made at this day by the Lord concerning the LIFE OF MEN AFTER DEATH. The angels said, "Why concerning the life after death? Who does not know that man lives after death?" I answered, "They know, and they do not know. They say that the man does not, but his soul, and that this lives as a spirit; and they entertain an idea concerning spirit as of wind or ether; and that the man does not live till the day of the last judgment, and that then the things of the body, which they had left in the world, although eaten up by worms, mice and fishes, would be again collected together, and be fitted together again into a body, and that men are thus to rise again." The angels said, "What is this? Who does not know that man lives as a man after death, with the difference only that he then lives a substantial man, and not a material one, as before; and that a substantial man sees a substantial man, just as a material man a material one; and that they know not one point of difference, except that they are in a more perfect state?" IV. The angels asked, "What do they know of our world, and of HEAVEN AND HELL?" I answered, that they knew nothing at all; but that it is, at this day, disclosed by the Lord, what the world is, in which angels and spirits live; thus what heaven is, and what hell is; and also that angels and spirits are in conjunction with men; besides many wonderful things concerning them. The angels were glad that it had pleased the Lord to disclose such things, that man might no longer, through ignorance, be in doubt concerning his immortality. V. Again I said, that it is at this day revealed by the Lord, that in your world there is another sun than in ours, and that the sun of your world is pure love, and that the sun of our world is pure fire; and that, therefore, all that proceeds from your sun, because it is pure love, partakes of life; and that all that proceeds from our sun, because it is pure fire, partakes nothing of life; and that thence is the distinction between SPIRITUAL AND NATURAL, which distinction, hitherto unknown, is also disclosed; from which it is made known whence the light is, which enlightens the human understanding with wisdom, and whence the heat is, which enkindles the human will with love. VI. Moreover, it is disclosed that there are three degrees of life, and that thence there are three heavens, and that the mind of man is distinguished into those degrees; and that thence man corresponds to the three heavens. The angels said, "Did they not know this before?" I answered, that they knew concerning degrees between more and less, but nothing concerning degrees between prior and posterior. VII. The angels asked, whether any thing more beside those had been revealed. I said that there had, many things more, which are concerning the LAST JUDGMENT; concerning the LORD, that He is the God of heaven and earth; that God is one both in person and essence, in whom is a Divine Trinity, and that He is the Lord; also concerning the NEW CHURCH to be instituted by Him, and concerning the DOCTRINE of that church; concerning the HOLINESS of the SACRED SCRIPTURE; that the APOCALYPSE also is revealed; and, moreover, concerning the INHABITANTS OF THE PLANETS; and concerning the EARTHS in the universe; besides many memorable and wonderful things from the spiritual world, by which many things that are of wisdom have been disclosed from heaven.

847. After these things, I said to the angels, that something more had been revealed in the world by the Lord. They asked what it was. I said, concerning TRULY CONJUGIAL LOVE, and concerning its spiritual delights. And the angels said, "Who does not know that the delights of conjugial love exceed the delights of all loves? And who cannot think, that all the blessedness, satisfactions and delights which can ever be conferred by the Lord, are collected into some love, since it corresponds to the love of the Lord and the church, and that the receptacle of them is truly conjugial love, which can receive and perceive them to the full sense?" I answered, that they do not know this, because they have not approached the Lord, and, therefore, have not shunned the lusts of the flesh, and so could not be regenerated; and truly conjugial love is solely from the Lord, and is given to those who are regenerated by Him; and these also are they who are received into the Lord's New Church, which is meant in the Revelation by the New Jerusalem. To this I added, that I was in doubt whether the people in the world at this day would believe that that love is in itself spiritual, and thence from religion, because they entertain only a corporeal idea concerning it; consequently, that, because it is according to religion, it is spiritual with the spiritual, natural with the natural, and merely carnal with adulterers.

848. The angels, on hearing these and the former things, rejoiced exceedingly; but they perceived sadness in me, and asked, "Whence is your sadness?" I said, that those secrets revealed by the Lord, although they exceed, in excellence and dignity, all the knowledges hitherto communicated, still are not reputed on earth as of any value. The angels wondered at this, and desired of the Lord that they might be permitted to look down into the world; and they looked down, and behold! mere darkness there. And it was said to them, that those secrets should be written on a paper, and be sent down to the earth, and they would see a prodigy. And it was done so; and behold, the paper on which those secrets were written, was sent down from heaven, and in its progress, while it was yet in the spiritual world, it shone like a star; but when it descended into the natural world, the light disappeared, and as it fell down, it became dark. And when it was sent down by the angels into companies, where were the learned and erudite from some of the clergy and laity, a murmur was heard from many, in which were these expressions: "What is this? Is it any thing? Of what concern is it, whether we know those things, or do not know them? Are they not fetuses of the brain?" And it appeared as if some took the paper and folded it, and rolled and unrolled it with their fingers; and also as if some tore it to pieces, and wished to trample it under their feet; but they were restrained by the Lord from that enormity. It was commanded the angels to take it back, and preserve, and keep it; and because the angels became sad, and thought how long this would be, it was said, *Even for a time, and times, and half a time*, Rev. xii. 14.

849. After this, I heard a hostile murmur from below, and at the same

time these words, "Do MIRACLES, AND WE WILL BELIEVE." And I replied, "Are not those things miracles?" And it was answered, "They are not." And I asked, "What miracles, then?" And it was said, "Manifest and reveal future events, and we will have faith." But I answered, "Such things are not given by the Lord, since, as far as man knows the future, so far his reason and understanding, with his prudence and wisdom, sink into indolence, become torpid, and decay." And again I asked, "What other miracles shall I do?" And they cried, "Do such as Moses did in Egypt." And I replied, "Perhaps you would harden your hearts against them, as Pharaoh and the Egyptians did." And they answered that they would not. And again I said, "Assure me that you would not dance around a golden calf and worship it, as the posterity of Jacob did, in the space of a month after they saw the whole of mount Sinai burning, and heard Jehovah himself speaking out of the fire; thus after a miracle which was the greatest of all. (*A golden calf, in the spiritual sense, is the pleasure of the flesh.*) And it was answered from below, "We will not be like the posterity of Jacob." But then I heard this said to them from heaven, "If ye believe not Moses and the prophets, that is, the Word of the Lord, ye will not believe from miracles, any more than the posterity of Jacob did in the desert, nor any more than they did, when they saw with their eyes the miracles done by the Lord himself, when He was in the world."

850. After this, I saw some ascending from below, whence those things were heard, who, addressing me in a grave tone, said, "Why did your Lord reveal those secrets, which you have just enumerated in a long series, to you who are a layman, and not to some one of the clergy?" To which I answered, that this was according to the good pleasure of the Lord, who prepared me for this office from my earliest youth. But yet I will ask you in return, "Why did the Lord, when He was in the world, choose fishermen for disciples, and not some of the lawyers, scribes priests or rabbies? Discuss this among yourselves, and conclude from judgment, and you will discover the reason." On hearing these words, a murmur was made, and after this, silence.

851. I foresee that many, who read the Relations after the chapters, will believe that they are inventions of the imagination; but I assert in truth, that they are not inventions, but were truly seen and heard; not seen and heard in any state of the mind buried in sleep, but in a state of full wakefulness. For it has pleased the Lord to manifest Himself to me, and to send me to teach those things which will be of his New Church, which is meant by the New Jerusalem in the Revelation; for which end He has opened the interiors of my mind or spirit, by which it has been given me to be in the spiritual world with angels, and at the same time in the natural world with men, and this now for twenty-seven years. Who in the Christian world would have known any thing concerning HEAVEN AND HELL, unless it had pleased the Lord to open in some one the sight of his spirit, and to show and teach? That such things as are described in the RELATIONS, appear in the heavens, is manifestly evident from the like things, which were seen by JOHN, and described in the Revelation, as also which were seen and described in the Word of the Old Testament by the PROPHETS. In the REVELATION are these: That he saw THE SON OF MAN in the midst of the seven candlesticks; that he saw a tabernacle, a temple, an ark and an altar in heaven; a book sealed with seven seals, the book open, and thence horses going forth; four animals around the throne; twelve thousand chosen out of each tribe; locusts ascending out of the abyss; a woman bringing forth a male child, and fleeing into the desert on account of the dragon; two beasts, one ascending out of the sea, the other out of the earth; an angel flying in the midst of heaven, having the everlasting gospel; a sea of glass mixed with fire; seven angels having the seven last plagues;

vials poured out by them, into the earth, into the sea, into the rivers, into the sun, into the throne of the beast, into the Euphrates, and into the air; a woman sitting upon a scarlet beast; the dragon cast out into a lake of fire and sulphur; a white horse; a great supper; a new heaven and a new earth; the holy Jerusalem coming down out of heaven, described as to the gates, the wall and its foundations; also a river of the water of life, and trees of life bearing fruit every month; beside many more things; all which were seen by JOHN, and seen while as to his spirit he was in the spiritual world, and in heaven. Beside the things which were seen by the apostles after the Lord's resurrection, as those which were seen afterwards by PETER, Acts xi.; and also those seen and heard by PAUL. Moreover, those which were seen by the PROPHETS in the Old Testament; as by EZEKIEL, that he saw four animals which were cherubs, Ezek. i. and x.; also a new temple and a new earth, and an angel measuring them, xl. to xlviii.; that he was carried away to Jerusalem, and saw there abominations; and also into Chaldea, viii. xi. The case was similar with ZECHARIAH; that he saw a man riding among the myrtle trees, Zech. i. 8; that he saw four horns, and afterwards a man with a measuring line in his hand, ii.; that he saw a flying roll, and an ephah, v. 1, 6; that he saw four chariots between two mountains, and horses, vi. 1, &c.: and likewise with DANIEL; that he saw four beasts ascending out of the sea, Dan. vii. 1, &c.; that he saw the Son of Man coming with the clouds of heaven, whose dominion will not pass away, and whose kingdom will not perish, vii. 13, 14; that he saw the battles of the ram and the he-goat, viii. 1, &c.; that he saw the angel Gabriel, and talked with him, ix.; that Elisha's boy saw chariots and horses of fire around Elisha, and that he saw them when his eyes were opened, 2 Kings vi. 17. From these and many other things in the Word, it is evident that the things which exist in the spiritual world have appeared to many, before and since the coming of the Lord what wonder that they should also now, when the church is commencing, and the New Jerusalem coming down out of heaven?

A THEOREM

PROPOSED BY A CERTAIN DUKE, AN ELECTOR IN GERMANY, WHO ALSO HAD THE HIGHEST ECCLESIASTICAL DIGNITY.

ONCE in the spiritual world, I saw a certain duke, an elector in Germany, who also had had the highest dignity in ecclesiastical affairs, and near him two bishops, and also two ministers; and at a distance I heard what they said among themselves. The electoral duke asked the four standing by him, whether they knew what makes the head of religion in Christendom. The bishops answered, "The head of religion in Chistendom is FAITH ALONE JUSTIFYING AND SAVING." He asked again, "Do you know what lies inwardly concealed in that faith? Open it, look into it, and tell." They answered, "That inwardly in it there lies concealed nothing else but THE MERIT AND RIGHTEOUSNESS OF THE LORD THE SAVIOR." To this the electoral duke said, "There is concealed in it, then, the Lord the Savior in his Human, in which He is called JESUS CHRIST; because He alone, in his Human, was righteousness." To this they said, "This certainly and inevitably follows." The electoral duke insisted, saying, "Open that faith and look into it further, and search well, whether there be any thing else therein." And the ministers said, "There is also concealed therein THE GRACE OF GOD THE FATHER." To which the electoral duke said, "Conceive and perceive rightly, and you will see, that there is the Grace of the Son with the Father, for He asks and intercedes. Wherefore, I tell you, since you confess, venerate and kiss that faith alone of yours, you will by all means confess, venerate and kiss the Lord the Savior alone in his Human; for, as was said above, He in his Human was and is RIGHTEOUSNESS. That He, in this also, is JEHOVAH AND GOD, I saw in the Sacred Letters, from these passages: *Behold the days will come, when I shall raise up to David a righteous Branch, who shall reign a King, and shall be prospered; and this is the name which they shall call Him*, JEHOVAH OUR RIGHTEOUSNESS, Jer. xxxiii. 15, 16: in Paul: *In Jesus Christ all the fulness of the Godhead dwelleth bodily*, Coloss. ii. 9: and in John: *Jesus Christ is* THE TRUE GOD *and eternal Life*, 1 John v. 20, 21. Wherefore, also, He is called the GOD OF FAITH, Phil. iii. 9"

INDEX OF THE RELATIONS.

I.

I HEARD some new comers conversing together about three divine persons from eternity; and then a certain one, who, in the world, had been a primate, opened the ideas of his thought concerning that mystery, saying, That it had been and was still his mind, that three in heaven sit upon high thrones; God the Father upon a throne of the finest gold, with a sceptre in his hand; God the Son at his right hand, upon a throne of the purest silver, with a crown upon his head; and God the Holy Ghost upon a throne of shining crystal, holding in his hand the dove, in which he appeared, when Christ was baptized; and that round about them, lamps, hanging in triple order, glittered from precious stones; and that at a distance, in the circus, stood innumerable angels adoring and glorifying. And, moreover, he spoke concerning the Holy Ghost, how he introduces faith, purifies and justifies. He said that many of his order favored his ideas; believing that I also, because I was a layman, should have faith in them. But then, leave of speaking being given to me, I said that, from my childhood, I had cherished the idea that God is one; wherefore I explained to him what the trinity involves; what a throne, sceptre and crown signify, when they, in the Word, are predicated of God. To which I added, that all who believe that there are three divine persons from eternity, cannot but believe that there are three Gods. And, moreover, that the divine essence is not divisible. *n.* 16.

II.

A discourse of the angels concerning God, that his Divine is Divine *Esse* in itself, and not from itself; and that it is One, the Same, Itself, and Indivisible; also, that God is not in place, but with those who are in place; and that his Divine Love appears to the angels as a sun, and that the heat thence in its essence is love, and the light thence in its essence, wisdom. *n.* 25.

That the proceeding divine attributes, which are creation, redemption and regeneration, are of one God, and not of three. *n.* 26.

III.

Since I perceived that a vast multitude of men are in the persuasion, that all things are of nature, and thence that nature is the creator of the universe, in a certain gymnasium, where there were such, I spoke with a certain ingenious one respecting these three things: 1. *Whether nature be of life, or whether life be of nature.* 2. *Whether the centre be of the expanse, or whether the expanse be of the centre.* 3. *Concerning the centre and expanse of nature and of life.* And that the centre of nature is the sun of the natural world, and the expanse of this, its world itself; and that the centre of life is the sun of the spiritual world, and the expanse of this, its world itself; which were canvassed on both sides, and finally it was shown which was true. *n.* 35.

IV.

That I was brought into a certain theatre of wisdom, where were assembled angelic spirits from the four quarters, upon whom it had been enjoined to canvass three arcana: 1. *What is the image of God, and what the likeness of God.* 2. *Why man is not born into the science of any love, when yet beasts and birds are born into the science of all their loves.* 3. *What the tree of life signifies, and the tree of the knowledge of good and evil.* And, moreover, that they should join those three together into one sentence, and refer this to the angels; which being done. the sentence was referred, and it was accepted by the angels. *n.* 48.

V.

That from evil spirits just above hell, there was heard, as it were, a noise of the sea, which was a tumult that existed among them, because they heard above them, that God Almighty had bound himself to order. And that some ascended thence and spoke to me sharply concerning that subject, saying that God, because He is almighty, is not bound to any order. And being questioned concerning order, I said, 1 That God is order itself. 2. That He created man from order, in order, and to order 3. That He created his rational mind according to the order of the spiritual world, and his body according to the order of the natural world. 4. That thence it is a law of order, that man from his little spiritual world, or *microüranus*, should govern his little natural world, or *microcosm;* as God, from his *macroüranus*, or the spiritual world, governs his *macrocosm*, or the natural world. 5. That thence more laws of order flow forth, some of which were added. What afterwards happened to those spirits is described *n.* 71.

VI.

Concerning the reasoning of some from Holland and Britain, in the spiritual world, concerning Imputation and Predestination. On one side, why God, because He is almighty, does not impute the righteousness of his Son to all, and thus make them redeemed; when yet, because He is almighty, He can make all the satans of hell angels of heaven; yea, if it be his good pleasure, He can make Lucifer, the dragon, and all the goats, archangels; and what need of but a single word for this? On the other side, that God is order itself, and that He can do nothing contrary to the laws of his order, because this would be to do contrary to Himself; besides other things, by which they sported among themselves concerning this subject. *n.* 72.

VII.

That afterwards I spoke with those who were in the faith of predestination, who deduced it from the absolute power or omnipotence of God; and that otherwise, the power of God would be less than that of a king, a monarch in the world, who can turn the laws of justice, as the palms of his hands, and act absolutely, as Octavius Augustus, and also absolutely as Nero. To which it was replied, that God created the world, and all and every thing of it, from Himself as order, and thus put order into every thing; and that the laws of his order are as many as the truths in the Word: and then were mentioned some of the laws of order, and what ones were on the part of God, and what on the part of man; and that they cannot be changed, because God is order itself; and that man was created an image of his order. *n.* 73

VIII.

That I spoke with persons assembled from the clergy and laity, concerning the Divine Omnipotence; who said, that omnipotence was unlimited, and that limited omnipotence was a contradiction. To which it was replied, that it is not a contradiction to act omnipotently according to the laws of justice with judgment; it is said also in David, that justice and judgment are the support of God's throne, Psalm .xxxix. 14; and that it is not a contradiction to act omnipotently according to the laws of love from wisdom; but that it is a contradiction, that God can act contrary to the laws of justice and love, and that this would be from no judgment and wisdom; and that such a contradiction the faith of the present church involves, that God can make the unjust just, and confer on the impious all the gifts of salvation, and the rewards of life; besides more concerning this faith, and concerning omnipotence. *n.* 74.

IX.

Once, when I was in meditation concerning the creation of the universe by God, I was led away in spirit to some wise ones, who at first complained of the ideas entertained by them in the world, which were concerning the creation of the universe out of chaos, and concerning creation out of nothing, because they obscure, pervert and destroy meditation concerning the creation of the universe by God. Wherefore, on being asked what my mind was, I delivered this: That it is vain to conclude any thing but what is fantastical, concerning the creation of the universe, unless it be known that there are two worlds, the spiritual and the natural; and that in each there is a sun; and that the sun of the spiritual world is pure love, in the midst of which is God, and that from it are all spiritual things, which in themselves are substantial; and that the sun of the natural world is pure fire, and that from it are all natural things, which in themselves are material; and that from these things being known, it may be concluded concerning the creation of the universe, that it is from God; and in what manner; which also was briefly delineated. *n.* 76.

X.

That some satans of hell desired to speak with the angels of heaven, for the purpose that they might convince them that all things are from nature, and that God is only a word, unless nature be meant. And it was permitted that they should ascend; and then some angels descended from heaven into the world of spirits, that they might hear them; who being seen, the satans ran furiously up to them, saying, "You are called angels, because you believe that there is a God, and that nature is not any thing respectively; and yet you believe those things, although it is contrary to all the senses. Which sense of your five feels any thing else than nature?" After these and many other bitter words, the angels recalled to their remembrance, that they now lived after death, and that they did not before believe even this. And then they made them see the beautiful and splendid things of heaven; and they said that these things were there, because all there believe in God. And afterwards they made them see the ugly and filthy things of hell, saying that these things were there, because all there believe in nature. The satans, from seeing those things, at first were convinced that there is a God, and that He created nature; but as they descended, the love of evil returned and closed up their understanding from above; which being closed up, they believed as before, that all things are of nature, and nothing of God. *n.* 77.

XI.

A type of the creation of the universe, to the life, was shown to me by the angels. I was brought into heaven, and it was given to see there all things which were of the animal kingdom, all which were of the vegetable kingdom, and all which were of the mineral kingdom, which were altogether similar to the objects of those three kingdoms in the natural world. And then they said, "All those things are created in a moment by God, and they subsist as long as the angels are in a state of love and faith as to thought; and that that instantaneous creation evidently testifies the creation of similar things, yea, a similar creation in the natural world, with the difference only, that natural things clothe spiritual, and that that clothing was provided by God for the sake of the generations of one from another, by means of which creation is perpetuated. Consequently, that the creation of the universe was effected in like manner as it is every moment in heaven. But still, that all things in the three kingdoms of nature, that are noxious and filthy, which are enumerated, were not created by God, but arose together with hell." *n.* 78.

XII.

A conversation with some, who in the world were celebrated for erudition, concerning the creation of the universe; who, speaking from the same ideas that they before entertained, said—one, that nature created itself; another, that nature collected its elements into vortexes, and that, from the collision of these, the earth was formed; and the third, that it was from chaos, which he equalled in magnitude to a great part of the universe; and that at first there burst forth thence the purest things, of which the sun and stars were formed; and that afterwards those less pure, of which the atmospheres, and lastly the gross things, of which the terraqueous globe consists. To the question, "Whence were human souls?" they said, that the ether brought itself together into little discrete balls, and that these infuse themselves into those who are about to be born, and make souls, and that after death they fly off to the former host in the ether, and thence return into others, according to the metempsychosis of the ancients. After this, a certain priest, by solid reasons for the creation of the universe by God, reduced all the things that were said to a flashy hodge-podge, and put them to shame, but still they retained their former deliriums. *n.* 79.

XIII.

With a certain satan, concerning God, concerning the angelic heaven, and concerning religion, who, because he knew no other than that he was still in the former world, said that God is the universe, and that the angelic heaven is the atmospherical firmament, and that religion is an amulet of the common people; besides many more foolish things. But when it was again brought to his. remembrance, that now he lived after death, and that before he did not believe that life, at that moment he confessed that he was insane; but as soon as he turned himself about, and went back, he was insane, just as before. *n.* 80.

XIV.

That in the night, I saw an *ignis fatuus* falling down to the earth, which by many is called a dragon. I observed the place where it fell. There was there sulphurous earth mixed with iron dust; and when, in the morning, I looked thither, I saw there two tents, and then presently a spirit fell down from heaven, to whom I went and asked why he fell down from heaven. He answered, that he was cast down by the angels of Michael, because he said that God the Father and his Son are two, and not one. And he said, that the whole angelic heaven believes that God the Father and his Son are one, as the soul and body are one; and that they confirm this by many things from the Word; and moreover from reason, that the soul of the son is only from the father; and that it is also thence in the body a likeness of the father. And he added, that he indeed confessed in heaven, as before on earth, that God is one; but because the confession of the mouth and the thought of the mind disagreed in this, they said that I did not believe in any God, because one dissipates the other. And he said that this was the cause of his being cast down. The next day, returning to the same place, I saw two statues of like dust, which was a mixture of sulphur and iron, instead of the two tents, one of which represented the faith of the present church, and the other its charity, both beautifully clothed; but the garments were induced by fantasies. But because they were of that dust, in consequence of rain sent down from heaven, they both began to boil and to blaze. *n.* 110.

XV.

That, in the spiritual world, it is not lawful for any one to speak otherwise than he thinks; if he does, that which is hypocritical is manifestly heard; and that, therefore, in hell no one can name *Jesus*, because Jesus signifies salvation. By this it was there proved, how many in the Christian world, at this day, believe that Christ, also as to his Human, is God. Wherefore, when many of the clergy and laity had assembled, it was proposed to them, that they should say DIVINE HUMAN; but still scarcely any could extract these two words together from the thought, and thus enunciate them. It was confirmed before them, by many things from the Word, that the Lord, as to the Human also, was God; as by those which are in Matt. xxviii. 18; John i. 1, 2, 14; xvii. 2; Colos. ii. 9; 1 John v. 20; and also elsewhere: but still they could not speak out Divine Human; and, what they wondered at, that neither could the Evangelical, although their orthodoxy teaches, *That, in Christ, God is Man and Man God*. and still more, that neither could the Monks, who yet most devoutly adore the body of Christ in the eucharist. From these things it was found, that Christians, at this day, as to the greater part, are interiorly either Arians or Socinians: and that these, if they adore Christ as God, are hypocrites. *n.* 111

XVI.

An altercation concerning the little treatise, "A Brief Exposition of the Doctrine of the New Church," published by me at Amsterdam; and concerning this there, especially, *That not God the Father, but the Lord God the Redeemer, is to be addressed and adored;* arguing, that still it is said in the Lord's prayer, *Our Father, who art in the heavens, hallowed be thy name; thy kingdom come;* consequently that God the Father is to be addressed. To settle which strife, I was sent for; and then I demonstrated, that God the Father cannot be addressed in his Divine, but in his Human; and because the Divine and the Human in Him are one Person, that the Lord is that Father; which also was confirmed from the Word; as well from the Word of the Old Testament, where the Son of God is called the Father of eternity, and in many places Jehovah the Redeemer, Jehovah Righteousness, and the God of Israel, as from the Word of the New Testament often; and thus that when the Lord God the Redeemer is addressed, the Father is addressed; and that then his name is hallowed, and his kingdom comes; besides more. *n.* 112.

XVII.

That I saw an army upon red and black horses, all in it turned as to their faces to the tails of the horses, and as to the hinder part of their heads to their heads, crying for battle against those who were riding upon white horses; and that that ludicrous army issued forth from the place which is called Armageddon, Rev. xvi. 16; and that it consisted of those, who in youth imbued the dogmas concerning justification by faith alone, and who afterwards, when they were promoted to eminent offices, rejected the things which are of faith and religion, from the internals of their mind to the externals of their body, where, finally, they vanished. Described as they appeared in Armageddon; and it was heard thence, that they wished to engage with the angels of Michael, which also was given, but at some distance from hence; and that here it was disputed between them concerning the meaning of the words in the Lord's prayer, *Our Father, who art in the heavens, hallowed be thy name; thy kingdom come.* And then it was said by the angels of Michael, that the Lord, the Redeemer and Savior, is Father to all in the heavens; since He taught, that the Father and He are one; that the Father is in Him, and He in the Father; and that he that seeth Him seeth the Father; that all things of the Father are in Him; also, that it is the will of the Father that they should believe in the Son, and that those who believe not the Son shall not see life, but that the anger of God will abide on them; also, that He has all power in heaven and in earth; and that He has power over all flesh; and moreover, that no one has seen, or can see, God the Father, but the Son alone, who is in the bosom of the Father; besides more. After this combat, the Armageddons being convinced, some of them were cast into the abyss, mentioned Revelation ix. and some of them were sent forth into a desert. *n.* 113.

XVIII.

That I was in a temple, in which there were no windows, but a large aperture in the roof, and that those assembled there conversed together about Redemption, saying unanimously, that redemption was made by the passion of the cross. But when they were in that conversation, a black cloud covered the aperture of the roof, whence it became dark in the temple; but that, a little afterwards, that cloud was dispersed by angels, that descended from heaven, who then sent down one of their number into the temple to instruct them about redemption. He said that the passion of the cross was not redemption, but that redemption was the subjugation of the hells, the establishment of order in the heavens, and thus the restitution of all things, which were in disorder, both in the spiritual world and in the natural world; and that without it no flesh could have been saved. And concerning the passion of the cross, he said, that by it was completed the inmost unition with the Father; and that when it is taken for redemption, many things unworthy of God, yea, abominable, follow as consequences; as that He passed sentence of condemnation upon the whole human race, and that the Son took it upon Himself, and that thus He propitiated the Father, and by intercession reduced Him to his divine essence, which is love and wisdom; betides many more things, which it is scandalous to attribute to God. *n.* 134.

XIX.

That the sun of the spiritual world was seen, in which Jehovah God is, in his Human: and then this was heard from heaven, THAT GOD IS ONE. But when this glided down into the spiritual world, it was turned according to the forms of the minds there, and at length into three Gods; which also one there reasoning confirmed by these things: That there is one who created all things, another who redeemed all, and a third who operates all things; also that there is one who imputes, another who mediates, and a third who inscribes those things on man, and thus puts in faith, by which he justifies him. But because the faith of three Gods had perverted the whole Christian church, from the perception given, I disclosed to them what, with the one God, is meant by Mediation, Intercession, Propitiation and Expiation; namely, that those four are attributes of the Human of Jehovah God; that because Jehovah God without the Human cannot approach man, nor be approached by man, *Mediation* signifies that the Human is what is intermediate; that *Intercession* signifies that it mediates perpetually; that *Propitiation* signifies that there is free access for every man to God, and that *Expiation* signifies that there is also for sinners; and all these things through the Human. *n.* 135.

XX.

That I entered into a gymnasium, where it was canvassed, how that is to be understood, which is said concerning the Son of God, that HE SITS AT THE RIGHT HAND OF THE FATHER. Concerning this there were various opinions; yet it was the opinion of all that the Son actually sits thus; but they were canvassing why it was so. Then some supposed that it was done on account of redemption; some that it was from love; some, that He might be a counsellor; some, that He might have honor from the angels; some, because it was given him to reign instead of the Father; some, that he might be heard with the right ear by those for whom He intercedes. Besides, they also canvassed, Whether the Son of God from eternity sits thus, or whether the Son of God born in the world. Having heard these things, I raised my hand, requesting that I might be permitted to say something, and to tell what is meant by sitting at the right hand of God. And I said, "The omnipotence of God, by means of the Human which he assumed, is meant; for by means of this He wrought redemption, that is, subjugated the hells, created a new angelic heaven, and instituted a new church." That this is meant by sitting at the right hand, I confirmed from the Word, in which power is signified by the right hand; and afterwards it was confirmed from heaven, by the appearance of a right hand over them, from the power of which, and the terror thence, they all became almost lifeless. *n.* 136.

XXI.

That, in the spiritual world, I was brought into a council-house, in which were assembled the celebrated ones who lived before the Nicene council, and were called Apostolic Fathers; and also the renowned ones who lived after that council; and I saw that some of the latter appeared with a beardless chin, and in wigs of women's hair neatly trimmed; but all the former in a bearded chin, and in natural hair. Before them stood a man, the judge and arbiter of the writings of this age, who commenced by a certain lamentation, saying, "A man from the laity has risen up, who has dragged down our faith out of its sanctuary, which yet is a star shining day and night before us; but this is done because that man is blind in the mysteries of that faith, and does not see in it the righteousness of Christ, and thus not the wonderful things of its justification; when yet that faith is in three divine persons, and thus in the whole God; and because he has transferred his faith to the second person, and not to this, but to his Human, it cannot be otherwise than that naturalism should spring thence." Those who lived after the Nicene council favored his speech, saying, "That it is impossible that there should be any other faith, and from any other source." But the Apostolic Fathers, who lived before that age, being indignant, related many things which are said in heaven concerning the Nicene and Athanasian faith, which may be seen. But because the president of the council was consociated as, to the spirit, with that writer in Leipsic, I addressed him, and demonstrated from the Word, that Christ, also as to the Human, is God; and also from the dogmatical book of the Evangelical, called FORMULA CONCORDIÆ, *That in Christ God is Man and Man God;* as also that the Augsburg Confession very highly approves of the worship of Him; besides more; at which he was silent, and turned himself away. Afterwards I spoke with a certain spirit, who was consociated with an eminent man in Gottenburg, who defiled the worship of the Lord with a still greater reproach. But at length those two reproaches were declared to be lies craftily invented for averting the wills, and deterring them from the holy worship of the Lord. *n.* 137.

XXII.

That there appeared a smoke ascending from the lower earth, and it was said that smokes are nothing else than falses in a heap. And then some angels had a desire of exploring what the falses were, which thus smoked; and they descended, and found four troops of spirits, two of which were of the learned and unlearned of the clergy, and two of the learned and unlearned of the laity, who all, among themselves, confirmed that an invisible God is to be worshipped, and that the worshippers then have holiness and audience; otherwise if a visible God should be worshipped. Holiness and audience from an invisible God they confirmed by various things; and that, therefore, they acknowledge three Gods from eternity, who are invisible. But it was shown, that the worship of an invisible God, and still more of three invisible ones, is no worship. To confirm this, Socinus and Arius, with some of their followers, who all had worshipped an invisible Divinity, were brought forth from below; who, when they spoke from the natural or external mind, said that there is a God, although He is invisible; but when their external mind was shut, and the internal was opened, and from this they were forced to make their confession concerning God, they said, "What is God? We have not seen his shape, nor heard his voice. What, then, is God, but an ideal entity or nature?" But they were instructed, that it had pleased God to descend and assume the Human, that they might see his shape and hear his voice; but this in their ears was to no purpose. *n.* 159.

XXIII.

First, concerning the stars in the natural world; that perhaps they might be of the same number as the angelic societies in heaven, since every society there sometimes shines as a star. Afterwards, I spoke with the angels concerning a certain way, which appears filled with innumerable spirits, and that it is the way by which all, who depart out of the natural world, pass into the spiritual world. To this way I went in company with angels; and we called from that way twelve men, and asked what they believed concerning heaven and hell, and concerning a life after death; and because they were recently from the world, and knew no otherwise than that they were still in the natural world, they answered from the idea which they brought with them THE FIRST, "That all who live morally come into heaven; and that no one comes into hell, because all live morally." THE SECOND, "That God governs heaven, and the devil hell; and because they are opposite, one calls good what the other calls evil; and that the man who is a dissembler, because he stands on the side of both, can live under the dominion of one equally as under the dominion of the other" THE THIRD, "That there is no heaven nor hell. Who has come thence and told?" THE FOURTH, "That no one could return thence and tell, because man, when he dies, is either a spectre or wind." THE FIFTH, "That we must wait till the day of the last judgment, and then they will tell, and you will know all about it." But when he said this, he laughed in his heart. THE SIXTH, "How can the soul of man, which is only wind, reënter its body, eaten up by worms, and be clothed with a skeleton either burnt up or reduced to dust." THE SEVENTH, "That men no more live after death than beasts and birds. Are not these equally rational?" THE EIGHTH, "I believe there is a heaven, but I do not believe there is a hell, because God is almighty, and is able to save all." THE NINTH, "That God, because He is gracious, cannot send any one to eternal fire." THE TENTH, "That no one can come into hell, because God sent his Son, who has made expiation for all, and taken away the sins of all. What can the devil do against that?" THE ELEVENTH, who was a priest, "That those only are saved who have obtained faith, and that election is according to the will of the Almighty." THE TWELFTH, who was a politician, "I do not say any thing about heaven and hell; but let the priests preach about them, that the minds of the common people may be kept bound, by an invisible bond, to the laws and rulers." On hearing these things, the angels were astonished; but they waked them up by instructing them, that they were now living after death; and he introduced them into heaven, but they did not stay there long, because it was found that they were merely natural, and that thence the hinder part of their heads was excavated; concerning which excavation and the cause of it, lastly, something is said, *n.* 160.

XXIV.

That there was heard a sound as of a mill, and that, following the sound, I saw a house full of chinks, into which there was an entrance open under ground, and in it a man collecting from the Word and books many things concerning JUSTIFICATION BY FAITH ALONE; and that scribes at his side were writing his collections upon paper; and to the question, what he was now collecting, he said this, that God the Father fell out of favor towards the human race, and that He, therefore, sent the Son to make expiation and propitiation. To which I answered, that this is contrary to Scripture, and contrary to reason, that God could fall out of favor; thus He would also fall out of his essence, and thus would not be God. And when I demonstrated this even to conviction, he grew warm, and commanded the scribes to cast me out. But when I went out of my own accord, he threw after me a book, which, by chance, his hand took hold of; and that book was the Word. *n.* 161.

XXV.

It was disputed among spirits, whether any one can see any genuine truth in the Word, unless he goes immediately to the Lord, who is the Word itself. But, because there were those who contradicted, an experiment was made; and then those who went to God the Father, did not see any truth; but all who went to the Lord saw During this disputation, some spirits ascended out of the abyss, of which Rev ix., where they canvass the mysteries of justification by faith alone, saying that they go to God the Father, and see their mysteries in clear light. But it was answered, that they see them in fatuous light, and that they have not even a single truth; at which being indignant, they brought forth from the Word many things which were true; but it was said to them, that they were true in themselves, but in them falsified. That it was so, was proved by their being led into a house, where there was a table, into which light from heaven flowed directly; and it was said to them, that they should write those truths, which they had brought forth from the Word, upon paper, and lay it upon that table; which being done, that paper, on which the truths were written, shone like a star; but when they came up and fixed their eyes upon it, the paper appeared blackened as by soot. And afterwards they were led to another similar table, upon which lay the Word encircled with a rainbow; which when a certain champion of the doctrine of faith alone touched with his hand, an explosion was made, as from a gun, and he was cast into a corner of the room, and lay as dead for the space of half an hour. From these things, they were convinced that all the truths, which were with them from the Word, were true in themselves, but falsified in them. *n.* 162.

XXVI.

That there are climates in the spiritual world, as in the natural world; and that thence also there are northern zones, where are snow and ice. Once being brought thither in spirit, I entered a temple then covered over with snow, illuminated within by lamps, where, behind the altar, there was seen a table, upon which was written this, THE DIVINE TRINITY, FATHER, SON AND HOLY GHOST, WHO ESSENTIALLY ARE ONE, BUT PERSONALLY THREE. And I heard a priest preaching about four mysteries of faith, respecting which the understanding is to be kept under the obedience of faith, which may be seen. After the discourse, the hearers thanked the priest for his sermon so full of wisdom. But when I asked them whether they understood any thing, they answered, "We caught all with full ears; why do you ask whether we understood? Is not the understanding amazed in such things?" To this the priest, being present, added.

"Because you have heard and not understood, you are blessed, since thence is your salvation," &c. *n.* 185.

XXVII.

That THE HUMAN MIND is distinguished into three regions, like the heaven in which angels are; and that theological things, with those who love truths because they are truths, reside in the highest region of the mind; and that under them, in the middle region, moral things, but under these, political things; and that the various sciences make the door. But that theological things, with those who do not love truths, sit in the lowest region, and mingle themselves there with man's own things, and thus with the fallacies of the senses; and that thence it is, that some cannot perceive theological things at all. *n.* 186.

XXVIII.

That I was brought to a place, where were those who are meant by THE FALSE PROPHET in the Revelation; and by those there I was invited to see their temple; and I followed and saw in it the image of a woman clothed in a scarlet robe, holding in her right hand a golden coin, and in her left a chain of pearls; but these things were induced by fantasy. But when the interiors of the mind were opened by the Lord, instead of the temple, there was seen a house full of chinks; and instead of the woman, there was seen a beast, such as is described, Revelation xiii. 2; and under the floor there a bog, in which lay the Word, deeply concealed. But presently, an eastern wind blowing up, the temple was carried away, and the bog dried up, and the Word appeared; and then, by the light from heaven, there appeared there a TABERNACLE, like that of Abraham, when the three angels came and told him concerning Isaac, who was about to be born; and afterwards, light being sent forth from the second heaven, instead of the tabernacle there appeared a TEMPLE, such as had been at Jerusalem; and after this, a light shone upon it from the third heaven, and then the temple disappeared, and there was seen a HOUSE ALONE, standing upon the foundation stone, where the Word was. But because too great sanctity then filled their minds, this light was withdrawn, and instead of it, light from the second heaven was let in, from which the view of the temple returned, and within in it that of the tabernacle. *n.* 187.

XXIX.

That there was seen a magnificent palace, in which there was a temple, and in this seats were placed in triple order; in it there was a council convoked by the Lord, in which they deliberated concerning THE LORD THE SAVIOR, and concerning the HOLY SPIRIT; and when as many of the clergy were present as there were seats, they entered the council; and because it was concerning the Lord, the first proposition was, WHO ASSUMED THE HUMAN IN THE VIRGIN MARY? And then the angel standing at the table read before them what the angel Gabriel said to Mary: THE HOLY SPIRIT SHALL COME UPON THEE, AND THE POWER OF THE MOST HIGH SHALL OVERSHADOW THEE; AND THE HOLY THING THAT SHALL BE BORN OF THEE SHALL BE CALLED THE SON OF GOD, Luke i. 35; and also from Matt. i. 20, 25. And moreover many things from the prophets, that Jehovah himself was about to come into the world, and that Jehovah himself is called Savior, Redeemer and Righteousness: from which it was concluded that Jehovah himself assumed the Human. Another deliberation concerning the Lord was, WHETHER THE FATHER AND THE LORD JESUS CHRIST ARE NOT THUS ONE, AS THE SOUL AND BODY ARE ONE; and this was confirmed from many passages in the Word, and also from the general creed of the present church; from which it was concluded, that the soul of the Lord was from God the Father, and thence that his Human is Divine; and that this is to be approached as the Father is approached, since Jehovah God by it sent Himself into the world, and made Himself visible to the eyes of men, and thus also accessible. The third deliberation followed, which was concerning THE HOLY SPIRIT; and then first the idea concerning three divine persons from eternity was shaken off, and it was proved from the Word, that the Holy Divine, which is called the Holy Spirit, proceeds out of the Lord from the Father. At length, from what was deliberated in this council, this conclusion was made: That in the Lord the Savior there is a Divine Trinity, which is the Divine from which, which is called the Father, the Divine

Human, which is called the Son, and the Divine Proceeding, which is called the Holy Spirit; and that thus there is one God in the church. After the council was ended, splendid garments were given to those who sat in it, and they were led into the new heaven. *n.* 188.

XXX.

That I saw in a certain stable great purses, in which there was silver in great plenty, and by them young men as guards; in the next room, modest virgins with a chaste wife; and also in another room, two infants; and at last a harlot and dead horses. And afterwards I was instructed what each of those things signified; and that by them was represented and described the Word, as it is in itself, and as it is at this day. *n.* 277.

XXXI.

That writing was seen, such as there is in the highest or third heaven, which consisted of inflected letters, with little horns turning upwards; and it was said that the Hebrew letters, in the most ancient time, were somewhat similar to them, when they were more inflected than they are at this day; and that the letter *h*, which was added to the names of Abram and Sarai, signifies *infinite* and *eternal*. They explained before me the sense of some words in Psalm xxxii. 2, from the letters only or syllables there, which is, *That the Lord is merciful also to those who do evil.* *n.* 278.

XXXII.

That before the Israelitish Word there was a Word, the prophetical books of which were called ENUNCIATIONS, and the historical, THE WARS OF JEHOVAH; and besides these, also one called the book of JASHER; which three also are named in our Word: and that that ancient Word was in the land of Canaan, Syria, Mesopotamia Arabia, Assyria, Chaldea, Egypt, Tyre, Zidon and Nineveh; but that this, because it was full of such correspondences as remotely signify celestial and spiritual things, which gave occasion to idolatries, of the Divine Providence disappeared. I heard that Moses copied out of that Word the things which he related concerning the Creation, Adam and Eve, the Flood, and concerning Noah, and concerning his three sons, but no further. That that same Word is still reserved with the people in GREAT TARTARY, and that they draw from it the precepts of their faith and life, was related to me in the spiritual world by the angels thence. *n.* 279.

XXXIII.

That those who are in the spiritual world cannot appear to those who are in the natural world, nor conversely; thus spirits and angels cannot appear to men, nor men to spirits and angels, on account of THE DISTINCTION BETWEEN SPIRITUAL AND NATURAL; or, what is the same, between substantial and material. It is from this origin that spirits and angels have altogether a different language, different writing, and also different thought, from what men have. That it is so, was made manifest by lively experience, which was done by their entering by turns to their companions, and returning to me, and thus comparing. Thence it was discovered, that there is not even one word of spiritual language similar to any word of natural language; and that their writing consisted of syllables, each of which involves the sense of some thing; and that the ideas of their thought do not fall into the ideas of natural thought. The cause of these distinctions is, that spirits and angels are in principles, but men in derivatives; or that the former are in prior things, from which, as causes, are posterior things, and men in posterior things from them. It was said that there is a similar distinction between the languages, writings and thoughts of the angels of the third heaven and the angels of the second. *n.* 280.

XXXIV.

Concerning THE STATE OF MEN AFTER DEATH, in general, and concerning the state of those who have confirmed themselves in falses, in particular. Concerning the latter and the former these things were observed: 1. That men are most commonly resuscitated the third day after death, and that then they know no otherwise than that they are still living in the former world. 2. That all flow into the world, which is in the middle between heaven and hell, which is called the world of spirits 3. That there they are transferred into various societies, and thus are explored as to their quality. 4. That there the good and faithful are prepared for heaven, and the evil and unfaithful for hell. 5. That after the preparation, which lasts some years, a way is opened for the good to some society in heaven, where they are to live for ever, but a way for the evil into hell; besides many more things. Afterwards hell is described as it is; and that there those are called satans, who are in falses from confirmation, and devils, who are in evils of life. *n.* 281.

XXXV.

That from the lower earth next above hell, I heard the vociferations, O HOW JUST! O HOW LEARNED! O HOW WISE! and because I wondered that there should be there also any just, learned and wise, I descended, and first went to the place where they were crying, O HOW JUST! and I saw there, as it were, a tribunal, and in it judges of injustice, who could dexterously pervert the laws, and turn judgments to the favor of any one whatever; and that thus their judgments were only arbitrary judgments; and when the sentences were carried out to the clients, then they cried a long way, *O how just!* Concerning these, the angels afterwards said, that such cannot see any thing at all of what is just. After a while, those judges were cast into hell, and their books were turned into placards, and, instead of judging, there was given to them the office of preparing paint, with which they daubed the faces of harlots, and thus turned them into beauties. *n.* 332.

XXXVI.

Afterwards, I went on to the place where it was cried, O HOW LEARNED! and I saw a company of those who reasoned, WHETHER IT BE SO OR NOT, and did not think, THAT IT IS SO; and thence they stopped at the first step concerning any subject whatever; and thus they only touched it from without, and did not enter: thus also concerning God, whether there be a God. That I might know for certain whether they were such, I proposed to them, *What will be the religion by which man is saved?* They replied that, 1. It is to be canvassed whether religion be any thing. 2. Whether one religion effect more than another. 3. Whether there be any eternal life, and thus whether there be any salvation. 4. Whether there be a heaven and a hell. And then they began to canvass the first, *Whether religion be any thing.* And they said that that needed so much investigation, that it could not be finished in the space of a year; and one among them said, that it could not in the space of a hundred years; to which I replied, that in the mean time they were without religion. But still they canvassed this first point so artfully, that the company standing by cried, *O how learned!* It was said to me by the angels, that such appear like carved images; and that afterwards they are sent out into deserts, where, among themselves, they prate and speak only vain things. *n.* 333.

XXXVII.

I went on further, to the third company, where I heard the cry, O HOW WISE! and I found that there were assembled those who cannot see whether truth be truth, but still can make whatever they please appear as truth, and thence are called CONFIRMERS. That they were such, I observed also from various answers to propositions, as that they could make it true that faith is the all of the church, and afterwards that charity is the all of the church, and also that faith and charity together are the all of the church; and because they confirmed whichever of them they liked, and adorned them with appearances so that they shone like truths, therefore the by-standers cried, *O how wise!* Afterwards, some ludicrous things, also, were proposed to them, that they might make them true; for they say that there is nothing true, except what man makes true. The ludicrous things were these: that light is darkness, and darkness light; and also that a crow is white, and not black; which two they made appear altogether as true: the confirmations of them may be seen there. Concerning them, it was said to me by the angels, that such do not possess even a grain of understanding, since all that is above the rational with them is shut up, and that all that is below the rational, open, and this can confirm whatever it likes, but cannot see any truth to be truth; wherefore, this is not the property of an intelligent man; but that to be able to see that the true is true, and the false is false, and to confirm it, is the property of an intelligent man. *n.* 334.

XXXVIII.

I spoke with spirits, who, in the natural world, were renowned for the fame of erudition, who then, among themselves, disputed about CONNATE IDEAS, whether men have any, as beasts have; and then a certain angelic spirit thrust himself in, and said, "You dispute about goats' hair. Men have no connate ideas, nor have beasts any connate:" at which words all grew warm: but afterwards, opportunity of speaking being given, he spoke first concerning beasts, that they have no connate ideas: the reason is, because they do not think, but only operate from instinct, which they have from their natural love, which makes what is analogous to will with them, flows immediately into the senses of their body, and excites that which agrees with and favors the love; and yet ideas are predicated only of thought. That beasts have only sensation, and no thought, he confirmed by various things, especially by the wonderful things which are known respecting spiders, bees and silk-worms, saying, "Does a spider think in its little head, when it forms its web, that it is to be so connected for the sake of these or those uses? Does a bee think in its little head, From these flowers I will suck honey, and from these wax; out of this I will build little cells in a continuous series, and in these I will put honey in abundance, that it may be sufficient also for the winter? besides more things. Does the silk-worm think in its little head, Now I will betake myself to spinning silk, and when I have spun it, then I shall fly off and sport with my companions, and provide for myself a posterity?" besides similar things with beasts and birds. Concerning men, he said, that every mother and nurse, and the father also, knows that infants recently born have no connate ideas, and that they have not any ideas before they have learned to think, and that then ideas rise up and are made according to every quality of the thought, which they had imbibed by instruction; and that this is the case, because man has nothing else born with him but a faculty for knowing, understanding and being wise, and an inclination for loving not only himself and the world, but also the neighbor and God. These things LEIBNITZ and WOLFIUS heard at a distance, and Leibnitz favored, but Wolfius did not. *n.* 335.

XXXIX.

Once a certain angelic spirit illustrated WHAT FAITH AND CHARITY ARE, and what their conjunction effects. He illustrated it by comparison with light and heat, which meet together in a third; because the light in heaven, in its essence, is the truth of faith, and the heat there, in its essence, is the good of charity; consequently that as light without heat, such as there is in the time of winter, strips the trees of leaves and fruits, so faith without charity; and that as light conjoined to heat, such as there is in the time of spring, vivifies all things, so faith conjoined to charity. *n.* 385.

XL.

That two angels descended, one from the eastern heaven, where they are in love, and the other from the southern heaven, where they are in wisdom, and spoke concerning the essence of the heavens, whether it were love, or whether wisdom; and they agreed that it is love and thence wisdom; consequently, that the heavens were created by God, from love by wisdom. *n.* 386.

XLI.

That after that, I entered a certain garden, where I was led around by a certain spirit, and at length to a palace, which was called THE TEMPLE OF WISDOM, which was quadrangular, the walls of crystal, the roof of jasper, the underpinning of various precious stones. And he said that no one could enter into it, unless he believe that that which he knows, understands and comprehends is respectively so little, that it is scarcely any thing. And because I believed it, it was given me to enter; and it was seen that the whole of it was constructed for the form of light. In that temple I related what I had lately heard from the two angels concerning love and wisdom; and they asked, 'Did they not also speak concerning the third, which is use?" And they said that love and wisdom without use, are only ideal entities, but that in use they become real, and that it is similar with charity, faith and good works. *n.* 387

XLII.

That one of the spirits of the dragon invited me to see the delights of his love ; and he led me to something like an AMPHITHEATRE, upon the benches of which sat satyrs and harlots. And then he said, "Now you will see our sport." And he opened a door, and let in, as it were, bullocks, rams, kids and lambs ; and presently, through another door, he let in lions, panthers, tigers and wolves, which rushed upon the flock and mangled and killed it; but all those things, which were seen, were induced by fantasies. Having seen this, I said to the dragon, "After a while, you will see this theatre turned into a lake of fire and sulphur." The sport being finished, the dragon went out, attended by his satyrs and harlots, and saw a flock of sheep, from which he inferred that a city of the Jerusalemites was in the neighborhood ; on seeing which, he was seized with the desire of taking it, and casting out the inhabitants ; but because it was surrounded with a wall, he intended to take it by stratagem. And then he sent one skilled in incantation, who spoke craftily with the citizens concerning faith and charity ; especially, which of them is the primary, and whether charity contributes any thing to salvation. But the dragon, enraged at the answer, went out and gathered together many of his crew, and began to besiege the city ; but when he was in the effort of taking and seizing it, fire from heaven consumed them, according to what was foretold in REVELATION xx. 8, 9. *n.* 388.

XLIII.

Once there was a paper sent down from heaven, in which there was an exhortation that they should acknowledge the Lord the Savior for the God of heaven and earth, according to his words, Matt. xxviii. 18. But two bishops, who were there, were consulted, what they should do ; who said that they should send the paper back to heaven, whence it came ; and when it was done, that society sunk down, but not very deep. The next day, some ascended thence and told what lot they underwent there, and also that there they went to the bishops and reproved them for their advice, and that they spoke many things concerning the state of the church at this day, and found fault with their doctrine concerning the Trinity, concerning justifying faith, concerning charity, and concerning other things which were of the orthodoxy of the bishops, and requested that they would desist from them, because they were contrary to the Word ; but to no purpose. And because they called their faith dead and also diabolical, according to James in his Epistle, one of the bishops took off the mitre from his head, and laid it down upon the table, saying that he would not take it up again, before he had punished the sarcastic speeches concerning his faith. But then there appeared a monster ascending from below, similar to the beast described in REVELATION xiii. 1, 2, which took up the mitre and carried it away. *n.* 389.

XLIV.

That I went to a certain house, where those who were assembled were arguing one with another, whether the good which a man does in the state of justification by faith, be the good of religion or not. There was an agreement, that by the good of religion is meant the good which contributes to salvation. But their opinion prevailed, who said, that all the good that man does, does not contribute any thing to salvation ; since no voluntary good of man can be conjoined with what is gratuitous, because salvation is bestowed freely ; that neither can any good from man be conjoined with the merit of Christ, by which alone salvation is given ; that neither can the operation of man be conjoined with the operation of the Holy Spirit, who does all things without the help of man. From which it was concluded, that good works, even in the state of justification by faith, contribute nothing to salvation, but faith alone. On hearing these things, two gentiles, who stood in the door, said to each other, "These have not any religion. Who does not know that to do good to the neighbor for the sake of God, thus from God and with God, is religion?" *n.* 390.

XLV.

I heard the angels lamenting that there was such SPIRITUAL INDIGENCE at this day in the church, that they know nothing more than that there are three divine persons from eternity, and that faith alone saves; and concerning the Lord, only the historical things; and that they are deeply ignorant of the things which are related in the Word concerning the Lord, his unity with the Father, his divinity and power. And they said that a certain angel was sent down by them to see whether there were such indigence at this day among Christians; and that he asked a certain one what his religion was. He answered, that it was faith. And that then he asked him about redemption, regeneration and salvation. He answered, that they all were of faith; and also concerning charity, that it is in faith; and who can do good from himself? To whom afterwards the angel said, "You have answered like one who plays with one tone of a pipe: I hear only faith; but if you know nothing else but that, you know nothing." And then he led him to his companions in a desert, where there was not even grass. Besides more. *n.* 391.

XLVI.

That I saw five gymnasiums surrounded with various light, and that with many I entered into the first, which was seen as if in flammeous light. Many were assembled there, and the president proposed that they should declare their opinions concerning CHARITY: and after they had begun, THE FIRST said, That his opinion was, that charity was morality inspired by faith. THE SECOND, That it was piety inspired by pity. THE THIRD, That it was to do good to every one, both good and bad. THE FOURTH, That it was in every way to serve one's relations and friends. THE FIFTH, That it was to give alms to the poor and to help the needy. THE SIXTH, That it was to build hospitals for the reception of invalids and orphans. THE SEVENTH, That it was to enrich temples and to do good to their ministers. THE EIGHTH, That it was the old Christian brotherhood. THE NINTH, That it was to forgive every one his trespasses. Each of them amply confirmed his opinion; which things, because they are many, cannot be transferred hither; wherefore they may be seen in the RELATION itself. After this, there was given to me, also, an opportunity of expressing my opinion; and I said, that charity was to act from the love of justice with judgment, in every work and duty, but from love not from any other source than from the Lord the Savior; and after this was demonstrated, I added, that all those things which were said above, by the nine celebrated men, concerning charity, were excellent examples of charity, provided they be done from justice with judgment; and because justice and judgment are from no other source than from the Lord the Savior, that they be done by man from Him. This was approved by most, in the internal man, but not as yet so in the external. *n.* 459.

XLVII.

That at a distance there was heard, as it were a gnashing of teeth, and intermixed with it, as it were a knocking; and I went towards the sounds, and saw a little house built of rushes glued together; and instead of the gnashing of teeth, and the sound of knocking, I heard within, in the little house, altercations about faith and charity, which of them was the essential of the church. And those who were for faith, brought forward their arguments, saying, that faith was spiritual, because from God, but charity natural, because from man. On the other hand, those who were for charity said, that charity was spiritual, and faith natural, unless it be conjoined to charity. To these things, a certain *syncratist*, wishing to settle the dispute, added, confirming that faith was spiritual and charity only natural. But it was said, that moral life was twofold, spiritual and natural, and that in the man who lives from the Lord, it is spiritual-moral, but in the man who does not live from the Lord, it is natural-moral, such as is given with the evil, and sometimes with the spirits in hell. *n.* 460.

XLVIII.

That in spirit I was brought into a certain garden, in the southern quarter, and that I saw some sitting there under a certain laurel, eating figs, whom I asked how they understood that man can do good from God, and yet still as from himself. And they answered, That God works good inwardly in man, but if man does it from his own will and from his own understanding, that he defiles it, so that it is no more good. But to that I said, that man is only an organ of life, and that if he believes in the Lord, he may do good of himself from Him; but if he does not believe in the Lord, and still more, if he does not believe in any God, he may do good of himself from hell; and further, that the Lord has given to man the free choice of doing from the one or from the other. That the Lord has given this freedom, was confirmed from the Word, in that he commanded man to love God and the neighbor, to produce the goods of charity as a tree produces fruits, and to do his commandments that he may be saved, and that every one would be judged according to his deeds; and that these and those things would not have been commanded, if man could not do good of himself from God. After these things were said, I gave them shoots from a certain vine, and the shoots in their hands put forth grapes; besides other things. *n.* 461.

XLIX.

That I saw a MAGNIFICENT DOCK, and in it vessels large and small, and upon the decks, boys and girls, who were waiting for turtles to rise up out of the sea; and when they emerged, I saw that they had two heads, one, which at pleasure they drew back into the shells of their body, and another, which appeared in form as a man, and from this they spoke with the boys and girls; and these, on account of their elegant discourses, caressed them and also gave them presents. These things being seen, it was explained by an angel what they signified, namely; that there are men in the world, and thence as many spirits after death, who say that God, with those who have got faith, does not see any thing that they think and do, but only looks at the faith, which he has hid in the interiors of their mind; and that those same persons, before the congregations in temples, bring forth holy things from the Word, altogether as others, but these from the greater head which appears as a man, in which they then insert the little one, or draw this into the body. That the same persons afterwards were seen in the air in a vessel with seven sails flying, and those in it in laurels and in purple garments, crying, that they were the heads of the wise of all the clergy; but the things seen were the images of pride flowing forth from the ideas of their mind. And when they were upon the earth, I spoke with them, first from reason, and afterwards from the Sacred Scripture; and by many things I demonstrated, that their doctrine was unsound, and, because contrary to the Sacred Scripture, from hell; but the arguments, by which I demonstrated those things, cannot be transferred hither, on account of their prolixity; wherefore they may be seen in the RELATION itself. Also, that afterwards they were seen in a sandy valley, in garments of rags, and girded as it were, with fishing nets around the loins, through which their nakedness appeared; and at last they were sent down into a society, which is next to the Machiavelians. *n.* 462.

L.

That there was called together a convention, which sat in a round temple, in which, at the sides, were altars, by which the members of the convention sat, but there was no primate there; wherefore, each one of himself rushed forth into the midst, and spoke out the feelings of his mind. And there was begun a discourse concerning FREE AGENCY IN SPIRITUAL THINGS. And THE FIRST, rushing forth, cried, That man had no more free agency in those things than Lot's wife, when she was turned into a statue of salt. THE SECOND, That he had no more than a beast or a dog. THE THIRD, That he had no more than a mole, or than an owl in the light of day. THE FOURTH, That if man had free agency in spiritual things, he would become a maniac, and believe himself to be as God, who can regenerate and save himself. THE FIFTH read from the book of the Evangelical, called FORMULA CONCORDIÆ, *That man has no more free agency in spiritual things than a stock or a stone, and that he has no ability at all concerning those things, to understand, think, will, and not even to apply and accommodate himself to receive what is spiritual;* besides more things, of which above, n. 464. After these things were said, there was also given to me an opportunity of speaking; and I spoke and said, "What else is man, without free agency in spiritual things, but a brute? And without it, to what purpose are all theological things?" But to this they replied, "Read our theological things, and you will not find therein any thing spiritual, and that this is so concealed within them, that not even a shadow of it appears. Wherefore, read what our theology teaches concerning justification, that is concerning the remission of sins, regeneration, sanctification and salvation; you will not see there any thing spiritual, because they flow in through faith, without any consciousness of man. It has also removed charity far from what is spiritual, and also repentance from contact with it. And besides, as to redemption, it attributes to God purely natural human properties, as that He concluded the human race under universal damnation; that the Son took that upon Himself, and that thus He propitiated the Father; and what else are intercession and mediation with the Father? From these things it is evident, that, in all our theology, there is nothing spiritual, and not even rational, but merely what is natural below them." But then suddenly a thunderbolt was heard from heaven, and the members of the convention, being thence terrified rushed forth, and each one fled into his own house. *n.* 503.

LI.

That I spoke with two spirits, one of whom loved what is good and true, and the other what is evil and false; and I found that both enjoyed a similar faculty of thinking rationally. But when he who loved what is evil and false was left to himself, I saw, as it were, that smoke ascended from hell and extinguished the lucidity which was above his memory; but when he who loved what is good and true was left to himself, I saw that, as it were, a gentle flame descended from heaven and illuminated the region of his mind above the memory, and thence also the things that were below it. Afterwards I spoke with him, who loved what is evil and false, concerning FREE AGENCY IN SPIRITUAL THINGS; and he, only at the mention of it, grew warm, and cried, that no one can move his foot or hand to do any spiritual good, nor his tongue and mouth to speak any spiritual truth, and thus that he cannot apply and accommodate himself to receive any such thing. Is not man in such things dead, and merely passive? How can what is dead and merely passive do good, and speak truth of itself? Does not our church also speak so? But the other, who loved what is good and true, concerning free agency in spiritual things, spoke thus: "What would the whole Word be without it? And what the church, what religion, what the worship of God, thus what the ministry, without it? And from the light of my understanding, I know that man, without that spiritual freedom, would not be man, but a beast; for that he is man, and not a beast, is from that freedom; and moreover, that man without free agency in spiritual things, would not have life after death, thus not eternal life, because not any conjunction with God; wherefore, to deny it is the part of those who are insane in spiritual things." Afterwards there was seen, as it were, a horned serpent upon a tree, which reached fruit thence to him who denied free agency in spiritual things; which being eaten, there appeared smoke ascending from hell, which extinguished the higher part of his rational mind as to light. *n.* 504.

LII.

There was heard a grating noise, as of two mill-stones striking against each other; and I went up to the beginning of the sound, and saw a house, in which were many little cells, in which the learned of this age were sitting and confirming justification by faith alone; and going up to one, I asked what he was now studying. He answered, "Concerning THE ACT OF JUSTIFICATION, which is the head of all things of doctrine in our orthodoxy." And I asked whether he knew any sign, when justifying faith enters, and when it has entered. And he said, that this was done passively, and not actively. To which I replied that, "If you take away what is active in it, you also take away what is receptive; and thus that act would be only something purely ideal, which is called an imaginary entity, and thus nothing more than the statue Lot's wife, tinkling from mere salt, when struck with a scribe's pen, or his finger nail." The man, growing warm, took a candlestick, in order to throw at me; but then, the light being extinguished, he threw it at his companion. *n.* 505.

LIII.

There were seen two flocks, one of sheep and the other of goats, but when they were viewed closely, instead of goats and sheep, men were seen; and it was perceived, that the flock of goats consisted of those who make faith alone saving, and the flock of sheep, of those who make charity and at the same time faith. To the question, Why there? those who were seen as goats said, That they were sitting as a council, since it was disclosed to them, that the saying of Paul, *That man is justified by faith, without the works of the law*, Rom. iii. 28, is not rightly understood; since by *faith* there, is not meant the faith at this day, but faith in the Lord the Savior; and by *the works of the law*, are not meant the works of the law of the decalogue, but the works of the Mosaic law, which were rituals; which also was demonstrated. And they said, that they had concluded that faith produces good works, as a tree produces fruit. Those who constituted the flock of sheep favored them; but then an angel, standing between the two flocks, cried to the flock of sheep, "Do not listen, because they have not receded from their former faith." And he divided the flock of goats into two, and said to those on the left hand, "Join yourselves to the goats; but I tell you beforehand, that a wolf is about to come, which will seize them and you with them." But then inquiry was made, how they understood, that faith produces good works, as a tree produces fruit; and it was found out, that their perception concerning the conjunction of faith and charity was altogether different from that comparison, and thus that it was a fallacious mode of speaking. When these things were understood, the flocks of sheep reunited themselves into one, as before, to which some of the goats adjoined themselves, confessing that charity is the essence of faith, and that thus faith separate from it, is only natural, but conjoined to it, it becomes spiritual. *n.* 506.

LIV.

A discourse with angels concerning the three loves, which are universal, and thence with every man; which are THE LOVE OF THE NEIGHBOR, OR THE LOVE OF USES which in itself is spiritual; THE LOVE OF THE WORLD, OR THE LOVE OF POSSESSING WEALTH, which in itself is material; and THE LOVE OF SELF, OR THE LOVE OF RULING OVER OTHERS, which in itself is corporeal; and that when those three loves are rightly subordinated with man, man is truly man, and that they are then rightly subordinated, when the love of the neighbor makes the head, the love of the world the body, and the love of self the feet: it is altogether otherwise when they sit with man contrary to order. And it was shown what man is when the love of the world makes the head, and what he is when the love of self; that then he is an inverted man; as to the interiors of his mind, a wild beast, and as to the exteriors of it, and thence of the body, a stage-player. After this, there was seen a certain devil ascending from below, having a dark face with a white circle around the head; and he said that he was *Lucifer*, although he was not; and that, in his internals, he was a devil, but in his externals an angel of light: and he told, that in externals, he was moral among the moral, rational among the rational, yea, spiritual among the spiritual; and that when he was in the world, he preached, and that then he uttered imprecations against evil doers of every kind, and that thence he was called *Son of the morning*; and, what he himself wondered at, that when he was upon the pulpit, he perceived no otherwise than that it was so, as he spoke; but otherwise when he was out of the temple. He said the reason was, because in the temple he was in his externals, and then only in the understanding, but out of the temple in his internals, and then in the will; and thus that the understanding elevated him into heaven, but the will draws him down into hell; but that the will prevails over the understanding, because the former disposes the latter at its beck and nod. After this, the devil, who pretended to be Lucifer, glided down into hell. *n.* 507.

LV.

There was seen a round temple, the roof of which was in the shape of a crown, the walls continuous windows of crystals, the gate of a pearly substance: in it there was a sort of pulpit, upon which was the Word encompassed with a sphere of light. In the middle of the temple there was a sacred recess, before which there was a veil but now withdrawn, in which there stood a cherub with a sword vibrating in his hand After these things were seen, they were explained before me, one by one, what they signified, which may be seen. Upon the gate there was this writing, NOW IT IS LAWFUL; which signified, that now it is lawful to enter intellectually into the mysteries of faith; and it was given me to perceive, that it was very dangerous to enter with the understanding into dogmas of faith, which are from one's own intelligence and thence in falses, and still more to confirm them from the Word; and that, therefore by the Divine Providence, the Word was taken away from the Roman Catholics, and that, with Protestants, it is shut up by their dogma, That the understanding is to be kept under obedience to their faith. But because the dogmas which are of the New Church are all from the Word, that in it, it is lawful to enter with the understanding, because they are continuous truths from the Word, which also shine before the understanding. This was what is meant by the writing upon the gate, NOW IT IS LAWFUL, and by the circumstance, that the veil of the sacred recess was withdrawn, within which there stood a cherub. After this, there was brought to me a paper from an infant, who was an angel in the third heaven, in which was written, ENTER HEREAFTER INTO THE MYSTERIES OF THE WORD, HITHERTO SHUT UP; FOR ALL ITS TRUTHS ARE SO MANY MIRRORS OF THE LORD. *n.* 508.

LVI.

That I was seized with a grievous disease, from the smoke which came in from the Jerusalem, which, in Rev. xi. 8, is called Sodom and Egypt; and that I was seen by those who were in that city as dead, saying thus one to another, that I was not worthy of burial, just as it is said concerning the two witnesses in the same chapter in the Revelation; and in the mean time I heard blasphemies in abundance, from the citizens, on account of my having preached repentance, and faith in the Lord Jesus Christ. But because judgment came upon them, I saw that that whole city fell down, and was overflowed with waters; and afterwards, that they were running about among the heaps of stones, and lamenting on account of their lot; when yet they had believed, that, by the faith of their church, they were born again and thus righteous; but it was said to them, that they were any thing else than such, since they had never performed any actual repentance, and that thence they did not know one damnable evil with them. Afterwards it was said to them from heaven, that faith in the Lord, and repentance, are the two means of regeneration and salvation; and that this was very well known from the Word, and moreover, from the decalogue, baptism, and the holy supper; concerning which see in the RELATION. *n.* 567.

LVII.

That all, who after death come into the spiritual world, at first for a time are kept in externals, in which they were in the natural world; and because most, while they are in externals, live morally, frequent temples, and pray to God, they believe that they shall certainly come into heaven; but they are instructed that every man after death successively puts off the external man, and the internal man is opened, and then the man is known, as he is in himself, since man is man from the will and understanding, and not only from action and speech; and that thence it is, that man can, in externals, appear as a sheep, although in internals he is as a wolf: and that he is such, in his internal man, unless he explore the evils of his will, and thence of the intention and repent of them; besides more. *n.* 568.

LVIII.

That every love breathes forth a delight, but that THE DELIGHTS OF LOVES are but little felt in the natural world, but manifestly in the spiritual world; and that in this they are sometimes turned into odors; and that then it is perceived what the delights are, and of what love; and that the delights of the love of good, such as are in the heavens, are perceived as fragrances in gardens and flower-beds; and on the other hand, the delights of the love of evil, such as are in hell, as stenches and stinks from bogs and privies; and that, because they are so opposite, the devils are tortured when they feel any sweet odor from heaven, and, on the other hand, the angels are tortured when they feel stinking ones from hell. That it is so, was confirmed by two examples. It is from this cause, that the oil of anointing was prepared from aromatics, and that it is said concerning Jehovah, that he smelled a grateful odor from the burnt-offerings; and on the other hand, that it was commanded the sons of Israel, that they should carry unclean things out of their camp, and that they should bury their excrements; for their camp represented heaven, and the desert out of it represented hell. *n.* 569.

LIX.

That a certain novitiate spirit, who in the world meditated much concerning heaven and hell, desired to know what is the quality of the one and the other, and that it was said to him from heaven, INQUIRE WHAT DELIGHT IS, AND YOU WILL KNOW. Wherefore, going away, he inquired, but, among spirits merely natural, in vain. But he was led to three companies, in order; to one, where they explored ends, and thence were called wisdoms; to another, where they investigated causes, and thence were called intelligences; and to a third, where they examined effects, and thence were called sciences; and by the latter and the former, he was instructed, that every angel, spirit and man has life from the delight of his love; and that the will and thought cannot move at all, except from the delight of some love; and that this is, to every one, that which is called good. And, moreover, that the delight of heaven is the delight of doing good, and that the delight of hell is the delight of doing evil. That he might be further instructed, a devil providentially ascended, and, before him, described the delights of hell, that they were the delights of revenging, of committing whoredom, of defrauding and of blaspheming; and that those things, when they are felt there as odors, are felt as balsams; whence he called them the delights of their nostrils. *n.* 570.

LX.

That there was seen a company of spirits praying to God, that He would send angels to instruct them concerning various things which are of faith, because in most things they hesitated, since churches differ so one from another, and all their ministers say, BELIEVE US; WE ARE THE MINISTERS OF GOD, AND WE KNOW. And there appeared angels, whom they questioned respecting charity and faith, respecting repentance, respecting regeneration, respecting God, respecting the immortality of the soul, and respecting baptism and the holy supper; to each of which the angels answered so that they fell into their understanding; saying further, that all that which does not fall into the understanding is like what is sown in the sand, which, however it is watered by the rain, still withers away; and that the understanding, closed up from religion, no longer sees any thing in the Word, from the light which is therein from the Lord; yea, that if one reads it, he becomes more and more blind in the things of faith and salvation. *n.* 621.

LXI.

How man, when he is prepared for heaven, enters it; namely, that, after preparation, he sees a way which leads to the society in heaven in which he is to live to eternity; and that, near the society, there is a gate which is opened; and that, after entrance, it is inquired whether there is in him similar light and similar heat, that is, similar good and truth, as in the angels of that society; which being found out, he goes about and inquires where his house is; for there is for every novitiate angel a new house, which being found, he is received and numbered as one among them. But those in whom there is not the light and heat, that is, the good and truth of heaven, have this hard lot, that, when they enter, they are miserably tortured, and from the torture cast themselves down headlong. This happens to them from the sphere of the light and heat of heaven, in the opposite of which they are; and they afterwards no longer desire heaven, but are consociated with their like in hell. Thence it is manifest, that it is vain to think that heaven is only an admission from favor, and that those who are admitted enjoy the joys there, as those who, in the world, enter into the house of a wedding. *n.* 622.

LXII.

That many, who believed that heaven was only an admission from favor, and, after admission, eternal joy, by permission ascended into heaven; but that, because they could not bear the light and heat, that is, the faith and love there, they cast themselves down headlong; and that then they were seen, by those who stood below, as dead horses. Among those who stood below, and saw them thus, there were boys with their master; and he instructed them what the appearing as dead horses signified, and then who they are who at a distance appear so; saying that they are those, who, when they read the Word, think materially, and not spiritually, concerning God, concerning the neighbor, and concerning heaven; and that those think materially concerning God who think from person concerning essence; concerning the neighbor, from the face and speech concerning quality; and concerning heaven, from place concerning the state of love there; but that those think spiritually who think concerning God from essence, and thence concerning person; concerning the neighbor from quality, and thence concerning the face and speech; and concerning heaven from the state of love there, and thence concerning place. And afterwards he taught them that a horse signifies the understanding of the Word; and because the Word, with those who think spiritually, when they read it, is a living letter, that therefore those appear, at a distance, as live horses; and, on the other hand, because the Word, with those who think materially, when they read it, is a dead letter, that these, therefore, at a distance, appear as dead horses. *n.* 623.

LXIII.

That there was seen an angel, with a paper in his hand, upon which was written, THE MARRIAGE OF GOOD AND TRUTH, descending from heaven into the world; and it was seen that that paper shone in heaven, but, in its descent, gradually less and less, until neither the paper nor the angel appeared, except only before some unlearned ones, who were in a simple heart: before these, the angel explained what the marriage of good and truth involves, namely, that all and each of the things, in the whole heaven and in the whole world, contain both at the same time, because good and truth in the Lord God the Creator make one; and that, therefore, there is not any where given any thing which by itself is good, nor any thing which by itself is true; consequently, that, in each and every thing, there is a marriage of good and truth, and in the church, a marriage of charity and faith, since charity is of good, and faith is of truth. *n.* 624.

LXIV.

That when I was in profound thought, concerning the second coming of the Lord, I saw heaven, from the east to the west, luminous, and heard from the angels a glorification and celebration of the Lord, but from the Word, as well the prophetical Word of the Old Testament, as the apostolical of the New. The passages themselves, by which the glorifications were made, may be seen in the RELATION. *n.* 625.

LXV.

That, in the north-eastern quarter, there are PLACES OF INSTRUCTION; and that those who receive instructions interiorly are there called disciples of the Lord. Once, when I was in the spirit, I asked the teachers there whether they knew the universals of heaven, and the universals of hell; and they answered, that the universals of heaven were three loves; the love of uses, the love of possessing the goods of the world from the love of doing uses, and truly conjugial love; and that the universals of hell were three loves opposite to those three, which are the love of ruling from the love of self, the love of possessing the goods of others from the love of self, and scortatory love. It is described, afterwards, what the first INFERNAL LOVE IS, WHICH IS THE LOVE OF RULING FROM THE LOVE OF SELF; that it is such with the laity, that, when the reins are given to it, they wish to rule over all things of the world, and, with the clergy, that they wish to rule over all things of heaven. That there is such fantasy with those who are in that love, was confirmed by the like in hell, where such are together in a certain valley, who entertain their minds with the fantasies that they are emperors of emperors, or kings of kings; and elsewhere that they are gods: and it was seen, that, at the sight of these, the former, who were of so lofty a mind, fell upon their knees and adored. That afterwards I spoke with two, one of whom was the prince of a certain society in heaven, and another who was the high-priest there; who said, that, with those in that society, there are magnificent and splendid things, because their love is not from the love of self, but from the love of uses; and that they are surrounded with honors, and that they accept them, not for the sake of themselves, but for the sake of the good of obedience. I then asked them, "How can any one know whether he does uses from the love of self or of the world, or from the love of uses, since all the three do uses? Let it be supposed that there is a society composed of mere satans, and a society composed of mere angels, and I can imagine that the satans, from the love of self and the world, would do as many uses in their society as the angels would in theirs: who, then, can know from which love the uses are?" To this the prince and priest replied, that "Satans do uses for the sake of fame, that they may be raised to honors and gain wealth, but angels do uses for the sake of uses; but these are discriminated from those especially by this, that every one who believes in the Lord, and shuns evils as sins, does uses from the Lord, and thus from the love of uses; but that every one who does not believe nor shun evils as sins, does uses from himself and for the sake of himself, thus from the love of self and the world." *n.* 661.

LXVI.

That I entered a certain grove, and saw two angels conversing together. I went up to them, and they were speaking of the lust of possessing all things of the world; and that many, who in actions appear moral and in conversation rational, are in the madness of that lust; and that that lust is turned into fantasies with those who indulge their ideas concerning it. And because every one is permitted to delight himself in his fantasy, in the spiritual world, provided he does no evil to another, that there are also congregations of such in the lower earth; and because it was known where they were, we descended and went in to them; and we saw that they were sitting at tables, upon which there was a great plenty of golden coin, saying that that was the wealth of all in the kingdom; but it was only an imaginary vision, which is called fantasy, by which they made that appearance. But when it was said to them that they were insane, being turned away from the tables, they confessed that it was so; but because that vision exceedingly delighted them, they could not do otherwise than go in by turns, and favor the allurements of their senses. To this they added, that if any one steals from another his goods, or does any other evil, he falls down into some prison under them, and is kept there to labor for food, clothing, and some little pieces of money; and if they also do evil there, they are deprived of those things and punished *n.* 662.

LXVII.

There was heard a dispute between an ambassador of a kingdom and two priests, WHETHER INTELLIGENCE AND WISDOM, AND THUS ALSO PRUDENCE, WERE FROM GOD, OR WHETHER FROM MAN. But it was perceived by some angels, that the priests inwardly, in themselves, believed in like manner as the ambassador, namely, that intelligence and wisdom, and thence prudence, were from man; wherefore, that it might be made manifest, the ambassador was requested to take off the garments of his office, and to put on the garments of the sacerdotal ministry; which being done, the ambassador began to confirm, by many things, that all intelligence, and also prudence, is from God. And afterwards the priests also were requested to take off their garments, and to put on the garments of political ministers; which being done, the priests spoke from their interior self, saying that all intelligence and prudence is from man. The cause of their speaking so was, because a spirit thinks himself to be such as the garment on him is. After this, those three became cordial friends; and, as they conversed together, they went the way which tended downwards; but afterwards I saw them returning. *n.* 663.

LXVIII.

It is treated first of those who in the Word are called THE ELECT; and that they are those, who, after death, are found to have lived a life of charity, and are separated from those who have not lived that life, and thus who are then ELECTED, and prepared for heaven. Wherefore, to believe only some, before their nativity or after it, to be elected and predestinated to heaven, and not all, because all are called, would be to accuse God of the inability of saving, and also of injustice. *n.* 664.

LXIX.

By a certain new comer it was said in heaven, that no one in the Christian world knows what CONSCIENCE is; and, because the angels did not believe it, they said to a certain spirit that he might, with a trumpet, call together the intelligent, and ask them whether they know what conscience is. And so it was done; and they came, and among them there were politicians, scholars, physicians and priests. And then, first, the POLITICIANS were asked what conscience was. They answered, that it was pain from fear, entertained before or afterwards, of the loss of honor or wealth; or that it was from a melancholic humor arising from undigested things in the stomach; besides more. Afterwards, they asked the SCHOLARS what they knew about conscience. They answered, that it was sadness and anxiety infesting the body, and thence the head, or the head and thence the body, from various causes, especially from this, that they applied the mind to one thing only, which is done especially when the reigning love suffers; whence sometimes are fantasies and deliriums, and with some brain-sick scruples in religious matters, which are called remorse of conscience. After these, the PHYSICIANS were asked what conscience was. And they said, that it was only a pain arising from various diseases, which in abundance they enumerated; and that they had cured many by means of drugs. The diseases from which the pains, which are called those of conscience, are derived, may be seen enumerated in the RELATION. At last the PRIESTS were asked what conscience was. They said, that it was the same with contrition, which precedes faith, and that they had cured it by the gospel; and, moreover, that there are conscientious persons of every religion, true as well as fanatical, who make to themselves scruples in the things of salvation, also in things indifferent. The angels, from hearing these things, perceived the truth, that no one knew what conscience was; wherefore, they sent down one from them to teach. He, standing in the midst of them, said, that conscience was not any pain, as they all imagined, but that it was a life according to religion; and that that life is especially with those who are in the faith of charity; and that those who have conscience speak from the heart what they speak, and do from the heart what they do, which he also illustrated by examples. Wherefore, when it is said of any one that he has a conscience, it is meant that he is just; and conversely. These things being said, those who were called together divided themselves into four phalanxes: those who understood and favored the words of the angel passed over into one; those who did not understand, but still favored, into another; those who would not understand, saying to each other, "What have we to do with conscience?" into a third; and those who scoffed, saying, "What is conscience but a blast of wind?" into the fourth. After this, the two latter phalanxes were seen to go aside to the left, and the two former to the right. *n.* 665.

LXX.

That I was led to the place where the ancient sophists, who were in Greece, resided, which place they called Parnassium; and it was said to me, that once in a while they send out some for the purpose of calling to them some new comers from the world, and of inquiring something about wisdom, how it is at this day on earth. And then two from the Christians were found and brought, who were presently asked, "WHAT NEWS FROM THE EARTH?" And they answered, that this there was new; that they had found men in the woods, perhaps left there in early childhood; and that they appeared from the face, indeed, as men, but that still they were not men; and that from them they concluded in the world, that man was no more than a beast, only that he could articulate sound, and thus speak; and that a beast could in like manner become wise, if it were endued with the faculty of expressing articulate sounds; besides more. The sophists, from hearing these things, concluded many things concerning wisdom, what changes it had undergone since their times, especially from this, that they do not know the distinction between the state of man and the state of a beast, and not even that man is only born the form of a man, and that by instructions he becomes man, and such a man as the instructions he receives; and that he becomes wise from truths, insane from falses, and inwardly a wild beast from evils; and that he is only born a faculty for knowing, understanding, and becoming wise, in order that he may be a subject into which God might inspire wisdom, from the first degree of it to the highest; saying further, that from the new comers they comprehended, that wisdom, which in their time was in its rising, is at this day in its setting. Afterwards, they instructed the new comers whence it is that man, created a form of God, could be turned into the form of the devil. But, concerning the latter and the former, the RELATION may be seen. *n.* 692.

LXXI.

That there was again a meeting appointed, in the place where the ancient sophists were, since they had heard from the emissaries that they had found three new comers from the earth, one who was a priest, another who was a politician, and a third who was a philosopher; who were brought up and presently asked, WHAT NEWS FROM

THE EARTH? And they replied, this is new; that they had heard that a certain man says that he speaks with angels and spirits; and that he relates many things concerning their state, and among them that man lives equally a man after death, with the difference only, that he is then clothed with a spiritual body, but before with a material body. On hearing which, they asked the PRIEST what he had thought about those things on earth. He replied, that because he had believed that man was not to live a man before the day of the last judgment, he, with the rest of his order, supposed his relations to have been visions, and afterwards fictions, and that at last he hesitated. Then he was asked, whether the inhabitants of the earth could not see, from reason, that man lives a man after death, and thus dissipate the paradoxical notions concerning the state of souls in the mean time, which are, that souls in the mean time fly about like winds in the universe, and continually expect the last judgment, that they may coalesce with their bodies; which lot would be worse than the lot of any beast. To which the priest replied, that they say, but they do not convince; and that they ascribe the coalition or reunion of souls with their bodies and skeletons in the sepulchre, to the omnipotence of God; and when they name omnipotence, and also faith, all reason is banished. Afterwards, the POLITICIAN, being questioned respecting the things heard, replied, that in the world he could not believe that man would live after death, since all of man lies dead in the sepulchre, and thus that that man saw spectres, and believed that they were angels and spirits; but that now, for the first time, he was convinced, by the senses themselves, that he lives a man as before, and that he was therefore ashamed of his former thoughts. The PHILOSOPHER related very similar things respecting himself, and respecting some of his school; and moreover, that he referred those things which he had heard, respecting the things seen and heard by that man, among the opinions and hypotheses which he had collected from the ancients and moderns. On hearing these things, the sophists were astonished, especially that Christians, who are in light above others from revelation, should be in such thick darkness respecting their life after death; when yet we, and the wise men of our time, knew and believed that life; saying further, that they observed that the light of wisdom, since that age, had let itself down from the interiors of the brain, even to the mouth under the nose, where it appears as the brightness of the lip, and thence the speech of the mouth as wisdom. To these things, some of the tyros added this: "O how stupid are the minds of the inhabitants of the earth at this day! I wish we had here the disciples of Heraclitus, who laughed at every thing, and the disciples of Democritus, who wept at every thing, and we should hear much laughing and much weeping." After this, there were given to the new comers copper plates, on which hieroglyphics were engraved, and they departed. *n.* 693.

LXXII.

That new comers from the world were found, and were brought to the city under Parnassium, and asked, WHAT NEWS FROM THE EARTH? And they answered, that in the world they had believed that after death there would be an entire rest from labors, and yet they heard, when they were coming hither, that there are here administrations, offices and employments, as in the former world, and thus that there is not rest. To this the wise ones there replied, "Thus you believed that now you are to live in mere idleness, when yet from idleness are produced languor, torpor, stupor and sleep of the mind, and thence of the whole body, which are death and not life. And then they were led around in the city, and to the administrators and workmen; on seeing which, they wondered that there should be such things, when yet they also believed that there would be some empty place, in which souls are to live before the new heaven and new earth exist. And they were instructed that all the things which here appear before the eyes are substantial, and are called spiritual, and that all things in the former world are material, and are called natural; and that this distinction is, because they are from another origin; namely, that all things which are in this world exist and subsist from a sun which is pure love, and all things which are in that world exist from a sun which is pure fire. And, moreover, they were instructed that in this world there are not only administrations, but also studies of every kind, and also writings and books. The new comers were gratified by these instructions; and when they were going away, there came some virgins with pieces of embroidery and netting, the works of their own hands, and gave these to them; and they sung before them an ode which expressed with angelic melody, the affection of the works of use with its delights. *n.* 694.

LXXIII.

That I was introduced into an assembly where some of the ancient philosophers were present, and was asked what they knew in my world concerning INFLUX. To which I answered, that they knew of no other than of an influx of the light and heat of their sun into the things which are of nature, as well into those which are animate as into those which are inanimate, and that they did not know any thing at all of the influx of the spiritual world into the natural, when yet from that influx are all the wonderful things which are beheld both in the animal kingdom there, and also in the vegetable kingdom, which are in part recounted: and because they do not know this influx, they confirm themselves in favor of nature, and become naturalists, and at length atheists. *n.* 695

LXXIV.

That I spoke with the followers of Aristotle, Descartes and Leibnitz, concerning PHYSICAL INFLUX, OCCASIONAL INFLUX, AND PREËSTABLISHED HARMONY; and I heard how each confirmed his hypothesis; and since they were not able to look into that subject with the understanding, above confirmations, but only below them, they ended the dispute by lot, which came out in favor of spiritual influx, which, in part, coincides with occasional influx. *n.* 696.

LXXV.

That I was brought into a certain gymnasium, in which the young are initiated into various things which are of wisdom, which was done by the discussion of some subject, which was proposed by the president there: and the subject of discussion then was, WHAT IS THE SOUL, AND OF WHAT QUALITY? There was a desk into which those ascended who were about to answer. And presently ONE ascended, saying, "That no one since the creation of the world has been able to find out what the soul is, and of what quality: but because they knew that the soul was in man, it was inquired whereabouts it was; and that there was one who thought that it resides with man in a certain little gland, which is called the pineal gland, and sits between the two brains in the head; and that he believed this at first; but because it was rejected by many, he also afterwards receded." After this, THE SECOND ascended, and said, "That he believed that the seat of the soul was in the head, since the understanding is there: but because he could not divine where it resided there, he acceded now to the opinion of those who said that its seat was in the three ventricles of the brain; now to that of those who said it was in the striated bodies there; now to that of those who said that it was in the medullary or cortical substance; and now to that of those who said that it was in the *dura mater;*" to which he added, "that he left it to every one to think what he likes." THE THIRD, ascending, said, "That the seat of the soul was in the heart and thence in the blood;" and this he confirmed from the Word, where it is said, *heart and soul.* THE FOURTH, afterwards ascending, said, "That from his childhood he had believed, with the ancients, that the soul was not in one part but in the whole, because it is a spiritual substance, of which place cannot be predicated, but impletion; and also because by soul is also meant life, and life is in the whole." THE FIFTH, ascending, said, "That he believed the soul to be something pure, like air or ether, and that he believed this, because they supposed that the soul would be such after it is separated from the body." But because the wise ones in the orchestra perceived that none of them knew what the soul was, they requested the president, who had proposed that problem, to descend and teach. He, therefore, descending, said, "That the soul was the very essence of man, and because an essence without a form is not any thing, that the soul is the form of the forms of man; and that this form is the truly human form, in which wisdom with its perceptions, and love with its affections, universally reside; and because you believed in the world that you would be souls after death, you are now souls;" besides more. And this was confirmed by this declaration in the book of Creation; *Jehovah breathed into the nostrils of Adam* THE SOUL OF LIVES, *and man was made into* A LIVING SOUL, Gen. ii. 7. *n.* 697.

LXXVI.

That there was seen an angel with a trumpet, by which he called together those celebrated for erudition among Christians, that they might tell what they had before believed in the world concerning THE JOYS OF HEAVEN, and concerning ETERNAL HAPPINESS. This was done, because it was said in heaven, that no one in the Christian world knew any thing about them. And after about an hour, there were seen six companies coming from the learned Christians, who being asked what they had known about the joys of heaven and about eternal happiness, THE FIRST COMPANY said, That they believed there would be only an admission into heaven, and then into its festive joys, as one is admitted into the house of a wedding and into its festivities. ANOTHER COMPANY said, That they believed there would be most pleasant intercourse and most agreeable conversations with angels. THE THIRD COMPANY said, That they believed there would be feasts with Abraham, Isaac and Jacob. THE FOURTH COMPANY said, That they believed them to be paradisiacal delights. THE FIFTH COMPANY That there would be supereminent dominions, most opulent riches, and more than roya magnificence. THE SIXTH COMPANY, That there would be a glorification of God and a festival enduring for ever. That, therefore, those learned ones might know whether those things, which they had believed to be the joys of heaven, were so, it was given them to enter into those their joys, and to each company by itself, in order that they might learn, by lively experience, whether the joys were imaginary, or whether real. This is the case with most who come from the natural world into the spiritual *n.* 731, 732, 733.

And then, presently, that company, which had supposed the joys of heaven to be most pleasant intercourse and agreeable conversations with angels, was let into the joys of their imagination; but because they were external joys, and not internal, after some days they were affected with weariness, and departed. *n.* 734.

Afterwards, those who had believed that the joys of heaven were feasts with Abraham, Isaac and Jacob, were let into things similar to them; but because they perceived that those joys were only external, and not internal, they became weary, and went away. *n.* 735.

The like was done with those who had believed the joys of heaven and eternal happiness to consist in supereminent dominions, most opulent riches, and more than royal magnificence. *n.* 736.

Likewise, also, with those who had believed heavenly joys, and thence eternal happiness, to be paradisiacal delights. *n.* 737.

Likewise, afterwards, with those who had believed heavenly joys and eternal happiness to be a perpetual glorification of God, and a festival enduring for ever. These at length were instructed what is meant in the Word by the glorification of God. *n.* 738.

Finally, the like was done with those who had believed that they should come into heavenly joys and eternal happiness, if they were only admitted into heaven; and that they should then have joys, in like manner, as those do who enter into the house of a wedding, and then, at the same time, into festivities. But because it was shown to them, by lively experience, that in heaven there are no joys, except for those who have lived the life of heaven, that is, the life of charity and faith; and that, on the other hand, heaven is torture to those who have led a contrary life, they withdrew, and consociated themselves with their like. *n.* 739.

Since it was perceived by the angels that as yet none in the natural world knew what the joys of heaven are, and thence what eternal happiness is, it was said to the angel of the trumpet, that he should choose ten from those who had been called together, and introduce them into a society of heaven, that they might see with their eyes, and perceive with their minds, what heaven is, and what the joys there are; and so it was done. And after admission, it was first given them to see the magnificent palace of the prince there. *n.* 740. Then the paradise near it. *n.* 741. Afterwards, the prince himself and his grandees in splendid garments. *n.* 742. Then, being invited to the table of the prince, they saw such an entertainment as no eye had ever seen on earth; and at the table they heard the prince instructing concerning heavenly joys and eternal happiness, that they essentially consist in internal blessedness, and from this in external enjoyments; and that internal blessedness derives its essence from the affection of use. *n.* 743. After dinner, by command of the prince, some wise ones of the society were sent for, who fully instructed them what and whence internal blessedness is, which is eternal happiness; and that this causes external enjoyments to be joys; besides more concerning the latter and the former. *n.* 745, 746. After these things, it was given them to see a wedding in that heaven, of which *n.* 747 to 749. And finally, to hear preaching. *n.* 750, 751. All which being seen and heard, full of knowledge concerning heaven, and joyful in heart, they descended. *n.* 752.

LXXVII.

It is treated there of REVELATION. That it has pleased the Lord to manifest Himself to me, and to open the interiors of my mind, and thus to give me to see the things which are in heaven and hell; and that thus he had disclosed secrets which, in excellence and dignity, exceed all the secrets hitherto disclosed; which are, I. That in all and every thing of the Word, there is a SPIRITUAL SENSE, which does not appear in the sense of the letter; and that, therefore, the Word was written by the correspondences of spiritual things with natural. II. That THE CORRESPONDENCES themselves, such as they are, have been manifested. III. And also concerning THE LIFE OF MEN AFTER DEATH. IV. Concerning HEAVEN AND HELL, what the one is, and what the other is; and also concerning BAPTISM and THE HOLY SUPPER. V. Concerning THE SUN in the spiritual world, that it is pure love from the Lord, who is in the midst of it, from which the proceeding light is wisdom, and the proceeding heat is love; and thus that faith and charity is thence; and that all things which proceed thence are spiritual, and thus alive; and that the sun of the natural world is pure fire, and thence that all things which are from this sun are natural, and thus dead. VI. That there are three degrees hitherto unknown. VII. And, moreover, concerning THE LAST JUDGMENT. That THE LORD THE SAVIOR IS THE GOD OF HEAVEN AND EARTH Concerning THE NEW CHURCH and its Doctrine. Concerning THE INHABITANTS OF THE PLANETS, and concerning THE EARTHS in the universe. *n.* 846. VIII. Moreover, concerning CONJUGIAL LOVE; and that it is spiritual with the spiritual, natural with the natural, and carnal with adulterers. *n.* 847. IX. That it was intuitively perceived by the angels, that although those secrets are more excellent than the secrets hitherto disclosed, still, by many at this day, they are regarded as trifles. *n.* 848. That there was heard a murmur from some in the lower earth, that they should not believe those things, unless MIRACLES were done; but that they received answer, that by miracles they would not believe any more than Pharaoh and the Egyptians; nor any more than the posterity of Jacob, when they danced around the golden calf in the desert; nor any more than the Jews themselves, when they saw the miracles done by the Lord himself. *n.* 849. XI. Finally, why the Lord revealed those secrets to me, and not rather to any one of the ecclesiastical order. *n.* 850.

That the things contained in THE RELATIONS which are after the chapters are true; and that similar things were seen and heard by the prophets before the coming of the Lord, and similar things by the apostles after his coming, as by Peter, Paul and especially by John in the Revelation; which things are recounted *n.* 851.

INDEX.

The figures refer to the numbers, including the notes, and not to the pages.

An Account of the Last Judgment and the Babylon Destroyed: showing that all the Predictions in the Apocalypse are at this day fulfilled. Being a Relation of Things Heard and Seen. From the Latin of EMANUEL SWEDENBORG. 12mo. Cloth, 75 cents. Paper, 30 cents.

Lectures on the Incarnation, Atonement, and Mediation of the Lord Jesus Christ. By CHAUNCEY GILES, Minister of the New Jerusalem Church. 12mo. Cloth, 50 cents. Paper, 25 cents.

*Concerning Heaven and its Wonders, and Con*cerning Hell. From Things Heard and Seen. By EMANUEL SWEDENBORG. 12mo. Cloth, $1.25. Boards, 50 cents.

The Catechism or Decalogue Explained as to its External and Internal Senses. Being Chapter V. of "The True Christian Religion." By EMANUEL SWEDENBORG. 12mo. Cloth, 50 cents.

*Swedenborg on the Athanasian Creed and Sub*jects connected with it. Being a translation of "De Fide Athanasiana." By EMANUEL SWEDENBORG. 12mo. Cloth, $1.25.

*On the White Horse, mentioned in the Apoca*lypse, Chapter XIX. With a Summary from the Arcana Cœlestia on the Subject of the Word, and its Spiritual or Internal Sense. From the Latin of EMANUEL SWEDENBORG. Paper.

*Angelic Wisdom Concerning the Divine Provi*dence. By EMANUEL SWEDENBORG. Originally published in Latin at Amsterdam in 1764. 12mo. Cloth, pp. 387, $1.25.

*Earths in the Universe. By Emanuel Sweden*BORG. 16mo. Paper, 25 cents.

*Of the New Jerusalem and its Heavenly Doc*trine as revealed from Heaven. To which are prefixed Some Observations Concerning the New Heaven and the New Earth. Translated from the Latin of EMANUEL SWEDENBORG. 16mo.

A Summary Exposition of the Internal Sense of the Prophetical Books of the Word of the Old Testament, and also of the Psalms of David. With a twofold Index. Translated from the Latin of EMANUEL SWEDENBORG. Paper, pp. 132, 25 cents.

Doctrines of the New Jerusalem. Embracing the Four Leading Doctrines, The New Jerusalem and its Heavenly Doctrine, The Doctrine of Charity, and Intercourse between the Soul and the Body. By EMANUEL SWEDENBORG. 12mo. Cloth, $1.75.

A Brief Exposition of the Doctrine of the New Church, which is meant by the New Jerusalem in the Apocalypse. Translated from the Latin of EMANUEL SWEDENBORG. Paper, 20 cents.

The Doctrine of the New Jerusalem Concerning the Lord. By EMANUEL SWEDENBORG. Paper, 25 cents.

*The Doctrine of the New Jerusalem on the Sub-*ject of Faith. Translated from the Latin of EMANUEL SWEDENBORG. Paper, 15 cents.

The Four Leading Doctrines of the New Church, signified by the New Jerusalem in the Revelation: being those concerning the Lord; the Sacred Scripture; Faith; and Life. By EMANUEL SWEDENBORG. 12mo. Cloth, $1.50.

Lectures on the Nature of Spirit and of Man as a Spiritual Being. By CHAUNCEY GILES, Minister of the New Jerusalem Church. 12mo. Cloth, $1.25. Paper, 60 cents.

Religion and Life. By James Reed. 12mo. Cloth, 75 cents.

Light on the Last Things. By William B. HAYDEN. 12mo. Cloth, $1.25.

Preparation for Death. Translated from the Italian of Alphonso, Bishop of S. Agatha. By Rev. ORBY SHIPLEY, M. A. Square crown 8vo. Tinted paper. Extra cloth, red edges. $1.75.

"But at the same time many of the pages of this book teem with rich spiritual matter, and many of the prayers may be well studied as models."—*Presbyterian Banner.*

"As to the contents, their merits have long since been settled, deeply and lovingly, in all hearts whose needs and tastes make welcome the precious ore outpoured for us through the long ages by those who have dug earnestly in the exhaustless mine of communion with God."—*Charleston Courier.*

Mizpah. Friends at Prayer. Containing a Prayer or Meditation for Each Day in the Year. By LAFAYETTE C. LOOMIS. 12mo. Beautifully printed on superfine tinted paper, within red lines. Fine cloth. $2. Extra cloth, gilt edges. $2.50.

"A beautifully printed volume with colored border. The plan of the work consists in 'an evening meditation' for each day of the year; with appropriate Scripture references for morning and evening. The meditations are well and piously written, and will, we doubt not, accomplish great good."—*The Lutheran Observer.*

Blunt's Key to the Holy Bible. A Key to the Knowledge and Use of the Holy Bible. By J. H. BLUNT, M. A., author of "Household Theology," etc. 16mo. Extra cloth. $1.

"Is a compact history of Holy Scripture, showing how, when and by whom it was written, with what purpose, what was its writers' inspiration, how it is to be interpreted, and what are the Apocrypha of the Old and New Testaments. There is an Appendix of peculiar Bible words, with their meanings, and a good Index. . . . On the whole, this is a singularly well-executed work, of great value in many respects."—*The Philada. Press.*

Pulpit Germs. Plans for Sermons. By Rev. W. W. WYTHE. 12mo. Tinted paper. Extra cloth. $1.50.

"This book is intended as an aid to clergymen in the preparation of their sermons—not as a labor-saving apparatus for drones, but as an incentive to study. It contains 455 texts, upon each of which the leading heads or skeletons of a discourse are supplied with occasional subdivisions under such heads. The utility of the work is obvious."—*San Francisco Times.*

"The book is unquestionably the best and most unexceptionable of its kind we have met with."—*The Prot. Churchman.*

Evidences of Natural and Revealed Theology. By CHAS. E. LORD. 8vo. Toned paper. Extra cloth. $3.50.

"This volume bears the marks of careful study and clear thinking. . . . The book is a calm, serious and valuable contribution to the theological literature of the age."—*N. Y. Observer.*

"Dr. Lord is a calm, clear and careful writer, and this volume is a valuable contribution to theological literature. . . . As a summary treatise upon natural and revealed theology, or as a manual for use in schools and higher institutions of learning, this book has few, if any, superiors. It will therefore be welcome to the general reader of religious works and useful to the cause of education."—*N. Y. Times.*

The Christian Worker; A Call to the Laity. By REV. C. F. BEACH. 16mo. Cloth. $1.

Moral Reforms, Suggested in a Pastoral Letter. With remarks on Practical Religion. By RT. REV. A. CLEVELAND COXE, Bishop of Western New York, and author of "Thoughts on the Services, etc. 12mo. Cloth. $1.

"This volume will be universally welcomed as a fuller and freer discussion of some of the more practical subjects of Christian life and duty, touched upon in the Bishop's Lenten Pastoral and that of the House of Bishops. . . .

"The book must have a large circulation, for its style and matter will make any one who begins it read it through."—*Utica Gospel Messenger.*

Heart Breathings; or, The Soul's Desire Expressed in Earnestness. A Series of Prayers, Meditations and Selections for the "Home Circle." By S. P. GODWIN. 18mo. Tinted paper. Fine cloth. 75 cents.

"A truly precious little volume, which will doubtless aid the devotions and cheer the way of many a Christian pilgrim."—*Protestant Churchman.*

True Protestant Ritualism. Being a Review of a book entitled "The Law of Ritualism." By the REV. CHARLES H. HALL, D. D., Rector of the Church of the Epiphany, Washington, D. C. 16mo. Cloth. $1.50.

"Dr. Hall has contributed one of the most comprehensive and comprehensible arguments upon the subject which has yet been written. It is well worth the careful perusal of all who are interested in this vexed question."—*Philada. Even. Bulletin.*

Divisions in the Society of Friends. By Thomas H. SPEAKMAN. 16mo. Fine cloth. 63 cents.

"The essay under notice furnishes in a compact form the reasons for the separation of the Society into different organizations."—*Balt. Gazette.*

Life of Philip Doddridge, D. D. With Notices of some of his Contemporaries, and Specimens of his Style. By D. H. HARSHA, M. A., author of "The Star of Bethlehem," etc. NEW EDITION. 12mo. Tinted paper. Extra cloth. $1.50.

"Doddridge is one of the purest and most elevated characters in English religious literature. An American minister, attracted by its excellence, made it a study, and reproduces it in the narrative here given. The work is fairly well executed, and the result is a valuable piece of Christian biography—a book the reading of which will give present pleasure and permanent spiritual advantage to any one who may be able to appreciate it."—*N. Y. Christian Advocate.*

The Threefold Grace of the Holy Trinity. By JOHN H. EGAR, B. D. 12mo. Toned paper. Extra cloth. $1.50.

"It is, in our opinion, one of the ablest and most original contributions to American scientific theology which have been made in our day, and we shall be disappointed if that is not the judgment of the best judges."—*The Amer. Churchman.*

Who is He? An Appeal to those who Regard with any doubt the name of Jesus. By S. F. SMILEY. 16mo. Cloth. 75 cents.

"We hail this little volume, and rejoice at its publication."—*The Episcopalian.*

"Every Friend, every Christian, and most especially every one who is *not* a Christian, should possess and read it."—*Friends' Review.*

Ecce Deus Homo; or, The Work and Kingdom of the Christ of Scripture. 12mo. Tinted paper. Extra cloth. $1.50.

"There is not a page of the book that is wearisome, tedious or dry. The reader feels that a superior intellect is not here weaving a web around him. Amid such terse, short, pithy sentences the light must shine, and misconception is quite impossible."—*The Episcopalian.*

. . . "It seems to be a clear, concise presentation of substantially the common doctrine of the Church on this subject."—*The Congregationalist.*

"We accept with pleasure, as a good statement of the Christian Church, nearly everything in the volume."—*The National Baptist.*

The Divine Teacher. Being the Recorded Sayings of our Lord Jesus Christ during His Ministry on Earth. Small 12mo. Tinted paper. Neat cloth. $1.25.

"The idea is excellent, the workmanship thoughtful, and the book will be a valuable aid to devotion. The little volume will be highly prized by those who are longing and seeking help that may bring them into closer fellowship with the Divine Master and Lord of the Church."—*British Quarterly Review.*

The Unconscious Truth of the Four Gospels. By W. H. FURNESS, D. D. 12mo. Tinted paper. Extra cloth. $1.25.

"A thoughtful and able work."—*N. Y. Even. Post.*

"A really healthy and refreshing religious book."—*The Liberal Christian.*

"One well worth a close perusal by all who have made the study of the New Testament a specialty."—*Chicago Even. Journal.*

Last Days of our Saviour. The Life of our Lord, from the Supper in Bethany to His Ascension into Heaven, in Chronological Order, and in the Words of the Evangelists. *For Passion Week.* Arranged by CHARLES D. COOPER, Rector of St. Philip's Church, Philadelphia. 16mo. Cloth. $1.

"We have examined this with great satisfaction."—*Boston Christian Witness.*

"The idea is an excellent one, and affords the best possible means of obtaining a correct acquaintance with the Man of Sorrows and the great Immanuel in the most interesting aspect of His life."—*Balt. Episcopal Methodist.*

The Reformation of the Church of England. Its History, Principles and Results. 1514–1547. By REV. JOHN BLUNT, M. A., F. S. A., etc. 8vo. Cloth. $6.

"It is distinctly a learned book. The author is not a secondhand retailer of facts; he is a painstaking, conscientious student, who derives his knowledge from original sources."—*London Times.*

The Divine Attributes. Including also the Divine Trinity. A Treatise on the Divine Love and Divine Wisdom, and Correspondence. From the "Apocalypse Explained" of Emanuel Swedenborg. 12mo. Extra cloth, $2.

Angelic Wisdom Concerning the Divine Love and Wisdom. By EMANUEL SWEDENBORG. From the original Latin as edited by Dr. J. F. I. Tafel. Translated by R. N. Foster. Demi 8vo. Extra cloth, $2.

Heaven and its Wonders, and Hell. From Things Heard and Seen. By EMANUEL SWEDENBORG. From the Latin edition of Dr. J. F. I. Tafel.
8vo. Extra cloth, $2.50.

*Angelic Wisdom Concerning the Divine Provi-*dence. By EMANUEL SWEDENBORG. From the original Latin as edited by Dr. J. F. I. Tafel. Translated by R. Norman Foster. Demi 8vo. Tinted paper. Extra cloth, $2.25.

True Christian Religion. Containing the entire Theology of the New Church, foretold by the Lord in Dan vii. 13 14 and Rev. xxi. 1, 2. By EMANUEL SWEDENBORG. From the Latin edition of Dr. J. F. I. Tafel. Translated by R. Norman Foster. 2 vols. demi 8vo. Tinted paper. Extra cloth, $5.

Life and Works of Emanuel Swedenborg. By W. WHITE. With Four Steel Plates. 8vo. Extra cloth, $5.

Life of Emanuel Swedenborg, with a Synopsis of his Writings. By W. WHITE.
12mo. Extra cloth, $1.50.

Life: Its Nature, Varieties and Phenomena. By LEO H. GRINDON, author of "Emblems," "Figurative Language," etc. First American Edition. 12mo. Extra cloth, $2.25.

Talks with a Child on the Beatitudes. By the author of "Talks with a Philosopher." 16mo. Fine cloth, 75 cents. Cloth, flexible, 50 cents.

"A volume written in a sweet, devout, simple and tender spirit, and calculated to edify the old as well as the young."—*Boston Ev. Transcript.*

"A charming little volume to place in the hands of young people."—*Boston Journal.*

Deus Homo : God-Man. By Theophilus Parsons. Crown 8vo. Extra cloth, $2.50.

"Perhaps no book has appeared from the scholars of the New Church that has promised more light to the inquirer or bestowed more satisfaction upon the reader." —*Historical Magazine.*

Emanuel Swedenborg as a Philosopher and a Man of Science. By R. L. Tafel. Crown 8vo. Extra cloth, $2.25.

"We invite our readers to peruse Prof. Tafel's book. Its reading will acquaint them with one of the greatest thinkers and one of the purest characters that ever lived."—*St. Louis Paper.*

Elements of Character. By Mary G. Ware, author of "Death and Life," etc. 16mo. Cloth, $1.25.

"This work is entitled to a place among the higher productions of American female literature."—*Harper's Magazine.*

Observations on the Growth of the Mind. By Sampson Reed. Seventh edition. 16mo. Extra cloth, $1.

"The title of the work expresses its character. It is an attempt to show *how the mind grows,* and after defining the essential character of the mind the author points out, in a most interesting and original manner, the actual development required."—*Boston Transcript.*

Observations on the Authenticity of the Gospels. By a Layman. Second edition. 16mo. Extra cloth, $1.

"A work that should be in everybody's library, and especially ought steps to be immediately taken to place it in the hands of every theological student in our land." —*Religious Magazine.*

"The author writes with vigor and clearness."—*North American Review.*

Sermons on the Lord's Prayer. By Henry A. Worcester. 12mo. Cloth, $1.25.

Mistaken; or, The Seeming and the Real. By LYDIA FULLER. 12mo. Fine cloth, $1.50.

*Moody Mike; or, The Power of Love. A Christ*mas Story. By FRANK SEWALL. Illustrated. 16mo. Extra cloth, $1.

Talks with a Philosopher on the Ways of God to Man. By the author of "Talks with a Child on the Beatitudes." 16mo. Cloth.

Lessons from Daily Life. By Emily E. Hildreth. 12mo. Tinted paper. Extra cloth, $1.

*The Other Life. By Dr. W. H. Holcombe, au*thor of "The Sexes," "In Both Worlds," etc. 12mo. Cloth.

Who was Swedenborg? By O. P. Hiller. 16mo. Paper cover, 25 cents. Cloth, 50 cents.

Letters to a Man of the World. By J. F. E. LE BOYS DES GUAYS, ex-sous Prefect in Department du cher. Revised edition. 16mo. Cloth, $1.50.

Doctrine of Life for the New Jerusalem; from the Commandments of the Decalogue. By EMANUEL SWEDENBORG. 24mo. Extra cloth, gilt, 75 cents.

Heroism. By Horace Field. 12mo. Extra cloth, $1.50.

Thoughts in my Garden. By Mary G. Ware, author of "Elements of Character," etc. 16mo. Cloth, $1.25.

Death and Life. By Mary G. Ware, author of "Thoughts in my Garden," etc. 16mo. Cloth, $1.25.

Words in Season. A Manual of Instruction, Comfort and Devotion for Family Reading and Private Use. By REV. HENRY B. BROWNING, M. A. 16mo. Toned paper. Extra cloth. $1.

"*Words in Season* is the title of a beautiful little volume of practical religious counsels of instruction, comfort and devotion for family reading and private use. It appears to be truly evangelical, and to be calculated, in style and spirit, to do the good at which it aims."—*Boston Congregationalist.*

"*Words in Season*, a thoughtful, sweet-toned manual for family reading and hours of devotion, prepared by an English minister of the Established Church. Spiritual souls will read it with comfort and strengthening."—*Chicago Advance.*

"A very good book."—*N. Y. Liberal Christian.*

www.ingramcontent.com/pod-product-compliance
Lightning Source LLC
LaVergne TN
LVHW021058110826
845150LV00001B/106

* 9 7 8 1 4 2 5 5 6 6 5 8 6 *